Lecture Notes in Computer Science 4985

Commenced Publication in 1973
Founding and Former Series Editors:
Gerhard Goos, Juris Hartmanis, and Jan van Leeuwen

Masumi Ishikawa   Kenji Doya
Hiroyuki Miyamoto   Takeshi Yamakawa (Eds.)

Neural Information Processing

14th International Conference, ICONIP 2007
Kitakyushu, Japan, November 13-16, 2007
Revised Selected Papers, Part II

 Springer

Volume Editors

Masumi Ishikawa
Hiroyuki Miyamoto
Takeshi Yamakawa
Kyushu Institute of Technology
Department of Brain Science and Engineering
2-4 Hibikino, Wakamatsu, Kitakyushu 808-0196, Japan
E-mail: {ishikawa, miyamo, yamakawa}@brain.kyutech.ac.jp

Kenji Doya
Okinawa Institute of Science and Technology
Initial Research Project
12-22 Suzaki, Uruma, Okinawa 904-2234, Japan
E-mail: doya@oist.jp

Library of Congress Control Number: Applied for

CR Subject Classification (1998): F.1, I.2, I.5, I.4, G.3, J.3, C.2.1, C.1.3, C.3

LNCS Sublibrary: SL 1 – Theoretical Computer Science and General Issues

ISSN   0302-9743
ISBN-10   3-540-69159-6 Springer Berlin Heidelberg New York
ISBN-13   978-3-540-69159-4 Springer Berlin Heidelberg New York

Typesetting: Camera-ready by author, data conversion by Scientific Publishing Services, Chennai, India
Printed on acid-free paper   SPIN: 12282913   06/3180   5 4 3 2 1 0

Preface

These two-volume books comprise the post-conference proceedings of the 14th International Conference on Neural Information Processing (ICONIP 2007) held in Kitakyushu, Japan, during November 13–16, 2007. The Asia Pacific Neural Network Assembly (APNNA) was founded in 1993. The first ICONIP was held in 1994 in Seoul, Korea, sponsored by APNNA in collaboration with regional organizations. Since then, ICONIP has consistently provided prestigious opportunities for presenting and exchanging ideas on neural networks and related fields. Research fields covered by ICONIP have now expanded to include such fields as bioinformatics, brain machine interfaces, robotics, and computational intelligence.

We had 288 ordinary paper submissions and 3 special organized session proposals. Although the quality of submitted papers on the average was exceptionally high, only 60% of them were accepted after rigorous reviews, each paper being reviewed by three reviewers. Concerning special organized session proposals, two out of three were accepted. In addition to ordinary submitted papers, we invited 15 special organized sessions organized by leading researchers in emerging fields to promote future expansion of neural information processing.

ICONIP 2007 was held at the newly established Kitakyushu Science and Research Park in Kitakyushu, Japan. Its theme was "Towards an Integrated Approach to the Brain—Brain-Inspired Engineering and Brain Science," which emphasizes the need for cross-disciplinary approaches for understanding brain functions and utilizing the knowledge for contributions to the society. It was jointly sponsored by APNNA, Japanese Neural Network Society (JNNS), and the 21st century COE program at Kyushu Institute of Technology.

ICONIP 2007 was composed of 1 keynote speech, 5 plenary talks, 4 tutorials, 41 oral sessions, 3 poster sessions, 4 demonstrations, and social events such as the Banquet and International Music Festival. In all, 382 researchers registered, and 355 participants joined the conference from 29 countries. In each tutorial, we had about 60 participants on the average. Five best paper awards and five student best paper awards were granted to encourage outstanding researchers. To minimize the number of researchers who cannot present their excellent work at the conference due to financial problems, we provided travel and accommodation support of up to JPY 150,000 to six researchers and of up to JPY to eight students 100,000.

ICONIP 2007 was jointly held with the 4th BrainIT 2007 organized by the 21st century COE program, "World of Brain Computing Interwoven out of Animals and Robots," with the support of the Japanese Ministry of Education, Culture, Sports, Science and Technology (MEXT) and Japan Society for the Promotion of Science (JSPS).

We would like to thank Mitsuo Kawato for his superb Keynote Speech, and Rajesh P.N. Rao, Frédéric Kaplan, Shin Ishii, Andrew Y. Ng, and Yoshiyuki Kabashima for their stimulating plenary talks. We would also like to thank Sven Buchholz, Eckhard Hitzer, Kanta Tachibana, Jung Wang, Nikhil R. Pal, and Tetsuo Furukawa for their enlightening tutorial lectures.

We would like to express our deepest appreciation to all the participants for making the conference really attractive and fruitful through lively discussions, which we believe would tremendously contribute to the future development of neural information processing. We also wish to acknowledge the contributions by all the Committee members for their devoted work, especially Katsumi Tateno for his dedication as Secretary. Last but not least, we want to give special thanks to Irwin King and his students, Kam Tong Chan and Yi Ling Wong, for providing the submission and reviewing system, Etsuko Futagoishi for hard secretarial work, Satoshi Sonoh and Shunsuke Sakaguchi for maintaining our conference server, and many secretaries and graduate students at our department for their diligent work in running the conference.

January 2008

Masumi Ishikawa
Kenji Doya
Hiroyuki Miyamoto
Takeshi Yamakawa

Organization

Conference Committee Chairs

General Chair	Takeshi Yamakawa (Kyushu Institute of Technology, Japan)
Organizing Committee Chair	Shiro Usui (RIKEN, Japan)
Steering Committee Chair	Takeshi Yamakawa (Kyushu Institute of Technology, Japan)
Program Co-chairs	Masumi Ishikawa (Kyushu Institute of Technology, Japan), Kenji Doya (OIST, Japan)
Tutorials Chair	Hirokazu Yokoi (Kyushu Institute of Technology, Japan)
Exhibitions Chair	Masahiro Nagamatsu (Kyushu Institute of Technology, Japan)
Publications Chair	Hiroyuki Miyamoto (Kyushu Institute of Technology, Japan)
Publicity Chair	Hideki Nakagawa (Kyushu Institute of Technology, Japan)
Local Arrangements Chair	Satoru Ishizuka (Kyushu Institute of Technology, Japan)
Web Master	Tsutomu Miki (Kyushu Institute of Technology, Japan)
Secretary	Katsumi Tateno (Kyushu Institute of Technology, Japan)

Steering Committee

Takeshi Yamakawa, Masumi Ishikawa, Hirokazu Yokoi, Masahiro Nagamatsu, Hiroyuki Miyamoto, Hideki Nakagawa, Satoru Ishizuka, Tsutomu Miki, Katsumi Tateno

Program Committee

Masumi Ishikawa, Kenji Doya

Track Co-chairs	Track 1: Masato Okada (Tokyo Univ.), Yoko Yamaguchi (RIKEN), Si Wu (Sussex Univ.) Track 2: Koji Kurata (Univ. of Ryukyus), Kazushi Ikeda (Kyoto Univ.), Liqing Zhang (Shanghai Jiaotong Univ.)

Track 3: Yuzo Hirai (Tsukuba Univ.), Yasuharu Koike (Tokyo Institute of Tech.), J.H. Kim (Handong Global Univ., Korea)
Track 4: Akira Iwata (Nagoya Institute of Tech.), Noboru Ohnishi (Nagoya Univ.), Se-Young Oh (Postech, Korea)
Track 5: Hideki Asoh (AIST), Shin Ishii (Kyoto Univ.), Sung-Bae Cho (Yonsei Univ., Korea)

Advisory Board

Shun-ichi Amari (Japan), Sung-Yang Bang (Korea), You-Shou Wu (China), Lei Xu (Hong Kong), Nikola Kasabov (New Zealand), Kunihiko Fukushima (Japan), Tom D. Gedeon (Australia), Soo-Young Lee (Korea), Yixin Zhong (China), Lipo Wang (Singapore), Nikhil R. Pal (India), Chin-Teng Lin (Taiwan), Lai-wan Chan (Hong Kong), Jun Wang (Hong Kong), Shuji Yoshizawa (Japan), Minoru Tsukada (Japan), Takashi Nagano (Japan), Shozo Yasui (Japan)

Referees

S. Akaho	S. Gruen	S. Koyama
P. Andras	K. Hagiwara	J.L. Krichmar
T. Aonishi	M. Hagiwara	H. Kudo
T. Aoyagi	K. Hamaguchi	T. Kurita
T. Asai	R.P. Hasegawa	S. Kurogi
H. Asoh	H. Hikawa	M. Lee
J. Babic	Y. Hirai	J. Liu
R. Surampudi Bapi	K. Horio	B-L. Lu
A. Kardec Barros	K. Ikeda	N. Masuda
J. Cao	F. Ishida	N. Matsumoto
H. Cateau	S. Ishii	B. McKay
J-Y. Chang	M. Ishikawa	K. Meier
S-B. Cho	A. Iwata	H. Miyamoto
S. Choi	K. Iwata	Y. Miyawaki
I.F. Chung	H. Kadone	H. Mochiyama
A.S. Cichocki	Y. Kamitani	C. Molter
M. Diesmann	N. Kasabov	T. Morie
K. Doya	M. Kawamoto	K. Morita
P. Erdi	C. Kim	M. Morita
H. Fujii	E. Kim	Y. Morita
N. Fukumura	K-J. Kim	N. Murata
W-k. Fung	S. Kimura	H. Nakahara
T. Furuhashi	A. Koenig	Y. Nakamura
A. Garcez	Y. Koike	S. Nakauchi
T.D. Gedeon	T. Kondo	K. Nakayama

K. Niki
J. Nishii
I. Nishikawa
S. Oba
T. Ogata
S-Y. Oh
N. Ohnishi
M. Okada
H. Okamoto
T. Omori
T. Omori
R. Osu
N. R. Pal
P. S. Pang
G-T. Park
J. Peters
S. Phillips
Y. Sakaguchi
K. Sakai
Y. Sakai
Y. Sakumura
K. Samejima
M. Sato
N. Sato
R. Setiono
T. Shibata
H. Shouno
M. Small
M. Sugiyama
I. Hong Suh
J. Suzuki
T. Takenouchi
Y. Tanaka
I. Tetsunari
N. Ueda
S. Usui
Y. Wada
H. Wagatsuma
L. Wang
K. Watanabe
J. Wu
Q. Xiao
Y. Yamaguchi
K. Yamauchi
Z. Yi
J. Yoshimoto
B.M. Yu
B-T. Zhang
L. Zhang
L. Zhang

Sponsoring Institutions

Asia Pacific Neural Network Assembly (APNNA)
Japanese Neural Network Society (JNNS)
21st Century COE Program, Kyushu Institute of Technology

Cosponsors

RIKEN Brain Science Institute
Advanced Telecommunications Research Institute International (ATR)
Japan Society for Fuzzy Theory and Intelligent Informatics (SOFT)
IEEE CIS Japan Chapter
Fuzzy Logic Systems Institute (FLSI)

Table of Contents – Part II

Statistical and Pattern Recognition Algorithms

Neuromorphic Hardware and Implementations

Robotics

Data Mining and Knowledge Discovery

Real World Applications

Cognitive and Hybrid Intelligent Systems

Bioinformatics

Neuroinformatics

Brain-Conputer Interfaces

Novel Approaches

Table of Contents – Part I

Computational Neuroscience

Learning and Memory

Neural Network Models

Supervised/Unsupervised/Reinforcement Learning

Statistical Learning Algorithms

Optimization Algorithms

Novel Algorithms

Motor Control and Vision

Interpolating Vectors:
Powerful Algorithm for Pattern Recognition

Kunihiko Fukushima

Kansai University, Takatsuki, Osaka 569–1095, Japan
`fukushima@m.ieice.org`
`http://www4.ocn.ne.jp/~fuku_k/index-e.html`

Abstract. This paper proposes the use of *interpolating vectors* for robust pattern recognition. Labeled reference vectors in a multi-dimensional feature space are first produced by a kind of competitive learning. We then assume a situation where interpolating vectors are densely placed along lines connecting all pairs of reference vectors of the same label. From these interpolating vectors, we choose the one that has the largest similarity to the test vector. Its label shows the result of pattern recognition. We applied this method to the *neocognitron* for handwritten digit recognition, and reduced the error rate from 1.48% to 1.00% for a blind test set of 5000 digits.

1   Introduction

This paper proposes a powerful algorithm for pattern recognition, which uses *interpolating vectors* for classifying patterns in a multi-dimensional feature space.

Various methods for classifying feature vectors have been proposed so far [1,2,3,4]. Many of them try to classify input patterns based on some kinds of similarities between test vectors (or input patterns) and labeled reference vectors (or code vectors), which have been produced from training vectors. Varieties of techniques have been proposed, for generating labeled reference vectors and/or finding a reference vector that has the largest similarity to the test vector.

In the method proposed in this paper, labeled reference vectors are first produced by a kind of competitive learning. Different from conventional methods, however, we do not simply search for a reference vector that has the largest similarity to the test vector. We assume a situation where virtual vectors, called *interpolating vectors*, are densely placed along the line segments connecting every pairs of reference vectors of the same label. From these interpolating vectors, we choose the one that has the largest similarity to the test vector. The label (or the class name) of the chosen vector is taken as the result of pattern recognition. Actually, we can get the same result with a simpler process.

To demonstrate the ability of this algorithm, we apply it to the *neocognitron*, which is a neural network model for robust visual pattern recognition [5,6], and show that the error rate can be further reduced by the use of interpolating vectors.

M. Ishikawa et al. (Eds.): ICONIP 2007, Part II, LNCS 4985, pp. 1–10, 2008.
© Springer-Verlag Berlin Heidelberg 2008

2 Interpolating Vectors

2.1 Reference Vectors

In visual pattern recognition, we assume a situation where the process of feature extraction has already been finished. Each input pattern, either training or test pattern, can be represented by a vector in a multi-dimensional feature space.

We define similarity s between arbitrary two vectors $\boldsymbol{x}$ and $\boldsymbol{y}$, using inner product $(\boldsymbol{x}, \boldsymbol{y})$ and norm $||\boldsymbol{x}|| = \sqrt{(\boldsymbol{x}, \boldsymbol{x})}$ of the vectors, by

$$s = \frac{(\boldsymbol{x}, \boldsymbol{y})}{||\boldsymbol{x}|| \cdot ||\boldsymbol{y}||} . \tag{1}$$

Each training vector has a label indicating the class to which the vector belongs. From a set of training vectors, we generate *reference vectors* for each class. Each reference vector has a label of the class name. A single reference vector usually represents a number of training vectors of a class. There can be more than one reference vectors for each class.

The learning progresses in two steps: an *initial learning* and an *adjusting phase*. In the initial learning, we produce reference vectors in such a way that each training vector of a class comes to have a largest similarity to a reference vector of the class. The generation of reference vectors is made by a kind of competitive learning. The learning starts from a state where there is no reference vector. When a training vector of a class is presented at first, it is adopted as a reference vector and is assigned a label of the class name.

If another training vector is presented afterward, the reference vector that has the largest similarity to the training vector is taken as the winner of the competition, provided that the similarity is larger than a certain threshold, θ_L.

If the label of the winner is the same as the class name of the training vector, the training vector is added to the reference vector of the winner, resulting in a modification of the reference vector. Namely, a reference vector $\boldsymbol{X}$ is produced by the total sum of all training vectors $\boldsymbol{x}^{(m)}$ that have made $\boldsymbol{X}$ a winner:

$$\boldsymbol{X} = \sum_m \boldsymbol{x}^{(m)} \tag{2}$$

If the label of the winner is different from that of the training vector, however, the reference vector, which became the winner and caused a wrong classification of this training vector, is not modified this time. A new reference vector is generated instead: the training vector itself is adopted as the new reference vector of the class. A new reference vector is also generated, if there is no reference vector whose similarity to the training vector is larger than the threshold θ_L.

The process of finding the winner is equivalent to the process of finding the nearest reference vector. Each reference vector has its own territory determined by the Voronoi partition of the feature space. Generation of a new reference vector causes a shift of decision borders in the feature space, and some of the training vectors of other classes, which have been classified correctly before, might be misclassified now. If this situation occurs, additional reference vectors have to be generated again to readjust the decision borders. Thus, the decision borders are gradually adjusted to fit the real borders between classes.

Since training vectors that are located near the center of the territory of a class have a large tendency of being correctly classified, a single reference vector usually represents a large number of training vectors. As a result, the number of reference vectors generated is much smaller than the number of training vectors. Since training vectors that are misclassified often come from near class borders, reference vectors come to be distributed more densely near class borders.

We repeat the presentation a training vector set until the generation of new reference vectors stops. Although a repeated presentation of the training vector set is required before the initial learning converges, the required number of repetition is not so large in usual cases for neocognitrons.

2.2   Interpolating Vectors

After having finished the initial learning, by which all reference vectors have been produced, we use the method of interpolating vectors.

The basic idea of the method is as follows. We assume a situation where virtual vectors, which are named *interpolating vectors*, are densely placed along the line segments connecting every pairs of reference vectors of the same label. From these interpolating vectors, we choose the one that has the largest similarity to the test vector. The label (or the class name) of the chosen vector is taken as the result of pattern recognition.

Actually, we do not need to generate infinite number of interpolating vectors. We just assume line segments connecting every pairs of reference vectors of the same label. We then measure distances (based on similarity) to these line segments from the test vector, and choose the nearest one. The label of the line segment shows the result of pattern recognition.

Mathematically, this process can be expressed as follows. Let $\boldsymbol{X}_i$ and $\boldsymbol{X}_j$ be two reference vectors of the same label. An interpolating vector $\boldsymbol{\xi}$ for this pair of reference vectors is given by a linear combination of them:

$$\boldsymbol{\xi} = p\frac{\boldsymbol{X}_i}{||\boldsymbol{X}_i||} + q\frac{\boldsymbol{X}_j}{||\boldsymbol{X}_j||}. \tag{3}$$

Similarity s between the interpolating vector $\boldsymbol{\xi}$ and a test vector $\boldsymbol{x}$ is

$$s = \frac{(\boldsymbol{\xi}, \boldsymbol{x})}{||\boldsymbol{\xi}|| \cdot ||\boldsymbol{x}||} = \frac{ps_i + qs_j}{\sqrt{p^2 + 2pqs_{ij} + q^2}}, \tag{4}$$

where

$$s_i = \frac{(\boldsymbol{X}_i, \boldsymbol{x})}{||\boldsymbol{X}_i|| \cdot ||\boldsymbol{x}||}, \qquad s_j = \frac{(\boldsymbol{X}_j, \boldsymbol{x})}{||\boldsymbol{X}_j|| \cdot ||\boldsymbol{x}||}, \qquad s_{ij} = \frac{(\boldsymbol{X}_i, \boldsymbol{X}_j)}{||\boldsymbol{X}_i|| \cdot ||\boldsymbol{X}_j||}. \tag{5}$$

Among various combinations of p and q, similarity s takes a maximum value

$$s_{\max} = \sqrt{\frac{s_i^2 - 2s_i s_j s_{ij} + s_j^2}{1 - s_{ij}^2}}. \tag{6}$$

We can interpret that $s_{\max}$ represents similarity between test vector $\boldsymbol{x}$ and the line segment that connects reference vectors $\boldsymbol{X}_i$ and $\boldsymbol{X}_j$ (Fig. 1). Among all line segments that connect every pairs of reference vectors of the same label, we choose the one that has the largest similarity to the test vector. The label (or the class name) of the chosen vector is taken as the result of pattern recognition.

Fig. 1. Largest similarity $s_{\max}$ between test vector $\boldsymbol{x}$ and the line segment connecting a pair of reference vectors $\boldsymbol{X}_i$ and $\boldsymbol{X}_j$ of the same label

In the search of the largest similarity, we allow p or q be negative, because this gives a better recognition rate. This means that line segments can extend beyond the reference vectors on both sides, and that the search is made, not only among *interpolating*, but also among *extrapolating* vectors (See Section 5).

If some parts of borders between classes are concave, however, some of the line segments might cross the concave borders and invade into the territory of other classes. Such line segments, whose example is illustrated by a dotted line in Fig. 2, will cause misclassification of the test vector. To find out and eliminate such line segments that are suspected of crossing class borders, we have an *adjusting phase* after having generated reference vectors in the initial learning.

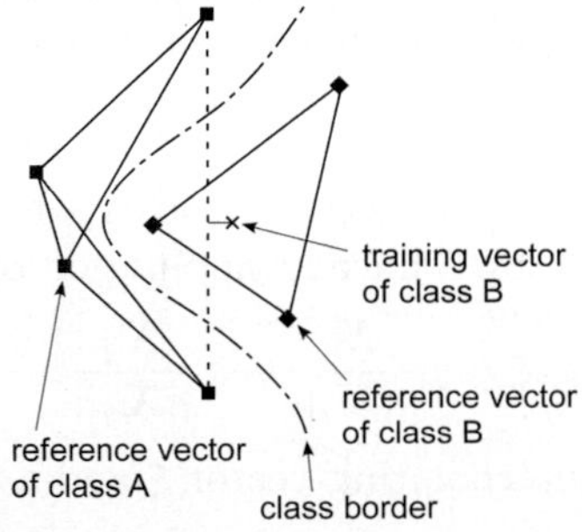

Fig. 2. Elimination of a line segment that crosses the concave boarder between classes. The training vector of class B ($\times$) is nearer to the line segment of class A (dotted line) than to line segments of class B.

During the adjusting phase, we test how the training vectors, which have been used to generate reference vectors, are classified. If a training vector is erroneously classified, we suspect that the line segment nearest to the training vector crosses the class border. We then eliminate the line segment. Sometimes, more than one line segments might be eliminated by a single training vector.

3   Use of Interpolating Vectors for the Neocognitron

3.1   Outline of the Neocognitron

The neocognitron to which the method of interpolating vectors is applied is
almost the same as the conventional neocognitron [6], except the highest stage
of the hierarchical network. As illustrated in Fig. 3(a), the network consists of 4
stages of S- and C-cell layers. The stimulus pattern is presented to input layer
U_0, and the result of pattern recognition appears in layer U_{C4}.

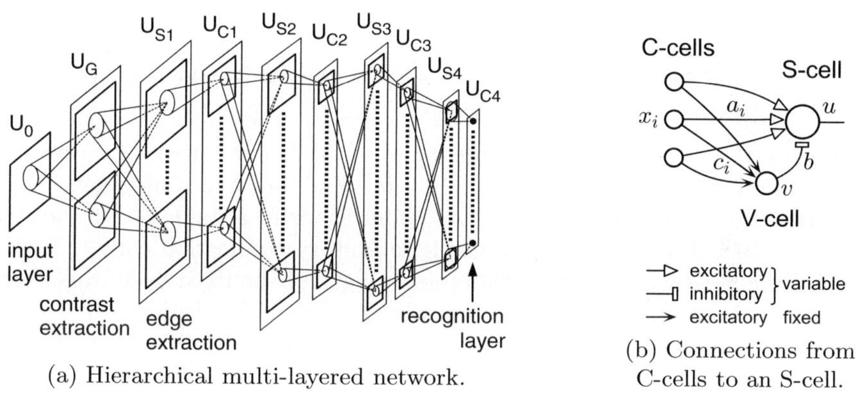

(a) Hierarchical multi-layered network.

(b) Connections from C-cells to an S-cell.

Fig. 3. The architecture of the neocognitron

S-cells have modifiable input connections, which are determined by learning.
They work as feature-extracting cells after having finished the learning. Each C-
cell receives fixed excitatory connections from a group of S-cells that extract the
same feature, but from slightly different positions. Even if the stimulus feature
shifts and another S-cell comes to respond instead of the first one, the same C-cell
keeps responding. Thus, C-cells absorb positional errors of features. The process
of tolerating shift by C-cells can also be interpreted as a blurring operation.

In the whole network, with its alternate layers of S- and C-cells, feature-
extraction by S-cells and toleration of positional shift by C-cells are repeated.
During this process, local features extracted in lower stages are gradually integrated into more global features. Since small amounts of positional errors of
local features are absorbed, an S-cell in a higher stage comes to respond robustly
to a specific feature even if the feature is slightly deformed or shifted.

Each layer is divided into sub-layers, called *cell-planes*, according to the features to which the cells responds. The cells in each cell-plane are arranged retino-
topically and share the same set of input connections.

3.2   S-cells of the Highest Stage

Since main differences from the conventional neocognitron [6] reside only in the
highest stage, we discuss here the characteristics of S-cells of U_{SL} ($L=4$).

Layer U_{SL}, like layers in other stages, contains not only S-cells but also V-cells, which send inhibitory signals to S-cells. Fig. 3(b) illustrates the connections converging to an S-cell. Let $u_{SL}(\boldsymbol{n}, k)$ be the output of an S-cell of the kth cell-plane, where $\boldsymbol{n}$ represents the location of the receptive field center of the cell. The outputs of the S-cell and the accompanied V-cell are given by

$$u_{SL}(\boldsymbol{n}, k) = \frac{\displaystyle\sum_{\kappa=1}^{K_{CL-1}} \sum_{|\boldsymbol{\nu}|<A_{SL}} a_{SL}(\boldsymbol{\nu}, \kappa, k) \cdot u_{CL-1}(\boldsymbol{n}+\boldsymbol{\nu}, \kappa)}{b_{SL}(k) \cdot v_L(\boldsymbol{n})}, \tag{7}$$

$$v_L(\boldsymbol{n}) = \sqrt{\sum_{\kappa=1}^{K_{CL-1}} \sum_{|\boldsymbol{\nu}|<A_{SL}} c_{SL}(\boldsymbol{\nu}) \cdot \left\{u_{CL-1}(\boldsymbol{n}+\boldsymbol{\nu}, \kappa)\right\}^2}, \tag{8}$$

where $a_{SL}(\boldsymbol{\nu}, \kappa, k)$ (≥ 0) is the strength of variable excitatory connection that the S-cell receives from C-cell $u_{CL-1}(\boldsymbol{n}+\boldsymbol{\nu}, \kappa)$ of the preceding stage. A_{SL} denotes the size of spatial spread of input connections to a single S-cell. Parameter $b_{SL}(k)$ (≥ 0) is the strength of variable inhibitory connection coming from the V-cell. Parameter $c_{SL}(\boldsymbol{\nu})$ represents the strength of the fixed excitatory connections to the V-cell, and is a monotonically decreasing function of $|\boldsymbol{\nu}|$.

Before applying the method of interpolating vectors, we first train U_{SL} using the same method as for the conventional neocognitron [6]. The initial learning of U_{SL} begins, after the training of lower stages (U_{S2} and U_{S3}) has been completely finished. The same set of training patterns as for the lower stages is used.

Every time when a training pattern is presented, competition occurs among all S-cells in the layer. The maximum-output S-cell is taken as a winner of the competition, provided that the output is larger than a certain threshold value, θ_L. If the winner of the competition has the same label as the training pattern, the winner becomes the *seed cell* [6] and learns the training pattern.

If the winner has a wrong label (or if there is no S-cell whose response is larger than the threshold θ_L), however, a new cell-plane is generated and is assigned a label of the class name of the training pattern.

Let cell $u_{SL}(\hat{\boldsymbol{n}}, \hat{k})$ be selected as a seed cell at a certain time. The variable connections $a_L(\boldsymbol{\nu}, \kappa, \hat{k})$ to this seed cell are increased by the following amount:

$$\Delta a_{SL}(\boldsymbol{\nu}, \kappa, \hat{k}) = c_{SL}(\boldsymbol{\nu}) \cdot u_{CL-1}(\hat{\boldsymbol{n}}+\boldsymbol{\nu}, \kappa). \tag{9}$$

The inhibitory connection $b_L(\hat{k})$ is determined directly from $a_L(\boldsymbol{\nu}, \kappa, \hat{k})$:

$$b_{SL}(\hat{k}) = \sqrt{\sum_{\kappa=1}^{K_{CL-1}} \sum_{|\boldsymbol{\nu}|<A_{SL}} \frac{\left\{a_{SL}(\boldsymbol{\nu}, \kappa, \hat{k})\right\}^2}{c_{SL}(\boldsymbol{\nu})}}. \tag{10}$$

3.3   Application of Interpolating Vectors to the Neocognitron

After having finished the conventional learning [6], we use interpolating vectors to analyze the response of U_{SL} and obtain a better recognition rate.

We define a *weighted* inner product of arbitrary two vectors $\boldsymbol{x}$ and $\boldsymbol{y}$ by

$$(\boldsymbol{x}, \boldsymbol{y}) = \sum_{|\boldsymbol{\nu}| < A_{SL}} c_{SL}(\boldsymbol{\nu})\, x(\boldsymbol{\nu})\, y(\boldsymbol{\nu}), \tag{11}$$

using $c_{SL}(\boldsymbol{\nu})\ (> 0)$, which represents the strength of fixed excitatory connections to a V-cell (See (8) and (9)), as the weight.

Let $\boldsymbol{x}$ be the vector representing input signals to an S-cell $u_{SL}(\boldsymbol{n}, k)$. In other words, the response of a preceding C-cell $u_{CL-1}(\boldsymbol{n}+\boldsymbol{\nu}, \kappa)$ is the $\boldsymbol{\nu}$th element of vector $\boldsymbol{x}$. Let $\boldsymbol{X}$ be the total sum of all training vectors to the S-cell, which can be expressed by the same equation as (2). Substituting (8), (9) and (10) in (7), and using the *weighted* inner product defined by (11), we have

$$u_{SL}(\boldsymbol{n}, k) = \frac{(\boldsymbol{X}, \boldsymbol{x})}{\|\boldsymbol{X}\| \cdot \|\boldsymbol{x}\|} = s. \tag{12}$$

We can interpret that the set of input connections to an S-cell (or a cell-plane) represents the *reference vector*. The response of the S-cell shows the similarity s between the test vector $\boldsymbol{x}$ and the reference vector $\boldsymbol{X}$.

Similarity s_{ij} between the ith and the jth reference vectors, namely between the ith and the jth cell-planes, is given by

$$s_{ij} = \frac{1}{b_{SL}(i) \cdot b_{SL}(j)} \sum_{\kappa=1}^{K_{CL-1}} \sum_{|\boldsymbol{\nu}| < A_{SL}} \frac{a_{SL}(\boldsymbol{\nu}, \kappa, i) \cdot a_{SL}(\boldsymbol{\nu}, \kappa, j)}{c_{SL}(\boldsymbol{\nu})} \tag{13}$$

We calculate s_{ij} for every pairs of cell-planes (or reference vectors) of the same label in advance, and store the values. We also put a mark, in the adjusting phase, to line segments that caused wrong classification of any training vectors and were suspected of crossing class borders. Then, we can easily calculate $s_{\max}$ from (6), because s_i and s_j are the responses of the ith and the jth S-cells. Among all pairs of S-cells that have the same label, we search the pair that gives the largest value of $s_{\max}$. In this search, we exclude the pairs that are marked as suspicious of crossing borders. The search is made, not at a single location $\boldsymbol{n}$, but from all S-cells that have receptive fields at different locations $\boldsymbol{n}$. The label of the S-cells thus selected represents the final result of pattern recognition.

4   Computer Simulation

We simulated a neocognitron with interpolating vectors on a computer. The scales and parameters of the network and the method of learning for lower stages of the network are almost the same as those for the conventional neocognitron [6]. We tested its ability to recognize patterns, using handwritten digits (free writing) randomly sampled from the ETL1 database, which was published by former Electrotechnical Laboratory, Tsukuba, Japan.

We show here the results of an experiment, where we used a training set randomly sampled 5000 patterns (500 patterns for each digit) and $\theta_L = 0.6$ (θ_L is

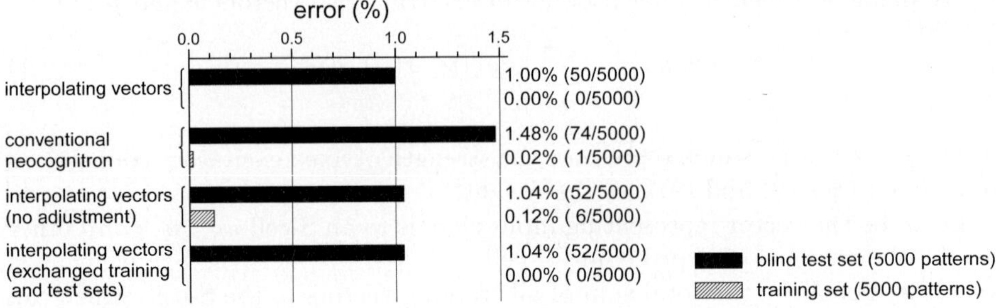

Fig. 4. Recognition errors under various conditions

Fig. 5. An example of the response of the neocognitron with interpolating vectors. The input pattern (U_0) is recognized correctly as '3' (U_{C4}).

the threshold of S-cells in the learning phase). Fig. 4 summarizes the recognition errors of the neocognitron under various conditions, which are discussed below.

When the method of interpolating vectors was used, the error rate was 1.00% (50/5000) with no rejection, for a blind test set of randomly sampled 5000 patterns, and 0% for the training set. The number of cell-planes (or reference vectors) generated in U_{S4} was 161, which was much smaller than the number of training patterns. The number of line segments was also reasonably small: it was 1312 after having finished the adjusting phase. The line segments deleted during the adjusting phase were 16.

Fig. 5 shows a typical response of the network that has finished the learning.

If the method of interpolating vectors was not used and the response of U_{S4} was analyzed by the method for the conventional neocognitron, the error rate was 1.48% (74/5000) for the blind test set.

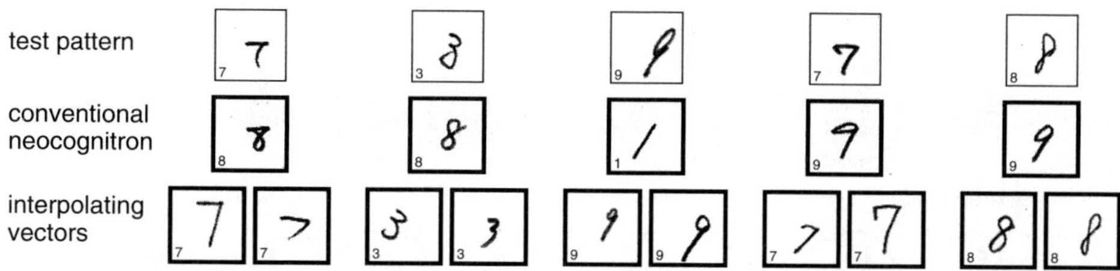

Fig. 6. Some examples of the test patterns (upper line) that were recognized, erroneously by the conventional neocognitron (middle line), but correctly by the use of interpolating vectors (bottom line)

Fig. 6 shows some examples of the test patterns that were recognized, erroneously by the conventional neocognitron, but correctly by the use of interpolating vectors. The figure shows which reference vectors (middle line: conventional neocognitron), and which line segments (bottom line: interpolating vectors), exhibited the largest similarity to the test patterns (top line). In this display, each reference vector is represented expediently by a training pattern that elicits the largest response from it.

Incidentally, if the adjusting phase, which eliminates suspicious line segments, was omitted, the error rate was 1.04% (52/5000) for the test sample, and 0.12% (6/5000) for the training set.

To see how the recognition rate is affected by the sampling of training and test patterns, we tried to exchange the training and the test sets. The error rate for the test set was 1.04% (52/5000). The effect of the exchange was very little.

Application to Other Systems Than Neocognitron: The application of the interpolating vectors is not limited to the neocognitron. To demonstrate this, we tried to apply it directory to the raw input patterns U_0, and compared it with the k-nearest neighbor method. The recognition errors by the k-nearest neighbor method for the blind test set were 16.40%, 15.48%, 14.98% and 15.14%, for $k = 1$, 3, 5 and 7, respectively. The error rates by the interpolating vectors with $\theta_L = 0.6$ were 13.00%. Although the error rate itself was not so small, because any preprocessing, such like normalization of location and size, had not been given to the test patterns, superiority of the interpolating vectors over the k-nearest neighbor method was clearly observed.

5   Discussions

This paper proposed the use of interpolating vectors for robust pattern recognition. To demonstrate its ability, we applied it to the neocognitron for handwritten digit recognition, and reduced the error rate from 1.48% to 1.00% for a blind test set of 5000 digits. The increase in computational cost is very small, because the number of reference vectors (or cell-planes) generated in the learning is much smaller than the number of training vectors (or training patterns).

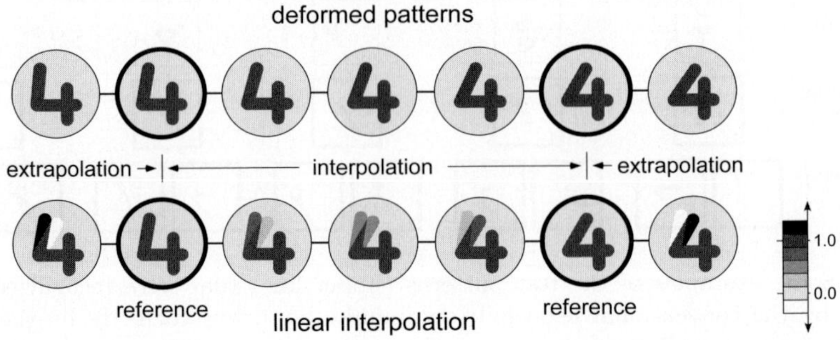

Fig. 7. The use of extrapolating vectors, together with interpolating vectors, improves the recognition rate further

The method of interpolating vectors is well suited to the neocognitron. In the neocognitron, S-cells of the highest stage (U_{S4}) analyze the response of the C-cell layer of the preceding stage (U_{C3}), which has been spatially blurred.

Intermediate deformed patterns between arbitrary two reference vectors (or reference patterns) can be well emulated by an interpolating vector (or an interpolating pattern) produced by a linear combination of the two vectors, especially when the patterns are spatially blurred (Fig. 7).

The same is true for extrapolating vectors. As was mentioned in section 2.2, a better recognition rate can be obtained if both *interpolating* and *extrapolating* vectors are used. Lower half of Fig. 7 shows a series of interpolating and extrapolating vectors produced by linear combinations from a pair of reference vectors. Upper half of the figure illustrates examples of deformed patterns generated from the same pair of reference vectors. The pattern at the upper left, for example, is deformed from the left reference vector, not in the direction to its partner, but in the opposite direction. This pattern has a much larger similarity to the extrapolating vector (pattern) at the lower left.

References

1. Cover, T.M., Hart, P.E.: Nearest neighbor pattern classification. IEEE Transactions on Information Theory IT-4, 515–516 (1968)
2. Gray, R.M.: Vector quantization. IEEE ASSP Magazine 1, 4–29 (1984)
3. Kohonen, K.: The Self-Organizing Maps. Springer, Heidelberg (1995)
4. Schölkoph, B., Sung, K., Burges, C., Girosi, F., Niyogi, P., Poggio, T., Vapnik, V.: Comparing support vector machines with Gaussian kernels to radial basis function classifiers. IEEE Trans. Signal Processing 45, 2758–2764 (1997)
5. Fukushima, K.: Neocognitron: a hierarchical neural network capable of visual pattern recognition. Neural Networks 1, 119–130 (1988)
6. Fukushima, K.: Neocognitron for handwritten digit recognition. Neurocomputing 51, 161–180 (2003); A computer program of this neocognitron in C language is available from Visiome Platform: `http://platform.visiome.neuroinf.jp/`

Multi-Scale Kernel Latent Variable Models for Nonlinear Time Series Pattern Matching

B. Venkataramana Kini[1] and C. Chandra Sekhar[2]

[1] Honeywell Technology Solutions Lab., Bangalore, India
[2] IIT Madras, Chennai, India

Abstract. In this paper we propose a method for nonlinear time series pattern matching: "Multi-Scale Kernel Latent Variable (MSKLV) models". The pattern matching methodology includes multi-scale analysis using wavelet decomposition of time series and finding latent vectors in the kernel feature space at different scales of wavelet decomposition. Latent vectors so obtained are matched for similarity with the corresponding latent vectors obtained for time series in the historical database. The proposed methodology is applied on time series generated in the evolving stages of disturbances of Tennesse Eastman challenge problem and MSKLV models are found to be superior to Multi-scale Latent Variable (MSLV) models.

1 Introduction

Dynamic behavior of real world systems can be represented by measurements along temporal dimension (time series). These time series are collected over long periods of time and stored in historical databases. Such historical database of time series is usually a source of large number of interesting behaviors that the system may have undergone in past. Human beings will be overwhelmed by the high dimensionality of the measurements and the complex dynamics of the system. The task of forecasting the time series involves predicting the time series for next few steps, which can usually provide the trends into near future. However, it is desirable to know higher level trends of the system. Usually, the higher level trends are known by domain experts to some extent. But this kind of knowledge is limited and subjective. Here the approach is towards matching the current system behavior represented by time series into past and retrieving the similar time series pattern matches. Analyzing the current system behavior, associating with some precursor events or extrapolating it into the future are the utilities of such retrieved similar time series.

Usually, such time series patterns are inherently non-stationary in nature. There will be nonlinear correlations between variables. The matching of such time series patterns calls for the feature extraction/modeling methods which can explicitly capture the non-stationary behavior and nonlinear correlations among variables, leading to retrieval of the relevant time series from historical time series database.

M. Ishikawa et al. (Eds.): ICONIP 2007, Part II, LNCS 4985, pp. 11–20, 2008.

Machine learning methods have been shown to be successful for several pattern classification, regression and data based latent variable modeling tasks. It should be noted that, the i.i.d. assumption is implicit in developing these methods. Hence, temporal aspect in the data is ignored. The state of the art kernel methods proposed in [8] are no different. These methods include the kernel formulation of the latent variable models such as Kernel Principal Component Analysis (KPCA) and Kernel Partial Least Squares (KPLS). However, an important advantage of the kernel methods is that they are capable of solving nonlinear problems mainly due to implicit nonlinear mapping of data from the input space to a higher dimensional feature space efficiently.

Wavelets are mathematical tools for analyzing time series. They have two advantages when applied to analyze time series: The wavelets are shown to approximately decorrelate the time series temporally for quite general classes of time series [9]. Usually, the interesting events in time series will happen at different scales. There may be abrupt changes and steady portions. These kind of patterns can be easily localized using multiresolution analysis capability of wavelets.

In this work, we propose a method to capture the nonstationary behavior of time series using wavelet domain analysis and nonlinear spatial correlations (i.e., among variables) using kernel latent variable models. We call these methods Multi-Scale Kernel Latent Variable (MSKLV) models. Specifically we propose the Multi-Scale Kernel Principal Component Analysis (MSKPCA) and Multi-Scale Kernel Partial Least Squares (MSKPLS). In general, these models can be utilized in modeling nonlinear dynamical systems. In this work, we utilize their capability for the purpose of nonlinear time series pattern matching.

The proposed models can be applied in different domains. For example, one may be interested in knowing what are the similar situations in the past compared to current scenario of stock market performance of a particular stock, what are the precursor events that led to current scenario, where it is likely headed towards, etc. An application in the process industry is pattern matching of time series generated in a chemical plant during the evolving stages of abnormality. It should be noted that in general, in these kind of problems, we cannot predefine the set of classes. Even if we could define classes, the training instances available from each class will be very small to train a classifier. In general, the user will be interested in knowing the similar situations in the past. Also, it is desirable to match reliably the time series in the early stages of some interesting behavior / abnormal event which is typically of short duration. In section 5, we show how MSKLV models can be applied in one such application.

In the next section, we give an overview the wavelet analysis and its advantages for time series applications. In section 3 we introduce the notation and bring out how kernel latent variable models can be utilized in modeling the nonlinear correlations between variables. In section 4 we give the proposed methodology for time series pattern matching. In section 5 we explain experiments carried out on Tennesse Eastman(TE) plant time series data and discuss the results.

2 Wavelet Analysis of Time Series

Wavelet transforms are popular in many engineering and computing fields. Wavelets can model irregular data patterns such as sharp jumps and dips, better than the Fourier transform and other standard statistical procedures, such as splines [11]. In the following overview of wavelet analysis, $\mathbf{R}$ denotes the real line and $L^2(\mathbf{R})$ denotes the space of square integrable real functions defined on $\mathbf{R}$. A wavelet $\psi(t) \in L^2(\mathbf{R})$ is a function with the following basic properties:

$$\int_{\mathbf{R}} \psi(t)dt = 0 \;\; and \;\; \int_{\mathbf{R}} \psi^2(t)dt = 1 \tag{1}$$

Wavelets can be used to create a family of time-frequency functions, $\psi_{\eta,\tau}(t) = \eta^{\frac{1}{2}}\psi(\eta t - \tau)$, via the dilation factor η and the translation τ. It is common to discretize these parameters dyadically as, $\eta = 2^m$, $\tau = 2^m k$, $(m, k) \in \mathbf{Z}^2$. We also require a scaling function $\phi(t) \in L^2(\mathbf{R})$ with the following basic properties:

$$\int_{\mathbf{R}} \phi(t)dt \neq 0 \;\; and \;\; \int_{\mathbf{R}} \phi^2(t)dt = 1 \tag{2}$$

Any signal can be decomposed into its contributions from multiple scales as a weighted sum of dyadically discretized orthonormal basis functions:

$$y(t) = \sum_{m=1}^{L} \sum_{k=1}^{N} d_{m,k}\psi_{m,k}(t) + \sum_{k=1}^{N} a_{L,k}\phi_{L,k}(t) \tag{3}$$

Widely used wavelets in time series analysis are Daubechies and Symmlet. More details can be found in [12]. The dyadic decomposition in discrete wavelet transform may not be suitable when wavelets are used for feature extraction, because of downsampling of the coefficients at coarser scales. This problem can be avoided by using Stationary Wavelet Transform (SWT), wherein at coarser scales we do integer discretization, without downsampling. The wavelet coefficients are no longer orthonormal to each other, leading to approximate decorrelation [3]. This overcomplete wavelet decomposition is convenient for feature extraction, including the Multi Scale Latent Variable models we are proposing for time series pattern matching. Figure 1 shows the stationary wavelet decomposition of a sample time series (explained in section 5) using $db4$ wavelet. It can be seen that detailed coefficients at scales d_5 and d_6 capture the non-stationary behavior in time series shown in Figure 2a. It should be noted that each of the variable time series is decomposed separately, and the correlation between variables is not considered. In next section, we introduce kernel latent variable models which explicitly model the nonlinear correlation between the variables.

3 Kernel Latent Variable Models

A latent variable model is a class of statistical models that relate a set of variables to a set of latent variables. These models find orthogonal directions (latent

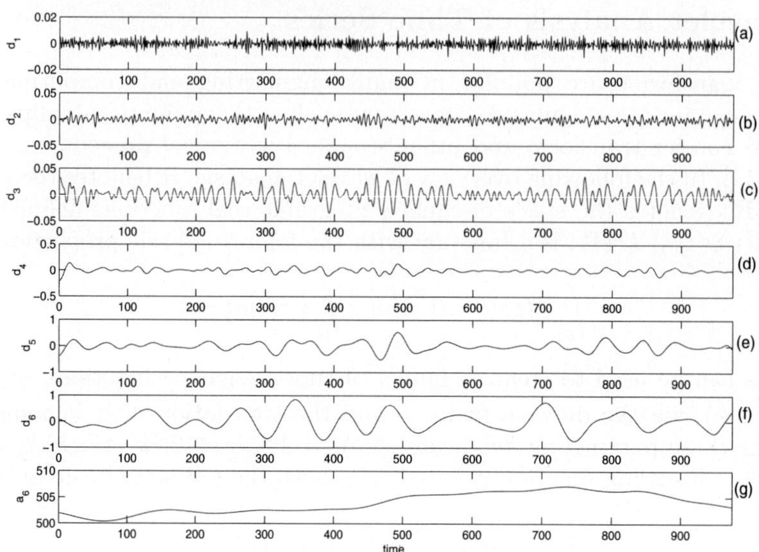

Fig. 1. Wavelet decomposition of sample time series into six scales: $d_1 - d_6$ are detailed coefficients at levels 1 to 6 (shown in (a)-(f)) and a_6 is approximate coefficient (shown in (g))

directions) of the coordinate system in which we describe the data. It is often the case that small number of latent directions are sufficient to account for most of the structure in data. Important among these latent variable models is Principal Component Analysis (PCA). There is a related class of techniques known as Partial Least Squares (PLS) which analyzes the association between two blocks (input and output) of observed variables in terms of their latent variables.

These techniques have been elegantly extended to the kernel feature space, namely, Kernel PCA (KPCA) [5] and Kernel PLS (KPLS) [6] for handling nonlinear correlations between variables by introducing the implicit nonlinear kernel mapping into some arbitrary high dimensional space. Moreover, these models solve essentially a linear problem in this higher dimensional space. These extensions of latent variable models have been successfully used in different feature extraction and model development tasks [10]. The limitation with these methods is that they assume data to be independently and identically distributed (i.i.d). But, time series data will have temporal dependency which we try to approximately decorrelate using wavelet domain analysis and apply kernel latent variable modeling techniques for handling nonlinear correlations among the variables.

Consider the time series of measurements from a system. Generally, for a physical system, we can segregate certain measured variables as input variables $\bar{\mathbf{x}} = [x_1 \ldots x_L]'$ and output variables $\bar{\mathbf{y}} = [y_1 \ldots y_M]'$. These variables are measured over time to give input matrix $X = \bar{\mathbf{x}}_1 \ldots \bar{\mathbf{x}}_T$ and output matrix $Y = \bar{\mathbf{y}}_1 \ldots \bar{\mathbf{y}}_T$. In PCA the input and output matrices are pooled together by

$\mathbf{z}_i = [\bar{\mathbf{x}}'_i, \bar{\mathbf{y}}'_i]'$ $i = 1 \ldots T$ during analysis. But PLS distinguishes between them and tries to model the relationship between input and output measurements.

3.1   Kernel PCA

In PCA we analyze the covariance matrix. Analogously in KPCA we analyze the covariance matrix in the feature space defined by $\Phi : \mathbf{R}^{L+M} \mapsto F$. The covariance matrix in F is:

$$C = \frac{1}{T} \sum_{i=1}^{T} \Phi(\mathbf{z}_i)\Phi(\mathbf{z}_i)' \tag{4}$$

It is shown in [5] that the principal components in this feature space can be obtained by eigen decomposition of kernel matrix $K = \Phi(\mathbf{z}_i)'\Phi(\mathbf{z}_j)$, $i, j = 1, 2, \ldots T$. Thus extracted eigen vectors model the structure in data. The dominant eigen vectors are represented by $B_{KPCA} = [\bar{\mathbf{v}}_1 \ldots \bar{\mathbf{v}}_{nlv}]$ where, $\bar{\mathbf{v}}$ represents an eigen vector of K and nlv is number of latent vectors retained to represent the structure of data.

3.2   Kernel PLS

Kernel Partial Least Squares(KPLS) is a method based on implicit nonlinear projection of input variables and finds latent variables by modeling the relationship between the nonlinearly mapped inputs and the output variables. Compared to Wald's PLS method, the KPLS uses transpose of input matrix. Hence XX' matrix is replaced by Kernel matrix, $K_{i,j} = \Phi(\mathbf{x}_i)'\Phi(\mathbf{x}_j)$, $i, j = 1 \ldots T$ and iterations are performed as in Wald's traditional PLS method, given below:

1. Randomly initialize output score vector $\mathbf{u}$
2. $\mathbf{t} = KK'\mathbf{u}$, $\mathbf{t} \leftarrow \mathbf{t}/\|\mathbf{t}\|$
3. $\mathbf{c} = Y'\mathbf{t}$
4. $\mathbf{u} = Y\mathbf{c}$, $\mathbf{u} \leftarrow \mathbf{u}/\|\mathbf{u}\|$
5. Repeat steps 2. - 4. until convergence
6. Deflate K and Y matrices: $K \leftarrow (I - \mathbf{t}\mathbf{t}')K(I - \mathbf{t}\mathbf{t}')$ and $Y \leftarrow Y - \mathbf{t}\mathbf{t}'Y$
7. Repeat steps 1 through 6, nlv times to obtain $U = [\mathbf{u}_1, \mathbf{u}_2 \ldots \mathbf{u}_{nlv}]$, and $T = [\mathbf{t}_1, \mathbf{t}_2 \ldots \mathbf{t}_{nlv}]$.

The overall matrix of regression which represents Kernel Latent Variable PLS model can be shown to be [6]: $B_{KPLS} = KU(T'KU)^{-1}T'Y$.

4   Time Series Pattern Matching Using MSKLV Models

The time series pattern matching algorithm retrieves the similar patterns from the database for a user provided multivariate query time series, Q. The stationary wavelet decomposition is applied for the time series of each variable in the query separately. Dominant coefficients are selected from last few detailed scales. Which scales are to be retained is decided based on the magnitude of wavelet coefficients. In our experiments, we found the detailed scales 5 and 6 to capture

Table 1. Algorithm for time series pattern matching using MSKLV model

<table>
<tr><td>

$[Similar\,Patterns]\;=\;MSKLV\,Model(Q,\;DB)$
1. Decompose each variable time series in Q with selected wavelet $= Q_w$
      (a) Choose the dominant detailed scales for analysis
      (b) Choose the important coefficients in those scales
2. Form latent variable analysis matrix/ces at each scale by the union of important coefficients of different variables
3. Apply the Latent variable model at each scale, retain latent vectors which capture 90% of variance
4. For each of the time series in the database DB, apply the procedure 1 through 3 (here same scale coefficients are selected)
      (a) Form Analysis matrix/ces at each scale
      (b) Apply the latent variable model at each scale
      (c) Find the corresponding similarity at each scale
     w.r.t Q found in step 3 using equation 5.
      (d) Overall similarity is found by summing similarities at different scales (using eqn 5)
5. The similarity values found in step 4 are ranked and top 10 matches are given as output of algorithm:
     "$Similar\,Patterns$"

</td></tr>
</table>

significant changes in time series. Figure 2b shows detailed coefficients at level 6 of decomposition using *db*4 wavelet. The coefficients which are above and below twice the standard deviation level (shown by horizontal lines in Figure 2b) represent the points of interesting changes as can be seen by dashed lines projected onto the original time series shown in Figure 2b. The same steps are carried out for time series of different variables. Union of these coefficients from the time series for different variables at the same scale are used in forming the analysis matrices for MSKLV models for time series pattern matching (in MSKPLS we have two matrices at each scale: input and output variable matrices). We develop an MSKLV model at dominant scales. The latent variable directions represent the signature for the query time series.

Similarly, wavelet decomposition is performed for each of the time series from the database (by retaining the same scale and position of coefficients as that of query time series), and the latent variable model at chosen scales of query time series is applied. The angular similarity between latent directions for each of the time series in the database is found out with respect to the query time series. The similarity metric in the latent variable space is given by:

$$S_{LV} = \sum_{s=1}^{scales} \sum_{i=1}^{nlv_s} cos(\theta_{s,i}) \tag{5}$$

where $\theta_{s,i}$ is the angle between i^{th} latent vector of query time series latent variable model at particular scale s and the corresponding latent vector of a time series data in the database at the same scale.

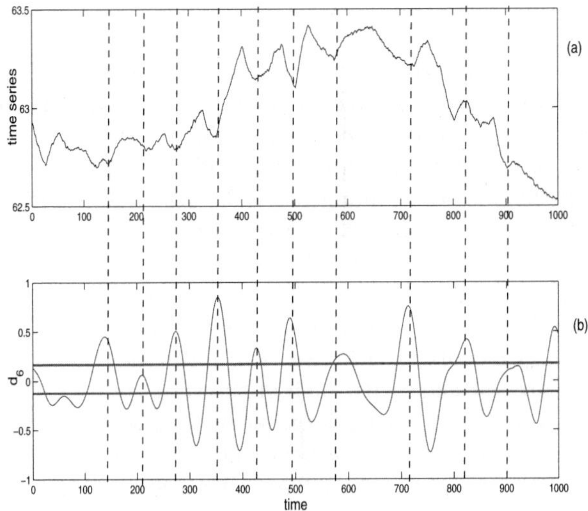

Fig. 2. The sharp changes in time series in (a) are captured by sixth scale detailed coefficients in (b)

5   Experiments and Discussion

In this paper, we apply the time series pattern matching algorithm developed in previous sections for the time series data generated using Tennesse Eastman challenge problem [4]. It resembles an actual chemical plant, has large number of process variables and is highly nonlinear. It allows simulation of a variety of disturbances (20 different disturbances, IDV(1) to IDV(20): 7 step disturbances, one slow drift, two sticking valve disturbances, 5 random variations, 5 unknown variations) which are similar to that found in real world plants.

Our focus is on matching the time series data generated during evolving/ incipient stages of abnormal events. In chemometrics literature, there are established methods for abnormality detection using latent variable [1] and multi-scale models [2]. In [7], the query time series is matched with the whole of historical database (containing both normal and abnormal data) by a moving window using PCA based angular similarity measure. This approach neither accounts for nonstationary behavior in time series, nor nonlinear correlations among variables. In this work, it is assumed that the abnormality is already detected using the established methods ([1], [2]) in evolving stages. The time series which represents the evolving stages of the abnormality is the query time series, and it is matched with the library of abnormal event time series from the historical database. We develop MSKLV model for query time series and for each time series in database, and find similarity based on the angle between latent vectors as explained in the algorithm given in Table 1. This will simplify the task of query matching over whole database and reduce computational cost significantly compared to procedure followed in [7].

The historical time series database is generated using simulations as suggested in [7]. There were 386 instances of disturbances with durations set randomly between 20 to 96 hours in the database, without any set point changes. After each disturbance, process is restored back to normal operation. The total time period for disturbance and relaxation period which brings the process to normal operation is 144 hours. Four query time series for each disturbance are generated after performing the set point changes: SP(1)-SP(4), amounting to total of 80 query time series. The set point change while generating query time series ensures that the generalization results of time series pattern matching are realistic compared to performance of the methods on real world data. The disturbance time is set randomly between 5 to 10 hours as compared to 20 to 96 hours while generating the disturbances in the historical database. These shorter duration query time series are matched with each of the time series in the database, with disturbance start point to the length of query time series using MSKLV model matching algorithm explained in Table 1. This process is repeated by moving the query time series across the disturbance time series for 5 minutes length of data. This process is repeated 100 times, covering about initial 18 hours of data from database. The average overall similarity of query time series with the disturbance time series in the database is the average of 100 such similarity values. For a given query time series, average similarity values with respect to different time series in the database are found, and the top 10 most similar time series matches are retrieved.

The wavelet function used in decomposing the time series is *db*4. The variable time series is decomposed into 6 scales. The fifth and sixth scales are used in the analysis and the dominant coefficients are chosen from sixth scale is shown in Figure 2b (above and below horizontal lines) for IDV(12) disturbance for agitator speed variable time series [4].

For MSKLV model, Gaussian kernel and polynomial kernel were used. The Gaussian kernel is seen to give better results. The *nlv* is chosen such that 90% of the variance in kernel matrix is retained.

The results of time series pattern matching are shown in Table 2. We use the evaluation measures precision, recall and F-measure used in information retrieval. Precision, P is ratio of intersection between relevant disturbance time series matches and total number of time series retrieved, to total number of time series retrieved. Similarly, recall, R is defined as ratio of intersection between relevant disturbance time series matches and total number of time series retrieved, to relevant disturbance time series matches retrieved. The F-measure combines these two measures: $F = 2(P * R)/(P + R)$.

We conducted experiments using MSPCA and MSPLS models for comparison. It can be seen that MSKPCA and MSKPLS models perform better for each kind of disturbance. Overall, the MSKPLS performs better with an average F-measure of 0.82 (0.78 with MSKPCA and less than 0.7 for MSPCA and MSPLS). It is to be noted that the five disturbances (3, 9, 11, 15 and 16) cannot be detected with high degree of accuracy [1], and for these disturbances the F-measure is found to be low for all models. Without considering these disturbances the average

Table 2. Performance comparison of different MSLV models on disturbances (1-20) query time series matching in terms of F-measure

model($\downarrow$) IDV($\rightarrow$)	1	2	3	4	5	6	7	8	9	10
$MSPCA$	0.82	0.75	0.37	0.85	0.67	0.77	0.63	0.72	0.29	0.56
$MSPLS$	0.88	0.79	0.32	0.88	0.68	0.73	0.78	0.82	0.39	0.59
$MSKPCA$	0.92	0.92	0.47	0.95	0.92	0.96	0.92	0.89	0.45	0.92
$MSKPLS$	0.97	0.98	0.38	0.99	0.94	0.97	0.92	0.96	0.54	0.93
model($\downarrow$) IDV($\rightarrow$)	11	12	13	14	15	16	17	18	19	20
$MSPCA$	0.55	0.68	0.57	0.73	0.34	0.22	0.77	0.75	0.47	0.76
$MSPLS$	0.45	0.75	0.78	0.72	0.38	0.56	0.76	0.69	0.48	0.69
$MSKPCA$	0.56	0.87	0.78	0.79	0.38	0.33	0.78	0.88	0.63	0.93
$MSKPLS$	0.49	0.99	0.96	0.99	0.56	0.22	0.89	0.92	0.64	0.96

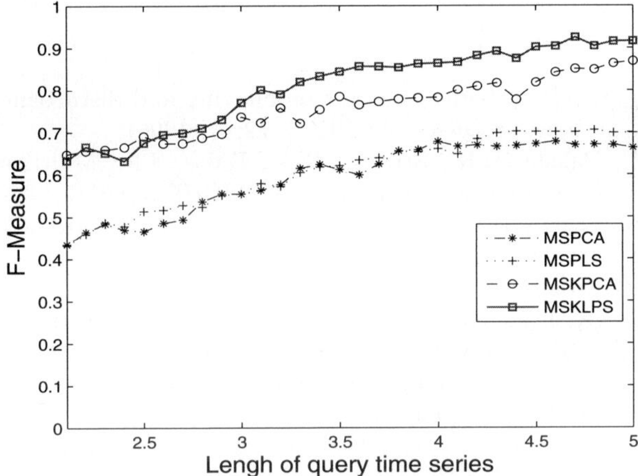

Fig. 3. F-measure for different pattern matching methods with increasing query length

F-measure is 0.95 with MSKPLS (0.89 with MSKPCA and less than 0.75 for MSPCA and MSPLS models). The higher accuracy of MSKPLS compared to MSKPCA may be due to explicit input-output modeling capability of MSKPLS.

A series of these experiments are conducted with increasing length of time series query. Figure 3 shows the average F-measure values for different models with increasing length (2 Hours to 5 Hours in steps of 10 minute length) of the query time series. It can be seen that the MSKPLS performs better than other models. With 2 hour length query time series, the average F-measure for MSKPLS and MSKPCA is approximately 0.65 which is greater than the corresponding value of 0.45 for MSPCA and MSPLS. Therefore, it can be inferred that multiscale kernel latent variable models perform better while matching the time series in the early stages of disturbances.

6   Conclusion and Future Work

In this paper the Multi Scale Kernel Latent Variable(MSKLV) models namely Multi Scale Kernel PCA (MSKPCA) and Multi Scale Kernel PLS (MSKPLS) are proposed for nonlinear time series pattern matching problem. We used multi-scale analysis method, wavelet decomposition, for capturing the non-stationary portions of time series and kernel latent variable models for modeling the non-linear correlation between variables. These methods are applied for the time series pattern matching of evolving disturbances of simulated chemical plant. It is found that the MSKLV models perform better (in terms of F-measure of greater than 90%) for time series pattern matching of TE challenge problem compared to other multi-scale models multi-scale PCA and PLS. Also, MSKLV methods can be reliably used for matching time series with short length.

References

1. Raich, A., Cinar, A.: Statistical process monitoring and disturbance diagnosis in multivariable contnous processes. AICHE J. 42(4) (1996)
2. Aradhye, H.B., Bakshi, B.R., Strauss, R.A., Davis, J.F.: Multiscale SPC using wavelets - theoretical analysis and properties. AICHE J. 49(4), 939–958 (2003)
3. Nason, G.P., Silverman, B.W.: The stationary wavelet transform and some statistical applications. In: Antoniadis, A., Oppenheim, G. (eds.) Wavelets and Statistics. Lecture Notes in Statistics, pp. 281–299 (1995)
4. Downs, J.J., Vogel, E.F.: A plant-wide industrial process control problem. Computers Chem. Engng. 17(3), 245–255 (1993)
5. Schölkopf, B., Smola, A.J., Müller, K.R.: Nonlinear component analysis as a kernel eigenvalue problem. Neural Computation 10(5), 1299–1319 (1998)
6. Rosipal, R., Trejo, L.J.: Kernel partial least squares regression in reproducing kernel hilbert space. JMLR 2, 97–123 (2001)
7. Singhal, A., Seborg, D.E.: Evaluation of a pattern matching method for the Tennessee Eastman challenge process. Journal of Process Control 16(6), 601–613 (2006)
8. Vapnik, V.N.: The Nature of Statistical Learning Theory. Springer, Berlin (1995)
9. Percival, D.B., Walden, A.T.: Wavelet methods for time series analysis. Cambridge Series in Statistical and Probabilistic Mathematics (2000)
10. Sohara, K., Kotani, M.: Application of kernel principal components analysis to pattern recognitions. In: Proceedings of the 41st SICE Annual Conference, pp. 750–752 (2002)
11. Chan, K., Fu, A.W.: Efficient time series matching by wavelets. In: Proceeding in 15th International conference on Data Engineering, pp. 126–133 (1999)
12. Strang, G., Nguyen, T.: Wavelets and Filter Banks. Wellesley-Cambridge Press (1997)

On-line Algorithm for Extraction of Specific Signals with Temporal Structure

Ewaldo Santana[1,2], André B. Cavalcante[3], Marcio de O. Santos[1], Allan Barros[3], and R.C.S. Freire[1]

[1] Federal University of Campina Grande. Campina Grande, PB, Brazil
[2] Faculdade Atenas Maranhense. São Luís, MA, Brazil
[3] Federal University of Maranhao. São Luís, MA, Brazil
ewaldosantana@ieee.org
allan@ufma.br

Abstract. Blind source separation techniques based on statistical independence criteria require a large number of data samples to estimate higher-order statistics. Thus, those techniques are not suitable to either on-line adaptive modeling. In this work we developed both an online and a batch algorithms for semi-blind extraction of a desired source signal with temporal structure from linear mixtures . Here, we do not assume that sources are statistically independent but we use an *a priori* information about the autocorrelation function of primary sources to extract the desired signal. Also, we develop an analytical framework to guarantee convergence of the online algorithm based on second-order statistics. Extensive computer simulations and real data applications confirm the validity and high performance of the proposed algorithms.

Keywords: On-line algorithm, ICA, BSS.

1   Introduction

Blind source separation (BSS) techniques based on statistical independence criteria such as Independent Component Analysis (ICA) require a large number of data samples to estimate higher-order statistics (HOS), density functions, entropies, so on [1]. Also, ICA assumes that the underlying sources must have non-Gaussian distributions. Thus, those techniques are not suitable to either on-line adaptive modeling, or extraction of arbitrarily distributed sources.

On the other hand, algorithms based only on second-order statistics (SOS) such as the Least Mean Square (LMS) [2] are very advantageous to on-line implementations. Further, SOS allows us to study algorithms' convergence behavior. And to our knowledge, there is no work which emphasizes the convergence of ICA algorithms. Therefore, it could be very interesting if we eliminate ICA limitations using an online SOS algorithm to extract arbitrarily distributed sources including Gaussian ones.

Indeed, some biomedical sources signal are characterizing by extremely low values of normalized kurtosis and due to nonstationarities, their distribution may change in time [3].

M. Ishikawa et al. (Eds.): ICONIP 2007, Part II, LNCS 4985, pp. 21–29, 2008.

In this work we propose an online algorithm based on the Barros and Cichocki's algorithm [4] that guarantees, under certain decorrelation constraints, the extraction of any arbitrarily distributed source. Also, we include an analysis of the algorithm's convergence along with results of simulations.

2   Methods

Let us denote the source signal vector at time k as $\mathbf{s}(k) = [s_1(k), \cdots, s_n(k)]^{\mathrm{T}}$. In the model, the observed vector $\mathbf{x}(k) = [x_1(k), \cdots, x_n(k)]^{\mathrm{T}}$ results for linearly mixing the source signals. Thus, this mixture can be written as $\mathbf{x}(k) = \mathbf{A}\mathbf{s}(k)$, where $\mathbf{A}$ is an n x n nonsingular matrix.

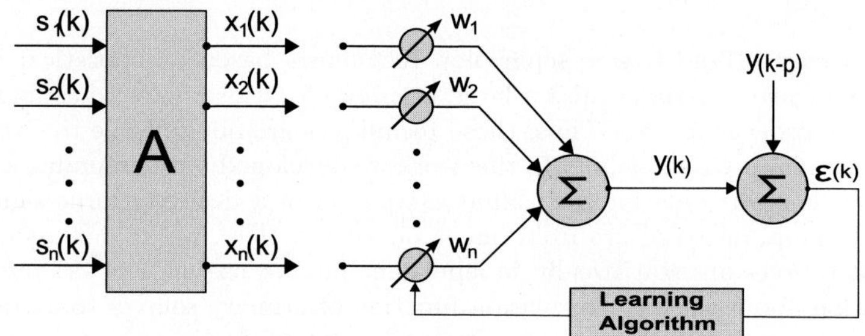

Fig. 1. Block diagram of model

We assume here that the source signals have temporal structure and different autocorrelation functions, but they are not necessarily statistically independent [4]. Let us suppose that for a specific time delay τ_i the following relations hold:

$$E[s_i(k)s_i(k - \tau_i)] \neq 0$$
$$E[s_i(k)s_j(k - \tau_i)] = 0 \quad \forall\, i \neq j. \tag{1}$$

For ease of use, throughout this paper, let us define the following notation: $\mathbf{x}_k = \mathbf{x}(k)$, $\mathbf{w}_k = \mathbf{w}(k)$, $\varepsilon_k = \varepsilon(k)$, $y_k = y(k)$ and $y_p = y(k - p)$.

To extract one source signal $s_i(k)$, we use a simple processing unit described as $y_k = \mathbf{w}_k^{\mathrm{T}}\mathbf{x}_k$, shown in Figure 1, where y_k is the output signal, $\mathbf{w}_k$ is the weight vector and

$$\varepsilon_k = y_k - y_p, \tag{2}$$

where p is a specific time delay.

Under these conditions, Barros and Cichocki [4] developed a batch algorithm which can extract one source signal from a mixture using the following learning rule:

$$\mathbf{w} = E[\mathbf{x}y_p], \qquad ||\mathbf{w}|| = 1. \tag{3}$$

The algorithm's output $y(k)$ equals one source signal $s_i(k)$ when the mean squared error $E[\varepsilon^2(k)]$ is minimum.

Defining a performance vector as

$$\mathbf{c} = \mathbf{A}^{\mathrm{T}}\mathbf{w}. \tag{4}$$

We obtain that at the convergence this is equal to:

$$\mathbf{c} = \mathbf{A}^{\mathrm{T}}\mathbf{w}_* = \beta \mathbf{e}_i, \tag{5}$$

where $\mathbf{w}_*$ is the optimal weight vector, β is a nonzero scalar and $\mathbf{e}_i = [\, e_1 \; e_2 \ldots e_n \,]$ is a canonical basis vector, that is, $e_i = \pm 1$ and $e_l = 0, \forall l \neq i$.
We can simplify that learning rule by noting that:

$$\begin{aligned}
\mathbf{w} &= \mathrm{E}[\mathbf{x}y_p] \\
&= \mathrm{E}[\mathbf{x}\mathbf{w}^{\mathrm{T}}\mathbf{x}_p] \\
&= \mathrm{E}[\mathbf{x}\mathbf{x}_p^{\mathrm{T}}]\mathbf{w}.
\end{aligned} \tag{6}$$

Now, we can define the matrix $\mathbf{R} = \mathrm{E}[\mathbf{x}\mathbf{x}_p^{\mathrm{T}}]$, and putting it before learning. Thus, we obtain a lower computational cost learning rule defined as

$$\mathbf{w}(k+1) = \mathbf{R}\mathbf{w}(k). \tag{7}$$

Eq. (7) define our proposal to a batch algorithm for semi-blind extraction of a desired signal (source of interest).

2.1   Learning Algorithm

In order to develop an online algorithm, we remember that from LMS algorithm we have the following learning rule [2],

$$\mathbf{w}_{k+1} = \mathbf{w}_k - \mu \varepsilon_k \mathbf{x}_k, \tag{8}$$

where the constant μ is the step size parameter controlling the stability and rate of convergence.
From Eq. (2) we see that,

$$\varepsilon_k = \mathbf{x}_k^{\mathrm{T}}\mathbf{w}_k - \mathbf{x}_p^{\mathrm{T}}\mathbf{w}_k. \tag{9}$$

Multiplying both side of Eq. (9) for $\mathbf{x}_k$, we obtain

$$\mathbf{x}_k \varepsilon = (\mathbf{x}_k\mathbf{x}_k^{\mathrm{T}} - \mathbf{x}_k\mathbf{x}_p^{\mathrm{T}})\mathbf{w}_k. \tag{10}$$

Substituting Eq. (10) into Eq. (8), we have the following learning rule to updating the weights:

$$\mathbf{w}_{k+1} = \mathbf{w}_k - \mu(\mathbf{x}_k\mathbf{x}_k^{\mathrm{T}} - \mathbf{x}_k\mathbf{x}_p^{\mathrm{T}})\mathbf{w}_k. \tag{11}$$

2.2 Convergence Behavior

In order to find the algorithm's convergence condition, let us define the deviation vector $\mathbf{v}_k = \mathbf{w}_k - \mathbf{w}^*$, where $\mathbf{w}^* = \mathrm{E}[\mathbf{x}_k\mathbf{x}_k^{\mathrm{T}}]\mathrm{E}[y_p\mathbf{x}_k]$ is the optimal weight. Assuming that $\mathbf{x}$ is white (of very common use in ICA), the matrix $\mathrm{E}[\mathbf{x}_k\mathbf{x}_k^{\mathrm{T}}] = \mathbf{I}$. This way, $\mathbf{w}^*$ is given by:

$$\mathbf{w}_* = \mathrm{E}[\mathbf{x}_k y_p] \tag{12}$$

Thus, Eq. (11) can be rewritten as:

$$\begin{aligned}
\mathbf{v}_{k+1} &= \mathbf{v}_k - \mu(\mathbf{x}_k\mathbf{x}_k^{\mathrm{T}} - \mathbf{x}_k\mathbf{x}_p^{\mathrm{T}})(\mathbf{v}_k - \mathbf{w}^*) \\
&= \mathbf{v}_k - \mu(\mathbf{x}_k\mathbf{x}_k^{\mathrm{T}} - \mathbf{x}_k\mathbf{x}_p^{\mathrm{T}})\mathbf{v}_k,
\end{aligned} \tag{13}$$

due $\mathbf{w}^* = \mathbf{0}$ in the v-axes.

Taking the expected value of Eq. (13) over k yields

$$\mathrm{E}[\mathbf{v}_{k+1}] = \left(\mathbf{I} - \mu\mathbf{R}_{kp}\right)\mathrm{E}[\mathbf{v}_k], \tag{14}$$

where $\mathbf{R}_{kp} = \mathrm{E}[\mathbf{x}_k\mathbf{x}_k^{\mathrm{T}}] - \mathrm{E}[\mathbf{x}_k\mathbf{x}_p^{T}]$.

Now, using the normal form $\mathbf{R}_{kp} = \mathbf{Q}\boldsymbol{\Lambda}\mathbf{Q}^{-1}$, where $\mathbf{Q}$ and $\boldsymbol{\Lambda}$ are the eigenvectors and eigenvalues matrices respectively, we can rewritten Eq. (14) as,

$$\begin{aligned}
\mathrm{E}[\mathbf{v}_{k+1}] &= \left(\mathbf{I} - \mu\mathbf{Q}\boldsymbol{\Lambda}\mathbf{Q}^{-1}\right)\mathrm{E}[\mathbf{v_k}] \\
&= \mathbf{Q}\mathbf{Q}^{-1}\mathrm{E}[\mathbf{v}_k] - \mu\mathbf{Q}\boldsymbol{\Lambda}\mathbf{Q}^{-1}\mathrm{E}[\mathbf{v_k}].
\end{aligned} \tag{15}$$

Let $\tilde{\mathbf{v}} = \mathbf{Q}^{-1}\mathbf{v}$ represents a rotation on weight vectors $\mathbf{v}$. This way,

$$\mathrm{E}[\mathbf{v}_{k+1}] = \mathbf{Q}\mathrm{E}[\tilde{\mathbf{v}}_k] - \mu\mathbf{Q}\boldsymbol{\Lambda}\mathrm{E}[\tilde{\mathbf{v}_k}]. \tag{16}$$

Multiplying both sides of Eq. (16) for $\mathbf{Q}^{-1}$ and after some mathematical manipulations we obtain,

$$\mathrm{E}[\tilde{\mathbf{v}}_{k+1}] = \left(\mathbf{I} - \mu\boldsymbol{\Lambda}\right)\mathrm{E}[\tilde{\mathbf{v}_k}], \tag{17}$$

which can be easily solved by induction. Starting with the initial guess $\tilde{\mathbf{v}}_0$ we obtain,

$$\mathrm{E}[\tilde{\mathbf{v}}_k] = \left(\mathbf{I} - \mu\boldsymbol{\Lambda}\right)^{\mathbf{k}}\tilde{\mathbf{v}_0}. \tag{18}$$

Thus, as k increases we see that the expected weight vector in (18) reaches the optimum solution (i.e., zero in the $\tilde{\mathbf{v}}$-axis system) only if the right side of the equation converges to zero [5]. This is satisfied by choosing μ so that,

$$0 < \mu < \frac{1}{\lambda_{max}}, \tag{19}$$

where λ_{max} is the maximum eigenvalue of $\mathbf{R}_{kp}$.

This means that if the condition given by equation (19) is met, the algorithm is seen to converge to the optimum solution:

$$\lim_{k\to\infty}[\mathbf{w}_k] = \mathbf{w}^* \tag{20}$$

3   Results

We have carried out tests intend to confirm the validity of the algorithms defined by the learning rules in Eq. (7) and Eq. (11), and to analyze the convergence behavior of the on-line algorithm defined in Eq. (11). We illustrate the performances by the following examples.

3.1   Example 1

Here, we tested the online algorithm which is given by Eq. (11). We have selected four statistically independent source signals as shown in Figure 2 and we mixed them by randomly generating mixing matrices. The electrocardiogram signal has been chosen as desired source in the extraction. For this, we have set the step size $\mu = 0.04$ and time delay $p = 1.28$ seconds.

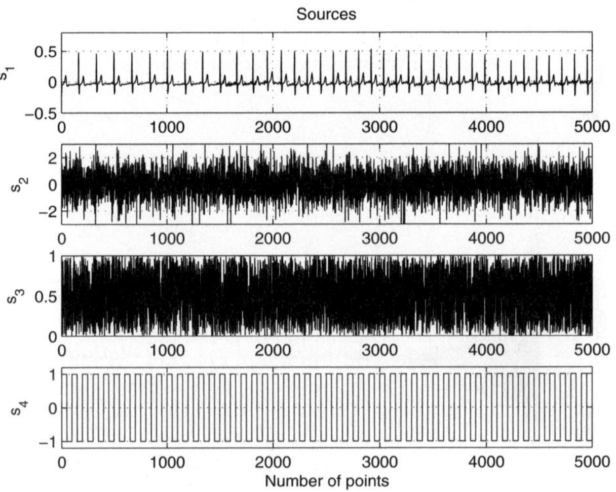

Fig. 2. Four statistically independent source signals. (s_1) Electrocardiogram signal. (s_2) Gaussian signal. (s_3) Uniformly distributed signal. (s_4) the square signal.

As results, the temporal behavior of the performance vector c defined by Eq. (10) and the output of the extraction algorithm are shown in Figures 3 and 4, respectively.

3.2   Example 2

In this example, we have tested the batch algorithm given by Eq. (7) for real-world data - the fetal magnetocardiography (fMCG) [6]. A total of 37 channels were available for analysis. Figure 5 shows ten seconds from five of these channels.

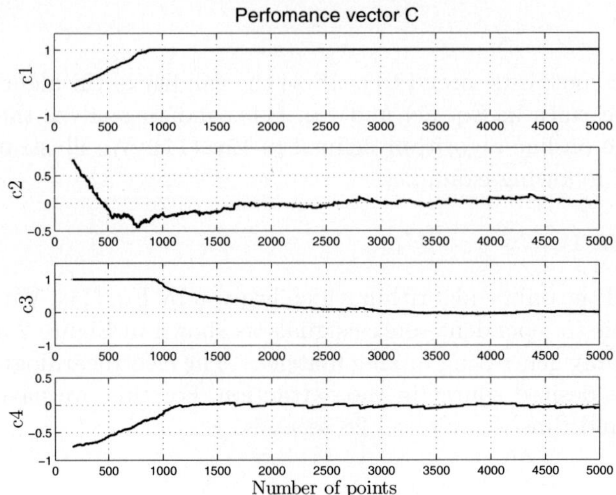

Fig. 3. Performance vector behavior

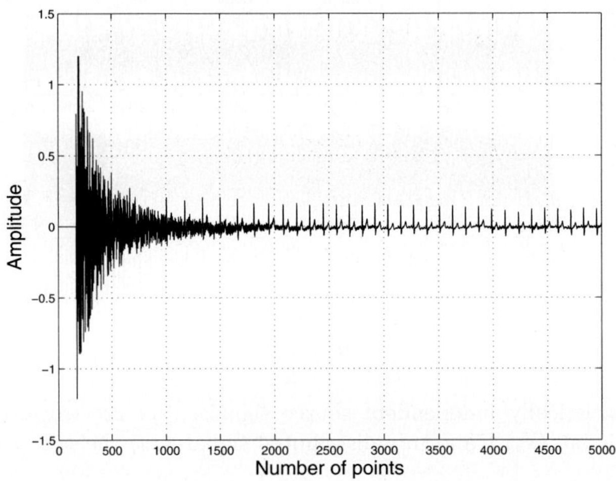

Fig. 4. Output of the on-line algorithm in a trial where we used $\mu = 0.04$ and $p = 1.28$ seconds.

We applied the proposed algorithm to extract both the fetal and maternal MCG. To estimate the appropriate time delays, we have analyzed the values of p, that maximize the autocorrelation function $\varsigma(p) = \mathrm{E}[x_j(t)x_j(t - p)]$, shown in Figure 6. Since the fetal heartbeat rate is normally higher than mother's, than the first peak in $p = 0.4$ seconds should corresponds to the fetal signal and the second one in $p = 0.8$ seconds, to the mother's. In Figure 7 one can see the extracted signals.

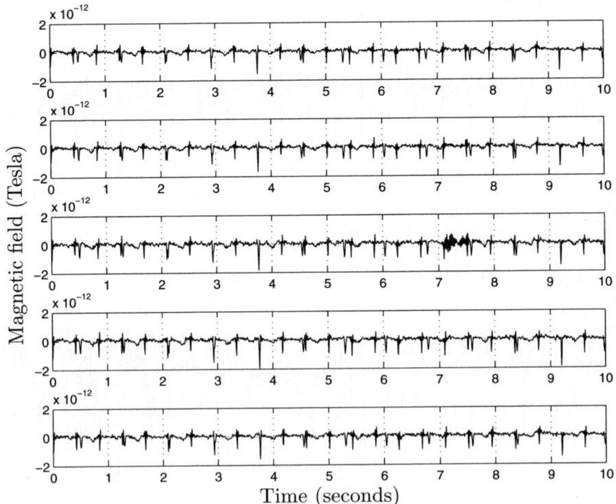

Fig. 5. Ten seconds of raw data, from five of the 37 channels of the fetal MCG contaminated by the signal from the maternal heart

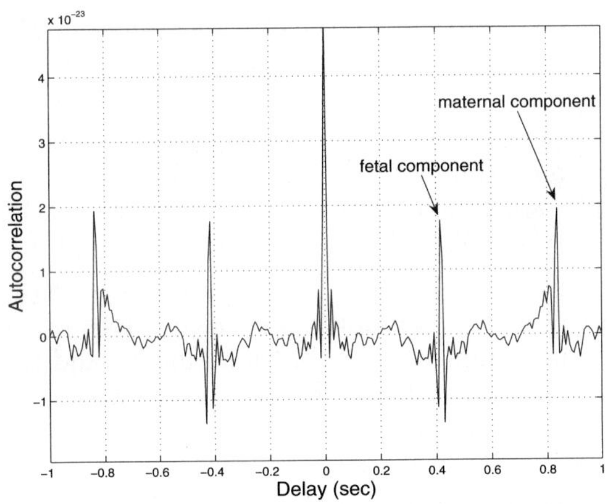

Fig. 6. Autocorrelation of one signal in Figure 5

4   Discussion

The simulations results show that the online and batch algorithms worked efficiently.

In the on-line case, since the Eq 19 holds, the convergence of the algorithm is guaranteed. In order to analyze the algorithm's convergence, one must observe the temporal behavior of the performance vector which is defined Eq. 4. In convergence, the performance vector tends towards one vector of canonical basis.

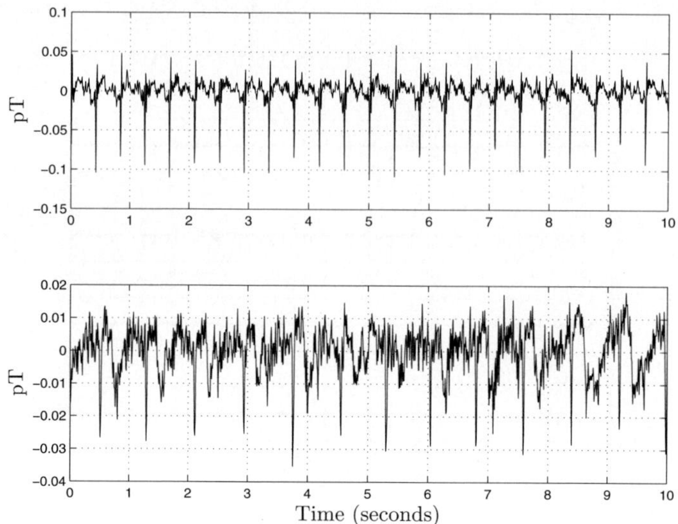

Fig. 7. Separated components. (a) from the fetal MCG. (b) from the maternal MCG

In example 1, the task is to extract the electrocardiogram signal from mixtures with other three sources using the on-line algorithm. The time delay $p = 165$ was chosen based on *a priori* knowledge of the electrocardiogram signal's period.

According to Figure 3, the performance vector approximating one of the canonical basis vectors around 1000 iterations. Furthermore, in Figure 4, the convergence is emphasized while the electrocardiogram signal is being recovered.

On the other hand, the batch algorithm clearly offers a lower computationally rule when compared to that proposed by Barros and Cichocki [4] due to the fact that now we need to calculate the matrix **R** once before learning.

Also, we can see in example 2 that this new rule is valid to extract the signal sources. Using the appropriated time delays the algorithm was able to recover both the fetal and maternal signals as shown in Figure 7. It is important to notice that the appropriate time delay was estimated as a pre-processing step by examining the autocorrelation function $\varsigma(p)$ in Figure 6, where the fetal and the maternal component is localized at 0.4 and 0.8 seconds, respectively.

Acknowledgments. We are indebted to Carlos Estombelo-Montesco, University of São Paulo, for his assistance.

This work was supported by the Brazilian agency FAPEMA.

References

1. Hyvarinen, A.: New Approximations of Differential Entropy for Independent component Analysis and Projection Pursuit. Advances in Neural Information Processing Systems 10, 273–279 (1995)
2. Haykin, S.: Adaptive Filter Theory. Prentice-Hall, Englewood Cliffs (1991)

3. Cichocki, A., Amari, S.: Adaptive Blind Signal and Image Processing: Learning Algorithms and Applications. John Willey and Sons, London (2002)
4. Barros, A.K., Cichocki, A.: Extraction of Specific Signals with Temporal Structure. Neural Computation 13, 1995–2003 (2001)
5. Widrow, B., Stearns, S.D.: Adaptive signal Processing. Prentice Hall, Englewood Cliffs (1985)
6. Araujo, D.B., Barros, A.K., Estombelo-Montesco, C., Zhao, H., Silva Filho, A.C.R., Baffa, O., Wakai, R., Ohnishi, N.: Fetal Source Extraction from magnetocardiographic recordings by Dependent Component Analysis. Phys. Med. Biol. 50, 4457–4464 (2005)

Modified Lawn Weed Detection: Utilization of Edge-Color Based SVM and Grass-Model Based Blob Inspection Filterbank

Ukrit Watchareeruetai, Yoshinori Takeuchi, Tetsuya Matsumoto,
Hiroaki Kudo, and Noboru Ohnishi

Department of Media Science, Graduate School of Information Science,
Nagoya University, Furo-cho, Chikusa-ku, Nagoya, 464-8603 Japan
{ukrit,takeuchi,matumoto,kudo,ohnishi}@ohnishi.m.is.nagoya-u.ac.jp,
http://www.ohnishi.m.is.nagoya-u.ac.jp

Abstract. We propose a lawn weed detection method modified from our previous work, i.e., Bayesian classifier based method. The proposed method employs features calculated from not only the edge-strength of weed/lawn textures but also color information of RGB. Instead of using Bayesian classifier, we exploit more sophisticated classifier, i.e., support-vector machine, for detecting weeds. After weed detection, the proposed method uses noise blob inspection for removing misclassified weed areas. The inspection process is based on a bank of directional filters modeled from characteristics of the edge of grass blade. Experimental results show that the performance of the proposed method outperforms the compared methods.

Keywords: Lawn weed detection, edge-color information, noise blob inspection, grass-edge model, directional filter.

1   Introduction

Using herbicide is one of the popular methods for controlling weeds because it is convenient and does not take too much time. Obviously, using a large amount of herbicide, however, causes environmental pollution and also increases the cost of weeds control. Therefore a weed control method with reduction of herbicide usage or a non-chemical method is preferred. Nowadays, with the advances of image processing techniques and robotics, an automatic weed control system becomes an alternative solution for this problem. Such the system uses a camera for capturing the field or lawn image, and sends the image to a processor for detecting weeds. If the processor found a weed in the image, it controls a nozzle system for selective spraying (sometimes called spot spraying), i.e., it sprays herbicide only onto the area of detected weeds, instead of spraying uniformly the entire area. Consequently, herbicide usage can be significantly reduced. Moreover, the system may not use any nozzle system for spraying but it is equipped a non-chemical weeding device for removing weeds, e.g., using a robot arm for picking up, or using flaming or electric current to destroy weeds.

M. Ishikawa et al. (Eds.): ICONIP 2007, Part II, LNCS 4985, pp. 30–39, 2008.

Up to now, there are some works about the methods for controlling weeds in lawn based on both image processing techniques and special sensors. Mashita et al. reported their development of microwave based sensor for discriminating weeds in lawn in summer [1]. In the same work, they also reported a technique that analyzes the intensity of red band for detecting weed in winter. In [2], Kawamura et al. reported the development of tactile and photo diode sensors for detecting lawn weeds. These two types of sensors were developed for detecting weeds in autumn and winter. They also proposed a detection method based on image processing techniques. The detection method was designed for detecting ears of weeds of some species, which form in spring and have different color from lawns. In [3], Otsuka and Taniwaki proposed a lawn weed detection method based on analysis of variance of weed/lawn surfaces. Their research, however, focused on only detection of broadleaf weeds. In [4], Ahmad et al. proposed a technique using three types of classical textural features, i.e., contrast, angular second moment, and inverse difference moment, and they did the detection in block-level instead of pixel-level. In [5], they also proposed another method based on gray-scale uniformity analysis. This method employs the difference of uniformity between weed and lawn surfaces for detecting weed. After the uniformity analysis, image enhancement and blob inspection are done by considering on its area and perimeter ratio, and multiple expansion and contraction are done. They showed that the method can accurately detect weeds of round shape and medium shape groups. In addition, they proposed a method for finding the center location of detected weeds by using a grouping technique [6,7].

Recently, we proposed two methods for detecting weeds in lawn [8]. The first method, called BC method, is based on well-known Bayesian classifier [9]. It uses two features calculated from the edge image. The second method is called morphological operation based method (denoted by MO). This method exploits morphological image processing operations, e.g., closing and opening [10], for segmenting weed area from background. In [11], the performance of the two detection methods and the gray-scale uniformity analysis method were evaluated and compared using two types of simulated automatic weeding systems and using four datasets taken from four different seasons. Moreover, we proposed the method based on a fast and simple color image processing technique for detecting weeds when the color of weed and lawn are clearly different, especially in winter [12]. This color based method outperforms the compared gray-scale based methods for a winter dataset. We also proposed the method for discriminating input image taken in winter from the image taken in the other seasons. This enables us to realize a hybrid system that automatically selects to use color based or gray-scale based methods, depending on input images.

In this work, we propose a method modified from our BC method by using both edge and color information and inspecting noise blobs based on grass-edge model filterbank. In Sect. 2, we explain the detail of the proposed method. Then, Sect. 3 shows the experimental results and discussion. Finally, we conclude the paper in Sect. 4.

2   Proposed Method

2.1   Modified Lawn Weed Detection Method Using Edge-Color Information

Bayesian classifier (BC) based weed detection method was designed from the assumption that the texture of weed and lawn surfaces are different; the weed surface is quite smooth, whereas lawn surface contains a lot of edges. The BC method uses two features extracted from edge image, i.e., mean and variance of edge strength, to measure the difference of weed/lawn surfaces. The features are calculated from each pixels in the edge image using a window of size $N \times N$. Then, each pixel is classified into weed or lawn classes using Bayesian classifier.

In this work, we not only use the edge based features but also add up color information from input image. We directly use features from RGB images, i.e., the intensities of red, green, and blue bands. In most related works, to make weed detection be generalized to any seasons, color information is not used as a feature in the detection and only gray-scale based information is used because of the similarity of weed and lawn colors [3,4,5,6,7,8,11]. In fact, although the colors of weed and lawn seem to be similar when they are observed by human eyes, they are slightly different when they are observed by a digital camera. Moreover, using color information may reduce the errors caused by the soil and shadow. In the soil and shadow areas, it is possible that their textures are similar to that of the weed areas; however, their colors are clearly different from the color of weeds. In this work, we adopt more sophisticated classifier, i.e., support-vector machine (SVM) [13], for distinguishing the difference in edge and color features. Using more features, SVM can exploit the kernel method to map input features into higher dimension space where input patterns from different classes can be separated. Here we use five-dimensional feature vector as input. Similar to the BC method, each pixel in the image is classified into weed or lawn classes by using trained SVM. After weed detection, noise blob inspection is done for removing noise blobs. The flowchart of the proposed method is shown in Fig. 1.

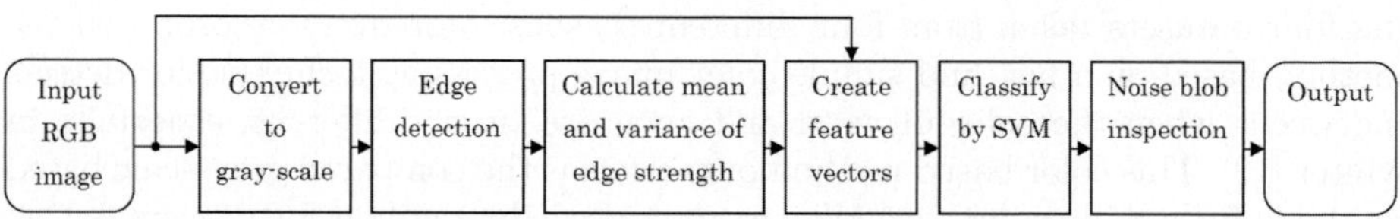

Fig. 1. Flowchart of the proposed system

2.2   Noise Blob Inspection Using Grass-Edge Model Filter

For detecting weeds in agriculture fields, many works attempt to detect only the known plant, i.e., the crop in the field, and consider the other unknown plants as weeds [14,15]. However, it is quite difficult to do that for detecting weeds in lawn fields, where the known plant is grass. As shown in Fig. 2(left), there are a

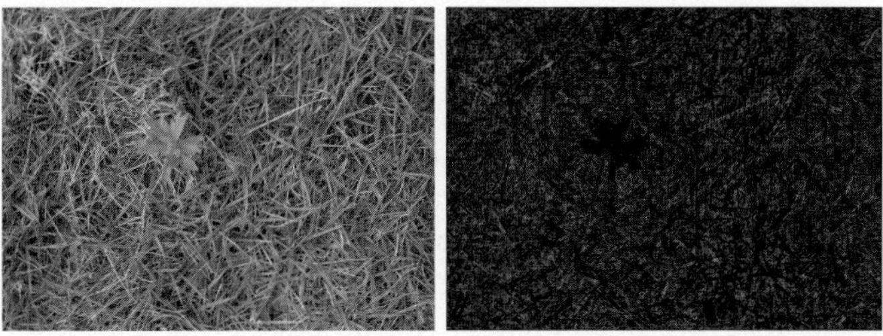

Fig. 2. Example of lawn weed image (left) and its edge image (scaled version) (right)

lot of grass blades in lawn areas. Each of them aligns in different directions, and these alignments seem to be in random-manner. Therefore no one proposes a model of grass blade and does detection in the way mentioned above. However, in this work, we try to model the edge of grass blades and design matching filters corresponding to the model. Figure 2(right) shows an example of edge image calculated by using Sobel operators [10]. We can see two nearly parallel lines caused from drastically changing at the border of grass blade, whereas the inside of the grass blade seems to have no edge due to its smoothness. Therefore there should be two peaks caused by two edge lines in the direction that is perpendicular to grass blade direction. This characteristic of the edge image can be used as a model of grass blade, i.e., composition of two peaks in cross section and two parallel lines in the grass blade direction.

From the model, we design a matching filter that has the same pattern as the edge of grass blade. The filter consists of one Gaussian distribution in the grass blade direction and two Gaussian distributions in the cross section of grass blade. Such the filter of zero degree direction is shown in Eq. 1. It is a separable filter [10].

$$G(x, y, \sigma_x, \sigma_y, d) = G(x, \sigma_x) \cdot G(y, \sigma_y, d), \tag{1}$$

$$G(x, \sigma_x) = exp\{-0.5 \cdot (\frac{x}{\sigma_x})^2\}, \tag{2}$$

$$G(y, \sigma_y, d) = exp\{-0.5 \cdot (\frac{y - \frac{d}{2}}{\sigma_y})^2\} + exp\{-0.5 \cdot (\frac{y + \frac{d}{2}}{\sigma_y})^2\}, \tag{3}$$

where the parameters x and y are coordinate of the filter and parameters σ_x and σ_y control the shape of Gaussian distributions of Eqs. 2 and 3, respectively. Parameter d controls distance between the peaks of two Gaussian distributions. Separated components (x and y components) of the proposed filter are shown in Fig. 3. To generalize the proposed filter to any direction θ, we replace x and y in the right terms of Eqs. 2 and 3 by x_θ and y_θ, respectively. The generalized form of the proposed filter can be written as Eq. 4. Figure 4 shows an example of the proposed filter of eight directions by the step of 22.5 degrees.

$$G(x, y, \sigma_x, \sigma_y, d, \theta) =$$
$$[exp\{-0.5 \cdot (\frac{x_\theta}{\sigma_x})^2\}] \times [exp\{-0.5 \cdot (\frac{y_\theta - \frac{d}{2}}{\sigma_y})^2\} + exp\{-0.5 \cdot (\frac{y_\theta + \frac{d}{2}}{\sigma_y})^2\}], \tag{4}$$

$$\begin{bmatrix} x_\theta \\ y_\theta \end{bmatrix} = \begin{bmatrix} cos\theta & sin\theta \\ -sin\theta & cos\theta \end{bmatrix} \begin{bmatrix} x \\ y \end{bmatrix}. \tag{5}$$

If the shape of the proposed filter matches an edge of grass blade, the filter should give higher response because the peaks of grass blade are multiplied with two peaks of the filter. However, when the shape of the filter does not match or the filter is convoluted to weed areas, the filter should give lower response because the peaks of the filter are multiplied with non-edge area. This characteristic of the proposed filter is exploited for discriminating noise blobs from real weed blobs. Figure 5 shows an example of filtering results of the edge image in Fig. 2(left).

In noise blob inspection, using Eq. 4, we generate a bank of n filters of various directions and shapes by changing the parameters θ, σ_x, σ_y, and d. This filter-bank is convoluted to some detected areas to calculate a feature. That feature is used for discriminating noise blobs from real weed blobs by thresholding method. The noise blob inspection is described as follows:

1. Apply closing operation to connect detected areas located in near distance.
2. Delete all blobs whose area is less than a threshold value Th_1.
3. Apply dilation operation to expand border of the remaining blobs.
4. Consider only the remaining blobs whose area is smaller than a threshold value Th_2, and convolute them with the proposed filterbank.
5. Calculate M_{ij}, i.e., the mean of intensity of the pixels located inside the jth blob convoluted by the ith filter ($i = 1, 2, 3, ..., n$, $j = 1, 2, 3, ..., m$, where m is the number of convoluted blobs).
6. Calculate VAR_j, i.e., the variance of M_{ij} over all n convoluted images.
7. Delete the jth blob if VAR_j is greater than a threshold value VAR_{max}.

The following is the reason that why we can discriminate noise blobs from weed blobs by using VAR_j. In weed areas, no filter matches to the edge of grass blade. Therefore, all values of M_{ij} are low, resulting in lower VAR_j. However, in lawn areas, there are both matched and mismatched filters. Some values of M_{ij} are high, whereas the others are low, resulting in higher VAR_j.

3   Experimental Results and Discussion

The database used in our experiments consists of four datasets taken from different seasons in Japan. It is the same database as used in [11,12]. Image size is 640×480 pixels. Each datasets contains 25 images for testing and five images for training. Five images from 25 test images contain no weed, whereas the remains of 20 images contain at least one weed. In the experiments, we combine all four datasets together. Therefore we get total 20 training images and 100 testing images. The total of weeds in the testing set is 188.

In this work, we used a support-vector machine implementation called LIB-SVM [16]. It provides support-vector machine source code for both classification

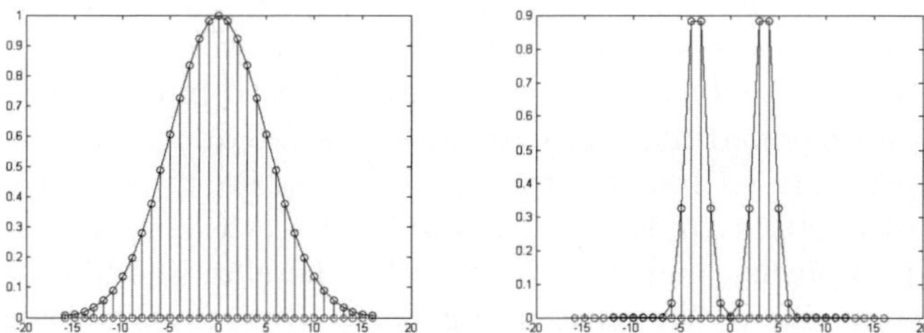

Fig. 3. Separated components of the grass-edge-model filter at direction of zero degrees. x component (left) and y component (right) are corresponding to Eqs. 2 and 3, respectively.

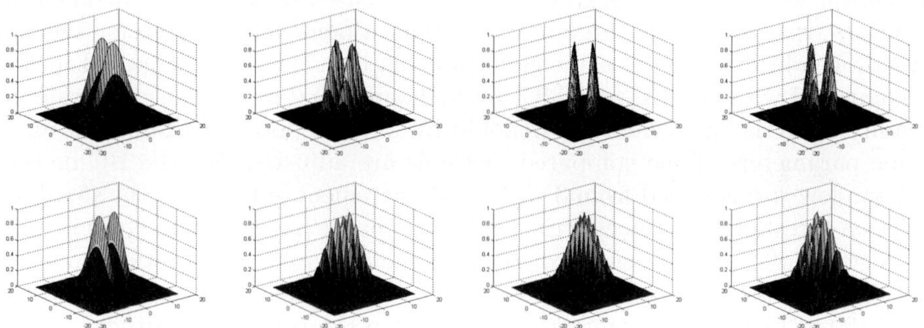

Fig. 4. Examples of eight directional grass-edge model filters. From top-left to bottom-right, the directions of filters are 0, 22.5, 45, 67.5, 90, 112.5, 135, and 157.5 degrees, respectively.

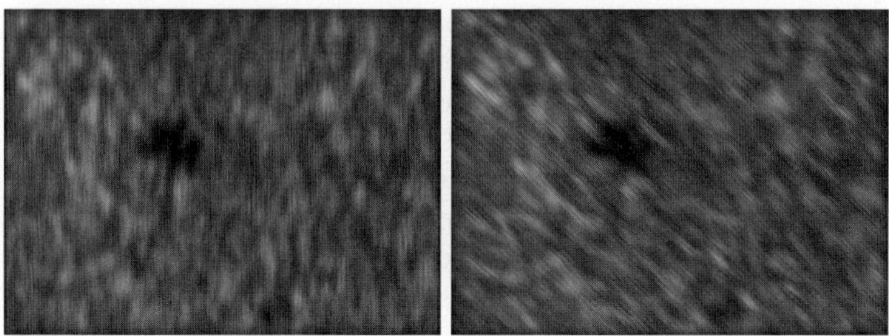

Fig. 5. Responses of the edge image in Fig. 2 filtered by the grass-edge model filters of 0 degree (left) and 45 degrees (right) directions. Note that the origin of x-y coordination is at the top-left.

and regression, and provides various types of kernel. Because training support-vector machine spends a lot of time if the number of training vectors is too high, we did not extract features from every pixels of the training images but extracted only from the pixels located at cross points of a sampling grid. The size of each blocks of the sampling grid used in this work is 16×16 pixels. By doing that, training time can be significantly reduced into an acceptable time, whereas it still preserved the characteristics of weed- and lawn-pattern models.

In the experiments, we used filterbank of the proposed filters of eight directions (0, 22.5, 45, 67.5, 90, 112.5, 135, and 157.5 degrees), three values of the distance d (8, 10, and 12 pixels), and $\sigma_x = 5$, $\sigma_y = 1$. Therefore the filterbank contains total 24 different filters. The filter size is 33×33 pixels. The threshold values Th_1, Th_2, and VAR_{max} are set to 100, 500, and 15, respectively. The type of SVM is C-SVM, the kernel type is RBF, parameters $C = 10$ and $\gamma = 0.1$. The window size used for calculating mean and variance of edge strength is varied from 3 to 15 with increment of two.

To evaluate performance of the proposed method, we simulate two types of automatic weeding systems. One is a chemical based weeding system. The other is an electrical spark discharge based system, a non-chemical system. The simulation conditions are the same conditions used in [11]. The proposed method is compared with the BC and MO methods proposed in [8] and gray-scale uniformity analysis based method (denoted by UA) proposed by Ahmad et al. [5]. Some parameters of the compared methods are adjusted. For the BC method, the window size is varied from 3 to 17 with increment of two, and the small area deletion threshold (for the electrical spark discharge based system only) is varied from 100 to 400 with increment of 100. For the MO method, structuring element is a circle of seven pixels in diameter, and small area deletion threshold is varied from 100 to 1400 with increment of 100. For the UA method, sensitivity is set to three, the window size is varied from 3 to 9 with increment of two, three pairs of blob inspection thresholds are used; (64, 81), (172, 218), and (466, 590).

In the comparison, performance of weed destruction (killed weed rate and the number of killed weeds), and accuracy performance (correct/false spray rate, the numbers of correct/false sprayed blocks, correct/false spark rate, the numbers of correct/false sparks) are considered as the main factors. To compare the performance of each set of parameters for finding the best one, we set an acceptable error, i.e., acceptable false sprayed blocks for the chemical based system and acceptable false sparks for the electrical spark discharge based system. Then we find the set of parameters that gives error smaller than the acceptable error and gives the best weed destruction performance. If there are two or more sets of parameters giving the same number of killed weeds, the set of parameters giving smaller error is considered to be better than the others. Figure 6(left) shows the comparison of parameters for the chemical based weeding system, whereas Fig. 6(right) shows that of the electrical spark discharge based system. Note that BC NR denotes the BC method with a noise removal step.

In the case of the chemical based system, it is quite difficult to compare the proposed method with the BC and MO methods because the error (# of false sprayed blocks) of the proposed method is in lower range than the BC and MO methods and it does not overlap with those of the BC and MO methods. However, it shows the characteristics of the proposed method; it gives accuracy

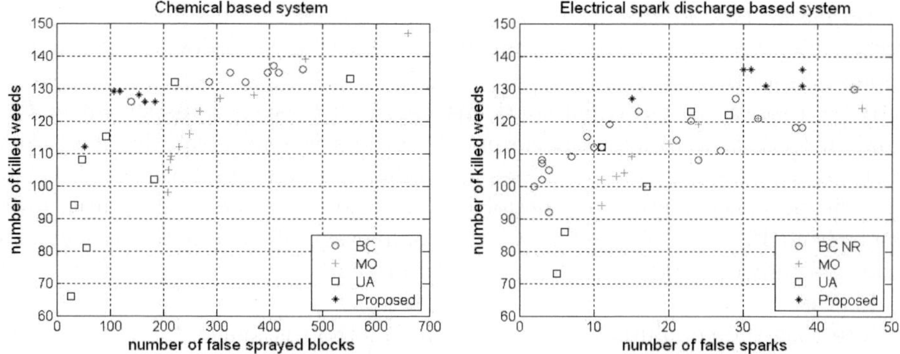

Fig. 6. Performance comparison of the chemical based system (left) and the electrical spark discharge based system (right). Each point shows weeding performance (# of killed weeds) and error (# of false sprayed block or # of false sparks) of each method with a set of parameters.

Table 1. Performance of all gray-scale methods with the best parameters for the chemical based system. The acceptable error (# of false sprayed blocks) is set to 210.

Method	# of killed weeds	Killed weed rate	# of sprayed blocks	# of correct sprayed blocks	# of false sprayed blocks	Correct spray rate	False spray rate	Herbicide reduction rate
BC	126	67.02%	3133	2993	140	95.53%	4.47%	95.10%
MO	105	55.85%	3751	3541	210	94.40%	5.60%	94.13%
UA	115	61.17%	3216	3123	93	97.11%	2.89%	94.48%
Proposed	129	68.61%	3451	3343	108	96.87%	3.13%	94.60%

Table 2. Performance of all gray-scale methods with the best parameters for the electrical spark discharge based system. The acceptable error (# of false sparks) is set to 20.

Method	# of killed weeds	Killed weed rate	# of spark	# of correct sparks	# of false sparks	Correct spark rate	False spark rate
BC NR	123	65.43%	415	399	16	96.14%	3.86%
MO	113	60.11%	201	181	20	90.05%	9.95%
UA	112	59.57%	265	254	11	95.85%	4.15%
Proposed	127	67.55%	538	523	15	97.21%	2.78%

better than those two methods. When we compare the proposed method with the UA method, it is clearly that the proposed method outperforms the UA method. It gives killed weed rate better than the UA method when we select an acceptable error (the number of false spray blocks) in low range. Table 1 shows the comparison of each methods when the acceptable error is set to 210. Clearly, the proposed method gives the best trade-off between weeding performance and error. Note that there is no significant difference in herbicide reduction rate among all four methods.

In the case of the electrical spark discharge based system, as shown in Fig. 6(right), the BC method outperforms the others when we set the acceptable error, i.e., the number of false sparks, to a value less than 15. However, it is clear that the proposed method outperforms the others when the acceptable error ranges from 15 to 50. Table 2 shows the comparison of each methods when the acceptable error is set to 20. The proposed method also gives the best trade-off in this case.

Note that the computational time of this method is longer than that of the other methods. The computational intense step is the weed detection by using SVM because there are a lot of support-vectors got from the training of SVM. Filtering using the proposed filterbank does not spend a lot of time because it is done only on specific areas, some selected blobs, instead of filtering on the entire image. Although increasing the number of filters in the filterbank slows down the proposed method, filtering with the proposed directional filters can be sped up by using separable filtering techniques proposed in [17,18].

4   Conclusion

In this paper, we have proposed the lawn weed detection method modified from the BC method. Instead of using only features from gray-scale image (the mean and variance of edge strength), we also use the color information as additional features. The classifier was changed to more sophisticated one, i.e., support-vector machine. Also noise blob inspection has been proposed for post-processing. It is based on the proposed directional filterbank design from the model of grass-edge. From the experiments, the performance of the proposed method outperforms the compared methods.

References

1. Mashita, T., Ito, A., Miwa, Y.: Developing of weeding robot (1): Manufacture of weed discrimination system on golf course. In: Proc. of JSPE, pp. 997–998 (1992) (in Japanese)
2. Kawamura, K., Mashita, T., Miwa, Y., Ito, A.: Developing of weeding robot (2): Development of weed detecting sensors on green area of golf course. In: Proc. of JSPE, pp. 443–444 (1993) (in Japanese)
3. Otsuka, A., Taniwaki, K.: Round leaf weed detection in lawn field using texture analysis. In: 55th JSAM Annual Meeting, pp. 235–236 (preprint, 1996) (in Japanese)
4. Ahmad, U., Kondo, N., Arima, S., Monta, M., Mohri, K.: Weed detection in lawn field using machine vision: utilization of textural features in segmented area. J. of JSAM 61(2), 61–69 (1999)
5. Ahmad, U., Kondo, N., Monta, M., Arima, S., Mohri, K.: Weed detection in lawn field based on gray-scale uniformity. Environmental Control in Biology 36(4), 227–237 (1998)

6. Ahmad, U., Kondo, N., Arima, S., Monta, M., Mohri, K.: Algorithm to find center-point of detected weed in lawn field. In: 57th JSAM Annual Meeting, pp. 355–356 (preprint, 1998)
7. Ahmad, U., Kondo, N., Arima, S., Monta, M., Mohri, K.: Weed center detection in lawn field using morphological image processing. J. of Society of High Technology in Agriculture 11(2), 127–135 (1999)
8. Watchareeruetai, U., Takeuchi, Y., Matsumoto, T., Kudo, H., Ohnishi, N.: Computer vision based methods for detecting weeds in lawns. Machine Vision and Applications 17(5), 287–296 (2006)
9. Theodoridis, S., Koutroumbas, K.: Pattern Recognition, 2nd edn. Academic Press, London (2003)
10. Gonzalez, R.C., Woods, R.E.: Digital Image Processing. Addison-Wesley, Reading (1992)
11. Watchareeruetai, U., Takeuchi, Y., Matsumoto, T., Kudo, H., Ohnishi, N.: Lawn weed detection methods using image processing techniques. In: IEICE Tech. Report of PRMU meeting, pp. 65–70 (2006)
12. Watchareeruetai, U., Takeuchi, Y., Matsumoto, T., Kudo, H., Ohnishi, N.: A lawn weed detection in winter season based on color information. In: Proc. of IAPR Conf. MVA 2007, pp. 524–527 (2007)
13. Cristianini, N., Shawe-Taylor, J.: An introduction to support vector machines and other kernel-based learning methods. Cambridge University Press, Cambridge (2000)
14. Hemming, J., Rath, T.: Computer-vision-based weed identification under field conditions using controlled lighting. J. of Agricultural Engineering Research 78(3), 233–243 (2001)
15. Lee, W.S., Slaughter, D.C., Giles, D.K.: Robotic weed control system for tomatoes. Precision Agriculture 1(1), 95–113 (1999)
16. Change, C.-C., Lin, C.-J.: LIBSVM: a library for support vector machines (2001), Software available at http://www.csie.ntu.edu.tw/~cjlin/libsvm
17. Areekul, V., Watchareeruetai, U., Tantaratana, S.: Fast Separable Gabor Filter for Fingerprint Enhancement. In: Zhang, D., Jain, A.K. (eds.) ICBA 2004. LNCS, vol. 3072, pp. 403–409. Springer, Heidelberg (2004)
18. Areekul, V., Watchareeruetai, U., Suppasriwasuseth, K., Tantaratana, S.: Separable Gabor Filter Realization for Fast Fingerprint Enhancement. In: Proc. of IEEE ICIP 2005, vol. III, pp. 253–256 (2005)

Reproduction and Recognition of Vowel Signals Using Single and Bagging Competitive Associative Nets

Shuichi Kurogi, Naoko Nedachi, and Yuki Funatsu

Kyushu Institute of Technology, Tobata, Kitakyushu 804-8550, Japan

Abstract. So far, it has been shown that the piecewise linear predictive coefficients obtained by the competitive associative net called CAN2 can provide a better performance in reproduction and recognition of vowel signals than the LPC (linear predictive coding) method which is widely used for speech processing. However, when a vowel signal involves a certain amount of observation noise, the performance becomes low. In this article, we introduce bagging CAN2 and show that it can reproduce and recognize vowel signals better than the conventional single CAN2. Furthermore, we suggest that the bagging CAN2 is useful for the analysis of vowel signals.

1   Introduction

The LPC (linear predictive coding) [1] is well known to be a powerful tool for processing speech signals, and we recently have shown that the piecewise linear predictive coefficients obtained by the competitive associative nets called CAN2 could reproduce and recognize vowel signals better than the LPC [2]. Here, the CAN2 is a neural net intended for learning efficient piecewise linear approximations of nonlinear functions [3] by means of using the competitive and associative schemes [4,5]. Its effectiveness has been shown in several applications; especially, a method using the CAN2 has been awarded the regression winner at the Evaluating Predictive Uncertainty Challenge held at NIPS2004 [6]. The net has also been applied to learning and analyzing chaotic and vowel time-series [7,8], showing that the chaotic and vowel time-series (see [9] for background) can be reproduced with high precision by the CAN2 with multiple units.

In this article, we focus on that the performance in reproduction and recognition of vowels becomes low when vowel signals involve a certain amount of observation noise. Thus, we introduce bagging CAN2 and show that it can reproduce and recognize vowels better than the conventional single CAN2. Furthermore, we show that the bagging CAN2 is useful for the analysis of vowel signals. Note that our analysis by the CAN2 will provide a relationship between the conventional LPC method and piecewise linear predictive coefficients obtained by the single CAN2 and the bagging CAN2.

2   CAN2 and Bagging

2.1   Single CAN2

Let $D^n \triangleq \{(\boldsymbol{x}_i, y_i) | i \in I^n\}$ be a given training dataset, where $I^n \triangleq \{1, 2, \cdots, n\}$ denotes the index set of the dataset, and $\boldsymbol{x}_i \triangleq (x_{i1}, x_{i2}, \cdots, x_{ik})^T$ and y_i denote an input

M. Ishikawa et al. (Eds.): ICONIP 2007, Part II, LNCS 4985, pp. 40–49, 2008.

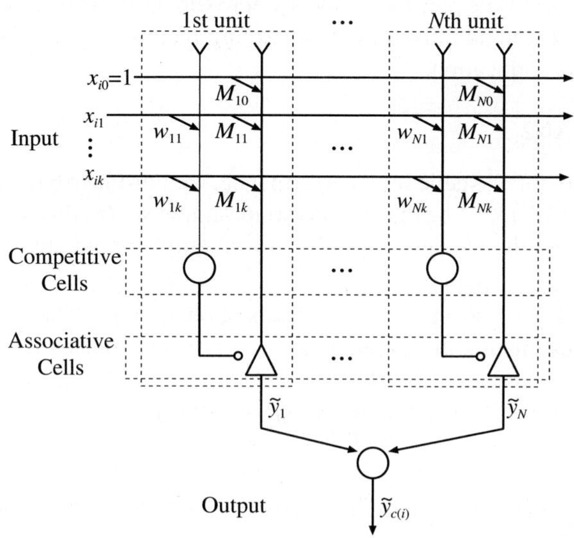

Fig. 1. Schematic diagram of the CAN2. For the input vector $\boldsymbol{x}_i = (x_{i1}, \cdots, x_{ik})^T$, the closest weight vector $\boldsymbol{w}_{c(i)}$ of the competitive cell is selected according to Eq.(3), and the associative output value $\widetilde{y}_{c(i)} = \boldsymbol{M}_{c(i)}\widetilde{\boldsymbol{x}}_i$ of this unit is sent to the output of the net

vector and the target scalar value, respectively. Note that $\boldsymbol{x}_i$ and y_i, respectively, correspond to $\boldsymbol{x}(t)$ and $y(t)$ of the vowel time-series introduced below. Here, we suppose the relationship given by

$$y_i \triangleq r_i + \epsilon_i = f(\boldsymbol{x}_i) + \epsilon_i, \tag{1}$$

where $r_i \triangleq f(\boldsymbol{x}_i)$ is a nonlinear function of $\boldsymbol{x}_i$, and ϵ_i represents noise. A (single) CAN2 has N units (see Fig. 1). The jth unit has a weight vector $\boldsymbol{w}_j \triangleq (w_{j1}, \cdots, w_{jk})^T \in \mathbb{R}^{k \times 1}$ and an associative matrix (or a row vector) $\boldsymbol{M}_j \triangleq (M_{j0}, M_{j1}, \cdots, M_{jk}) \in \mathbb{R}^{1 \times (k+1)}$ for $j \in I^N \triangleq \{1, 2, \cdots, N\}$. The CAN2 approximates the above function $f(\boldsymbol{x}_i)$ by

$$\widehat{y}_i \triangleq \widehat{f}(\boldsymbol{x}_i) \triangleq \widetilde{y}_{c(i)} \triangleq \boldsymbol{M}_{c(i)}\widetilde{\boldsymbol{x}}_i, \tag{2}$$

where $\widetilde{\boldsymbol{x}}_i \triangleq (1, \boldsymbol{x}_i^T)^T \in \mathbb{R}^{(k+1) \times 1}$ denotes the (extended) input vector to the CAN2, and $\widetilde{y}_{c(i)} = \boldsymbol{M}_{c(i)}\widetilde{\boldsymbol{x}}_i$ is the output value of the $c(i)$th unit of the CAN2. The index $c(i)$ indicates the unit who has the weight vector $\boldsymbol{w}_{c(i)}$ closest to the input vector $\boldsymbol{x}_i$, or

$$c(i) \triangleq \underset{j \in I^N}{\operatorname{argmin}} \|\boldsymbol{x}_i - \boldsymbol{w}_j\|. \tag{3}$$

The above function approximation partitions the input space $V \in \mathbb{R}^k$ into the Voronoi (or Dirichlet) regions

$$V_j \triangleq \{\boldsymbol{x} \mid j = \underset{i \in I^N}{\operatorname{argmin}} \|\boldsymbol{x} - \boldsymbol{w}_i\|\}, \tag{4}$$

for $j \in I^N$, and performs piecewise linear approximation of the function $f(\boldsymbol{x})$. Note that we have developed an efficient batch learning method (see [3] for details), which we also use in this application.

2.2 Bagging CAN2

In order mainly to obtain stable high performance, we introduce bagging method to the CAN2 as follows; let $D_j^{\alpha n*}$ be the jth bootstrap sample set (multiset, or bag) involving αn elements, where the elements in $D_j^{\alpha n*}$ are resampled randomly with replacement from the given training dataset D^n, where $j \in I^b \triangleq \{1, 2, \cdots, b\}$, $\alpha > 0$, and we use $\alpha = 0.7$ and $b = 20$ in the experiments shown below. The bagging (bootstrap aggregation) for estimating the target value $r_i = f(\boldsymbol{x}_i)$ is done by the mean given by

$$\hat{y}_i^{b*} \triangleq \frac{1}{b} \sum_{j \in I^b} \hat{y}_i^j, = \boldsymbol{M}_i^{b*} \tilde{\boldsymbol{x}}_i \tag{5}$$

where $\hat{y}_i^j \triangleq \hat{y}^j(\boldsymbol{x}_i)$ denotes the prediction by the jth CAN2 which has learned $D_j^{\alpha n*}$, and

$$\boldsymbol{M}_i^{b*} = \frac{1}{b} \sum_{j \in I^b} \boldsymbol{M}_{c^j(i)}. \tag{6}$$

Here $c^j(i)$ indicates the unit in the jth CAN2 who has the weight vector closest to $\boldsymbol{x}_i$. Thus, bagging prediction is also a piecewise linear approximation of $y_i = f(\boldsymbol{x}_i)$, whose piecewise linear regions V_i^* are the minimum regions which are surrounded by the boundary of the Voronoi regions of the multiple CAN2s used for the bagging.

3 Models of Vowel Generation

The conventional model of the vowel generation is depicted in Fig. 2 (a), where the voiced source signal $s(t)$ is assumed to be a periodic impulse train, and the vocal tract as an articulator is modeled by an auto-regressive (AR) model given by $y(t) = \boldsymbol{a}^T \boldsymbol{x}(t) + s(t)$, where $\boldsymbol{a} = (a_1, a_2, \cdots, a_k)^T \in \mathbb{R}^{k \times 1}$ is a k-dimensional coefficient column vector and $\boldsymbol{x}(t) = (y(t-1), y(t-2), \cdots, y(t-k))^T$. Note that, using the time-delay operator z^{-1}, the above equation is also represented by

$$y(t) = \frac{s(t)}{1 - \sum_{j=1}^k a_j z^{-j}} = \frac{s(t)}{1 + H_1(z)} \tag{7}$$

On the other hand, a number of recent studies suggest that a vowel signal exhibits a deterministic chaos, which indicates that the vowel signal without noise is represented by $y_s(t) = f(\boldsymbol{x}_s(t))$, where $f(\boldsymbol{x}_s(t))$ is a nonlinear function of $\boldsymbol{x}_s(t) = (y_s(t-1), y_s(t-2), \cdots, y_s(t-k))$. When the observed data $y(t)$ involves observation noise $e(t)$, or $y(t) = y_s(t) + e(t)$, we have

$$y(t) = f(\boldsymbol{x}(t)) + \epsilon(t) \tag{8}$$

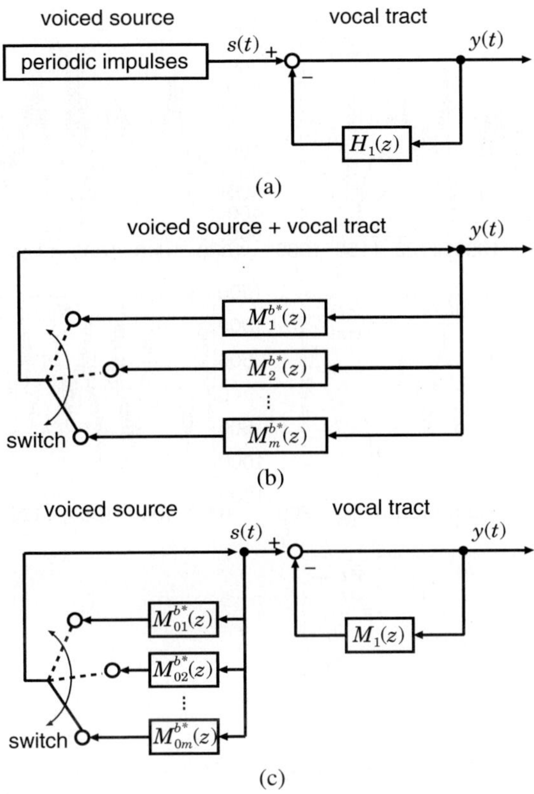

Fig. 2. (a) Conventional, (b) bagging CAN2 based, and (c) combined models of vowel generation

where $\epsilon(t) = e(t) + f(\boldsymbol{x}_s(t)) - f(\boldsymbol{x}(t))$ represents the term involving error and noise.

By means of replacing $\boldsymbol{x}_i = \boldsymbol{x}(t)$ and $y_i = y(t)$ in Eq.(1) and then applying the bagging method, the bagging CAN2 approximates the above function as

$$\widehat{y}(t) = \begin{cases} \boldsymbol{M}_1^{b*}\widetilde{\boldsymbol{x}}(t), & \boldsymbol{x}(t) \in V_1^* \\ \boldsymbol{M}_2^{b*}\widetilde{\boldsymbol{x}}(t), & \boldsymbol{x}(t) \in V_2^* \\ \vdots & \vdots \\ \boldsymbol{M}_m^{b*}\widetilde{\boldsymbol{x}}(t), & \boldsymbol{x}(t) \in V_m^*. \end{cases} \tag{9}$$

where m represents the number of all piecewise linear regions. Thus, the CAN2 based model can be depicted as shown in Fig. 2(b), where $M_i^{b*}(z) = \sum_{j=1}^{k} M_{ij}^{b*} z^{-j}$.

Here, keeping the consistency of the conventional model, a model of the vowel generation using the bagging CAN2 can be depicted as shown in Fig. 2(c), where the model of the vocal tract is supposed to be linear although it has a possibility to be nonlinear. We may be able to examine the nonlinearity of the vocal tract by means of examining the three models in Fig. 2, which will be the subject of our future research study.

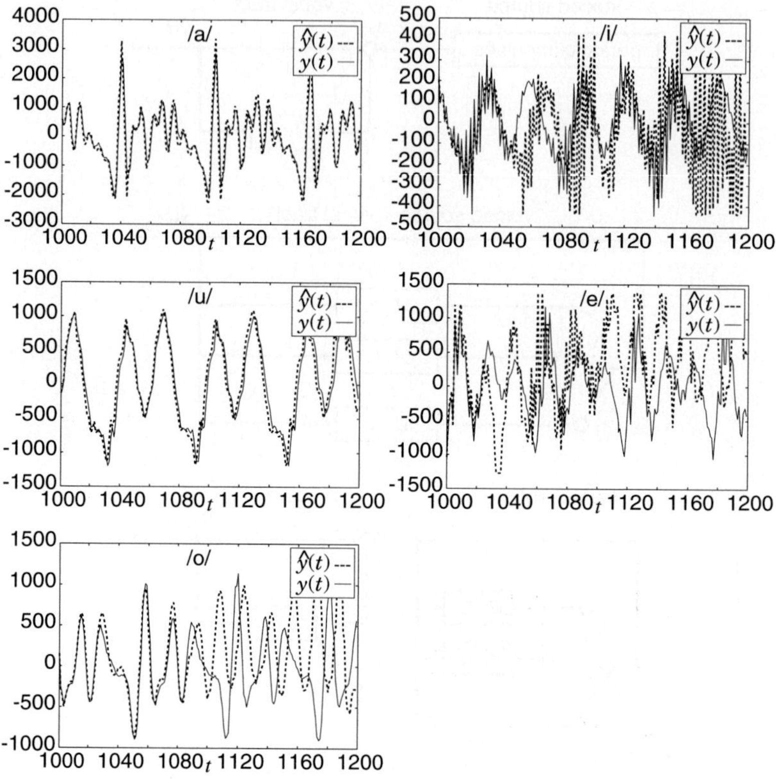

Fig. 3. Example of vowel signals /a/, /i/, /u/, /e/, /o/ reproduced via multi-step prediction using a single CAN2 with $k = 9$ and $N = 33$ after learning the vowel signal $y(t)$ for $t = 0, 1, 2, \cdots, 999$

4   Analysis of Vowel Signals Using the CAN2

4.1   Reproduction of Vowel Signals

The vowel signals reproduced by the single CAN2 after learning the vowel signal $y(t)$ for $t = 0, 1, 2, \cdots, 999$ of (Japanese) vowels /a/, /i/, /u/, /e/, /o/, respectively, are shown in Fig. 3. Here, the embedding dimension $k = 9$ and the number of units $N = 33$ are tuned to be selected for a good performance for all vowels. Especially, the performance of the reproduction for /i/ and /e/ could not be improved by means of using different k and N. The performance for /o/ can be improved with $k = 10$, which however provided worse performance for /a/ and /i/. Note that the vowel signals used in [2] are reproduced very well, but it does not involve high frequency fluctuations as shown in /i/ and /e/, which seem to cause the worse performance for the vowel signals used in this article. Furthermore, these high frequency components are considered to be not important for vowel recognition because the signals in [2] can be recognized very well without such components. Here, note that the sampling rate of the data used in [2] is 8kHz, while

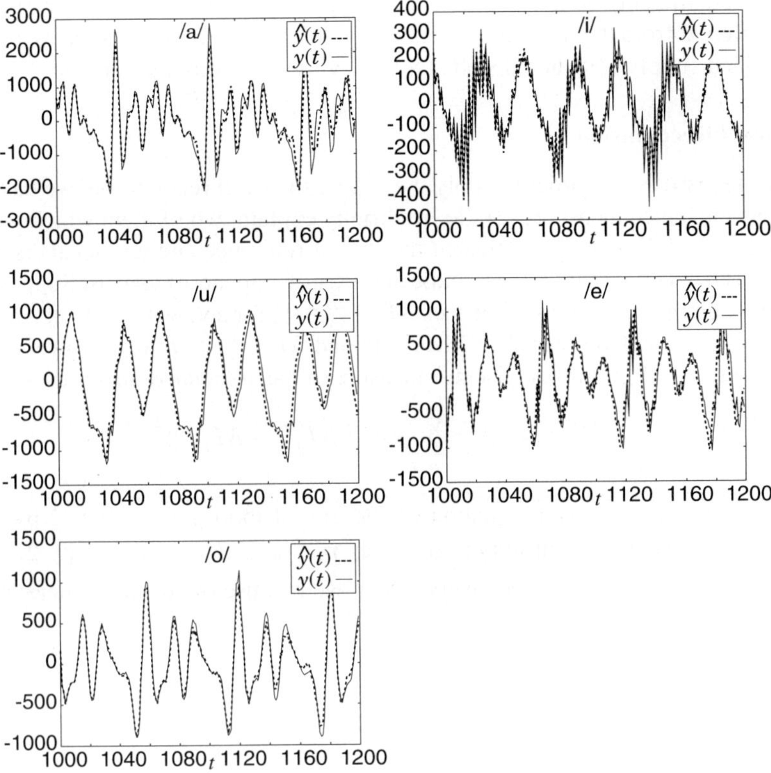

Fig. 4. Example of vowel signals /a/, /i/, /u/, /e/, /o/ reproduced via multi-step prediction using a bagging CAN2 with $k = 54$ and $N = 6$ after learning $y(t)$ for $t = 0, 1, 2, \cdots , 999$. The SNR (signal-to-noise ratio) are 9.30, 9.45, 11.10, 5.96, 15.96 for /a/, /i/, /u/, /e/, /o/, respectively.

it is 45kHz in this article and we further successively resampled a datum from every 6 sampled data, so the actual sampling frequency of the data in this article is $45/6 = 7.5$kHz, and they may involve the alias noise caused by the high frequency components. Thus, with an 8kHz sampler involving a low pass filter for removing the alias noise, we may be able to obtain a better reproduction performance, but we show that we can improve the performance by the bagging CAN2.

Namely, the bagging CAN2 with $k = 54$ and $N = 6$ has reproduced vowel signals very well as shown in Fig. 4, where we can see that the high frequency components in the reproduced data disappear as the time increases, but the overall reproduction seem to be achieved very well. Thus, the bagging CAN2 is considered to have obtained almost all information on the vowel signals, such as not only phoneme but also pitch, individuality, and so on. Especially, it is interesting that the bagging CAN2 stores the information on the vowels into the (piecewise) linear models or the associative matrices which may be directly related to the physical structures of the speaker, such as the transfer function of the vocal tract modeled by the associative matrix (the linear predictive coefficient) obtained by the CAN2 with a single unit as described above. This is different from the high-quality codec (code/decode) methods, such as waveform coders which simply code and decode for achieving high compression rate.

4.2 Vowel Recognition

Distance measures: In order to apply the CAN2 to vowel recognition, we have introduced three distance measures [2]. So, we briefly explain two of them which we use in this article. Let S^{ref} and S^{test} represent the sets of reference and test speakers, respectively, and $V = \{/a/, /i/, /u/, /e/, /o/\}$ indicates a set of (Japanese) vowels. Suppose that a CAN2 has obtained associative matrices $\boldsymbol{M}_i^{s,u}$ $(i \in I)$ for a vowel $u \in V$ of a reference speaker $s \in S^{\text{ref}}$, and another CAN2 has obtained $\boldsymbol{M}_j^{t,v}$ $(j \in I)$ for a vowel $v \in V$ of a test speaker $t \in S^{\text{test}}$. First, a distance measure of the associative matrices is given by

$$L^M(t, v, s, u) \triangleq \sum_{j \in I} \min_{i \in I} \left\| \boldsymbol{M}_j^{t,v} - \boldsymbol{M}_i^{s,u} \right\|^2 . \tag{10}$$

Next, from the characteristic equation of the closed loop gain of Fig. 2(b), or $1 - \sum_{j=1}^k M_{ij}^{b*} z^{-i} = 0$, we can obtain the poles $\boldsymbol{p}_{i,l}^{s,u}(i \in I, l \in K \triangleq \{1, 2, \cdots, k\})$ and $\boldsymbol{p}_{j,m}^{t,v}(j \in I, m \in K)$, respectively. Then, we can use the distance measure given by

$$L^P(t, v, s, u) \triangleq \sum_{j \in I} \min_{i \in I} \left(\sum_{m \in K} \min_{l \in K} \left\| \boldsymbol{p}_{j,m}^{t,v} - \boldsymbol{p}_{i,l}^{s,u} \right\|^2 \right) \tag{11}$$

With one of the above distance measures, $L = L^M$ or L^P, we can decide that the vowel v of a test speaker t is recognized as

$$v^{recog}(t, v) = \operatorname*{argmin}_{u \in V} \min_{s \in S^{\text{ref}}} L(t, v, s, u). \tag{12}$$

Vowel recognition via single and bagging CAN2s: For examining the performance of the distance measures introduced in the previous section, we have prepared vowel signals for 6 speakers, $S = \{\text{HF}, \text{YKi}, \text{YKo}, \text{TS}, \text{YT}, \text{KY}\}$. We execute the recognition test by means of leave-one-out method. Namely, we choose a speaker as test speakers, $S^{\text{test}} = \{s | s \in S, |S^{\text{test}}| = 1\}$, and the rest for reference speakers, $S^{\text{ref}} = S \backslash S^{\text{test}}$, and then we have the correct recognition rate by summing up the score of the number of correctly recognized vowels for every speaker as test speaker. Thus, 5 vowels for 6 speakers, or the total 30 vowels, are tested. Here, we should note that we have used $y(t)$ for $t = 0, 1, 2, \cdots, 149$ for training and $y(t)$ for $t = 150, 151, \cdots, 299$ for testing, where the training and test duration $T = 150[1/7.5\text{kHz}]$ indicates $20(= 150/7.5)\text{ms}$.

The recognition rate for four methods is shown in Table 1. From the table, we can see that L^M by the single CAN2 with $N = 1$ and $k = 9$, which is identical to the conventional LPC method, has achieved a good correct recognition rate 83%. Furthermore, L^P of the single CAN2 ($N = 1$, $k = 9$) has worse recognition rate 67%, while L^P of the bagging CAN2 ($N = 1$, $k = 9$) achieved 83%. In order to examine the difference, we show the poles of YT in Fig. 5 and Fig. 6.

Table 1. Correct recognition rate of vowels, R_v, via using $y(t)$

	specification of CAN2	R_v
L^M	single, $N = 1$, $k = 9$	83% (25/30)
L^p	single, $N = 1$, $k = 9$	67% (20/30)
L^p	bagging, $N = 1$, $k = 9$	83% (25/30)
L^p	bagging, $N = 6$, $k = 27$	90% (27/30)

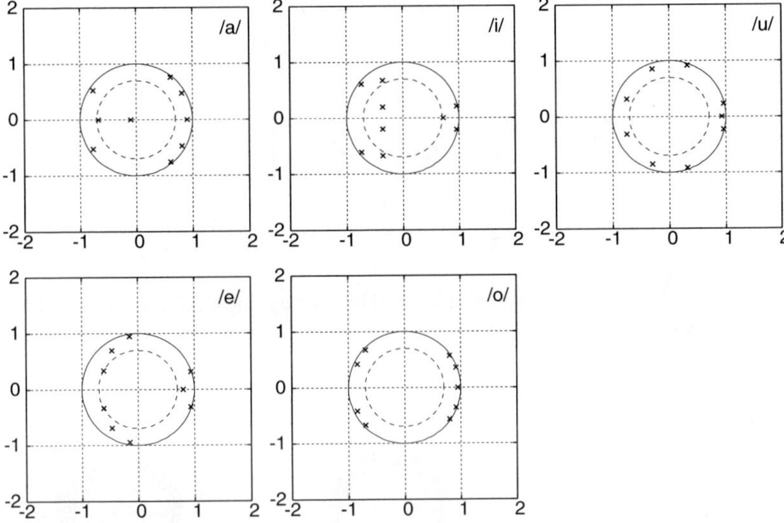

Fig. 5. Example of the poles obtained by the single CAN2 with $N = 1$ and $k = 9$ for the reference speaker YT. The horizontal and the vertical axes, respectively, represent the real and the imaginary parts of the poles. The crosses denote the poles, and the solid and the dotted circles with the radii 1 and 0.7, respectively, indicate unity (0dB) and half-power ($-$3dB) gains.

From these figures, we can see that the poles in Fig. 6 seem to be clustered around the 9 poles for each vowel in Fig. 5. Furthermore, the variation of the clustered poles for /u/ and /o/ in Fig. 6 is small, but the variation of the clusters for /a/, /i/ and /e/ is large. This relationship of the magnitude of the variation for each vowel, however, was different from speaker to speaker, but the variation of the poles of the bagging CAN2 is considered to contribute to the recognition rate of the bagging CAN2 higher than the single CAN2 with the distance measure L^p. So far, we could not have obtained a good explanation why L^M of the single CAN2 with $N = 1$ and $k = 9$ achieves the same recognition rate, 83%, as L^p not with the single CAN2 but with the bagging CAN2, which we will examine in the future research study. From the bottom of Table 1, we can see L^p by the bagging CAN2 with $N = 6$ and $k = 27$ achieves the highest recognition rate 90%. Here, we should explain several points. First, the embedding dimension $k = 27$ is different from $k = 54$ used in Fig. 4. This is because $k = 27$ is enough for

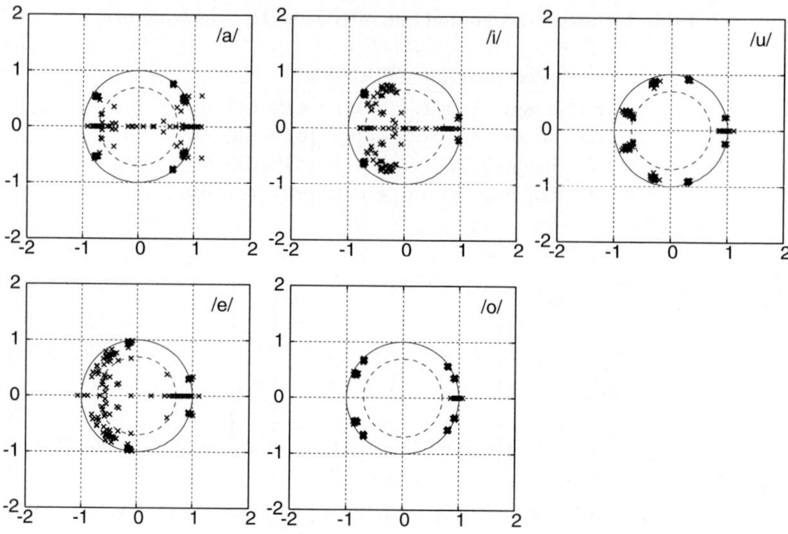

Fig. 6. Example of the poles of the vowels obtained by the bagging CAN2 with $N = 1$ and $k = 9$ for the reference speaker YT

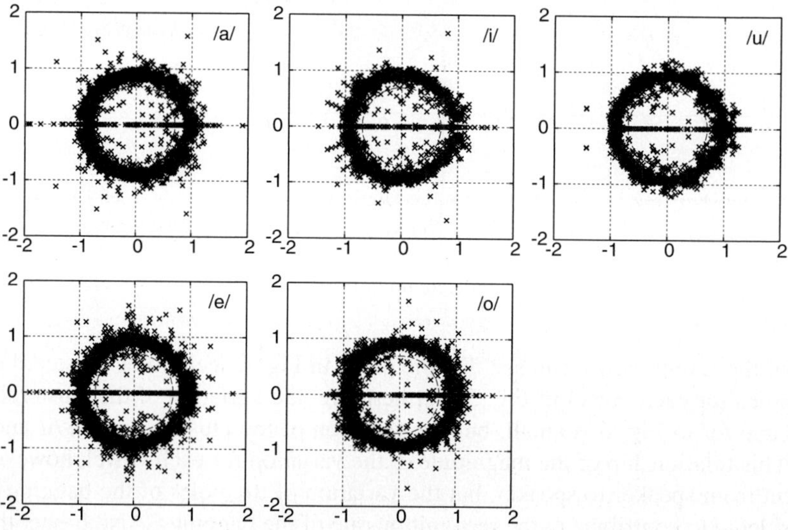

Fig. 7. Example of the poles obtained by the bagging CAN2 with $N = 6$ and $k = 27$ for the reference speaker YT

learning 150 data while $k = 54$ is good for learning 1000 data for reproducing 200 data as shown in Fig. 4. Furthermore, we restrict the range of the magnitude r_i and the angle θ_i of the pole $p_i = r_i \exp(j\theta_i)$, as $0.7 \leq r_i \leq 1.1$, and $1° \leq \theta_i \leq 179°$ for calculating the distance measure L^p, where $j^2 = -1$. Moreover, we use the poles p_i of each CAN2 involved in the bagging CAN2, because it is not so easy to obtain the piecewise region V_i^* and M_i^{b*} of the bagging CAN2. Although we can plot the poles as shown in in Fig. 7, we could not have characterized the difference of the configuration of the poles for each vowel, while we can say that these poles have derived the highest recognition rate. We would like to analyze the reason in our future research study.

5   Conclusion

We have introduced the bagging CAN2 for dealing with vowel signals involving a certain level of observation noise, and shown that the bagging CAN2 can learn and reproduce the vowel signals better than the single CAN2. We have applied the bagging CAN2 as well as the single CAN2 to modeling vowel generation and vowel recognition. The present research study using the CAN2 which learns efficient piecewise linear approximations of nonlinear functions may provide a novel approach to the speech processing and analysis, which, however, may be a natural extension of the conventional LPC research studies. We would like to continue this approach much more in the future.

Acknowledgment

We would like to note that our research on the CAN2 is partially supported by the Grant-in-Aid for Scientific Research (B) 16300070 of the Japanese Ministry of Education, Science, Sports and Culture.

References

1. Markel, J.D., Gray Jr., A.H.: Linear Prediction of Speech. Springer, Heidelberg (1976)
2. Kurogi, S., Nedachi, N.: Reproduction and Recognition of Vowels Using Piecewise Linear Predictive Coefficients Obtained by Competitive Associative Nets. In: Proc. of SICEICCAS 2006 (2006)
3. Kurogi, S., Ueno, T., Sawa, M.: A batch learning method for competitive associative net and its application to function approximation. In: Proc. of SCI 2004, vol. V, pp. 24–28 (2004)
4. Ahalt, A.C., Krishnamurthy, A.K., Chen, P., Melton, D.E.: Competitive learning algorithms for vector quantization. Neural Networks 3, 277–290 (1990)
5. Kohonen, T.: Associative Memory. Springer, Heidelberg (1977)
6. http://predict.kyb.tuebingen.mpg.de/pages/home.php
7. Kurogi, S., Ueno, T., Tanaka, K.: Asymptotic optimality of competitive associative net and its application to chaotic time series prediction. In: Proc. of JNNS 2002, pp. 283–284 (2002)
8. Kurogi, S., Sawa, M.: Analysis of vowel time series via competitive associative nets. In: Proc. of JNNS 2003, pp. 54–55 (2003)
9. Aihara, K.: Theories and Applications of Chaotic Time Series Analysis. Sangyo Tosho, Tokyo (2000)

Orientation Recognition of Iris Pattern

Takeshi Kawasaki, Hironobu Takano, and Kiyomi Nakamura

Graduate School of Engineering, Toyama Prefectural University
5180, Kurokawa, Imizu, Toyama 939-0398, Japan

Abstract. An iris recognition system that employs a rotation spreading neural network (R-SAN net) has been proposed. R-SAN net is suitable for the orientation recognition of concentric circular patterns such as the iris pattern. The orientation recognition characteristics of R-SAN net for the iris pattern have been investigated. However, it has not yet been understood how the orientation recognition performance of R-SAN net is better than that of other methods employed for orientation recognition.

In this study, we evaluated the effectiveness of the orientation recognition performance of R-SAN net by comparing its orientation recognition characteristics with those of the moment (MO) method. The standard deviation of the orientation recognition error in the MO method is larger than that in R-SAN net. For an arbitrary input orientation, R-SAN net showed a fairly good orientation recognition performance as compared to the MO method.

1   Introduction

An iris recognition system that employs a rotation spreading neural network (R-SAN net) has been proposed [1], [2]. For orientation recognition, R-SAN net requires a two-dimensional input pattern to be converted from the Cartesian coordinate system to the polar coordinate system. Thus, R-SAN net is suitable for the orientation recognition of concentric circular patterns such as the iris pattern. In personal authentications through cellular phones, a change in the rotation of the iris pattern occurs due to the use of an unfixed camera, and this causes a decrease in the iris recognition rate. In order to solve such problems, the change in the rotation is corrected by using the recognized rotation angle obtained by R-SAN net. The correction of the change in the rotation prevents the decrease in the iris recognition rate. In the previous study, the orientation recognition characteristics of R-SAN net were investigated. However, it has not yet been understood how the orientation recognition performance of R-SAN net is better than that of other methods employed for orientation recognition.

In this study, we evaluated the effectiveness of the orientation recognition performance of R-SAN net by comparing its orientation recognition characteristics with those of the moment (MO) method, which is a typical technique employed for orientation recognition.

2   Orientation Recognition by R-SAN Net

2.1   Outline of R-SAN Net

The structure of R-SAN net is shown in Fig.1. R-SAN net consists of orientation and shape recognition systems. In the operation of this network, the input pattern (300×300

M. Ishikawa et al. (Eds.): ICONIP 2007, Part II, LNCS 4985, pp. 50–56, 2008.

pixels) is converted into a pattern in polar coordinates. This transformed pattern is input to the spreading layer and a spread pattern is obtained.

In the learning process, the orientation memory matrix is obtained by generalized inverse learning. In the recollection process, the output of orientation recognition neurons is obtained by multiplying the spread pattern and the orientation memory matrix. The orientation is recognized from the output of the orientation recognition neurons by using the population vector (PV) method.

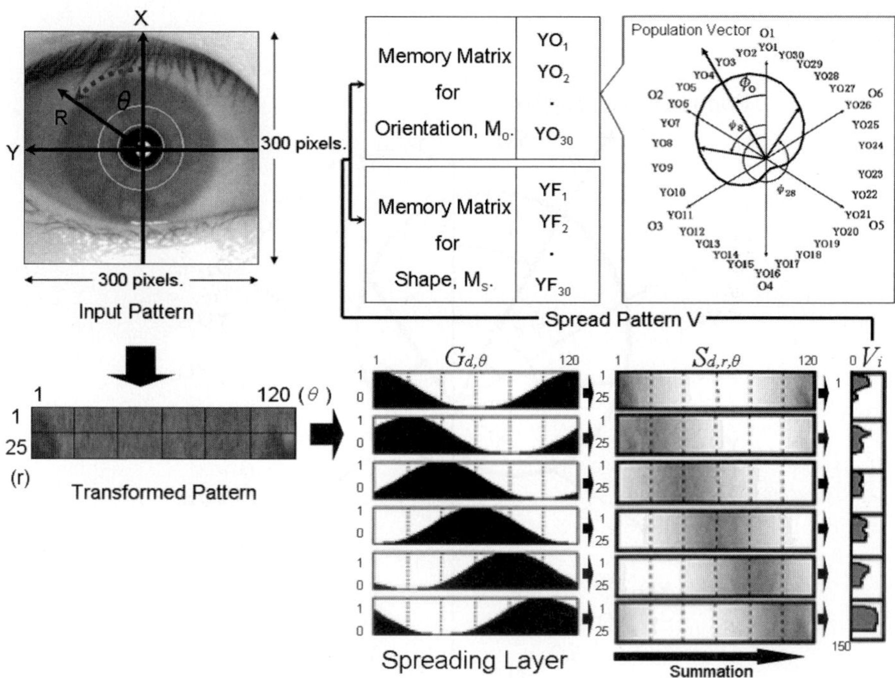

Fig. 1. Structure of R-SAN net

2.2 PV Method

The orientation recognition of the iris pattern is realized by using the PV method along with the output of the orientation recognition neurons [3]. This method provides the orientation of an object by synthesizing the continuous spectra of the outputs of the orientation recognition neurons. The arrangements of the orientation recognition neurons and the population vector are shown in Fig.2. Each orientation recognition neuron YO_i has a representative orientation ψ_i that characterizes the best orientation for the optimal response in Eq.(1). The length of the vector is proportional to the neuron's output. The population vector orientation ϕ is calculated by the vectorial summation of 30 orientation neurons arranged at intervals of $12°$, as shown in Eqs.(2) and (3).

$$\psi_i = \frac{2\pi}{30} \times (i-1)[rad] \qquad (i = 1, 2, \cdots, 30) \tag{1}$$

$$x = \sum_{i=1}^{30} YO_i \cos\psi_i \quad , \quad y = \sum_{i=1}^{30} YO_i \sin\psi_i \tag{2}$$

$$\phi = \tan^{-1}\left(\frac{y}{x}\right) \tag{3}$$

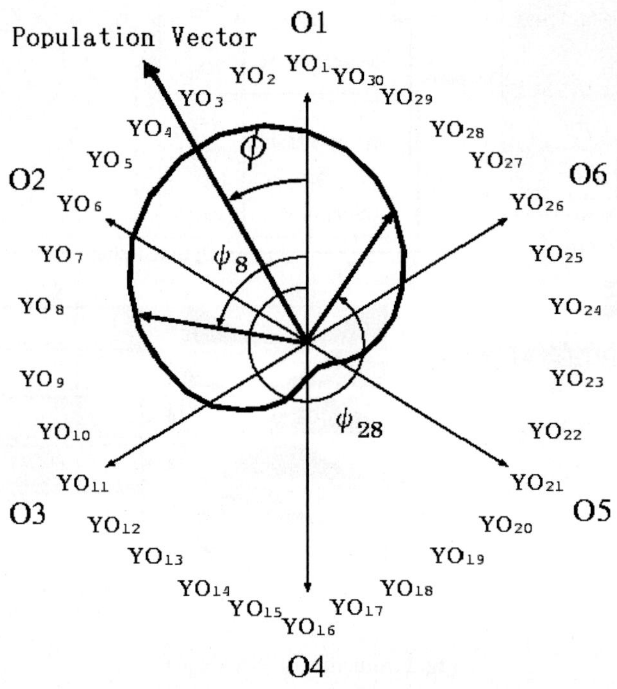

Fig. 2. Orientation recognition with the PV method

2.3 Process of Orientation Recognition Using R-SAN Net

The process of orientation recognition using R-SAN net is performed as follows. In the learning process, the iris pattern is captured by a CCD camera. The original pattern for learning and recollection processes is a gray-scale pattern of 300×300 pixels. The origin for the polar and Cartesian coordinates is the central position of the pupil. The transformed pattern is obtained by sampling the original pattern in polar coordinates (r, θ) at intervals of $3°$ for θ and at equal intervals ranging from 30 to 55 pixels for r, excluding the pupil region. Next, the spread pattern is obtained by multiplying the transformed pattern with the spreading weight, which is a periodic Gaussian function in the

θ-direction. The summation of each pixel value of the spread pattern in the θ-direction provides the spread pattern vector. The orientation memory matrix is obtained by associating the spread pattern vector with the desired outputs of the orientation recognition neurons.

In the recollection process, the spread pattern vector is obtained in a manner identical to that of the learning process. The outputs of the orientation recognition neurons are obtained by multiplying the spread pattern and orientation memory matrix. The orientation of the input iris pattern is recognized by using the PV method along with the outputs of the orientation recognition neurons.

3   Orientation Recognition Using the MO Method

3.1   Moment Characteristics

The moment characteristics are one of the important factors for representing the shape of an object [4], [5]. The second-order moment around the center of gravity describes the degree of concentration. The moment characteristics around an arbitrary axis of an object show the degree of extension. In the MO method, the direction along which the object extends is used to define the orientation angle.

3.2   MO Method

In the present study, the orientation recognition characteristics of R-SAN net are compared with those of the MO method. The orientation recognition performed using the MO method is as follows.

The $(p + q)$-order moment M_{pq} of pattern $f(m, n)$ around the center of gravity is given by Eq.(4). When the center of gravity (m_G, n_G) is set as the origin $(0, 0)$, the $(i + j)$-order moment μ_{ij} is given by Eq.(5). In addition, the second-order moment μ_θ around the straight line passing through the origin with an inclination θ is defined by Eq.(6). The angle θ for the minimum value of μ_θ defines the principal axes of inertia and represents the direction along which the object expands. The orientation of the object is calculated by using θ, as shown in Eq.(7).

$$M_{pq} = \sum_m \sum_n (m - m_G)^p (n - n_G)^q f(m, n) \tag{4}$$

$$\mu_{ij} = \sum_m \sum_n m^i n^j f(m, n) \tag{5}$$

$$\mu_\theta = \sum_m \sum_n (m \cos \theta - n \sin \theta)^2 f(m, n) \tag{6}$$

$$\theta = \frac{1}{2} \tan^{-1} \left(\frac{2\mu_{11}}{\mu_{20} - \mu_{02}} \right) \tag{7}$$

3.3 Process of Orientation Recognition Using MO Method

The orientation recognition of the iris pattern by using the MO method is as follows. In the learning process, the iris image is extracted from the original image from a radius of 30 to 55 pixels, excluding the pupil region. The MO method provides the iris orientation by using the extracted image of the iris pattern. The orientation of the iris image is obtained by calculating the second-order moment around the center of gravity. The calculated orientation is stored as the criteria angle θ_L of the registered iris. In the recognition process, the recognized orientation θ_{MO} of the iris image is obtained by subtracting the registered angle θ_L calculated in the learning process from the orientation angle θ_R calculated in the recognition process, as shown in Eq.(8).

$$\theta_{MO} = \theta_R - \theta_L \tag{8}$$

4 Orientation Recognition Experiment

4.1 Experimental Method

In order to evaluate the orientation recognition performance of R-SAN net and the MO method, the orientation recognition experiment was conducted by using 35 iris patterns. In the recognition process, the iris image was recaptured. The orientation recognition results were obtained by rotating the iris pattern at intervals of $10°$ based on the pupil center. For the p-th input of the iris pattern at θ_i, the recognized orientation errors $E_{o,\theta_i,p}^{R-SAN}$ (in R-SAN net) and $E_{o,\theta_i,p}^{MO}$ (in the MO method) are calculated by Eqs.(9) and (10), respectively. The average $\bar{E}_{o,\theta_i}^{R-SAN}$ and standard deviation $SD(E_{o,\theta_i}^{R-SAN})$ in R-SAN net and the average $\bar{E}_{o,\theta_i}^{MO}$ and standard deviation $SD(E_{o,\theta_i}^{MO})$ in the MO method are calculated for each input angle θ_i $(= 0°, 10°, \cdots, 360°)$ for all the iris patterns $(p = 1, 2, \cdots, 35)$. The average $\bar{E}_o^{R-SAN}$ and standard deviation $SD(E_o^{R-SAN})$ in R-SAN net and the average $\bar{E}_o^{MO}$ and standard deviation $SD(E_o^{MO})$ in the MO method are calculated by using $E_{o,\theta_i,p}^{R-SAN}$ and $E_{o,\theta_i,p}^{MO}$ in all values of θ_i $(= 0°, 10°, \cdots, 360°)$ and p $(= 1, 2, \cdots, 35)$. These values are used for the evaluation of the orientation recognition performance.

$$E_{o,\theta_i,p}^{R-SAN} = \phi_{\theta_i,p} - \theta_i \qquad (\theta_i = 0°, 10°, \cdots, 360°, p = 1, 2, \cdots, 35) \tag{9}$$

$$E_{o,\theta_i,p}^{MO} = \theta_{MO,\theta_i,p} - \theta_i \qquad (\theta_i = 0°, 10°, \cdots, 360°, p = 1, 2, \cdots, 35) \tag{10}$$

4.2 Orientation Recognition Result

The orientation recognition characteristics of R-SAN net are shown in Fig.3. The horizontal axis represents the input orientation angle θ_i of the iris pattern, and the vertical axis denotes the recognized orientation angle. The characteristics for ideal orientation recognition are represented by a solid line. The circle shows the average $\bar{E}_{o,\theta_i}^{R-SAN}$ of the recognized orientations of 35 iris patterns. The vertical bar shows the standard deviation $SD(E_{o,\theta_i}^{R-SAN})$. The recognition result for R-SAN net shows good linearity between the

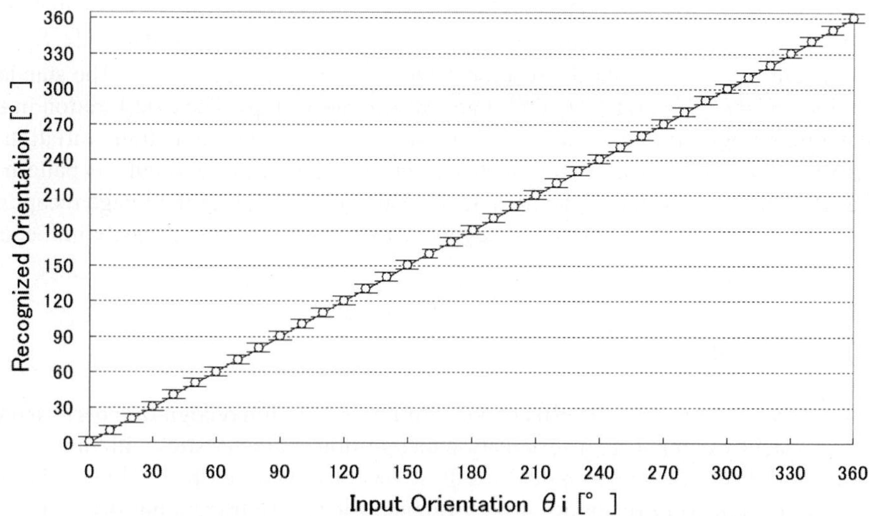

Fig. 3. Orientation recognition characteristics obtained using R-SAN net

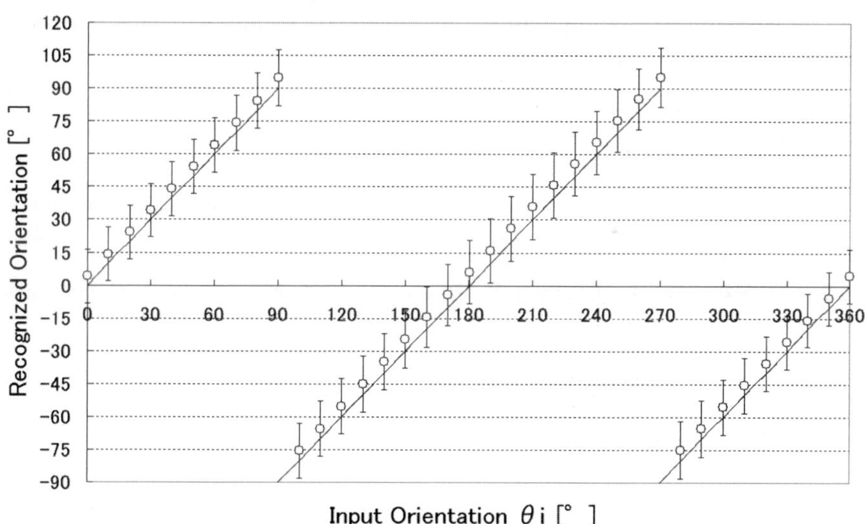

Fig. 4. Orientation recognition characteristics obtained using the MO method

orientations of the input and recognized iris patterns. The average $\bar{E}_o^{R-SAN} \pm$ standard deviation $SD(E_o^{R-SAN})$ is $0.46° \pm 2.88°$. R-SAN net can correctly recognize the iris orientations for arbitrary input orientations.

The orientation recognition characteristics of the MO method are shown in Fig.4. The horizontal axis represents θ_i for the iris pattern, and the vertical axis denotes the recognized orientation angle. The characteristics for ideal orientation recognition are represented by a solid line. The circle shows the average $\bar{E}_{o,\theta_i}^{MO}$ of the recognized orientations of 35 iris patterns. The vertical bar shows the standard deviation $SD(E_{o,\theta_i}^{MO})$. The average $\bar{E}_o^{MO} \pm$ standard deviation $SD(E_o^{MO})$ is $4.87° \pm 12.99°$. The standard deviations $SD(E_{o,\theta_i}^{MO})$ and $SD(E_o^{MO})$ are considerably large. The deterioration in the orientation recognition performance of the MO method is due to a slight variation in the pixel value, which results from a change in the rotation of the input iris pattern or a change in the pixel value of the iris pattern that occurred during the image recapture. Thus, it is clarified that orientation recognition by the MO method is easily influenced by a slight change in the pixel values.

5   Conclusion

In this study, we evaluated the effectiveness of the orientation recognition performance of R-SAN net by comparing its orientation recognition characteristics with those of the MO method. From the experimental result, it was observed that R-SAN net exhibited fairly good orientation recognition performance for an arbitrary input orientation as compared to the MO method. The MO method is vulnerable to slight changes in pixel values. The orientation of the iris pattern was correctly recognized by R-SAN net for arbitrary input orientations.

In a future study, we will investigate the orientation recognition characteristics for the iris pattern captured by a rotating camera.

References

1. Yoshikawa, T., Nakamura, K.: Evaluation of recognition ability and inside parameters for spreading associative neural network. IEICE Trans. Inf. & Syst. J83-D-II(5), 1332–1343 (2000)
2. Takano, H., Kobayasi, H., Nakamura, K.: Rotation invariant iris recognition method adaptive to ambient lighting variation. IEICE Trans. Inf. & Syst. E90-D, 955–962 (2007)
3. Georgopoulus, A.P., Kalaska, J.F., Caminiti, R., Massey, J.T.: On the relations between the direction of two-dimensional arm movements and cell discharge in primate motor cortex. J. Neurosci. 2, 1527–1537 (1982)
4. Gonzalez, R.C., Woods, R.E.: Digital image processing, pp. 514–518. Addison-Wesley, Reading (1992)
5. Ozaki, H., Taniguti, K.: Image processing, pp. 215–218. Kyoritsu Shuppan CO., LTD. (1983)

Clustering Based on LVQ and a Split and Merge Procedure

Fujiki Morii

Dept. of Information and Computer Sciences,
Nara Women's University, Nara 630-8506, Japan
fmorii@ics.nara-wu.ac.jp

Abstract. Although learning vector quantization (LVQ) based on learning concept is a typical clustering method, we cannot necessarily obtain satisfactory classification results for linearly separable data. In this paper, a new clustering method based on LVQ and a split and merge procedure is proposed to realize reliable classification. Introducing a criterion of whether or not there is only one cluster in each class after clustering by LVQ, split subclasses in a class are merged into appropriate neighboring classes except one subclass. And the validity of the classification result is checked. Under several classification experiments, the performance of the proposed method is provided.

1   Introduction

An important and fundamental research issue for pattern recognition, image processing and data mining is clustering [1-9], whose aim is to classify unlabeled data forming clusters to classes correctly. In this paper, a new clustering method based on learning vector quantization (LVQ) [1-3] and a split and merge procedure is investigated.

Focusing on split and merge procedures for classification, Ueda et al. [10,11] provide remarkable results on parameter estimations of mixture models, where split and merge procedures are incorporated into the EM algorithm and the Variational Bayesian learning to avoid local minima of object functions.

The ideal of clustering is to classify data without any external restrictions. Although it is assumed that the number of clusters is provided, the K-Means algorithm (KMA) [8,9] and LVQ are typical algorithms for clustering, where KMA is derived from the viewpoint of minimizing the sum of squared-error distortion and LVQ is derived on the basis of learning concept. The value of the distortion function in KMA like the EM algorithm depends on initial cluster centers, and a local minimum may be captured. To avoid its defect and acquire the global minimum, a split and merge procedure is introduced into vector quantization (VQ) by Kaukoranta et al. [12], where VQ being almost equivalent to KMA is used for data compression. By using KMA with the split and merge procedure, i.e., Kaukoranta's method, we may obtain the minimum distortion or its approximations.

M. Ishikawa et al. (Eds.): ICONIP 2007, Part II, LNCS 4985, pp. 57–66, 2008.

However, when there are big differences among statistical distributions of class data, even KMA attaining the minimum distortion reveals bad classification results, which are well known and stated in the research book [9]. Although KMA provides good classification with the high possibility, clustering by the criterion of minimizing the distortion cannot necessarily find correct clusters, especially for those distributions. The motivation of this research is to recover those bad situations.

Fig.1 shows a typical bad classification result by KMA, where data are divided into three regions by three lines, and those cluster centers seem to attain the minimum squared-error distortion. Concerning the detail of the data, refer Section 3. Table 1 shows three of the sum of squared-distortion D_{KMA}, D_{CEN} and D_{OPT}, where D_{KMA} may be the minimum distortion by KMA, D_{CEN} is the distortion by correct centroids of clusters and the Voronoi partition, and D_{OPT} is the distortion by the optimum partition with no classification error. Note that $D_{OPT} > D_{KMA}$.

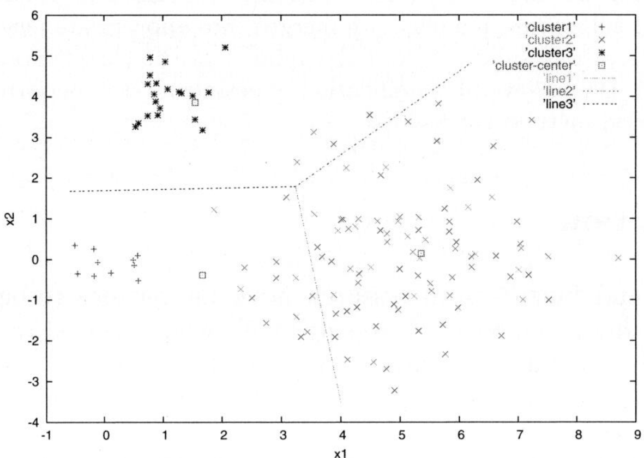

Fig. 1. A typical bad classification result by KMA with $K = 3$

Table 1. Comparison of the distortion D_{KMA}, D_{CEN} and D_{OPT}

	D_{KMA}	D_{CEN}	D_{OPT}
Distortion	373.0	397.8	412.9

After classifying data by an appropriate method such as Kaukoranta's method and obtaining good cluster centers, in order to deal with these bad situations too, LVQ started with those cluster centers is applied to the data, and a new split and merge procedure and another classification criterion being not the distortion criterion are introduced. KMA and LVQ are relations just like brothers. LVQ in comparison with KMA seems to have the high possibility of acquiring correct centroids of clusters. Hence we adopt LVQ in this paper.

By classifying the data by LVQ, suppose that we obtain samples classified into K classes. A method determining whether or not there is only a cluster in each class is introduced, where LVQ is applied to samples in each class again, and a measure of splitting a class into subclasses is introduced. When it is determined that the class must be split into subclasses, by comparing the dissimilarities between samples in the subclasses and samples in adjacent classes, the other subclasses except one subclass are merged into appropriate adjacent classes. This classification method by LVQ is a LVQ type version of the method by KMA [13].

This procedure is described in Section 2 in detail. In Section 3, several experimental results by this clustering method using LVQ and the split and merge procedure are shown for data composed from pseudo random numbers [14].

2 Clustering Based on LVQ and a Split and Merge Procedure

Let us consider classification of linearly separable data, where a set X of n samples $\boldsymbol{x}_i = (x_{i1}, \ldots, x_{iD}), i = 1, \ldots, n$ is partitioned into K disjoint subsets (classes) $X_k, k = 1, \ldots, K$.

Assume that we obtain appropriate cluster centers which satisfy the minimum squared-error distortion or its approximation by using random initialization or a classification method such as Kaukoranta's method. Subsequently, to realize more reliable classification, a clustering method based on LVQ and a split and merge procedure shown below is excuted.

(LVQ Algorithm)
(LVQ1) Set initial values of cluster centers $\{\boldsymbol{c}_k(1), k = 1, \ldots, K\}$. Repeat (LVQ2) and (LVQ3) for $t = 1, 2, \ldots$ untill convergent.
(LVQ2) Set

$$\boldsymbol{c}_l(t) = \arg \min_{1 \leq k \leq K} \parallel \boldsymbol{x}(t) - \boldsymbol{c}_k(t) \parallel . \tag{1}$$

(LVQ3) Compute

$$\boldsymbol{c}_l(t + 1) \leftarrow \boldsymbol{c}_l(t) + \alpha(t)[\boldsymbol{x}(t) - \boldsymbol{c}_l(t)], \tag{2}$$

and determine $\boldsymbol{x}(t) \in$ class X_l.
(End of LVQ)

In the LVQ algorithm, we use $\boldsymbol{x}(1) = \boldsymbol{x}_1, \cdots, \boldsymbol{x}(n) = \boldsymbol{x}_n, \boldsymbol{x}(n + 1) = \boldsymbol{x}_1, \cdots,$ $\boldsymbol{x}(2n) = \boldsymbol{x}_n, \boldsymbol{x}(2n + 1) = \boldsymbol{x}_1, \cdots,$ and a learning rate $\alpha(t) = \text{constant}/t$.

Next, for classes $X_k, k = 1, \ldots, K$ classified by LVQ, let us consider a criterion determining whether or not there is only a cluster in each class by using LVQ again.

After classifying the samples in X by using LVQ, assume that we obtain classes $\{X_k\}$ and cluster centers $\{\boldsymbol{c}_k\}$. When it is determined that there is only a cluster in each X_k, the processing of clustering stops. However, if it is determined that there are two or more clusters in X_k, only a correct subcluster must survive in X_k by splitting X_k and merging other incorrect subclusters into adjacent classes. A method to dissolve this issue is proposed and investigated, where LVQ is used for the samples in each X_k again, and a split and merge procedure is applied to X_k and the subclasses of X_k.

After LVQ with $K = m$ for $2 \leq m \leq M$ is applied to the samples in X_k, X_k is split into m subclasses, whose subclasses and their cluster centers are denoted by $\{X_{k,p}^{(m)}, p = 1, \ldots, m\}$ and $\{c_{k,p}^{(m)}, p = 1, \ldots, m\}$, respectively. In the ordinary situations of clustering, 2 or 3 as the value of M is used.

The squared-distortion for X_k is defined as

$$D_k^{(m=1)} = \sum_{x_i \in X_k} \|x_i - c_k\|^2. \tag{3}$$

Under the definition of the distortion for $X_{k,p}^{(m)}$ by

$$D_{k,p}^{(m)} = \sum_{x_i \in X_{k,p}^{(m)}} \|x_i - c_{k,p}^{(m)}\|^2, \ m = 2, \ldots, M, \tag{4}$$

the distortion for $X_k^{(m)}$, which means X_k with m subclasses, is provided as

$$D_k^{(m)} = \sum_{p=1}^{m} D_{k,p}^{(m)}. \tag{5}$$

Let us introduce a measure of splitting X_k given by

$$\rho_k(m) = D_k^{(m)}/D_k^{(m-1)}, \ m = 2, \ldots, M. \tag{6}$$

The abrupt decrease of $\rho_k(m)$ on m states that X_k should be split into m subclasses when X_k has m clusters. Consider the situation that for the partition of X_k into $m-1$ subclasses, each cluster center does not become a correct representative of the cluster in the subclass, but for the partition of X_k into m subclasses, each cluster center has the high possibility of becoming a correct representative. Then, the value of $D_k^{(m)}$ decreases abruptly in comparison with the value of $D_k^{(m-1)}$. This matter is demonstrated through classification experiments shown in Section 3.

Calculating

$$\rho_k(m^*) = \min_m \{\rho_k(m), \ m = 2, \ldots, M\}, \tag{7}$$

for a predetermined value ζ, if

$$\rho_k(m^*) < \zeta, \tag{8}$$

we split X_k into m^* subclasses. Otherwise, X_k is not split. The value of ζ is usually chosen on the basis of some experiential results, and the small value of ζ lowers the possibility of splitting.

When the class X_k must be split into the subclasses $\{X_{k,p}^{(m^*)}, p = 1, \ldots, m^*\}$ and the cluster centers $\{\boldsymbol{c}_{k,p}^{(m^*)}, p = 1, \ldots, m^*\}$ of $\{X_{k,p}^{(m^*)}\}$ are obtained by LVQ, only one subclass becomes the new class X_k renewing the old X_k and the other $m^* - 1$ subclasses must be merged into adjacent classes.

Let us define the dissimilarity between $X_{k,p}^{(m^*)}$ and the classes being adjacent to X_k as

$$d(X_{k,p}^{(m^*)}) = \min_{\boldsymbol{x}_i \in X_{k,p}^{(m^*)}, \boldsymbol{x}_j \in X_l, l \neq k} d(\boldsymbol{x}_i, \boldsymbol{x}_j), \tag{9}$$

where $d(\cdot, \cdot)$ expresses the Euclidean distance. Then, the subclass $X_{k,p^*}^{(m^*)}$ given by

$$\hat{d}(X_{k,p^*}^{(m^*)}) = \max_p \{d(X_{k,p}^{(m^*)}), \ p = 1, \ldots, m^*\} \tag{10}$$

becomes the new class X_k. The other subclass $X_{k,p}^{(m^*)}$ being $p \neq p^*$ are merged into the adjacent classes satisfying (9).

(Validity of classification)
After the classification by the split and merge procedure, the validity of the classification result must be checked. When there is only one cluster in each class X_k by using (8), the classification result is adopted. When otherwise, we do not adopt the classification result and the processing process is outputted.

When happening the inconsistency of processing, for example the exchange of subclasses in different classes, the classification result is not adopted.

3   Clustering Experiments

Let us consider the data shown by Fig.2, whose data are composed from three clusters. Cluster 1 is composed from 10 pseudo random numbers with mean $(x_1, x_2) = (0.086, -0.113)$, variance$(x_1, x_2) = (0.167, 0.076)$. Cluster 2 is composed from 100 pseudo random numbers with mean$(x_1, x_2) = (4.98, 0.163)$, variance$(x_1, x_2) = (1.78, 2.23)$. Cluster 3 is composed from 20 pseudo random numbers with mean$((x_1, x_2) = (1.10, 4.04)$, variance$(x_1, x_2) = (0.17, 0.306)$. Then the centroids for the clusters are provided by $(0.0861, -0.113)$, $(4.98, 0.163)$ and $(1.10, 4.04)$.

Fig.3 shows the classification result by LVQ. We obtain $\boldsymbol{c}_1 = (0.695, -0.0738)$, $\boldsymbol{c}_2 = (5.24, 0.132)$ and $\boldsymbol{c}_3 = (1.28, 3.98)$ as the cluster centers. Then, 11 samples among 130 samples are misclassified. The classification result is summarized by Table 2.

Selecting $M = 3$ as the maximum number of subclasses, let us split each class into m subclasses by using LVQ with $K = m$. Partition results of the classes $\{X_k\}$ by LVQ with $m = 2, 3$ are shown by Table 3 and Table 4.

The distortions $\{D_k^{(m)}\}$ for $\{X_k\}$ and $\{X_k^{(m)}\}$ calculated from (3) and (5) are provided in Table 5. Table 6 shows the splitting measures $\{\rho_k^{(m)}\}$ by (6).

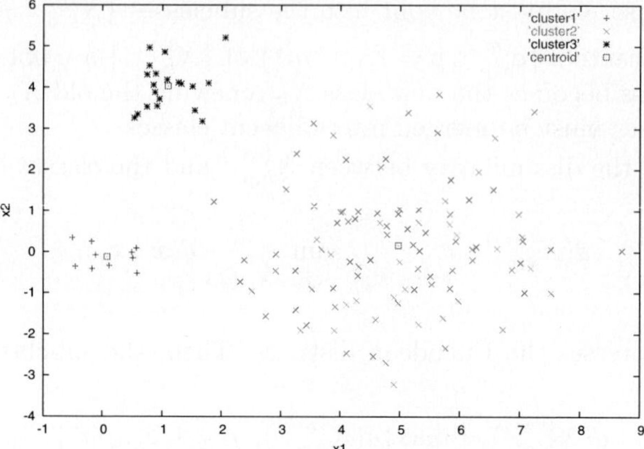

Fig. 2. Data composed from 3 clusters

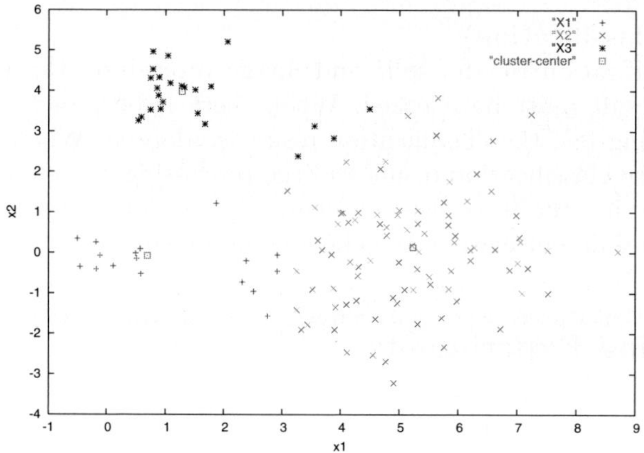

Fig. 3. Classification by LVQ with $K = 3$

Focusing on the values of $\{\rho_k^{(m)}\}$ in Table 6, we recognize that the values of $\rho_{k=1}^{(m=2)}$ and $\rho_{k=3}^{(m=2)}$ are very small. When $\zeta \approx 0.35$ in (8) is settled, it is determined that $m^* = 2$ and the classes X_1 and X_3 must be split into two subclasses, respectively.

Next, based on (10), appropriate subclasses among $\{X_{k,p}^{(m^*=2)}, k = 1, p = 1, 2\}$ and $\{X_{k,p}^{(m^*=2)}, k = 3, p = 1, 2\}$ must be merged into adjacent classes. The dissimilarities between the subclasses and the adjacent classes, and $\{d(X_{k,p}^{(m^*=2)})\}$ of (9) are provided by Table 7. From Table 7, $X_{1,2}^{(m^*=2)}$ is merged into X_2, and $X_{3,2}^{(m^*=2)}$ is merged into X_2.

Fig.4 shows the situation of classification by applying LVQ with $m^* = 2$ to each X_k. The class X_1 is split into two subclasses $X_{1,1}, X_{1,2}$. The right

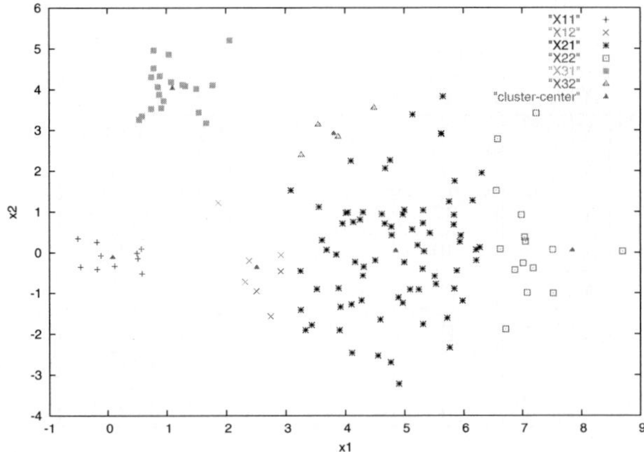

Fig. 4. Classification by LVQ for $K = 3$ and $m^* = 2$

Table 2. Classification result by LVQ

Class	Number	Cluster center
X_1	17	$\boldsymbol{c}_1 = (0.695, -0.0738)$
X_2	89	$\boldsymbol{c}_2 = (5.24, 0.132)$
X_3	24	$\boldsymbol{c}_3 = (1.28, 3.98)$

Table 3. Partition results by LVQ with $m = 2$

Subclass	Number	Cluster center
$X_{1,1}^{(m=2)}$	10	$\boldsymbol{c}_{1,1}^{(m=2)} = (0.0866, -0.110)$
$X_{1,2}^{(m=2)}$	7	$\boldsymbol{c}_{1,2}^{(m=2)} = (2.51, -0.363)$
$X_{2,1}^{(m=2)}$	74	$\boldsymbol{c}_{2,1}^{(m=2)} = (4.85, -0.0461)$
$X_{2,2}^{(m=2)}$	15	$\boldsymbol{c}_{2,2}^{(m=2)} = (7.85, 0.0548)$
$X_{3,1}^{(m=2)}$	20	$\boldsymbol{c}_{3,1}^{(m=2)} = (1.10, 4.04)$
$X_{3,2}^{(m=2)}$	4	$\boldsymbol{c}_{3,2}^{(m=2)} = (3.81, 2.91)$

subclass $X_{1,2}$ is merged into the class X_2. The class X_3 is split into two subclasses $X_{3,1}, X_{3,2}$. The right subclass $X_{3,2}$ is merged into the class X_2.

The final classification result is provided by the same figure as Fig.2. We recognize that the perfect classification for the data is realized with no error.

Lastly, the validity of the final classification result must be checked. According to (5)-(10), we apply LVQ with $K = m(2 \leq m \leq M)$ to the samples classified as Fig.2. We obtain Table 8 and Table 9. From Table 9 and (8), it is concluded that there is one cluster in each classified class.

Table 4. Partition results by LVQ with $m = 3$

Subclass	Number	Cluster center
$X_{1,1}^{(m=3)}$	6	$c_{1,1}^{(m=3)} = (-0.222, -0.0676)$
$X_{1,2}^{(m=3)}$	4	$c_{1,2}^{(m=3)} = (0.652, -0.143)$
$X_{1,3}^{(m=3)}$	7	$c_{1,3}^{(m=3)} = (2.52, -0.355)$
$X_{2,1}^{(m=3)}$	37	$c_{2,1}^{(m=3)} = (4.55, -0.967)$
$X_{2,2}^{(m=3)}$	40	$c_{2,2}^{(m=3)} = (5.37, 1.31)$
$X_{2,3}^{(m=3)}$	12	$c_{2,3}^{(m=3)} = (7.99, -0.171)$
$X_{3,1}^{(m=3)}$	19	$c_{3,1}^{(m=3)} = (1.07, 4.08)$
$X_{3,2}^{(m=3)}$	1	$c_{3,2}^{(m=3)} = (2.34, 3.67)$
$X_{3,3}^{(m=3)}$	4	$c_{3,3}^{(m=3)} = (3.81, 2.91)$

Table 5. Distortions $\{D_k^{(m)}\}$ for $\{X_k\}$ and $\{X_k^{(m)}\}$

	$D_k^{(m=1)}$	$D_k^{(m=2)}$	$D_k^{(m=3)}$
$k = 1$	35.6	7.83	6.49
$k = 2$	306.8	250.0	142.6
$k = 3$	41.2	11.1	10.7

Table 6. Splitting measures $\{\rho_k^{(m)}\}$.

	$\rho_k^{(m=2)}$	$\rho_k^{(m=3)}$
$k = 1$	0.22	0.83
$k = 2$	0.82	0.57
$k = 3$	0.27	0.96

Table 7. Dissimilarity table

Subclass	X_1	X_2	X_3	$d(X_{k,p}^{(m^*)})$
$X_{1,1}^{(m^*=2)}$		2.66	3.09	$d(X_{1,1}^{(m^*)=2}) = 2.66$
$X_{1,2}^{(m^*=2)}$		0.333	1.82	$d(X_{1,2}^{(m^*)=2}) = 0.333$
$X_{3,1}^{(m^*=2)}$	1.97	2.18		$d(X_{3,1}^{(m^*)=2}) = 1.97$
$X_{3,2}^{(m^*=2)}$	1.82	0.628		$d(X_{3,2}^{(m^*)=2}) = 0.628$

Table 8. Validity: Distortions $\{D_k^{(m)}\}$ for $\{X_k\}$ and $\{X_k^{(m)}\}$

	$D_k^{(m=1)}$	$D_k^{(m=2)}$	$D_k^{(m=3)}$
$k = 1$	2.43	0.995	0.693
$k = 2$	401.0	260.0	195.9
$k = 3$	9.52	5.44	3.94

Table 9. Validity: Splitting measures $\{\rho_k^{(m)}\}$

	$\rho_k^{(m=2)}$	$\rho_k^{(m=3)}$
$k = 1$	0.410	0.697
$k = 2$	0.648	0.753
$k = 3$	0.571	0.725

4 Conclusion

We proposed a new clustering method based on LVQ and the split and merge procedure to improve the classification performance of the ordinary LVQ algorithm. After introducing the splitting measure and the dissimilarity measure for merging, the classification method proposed in this paper was applied to the data that reveal the typical bad performance by the ordinary LVQ algorithm. Under some classification experiments, the performance of this method was investigated. As a future issue, we would like to develop this method to a general and robust method under the consideration of research results by the papers [10,11,12,13]. And it is also an important issue to estimate the number of clusters correctly.

References

1. Kohonen, T.: Self-Organizing Maps, 2nd edn. Springer, Berlin (1997)
2. Pal, N.R., Bezdek, J.C., Tsao, C.-K.: Generalized Clustering Networks and Kohonen's Self-Organizing Scheme. IEEE Trans. Neural Network 4(4), 549–557 (1993)
3. Miyamoto, S.: Intoduction of Cluster Analysis: Theory and Applications of Fuzzy Clustering. Morikita-Syuppan (1999) (in Japanese)
4. Duda, R.O., Hart, P.E., Stork, D.G.: Pattern Classification, 2nd edn. John Wiley & Sons, INC., Chichester (2001)
5. Jain, A.K., Dubes, R.C.: Algorithms for Clustering Data. Prentice-Hall, Englewood Cliffs (1988)
6. Gordon, A.D.: Classification, 2nd edn. Chapman & Hall/CRC, Boca Raton (1999)
7. Bezdek, J.C.: Pattern Recognition with Fuzzy Objective Function Algorithms. Plenum Press, NY (1981)
8. MacQueen, J.: Some Methods for Classification and Analysis of Multivariate Observations. In: Proc. 5th Berkeley Symp. on Math. Stat. and Prob. 1, pp. 281–297. Univ. of California Press, Berkeley and Los Angeles (1967)
9. Linde, Y., Buzo, A., Gray, R.M.: An Algorithm for Vector Quantizer Design. IEEE Trans. Commun. 28, 84–95 (1980)
10. Ueda, N., Nakano, R.: EM Algorithm with Split and Merge Operations for Mixture Models. Systems and Computers in Japan 31(5), 930–940 (2000)
11. Ueda, N., Ghahramani, Z.: Bayesian model search for mixture models based on optimizing variational bounds. Neural Networks 15, 1223–1241 (2002)

12. Kaukoranta, T., Franti, P., Nevalainen, O.: Iterative split-and-merge algorithm for vector quantization codebook generation. Optical Engineering 37(10), 2726–2732 (1998)
13. Morii, F., Kurahashi, K.: Clustering by the K-means algorithm using a split and merge procedure. In: Proc. of SCIS and ISIS 2006, pp. 1767–1770 (2006)
14. Press, W.H., Flannery, B.P., Teukolsky, S.A., Vetterling, W.T.: Numerical Recipes in C. Cambridge University Press, Cambridge (1988)

Experimental Analysis of Exchange Ratio in Exchange Monte Carlo Method

Kenji Nagata[1] and Sumio Watanabe[2]

[1] Department of Computational Intelligence and Systems Science, Tokyo Institute of Technology, MailBox R2-5,4259, Nagatsuta, Midori-ku, Yokohama, 226-8503 Japan
`kenji.nagata@cs.pi.titech.ac.jp`
[2] P&I Lab., Tokyo Institute of Technology
`swatanab@pi.titech.ac.jp`

Abstract. In hierarchical learning machines such as neural networks, Bayesian learning provides better generalization performance than maximum likelihood estimation. However, its accurate approximation using a Markov chain Monte Carlo (MCMC) method requires huge computational cost. The exchange Monte Carlo (EMC) method was proposed as an improved algorithm of MCMC method. Although its effectiveness has been shown not only in Bayesian learning but also in many fields, the mathematical foundation of EMC method has not yet been established. In our previous work, we analytically clarified the asymptotic behavior of average exchange ratio, which is used as a criterion for designing the EMC method. In this paper, we verify the accuracy of our result by comparing the theoretical value of average exchange ratio with the experimental value, and propose the method to check the convergence of EMC method based on our theoretical result.

1   Introduction

A lot of learning machines with hierarchical structures such as neural networks and hidden Markov models are widely used for pattern recognition, gene analysis and many other applications. For these hierarchical learning machines, Bayesian learning is proven to provide better generalization performance than maximum likelihood estimation [1] [13][14].

In Bayesian learning, we need to compute the expectation over a Bayesian posterior distribution, which cannot be performed exactly. Therefore, Bayesian learning requires some approximation methods. One of the well-known approximation methods is the Markov chain Monte Carlo (MCMC) method. The MCMC method is well-known algorithm to generate a sample sequence which converges to a target distribution. However, it requires huge computational cost because of slow convergence of a sample sequence, in particular, in the Bayesian posterior distribution for a hierarchical learning machine.

Recently, various improvements of MCMC method have been developed based on the idea of extended ensemble, which are surveyed in [7]. Multicanonical method [3] and simulated tempering [9] belong to this category called extended

M. Ishikawa et al. (Eds.): ICONIP 2007, Part II, LNCS 4985, pp. 67–76, 2008.

ensemble methods. This idea gives us a general strategy to overcome the problem of slow convergence of a conventional MCMC method. The exchange Monte Carlo (EMC) method is well known as one of the extended ensemble methods [5]. This method is to generate a sample sequence from a joint distribution which consists of many distributions with different temperatures. Its algorithm is made of two steps of MCMC simulations. One is the conventional update of MCMC simulation for each distribution. The other is the probabilistic exchange process between two neighboring sequences. The EMC method has been successfully applied to not only Bayesian learning in hierarchical learning machines [8] but also an optimization problem [6][11] and a protein-folding problem [12].

When we design the EMC method, the setting of temperatures is very important to make this algorithm efficient [4]. The values of temperature have close relation to the exchange ratio and its average, which is the acceptance ratio of exchange process. Although the average exchange ratio is used as a criterion for the setting of temperatures, the mathematical property of average exchange ratio has not been clarified. In our previous work, we mathematically clarified the asymptotic behavior of average exchange ratio, and propose the optimal setting of temperatures for the EMC method.

In this paper, we verify our theoretical result by comparing the theoretical value of average exchange ratio with the experimental value. Moreover, we propose the method to check the convergence of EMC method based on our theoretical result.

This paper consists of five chapters. In Chapter 2, we explain the framework of EMC method and the design of EMC method. In Chapter 3, the main result of analysis for the EMC method is described. Discussion and Conclusion are followed in Chapter 4 and 5.

2   Background

2.1   Exchange Monte Carlo Method

In this section, we introduce the well-known EMC method.

Suppose that $w \in R^d$ and our aim is to generate a sample sequence from the following target probability distribution with an energy function $f(w)$ and a probability distribution $\varphi(w)$,

$$p(w) = \frac{1}{Z(n)} \exp(-nf(w))\varphi(w),$$

where $Z(n)$ is the normalization constant. In Bayesian learning, we need to generate a sample sequence from a Bayesian posterior distribution in order to estimate the expectation. Then, the number n, the function $f(w)$ and the probability distribution $\varphi(w)$ respectively correspond to the number of training data, Kullback information between a true distribution and a learning machine, and the prior distribution of parameters. The EMC method treats a compound system which consists of K non-interacting sample sequences from the system concerned. The k-th sample sequence $\{w_k\}$ converges to the following probability distribution,

$$p(w|t_k) = \frac{1}{Z(nt_k)} \exp(-nt_k f(w))\varphi(w) \quad (1 \leq k \leq K),$$

where $t_1 < t_2 < \cdots < t_K$ is called "inverse temperatures" (in this paper, we call "temperatures" hereafter). Given a set of temperatures $\{t\} = \{t_1, \cdots, t_K\}$, the joint distribution for finding $W = \{w_1, w_2, \cdots, w_K\}$ is expressed by a simple product formula, $p(W) = \prod_{k=1}^{K} p(w_k|t_k)$. The EMC method is based on two types of updating in constructing a Markov chain. One is conventional updates based on the Metropolis algorithm for each target distribution $p(w_k|t_k)$. The other is the position exchange between two neighboring sequences, that is, $\{w_k, w_{k+1}\} \to \{w_{k+1}, w_k\}$. The transition probability u is determined by the detailed balance condition for the simultaneous distribution $p(W)$ as follows,

$$u = \min(1, r)$$
$$r = \frac{p(w_{k+1}|t_k)p(w_k|t_{k+1})}{p(w_k|t_k)p(w_{k+1}|t_{k+1})} = \exp(n(t_{k+1} - t_k)(f(w_{k+1}) - f(w_k))). \qquad (1)$$

Hereafter, we call u "exchange ratio".

Consequently, the following two steps are carried out alternately:

1. Each sequence is generated simultaneously and independently for a few iterations by a conventional MCMC method.
2. Two positions are exchanged with the exchange ratio u.

The advantage of EMC method is to accelerate the convergence of sample sequence compared to the conventional MCMC method. The conventional MCMC method requires huge computational cost to generate sample sequence from a target distribution because this algorithm is based on local updating. The EMC method can realize the efficient sampling by preparing a simple distribution such as a normal distribution, which is easy for sample sequence to converge. In practice, we set the temperature of a target distribution as $t_K = 1$, and $\varphi(w)$ is sought to be a simple distribution that is easy to sample from and $t_1 = 0$.

2.2   Exchange Ratio of EMC Method

When we design the EMC method, the setting of temperatures is very important to make the EMC method efficient. As we can see in Eq.(1), temperature has close relation to the exchange ratio. Therefore, temperature is very important parameter in adjusting the exchange ratio and its average.

For the efficient EMC method, each sample needs to wander over the whole temperature region. Moreover, the time for a sample to move from end to end (from t_1 to t_K) is good to be short. Therefore, it is not efficient for the interval of neighboring temperatures to be large, which leads to the low average exchange ratio. On the contrary, in order to make the average exchange ratio higher, the interval of neighboring temperatures has to be smaller, that is, the total number K of temperatures needs to be large. Therefore, this setting is not efficient because it needs huge cost to generate the sample from each distribution. Consequently, the set of temperatures needs to be optimized so that the average exchange ratios for any neighboring temperatures becomes not low and not too high.

As above mentioned, the average exchange ratio is used as a criterion for the setting of temperatures. However, the theoretical property of average exchange ratio has not been clarified. Hence, in order to obtain the value of average exchange ratio, we have to carry out EMC simulations. Moreover, there is the problem that the accuracy of experimental average exchange ratio is not clear because EMC method is based on a probabilistic algorithm.

In our previous work, we analytically clarified the asymptotic behavior of average exchange ratio in the low temperature limit, $n \to \infty$ [10]. This result gives us a criterion for optimizing the set of temperatures and for checking the convergence of EMC simulations. However, the accuracy of this theoretical result has not been clarified experimentally.

In this paper, we verify the accuracy of our result by comparing the theoretical value of average exchange ratio with the experimental value, and propose the method to check the convergence of EMC method based on our theoretical result.

3   Our Previous Work

In this section, we introduce the theoretical result of our previous study [10].

We assume that $t > 0$ and $t + \Delta t > 0$, and consider the EMC method between the following two distributions,

$$p_1(w) = \frac{1}{Z(nt)} \exp(-ntf(w))\varphi(w)$$

$$p_2(w) = \frac{1}{Z(n(t + \Delta t))} \exp(-n(t + \Delta t)f(w))\varphi(w),$$

where the interval Δt of two temperatures is not necessarily small. As we can see in Eq.(1), the exchange ratio u is a function of each sample w_1 and w_2. Hence, we define the average exchange ratio J as the expectation of exchange ratio over the joint distribution $p_1(w_1) \times p_2(w_2)$ as follows,

$$J = \int \int u p_1(w_1) p_2(w_2) dw_1 dw_2.$$

Note that the average exchange ratio J is a function of the temperature t and the interval Δt of two temperatures.

In a lot of learning machines with hierarchical structures, the Bayesian posterior distribution does not converge to the normal distribution as $n \to \infty$ because the Hessian of log likelihood $f(w)$ is not positive definite. We can assume $f(w) \geq 0$ and $f(w_0) = 0(\exists w_0)$ without loss of generality.

The zeta function of $f(w)$ and $\varphi(w)$ is defined by

$$\zeta(z) = \int f(w)^z \varphi(w) dw,$$

where z is a one complex variable. Then $\zeta(z)$ is a holomorphic function in the region of $Re(z) > 0$, and can be analytically continued to the meromorphic function on the entire complex plane, whose poles are all real, negative, and rational numbers [2]. We also define the rational number $-\lambda$ as the largest pole of zeta function $\zeta(z)$ and the natural number m as its order. If the Hessian matrix $\left(\frac{\partial^2 f(w)}{\partial w_i \partial w_j}\right)$ is positive definite for arbitrary w, it holds that $\lambda = \frac{d}{2}$, $m = 1$. Otherwise, λ and m can be calculated by using the resolution of singularities in algebraic geometry [2]. In fact, there are some studies to calculate the value λ and m for a certain energy function $f(w)$ and a probability distribution $\varphi(w)$ [14].

Under these conditions, we proved the following theorem about the average exchange ratio.

Theorem 1. *The average exchange ratio J converges to the following value as $n \to \infty$,*

$$J \to \begin{cases} \left(1 + \frac{\Delta t}{t}\right)^\lambda \frac{2\Gamma(2\lambda)}{\Gamma(\lambda)^2} g(\lambda, \frac{\Delta t}{t}) & \text{(if } \Delta t \geq 0) \\ \left(1 - \frac{\Delta t}{t + \Delta t}\right)^\lambda \frac{2\Gamma(2\lambda)}{\Gamma(\lambda)^2} g(\lambda, -\frac{\Delta t}{t + \Delta t}) & \text{(if } \Delta t < 0), \end{cases}$$

where $g(\lambda, \frac{\Delta t}{t})$ is defined by

$$g\left(\lambda, \frac{\Delta t}{t}\right) = \int_0^1 \frac{s^{\lambda - 1}}{(1 + \frac{\Delta t}{t} + s)^{2\lambda}} ds.$$

The condition $n \to \infty$ means that the coefficients, nt and $n(t + \Delta t)$, of exponential part in the distributions $p_1(w)$ and $p_2(w)$ also go to infinity. Hence, if the value t is equal to or smaller than order of $\frac{1}{n}$, our theorem cannot be applied to these distributions.

Although the range of temperature which our theorem is applicable is limited, we clarify the average exchange ratio quantitatively. According to Theorem 1, the average exchange ratio is expressed by a function of the term $\frac{\Delta t}{t}$ or $\frac{\Delta t}{t + \Delta t}$. Hence, in order to make the average exchange ratio constant over the various temperatures, the set of temperatures should be set as the values $\frac{\Delta t}{t}$ are constant over the various temperatures. Then, the set $\{t_k\}$ of temperatures becomes a geometric progression. Consequently, we can see by Theorem 1 that the set of temperatures should be set as a geometric progression in order to make the average exchange ratio constant over the various temperatures.

4   Experiments

In this section, we show the experimental results to verify the accuracy of our theoretical study.

4.1   Setting

Setting of Target Distribution. Let w be set as $\{w = (A, B)\}$, where A and B are respectively an $H \times M$ matrix and an $N \times H$ matrix. Then, the dimension d of w is $d = (M + N)H$. In our experiment, we considered the sampling from the following target distribution, $p(w) = \frac{1}{Z(n)} \exp(-nf(w))\varphi(w)$. Let the function $f(w)$ be given by $f(w) = ||BA - B_0 A_0||^2$, where A_0 and B_0 are respectively an $H_0 \times M$ matrix and an $N \times H_0$ matrix. This setting corresponds to Bayesian learning in the reduced rank regression [1]. Here, M, N, H_0 and H respectively show the numbers of input units, output units, hidden units for a true structure, and hidden units for a learning machine. The number n was set as 1000 and the probability distribution $\varphi(w)$ was defined by the d-dimensional normal distribution whose mean and variance are respectively 0 and 10. The elements of matrix A_0 and B_0 were randomly chosen from the standard normal distribution.

In our experiment, we simulated the following two cases,

1. $M = N = 10$, $H_0 = 2$ and $H = 6$,
2. $M = N = 20$, $H_0 = 4$ and $H = 12$.

In these cases, the value λ can be analytically calculated as follows [1], and each value becomes 32 and 128.

Setting of EMC Method. Our theoretical result claims that the set of temperatures should be set as a geometric progression in order to make the average exchange ratio constant over the various temperatures. Therefore, in our experiment, we set each temperature $\{t_1, \cdots, t_K\}$ as follows,

$$t_k = \begin{cases} 0 & (\text{if } k = 1) \\ (1.125)^{-K+k} & (\text{otherwise}). \end{cases}$$

The total number K of temperatures was set as 145 in case 1 and 165 in case 2. As a criterion for the iteration of EMC, we define "Monte Carlo Step (MCS)". Let 1 MCS means once simulating Step 1 and Step 2 for EMC algorithm. In Step 1, we used the Metropolis algorithm as a conventional MCMC method. The iteration for Step 1 was set as one. In Step 2, the rule for selecting exchange pairs was

$$\{(w_1, w_2), (w_3, w_4), \cdots, (w_{K-2}, w_{K-1})\} \text{ if MCS is odd,}$$
$$\{(w_2, w_3), (w_4, w_5), \cdots, (w_{K-1}, w_K)\} \quad \text{otherwise.}$$

Average Exchange Ratio. In these settings, the value of $\frac{\Delta t}{t}$ is 0.125. From the value of $\frac{\Delta t}{t}$ and λ, we calculate the theoretical value of average exchange ratio using numerical integration. As a result, we obtain the theoretical value 0.638955 for case 1 and 0.346667 for case 2. For numerically calculating the

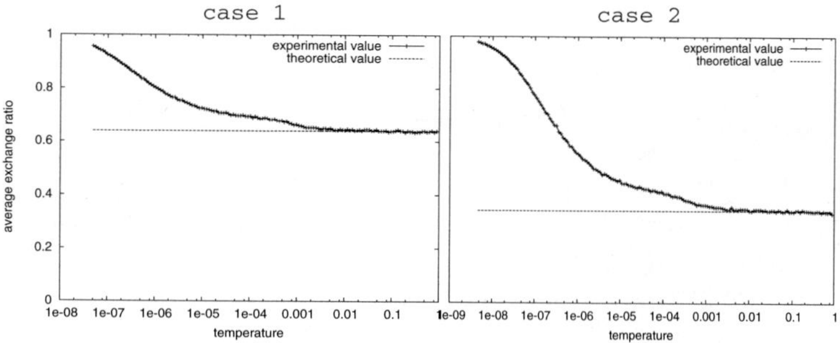

Fig. 1. The experimental value of average exchange ratio against the value of temperature. Horizontal lines show the theoretical value.

average exchange ratio, let the average exchange ratio $J(t_k)$ $\{k : 1 \leq k \leq K-1\}$ be defined as follows,

$$J(t_k) = \frac{1}{\text{MCS}} \sum_{i=1}^{\text{MCS}} r_i(t_k),$$

$$r(t_k) = \begin{cases} 1 \text{ (if the exchange between } w_k \text{ and } w_{k+1} \text{ is accepted)} \\ 0 \text{ (otherwise).} \end{cases}$$

4.2   Experimental Results

Under these settings, we simulated some experiments.

Firstly, we verified the accuracy of our theorem. Figure 1 shows the experimental result of average exchange ratio. The horizontal axis shows the value of temperature and the vertical one the average exchange ratio. In this experiment, we set MCS 100000. In these figures, there are horizontal lines, which show the theoretical values of average exchange ratio. As we above mentioned, our theorem is applicable to the distributions which has temperature larger than order of $\frac{1}{n}$. Hence, in the range [0.001 : 1] of temperature, the experimental value of average exchange ratio can be seen to be equal to the theoretical value for any temperatures. On the contrary, in the other range [0 : 0.001], the experimental value of average exchange ratio is larger than the theoretical value.

Secondly, we studied the behavior of average exchange ratio as MCS increases. Figure 2 shows the average exchange ratios for some temperatures $t = \{1.125^{-1}, 1.125^{-11}, 1.125^{-21}, 1.125^{-31}, 1.125^{-41}\}$. Note that $1.125^{-41} \cong 0.008 > 0.001$. This means that all the values of average exchange ratios in Figure 2 finally converge to the theoretical value because of the above experimental result. The horizontal axis shows the value of MCS and the vertical one the average exchange ratio. The horizontal lines on these figures show the theoretical values. From these figures, we can see that any average exchange ratios begin to converge to the theoretical value in a certain MCS, about 600 MCS in case 1 and about 1200 MCS in case 2.

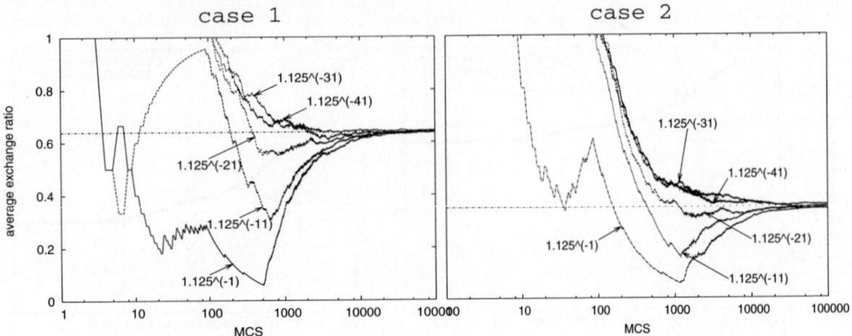

Fig. 2. The experimental value of average exchange ratio against MCS. Horizontal lines show the theoretical value. The value of temperature for each graph is 1.125^{-1}, 1.125^{-11}, 1.125^{-21}, 1.125^{-31} and 1.125^{-41}.

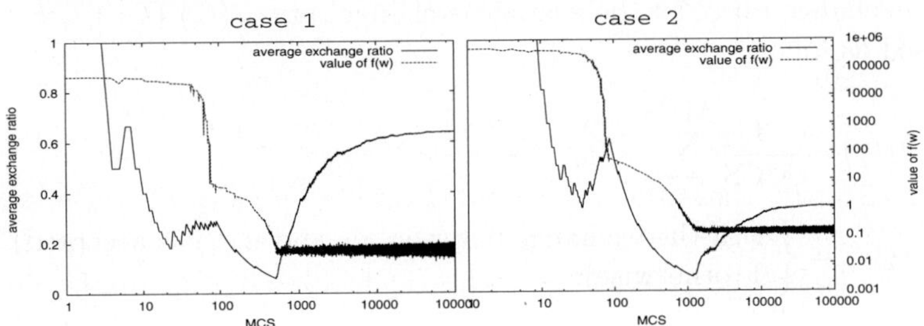

Fig. 3. A comparison between the average exchange ratio and the value of function $f(w)$ against MCS

In order to clarify this point more clearly, we compared the average exchange ratio with the value of function $f(w)$. Figure 3 shows the comparison between the average exchange ratio and the function $f(w)$. The horizontal axis shows the value of MCS and vertical ones the average exchange ratio of the temperature $t = 1.125^{-1}$ and the value of function $f(w)$ of temperature $t = 1$. By comparing these functions, the MCS when the value of function $f(w)$ converges and the MCS when the average exchange ratio begins to converge are almost equal. Therefore, we can check the convergence of function $f(w)$ by monitoring the value of average exchange ratio. This fact can be used as a criterion for checking the convergence of EMC method.

5   Discussion

In this paper, we clarified the accuracy of our theoretical result by comparing the theoretical value of average exchange ratio to the experimental value and proposed the method to check the convergence of EMC method.

In the first experiment, we verified the fact that the experimental value of average exchange ratio is almost equal to the theoretical value, and that the average exchange ratios are almost constant over the various temperatures by setting the temperatures as a geometric progression. On the contrary, in the small value of temperature, the average exchange ratio is larger than the theoretical value.

In general, the behavior of average exchange ratio depends on the two distributions, $p(w|t = 0)$ and $p(w|t = 1)$. For our experience, if the peak(s) of the distribution $p(w|t)$ change as the value t of temperature increases from 0 to 1, the average exchange ratio rapidly decreases in certain temperature(s) by setting the temperatures as a geometric progression, which leads to inefficient EMC method. In our experiment, there is no temperature where the average exchange ratio rapidly decreases. This means that EMC method can work efficiently for Bayesian learning in reduced rank regression.

In the second experiment, we verified that the experimental values of average exchange ratios for any temperatures begin to converge to the theoretical value in a certain MCS, and that the value of function $f(w)$ also converges in this MCS. Based on these facts, we proposed the method to check the convergence of EMC method.

When discussing the convergence of EMC method, there are the following two problems, One is how many samples should be rejected in order to reduce the influence of initial value? The other is how many samples should be generated in order to approximate a target distribution accurately? These two problems are very important to generate a sample sequence from a target distribution accurately. Our proposed method, which is to monitor the average exchange ratios for some temperatures, is to overcome the problem 1. In general, a method to monitor the value of function $f(w)$ is often used in order to address the problem 1. However, it is not easy to check the convergence by this method because the value of function $f(w)$ after a sample converges is generally unknown. On the contrary, since the theoretical value of average exchange ratio is clarified, it is easy to check the convergence by our proposed method. Moreover, although the theoretical value cannot be calculated because the value of λ is unknown, our proposed method can be applied to checking the convergence by using the property that the average exchange ratios are almost constant over the various temperatures by setting the temperatures as a geometric progression. On the other hand, as a method to address the problem 2, a method to count the total samples which move from t_1 to t_K in a temperature space is often used. This method is considered to have close relation to the average exchange ratio for all temperatures. Hence, our theoretical result can be applied to addressing the problem 2, which should be addressed as a future work.

6   Conclusion

In this paper, we clarified the accuracy of our theoretical result by comparing the theoretical value of average exchange ratio to the experimental value. As a result, the following properties are verified that the experimental value of average exchange ratio is almost equal to the theoretical value, that the average exchange ratios are almost constant over the various temperatures by setting the temperatures as a geometrical progression, and that the experimental values of average exchange ratios for any temperatures begin to converge to the theoretical value in a certain MCS. Moreover, from these properties, we proposed the method to check the convergence of EMC method. As the future works, constructing the design of EMC method and applying these results to the practical problem should be addressed.

Acknowledgment. This work was partially supported by the Ministry of Education, Culture, Sports, Science and Technology, Grant-in-Aid for JSPS Fellows 18-5809, and for Scientific Research 18079007, 2007.

References

1. Aoyagi, M., Watanabe, S.: Stochastic complexities of reduced rank regression in Bayesian estimation. Neural Networks 18(7), 924–933 (2005)
2. Atiyah, M.F.: Resolution of singularities and division of distributions. Communications of Pure and Applied Mathematics 13, 145–150 (1970)
3. Berg, B.A., Neuhaus, T.: Multicanonical algorithms for first order phase transitions. Physics Letter B 267(2), 249–253 (1991)
4. Hukushima, K.: Domain Wall Free Energy of Spin Glass Models: Numerical Method and Boundary Conditions. Physical Review E 60, 3606–3613 (1999)
5. Hukushima, K., Nemoto, K.: Exchange Monte Carlo Method and Application to Spin Glass Simulations. Journal of Physical Society of Japan 65(6), 1604–1608 (1996)
6. Hukushima, K.: Extended ensemble Monte Carlo approach to hardly relaxing problems. Computer Physics Communications 147, 77–82 (2002)
7. Iba, Y.: Extended Ensemble Monte Carlo. International Journal of Modern Physics C 12, 623–656 (2001)
8. Liang, F.: An effective Bayesian neural network classifier with a comparison study to support vector machine. Neural Computation 15, 1959–1989 (2003)
9. Marinari, E., Parisi, G.: Simulated tempering: a new Monte Carlo scheme. Europhysics Letters 19(6), 451–455 (1992)
10. Nagata, K., Watanabe, S.: Analysis of Exchange Ratio for Exchange Monte Carlo Method. In: Proc. of the First IEEE Symposium on Foundation of Computational Intelligence (FOCI 2007), pp. 434–439 (2007)
11. Pinn, K., Wieczerkowski, C.: Number of Magic Squares from Parallel Tempering Monte Carlo. International Journal of modern Physics 9(4), 541–546 (1998)
12. Sugita, Y., Okamoto, Y.: Replica-exchange molecular dynamics method for protein folding. Chemical Physics Letters 314(1-2), 141–151 (1999)
13. Watanabe, S.: Algebraic Analysis for Nonidentifiable Learning Machines. Neural Computation 13, 899–933 (2001)
14. Yamazaki, K., Watanabe, S.: Singularities in mixture models and upper bounds of stochastic complexity. Neural networks 16(7), 1029–1038 (2003)

Video Restoration with Motion Prediction Based on the Multiresolution Wavelet Analysis

Kei Akiyama[1,2,5], Zhi-wei Luo[3,2], Masaki Onishi[4,2],
Shigeyuki Hosoe[2], Kouichi Taji[1], and Yoji Uno[1]

[1] Nagoya University, Graduate School of Engineering,
Furo-cho, Chikusa-ku Nagoya, 464-8603 Japan
{k_akiyama, taji, uno}@nuem.nagoya-u.ac.jp
[2] Bio-mimetic Control Research Center, RIKEN
2271-130, Anagahora, Shimoshidami, Moriyama-ku Nagoya, 463-0003 Japan,
hosoe@bmc.riken.jp
[3] Kobe University, Faculty of Engineering,
1-1 Rokkohdai-cho, Nada-ku, Kobe, 657-8501, Japan,
luo@gold.kobe-u.ac.jp
[4] Information Technology Research Institute, AIST
1-1-1 Umezono, Tsukuba, 305-8568, Japan
onishi@ni.aist.go.jp
[5] Hitachi Global Storage Technologies Japan, Ltd.
1 Kirihara-cho, Fujisawa, 252-8588, Japan

Abstract. We propose a novel method for image sequence restorations. It is based on the wavelet domain image restoration method proposed by Belge et al. for static images [1]. In this paper, by combining the iteration procedure in the Belge's method with the renewing process for sequentially given images and by employing Kalman filer for predicting the foreground movement of the images in the wavelet domain, considerable reduction of the computational cost is shown to be achievable. This is verified by computer simulations on artificially degraded images.

Keywords: Multiresolution wavelet analysis, Video restoration, Motion dynamics, Nonlinear optimization.

1 Introduction

A video sequence acquired by a camera often contains blur and/or disturbance by various causes. In many applications like image surveillance or broadcasting, these degradation factors need to be automatically removed in order to facilitate higher level recognitions. So far many restoration methods have been proposed especially for static images [1,2]. In recent years the number of restoration method for video sequences is gradually increasing. Pizurica et al. proposed a method [3] which combines spatially adaptive noise filtering in the wavelet domain and temporal filtering in the signal domainD Rares et al. presented an algorithm dealing with degradation related to severe artifacts [4]. In [5,6], Kornprobst et al. proposed some restoration methods utilizing motion compensation.

M. Ishikawa et al. (Eds.): ICONIP 2007, Part II, LNCS 4985, pp. 77–86, 2008.

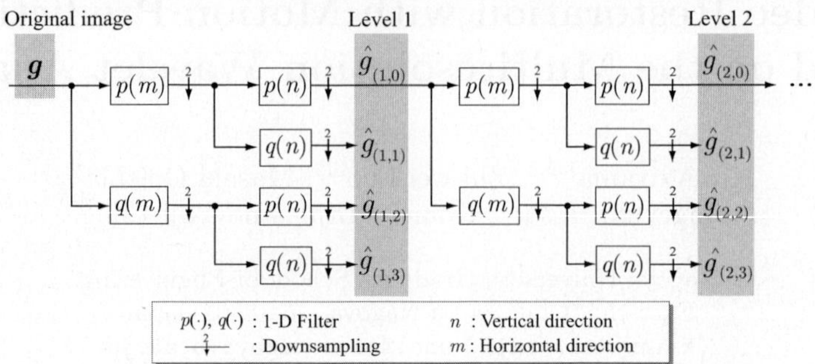

Fig. 1. Block diagrams for the multiresolution wavelet decomposition of an image

For further references, please see [7,8]. With these developments, however, to handle the degradation like optical blur and disturbance which happens more frequently in real environment, more work is needed for restoration.

In this paper, we propose a restoration method for video sequences which are degraded by optical blur and noise. In our previous work [9], we proposed a video restoration method by extending Belge et al.'s restoration method for static images to video case. This method could reduce the computational cost compare to the method of [1] by modeling a class of image sequences by a state equation and predicting future frames based on it. However, there was yet a room for further improvement since we had to execute a multiresolution wavelet reconstruction (MWR, to be described) for making a prediction of the future image in state space. In the present paper, we propose an improved method. Here the prediction of the future image is directly realized in the wavelet domain. This contributes not only reducing the above redundancy but also making the prediction more efficient by utilizing the property of multiresolution wavelet decomposition (MWD) images. We verify our method by computer simulation of an artificially degraded image sequence.

2 Image Restoration Using Multiresolution Wavelet Decomposition

2.1 Multiresolution Wavelet Decomposition

Let g be a lexicographically ordered static image. The block diagram of the MWD of g is shown in Fig. 1. In the figure $p(\cdot)$ and $q(\cdot)$ generally represent an 1-D low-pass and high-pass filter, respectively. From the input image, four down-sampled images are obtained [1]. Furthermore, by repeating the decomposition, we can get multiresolution images [10]. An MWD image $\hat{g}$ calculated by L level MWD is presented as

$$\hat{g} := \left(\hat{g}_{(L,0)}^T, \cdots, \hat{g}_{(L,3)}^T, \hat{g}_{(L-1,1)}^T, \cdots, \hat{g}_{(1,3)}^T \right)^T . \tag{1}$$

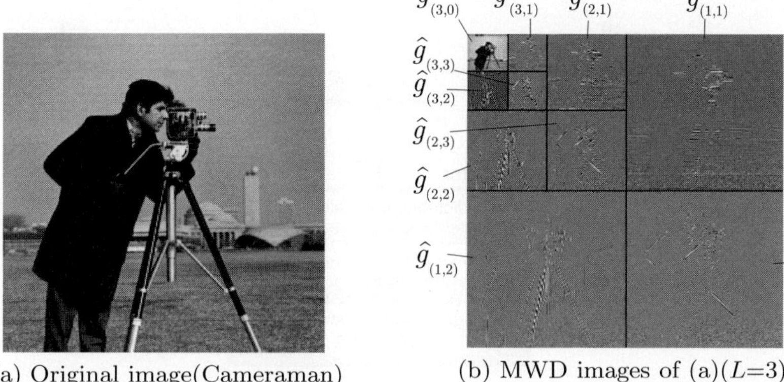

(a) Original image(Cameraman)   (b) MWD images of (a)(L=3)

Fig. 2. An example of the MWD images

An MWD result for the image 'Cameraman' is shown in Fig. 2 as an example. In Fig. 2(b), component $\hat{g}_{(3,0)}$ represents a scaled down image of the original one and other components $\hat{g}_{(l,j)}$ correspond to extracting the 1-D features (horizontal, vertical and diagonal) of the original image. Note that the number of the total pixels is unchanged during the decomposition. Since the decomposition operation has the orthogonal property, we can get the reconstruction operation and it can completely recapture the original image from the decomposed one. We call it the wavelet multiresolution reconstruction (MWR).

2.2 Degradation Process and Its Restoration for MWD Images

Given the low-resolution image sequence $g = \{g^{[1]}, g^{[2]}, \cdots, g^{[K]}\}$ of the original image sequence $f = \{f^{[1]}, f^{[2]}, \cdots, f^{[K]}\}$ of length K. The sequences $\hat{g} = \{\hat{g}^{[1]}, \hat{g}^{[2]}, \cdots, \hat{g}^{[K]}\}$ and $\hat{f} = \{\hat{f}^{[1]}, \hat{f}^{[2]}, \cdots, \hat{f}^{[K]}\}$ denote respectively the MWD of g and f. In this paper, we consider a restoration problem for a given degraded MWD image sequence $\{\hat{g}^{[1]}, \cdots, \hat{g}^{[K]}\}$ which is degraded from its original image sequence $\{\hat{f}^{[1]}, \cdots, \hat{f}^{[K]}\}$, where the superscripts denote the frame number. First, we formulate a degradation process for MWD images [1] by

$$\hat{g}^{[k]} = \hat{H}\hat{f}^{[k]} + \hat{u}^{[k]}. \tag{2}$$

In equation(2), the vector $\hat{u}^{[k]}$ is an additive noise and the matrix $\hat{H}$ represents an linear distortion or optical blur, which can be assumed to be constant with respect to frames since the change is sufficiently small.

When considering a restoration for the degradation process of equation (2), one natural way would be to apply some of the known restoration procedures to each frames one by one, regarding them as static images, and then make necessary modifications to make the computation more efficient and improve

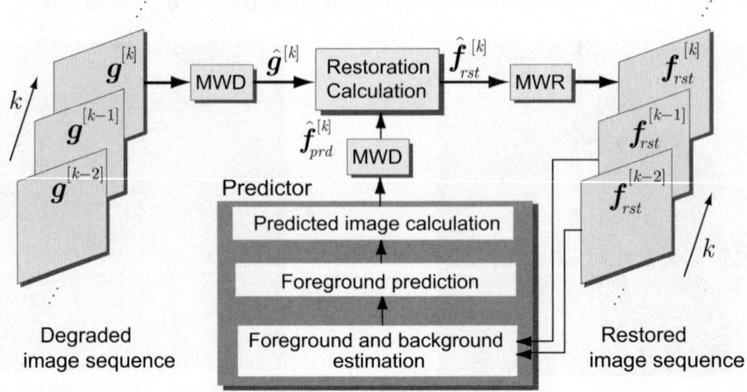

Fig. 3. Block diagram of the image sequence restoration [9]

restoration by considering relationships existing among the frames. In this paper, we follow this way. As a basic restoration method for static images, the one proposed by Berge et al. will be used. The method has been derived by considering minimization of the cost function given by

$$J_k\left(\hat{\boldsymbol{f}}^{[k]}, \lambda\right) = \left\|\hat{\boldsymbol{g}}^{[k]} - \hat{\boldsymbol{H}}\hat{\boldsymbol{f}}^{[k]}\right\|_2^2 + \lambda_{(L,0)}\left\|\hat{f}_{(L,0)}^{[k]}\right\|_p^p + \sum_{l=1}^{L}\sum_{j=1}^{3}\lambda_{(l,j)}\left\|\hat{f}_{(l,j)}^{[k]}\right\|_p^p. \quad (3)$$

The first term of equation (3) represents the closeness of the original image. The second and the third terms express the closeness to the statistical prior knowledge of the natural image in the wavelet domain. Lambdas are the regularization parameters. The optimal restored images can be calculated by a numerical optimization [1]. The algorithm can realize the edge preserving restoration by assigning different parameters to each decomposed image.

However, generally the calculation will become very huge since we have to repeat iterative computations with big size matrices for every frames. To cope with this problem, in [9] by combining the iterative procedure in the Berge's method with the renewing process for sequentially given images and employing Kalman filter, we showed that considerable reduction of the calculation cost can be realized. The block diagram is shown in Fig. 3. In the 'Restoration Calculation' box, the optimal restored image (denoted by $\hat{\boldsymbol{f}}_{rst}^{[k]}$) is calculated by using the following modified equation of the optimization method in [1]:

$$\left(\hat{\boldsymbol{H}}^T\hat{\boldsymbol{H}} + \frac{p}{2}\boldsymbol{D}_{prd}^{[k]}\right)\hat{\boldsymbol{f}}_{rst}^{[k]} = \hat{\boldsymbol{H}}^T\hat{\boldsymbol{g}}^{[k]} \quad (4)$$

$$\boldsymbol{D}_{prd}^{[k]} = \text{diag}\left[\frac{\lambda(i)}{(|\hat{\boldsymbol{f}}_{prd}^{[k]}(i)|^2 + \beta)^{1-p/2}}\right]_{i=1}^{N^2}. \quad (5)$$

Notice that instead of restored image $f_{rst}^{[k]}$ in [1] its predicted image $f_{prd}^{[k]}$ is used here. Predicted image $f_{prd}^{[k]}$ is computed in the 'Predictor' box. To carry out the computations in Predictor box we had made the following assumptions.

A1 An original image sequence consists of a foreground and a background.
A2 The change of the background is small enough to be set as a static image.
A3 The change of the foreground can be formulated or approximated by a known dynamic equation.
A4 The foreground is assumed to be a single rigid body and maintain its orientation.

With the assumptions **A1** and **A2**, we can utilize the restoration result of previous frame directly as an initial estimation of the background for each frame. On the other hand, we can predict a new position of the foreground from the previous restoration result and the information about motion dynamics (**A3**) by using Kalman filter.

This algorithm can reduce the calculation cost for an image sequence restoration compared to the frame by frame optimization based on Belge et al.'s method, while the qualities of the restoration results being almost unaffected. However, yet some redundant calculations are included because it needs MWR calculations of restored images for the sake of making prediction for next frames, and again calculate MWD after a predicted image is obtained. If we could get a predicted image directly in the wavelet domain, the redundancy of this algorithm can be reduced. We state this modified image sequence restoration method in the next section.

3   Video Restoration Algorithm in Wavelet Domain

At first, we show the overall sketch to our new video restoration algorithm in wavelet domain (Fig. 4). In the following, the restoration image and the predicted image of $\hat{f}$ will be represented as $\hat{f}_{rst} = \{\hat{f}_{rst}^{[1]}, \hat{f}_{rst}^{[2]}, \cdots, \hat{f}_{rst}^{[K]}\}$ and $\hat{f}_{prd} = \{\hat{f}_{prd}^{[1]}, \hat{f}_{prd}^{[2]}, \cdots, \hat{f}_{prd}^{[K]}\}$ respectively. According to the structure of MWD, $\hat{f}^{[k]}$ (similarly for $\hat{f}_{rst}^{[k]}$ or $\hat{f}_{prd}^{[k]}$) will be represented as

$$\hat{f}^{[k]} := \left(\hat{f}_{(L,0)}^{[k]T}, \cdots, \hat{f}_{(L,3)}^{[k]T}, \hat{f}_{(L-1,1)}^{[k]T}, \cdots, \hat{f}_{(1,3)}^{[k]T} \right)^T .$$

Step 1 Initialization. Let

$$\hat{f}_{prd}^{[1]} = \hat{g}^{[1]},$$

$\hat{f}_{rst}^{[1]}$ is given by (4) and (5),

$$\hat{f}_{prd}^{[2]} = \hat{f}_{rst}^{[1]},$$

$\hat{f}_{rst}^{[2]}$ is given by (4) and (5).

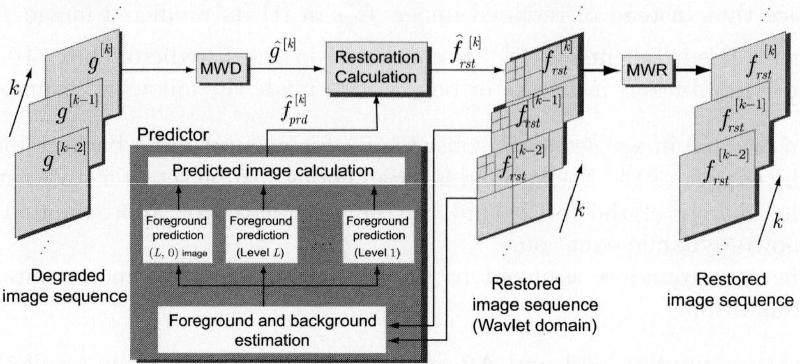

Fig. 4. Block diagram of the proposed method for kth frame

Step 2 With using $\hat{\boldsymbol{f}}_{rst}^{[k-1]}$ and $\hat{\boldsymbol{f}}_{rst}^{[k]}$, for all

$$(l, j) = (L, 0), (L, 1), (L, 2), (L, 3), (L-1, 1), \cdots, (1, 3),$$

compute the followings in turn

$$\hat{\boldsymbol{f}}_{fg(l,j)}^{[k]} \quad : \text{foreground (Sec. } \mathbf{3.2}),$$

$$\hat{\boldsymbol{f}}_{bg(l,j)}^{[k]} \quad : \text{background (Sec. } \mathbf{3.2}),$$

$$\hat{\boldsymbol{f}}_{bd(l,j)}^{[k]} \quad : \text{background domain (Sec. } \mathbf{3.2}),$$

$$\boldsymbol{v}_{(L,0)}^{[k]}, \text{ and } \boldsymbol{v}_{l}^{[k]} \ (l = L, L-1, \cdots, 1).$$

Step 3 Compute the prediction of $\boldsymbol{v}_{l}^{[k+1]}$ using Kalman filter for (11).
Step 4 Compute

$$\hat{\boldsymbol{f}}_{bd(l,j)}^{[k+1]} \quad \text{and} \quad \hat{\boldsymbol{f}}_{fg(l,j)}^{[k+1]} \ (\text{by (8)}),$$

$$\hat{\boldsymbol{f}}_{prd(l,j)}^{[k+1]} \quad \text{by inserting estimated } \hat{\boldsymbol{f}}_{fg(l,j)}^{[k+1]} \text{ into } \hat{\boldsymbol{f}}_{bg(l,j)}^{[k]}.$$

Step 5 Compute $\hat{\boldsymbol{f}}_{rst}^{[k]}$ by (4) and (5).
Step 6 Compute $\boldsymbol{f}_{rst}^{[k]}$ by MWR.
Step 7 If $k = K$, stop. Othewise $k = k+1$ and go to **Step 2**.

In executing the algorithm if it happens that we can not continue computation
by the frame out of the moving object or by a sudden change of the background
we have to cancel the prediction till the next movement is observed.

3.1 Definition of the Dynamics for the MWD Image Sequence

Based on the above assumptions made in **2.2**, we model the dynamics of an
original MWD image sequence as follows. First, we define the variables as in

Table 1. Definition of the variables for kth frame

Item name	Definition
$\hat{f}^{[k]}$	Original image
$\hat{f}_{bd}^{[k]}$	Original background domain (0: foreground, 1: others)
$\hat{f}_{bg}$	Original background image
$\hat{f}_{fg}^{[k]}$	Original foreground image
$\hat{g}^{[k]}$	Degraded image

Table 1. By these definitions, each component of the original MWD image sequence is represented as:

$$\hat{f}_{(l,j)}^{[k]} = \left\{ I_{(N/2^l)^2} - \mathrm{diag}\left[\hat{f}_{bd(l,j)}(i)\right]_{i=1}^{(N/2^l)^2} \right\} \cdot \hat{f}_{bg(l,j)}^{[k]} + \hat{f}_{fg(l,j)}^{[k]}. \qquad (6)$$

$$((l,j) = (L,0) \ \text{and} \ l=1,\cdots,L, \ j=1,2,3)$$

We introduce a transition of a foreground between kth and $k+1$th frames. For this, a motion of a foreground object is described by

$$\begin{bmatrix} \boldsymbol{v}_l^{[k+1]} \\ \boldsymbol{a}_l^{[k+1]} \end{bmatrix} = \begin{bmatrix} I_2 & I_2 \\ 0_{2\times 2} & I_2 \end{bmatrix} \begin{bmatrix} \boldsymbol{v}_l^{[k]} \\ \boldsymbol{a}_l^{[k]} \end{bmatrix}, \qquad (7)$$

where $\boldsymbol{v}_l^{[k]}$ and $\boldsymbol{a}_l^{[k]}$ are velocity and acceleration per a frame of a characteristic point for each decomposed image of kth frame, respectively. I_2 denotes a 2×2 identity matrix. Equation (7) represents an uniform accelerated motion on a 2-D plane. In correspondence with the difference of the initial condition, the various movement (straight lines or parabola-shaped motions in the 2-D plane, for example) can be described in this way. Since from assumption **A4**, the distance between each element of $\hat{f}_{bd(l,j)}^{[k]}$ and its corresponding element of $\hat{f}_{bd(l,j)}^{[k+1]}$ remains the same, the relationship between $\hat{f}_{bd(l,j)}^{[k]}$ and $\hat{f}_{bd(l,j)}^{[k+1]}$ is written by

$$\hat{f}_{bd(l,j)}^{[k+1]}((n-1)N+m)$$
$$= \hat{f}_{bd(l,j)}^{[k]}\left(\left[\left\{(n-v_{lv}^{[k+1]}) \bmod N/2^l\right\}-1\right]N/2^l+\left\{(m-v_{lh}^{[k+1]}) \bmod N/2^l\right\}\right). \qquad (8)$$
$$(n = 1,\cdots,N/2^l, \ m = 1,\cdots,N/2^l)$$

Equation (8) can be expressed using a matrix $\boldsymbol{T}_l(\boldsymbol{v}_l^{[k]})$ as follows:

$$\hat{f}_{bd(l,j)}^{[k+1]} = \boldsymbol{T}_l\left(\boldsymbol{v}_l^{[k+1]}\right) \hat{f}_{bd(l,j)}^{[k]} \qquad (9)$$

$$\boldsymbol{T}_l\left(\boldsymbol{v}_l^{[k+1]}\right) = \mathrm{diag}\left(C_{lh}^{v_{lh}^{[k+1]}},\ldots,C_{lh}^{v_{lh}^{[k+1]}}\right) \cdot C_{lv}^{v_{lv}^{[k+1]}}. \qquad (10)$$

We call $\boldsymbol{T}_l\left(\boldsymbol{v}_l^{[k+1]}\right)$ the transition matrix of level l. C_{lv} and C_{lh} in equation (10) are an $(N/2^l)^2 \times (N/2^l)^2$ dimension block circulant matrix and $N/2^l \times N/2^l$

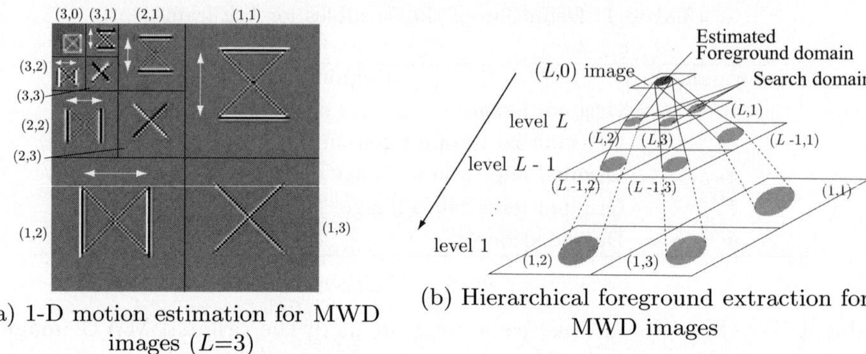

(a) 1-D motion estimation for MWD images ($L=3$)

(b) Hierarchical foreground extraction for MWD images

Fig. 5. Motion estimation for MWD images

dimension circulant matrix respectively, which are the same as in [9]. The transition of foreground image $\hat{f}_{fg(l,j)}^{[k+1]}$ can also be described exactly in the same way as in (9).

3.2   Foreground Extraction and Motion Prediction

First, we estimate optical flow for $(L,0)$ image by taking squared error between local areas of $k-1$th and kth frames. To avoid mismatching, squared errors over a certain threshold would not be recognized as a motion. Second, we extract the foreground object domain, in which the optical flows are similar each other. To detect a motion vector $\boldsymbol{v}_{(L,0)}^{[k]}$ of the foreground object, we take an average of the flows within the foreground object domain.

Since from the properties of MWD, $(L,1)$, $(L,2)$ and $(L,3)$ images are reflecting the vertical, horizontal and diagonal characteristics of an original image more strongly [11], we will use them to detect motions along one direction only. We detect motion of these three images for each one dimension ($(L,1)$ for horizontal direction, $(L,2)$ for vertical direction and $(L,3)$ for diagonal direction) (Fig. 5(a)) within the corresponding domain detected by $(L,0)$ image, and extract foreground objects of each image. Then, we take averages of the motion within the foreground object domains for $(L,1)$ and $(L,2)$ images and assign these values to the motion vector $\boldsymbol{v}_L^{[k]}$. Repeat the above process from level $L-1$ to level 1, and detect the motion vector for each level. Motion search in each level is done within the foreground object domain detected in the upper level (Fig. 5(b)). By this hierarchical searching method, calculation cost can be smaller than the full searching method. The motion vector for level l is denoted as $\boldsymbol{v}_l^{[k]} := (v_{lv}^{[k]}, v_{lh}^{[k]})$, of which $v_{lv}^{[k]}$ and $v_{lh}^{[k]}$ are results of the 1-D (vertical and horizontal) motion estimations. $(l,3)$ images are not used for motion estimations, since they may be strongly affected by noise in the original image [11].

Now, with the detected motion vector $\boldsymbol{v}_l^{[k]}$ as above and with the assumed model (7) for the movement of the foreground object, we can get a prediction

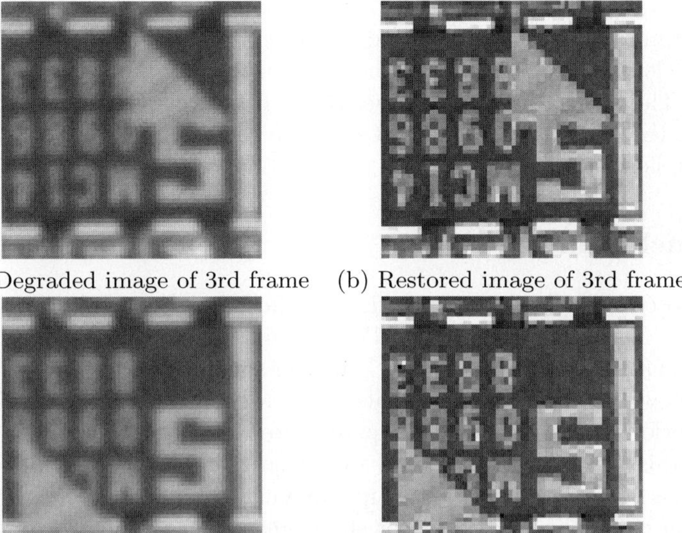

(a) Degraded image of 3rd frame   (b) Restored image of 3rd frame

(c) Degraded image of 10th frame   (d) Restored image of 10th frame

Fig. 6. Simulation result of the proposed method (3rd and 10th frames)

concerning the foreground location of the next frame image, by constructing a Kalman filter for

$$
\begin{cases}
\begin{bmatrix} \boldsymbol{v}_l^{[k+1]} \\ \boldsymbol{a}_l^{[k+1]} \end{bmatrix} = \begin{bmatrix} I_2 & I_2 \\ 0_{2\times 2} & I_2 \end{bmatrix} \begin{bmatrix} \boldsymbol{v}_l^{[k]} \\ \boldsymbol{a}_l^{[k]} \end{bmatrix} + \boldsymbol{w}_{(l,j)}^{[k]} \\[2em]
\begin{bmatrix} v_{lv}^{[k]} \\ v_{lh}^{[k]} \end{bmatrix} = \begin{bmatrix} I_2 & 0_{2\times 2} \end{bmatrix} \begin{bmatrix} \boldsymbol{v}_l^{[k]} \\ \boldsymbol{a}_l^{[k]} \end{bmatrix} + \boldsymbol{n}_{(l,j)}^{[k]}.
\end{cases}
\tag{11}
$$

4   Simulation

We performed a simulation of the proposed method with known degradation parameters and we verified the performance of the proposed method. We generated an artificial image sequence in 64×64 pixels and 10 frames. We used a test image 'Text' for the background and a triangle object with changing pixel value for the foreground. The foreground was supposed to move with constant velocity. We made the original image sequence $\boldsymbol{f}^{[k]}$ by equation (6) and calculted its degraded image sequence $\boldsymbol{g}^{[k]}$ by equation (1). We considered an optical blur for $\boldsymbol{H}$ in equation (1) and used a Gauss function of the variance $\sigma^2 = 1.2$ with the 7×7 discretized elements. The disturbance $\boldsymbol{u}^{[k]}$ was assumed to be a Gaussian noise of average zero and the SN ratio of 30dB independently for each frames. In the restoration calculation, the level of the wavelet multiresolution decomposition (L) was assumed to be three and we selected the three tap wavelet [11].

The degraded and the restored images for some frames are shown in Fig. 6. In both frames, the background and the foreground of the restored images could be much clearly recognized than the original degraded images by the proposed method. The total calculation time for 10 frames was 90 sec. and the prediction time (Steps 2–5) was about10 sec. The calculation time for our prediction algorithm is sufficiently short.

5   Conclusion

We proposed an effective restoration method for degraded video sequence in this paper. The dynamics of the MWD image sequence is modeled and a novel calculation algorithm is proposed. Computer simulation for an artificial image sequence shows favorable result qualitatively. More quantitative verifications such as calculation time or restoration quality are remained for future works.

Since this formulation is based on several restrictive assumptions, further extension is needed such as for multiple moving objects, more complex movement other than parabolic translation or shape change in an image sequence.

References

1. Belge, M., Kilmer, M.E., Miller, E.L.: Wavelet domain image restoration with adaptive edge-preserving regularization. IEEE Trans. on IP 9(4), 597–608 (2000)
2. Osher, S., Ruden, L.I., Fatemi, E.: Nonlinear total variation based noise removal algorithms. Phisical Riview D 60, 259–268 (1992)
3. Pizurica, A., Zlokolika, V., Philips, W.: Combined wavelet domain and temporal video denoising. In: Proc. IEEE Intl. Conf. on Advanced Video and Signal based Surveillance (AVSS) (2003)
4. Rares, A., Reinders, M.J.T., Biemond, J., Lagendijk, R.L.: A spatiotemporal image sequence restoration algorithm. In: Proc. IEEE Intl. Conf. on IP (2002)
5. Kornprobst, P., Deriche, R., Aubert, G.: Image sequence restoration: A PDE based coupled method for image restoration and motion segmentation. In: Burkhardt, H., Neumann, B. (eds.) ECCV 1998. LNCS, vol. 1407, p. 548. Springer, Heidelberg (1998)
6. Gangal, A., Kayikçiouglu, T., Dizdariglu, B.: An improved motion-compensated restoration method for damaged color motion picture films. Signal Processing: Image Communication 19(4), 353–368 (2004)
7. Gee, T.F., Karnowski, T.P., Tobin Jr., K.W.: Multiframe combination and blur deconvolution of video data. In: Proc. SPIE Image and Video Communications and Processing, vol. 3974, pp. 788–795 (2000)
8. Selesnick, I.W., Li, K.Y.: Video denoising using 2d and 3d dual-tree complex wavelet transforms. In: Proc. SPIE Wavelets: Appl. Signal Image Processing X, vol. 5207, pp. 607–618 (2003)
9. Akiyama, K., Luo, Z.W., Onishi, M., Hosoe, S.: Restoration of degraded moving image for predicting a moving object. IEE J. Trans. EIS 127(7) (2007) (in Japanese)
10. Mallat, S.: A theory for multiresolution signal decomposition: the wavelet representation. IEEE Trans. on PAMI 11(7), 674–693 (1989)
11. Daubechies, I.: Ten Lectures on Wavelets. SIAM, Philadelphia (1992)

Fundamental Analysis of a Digital Spiking Neuron for Its Spike-Based Coding

Hiroyuki Torikai

Graduate School of Engineering Science, Osaka University
torikai@sys.es.osaka-u.ac.jp

Abstract. A *digital spiking neuron* (DSN) is a wired system of shift registers. By adjusting the parameters (e.g., number of registers and wiring pattern), the DSN can generate spike-trains having various inter-spike-intervals. In this paper we present some basic relations between parameters of the DSN and characteristics of the spike-train. We also discuss that the presented results will be fundamental to consider ISI-based coding abilities of the DSN.

1   Introduction

Various simplified spiking neuron models have been proposed and their dynamics have been investigated intensively (see [1]-[8] and references therein). Using such spiking neuron models, pulse-coupled neural networks (PCNNs) have been constructed and their possible functions and application potentials have been investigated, e.g., image processing based on synchronization of spike-trains [6]-[8]. Inspired by such spiking neuron models, we have proposed a *digital spiking neuron* (DSN) [9][10] as shown in Fig.1. Depending on parameters (i.e., number of registers and wiring pattern among the registers), the DSN can generate spike-trains with various patterns of inter-spike-intervals. One of the biggest motivations for considering the DSN is that the parameters of the DSN can be dynamically adjusted in real electrical circuits such as *field programmable gate array* (FPGA). This means that DSN is suitable for on-chip learning. It should be note that it is troublesome to realize dynamical parameter adjustment (e.g., conductance and nonlinearity) of spiking neurons that are implemented in analog integrated circuits. Previous results on the DSN include the followings.

(a) A learning algorithm for the DSN was proposed in order to approximate spike-trains generated by analog neuron models [11]. The results suggest that the DSN may be able to approximate dynamics of neuron models as well as biological neurons. Hence the results may contribute to develop communication interface with biological neurons, e.g., a digital circuitry that can mimic spike-based communication protocols of neurons.

(b) Another learning algorithm for the DSN was proposed in order to generate spike-trains whose characteristics are suitable for ultra-wide band (UWB) impulse-radio technologies [10]. The results may contribute to develop a bio-inspired spike-based engineering system, e.g., UWB sensor network with bio-inspired learning abilities.

(c) Some spike-based coding abilities of the DSN have been clarified [9][12]. Also, a PCNN of DSNs has been constructed and its application potentials (e.g., spike-based multiplex communication) have been studied.

M. Ishikawa et al. (Eds.): ICONIP 2007, Part II, LNCS 4985, pp. 87–96, 2008.
© Springer-Verlag Berlin Heidelberg 2008

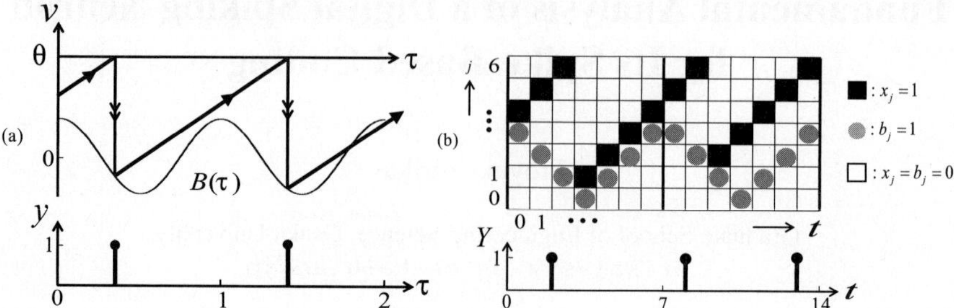

Fig. 1. (a) Analog spiking neuron model. Integrate-and-fire behavior of analog potential v for continuous-time τ [1]-[4]. (b) Digital spiking neuron. Shift-and-reset behavior of digital state x_j for discrete-time t [9][10].

In this paper we present some basic relations between parameters of the DSN and characteristics of the spike-train. Such results have not been shown in the previous works. We also discuss that the presented results will be fundamentals to develop applications of the DSN such as the spike-based coding.

2   Digital Spiking Neuron

In this section we introduce our *digital spiking neuron* (DSN) proposed in Refs. [9][10]. The DSN operates on a discrete time $t = 0, 1, 2, \cdots$. Fig.2(a) shows the DSN. First, let us consider the p-cells that are usual shift registers. Let the number of p-cells be denoted by M, where $M \geq 1$. Let $i \in \{0, 1, \cdots, M - 1\}$ be an index for the p-cell. The p-cell has a digital state $p_i \in \{0, 1\} \equiv B$, where "$\equiv$" denotes "*definition*" throughout this paper. The p-cells are ring-coupled and their dynamics is described by

$$p_i(t + 1) = p_{i+1 \ (\mathrm{mod}M)}(t). \tag{1}$$

For convenience, initial states of the p-cells are fixed as follows: $p_i(0) = 1$ for $i = Int(\frac{M-1}{2})$, and $p_i(0) = 1$ otherwise, where $Int(\alpha)$ gives the integer part of α. Then the p-cells oscillate periodically with period M. In order to consider dynamics of the DSN, we introduce a state vector $\boldsymbol{P}(t) \equiv (p_0(t), \cdots, p_{M-1}(t))^t \in \boldsymbol{B}^M$. Second, let us consider the reconfigurable wirings from p-cells to x-cells. Let the number of x-cells be denoted by N, where $N \geq M$. Let $j \in \{0, 1, \cdots, N - 1\}$ be an index for the x-cell. In the dotted box of Fig.2(a), the left terminals are denoted by $\{p_0, \cdots, p_i, \cdots, p_{M-1}\}$ and the right terminals are denoted by $\{b_0, \cdots, b_j, \cdots, b_{N-1}\}$. Each left terminal p_i has one wiring and each right terminal b_j can accept any number of wirings. In order to describe pattern of the wirings, let us define an $N \times M$ matrix $\boldsymbol{A}$ whose elements are $a(j, i) = 1$ if p_i is wired to b_j, and $a(j, i) = 0$ otherwise. The matrix $\boldsymbol{A}$ is referred to as a *wiring matrix*. In the case of Fig.2(a), the wiring matrix is given by $a(i, i) = 1$ for all i and $a(i, j) = 0$ for $i \neq j$. The right N terminals output a signal vector $(b_0(t), b_1(t), \cdots, b_{N-1}(t))^t \equiv b(t) \in \boldsymbol{B}^N$ which is given by

$$b(t) = \boldsymbol{A}\boldsymbol{P}(t). \tag{2}$$

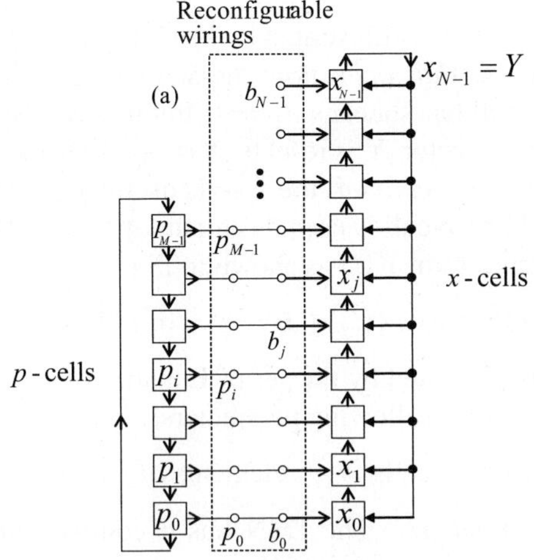

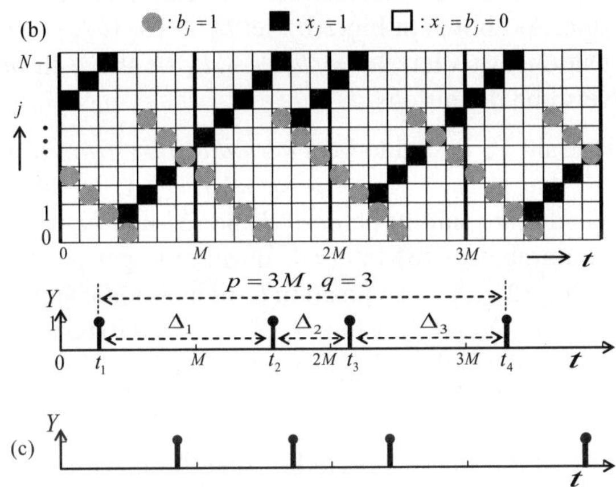

Fig. 2. (a) Digital spiking neuron. $M = 7$ and $N = 10$. (b) Basic dynamics. The initial state is $x_7(0) = 1$. p is the period and q is the ISI-number. (c) Co-existing spike-train. The initial state is $x_3(0) = 1$.

The signal $b(t)$ is referred to as a *base signal* and is to be periodic with period M as illustrated by gray circles in Fig.2(b). Third, let us consider the x-cells that are specialized shift registers. Each x-cell has a digital state $x_j \in B$. The x-cell has three digital inputs (b_j, x_{N-1}, x_{j-1}) for $j \geq 1$ and has two digital inputs (b_j, x_{N-1}) for $j = 0$. If $x_{N-1}(t) = 0$, the x-cell operates $x_j(t+1) = x_{j-1}(t)$ for $j \geq 1$ and operates $x_j(t+1) = 0$ for $j = 0$. If $x_{N-1}(t) = 1$, the x-cell operates $x_j(t+1) = b_j(t)$ for all j. Let us define a state vector of the x-cells: $(x_0(t), \cdots, x_{N-1}(t))^t \equiv X(t) \in B^N$. Then, using a shift operator $S((x_0, \cdots, x_{N-1})^t) = (0, x_0, \cdots, x_{N-2})^t$, the dynamics of the x-cells is described by

$$X(t+1) = \begin{cases} S(X(t)) & \text{if } x_{N-1}(t) = 0 \text{ (Shift)}, \\ b(t) & \text{if } x_{N-1}(t) = 1 \text{ (Reset)}. \end{cases} \tag{3}$$

Basic dynamics of the x-cells is illustrated by black boxes in Fig.2(b). If $x_{N-1} = 0$, the DSN is governed by the *shift operation*: the state $x_j = 1$ is shifted upward. At $t = t_1$, the $(N-1)$-th x-cell has state $x_{N-1} = 1$. In this case the DSN is governed by the *reset operation*: the state vector $\boldsymbol{X}$ is reset to $\boldsymbol{X}(t_1+1) = \boldsymbol{b}(t_1) = (0, 1, 0, \cdots, 0)^t$. Repeating such *shift-and-reset behavior*, the x-cells oscillate as shown in Fig.2(b). The state x_{N-1} of the $(N-1)$-th x-cell is used as an output Y of the DSN. Then the DSN outputs a discrete-time spike-train $Y(t)$ as shown in Fig.2(b):

$$Y(t) \equiv x_{N-1}(t) \in \boldsymbol{B}, \quad t = 0, 1, 2, \cdots . \tag{4}$$

As a result the DSN is governed by the set of Equations (1), (2), (3) and (4). Also, the DSN is characterized by the following parameters:

$$\text{\# of } p\text{-cells } M, \quad \text{\# of } x\text{-cells } N, \quad \text{elements } a(j, i) \text{ of wiring matrix } \boldsymbol{A}$$

where "#" denotes "*the numbers.*" The DSN has a controllable initial state vector $\boldsymbol{X}(0) = (x_0(0), x_1(0), \cdots, x_{N-1}(0))^t$ of the x-cells. In this paper we assume that only one element of $\boldsymbol{X}(0)$ is 1. The black boxes in Fig.2(b) show a trajectory of $\boldsymbol{X}$ under such an assumption. As shown in Fig.2(b), let $t_n \in \{0, 1, 2, \cdots, \}, n = 1, 2, 3, \cdots$ be the n-th spike position. Also let $\Delta_n = t_{n+1} - t_n$ be the n-th *inter-spike-interval* (ISI). Here let us give some definitions.

Definition 1. A spike-train Y_* is said to be a *periodic spike-train* if there exist positive integers p and q such that $t_{n+q} = t_n + p$ for all $n \geq 1$. In this case, the possible minimum integers p and q are said to be *period* and *ISI-number* of the periodic spike-train Y_*. q means the number of ISI-intervals during the period $0 \leq t \leq p$, and the period is to be $p = \sum_{n=1}^{q} \Delta_n$. A spike position t_* of a periodic spike-train Y_* is said to be a *periodic spike position*. A spike position $t_1 = t_e$ is said to be an *eventually periodic spike position* if t_e is not a periodic spike position but t_n is a periodic spike position for some $n \geq 2$.

The spike-train $Y(t)$ in Fig.2(b) is a periodic spike-train with period $p = 3M$ and ISI-number $q = 3$, where $M = 7$. The DSN can exhibit the following phenomena.

- The DSN has the finite states $\boldsymbol{P}$ and $\boldsymbol{X}$ operating on the discrete-time t. Then the DSN oscillates periodically and generates a periodic spike-train Y_* in a steady state. The periodic spike-train Y_* can have various patterns of ISIs $(\Delta_1, \Delta_2, \cdots, \Delta_q)$.
- The periodic spike-trains $Y(t)$ in Fig.2(b) and (c) are caused by different initial states $x_7(0) = 1$ and $x_3(0) = 1$, respectively. Such phenomenon is referred to as *co-existence for initial state*. The DSN can have multiple co-existing periodic spike-trains and generates one of them depending on the initial state $\boldsymbol{X}(0)$.
- The DSN may have an eventually periodic spike position depending on parameter values. The existence of an eventually periodic spike position implies existence of a transient phenomenon.

3   Analysis of Various Spike-Trains

In order to consider dynamics of the spike position t_n, let us define the following *base index function* $\beta(t) \equiv j$ such that $b_j(t) = 1$. Fig.3(a) shows the base index function $\beta(t)$

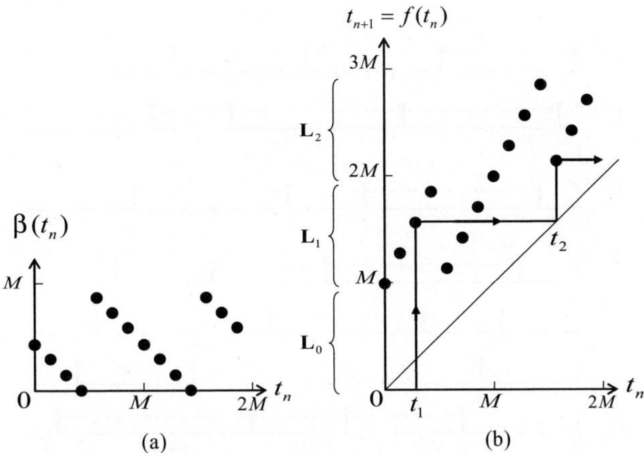

Fig. 3. Maps corresponding to the DSN in Fig.2(a). (a) Base index function $\beta(t)$. (b) Spike position map f.

corresponding to the DSN in Fig.2(a). The base index function $\beta(t)$ can be regarded as a trajectory of the gray circle (i.e., the state "$b_j(t) = 1$") in Fig.2(b). The shape of $\beta(t)$ is determined by the wiring matrix A as follows:

$$\beta(t) = j \;\; \text{such that} \;\; a(j, M + \gamma - t \, (\text{mod} M)) = 1 \;\;\; \text{for } 0 \le t \le M - 1 \qquad (5)$$

where $\beta(t + M) = \beta(t)$. Using the base index function $\beta(t)$, the dynamics of the spike position t_n is described by the following *spike position map*:

$$t_{n+1} = f(t_n) \equiv t_n + N - \beta(t_n), \quad f : L \to L \equiv \{0, 1, 2, \cdots\}. \qquad (6)$$

Fig.3(b) shows the spike position map f corresponding to the DSN in Fig.2(a). The first spike position t_1 of the spike position map f is determined by the initial state of the x-cells as follows:

$$t_1 = j \;\; \text{such that} \;\; x_{N-1-j}(0) = 1. \qquad (7)$$

We emphasize that the shape of the spike position map f is determined by the wiring matrix A which describes pattern of the reconfigurable wirings of the DSN (see Fig.2(a)). That is, various shapes of f (i.e., various dynamics of the spike position t_n) can be realized by adjusting the wiring matrix A. In the following part, we give some new results by focusing on a simple form of A.

Let us focus on the following parameter case hereafter:

$$M \ge 1, \quad N = Int(\tfrac{3M-1}{2}), \quad a(j, i) = \begin{cases} 1 \text{ for } i = j, \\ 0 \text{ otherwise.} \end{cases} \qquad (8)$$

In this case the DSN is characterized by one parameter: the number M of the p-cells. For short, let us refer to M as a *system size* hereafter. The DSN in Fig.2(a) satisfies the condition in Equation (8) with the system size $M = 7$. We can see in Fig.2(a) that

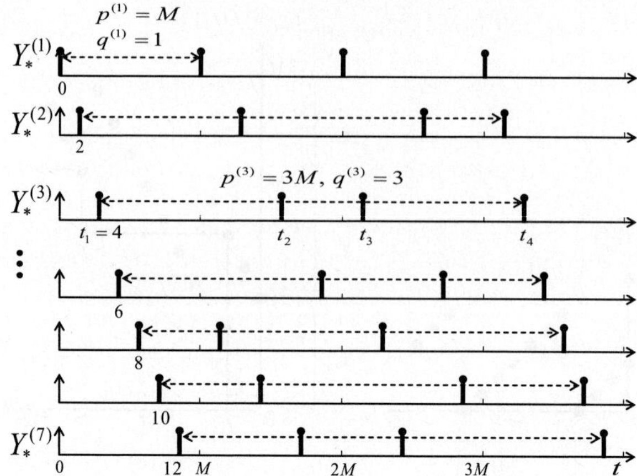

Fig. 4. The co-existing periodic spike-trains under the parameter condition in Equation (8) with the system size $M = 14$. The number S of co-existing periodic spike-trains is 7.

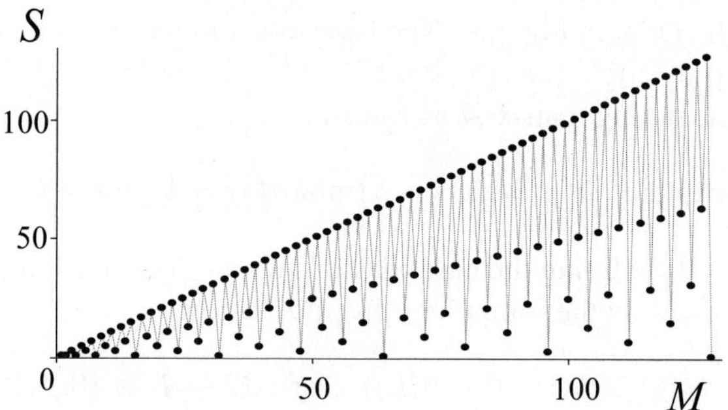

Fig. 5. Characteristics of the number S of co-existing periodic spike-trains

the pattern of wirings is simple: each right terminal p_i is wired to each left terminal b_i straightly. Under the condition in Equation (8), the spike position map f is given by

$$f(t_n) = \begin{cases} 2t_n + M & \text{for } 0 \le t_n \le \gamma, \\ 2t_n & \text{for } \gamma + 1 \le t_n \le M - 1, \end{cases} \qquad f(t_n + M) = f(t_n) + M. \quad (9)$$

Fig.3(b) shows this spike position map f for $M = 7$. As shown in this figure, let us define the sets $\boldsymbol{L}_k \equiv \{kM, \ kM + 1, \ kM + 2, \ \cdots, \ kM + M - 1\}$, where $k = 0, 1, 2, \cdots$. Then we can confirm $f(\boldsymbol{L}_k) \subseteq \boldsymbol{L}_{k+1}$, where $f(\boldsymbol{L}_k)$ represents the set $\{f(t) \mid t \in \boldsymbol{L}_k\}$ of images of f. This means that the spike-train $Y(t)$ has one spike in each set $\boldsymbol{L}_k$, i.e.,

$$t_n \in \boldsymbol{L}_{n-1} \quad \text{for all} \quad n = 1, 2, 3, \cdots. \quad (10)$$

From Equation (10), we can restrict the following first spike position into $t_1 \in \boldsymbol{L}_0$. Let us refer to $\boldsymbol{L}_0$ as an *initial state set*. In addition, from Equation (10), we can have the relation $p = Mq$. In the case of Fig.2(b), we can confirm $q = 3$ and $p = 3M$.

3.1   Number of Periodic Spike-Trains

Fig.4 shows all the co-existing periodic spike-trains of the DSN for the system size $M = 14$. Let us consider the following quantity:

$$S \equiv \# \text{ of co-existing periodic spike-trains for the initial state } X(0).$$

In the case of Fig.4, $S = 7$. Fig.5 shows characteristics of S for the system size M, that can be given by a function of M as shown below. Let M_0 be the maximum odd divisor of M and let M be decomposed into even and odd components:

$$M = 2^r M_0, \quad r \in \{0, 1, 2, \cdots\}, \quad M_0 \in \{1, 3, 5, \cdots\}. \tag{11}$$

In the case of Fig.4, $M_0 = 7$ and $r = 1$. Let us divide the initial state set L_0 into the following two disjoint subsets L_p and L_e:

$$L_p \equiv \{0, \; 2^r, \; 2^r 2, \; \cdots, \; 2^r(M_0 - 1)\}, \qquad L_e \equiv L_0 - L_p. \tag{12}$$

In the case of Fig.4, $L_p = \{0, 2, \cdots, 12\}$ and $L_e = \{1, 3, \cdots, 13\}$. We can generalize this results into the following properties for any given system size M.

- The number S of co-existing periodic spike-trains is M_0.
- L_p is a set of all the periodic spike positions in the initial state set L_0.
- L_e is a set of all the eventually periodic spike positions in L_0.

Proof of these properties will be given in a journal paper.

3.2   Period and ISI-Number

Here let us consider periods and ISI-numbers of the co-existing spike-trains. Let us give some definitions (see Fig.4).

Definition 2. Let the S pieces of co-existing periodic spike-trains be denoted by $\{Y_*^{(1)}, Y_*^{(2)}, \cdots, Y_*^{(S)}\}$ in the order of the first spike position t_1. Let the period and the ISI-number of each spike-train $Y_*^{(s)}$ be denoted by $p^{(s)}$ and $q^{(s)}$, respectively, where $s \in \{1, 2, \cdots, S\}$. Let the least common multiple of the periods $\{p^{(s)}\}$ be denoted by P and let it be referred to as a *common period*. Let the least common multiple of the ISI-numbers $\{q^{(s)}\}$ be denoted by Q and let it be referred to as a *common ISI-number*.

The set $\{Y_*^{(s)}\}$ of co-existing periodic spike-trains can be characterized by the common period P and the common ISI-number Q. In the case of Fig.4, the common period is $P = 3M$ and the common ISI-number is $Q = 3$. Fig.6 shows characteristics of Q for the system size M, that can be given by a function of M as shown below. As a preparation, let us define the following function $K(l)$ for a positive odd integer l:

$$K(l) \equiv \min\{z \mid z \in \{1, 2, \cdots, l\}, \; 2^z - 1 \; (\bmod \; l) = 0\}. \tag{13}$$

For example $K(7) = 3$. Let the system size M be given. Let a periodic spike position $t_1 \in L_p$ be the first spike position of a periodic spike-train $Y_*^{(s)}$. Let a fraction $\frac{t_1}{M}$ be reduced into an irreducible fraction $\frac{m'}{M'}$. Then we can give the following properties.

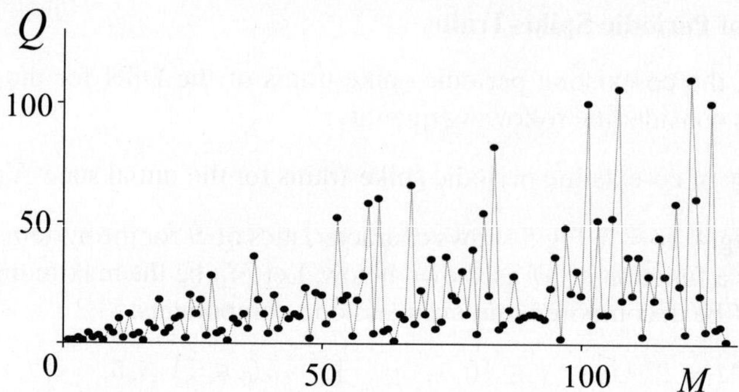

Fig. 6. Characteristics of the common ISI-number Q

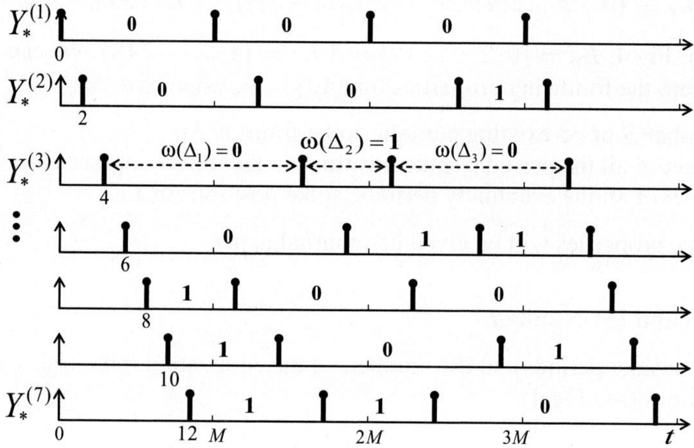

Fig. 7. ISI coding. The parameters satisfy the condition in Equation (8) with the system size $M = 14$. The spike-trains are identical with that in Fig.4. The periodic spike-trains have one-to-one relation to all the 3-bit binary numbers except for $(1, 1, 1)$.

- The period $p^{(s)}$ and the ISI-number $q^{(s)}$ of the spike-train $Y_*^{(s)}$ are given by $MK(M')$ and $K(M')$, respectively.
- The common period P and the common ISI-number Q of the co-existing periodic spike-trains $\{Y_*^{(s)}\}$ are given by $MK(M_0)$ and $K(M_0)$, respectively.

Proof of these properties will be given in a journal paper. In the case of Fig.4, $Y_*^{(1)}$ has the first spike position $t_1 = 0$. The fraction $\frac{0}{14}$ can be reduced into an irreducible fraction $\frac{0}{1}$ and then $Y_*^{(1)}$ has period $p^{(1)} = MK(1) = M$ and ISI-number $q^{(1)} = K(1) = 1$. $Y_*^{(3)}$ has the first spike position $t_1 = 4$. The fraction $\frac{4}{14}$ can reduced into an irreducible fraction $\frac{2}{7}$ and then $Y_*^{(3)}$ has period $p^{(3)} = MK(7) = 3M$ and ISI-number $q^{(3)} = K(7) = 3$. The common period and the common ISI-number can be given by $P = MK(7) = 3M$ and $Q = K(7) = 3$, respectively.

3.3   Inter-Spike-Interval Coding

Fig.7 shows the co-existing periodic spike-trains for the system size $M = 14$. As shown in this figure, let us consider an ISI coding:

$$\omega(\Delta_n) = 0 \ \text{ for } \ \Delta_n \geq M, \qquad \omega(\Delta_n) = 1 \ \text{ for } \ \Delta_n \leq M - 1. \tag{14}$$

Using the ISI coding, the periodic spike-train $Y_*^{(3)}$ in Fig.7 is coded by a 3-bit digital sequence $(\omega(\Delta_1), \omega(\Delta_2), \omega(\Delta_3)) = (0, 1, 0)$. We refer to this sequence as a *ISI code*. In the case of Fig.7, the common ISI-number is $Q = 3$ and each spike-train $Y^{(s)}$ is coded by a 3-bit ISI code. We can see that the set $\{Y_*^{(s)}\}$ of co-existing periodic spike-trains can have one-to-one relation to the set of 3-bit binary numbers except for $(1, 1, 1)$. For general system size M, recalling Theorem 2, the common ISI-number is to be $Q = K(M_0)$. In this case the co-existing periodic spike-trains are coded by Q-bit ISI codes $(\omega(\Delta_1), \omega(\Delta_2), \cdots, \omega(\Delta_Q))$. We can give the following property for a given system size M.

- Let M be given. A periodic spike-train $Y_*^{(s)}$ having a first spike position $t_1 \in L_p$ is coded by a Q-bit ISI code $(\omega(\Delta_1), \omega(\Delta_2), \cdots, \omega(\Delta_Q))$ such that

$$\sum_{n=1}^{Q} 2^{Q-n}\omega(\Delta_n) = \frac{2^Q-1}{M}t_1. \tag{15}$$

Proof of this property will be given in a journal paper. Equation (15) suggests that the set of co-existing periodic spike-trains can have one-to-one relation to a set of some Q-bit binary numbers, where the binary number representation of $\frac{2^Q-1}{M}t_1$ is identical with the ISI code $(\omega(\Delta_1), \omega(\Delta_2), \cdots, \omega(\Delta_Q))$. In the case of $Y_*^{(3)}$ in Fig.7, we can confirm that the binary number representation of $\frac{2^Q-1}{M}t_1 = \frac{7}{14}4 = 2$ is $(0, 1, 0)$ which is identical with the ISI code.

Discussion: Ref. [9] proposes a pulse-coupled network of DSNs and its application to a multiplex communication system, where the DSN is used to code binary information into spike-train. The theorems in this paper will be mathematical basis to investigate such an application as follows.

(i) The number S of co-existing periodic spike-trains corresponds to the number of binary numbers (informations) that can be coded into the spike-train.

(ii) The common ISI-number Q corresponds to the code length.

(iii) Equations (7) and (15) show relation between the initial state $X(0)$ and the ISI code. These equations suggest that the DSN can code a binary number (information) into the spike-train by adjusting the initial state (which can be regarded as an input) appropriately.

We note that Ref. [9] analyzes the DSN for a very limited parameter case, and this paper generalizes the analysis.

4   Conclusions

We have introduced the *digital spiking neuron* (DSN) and clarified the basic relations between parameter of the DSN and characteristics of the spike-train, e.g., the number of co-existing periodic spike-trains, their initial states, their periods, and their ISI-numbers. We have also clarified the relation between the initial state of the spike-train and its corresponding ISI code, and have shown that the set of co-existing periodic spike-trains can have one-to-one relation to a set of some binary numbers. Then we have discussed that the presented results will be fundamental to study coding functions of the DSN. Future problems include: (a) analysis of the DSN for various cases of wiring matrix; (b) synthesis of a pulse-coupled neural network of DSNs with interesting functions; and (c) development of on-chip learning algorithms for the DSN and/or its pulse-coupled neural network.

Acknowledgement

The author would like to thank Professor Kazuyuki Aihara of Tokyo Univ. and Professor Masato Okada of Tokyo Univ. for valuable discussions. The author would like to thank Professor Toshimitsu Ushio of Osaka Univ. and Professor Toshimichi Saito of Hosei Univ. for valuable advises.

References

1. Perez, R., Glass, L.: Bistability, period doubling bifurcations and chaos in a periodically forced oscillator. Phys. Lett. 90A(9), 441–443 (1982)
2. Izhikevich, E.M.: Dynamical systems in neuroscience. MIT Press, Cambridge (2006)
3. Torikai, H., Saito, T.: Synchronization phenomena in pulse-coupled networks driven by spike-train inputs. IEEE Trans. Neural Networks 15(2), 337–347 (2004)
4. Lee, G., Farhat, N.H.: The bifurcating neuron network 2. Neural networks 15, 69–84 (2002)
5. Eckhorn, R.: Neural mechanisms of scene segmentation: recordings from the visual cortex suggest basic circuits for linking field models. IEEE Trans. Neural Networks 10(3), 464–479 (1999)
6. Hopfield, J.J., Herz, A.V.M.: Rapid local synchronization of action potentials: Toward computation with coupled integrate-and-fire neurons. Proc. Natl. Acad. Sci. USA 92, 6655–6662 (1995)
7. Campbell, S.R., Wang, D., Jayaprakash, C.: Synchrony and desynchrony in integrate-and-fire oscillators. Neural computation 11, 1595–1619 (1999)
8. Nakano, H., Saito, T.: Grouping synchronization in a pulse-coupled network of chaotic spiking oscillators. IEEE Trans. Neural Networks 15(5), 1018–1026 (2004)
9. Torikai, H., Hamanaka, H., Saito, T.: Reconfigurable Digital Spiking Neuron and its Pulse-Coupled Network: Basic Characteristics and Potential Applications. IEEE Trans. CAS-II 53(8), 734–738 (2006)
10. Torikai, H.: Basic Characteristics and Learning Potential of a Digital Spiking Neuron. IEICE Trans. Fundamentals (to appear, 2007)
11. Torikai, H., Funew, A., Saito, T.: Approximation of Spike-trains by Digital Spiking Neuron. In: Proc. of IJCNN, paper #1698 (2007)
12. Kabe, T., Torikai, H., Saito, T.: Synchronization via multiplex spike-trains in digital pulse-coupled networks. In: King, I., Wang, J., Chan, L.-W., Wang, D. (eds.) ICONIP 2006. LNCS, vol. 4234, pp. 1141–1149. Springer, Heidelberg (2006)

A 160×120 Edge Detection Vision Chip for Neuromorphic Systems Using Logarithmic Active Pixel Sensor with Low Power Dissipation

Jae-Sung Kong, Dong-Kyu Sung, Hyo-Young Hyun, and Jang-Kyoo Shin

Department of Electronics, Kyungpook National University, 1370 Sankyuk-Dong, Buk-Gu, Daegu 702-701, South Korea
{kongjs, dksung}@ee.knu.ac.kr, hyhyun@knu.ac.kr, jkshin@ee.knu.ac.kr

Abstract. In this paper, a vision chip for edge detection based on the structure of a biological retina is introduced. The chip processes an image in a bio-inspired vision mechanism; therefore, it is proper for the neuromorphic systems. Logarithmic active pixel sensor (APS) was applied to the vision chip. By applying a MOS-type photodetector to the logarithmic APS, we could achieve sufficient output swing for the vision chip in natural illumination condition. A correlated-double sampling technique was applied to the chip for noise suppression. In addition, a CMOS buffer circuit is commonly used for both raw and smoothed images by using additional switches. This structure helps reduce the total number of MOSFETs for a unit-pixel and noise. A vision chip with a 160×120 pixel array was fabricated using a 0.35 μm double-poly four-metal CMOS technology, and its operation was successfully demonstrated.

1 Introduction

Vision systems, which have image sensors and subsequent processing units for a particular purpose, do not use a raw image from an image sensor such as charge-coupled devices (CCD) or complementary metal-oxide-semiconductor (CMOS) image sensors (CIS)[1, 2]. Indeed, they use a filtered image to improve its performance and reduce error rate. In particular, Laplacian filtering, which sends enhanced signal at the edge of an image, is used in many image processing fields such as pattern recognition and the treatment of noisy images (e.g. medical images, silhouettes, and infrared red images) [3-4]. Until now, computer vision systems, which use a CCD camera for capturing an incident image and a general purpose computer for acquisition of useful data from the captured image, have been used as an approach of vision systems. However, these systems are limited in terms of size, power consumption, and speed regarding real applications because they consist of two separate modules for image capturing and processing which do not interact. Recently, bio-inspired vision chips have been developed to overcome these problems [5-13]. The vision chips, which mimic the structure and functions of the human retina, offer several advantages including compact size, high speed, low power dissipation, and dense system integration.

M. Ishikawa et al. (Eds.): ICONIP 2007, Part II, LNCS 4985, pp. 97 – 106, 2008.

In order to implement real-time image processing in hardware, first, the time dissipation for image capturing should be minimized. Conventional APS requires light integration time for charge accumulation. In dim illumination condition, this time loss exceedingly increases and it limits continuous operation. On the other hand, logarithmic APS continuously sends output; thus, the combination of the logarithmic APS and the signal processing mechanism of a biological retina helps materialize a high-speed bio-inspired vision chip. Logarithmic APSs have advantages in a wide dynamic range and continuous output. However, they suffer from narrow output swing and low signal-to-noise ratio (SNR), compared with charge accumulation-type APSs [14-16]. In particular, conventional correlated-double sampling (CDS) technique is not adequate for these logarithmic APSs, because they have not a proper reference for pixel noise. Previously reported vision chips based on a logarithmic APS showed limitations in required illumination conditions and SNR due to these mentioned problems [14-16]. In this paper, we applied a metal-oxide-semiconductor (MOS)-type photodetector to the logarithmic APS to achieve a sufficient output swing in natural illumination condition. In order to increase SNR, a CDS technique was applied using a special circuit for a current-reference.

In particular, the vision chips require a resistive network, which functions as Gaussian filtering in digital image processing and a specialized circuit structure for acquisition of both raw and smoothed images [5-13]. These additional circuits can cause additional area consumption, power dissipation and noise. In particular, the design of the structure, as well as the other circuits, is very important for improvement of their final output image quality. Previously, two structures have been used. One type is a voltage division type [6, 8]. The other uses two analog buffers to achieve raw and smoothed images [7, 10]. These structures have their own disadvantages in power and area consumption, signal aliasing and additional noise. To overcome these challenges, a switch-selective resistive network was applied.

2   Theory

2.1   The Principle of Edge Detection

Figure 1(a) shows the structure of a biological retina, which consists of photoreceptors (rods and cones), horizontal cells, bipolar cells, amacrine cells, and ganglion cells. The information falling on the photoreceptors is not sent directly to the brain through the optic nerves, but is instead first processed in a number of ways by a variety of interactions among neurons within the retina. Photoreceptors, horizontal cells and bipolar cells are related to edge extraction and ganglion cells are related to signal digitization [17].

Figure 1(b) shows a simple example of edge extraction. The x-axis represents the position and the y-axis represents the normalized outputs of the photoreceptors, horizontal cells, and bipolar cells, respectively. If a bright light is projected only on the right-hand side of the photoreceptor array, the output of each photoreceptor sends a high-level signal. On the other hand, when a dim light is projected on the left-hand side of the photoreceptor array, the output of each photoreceptor sends a low-level signal. Horizontal cells receive signals from the photoreceptors and spatially smooth them. Edge signals, resulting from the differences between outputs of photoreceptors and horizontal cells, are yielded through the bipolar cells. The smoothing function, so-called lateral inhibition, is mainly characterized by the resistive properties of the horizontal cells. If the diffusion length, the number of pixels that contributes to the smoothing function, is large, many pixels will be needed to represent the edge signal. A large diffusion length is directly related to a decrease of the spatial resolution. The difference between the outputs of the photoreceptors and the horizontal cells is directly related to the output of the bipolar cells. Generally, the gain of the electrical circuit for the bipolar cells is constant. In that case, the difference between the outputs of the photoreceptor and the horizontal cell will be the most important factor in deciding the magnitude of an edge.

The major advantage of the retinal structure is the speed of operation for edge extraction because all operations which contain the image capturing, smoothing, and differencing are done in a parallel manner. Another advantage is that each function of the structure is simple enough to realize in an electrical circuit; thus, the entire system size can be reduced.

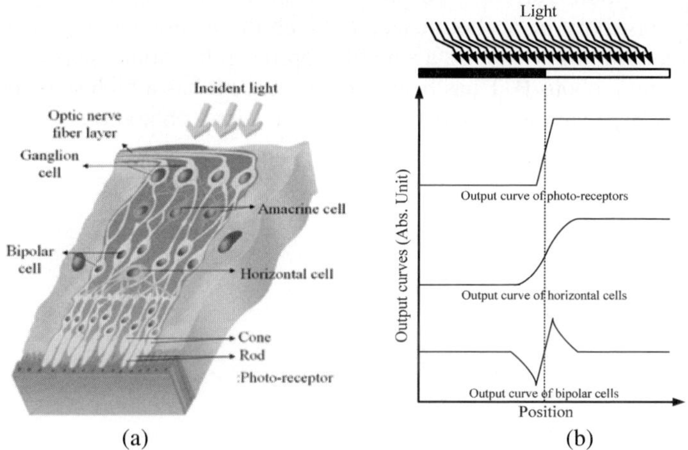

Fig. 1. (a) Structure of biological retina, (b) Principle of edge detection

2.2 Modeling of Retinal Structure in Electrical Devices

Photoreceptors, horizontal cells, and bipolar cells in the retina are the three key elements to embody in the vision chip for edge detection [5-13]. First, a raw image is necessary to extract the edge information. CCDs are useful for sensing the incident image in high quality. However, they require a special process for fabrication; thus, it is impossible to embed other circuits for image processing. The problem of on-chip integration can be solved by using CIS. The function of horizontal can be embodied by using the resistive network, which has been proposed by Mead's research group in which all the photo-sensors in unit pixels are connected in horizontal and vertical through resistive circuits [2]. The current flow from the higher potential area to the lower potential area contributes to the image smoothing. Smooth processing is done in spatially parallel manner;

therefore, the mechanism is proper for real-time applications. The function of bipolar cells can be embodied by using differential circuits. In addition, addressing circuits and noise suppression circuits are necessary for practical design.

3   Implementation

3.1 MOS-Type Photodetector

Previous logarithmic APSs have used a photodiode or a photo-BJT as a photodetector [14-16]. They suffer from a narrow output swing range or large area consumption.

Several approaches have been introduced in order to enlarge their output swing. One method increases the resistivity of its diode-connected MOSFET. The disadvantage of this approach is that the increased resistivity is directly related to the amount of noise. By attaching an amplifier (which has a gain of over one) to the logarithmic APS, its output swing can be enlarged. The idea, however, is also not a proper approach, because the amplifier enlarges noise as well as signal. The other approach is to increase the photo-current. The photo-current can be increased by enlarging the size or the sensitivity of a photodetector. Since the enlargement of a photodetector reduces resolution, it may not be a suitable approach. In another approach to enhance the photo-current, photo-BJT has been used, because it has a high sensitivity. It, however, requires large area for fabrication compared with a photodiode.

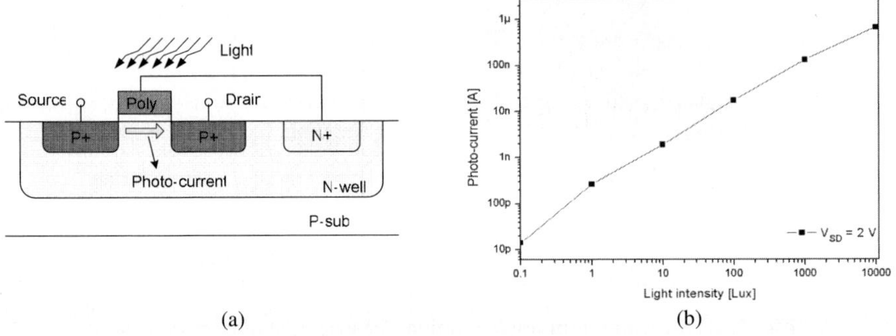

Fig. 2. MOS-type photodetector. (a) Circuit structure. (b) Photocurrent-illumination curve at $V_{SD} = 2V$.

We applied a MOS-type photodetector, which is embodied by connecting the gate and the body of a p-type MOSFET, to a logarithmic APS. The channel potential of the MOS-type photodetector varies according to the incident light intensity [18]. The MOS-type photodetector has several advantages, it has a high photo-sensitivity, and furthermore it is compatible with standard CMOS process. In addition, since it has a simple structure, it requires a small area of silicon die. Figure 2 shows the structure of a MOS-type photodetector and its photocurrent-illumination characteristic curves.

By using the MOS-type photodetector in a logarithmic APS, a large output swing could be achieved with a small area occupation.

3.2 Logarithmic APS and Simplified CDS

Conventional CISs use a CDS for noise suppression. However, logarithmic APS rarely used the CDS, because a proper noise-reference could not be achieved. Particularly, previously proposed logarithmic APS with noise reduction function were not adequate for the bio-inspired vision chip because of their complex structure, large area consumption, and sequential way of operation [14-16]. In order to apply a logarithmic APS to a bio-inspired vision chip, mentioned problem should be concerned.

Simplified CDS (SCDS), which was proposed by Kavadias, is a very effective method for noise reduction [19]. SCDS consists of 5 switches (SW1s and SW2s), one capacitor (C1), and two MOSFETs (MP3 and MP4). The key advantage of SCDS is that the circuit only requires one capacitor. Therefore, we can easily minimize area consumption. Compared with the SCDS, conventional CDSs use 2 capacitors for memorizing both the image and reference signals. A detailed operation of SCDS can be found in the Refs [8, 19].

Figure 3 shows the circuit schematic. Logarithmic APS, which consists of MOSFETs MPD, MN2 and MN3, continuously sends a voltage output according to the incident light intensity. MPD represents the MOS-type photodetector. MP1 offers a constant current source for a noise reference. In order to reduce the current variation due to the process variation, the MP1 was divided into 5 MOSFETs, and then they were spread over neighboring pixels. The reference current and the light-induced current are selected by VMODSL. MN1 and MP2 are switches. The area occupation could be reduced by using different types of MOSFETs for signal selection. Two diode-connected MOSFET, MN2 and MN3, were used for the current-voltage conversion. We have achieved the optimum results in output swing and FPN reduction when the number of the diode-connected MOSFETs is two by using SPICE simulation.

The light-induced voltage and the reference voltage are respectively sampled when the SW1 and SW2 are turned on at the drain node of MN2, and then these two signals are subtracted. Figure 4 shows its timing diagram.

3.3 Pixel-Level Adaptive Resistive Circuit (PLARC)

In order to improve an output image, a proper resistive circuit is required. Mead proposed a resistive network using linear resistors [2]. A linear resistor requires large area to make it by using standard CMOS process; thus, we should found another resistive circuit. A resistive circuit using a single MOSFET was also concerned in Refs. [7], [10]. The gate bias for the MOSFET was globally applied a single voltage. The results showed information loss due to the regionally improper bias condition.

The proposed resistive circuit is represented in Figure 3. The circuit consists of 4 MOSFETs, MP5, MN4, MN5, and MN6. The source/drain nodes of MP5 are respectively interconnected between itself and its neighboring pixel. The states of these nodes are exchanged according to potentials of these two pixels. The biasing circuit which consists of MN4, MN5, and MN6 keeps the source-gate potential difference on at particular level although source and drain potentials regionally varies. The uniform source-gate potential difference keeps the resistivity of resistive circuits at a certain value. It helps reduce information loss. The size of our proposed circuit was 13.5×17 μm^2 by using a 0.35 μm double-poly four-metal (2P4M) standard CMOS process.

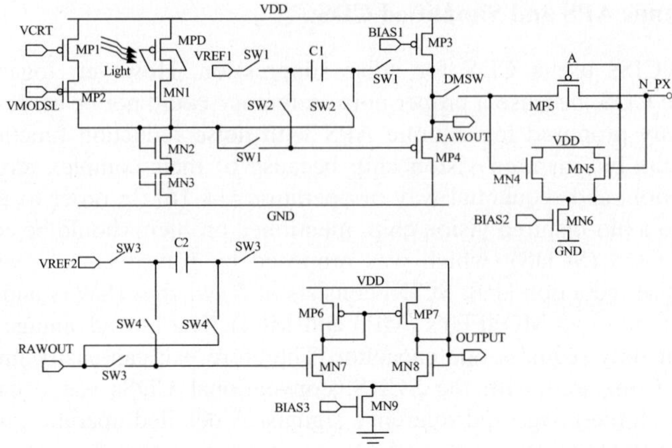

Fig. 3. Circuit schematic

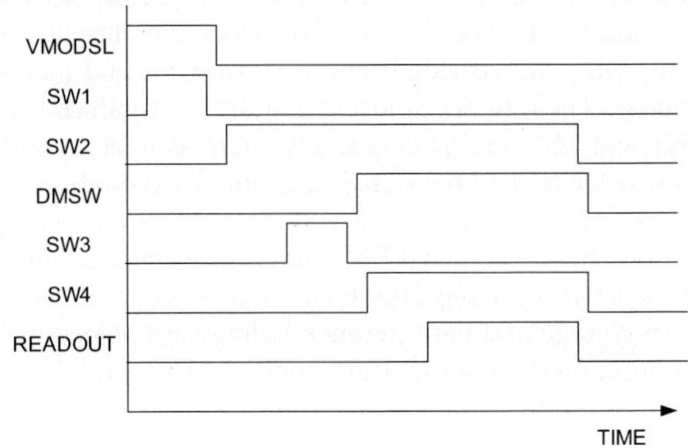

Fig. 4. Timing diagram

3.4 Switch-Selective Resistive Network

The proposed edge detection circuit uses only one source follower circuit, which consists of MP3 and MP4, for both raw and smoothed images [12]. Each image can be selected by a switch DMSW. This switch was embedded in each unit-pixel to connect a neighboring pixel via a resistive circuit; i.e. the node RAWOUT sends a raw image when the switch is open. RAWOUT, otherwise, sends a smoothed image when the switch is closed. The first advantage of this structure is low power dissipation, because the switch does not require extra current for its operation. Raw and smoothed images can be achieved at the same node; thus there is no additional noise between these two images. This is the second advantage. The third advantage is that the structure requires less area. The proposed circuit requires only a small additional switch. It is very area-effective method compared with a vertical resistive circuit or buffers of previous types [6, 9, 10]. The fourth advantage is that there is no aliasing problem between the raw and the smoothed images, because the resistive network is physically disconnected when the switches are open. The other advantage is that the characteristic of resistive network is easily controlled, due to their simple structure. This advantage helps apply various resistive circuits to the vision chip in order to obtain a proper image for a particular purpose. Structural disadvantages include additional switching noise and control complexity, but they are not serious problems. The differential circuit extracts the edge signal from the raw and the smoothed images by switching SW3 and SW4. Figure 4 shows the timing diagram for the proposed circuit.

3.5 Circuit Arrangement: Pseudo 2-D Structure for Resolution Improvement

Conventional vision chips are built 2-dimensional (2-D) resistive network for high operation speed and mimicking a more retina-like model. A unit-pixel of this kind chip contains a photodetector, a noise suppression circuit, resistive circuits and a differential circuit. Particularly, both the noise suppression and the differential circuit require a capacitor for storage of analog data. Thus, the unit-pixel requires large area, approximately 100×100 μm^2 [6-9]. For the reason of area consumption, this type of vision chip suffers from critical lack of resolution. Figure 5(a) shows the structure of a vision chip with 2-D resistive network.

We have tried to solve this problem by restructuring circuits for photo-sensing and image processing. Figure 5(b) shows our structure. The signal processing circuits were separated from photo-sensing circuit; then the signal processing circuits were used in row-parallel. This structure has two advantages and disadvantages, respectively. The advantages are high resolution and low power dissipation. High resolution is caused by the small size of a unit-pixel. Lower power dissipation is caused by less current paths through the overall chip. The disadvantages are possibility of data loss and low operation speed. Data loss can be appeared at horizontal or vertical edges according to the direction of resistive network. However, this problem can be compensated when the resolution is sufficiently improved. The other disadvantage of low operation speed can be a problem when the illumination condition is dim because of their long exposure time; however, the problem can be minimized when the proposed logarithmic APS is used.

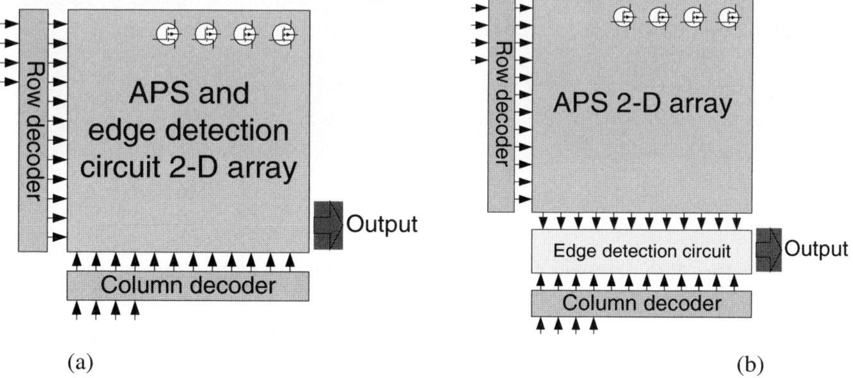

Fig. 5. Structures of a bio-inspired CMOS vision chip. (a) Conventional structure with 2-D resistive network. (b) Resolution-improved structure.

4 Measurement

The bio-inspired vision chip with 160×120 pixels was fabricated by using a 0.35 µm 2P4M standard CMOS technology. The chip size was 5×5 mm^2. The chip contained 144 pads for input/output (I/O), a 2-D logarithmic APS array, two decoders for pixel selection, and a one-dimensional (1-D) edge detection circuit. An optical lens (focal length of 16 mm, f number of 1.4) was mounted in a C-mount format for the projection of an input image onto the chip surface. Figure 6 shows the layout of the fabricated chip.

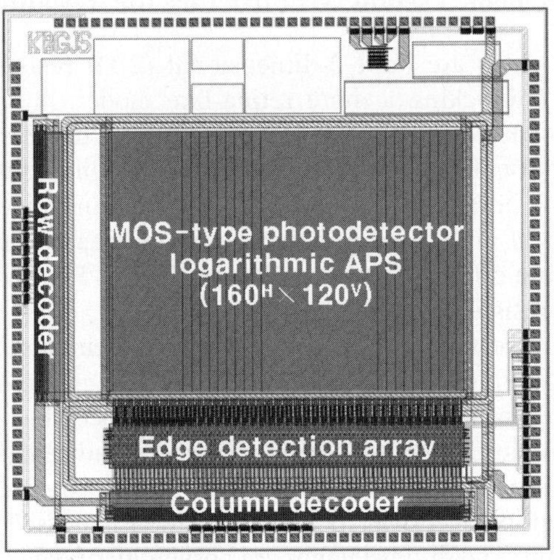

Fig. 6. Layout of the fabricated chip

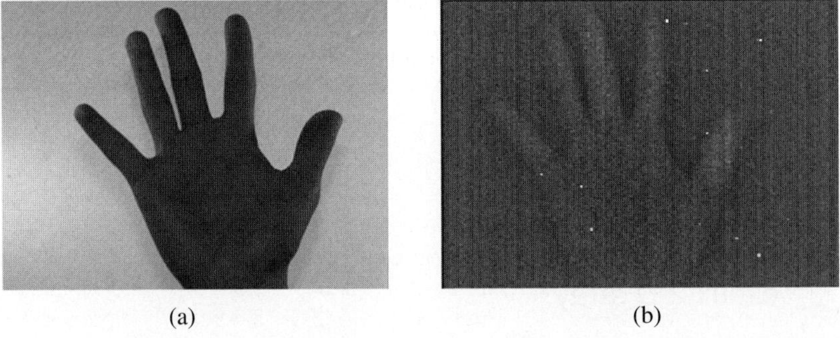

(a)   (b)

Fig. 7. Experimental results. (a) Input image, (b) Output Image.

Figure 7(a) and (b) show an input image and an output image, respectively. The output swing was approximately 100 mV for the second order of contrast difference. Over 300 mV of maximum swing was measured for an edge over 5 decades. The average noise of a final image was approximately 10.6 mV. Compared with previous results using a logarithmic APS, it is very improved results. The operation speed of the vision chip is also improved compared with chips using a charge-accumulation type APS. For our chip, the required operation time containing noise reduction and edge detection was only 600 micro-seconds. This time may be reduced by optimizing the circuit. In the case of the illumination condition of a thousand lx, a commercial CMOS APS requires at least several milliseconds for charge accumulation, but our chip could send information in real-time. It helps detect and search a region-of-interest (ROI) for real applications. Approximately 25.6 mW of power consumption was investigated.

5 Conclusion

Previously, many silicon retina chips have been introduced. Their parallel signal processing based on a biological retina is proper for neuromorphic systems. However, the photo-sensor based on charge-accumulation limits their functional advantage of continuity. In order to overcome this problem, several silicon retinas based on logarithmic APS have been proposed; however, their results suffered from low SNR and small output swing for real applications.

In this paper, a vision chip using MOS-type photodetector logarithmic APS with low power dissipation and low noise was introduced. By using the logarithmic APS and SCDS, low noise image could be continuously obtained. Higher quality of final output image could be obtained by using PLARC, compared with previous results. SSRC helped reduce noise and power consumption. In addition, the resolution of the proposed vision chip could be largely improved without extra cost-increase by using the pseudo 2-D structure. The proposed vision chip has been fabricated by using a 0.35 μm 2P4M standard CMOS process, and then successfully demonstrated. By applying the proposed vision chip to neuromorphic systems, real-time and robust computation with a compact hardware would be achieved.

Acknowledgement. This research was supported as a Brain neuroinformatics research program by Korean Ministry of Commerce, Industry, and Energy.

References

1. Moini, A.: Vision Chips or Seeing Silicon. CHiPTec (1997)
2. Mead, C.A.: Analog VLSI and Neural Systems. Addison-Wesley, Reading (1989)
3. Gonzalez, R.C., Woods, R.E.: Digital Image Processing. Addison-Wesley, Reading (1993)
4. Kim, W.-C., Kim, J.-H., Lee, M., Shin, J.-K., Yang, H.-S., Yonezu, H.: Smooth Pursuit Eye Movement System using Artificial Retina Chip and Shape Memory Alloy Actuator. IEEE Sensors Journal 5, 501–509 (2005)
5. Wu, C.-Y., Chiu, C.-F.: A New Structure of the 2-D Silicon Retina. IEEE J. Solid-State Circuit 30, 890–897 (1995)
6. Kameda, S., Honda, A., Yagi, T.: Real Time Image Processing with an Analog Vision Chip System. International Journal of Neural Systems 9, 423–428 (1999)
7. Sawa, S., Nishio, K., Furukawa, Y., Shin, J.-K.: Analog Integrated Circuit for Edge Detection with Wide Dynamic Range Based on Vertebrate Outer Retina. Intelligent Automation and Soft Computing 12, 233–305 (2006)

8. Suh, S.-H., Kim, J.-H., Kong, J.-S., Shin, J.-K.: Vision Chip for Edge Detection with a Function of Pixel FPN reduction. J. of the Korean Sensors Society 14, 191–197 (2005)
9. Park, J.-H., Kim, J.-H., Suh, S.-H., Shin, J.-K., Lee, M., Choi, P., Yagi, T.: A Complementary Metal-Oxide-Semiconductor Vision Chip for Edge Detection and Motion Detection with a Function for Output Offset Cancellation. Optical Review 12, 15–19 (2005)
10. Kim, J.-H., Kong, J.-S., Suh, S.-H., Lee, M., Shin, J.-K., Park, H.B., Choi, C.A.: A Low Power Analog CMOS Vision Chip for Edge Detection Using Electronic Switches. ETRI Journal 27, 539–544 (2005)
11. Kong, J.-S., Kim, S.-H., Sung, D.-K., Shin, J.-K., Lee, M.: A 160X120 Light-Adaptive CMOS Vision Chip for Edge Detection Based on a Retinal Structure Using a Saturating Resistive Network. ETRI Journal 29, 59–69 (2007)
12. Kong, J.-S., Kim, S.-H., Shin, J.-K., Lee, M.: An Artificial Retina Chip Using Switch-Selective Resistive Network for Intelligent Sensor Systems. In: Huang, D.-S., Li, K., Irwin, G.W. (eds.) ICIC 2006. LNCS (LNBI), vol. 4115, pp. 702–710. Springer, Heidelberg (2006)
13. Kong, J.-S., Suh, S.-H., Kim, S.-H., Shin, J.-K., Lee, M.: A Bio-Inspired 128X128 Complementary Metal-Oxide-Semiconductor Vision Chip for Edge Detection with Signal Processing Circuit Separatd from Photo-Sensing Circuit. Optical Review 12, 320–325 (2006)
14. Loose, M., Meier, K., Schemmel, J.: A Self-Calibrating Single-Chip CMOS Camera with Logarithmic Response. IEEE J. of Solid-State Circuits 36, 586–596 (2001)
15. Lai, L.-W., Lai, C.-H., King, Y.-C.: Novel Logarithmic Response CMOS Image Sensor with High Output Voltage Swing and In-Pixel Fixed-Pattern Noise Reduction. IEEE Sensors J. 4, 122–126 (2004)
16. Kavadias, S., Dierickx, V., Schelffer, D., Alaerts, A., Uwaerts, D., Mogaerts, J.: A Logarithmic Response CMOS Image Sensor with On-Chip Calibration. IEEE J. of Solid-State Circuits 35, 1146–1152 (2000)
17. Kandel, E.R., Schwartz, J.H., Jessell, T.M.: Principles of Neural Science, 3rd edn. Appleton & Lange Norwalk, CT
18. Zhang, W., Chan, M.: A High Gain N-well/gate Tied PMOSFET Image Sensor Fabricated from a Standard CMOS Process. IEEE Trans. on Electron Devices 48, 1097–1102 (2001)
19. Kavadias, S.: Offset-Free Column Readout Circuit for CMOS Image Sensors. Electronics Letters 35, 2112–2113 (1999)

A Robot Vision System for Collision Avoidance Using a Bio-inspired Algorithm

Hirotsugu Okuno and Tetsuya Yagi

Osaka University, 2-1 Yamadaoka, Suita, Osaka, Japan

Abstract. Locusts have a remarkable ability of visual guidance that includes collision avoidance exploiting the limited nervous networks in their small cephalon. We have designed and tested a real-time intelligent visual system for collision avoidance inspired by the visual nervous system of a locust. The system was implemented with mixed analog-digital integrated circuits consisting of an analog resistive network and field-programmable gate array (FPGA) circuits so as to take advantage of the real-time analog computation and programmable digital processing. The response properties of the system were examined by using simulated movie images, and the system was tested also in real-world situations by loading it on a motorized miniature car. The system was confirmed to respond selectively to colliding objects even in complex real-world situations.

1   Introduction

The ability to avoid collisions is important for autonomous robots and vehicles. Although visually guided collision avoidance has been studied intensively by employing charge-coupled device (CCD) cameras and digital processing devices, it is still difficult for conventional digital systems to realize real-time computation with compact hardware system because visual signal processing requires a large amount of computation.

In contrast, insects have a remarkable ability of visual guidance that includes collision avoidance exploiting the limited nervous networks in their small cephalon. The comparatively simple nervous networks of insects enable researchers to specify the functions and activities of an individual neuron and those of well-defined neural circuits [1][2]. Based on this background, artificial visual systems that imitate some features of the nervous system of flies have been developed to demonstrate the advantages of such bio-inspired systems in robotic vision [3].

Locusts have attracted attention for their ability to avoid collisions through the use of monocular cues. A neuron called the lobula giant movement detector (LGMD) has been identified as being responsible for triggering avoidance behavior in the locust visual nervous system [4][5], and a network model of the neuronal circuit has been proposed [6]. Algorithms based on the model have been implemented on a personal computer (PC) [7]–[9], and a digital very large-scale integrated (VLSI) vision chip has been designed to mimic the collision avoidance response of the locust neuronal circuit [10][11].

M. Ishikawa et al. (Eds.): ICONIP 2007, Part II, LNCS 4985, pp. 107–116, 2008.

In the previous study, we have proposed a network model to implement the LGMD neurons with a mixed analog-digital integrated circuits and demonstrated that the system gave rise to responses similar to that of LGMD neurons using simulated video movies [12].

In the present study, the system has been implemented with a neuromorphic silicon retina [13] and field-programmable gate array (FPGA) circuits so as to take advantage of the real-time analog computation and programmable digital processing. The system was applied to control a motorized miniature car avoiding collision in real-time.

2   Algorithm for Collision Avoidance

2.1   Computational Model for Collision Avoidance

The system implemented in this study is inspired by the computation that takes place in locust visual neurons. The neuronal network model of the visual circuit for collision avoidance has been proposed by Rind et al. [6].

The computation carried out in the neuronal network model can be diagramed as shown in Fig.1 (a). The input unit of the model generates a transient response to light (indicated as signal "E" in Fig.1), which is mainly induced by the motion of edges. Then, signal E is spread to adjacent pixels after a certain delay, resulting in signal "I" in Fig.1 (a). Here, E and I correspond respectively to the excitatory signal and the inhibitory signal of the original neuronal network model. The spatial profile of signals E and I is shown in Fig.1 (b). The output of each pixel, which is indicated as "S" in Fig.1 (a), is given by:

$$S = \begin{cases} 0 & (E < I) \\ E - I & (E \geq I) \end{cases} \tag{1}$$

The final output of the model is given by:

$$final\ output = \sum_{pixel} S \tag{2}$$

The fundamental computation required for generating the collision avoidance signal is the critical competition between excitatory signal E induced by the moving edge and inhibitory signal I spreading laterally. If the surrounding edge of the object moves fast enough to get away from the skirt of signal I, the S units are excited and the final output unit generates a large response. Otherwise, the excitatory signal is cancelled or suppressed by the inhibitory signal, resulting in no or weak response in the final output.

2.2   Monocular Cues for Approach Detection

Fig.2 depicts how an approaching object is projected onto the retinal surface. D is the diameter of an object and $d(t)$ is the distance of the object from a lens

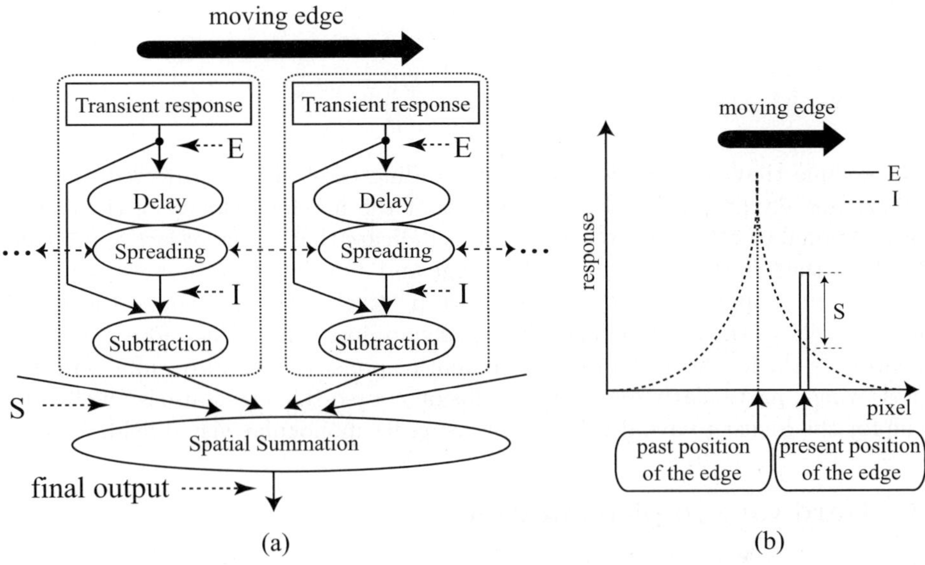

Fig. 1. (a) Visual signal flow diagram of the locust neuronal circuit for collision avoidance. (b) Spatial profile of E and I signals. An edge motion induces an instant localized response (solid line) and broad response with a delay (dashed line).

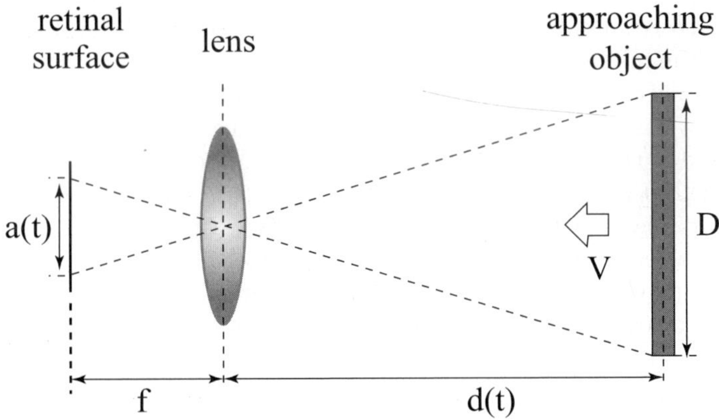

Fig. 2. Diagram of an approaching object focused by a lens onto a retinal surface. On the retinal surface, both the length and the moving velocity of the surrounding edge of the projected image increase drastically at close range.

with focal length f. Now, consider that the object is approaching the lens at constant velocity V along the optical axis of the lens. In this case, the diameter of the object's image projected onto the retinal surface and its derivative with respect to time are given by:

$$a(t) = \frac{fD}{d(t)} \tag{3}$$

$$\dot{a}(t) = -\frac{fDV}{d(t)^2} \tag{4}$$

We assume that the length of the surrounding edge of the projected image is approximately proportional to $a(t)$ and that the moving velocity of the edge is proportional to $\dot{a}(t)$. The above equations indicate that as the object approaches the lens, the length of the surrounding edge and its velocity on the retinal surface increase in proportion to d^{-1} and d^{-2}, respectively. In other words, the length and velocity of the edge increase drastically at close range. Therefore, the visual neurons of the locusts generate a prominent response to an approaching object at close range, particularly for a direct collision course. This response is an effective cue for the locust to avoid collision by using its monocular visual field.

3   Hardware Implementation

3.1   System Architecture

We have implemented the fundamental architecture of the collision avoidance circuit depicted in the previous section by using a mixed analog-digital system consisting of a silicon retina and FPGA circuits (Fig.3). In the system developed here, the lateral spread of the inhibitory signal is achieved by using the resistive network. This is an efficient architecture for realizing the lateral spread of the signal since the inhibitory signal is conducted passively and instantaneously over the resistive network. However, it is not appropriate to implement the delay of the inhibitory signal by using the analog circuit since in order to realize the delay time required in the present situation, the capacitor occupies a significantly large area on the chip when fabricated in the analog VLSI. Accordingly, the delay of the inhibitory signal is configured with the FPGA circuit.

The silicon retina used here has 100×100 pixels, each of which is composed of an active pixel sensor (APS), resistive networks, and differential amplifiers [14]. The architecture of the chip has been originally designed by Kameda and Yagi [13].

3.2   Visual Signal Flow

The transient response to light is obtained by the differential amplifiers in the silicon retina circuit, which subtract consecutive image frames received by the APS array. The resistive network connecting neighboring pixels is used to generate the lateral spread inhibitory signals. The signal that is smoothed by the resistive network of the silicon retina has skirts with a decaying spatial profile on both sides, as shown in Fig.1 (b). The size of the smoothing filter, or in other words, the degree of exponential decay of the smoothed image, can be easily controlled by an externally applied voltage to registers R_s because the resistive network of

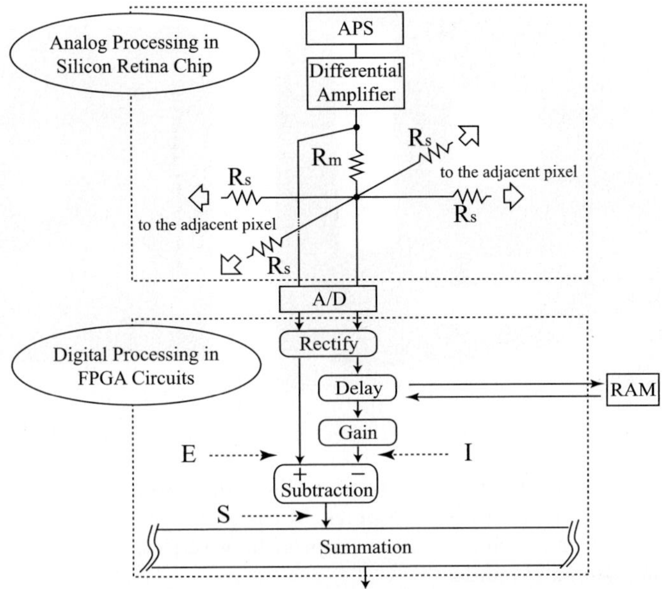

Fig. 3. Block diagram of the system implemented using FPGA circuits and a silicon retina. The lateral spread is realized by exploiting the analog resistive network in the silicon retina. This implementation reduces the computational cost in the subsequent processing. The delay, subtraction, and summation are realized in the FPGA with RAM.

the silicon retina is implemented with metal-oxide-semiconductor (MOS) transistors [13]. The delay in the inhibitory signal is generated in the FPGA circuits using random access memory (RAM). The difference between V_E and V_I gives V_S in each pixel. The V_S values of all pixels are summed up to obtain the final output of this system. The amplitude and delay time of the inhibitory signal can be controlled in the FPGA circuits.

4   System Response

4.1   Response Property

The responses of the system to moving images have been examined in the environment as shown in Fig.4(a). In this experiment, a movie simulating an approaching object is created on a computer and presented on a liquid crystal display (LCD) monitor. The frame sampling time of the silicon retina is set to 33 ms.

Fig.5 shows the system response to varied edge velocity. Here, the edge velocity refers to the velocity of a moving edge of an image projected onto the acceptance surface. Black and outline circles plot the responses with inhibitory signal with

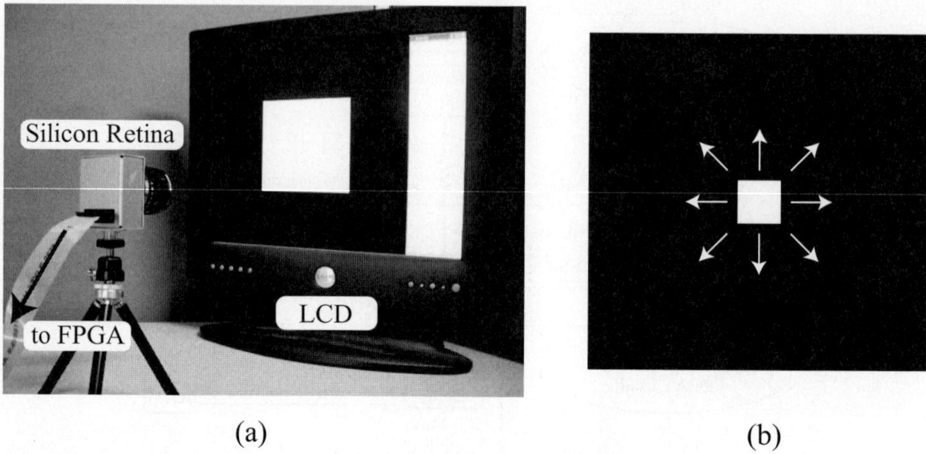

(a)   (b)

Fig. 4. (a)Experimental environment to test the system response. Movie images are presented on an LCD monitor. The response of the system was recorded by a PC via Ethernet. (b)Movie image simulating an approaching object. The white rectangle in the center of the screen expands.

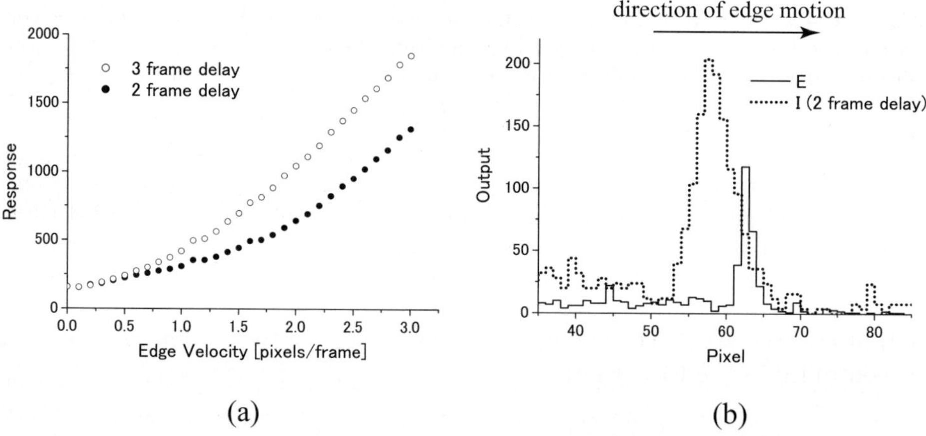

(a)   (b)

Fig. 5. (a)System response to varied edge velocity. Movie images in which a black-and-white edge moves sideways used as visual stimuli. (b)Spatial profile of E and I signals along the 50th row.

delay of 2 frames and 3 frames, respectively. The slope of each response increases at a certain edge velocity; the velocity get slower as the delay lengthens. The change in the slope can be explained by Fig.5(b) which shows the spatial profile of E and I signals along the 50th row. If signal E moves fast enough to get out of the influence of inhibitory signal I in the time of delay, the effect of the inhibition reduces. Therefore, the slope of the system response with delay of 2 frames and 3 frames increases at about 1.2 pixels/frame and 1.8 pixels/frame, respectively.

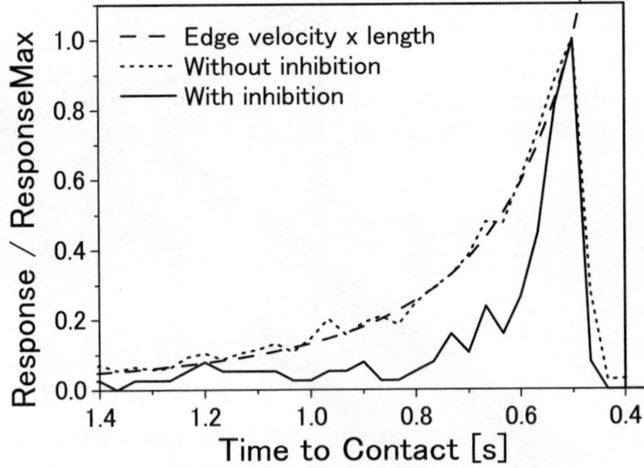

Fig. 6. System response to an approaching object. In the movie image displayed here, it is assumed that an object in front of the retina approaches straight-on with a uniform velocity. The solid line plots the response of the system with inhibition, and the dotted line plots the response of the system without inhibition. The dashed line plots the product of the edge velocity and the edge length.

Fig.6 shows the system response to the movie shown in Fig.4(b). In the figure, the comparison between the response of the system with inhibition (solid line) and that without inhibition (dotted line) is illustrated. The amplitude of the output is normalized with the maximum response. Without inhibition, the output of the model is approximately proportional to the product of the edge length and the edge velocity because the number of pixels stimulated by the moving edge is proportional to the product. However, with inhibition, the model responds to the approaching object only at close range.

4.2   Response in Real-World Situations

The system response has been examined in real-world situations as shown in Fig.7. In this setting, a motorized miniature car loaded with a silicon retina moves toward a beverage can placed on a direct collision course, passing two beverage cans placed on a non collision course.

Fig.8 shows the system response when the miniature car moves forward in the test environment. The solid line plots the response of the system with inhibition, and the dotted line plots the response of the system without inhibition. When the car is distant from the colliding object, the response with inhibition keeps relatively low amplitude compared with that without inhibition. However, when the colliding object reaches at close range, the response with inhibition increases drastically because the excitatory signal induced by the edge moves fast enough to get away from the influence of the inhibitory signal, just as expected by the simulation. Small bumpy responses are mainly caused by objects on a non collision course.

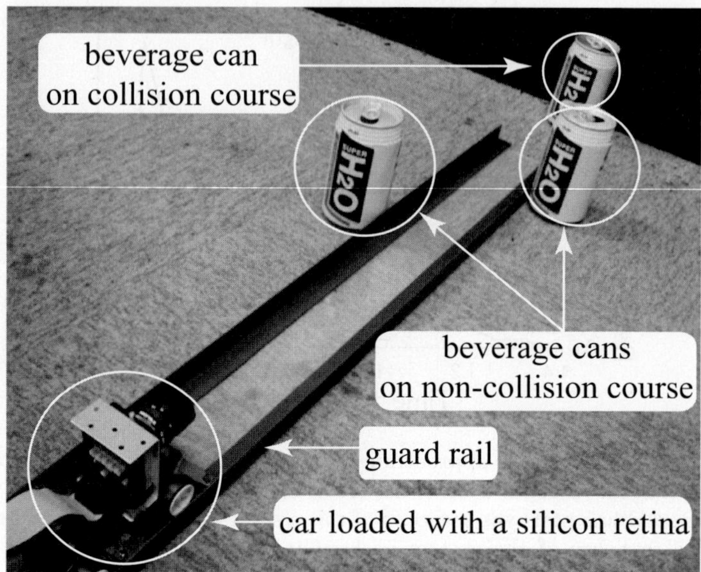

Fig. 7. Experimental environment to test the system response in a real-world situation. A motorized miniature car loaded with a silicon retina moves toward a beverage can. Two other beverage cans are also placed respectively on either side of the collision course.

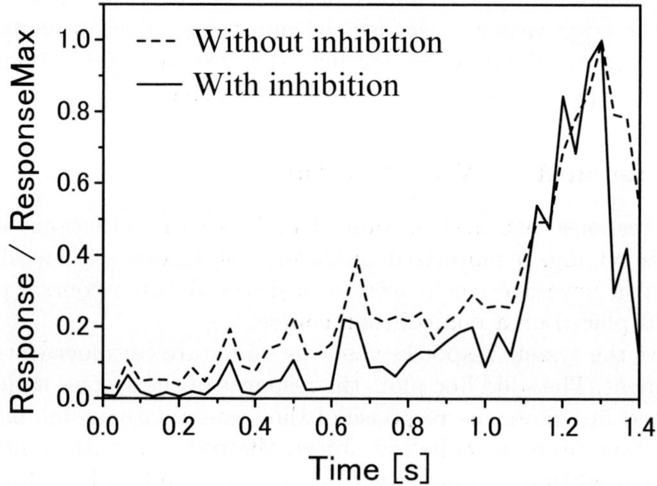

Fig. 8. System response when silicon retina moves forward in the environment as shown in Fig.7. The solid line plots the response of the system with inhibition, and the dotted line plots the response of the system without inhibition.

The brake of the miniature car is designed to operate when the system response exceeds a particular value. Because the colliding object cause a much larger response than that of non colliding object, the system was successful in generating a stop signal only to a colliding object, and consequently the car stopped just before the collision.

5   Discussion

In the present study, we have implemented a real-time vision system for collision avoidance inspired by neuronal circuits of locusts.

Conventional digital computation often encounters the limitations of excessive power consumption, large-scale hardware, and high cost of computation in terms of sensory information processing [15]. However, its programmable architecture enables a variety of image processing techniques to be executed.

In contrast, the analog VLSI circuits execute parallel computation by using their physical properties of built-in circuits, and the results of the computation are instantaneously obtained in the form of a voltage or current distribution. Therefore, the analog VLSI circuits can provide a high computational efficiency in sensory information processing, although the computation is not as flexible as that performed by its digital counterparts.

The implemented system consists of the analog VLSI silicon retina [14] and FPGA circuits so as to take advantage of the properties of both analog and digital technologies.

The system was successful in responding selectively to colliding objects even in complex real-world situations. The key to the selective response is the velocity of image edges on the retina. As can be seen from Fig.5, the sensitivity to slowly traveling edges is designed to be low. Therefore, the system response is suppressed when approaching objects are distant points. However, as the objects approach, the edge velocity increases in proportion to d^2 as indicated in equation (4), and accordingly, the system responds strongly to the objects at close range. In addition, the increase of edge length also contributes to enhancing the response.

In contrast to colliding objects, non-colliding objects fade out from the field of view at a much distant point, and as a consequence the edge velocity does not increase significantly. Therefore, the system can respond to colliding objects without responding to non colliding objects.

References

1. Reichardt, W., Poggio, T.: Visual control of orientation behaviour in the fly Part I. Q. Rev. Biophys. 9, 311–375 (1976)
2. Poggio, T., Reichardt, W.: Visual control of orientation behaviour in the fly Part II. Q. Rev. Biophys. 9, 377–438 (1976)
3. Franceschini, N.: Visual guidance based on optic flow: a biorobotic approach. J. Physiol. Paris 98, 281–292 (2004)

 4. Hatsopoulus, N., Gabbiani, F., Laurent, G.: Elementary computation of object approach by a wide-field visual neuron. Science 270, 1000–1003 (1995)
 5. Rind, F.C.: Intracellular characterization of neurons in the locust brain signalling impending collision. J. Neurophysiol. 75, 986–995 (1996)
 6. Rind, F.C., Bramwell, D.I.: Neural network based on the input organization of an identified neuron signaling impending collision. J. Neurophysiol. 75, 967–984 (1996)
 7. Blanchard, M., Rind, F.C., Verschure, P.F.M.J.: Collision avoidance using a model of the locust LGMD neuron. Robot. Auton. Sys. 30, 17–38 (2000)
 8. Bermudez, S., Verschure, P.: A Collision Avoidance Model Based on the Lobula Giant Movement Detector(LGMD) neuron of the Locust. In: Proceedings of the IJCNN, Budapest (2004)
 9. Yue, S., Rind, F.C., Keil, M.S., Cuadri, J., Stafford, R.: A bio-inspired visual collision detection mechanism for cars: Optimisation of a model of a locust neuron to a novel environment. NeuroComputing 69, 1591–1598 (2006)
10. Cuadri, J., Linan, G., Stafford, R., Keil, M.S., Roca, E.: A bioinspired collision detection algorithm for VLSI implementation. In: Proceedings of the SPIE conference on Bioengineered and Bioinspired System 2005 (2005)
11. Laviana, R., Carranza, L., Vargas, S., Liñán, G., Roca, E.: A Bioinspired Vision Chip Architecture for Collision Detection in Automotive Applications. In: Proceedings of the SPIE conference on Bioengineered and Bioinspired System 2005 (2005)
12. Okuno, H., Yagi, T.: Bio-inspaired real-time robot vision for collision avoidance. Journal of Robotics and Mechatronics (in press)
13. Kameda, S., Yagi, T.: An analog VLSI chip emulating sustained and transient response channels of the vertebrate retina. IEEE Trans. on Neural Networks 14, 1405–1412 (2003)
14. Takami, R., Shimonomura, K., Kameda, S., Yagi, T.: A novel pre-processing vision system employing neuromorphic 100x100 pixel silicon retina. In: Proc. 2005 IEEE Intl. Symp. on Circuits and Systems, Kobe, Japan, pp. 2771–2774 (2005)
15. Indiveri, G., Douglas, R.: Neuromorphic Vision Sensors. Science 288, 1189–1190 (2000)

Analog CMOS Circuits Implementing Neural Segmentation Model Based on Symmetric STDP Learning

Gessyca Maria Tovar[1], Eric Shun Fukuda[2], Tetsuya Asai[1], Tetsuya Hirose[1], and Yoshihito Amemiya[1]

[1] Hokkaido University, Kita 14, Nishi 9, Kita-ku, Sapporo, 060-0814 Japan
gessyca@sapiens-ei.eng.hokudai.ac.jp,
http://sapiens-ei.eng.hokudai.ac.jp/
[2] Tokyo University, Kashiwanoha 5-1-5, Kashiwa-shi, Chiba 277-8561, Japan

Abstract. We proposed a neural segmentation model that is suitable for implementation in analog VLSIs using conventional CMOS technology. The model consists of neural oscillators mutually couple through synaptic connections. The model performs segmentation in temporal domain, which is equivalent to segmentation according to the spike timing difference of each neuron. Thus, the learning is governed by symmetric spike-timing dependent plasticity (STDP). We numerically demonstrate basic operations of the proposed model as well as fundamental circuit operations using a simulation program with integrated circuit emphasis (SPICE).

1 Introduction

The human brain has the ability to group elements from multiple sensory sources. Synchronous activity has been observed in many parts of the brain, e.g., in the visual and auditory cortex. These discoveries have triggered much interest in exploring oscillatory correlation to solve the problems of neural segmentation. Many neural models that perform segmentation have been proposed, e.g., [1,2,3], but they are often difficult to implement on practical integrated circuits. A neural segmentation model called LEGION (Locally Excitatory Globally Inhibitory Oscillator Networks) [4], can be implemented on LSI circuits [5]. However, the LEGION model fails to work in the presence of noise. Our model solves this problem by including spike-timing dependent plasticity (STDP) learning with all-to-all connections of neurons.

In this paper, we present a simple neural segmentation model that is suitable for analog CMOS circuits. The segmentation model is suitable for applications such as figure-ground segmentation and the cocktail-party effect, etc.

The model consists of mutually coupled (all-to-all) neural oscillators that exhibit synchronous (or asynchronous) oscillations. All the neurons are coupled with each other through positive or negative synaptic connections. Each neuron accepts external inputs, e.g., sound inputs in the frequency domain, and oscillates (or does not oscillate) when the input amplitude is higher (or lower) than a

M. Ishikawa et al. (Eds.): ICONIP 2007, Part II, LNCS 4985, pp. 117–126, 2008.

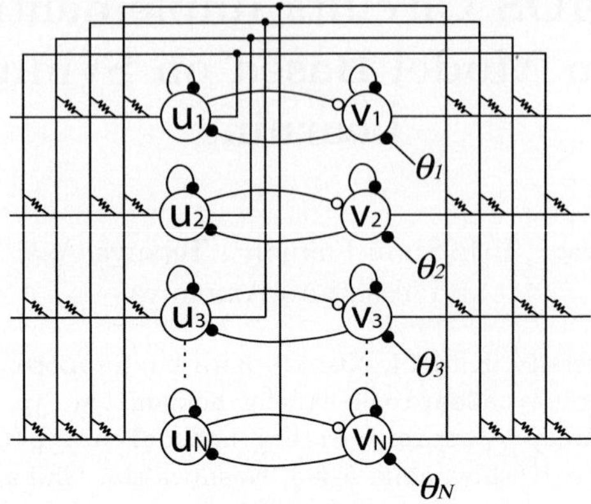

Fig. 1. Network construction of segmentation model

given threshold value. The basic idea is to strengthen (or weaken) the synaptic weights between synchronous (or asynchronous) neurons, which may result in phase-domain segmentation. The synaptic weights are updated based on symmetric STDP using Reichardt's correlation neural network [6] which is suitable for analog CMOS implementation.

2   The Model and Basic Operations

Our segmentation model is illustrated in Fig. 1. The network has N neural oscillators consisting of the Wilson-Cowan type activator and inhibitor pairs (u_i and v_i) [7]. All the oscillators are coupled with each other through resistive synaptic connections, as illustrated in the figure. The dynamics are defined by

$$\tau \frac{du_i}{dt} = -u_i + f_{\beta_1}(u_i - v_i) + \sum_{j \neq i}^{N} W_{ij}^{\mathrm{uu}} u_j, \tag{1}$$

$$\frac{dv_i}{dt} = -v_i + f_{\beta_2}(u_i - \theta_i) + \sum_{j \neq i}^{N} W_{ij}^{\mathrm{uv}} u_j, \tag{2}$$

where τ represents the time constant, N the number of oscillators, θ_i the external input to the i-th oscillator. $f_{\beta_i}(x)$ represents the sigmoid function defined by $f_{\beta_i}(x) = [1 + \tanh(\beta_i x)]/2$, W_{ij}^{uu} the connection strength between the i-th and j-th activators and W_{ij}^{uv} the strength between the i-th activator, and the j-th inhibitor. The operation of the model and the simulations of nullclines and trajectory are explained in [8].

According to the stability analysis in [7], the i-th oscillator exhibits excitable behaviors when $\theta_i < \Theta$ where $\tau \ll 1$ and $\beta_1 = \beta_2$ ($\equiv \beta$), where Θ is given by

$$\Theta = u_0 - \frac{2}{\beta} \tanh^{-1}(2v_0 - 1), \tag{3}$$

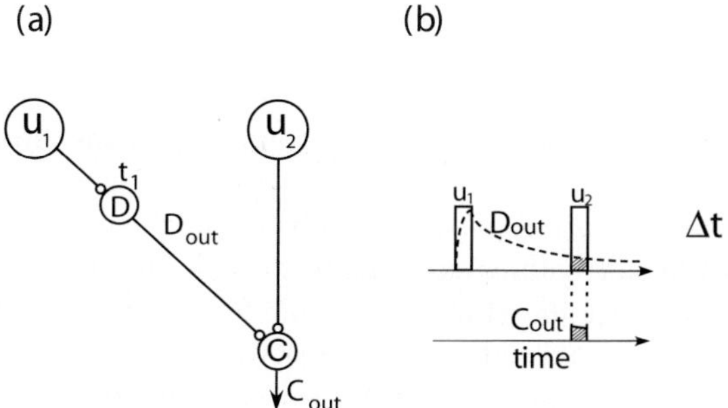

Fig. 2. Reichardt's correlation network

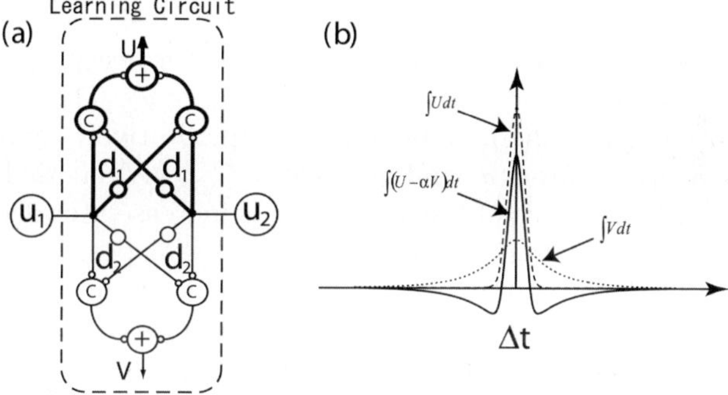

Fig. 3. Learning characteristic: Reichardt's correlation

$$u_0 \equiv \frac{1 - \sqrt{1 - 4/\beta}}{2},$$

$$v_0 \equiv u_0 - \frac{2}{\beta} \tanh^{-1}(2u_0 - 1),$$

and exhibits oscillatory behaviors when $\theta_i \geq \Theta$, if W_{ij}^{uu} and W_{ij}^{uv} for all i and j are zero.

Suppose that neurons are oscillating ($\theta_i \geq \Theta$ for all i) with different initial phases. The easiest way to segment these neurons is to connect the activators belonging to the same (or different) group with positive (or negative) synaptic weights. In practical hardware, however, the corresponding neuron devices have to be connected by special devices having both positive and negative resistive properties, which prevents us from designing practical analog circuits. Therefore, we simply use positive synaptic weights between activators and inhibitors, and do not use negative weights. When the weight between the i-th and j-th activators (W_{ij}^{uu}) is positive and W_{ij}^{uv} is zero, the i-th and j-th activators will be synchronized. Contrarily, when the weight between the i-th activator and the j-th inhibitor (W_{ij}^{uv}) is positive and W_{ij}^{uu} is zero, the i-th and j-th activators will exhibit asynchronous oscillation because the j-th inhibitor (synchronous to the i-th activator) inhibits the j-th activator.

The synaptic weights (W_{ij}^{uu} and W_{ij}^{uv}) are updated based on our assumption; one neural segment is represented by synchronous neurons, and is asynchronous with respect to neurons in the other segment. In other words, neurons should be correlated (or anti-correlated) if they received synchronous (or asynchronous) inputs. These correlation values can easily be calculated by using Reichardt's correlation neural network [6] which is suitable for analog circuit implementation [9]. The basic unit is illustrated in Fig. 2(a). It consists of a delay neuron (D) and a correlator (C). A delay neuron produces blurred (delayed) output D_{out} from spikes produced by activator u_1. The dynamics are given by

$$d_1 \frac{dD_{\mathrm{out}}}{dt} = -D_{\mathrm{out}} + u_1, \tag{4}$$

where d_1 represents the time constant. The correlator accepts D_{out} and spikes produced by activator u_2 and outputs $C_{\mathrm{out}} = D_{\mathrm{out}} \times u_2$. The conceptual operation is illustrated in Fig. 2(b). Note that C_{out} qualitatively represents correlation values between activators u_1 and u_2 because C_{out} is decreased (or increased) when Δt, inter-spike intervals of the activators, is increased (or decreased). Since this basic unit can calculate correlation values only for positive Δt, we use two basic units, which we call a unit pair, as shown by thick lines in Fig. 3(a). The output (U) is thus obtained for both positive and negative Δt by summing the two C_{out}s. Through temporal integration of U, we obtain impulse responses of this unit pair. The sharpness is increases as $d_1 \to 0$. Introducing two unit pairs with different time constants, i.e., d_1 and d_2 ($\gg d_1$), one can obtain those two impulse responses (U and V) simultaneously. The impulse responses (U and V) are plotted in Fig. 3(b) by a dashed and a dotted line, respectively. The weighted subtraction ($U - \alpha V$) produces well-known Mexican hat characteristics, as shown in Fig. 3(b) by a solid line. We use this symmetric characteristic for the weight updating as a spike-timing dependent plasticity (STDP) in the oscillator network.

Our learning model is shown in Fig. 4(a). The learning circuit is located between two activators u_1 and u_2. The two outputs (U and V) of the learning circuit are given to interneuron W which performs subtraction $U - \alpha V$. According to our above assumptions for neural segmentation, when $U - \alpha V$ is positive, the weight between activators u_1 and u_2 (illustrated by a horizontal resistor symbol in Fig. 4(a)) is increased because the activators should be correlated. On the other hand, when $U - \alpha V$ is negative, the weight between activator u_1 and inhibitor v_2 (illustrated by a slant resistor symbol in Fig. 4(a)) is increased because activators u_1 and u_2 should be anti-correlated. To this end, the output of interneuron W is given to two additional interneurons (f_{uu} and f_{uv}). The input-output characteristics of these interneurons are shown in Figs. 4(b). Namely, f_{uu} (or f_{uv}) increases linearly when positive (or negative) $U - \alpha V$ increases, but is zero when $U - \alpha V$ is negative (or positive). Those positive outputs (f_{uu} and f_{uv}) are given to the weight circuit to modify the positive resistances. The dynamics

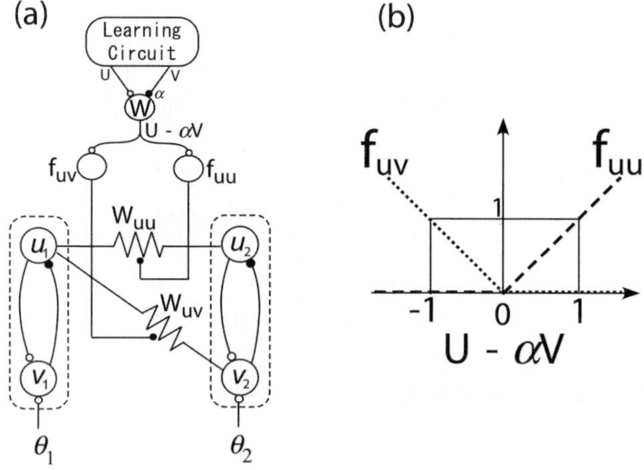

Fig. 4. STDP learning Model

of the "positive" weight between activators u_i and u_j is given by

$$\frac{dW_{ij}^{\mathrm{uu}}}{dt} = -W_{ij}^{\mathrm{uu}} + f_{\mathrm{uu}}, \tag{5}$$

and the "positive" weight between activator u_i and inhibitor v_j is

$$\frac{dW_{ij}^{\mathrm{uv}}}{dt} = -W_{ij}^{\mathrm{uv}} + f_{\mathrm{uv}}. \tag{6}$$

We carried out numerical simulations with $N = 6$, $\tau = 0.1$, $\beta_1 = 5$, $\beta_2 = 10$, $d_1 = 2$, $d_2 = 0.1$ and $\alpha = 1.2$. Time courses of activators u_i ($i = 1 \sim 6$) are shown in Fig. 5. Initially, the external inputs θ_i ($i = 1 \sim 6$) were zero ($< \Theta$), but θ_i for $i = 1 \sim 3$ and $i = 4 \sim 6$ were increased to 0.5 ($> \Theta$) at $t = 10$ s and 20.9 s, respectively. We observed that $u_{1\sim3}$ and $u_{4\sim6}$ were gradually desynchronized without breaking synchronization amongst neurons in the same group, which indicated that segmentation of neurons based on the input timing was successfully achieved.

3   CMOS Unit Circuits and Operations

The construction of a single neural oscillator is illustrated in Fig. 6. The oscillator consists of two differential pairs (m_3-m_4 and m_8-m_9), two current mirrors (m_1-m_2 and m_6-m_7), bias transistors (m_5 and m_10); and two additional capacitors (C_1 and C_2). To explain the basic operation of the neural oscillator, let us suppose that W_{uu} and W_{uv} in Eqs. (1) and (2) are zero. Now in Eq. (1), when u is larger than v ($u > v$) u tends to increase and approach to 1 (vdd), on the contrary, when u is lower than v ($u < v$) u tends to decrease and approach to

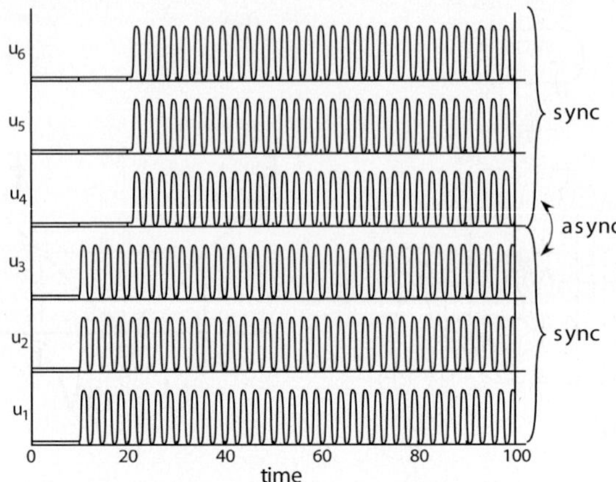

Fig. 5. Numerical simulation results

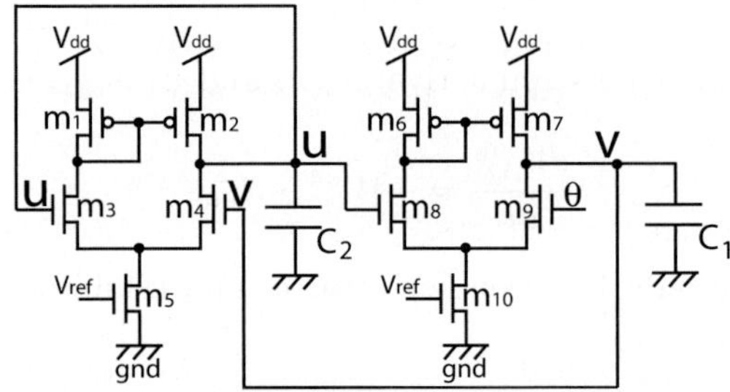

Fig. 6. Unit circuits for neural segmentation

0 (gnd). The same analysis can be apply to Eq. (2). When u is larger than θ ($u > \theta$) v tends to increase approaching to (vdd), and, when u is lower than θ ($u < \theta$) v tends to decrease and approaching to (gnd).

The nullclines (steady state voltage) of a single neuron circuit were simulated in [8]. Transient simulation results of the neuron circuit are shown in Fig. 7. The parameter used for the transistors were obtained from MOSIS AMIS 1.5-μm CMOS process. All transistor sizes were fixed at $L = 1.6$ μm and $W = 4$ μm, the capacitors (C_1 and C_2) were set at 0.1 pF, and the differential amplifier's V_{ref} was set at 0.7 V, and the supply voltage was set at 5 V. Time courses of the activator unit (u) and (v) are shown. Initially, θ was set at 0.5 V (in relaxing state), and neither u nor v oscillated, instead u they are in equilibrium. Then θ was increased to 2.5 V at $t = 5$ μs, and both u and v exhibited oscillations with small phase difference between them. Again, θ was set at 0.5 V at $t = 10$ μs and u relaxed, and v to a high value (around V_{dd}) and decreases with time until it reach equilibrium, as expected.

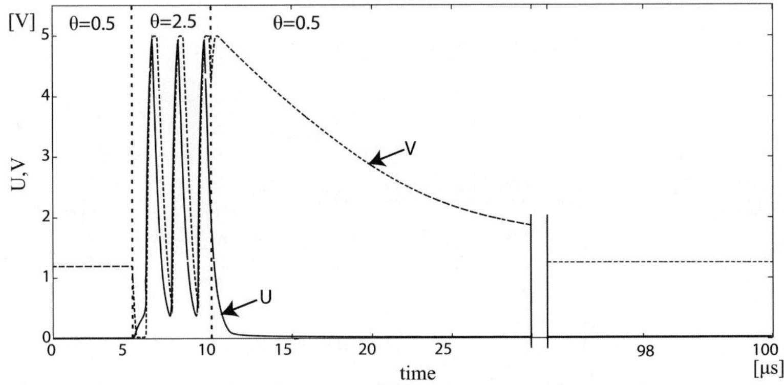

Fig. 7. Simulation results of neural oscillator

A circuit implementing Reichardt's basic unit shown in Fig. 2(a) is shown in Fig. 8. Bias current I_1 drives m$_6$. Transistor m$_5$ is thus biased to generate I_1 because m$_5$ and m$_6$ share the gates. When m$_3$ is turned on (or off) by applying V_{dd} (or 0) to u_1, I_1 is (or is not) copied to m$_1$. Transistors m$_1$ and m$_2$ form a current mirror, whereas m$_2$ and m$_4$ form a pMOS source-common amplifier whose gain is increased as $V_{b1} \rightarrow 0$. Since the parasitic capacitance between the source and drain of m_2 is significantly amplified by this amplifier, temporal changes of u_1 are blurred on the amplifier's output (D_{out}). Therefore this "delayer" acts as a delay neuron in Fig. 2(a). A correlator circuit consists of three differential amplifiers (m_{12}-m_{13}, m_{14}-m_{15} and m_{16}-m_{17}), a pMOS current mirror (m_{19}-m_{20}), a bias transistor (m_{18}) and a bias current source (I_2). In this circuit, m_{12}, m_{14} and m_{17} are floating gate transistors. They reduce voltages of D_{out} and u_2 to $D_{out}/10$ and $u_2/10$ because the input gate sizes were designed to 'capacitively' split the input voltages with the ratio of 1:10. The output current of differential pair m_{14}-m_{15} is:

$$I_{out} = I_2 f(D_{out}/10) f(u_2/10), \qquad (7)$$

where $f(x)$ is the sigmoid function given by $f(x) = 1/(1 + e^{-x})$. Current I_{out} is regulated by the bias transistor m_{18}. The result is copied to m_{20} through current mirror m_{19}-m_{20}. This operation corresponds to that of a correlator in Fig. 2(a).

We carried out circuit simulations of the above circuits. The parameter sets we used for the transistors were obtained from MOSIS AMIS 1.5-μm CMOS process. Transistor sizes of all nMOS and pMOS m$_9$, m$_{10}$ and m$_{18}$ were fixed at $L = 1.6$ μm and $W = 4$ μm pMOS transistors m$_1$, m$_2$, m$_{19}$ and m$_{20}$ were fixed at $L = 16$ μm and $W = 4$ μm. The supply voltage was set at 5 V.

Simulation results of our STDP circuits are shown in Fig. 9. Parameters V_{b1}, V_{b2} and V_{b3} were set at 0.41 V, 0.7 V and 4.1 V, respectively. The value of V_{b1} was chosen so that the delayer makes a reasonable delay. Horizontal axes (Δt) in Fig. 9 represent time intervals of input current pulses (spikes). Voltage

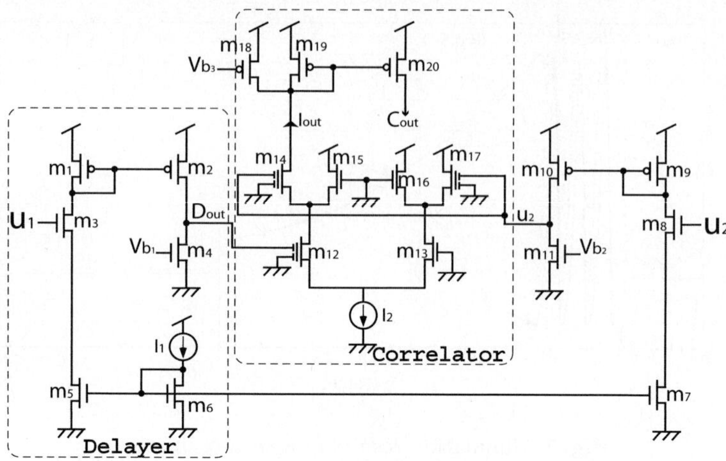

Fig. 8. STDP circuit

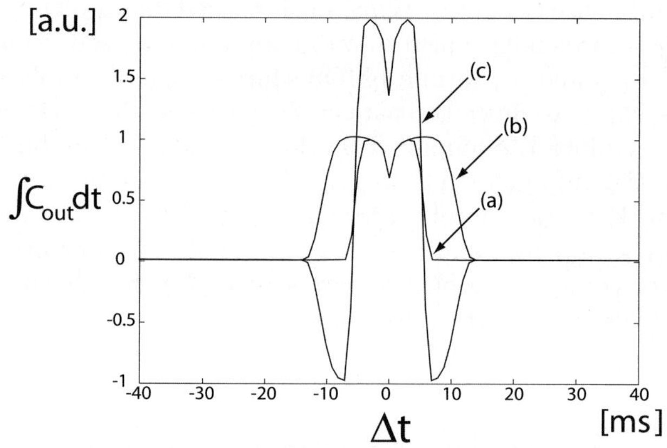

Fig. 9. STDP characteristics

pulses (amplitude: 5 V, pulse width: 10 ms) were applied as u_1 and u_2 in Fig. 8. We integrated C_{out} during the simulation and plotted normalized values [(a) in Fig. 9]. Then we changed the value of V_{b_1} to 0.37 V. The lowered V_{b1} reduced the drain current of m4 and made the delay larger. Again, C_{out} was integrated and normalized. The result is plotted [(b) in Fig. 9]. By subtracting (b) from tripled (a), we obtained the STDP learning characteristic (c) in Fig. 9.

Simulations for testing the synaptic weights of two coupled neural oscillators were made. Figure 10(a) shows the two oscillators with all the synaptic connections. The oscillation of neurons u_1 and u_2 without applying any connection between them ($V_{gs}=0$ V for W_{uu} and W_{uv}) are shown in Fig. 10(b) where the neurons oscillated independently. nMOS transistors with $L = 1.6$ μm and $W = 4$

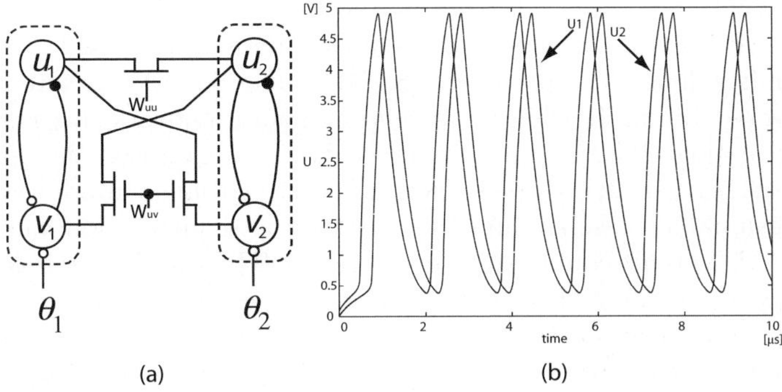

Fig. 10. (a) Coupled neural oscillators (b) u_1 and u_2 oscillations

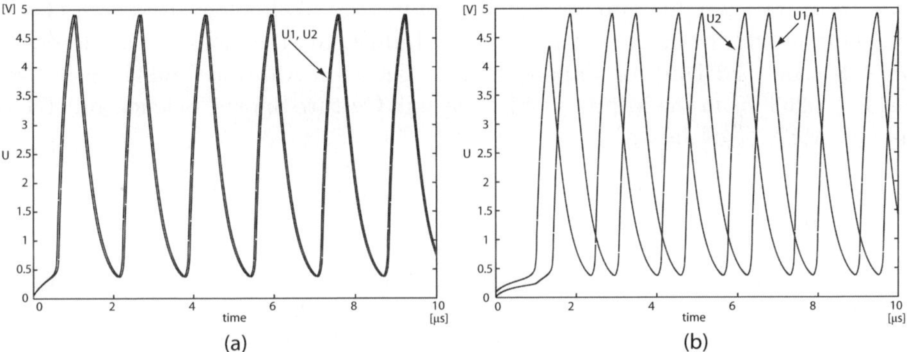

Fig. 11. Oscillation of neurons u_1 and u_2 when (a)excitation is applied and (b) inhibition is applied

μm were used as synaptic weight W_{uu} and W_{uv}, Fig. 10(a) shows the excitatory connection W_{uu} between neurons u_1 and u_2, and inhibitory connections W_{uv} between neurons $u_{1,2}$ and $v_{2,1}$. The oscillations of neurons u_1 and u_2 when applying an excitation through W_{uu} (the gate voltage of W_{uu} was set at 1 V and 0 V for W_{uv}) are shown in Fig. 11(a), in this case both neurons synchronized. On the contrary, when applying an inhibition through W_{uv} (the gate voltage of W_{uv} was set at 0.6 V and 0 V for W_{uu}) the neurons oscillated asynchronously as shown in Fig. 11(b).

4   Conclusion

In this paper, we proposed a neural segmentation model that is suitable for analog VLSIs using conventional CMOS technology. In order to facilitate the implementation of the model, instead of employing negative connections required for anti-correlated oscillation among different segments, we introduced positive connections between activators and inhibitors among different neuron units. Moreover, we proposed a novel segmentation method based on a symmetric spike-timing dependent plasticity (STDP). The STDP characteristics were produced by combining Reichard's correlation neural networks because they are suitable for analog CMOS implementation. We demonstrated the operation of the segmentation network through numerical simulations. In addition we proposed and evaluated basic circuits for constructing segmentation hardware. We showed that the circuit could produce symmetric STDP characteristics. Finally, we confirmed operations of synchronization or desynchronization of two neuron circuits by connecting them with standard synaptic circuits (single MOS transistors). Our next target is to set up the entire segmentation network.

Acknowledgments

This study was partly supported by the Industrial Technology Research Grant Program in '04 from New Energy and Industrial Technology Development Organization (NEDO) of Japan, and a Grant-in-Aid for Young Scientists [(B)17760269] from the Ministry of Education, Culture Sports, Science and Technology (MEXT) of Japan.

References

1. Han, S.K., Kim, W.S., Kook, H.: Temporal segmentation of the stochastic oscillator neural network. Physical Review E 58, 2325–2334 (1998)
2. von der Malsburg, Ch., Buhmann, J.: Sensory segmentation with coupled neural oscillators. Biological Cybernetics 67, 233–242 (1992)
3. von der Malsburg, Ch., Schneider, W.: A neural cocktail-party processor. Biological Cybernetics 54, 29–40 (1986)
4. Wang, D.L., Terman, D.: Locally excitatory globally inhibitory oscillator networks. IEEE Trans. on Neural Networks 6(1), 283–286 (1995)
5. Ando, H., Morie, T., Nagata, M., Iwata, A.: An Image Region Extraction LSI Based on a Merged/Mixed-Signal Nonlinear Oscillator Network Circuit. In: European Solid-State Circuits Conference (ESSCIRC 2002), Italy, September 2002, pp. 703–706 (2002)
6. Reichardt, W.: Principles of Sensory Communication, p. 303. Wiley, New York (1961)
7. Asai, T., Kanazawa, Y., Hirose, T., Amemiya, Y.: Analog reaction-diffusion chip imitating the Belousov-Zhabotinsky reaction with Hardware Oregonator Model. International Journal of Unconventional Computing 1(2), 123–147 (2005)
8. Tovar, G.M., Fukuda, S.E., Asai, T., Hirose, T., Amemiya, Y.: Neuromorphic CMOS circuits implementing a novel neural segmentation model based on symmetric STDP learning. In: 2007 International Joint Conference on Neural Networks, Florida, USA, August 12-17 (2007)
9. Asai, T., Ohtani, M., Yonezu, H.: Analog MOS circuits for motion detection based on correlation neural networks. Japanese Journal of Applied Physics 38(4B), 2256–2261 (1999)

Power Quality Control of Hybrid Wind Power Generation System Using Fuzzy-Robust Controller

Hee-Sang Ko[1], Min-Jae Kang[2], Chang-Jin Boo[2], Chong-Keun Jwa[2], Sang-Soo Kang[2], and Ho-Chan Kim[2]

[1] Wind Energy Research Center, Korea Institute of Energy Research, Daejeon, 305-343, Korea
hee-sang@ieee.org
[2] Faculty of Electrical and Electronic Engineering, Cheju National University, Jeju, 690-756, Korea
{minjk, boo1004, keunjc, rkdtkdtn, hckim}@cheju.ac.kr

Abstract. This paper proposes a modeling and controller design approach for a wind-diesel hybrid generation system that includes a wind-turbine and dump load. The proposed control scheme is based on the Takagi-Sugeno (TS) fuzzy model and the sliding mode nonlinear control. The TS fuzzy model expresses the local dynamics of a nonlinear system through sub-systems partitioned by linguistic rules. Thus, the TS fuzzy model provides a mechanism to take an advantage of the advances in modern control theory in designing a nonlinear controller. In the simulation study, the proposed controller is compared with a proportional-integral (PI) controller. Simulation results show that the proposed controller is more effective against disturbances caused by wind speed and load variation than the PI controller, and thus it contributes to a better quality wind-hybrid power generation system.

1 Introduction

The drawback of wind power generation is its dependence on nature — power output varies widely due to changes in wind speed, which are difficult to model and predict. Excessive fluctuation of power output negatively influences the quality of electricity, particularly frequency and voltage, in small-scale system such as in islands and in remote areas [1,2]. A hybrid system is generally composed of a wind-turbine coupled with an induction generator, an energy storage system, a dump load, and a backup diesel engine-driven synchronous generator for operation when wind power is insufficient. There can be several possible modes of operation [2-4].

This paper considers a mode where both the wind turbine-induction generator unit and the dump load operate in parallel. In this mode, wind-generated power is sufficient to supply loads and the diesel engine is disconnected from the synchronous generator. The synchronous generator acts as a synchronous condenser, to generate or absorb the reactive power that contributes to its terminal voltage in stabilizing the system. The dump load is applied to the frequency control by absorbing the excess active power in the network. Since no dynamic model of a wind-dump load system

M. Ishikawa et al. (Eds.): ICONIP 2007, Part II, LNCS 4985, pp. 127–136, 2008.

has been reported, this paper develops a novel nonlinear dynamic model of a wind-dump load system.

The nonlinear model is reduced for the purpose of designing the controller. With a reduced-order model, the proposed controller is designed based on the sliding mode control and the TS fuzzy model [5]. The TS fuzzy model provides a simple and straightforward way to decompose the task of modeling and controller design into a group of local tasks, which tend to be easier to handle and, in the end, the TS fuzzy model also provides the mechanism to blend these local tasks together to deliver the overall model and control design. Therefore, by employing the TS fuzzy model, we devise a control methodology to take advantage of the advances of modern control.

2 System Model

A wind-dump load hybrid system consists of a wind turbine, an induction generator (IG), a diesel engine (DE), a synchronous generator (SG), a dump load, and a load. The DE is disconnected from the SG by an electromagnetic clutch. A three-phase dump load is used with each phase consisting of seven transistor-controlled resistor banks [6]. Fig. 1 shows the structure of a wind-dump load system: e_{fd} is the excitation field voltage, f is the frequency, V_b is the bus voltage, C_a is the capacitor bank, P_{dump} is the required dump load power, and r_{dump} is the dump load resistance.

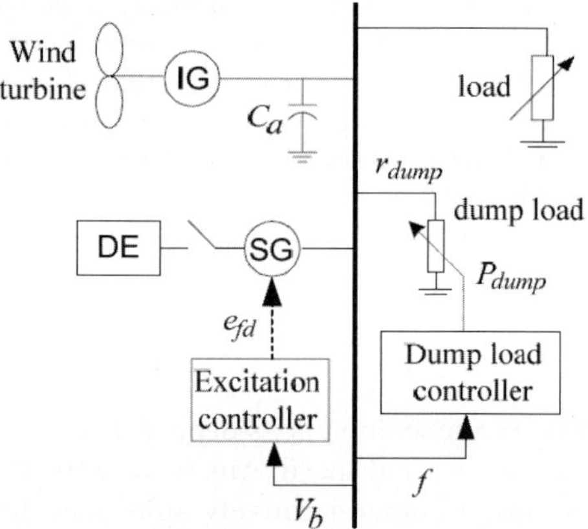

Fig. 1. The overall control structure of a wind-dump load system

3 Fuzzy-Robust Controller Design

The proposed controller is deigned based on the state feedback approach. In practical systems, it is difficult or impossible to measure all states as required. Therefore, special considerations are needed when a controller is designed, based on state feedback.

In this paper, two considerations are made for a controller design: first, a reduced-order nonlinear model is derived to describe the nonlinear system with only target states, which are easily measurable. Second, an extended state-space model is presented to overcome a non-zero final state problem because the state feedback approach is usually based on the zero final states. For a non-zero final state, an output feedback and a state observer approach are normally used [7]. The design procedure presented in this paper, however, is simpler than the output feedback and state observer approaches.

Fig. 2 depicts the input and output relationship of the wind-dump load system from the control point of view. The control inputs are the excitation field voltage (u_1) of the SG and the dump load resistance (u_2). The measurements are the voltage amplitude (y_1) and the frequency (y_2) of the AC bus. The wind speed (v_1) and load (v_2) are considered to be disturbances. The wind turbine generator and the dump load run in parallel, serving the load. From the control point of view, this is a coupled 2×2 multi-input-multi-output nonlinear system, since every input controls more than one output and every output is controlled by more than one input.

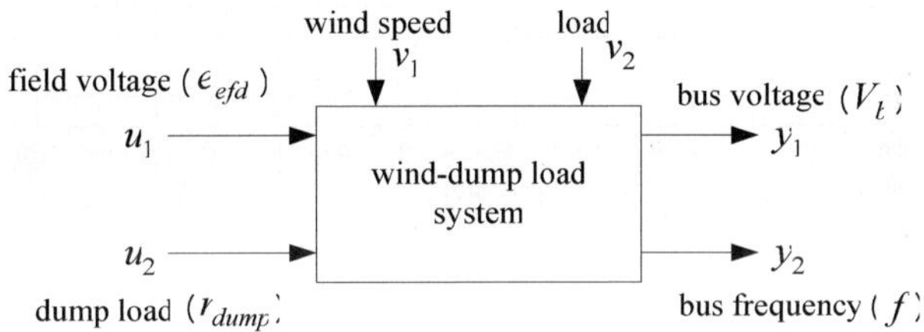

Fig. 2. The wind-dump load control system

3.1 Generator and Dump Load Model

The models of the generators are based on the standard Park's transformation [8] that transforms all stator variables to a rotor reference frame described by a direct and quadratic (d-q) axis.

Fig. 3 is the three-phase dump load, where each phase consists of 7 transistor-controlled resistor banks with binary resistor sizing in order to minimize quantum effects and provide more-or-less linear resolution.

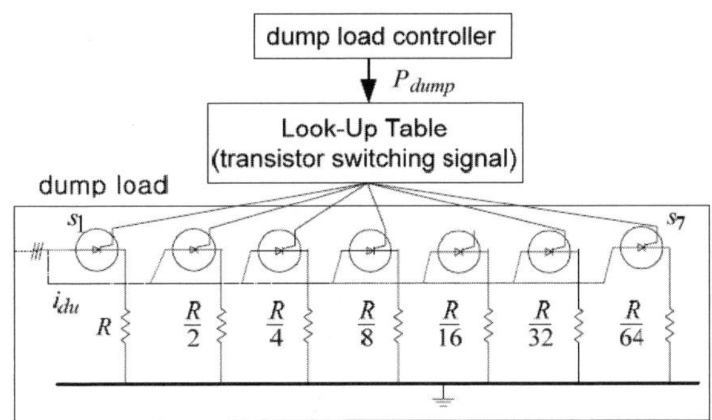

Fig. 3. The structure of the dump load with binary resistor sizing

Fig. 4 shows how the transistors are switched to meet the required power. For example, based on the rated AC line voltage of 230V and per-phase resistance of R (=120Ω), if the required dump load power from the dump load controller is 880W, step-2 is identified, and only switch S2 is turned ON.

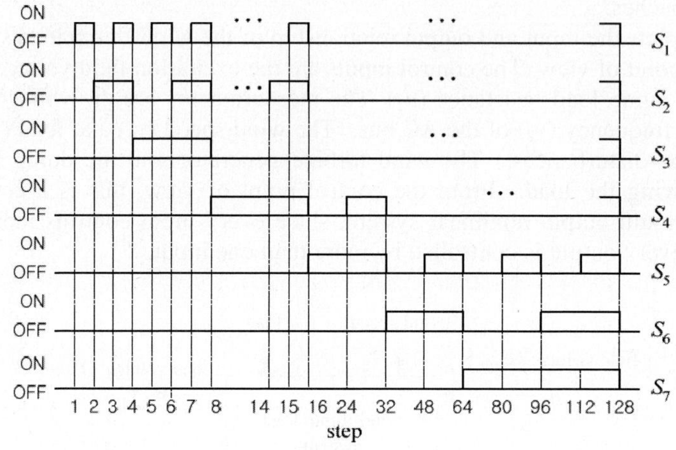

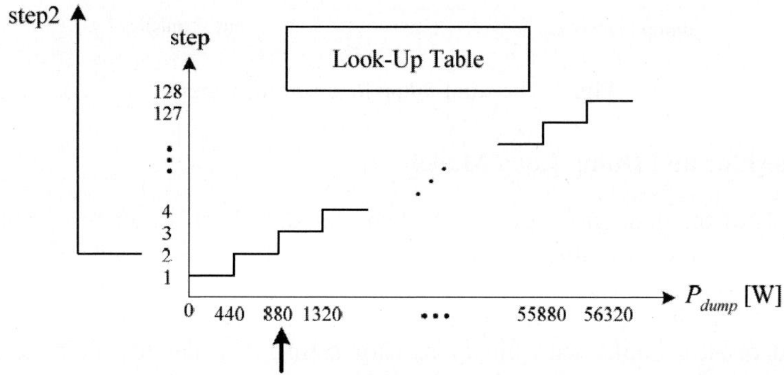

Fig. 4. Transistor switching signal

3.2 Reduced-Order Model

The nonlinear mathematical model of the wind-dump load system [6] is reduced to the following second-order model, to be used for a controller design:

$$\dot{\omega}_s = \frac{1}{J_s}\left(-D_s\omega_s - T_s\right),\ \dot{\psi}_f = \frac{1}{\tau'_{do}}\left(-\psi_f + L_{md}i_{sd}\right) + e_{fd} \tag{1}$$

The reduced-order model (1) can be slightly modified to present dump load effect in the system by noting that the air gap torque of the synchronous generator T_s can be represented as

$$T_s = P/\omega_s = \left(P_{dump} + P_{load} - P_{ind}\right)/\omega_s \tag{2}$$

where P_{dump}, P_s, and P_{ind} are the power of dump load, the synchronous generator, and the induction generator, respectively, and ω_s is the angular speed, which is proportional to frequency f. Applying (2) into (1), the reduced-order model becomes

$$\dot{\omega}_s = \frac{1}{J_s}\left(-D_s\omega_s + \frac{P_{ind}-P_{load}}{\omega_s} - \frac{1}{\omega_s}P_{dump}\right), \quad \dot{\psi}_f = \frac{1}{\tau'_{do}}\left(-\psi_f + L_{md}i_{sd}\right) + e_{fd} \tag{3}$$

In (3), flux linkage ψ_f can be modified in terms of the bus voltage and the frequency. This is because, in local operating point, the following assumption can be made such that the rate of change of voltage is a linear combination of the rate of change of rotor flux and angular speed of the SG:

$$\dot{V}_b = \eta_1\dot{\psi}_f + \eta_2\dot{\omega}_s \tag{4}$$

where $\eta_1 = \partial V_b/\partial\psi_f$ and $\eta_2 = \partial V_b/\partial\omega_s$. Here, η_1 and η_2 are approximated as 1 [p.u.]. Therefore, from (3) and (4) the final reduced-order model is derived as

$$\dot{x}(t) = Ax(t) + Bu(t), \; y(t) = Cx(t) \tag{5}$$

where $x(t) = \begin{bmatrix} V_b & \omega_s \end{bmatrix}^T$, $u(t) = \begin{bmatrix} e_{fd} & P_{dump} \end{bmatrix}^T$, and

$$A = \begin{bmatrix} 1 & 1 \\ 0 & 1 \end{bmatrix}\begin{bmatrix} -\dfrac{L_f}{T'_{do}L_{md}\omega_s} & \dfrac{L_f}{T'_{do}\omega_s L_{md}}\left(L_d i_{sd} - \dfrac{r_a i_{sq}}{\omega_s}\right) \\ \dfrac{P_{ind}-P_{load}}{J_s V_b \omega_s} & -\dfrac{D_s}{J_s} \end{bmatrix}, \quad B = \begin{bmatrix} 1 & -\dfrac{1}{J_s\omega_s} \\ 0 & -\dfrac{1}{J_s\omega_s} \end{bmatrix}, \quad C = \mathbf{I}_2.$$

Note that the model (5) is in the linear form for fixed system matrices A, B and C. However, matrices A and B are not fixed, but changes as functions of state variables, thus making the model nonlinear. Therefore, even though the reduced-order model is used to design a controller, the TS fuzzy-model based controller can be designed taking into account model imperfections and uncertainties. The proposed controller is designed in the following sub-sections.

3.3 Fuzzy-Robust Controller

The main feature of the Takagi-Sugeno fuzzy model expresses the local dynamics of a nonlinear system through linear sub-systems partitioned by linguistic rules. Therefore, by employing the TS fuzzy model, modern linear control theory can be utilized in devising a control methodology for the nonlinear system. In this paper, three linear sub-systems are considered as the state-space model:

$$\dot{x}(t) = A_i x(t) + B_i u(t), \quad y(t) = C_i x(t), \quad i = 1,2,3 \tag{6}$$

where $A_i \in \mathfrak{R}^{n\times n}$, $B_i \in \mathfrak{R}^{n\times m}$, and $C_i \in \mathfrak{R}^{p\times n}$. Here, n, m, and p are the number of states, inputs, and outputs, respectively. It can be seen from the reduced model (5) that $n=m=p=2$. The sub-systems are obtained by partitioning the state-space into overlapping ranges of low, medium, and high states. For each sub-space, different model

(i=1, 2, 3) is applied. The degree of membership function for each state-space is depicted in Fig. 5. Here, $LP(i=1)$, $BP(i=2)$, and $HP(i=3)$ stand for possible low, most possible, and possible high membership functions, respectively. Even if the sub-systems are linear model, the composite system represents the nonlinear system.

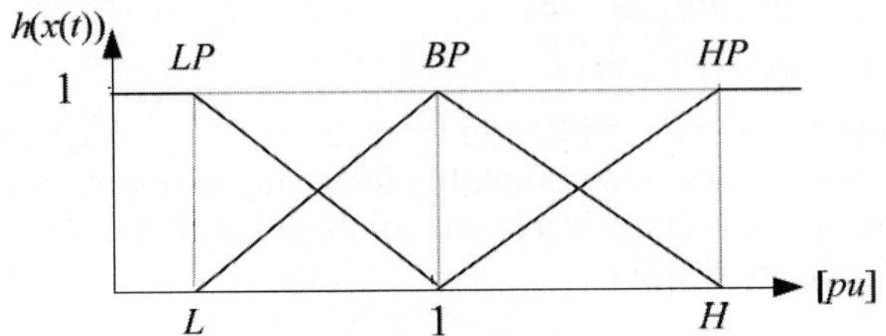

Fig. 5. The membership function for states

When the three controllers are obtained for each sub-system, each control input is weighted by its own membership function shown in Fig. 5. The fuzzy-robust controller output is obtained by deffuzification as

$$u_{FR}(t) = \left(\sum_{i=1}^{3} h_i(x(t)) u_i(t) \right) \Big/ \left(\sum_{i=1}^{3} h_i(x(t)) \right) \tag{7}$$

where $u_{FR}(t)$ is the fuzzy-robust controller output, $u_i(t)$ is the controller output for each linear sub-system, and $h_i(x(t))$ is the membership value of each linear system.

3.4 Sliding Mode Controller

The final states may not be zero but constants, such as in the system under study. Therefore, the modified state vector with the additional state $x_r(t) \in \mathfrak{R}^p$ [7] is obtained as follows:

$$\tilde{x}(t) = \begin{bmatrix} x_r(t) & x(t) \end{bmatrix}^T \tag{8}$$

where $x_r(t) = \int (r(t) - y(t)) dt$ and $r(t) = ref = 1$, and $\tilde{x}(t) \in \mathfrak{R}^{p+n}$ is the augmented state and the associated augmented system is represented as

$$\dot{\tilde{x}}(t) = \tilde{A}\tilde{x}(t) + \tilde{B}u(t) \tag{9}$$

where $\tilde{A} \in \mathfrak{R}^{(p+n)\times(p+n)}$, $\tilde{B} \in \mathfrak{R}^{(p+n)\times m}$ and with matrix A, B, and C of ith sub-system

$$\tilde{A} = \begin{bmatrix} 0 & -C \\ 0 & A \end{bmatrix}, \quad \tilde{B} = \begin{bmatrix} 0 \\ B \end{bmatrix} \tag{10}$$

The proposed controller can then be designed with (9). The motivation to utilize the sliding mode control design is to enable robust control design utilizing multiple linear systems [9]. The controller for each linear sub-system (9) can be obtained as

$$u(t) = -(S\tilde{B})^{-1}(S\tilde{A} - \xi S)\tilde{x}(t) \tag{11}$$

where S is the hyperplane system matrix and where $\xi \in \Re^{m \times m}$ is a stable design matrix. The overall proposed control scheme is given in Fig. 6. Here, $u_F(t)$ is the final control input in the form

$$u_F(t) = r(t) + u_{FR}(t) \tag{12}$$

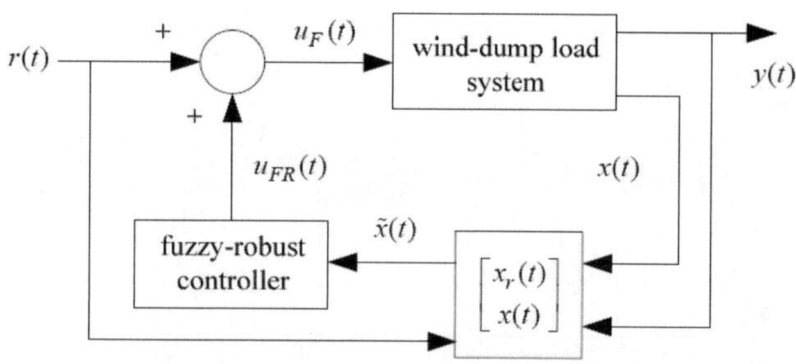

Fig. 6. The overall wind-dump load control scheme

4   Evaluation by Simulation

4.1   System Parameters

The system under study consists of a fixed wind turbine, an induction generator (IG) rated at 55kW, a 50kW turbocharged diesel engine (DE) driving a 55kVA brushless synchronous generator (SG). Nominal system frequency is 50Hz, and the rated line AC voltage is 230V [6]. The dump load consists of seven transistor-controlled resistor banks, rated at 55kW. Load is rated at 40kW. The rated wind speed is 7.25m/s. This section describes a simulation performance that tests the proposed controller. The augmented system state $\tilde{x}(t)$ is defined as

$$\tilde{x}(t) = \begin{bmatrix} x_{r,1}(t) & x_{r,2}(t) & x_1(t) & x_2(t) \end{bmatrix}^T \tag{13}$$

where x_1 and x_2 stand for voltage and frequency, respectively.

Three linear models are obtained from (5) applying $L=0.5$ and $H=1.5$ for both V_b and f. For controller design parameters, the diagonal matrix Q is with $Q_{11}=Q_{33}=2000$ and $Q_{22}=Q_{44}=4000$, and the diagonal matrix ξ is with $\xi_{11}=\xi_{22}=80$. The rest of the terms equal zero. The tuned PI controller gains are $P_{gov}=20$, $I_{gov}=60$, and $P_{efd}=30$, $I_{efd}=90$.

4.2   Wind-Dump Load Control

Wind speed is shown in Fig. 7. For the simulation task, a step load change is applied at 5 seconds from the initial loading of 35kW to 27kW. In the following figures, the proposed fuzzy-robust controller is referred to as SMLQR for comparison with the PI controller. Fig. 8 shows the power in the IG, the load, and the dump load. In this case, when the load decreases, the dump load dissipates the excess power in the network. The proposed control scheme improves the bus frequency performance compared to the PI controller as shown in Fig. 9. In this system, the SG is used as a synchronous condenser. By controlling the field excitation, the SG can be made to either generate or absorb reactive power to maintain its terminal voltage. Fig. 10 shows the reactive power from the SG. Fig. 11 shows the bus voltage performance.

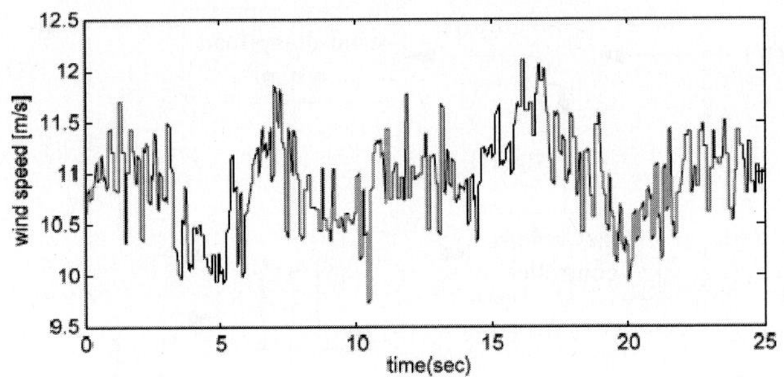

Fig. 7. Wind speed

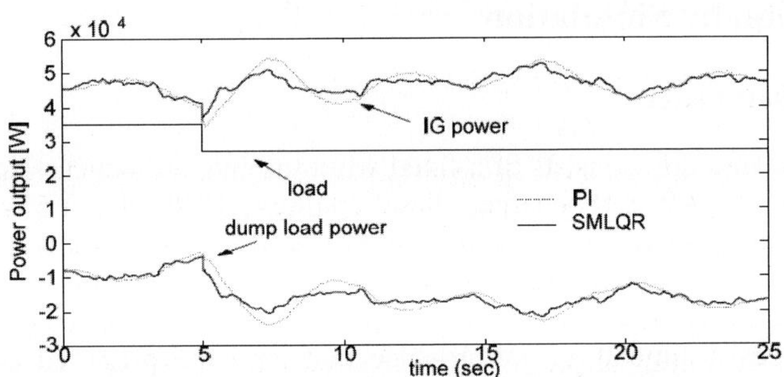

Fig. 8. Power outputs of IG, load, and dump load

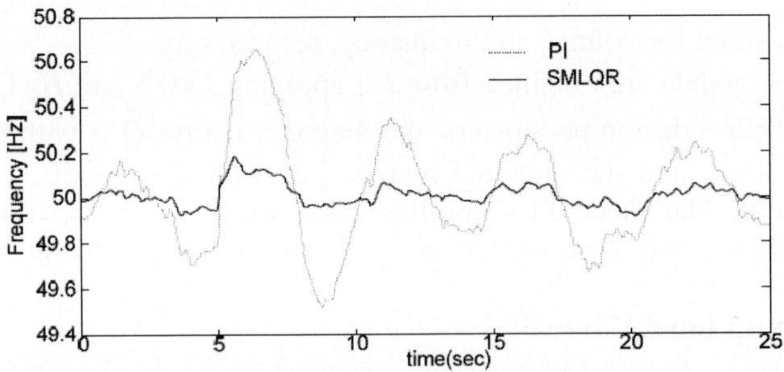

Fig. 9. Frequency performance

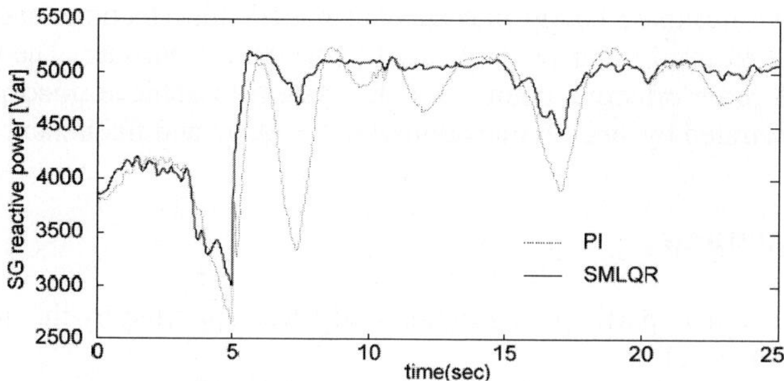

Fig. 10. Reactive power output from the SG

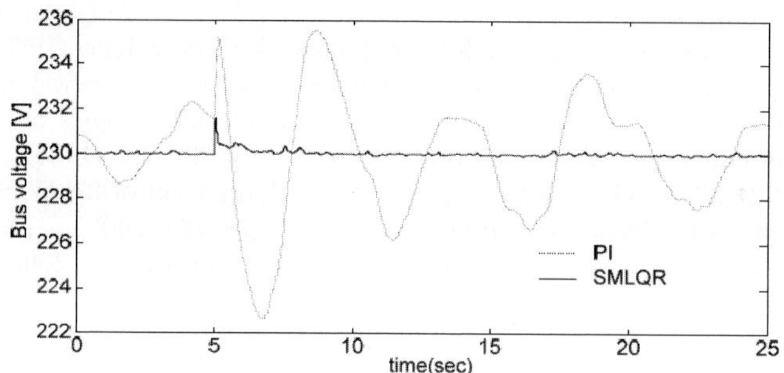

Fig. 11. Bus voltage performance

In SMLQR, the improvement of frequency and voltage with respected to the PI controller is 51.922% and 52.511% in per unit, respectively. The fuzzy-robust controller achieves better performance compared to the PI controller. The maximum voltage and frequency deviations are less than 1%. However, the voltage performance of the PI controller shows slow damping. Such poor performance is caused by the neglect of the interaction of variables between the PI controller loops [7]. Clearly, a control method is required that handles a multi-input-multi-output system. In the proposed controller, all performances are smooth and damped. Therefore, the fuzzy-robust controller provides more effective mechanism for multi-input-multi-output nonlinear system.

5 Conclusions

In this paper, the modeling of a wind-dump load system has been presented for power quality analysis, and the proposed control scheme is derived based on the Takagi-Sugeno (TS) fuzzy model and the sliding mode control. The proposed state-space model provides a new means for a controller design, especially when system states are not fully measurable or a non-zero final state. By employing the TS fuzzy model that represents a nonlinear system with several linear sub-systems, combined by linguistic rules, and by using the sliding mode control for each sub-system, the TS fuzzy model based controller can be designed taking into account model imperfections and uncertainties even though the reduced-order model is used to design a controller. The proposed controller provides more effective control for the system to achieve good power quality, which is demonstrated by smooth transition of bus voltage and frequency.

Acknowledgement

The part of researchers participating in this study are supported by the grant from "the 2nd phase BK21 project".

References

1. Feris, L.L.: Wind Energy Conversion System. Prentice Hall, New Jersy (1990)
2. Hunter, R., Elliot, G.: Wind-Diesel Systems. Cambridge University, New York (1994)
3. Uhlen, K., Foss, B.A., Gjosaeter, O.B.: Robust Control and Analysis of A Wind-Diesel Hybrid Power Plant. IEEE Trans. on Energy Conversion 9, 701–708 (1994)
4. Chedid, R.B., Karaki, S.H., Chadi, E.C.: Adaptive Fuzzy Control for Wind-Diesel Weak Power Systems. IEEE Trans. on Energy Conversion 15, 71–78 (2000)
5. Tanaka, K., Wang, H.O.: Fuzzy Control Systems Design and Analysis. John Wiley & Sons, New York (2001)
6. Ko, H.S., Jatskevich, J.: Power Quality Control of Hybrid Wind Power Generation System Using Fuzzy-LQR Controller. IEEE Transaction on Energy Conversion (submitted for publication)
7. Ogata, K.: Modern Control Engineering. Prentice-Hall, Upper Saddle River (1997)
8. Krause, P.C., Wasynczuk, O., Sudhoff, S.D.: Analysis of Electrical Machinery. McGraw-Hill, New York (1986)
9. Utkin, I., Guldner, J., Shi, J.: Sliding Modes in Electromechanical Systems. Taylor and Francis, Philadelphia (1999)

A New Hardware Friendly Vector Distance Evaluation Function for Vector Classifiers

Hiroomi Hikawa and Kaori Kugimiya

Oita University, Oita, 870-1192 Japan

Abstract. This paper proposes a new vector distance evaluation function for vector classifications. The proposed distance evaluation function is the weighted sum of the differences between vector elements. The weight values are determined according to whether the input vector element is in the neighborhood of the prototype vector element or not. If the element is not within the neighborhood, then the weight is selected so that the distance measure is less significant The proposed distance measure is applied to a hardware vector classifier system and its feasibility is verified by simulations and circuit size evaluation. These simulations and evaluations reveal that the performance of the classifier with the proposed method is better than that of the Manhattan distance classifier and slightly inferior to Gaussian classifier. While providing respectable performance on the classification, the evaluation function can be easily implemented in hardware.

1 Introduction

Pattern classification covers very wide applications, such as face recognition, character recognition, voice recognitions, etc. In the above mentioned applications, given patterns or data are treated as vectors. The vectors could be a sequence of sampled voice data, feature vectors generated from the given images. Then a vector classification is carried out to identify the class to which the given pattern belongs. The vector classification is a mapping process of a D-dimensional space vectors into a finite set of clusters, each of which represents a particular class. Each cluster is associated with a reference prototype $\mathbf{v_i}$ that is center of the cluster, and a set of the prototypes is called as a codebook $\nu = \{\mathbf{v}^{(1)}, \mathbf{v}^{(2)}, \cdots, \mathbf{v}^{(C)}\}$. A vector classification algorithm encodes an input vector with the closest prototype that minimizes the distance to the input vector $\mathbf{x}$.

$$\mathbf{s}^{(*)} = \arg \min_{\mathbf{v_j} \in \nu} d(\mathbf{x}, \mathbf{v_j}) \tag{1}$$

where, $d(\mathbf{x}, \mathbf{v_j})$ is the distance between $\mathbf{x}$ and $\mathbf{v_j}$. $\mathbf{x}$ and $\mathbf{v}$ are D-dimensional vectors, $\mathbf{x} = \{x_1, x_2, \cdots, x_D\}$, $\mathbf{v_s} = \{m_1^{(c)}, m_2^{(c)}, \cdots, m_D^{(c)}\}$. Not only in the pattern classification, but also the distance measure plays an important roles in various field such as, data mining including self organizing maps, vector quantization, etc.

M. Ishikawa et al. (Eds.): ICONIP 2007, Part II, LNCS 4985, pp. 137–146, 2008.

Many applications use Euclidian metrics to measure the distance between two vectors.

$$d_E(\mathbf{x}, \mathbf{v_c}) = \sqrt{(x_1 - m_1^{(c)})^2 + (x_2 - m_2^{(c)})^2 + \cdots (x_D - m_D^{(c)})^2} \qquad (2)$$

In hardware point of view, Manhattan distance is more desirable as it does not require square root function.

$$d_M(\mathbf{x}, \mathbf{v_c}) = \sum_{i=1}^{D} \mid x_i - m_i^{(c)} \mid \qquad (3)$$

Gaussian classifiers with the following function is widely used in the pattern recognitions and radial basis function (RBF) networks.

$$d_G(\mathbf{x}, \mathbf{v_c}) = \exp(-\frac{\sum_{i=1}^{D}(x_i - m_i^{(c)})^2}{2\sigma^2}) \qquad (4)$$

The vector distance is evaluated by using the nonlinear function. $d_G(\mathbf{x}, \mathbf{v})$ reaches its largest value if the input vector is at the center of the cluster.

As equations (2) $\sim$ (4) show, the conventional distance measure treat all vector elements with an identical weight. However, the relative importance of each vector element varies and improvement on the classification performance can be achieved by taking into account the relative importance of the vector elements. In [1], a new weighted distance measure has been proposed, in which the variances and mean values of vector elements of sample vectors are utilized to determine the weight factors.

On the other hand, in spite of its formal simplicity, the computational cost involved by (1) to associate a given input pattern with the best-matching prototype, can be remarkable at run time, especially in high-dimensional domains or when the code book is very large. The time required by an exhaustive-search process may be impractical for most real-world problems. Many research tackled this drawback by direct hardware implementations of the quantization math [2]-[5].

This paper proposes a new vector distance evaluation function that can be implemented in hardware with low hardware cost. The function is an weighted sum of the element distance, which is a modified version of the Manhattan distance measure. The weight value is selected according whether the input vector element is within the neighbor of the prototype vector element or not. If the input vector is not within the neighbor, the distance value is made less significant. As the proposed method requires no multipliers, or complicated function, it is suitable for the hardware implementation.

The proposed distance measure is applied to a hardware vector classifier to evaluate the performance improvement on the pattern classification, and the additional hardware cost. This paper is organized as follows: Section 2 describes the new distance measure function. In section 3, the hardware vector classifier with the proposed method is discussed. The feasibility of the method is verified by simulations. Results of the simulations are presented in section 4. Then the classifiers are designed by using VHDL, and their hardware costs are evaluated in section 5 followed by conclusions in Section 6.

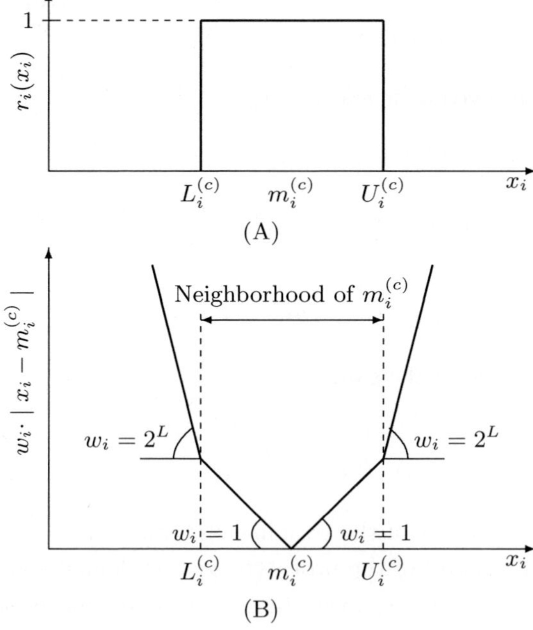

Fig. 1. Evaluation functions, (A) range check, (B) proposed method

2   New Vector Distance Measure Function

The Manhattan distance measure in (3) is modified by introducing the weighting on each $\mid x_i - m_i^{(c)} \mid$ calculation. The proposed vector measure function is,

$$d_N(\mathbf{x}, \mathbf{m}) = \sum_{i=1}^{D} w_i \mid x_i - m_i^{(c)} \mid \tag{5}$$

where w_i is the weight, and its magnitude is selected from two values adaptively according to whether the input vector element is within the neighbor of the prototype vector element $m_i^{(c)}$ or not.

$$w_i = \begin{cases} 1 & \text{if } x_i \text{ is within the neighbor of } m_i^{(c)} \\ 2^L & \text{otherwise} \end{cases} \tag{6}$$

where, L is an integer that determines the magnitude of the weight, which is a power of two value, so that no actual multiplier is necessary.

The prototype vectors and their neighborhoods are defined from the training vectors. First, the data processed by the proposed system, including the training vectors are normalized as follows,

$$x_i = \hat{x}_i / X_i \tag{7}$$

where, $\hat{x}_i$ is a raw sample data and X_i is the largest value among all i-th vector element, $X_i = \max_c \ x_i^{(c)}$. From the training data set, X_i is obtained in the training phase.

Here, the training vector is expressed as,

$$\boldsymbol{T^{(c)}} = \{\xi_1^{(c)}, \xi_2^{(c)}, \cdots, \xi_D^{(c)}\} \in \Re^D \tag{8}$$

where, $\xi_i^{(c)}$ is i-th training vector element belonging to class c. Class c prototype vector is defined as

$$\mathbf{v^{(c)}} = \{m_1^{(c)}, m_2^{(c)}, \cdots, m_D^{(c)}\} \in \Re^D \tag{9}$$

$m_i^{(c)}$ is the mean value of the samples,

$$m_i^{(c)} = \frac{\sum_{i=1}^{M^{(c)}} \xi_i^{(c)}}{M^{(c)}} \tag{10}$$

where, $M^{(c)}$ is the number of the training vectors.

Then the neighborhood of the prototype vector elements are defined by $U_i^{(c)}$, $L_i^{(c)}$, which are the upper and lower limit of the neighborhood of the cluster c vector element i, respectively.

$$U_i^{(c)} = \mu_i^{(c)} + \alpha \cdot \sigma_i^{(c)}, \tag{11}$$
$$L_i^{(c)} = \mu_i^{(c)} - \alpha \cdot \sigma_i^{(c)} \tag{12}$$

$\sigma_i^{(c)}$ is the standard deviation of the vector elements and α is a coefficient to adjust the range. To test if the input vector element x_i is within the neighborhood or not, following range check function is employed.

$$r_i^{(c)}(x_i) = \begin{cases} 1 & \text{if} \ \ U_i^{(c)} > x_i > L_i^{(c)} \\ 0 & \text{otherwise} \end{cases} \tag{13}$$

Fig. 1(A) shows the function of the range check. As the figure shows, the function is a crisp function, which can be considered as the binary quantized Gaussian function. In [8], the classifier using the range check method has been proposed. Using eq.(13), the equation (6) is rewritten as,

$$w_i = \begin{cases} 1 & \text{if} \ \ r_i^{(c)}(x_i) = 1 \\ 2^L & \text{otherwise} \end{cases} \tag{14}$$

The evaluation function realized by the eq. (14) is depicted in Fig. 1(B).

If the input vector element is not in the neighborhood, the larger weight value 2^L is assigned to that element difference, resulting that the distance is made larger than the actual distance. As eq. (1) shows, in the classifying process, the smaller the distance, the more the possibility of the input vector belonging to

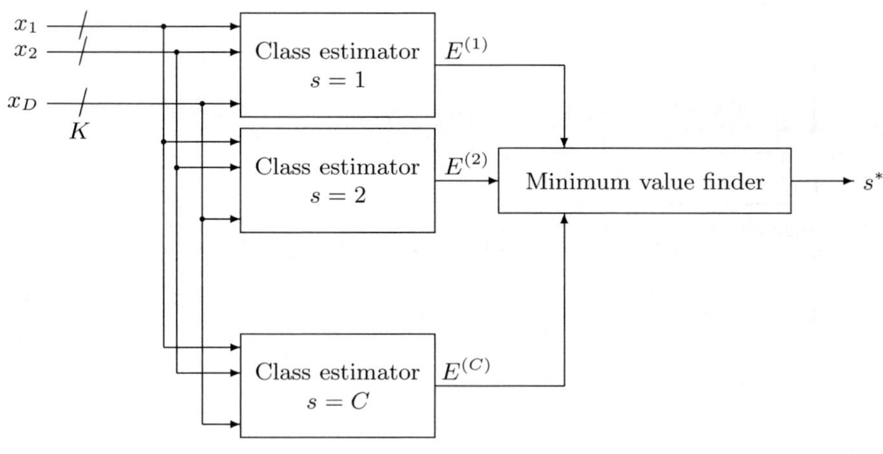

Fig. 2. Vector classification system

that cluster increases. Thus the assignment of the large weight decreases the possibility of the vector having the smallest distance to the prototype vector.

3   Vector Classifiers Based on the Proposed Distance Measure

The proposed vector distance measure described in Section 2 is applied to the hardware vector classifier. The block diagram of the classifier is shown in Fig. 2. The system consists of class estimators and a minimum value finder circuit.

3.1   Class Estimator

The class estimator output $E^{(c)}$ is given by calculating the weighted sum of the element distance as shown in Fig. 3.

$$E^{(c)} = d_N(\mathbf{x}, \mathbf{m}^{(\mathbf{c})}) \tag{15}$$

The class estimator consists of D subtractors, absolute circuits, range check circuits, 2:1 multiplexers, and an adder. While the absolute values of the difference between the input vector and prototype vector elements, $|\, x_i - m_i\,|$ are calculated, the range check circuit checks if the input x_i is in the neighborhood by comparing it with the upper and the lower limit values. If the input is in the neighborhood, then the absolute value $|\, x_i - m_i\,|$ is selected and fed to the adder, otherwise $2^L \times |\, x_i - m_i\,|$ is sent to the adder. In this way eq. (14) is realized. It should be noted that the multiplication with 2^L requires no hardware as it can

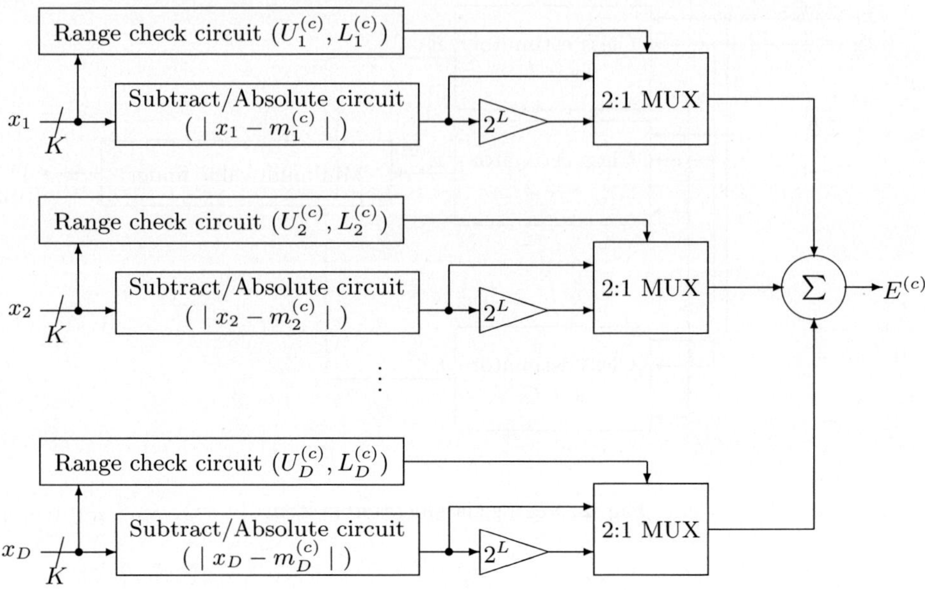

Fig. 3. Class estimator with the proposed vector distance measure

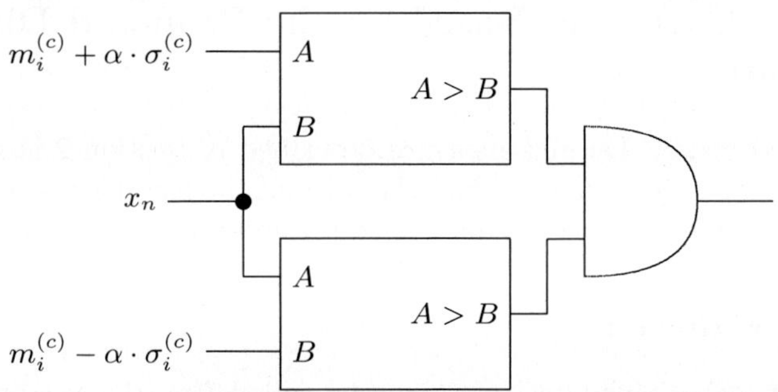

Fig. 4. Range check circuit

be implemented by the bit-shift wiring. The output $E^{(c)}$ is given as the sum of the multiplexer outputs.

3.2   Range Check Circuit

The range check circuit shown in Fig. 4 performs the range test given by equation (13). Comparator becomes active and yields '1' if the input element is between the upper and lower limit.

3.3   Class Identification

As described by the previous section, $E^{(c)}$ becomes smaller as the input vector is closer to the prototype vector of class c. Winner-takes-all competition by the minimum finder circuit is employed for the final classification. The minimum finder circuit searches for the minimum output from the class estimators, which is the winner and the class assigned to that estimator is given as the recognition results.

Each class uses a single estimator in the classifier shown in Fig. 2 as it is assumed that each class can be associated with a single clusters. However, in the case where classes are made of multiple clusters, then each class must have multiple estimators.

4   Simulations

The classifier system is described by C and the classification performance is examined.

4.1   Data Set

This section presents performance of the proposed algorithm on three data sets, i.e., IRIS [7], THYROID [6] and WINE [6] data set. They are different in terms of the data structure and the dimensionality of the feature vectors.

The IRIS data set [7] is frequently used as an example of the problem of pattern recognition. The data set consists of four features belonging to three physical classes. The features are; sepal length, sepal width, petal length and petal width. The four dimensional vector is classified into three classes, i.e., Iris Setosa, Iris Versicolour, and Iris Virginica. This data set contains 50 samples per class, totaling 150 samples.

The THYROID data set consists of five features belonging to three physical classes. This data set was obtained by recording the results of five laboratory tests conducted to determine if a patient has hypothyroidism, hyperthyroidism, or normal thyroid function.

The WINE data set consists of 13 features belonging to three physical classes. This data set was obtained by chemical analysis of wine produced by three different cultivators from the same region of Italy. This data set contains 178 feature vectors with 59 in class 1, 71 in class 2 and 48 in class 3.

All vectors in the data sets are normalized beforehand according to eq. (7).

4.2   Simulation Procedure

Following procedure is repeated 100 times and the average classification rate is used for the evaluation so that classification performance can be accurately checked.

Table 1. Recognition rate

Neuron type	IRIS	THYROID	WINE	Average
Gaussian	94.0 %	96.4 %	94.9 %	95.1 %
Manhattan	91.5 %	94.3 %	95.2 %	93.7 %
[1]	94.9 %	94.3 %	93.4 %	94.2 %
[8]	93.5 %	94.6 %	92.8 %	93.6 %
($M = 1$)	$\alpha = 2.4$	$\alpha = 2.4$	$\alpha = 2.0$	
Proposed	93.6 %	95.4 %	95.7 %	94.9 %
($L = 2$)	$\alpha = 2.5$	$\alpha = 3.0$	$\alpha = 2.0$	

Table 2. Circuit size and speed of the hardware classifier for IRIS data set

Classifier type	Gate count	Maximum delay
Manhattan	6,088	5.857 ns
[1]	14,233	5.857 ns
Proposed	8,582	5.857 ns

1. For each class, the quarter of the sample data set is randomly selected, and used as "learning data". The remaining data is used as "evaluation data".
2. Using the learning data, the prototype vectors $\mathbf{v}^{(c)}$, the upper and lower limits $U_i^{(c)}$, $L_i^{(c)}$ are defined. Then, classification rate is obtained by classification test using the evaluation data.

After the trials, the average recognition rate is used for the evaluation.

4.3   Simulation Results

The simulation results of the classifier with the proposed method is shown in Table 1. The recognition rates of the Gaussian classifier, classifier using the vector distance measure proposed in [1] and classifier with the range check circuit proposed in [8], are also obtained by the simulations and shown in the same table.

The table shows that the recognition rate of the proposed method is slightly worse than the Gaussian classifier but better than other types of classifiers.

5   Circuit Size Evaluation

The vector classifiers with the proposed method, Manhattan distance, and the measure proposed in [1], are described by VHDL, and the circuit size and speed evaluations are carried out. The correctness of the VHDL design is verified by confirming that VHDL simulation results and the C simulation results are identical. The circuit size and speed of the system are estimated by XILINX tool,

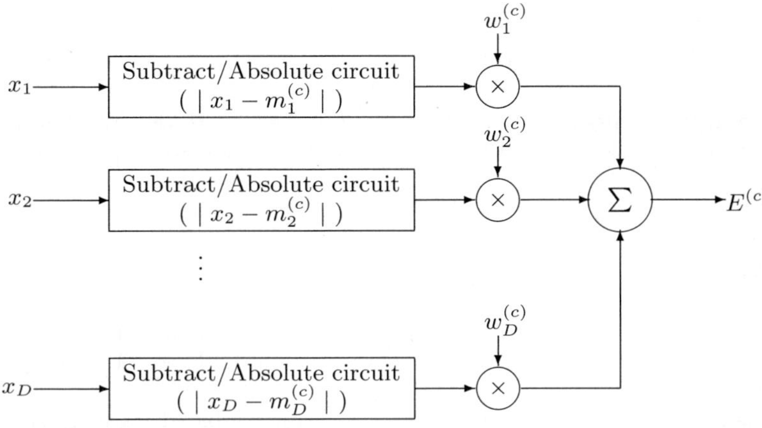

Fig. 5. Configuration of the class estimator using the vector distance measure in [1]

assuming that the design is implemented on XILINX Virtex-E device, XCV400-FG676-8. Circuit size and maximum delay of the proposed system targeting the IRIS data are summarized in Table. 2. As the classifier is realized as a combinatorial digital circuits, the maximum delay is used for the speed evaluation.

The circuit size of the proposed classifier is slightly larger than that of the Manhattan classifier and its size is less than half of the classifier using the distance measure proposed in [1]. As shown in Fig. 5, the class estimator using the distance measure in [1] uses numerical multipliers. The use of multipliers increases the total hardware cost of the system. Due to the complex function required by the Gaussian function, it is easily expected that the hardware cost of the Gaussian classifier is much higher than the classifiers listed in the table.

With regard to the speed, all systems can process all three data within 6 ns with the above mentioned FPGA.

6   Conclusions

This paper has proposed a new vector distance measure function, that is suitable for hardware implementation. The proposed method employs weighting on the vector element difference. The weight values are determined so that the element evaluation is made less significant if the element is outside the neighborhood of the prototype vector element. The proposed distance measure function is applied to the hardware vector classifier system.

The algorithm and its hardware configuration have been described followed by computer simulations to evaluate its performance. It has been revealed that the performance of the classifier with the proposed method is better than Manhattan distance and close to that of the Gaussian classifier. Even though the classification performance of the proposed method is slightly inferior to the Gaussian classifier, the smaller hardware cost of the proposed method is the great advantage over the Gaussian classifier.

Acknowledgements. This work was supported by KAKENHI, Grant-in-Aid for Scientific Research (C) (19500153) from Japan Society for the Promotion of Science (JSPS).

References

1. Kawahara, K., Shibata, T.: A New Distance Measure Employing Element-Significance Factor for Robust Image Classification. In: Proc. EUSIPCO 2005 (September 2005)
2. Lipman, A., Ynag, W.: VLSI hardware for example-based learning. IEEE Trans. VLSI Syst. 5, 320–328 (1997)
3. Rovetta, S., Zunino, R.: Efficient training of neural gas vector quantizers with analog circuit implementation. IEEE Trans. Circuits Syst. II 46, 688–698 (1999)
4. Bracco, M., Ridella, S., Zunino, R.: Digital Implementation of Hierarchical Vector Quantization. IEEE Trans. Neural Networks 14(5), 1072–1083 (2003)
5. Moritake, Y., Hikawa, H.: Category Recognition System Using Two Ultrasonic Sensors and Combinational Logic Circuit (Japanese). IEICE Transactions on Fundamentals J87-A(7), 890–898 (2004)
6. University of California at Irvine web site, `http://wwww.ics.uci.edu/~mlearn/MLRepository.html`
7. Fisher, R.A.: The use of multiple measurements in taxonomic problems. Annals of Eugenics 7(2), 170–188 (1936)
8. Matsubara, S., Hikawa, H.: Hardware Friendly Vector Quantization Algorithm. In: Proc. IEEE ISCAS 2005, pp. 3623–3626 (2005)

Intelligent Behavior Generation of Benevolent Agents with a Stochastic Model of Emotion

Sajal Chandra Banik, Keigo Watanabe, and Kiyotaka Izumi

Department of Advanced Systems Control Engineering
Graduate School of Science and Engineering
Saga University, 1-Honjomachi, Saga 840-8502, Japan
baniksajal@yahoo.com, {watanabe, izumi}@me.saga-u.ac.jp

Abstract. This paper deals with the implementation of emotions in a benevolent multi-agents system performing a specified task in a group to develop intelligent behavior and easier form of communication. The task is assigned by the user of the system and the user also evaluates the overall performance of the system according to his demand criteria. The overall group performance depends on the individual performance, group communication and synchronization of cooperation. With the emotional capability, each agent can distinguish the changed environment, can understand colleague's state, enables adaptation and reacts with changed world. The behavior of an agent is derived from the dominating emotion in an intelligent manner. A stochastic model based on Markov theory is developed to model the emotional state of agent.

Keywords: Emotion, Benevolent agent, Stochastic model, Colleague robot, Distributed job, Emotional embodied intelligence.

1   Introduction

Nowadays, robots are being used as multi-purpose tools like: service robots, pet robots, industrial robots, medical robots, etc. and day by day, their fields of application are increasing. Robot may need to work in a mixed-agents system where human (worker) and robots work together and need more interactions. An emotion based interaction among the agents can be easier and faster methods for communications. In [1], Ortony et al. stated that it is important for artificial intelligence to be able to reason about emotions-especially for natural language understanding, cooperative task solving and planning. For a human team, a lot of emphasis is given on the emotional state of the members of a team and on the understanding each others' emotions and thus keeping all motivated to the general goals [2], [3]. Emotions act like a value system which can be very beneficial for a multiagent system in situation where the individual needs to think and act rapidly. Also an advantage can be had by attitudinal communication or emotional information exposing to teammates automatically using low cost channels. By using these emotional information, action selection of other agents can be selected resulting greater synchronization and better team performance.

M. Ishikawa et al. (Eds.): ICONIP 2007, Part II, LNCS 4985, pp. 147–156, 2008.
© Springer-Verlag Berlin Heidelberg 2008

We consider agents as benevolent because they have desire to assist each other and user's interest is their best interest. Agents also try to maintain a certain level of group performance expected by the owner. The task to be performed is assigned by the user of the system and time to time evaluates the performance. The choice of behavior of an agent depends on: work load, the current emotional state of each robot, response of colleague robot and performance evaluation. In this paper, we apply the rationality (the reasoning) of emotions and their internal mechanism to a multi-agents system. Section 2 describes the related works where some researchers have applied emotions to control robots and multiagent system. Section 3 clearly describes the purpose of the research work, the system where emotion is applying to control the robot team and the control strategy. Description of simulation software and its application to simulate emotionally based behavior is given in Section 4. Finally, Section 5 concludes with advantages of the emotionally biased control method as well as discusses the limitations with some open issues.

2   Related Work

Artificial emotion is increasingly used in designing autonomous robotics agents, by making robots to experience emotionally with the changed environment or to make interaction with other agents [4], [5]. Oliveira and Sarmento presented an agent architecture that includes several emotional-like mechanisms, namely: emotion evaluation function, emotion-biased processing, emotional tagging and mood congruent memory which are intended to increase the performance and adaptability of agents operating in real time environment [6]. Shibata et al. [7] created an emotional architecture to generate cooperative behavior among the robots working in a team. The generated behavior of each robot depends on its own experience from the environment and the observed behavior of other robots. In our research work, the topics are related to cooperation between job distributed robot teams, computational architecture for modeling emotions, use of emotion for control and avoiding stagnation.

Schneider-Fontan and Mataric included an emotional model for using in communication for the minimization of interference [8]. In [9], Murphy et al. developed a multiagent control approach for interdependent tasks which imbues the agents with emotions and allows a satisfactory behavior to emerge. It mainly focused on interdependent tasks where one robot must wait upon a real resource to be transferred from one robot to the other. Our work in this article is different in task mode (job is distributed to each agent, but each one is capable to do other one's job if necessary) and emotion is generated based on Markov modeling theory [10]. The benevolent characters are created among the agents according to the demand of the user of the system. Different emotional characters can be obtained through the tuning of the transition probabilities of Markovian emotion model. In [11], Kolja and Martin developed an emotional core based on hidden Markov model which has a very close relation with our work in case of emotion modeling.

Adamatzky [12] has demonstrated a space-time dynamics of emotions with cellular automation (CA) models of affective solutions, where chemical species in the solution represent happiness, anger, fear, confusion and sadness. Here, emotions were considered as abstract entities without any connection to goals and attitudes and the entities changed their emotions as a result of observation of other's emotions. He found happiness is the most common and predominant affective state in the evolution of CA model. In our case, the emotion is also discrete state with intensity level, but the carriers (agents) of emotion are performing tasks with some behavioral actions having a specific goal. Each of the emotions (in our case: joy, anger, fear and sad) can act as dominating affective state depending on its intensity level.

3   Approach

We have considered benevolent agent to generate behavior with emotional reasoning. A benevolent agent is having a desire to promote happiness of others and generous in assistance to other by maintaining a level of self performance. This section describes cooperative distributed job among the benevolent agents, control architecture and emotional model that has been applied for dominating emotion generator.

3.1   Control and Communication Strategy

We have considered two robots working in a group as benevolent agents that always try to satisfy/make happy the user as well as the colleague. One robot is engaged to clean the center part of a floor by pushing laid objects (balls) to the wall side and another (colleague robot) is engaged to pick up the objects from the wall side simultaneously. But in case of any inability of one robot (due to over workload with respect to time limit or if battery operated and power shortage occurred or any other causes), the other one can also help in colleague's task following a *task sharing* approach. As a result, the process is continued targeting to finish the assigned task in time maintaining a constant level of performance. The workload (which is a function of time limit, number of laid objects on the floor and area to be cleaned) is assigned by the user of the system and this workload is one of the major issues that affects on emotional state of agents.

The architecture of control and communication mechanism is based on four basic subsystems: perception, motivation, emotion generator and behavior selection subsystems as shown in Fig. 1. The world (or environment) is perceived by the perception subsystem through some parameters. The motivation subsystem selects the present need (or goal) to be satisfied through the subsequent analysis of the perceived parameters and emotion.

The behavior subsystem selects two things at a time: one is the behavior to be performed by itself which is best suited with the present need and the other is an interaction command to express its emotional state and situation to the external agent (colleague). In response to the command, colleague robot sends a feedback to its perception subsystem. For the task described before, we have

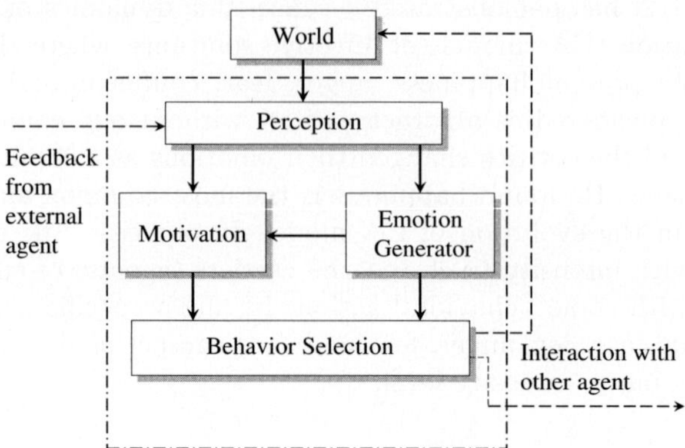

Fig. 1. A simplified view of control and communication mechanism

identified some fundamental behaviors such as: cleaning, collecting, assisting, seeking help, charging and pausing.

3.2   Emotional Model

The stochastic approach of emotion model is described in this section which is used to generate the benevolent characters among the agents and also the updating process of emotion inducing factors is described.

Stochastic model of emotion. In reality, it is very complex task to define different emotions and to model them. In our case, the emotional model consists of four basic emotions [13]: joy, anger, fear and sad. These emotions are defined as follows for our case:

- *Joy*: A robot is in joy state when the robot has high energy level to perform task and workload is normal, where workload is defined as:

$$Workload = f(time, workspace\_area, no.\_of\_balls)$$

- *Angry*: Angry is activated when getting high workload with low energy level.
- *Fear*: Fear state increases with probability of failure to obtain the goal
- *Sad*: It increases with ignoring the help messages (recruitment call of other robots). This is an emotional state of becoming sorry for ignoring help messages.

In our model, we have not included calm (normal) state because we assume that if overall working state (workload, working condition, colleague's response, etc.) is normal to a agent, then the agent is in happy state and motivated to continue its task. An application of Markov modeling theory for our purposes is described by Markovian emotion model as shown in Fig. 2. We have applied it for pure agents emotion due to its memoryless property as behaviors and commands are highly dependent on emotional present state than the history

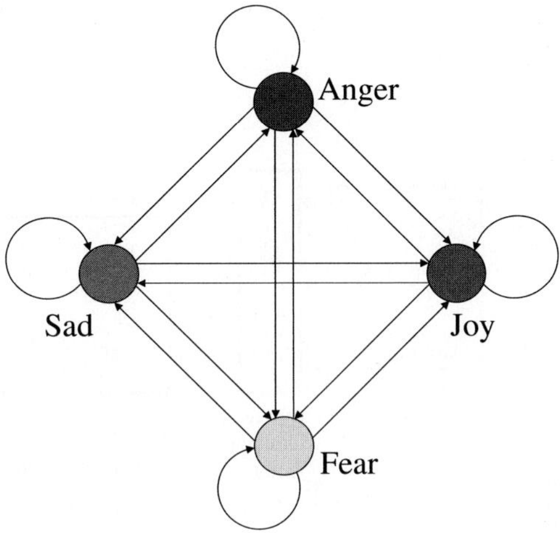

Fig. 2. A Topological view of Markovian emotion model

of arriving the state. The Markovian emotion model with four states can be expressed as follows:

$$X_{k+1} = AX_k \tag{1}$$

with emotional state points

$$\Omega = \{Joy, Anger, Fear, Sad\} \tag{2}$$

where X_k represents the current emotional state and A is the emotional state transition matrix (so called stochastic matrix) which can be expressed as follows:

$$A = \begin{bmatrix} P_{joy/joy} & P_{joy/anger} & P_{joy/fear} & P_{joy/sad} \\ P_{anger/joy} & P_{anger/anger} & P_{anger/fear} & P_{anger/sad} \\ P_{fear/joy} & P_{fear/anger} & P_{fear/fear} & P_{fear/sad} \\ P_{sad/joy} & P_{sad/anger} & P_{sad/fear} & P_{sad/sad)} \end{bmatrix} \tag{3}$$

In the Markovian emotion model, the nodes represent the emotional states and the arcs/arrows indicate the probability of getting out of states to the directed state. The arc/arrow values are set to initial values (e.g. $q_1, q_2, \ldots, q_{16}$) which give the initial state transition matrix of Markov model. These values can be modified later on with the influence of emotion inducing factors: α, β, γ and δ for joy, anger, fear and sad respectively. In this model, there are four types of transition probabilities from each of the present state. For example, the probability of state transition (arc/arrow values) from joy to other states can be expressed by following equations:

$$P_{anger/joy} = q_2 + (\beta - \alpha)q_2$$
$$P_{fear/joy} = q_3 + (\gamma - \alpha)q_3$$

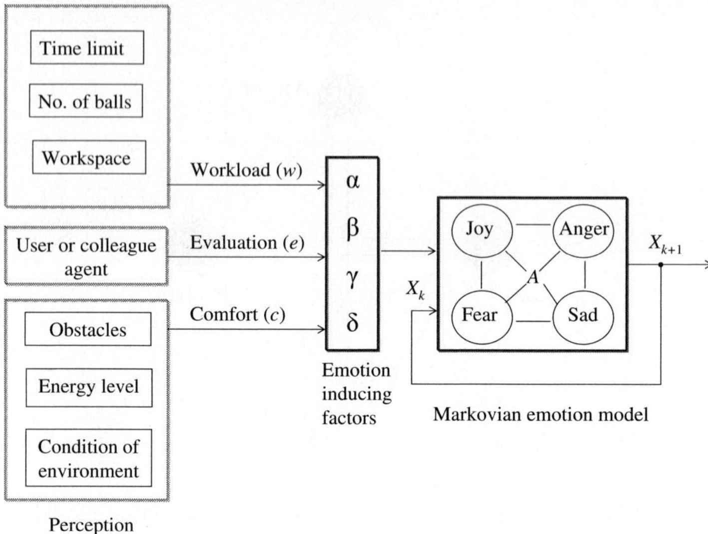

Fig. 3. The perception and emotional state generator

$$P_{sad/joy} = q_4 + (\delta - \alpha)q_4$$
$$P_{joy/joy} = 1 - (P_{anger/joy} + P_{fear/joy} + P_{sad/joy}) \tag{4}$$

where q_2, q_3 and q_4 are the initial arrow values for $P_{anger/joy}$, $P_{fear/joy}$ and $P_{sad/joy}$ respectively. These new values are used to obtain the updated state transition matrix. More details of the model and computational procedures are given in [10], [14].

Updating of emotion inducing factors. In a sense, the emotion factors reflect the total environmental conditions surrounding the agents. The emotion inducing factors are updated through the information from inputs, e.g. from sensors, user, response of colleague or internal events (see Fig. 3). Here, we can see that the input variables affect on the emotion inducing factors (α, β, γ and δ) and thus affect on the emotional state generated by the Markovian emotion model. All the environmental variables are grouped into three variables: workload (w), comfort (c) and evaluation (e). Each of them is scaled as 0 to 10 indicating low to high. For each of the emotion factors, we have used a second order polynomial in the three dimensional space of (w, c, e) for approximate mapping of emotion factors from input variables. The coefficients of the polynomial are individuality factors that vary from agent to agent. The user of the agent can design the benevolent characters by manipulating the individuality factors through the approximation of emotion factors with response surface method (RSM). For this, we have selected central composite design (CCD) in which approximated value of emotion factors at 15 points in the three dimensional space can generate the individuality factors of an agent to create emotional based behavior (see Fig. 4).

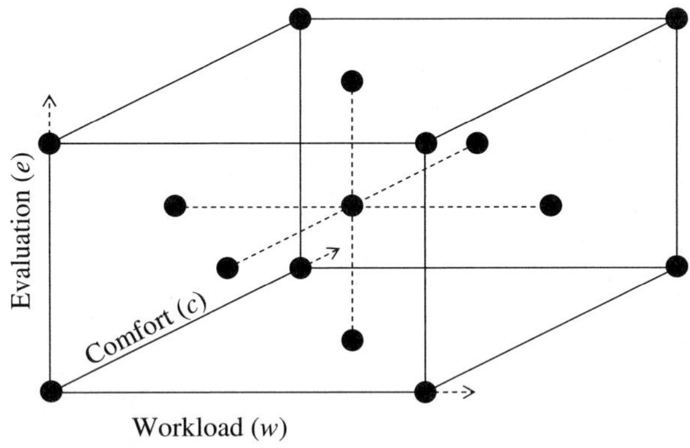

Fig. 4. The central composite design in 3D space (w, c, e)

4   Simulation Results

We have performed simulation in Matlab environment using *KiKS* (a Khepera simulator) which can simulate in a very realistic way [15]. Two robots are considered for simulation which we call as: *Cleaner* and *Collector*. The *Cleaner* is able to push the balls (as laid objects on the floor) to wall side and the *Collector* has the wall following character to collect the balls. But it is also able to help in cleaning floor and vice versa, if necessary. The workload is assigned as: workspace 600 mm × 600 mm , no. of objects 20 and time limit 120 sec. The user of the system tuned the individuality factors in such a way that, the robot

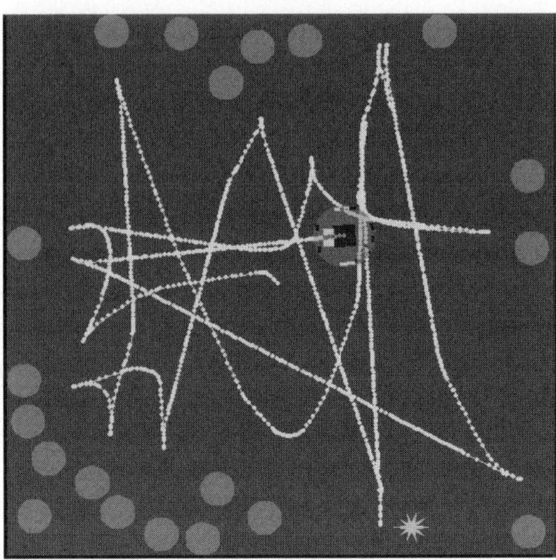

Fig. 5. Floor cleaning and power source searching behavior of a robot

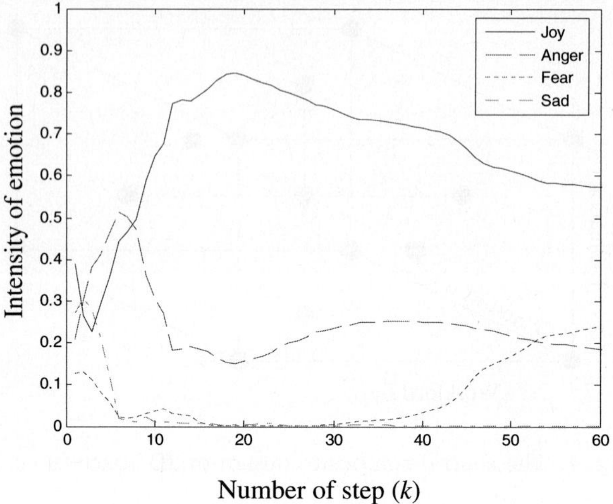

Fig. 6. Plot of emotion intensity vs. step

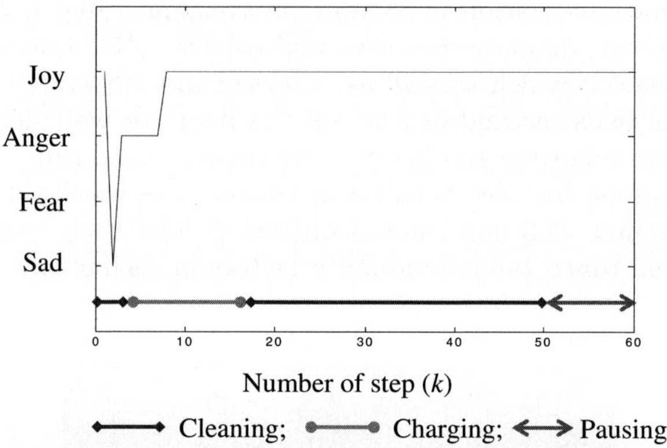

Fig. 7. Plot of dominating emotion vs. step with action state

can stay in joy state even in high workload (it means the agent like to work more being in joy mode). In Fig. 5, it is shown that the *Cleaner* robot was able to complete cleaning within the time limit.

The simulation starts with the following initial stochastic matrix and emotional state:

$$A = \begin{bmatrix} 0.7 & 0.2 & 0.10 & 0.15 \\ 0.1 & 0.6 & 0.05 & 0.15 \\ 0.1 & 0.1 & 0.80 & 0.10 \\ 0.1 & 0.1 & 0.05 & 0.60 \end{bmatrix} \tag{5}$$

$$X_0 = [0.5 \; 0.1 \; 0.1 \; 0.3]^T \tag{6}$$

In Fig. 6, we can see the trend of emotional change in which the intensity of emotion is developed from a belief model based on probability. The trend (increasing or decreasing of emotional intensity) is very important in selecting behavior or action to be performed. When the joy state is decreasing and anger state is increasing rapidly, the robot stop cleaning and started to search power source and recharged (see Fig. 7). After that, it again started its usual work (cleaning). After completing the cleaning, the robot rest a while. Here, we can see that the robot is able to select behaviors with the changing of emotional state.

5   Conclusion

The aim of this work has been to develop intelligent behavior among benevolent agents by using the rationality of emotions. Although emotion generation and modelling is very complex task, we have used Markovian emotion model emphasizing the present state.

A benevolent agent can be created in affective way by designing the individuality factors according to the user's consent. If the agent is taught the work and duties of user, then the user's position may be replaced by the agent (in case of leave or unable to work for any other reason) to work with the same environment with the same emotional behavior of the user. The behavior also depends on emotional intensity which is not yet considered because it is very tough to find out the initial stochastic matrix and emotional state which will suit with the real environment. It is also possible to develop a localized emotional field for working environment which can be used for path planning. These are the pending issues to be considered for future work.

References

1. Ortony, A., Clore, G.L., Collins, A.: The cognitive structure of emotions. Cambridge University Press, Cambridge (1990)
2. Katzenbach, J., Smith, D.K.: The wisdom of teams. Harper Business (1994)
3. Jennings, J.: The teamwork: United in victory. Silver Burdett Press, Englewood Cliffs (1990)
4. Breazeal, C., Scassellati, B.: Infant-like social interactions between a robot and a human caretaker. Adaptive Behavior 8(1), 47–72 (2000)
5. Velásquez, J.D.: A computational framework for emotion-based control. In: Workshop on Grounding Emotion in Adaptive System, Conference on Simulation of Adaptive Behavior (1998)
6. Oliveira, E., Sarmento, L.: Emotional advantage for adaptability and autonomy. In: Proceedings of the 2nd International Joint Conference on Autonomous Agents and Multiagent system, pp. 305–312 (2003)
7. Shibata, T., Ohkawa, K., Tanie, T.: Spontaneous behavior of robots for cooperation of emotionally intelligent robot system. In: IEEE Proceedings on International Conference on Robotics and Automation, vol. 3, pp. 2426–2431 (1996)
8. Schneider-Fontan, M., Mataric, M.: Territorial multi-robot task division. IEEE Trans. on Robotics and Automation 14, 815–822 (1998)

9. Murphy, R.R., Lisetti, C.L., Tardif, R., et al.: Emotion-based control of cooperating heterogeneous mobile robots. IEEE Trans. on Robotics and Automation 18(5), 744–757 (2002)
10. Arun, C.: A computational architecture to model human emotions. In: Proceedings of International Conference on Intelligent Information System, pp. 86–89 (1997)
11. Kolja, K., Martin, B.: Towards an emotion core based on a Hidden Markov Model. In: 13th IEEE International Workshop on Robot and Human Interactive Communication, pp. 119–124 (2004)
12. Adamatzky, A.: On patterns in affective media. Int. J. of Modern Physics C 14(5), 673–687 (2003)
13. Oatley, K.: Best laid schemes: The psychology of emotions. Cambridge University Press, Cambridge (1992)
14. Trivedi, K.S.: Probability and statistics with reliability, queuing, and computer science application. Prentice-Hall, Englewood Cliffs (1982)
15. Theodor, S.: KiKS is a Khepera Simulator (2001)

Design Principles and Constraints Underlying the Construction of Brain-Based Devices

Jeffrey L. Krichmar and Gerald M. Edelman

The Neurosciences Institute, 10640 John Jay Hopkins Drive, San Diego, California, USA
`{krichmar, edelman}@nsi.edu`

Abstract. Without a doubt the most sophisticated behavior seen in biological agents is demonstrated by organisms whose behavior is guided by a nervous system. Thus, the construction of behaving devices based on principles of nervous systems may have much to offer. Our group has built series of brain-based devices (BBDs) over the last fifteen years to provide a heuristic for studying brain function by embedding neurobiological principles on a physical platform capable of interacting with the real world. These BBDs have been used to study perception, operant conditioning, episodic and spatial memory, and motor control through the simulation of brain regions such as the visual cortex, the dopaminergic reward system, the hippocampus, and the cerebellum. Following the brain-based model, we argue that an intelligent machine should be constrained by the following design principles: (i) it should incorporate a simulated brain with detailed neuroanatomy and neural dynamics that controls behavior and shapes memory, (ii) it should organize the unlabeled signals it receives from the environment into categories without a priori knowledge or instruction, (iii) it should have a physical instantiation, which allows for active sensing and autonomous movement in the environment, (iv) it should engage in a task that is initially constrained by minimal set of innate behaviors or reflexes, (v) it should have a means to adapt the device's behavior, called value systems, when an important environmental event occurs, and (vi) it should allow comparisons with experimental data acquired from animal nervous systems. Like the brain, these devices operate according to selectional principles through which they form categorical memory, associate categories with innate value, and adapt to the environment. This approach may provide the groundwork for the development of intelligent machines that follow neurobiological rather than computational principles in their construction.

Keywords: embodiment, neural modeling, neuroanatomy, value systems.

1 Introduction

Although much progress has been made in the neurosciences over the last several decades, the study of the nervous system is still a wide open area of research with many unresolved problems. This is not due to a lack of first-rate research by the neuroscience community, but instead it reflects the complexity of the problems. Therefore, novel approaches to the problems, such as computational modeling and

M. Ishikawa et al. (Eds.): ICONIP 2007, Part II, LNCS 4985, pp. 157–166, 2008.

robotics, may be necessary to achieve a better understanding of brain function. Moreover, as models and devices become more sophisticated and more biologically realistic, the devices themselves may approach the complexity and adaptive behavior that we associate with biological organisms and may find their way in practical applications. In this review, we will outline what we believe are the design principles necessary to achieve these goals (Krichmar and Edelman, 2005; Krichmar and Reeke, 2005). We will illustrate how these principles have been put into practice by describing two recent brain-based devices (BBDs) from our group.

2   Brain-Based Modeling Design Principles

2.1   Incorporate a Simulated Brain with Detailed Neuroanatomy and Neural Dynamics

Models of brain function should take into consideration the dynamics of the neuronal elements that make up different brain regions, the structure of these different brain regions, and the connectivity within and between these brain regions. The dynamics of the elements of the nervous system (e.g. neuronal activity and synaptic transmission) are important to brain function and have been modeled at the single neuron level (Borg-Graham, 1987; Bower and Beeman, 1994; Hines and Carnevale, 1997), network level (Izhikevich et al., 2004; Pinsky and Rinzel, 1994), and synapse level in models of plasticity (Bienenstock et al., 1982; Song et al., 2000; Worgotter and Porr, 2005). However, structure at the gross anatomical level is critical for function, and it has often been ignored in models of the nervous system. Brain function is more than the activity of disparate regions; it is the interaction between these areas that is crucial as we have shown in a number of devices, Darwins IV through XI (Edelman et al., 1992; Fleischer et al., Krichmar and Edelman, 2005; Krichmar et al., 2005b; Seth et al., 2004). Brains are defined by a distinct neuroanatomy in which there are areas of special function, which are defined by their connectivity to sensory input, motor output, and to each other.

2.2   Organize the Signals from the Environment into Categories without a Priori Knowledge or Instruction

One essential property of BBDs, is that, like living organisms, they must organize the unlabeled signals they receive from the environment into categories. This organization of signals, which in general depends on a combination of sensory modalities (e.g. vision, sound, taste, or touch), is called *perceptual categorization*. Perceptual categorization in models (Edelman and Reeke, 1982) as well as living organisms makes object recognition possible based on experience, but without *a priori* knowledge or instruction. A BBD selects and generalizes the signals it receives with its sensors, puts these signals into categories without instruction, and learns the appropriate actions when confronted with objects under conditions that produce responses in value systems.

2.3 Active Sensing and Autonomous Movement in the Environment

Brains do not function in isolation; they are tightly coupled with the organism's morphology and environment. In order to function properly, an agent, artificial or biological, needs to be situated in the real world (Chiel and Beer, 1997; Clark, 1997). Therefore, models of brain function should be embodied in a physical device and explore a real as opposed to a simulated environment. For our purposes, the real environment is required for two reasons. First, simulating an environment can introduce unwanted and unintentional biases to the model. For example, a computer generated object presented to a vision model has its shape and segmentation defined by the modeler and directly presented to the model, whereas a device that views an object hanging on a wall has to discern the shape and figure from ground segmentation based on its on active vision. Second, real environments are rich, multimodal, and noisy; an artificial design of such an environment would be computationally intensive and difficult to simulate. However, all these interesting features of the environment come for "free" when we place the BBD in the real world. The modeler is freed from simulating a world and need only concentrate on the development of a device that can actively explore the real world.

2.4 Engage in a Behavioral Task

It follows from the above principle that a situated agent needs to engage in some behavioral task. Similar to a biological organism, an agent or BBD needs a minimal set of innate behaviors or reflexes in order to explore and initially survive in its environmental niche. From this minimal set, the BBD can learn, adapt and optimize its behavior. How these devices adapt is the subject of the next principle, which describes value systems (see section 2.5). This approach is very different from the classic artificial intelligence or robotic control algorithms, where either rules or feedback controllers with pre-defined error signals need to be specified *a priori*. In the BBD approach, the agent selects what it needs to optimize its behavior and thus adapts to its environment.

A second and important point with regard to behavioral tasks is that they give the researcher a metric by which to score the BBD's performance. Moreover, these tasks should be made similar to experimental biology paradigms so that the behavior of the BBD can be compared with that of real organisms (see section 2.6).

2.5 Adapt Behavior When an Important Environmental Event Occurs

Biological organisms adapt their behavior through value systems, which provide non-specific, modulatory signals to the rest of the brain that bias the outcome of local changes in synaptic efficacy in the direction needed to satisfy global needs. Stated in the simplest possible terms, behavior that evokes positive responses in value systems biases synaptic change to make production of the same behavior more likely when the situation in the environment (and thus the local synaptic inputs) is similar; behavior that evokes negative value biases synaptic change in the opposite direction. Examples of value systems in the brain include the dopaminergic, cholinergic, and noradrenergic systems (Aston-Jones and Bloom, 1981; Hasselmo et al., 2002; Schultz et al., 1997) which respond to environmental cues signalling reward prediction, uncertainty, and novelty. Theoretical models based of these systems and their effect on brain function have been developed (Doya, 2002; Friston et al., 1994; Montague et al., 1996; Yu and Dayan, 2005) and embedded in real world behaving devices (Arleo et al., 2004; Krichmar and Edelman, 2002; Sporns and Alexander, 2002).

2.6 Comparisons with Experimental Data Acquired from Animal Models

The behavior of BBDs and the activity of their simulated nervous systems must be recorded to allow comparisons with experimental data acquired from animals. The comparison should be made at the behavioral level, the systems level, and the neuronal element level. These comparisons serve two purposes: First, BBDs are powerful tools to test theories of brain function. The construction of a complete behaving model forces the designer to specify theoretical and implementation details that are easy to overlook in a purely verbal description and it forces those details to be consistent among them. The level of analysis permitted by having a recording of the activity of every neuron and synapse in the simulated nervous system during its behavior is just not possible with animal experiments. The results of such situated models have been compared with rodent hippocampal activity during navigation, basal ganglia activity during action selection, and attentional systems in primates (Burgess et al., 1997; Guazzelli et al., 2001; Itti, 2004; Prescott et al., 2006). Second, by using the animal nervous system as a metric, designers can continually make the simulated nervous system closer to that of the chosen model animal. This should eventually allow the creation of practical devices approaching the sophistication of living organisms.

3 Illustrative Examples of Brain-Based Devices

In this section, we will use our group's two most recent BBDs as illustrative examples of the above principles. The first example, embodied in Darwin X and XI (Fleischer et al., 2007, Krichmar et al., 2005a; Krichmar et al., 2005b), is a BBD that develops spatial and episodic memory by incorporating a detailed model of the hippocampus and its surrounding regions. The second example is a BBD capable of predictive motor control based on a model of cerebellar learning (McKinstry et al., 2006).

3.1 An Embodied Model of Spatial and Episodic Memory

Darwin X and XI were used to investigate the functional anatomy specific to the hippocampal region during a memory task. Darwin X and XI incorporate aspects of the anatomy and physiology of the hippocampus and its surrounding regions, which are known to be necessary for the acquisition and recall of spatial and episodic memories. The simulated nervous system contained 50 neural areas, 90,000 neuronal units, and 1.4 million synaptic connections. It included a visual system, a head direction system, a hippocampal formation, a basal forebrain, a value or reward system, and an action selection system. Darwin X used camera input to recognize the category and position of distal objects and odometry to construct head direction cells.

Darwin X successfully demonstrated the acquisition and recall of spatial and episodic memories in a maze task similar to the Morris water maze (Morris, 1984) by associating places with actions. The association was facilitated by a dopaminergic value system based on the known connectivity between CA1 and nucleus accumbens and frontal areas (Thierry et al., 2000). The responses of simulated neuronal units in the hippocampal areas during its exploratory behavior were comparable to neuronal responses in the rodent hippocampus; i.e., neuronal units responded to a particular location within Darwin X's environment (O'Keefe and Dostrovsky, 1971).

Darwin XI was tested on a plus maze in which it approached a goal arm from different start arms (see Fig. 1A). In the task, a journey corresponded to the route from a particular starting point to a particular goal. Darwin XI was constructed on Darwin X's platform, but added artificial whiskers for texture discrimination, an internal compass for determining head direction, and a laser range finder for estimating position.

During maze navigation, journey-dependent place fields, whose activity differed in different journeys through the same maze arm, were found in the recordings of simulated CA1 neuronal units (See Fig. 1B). Neuronal units in Darwin XI's CA1 area developed place fields through experience-dependent plasticity while traversing the

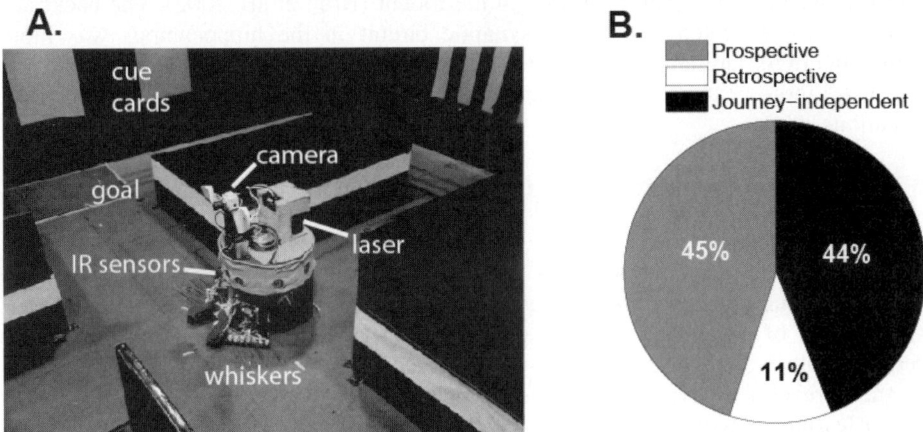

Fig. 1. A. Darwin XI at the choice point of its plus-maze environment. Darwin XI began a trial alternatively at the east arm or west arm and used its whiskers to follow the maze arm until it reached the intersection. In this trial, Darwin XI was given a reward stimulus if it chose the North goal arm. Motor area activity in Darwin XI's neural simulation was used to decide which goal arm to traverse. Darwin XI sensed patterns of pegs with its whiskers, sensed color cue cards with its camera, developed head direction cells from an internal compass, and got range information from a laser. **B.** Place fields emerged in Darwin XI's simulated hippocampus as a result of its experience in the environment. Over half of these place fields were journey-dependent; Retrospective - active in the goal arm when it arrived there from a particular start arm, or Prospective - active in the start arm prior to choosing a particular goal arm. Adapted from Fleischer et al., 2007.

plus maze. Of 2304 CA1 neuronal units (576 CA1 neuronal units per subject, four Darwin XI subjects), 384 had journey-dependent fields, and 303 had journey-independent fields. This roughly equal distribution of journey-dependent and journey-independent fields in hippocampal place units is similar to findings in rodent hippocampus (Ferbinteanu and Shapiro, 2003). The journey-dependent responses were either retrospective, where activity was present in the goal arm, or prospective, in which activity was present in the start arm.

Darwin X and XI took into consideration the macro- and micro-anatomy between the hippocampus and cortex, as well as the within the hippocampus. In order to identify different functional hippocampal pathways and their influence on behavior, we developed two novel methods for analyzing large scale neuronal networks: 1) Backtrace - tracing functional pathways by choosing a unit at a specific time and recursively examining all neuronal units that led to the observed activity in this reference unit (Krichmar et al., 2005a), and 2) Granger Causality - a time series analysis that distinguishes causal interactions within and between neural regions (Seth, 2005). These analyses allowed us to examine the information flow through the network and highlighted the importance of the perforant pathway from the entorhinal cortex to the hippocampal subfields in producing associations between the position of the agent in space and the appropriate action it needs to reach a goal. This functional pathway has recently been identified in the rodent (Brun et al., 2002). The backtrace analysis also revealed that the tri-synaptic circuit in the hippocampus was more influential in unfamiliar environments and in journey-dependent place responses. This suggests more extensive hippocampal involvement in difficult or contextual situations.

3.2   A Model of Predictive Motor Control Based on Cerebellar Learning and Visual Motion

Recently, our group constructed a BBD which included a detailed model of the cerebellum and cortical areas that respond to visual motion (McKinstry et al., 2006). One theory of cerebellar function proposes that the cerebellum learns to replace reflexes with a predictive controller (Wolpert et al., 1998). Synaptic eligibility traces in the cerebellum have recently been proposed as a specific mechanism for such motor learning (Medina et al., 2005). We tested whether a learning mechanism, called the delayed eligibility trace learning rule, could account for the predictive nature of the cerebellum in a real-world, robotic visuomotor task.

The BBD's visuomotor task was to navigate a path designated by orange traffic cones (see Fig. 2A). The platform for this task was a Segway Robotic Mobility Platform modified to have a camera, a laser range finder, and infrared proximity detectors as inputs. The BBD's nervous system contained components simulating the cerebellar cortex, the deep cerebellar nuclei, the inferior olive, and a cortical area *MT*. The simulated cortical area *MT*, which responds to visual motion, was constructed based on the suggestion that the visual system makes use of visual blur for determining motion direction (Geisler, 1999; Krekelberg et al., 2003). The simulated nervous system contained 28 neural areas, 27,688 neuronal units, and 1.6 million synaptic connections. Using an embedded Beowulf computer cluster of six compact personal computers, it took roughly 40 ms to update all the neuronal units and plastic

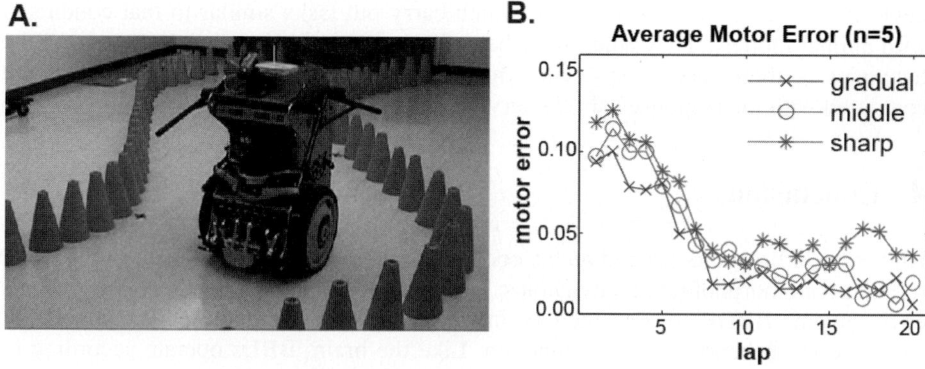

Fig. 2. A. The cerebellar BBD was constructed on a Segway Robotic Mobility Platform (RMP). The device navigated a pathway dictated by traffic cones. The middle course is shown in the figure. The device was also tested on a sharp course, in which the device was required to turn at right angles, and a gradual course, in which the device was required to turn slightly. Collisions were detected by a bank of IR sensors on the lower front region of the device. Visual optic flow was constructed from camera input. **B.** The mean motor error of five subjects during training on the gradual, middle, and sharp courses is shown in the plot. The magnitude of the motor error reflected the average per lap IR responses to the cones, where IR values ranged from 0 (no object in range) to 1 (an object within 1 inch or less of the IR detector). Adapted from McKinstry et al., 2006.

connections in the model for each simulation cycle. Initially, path traversal relied on a reflexive movement away from obstacles that was triggered by infrared proximity sensors when the BBD was within 12 inches of a cone. This resulted in clumsy, crooked movement down the path. The infrared sensor input was also the motor error signal to the cerebellum via simulated climbing fiber input. Over time, the cerebellar circuit predicted the correct motor response based on visual motion cues preventing the activation of the reflex and resulting in smooth movement down the center of the path (see Fig. 2B). The system learned to slow down prior to a curve and to turn in the correct direction based on the flow of visual information. The system adapted to and generalized over different courses having both gentle and sharp angle bends.

The experiments, which depended both on the dynamics of delayed trace eligibility learning and on the architecture of the cerebellum, demonstrated how the cerebellum can predict impending errors and adapt its movements. Moreover, by analyzing the responses of the cerebellum and the inputs from the simulated area *MT* during the device's behavior, we were able to predict the types of signals the nervous system might select to adapt to such a motor task. The BBD's nervous system categorized the motion cues that were predictive of different collisions and associated those categories with the appropriate movements. The neurobiologically inspired model described here prompts several hypotheses about the relationship between perception and motor control and may be useful in the development of general-purpose motor learning systems for machines.

As with other BBDs in the Darwin series, Darwin X, XI, and the Segway cerebellar model, follow the brain-based modeling principles. They are physical devices embedded in the real world, which carry out tasks similar to that conducted with animal models. They adapt their behavior based on their value systems, and the dynamics of their nervous systems, which are recorded during their behaviour, are compared with the responses of real nervous systems.

4 Conclusions

Higher brain functions depend on the cooperative activity of an entire nervous system, reflecting its morphology, its dynamics, and its interaction with its phenotype and the environment. BBDs are designed to incorporate these attributes in a manner that allows tests of theories of brain function. Like the brain, BBDs operate according to selectional principles through which they form categorical memory, associate categories with innate value, and adapt to the environment. Such devices also provide the groundwork for the development of intelligent machines that follow neurobiological rather than computational principles in their construction.

Acknowledgements

This work was supported by grants from the Office of Naval Research, the Defense Advanced Research Programs Agency, and the Neurosciences Research Foundation.

References

1. Arleo, A., Smeraldi, F., Gerstner, W.: Cognitive navigation based on nonuniform Gabor space sampling, unsupervised growing networks, and reinforcement learning. IEEE Trans. Neural Net. 15, 639–652 (2004)
2. Aston-Jones, G., Bloom, F.E.: Nonrepinephrine-containing locus coeruleus neurons in behaving rats exhibit pronounced responses to non-noxious environmental stimuli. J. Neurosc. 1, 887–900 (1981)
3. Bienenstock, E.L., Cooper, L.N., Munro, P.W.: Theory for the development of neuron selectivity: orientation specificity and binocular interaction in visual cortex. J. Neurosc. 2, 32–48 (1982)
4. Borg-Graham, L.: Modeling the electrical behavior of cortical neurons - simulations of hippocampal pyramidal cells. In: Cotterill, R.M.J. (ed.) Computer Simulation in Brain Science, Cambridge University Press, Cambridge (1987)
5. Bower, J.M., Beeman, D.: The Book of GENESIS: Exploring Realistic Neural Models with the GEneral NEural SImulation System. TELOS/Springer-Verlag (1994)
6. Brun, V.H., Otnass, M.K., Molden, S., Steffenach, H.A., Witter, M.P., Moser, M.B., Moser, E.I.: Place cells and place recognition maintained by direct entorhinal-hippocampal circuitry. Science 296, 2243–2246 (2002)
7. Burgess, N., Donnett, J.G., Jeffery, K.J., O'Keefe, J.: Robotic and neuronal simulation of the hippocampus and rat navigation. Philos. Trans. R Soc. Lond. B Biol. Sci. 352, 1535–1543 (1997)
8. Chiel, H.J., Beer, R.D.: The brain has a body: adaptive behavior emerges from interactions of nervous system, body and environment. Trends Neurosci. 20, 553–557 (1997)

9. Clark, A.: Being there. Putting brain, body, and world together again. MIT Press, Cambridge (1997)

10. Doya, K.: Metalearning and neuromodulation. Neural Netw. 15, 495–506 (2002)

11. Edelman, G.M., Reeke, G.N., Gall, W.E., Tononi, G., Williams, D., Sporns, O.: Synthetic neural modeling applied to a real-world artifact. Proc. Natl. Acad. Sci. USA 89, 7267–7271 (1992)

12. Edelman, G.M., Reeke Jr., G.N.: Selective networks capable of representative transformations, limited generalizations, and associative memory. Proc. Natl. Acad. Sci. USA 79, 2091–2095 (1982)

13. Ferbinteanu, J., Shapiro, M.L.: Prospective and retrospective memory coding in the hippocampus. Neuron 40, 1227–1239 (2003)

14. Fleischer, J.G., Gally, J.A., Edelman, G.M., Krichmar, J.L.: Retrospective and prospective responses arising in a modeled hippocampus during maze navigation by a brain-based device. Proc. Natl. Acad. Sci. USA 104, 3556–3561 (2007)

15. Friston, K.J., Tononi, G., Reeke, G.N., Sporns, O., Edelman, G.M.: Value-dependent selection in the brain: simulation in a synthetic neural model. Neuroscience 59, 229–243 (1994)

16. Geisler, W.S.: Motion streaks provide a spatial code for motion direction. Nature 400, 65–69 (1999)

17. Guazzelli, A., Bota, M., Arbib, M.A.: Competitive Hebbian learning and the hippocampal place cell system: modeling the interaction of visual and path integration cues. Hippocampus 11, 216–239 (2001)

18. Hasselmo, M.E., Hay, J., Ilyn, M., Gorchetchnikov, A.: Neuromodulation, theta rhythm and rat spatial navigation. Neural Netw. 15, 689–707 (2002)

19. Hines, M.L., Carnevale, N.T.: The NEURON simulation environment. Neural Comput. 9, 1179–1209 (1997)

20. Itti, L.: Automatic foveation for video compression using a neurobiological model of visual attention. IEEE Trans. Image Process 13, 1304–1318 (2004)

21. Izhikevich, E.M., Gally, J.A., Edelman, G.M.: Spike-timing dynamics of neuronal groups. Cereb Cortex 14, 933–944 (2004)

22. Krekelberg, B., Dannenberg, S., Hoffmann, K.P., Bremmer, F., Ross, J.: Neural correlates of implied motion. Nature 424, 674–677 (2003)

23. Krichmar, J.L., Edelman, G.M.: Machine psychology: autonomous behavior, perceptual categorization and conditioning in a brain-based device. Cereb Cortex 12, 818–830 (2002)

24. Krichmar, J.L., Edelman, G.M.: Brain-based devices for the study of nervous systems and the development of intelligent machines. Artif. Life 11, 63–77 (2005)

25. Krichmar, J.L., Nitz, D.A., Gally, J.A., Edelman, G.M.: Characterizing functional hippocampal pathways in a brain-based device as it solves a spatial memory task. Proc. Natl. Acad. Sci. USA 102, 2111–2116 (2005a)

26. Krichmar, J.L., Reeke, G.N.: The Darwin Brain-Based Automata: Synthetic Neural Models and Real-World Devices. In: Reeke, G.N., Poznanski, R.R., Lindsay, K.A., Rosenberg, J.R., Sporns, O. (eds.) Modeling in the Neurosciences: From Biological Systems to Neuromimetic Robotics, pp. 613–638. Taylor & Francis, Boca Raton (2005)

27. Krichmar, J.L., Seth, A.K., Nitz, D.A., Fleischer, J.G., Edelman, G.M.: Spatial navigation and causal analysis in a brain-based device modeling cortical-hippocampal interactions. Neuroinformatics 3, 197–221 (2005b)

28. McKinstry, J.L., Edelman, G.M., Krichmar, J.L.: A cerebellar model for predictive motor control tested in a brain-based device. Proc. Natl. Acad. Sci. USA (2006)

29. Medina, J.F., Carey, M.R., Lisberger, S.G.: The representation of time for motor learning. Neuron 45, 157–167 (2005)
30. Montague, P.R., Dayan, P., Sejnowski, T.J.: A framework for mesencephalic dopamine systems based on predictive Hebbian learning. J. Neurosci 16, 1936–1947 (1996)
31. Morris, R.: Developments of a water-maze procedure for studying spatial learning in the rat. J. Neurosci. Methods 11, 47–60 (1984)
32. O'Keefe, J., Dostrovsky, J.: The hippocampus as a spatial map. Preliminary evidence from unit activity in the freely-moving rat. Brain Res. 34, 171–175 (1971)
33. Pinsky, P.F., Rinzel, J.: Intrinsic and network rhythmogenesis in a reduced Traub model for CA3 neurons. J. Comput. Neurosci. 1, 39–60 (1994)
34. Prescott, T.J., Montes Gonzalez, F.M., Gurney, K., Humphries, M.D., Redgrave, P.: A robot model of the basal ganglia: Behavior and intrinsic processing. Neural Netw. 19, 31–61 (2006)
35. Schultz, W., Dayan, P., Montague, P.R.: A neural substrate of prediction and reward. Science 275, 1593–1599 (1997)
36. Seth, A.K.: Causal connectivity of evolved neural networks during behavior. Network 16, 35–54 (2005)
37. Seth, A.K., McKinstry, J.L., Edelman, G.M., Krichmar, J.L.: Active sensing of visual and tactile stimuli by brain-based devices. International Journal of Robotics and Automation 19, 222–238 (2004)
38. Song, S., Miller, K.D., Abbott, L.F.: Competitive Hebbian learning through spike-timing-dependent synaptic plasticity. Nat. Neurosci. 3, 919–926 (2000)
39. Sporns, O., Alexander, W.H.: Neuromodulation and plasticity in an autonomous robot. Neural Netw. 15, 761–774 (2002)
40. Thierry, A.M., Gioanni, Y., Degenetais, E., Glowinski, J.: Hippocampo-prefrontal cortex pathway: anatomical and electrophysiological characteristics. Hippocampus 10, 411–419 (2000)
41. Wolpert, D., Miall, R., Kawato, M.: Internal models in the cerebellum. Trends in Cognitive Sciences 2, 338–347 (1998)
42. Worgotter, F., Porr, B.: Temporal sequence learning, prediction, and control: a review of different models and their relation to biological mechanisms. Neural Comput. 17, 245–319 (2005)
43. Yu, A.J., Dayan, P.: Uncertainty, neuromodulation, and attention. Neuron 46, 681–692 (2005)

Finding Exploratory Rewards by Embodied Evolution and Constrained Reinforcement Learning in the Cyber Rodents

Eiji Uchibe[1] and Kenji Doya[1,2,3]

[1] Okinawa Institute of Science and Technology, Okinawa 904-2234, Japan
{uchibe,doya}@oist.jp
[2] Nara Institute of Science and Technology, Nara, Japan
[3] ATR Computational Neuroscience laboratories, Japan

Abstract. The aim of the Cyber Rodent project [1] is to elucidate the origin of our reward and affective systems by building artificial agents that share the natural biological constraints: self-preservation (foraging) and self-reproduction (mating). This paper shows a method to evolve an agent's exploratory reward by combining a framework of embodied evolution and the algorithm of constrained policy gradient reinforcement learning. Biological constraints are modeled by the average criteria, and the exploratory reward is computed from its own sensor information. The agent in which a part of constraints are satisfied is allowed to mate with another agent. If a mating behavior is successfully made between two agents, one of genetic operations is applied according to fitness values to improve the exploratory rewards. Through learning and embodied evolution, a group of agents obtain appropriate exploratory rewards.

1 Introduction

In application of reinforcement learning algorithms to real world problems, the design of reward function plays an important role for successful achievement of the task. To elucidate the origin of reward, we have developed wheel-based mobile robots named Cyber Rodents (CRs) [1]. Especially, the main goal of the Cyber Rodent project is to study the adaptive mechanisms of artificial agents under the same fundamental constraints as biological agents, namely self-preservation and self-reproduction. The self-preservation is the capability to forage (capture and recharge from external battery packs in the environment) and the self-reproduction is that two CRs exchange data and program via an infrared (IR) communication port. We have already summarized a part of our study on learning and evolution [1]. Furthermore, our research group recently showed several important topics such as a reinforcement learning algorithm [2] enhanced by the theory of natural gradient [3], evolution of hierarchical control architectures [4], and evolution of communication [5].

In this paper, the design of reward functions is discussed. If rewards are zero everywhere except for a few points that correspond to important events, a long

M. Ishikawa et al. (Eds.): ICONIP 2007, Part II, LNCS 4985, pp. 167–176, 2008.

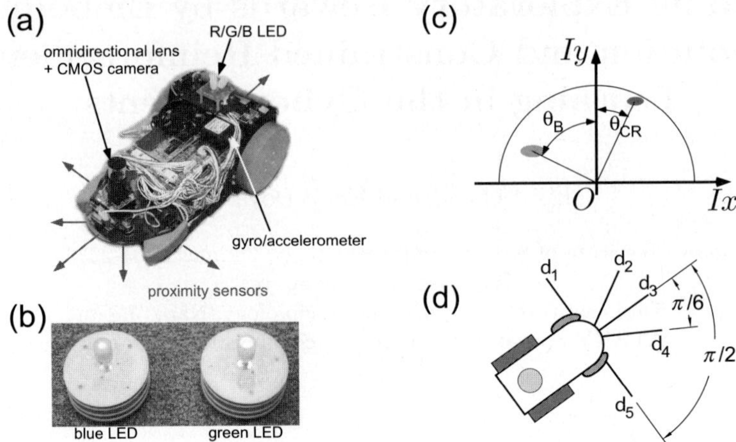

Fig. 1. Our experimental system. (a) hardware of the Cyber Rodent. (b) Battery pack with blue/green LED. (c) Image coordinate system $O\text{-}I_xI_y$ and two angles θ_B and θ_{CR} to the nearest battery and CR are detected. (d) Five proximity sensors $d_1,\ldots,d_5$ mounted in front. Each proximity sensor measures a distance of up to 30 [cm].

learning time is required. On the contrary, the dense reward functions which give non-zero rewards most of the time accelerate the efficiency of learning. One possible solution is to use an intrinsic exploratory reward computed from agent's internal information such as sensor outputs because it gives plenty information about the environment. This idea is categorized into a framework called "Intrinsically Motivated Reinforcement Learning" (IMRL) [6]. In this paper, we propose a method to find the appropriate exploratory reward by the framework of embodied evolution [7]. Each CR has its own parameterized exploratory reward and multiple extrinsic rewards. As a basic learning component, the Constrained Policy Gradient Reinforcement Learning (CPGRL) algorithm [8] is applied to maximize the average of the exploratory reward under the constraints given by the extrinsic rewards. The objective of embodied evolution is to find the appropriate exploratory reward by a group of CRs. Preliminary real experiments are conducted, and a discussion is given.

2   Cyber Rodent Hardware

Before getting into detail of our embodied evolution, a hardware system is explained briefly. Fig. 1 (a) shows a hardware of the Cyber Rodent (CR) [1]. Its body is 22 [cm] in length and 1.75 [kg] in weight. The CR is endowed with a variety of sensory inputs, including an omni-directional CMOS camera, an IR range sensor, seven IR proximity sensors, gyros, and accelerometer. Its motion system consists of two wheels that allow the CR to move at a maximum speed of 1.3 [m/s]. To represent an internal state, a three-color LED (red, blue and green) is mounted on the tail.

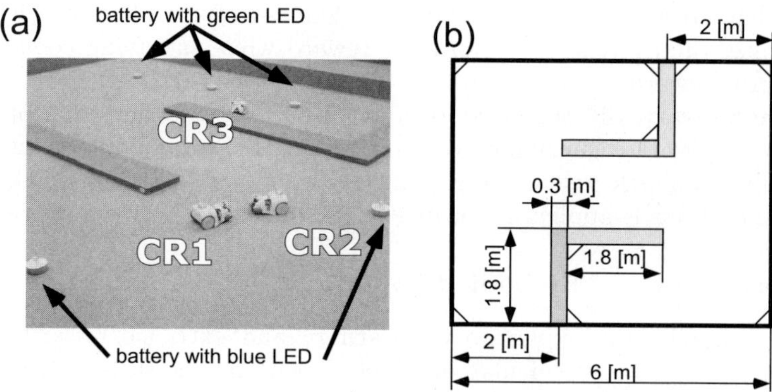

Fig. 2. Embodied evolution using three CRs

Fig. 1 (b) shows a blue battery and a green battery (battery pack equipped with blue and green LED, respectively). Although there exist two types of batteries, the CR can not distinguish between them. LED is lighting if the battery is charged enough. Therefore, the CRs can find the charged battery by using the visual information.

An image coordinate system $O\text{-}I_x I_y$ of the omni-directional CMOS camera is shown in Fig. 1 (c). The battery pack is recognized as a color blob in the image, and the size of the blob N_B and an angle θ_B are utilized. In addition, another CR is also detected if the LED on the tail is turned on. As a result, the angle θ_{CR} and the size of the blob N_{CR} can be used to represent the relative position of another CR. Fig. 1 (d) shows the location of the five proximity sensors. The relative angle θ_D and distance $d_{\min}$ to the nearest obstacle are estimated from these proximity sensors.

3   Embodied Evolution

3.1   Basic Framework of Embodied Evolution

Watson *et al.* defined embodied evolution as evolution taking place in a population of embodied robots [7]. As opposed to standard centralized evolution, embodied evolution can be regarded as natural evolution in the engineering sense. A major difference between Watson's embodied evolution and ours is a capability of behavior learning in each agent.

Fig.2 (a) shows a snapshot of actual embodied evolution in this study. There exist three CRs (CR1, CR2, and CR3), many battery packs and four obstacles in the environment. The size of the experimental field surrounded by the wall is 6 [m] × 5 [m] as shown in Fig.2 (b). The j-th CR has one exploratory reward r_1^j and multiple extrinsic rewards r_i^j $(i = 2, \ldots, m)$ that give constraints to the policy. The exploratory reward is coded by the parameter vector $\boldsymbol{w}^j$, and it is calculated from $\boldsymbol{w}^j$ and sensor outputs. On the contrary, extrinsic rewards usually characterize environmental events. The objective of behavior learning is to maximize the average of exploratory reward while satisfying constraints on the extrinsic rewards.

On the contrary, the objective for a group of CRs is to find appropriate exploratory rewards for surviving. When a mating behavior between two CRs is successfully made, they share $\boldsymbol{w}$ and fitness values explained later. One of two genetic operations is applied according to the difference between fitness values.

3.2   Formulation of Embodied Evolution

For the j-th CR, the exploratory reward r_1^j and extrinsic rewards r_i^j ($i = 2,\ldots,m$, $j = 1,2,3$) are calculated, which depend on the state and the action. Let $r_i^j = r_i^j(\boldsymbol{x}, \boldsymbol{u})$ and $\boldsymbol{r}^j = [r_1^j\ r_2^j\ \cdots\ r_m^j]^\top$ denote respectively the immediate reward given to the j-th CR and its vectorized representation. The operation $^\top$ means the vector/matrix transpose. The average reward is defined by

$$g_i^j(\boldsymbol{\theta}^j) = \lim_{T \to \infty} \mathrm{E}_{\boldsymbol{\theta}^j}\left[\frac{1}{T}\sum_{t=1}^{T} r_{i,t}^j\right], \quad i = 1,\ldots,m, \quad j = 1,2,3 \tag{1}$$

where $\boldsymbol{\theta}^j$ is a policy parameter of the j-th CR. $r_{i,t}^j$ represents the i-th reward given to the j-th CR at time t. The objective for the CR is to solve the optimization problem under the inequality constraints as follows:

$$\max_{\boldsymbol{\theta}^j} g_1^j(\boldsymbol{\theta}^j), \quad \text{s.t.} \quad g_i^j(\boldsymbol{\theta}^j) \geq G_i^j, \quad i = 2,\ldots,m, \quad j = 1,2,3, \tag{2}$$

where G_i^j is a threshold for controlling a level of the constraint. In other words, the objective is to find the policy parameter $\boldsymbol{\theta}^j$ that maximizes an average reward under the constraints determined by the extrinsic rewards. It is noted that the inequality constraints determined by (1) and (2) are also the functions of the average rewards. This reinforcement learning algorithm under constraints is introduced in section 4.

In this study, three extrinsic rewards are considered to specify *biological* constraints. The first reward is for foraging behaviors defined by

$$r_2^j = \begin{cases} 1 & \text{if the CR catches the blue or green LED} \\ -0.1 & \text{if the internal battery level is below a certain threshold} \\ 0 & \text{otherwise,} \end{cases}$$

for all j. When the CR catches the battery pack, a re-charging behavior is executed automatically. A single re-charging session is limited to three minutes. After re-charging, the hand-coded behavior is automatically executed to release the battery and to go search for another one for a while. The next reward is for mating behaviors defined by

$$r_3^j = \begin{cases} 1 & \text{if mating behavior is realized between the j-th CR and another,} \\ 0 & \text{otherwise.} \end{cases}$$

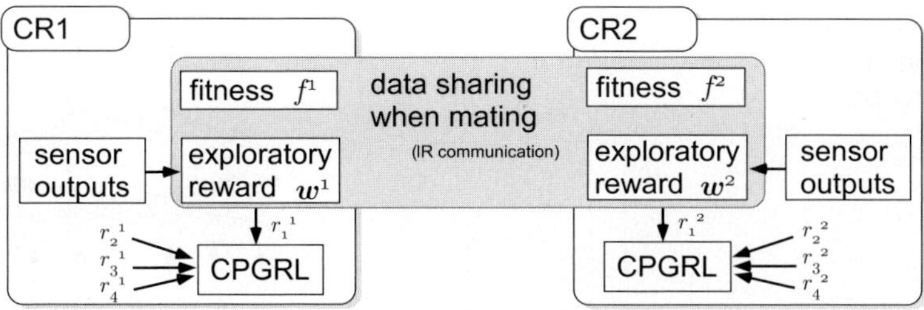

Fig. 3. Data sharing between two CRs when the mating behavior is successfully made. CR1 receives w^2 and fitness values of the CR2, and vice versa.

Since successful mating behavior is essential to the survival of all sexually reproducing organisms, a mating behavior learned from this reward is important. The CR attempts to establish the IR communication link when another CR is detected. The last reward is for avoiding behaviors defined by

$$r_4^j = \begin{cases} -0.1 & \text{if the } j\text{-th CR makes a collision with the obstacles} \\ 0 & \text{otherwise.} \end{cases}$$

A collision is estimated by the change of the reading from the accelerometer and the odometry of the wheels.

The average rewards can be estimated by the CPGRL (see (4)). If the constraints on r_2^j and r_4^j are satisfied, the red LED on the tail is turned on. As a result, another CR has a chance to find the CR that can mate. In Fig. 2, CR1 and CR2 try to mate with each other. On the other hand, the LED of CR3 is turned off because the constraint on r_4^j is violated due to a collision with the obstacle.

The exploratory reward r_1^j is computed from sensor outputs, and it is tuned after successful mating is achieved between two CRs. In current experiments, we encode in the CR's "genes" the strength of the exploratory reward for finding another CR with a red tail lamp in mating mode and charged batteries, in vision as follows:

$$r_1^j = 0.01 \exp\left\{ -\left(\frac{(1 - w_3^j)\,\theta_{\mathrm{CR}}}{w_1^j} \right)^2 - \left(\frac{w_3^j\,\theta_{\mathrm{B}}}{w_2^j} \right)^2 \right\}, \tag{3}$$

where θ_{CR} and θ_{B} are the nearest angles to another CR and battery, respectively. The shape of r_1^j is controlled by the three dimensional parameter vector $w^j = [w_1^j\ w_2^j\ w_3^j]^\top$ where inequalities are introduced: $w_1^j, w_2^j > 0$ and $0 < w_3^j < 1$. If the CR does not use this visual exploratory reward, it is extremely difficult for the CR to engage in mating or foraging. On the other hand, if the visual reward is too strong, the CR can end up satisfied by just watching other mates without actually start mating or foraging.

As a genetic operation, we adopt a mutation and a crossover based on BLX-α [9] according to the difference of fitness values. Suppose the operations between

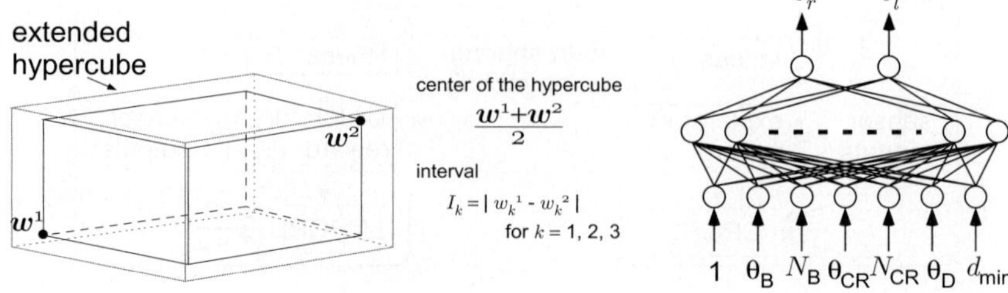

Fig. 4. Basic idea of BLX-α

Fig. 5. Neural network with 12 hidden units

CR1 and CR2 shown in Fig. 3. If $f^1 > f^2$, the mutation operator is applied to w^1, where the mutation operator is simply realized by adding a Gaussian noise with zero mean and 0.4 variance. Otherwise, the crossover operator is applied, illustrated in Fig. 4. BLX-α uniformly picks parameter values from points that lie on an interval that extends αI on either side of the interval I between parents.

As a fitness function, three fitness values are introduced: (1) f^j_{battery}: the number of captured battery packs per 10 minutes, (2) $f^j_{\text{collision}}$: the number of collisions per 10 minutes, and (3) f^j_{mating}: the number of successful mating per 10 minutes to measure the running performance. In this experiment, $f^j = f^j_{\text{battery}} + f^j_{\text{mating}}$ is used to select the genetic operation.

3.3   Stochastic Policy

To apply the policy gradient reinforcement learning, a stochastic policy must be considered. In other words, the CR observes a state $x \in \mathbb{X}$ and executes an action $u \in \mathbb{U}$ with probability $\mu_{\theta^j}(x, u)$ at each time step, where $\mu_{\theta^j} : \mathbb{X} \times \mathbb{U} \to [0, 1]$ is a stochastic policy parameterized by the n-dimensional vector $\theta^j \in \mathbb{R}^n$.

To represent the policy, a three-layer neural network with 12 hidden units are used shown in Fig. 5. The number of units in the input layer is seven. The output layer consists of two units that correspond to velocities of left and right wheels (v_l and v_r). By adding a Gaussian noise with zero mean and 0.4 variance, the stochastic policy is realized. As a result, all connections weights are stored in the policy parameter θ^j.

4   Constrained Policy Gradient Reinforcement Learning

4.1   Gradient Estimates by Policy Gradient Reinforcement Learning

In this section, the Constrained Policy Gradient Reinforcement Learning (CP-GRL) algorithm [8] is introduced as a basic component of our system. Fig. 6 illustrates the CPGRL system based on the actor-critic architecture [2]. Since the same algorithm is applied, the superscript j is omitted in section 4. It consists

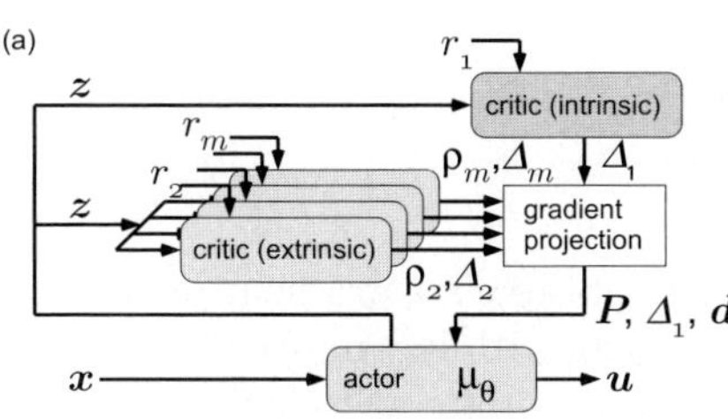

(b) **while** $k < N_K$

1. set $z_0 = 0$ and $\Delta_i = 0$ for all i.
2. **while** $t < N_T$
   (a) observe x_t and execute u_t.
   (b) receive the rewards r_t
   (c) estimate the average rewards and their gradients.
3. store the estimated average rewards
4. update the policy parameter.

Fig. 6. Actor-critic architecture for learning from intrinsic and extrinsic rewards. (a) Block diagram. (b) Algorithm. N_K and N_T denote the number of episodes and steps, respectively.

of one actor, multiple critics, and a gradient projection module that computes a projection onto a feasible region, which is the set of points satisfying all the inequality constraints (2). Based on the immediate reward r_i, each critic outputs ρ_i, an estimate of the long-term average reward g_i, and Δ_i, its gradient with respect to the policy parameters. Actor selects the action u according to the stochastic policy $\mu_\theta(x, u)$.

The PGRL algorithms have recently been re-evaluated since they are well-behaved with function approximation. There exist several methods to compute the gradient of the average reward Δ_i. In the current implementation, we choose the actor-critic method [10]. According to the current state and action, the function ψ_t at time t is defined by $\psi_t(x_t, u_t) \triangleq \partial \ln \mu_\theta(x_t, u_t)/\partial \theta$.

The CR interacts with the environment, producing a state, action, reward sequence. After receiving experiences $(x_t, u_t, x_{t+1}, u_{t+1}, r_{t+1})$, an eligibility traces $z_t \in \mathbb{R}^n$ is updated by $z_{t+1} = \beta z_t + \psi_t(x_t, u_t)$ where $\beta \in [0, 1)$ is a discount factor that controls the variance of the gradient estimate. Since z_t is independent of the reward functions, z_t can be used for estimating gradients of different average rewards. Then, all the gradients are updated in the same manner. For all $i = 1, \ldots, m$, the gradient of the long-term average reward is estimated by

$$\Delta_{i,t+1} = \Delta_{i,t} + \frac{1}{t+1} \left[Q_i(x_t, u_t)\psi(x_t, u_t) - \Delta_{i,t} \right],$$

where $Q_i(x, u) = v_i^\top \psi(x, u)$ is an estimated state-action value function parameterized by the weight vector v_i. The learning rule to train v_i is given by the standard temporal difference method, $v_{i,t+1} = v_{i,t} + \alpha_r \delta_{i,t} z_{t+1}$, where the temporal difference $\delta_{i,t}$ is defined by

$$\delta_{i,t} = r_{i,t+1} - \rho_{i,t+1} + v_{i,t}^\top \left[\psi_{t+1}(x_{t+1}, u_{t+1}) - \psi_t(x_t, u_t) \right].$$

Konda's actor-critic requires an additional learning mechanism to approximate $Q_i(x, u)$, but it can utilize the Markov property as opposed to naive policy gradient algorithms. The estimate of the average reward r_i is updated by

$$\rho_{i,t+1} = \rho_{i,t} + \alpha_r (r_{i,t+1} - \rho_{i,t}), \tag{4}$$

where α_r is a positive step-size meta-parameter.

4.2　Gradient Projection

After the average rewards and their gradients are obtained, a gradient projection method is applied to solve the maximization problem with inequality constraints. When k-th episode ends, the policy parameters are update as follows:

$$\boldsymbol{\theta}_{k+1} = \boldsymbol{\theta}_k + \alpha_1 \boldsymbol{P}\boldsymbol{\Delta}_1 - \alpha_e \boldsymbol{d} \tag{5}$$

where α_1, α_e are learning rates, $\boldsymbol{P}$ is a matrix that projects $\boldsymbol{\Delta}_1$ into the subspace tangent to the active constraints, and $\boldsymbol{d}$ is a restoration move for the violating constraints.

To estimate $\boldsymbol{P}$ and $\boldsymbol{d}$, a set of indices of the active inequality constraints is defined by $\mathcal{A} = \{i \mid \rho_i - G_i \le 0, \ i = 2, \ldots, m\}$, and let $a = |\mathcal{A}|$ denote the number of active constraints. $\mathcal{A}$ is called an active set. If no constraints are active (the case $a = 0$), the solution lies at the interior of the feasible region. In this case, $\boldsymbol{P}$ and $\boldsymbol{d}$ are set to the identity matrix and zero vector, respectively. Hereafter, the case $a \ne 0$ is considered. With the outputs from the multiple critics, we define $\boldsymbol{g}_\mathcal{A} \triangleq [\rho_{i_1} - G_{i_1} \ \cdots \ \rho_{i_a} - G_{i_a}]^\top$ and $\boldsymbol{N}_\mathcal{A} \triangleq [\boldsymbol{\Delta}_{i_1} \ \cdots \ \boldsymbol{\Delta}_{i_a}]$ where i_a is an index to count the element in $\mathcal{A}$. The projection matrix and restoration move are given by

$$\boldsymbol{P} = \boldsymbol{I} - \boldsymbol{N}_\mathcal{A} \left(\boldsymbol{N}_\mathcal{A}^\top \boldsymbol{N}_\mathcal{A}\right)^{-1} \boldsymbol{N}_\mathcal{A}^\top, \quad \boldsymbol{d} = \boldsymbol{N}_\mathcal{A} \left(\boldsymbol{N}_\mathcal{A}^\top \boldsymbol{N}_\mathcal{A}\right)^{-1} \boldsymbol{g}_\mathcal{A}. \tag{6}$$

It should be noted that $\boldsymbol{Pd} = \boldsymbol{0}$. It is noted that the situation where $\boldsymbol{P}\boldsymbol{\Delta}^1 = \boldsymbol{0}$ must be considered because it may be possible to modify the parameters. This can be detected by using Lagrange multipliers $\boldsymbol{\lambda} = \left(\boldsymbol{N}_\mathcal{A}^\top \boldsymbol{N}_\mathcal{A}\right)^{-1} \boldsymbol{N}_\mathcal{A}^\top \boldsymbol{\Delta}_1$. If $\boldsymbol{\lambda}$ has no negative components, we have a solution and terminate. Otherwise, the active set is re-evaluated by $\mathcal{A} \leftarrow \mathcal{A} \backslash \{r\}$ where $r = \mathrm{argmax}_{l \in \mathcal{A}} \lambda_l$. After deleting one constraint from $\mathcal{A}$, $\boldsymbol{P}$ and $\boldsymbol{d}$ are calculated again.

5　Experimental Results

We conducted three experimental runs. The parameter vectors for the exploratory rewards are initialized by $\boldsymbol{w}^1 = [1 \ 3 \ 0.5]^\top$, $\boldsymbol{w}^2 = [3 \ 2 \ 1]^\top$, and $\boldsymbol{w}^3 = [2 \ 1 \ 0]^\top$. Thresholds are set as $G_2^j = 0.0$, $G_3^j = 0.2$, and $G_4^j = 0.0$. These values are determined by conducting preliminary experiments.

Fig. 7 (a) shows the number of collisions with obstacles per 10 minutes. After about 50 minutes, CR1 and CR3 learned avoiding behaviors while it took about 70 minutes for CR2 to learn avoiding behaviors. Due to slow learning of the policy gradient algorithm, it took long time to obtain avoiding behaviors as compared with our previous studies. Figure 7 (b) shows the number of captured battery packs per 10 minutes. After about 130 minutes, all CRs obtained foraging

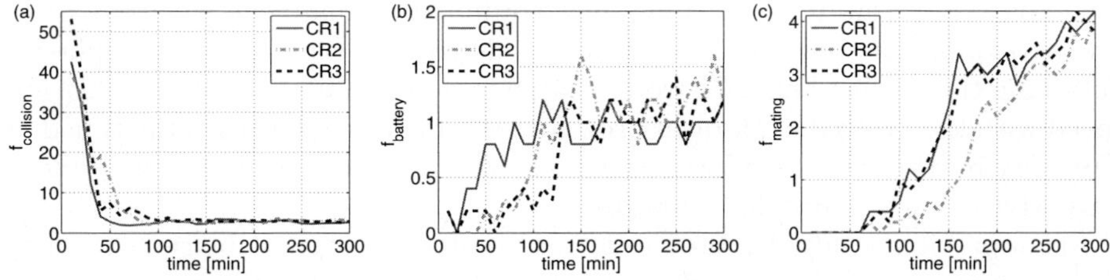

Fig. 7. Comparison of the average fitness values for three runs. (a) average $f_{\text{collision}}$. (b) average f_{battery}. (c) average f_{mating}.

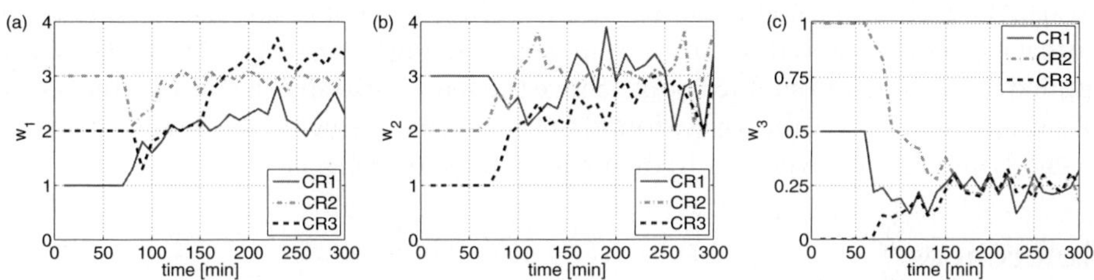

Fig. 8. Evolution of the weight values for three runs. (a) w_1, (b) w_2, and (c) w_3.

behaviors. Figure 7 (c) shows the number of successful mating behaviors per 10 minutes. The speed of improvement of f_{mating} of the CR2 was slow and it was related to the improvement of f_{battery} because mating behaviors were not allowed until two constraints were satisfied.

Fig. 8 compares evolutions of the weight vectors used in the exploratory rewards. As mentioned before, w is updated when a mating behavior is successfully achieved. Therefore, weight vectors were constant at the early stage of experiments. Interestingly, w_3 slowly converged to 0.25 shown in Fig. 8 (c). It suggests that θ_B was not so important as θ_{CR} for exploration. The reason for this is that the CR had many chances to find one of the battery packs because the number of them is greater than that of the CRs. In addition, a large supplementary reward related to the nearest battery pack prevents the CR from approaching it. On the other hand, a successful mating behavior is not sensitive to the distance between two CRs because of the property of IR communication. In this case, watching another CR is regarded as an appropriate strategy for mating. Therefore, it is concluded that appropriate exploratory rewards were obtained through embodied evolution.

5.1 Discussion

This paper proposed a method to find the exploratory reward evolved by a group of the real mobile robot. It is noted that maximization of the average of the exploratory reward is meaningless from a viewpoint of designers because the CR without constraints just wander over the environment. By considering the constraints, the exploratory reward is meaningful. In order to evaluate the efficiency of the evolved exploratory rewards, several hand-coded reward functions were applied for obtaining the mating behavior from scratch in a new environment. The learning speed with the evolved exploratory reward was similar to that with the tuned exploratory reward. If the exploratory reward was not used, the CR failed to learn purposive behaviors after 300 minutes.

In our previous study [1], three issues are pointed out in embodied evolution: (1) how to estimate the other's (and own) fitness, (2) how to select the mating partner, and (3) how to mix the genes of two agents. The first point is simply realized by IR communication, but it should be realized via a non-verbal communication [5]. The second point is implicitly solved by the framework of embodied evolution. In other words, the CR with good foraging and avoiding behaviors has many chances to mate with another, and it means that mating is made between good CRs. BLX-α is applied to implement the third point. Since the search space of the parameter vector w is very small, good values were found in the real experiments. More sophisticated methods should be developed to deal with a huge search space.

References

1. Doya, K., Uchibe, E.: The Cyber Rodent Project: Exploration of adaptive mechanisms for self-preservation and self-reproduction. Adaptive Behavior 13, 149–160 (2005)
2. Sutton, R.S., Barto, A.G.: Reinforcement Learning. MIT Press/Bradford Books (1998)
3. Morimura, T., Uchibe, E., Doya, K.: Utilizing the natural gradient in temporal difference reinforcement learning with eligibility traces. In: Proc. of the 2nd International Symposium on Information Geometry and its Application, pp. 256–263 (2005)
4. Elfwing, S., Uchibe, E., Doya, K., Christensen, H.I.: Evolutionary development of hierarchical learning structures. IEEE Transactions on Evolutionary Computation 11(2), 249–264 (2007)
5. Sato, T., Uchibe, E., Doya, K.: Learning how, what, and whether to communicate: emergence of protocommunication in reinforcement learning agents. Journal of Artificial Life and Robotics 12 (to appear, 2007)
6. Singh, S., Barto, A.G., Chentanez, N.: Intrinsically motivated reinforcement learning. In: Saul, L.K., Weiss, Y., Bottou, L. (eds.) Advances in Neural Information Processing Systems 17, pp. 1281–1288. MIT Press, Cambridge (2005)
7. Watson, R.A., Ficici, S.G., Pollack, J.B.: Embodied evolution: Distributing an evolutionary algorithm in a population of robots. Robotics and Autonomous Systems 39, 1–18 (2002)
8. Uchibe, E., Doya, K.: Constrained reinforcement learning from intrinsic and extrinsic rewards. In: Proc. of the International Conference of Development and Learning (2007)
9. Eshelman, L.J., Schaffer, J.D.: Real-coded genetic algorithms and interval-schemata. In: Foundations of Genetic Algorithms 2, pp. 187–202. Morgan Kaufmann, San Francisco (1993)
10. Konda, V.R., Tsitsiklis, J.N.: Actor-critic algorithms. SIAM Journal on Control and Optimization 42(4), 1143–1166 (2003)

Context-Dependent Adaptive Behavior Generated in the Theta Phase Coding Network

Hiroaki Wagatsuma[*] and Yoko Yamaguchi

Laboratory for Dynamics of Emergent Intelligence, RIKEN BSI,
2-1 Hirosawa, Wako-shi, Saitama
{waga, yokoy}@brain.riken.jp

Abstract. The real world changes in space over time. Our brains need real-time interaction with the external world and will update various internal representations even when events happen only one-time. Such one-time experiences are evaluated in relation to what happens for us in joy and sorrow. Recent brain studies suggest that the dynamic coordination of different representations in brain areas is governed by the synchronization of the brain oscillation, such as theta rhythms. In the rodent hippocampus, the temporal coding mechanism with the theta rhythm, theta phase coding, provides the ability to encode and retrieve behavioral sequences even in the one-time experience, by using successive firing phases in every theta cycle. We here extended the theory to the large-scale brain network and hypothesized that the phase coding not only represents the current behavioral context, but also properly associates it with the evaluation of what happened in the external environment. It is necessary for the animal to predict events in the near future and to update the current and next executive action. In a maze task on our robotic platform, the acquisition of spatial-temporal sequences and spatial-reward associations were demonstrated, even in few trials, and the association contributes to the current action selection. This result suggests that theta rhythms may contribute to coordinate different neural activities to enable contextual decision-making in the real environment.

Keywords: hippocampus, amygdala, prefrontal cortex, place cells, cognitive map, theta phase precession, reward-evaluation, action-selection, Khepera-robot.

1 Introduction

Contextual decision-making may require the dynamic coordination of different brain regions: the hippocampus, representing the current behavioral-spatial context, the amygdala, with its evaluation function, and the prefrontal cortex, functioning as the central executive. Based on experimental studies in spatial maze tasks, the prefrontal cortex is thought to integrate spatial information encoded in the hippocampus and positive/negative reward anticipation in the amygdala to execute an appropriate behavior [1,2]. Experimental data demonstrated highly synchronous neural activities in these brain regions in the range of the theta rhythm [3], and recent studies suggest that

---

[*] Corresponding author.

M. Ishikawa et al. (Eds.): ICONIP 2007, Part II, LNCS 4985, pp. 177–184, 2008.

the dynamic coordination of distant brain regions is governed by theta rhythms [4]. The question remains as to how rhythmic activities in different regions cooperate together on the real-time scale of cognition and behavior to solve spatial tasks. Wagatsuma and Yamaguchi [5,6,7] have proposed the temporal coding mechanism mediated by the hippocampal theta rhythm, called theta phase coding, which enables the encoding of temporal sequences of one-time behavioral experiences and distinguishes between different behavioral contexts by using successive firing phases in every theta cycle. However, it remains unclear whether the computational theory is extensively available for the real-time cognitive map formation and contextual-decision making in the real world environment.

2 Hypothesis

We hypothesized that the hippocampal-amygdala-prefrontal network is mediated by theta rhythms used to encode spatial-temporal sequences in the hippocampal network, to associate amygdaloid reward information with spatial context, and to update executive actions in the prefrontal cortex. We called the neural network model, a part of the whole brain network that is described by neural oscillators, the theta phase coding network. Our robotic platform is a combination of the real-time neural network simulator with mobile robot devices that allow us to monitor the robot's adaptive behaviors in the radial maze task, called the win-stay task. The spatial maze task in our experiments is designed as a radial maze with four arms having a food target located at the end of an arm. The ability to learn the food location after a few trial visits to the arm-ends and the acquisition of necessary representations in those brain regions are examined.

3 Robotic Platform

Our robotic platform consists of a robot, as input/output devices in the real world, and neural network models of the hippocampus (HPC), amygdala (AMG), prefrontal cortex (PFC), nucleus accumbens (NAC) and pre-motor cortex (MOT), as shown in Fig 1A. Note that our hippocampal network conventionally includes the sensory cortex and the entorhinal cortex. In the theta phase coding network, the HPC, AMG and PFC are individually a network of neural units uniformly coupled to a sustained oscillation of the theta rhythm, as the local-field potential (LFP), so that all the units' activities in the same network are modulated by the same rhythm. The basic structure and mathematical description is consistent with our previous models [5,6,7]. The learning property among neural units within each network (or between different networks) is given by the Hebbian synaptic plasticity with a time window of ~50ms [8,9]. We then assume a phase difference among local field potential (LFP) theta rhythms in different networks, as schematically shown in Fig 1B. According to these assumptions, it is possible to connect neural units on demand in the task, for example, the hippocampal representation of the temporal sequence that the robot visits sequentially, and also the sequence-reward association so that the reward information

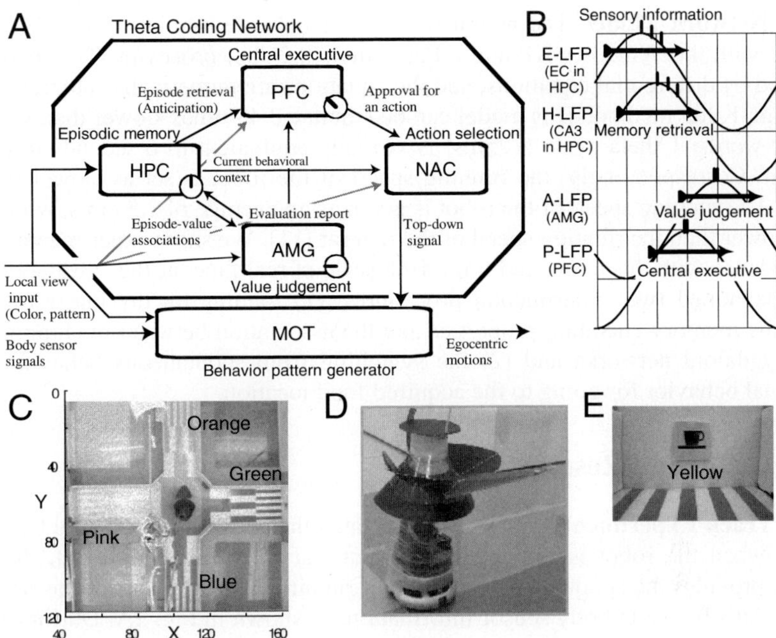

Fig. 1. (A) Schematic illustration of the neural network model. Each network has multiple neural units, and a theta rhythmic unit (LFP) is denoted by the circle with bar (representing a timer). (B) The phase relationship among LFP-units in individual networks, modulating all units in individual networks. (C) The top-view of the radial maze task. Each arm is colored and patterned differently. (D) The robot, with a cowboy hat. The robot's position and direction is respectively obtained from the hat and the brim. (E) The food tag with the yellow color.

is associated only with the termination of the temporal sequence. This gives the correct predictive information, because the unit representing the food existence activates only in the retrieval of the temporal sequence representing the robot approaching the food location, not for going out of the desired location. Thus, the temporal coding scheme overcomes the stimulus–response scheme.

Robotic Device and the Environment. We use a commercial robot system, Khepera, provided by the K-team Corporation, to communicate with neural network models. A monitoring CCD camera is fixed to the ceiling just above in the center, and signals are sent to a computer for calculating the robot's position in the environment. The CCD real-time capturing is obtained through software working with MATLAB [10]. The radial maze with four arms is placed in a square area of 120 x 120 cm (Fig 1C). Each arm has a 50 cm length and 20cm width, which allows the 6 cm-radius robot body to smoothly enter and turn within the arms (Fig. 2D). The floor is colored differently and patterned with various stripes. At the end of a few of the arms, a yellow tag is on the wall (Fig.2E) to identify where the food location is.

Neural Network Model. The neural network models are running on the MATLAB on a PC with the Windows XP and a Pentium-4 (3.2Ghz) processor. The models are described by differential equations, and the equations are numerically integrated using the Runge-Kutta method. This model can be simulated 48 times slower than real time. In other words, 1 theta cycle (125ms) is virtually equivalent to 6 seconds in this experiment. Correspondingly, the running speed of the robot is set as slower than the real rat. The running speed of the robot is given as an average of 2.5 cm/s, which is 36 times slower than the running speed of the real rat [11]. We show experimental results in accordance with this converted time, 1/48 scale of real time, as the "virtual time".

We examined two experimental procedures: (1) running on the linear track, for testing the memory encoding properties and the association between the hippocampal and amygdaloid networks and (2) the switching from spontaneous behavior to the intentional behavior for going to the acquired food location.

4   Experimental Results

Linear Track Experiment. First, we investigated the ability to encode the behavioral episode when the robot is running on a linear track. In this experiment, the MOT network provides the spontaneous behavior of running along the corridor as an avoidance of walls by using body sensor information, as shown in Fig. 2A. During running in the arm, color patterns in different areas allow sensory units in HPC, S1, S2 and S3 (Fig. 2B), to activate sequentially. All sensory inputs are terminated at the end of the arm. Depending on the onset of those inputs, the hippocampal unit starts to oscillate, interacting with the theta rhythm in this network, H-LFP. Observing the population

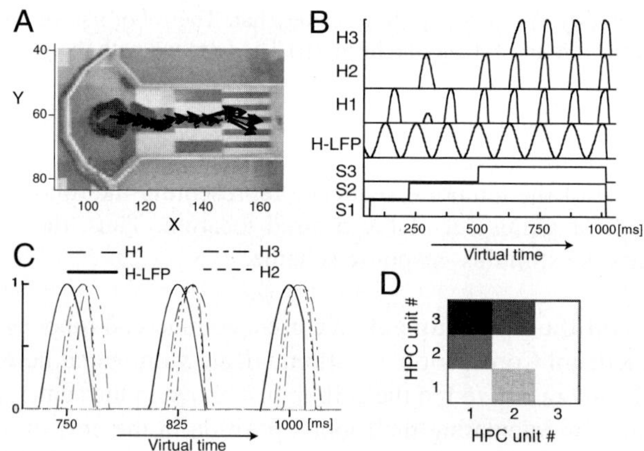

Fig. 2. (A) The superimposed image of the linear track with the running trajectory in the first trial. (B) The population activity of the CA3 units in HPC (H1-3). Activities of sensory units (S1-3) are projected to the entorhinal units in HPC, generating the phase precession pattern. Finally, CA3 units inherit the temporal firing pattern and modify their synaptic connections by the Hebbian plasticity. (C) The robust phase relationship among CA3 units during the theta phase precession. (D) The resultant synaptic connections among the units after the first running trial. It forms the asymmetric connection ($w_{ij}^{CA3} \equiv 0, {}^{\forall} i = j$), with high values in the upper half.

activity, we see that the unit's firing phase systematically changes in advance, and the phase relationship among units is maintained in the same sequential order (Fig. 2C). This enables the hippocampal recurrent network to encode the behavioral sequence, S1→S2→S3, in the one-time trial, by using the combination between the phase precession and the Hebbian synaptic plasticity with the asymmetric time window ~50ms [8,9]. The robust phase relationship and the repetition of the firing pattern, experimentally known as "theta phase precession" [11,12], gives the asymmetric connections representing the behavioral sequence, as shown in Fig. 2D.

We next observed the association between HPC and AMG units. The assumption is that an AMG unit responds to the yellow color on wall when the yellow pixels exceed a certain level, representative of the food signal, approximately 7cm from the wall. However, the unit activates without the direct food signal if associated with HPC units properly acquired in the second trial (Fig. 3A). Figure 3B shows how the networks acquired this predictive representation in detail. In the first trial, HPC units

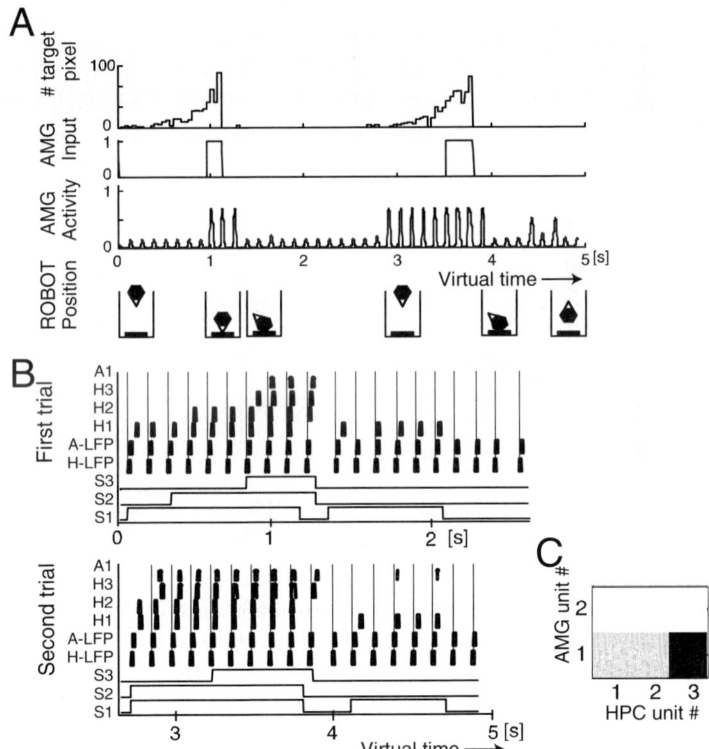

Fig. 3. (A) The food signal response of an AMG unit (A1) and its predictive activity. (B) Temporal activities of the CA3 units in HPC (H1-3) and an AMG unit (A1) both in the first and second trials. A1 fires just after the H3 firing, as phase locking. (C) The resultant connection between HPC and AMG units after the second trial. A connection from H3 to A1 only has a high value.

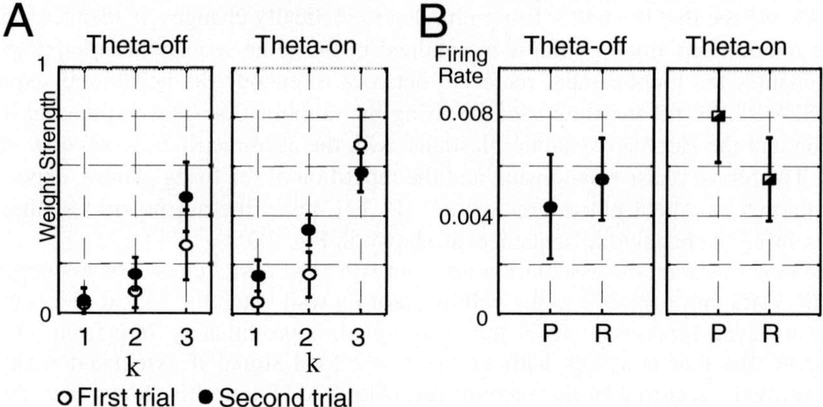

Fig. 4. (A) Statistical analysis of resultant connections between HPC and AMG units both in the first and second trials in different conditions (see text). The abscissa, k, denotes the HPC unit number. The mean and standard deviation in the experimental data (10 data sets) is plotted. (B) Firing rates in the predictive (P) and retrospective (R) firings. Firing rate is defined by $\int_T f(t)/T$, where T is the whole time either approaching the food or leaving the food location, and $f(t)$ is the AMG activity when the value exceeds 0.5 (see Fig. 3A).

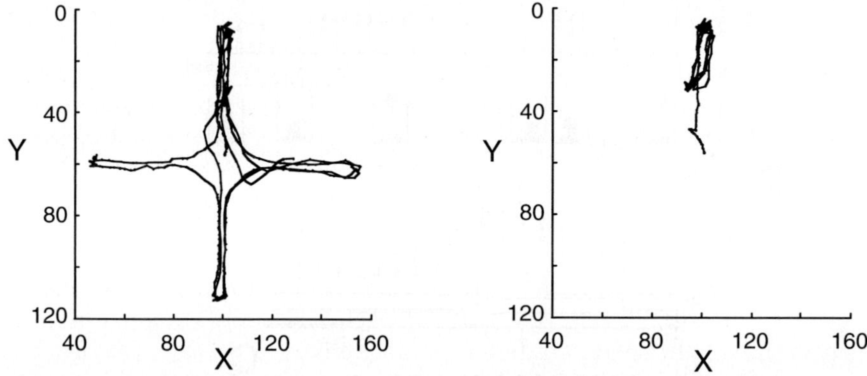

Fig. 5. Behavioral trajectories in the radial maze in conditions with (right) and without (left) the top-down signal. In the right, the robot repeatedly visits the same arm after it found the food. Note that the right figure shows the trajectory in the preferable arm.

generate the phase precession pattern, H1→H2→H3, in every theta cycle, forming the asymmetric connections among units. The A1 unit fires when the food signal is coming directly. In addition, the firing timing is properly controlled to fire just after the H3 firing. Therefore, the H3 selectively connects to the A1 unit, as shown in Fig. 3C. This allows the A1 unit to fire predictively when the robot starts to enter the arm in the second trial by the association between H3 and A1. When the robot enters the arm, the hippocampal network retrieves the previous behavioral sequence, as successive firing phases, representing the going-in behavior, while the same sequence is not activated when the robot is going out of the food location. Figure 4 shows statistical analyses of the formation of the HPC-AMG association and predictive firing profile, compared with the condition without the theta rhythm in AMG, called the "theta-off" condition. In the normal "theta-on" condition, the H3 unit selectively connects to the A1 unit, even after the first trial (Fig. 4A; right). In contrast, in the theta-off condition it is difficult to form the proper connection only one time, because the AMG units independently fire without the phase locking with HPC units. The H3-A1 connection seems to increase weakly by chance in a trial-to-trial manner (Fig. 4A; left). Figure 4B shows AMG firing activities in the second trial. The predictive AMG firing is clearly observed in the theta-on condition, while the predictive firing in the theta-off condition is weak compared with its retrospective firing (in going-out of the food). Retrospective firing is also observed in the theta-on condition, because the temporal sequence is occasionally retrieved when the robot is going out, which is triggered by some sensory inputs.

Radial Maze Task (Win-stay) Experiment. Secondly, we investigated the ability to solve the win-stay task in the radial maze. This task is known as the key experiment to test the hippocampal memory function. Rats easily learn to go to the target arm with the food from the center of the maze, while rats with the hippocampal area removed from their brains are hardly able to learn the task. In this experiment, we compared the normal condition with the condition without the top-down signal from the prefrontal cortex through the nucleus accombens (NAC here; see Fig. 1A). In our model, the AMG predictive signals enhance to PFC-HPC associations, as updating executive memories in PFC, and increase PFC-HPC firing synchrony to open the gate in the NAC sending the top-down signal to the MOT network [13]. Receiving the top-down signal, the MOT switches to an intentional behavior from a spontaneous behavior. The intentional behavior is given by the change of motor programs, as the dominant input is either body sensor inputs or preferable color inputs. Figure 5 shows an example of spontaneous behaviors without top-down signals (left in the figure) and the behavior after the transition to the intentional mode by the top-signal (right in the figure). The former exhibits visiting every arm without any preference, while in the latter case the robot visits the same arm that obtained the food signal in the arm-end repeatedly and with strict adherence. This clearly demonstrated the acquisition of the behavioral solution in the win-stay task.

5   Concluding Remarks

By using our robotic platform interacting with the real world in the real-time, our experimental results demonstrated that the theta phase coding network enables the encoding of spatial-temporal sequences in the hippocampal network and spatial-reward associations in the hippocampal-amygdala network, even after only a few trials. In the experiment of the radial maze task, an executive function of the prefrontal cortex is observed. The question of whether the other adaptive behavior, for instance the win-shift task, finding the other food arms flexibly, etc, will be investigated in further investigations. The theta-rhythm based synchrony between the striatum (or nucleus accumbens) and hippocampus, recently reported in a maze task [14], is also deeply of interest. The present results suggest that theta rhythms may contribute to coordinate distant neural activities to enable the contextual decision-making in the real environment in a small number of trials, which is crucial for survival.

Acknowledgments. The authors would like to thank Tatsuya Ikeda for valuable technical supports and Kentaro Someya for the assistance of robot experiments. This work was supported by JSPS KAKENHI (19650073).

References

1. Jones, M.W., Wilson, M.A.: Phase precession of medial prefrontal cortical activity relative to the hippocampal theta rhythm. Hippocampus 15(7), 867–873 (2005)
2. Siapas, A.G., Lubenov, E.V., Wilson, M.A.: Prefrontal phase locking to hippocampal theta oscillations. Neuron 46(1), 141–151 (2005)
3. Seidenbecher, T., Laxmi, T.R., Stork, O., Pape, H.C.: Amygdalar and hippocampal theta rhythm synchronization during fear memory retrieval. Science 301(5634), 846–850 (2003)
4. Yamaguchi, Y., Sato, N., Wagatsuma, H., Wu, Z., Molter, C., Aota, Y.: A unified view of theta-phase coding in the entorhinal-hippocampal system. Current Opinion in Neurobiology 17(2), 1–8 (2007)
5. Wagatsuma, H., Yamaguchi, Y.: Cognitive map formation through sequence encoding by theta phase precession. Neural Computation 16(12), 2665–2697 (2004)
6. Wagatsuma, H., Yamaguchi, Y.: Disambiguation in spatial navigation with theta phase coding. Neurocomputing 69, 1228–1232 (2006)
7. Wagatsuma, H., Yamaguchi, Y.: Neural dynamics of the cognitive map in the hippocampus. Cognitive Neurodynamics 1(2), 119–141 (2007)
8. Levy, W.B., Steward, O.: Temporal contiguity requirements for long-term associative potentiation/depression in the hippocampus. Neuroscience 8(4), 791–797 (1983)
9. Bi, G.Q., Poo, M.M.: Synaptic modifications in cultured hippocampal neurons: dependence on spike timing, synaptic strength, and postsynaptic cell type. Journal of Neuroscience 18(24), 10464–10472 (1998)
10. Kobayashi, K.: MATLAB Utilization Book, pp. 190–211. Shuwa System Co., Ltd., Tokyo (2001) [In Japanese]
11. O'Keefe, J., Recce, M.L.: Phase relationship between hippocampal place units and the EEG theta rhythm. Hippocampus 3(3), 317–330 (1993)
12. Skaggs, W.E., McNaughton, B.L., Wilson, M.A., Barnes, C.A.: Theta phase precession in hippocampal neuronal populations and the compression of temporal sequences. Hippocampus 6(2), 149–172 (1996)
13. O'Donnell, P., Grace, A.A.: Synaptic interactions among excitatory afferents to nucleus accumbens neurons: hippocampal gating of prefrontal cortical input. Journal of Neuroscience 15(5), 3622–3639 (1995)
14. DeCoteau, W.E., Thorn, C., Gibson, D.J., Courtemanche, R., Mitra, P., Kubota, Y., Graybiel, A.M.: Learning-related coordination of striatal and hippocampal theta rhythms during acquisition of a procedural maze task. Proc. Natl. Acad. Sci. USA 104(13), 5644–5649 (2007)

Computational Modeling of Human-Robot Interaction Based on Active Intention Estimation

Takashi Omori[1], Ayami Yokoyama[1], Hiroyuki Okada[1],
Satoru Ishikawa[2], and Yugo Nagata[3]

[1] Tamagawa University, 6-1-1 Tamagawagakuen, Machida-shi, Tokyo 194-8610 Japan
[2] Hokusei Gakuen University, 2-3-1 Ohyachi-Nishi, Atsubetu-ku,
Sapporo 004-8631 Japan
[3] Tokyo University, 3-8-1 Komaba,Meguro-ku,Tokyo 153-8902 Japan
`omori@lab.tamagawa.ac.jp`
`http://www.tamagawa.ac.jp`

Abstract. In human interaction with a robot, estimation of the other's intention is thought of as an indispensable factor for achievement of a precise self action. But estimation of the other's intention is heavy loaded information processing, and we don't think humans are always doing it. So, in this paper, we propose a light loaded computational algorithm that achieves human-robot interaction without intention estimation in the self agent. In the method, the self agent assumes the other agent to estimate intention, and searches for an action that is easy to be interpreted by the other agent. We evaluated the effectiveness of the proposed model by computer simulation on a hunter task. This method should be positioned as one of the possible variations of intention-based interaction.

Keywords: Intention estimation, Human-robot interaction, Computational model.

1   Introduction

Recent progress in robotics has resulted in robots with smooth physical actions and human-shaped bodies, and it is now becoming required for robots to have the intelligence to change their behavior based on situations in their environments. However, the range of environments in which robots are expected to work is wide, and it is desirable for robots to be aware of the mental states of the humans around them in addition to the usual physical environment. However, the current level of human-machine interaction by robots is insufficient for achieving smooth collaboration with humans. We consider the major reason for the insufficiency to be a lack of a computational model for action decision that includes human mental factors.

In the usual methods of robot programming, behaviors and actions of robots are designed and encoded by human programmers in advance of their real use. As the range of environments and required action variations is quite wide in robots

M. Ishikawa et al. (Eds.): ICONIP 2007, Part II, LNCS 4985, pp. 185–192, 2008.
© Springer-Verlag Berlin Heidelberg 2008

due to their large freedom of motion, we can only achieve robot behavior by choosing an action sequence from a prepared action list depending on situations of the moment. And each of the actions needs a setting of parameters to fit itself to its environment.

For human-robot collaboration, the most reliable way for a human to direct a robot is through explicit instruction by language or a controlling instrument like a remote control. But these methods are not effective for achieving smooth collaboration because the behavior of instructing itself disturbs smooth and continuous action sequences for collaborative work. Of course, robots can determine their own behavior when their working situation is constrained. But the strategy of constraining the robot working situation itself contradicts the concept of general purpose use that is increasingly expected of robots.

Model-free reinforcement learning [1] is a method often used for robot action decision in collaborative settings (e.g. [2]). The method is based on trial-and-error learning in each point of state space and requires many trials. But as a rather small number of trials are permitted in real world human-robot interaction even in new situations, the strategy of action decision through reinforcement learning is not practical. We need a model of action decision that requires a small number of or no trials for interaction with a human that has hidden mental states.

Determining robot behavior by estimating the implicit intentions of the user, not by explicit command, is one of the most effective ways for the achievement of flexible and effective interaction between robots and human users. The key technical issue for its accomplishment is a method of user intention estimation and a computational modeling of robot action decision based on the estimation. When we consider embodiment nature of robots and the wide variation in their working environments, what is important and worth to striving for is the estimation of a user's intentions based on nonverbal actions rather than an interpretation of a user's intentions by language instructions.

Intention can be defined as a hidden variable that dominates a user's behavior like a goal or a plan. A basic strategy for its estimation is observation of a user's behavior and optimization of hidden variables using evaluation functions. For example, Nagata et al. have developed a method to estimate the value of a hidden variable by maximizing a likelihood of behavior under an assumption that self and other have the same action decision function [3]. In the study, Nagata called the strategy of estimating the other's intention from the other's observed behavior level one (Lv.1), and proposed a more complex strategy of level two (Lv.2), in which the self agent estimates how the agent itself is estimated by the other agent, and demonstrated its effectiveness by a computer simulation. However, the computational load of the Lv.2 strategy is larger than Lv.1, and we don't think humans use the strategy in daily life so often. Our daily behavior decision-making is more intuitive and we believe there should be a simpler and lighter loaded strategy that doesn't require precise observation of the other's behavior and estimation of his/her intention.

So, in this study, we try computational modeling of action decision based on the estimation of the other's intentions using the action decision function of self, and introduce a simpler model that doesn't estimate the other's intention but will still be effective as Lv.2, which we call level zero star (Lv.0*). We demonstrate the effectiveness of the Lv.0* model by computer simulation on a hunter task.

2   Collaboration and Passive Intention Estimation

Intention estimation is one of the most important factors for achievement of social communication. When we communicate with another person, we observe the situation and the behavior of the person, estimate the intention of the person using our own experiences, as in "I behave like this when I have this intention." We then decide on an action for ourselves based on the estimation. But in most conventional studies, methods of intention estimation were passive, one-way observation of the other's situation and behavior by the self (e.g. [4][5]). We call the passive strategy level one (Lv.1). With the Lv.1 strategy, we can achieve the proper action decision of the self by adapting to the other's intention. But so far as we use Lv.1, we can't achieve "social leading," in which we implicitly induce other people to change their behavior as is convenient for us.

And in a case in which the other person also takes a Lv.1 strategy, mutual estimation of each other's intentions and simultaneous target change may happen. But as the Lv.1 strategy assumes others not changing their target, the target change will cause ineffective interaction. For this problem, Nagata et al. have proposed a level two (Lv.2) strategy and a meta system for strategy change [3]. In the Lv.2 strategy, the Lv.2 self agent evaluates how the agent itself is estimated by the other Lv.1 agent and decides its action based on the evaluation. In the meta system for strategy change, the self agent changes its strategy when the performance of the current strategy is not good in correspondence to a type of other agent strategy.

3   Active Intention Leading in Collaboration

So in this study, we consider a new method of interaction in which the self agent actively approaches another agent to induce action by the other agent that is convenient for the self. To induce the desired action of the other, the self must create a sequence of actions that is easy to be interpreted by the other. Though such a method requires a load for the planning of self action, the interaction is expected to be effective because it doesn't require time for observation of the other agent. In this study, we call this type of action decision strategy "active intention leading (AIL)."

Figure 1 shows a conceptual diagram of AIL. We consider the following process of interaction in AIL where the self agent (A) decides its intention at first, (B) searches for an action whose goal can be most easily observed by other Lv.1 agent and conducts it. Then (C), the action is observed by the other Lv.1 agent and affects its intention decision. When the other agent makes a collaborative decision, the decided intention should be one that is also convenient for the self agent. The intention is expected to appear as an action of the other agent

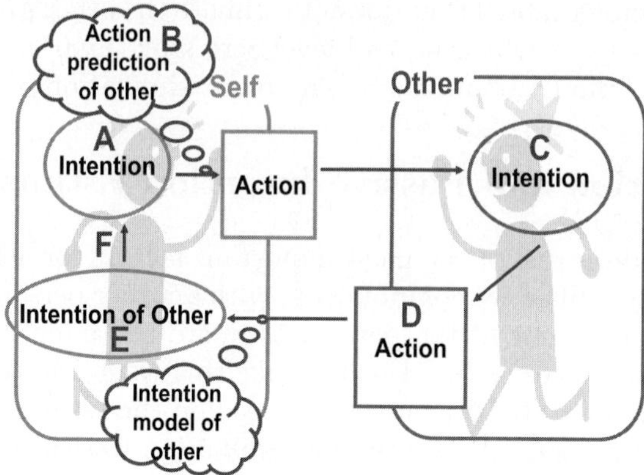

Fig. 1. Conceptual diagram of active intention understanding

(D), and the self agent can achieve an efficient interaction without making any observation or estimation of the other as the result. As the explicit action by the self (B) is also easy to observe, a computational load for observation by the other agent is expected to be lighter and the decision (D) by other agent is expected to be made more quickly. We call this strategy level zero star (Lv.0*). Lv.0* assumes the other to take the Lv.1 strategy.

On the other hand, conventional passive intention estimation can be explained as follows in Fig. 1. There is an intention of the other agent (C), it appears in the form of action (D), the self agent observes and estimates the intention (E) and it is reflected in the intention decision making of the self agent (F). In this case, the other is assumed to be an agent that doesn't estimate others, the level zero agent (Lv.0), or the Lv.2 agent that expect others to decide the goal of the moment.

4   Behavior Evaluation by Hunter Task

4.1   Hunter Task

To evaluate the effectiveness of the Lv.0* strategy, we conducted a computer simulation with a hunter task (Fig. 2). In this task, there were two hunters (H_A, H_B in the figure) and two identifiable prey (P_1, P_2 in the figure) in a grid world with torus organization. For each of the hunters, the other hunter is the other agent. In each time step, each of the hunters moved up, down, left or right one grid, and the prey moved one grid randomly with a probability of Up 20.

We prepared two conditions, Task 1 and Task 2. In Task 1, one of the hunters took the Lv.2 strategy and another took the Lv.1 strategy, the passive one. We evaluated the smoothness of the task solving process by a number of steps that were necessary to reach the solving condition from the initial layout of hunters and prey. When the step number is small, we can know the hunters have chased the prey without collision or mutual concession.

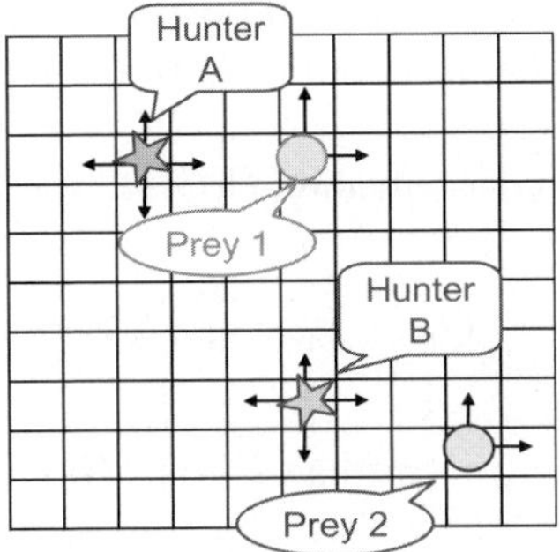

Fig. 2. Hunter task environment

In Task 2, one of the hunters took the Lv.0* strategy and the other took the Lv.1 strategy. With this combination of strategies, we can expect the Lv.1 agent to passively estimate the targeting prey of the Lv.0* agent faster than in Task 1, and to achieve the task solving state with shorter steps. When we compare the steps of Task 1 and Task 2 for the same initial layout of hunters and prey, we can know the effectiveness of the strategies used for the action decision.

4.2   Computational Model of Lv.X Strategy

In the hunter task, the estimation of the other's intention corresponds to guessing the prey targeted by the other hunter from its behavior. Its basic method is a use of probability distribution function $P(a_s, s_s, G_s)$ that decide a self action a_s from a relative self position s_s to a targeted prey G_s. When a self hunter chases its prey, the hunter decides its action a_s by the following equation. It corresponds to the level zero (Lv.0) strategy:

$$a_s = \underset{a}{\mathrm{argmax}}\, P(a|s_s, G_s) \tag{1}$$

In the Lv.1 strategy, the self hunter estimates the target of the other hunter $\tilde{G}_o$ by inputting the position information s_o and action information a_o of the other agent to the action decision function of the self.

$$\tilde{G}_o = \underset{G}{\mathrm{argmax}}\, P(G|s_o, a_o) \tag{2}$$

Once the targeted prey of the other hunter is estimated, the corresponding prey for the self agent is decided by a task requirement, and a self action a_s that is associated with the highest probability is calculated using the action decision function.

$$G_s = f(s_s, s_o, \tilde{G}_o) \tag{3}$$

$$a_s = \underset{a}{\mathrm{argmax}}\, P(a|s_s, G_s) \tag{4}$$

From our intuition, the Lv.2 strategy is a one step deeper inference of the other's internal state. But its computation can be achieved by a similar computation to that of Lv.1. The difference is a use of self position s_s and action history a_s information that are assumed to be observed from the other agent view position.

$$\tilde{G}_s = \underset{G}{\mathrm{argmax}}\, P(G|s_s, a_s) \tag{5}$$

$$G_o = f(s_o, s_s, \tilde{G}_s) \tag{6}$$

$$a_s = \underset{a}{\mathrm{argmax}}\, P(a|s_s, \tilde{G}_s) \tag{7}$$

Different from the Lv.1 and Lv.2 strategy computations, the Lv.0* agent doesn't observe either of the self's or the other's action and state information. But the Lv.0* agent uses just the self action decision function to search for the most appealing, easy to estimate from others, action for the other Lv.1 agent.

$$G_s = \underset{G}{\mathrm{argmax}}\, P(G|s_s) \tag{8}$$

$$\tilde{G}_o = g(s_s, G_s) \tag{9}$$

$$a_s = \underset{a}{\mathrm{argmax}}(P(G_s|s_s, a_s) - P(\tilde{G}_o|s_s, a_s)) \tag{10}$$

4.3   Computer Simulation

4.3.1   Task1

Nagata et al. have evaluated the number of steps for all of Lv.1, Lv.2, and Lv.0 combinations in the hunter tasks, and revealed that at least one of the hunters must be Lv.1 to achieve effective task solution [6]. It suggests the effectiveness of the other's intention estimation for collaborative tasks. But when both of the hunters took the Lv.1 strategy, the step number increased because of an explosion of unexpected target change by mutual estimation of the other's target.

4.3.2   Task2

Figure 3 shows the number of average steps for a combination of Lv.0*-Lv.1 hunters in Task 2. The performance was compared to that of the Lv.2-Lv.1 combination in Task 1 (Fig. 4). Figure 4 shows the average steps for 100 initial layouts. The horizontal axis shows steps for the Lv.0*-Lv.1 combination and the vertical axis shows steps for the Lv.2-Lv.1 combination. Each point corresponds to the 100 initial layouts.

From the results, the Lv.0* agent showed more performance improvement than the Lv.2 agent in 68 cases. In some cases, we observed large improvement. The initial layouts of those cases were that both hunters were located at the same distance from both prey and it was difficult for the other agent to judge which prey the self agent was chasing if the self agent approached its target in the shortest course. In this case, the AIL strategy was quite effective. In contrast,

Strategic combination	Number of average steps
Lv0-Lv1	48.2
Lv1-Lv1	76.3
Lv2-Lv1	33.6
Lv0*-Lv1	35.2

Fig. 3. Number of average steps for each strategic combination

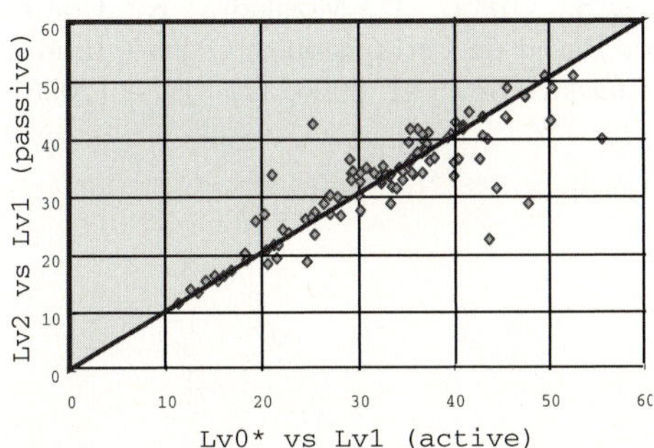

Fig. 4. Distribution of average steps in 100 initial allocations

we observed some cases where the performance degraded drastically. In these cases, the two preys were located very near and far from the hunters, and moved similarly. It was difficult for the AIL agent to take differentiable action for target identification by others.

5   Conclusion

In this study, we proposed an active intention leading (AIL) strategy for effective collaboration by agents and demonstrated that the AIL strategy is as effective as the passive intention estimation-based method with lower computational load. Though the active method was effective in many cases, we also found some cases where the active strategy was not effective. To resolve collaboration tasks that are typically represented by the hunter task, we need a choice of strategy that most fits the situation of the moment.

References

1. Sutton, R.S., Barto, A.G.: Reinforcement Learning: An Introduction. MIT Press, Cambridge (1998)
2. Ikenoue, S., Asada, M., Hosoda, K.: Cooperative behavior acquisition by asynchronous policy renewal that enables simultaneous learning in multiagent environment. In: Proceedings of the 2002 IEEE/RSJ Intl. Conference on Intelligent Robots and Systems, pp. 2728–2734 (2002)

3. Nagata, Y., Ishikawa, S., Omori, T., Morikawa, K.: Computational Model of Co-operative Behavior: Adaptive Regulation of Goals and Behavior. In: Proceeding of the Second European Cognitive Science Conference (EuroCogSci 2007), pp. 202–207 (2007)
4. Tohyama, S., Omori, T., Oka, N., Morikawa, K.: Identification and learning of other's action strategies in cooperative task. In: Proc. of 8th International Conference on Artificial Life and Robotics, pp. 40–43 (2003)
5. Ogawara, K., Sakita, K., Ikeuchi, K.: Action Support by a Robot System based on Intention Interpretation from Gaze Motion (in Japanese). In: Interaction 2005, IPSJ Symposium, pp. 103–110 (2005)
6. Nagata, Y., Ishikawa, S., Omori, T., Morikawa, K.: Computational Modeling of Cooperative Behavior Based on Estimation of Other's Intention. In: Proceedings of the 20th Annual Conference of JSAI, 2006, vol. IB4-2 (2006) (in Japanese)

Interpolation and Extrapolation of Motion Patterns in the Proto-symbol Space

Tetsunari Inamura[1,2] and Tomohiro Shibata[3]

[1] National Institute of Informatics, Tokyo, Japan
[2] The Graduate University for Advanced Studies, Kanagawa, Japan
`inamura@nii.ac.jp`,
`http://www.iir.nii.ac.jp/`
[3] Nara Institute of Science and Technology, Nara, Japan
`tom@is.naist.jp`,
`http://hawaii.naist.jp/~tom/`

Abstract. We propose a new method for interpolation and extrapolation of motion patterns in proto-symbol spaces. The proto-symbol space is a topological space which abstracts motion patterns by utilizing continuous hidden Markov models, and the mimesis model that recognizes/generates known/unknown motion patterns by using this topological space. An interpolation algorithm for the proto-symbol space has already been proposed, but it had a mathematical problem. Furthermore, extrapolation of motion patterns was not defined, and could not be calculated. In the new method, the synthesis of proto-symbols is done separately for state transition probabilities and output probabilities, and the synthesis of the state transition probabilities is done in the time domain. Experiments in a simulation environment demonstrate the feasibility of this method.

1   Introduction

Inamura *et al.* proposed the mimesis model [1] for imitation learning by humanoid robots. The mimesis model was inspired by the concept of the mirror neuron system [2][3][4] which has received a deal of attention in neuroscience. In their model, a continuous hidden Markov model (CHMM) was used to recognize, abstract and generate of motion patterns. Motion patterns were transformed into the locations of proto-symbols in a topological space, called the proto-symbol space [5], which was constructed by a non-metric multi-dimensional scaling method [6] with the distance among learned CHMMs measured by the Kullback-Leibler divergence [7]. Even unknown motion patterns was able to be modeled as a location of a proto-symbol in the proto-symbol space. Novel motion patterns were generated by synthesizing known proto-symbols. Generating such a novel motion in the proto-symbol space was easily performed by a user with the help of a user interface in which the proto-symbol space was visually presented as shown in Fig.2. The user was able to select proto-symbols and specify the internal dividing point of the proto-symbols in an intuitive way. The dividing point was then transformed into a CHMM that generated a novel motion pattern, which was then used as a rough kinematic pattern. There are several interpolation methods for motion patterns [8][9][10], but the advantage of the

M. Ishikawa et al. (Eds.): ICONIP 2007, Part II, LNCS 4985, pp. 193–202, 2008.

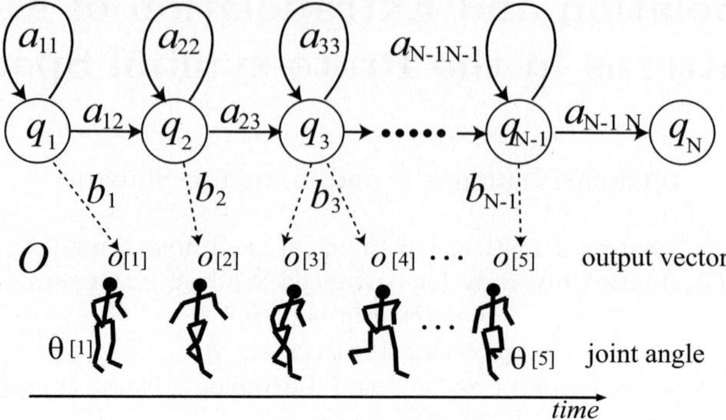

Fig. 1. Continuous hidden Markov model used in the previous work [5]

mimesis model is that not only synthesis but also recognition is possible. Interpolation can be interpreted an internal dividing point between two locations of proto-symbols, and recognition can be interpreted in a way that a given motion pattern is transformed into an internal dividing point.

There were, however, two big problems with the former mimesis model. One was the interpolation algorithm. The motion pattern generated by interpolating known proto-symbols generally became smaller compared with the original motion patterns associated with the proto-symbols. For example, when a stretching motion in which hands were held up higher than shoulders and a motion without any hand motions were interpolated, the newly synthesized hand positions were not be able to become higher than in the original stretching motion. The other problem was more critical: extrapolation could not be done. The reason is as follows. One of the target features for interpolating proto-symbols was the state transition probabilities of the CHMM. If we were to extrapolate them, the resultant state transition probabilities would often be out of the range from 0 to 1, which means they violated a basic property of probability. To synthesize a variety of motion patterns solely through the interpolation of finite motion patterns, a huge number of motion patterns must be used, and thus extrapolation of motion patterns is needed for synthesis of novel motion patterns.

The organization of this paper is as follows. In section 2, we introduce the proto-symbol space that is the outcome of the previous work, and touch on the remaining problems. Section 3 proposes new algorithms for interpolation and extrapolation. Simulation results are shown in section 4. We discuss our method and future work in section 5.

2   Proto-symbol Space for Recognition and Generation of Unknown Motion Patterns

2.1   Construction of the Proto-symbol Space

The CHMM is one of the most famous tools for recognition of time series data, especially in speech recognition research. The left-to-right model [11] is adopted as shown in Fig.1, which is also a common speech recognition model. The CHMM consists of a set of parameter $\lambda = \{Q, \pi, A, B\}$, where $Q = \{q_1, \cdots, q_N\}$ is a finite set of states, π is the initial distribution probability of state transition, $A = \{a_{ij}\}$ is a state transition probability matrix from q_i to q_j, and $B = \{b_i\}$ is a vector of output probabilities of $o[t]$ at q_i, corresponding to the joint angle vector $\theta[t]$ at a discrete time t. The CHMM can abstract and generate motion patterns, and it can also be used for generating time series data [5]. We assume that the number of state nodes N is the same over every CHMM and Left-to-Right model is used; hence the set of $\mathcal{P} = \{a_{ij}, b_i\}$ determines the behavior of the stochastic process; $\mathcal{P}$ is called a proto-symbol. The proto-symbol space is a topological space that represents the relationship between continuous motion patterns as locations of proto-symbols. The location of the proto-symbols is assigned by a multi-dimensional scaling (MDS) [6] with the distance between CHMMs measured with the Kullback-Leibler divergence [7].

2.2   Distance Between CHMMs

The Kullback-Leibler divergence between two CHMMs λ_1 and λ_2 is calculated by

$$D(\lambda_1, \lambda_2) = \frac{1}{2} \sum_i \frac{1}{T_1^i} \{\log P(O_1^i|\lambda_1) - \log P(O_1^i|\lambda_2)\}$$

$$+ \frac{1}{2} \sum_i \frac{1}{T_2^i} \{\log P(O_2^i|\lambda_2) - \log P(O_2^i|\lambda_1)\}, \tag{1}$$

where $P(O|\lambda)$ is the likelihood that is the probability of a particular output motion pattern $O = \{o[1], \cdots, o[T]\}$ from a CHMM λ. O_1^i and O_2^i are the i-th motion patterns that are learning samples for CHMM λ_1 and λ_2, respectively, and T_1^i and T_2^i are the durations of O_1^i and O_2^i, respectively [12].

The MDS accepts the distance among items and outputs the location of each item x in a Euclidean space. Let the distance between the i-th item and j-th item be f_{ij} by Eq. (1), and let the Euclidean distance between the i-th item x_i and j-th item x_j be d_{ij}. Then, the objective of the MDS is to calculate the appropriate x_i by minimizing the criterion $S^2 = \sum_{i,j}(f_{ij} - d_{ij})^2$.

x corresponds to the location of the proto-symbol in the proto-symbol space. Figure 2 shows an example proto-symbol space constructed using six categories of motion patterns.

2.3   Problems

In the previous study on the proto-symbol space [5], motion patterns were created by interpolating of the locations of the proto-symbols. More specifically, to create a new proto-symbol $\hat{\mathcal{P}} = \{\hat{a}_{ij}, \hat{b}_i\}$ whose location is a dividing point between the location of $\mathcal{P}_1 = \{a_{ij}^{(1)}, b_i^{(1)}\}$ and the location of $\mathcal{P}_2 = \{a_{ij}^{(2)}, b_i^{(2)}\}$ with fraction $(1 - \alpha) : \alpha$, the following equations were used.

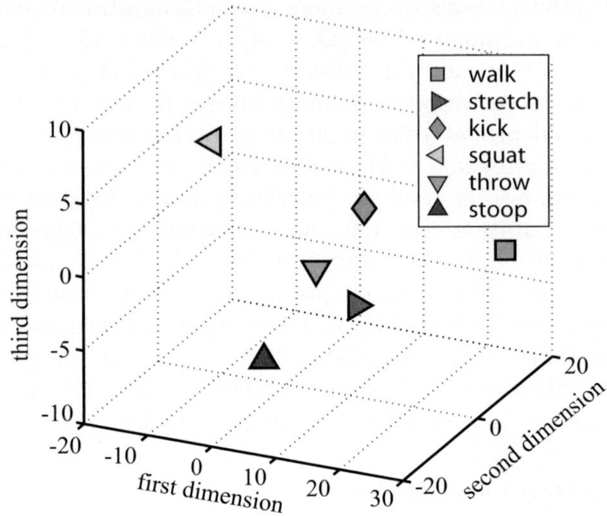

Fig. 2. An example of the proto-symbol space

$$\hat{a}_{ij} = \alpha a_{ij}^{(1)} + (1 - \alpha) a_{ij}^{(2)} \tag{2}$$

$$\hat{b}_i = \sum_{m=1}^{M} \left[\alpha c_{im}^{(1)} \mathcal{N}(\boldsymbol{\mu}_{im}^{(1)}, \boldsymbol{\sigma}_{im}^{(1)}) + (1 - \alpha) c_{im}^{(2)} \mathcal{N}(\boldsymbol{\mu}_{im}^{(2)}, \boldsymbol{\sigma}_{im}^{(2)}) \right], \tag{3}$$

where M is the number of Gaussian distributions at each node, and c_{im}, $\boldsymbol{\mu}_{im}$, and $\boldsymbol{\sigma}_{im}$ respectively indicate the mixing coefficient, mean vector and variance vector for the m-th Gaussian distribution at the i-th node. The mean of multiple stochastic generations from an HMM which uses $\{\hat{a}_{ij}, \hat{b}_i\}$ is calculated for motion generation. The whole motion generation algorithm is described in [13].

Equation (2) shows that the state transition probabilities are directly interpolated; thus its definition is mathematically vague. Moreover, it cannot be used for extrapolation. For example, a meaningless CHMM with negative state transition probabilities may be generated by extrapolating from a CHMM that has high state transition probabilities to another CHMM that has low state transition probabilities.

The reason motion patterns synthesized by interpolation generally become smaller compared with the original motion is as follows. In the previous method, interpolation of motion patterns corresponded to creation of an internal dividing point between two locations of the proto-symbols. Therefore, the coefficients in Eq. (2) and Eq. (3) were always less than 1, and the joint angles were always less than the original angles. This kind of interpolation is not sufficient for flexible motion synthesis. It is desirable to keep and synthesize joint angle values in the interpolation process.

3   New Method for Interpolation and Extrapolation of Proto-symbols

As described in the previous section, the main difficulty of the previous method for interpolation and extrapolation of proto-symbols is that the outcome did not satisfy the properties of the probability space. To overcome this difficulty, we propose a new method. There are two key aspects: One is that the state transition probabilities and the output probabilities are separately operated upon. The other is that the state transition matrices are calculated in a different domain, i.e., the time domain. Because we employ the left-to-right model, the expected stay period s_i in a state q_i can be calculated as

$$s_i = \sum_{n=1}^{\infty} n(1 - a_{ii})a_{ii}^{n-1} = \frac{1}{1 - a_{ii}}, \tag{4}$$

where a_{ii} indicates a probability that a self-transition occurs for q_i. By assuming that two CHMMs have the same the number of states, state-wise synthetic operations can be calculated, and the resulting expected stay period can then be transformed into a state transition probability.

3.1   Interpolation

Consider a motion pattern that is a interpolation of two proto-symbols $\mathcal{P}^{(1)} = \{a^{(1)}, b^{(1)}\}$ and $\mathcal{P}^{(2)} = \{a^{(2)}, b^{(2)}\}$ with a fraction $(1 - \alpha) : \alpha$ $(0 \leq \alpha \leq 1)$. To synthesize two proto-symbols, an internal dividing point that divides the line between two locations of the proto-symbols is used. The expected stay period $\hat{s}_i$ in state q_i is calculated as

$$\hat{s}_i = \alpha s_i^{(1)} + (1 - \alpha)s_i^{(2)}. \tag{5}$$

The Inverse transform from the expected stay period into the state transition probability $\hat{a}_{ii}$ in state q_i is calculated as

$$\hat{a}_{ii} = \frac{\hat{s}_i - 1}{\hat{s}_i}, \tag{6}$$

where

$$\hat{s}_i = \frac{\alpha}{1 - a_{ii}^{(1)}} + \frac{1 - \alpha}{1 - a_{ii}^{(2)}}. \tag{7}$$

Next, consider the interpolation of the output probability of proto-symbols. Here, for simplicity, we do not employ Gaussian mixture modes and use instead a single Gaussian model for the output such that an intuitive synthesis of joint angle vectors can be achieved just by using the mean and variance vectors of a Gaussian distribution.

Consequently, the interpolation process of the output probabilities is calculated as

$$\hat{\boldsymbol{\mu}}_i = \alpha \boldsymbol{\mu}_i^{(1)} + (1 - \alpha)\boldsymbol{\mu}_i^{(2)}, \tag{8}$$

$$\hat{\boldsymbol{\sigma}}_i = \alpha \boldsymbol{\sigma}_i^{(1)} + (1 - \alpha)\boldsymbol{\sigma}_i^{(2)}. \tag{9}$$

3.2 Extrapolation

Consider a proto-symbol P at an external dividing point a distance $\beta(\geq 1)$ from a proto-symbol $\mathcal{P}^{(1)} = \{a^{(1)}, b^{(1)}\}$ along a line segment passing through a proto-symbol $\mathcal{P}^{(2)} = \{a^{(2)}, b^{(2)}\}$, where the distance between P1 and P2 is defined as 1.

The State transition probability is one of the extrapolation targets. The expected stay period $\hat{s}_i$ in state q_i is calculated as

$$\hat{s}_i = (1 - \beta)s_i^{(1)} + \beta s_i^{(2)}. \tag{10}$$

Note that the condition

$$1 \leq \beta < \frac{1}{1 - \gamma} \tag{11}$$

is necessary for Eq. (10) when $s_i^{(2)} < s_i^{(1)}$ where γ is defined as

$$\gamma \equiv \frac{s_i^{(2)} - 1}{s_i^{(1)} - 1}, \tag{12}$$

because $\hat{s}_i \geq 1$ is derived from Eq. (4). Equations (11) and (12) involves that the each expected stay period is not allowed to be significantly different.

Regarding the output probability, two proto-symbols are extrapolated as follows:

$$\hat{\boldsymbol{\mu}}_i = (1 - \beta)\boldsymbol{\mu}_i^{(1)} + \beta\boldsymbol{\mu}_i^{(2)}, \tag{13}$$

$$\hat{\boldsymbol{\sigma}}_i = (1 - \beta)\boldsymbol{\sigma}_i^{(1)} + \beta\boldsymbol{\sigma}_i^{(2)}. \tag{14}$$

3.3 Generalization of Interpolation and Extrapolation

The motion pattern synthesis algorithms are essentially the same as the previous one. The only difference is whether negative coefficients are used or not. Not only synthesis using dyadic proto-symbols but also synthesis using three or more points can be easily achieved. Thus, we can derive a general algorithm to synthesize m proto-symbols $(\mathcal{P}_1, \cdots, \mathcal{P}_m)$. When mixing coefficients $c_1, \cdots, c_m$ to which negative values could be assigned are given, the expected stay period in the state q_i is calculated as

$$\hat{s}_i = \sum_{j}^{m} c_j s_i^j. \tag{15}$$

Note that the condition

$$\sum_{j}^{m} c_j \frac{1}{1 - a_{ii}^{(j)}} \geq 1 \tag{16}$$

is necessary for the coefficients c_j, because we require that $\hat{s}_i \geq 1$.

Regarding the output probability $\hat{b}$ of the synthesized proto-symbol, the mean vector $\hat{\boldsymbol{\mu}}_i$ and the variance vector $\hat{\boldsymbol{\sigma}}_i$ are calculated as

$$\hat{\boldsymbol{\mu}}_i = \sum_j^m c_j \boldsymbol{\mu}_i^{(j)}, \quad \hat{\boldsymbol{\sigma}}_i = \sum_j^m c_j \boldsymbol{\sigma}_i^{(j)}. \tag{17}$$

With the definition of the generalized synthesis, interpolation and extrapolation are able to be regarded as a particular bit of synthesis when Eq. (5) or Eq. (10) is satisfied.

4 Experiments

The experimental motion patterns corresponded to time-series data of the joint angle vectors of a human and a simulated humanoid robot. The humanoid robot has 20 degrees of freedom (DOF): 3 for each shoulder, 1 for each elbow, 3 for each leg, 1 for each knee, and 2 for each ankle. All simulations were kinematic. Using a motion capturing system, we recorded two kinds of motion patterns (punching and squatting) with a sampling time of 33 [ms] for about 3 [s]. Figures 3 and 4 show representative recorded motion patterns. These two behaviors were used in the following experiments.

4.1 Interpolation Experiment

Fig. 5 shows an example motion pattern synthesized by interpolating the punching and squatting behaviors where α was set to 0.5 described in section 3.1. Fig. 6 shows an example motion pattern by generalized synthesis where both c_1 and c_2 were set to 1.0 for the same two motion patterns by Eq. (15) to Eq. (17)). The former condition is equivalent to a condition where both c_1 and c_2 were set to 0.5 for generalized synthesis. Both figures demonstrate that our interpolation method blends the behaviors as expected. Even though the mixing rates are the same for both cases, the behavior differ in how the synthesized behavior preserves the joint amplitude of each original behavior. This fact can be easily seen in Fig. 8.

4.2 Extrapolation Experiment

Fig.7 shows an example motion pattern synthesized by extrapolating the punching and squatting behaviors using Eq. (10) to Eq. (14) with $\beta = 1.5$ (the distance between the punching and squatting behavior is 1.0). Although there was no bending motion at the pitch joint of the right leg in the original punching behavior, a warped motion exists in the extrapolated motion pattern (Fig.8, left). This motion is in the opposite direction to the squatting motion, which clearly demonstrates the effect of the extrapolation. In addition, the same effect could be observed in the left knee joint. Although the left knee stayed almost straight without any bending motion in the extrapolated motion pattern, it bent both in the original punching and squatting behaviors (Fig.8, right).

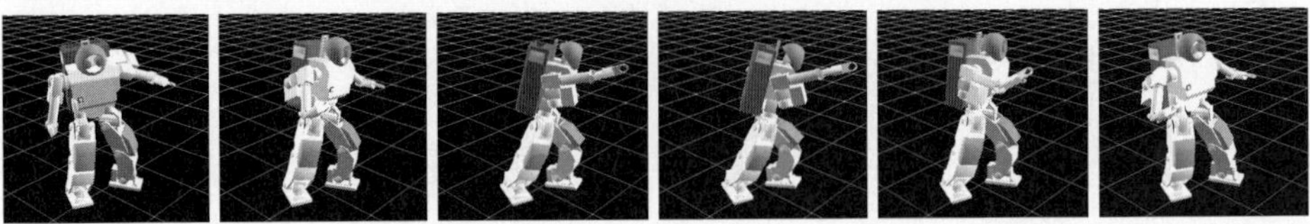

Fig. 3. Punching behavior as a known motion pattern

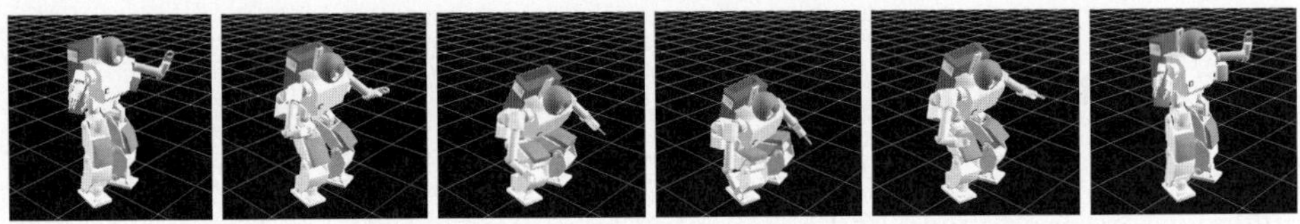

Fig. 4. Squat behavior as a known motion pattern

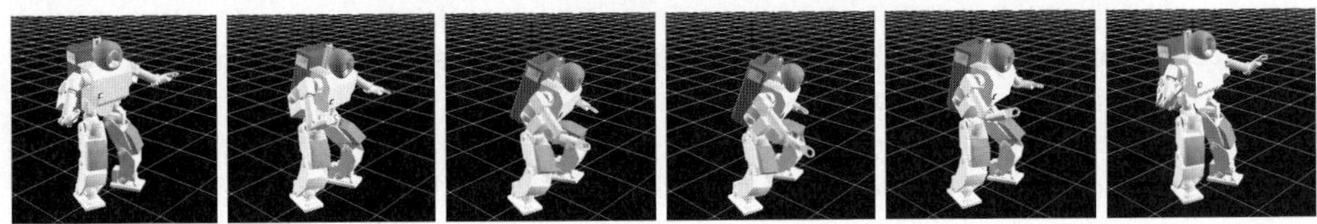

Fig. 5. Interpolation between squat and punch (mixing coefficient of each motion was 0.5)

Fig. 6. Interpolation between squat and punch (mixing coefficient of each motion was 1.0)

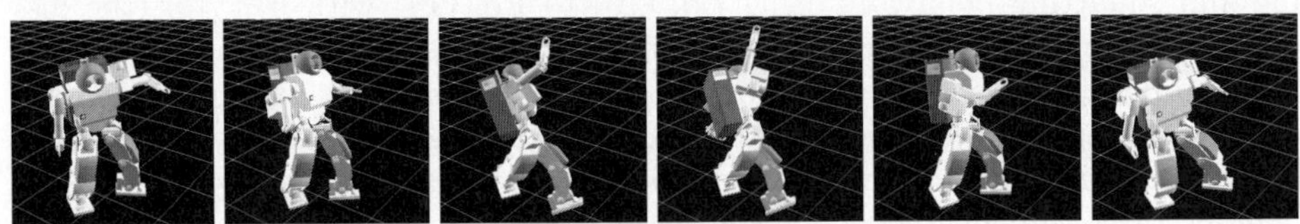

Fig. 7. Extrapolated motion pattern from squat to punch

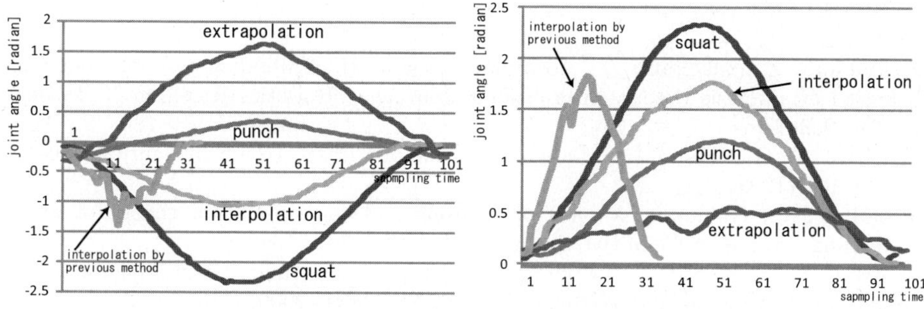

Fig. 8. Joint angle patterns of the pitch axis of right leg (left), and left knee (right)

To show the effectiveness of our method quantitatively, Fig.8 plots the time-series pattern for the pitch joint of the right leg and the left knee joint.

5   Discussion and Conclusion

The feasibility of the proposed method utilizing the expected stay period is clearly shown in Fig. 8 for the duration of the generated motion patterns. Although the duration of the motion synthesized by the previous algorithm was quite shorter than the original motions, the duration of motions synthesized by the proposed algorithm were nearly equal to the original motions. In this study, the synthesis of joint angle vectors was done by the interpolating and extrapolating the mean vector and variance vector of the output probability of proto-symbols. The following problems, however, still remained to be addressed.

Synthesis of variances: Synthesizing mean vectors of output probabilities makes sense since it corresponds to synthesizing representative joint angles. In contrast, the meaning of synthesizing the variance vectors is unclear. We need to make the proto-symbol more general to deal with not only joint angles but also other variable quantities such as joint velocity.

Component-wise synthesis of proto-symbols: The motion patterns are synthesized with Eq. (15) to Eq. (17), in which the mixing coefficients were the same for the state transition probability and the output probability. Figures 5 and 6 show an interesting difference caused by having different mixing coefficients whose mixing rates were the same. Because the state transition probability and the output probability are relevant to the period and amplitude of motion, respectively, it would be interesting to investigate what would happen if their mixing rates could be set independently.

Synthesis of the expected stay period: Equations (11) and (12) imposes that the expected stay period are not significantly different. Additionally, the number of states of each CHMM is assumed to be the same. Resolving these constraints is also our future work.

References

1. Inamura, T., Nakamura, Y., Toshima, I., Tanie, H.: Embodied symbol emergence based on mimesis theory. International Journal of Robotics Research 23(4), 363–378 (2004)
2. Rizzolatti, G., Arbib, M.A.: Language within our grasp. Trends in NeuroScience 21, 188–194 (1998)
3. Gallese, V., Goldman, A.: Mirror neurons and the simulation theory of mind-reading. Trends in Cognitive Sciences 2(12), 493–501 (1998)
4. Arbib, M.A., Billard, A., Iacoboni, M., Oztop, E.: Synthetic brain imaging: grasping, mirror neurons and imitation. Neural Networks (2000)
5. Inamura, T., Tanie, H., Nakamura, Y.: From stochastic motion generation and recognition to geometric symbol development and manipulation. In: International Conference on Humanoid Robots (2003) (CD-ROM)
6. Schiffman, S.: Introduction to Multidimensional Scaling: Theory, Methods, and Applications. Academic Press, London (1981)
7. Kullback, S.: Information Theory and Statistics. Wiley, Chichester (1959)
8. Hoshino, K.: Interpolation and extrapolation of repeated motions obtained with magnetic motion capture. IEICE Trans. Fundamentals of Electronics, Communications and Computer Sciences E87-A(9), 2401–2407 (2004)
9. Liu, C.K., Popovic, Z.: Synthesis of complex dynamic character motion from simple animations. In: SIGGRAPH, pp. 408–416 (2002)
10. Yamane, K., Kuffner, J.J., Hodgins, J.K.: Synthesizing animations of human manipulatioin tasks. ACM Transactions on Graphics 23(3), 532–539 (2004)
11. Young, S., Kershaw, D., Odell, J., Ollason, D., Valtchev, V., Woodland, P.: The HTK Book. Microsoft Corporation (2000)
12. Rabiner, L.R., Juang, B.H.: A probabilistic distance measure for hidden markov models. AT&T Technical Journal 1(64), 391–408 (1985)
13. Inamura, T., Tanie, H., Nakamura, Y.: Keyframe compression and decompression for time series data based on the continuous hidden markov model. In: Proc. of Int'l Conf. on Intelligent Robots and Systems, pp. 1487–1492 (2003)

Symbolic Memory of Motion Patterns by an Associative Memory Dynamics with Self-organizing Nonmonotonicity

Hideki Kadone and Yoshihiko Nakamura

Department of Mechano-Informatics
Graduate School of Information Science and Technology
University of Tokyo
7-3-1, Hongo, Bunkyoku, Tokyo, Japan
{kadone, nakamura}@ynl.t.u-tokyo.ac.jp

Abstract. We previously proposed a memory system of motion patterns [4] using an assotiative memory model. It forms symbolic representations of motion patterns based on correlations by utilizing bifurcations of attractors depending on the parameter of activation nonmonotonicity. But the parameter had to be chosen appropreately to some degree by manual. We propose here a way to provide the paremeter with self-organizing dynamics along with the retrieval of the associative momory. Attractors of the parameter are discrete states representing the hierarchical correlations of the stored motion patterns.

1 Introduction

Symbols are important for intelligent systems. Extracting important information from specific memories and experiences and memorizing them as abstract symbols enable one to apply the acquired information to other different situations. Based on this point of view, the authors[4] proposed a memory system for motion patterns of humanoid robots, which forms emergent abstract representations of motions and maintains the representations in abstract-specific hierarchical manner, based on the inherent global cluster structure of the motion patterns. The proposed memory system(Fig.1) consists of transforming the motion patterns into feature vectors, storing them into the connection weights by Hebb rule, and retrieval in the dynamics of the associative model parameterized by the nonmonotonicity of the activation function. Feature vectors clarify the global structure of motion patterns. Nonmonotonic associative model forms abstract representations integrating the clusters, and maintains abstract-specific hierarchy by bifurcations of attractors depending on the parameter of nonmonotonicity(Fig.2). The integrating dynamics was originally discussed by [1] and then by other researches[2],[6],[8] for sigmoid networks. In [5], the authors gave a mathematical explanation of the above nonmonotonic associative memory dynamics. However, the nonmonotonicity parameter had to be chosen appropriately to some degree by manual. We propose here a way to provide the

M. Ishikawa et al. (Eds.): ICONIP 2007, Part II, LNCS 4985, pp. 203–213, 2008.

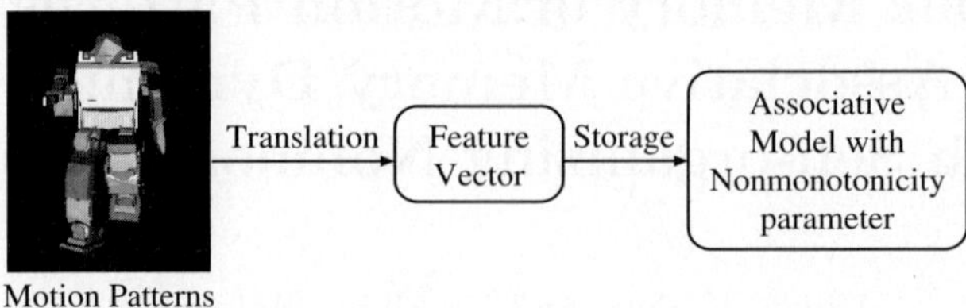

Fig. 1. Memory system for motions of humanoid robots

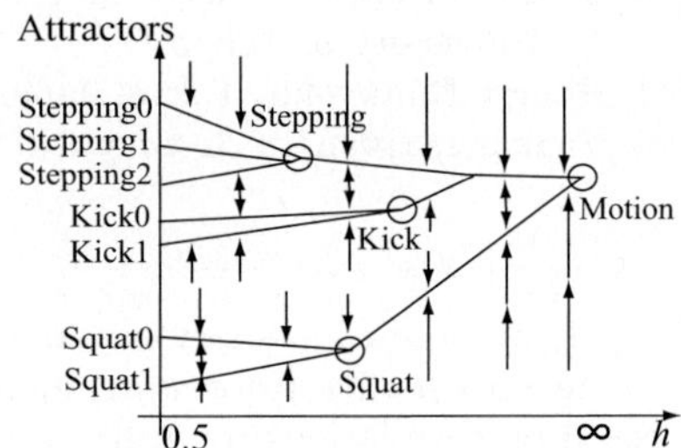

Fig. 2. Representation of hierarchy by bifurcations of attractors and basins proposed in our previous research

parameter with self-organizing dynamics along with the retrieval of the associative memory. The system automatically finds out the hierarchy of the correlations in the stored data, and forms attractors at the centers of clusters. The attractors of the nonmonotonicity parameter are discrete states representing the discrete levels of hierarchical correlations in the stored patterns. We will show the simulation results when feature vectors of motion patterns are stored, where symbolic attractors of motions and attractors of nonmonotonicity parameter are formed according to the initial values of the nonmonotonicity parameter.

There are some related researches. Okada et al.[10] proposed a model for self-organizing symbol acquisition of motions by combining Kohonen's self organizing map[7] and a polynomial dynamical system. Since Kohonen's map uses elements distributed on grids, the map is restricted in low dimensional spaces as the computational cost increases exponentially with the dimension of the map space. Sugita et al.[14] proposed a system that connects symbols and robot motions by connecting two recurrent neural networks using a parameter called parametric bias, which self-organizes to represent the connection structure. However the use of BPTT would restrict the number of neurons to small ones. Shimozaki et al.[13] proposed a model that self-organizes spatial and temporal information using nonmonotonic associative memory, where it is needed to tune the connection weights. Omori et al.[11] proposed PATON, which forms symbols as orthogonal patterns from nonorthogonal physical patterns. Oztop et al.[12] proposed HHOP, which suppresses the effects of correlations in the stored data by incorporating three body interactions between the neurons, and applied it to imitation learning by a robotic hand. These methods were not capable of representing the hierarchy of stored data by parameters.

2 Hierarchical Associative Memory with Self-organizing Nonmonotonicity

2.1 Model

We use an associative memory model in continuous space and time. N is the number of neurons, u_i is the states of each neuron, y_i is the output of each neuron, f is the activation function and g is the output function. f is the nonmonotonic function described by the following equation[9], in nonmonotonic networks.

$$f_h(u_i) = \frac{1 - \exp(-cu_i)}{1 + \exp(-cu_i)} \frac{1 + \kappa \exp(c'(|u_i| - h))}{1 + \exp(c'(|u_i| - h))} \tag{1}$$

The activation function f is parameterized by (κ, h) as shown in Fig.3 and approximates sigmoid as $\kappa \to 1$ or $h \to \infty$. Here, we fix $\kappa = -1$. h is shown to be the parameter of f, by the suffix. The output function g is a sign function.

The dynamics of the associative memory model is

$$\tau \dot{\boldsymbol{u}} = -\boldsymbol{u} + W \boldsymbol{f}_h(\boldsymbol{u}) \tag{2}$$

$$\boldsymbol{y} = \boldsymbol{g}(\boldsymbol{u}) , \tag{3}$$

where $\boldsymbol{u} \in R^N$ is the state vector composed of u_i and $\boldsymbol{y} \in R^N$ is the output vector composed of y_i. $W \in R^{N \times N}$ is the connection weight matrix and τ is the time constant. $\boldsymbol{f}_h$ and $\boldsymbol{g}$ are defined as vector functions calculating (1) and g for each element of the vector respectively.

W is determined by the simplest Hopfield type [3] covariance learning. When p storage patterns $\boldsymbol{\xi}_1, \boldsymbol{\xi}_2, \cdots, \boldsymbol{\xi}_p \in \{-1, 1\}^N$ are given,

$$W = \frac{1}{N} \sum_{\mu=1}^{p} \boldsymbol{\xi}_\mu \boldsymbol{\xi}_\mu^{\mathrm{T}} - \alpha I , \tag{4}$$

where α is a real value and I is an identity matrix.

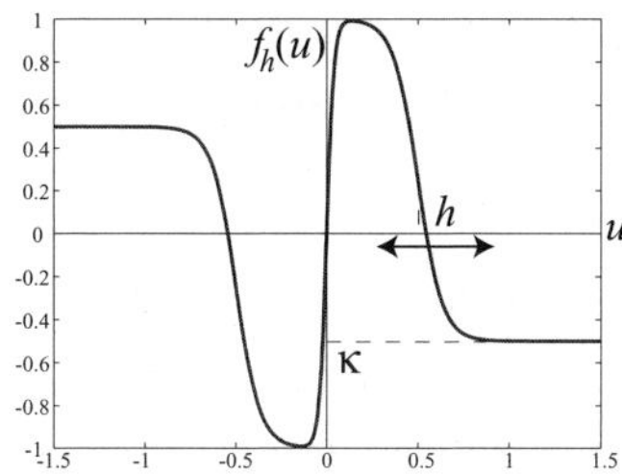

Fig. 3. Non-monotonic activation function

2.2 Hierarchically Correlated Storage Patterns and Hierarchically Bifurcating Attractors[5]

Kadone et al.[5] gave a theoretical description of the bifurcations of attractors in associative memory dynamics depending on the parameter of nonmonotonicity when storage patterns have hierarchical correlation, as an explanation of their simulations in which motion patterns are stored. We briefly summarize their results in this subsection.

Hierarchically correlated stored patterns are represented by a tree structure. Refer to Fig.6 in [5] for the image of the tree structure. Let us consider the case where a pattern at around the center of a certain cluster A in the tree structure becomes an attractor. For the storage patterns $\boldsymbol{\xi}_\mu$ and the state of neurons $\boldsymbol{u}$, a division into three is defined so as to separate the part belonging to the layer in consideration (N_a-dim), the part belonging to the upper layers (N_p-dim) and the part belonging to the lower layer (N_c-dim).

$$\boldsymbol{\xi}_\mu = [\boldsymbol{\xi}_{\mu,p}^{\mathrm{T}} \ \boldsymbol{\xi}_{\mu,a}^{\mathrm{T}} \ \boldsymbol{\xi}_{\mu,c}^{\mathrm{T}}]^{\mathrm{T}} \ , \ \boldsymbol{u} = [\boldsymbol{u}_p^{\mathrm{T}} \ \boldsymbol{u}_a^{\mathrm{T}} \ \boldsymbol{u}_c^{\mathrm{T}}]^{\mathrm{T}} \tag{5}$$

$\boldsymbol{\xi}_*^{\perp}$ is a pattern vector perpendicular to $\boldsymbol{\xi}_*$, where half of the elements of the vector is reversed. p_A is the number of storage patterns in the cluster A in consideration. With these assumptions, the following $\boldsymbol{u}^*$ is an attractor on $h \simeq \gamma^*$

$$\boldsymbol{u}^* = \begin{bmatrix} \gamma^* \boldsymbol{\xi}_{A,p} - \alpha \boldsymbol{\xi}_{A,p}^{\perp} \\ (\gamma^* - \alpha)\boldsymbol{\xi}_{A,a} \\ \gamma^* \bar{\boldsymbol{\xi}}_{A,c} - \alpha \boldsymbol{g}(\bar{\boldsymbol{\xi}}_{A,c}) \end{bmatrix} \ , \tag{6}$$

where

$$\gamma^* = (N_a + N_c O(1/\sqrt{p_A}))p_A/N \tag{7}$$

$$\bar{\boldsymbol{\xi}}_A = (1/p_A)\Sigma_{\mu \in A}\boldsymbol{\xi}_\mu \tag{8}$$

$$\boldsymbol{\xi}_{A,p} = \boldsymbol{g}(\bar{\boldsymbol{\xi}}_{A,p}) \tag{9}$$

$$\boldsymbol{\xi}_{A,a} = \boldsymbol{g}(\bar{\boldsymbol{\xi}}_{A,a}) \tag{10}$$

The output pattern on $\boldsymbol{u}^*$ is,

$$\boldsymbol{g}(\boldsymbol{u}^*) = [\boldsymbol{\xi}_{A,p}^{\mathrm{T}} \ \boldsymbol{\xi}_{A,a}^{\mathrm{T}} \ \boldsymbol{g}(\bar{\boldsymbol{\xi}}_{A,c})^{\mathrm{T}}]^{\mathrm{T}} \ , \tag{11}$$

which is at around the center of the cluster A. Also, by setting $N_c = 0, p_A = 1$, we can consider the case where the outputs from the attractors coincide with storage patterns.

2.3 Self-organizing Nonmonotonic Activation Function

In the previous subsection, we described the equilibrium points. Here, we first consider the retrieval process into the equilibrium points. In associative memory dynamics, the state is first attracted into the direction of large correlation of the storage patterns [8] with the current state, and the amplitudes of the activations become large in the subspace of large correlation. As the amplitudes of the activations become large, the output of the neurons become to be reversed by the nonmonotonic activation function. As the half number of neurons in the subspace of the large correlation are reversed, they become not to effect on the associative dynamics[5]. Then, the state is attracted into the average direction of the stored patterns in the subspace of second largest correlation with the current state, which is the direction of the center of cluster A. Therefore, by defining $\boldsymbol{u}_\gamma$ as an replacement of γ^* in the attractor (6) by a parameter γ

$$\boldsymbol{u}_\gamma = \begin{bmatrix} \gamma\boldsymbol{\xi}_{A,p} - \alpha\boldsymbol{\xi}_{A,p}^\perp \\ (\gamma - \alpha)\boldsymbol{\xi}_{A,a} \\ \gamma\bar{\boldsymbol{\xi}}_{A,c} - \alpha\boldsymbol{g}(\bar{\boldsymbol{\xi}}_{A,c}) \end{bmatrix} \, , \tag{12}$$

the state $\boldsymbol{u}$ transits from $\boldsymbol{u}(0)$ to $\boldsymbol{u}_h$, where $\gamma = h$. Next, on $\boldsymbol{u} = \boldsymbol{u}_h$, since $W\boldsymbol{f}_h(\boldsymbol{u}_h) = \boldsymbol{u}^*$ the dynamics (2) degenerates into

$$\tau\dot{\boldsymbol{u}} = -\boldsymbol{u}_h + \boldsymbol{u}^* \, , \tag{13}$$

which means that there exists a flow towards $\boldsymbol{u}^*$ on $\boldsymbol{u}_h$. Therefore, the state transits from $\boldsymbol{u}(0)$ to $\boldsymbol{u}_\gamma$ and then to $\boldsymbol{u}^*$, where $\gamma = \gamma^*$ (Fig.4). Note that it does not necessarily mean that $\boldsymbol{u}^*$ is an attractor when $h \neq \gamma^*$.

From the above discussion, we can expect a pattern at the center of the cluster A in consideration to be an attractor, by estimating γ from the state $\boldsymbol{u}$ and making h to trace γ, which would bring h from $h(0)$ to γ and then to γ^*. In $\boldsymbol{u}_\gamma$ of (12), the amplitudes of the upper two rows are about γ and the amplitudes of the lower row scatters with small order since they are the average of the subspace of the small correlations by definition. Hence we determine the estimation $\hat{\gamma}$ of γ by the following

$$\hat{\gamma} = \sigma_2 \frac{\sum_{i=1}^{N} k(u_i, \sigma_1 h)|u_i|}{\sum_{i=1}^{N} k(u_i, \sigma_1 h)} \, , \tag{14}$$

where $k(u_i, \sigma_1 h)$ is a function that gives 1 when the absolute value of u_i is larger than $\sigma_1 h$, and 0 otherwise. σ_2 is a parameter that compensates that the second row of (12) is smaller by α than γ. The dynamics of the nonmonotonicity parameter is given by the following

$$\tau\dot{h} = -h + \hat{\gamma} \, , \tag{15}$$

which evolves with the associative memory dynamics (2).

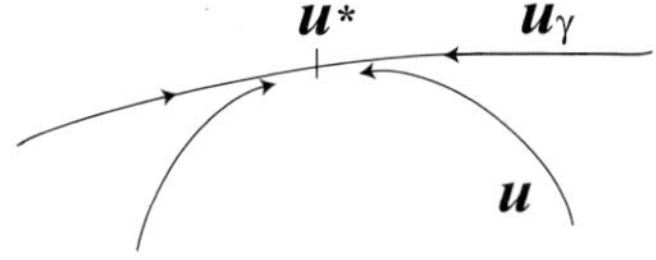

Fig. 4. Flow of the state $\boldsymbol{u}$

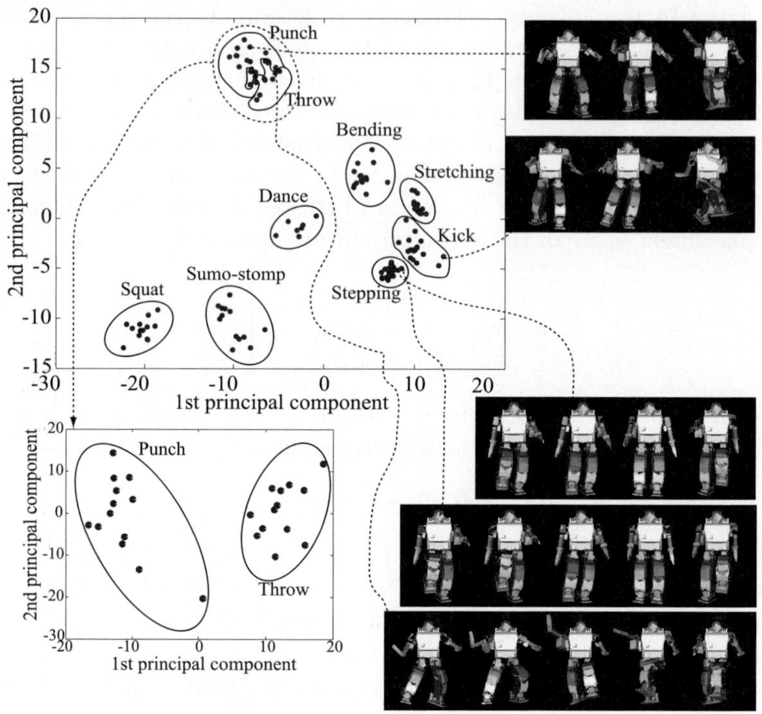

Fig. 5. Cluster structure in feature vector $\boldsymbol{m}_i$ space

3 Hierarchical Memory Integration for Motion Patterns with Self-organizing Nonmonotonicity

3.1 Feature Vectors of Motion Patterns[4]

Let $\boldsymbol{\theta}_i[k] \in R^{20}$ be the angular vector of humanoid robot motion i at time k. Motions we use are, 28 "Stepping"s, 15 "Stretching"s, 7 "Dance"s, 19 "Kick"s, 14 "Punch"s, 13 "Sumo-stomp"s, 13 "Squat"s, 13 "Throw"s, 15 "Bending"s, 137 motions in total that are obtained from motion capture. Sampling time is 0.033[ms]. Suffix i of $\boldsymbol{\theta}_i[k]$ is an index for these, for example "Stepping0".

$M_i(l) \in R^{20 \times 20}$ is an auto-correlation matrix of the time sequence of $\boldsymbol{\theta}_i[k]$,

$$M_i(l) = \frac{1}{T} \sum_{k=1}^{T} \boldsymbol{\theta}_i[k]\boldsymbol{\theta}_i^{\mathrm{T}}[k-l] \tag{16}$$

Feature vector of motion i is obtained by arranging the elements of matrix $M_i(l)$ into a column vector $\boldsymbol{m}_i(l) \in R^{400}$. Fig.5 shows the plots of $\boldsymbol{m}_i(l=2)$ by principal component analysis with some samples of motion sequences. Cluster structures can be seen clearly, except for "Punch" and "Throw". This is because

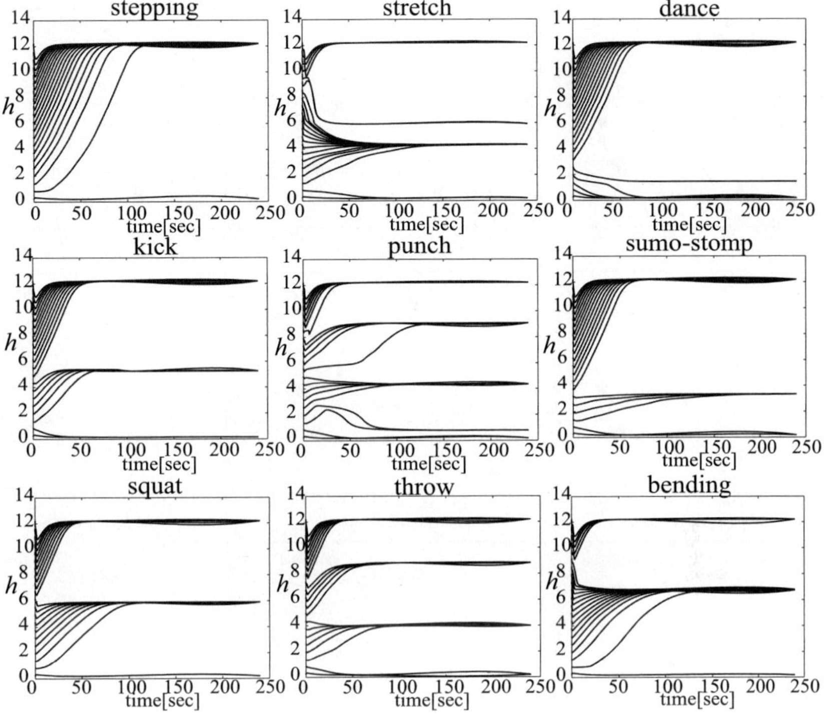

Fig. 6. Time evolution of h by (15) for representatives of each kind of motions

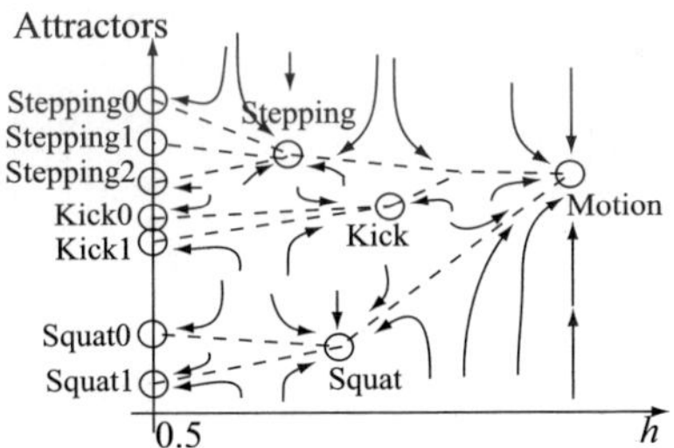

Fig. 7. Representation of hierarchy by bifurcations of attractors and basins with self-organizing nonmonotonicity, compared to Fig.2.

of executing PCA for all motions at one time. Executing PCA alone for these overlapping clusters results in clear cluster structures (Fig.5: Bottom Left).

In order to store these feature vectors into the associative networks, they are quantized into bit patterns whose elements are $\{-1, 1\}$. By quantizing $\boldsymbol{m}_i \in R^{400}$ with 10 bits for each real value, quantized pattern $\boldsymbol{\xi}_i \in \{-1, 1\}^{4000}$ is obtained. These quantized patterns have hierarchical correlations.

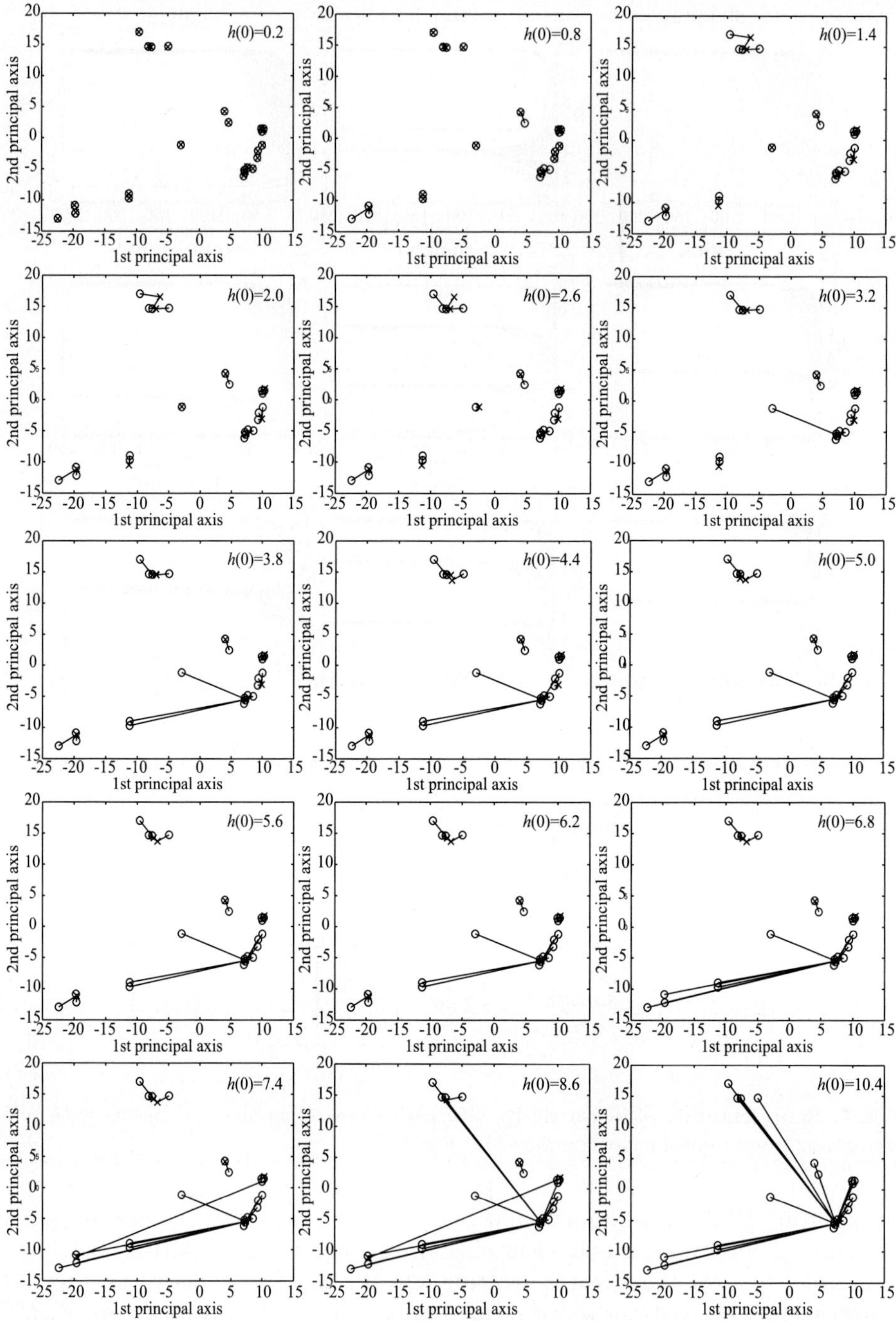

Fig. 8. Correspondences between initial states ('o') and attractors ('x') for various initial values of h, shown in the same space as Fig.5 top

3.2 Symbol Formation of Motion Patterns by Self-organizing Nonmonotonic Activation Function

The storage patterns are the quantized feature vectors of motion patterns obtained by the way described in the previous subsection. They are stored into the network by (4), and the dynamics (2)(15) are simulated to investigate the attractors. The number of neurons is $N = 4000$, the parameter of the function k of (14) is $\sigma_1 = 0.6$, and $\sigma_2 = 1.08$. σ_1 and σ_2 are chosen by some trials. Some of the storage patterns are given as the initial states of $\boldsymbol{u}$, and the initial values of h are given from 0.2 to 11.6 with the interval of 0.6. Fig.6 shows the time evolutions of h for representatives of each kind of motion. They are entrained into some discrete attractors. The time evolution of h is almost the same for the same kinds of motions. Fig.8 shows, in the same PCA space as Fig.5, the correspondences between the initial states $\boldsymbol{u}(0)$ and the attractors. Symbolic attractors are formed at $h(0) = 0.8$ for "bending" and "squat", at $h(0) = 1.4$ for "kick", "stretching", "punch", "throw" and "sumo-stomp". At larger $h(0)$s, symbolic attractors are formed that hierarchically integrates the larger clusters.

By comparing Fig.6 and Fig8, we can see correspondences between the attractors of h and the cluster integration, an image of which is shown in Fig.7. For example "kick" in Fig.6 shows three level attractors, for $h(0)$ of (0.2,0.8), (1.4,4.4) and (5.0,10.4). In Fig.8, they correspond to retrieval of the storage patterns, the symbolic patterns integrating the same kinds of motions and the symbolic pattern integrating all the patterns. Other pattens except "stepping" have similar properties. "stepping" have two attractors in Fig.6, which correspond to retrieval of the storage patterns and the symbolic pattern integrating all the patterns.

4 Conclusion

We proposed a method to automatically find out the hierarchy of the correlations in the stored data, and form attractors at the centers of clusters, by providing the parameter of nonmonotonicity with dynamics, that evolves through time along with the retrieval in the associative dynamics. This method has its base on an estimation of the nonmonotonicity utilizing the vector fields that drives the states towards the centers of clusters when larger correlations in the upper level cluster than the one in consideration is suppressed by the nonmonotonicity, during the retrieval. Storing the feature vectors of motion patterns, it forms attractors hierarchically corresponding to the storage patterns and symbols of motions, reflecting the hierarchical correlations and clusters of motion patterns, depending on the initial values and therefore attractors of the nonmonotonicity. The attractors of the nonmonotonicity parameter are discrete states representing the discrete levels of hierarchical correlations in the stored motion patterns.

Future scope can be a connection to motion generation and control mechanisms. To generate embodied symbols by our methods, we need a motion control mechanism that generates clusters of motions in some space. Another way may include storing the pairs of motion patterns and control patterns like proposed by Oztop et al.[12]. By using our neural network, we may be able to generate motions from symbolic attractors and provide interactions between symbols and bodily situations.

Acknowledgment

This research was supported by Category(S) (15100002) of Grant-in-Aid for Scientific Research, Japan Society for the Promotion of Science.

References

1. Amari, S.: Neural Theory of Association and Concept-Formation. Biological Cybernetics 26, 175–185 (1977)
2. Griniasty, M., Tsodyks, M.V., Amit, D.J.: Conversion of Temporal Correlations Between Stimuli to Spatial Correlations Between Attractors. Neural Computation 5, 1–17 (1993)
3. Hopfield, J.J.: Neural networks and physical systems with emergent collective computational abilities. Proceedings of the National Academy of Sciences of U.S.A. 79, 2554–2558 (1982)
4. Kadone, H., Nakamura, Y.: Symbolic Memory for Humanoid Robots Using Hierarchical Bifurcations of Attractors in Nonmonotonic Neural Networks. In: Proc. of the 2005 IEEE/RSJ International Conference on Intelligent Robots and Systems, pp. 2900–2905 (2005)
5. Kadone, H., Nakamura, Y.: Hierarchical Concept Formation in Associative Memory Models and its Application to Memory of Motions for Humanoid Robots. In: 2006 IEEE-RAS International Conference on Humanoid Robots (Humanoids 2006), Genoa, December 4-6, pp. 432–437 (2006)
6. Kimoto, T., Okada, M.: Mixed States on neural network with structural learning. Neural Networks 17, 103–112 (2004)
7. Kohonen, T.: Self-Organized Formation of Topologically Correct Feature Maps. Biological Cybernetics 43, 59–69 (1982)
8. Matsumoto, N., Okada, M., Sugase, Y., Yamane, S.: Neuronal Mechanisms Encoding Global-to-Fine Information in Inferior-Temporal Cortex. Journal of Computational Neuroscience 18, 85–103 (2005)
9. Morita, M.: Associative Memory with Nonmonotone Dynamics. Neural Networks 6, 115–126 (1993)
10. Okada, M., Nakamura, D., Nakamura, Y.: Self-organizing Symbol Acquisition and Motion Generation based on Dynamics-based Information Processing System. In: Proc. of the second International Workshop on Man-Machine Symbiotic Systems, pp. 219–229 (2004)
11. Omori, T., Mochizuki, A., Mizutani, K., Nishizaki, M.: Emergence of symbolic behavior from brain like memory with dynamic attention. Neural Networks 12, 1157–1172 (1999)
12. Oztop, E., Chaminade, T., Cheng, G., Kawato, M.: Imitation Bootstrapping: Experiments on a Robotic Hand. In: Proceedings of 2005 IEEE-RAS International Conference on Humanoid Robots (Humanoids 2005), pp. 189–195 (2005)

13. Shimozaki, M., Kuniyoshi, Y.: Integration of Spatial and Temporal Contexts for Action Recognition by Self Organizing Neural Networks. In: Proc. of the 2003 IEEE/RSJ International Conference on Intelligent Robots and Systems, pp. 2385–2391 (2003)
14. Sugita, Y., Tani, J.: Learning Semantic Combinatoriality from the Interaction between Linguistic and Behavioral Processes. Adaptive Behavior 13, 33–52 (2005)

From Biologically Realistic Imitation to Robot Teaching Via Human Motor Learning

Erhan Oztop[1,2], Jan Babic[2,3], Joshua Hale[1,2], Gordon Cheng[1,2],
and Mitsuo Kawato[1,2]

[1] JST, ICORP, Computational Brain Project,
4-1-8 Honcho Kawaguchi, Saitama, Japan
[2] ATR Computational Neuroscience Laboratories,
2-2-2 Hikaridai, Seika-cho, Soraku-gun Kyoto, 619-0288, Japan
[3] Jozef Stefan Institute, Department of Automation, Biocybernetics and Robotics, Jamoua 39,
1000, Ljubljana, Slovenia
{erhan, jan, jhale, gordon, kawato}@atr.jp

Abstract. Understanding mechanisms of imitation is a complex task in both human sciences and robotics. On the one hand, one can build systems that analyze observed motion, map it to their own body, and produce the motor commands to needed to achieve the inferred motion using engineering techniques. On the other hand, one can model the neural circuits involved in action observation and production in minute detail and hope that imitation will be an emergent property of the system. However if the goal is to build robots capable of skillful actions, midway solutions appear to be more appropriate. In this direction, we first introduce a conceptually biologically realistic neural network that can learn to imitate hand postures, either with the help of a teacher or by self-observation. Then we move to a paradigm we have recently proposed, where robot skill synthesis is achieved by exploiting the human capacity to learn novel control tasks.

1 Ways of Learning to Become an Imitator

In this article, we address the pragmatic nature of actions without considering their meanings, although we do not deny the fact that goal extraction and imitation with respect to such goals are important topics in robotics. A generic computational framework for imitation and its application to robotics can be found in [1, 2]. In humans, imitation has been the focus of extensive research both in developmental psychology and cognitive neuroscience [3]. An important but overlooked issue in models of human imitation is the effect of the limb to be imitated [4]. Whole body imitation, for example, poses very different challenges to the human brain compared to hand gesture imitation, because hands are visible to their operators during most actions. We argued in [5] that self-observation serves as a simple and effective means to bootstrap the ability to imitate certain actions, which we discuss next.

1.1 Imitation Through Auto-Associative Memories

(Auto-)associative memories [6] are computational models that can store and retrieve a set of patterns. The attractive point of an associative memory is that a partial

M. Ishikawa et al. (Eds.): ICONIP 2007, Part II, LNCS 4985, pp. 214–221, 2008.

representation of a stored pattern is used as the key to retrieve the whole pattern. Within this framework it is possible to postulate how imitation can be learned. When the system (a learning robot or an infant) generates motor commands the representation of this command and the sensed effects can be combined and stored in the associative memory as a single memory pattern. Then at a later time when the system is faced with a stimulus that partially matches one of the stored patterns the associated motor command can be retrieved. This motor command can be used to mimic the observed movement. This line of thought has also been explored by other researchers [7]. The *Hopfield* network [8] is a classical example of an auto-associative memory, which is composed of units that are fully interconnected. Hopfield networks do not perform well when the patterns to be stored have high overlap. Therefore, we proposed an extension of the Hopfield network, which utilized second order correlations between the memory 'bit' patterns(the Higher Order Hopfield net (HHOP)) [5, 9] and thus is less susceptible to overlapping patterns. The HHOP representation is bipolar (i.e. -1, +1). Each unit of HHOP receives input from all *products* of the other. The output of a unit (S_i) is given by $S_i = \mathrm{sgn}(\sum_{jk} w_{ijk} S_j S_k)$ where sgn(.) is the sign of its argument (sgn(0)=1 by definition).The weights are calculated with $w_{ijk} = \sum_{p} \xi_i^p \xi_j^p \xi_k^p / N$ where p runs over the patterns to be stored and ξ_k^p refers to the kth bit of the pattern p. The running of the network is asynchronous. Given initial assignments to S_i's the network is run by choosing a random unit and applying the update rule until convergence is reached. If the initial loaded pattern is close to one of the stored patterns then the network converges to that pattern.

1.2   Testing Imitation Bootstrapping

For testing the proposal of imitation through associative memory we used the Gifu Hand III (Dainichi Co. Ltd., Japan) robotic hand which consists of a thumb and four fingers. The 20 joints (16 DOFs) of the robot hand approximate the motion a human hand. The experimental environment is set up using three computers.

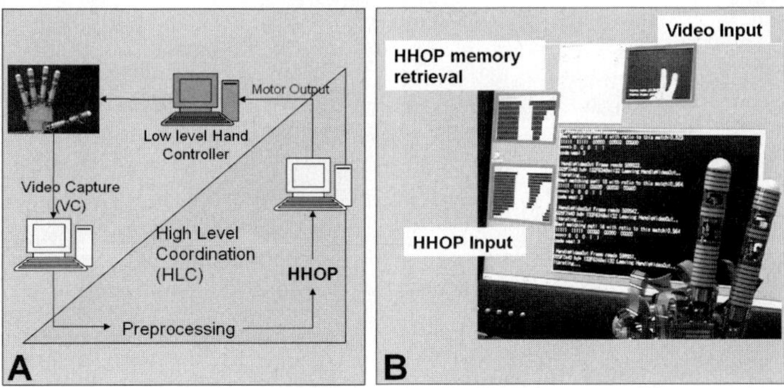

Fig. 1. (A) The general setup for realtime control of the Gifu Hand. (B) The system in imitation mode.

The video capture computer (VC) is connected to a video camera and a video capture board. The task of VC is solely to capture and send out the captured frames to the High Level Coordinator (HLC) at 30 frames/second (color 320x240 pixels/frame). HLC preprocess the incoming video and prepares the inputs for HHOP. HLC also runs the HHOP network and sends the resulting motor command to the Low Level Hand Control Server, which implements a PD servo driving the Gifu Hand to the desired postures (see Fig. 1A). To test the imitation system, we used static hand postures. To avoid extensive preprocessing the visual field was assumed to have a segmented hand image so the system saw hand postures over a black background. The input video was converted to grayscale and smoothed. The hand image was scaled to a standard size and then thresholded to obtain a binary image of the appropriate size for the HHOP network (see Fig. 1B). In this study the result of the preprocessing is directly connected to the HHOP network for a simple implementation; on the other hand, one could also use a feature based representation where one might expect a better imitation system. However, in this study the concern was not to provide a robust imitation, but rather to present a connectionist framework which may be thought of as a model for biological imitation. Therefore general pattern recognition (*i.e.,* engineering) techniques were avoided in order to maintain close parallels with biological systems.

1.3 Imitation Bootstrapping Results

We applied two types of learning. The first one corresponds to the self-observation hypothesis, where the video camera was directed at the Gifu Hand while the Gifu Hand executed motor patterns and 'watched' itself. The motor patterns and the resulting processed video images were associated using HHOP. The second type of learning corresponds to the supervised social (assisted) learning, where the Gifu Hand presented a hand posture and 'asked' the 'caregiver' to imitate it. When the set of patterns were exhausted, the HHOP associated the observed (caregiver's) hand postures with the motor patterns of the Gifu Hand. Both forms of learning resulted in an associative memory that can mediate imitation (see Fig. 2). The imitation with assisted learning was more robust to variations in the demonstrator's hand shapes. This

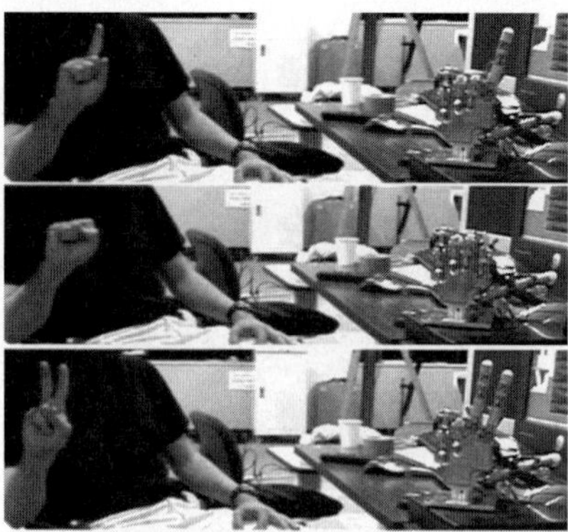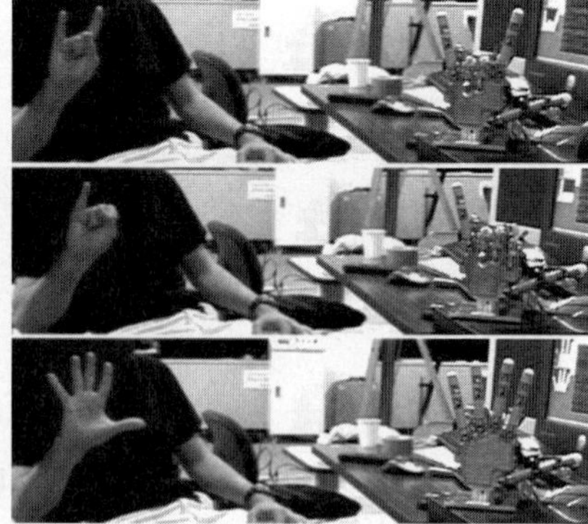

Fig. 2. Imitation of a selection of hand postures. The system became an imitator by self-observation and Hebbian-like association (adapted from [adapted from 5]).

was expected since self-observation relied only on the vision of the robot hand. Since the human and the robot fingers have different geometry, the response to human fingers is presumably less than it would be for say, a robot demonstrator. For a more detailed analysis of the results readers are referred to [5].

This experiment demonstrates how imitative abilities can be bootstrapped using biologically plausible computational structures. The future work must address the scalability of the system in terms of action complexity and the total number of actions to be imitated.

2 Human Motor Learning for Robot Training

Human motor learning ability is unprecedented, not only in controlling body parts but external tools as well. Using a computer mouse, driving a car, and snowboarding are clear examples. The cortical representation of one's body is generally referred as the *body schema*. Accumulating evidence suggests that the body schema is very plastic and subsumes the tools that one uses to manipulate the environment [10, 11]. Motivated by this line of thought, we have proposed the notion that robot skills can be acquired if the robot can be integrated into the body schema. To realize this goal, the robot was interfaced with a human subject so that this human could operate the robot as a novel tool. Importantly, the feedback from the robot is sent back to the human in a form such that motor learning can be performed with little conscious effort. In what follows, we present two on-going projects where robot skills are acquired using the paradigm introduced here.

2.1 Ball Swapping Task

The ball swapping task was defined as the manipulation of two balls (Chinese healing/health balls) such that the initial positions of the balls are swapped as in illustrated in Fig.3.After a short period of practice, this rotation of the so-called Chinese healing/health balls becomes an easy task for humans. Usually the task can be executed at 1-2.5 Hz depending on experience, often requiring palm and thumb articulation.

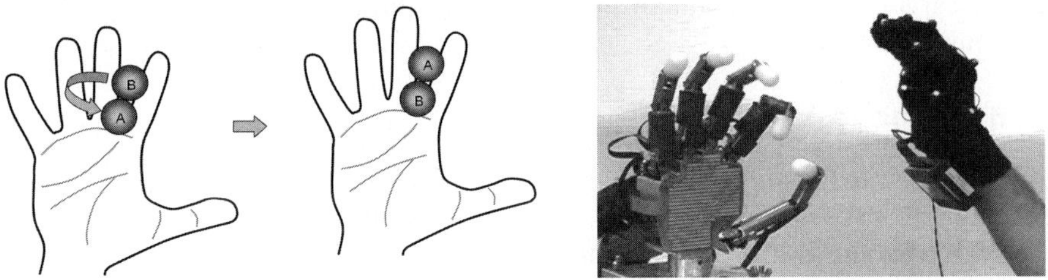

Fig. 3. The ball swapping task consists of finger movements for swapping the position of the balls without dropping them (Left). An instance of the real-time robot control via motion capture is shown (Right) (adapted from [17]).

At the outset it was not possible to predict whether the task could be completed with the robotic hand we have introduced above (the Gifu Hand). The real-time control of the robotic hand by the human operator was achieved using an active-marker motion-capture system (Visualeyez -PhoeniX Technologies Inc.).

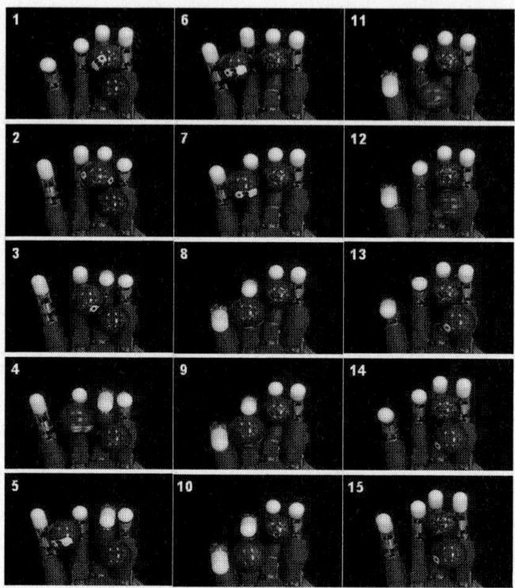

Fig. 4. Frames illustrating the ball swapping task performed by the robot hand using the skill transferred from the human performance. (adapted from [12])

The key factor here is that the control of the hand was achieved by motion capturing human finger movements, enabling transparent control of the robot hand. The subjects could control the robot hand as if it were their own. This suggested that the robot hand is subsumed in the body schema of the operator. After this stage, a human subject was asked to operate the robot hand in order to complete one cycle of the ball swapping task. This was not easy to learn, as the feedback provided to the subject was only visual, despite the task being at large a tactile manipulation task. However a week of training (2 hours per day) was enough for the subject to obtain a robust ball swapping trajectory as shown in Fig. 4. The details of the implementation and the subject learning can be found in [12]. We next present a more ambitious project within this framework.

2.2 Balancing Task

In autonomous humanoid robot applications balancing is crucial. While the robot is performing a task with say, its arms and hands, it has to simultaneously keep its balance. Balancing is therefore an integral part of a humanoid control system. To demonstrate that human learning is an effective tool for robotics research, we consider balancing as a target task to be learned. Typically, human to robot motion transfer is achieved by capturing human motion data and, after certain manipulations, playing it back on the robot. This can be understood as an open loop approach as shown on the left panel of Fig. 5, where, in order to keep the robot balanced the motion of the human is passed through a fixed transformation and sent to the robot. As this is a dynamic task and the human subject does not have any feedback information from the robot, possibly the visual appearance of the robot, it is a difficult task to learn. Rather than asking subjects to learn this task, researchers often work on tuning the transformation applied to the human motion data.

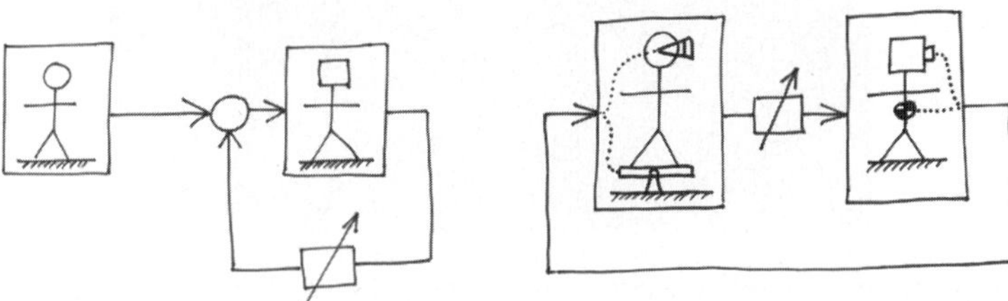

Fig. 5. Left: a typical way of using human motion to synthesize a robot behavior can be considered as an open loop system. Right: the new paradigm we propose considers the human as a part of the main control loop.

The paradigm we are proposing can be considered as a closed loop approach where the human subject is included in the main control loop as shown on the right panel of Fig. 5. In effect the human acts as the adaptive component of the control system. While controlling the robot, the (partial) state of the robot is fed back to the human subject. Visual feedback consists of feeding the robot's visual field to the eyes of the human operator. The dynamics of the center-of-mass of the robot is fed back to the operator by controlling the orientation of the platform the subject is standing on. We are content that humans will be able to balance the robot within this framework. This balancing performance can therefore be used to *learn* a transformation that will mimic human's control policy such that the center-of-mass feedback will become negligible, meaning that the platform will stay more or less flat, even though the subject makes actions that would change the center-of-mass of the robot as it will be compensated by the learned transformation.

2.2.1 The Pilot Experiment

For testing the proposed paradigm, we have set up a simplified version of the balancing task described above. In particular, the feedback to the subject was restricted to vision and the controlled robot was simulated. As with the ball swapping task, real-time motion capture was used to control the robot/simulator. The feedback was provided as a 2D representation of the support polygon and the projection of the center-of-mass of the simulated robot onto the floor. The task of the human subject was to keep the center-of-mass in the support polygon (see Fig. 6).

The information regarding the support polygon and the center-of-mass was calculated within a humanoid-robot software-platform that we have developed [13]. The platform provides a software-level interface to various data structures which organizes sensing information, provides access to automatically computed variables such as center-of-mass locations, Jacobian matrices, and force measurements.

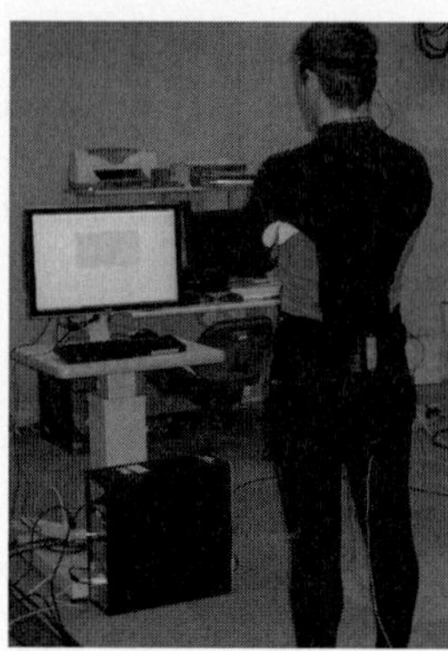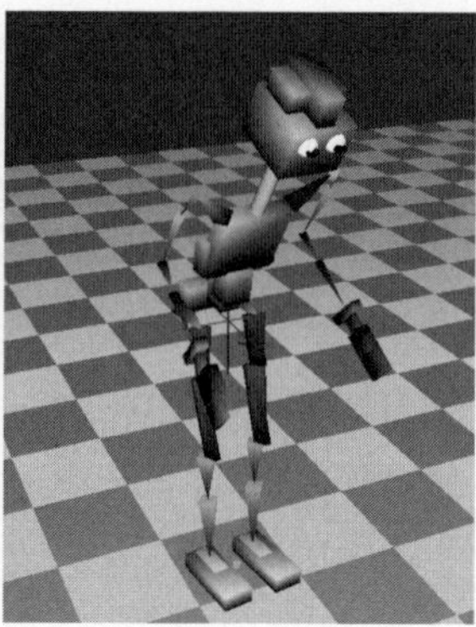

Fig. 6. On the left a session from the pilot experiment is shown. The subject is asked to perform various actions (*e.g.,* squatting) while keeping the center-of-mass of the robot (indicated as a dot on the screen) in the support polygon of the robot (shown as the green polygonal area on the screen). On the right, the humanoid robot simulation provided by the humanoid-robot software platform is shown. The movement of the subject is transferred to the robot as a set of desired joint angles. The simulator runs a PD-control servo and simulates the dynamics of the robot. It computes the center-of-mass and the information related to the support of the robot by its feet. This information is then fed back to the human as a dot and polygon drawn on the display in front of the subject.

For the dynamic balancing task, the robot control software accepted target joint angles over a network interface, and provided these to the actual robot or to the robot simulator. The feedback that we provided to the human subject in the pilot study was the location of the robot's center of mass projected onto the floor and the area occupied by the robot's feet, which was computed by the humanoid-robot software platform.

Using this simplified experimental setup, human subjects were able to control the simulation of an actual human-sized humanoid robot [13] and a small scale humanoid robot (Hoap 2, Fujitsu Automation) using real-time motion-capture based control and the visual display feedback (see Figure 6). In a few hours the subject was able to keep the simulated robot balanced while performing a number of basic motions including standing, squatting and reaching. For the subject this task was easier and much faster to learn compared to the ball swapping task because, the task did not require dynamics, i.e. the subject could perform the required tasks slowly in a statically stable way. Current work is addressing more complex motions and testing the system on the real robot.

3 Conclusion

In this article, we have reviewed how imitation ability can be bootstrapped within the framework of auto-associative memories. The approach avoided pure engineering approaches and detailed neural modeling, but instead proposed the auto-associative memory approach as a mid-way solution to imitation learning. The HHOP network used was a connectionist architecture with a Hebbian-type adaptation rule. So, it can be considered as a biologically plausible model of imitation, which at the same time can be implemented on robotic platforms.

The relationship between brain and robotics is reciprocal as we demonstrated through two studies utilizing human motor learning. The first study showed how dexterous hand manipulation can be achieved for a robot hand, and the second study, although currently at a pilot stage, indicates that a balance controller for a full body humanoid robot can be obtained within the same framework. Brain-machine interface (BMI) is a new and fast growing research area of (biomedical) robotics. In BMI framework signals recorded from subjects' brain activity are processed and converted into control signals that are sent to artificial devices. The latter two projects outlined, could be considered as 'soft' brain-machine interfacing as the signals from the brain (neural representations of the feedback sensed by the subject) are converted to control signals by the subject so to move the external device (robot) to fulfill a desired goal. Therefore our study should benefit to and from BMI research.

Acknowledgments. This work was supported by JST-ICORP Computational Brain Project.

References

1. Schaal, S., Ijspeert, A., Billard, A.: Computational approaches to motor learning by imitation. Philos. Trans. R Soc. Lond. B Biol. Sci. 358(1431), 537–547 (2003)
2. Billard, A., Epars, Y., Calinon, S., Schaal, S., Cheng, G.: Discovering optimal imitation strategies. Robotics and Autonomous Systems 47(2-3), 69–77 (2004)
3. Meltzoff, A.N., Decety, J.: What imitation tells us about social cognition: a rapprochement between developmental psychology and cognitive neuroscience. Philos. Trans. R Soc. Lond. B Biol. Sci. 358(1431), 491–500 (2003)
4. Chaminade, T., Meltzoff, A.N., Decety, J.: An fMRI study of imitation: action representation and body schema. Neuropsychologia 43(1), 115–127 (2005)
5. Oztop, E., Chaminade, T., Cheng, G., Kawato, M.: Imitation Bootstrapping: Experiments on a Robotic Hand. In: IEEE-RAS International Conference on Humanoid Robots, Tsukuba, Japan (2005)
6. Hassoun, M.: Associative Neural Memories: Theory and Implementation. Oxford University Press, Oxford (1993)
7. Kuniyoshi, Y., Yorozu, Y., Inaba, M., Inoue, H.: From Visuo-Motor Self Learning to Early Imitation - A Neural Architecture for Humanoid Learning. In: International Conference on Robotics & Automation, IEEE, Taipei, Taiwan (2003)
8. Hopfield, J.J.: Neural networks and physical systems with emergent collective computational abilities. Proc. Natl. Acad. Sci. USA 79(8), 2554–2558 (1982)
9. Oztop, E.: A New Content Addresable Memory Model Utilizing High Order Neurons, in Computer Engineering, Master Thesis, Middle East Technical University, Ankara (1996)
10. Iriki, A., Tanaka, M., Iwamura, Y.: Coding of modified body schema during tool use by macaque postcentral neurones. Neuroreport 7(14), 2325–2330 (1996)
11. Obayashi, S., Suhara, T., Kawabe, K., Okauchi, T., Maeda, J., Akine, Y., Onoe, H., Iriki, A.: Functional brain mapping of monkey tool use. Neuroimage 14(4), 853–861 (2001)
12. Oztop, E., Lin, L.H., Kawato, M., Cheng, G.: Extensive Human Training for Robot Skill Synthesis: Validation on a Robotic Hand. In: IEEE International Conference on Robotics and Automation, Roma, Italy (2007)
13. Cheng, G., Hyon, S., Morimoto, J., Ude, A., Jacobsen, S.: CB: A humanoid research platform for exploring neuroscience. In: IEEE-RAS International Conference on Humanoid Robots, Genova, Italy (2006)

Vowel Imitation Using Vocal Tract Model and Recurrent Neural Network

Hisashi Kanda, Tetsuya Ogata, Kazunori Komatani, and Hiroshi G. Okuno

Graduate School of Informatics, Kyoto University,
Engineering Building #10, Sakyo, Kyoto 606-8501, Japan
{hkanda, ogata, komatani, okuno}@kuis.kyoto-u.ac.jp,
http://winnie.kuis.kyoto-u.ac.jp/index-e.html

Abstract. A vocal imitation system was developed using a computational model that supports the *motor theory of speech perception*. A critical problem in vocal imitation is how to generate speech sounds produced by adults, whose vocal tracts have physical properties (i.e., articulatory motions) differing from those of infants' vocal tracts. To solve this problem, a model based on the *motor theory of speech perception*, was constructed. Applying this model enables the vocal imitation system to estimate articulatory motions for unexperienced speech sounds that have not actually been generated by the system. The system was implemented by using Recurrent Neural Network with Parametric Bias (RNNPB) and a physical vocal tract model, called Maeda model. Experimental results demonstrated that the system was sufficiently robust with respect to individual differences in speech sounds and could imitate unexperienced vowel sounds.

1   Introduction

Our final goal is to clarify the development process in the early-speech period of human infants. In this paper, we mainly focus on their vowel imitation using computational model that supports the *motor theory of speech perception*. The target are primitive utterances such as cooing[1] or babbling[2] before infants utter first words.

Human infants can acquire spoken language through vocal imitation of their parents. Despite their immature bodies, they can imitate their parents' speech sounds by generating those sounds repeatedly by trial and error. This is closely related to the cognitive development. Recently, many researchers have designed robots that duplicate the imitation process of human infants in terms of the constructive approach.

Typical methods of vocal imitation using vocal tract models first segment speech signals into multiple units of phonemes and then learn the corresponding vocal tracts shapes. To imitate a target signal, these fixed units are concatenated in an appropriate order. Therefore, it is necessary to interpolate adjacent units that are individually learned. This does not, however, reflect the articulatory mechanism of humans. Articulatory motions for the same phoneme are dynamically changed according to the context of continuous speech (e.g. coarticulation). This effect derives from a physical constraint

---

[1] The murmuring sound of a dove or a sound resembling it.
[2] A meaningless confusion of words or sounds.

M. Ishikawa et al. (Eds.): ICONIP 2007, Part II, LNCS 4985, pp. 222–232, 2008.

that articulatory motions should be continuous. Therefore, we should reflect this constraint in vocal imitation.

In this study, we propose a speech imitation model based on the *motor theory of speech perception* [1], which was developed to explain why speech sound (in the form of phonemes) is characterized by motor articulation information. The model captures sounds not as a set of phonemes but as temporal dynamics. To apply this model, we use Recurrent Neural Network with Parametric Bias (RNNPB) [2] and an anatomic vocal tract model, called Maeda model, to recreate physical constraints. There are other learning and generating models, for example, HMM, etc. However, these models require the adequate design of structure preliminarily and huge amounts of data for learning.

In the remainder of this paper, section 2 introduces the *motor theory of speech perception*. Section 3 describes the vocal tract model and RNN model used as the learning method. Section 4 describes our imitation model and system. Section 5 gives the results of some experiments with our proposed method. Section 6 discusses the adequacy and generalization capabilities of our system as an imitation model, and section 7 concludes the paper.

2   Motor Theory of Speech Perception

In this section, we describe the *motor theory of speech perception* with consideration of the association between speech perception and production in speech communication.

Speech is formed by complex cooperative action of the articulatory organs transforming a sequence of discrete phonetic units into continuous sounds. As a result, speech has a complicated configuration, and no acoustic invariants corresponding with phonemes have ever been found [3]. Nevertheless, human beings can hear the intended phonetic gestures of a speaker. The *motor theory of speech perception* was proposed as an answer to this question. This theory insists on the following two propositions.

1. Speech perception is active processing for the listener, and there is a special sensory mechanism for speech sound, called "speech mode."
2. Speech perception is executed through the speech production process.

In other words, we can make sense out of what we hear because we guess how the sounds are produced. Although this motor theory has been controversial, recent neuro-imaging studies seem to support the idea of perception as an active process involving motor cognition [4, 5].

Starting from the *motor theory of speech perception*, we propose that the motor information in speech, which enables the recovery of articulatory motions, enables the vocal imitation required for infants to learn spoken vocabulary. This function is essential for subsequent processes such as word identification.

3   Vocal Imitation System

3.1   Overview of Our Imitation Process

In this section, we present an overview of our system imitating the sound of a human voice. As illustrated in Fig. 1, our imitation process consists of three phases: learning, association, and generation. The system executes the following tasks.

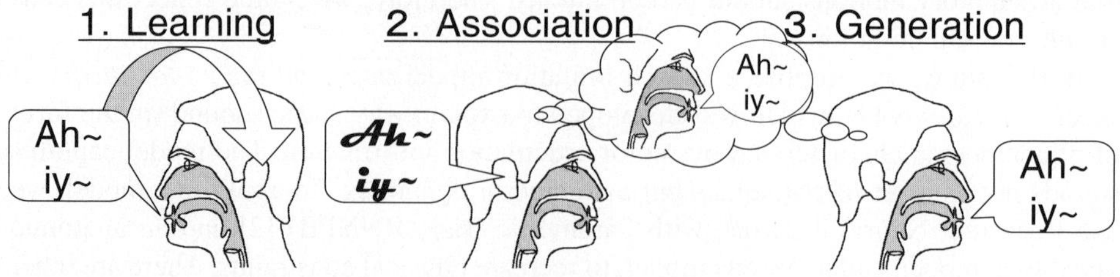

Fig. 1. Imitation process

1. Learning (Babbling)
   The vowel imitation system make articulatory motions to produce sounds, and it acquires the mapping between motions and sounds. This phase corresponds to babbling in infants.
2. Association (Hearing parents' speech sounds)
   In this phase, a speech sound is input to the system. The system associates the sounds with an articulation producing the same dynamics as the heard sound.
3. Generation (Vocally imitating heard sounds)
   Finally, the system use the articulatory motion to produce a imitation speech sound.

In this process, one problem is how to get an appropriate articulation from a speech sound input. We need a method of connecting an articulatory motion with the corresponding sound dynamics. To solve this problem, we use the method proposed by Yokoya et al. [6], which connects a robot motion with an object motion via RNNPB, to connect articulatory motions with sound dynamics.

3.2 Physical Vocal Tract Model

A speech production model simulating the human vocal tract system incorporates the physical constraints of the vocal tract mechanism. The parameters of the vocal tract with physical constraints are better for continuous speech synthesis than acoustic parameters such as the sound spectrum. This is because the temporal change of the vocal tract parameters is continuous and smooth, while that of the acoustic parameters is complex, and it is difficult to interpolate the latter parameters between phonemes.

In this study, we use the vocal tract model proposed by Maeda [7]. This model has seven parameters determining the vocal tract shape (Jaw position, Tongue dorsal position, Tongue dorsal shape, Tongue tip position, Lip opening, Lip protrusion and Larynx position), which were derived by principal components analysis of cineradiographic and labiofilm data from French speakers. Although there are other speech production models, such as PARCOR [8] and STRAIGHT [9], we think that Maeda model, with physical constraints based on anatomical findings, is the most appropriate, because of our aim to simulate the development process of infants' speech.

Each Maeda parameter takes on a real value between -3 and 3 and may be regarded as a coefficient weighting an eigenvector. The sum of these weighted eigenvectors is a vector of points in the midsagittal plane, which defines the outline of the vocal tract shape. The resulting vocal tract shape is transformed into an area function, which is

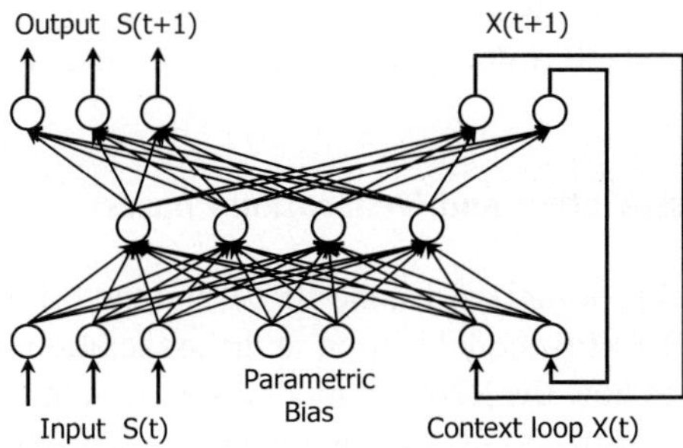

Fig. 2. RNNPB model

then processed to obtain the acoustic output and spectral properties of the vocal tract during speech.

3.3   Learning Algorithm

This subsection describes a method that enables our imitation model to learn temporal sequence dynamics. For this method, we apply the FF-model (forwarding forward model) proposed by Tani [2], which is also called RNN with Parametric Bias (RNNPB).

RNNPB model. The RNNPB model has the same architecture as the Jordan-type RNN model [10], except for the PB nodes in the input layer. Unlike the other input nodes, those PB nodes take a constant value throughout each time sequence. Figure 2 shows the network configuration of the RNNPB model. The RNNPB model works as a prediction system: its input data is current sensory state $S(t)$ and its output data is predicted sensory state $S(t+1)$ in the next step. The context layer has a loop that inputs current output as input data in the next step.

After learning time sequences using the back propagation through time (BPTT) algorithm [11], the RNNPB model self-organizes the PB values at which the specific properties of each individual time sequence are encoded. As a result, the RNNPB model self-organizes a mapping between the PB values and the time sequences. In our study, input data $S(t)$ are articulatory and sound parameters in time t, and one pair of the PB values represents a time sequence of an articulatory motion and sound by the motion.

Learning of PB Vectors. The learning algorithm for the PB vectors is a variant of the BPTT algorithm. The length of each sequence is denoted by T. For each of the articulatory parameters outputs, the backpropagated errors with respect to the PB nodes are accumulated and used to update the PB values. The update equations for the ith unit of the parametric bias at t in the sequence are as follows:

$$\delta\rho_i = \varepsilon \cdot \sum_{t=0}^{T} \delta_i(t), \tag{1}$$

$$p_i = sigmoid(\rho_i), \tag{2}$$

where ε is a coefficient. In Eq. 1, the δ force for updating the internal values of the PB p_i is obtained from the summation of the delta error δ_i. The delta error δ_i is backpropagated from the output nodes to the PB nodes: it is integrated over the period from the 0 to T steps. Then, the current PB values are obtained from the sigmoidal outputs of the internal values.

3.4   Calculation in Association and Generation Phases

After the RNNPB model is organized via the BPTT and the PB values are calculated in the learning phase, the RNNPB model is used in the association and generation phases. This subsection describes how the RNNPB model is used in the latter two phases.

The association phase corresponds to how infants recognize the sound presented by parents, i.e., to how the PB values are obtained. The PB values are calculated from Eq. 1 and 2 by the organized RNNPB without updating the connection weights. At this point, however, there is no vocal tract data because the system is only hearing sounds without articulating them, unlike in the learning phase. The initial vocal tract values (all zero in this paper) are input to the motion input layer in step 0, and the outputs are calculated forward in the closed-loop mode from step 1. More generally, the outputs in the motion output layer in step $t - 1$ are the input data in the motion input layer in step t. Put simply, the motion input layer plays the same role as the context layer does.

The sound generation phase corresponds to what articulation values are calculated. The motion output of the RNNPB model is obtained in a forward calculation without updating the connection weights. The PB values obtained in the association phase are input to the RNNPB in each step.

4   Model and System

4.1   Experimental System

In this subsection, we describe our experimental system, which is illustrated Fig.3. This system model was used to verify the relation between vocal imitation and the phoneme acquisition process according to the *motor theory of speech perception*. To simplify the system, we purposely used a simple vocal tract model and target vowel sound imitation.

In the learning phase, several articulatory motions are put into Maeda model, and learn temporal sequence dynamics of an articulatory motion and the speech sound for the motion by RNNPB. We first decide arbitrarily motion parameters: initial values of each motion parameters are all zero, and we produce sequences of vocal tract parameters by interpolating some vowel parameters, which are already known. Second, the sequences are put into Maeda model to produce the corresponding sounds, which are then transformed into temporal sound parameters. Finally, the RNNPB learns each set of the vocal tract and sound parameters, which are normalized and synchronized. The size of the RNNPB model and the time interval of the sequence data differed according to the experiment. In the association phase, speech sound data are put into the system. The corresponding PB values are calculated for the given sound sequence by the organized RNNPB to associate the articulatory motion for the sound data. In the generation phase, the system generates these imitation sounds by inputting the PB values obtained in the association phase into the organized RNNPB.

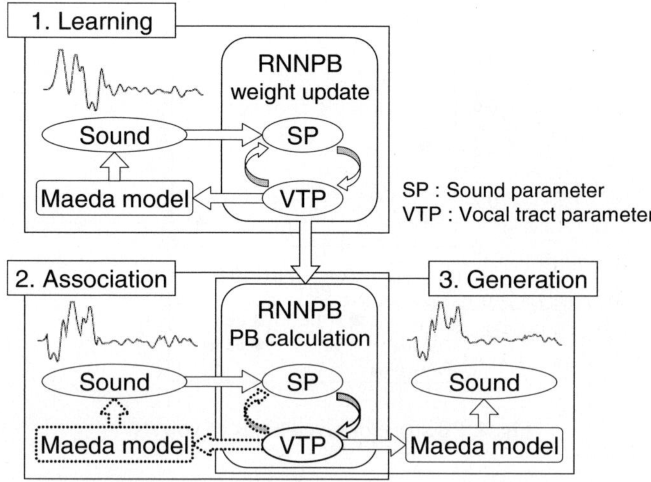

Fig. 3. Diagram of the experimental system

4.2 Sound Parameters

To convert a speech waveform into feature parameters, we use the Mel-Frequency Cepstrum Coefficient (MFCC), which is based on the known frequency variation of the human ear's critical bandwidths. Filters spaced linearly at low frequencies and logarithmically at high frequencies capture the phonetically important characteristics of speech.

In the experiments, the speech signals were single channel, with a sampling frequency 10kHz. They were analyzed using a Hamming window with a 40-ms frame length and a 17-ms frame shift, forming five-dimensional MFCC feature vectors. The number of mel filterbanks was 24. In addition, Cepstrum Mean Subtraction (CMS) [12] was applied to reduce linear channel effects.

4.3 Vocal Tract Parameter

In the experiments, we applied Maeda model - with six parameters except for Larynx position. When Maeda model produces vowel sounds, the seventh parameter has a steady value. In the generation phase, it is possible for the vocal tract parameters produced by the RNNPB to temporally fluctuate without human physical constraints. This occurs if the system does not easily associate the articulation for an unexperienced sound. Therefore, to help prevent extraordinary articulation, we execute temporal smoothing of the vocal tract parameters produced by the RNNPB. Concretely, the vocal tract parameters in each step are calculated by averaging those of the adjacent steps.

5 Experiments

5.1 Learning of Intermediate Vowel Sounds

First, we carried out this experiment to confirm how our system deal with intermediate vowel sounds. For the experiment, RNNPB was organized on the following conditions:

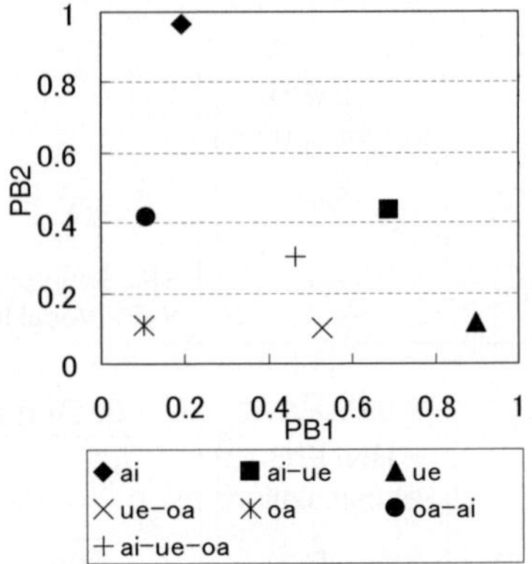

Fig. 4. PB space of seven kinds of vowels

the input and output layers had 11 units, the hidden layer had 20 units, the context layer had 10 units, and the PB layer had two units. The learning data consisted of three kinds vowel sounds: $/ai/$, $/ue/$, $/oa/$, and four kinds of intermediate vowels of the three: $/ai-ue/$, $/ue-oa/$, $/oa-ai/$, $/ai-ue-oa/$ (380 ms, 20 ms/step).

Figure 4 shows the resulting PB space, consisting of seven learned sounds. The result shows that the PB values of intermediate vowels were mapped between each original vowel combinations, and that the organized RNNPB got topological structure for Maeda model.

5.2   Model Verification by Two Continuous Vowels

Second, we carried out this experiment to verify the adequacy of our system by comparing the use of sound and articulatory information with the use of only sound information.

For the experiment, we organized two RNNPBs. One, called RNNPB–1, learned only the MFCC parameters as sound information. The input and output layers had five units, the hidden layer had 20 units, the context layer had 10 units, and the PB layer had two units. The other, called RNNPB–2, learned both the MFCC and vocal tract parameters as sound and articulatory information. The input and output layers had 11 units, the hidden layer had 20 units, the context layer had 15 units, and the PB layer had two units. The hierarchical structure of the two of RNNPBs were made a heuristic decision on as their learning performance were best. Because a mere increase of the number of whole units can not always improve RNNPB's generalization capability. The learning data consisted of the following vowels: $/ai/$, $/iu/$, $/ue/$, $/eo/$, and $/oa/$ (380 ms, 20 ms/step), produced by Maeda model. In the association phase, We inputted MFCC parameters, which were produced by recording the speech sounds of two speakers, into each

Table 1. Vocal tract parameters of vowel $/a/$, $/o/$ for Maeda model

Parameter number	1	2	3	4	5	6
$/a/$	-1.5	2.0	0.0	-0.5	0.5	-0.5
$/o/$	-0.7	3.0	1.5	0.0	-0.6	0.0

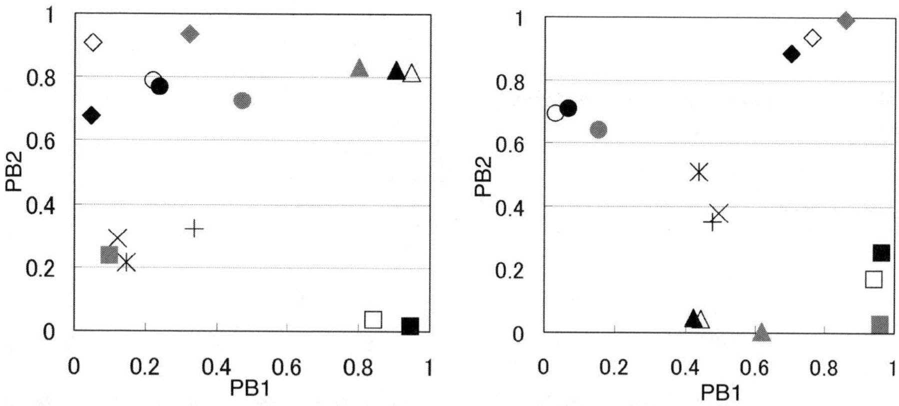

(a) PB space of RNNPB–1, using only sound information.

(b) PB space of RNNPB–2, using both sound and articulatory information.

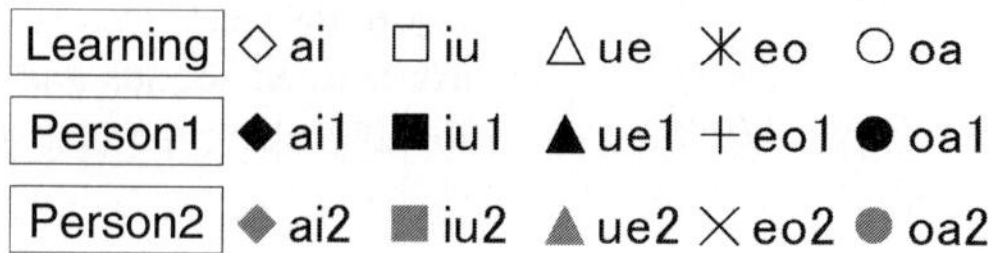

Fig. 5. PB space

organized RNNPB. Each RNNPB obtained the PB values from each set of sound data. The recording data used the same vowels as those in the learning data. In the following, we describe the association data of one person with the additional character '1', e.g., $/ai_1/$, and that of the other person with the additional character '2', e.g., $/ai_2/$. Figure 5 shows the PB space acquired by each organized RNNPB. The two parametric values in the RNNPBs correspond to the X–Y axes in the space. The characteristics of each space are as follows.

PB Space Acquired by RNNPB–1, 2. Figure 5(a) shows the PB space when only sound information was used. Although some of the PB values for the same vowel sounds were closely mapped, $/ai/$ and $/oa/$ was not clearly classified, and RNNPB–1 had $/iu_2/$ confused with $/eo/$. Meanwhile, Fig. 5(b) shows the PB space when both sound and articulatory information was used. The PB values for the same vowel sounds, including the learning data, were mapped with sufficient dispersion. We confirmed that RNNPB–2 could recognize the vowel sounds correctly. As we can see from table 1, there are sharp differences between vocal tract parameters of $/a/$ and $/o/$, which are acoustically similar. In fact, it is said that articulation information helps human beings to recognize speech sounds.

5.3   Imitation of Two Continuous Vowels

Third, we carried out an experiment to verify the adequacy of our imitation model by having it imitate both experienced and unexperienced sounds.

Table 2. Recording of two continuous vowels

Experienced	Unexperienced		
/ai/	/au/	/ae/	/ao/
/iu/	/ia/	/ie/	/io/
/ue/	/ua/	/ui/	/uo/
/eo/	/ea/	/ei/	/eu/
/oa/	/oi/	/ou/	/oe/

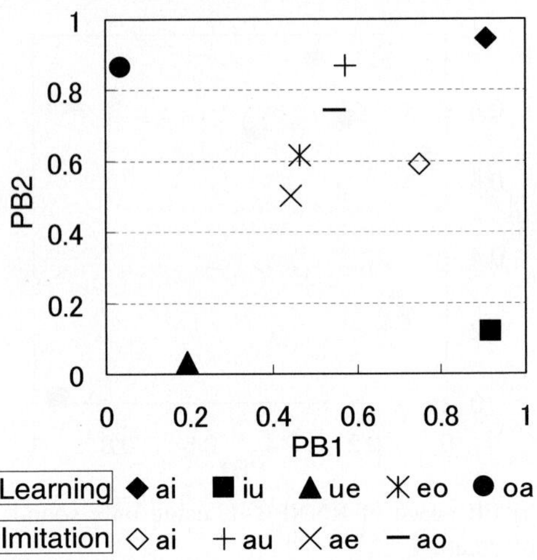

Fig. 6. PB space for two continuous vowels: five learned sounds and the four associated sounds, where the first vowel was /a/

In the learning phase, we organized the following RNNPB: the input and output layers had 11 units, the hidden layer had 20 units, the context layer had 15 units, and the PB layer had two units. The RNNPB learned the MFCC and vocal tract parameters of the learning data (/ai/, /iu/, /ue/, /eo/, and /oa/, 320 ms and 20 ms/step), produced by Maeda model. In the association phase, we inputted the MFCC parameters, generated by recording the speech sounds of a person, into the organized RNNPB, and we obtained the PB values for each of the sounds. Table 2 summarizes the recording two continuous vowels sounds. In the generation phase, we used the PB values to reproduce each of the recording sounds.

Figure 6 shows the resulting PB space, consisting of five learned sounds and four associated sounds, where the first vowel was /a/. Figure 7 shows the time series variation of the MFCC parameters for the original and imitation sounds /ai/ and /au/, as examples of an experienced sound and an unexperienced sound, respectively. The vertical axis represents the MFCC value, and the horizontal axis represents time [x 20 ms]. We could confirm that the imitation sound /ai/ reproduced the original sound. On the other hand, although the imitation sound /au/ differed from the original sound in the last part, the sound was reproduced to a differentiable extent. Most of the imitation sounds were similar to the original ones.

6   Discussion

As we can see from Fig 5, RNNPB–1, which used only sound information, acquired PB values that were affected by acoustic similarities in the sound data, and it made mistakes in recognizing the sounds. On the other hand, despite of the differences between the two speakers, RNNPB–2, which used both sound and articulation information, acquired PB

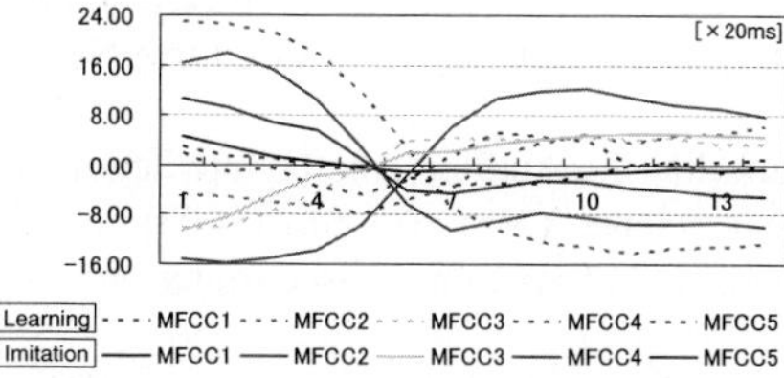
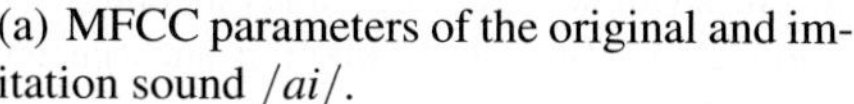

(a) MFCC parameters of the original and imitation sound /*ai*/.

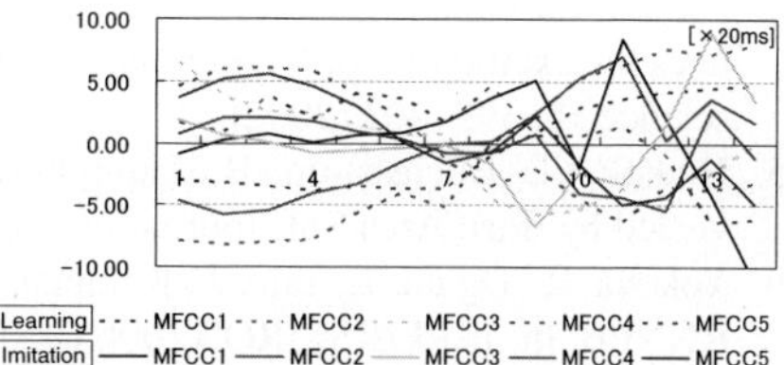

(b) MFCC parameters of the original and imitation sound /*au*/.

Fig. 7. MFCC parameters

values that were mapped closely to the same sounds, and it robustly recognized the sounds. These results show that articulation information helps human beings to recognize speech sounds, thus supporting the *motor theory of speech perception*. We have thus confirmed the adequacy of our imitation model for targeting language acquisition in infants.

7   Conclusions

We have proposed a vocal imitation system focused on the physical constraints of the human vocal tract and on treating speech sounds as dynamic sequences. Through experiments, we have verified the properties and the imitation capability of the system. The results show that the system could robustly recognize speech sounds without exhibiting the effects of differences between two speakers, and it could imitate experienced sounds accurately. In the case of imitating unexperienced sounds, two continuous vowels could reproduced accurately.

Our future work include extracting phonemes from speech sounds through an automatic tuning method for the RNNPB parameters.

Acknowledgements

This research was partially supported by the Ministry of Education, Science, Sports and Culture, Grant-in-Aid for Young Scientists (A) (No. 17680017, 2005-2007), Grant-in-Aid for Exploratory Research (No. 17650051, 2005-2006), and Kayamori Foundation of Informational Science Advancement.

References

1. Liberman, A.M., Cooper, F.S., et al.: A motor theory of speech perception. In: Proc. Speech Communication Seminar, Paper-D3, Stockholm (1962)
2. Tani, J., Ito, M.: Self-organization of behavioral primitives as multiple attractor dynamics: A robot experiment. IEEE Transactions on SMC Part A 33(4), 481–488 (2003)
3. Minematsu, N., Nishimura, T., Nishinari, K., Sakuraba, K.: Theorem of the invariant structure and its derivation of speech gestalt. In: Proc. Int. Workshop on Speech Recognition and Intrinsic Variations, pp. 47–52 (2006)

4. Fadiga, L., Craighero, L., Buccino, G., Rizzolatti, G.: Speech listening specifically modulates the excitability of tongue muscles: a TMS study. European Journal of Cognitive Neuroscience 15, 399–402 (2002)
5. Hickok, G., Buchsbaum, B., Humphries, C., Muftuler, T.: Auditory-motor interaction revealed by fmri. Area Spt. Journal of Cognitive Neuroscience 15(5), 673–682 (2003)
6. Yokoya, R., Ogata, T., Tani, J., Komatani, K., Okuno, H.G.: Experience based imitation using RNNPB. In: IEEE/RSJ IROS 2006 (2006)
7. Maeda, S.: Compensatory articulation during speech: Evidence from the analysis and synthesis of vocal tract shapes using an articulatory model. In: Speech production and speech modeling, pp. 131–149. Kluwer Academic Publishers, Dordrecht (1990)
8. Kitawaki, N., Itakura, F., Saito, S.: Optimum coding of transmission parameters in parcor speech analysis synthesis system. Transactions of the Institute of Electronics and Communication Engineers of Japan (IEICE) J61-A(2), 119–126 (1978)
9. Kawahara, H.: Speech representation and transformation using adaptive interpolation of weighted spectrum: vocoder revisited. In: IEEE Int. Conf. on Acoustics, Speech and Signal Processing (ICASSP), vol. 2, pp. 1303–1306 (1997)
10. Jordan, M.: Attractor dynamics and parallelism in a connectionist sequential machine. In: Eighth Annual Conference of the Cognitive Science Society, Erlbaum, Hillsdale, NJ, pp. 513–546 (1986)
11. Rumelhart, D., Hinton, G., Williams, R.: Learning internal representation by error propagation. MIT Press, Cambridge (1986)
12. Atal, B.S.: Effectiveness of linear prediction characteristics of the speech wave for automatic speaker identification and verification. Journal of the Acoustical Society of America 55, 1304–1312 (1972)

Policy Learning for Motor Skills

Jan Peters[1,2] and Stefan Schaal[2,3]

[1] Max-Planck Institute for Biological Cybernetics, Spemannstr. 32, 72074 Tübingen
[2] University of Southern California, Los Angeles, CA 90089, USA
[3] ATR Computational Neuroscience Laboratory, Soraku-gun Kyoto 619-0288, Japan

Abstract. Policy learning which allows autonomous robots to adapt to novel situations has been a long standing vision of robotics, artificial intelligence, and cognitive sciences. However, to date, learning techniques have yet to fulfill this promise as only few methods manage to scale into the high-dimensional domains of manipulator robotics, or even the new upcoming trend of humanoid robotics, and usually scaling was only achieved in precisely pre-structured domains. In this paper, we investigate the ingredients for a general approach policy learning with the goal of an application to motor skill refinement in order to get one step closer towards human-like performance. For doing so, we study two major components for such an approach, i.e., firstly, we study policy learning algorithms which can be applied in the general setting of motor skill learning, and, secondly, we study a theoretically well-founded general approach to representing the required control structures for task representation and execution.

1   Introduction

Despite an increasing number of motor skills exhibited by manipulator and humanoid robots, the general approach to the generation of such motor behaviors has changed little over the last decades [15]. The roboticist models the task as accurately as possible and uses human understanding of the required motor skills in order to create the desired robot behavior as well as to eliminate all uncertainties of the environment. In most cases, such a process boils down to recording a desired trajectory in a pre-structured environment with precisely placed objects. If inaccuracies remain, the engineer creates exceptions using human understanding of the task. While such highly engineered approaches are feasible in well-structured industrial or research environments, it is obvious that if robots should ever leave factory floors and research environments, we will need to reduce or eliminate the strong reliance on hand-crafted models of the environment and the robots exhibited to date. Instead, we need a general approach which allows us to use compliant robots designed for interaction with less structured and uncertain environments in order to reach domains outside industry. Such an approach cannot solely rely on human knowledge but instead has to be acquired and adapted from data generated both by human demonstrations of the skill as well as trial and error of the robot.

The tremendous progress in machine learning over the last decades offers us the promise of less human-driven approaches to motor skill acquisition. However, despite offering the most general way of thinking about data-driven acquisition of motor skills, generic machine learning techniques, which do not rely on an understanding of motor

M. Ishikawa et al. (Eds.): ICONIP 2007, Part II, LNCS 4985, pp. 233–242, 2008.

systems, often do not scale into the domain of manipulator or humanoid robotics due to the high domain dimensionality. Therefore, instead of attempting an unstructured, monolithic machine learning approach to motor skill aquisition, we need to develop approaches suitable for this particular domain with the inherent problems of task representation, learning and execution addressed separately in a coherent framework employing a combination of imitation, reinforcement and model learning in order to cope with the complexities involved in motor skill learning. The advantage of such a concerted approach is that it allows the separation of the main problems of motor skill acquisition, refinement and control. Instead of either having an unstructured, monolithic machine learning approach or creating hand-crafted approaches with pre-specified trajectories, we are capable of aquiring skills, represented as policies, from demonstrations and refine them using trial and error. Using learning-based approaches for control, we can achieve accurate control without needing accurate models of the complete system.

2   Learning of Motor Skills

The principal objective of this paper is to find the foundations for a general framework for representing, learning and executing motor skills for robotics. As can be observed from this question, the major goal of this paper requires three building blocks, i.e., (i) appropriate representations for movements, (ii) learning algorithms which can be applied to these representations and (iii) a transformation which allows the execution of the kinematic policies in the respective task space on robots.

2.1   Essential Components

We address the three essential components, i.e., representation, learning and execution. In this section, we briefly outline the underlying fundamental concepts.

Representation. For the representation of motor skills, we can rely on the insight that humans, while being capable of performing a large variety of complicated movements, restrict themselves to a smaller amount of primitive motions [14]. As suggested by Ijspeert et al. [4], such primitive movements (or basic skills) can be represented by nonlinear dynamic systems. We can represent these in the differential constraint form given by $A_{\theta_i}(x_i, \dot{x}_i, t)\ddot{x} = b_{\theta_i}(x_i, \dot{x}_i, t)$, where $i \in \mathbb{N}$ is the index of the motor primitive in a library of movements, $\theta_i \in \mathbb{R}^L$ denote the parameters of the primitive i, t denotes time and $x_i, \dot{x}_i, \ddot{x}_i \in \mathbb{R}^n$ denote positions, velocities and accelerations of the dynamic system, respectively. In the simplest case, A_{θ_i} could be an identity matrix and b_{θ_i} would be a desired task-spac acceleration. In more complicated cases, it could implicitly describe the task, see [8]. Note, that this dynamic system describes a task in its task space and *not necessarily* in the joint-space of the robot (which we denote by q).

Learning. Learning basic motor skills[1] is achieved by adapting the parameters θ_i of motor primitive i. The high dimensionality of our domain prohibits the exploration of the complete space of all admissible motor behaviors, rendering the application of

---

[1] Learning by sequencing and parallelization of the motor primitives (also referred to as basic skills) will be treated in future work.

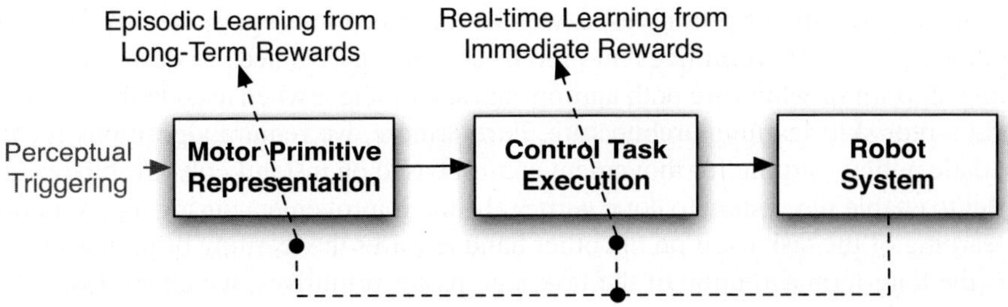

Fig. 1. This figure illustrates our general approach to motor skill learning by dividing it into motor primitive and a motor control component. For the task execution, fast policy learning methods based on observable error need to be employed while the task learning is based on slower episodic learning. The motor primitive yields a kinematic reference signal while the control task yields a motor command.

machine learning techniques which require exhaustive exploration impossible. Instead, we have to rely on a combination of supervised and reinforcement learning in order to aquire motor skills where the supervised learning is used in order to obtain the initialization of the motor skill while reinforcement learning is used in order to improve it. Therefore, the aquisition of a novel motor task consists out of two phases,i.e., the 'learning robot' attempts to reproduce the skill acquired through supervised learning and improve the skill from experience by trial-and-error, i.e., through reinforcement learning.

Execution. The execution of motor skills adds another level of complexity. It requires that a mechanical system $u = M(q, \dot{q}, t)\ddot{q} + F(q, \dot{q}, t)$, with a kinematic mapping to the task $x_i = f_i(q, \dot{q}, t)$ can be forced to execute each motor primitive $A_i\ddot{x}_i = b_i$ in order to fulfill the skill. Here, M denotes the inertia matrix and F Coriolis, centrifugal and gravitational forces. The motor primitive can be viewed as a mechanical constraint acting upon the system, enforced through accurate computation of the required forces based on analytical models. However, in most cases it is very difficult to obtain accurate models of the mechanical system. Therefore it can be more suitable to find a policy learning approach which replaces the control law based on the hand-crafted rigid body model. In this paper, we will follow this approach which forms the basis for understanding motor skill learning.

2.2   Resulting Approach

As we have outlined during the discussion of our objective and its essential components, we require an appropriate general motor skill framework which allows us to separate the desired task-space movement generation (represented by the motor primitives) from movement control in the respective actuator space. Based on the understanding of this transformation from an analytical point of view on robotics, we present a learning framework for task execution in operational space. For doing so, we have to consider two components, i.e., we need to determine how to learn the desired behavior represented by the motor primitives as well as the execution represented by the transformation of the motor primitives into motor commands. We need to develop scalable learning algorithms which are both appropriate and efficient when used with the chosen general motor skill learning architecture. Furthermore, we require algorithms for fast immediate policy learning for movement control based on instantly observable rewards in order to enable the system to cope with real-time improvement during the execution. The learning of the task itself on the other hand requires the learning of policies which define the long-term evolution of the task, i.e., motor primitives, which are learned on a trial-by-trial basis with episodic improvement using a teacher for demonstration and reinforcement learning for self-improvement. The resulting general concept underlying this paper is illustrated in Figure 1.

The resulting approach is related to approaches in neuroscientific models. It allows relating to both the the optimization based approaches (which have resulted in models like minimum jerk or minimum-torque change) as well as as to dynamic systems approaches (e.g., the VITE-FLETE model), see [13] for further information.

3   Policy Learning Approaches for Motor Skills

As outlined before, we need two different styles of policy learning algorithms, i.e., methods for long-term reward optimization and methods for immediate improvement. We can unify this goal by stating a cost function

$$J(\boldsymbol{\theta}) = \int_{\mathbb{T}} p_{\boldsymbol{\theta}}(\boldsymbol{\tau}) \, r(\boldsymbol{\tau}) \, d\boldsymbol{\tau}, \tag{1}$$

where $\boldsymbol{\tau}$ denotes a path, e.g., $\boldsymbol{\tau} = [\boldsymbol{x}_{1:n}, \boldsymbol{u}_{1:n}]$ with states $\boldsymbol{x}_{1:n}$ and actions $\boldsymbol{u}_{1:n}$, $r(\boldsymbol{\tau})$ denotes the reward along the path, e.g., $r(\boldsymbol{\tau}) = \sum_{t=1}^{n} \gamma^{t} r_{t}$ and $p_{\boldsymbol{\theta}}(d\boldsymbol{\tau})$ denotes the path probability density $p_{\boldsymbol{\theta}}(d\boldsymbol{\tau}) = p(\boldsymbol{x}_1) \prod_{t=1}^{n-1} p(\boldsymbol{x}_{t+1}|\boldsymbol{x}_t, \boldsymbol{u}_t) \pi(\boldsymbol{u}_t|\boldsymbol{x}_t; \boldsymbol{\theta})$ with a first-state distribution $p(\boldsymbol{x}_1)$, a state transition $p(\boldsymbol{x}_{t+1}|\boldsymbol{x}_t, \boldsymbol{u}_t)$ and a policy $\pi(\boldsymbol{u}_t|\boldsymbol{x}_t; \boldsymbol{\theta})$. Note, that $p_{\boldsymbol{\theta}}(\boldsymbol{\tau}) r(\boldsymbol{\tau})$ is an improper distribution, i.e., does not integrate to 1. The policy $\pi(\boldsymbol{u}_t|\boldsymbol{x}_t; \boldsymbol{\theta})$ is the function which we intend to learn by optimizing its parameters $\boldsymbol{\theta} \in \mathbb{R}^N$. Many policy learning algorithms have started optimize this cost function, including policy gradient methods [1], actor-critic methods [16,6], the Natural Actor-Critic [10,11,12] and Reward-Weighted Regression [9]. In the remainder of this section, we will sketch a unified approach to policy optimization which allows the derivation of all of the methods above from the variation of a single cost function. This section might appear rather abstract in comparison to the rest of the paper; however, it contains major novelties as it allows a coherent treatment of many previous and future approaches.

3.1   Bounds for Policy Updates

In this section, we will look at two problems in policy learning, i.e., an upper bound and a lower bound on policy improvements. The upper bound outlines why a greedy operator is not a useful solution while the lower bound will be used to derive useful policy updates.

Upper Bound on Policy Improvements. In the stochastic programming community, it is well-known that the greedy approach to policy optimization suffers from the major drawback that it can return only a biassed solution. This drawback can be formalized straighforwardly by showing that if we optimize $J(\boldsymbol{\theta})$ and approximate it by samples, e.g., by $\hat{J}_S(\boldsymbol{\theta}) = \sum_{s=1}^{S} p_{\boldsymbol{\theta}}(\boldsymbol{\tau}_s) r(\boldsymbol{\tau}_s) \approx J(\boldsymbol{\theta})$, we obtain the fundamental relationship

$$E\{\max_{\boldsymbol{\theta}} \hat{J}_S(\boldsymbol{\theta})\} \geq \max_{\boldsymbol{\theta}} E\{\hat{J}_S(\boldsymbol{\theta})\}, \tag{2}$$

which can be shown straightforwardly by first realizing the that the maximum is always larger than any member of a sample. Thus, a subsequent expectation will not change this fact nor the subsequent optimization of the lower bound. Thus, a policy which is optimized by doing a greedy step in parameter space is guaranteed to be biased in the presence of errors with a bias of $b_S(\boldsymbol{\theta}) = E\{\max_{\boldsymbol{\theta}} \hat{J}_S(\boldsymbol{\theta})\} - \max_{\boldsymbol{\theta}} E\{\hat{J}_S(\boldsymbol{\theta})\} \geq 0$. However, we can also show that the bias decreases over the number of samples, i.e., $b_S(\boldsymbol{\theta}) \geq b_{S+1}(\boldsymbol{\theta})$, and converges to zero for infinite samples, i.e., $\lim_{S \to \infty} b_S(\boldsymbol{\theta}) = 0$ [7]. This optimization bias illustrates the deficiencies of the greedy operator: for finite data any policy update is problematic and can result into unstable learning processes with oscillations, divergence, etc as frequently observed in the reinforcement learning community [2,1].

Lower Bound on Policy Improvements. In other branches of machine learning, the focus has been on lower bounds, e.g., in Expectation-Maximization (EM) algorithms. The reasons for this preference apply in policy learning: if the lower bound also becomes an equality for the sampling policy, we can guarantee that the policy will be improved. Surprisingly, the lower bounds in supervised learning can be transferred with ease. For doing so, we look at the scenario (suggested in [3]) that we have a policy $\boldsymbol{\theta}'$ and intend to match the path distribution generated by this policy to the success weighted path distribution, then we intend to minimize the distance between both distributions, i.e., $D(p_{\boldsymbol{\theta}'}(\boldsymbol{\tau}) \| p_{\boldsymbol{\theta}}(\boldsymbol{\tau}) r(\boldsymbol{\tau}))$. Surprisingly, this results into a lower bound using Jensen's inequality and the convexity of the logarithm function. This results into

$$\log J(\boldsymbol{\theta}') = \log \int \frac{p_{\boldsymbol{\theta}}(\boldsymbol{\tau})}{p_{\boldsymbol{\theta}}(\boldsymbol{\tau})} p_{\boldsymbol{\theta}'}(\boldsymbol{\tau}) r(\boldsymbol{\tau}) \, d\boldsymbol{\tau}, \tag{3}$$

$$\geq \int p_{\boldsymbol{\theta}}(\boldsymbol{\tau}) r(\boldsymbol{\tau}) \log \frac{p_{\boldsymbol{\theta}'}(\boldsymbol{\tau})}{p_{\boldsymbol{\theta}}(\boldsymbol{\tau})} \, d\boldsymbol{\tau} \propto -D(p_{\boldsymbol{\theta}'}(\boldsymbol{\tau}) \| p_{\boldsymbol{\theta}}(\boldsymbol{\tau}) r(\boldsymbol{\tau})), \tag{4}$$

where $D(p_{\boldsymbol{\theta}'}(\boldsymbol{\tau}) \| p_{\boldsymbol{\theta}}(\boldsymbol{\tau})) = \int p_{\boldsymbol{\theta}}(\boldsymbol{\tau}) \log(p_{\boldsymbol{\theta}}(\boldsymbol{\tau}) / p_{\boldsymbol{\theta}'}(\boldsymbol{\tau})) d\boldsymbol{\tau}$ is the Kullback-Leibler divergence, i.e., a distance measure for probability distributions. With other words, we have the lower bound $J(\boldsymbol{\theta}') \geq \exp(D(p_{\boldsymbol{\theta}'}(\boldsymbol{\tau}) \| p_{\boldsymbol{\theta}}(\boldsymbol{\tau}) r(\boldsymbol{\tau})))$, and we can minimize

$$J_{\mathrm{KL}} = D(p_{\boldsymbol{\theta}'}(\boldsymbol{\tau}) \| p_{\boldsymbol{\theta}}(\boldsymbol{\tau}) r(\boldsymbol{\tau})) = \int p_{\boldsymbol{\theta}}(\boldsymbol{\tau}) r(\boldsymbol{\tau}) \log \frac{p_{\boldsymbol{\theta}}(\boldsymbol{\tau}) r(\boldsymbol{\tau})}{p_{\boldsymbol{\theta}'}(\boldsymbol{\tau})} \, d\boldsymbol{\tau} \tag{5}$$

without the problems which have troubled the reinforcement learning community when optimizing the upper bound as we are guaranteed to improve the policy. However, in many cases, we might intend to punish divergence from the previous solution. In this case, we intend to additionally control the distance which we move away from our previous policy, e.g., minimize the term $J_+ = -D\left(p_{\boldsymbol{\theta}}\left(\boldsymbol{\tau}\right)||p_{\boldsymbol{\theta}'}\left(\boldsymbol{\tau}\right)\right)$. We can combine these into a joint cost function

$$J_{\mathrm{KL}+} = J_{\mathrm{KL}} + \lambda J_+, \tag{6}$$

where $\lambda \in \mathbb{R}^+$ is a positive punishment factor with $0 \le \lambda \le J(\boldsymbol{\theta})$. Note that the exchange of the arguments is due to the fact that the Kullback-Leibler divergence is unsymmetric. This second term will play an important rule as both baselines and natural policy gradients are a directly result of it. The proper determination of λ is non-trivial and depends on the method. E.g., in policy gradients, this becomes the baseline.

3.2   Resulting Approaches for Policy Learning

We now proceed into deriving three different methods for lower bound optimization, i.e., policy gradients, the natural actor-critic and reward-weighted regression. All three of these can be derived from this one perspective.

Policy Gradients Approaches. It has recently been recognized that policy gradient methods [2,1] do not suffer from the drawbacks of the greedy operator and, thus, had a large revival in recent years. We can derive policy gradient approaches straightforwardly from this formulation using the steepest descent of the first order taylor extension

$$\boldsymbol{\theta}' = \boldsymbol{\theta} + \alpha(\boldsymbol{\nabla} J_{\mathrm{KL}} - \lambda\boldsymbol{\nabla} J_+) \tag{7}$$

$$= \boldsymbol{\theta} + \alpha \int p_{\boldsymbol{\theta}}\left(\boldsymbol{\tau}\right)\left(r\left(\boldsymbol{\tau}\right) - \lambda\right)\boldsymbol{\nabla}\log p_{\boldsymbol{\theta}'}\left(\boldsymbol{\tau}\right)d\boldsymbol{\tau}, \tag{8}$$

where α is a learning rate. This is only true as for the first derivative $\boldsymbol{\nabla} D\left(p_{\boldsymbol{\theta}}\left(\boldsymbol{\tau}\right)||p_{\boldsymbol{\theta}'}\left(\boldsymbol{\tau}\right)\right) = \boldsymbol{\nabla} D\left(p_{\boldsymbol{\theta}'}\left(\boldsymbol{\tau}\right)||p_{\boldsymbol{\theta}}\left(\boldsymbol{\tau}\right)\right)$. The punishment factor from before simply becomes the baseline of the policy gradient estimator. As $\boldsymbol{\nabla}\log p_{\boldsymbol{\theta}'}\left(\boldsymbol{\tau}\right) = \sum_{t=1}^{n-1}\boldsymbol{\nabla}\log\pi(\boldsymbol{u}_t|\boldsymbol{x}_t;\boldsymbol{\theta})$, we obtain the straightforward gradient estimator also known as REINFORCE, policy gradient theorem or GPOMDP, for an overview see [1]. The punishment term only constrains the variance of the policy gradient estimate and vanishes as $\boldsymbol{\nabla} J_{\mathrm{KL}+} = \boldsymbol{\nabla} J_{\mathrm{KL}}$ for infinite data. However, this policy update can be shown to be rather slow [5,10,11,12].

Natural Policy Gradient Approaches. Suprisingly, the speed update can be improved significantly if we punish higher order terms of J_+, e.g., the second term of the taylor expansion yields

$$\boldsymbol{\theta}' = \mathrm{argmax}_{\boldsymbol{\theta}'}(\boldsymbol{\theta}' - \boldsymbol{\theta})^T(\boldsymbol{\nabla} J_{\mathrm{KL}} - \lambda\boldsymbol{\nabla} J_+) - \frac{1}{2}\lambda(\boldsymbol{\theta}' - \boldsymbol{\theta})^T\boldsymbol{\nabla}^2 J_+(\boldsymbol{\theta}' - \boldsymbol{\theta}) \tag{9}$$

$$= \lambda\left(\boldsymbol{\nabla}^2 J_+\right)^{-1}\left(\boldsymbol{\nabla} J_{\mathrm{KL}} - \lambda\boldsymbol{\nabla} J_+\right) = \lambda\boldsymbol{F}^{-1}g_1, \tag{10}$$

where $\boldsymbol{F} = \boldsymbol{\nabla}^2 D\left(p_{\boldsymbol{\theta}}\left(\boldsymbol{\tau}\right)||p_{\boldsymbol{\theta}'}\left(\boldsymbol{\tau}\right)\right) = \boldsymbol{\nabla}^2 D\left(p_{\boldsymbol{\theta}'}\left(\boldsymbol{\tau}\right)||p_{\boldsymbol{\theta}}\left(\boldsymbol{\tau}\right)\right) = \boldsymbol{\nabla}^2 J_+$ is also known as the Fisher information matrix and the resulting policy update g_2 is known as the Natural Policy Gradient. Surprisingly, the second order term has not yet been expanded and no Natural second-order gradient approaches are known. Thus, this could potentially be a great topic for future research.

EM-Policy Learning.   In a very special case, we can solve for the optimal policy parameters, e.g, for policy which are linear in the log-derivatives such as

$$\nabla \log \pi(\boldsymbol{u}_t | \boldsymbol{x}_t; \boldsymbol{\theta}) = \boldsymbol{A}\left(\boldsymbol{x}_t, \boldsymbol{u}_t\right) \boldsymbol{\theta} + \boldsymbol{b}\left(\boldsymbol{x}_t, \boldsymbol{u}_t\right), \tag{11}$$

it is straightforward to derive an EM algorithm such as

$$\boldsymbol{\theta}' = \alpha^{-1}\beta, \tag{12}$$

$$\boldsymbol{\alpha} = \int p_{\boldsymbol{\theta}}\left(\boldsymbol{\tau}\right)\left(r\left(\boldsymbol{\tau}\right) - \lambda\right) \sum_{t=1}^{n} \boldsymbol{A}\left(\boldsymbol{x}_t, \boldsymbol{u}_t\right) d\boldsymbol{\tau}, \tag{13}$$

$$\boldsymbol{\beta} = \int p_{\boldsymbol{\theta}}\left(\boldsymbol{\tau}\right)\left(r\left(\boldsymbol{\tau}\right) - \lambda\right) \sum_{t=1}^{n} b\left(\boldsymbol{x}_t, \boldsymbol{u}_t\right) d\boldsymbol{\tau}. \tag{14}$$

This type of algorithms can result into very fast policy updates if applicable. It does not require a learning rate and is guaranteed to converge to at least a locally optimal solution.

3.3   Sketch of the Resulting Algorithms

Thus, we have developed two different classes of algorithms, i.e., the Natural Actor-Critic and the Reward-Weighted Regression.

Natural Actor-Critic.   The Natural Actor-Critic algorithms [10,11] instantiations of the natural policy gradient previously described with a large or infinite horizon n. They are considered the fastest policy gradient methods to date and "the current method of choice" [1]. They rely on the insight that we need to maximize the reward while keeping the loss of experience constant, i.e., we need to measure the distance between our current path distribution and the new path distribution created by the policy. This distance can be measured by the Kullback-Leibler divergence and approximated using the Fisher information metric resulting in a natural policy gradient approach. This natural policy gradient has a connection to the recently introduced compatible function approximation, which allows to obtain the Natural Actor-Critic. Interestingly, earlier Actor-Critic approaches can be derived from this new approach. In application to motor primitive learning, we can demonstrate that the Natural Actor-Critic outperforms both finite-difference gradients as well as 'vanilla' policy gradient methods with optimal baselines.

Reward-Weighted Regression.   In contrast to Natural Actor-Critic algorithms, the Reward-Weighted Regression algorithm [9] focuses on immediate reward improvement, i.e., $n = 1$, and employs an adaptation of the expectation maximization (EM) policy learning algorithm for reinforcement learning as previously described instead of a gradient based approach. The key difference here is that when using immediate rewards, we can learn from our actions directly, i.e., use them as training examples similar to a supervised learning problem with a higher priority for samples with a higher reward. Thus, this problem is a reward-weighted regression problem, i.e., it has a well-defined solution which can be obtained using established regression techniques. While

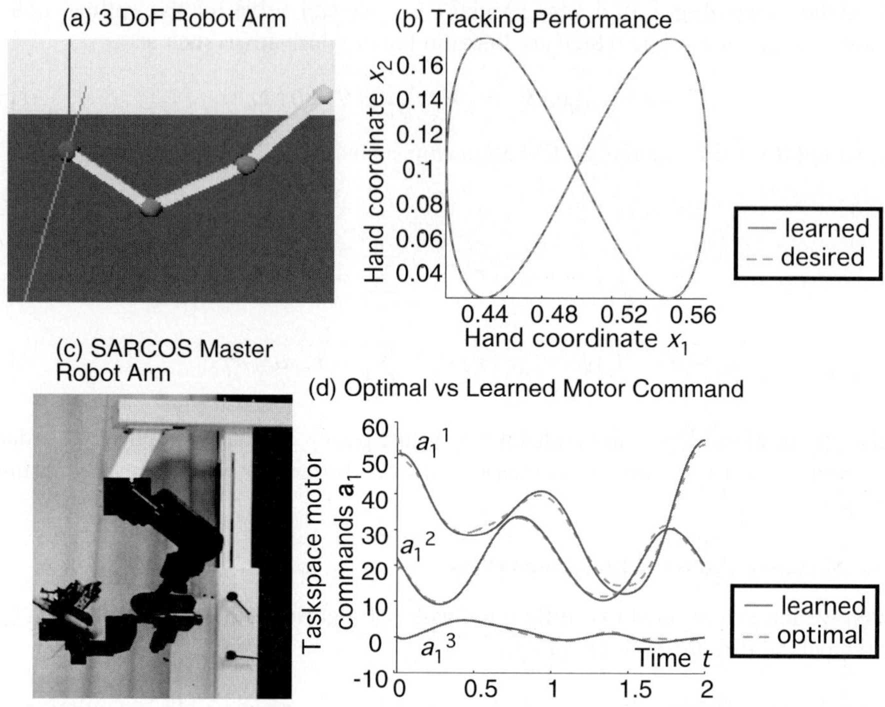

Fig. 2. Systems and results of evaluations for learning operational space control: (a) screen shot of the 3 DOF arm simulator, (c) Sarcos robot arm, used as simulated system and for actual robot evaluations in progress. (b) Tracking performance for a planar figure-8 pattern for the 3 DOF arm, and (d) comparison between the analytically obtained optimal control commands in comparison to the learned ones for one figure-8 cycle of the 3DOF arm.

we have given a more intuitive explanation of this algorithm, it corresponds to a properly derived maximization-maximization (MM) algorithm which maximizes a lower bound on the immediate reward similar to an EM algorithm. Our applications show that it scales to high dimensional domains and learns a good policy without any imitation of a human teacher.

4   Robot Application

The general setup presented in this paper can be applied in robotics using analytical models as well as the presented learning algorithms. The applications presented in this paper include motor primitive learning and operational space control.

4.1   Learning Operational Space Control

Operational space control is one of the most general frameworks for obtaining task-level control laws in robotics. In this paper, we present a learning framework for operational

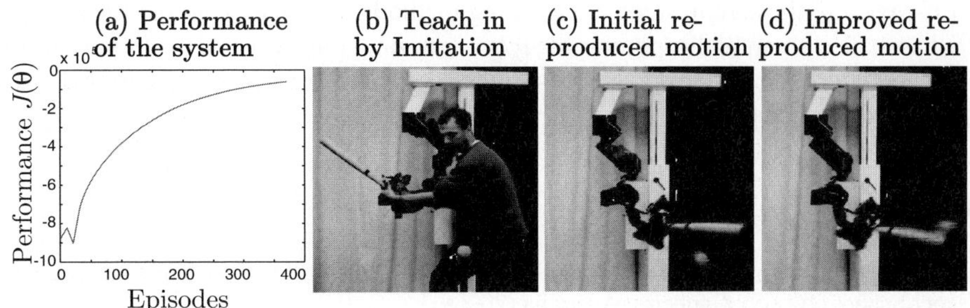

Fig. 3. This figure shows (a) the performance of a baseball swing task when using the motor primitives for learning. In (b), the learning system is initialized by imitation learning, in (c) it is initially failing at reproducing the motor behavior, and (d) after several hundred episodes exhibiting a nicely learned batting.

space control which is a result of a reformulation of operational space control as a general point-wise optimal control framework and our insights into immediate reward reinforcement learning. While the general learning of operational space controllers with redundant degrees of freedom is non-convex and thus global supervised learning techniques cannot be applied straightforwardly, we can gain two insights, i.e., that the problem is locally convex and that our point-wise cost function allows us to ensure global consistency among the local solutions. We show that this can yield the analytically determined optimal solution for simulated three degrees of freedom arms where we can sample the state-space sufficiently. Similarly, we can show the framework works well for simulations of the both three and seven degrees of freedom robot arms as presented in Figure 2.

4.2   Motor Primitive Improvement by Reinforcement Learning

The main application of our long-term improvement framework is the optimization of motor primitives. Here, we follow essentially the previously outlined idea of acquiring an initial solution by supervised learning and then using reinforcement learning for motor primitive improvement. For this, we demonstrate both comparisons of motor primitive learning with different policy gradient methods, i.e., finite difference methods, 'vanilla' policy gradient methods and the Natural Actor-Critic, as well as an application of the most successful method, the Natural Actor-Critic to T-Ball learning on a physical, anthropomorphic SARCOS Master Arm, see Figure 3.

5   Conclusion

In conclusion, in this paper, we have presented a general framework for learning motor skills which is based on a thorough, analytically understanding of robot task representation and execution. We have introduced a general framework for policy learning which allows the derivation of a variety of novel reinforcement learning methods including the Natural Actor-Critic and the Reward-Weighted Regression algorithm. We demonstrate the efficiency of these reinforcement learning methods in the application of learning to hit a baseball with an anthropomorphic robot arm on a physical SARCOS master arm using the Natural Actor-Critic, and in simulation for the learning of operational space with reward-weighted regression.

References

1. Aberdeen, D.: POMDPs and policy gradients. In: Proceedings of the Machine Learning Summer School (MLSS), Canberra, Australia (2006)
2. Aberdeen, D.A.: Policy-Gradient Algorithms for Partially Observable Markov Decision Processes. PhD thesis, Australian National Unversity (2003)
3. Dayan, P., Hinton, G.E.: Using expectation-maximization for reinforcement learning. Neural Computation 9(2), 271–278 (1997)
4. Ijspeert, A., Nakanishi, J., Schaal, S.: Learning attractor landscapes for learning motor primitives. In: Becker, S., Thrun, S., Obermayer, K. (eds.) Advances in Neural Information Processing Systems, vol. 15, pp. 1547–1554. MIT Press, Cambridge (2003)
5. Kakade, S.A.: Natural policy gradient. In: Advances in Neural Information Processing Systems, Vancouver, CA, vol. 14 (2002)
6. Konda, V., Tsitsiklis, J.: Actor-critic algorithms. Advances in Neural Information Processing Systems 12 (2000)
7. Peters, J.: The bias of the greedy update. Technical report, University of Southern California (2007)
8. Peters, J., Mistry, M., Udwadia, F., Cory, R., Nakanishi, J., Schaal, S.: A unifying methodology for the control of robotic systems. In: Proceedings of the IEEE/RSJ International Conference on Intelligent Robots and Systems (IROS), Edmonton, Canada (2005)
9. Peters, J., Schaal, S.: Learning operational space control. In: Proceedings of Robotics: Science and Systems (RSS), Philadelphia, PA (2006)
10. Peters, J., Vijayakumar, S., Schaal, S.: Reinforcement learning for humanoid robotics. In: Proceedings of the IEEE-RAS International Conference on Humanoid Robots (HUMANOIDS), Karlsruhe, Germany (September 2003)
11. Peters, J., Vijayakumar, S., Schaal, S.: Natural actor-critic. In: Gama, J., Camacho, R., Brazdil, P.B., Jorge, A.M., Torgo, L. (eds.) ECML 2005. LNCS (LNAI), vol. 3720, pp. 280–291. Springer, Heidelberg (2005)
12. Richter, S., Aberdeen, D., Yu, J.: Natural actor-critic for road traffic optimisation. In: Schoelkopf, B., Platt, J.C., Hofmann, T. (eds.) Advances in Neural Information Processing Systems, vol. 19, MIT Press, Cambridge (2007)
13. Schaal, S.: Dynamic movement primitives - a framework for motor control in humans and humanoid robots. In: Proceedings of the International Symposium on Adaptive Motion of Animals and Machines (2003)
14. Schaal, S., Ijspeert, A., Billard, A.: Computational approaches to motor learning by imitation. In: Frith, C.D., Wolpert, D. (eds.) The Neuroscience of Social Interaction, pp. 199–218. Oxford University Press, Oxford (2004)
15. Sciavicco, L., Siciliano, B.: Modeling and control of robot manipulators. MacGraw-Hill, Heidelberg (2007)
16. Sutton, R.S., McAllester, D., Singh, S., Mansour, Y.: Policy gradient methods for reinforcement learning with function approximation. In: Solla, S.A., Leen, T.K., Mueller, K.-R. (eds.) Advances in Neural Information Processing Systems (NIPS), Denver, CO, MIT Press, Cambridge (2000)

Task Learning Based on Reinforcement Learning in Virtual Environment

Tadashi Tsubone, Kenichi Kurimoto, Koichi Sugiyama, and Yasuhiro Wada

Department of Electrical Engineering, Nagaoka University of Technology
tsubone@vos.nagaokaut.ac.jp

Abstract. As a novel learning method, reinforced learning by which a robot acquires control rules through trial and error has gotten a lot of attention. However, it is quite difficult for robots to acquire control rules by reinforcement learning in real space because many learning trials are needed to achieve the control rules; the robot itself may lose control, or there may be safety problems with the control objects. In this paper, we propose a method in which a robot in real space learns a virtual task; then the task is transferred from virtual to real space. The robot eventually acquires the task in a real environment. We show that a real robot can acquire a task in virtual space with an input device by an example of an inverted pendulum. Next, we verify availability that the acquired task in virtual space can be applied to a real world task. We emphasize the utilization of virtual space to effectively obtain the real world task.

1   Introduction

A robot can perform complicated operations by control rules designed and planned by engineers. However, for an intelligent robot to coexist with humans in daily life and perform assigned tasks with sufficient accuracy, it needs to adapt to the manipulation according to the dynamic alteration of the environment. Recently, reinforcement learning [1] has gotten a lot of attention as a learning method by which a robot can autonomously obtain information from environments and actions. Reinforcement learning has been applied to various robot control researches [2] [3]. The robot tries to acquire optimal control rules through trial and error learning during the reinforcement learning. However, in a real world environment, robots have difficulties in learning a task by trial and error such as reinforcement learning. For example: 1) Restoring the environment to the initial state for learning is difficult because the number of learning needed to acquire adequate actions may exceed several thousands. 2) In the learning process, there are safety problems with the robot itself, as well as concerns about damage to operational objects and harm to humans since robot movement is not stable. To solve these problems we propose a novel method to acquire a task by trial and error learning in which a robot in the real world learns a task in virtual space through an input device connected to the real world and virtual space. After this, the robot can achieve the real task almost without learning in the

M. Ishikawa et al. (Eds.): ICONIP 2007, Part II, LNCS 4985, pp. 243–253, 2008.

real world. Since various tasks can be realized in the virtual space, the robot obtains them by changing the virtual space environment with relatively little effort. This means that the first problem above can be easily solved by the approach. Moreover, the second problem above can be tolerated due to the robot handling virtual control objects. In this paper, after reviewing related previous works, we explain our proposed approach. First, we show that a real robot can learn to control an inverted pendulum in virtual space. Next, the robot that acquires a virtual task can successfully control the inverted pendulum in the real world with fewer learning trials. Virtual space learning effectively acquires the real task by using reinforcement learning.

2   Utilization of Virtual Space to Acquire Real World Tasks

The following are examples of the utilization of virtual space for a robot system: 1) Utilization of engineering for robot mechanism (ex., consideration of layout or component parts) 2) Evaluation of robot control software 3) Teaching tools for robot control Several simulation softwares have been proposed for humanoid or mobile robots to satisfy the second utility above. Simulation softwares can enhance the development or the verification of the robot itself and the control rules by using virtual space. OpenHRP (Open Architecture Humanoid Robotics Platform) [4][5] and Dynamic Simulation [6] are typical examples. OpenHRP is a distributed architecture that can simulate in real time by operating a schedule client. OpenHRP is composed of a schedule client and various other clients who provide such functions as kinetics calculations and control. These systems are effective because control program bugs can be found in the simulator without involving the real robot. Therefore, we can minimize danger to people or the robots surroundings if it loses control. In the third utility, research has been done on teaching in assembly operations [7][8]. Computer programs for such operations are automatically produced after teaching data are extracted from actions performed by human operators in virtual space. Operators can edit and modify the extracted teaching data on a computer display to adapt to the real world. A virtual environment effectively develops a robot control system. In previous research on the utilization of virtual space, the robot system itself existed in virtual space where it manipulated the task. Our proposed method differs from previous research because the real robot (the robot in the real world is called a real robot) interacts with a virtual environment to achieve a virtual task. We propose a method where a real robot utilizes a virtual environment to obtain a real task.

3   Method Where Real Robots Utilize Virtual Environments to Obtain Real Tasks

The proposed method has two stages. In the first stage, the real robot learns the virtual task through an input device connected to virtual space (Figure 1),

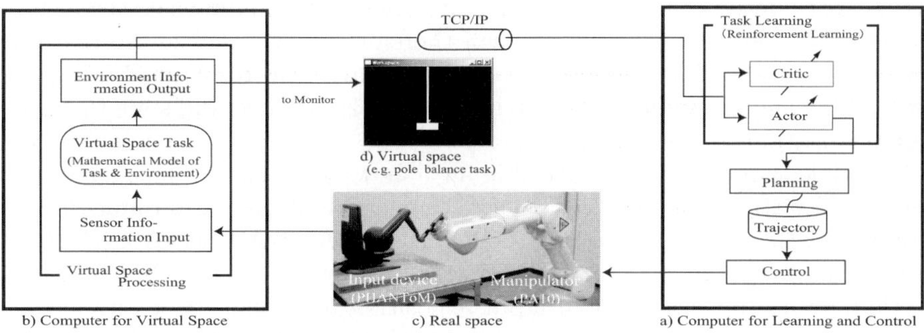

Fig. 1. Task learning system in virtual space

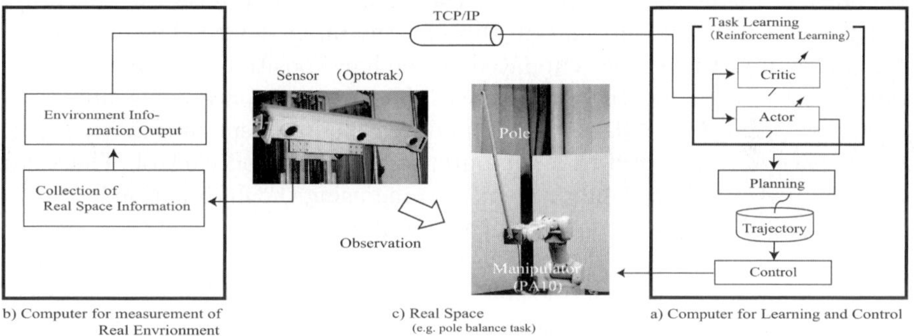

Fig. 2. Task learning system in real space

providing an opportunity to learn the task as if in the real world. In the second stage, the real robot learns the real task based on control rules acquired in the first stage (Figure 2). As mentioned above, there are several problems in trial and error learning such as reinforcement learning in real space. The utilization of virtual space allows the real robot to obtain the real task and avoid these problems. Moreover, we expect the following merits by using this approach. First, the robot can learn a huge variety of environmental alterations because virtual environment parameters can be arbitrarily and easily changed. The robot must experience various environments to autonomously adapt to them. In virtual space, the robot can learn iteratively and easily in situations whose realization is difficult in the real world. A simulation learning system is another idea where both the robot and the task exist in virtual space. However, if the robot mechanism is changed, we need to remodel the robot. At present the robot actuator by electric servomotor is general. But recently, the development of soft actuators has actively progressed [9] because soft robot systems, which pose no threat to humans, are required in welfare and caregiving fields. It is hard to simulate robot systems with soft actuators by computer. Robot system modeling with a soft actuator is very difficult because of the hysteresis of the air pressure actuator [10] or the nonlinear spring property. Robot modeling in virtual space does not need to use a real robot, and the differences between real and virtual robots are ignored. We can therefore quickly realize the real robot that acquire the task rule. The proposed approach features the following effective points: flexible environment setting, safe task learning, and smooth transfer (easy realization) to the real world.

1) Task learning in virtual space Figure 1 shows a system in which a real robot can learn a virtual task. The real robot is a general purpose arm robot PA10-7C (Mitsubishi Heavy Indusries, LTD.). We used PHANToM (SensAble Technologies, LTD.) as the device that connects real and virtual space. PHANToM is a haptic interface device that can input a position to virtual space and feedback force to real space. In this paper, even though we used PHANToM as an input device, in the future the system will feature the potential to be applied to tasks that need to interact with haptic sense. The robot can manipulate the input device shown in Figure 1. A computer for the virtual space receives the arm robot's hand position as robot information through the input device. The environment information in virtual space is updated by the hand position using mathematical models for the task and the environment. The virtual space is visualized on a monitor by using OpenGL [11]. The updated environment information in the virtual space is transferred to a computer for learning and control. The virtual task is learned based on reinforcement learning using the information in the task learning part of the computer for learning and control.

2) Task learning system in real space Figure 2 shows a system for the learning real task by the real robot. The environment information in real space is measured in a computer for state measurement by a three-dimensional position measurement system OPTOTRAK (Northern Digital Inc.), which gauges three-dimensional positions by tracing markers attached to the hand of the robot or the control object. Measured data is transferred to the computer for learning and control through a TCP/IP network. The real task is learned based on reinforcement learning using the information in the task learning part of the computer for learning and control. However, the robot has learned the virtual task and almost completed it using the acquired control rules in virtual space. Learning the real task is tuned exactly according to the difference between the real task and the mathematical model in virtual space. Finally, the robot is perfectly controlled by the tuned control rules.

4   Experiment Results of an Inverted Pendulum

4.1   An Inverted Pendulum

We show control results of an inverted pendulum by the proposed approach. The inverted pendulum's goal is to maintain the inverted state of the pendulum by moving a bogie toward the X-axis (Figure 3). The mathematical model in virtual space is denoted as follows [12]:

$$\dot{\theta}_{i+1} = (1 - \alpha_1)\,\dot{\theta}_i + \frac{g \triangle t}{l}\left(\sin(\theta_i) + \frac{\ddot{x}\cos(\theta_i)}{g}\right) \tag{1}$$

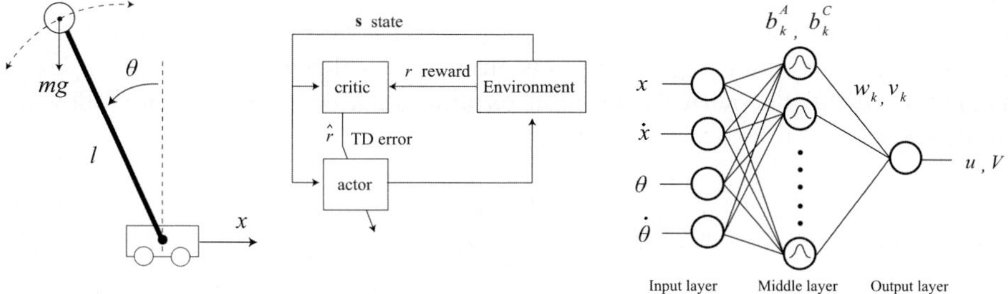

Fig. 3. Pole balance task **Fig. 4.** Actor-critic architecture **Fig. 5.** Actor-critic network representation

where θ_i, $\dot{\theta}_i$ and $\ddot{x}$ show the angle of the pendulum at time i, the angular velocity, and the acceleration of the bogie, respectively. We use the following parameter values: viscosity $\alpha_1 = 0.01$, time step $\Delta t = 0.02$s, gravitational acceleration $g = 9.81$m/s^2, and pendulum length $l = 0.9$m.

4.2 Learning Control of the Inverted Pendulum

In this paper the inverted pendulum is controlled based on reinforcement learning, the actor-critic algorithm (shown in Figure 4) [13]. In critic, state value is learned as error prediction $\hat{r}$ in equation (2) to become zero. The actor learns to select action as rewards increase:

$$\hat{r} = r\left(\mathbf{s}\left(t\right)\right) + \gamma V\left(\mathbf{s}\left(t\right)\right) - V\left(\mathbf{s}\left(t-1\right)\right) \tag{2}$$

where $r\left(\mathbf{s}\left(t\right)\right)$ is the reward at time t, γ is a discount factor, and $V\left(\mathbf{s}\left(t\right)\right)$ is value estimated by the critic. State variable $\mathbf{s}$ is denoted by four dimensions: $\left\{\theta, \dot{\theta}, x, \dot{x}\right\}$. Reward is expressed as follows:

$$r\left(\mathbf{s}\left(t\right)\right) = \begin{cases} 0 & |x| \leq 0.15[\text{m}] \text{ and } |\theta| \leq 12[^\circ] \\ -1 & \text{otherwise} \end{cases} \tag{3}$$

1) Critic:

The critic and actor are represented by the Adaptive Gaussian Softmax Basis Function [2]. Figure 5 shows a critic network using AGSBF. The critic's output is computed by the following equation. A $k-$th activating function is denoted as

$$a_k\left(\mathbf{s}\left(t_n\right)\right) = \exp^{-\frac{1}{2}\|M_k\left(\mathbf{s}\left(t_n\right) - \mathbf{c}_k\right)\|^2} \tag{4}$$

where c_k and M_k show a center and a variance matrix of the activating function, respectively. A base function is given as:

$$b_k\left(\mathbf{s}\left(t_n\right)\right) = a_k\left(\mathbf{s}\left(t_n\right)\right) / \sum_{l=1}^{K} a_l\left(\mathbf{s}\left(t_n\right)\right) \tag{5}$$

The base functions are successively arranged in learning. A new base function is arranged when error exceeds threshold e_{max} and activation values for all units are less than threshold a_{min}. The new unit is initialized as $\mathbf{c}_k = \mathbf{s}(t_n)$, $M_k = \mathrm{diag}(\mu^C)$, $v_k = 0$. The network's weight parameters are updated by the following equations:

$$\triangle v_k = \beta \hat{r}(t_n) e_k^C(t_n) \tag{6}$$

$$e_k^C(t_n) = \gamma \lambda e_k^C(t_{n-1}) + b_k^C(t_n) \tag{7}$$

where β and e_k^C denote a learning coefficient and eligibility trace [14], respectively. The following are the parameter values used in the experiment: $\beta = 0.3$, $\lambda = 0.8$, $a_{min} = 0.5$, $e_{max} = 0.0001$, $\mu^C = (50, 10, 50, 20)$.

2) Actor

The output of actor u, which is the distance of the robot arm movement, is computed by the following equation:

$$u(\mathbf{s}(t_n)) = u^{max} g\left(\sum_k w_k b_k^A(\mathbf{s}(t_n)) + \sigma(t_n)\varepsilon(t_n)\right) + u_b \tag{8}$$

where b_k^A is a base function, output u is saturated at maximum value u^{max} by a sigmoidal function, u_b is a biased output, and $\varepsilon(t_n)$ is a kind of noise for exploration. The weight values are updated by the next equations:

$$\triangle w_k = \alpha \hat{r}(t_n)\sigma(t_n)\varepsilon(t_n) e_k^A(t_n) \tag{9}$$

$$e_k^A(t_n) = \gamma \lambda e_k^A(t_{n-1}) + b_k^A(t_n) \tag{10}$$

where α and e_k^A show a learning coefficient and eligibility trace, respectively. A gaussian-typed noise is used as the exploration noise in equation (8), and noise magnitude $\sigma(t_n)$ is determined according to estimation function $V(t_n)$ to explore the smaller areas for the high estimation value of action:

$$\sigma(t_n) = \min[1, \max[0, -V(t_n)]] \tag{11}$$

The following parameter values were used in the experiment: $\alpha = 0.3$, $\lambda = 0.8$, $a_{min} = 0.5$, $e_{max} = 0.0001$ and $\mu^A = (50, 10, 50, 20)$.

3) Trajectory planning

Robot hand trajectory is planned based on the minimum jerk criterion [15] as follows:

$$x(t) = x_0 + (x_0 - x_f)\left(15\tau^4 - 6\tau^5 - 10\tau^3\right) \tag{12}$$

where $\tau = t/t_f$, x_0, x_f and t_f show starting point, final point, and movement duration, respectively. The final point, x_f, can be calculated by the sum of distance u and starting point x_0. In the paper, the duration of point to point movement is 100 msec, and the robot arm is controlled every 20 msec according to the planned point to point movement.

4.3   Task Learning in Virtual Space

The task is learned in virtual space. 1) Experimental conditions

The initial angle θ of the pendulum is given according to a Gaussian distribution with mean $0°$ and standard deviation $1°$, and initial angular velocity $\dot{\theta}$ is set to $0°$/sec. The successful trial is defined as maintaining the inverted pendulum for 10 minutes. When the number of continuous successful trials exceeds five, the experiment is terminated.

2) Experimental results

We performed the experiments three times. In all three experiments the pendulum was kept for more than 10 minutes. The average number of learning trials to achieve the experiment's termination conditions was 2128. We show an example of the results. Figure 6 shows TD error development to trail. The $x-$ and $y-$axes denote the number of learning trials and the TD error, respectively. We observed that the TD error converges to 0. Figure 7 shows the relation of the holding time of the inverted pendulum and the number of learning trials. The $x-$ and $y-$axes denote the number of learning trials and the holding time, respectively. After about 2100 trials, the robot arm could maintain the inverted pendulum for 10 minutes. The tilted pendulum was controlled vertically from the beginning for 15 sec and then periodically controlled to keep it near the origin in small amplitude less than 1 cm. These results show that the real robot can learn a virtual task with the input device.

4.4   Task Acquisition in Real Space

Task acquisition in real space was performed using the actor and critic obtained in virtual task learning.

1) Experimental conditions

A successful trial is defined as one that maintained the inverted pendulum for 10 minutes. When the number of continuous successful trials exceeded five, the experiment is terminated.

2) Experimental results

We performed the experiments three times. In all three experiments the pendulum was kept for more than 10 minutes. The average number of learning trials was 11 before the experiment's termination conditions were satisfied. Figure 8 shows an example of the relation of the holding time of the inverted pendulum and the number of learning trials. The $x-$ and $y-$axes denote the same data as Figure 7. The solid line (virtual) in Figure 8 shows the holding time of the pendulum when using the actor and critic obtained in the virtual task learning as initial states. Just after starting real task learning, the robot arm could maintain the inverted pendulum for 10 minutes. The control results of the pendulum for the first minute in successful trials are shown in Figure 9. The upper and bottom parts of the figure show the transitions of the robot arm position and the angle of the pendulum, respectively. The tilted pendulum is recovered just after starting and then periodically controlled to keep it near the origin at an constant amplitude. These results show that a virtual learning task can be effectively transferred to a real world task when actions learned in virtual space are

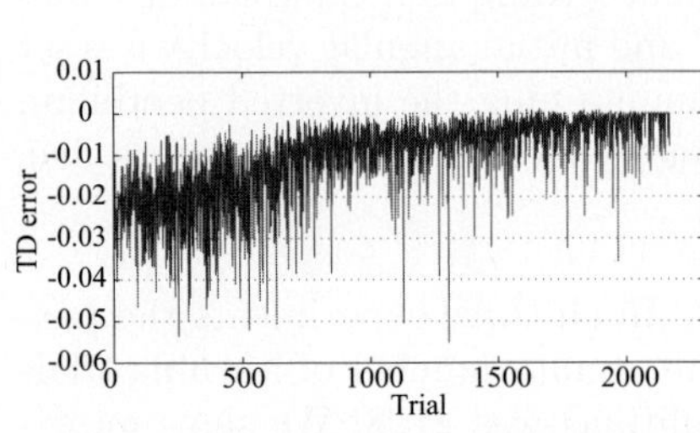

Fig. 6. TD error

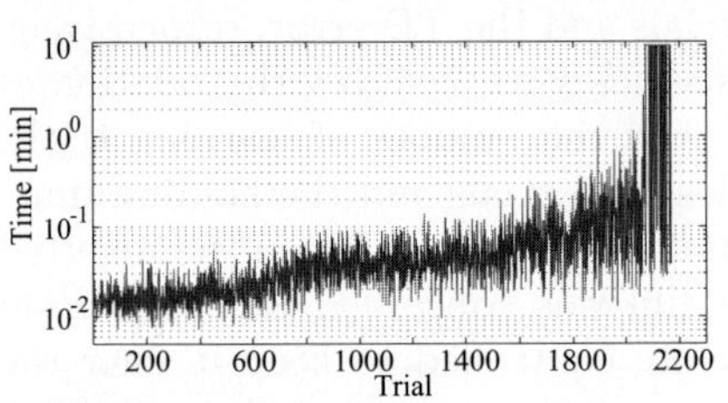

Fig. 7. Learning results in virtual space

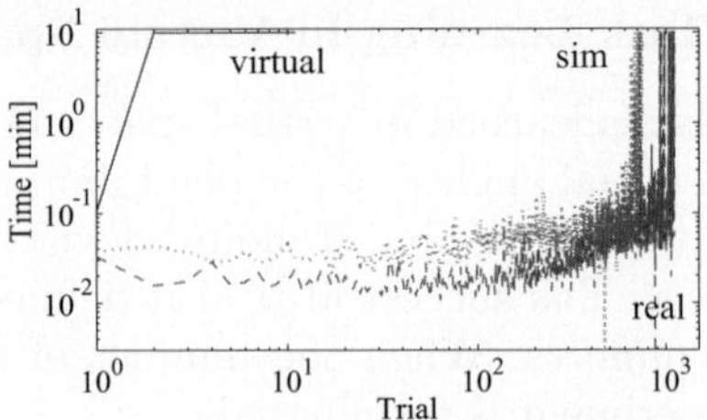

Fig. 8. Learning results in real space

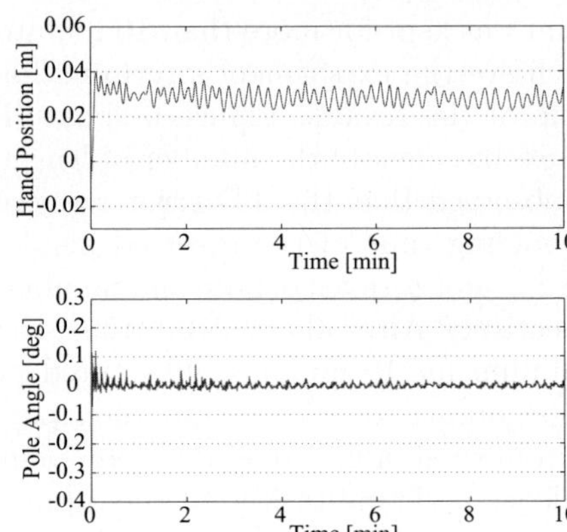

Fig. 9. Control results of hand position and pendulum angle in real space

applied to real world space using the proposed approach. Scant learning trials are needed in the above results when the virtual learning task is transferred to the real world task, probably because the mathematical model in virtual space closely resembles real dynamics.

5 Discussion: Comparison When Virtual Space is Not Used

To verify the effectiveness of virtual space use for the real robot in real task learning, we compared virtual space use with a case that didn't use virtual space in the following two experiments.

1) Only real space is used for task learning.

2) First, the task is learned in computer simulations, and then it is learned in real space. The robot system and the task environment exist in computer simulations.

In a sense the first method is conventional. The task is acquired in real space through the first trial to the final. The pendulum is manually returned to the initial state. In the second method, we ignore the position error and the time lag of the robot control because we assume that control is performed perfectly. The learned actor and critic are applied to the real task.

A. Experimental conditions

The parameter values for the actor and critic are identical to the virtual task learning experiment. Initial angle is set by Gaussian distribution with mean $0°$ and standard deviation $1°$, and the initial angular velocity is set to $0°/\text{sec}$. A successful trial is defined as maintaining the inverted pendulum for 10 minutes. When the number of continuous success trials exceeds five, the experiment is terminated.

Table 1. The number of trials which are necessary to acquire task in real space

Learning approach	Virtual→ Real (proposed approach)	Simulation → Real	Just Real
Number of trials	about 12	about 800	about 1200

B. Experimental results

The above experiments were performed three times. The task was achieved every time. In the first experiment, the average number of learning trials was 1225, and in the second experiment it took 808 trials. A dashed line (real) in Figure 8 shows the holding time of the pendulum in the real world after learning was performed in real space. It took about 1,200 trials to achieve the real task. A dotted line (sim) in the figure shows the holding time of the pendulum in the real world after learning was performed in the computer simulation. About 800 trials were required. Table 1 shows the number of learning trials until the robot obtains the task in the real world in each approach. About 1,200 trials were needed to complete the task when learning was only performed in real space. However, the proposed virtual space approach needed no learning trial. The computer simulation approach took less than about half of the number of learning trials for the case of only real space; however, it was inferior to the proposed approach. Since the task rule was located by the computer simulation before the real task was learned, the almost proper actor and critic had already been obtained before the learning performance in real space. Therefore, faster learning was naturally expected in comparison to learning only using the real task. We infer that robot dynamics is responsible for the difference between the proposed approach using virtual space and the computer simulation approach. The same mathematical inverted pendulum model for virtual space and simulations was used, so the difference does not depend on pendulum dynamics. We suppose that an ideal robot can be completely controlled with no time lag. However, in fact the robot cannot be controlled perfectly because of the increasing time of electric motors, etc. In the simulation approach, it apparently takes additional time to learn the real characteristics of robot dynamics. From these results, the proposed approach, which dramatically reduces the number of learning trials in real space, can be expected to smoothly shift to real space by the proposed approach because the differences between real and virtual robots need not be considered.

6 Conclusion

In this paper we proposed a novel approach for task learning by reinforcement learning that uses virtual space by which a real task is effectively and safely learned. We show one example where the real robot can control the inverted pendulum in virtual space using an input device. Then we show that the real task can be effectively obtained by applying the rules acquired in virtual task learning to real task learning. This means that the proposed approach, which first learns the virtual task and then shifts to real space, is quite a useful approach when the real robot has to learn and acquire tasks by trial and error. In the approach, it is possible to use force feedback controlled by a system that includes a haptic interface device such as PHANToM. In the future, we will discuss the effectiveness of a system that includes force feedback control.

References

[1] Barto, A.G., Sutton, R.S., Anderson, C.W.: Neuronlike adaptive elements that can solve difficult learning control problems. IEEE Transaction on Systems, Man and Cybernetics 3(5), 834–846 (1983)

[2] Morimoto, J., Doya, K.: Reinforcement learning of dynamic motor sequence: Learning to stand up. In: IEEE International Conference on Intelligent Robots and Systems, vol. 3, pp. 1721–1726 (1998)

[3] Morimoto, J., Cheng, G., Atkenson, C.G., Zeglin, G.: A Simple Reinforcement Learning Algorithm For Biped Walking. In: IEEE International Conference on Robotics and Automation 2004, vol. 3, pp. 3030–3035 (2004)

[4] Kanehiro, F., Miyata, N., Kajita, S., Fujiwara, K., Hirukawa, H., Nakamura, Y., Yamane, K., Kohara, I., Kawamura, Y., Sankai, Y.: Virtual humanoid robot platform to develop controllers of real humanoid robots without porting. In: IEEE International Conference on Intelligent Robots and Systems, vol. 2, pp. 1093–1099 (2001)

[5] Kanehiro, F., Hirukawa, H., Kajita, S.: OpenHRP: Open Architecture Humanoid Robot Platform. International Journal of Robotics Research 23(2), 155–165 (2004)

[6] Khatib, O., Brock, O., Chang, K.S., Conti, F., Ruspini, D., Sentis, L.: Robotics and interactive simulation. Communications of the ACM 45(3), 46–51 (2002)

[7] Ogata, H., Takahashi, T.: Robotic assembly operation teaching in a virtual environment. IEEE Transactions on Robotics and Automation 10(3), 391–399 (1994)

[8] Onda, H., Hirukawa, H., Takase, K.: Assembly motion teaching system using position/force simulator -extracting a sequence of contact state transition. In: IEEE International Conference on Intelligent Robots and Systems, vol. 1, pp. 9–16 (1995)

[9] Konyo, M., Tadokoro, S., Takamori, T., Oguro, K.: Artificial tactile feel display using soft gel actuators. In: IEEE International Conference on Robotics and Automation, vol. 4, pp. 3416–3421 (2000)

[10] Caldwell, D.G., Tsagarakis, N., Badihi, D., Medrano-Cerda, G.A.: Pneumatic muscle actuator technology a light weight power system for a humanoid robot. In: IEEE International Conference on Robotics and Automation, vol. 4, pp. 3053–3058 (1998)

[11] http://www.opengl.org/

[12] Atkeson, C.G., Schall, S.: Robot learning from demonstration. In: 14th International Conference on Machine Learning, pp. 12–20 (1997)
[13] Sutton, R.S., Barto, A.G.: Reinforcement Learning: An Introduction, A Bradford Book, MIT Press (1998)
[14] Singh, S.P., Sutton, R.S.: Reinforcement learning with replacing eligibility traces. Machine Learning 22(1-3), 123–158 (1996)
[15] Flash, T., Hogan, N.: The coordination of arm movements: an experimentally confirmed mathematical model. Journal of Neuroscience 5(7), 1688–1703 (1985)

Resolving Hidden Representations

Cheng-Yuan Liou* and Wei-Chen Cheng

Department of Computer Science and Information Engineering
National Taiwan University
Republic of China
cyliou@csie.ntu.edu.tw

Abstract. This paper presents a novel technique to separate the pattern representation in each hidden layer to facilitate many classification tasks. This technique requires that all patterns in the same class will have near represention and the patterns in different classes will have distant represention. This requirement is applied to any two data patterns to train a selected hidden layer of the MLP or the RNN. The MLP can be trained layer by layer feedforwardly to accomplish resolved representations. The trained MLP can serve as a kind of kernel functions for categorizing multiple classes.

1 Background

The study in [7] points out that an unresolved (ambiguous) representation in a lower hidden layer cannot be corrected by tuning any weights of its successive (higher) layers using the BP algorithm. This paper presents a novel technique to obtain resolved representations layer by layer feedforwardly to accomplish distinctive representations for different classes.

Geometrically, the functions of the neurons in a hidden layer are the decision hyperplanes in its lower layer space. These hyperplanes partition the whole space and generate the coding (representation) of data in this layer [7]. The partitioned space provides the finest coding areas [7] for its all higher layers. The data patterns included in each finest area has a code as the output of this layer. An ambiguous representation maps two data in different classes to the same data code in a layer. The BP algorithm cannot resolve this incorrect representation by training the weights of any higher layers. This suggested a feedforward tuning method should be developed.

Since a large number of neurons in a hidden layer can map data into high dimensional space, one can utilize this high representation space to accomplish many difficult classification tasks, such as SVM [2]. SVM is designed for resolving *two* classes. It can locate optimal separation boundary in the space by employing a selected kernel function. We show how to operate the SIR [9] in the MLP to accomplish the task for classifying *multiple* classes. We also show how to operate the SIR in the BP algorithm and the RNN algorithm additively.

---

* Supported by National Science Council and College of EECS 95R0036-07 NTU.

M. Ishikawa et al. (Eds.): ICONIP 2007, Part II, LNCS 4985, pp. 254–263, 2008.
© Springer-Verlag Berlin Heidelberg 2008

2   Method

2.1   Architecture

Suppose there are total P data patterns, $\{\mathbf{x}^p, p = 1, .., ..P\}$, in K different classes, $\{C_1, .., C_k, \ldots, C_K\}$. Assume the network has total $L + 1$ layers including input and output layers. There are $L - 1$ hidden layers. Let the dimension (number of neurons) of input layer be n_0, the dimension of output layer be $n_L = K$ and the dimension of each hidden layer excluding the bias be $n_1, n_2, \ldots n_{L-1}$. The first layer with n_1 neurons is connected to the input layer. Neighborhood layers connect with each other by synapse weights, $W^{(m)}$. $W^{(m)}$ is the weight matrix of the mth layer. $W^{(m)}$ is a n_m by $(n_{m-1} + 1)$ matrix. The element in ith row and jth column is written as $w_{ij}^{(m)}$. $\mathbf{y}^{(p,m)}$ is the output column vector of the mth layer when the input layer, receives the pth data pattern, $\mathbf{x}^p$. Each neuron's output needs to go through an activation function and the activation function we used in this paper is

$$f\left(v\right) = \tanh\left(av\right) \text{ and } \frac{df\left(v\right)}{dv} = a\left(1 - f\left(v\right)\right)\left(1 + f\left(v\right)\right), \tag{1}$$

where a is an adjustable parameter. The output of this activation function is in between the range $[-1, 1]$. a controls the slope of output change. The input of the activation function or the so-called induced local field of the neuron is

$$v_i^{(p,m)} = \sum_{j=0}^{n_{m-1}} w_{ij}^{(m)} y_j^{(p,m-1)}, \tag{2}$$

where $y_0^{(p,m-1)}$ is corresponding to a bias term, p denotes the pth data pattern $\mathbf{x}^p$, and i denotes the ith neuron in the mth layer. The output of the neuron is the value of induced local field passing through the non-linear activation function (1),

$$\mathbf{y}^{(p,m)} = f\left(\mathbf{v}^{(p,m)}\right). \tag{3}$$

The column vector $\mathbf{y}^{(p,0)}$ corresponds to input $\mathbf{x}^p$. In the BP algorithm [12], the output is calculated in the feed-forward pass and compared to the desired output. Then the error is back-propagated to adjust the synaptic weights. The desired output $\mathbf{d}^p$ of each class is determined by logistic function

$$d_k^p = \begin{cases} 1 \text{ when the pattern } \mathbf{x}^p \text{ belongs to } C_k; \\ 0 \text{ when the pattern } \mathbf{x}^p \text{ does not belongs to } C_k \end{cases}, \tag{4}$$

where $\mathbf{d}^p$ is a K-dimensional vector. The neural network decides the class of pth data entry, $\mathbf{x}^p$, by the output $\mathbf{y}^{(p,L)}$. If

$$y_k^{(p,L)} > y_j^{(p,L)}, \text{ for all } j \neq k, \tag{5}$$

then $\mathbf{x}^p$ is classified as C_k. The energy function used in the BP is

$$E^{BP} = \frac{1}{2} \sum_p \left\|\mathbf{y}^{(p,L)} - \mathbf{d}^p\right\|^2. \tag{6}$$

The study in [7] showed that the persistent error of the MLP classifier is due to the ambiguous binary representation in any lower hidden layer. The SIR method [9] provides a way to feedforwardly resolve the ambiguous representation in a low layer. We review the SIR method.

2.2   SIR Method

Two energy functions [9] have been proposed to address the discrimination respresentation of the output according to the class of data pattern. The repelling energy function for pattern separation that enlarges the distance between the output of two data entries at layer m is:

$$E_{pq}^{rep} = \frac{-1}{2} \left\| \mathbf{y}^{(p,m)} - \mathbf{y}^{(q,m)} \right\|, \tag{7}$$

and the attracting energy function for pattern completion that reduces the distance between the output at layer m is:

$$E_{pq}^{att} = \frac{1}{2} \left\| \mathbf{y}^{(p,m)} - \mathbf{y}^{(q,m)} \right\|. \tag{8}$$

We define a $P \times P$ discrimination matrix $D^{(m)}$,

$$D_{pq}^{(m)} = \begin{cases} 1 & \text{when both } \mathbf{x}^p \text{and } \mathbf{x}^q \text{ belong to the same class;} \\ 0 & \text{no effect;} \\ -\beta & \text{when } \mathbf{x}^p \text{and } \mathbf{x}^q \text{ belong to different classes,} \end{cases} \tag{9}$$

where β is a parameter controlling the preference of attracting or repelling forces in the algorithm. Combine equation (7) and (8) into a total energy function

$$E^{SIR(m)} = \sum_p \sum_q E_{pq}^{SIR(m)} = \sum_p \sum_q \frac{D_{pq}^{(m)}}{2} \left\| \mathbf{y}^{(p,m)} - \mathbf{y}^{(q,m)} \right\|. \tag{10}$$

$D_{pq}^{(m)}$ designates the required representations of the outputs of neurons in the mth layer for different class patterns. If $D_{pq}^{(m)}$ is not zero, then the representations of patterns $\mathbf{x}^p$ and $\mathbf{x}^q$ at layer m will be forced to change by the SIR force. If $D_{pq}^{(m)}$ is zero, then SIR does not affect the representations of patterns $\mathbf{x}^p$ and $\mathbf{x}^q$ at layer m. The direct way to achieve this goal is to minimize the overall energy. The network's energy function is written as:

$$E = \gamma E^{BP} + (1 - \gamma) E^{SIR(m)}, \tag{11}$$

and the updating function of weight is

$$w_{ij}^{(m)} \longleftarrow w_{ij}^{(m)} - \eta \frac{\partial E}{\partial w_{ij}^{(m)}}, \ m = 0, \ldots, L. \tag{12}$$

Therefore the hidden layers below the mth layer do not merely follow the delta rule to minimize the output error (6). There is another discrimination force that additively assists the network converge towards a better representation. In (11), γ dictates the competition between error function satisfaction and good representation. If γ is closer to one, that means the neural network prioritize the satisfaction of desired output. If γ is closer to 0, that means the neural network favors the satisfaction of $D^{(m)}$'s representation. At training stage, γ is usually big and close to one, and it gradually reduces to a constant number, for example, 0.5. The following sections demonstrate how to operate the SIR to assist and improve the MLP.

2.3 Setting Discrimination Matrix $D^{(m)}$

$D^{(m)}$ is a matrix that controls the neural network internal representation. We explain how to operate the elements of the matrix $D^{(m)}$ to save computation. Let r be a variable representing the influence radius. This variable represents the radius we apply SIR to the data patterns. As the training time increases, r gradually decreases to the minimum distance among the different classes of data. After certain amount of time in training, we reduce r linearly and recalculate $D^{(m)}$

$$D_{pq}^{(m)} = \begin{cases} 1 & \text{if } \|\mathbf{x}^p - \mathbf{x}^q\| \leq r, \text{ and both } \mathbf{x}^p \text{and } \mathbf{x}^q \text{ belong to the same class;} \\ 0 & \text{if } \|\mathbf{x}^p - \mathbf{x}^q\| > r; \\ -\beta & \text{if } \|\mathbf{x}^p - \mathbf{x}^q\| \leq r, \text{ and } \mathbf{x}^p \text{ and } \mathbf{x}^q \text{ belong to different classes} \end{cases}$$

$$(13)$$

Figure 1 provides an illustration for the above setting. For each class of data, we pick a point, the circle centered at the point has radius r. Initially, r is very large and decreases as training goes by and so does the circle. The solid line between points means that $D_{pq}^{(m)} = 1$, dotted line for $D_{pq}^{(m)} = -\beta$ and if there is no line, $D_{pq}^{(m)} = 0$. With this setting, $D^{(m)}$ contains a large number of zero elements $D_{pq}^{(m)} = 0$ and we can save computations. The measurement of r and choice of $D_{pq}^{(m)}$ are based on the calculation in input space. Figure 1 (a,b,c,d) shows the operation area of SIR as the training proceeds.

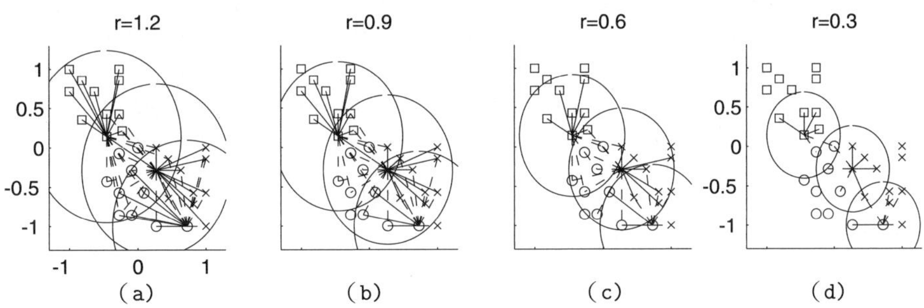

Fig. 1. The conceptual diagram shows how to train SIR. The r will be gradually reduced.

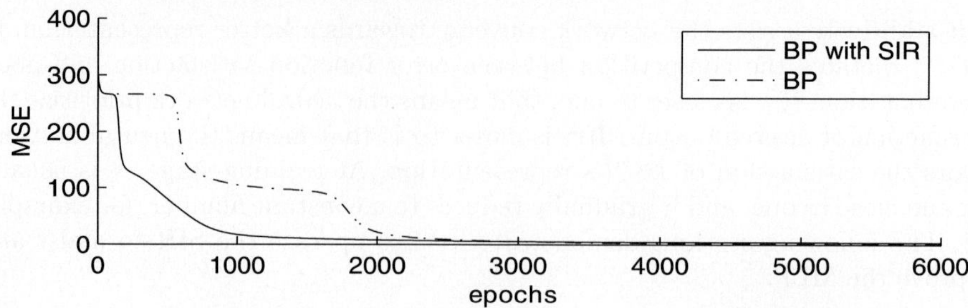

Fig. 2. The result of testing with fisheriris dataset. Number of hidden neurons, $n_1 = 20$. The figure shows that BP with the assistance of SIR can effectively accelerates classification and lower MSE is achieved in less epochs.

3   Experimental Results

3.1   Experiment on Iris Dataset

Fisheriris data set [14] has 150 data entries of four dimensions including sepal length, sepal width, petal length and petal width. There are three classes: Iris Setosa, Iris Versicolour and Iris Virginica; we randomly pick 2/3 of the data (100 entries) for training and the other 1/3 (50 entries) for testing. Both BP and SIR methods have training accuracy 100% and testing accuracy 94%. Both methods use exactly the same initial weight ranged in $[-0.01, 0.01]$ and no momentum term is included. The network contains a hidden layer of 20 neurons, a 4 dimension input layer, $n_0 = 4$ and a 3 dimension output layer, $n_L = 3$. The SIR takes effect in the hidden layer. Figure 2 is the training curve. The MSE in the figure is the E^{BP} in equation (11). We see the SIR reduces the epochs required for backpropagation to find the minimum value. Since this is a supervised problem, we set $D_{ij}^{(1)} = 1$ if i and j are of the same class and set $D_{ij}^{(1)} = -\beta$ otherwise. The parameters for SIR are set to be $\beta = 0.3$, $\gamma = 0.5$. SIR helps the backpropagation to escape from local minimum or to prevent from falling into a local minimum. Besides, the computational time of SIR is proportional to the square of the number of input patterns and is proportional to the input dimension. Therefore the computational complexity is $O\left(P^2 n_0\right)$. The weight is small initially, so the $E^{SIR(1)}$ in equation (11) is close to 0 and has little effect. E^{BP} is at dominance by the time. As time goes by, the weight increases and so does the effect of $E^{SIR(1)}$.

Besides, we randomly choose 100 entries from the iris dataset that includes all three classes and use them to train the multilayer perceptrons network. The structure of network is shown on the upper half of figure 3. Figure 3 shows the representation of the hidden layer during the training. There are 2 hidden neurons at layer 2 and 4 and all layers use the SIR's energy function. Therefore the total energy is

$$\gamma E^{BP} + \frac{(1-\gamma)}{2} E^{SIR(2)} + \frac{(1-\gamma)}{2} E^{SIR(4)}. \tag{14}$$

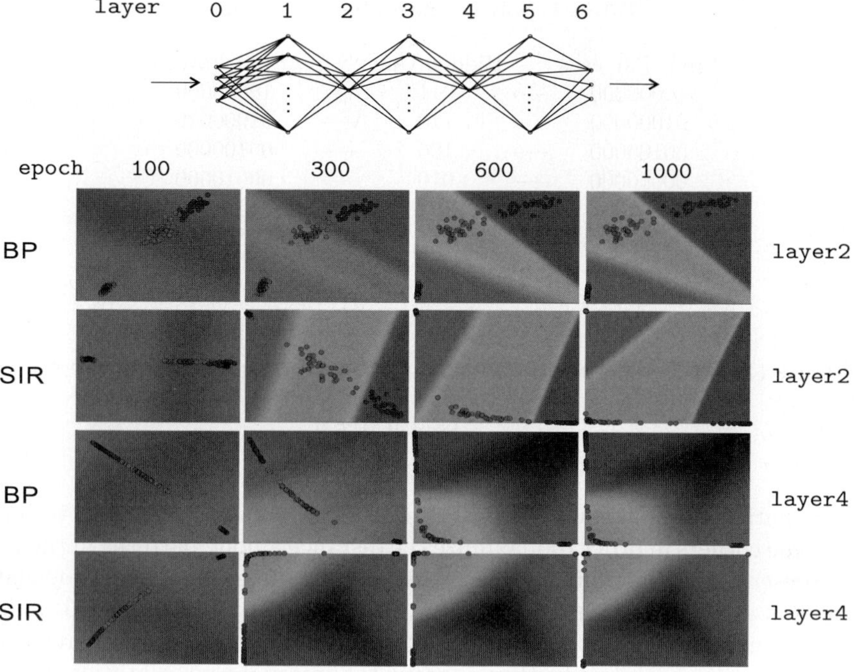

Fig. 3. The representation of hidden layer. BP means back-propagation. SIR means the model trained by (11).

Circles in the figure represent the output position of data in the hidden layer and the color represents the corresponding class of the data. The three classes are represented by red, green and blue. The background color represents the corresponding output of the network, that is to say, how the space is divided. Red means the output is $\begin{bmatrix} 1 & -1 & -1 \end{bmatrix}^{T}$. We can see that the hidden neuron at layer 4 uses SIR for 1000 epochs, the patterns has output close to ± 1 at this layer.

3.2   Experiment on the Encoding Problem

Ackley and Hinton [1] rose the question that map a set of orthogonal input patterns onto a set orthogonal input patterns through a hidden layer which has small number of neurons, the internal representation of the hidden layer must be coding *efficient* [6]. Rumelhart *et al.* [12] used backpropagation to map eight independent input patterns to themselves through a hidden layer of three neurons to get a 3 bit internal representation. They pointed out that the multilayer perceptrons used an intermediate value 0.5 as the representation to solve this problem.

"... by our learning system on this example. It is of some interest that the system employed its ability to use intermediate values in solving this problem. It could, of course, ..."[12]

Table 1. Solving the encoding problem

Input Patterns		Hidden Unit		Output Patterns
10000000	$\longrightarrow$	011	$\longrightarrow$	10000000
01000000	$\longrightarrow$	110	$\longrightarrow$	01000000
00100000	$\longrightarrow$	100	$\longrightarrow$	00100000
00010000	$\longrightarrow$	010	$\longrightarrow$	00010000
00001000	$\longrightarrow$	101	$\longrightarrow$	00001000
00000100	$\longrightarrow$	111	$\longrightarrow$	00000100
00000010	$\longrightarrow$	000	$\longrightarrow$	00000010
00000001	$\longrightarrow$	001	$\longrightarrow$	00000001

We use (11) to assist the adjustment of internal representation. We set

$$D_{pq}^{(1)} = \begin{cases} -1 \text{ if } p \neq q \\ 0 \ \text{ if } p = q \end{cases}.$$
(15)

100 simulation results show that the internal representations are close to binary hypercube corners in order to maximize the distance among patterns in the internal representation. The force to change weights in the original backpropagation diminishes as the output error decreases. Besides, the application of (6) in layer weight adjustment is only for reducing the energy of multilayer perceptrons. Using (10), we can always further improve the internal representation even the E^{BP} is close to 0. Table 1 lists an example using (11). The result never has the value 0.5 as mentioned in [1]. The 0 in the table actually represents -1. We use 0 in the table for convenience.

3.3   Recurrent Neural Networks

Using trained recurrent neural networks (RNN) to recognize finite state machine has been proposed in [3][4][8][10][11]. Conversely, hierarchical cluster analysis was used for analyzing RNN. The basic assumption for the FSM extraction from a trained RNN is that states should cluster together in the state space[3]. A widely used technique to discretize the continuous states of RNN is quantization methods. Here we propose a method need not use the assumption and the method directly operate the state representations in state space. This method is essentially different from other methods.

Data Description. Tomita [13] studied a set of regular languages. Definition of the set is listed in table 2. We randomly generate a lot of strings and by examining the definition in table 2, the corresponding outputs are generated. For example, 101011 has corresponding output 010100 in language 2 and 10110 has corresponding output 01000. Each language generates 100 strings of length 10 and to make the number of 0's and 1's in those strings be the same.

Network Framework. The basic structure is illustrated in figure 4. The output of layer 2 will be copied to context layer. This structure is a variance of the one proposed in [4].

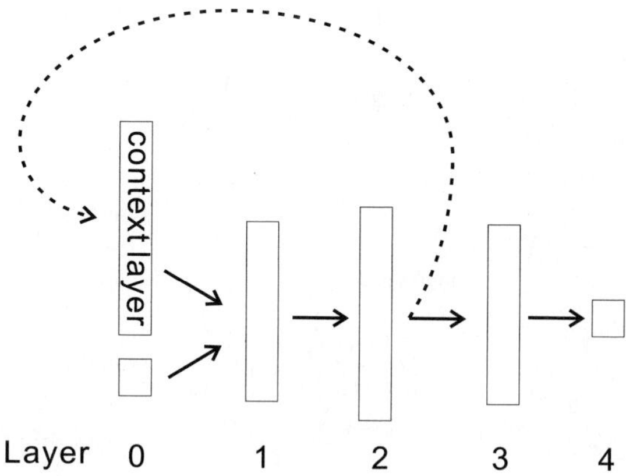

Fig. 4. The architecture of RNN used to learn DFA

Table 2. Tomita Language

Language	Definition	$(n_0, n_1, n_2, n_3, n_4)$
1	1^*	$(1, 10, 2, 5, 1)$
2	$(10)^*$	$(1, 10, 2, 5, 1)$
3	Any string without an odd number of consecutive 0's after an odd number of consecutive 1's.	$(1, 10, 4, 5, 1)$
4	Any string does not have more than 3 consecutive 0's.	$(1, -, 3, 5, 1)$
5	Any string has an even number of (01)'s or (10)'s.	$(1, 10, 4, 5, 1)$
6	Any string such that the difference between the number of 1's and 0's is a multiple of 3.	$(1, 10, 4, 5, 1)$
7	0*1*0*1*	$(1, 10, 4, 5, 1)$

Training Method. Choose one input symbol (0 or 1) from an input sequence and a output symbol (0 or 1). This out symbol indicates whether the input sequence conforms the grammar up to this input symbol. The network weights are adjusted by backpropagation through time. In forward pass, calculate the state and output bit from the current input and previous state. The network needs to minimize the error between the network output bits and the desired output sequence at all points of time. We define configuration matrix $D^{(2)}$ to be a matrix and its column and row represents points of time.

$$D_{t_1 t_2}^{(2)} = \begin{cases} 1 & \text{if network is in the same state in } t_1 \text{ and } t_2. \\ 0 & \text{the relation is unknown.} \\ -\beta & \text{if the network is in different state in } t_1 \text{ and } t_2. \end{cases} \qquad (16)$$

Hopcroft points out that two states are the same if and only if they generate exactly the same output for all possible future inputs [5]. Taking advantage of this point, we can estimate which states may be the same but we cannot be sure about all possible inputs for now. We use an approximate approach by defining the depth dp to be a positive integer. If two states generates the same output

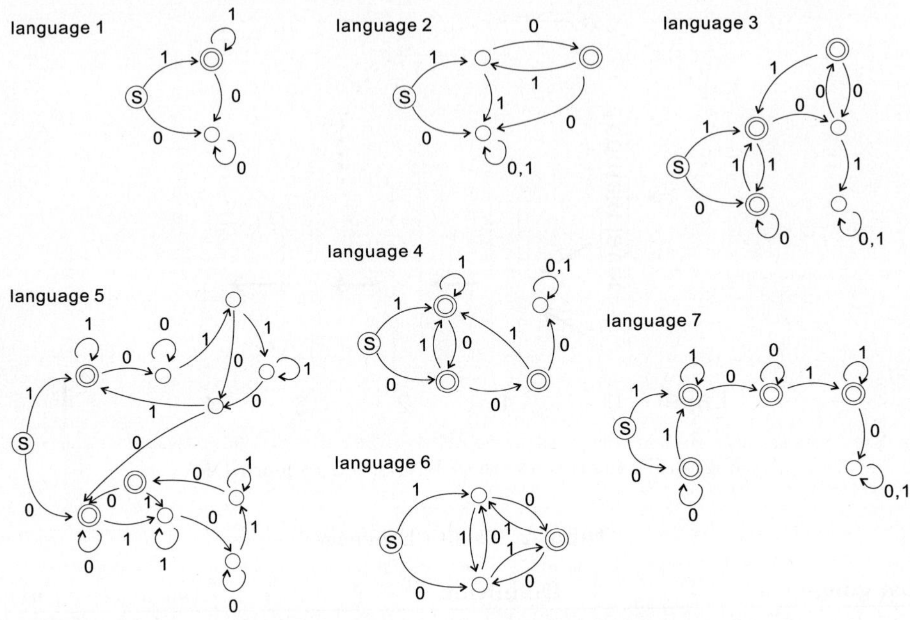

Fig. 5. FSMs learned by RNN with SIR

for all input of length dp, then we assume they are the same state. Therefore the $D_{t_1 t_2}^{(2)}$ is determined by:

$$
D_{t_1 t_2}^{(2)} = \begin{cases} 1 & \text{if network in state } t_1 \text{ and } t_2 \\ & \text{have the same output for } dp \text{ steps for all input.} \\ -\beta & \text{if the network in state } t_1 \text{ and } t_2 \\ & \text{have different output for any of } dp \text{ steps for any input.} \end{cases} \tag{17}
$$

Initial state is randomized and the initial weights are chosen randomly from $[-0.25, 0.25]$ by uniform distribution. Number of neurons used by each language is listed in the last column of Table 2. The dash, $-$, means we don't use that layer. At beginning, $\gamma = 1$. After training the network with 10000 epochs of all training sequences, γ linearly decreases to 0.7. The learning rate is set to 0.1, dp is set to 5 and there is no momentum term. The FSM learned by the network is shown in Fig. 5. The S in circle indicates that it is an initial state. Two concentric circles indicate that the FSM accepts this string and stops. A single circle indicates the FSM rejects this string and stops. The number 0 and 1 on the state transition line is the input symbol. Those FSMs can completely explain the relationship between the input and output of the training data. Those data are noise-free. Therefore if the E^{BP} does not fall to approximately zero, we know the network energy has stuck in local minimum. If this happens, we re-initialize the weights and re-train the network.

This paper shows how to operate the SIR to improve the backpropagation algorithm. The experiment results demonstrate that this method can reduce the problem of ambiguity and assist the learning of neural network efficient. We also propose using this technique to correct the state representation of the recurrent neural network and force the internal representation to be binary states. Hence we can train a recurrent neural network to learn a finite state machine and states can be easily extracted.

References

1. Ackley, D.H., Hinton, G.E., Sejnowski, T.J.: A Learning Algorithm for Boltzmann Machines. Cognitive Science 9, 147–169 (1985)
2. Boser, B.E., Guyon, I.M., Vapnik, V.N.: A Training Algorithm for Optimal Margin Classifier. In: Proceedings of the Fifth Annual Workshop on Computational learning theory, pp. 144–152 (1992)
3. Cleeremans, A., Servan-Schreiber, D., McClelland, J.L.: Finite State Automata and Simple Recurrent Networks. Neural Computation 1, 372–381 (1989)
4. Elman, J.L.: Finding Structure in Time. Cognitive Science 14, 179–211 (1990)
5. Hopcroft, J.E., Ullman, J.D.: Introduction to Automata Theory, Languages, and Computation. Addison-Wesley, Reading (1979)
6. Liou, C.Y., Lin, S.L.: The Other Variant Boltzmann Machine. In: International Joint Conference on Neural Networks, IJCNN, Washington, D.C., USA, June 18-22, pp. 449–454 (1989)
7. Liou, C.Y., Yu, W.J.: Ambiguous Binary Representation in Multilayer Neural Network. In: Proceedings of ICNN, Perth, Australia, November 27 - December 1, vol. 1, pp. 379–384 (1995)
8. Liou, C.Y., Yuan, S.K.: Error Tolerant Associative Memory. Biological Cybernetics 81, 331–342 (1999)
9. Liou, C.Y., Chen, H.T., Huang, J.C.: Separation of Internal Representations of the Hidden Layer. In: Proceedings of the International Computer Symposium, ICS, Workshop on Artificial Intelligence, Chiayi, Taiwan, pp. 26–34 (2000)
10. Liou, C.Y., Lin, S.L.: Finite Memory Loading in Hairy Neurons. Natural Computing 5, 15–42 (2006)
11. Liou, C.Y.: Backbone Structure of Hairy Memory. In: Kollias, S., Stafylopatis, A., Duch, W., Oja, E. (eds.) ICANN 2006. LNCS, vol. 4131, pp. 688–697. Springer, Heidelberg (2006)
12. Rumelhart, D.E., Hinton, G.E., Williams, R.J.: Learning Internal Representations by Error Propagation. In: Rumelhart, D.E., McClelland, J.L. (eds.) Parallel Distributed Processing: Explorations in the Microstructure of Cognition, vol. 1, pp. 318–362. MIT Press, Cambridge (1986)
13. Tomita, M.: Dynamics Construction of Finite-State Automata from Examples Using Hill-Climing. In: Proceedings of the Fourth Annual Conference of the Cognitive Science Society, pp. 105–108 (1982)
14. http://www.ics.uci.edu/~mlearn/MLRepository.html

Using Genetic Algorithm to Balance the D-Index Algorithm for Metric Search

Tao Ban

Information Security Research Center, National Institute of Information and Communications Technology, 4-2-1 Nukui-Kita Koganei, Tokyo, 184-8795 Japan

Abstract. The Distance Index (D-index) is a recently introduced metric indexing structure which capable of state-of-the-art performance in large scale metric search applications. In this paper we address the problem of how to balance the D-index structure for more efficient similarity search. A group of evaluation functions measuring the balance property of a D-index structure are introduced to guide the construction of the indexing structure. The optimization is formulated in a genetic representation that is effectively solved by a generic genetic algorithm (GA). Compared with the classic D-index, balanced D-index structures show a significant improvement in reduction of distance calculations while maintaining a good input-output (IO) performance.

1 Introduction

Similarity search has become a heated topic of great interest regarding both research and commercial applications. Various applications now use similarity search as either an essential preprocessing step or a kernel algorithm. In this paper, we discuss general similarity search problems where the only information available among objects is pairwise distances measured by some distance function. The data domain together with the similarity measure are generally abstracted as the following metric space model:

Let $\mathbb{D}$ be the data domain, $d : \mathbb{D} \times \mathbb{D} \to \mathcal{R}$ is a distance on $\mathbb{D}$, the tuple $\mathcal{M} = (\mathbb{D}, d)$ is called a *metric space,* if for all $\boldsymbol{x}, \boldsymbol{y}, \boldsymbol{z} \in \mathbb{D}$, the following conditions hold.

$$d(\boldsymbol{x}, \boldsymbol{y}) \geq 0 \qquad\qquad \mathrm{non - negativity} \qquad\qquad (1)$$

$$d(\boldsymbol{x}, \boldsymbol{y}) = 0 \Leftrightarrow \boldsymbol{x} = \boldsymbol{y} \qquad\qquad \mathrm{identity} \qquad\qquad (2)$$

$$d(\boldsymbol{x}, \boldsymbol{y}) = d(\boldsymbol{y}, \boldsymbol{x}) \qquad\qquad \mathrm{symmetry} \qquad\qquad (3)$$

$$d(\boldsymbol{x}, \boldsymbol{y}) + d(\boldsymbol{y}, \boldsymbol{z}) \geq d(\boldsymbol{x}, \boldsymbol{z}) \qquad\qquad \mathrm{triangular\ \ inequality} \qquad\qquad (4)$$

Given a metric space, a metric query is generally defined by a query object $\boldsymbol{q}$ and a similarity condition. For brevity, in this paper we only discuss the range query which is known as the most basic query type. A range query is defined by a query object $\boldsymbol{q} \in \mathbb{D}$ and a radius $r \in \mathbb{R}$. The response set of $\mathbb{Q}(\boldsymbol{q}, r, \mathbb{X})$ from a finite set $\mathbb{X} \subset \mathbb{D}$ is

$$\mathbb{R}(\boldsymbol{q}, r, \mathbb{X}) = \{\boldsymbol{x}_i | d(\boldsymbol{q}, \boldsymbol{x}_i) \leq r, \boldsymbol{x}_i \in \mathbb{X}\}. \qquad\qquad (5)$$

Most real world applications can be modeled as metric spaces. The goal when designing a *metric search* algorithm is to build a data structure for a finite set $\mathbb{X} \subset \mathbb{D}$, so that given a query object $\boldsymbol{q}$, the response set can be found efficiently—both in terms

M. Ishikawa et al. (Eds.): ICONIP 2007, Part II, LNCS 4985, pp. 264–273, 2008.

of the cutoff of distance computations as well as the reduction of input-output (IO) operations. Many metric indexing structures now available now; there are, to name a few, the metric tree approaches such as the Vantage Point tree (VPT) [1], Generalized Hyperplane tree (GHT) [2], and Metric tree (MTree) [3], and methods which exploit pre-computed distances such as AESA [4] and LEASA [5].

Similarity hashing methods known as Distance Index (D-index) [6] and its descendants incorporate multiple principles for search efficiency. With a novel clustering technique and the pivot-based distance searching strategy, D-index performs well in terms of reduction of distance calculations and offers a good IO management capability. The main idea of D-index is as follows. At individual levels, objects are hashed into separable buckets which are search-separable up to some predefined value ρ. Hence the structure supports easy insertion and a bounded search cost because at most one bucket per level needs to be accessed for queries with $r \leq \rho$. Furthermore, the pivot filtering strategy [4,5] is applied to significantly reduce the number of distance computations in the accessed buckets.

D-index has built a good framework for metric search especially for queries with comparatively small radii. In this paper, we try to further improve its search performance by optimizing the indexing structure. As noted in [6], a more balanced data distribution in the D-index structure improves search performance. Unfortunately, the classic D-index does not support balanced formulation. Our main idea is to use some optimization technique to guide the construction of the D-index structure. This optimization depends on the novel introduction of evaluation functions which measure the balance property of the structure. Another contribution of this paper is that the proposed optimization method allow us to automate the pivot selection procedure of D-index and obtain a well balanced indexing structure without much manual interruption. The D-index performance is further enhanced by sharing pivots among different search levels.

2   Metric Searching by D-index

In the following, we provide an overview of D-index [6].

2.1   Hashing the Dataset

In D-index, the ρ-split functions are defined to hash objects into search-separable clusters. An example is the bps (ball-partitioning split) function. With a predefined *separability parameter* ρ, a bps uniquely determines the belongingness of an object $o \in \mathcal{D}$:

$$bps^{1,\rho}(\boldsymbol{o}_i) = \begin{cases} 0 & \text{if } d(\boldsymbol{o}_i, \boldsymbol{p}) \leq d_m - \rho \\ 1 & \text{if } d(\boldsymbol{o}_i, \boldsymbol{p}) > d_m + \rho \\ - & \text{otherwise} \end{cases} \tag{6}$$

where $\boldsymbol{p}$ is a *pivot* and d_m the median of the distances from $\boldsymbol{p}$ to all $\boldsymbol{o}_i \in \mathbb{D}$. The superscript 1 denotes the order of the split function; i.e. the number of pivots involved. The subset characterized by the symbol '$-$' is called the *exclusion set*, noted as $\mathbb{E}$. The subsets noted by $\mathbb{S}_{[0]}^{1,\rho}(\mathbb{D})$ and $\mathbb{S}_{[1]}^{1,\rho}(\mathbb{D})$ are called *separable sets* according to the following *separable property*:

$$d(\boldsymbol{o}_i, \boldsymbol{o}_j) > 2\rho, \quad \text{for all } \boldsymbol{o}_i \in \mathbb{S}_{[0]}^{1,\rho}(\mathbb{D}), \boldsymbol{o}_j \in \mathbb{S}_{[1]}^{1,\rho}(\mathbb{D}). \tag{7}$$

To partition the dataset into more separable sets, higher order ρ-split functions are composed by combining multiple first order ρ-split functions. Given m *bps* split functions, the join m-order split function is denoted as $bps^{m,\rho}$, and the return value can be seen as a string $b = [b_1, b_2, \cdots, b_n]$, where $b_i \in \{0, 1, -\}$. The following hashing operator $\langle \cdot \rangle$ returns an integer value in the range $[0, \cdots, 2^m]$ for any string.

$$\langle b \rangle = \begin{cases} 2^m, & \text{if } \exists j \ b_j = - \\ [b_1, b_2, \cdots, b_m]_2 = \sum_{j=1}^{m} 2^{m-j} b_j, & \text{otherwise.} \end{cases} \tag{8}$$

Thus through the ρ-split function and the hashing function, a mapping is defined from $o_i \in \mathcal{D}$ to an integer $i \in [0, 2^m]$. The objects are grouped in 2^m separable subsets and an exclusion set with the separable property still holds.

The *bps* function is defined by multiple pivots and the associated median distances. D-index applies *incremental selection* to select pivots. At the beginning, a set $P = \{p_1\}$ with a maximized μ_1 is chosen from the objects, where μ_i is the expectation of the inter-object distances in the feature space defined by the pivots, formally,

$$\mu_i = \mathop{E}_{x \in \mathbb{D}, y \in \mathbb{D}} \mathop{\max}_{s=1}^{i-1} (|d(\boldsymbol{x}, \boldsymbol{p}_s) - d(\boldsymbol{y}, \boldsymbol{p}_s)|). \tag{9}$$

At step i, with the previously selected pivot set fixed, p_i is chosen from the dataset with the maximal μ_i. The process is repeated until a desired number of pivots are determined.

2.2 Insertion and Search Operations

The insertion algorithm is applied to build the D-index structure storing the dataset into a file. Starting with the first level, the algorithm tries to insert object, o_N, into a separable bucket. At a certain level, if o_N drops into the region of a separable bucket, it is assigned to the bucket and the algorithm terminates. If the algorithm fails for all levels, o_N is placed in the global exclusion set $\mathbb{E}_H$. In any case, the insertion algorithm selects exactly one bucket to store the object.

Given a D-index structure, the search algorithm guides the search procedure. For brevity, we only discuss the range search algorithm with $r \leq \rho$. Refer to [6] for fully specified general range search and nearest neighbor search algorithms. For a range query $\mathbb{R}(\boldsymbol{q}, r)$ with $r \leq \rho$, $bps_h^{m_h, 0}(q)$ always produces a value smaller than 2^{m_h} since ρ is set to zero. Consequently, at most one separable bucket is accessed at each level. In the simple range search algorithm, we assume all levels are accessed as well as the global exclusion bucket. This algorithm requires $H + 1$ bucket accesses, which is the upper bound to the more sophisticated algorithm specified in [6].

In D-index, special techniques are applied to speed up the search within a bucket. Generally, a bucket structure consists of a header plus a dynamic list of fixed-size blocks accommodating the object dataset. In the header, information on the pivots as well as the distances from all the objects in the bucket to these pivots is stored. Thus, the following *pivoting rule* [4] can be applied to avoid unnecessary distance computations in the bucket. Let p_i be a pivot and x be an object in the bucket. Then for $Q = R(q, r)$,

$$|d(x, p) - d(q, p)| > r \Rightarrow d(q, x) > r. \tag{10}$$

This pivoting rule follows directly from the triangular inequality. Note that when the objects in the bucket are all pruned by the pivoting rule, bucket access can be reduced.

3   Criteria to Measure the Balance Property of the D-index

The incremental selection method does not support fully automated pivot selection: the number of pivots at the individual levels of D-index are adjusted manually or heuristically. This may impose difficulties for users without domain knowledge. Moreover, it also does not support a balanced indexing structure, so the search performance may degenerate. In this section we discuss how to build a balanced D-index structure to improve search efficiency. To build such a structure, we should have some kind of measurement to evaluate the balance property of a given D-index structure.

The expected number of distance calculations for all possible searches appears to be the best measure of the performance of an indexing structure. However, note that this measurement is only available after the D-index structure is built: when the pivot filtering technique is applied to prune the objects, it is difficult to produce a theoretical estimation for the distance computations. Fortunately, we can instead use the number of visited objects during the search to estimate the computational cost because of the following observations. First, the number of distance computations is generally directly proportional to the number of visited objects during the search. Second, if the pivot filtering technique is not used, the number of visited objects will equal the number of distance computations. Last, for certain applications, the computational cost for pivoting is comparable with that of distance computation and cannot be ignored. In what follows we discuss three evaluation criteria.

3.1   Statistics-Based Objective Function

Let the number of samples in the dataset be N. For the hth level of the D-index structure, denote the number of samples in the jth separable set as s_{hj}, $j = 1 \ldots, 2^{m_h-1}$, and the size of the exclusion set as e_h. For a range query with a radius $r \leq \rho$, the expected number of objects to be visited, V_h, on the level can then be computed by

$$V_h(\alpha) = \sum_{l=0}^{2^{m_h}-1} \frac{s_{hl}}{N}(s_{hl} + \alpha e_h) + \frac{e_i}{N}\left(\alpha e_h + \frac{1}{2^{m_h}} \sum_{l=0}^{2^{m_h}-1} s_{hl}\right), \qquad (11)$$

where $\alpha \in [0, 1]$ denotes the ratio of objects that should be visited in the exclusion set. The first term on the right side of (11) stands for the expected distance computations for query objects dropping into the separable sets, and the second term stands for the estimated distance computations for query objects dropping into the exclusion set.

As we can see from (11), for a fixed α, the number of pruned objects at level h is

$$R_h(\alpha) = E_{h-1} - V_h(\alpha). \qquad (12)$$

By maximizing $R_h(\alpha)$, we can then expect better eliminating performance at level h. R_h is a function of α: with an α value close to 1, there will be few objects in the exclusion set, while for an α value close to 0 most objects will be assigned to the exclusion set. Thus, by setting α we can adjust the tendency of the algorithm to assign objects to the exclusion set. In this paper, we adopt the following strategy. We denote the expected number of levels for a D-index structure as H, and set α to h/H for the hth level. By maximizing $R_h(h/H)$ at the hth level, we can optimize the balance property of the D-index structure as well as control the number of levels in the D-index structure.

3.2 Objective Function Based on Worst Case Analysis

The second objective function is derived from the worst case analysis. In the worst case, at each level of the D-index structure, the algorithm would visit the largest separable set. That is, the maximal visited objects for a range query with $r \leq \rho$ will be

$$V_{\mathrm{m}} = E_H + \sum_{h=1}^{H} \max_{l=0}^{2^{m_h}-1} s_{hl}. \tag{13}$$

Similar to (11), this global function can be easily adopted to evaluate split functions on an individual level. To achieve this, we define the following objective function:

$$P_h = \sum_{l=0}^{2^{m_h}-1} s_{hl} \Big/ \max_{l=0}^{2^{m_h}-1} s_{hl}. \tag{14}$$

Maximizing (14) is equivalent to minimizing the portion of the objects to be visited in the worst case at the hth level. Thus from (13), we can compute an upper bound on the number of visited objects to answer a range query with $r \leq \rho$.

3.3 Heuristics-Based Objective Function

The last objective function comes from the following well-known arithmetic-geometric means inequality. Let $a_1, \ldots, a_L$ be a set of positive real numbers, where L is a positive integer. The arithmetic mean of the numbers is defined as $(a_1 + \cdots + a_L)/L$, whereas their geometric mean is $(a_1 \cdots a_L)^{1/L}$. The following inequation always holds

$$(a_1 + \cdots + a_L)/L \geq (a_1 \cdots a_L)^{1/L}. \tag{15}$$

Here we consider the set of cardinal numbers of all possible separable sets on the hth level. Assume $s_{hj} > 0$ for $j = 0, \cdots, 2^{m_h}-1$ with $\sum_j s_{hj} = C$, where C is a constant number. From inequality (15), we can see that the more evenly the objects scatter into the separable sets, the larger the geometric mean of s_{hl}. Thus, we can define the following objective function based on the arithmetic-geometric means inequality:

$$O_h = \frac{1}{2^{m_h}} \sum_{l=0}^{2^{m_h}-1} \log(s_{hl} + 1). \tag{16}$$

Here, the objective function is presented in logarithmic form for better scaling.

4 GA-Based Optimization

With the objective functions, we can apply suitable optimization techniques to balance the D-index structure. Note that the objective functions and the variables here are all discontinuous, which prevents application of many of the popular optimization techniques. Fortunately, GAs are a branch of optimization methods suitable for optimizing both combinatorial and continuous problems.

A typical genetic algorithm requires the definition of two things [7]: (1) a genetic representation of the solution domain, and (2) a fitness function to evaluate the solution domain. The second requirement is easily satisfied with the evaluation criterion defined in the previous section. Here we show how to format the problem in a genetic representation. The split function at the hth level in a D-index structure is defined by a group of pivots and their median distances. Suppose we are given a pool of W candidate pivots with good pivoting ability. The goal of the pivot selection algorithm is to select a subset from the pool that yields a balanced scattering over the separable sets. Here the candidates can be a preselected subset of the dataset or possibly all objects in the domain. We can then code the solution of the pivot selection problem in a genetic form trough the following steps. The solution is an array of bits $\mathcal{W} = [w_1, \cdots, w_W]$, with

$$w_i = \begin{cases} 1 & \text{if object } p_i \text{ is selected as a pivot,} \\ 0 & \text{otherwise.} \end{cases} \tag{17}$$

The problem can be solved by following the standard process of a GA. *Initialization:* Many individual solutions are randomly generated to form an initial population. *Selection:* In each successive generation, a proportion of the existing population is selected to breed a new generation. *Reproduction:* From the selected population, a second-generation population of solutions is generated through the two genetic operators: crossover and/or mutation. *Termination:* This generational process is repeated until the highest ranking solution's fitness is close to reaching or has reached a plateau such that successive iterations no longer produce better results.

We can reduce the number of genes to alleviate the computational cost of a GA and speed up its convergence. Recall that the incremental pivot selection algorithm is able to choose a set of pivots with good pivoting ability. We apply this algorithm to select a pool of candidates and then use a GA to select the active genes from the pool. Given a predefined candidate set size, n_p, we can define the following D-index algorithm, as shown in Table 1, which uses a GA algorithm to balance the structure. As specified in lines 3 through 7, at a certain level of the D-index structure, we first select a group of pivots through the incremental selection algorithm and then apply the GA method to select the most appropriate subset of pivots to form a balanced structure. To reduce the total number of pivots selected, we make the pivots at former levels reusable: the pivot set used at the hth level is formed by appending each pivot set ever selected up to level $h - 1$ with the incremental selection algorithm. The algorithm returns pivot set $\mathcal{P}_h$ for individual levels and a set $\mathcal{P}$ of all selected pivots.

5   Experiments

This section presents numerical results obtained with the balanced D-index. Several different approaches are also examined: the original D-index, MTree, VPT, and GHT.

5.1   Datasets

In the experiments, datasets with a variety of data distributions and distance functions are explored. Specifically, we use the following metric datasets. **KDD dataset:** The

Table 1. GA-based Pivot Selection for D-index

1 $\mathbb{P} \leftarrow \mathbb{P}_0 \leftarrow \emptyset;\ \ \mathbb{E}_0 \leftarrow \mathbb{X};\ \ \ h \leftarrow 0;$	// Initialization
2 **do**	// Repeat until $\mathbb{E}_h$ cannot be further divided
3 $\quad h \leftarrow h + 1;$	
4 $\quad \mathbb{P}'_h \leftarrow$ **IncrSelection**$(\mathbb{E}_{h-1}, \mathbb{P}, n_p);$	// Append the pivot set
5 $\quad \mathbb{P}_h \leftarrow$ **GA** $(\mathbb{P}'_h, f);$	// Use GA to optimize the pivot set
6 $\quad E_h \leftarrow$ **GetExclusion**$(\mathbb{E}_{h-1}, \mathbb{P}_h);$	// Update the exclusion set
7 $\quad \mathbb{P} \leftarrow \mathbb{P} \cap \mathbb{P}_h;$	// Pivot set includes all used pivots
8 **while** $\mathbb{E}_h \neq \mathbb{E}_{h-1}$	
9 **return** $\mathbb{P}, \mathbb{P}_h, h = 1, \cdots;$	

KDD dataset [10] contains simulated intrusions in a military network environment. It has 34 continuous and 7 categorical features. The distance between records is defined as the sum of the Euclidean distance with respect to continuous features and the Hamming distance with respect to categorical features. **WL dataset:** The word list dataset [8] consists of more than $60,000$ frequently used English words. The similarity between two words is measured by the *edit distance*: the number of operations required to transform one of them into the other. **CH dataset:** The color histogram dataset [9] includes the color histogram features of 68,040 photo images from various categories. The similarity is measured by the Euclidian distance between color histograms. **MAWD dataset:** The Microsoft Anonymous Web dataset [10] was created by sampling and processing the www.microsoft.com logs. For each user, the data lists all the areas out of a total of 17 in the web site that the user visited within a one-week time frame. If we let A_i be the set of areas a user has visited, the similarity between the behavior of two users, u_i and u_j, is measure by the Jaccard distance between A_i and A_j.

5.2 Performance Comparison

For all the datasets, subsets consisting of 10,000 objects are indexed in the indexing structures. The index structures are tested by 100 range queries with queries differing from the indexed objects. To get the results, we run the experiments 30 times and report the averaged results. The maximal query radii are selected to keep the response set size at about 20% of the dataset. Significance testing of the differences in performance between the balanced D-index structures and the classic D-index are done as follows. Paired t-tests are performed on the visiting operations, distance computations, and IO accesses required by each of the balanced D-index structures and the classic D-index at a confidence interval of 99%. In the t-test result curves, a value of 1 means the balanced structure has better performance than the classic D-index, a value of -1 stands for inferior performance, and a value of 0 means that the null hypothesis that there is no much difference between the two indexing structures is true.

First, we focus on the visiting operations of D-index structures built according to different objective functions, with the classic D-index serving as a baseline. In Figure 1, we show the curves of the visited objects against the search radius. We can learn three things from the figures. First, optimization of the indexing structure can effectively reduce the number of objects visited during the search. When the search radius is small

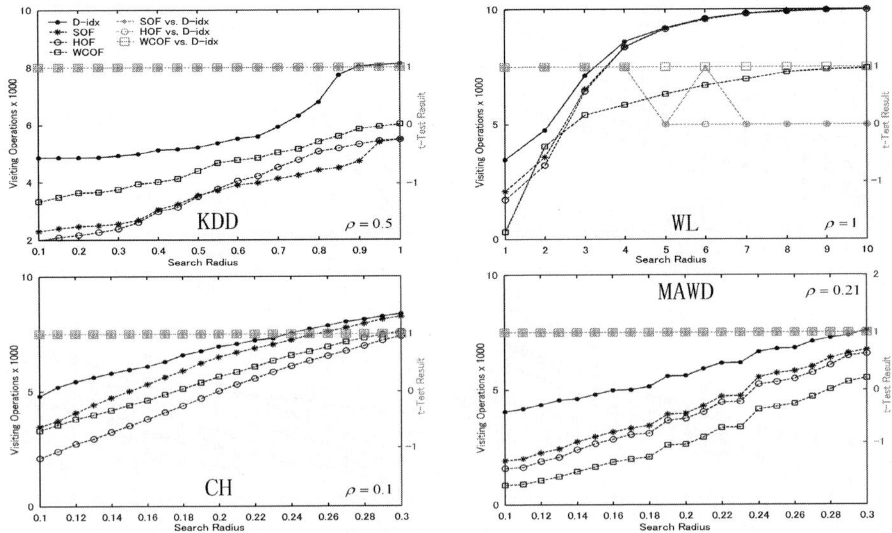

Fig. 1. Evaluation of the visiting operations

the improvement is significant: the best D-index structure will have only half as many visiting operations as the classic D-index structure. Second, the performance of each proposed objective function depends on the property of the metric space. The statistics-based objective function (SOF) is best for the KDD dataset. The worst case analysis objective function (WCOF) shows the best performance for the WL and MAWD datasets. The heuristics-based objective function (HOF) performs best on the CH dataset. Thus, for a given dataset, we should check all the three objective functions and select the most appropriate one to build the D-index structure. Last, the performance of a D-index structure is fairly stable against the increment in search radius. A good structure for a small search radius will also be effective for a large search radius. Because of this property, we can evaluate the relative performance of different D-index implementations with a fixed search radius. Reduction of distance calculations is a widely used criterion to evaluate a metric indexing method. Figure 2 shows the curves of distance calculations against the search radius. The results for VPT, GHT, and MTree are also shown for reference. As we expected, the curves for the D-index structures show characteristics similar to those in Figure 1. This verifies our claim that for a D-index structure the number of distance calculations will not necessarily be directly proportional to the number of visited objects. For all the metric search structures, the pruning effect diminishes as the search radius increases. Compared with other metric indexing algorithms, D-index shows better pruning performance, especially for small search radii. When the search radius increases, the classic D-index degenerates and shows pruning ability comparable with that of other indexing methods. With the structure balanced by the proposed method, D-index outperforms other methods even for rather large search radii. As mentioned, the number of disk accesses is another useful evaluation criterion for metric search methods. We show the curves of disk accesses against the search radius in Figure 3. We only show the results for D-index and MTree because other methods do

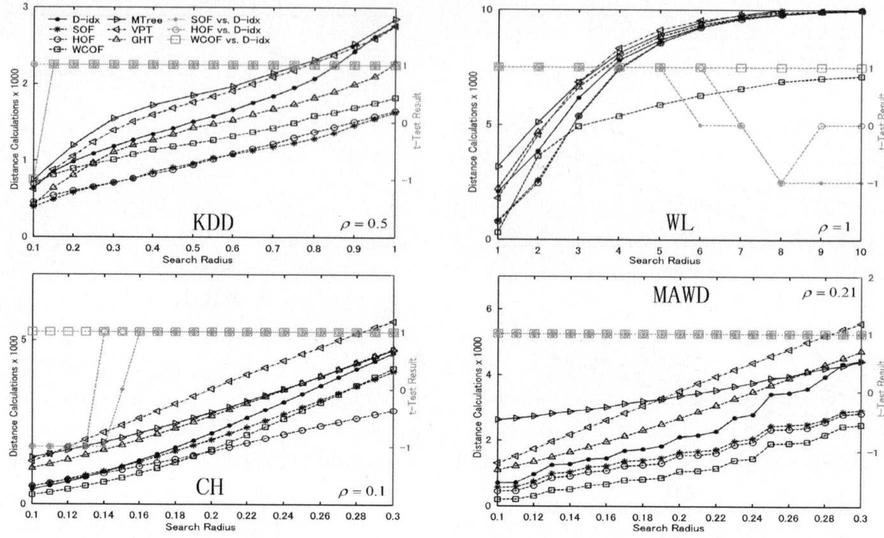

Fig. 2. Evaluation of the distance calculations

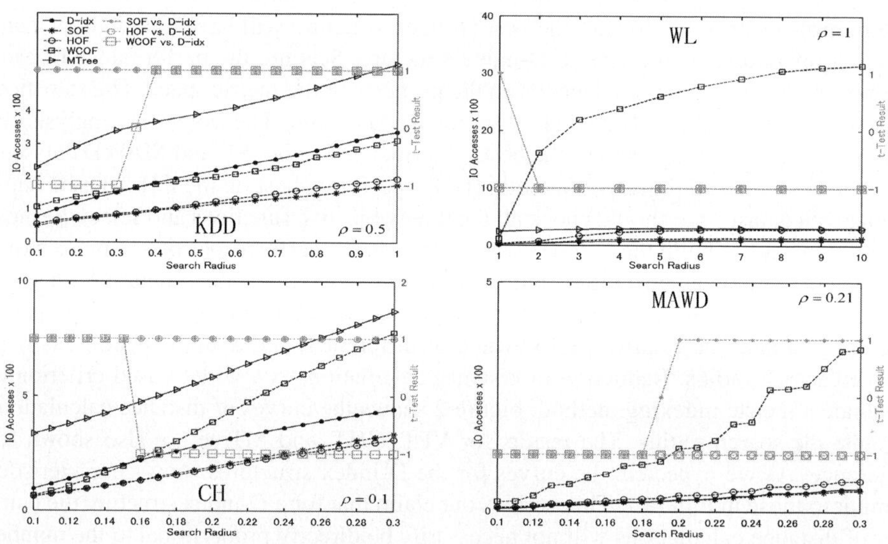

Fig. 3. Evaluation of the IO accesses

not comprise IO management functions. For all the experiments, the size of each disk page is 1,024 bytes. These results show that in most cases the D-index structures have a relatively efficient IO management ability. The D-index structures built according to the statistics-based objective function and heuristic-based function perform approximately as well as the classic D-index. For the MAWD dataset and WL dataset, the worst case analysis objective function trades off IO management performance against the reduction of distance computations.

6   Conclusions

In this paper, we focused on how to balance the D-index structure for better metric search performance. Using three functions—one statistics based, one heuristic based, and one based on worst case analysis—we evaluated the balance property of individual D-index levels. A GA algorithm optimizing these functions was then applied to guide the construction of the D-index structure.

The D-index showed the following properties. First, the number of visited objects during search coincided with the distance calculations. Thus, either of these measures can be used to guide the construction of a D-index structure with better searching performance. Second, balancing the D-index structure can help to improve the pruning ability of the search algorithm. With a balanced structure, D-index showed better pruning performance for all search radii than any of the other indexing approaches we examined. Last, the worst case analysis objective function performed best for datasets with discrete distances, but at a cost of an increased number of IO accesses; the statistics-based and heuristic-based objective functions showed improved pruning ability with an IO cost comparable with that of the classic D-index.

References

1. Yianilos, P.N.: Data structures and algorithms for nearest neighbor search in general metric spaces. In: ACM-SIAM Symposium on Discrete Algorithms, pp. 311–321 (1993)
2. Uhlmann, J.K.: Satisfying general proximity/similarity queries with metric trees. Information Processing Letters 40(4), 175–179 (1991)
3. Ciaccia, P., Patella, M., Zezula, P.: M-tree: an efficient access method for similarity search in matric spaces. In: Proceedings of the 23rd International Conference on Very Large Data Bases (VLDB 1997), pp. 426–435 (1997)
4. Vidal, E.: New formulation and improvements of the nearest-neighbor approximating and eliminating search algorithm (AESA). Pattern Recognition Letters 15(1), 1–7 (1994)
5. Micó, M.L., Oncina, J., Vidal, E.: A new version of the nearest-neighbor approximating and eliminating search algorithm (AESA) with linear preprocessing time and memory requirements. Pattern Recognition Letters 15(1), 9–17 (1994)
6. Dohnal, V., Gennaro, C., Savino, P., Zezula, P.: D-Index: distance searching index for metric sata sets. Multimedia Tools and Applications 21(1), 9–33 (2003)
7. Schmitt, L.M.: Theory of Genetic Algorithms. Theoretical Computer Science 259, 1–61 (2001)
8. Data available at http://www.net-comber.com/wordurls.html
9. Ortega, M., Rui, Y., et al.: Supporting ranked Boolean similarity queries in MARS. IEEE Transaction on Knowledge and Data Engineering 10(6), 905–925 (1998)
10. Data available at http://www.ics.uci.edu/~mlearn/MLRepository.html

Spherical and Torus SOM Approaches to Metabolic Syndrome Evaluation

Peter K. Kihato[1], Heizo Tokutaka[2], Masaaki Ohkita[1], Kikuo Fujimura[1],
Kazuhiko Kotani[3], Yoichi Kurozawa[3], and Yoshio Maniwa[4]

[1] Tottori University, Faculty of Engineering,
[2] SOM Japan Inc.,
[3] Tottori University, Faculty of Medicine,
[4] Futaba clinic
kamitazv@yahoo.co.uk, tokutaka@somj.com,
mohkita@ele.tottori-u.ac.jp, kakotani@grape.med.tottori-u.ac.jp,
kurozawa@grape.med.tottori-u.ac.jp, maniwayo@gold.ocn.ne.jp

Abstract. One of the threatening trends of health to the youth in recent years has been the metabolic syndrome. Many associate this syndrome to how big the fatty tissue around the belly is. Self-organizing maps (SOM) can be viewed as a visualization tool that projects high-dimensional dataset onto a two-dimensional plane making the complexity of the data be simplified and in the process disclose much of the hidden details for easy analyzes, clustering and visualization. This paper focuses on the analysis, visualization and prediction of the syndrome trends using both spherical and Torus SOM with a view to diagnose its trends, inter-relate other risk factors as well as evaluating the responses obtained from the two approaches of SOM.

Keywords: Metabolic syndrome, Self Organizing Maps (SOM), Visualization.

1   Introduction

Metabolic syndrome is a symptom of body disorder (medical) that causes the various organs to malfunction. The malfunctioning organs can lead to diseases like cardiovascular or diabetes to mention a few. The syndrome is believed to be associated with the eating and less physical exercises habits, where the body mass to height factor is taken as a scalar quantity.

The concept that big belly members of the society endanger themselves in relation to this syndrome cannot be overemphasized. Unfortunately many end up digging their grave through psychological implications and not due to their Body Mass Index (BMI).

SOM is a mapping routine where multi-dimensional data is mapped onto one, or two-dimensional surface for easy visualization, clustering and hence analysis and interpretation of the original complex data. SOM can be used to visualize and analyze the health behavior patterns of an individual. Clinical Doctors can then use the charts to help the examinees visualize their degree of health. The Doctors can as well predict the consequences well in advance and hence save the member from being affected.

Evaluation of this syndrome through SOM gives us a method of analyzing, visualizing and predicting its trends. This in effect if shared with the examinee becomes

M. Ishikawa et al. (Eds.): ICONIP 2007, Part II, LNCS 4985, pp. 274–284, 2008.

not only a useful tool to the Doctor but also a health conduit to solving any health issue and thereby preventing examinees from being affected by the secondary disease "psychology".

A health evaluation system based on spherical and torus SOM was constructed based on health checkup data from examinees. Here four parameters were used namely BMI, high blood pressure (H-BP), blood glucose level (GLU) and triglyceride (TG).

2 Self-organizing Maps (SOM)

Kohonen's SOM [1] is an Artificial Neural Network (ANN) used to map high dimensional data onto a low 2D-representation space. The network consists of a neural processing elements (nodes) usually arranged on a rectangular or hexagonal grid where each node is connected to the input. The goal is to group similar nodes close together in certain areas of the value range. The resultant maps are organized in such a way that similar data are mapped on the same node or to neighboring nodes on the map. This leads to a special clustering of similar input patterns in neighboring parts of the SOM and the clusters that appear on the map are themselves organized. SOM uses a distribution preserving property which has the ability to allocate more nodes to input patterns that appear more frequently during the training phase of the network configuration. Thus the topology of the n-dimensional space is captured by the SOM and reflected in the ordering of its nodes. The input data is thus projected onto a lower dimension space while roughly preserving the order of the data in its original space. The learning process is unsupervised meaning that the training patterns have no category information that follows them.

2.1 Best Matching Unit (BMU)

SOM is trained iteratively with each training step sampling input vector $\mathbf{x}$ and the distance between it and all the weight vectors ($\mathbf{m}_i$) of the lattice are calculated joined by scalar weights w_{ij}. The node whose weight vector is closest to the input vector is the BMU denoted here as c:

$$\|x - m_c\| = \min_i \{\|x - m_i\|\},\tag{1}$$

where $\|.\|$ is the Euclidean distance measure, $\mathbf{m}_i$ reference vector of each node on the lattice and $\mathbf{m}_c$ the winner node vector. After the winning node c is selected, the weights of the nodes in a neighborhood (defined) are adjusted so that similar input patterns are more likely to select this node again. This is achieved through computation:

$$\mathbf{m}_i(t + 1) = \mathbf{m}_i(t) + \alpha(t)h_{ci}(t)[\mathbf{x}(t) - \mathbf{m}_i(t)],\tag{2}$$

$h_{ci}(t)$ is the neighborhood kernel around the winner unit c which is often taken to be Gaussian,

$$h_{ci}(t) = \exp\left(-\|r_i - r_c\|^2 \Big/ 2\sigma^2(t)\right)$$
(3)

where $0 < \alpha < 1$ is the learning rate factor, t, the discrete-time index of the variables, r_i and r_c, vectorial locations in the display grid and σ, the width of the neighborhood function which decreases monotonically with the regression steps.

If the learning rate is taken as a linear function,

$\alpha(t) = A/(t + B)$, where 'A' and 'B' are suitably selected constants.

2.2 Torus SOM

This is one of the modes of representing the plane lattice that gives an outlook of a torus. It gives both a better view of the input data as well as a closer links to edge nodes.

The unified distance matrix (U-matrix) [Ultsch 99], [2, 3, 4] Torus makes the 2D visualization of multivariate data possible using SOM's code vectors as data source. This is achieved by using topological relations property among nodes after the learning process. The algorithm generates a matrix where each input parameter is a distance measure between two adjacent nodes, thereby being able to visualize a multivariant dataset in a two dimensional display.

Fig. 1 shows a U-matrix representation of male examinees dataset. Darker gray areas represent less population of examined members and can then be viewed as boundary health status points between the clusters. Lightest gray zones are densely populated regions of the clusters i.e. more members. Included in the map are the percentage metabolic points.

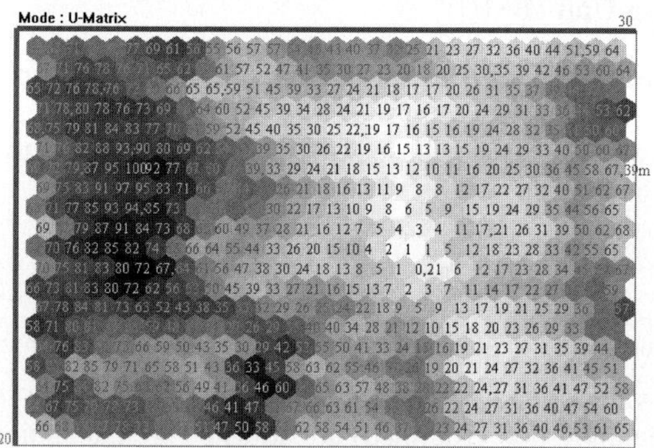

Fig. 1. Male Examinee U-Matrix SOM

2.3 Spherical SOM

Spherical surface SOM [5, 6] with a uniform phase expression is applied to metabolic syndrome. Using the same data for the examinees, "blossom" [8] was used as a tool to construct the SOM. Fig. 2 is a trained spherical SOM from male data. Gray scaling is used for the population density of the examinees. On the smooth face of the sphere, nodes are implanted. These are the trained nodes representing the examinees' health check data. Added to each node is the degree of metabolic risk ranging from 0 to 5. Fig. 2 (a) shows light gray portion of the sphere. This indicates densely populated zone (s) or cluster of examinees. Selected members from a certain Doctor 'A' have also been matched to the trained SOM. Dark gray areas as shown in Fig. 2 (b) indicate scarce population and it happens to be the higher metabolic risk zone (s).

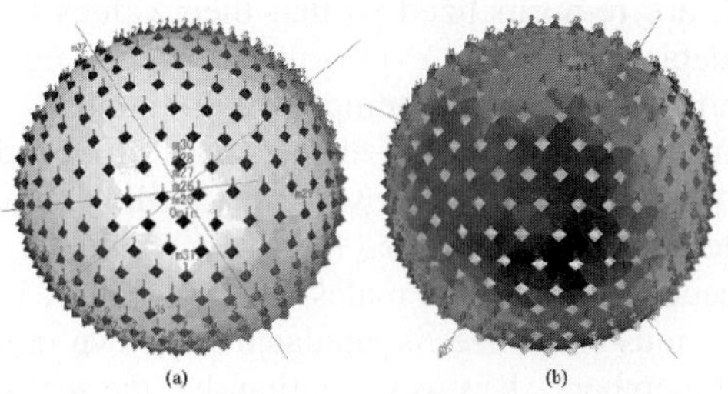

Fig. 2. Spherical SOM

3   Physical Examination

Patients need physical examination particularly if they feel insecure or fall sick. For the sake of the metabolic syndrome analysis, various members of a company were done physical examination. To perform the syndrome analysis the following health parameter were set as standards.

BMI (Kg/m^2):   Over 25
H-BP: Over 140 mmHG
GLU: Over 110 mg/dl
TG: Over 150 mg/dl

3.1   Data Pre-processing

Before the multi-dimensional data is applied to SOM, normalization of the data needs to be done. This is due to the fact that the incoming data has different dimensions. Normalizing it causes the data to be taken as emerging from one source. For the normalization of the physical test data, let us take the minimum value of any input parameter as L, maximum value as H, actual data as X, and normalized value as Y.
   Thus, if (X < L);

$$Y = X/L \tag{4}$$

If (L $\leq$ X $\leq$ H);

$$Y = 1 \tag{5}$$

If (X > H);

$$Y = X/H \tag{6}$$

However after normalizing the data, some parameters seem to have high-normalized values causing the frequency distribution curve [7] for the normalized data to be more on the higher side. In some situations majority of the input data seems to be higher than the normal. It is due to this abnormality that a ceiling value is decided for each input parameter. Any normalized value greater than the ceiling value is given the ceiling value.

Metabolic stage happens to be physical test data beyond the normal values. Taking the normal values to fall within those represented by equation (5), the four items BMI, H-BP, GLU and TG, are re-normalized so that their values fall within the standard way of normalizing data. Thus Data (Y-1) is re-normalized again to a new Y. In this contribution equation (4) type of data is temporarily omitted.

Frequency distribution for every input element was produced to obtain the ceiling value of the new Y of Equation (6). As shown in [7], ceiling values for all the elements were decided. Female ceiling scale values for BMI, H-BP, GLU and TG were 1.25, 1.3, 1.55 and 2.3 respectively, while the males' were 1.25, 1.3, 1.85 and 3 respectively. Data obtained from various examinees is tabulated as shown in table 1 being a sample of the male examined members. It is worth noting that the scaling parameters for both male and female stand different due to respective population densities. After normalizing the data, the next stage is training the data using SOM trainers.

3.2 Metabolic Syndrome Points (MSP)

Weight factor for all the elements was taken as 1. Normally the weight of each element is based on the importance of the element to the health state. Health mark point can be expressed by Equation (7), where a mark point is rounded off and where WV_n is the worst value of test data for particular parameter, NV normal value, X_{ni}, the data of examinee, n the number of parameters being examined while 'i' is the count of metabolic examinee.

$$\text{Health mark-point (MK)}_i = \frac{\sqrt{\sum_{n=1}^{n}(WV_n - NV)^2} - \sqrt{\sum_{n=1}^{n}(X_{ni} - NV)^2}}{\sqrt{\sum_{n=1}^{n}(WV_n - NV)^2}} \times 100 \tag{7}$$

MSP for torus type of SOM is 100-MK which is the deficiency of health. Spherical SOM MSP are taken as (100-MK)*5/100 for clarity on the map.

3.3 Color Coded SOM

After the learning process, the nodes can be colored according to each input item value in the code vector. A colored SOM can be used to visualize emerging patterns of the data distribution within the clusters. Fig. 3 shows a female examinees' torus SOM with the nodes colored depending on the metabolic risk condition.

A component map gives a better view of the contribution that input parameter has on the overall output SOM. Colored component maps are an added advantage to the

Table 1. Male normalized samples (Norm)

Male data Samples	BMI	BMI	BMI	H–BP	H–BP	H–BP	GLU	GLU	GLU	TG	TG	TG	L–BP	L–BP	L–BP	HCHO	HCHO	HCHO
	Kg/(m)^2		Norm	mmHg		Norm	mg/dl		Norm	mg/dl		Norm	mg/dl		Norm	mg/dl		Norm
Upper limit	24.2			139			109			150			89	89		200		
Lower limit	13			80			50			20			0	0		40		
Ceiling scale	1.2			1.26			1.6			2			1.14			1.25		
M1	27.4383	1.134	0.669	144	1.036	0.138	94	1	0	825	2	1	88	1	0	36	0.9	0.44444
M2	27.8452	1.151	0.753	190	1.26	1	317	1.6	1	777	2	1	100	1.124	0.8828	33	0.825	0.84848
M3	23.5014	1.000	0	140	1.007	0.028	142	1.3	0.505	773	2	1	100	1.124	0.8828	35	0.875	0.57143
M4	21.5943	1.000	0	126	1	0	113	1.04	0.061	769	2	1	84	1	0	49	1	0
M5	23.7963	1.000	0	140	1.007	0.028	98	1	0	673	2	1	104	1.14	1	36	0.9	0.44444

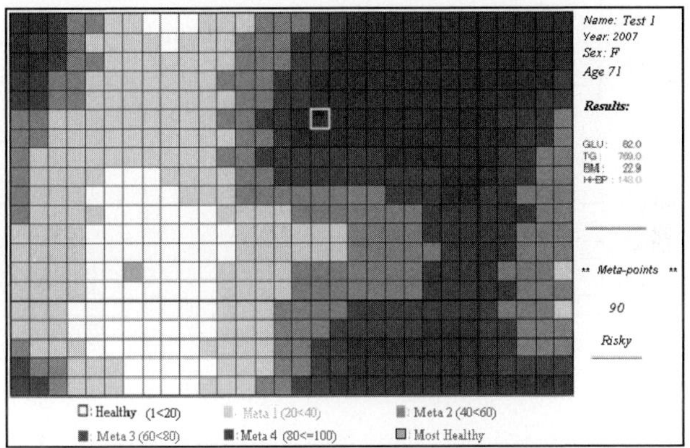

Fig. 3. Torus SOM Checkup Tool (Female)

user. Fig. 4 shows a unified component map with various distinct color-coding for each parameter. BMI has three distinct color codes while the other three input items have two each.

Additional color codes are those representing healthy examinees (clear) and Gray representing the gray scaling indicating the strength of the bonding between the various input parameters. This approach gives the viewer a better visualization of the input data and hence an alternative method to interpret the input data.

4   Analysis and Visualization of the Results

Originally there were 4000 female and 3000 male examinees. To remove healthy members from syndrome list, a re-normalization procedure was to be carried out. There-normalization process takes two folds; No_cut and B0s02cut formats; No_cut metabolic syndrome members were those with any trace of increase from 0 in any of the four elements. This gave 2910 and 1764 respectively. The B0s02cut case reduced the members further to 2564 and 1375 respectively. B0s02cut removed the boundary

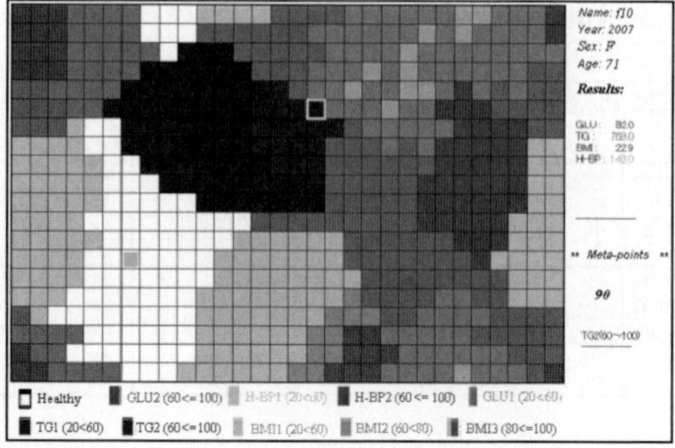

Fig. 4. Component Map SOM (Female)

Table 2. Metabolic syndrome check data

Sex	Age	B MI	H–BP	TG	GLU	Meta_Doc	Meta_SOM	No_cut	B0s02 cut
f1	56	24.2	122	37	103	0	0	0	0
f11	71	27.7	156	76	98	0	0	68	70
f12	75	22.7	134	51	146	0	0	63	63
f13	57	30.9	142	146	100	1	1	91	90
f4	38	20.4	116	131	84	0	0	1	0
f5	60	20.1	130	67	90	0	0	0	0
m30	43	22.2	130	91	93	0	0	0	0
m31	78	21.5	140	84	95	0	0	1	0
m32	68	25.8	124	55	92	0	0	25	24
m33	72	25.6	150	59	100	0	0	36	20
m38	67	26.5	150	77	125	1	0	52	51
m39	71	25.6	124	327	111	1	1	77	70

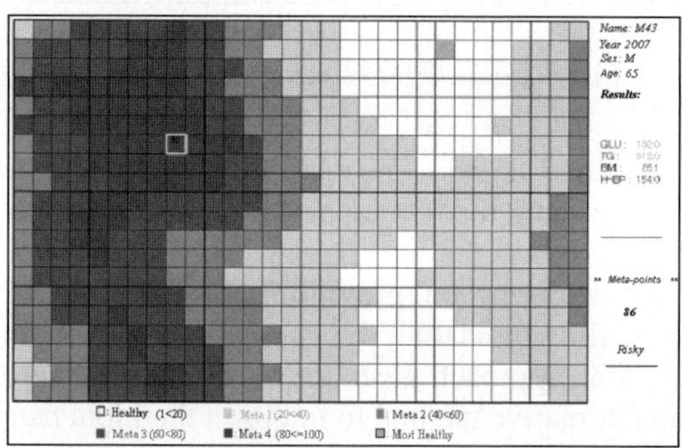

Fig. 5. Male Torus SOM Checkup Tool (Male)

members where the cutoff point was BMI being 0 and summation of the other three elements being greater than 0.2. To represent the whole spectrum of examinees, 20 healthy members were included in each input data.

Referring to Figs. 3 to 6 the following can be observed:

- Male examinees show risky trends mainly due to H-BP, TG and GLU with TG and GLU being the main risky elements.

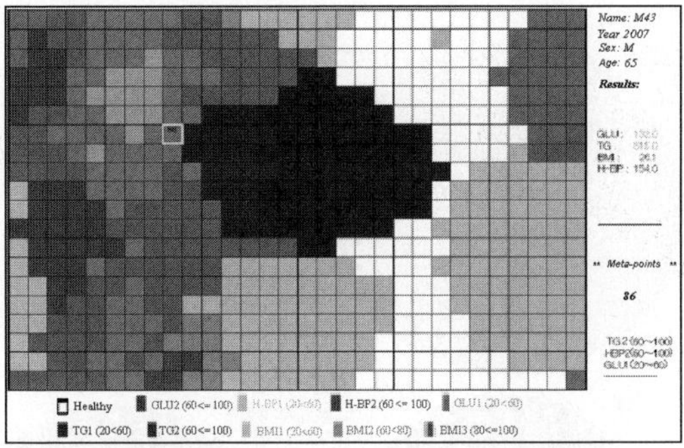

Fig. 6. Component Map (Male)

Fig. 7. Healthy Zone Component Maps

- Female examinees risky elements are BMI, H-BP and TG with the main risky element being BMI. All the same there seems to have a general problem across the board.
- Examinee's health-check details: raw data, metabolic syndrome risk points and the degree of risk on each input item.

Table 2 gives sampled data of female-male examinees with physician and SOM results indicated as Meta_Doc and Meta_SOM respectively. Examinee m38 risk factor is not as high as that of m39 or that of f13.

Figs. 7 and 8 show the spherical Component maps of the trained male examinee data where individual's health can be analyzed using this "blossom" tool [8]. It is of importance to maintain same location as one varies the type of input parameter for an examinee on the spherical SOM. The contribution each input item has on the overall metabolic syndrome is evident ranging from dark blue (least) to red (highest) risk. Fig. 7 displays a healthy zone whereas Fig. 8 has higher risk factors such as BMI.

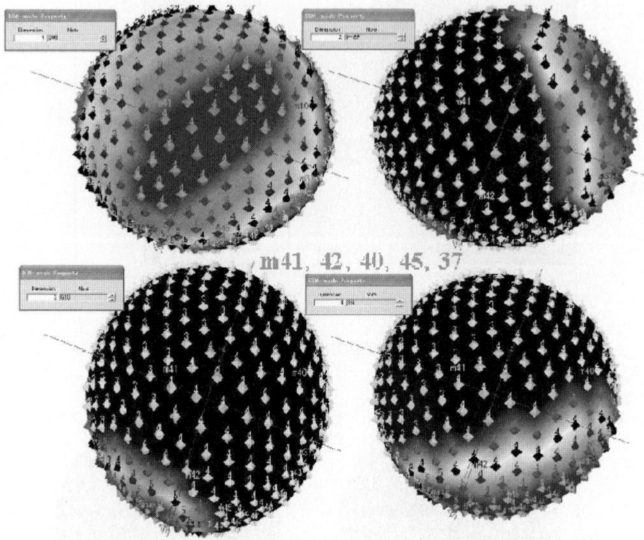

Fig. 8. Risky Zone Component Maps

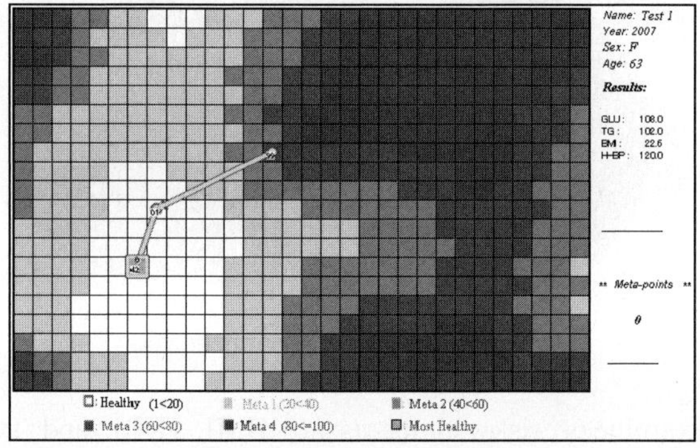

Fig. 9. Female Metabolic Traces

5   Metabolic Syndrome Prediction

Figs. 9 and 10 show examinees' health check details and projected patterns over a specified period. Using a database, the metabolic profiles can be displayed whenever a physician so requires. The examinee can observe the projected patterns and hence be ready to accommodate the suggestions laid down. Referring to random sampled examinee's data shown in Fig. 9, we notice the syndrome has ceased giving a sigh of relief to the examinee while that of Fig. 10 has deteriorated due to H-PB and TG.

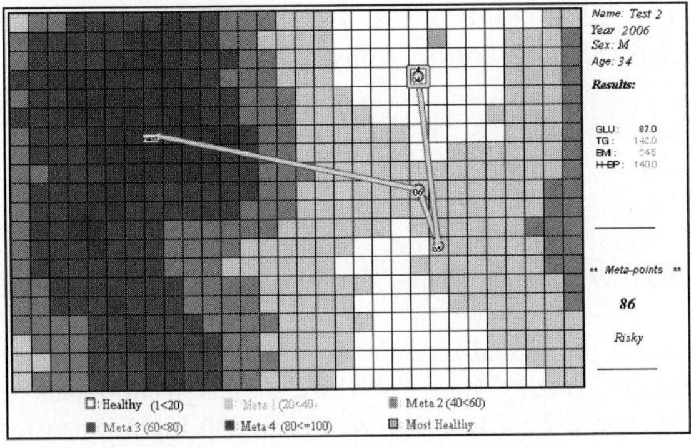

Fig. 10. Metabolic predictions Tool (Male)

6   Conclusions

A metabolic syndrome evaluation system has been presented. The two groups of examinees have different trends of the syndrome with the females being more affected by BMI and H-BP whereas H-BP and TG mainly affect the male counterparts. TG is seen to be a more risky element across the two groups.

Table 2 indicates that the physician has a second opinion to his deductions. The clustering done on the input data reviews some relationships that could not initially be identified.

Using a database for the syndrome for the examinees, their health check trends can be monitored closely. The physician becomes more equipped with past data at a glance. Predicted profile as well as expected cause of the syndrome risk is made possible again using the previous information.

Secondary effects based on psychological impact cannot be overlooked. Many examinees may have joined the risky zone due to the beliefs that go with the syndrome.

Much information within this area needs to be analyzed so that the affected members are given precise information about their health condition. With this type of visualization method, Physicians can have an alternative approach to giving their patients a sight of their health status and also their health trends. This in effect would make the patient share with the Doctor any health decision needed. The recovery period may as well be improved.

Majority of the affected members are the prime movers of the economy of their countries. An alternative definition and approach to this hypothesis should be sort to give patients enough details of their health if possible.

Further research on the syndrome trends will include Low Blood Pressure (L-BP) and HDL cholesterol levels.

Acknowledgements

The progress made on the syndrome research has encompassed other members whose contributions cannot be overemphasized. These members include; Mr. J. Endou,

Mr. K. Awaji, Prof. T. Shimizu, Prof. M. Tanaka all from Department of Information and Knowledge Engineering, Tottori University and SOM Japan Inc. members to mention a few.

References

[1] Kohonen, T.: Self-Organizing Maps. Springer series in information Sciences, vol. 30 (2001)

[2] Ultsch, A.: Maps for the Visualization of high-dimensional Data Spaces. In: Proceedings Workshop on Self-Organizing Maps (WSOM 2003), Kyushu, Japan, pp. 225–230 (2003)

[3] Ultsch, A.: U-Matrix: a Tool to visualize Clusters in high dimensional Data, Technical Report No. 36, Dept. of Mathematics and Computer Science, University of Marburg, Germany (2003)

[4] Ultsch, A.: Data mining and Knowledge Discovery with Emergent Self-Organizing Feature Maps for Multivariate Time. In: Kohonen Maps, pp. 33–46 (1999)

[5] Ritter, H.: Self-Organizing Maps on non-Euclidean Spaces. In: Oja, E., Kaski, S. (eds.) Kohonen Maps, pp. 95–110. Elsevier, Amsterdam (1999)

[6] Nakatsuka, D., Oyabu, M.: Application of Spherical SOM in Clustering. In: Proceedings of Workshop on Self-Organizing Maps (WSOM 2003), pp. 203–207 (2003)

[7] Kurosawa, H., Maniwa, Y., Fujimura, K., Tokutaka, H., Ohkita, M.: Construction of checkup system by Self-Organizing Maps. In: Proceedings of workshop on Self-Organizing Maps (WSOM 2003), pp. 144–149 (2003)

[8] SOM Japan Inc., http://www.somj.com/

A Kolmogorov-Smirnov Correlation-Based Filter for Microarray Data

Jacek Biesiada[1] and Włodzisław Duch[2]

[1] Division of Computer Methods, Department of Electrotechnology, The Silesian University of Technology, ul. Krasińskiego 8, 40-019 Katowice, Poland
Jacek.Biesiada@polsl.pl
Division of Biomedical Informatics, Cincinnati Children Hosptial Medical Center, 3333 Burnet Ave, Cincinnati, Ohio 45229-3039, USA
[2] Department of Informatics, Nicolaus Copernicus University, Grudziądzka 5, Toruń, Poland
Google: Duch

Abstract. A filter algorithm using F-measure has been used with feature redundancy removal based on the Kolmogorov-Smirnov (KS) test for rough equality of statistical distributions. As a result computationally efficient K-S Correlation-Based Selection algorithm has been developed and tested on three high-dimensional microarray datasets using four types of classifiers. Results are quite encouraging and several improvements are suggested.

1 Introduction

Feature ranking and feature selection algorithms applicable to large data mining problems with very high number of features that are potentially irrelevant for a given task are usually of the filter type [1]. Filter algorithms remove features that have no chance to be useful in further data analysis, independently of particular predictive system (predictor) that may be used on this data. In the simplest case feature filter is a function returning a relevance index $J(\mathcal{S}|\mathcal{D}, C)$ that estimates, given the data $\mathcal{D}$, how relevant a given feature subset $\mathcal{S}$ is for the task C (usually classification, association or approximation of data). Since the data and the task are usually fixed and only the subsets $\mathcal{S}$ vary, the relevance index will be written as $J(\mathcal{S})$. This index may result from a simple calculation of a correlation coefficient or entropy-based index, or it may be computed using more involved algorithmic procedures (for example, requiring creation of partial decision tree, or finding nearest neighbors of some vectors). For large problems simpler indices have an obvious advantage of being easier to calculate, requiring an effort on the order of $O(n)$, while more sophisticated procedures based on distances may require $O(n^2)$ operations.

Relevance indices may be computed for individual features $X_i, i = 1 \ldots N$, providing indices that establish a ranking order $J(X_{i_1}) \leq J(X_{i_2}) \cdots \leq J(X_{i_N})$. Those features which have the lowest ranks are subsequently filtered out. For independent features this may be sufficient, but if features are correlated many of them may be redundant. Ranking does not guarantee that a small subset of important features will be found. In pathological situations a single best feature may not even be a member of the best pair of features [2]. Adding many redundant features may create instable behavior

M. Ishikawa et al. (Eds.): ICONIP 2007, Part II, LNCS 4985, pp. 285–294, 2008.

of some predictive algorithms, with chaotic changes of results for a growing number of features. This is a major problem especially for small sample data with very large dimensionality, but has been also observed with large datasets [3]. However, methods that search for the best subset of features may first use filters to remove irrelevant features and then use the same ranking indices on different subsets of features to evaluate their usefulness.

Despite these potential problems in practical applications filter methods for ranking are widely used and frequently give quite good results. There is little empirical experience in matching filters with predictive systems. Perhaps different types of filters could be matched with different types of predictors, but so far no theoretical arguments or strong empirical evidence has been given to support such claim. The value of the relevance index should be positively correlated with accuracy of any reasonable predictor trained for a given task C on the data $\mathcal{D}$ using the feature subset $\mathcal{S}$.

Although filter methods do not depend directly on the predictors obviously the cut-off threshold for relevance index to reject features may either be set arbitrarily at some level, or by evaluation of feature contributions by the predictor. Features are ranked by the filter, but how many best features are finally taken is determined using the predictor. This approach may be called "filtrapper" or "frapper" [1], and it is not so costly as the original wrapper approach, because evaluation of predictor's performance (for example by crossvalidation tests) is done only after ranking for a few pre-selected feature sets. The threshold for feature rejection is a part of the model selection procedure and may be determined using crossvalidation calculations. To avoid oscillations only those features that really improve the training results should be accepted. This area between filters and wrappers seems to be rather unexplored.

In the next section a new relevance index based on the Kolmogorov-Smirnov (KS) test to estimate correlation between the distribution of feature values and the class labels is introduced (used so far only for datasets with small number of features [4]). Correlation-based filters are very fast and easily compete with information-based filters. In section three empirical comparisons between KS filter, Pearson's correlation based filter and other filters based on information gain are made on three widely used microarray datasets [5], [6], [7].

2   Theoretical Framework

2.1   Correlation-Based Measures

Pearson's linear correlation coefficient is very popular in statistics [8]. For feature X with values x and classes C with values c treated as random variables it is defined as

$$\varrho(X, C) = \frac{\sum_i (x_i - \bar{x}_i)(c_i - \bar{c}_i)}{\sqrt{\sum_i (x_i - \bar{x}_i)^2 \sum_j (c_i - \bar{c}_i)^2}}. \tag{1}$$

$\varrho(X, C)$ is equal to ± 1 if X and C are linearly dependent, and zero if they are completely uncorrelated. The simplest test estimating probability that two variables are related given the correlation $\varrho(X, C)$ is [8]:

$$P(X \sim C) = \text{erf}\left(|\varrho(X,C)|\sqrt{N/2}\right), \tag{2}$$

where erf is the error function. Thus for $N = 1000$ samples linear correlation coefficients as small as 0.02 really signify probabilities of correlation around 0.5.

The feature list ordered by decreasing values of $P(X \sim C)$ provides feature ranking. Similar approach is also taken with χ^2 statistics, but the problem in both cases is that for larger values of χ^2 or correlation coefficient probability $P(X \sim C)$ is so close to 1 that ranking becomes impossible due to the finite numerical accuracy of computations. Therefore initial threshold for $P(X \sim C)$ may be used in ranking only to determine how many features are worth keeping, although more reliable estimations may be done using crossvalidation or wrapper approaches.

Information theory is frequently used to define relevance indices. Mutual Information (MI) is defined as $MI(f,C) = H(f) + H(C) - H(f,C)$, where the entropy and joint entropy are:

$$H(f) = -\sum_i P(f_i) \log(P(f_i)); \quad H(C) = -\sum_i P(C_i) \log P(C_i) \tag{3}$$

and

$$H(f,C) = -\sum_{i,j} P(f_i, C_j) \log P(f_i, C_j) \tag{4}$$

Symmetrical Uncertainty (SU) Coefficient is defined as [8]:

$$SU(f,C) = 2\left[\frac{MI(f,C)}{H(f) + H(C)}\right] \tag{5}$$

If a group of k features has already been selected, correlation coefficient may be used to estimate correlation between this group and the class, including inter-correlations between the features. Denoting the average correlation coefficient between these features and classes as $r_{kc} = \bar{\varrho}(\mathbf{X}_k, C)$ and the average between different features as $r_{kk} = \bar{\varrho}(\mathbf{X}_k, \mathbf{X}_k)$ the relevance of the feature subset may be defined as:

$$J(\mathbf{X}_k, C) = \frac{k r_{kc}}{\sqrt{k + (k-1)r_{kk}}}. \tag{6}$$

This formula has been used in the Correlation-based Feature Selection (CFS) algorithm [9] adding (forward selection) or deleting (backward selection) one feature at a time. Non-parametric, or Spearman's rank correlation coefficients may be useful for ordinal data types.

F-score is another useful index that may be used for ranking [10]:

$$F(C, f_i) = \frac{1}{(K-1)\sigma_i^2} \sum_k n_k \left(\bar{f}_{ik} - \bar{f}_i\right)^2 \tag{7}$$

where n_k is the number of elements in class k, $\bar{f}_{ik}$ is the mean and σ_{ki}^2 is the variance of feature f_i in this class. Pooled variance for feature f_i is calculated from:

$$\sigma_i^2 = \sigma^2(f_i) = \frac{1}{(n-K)} \sum_k (n_k - 1)\sigma_{ik}^2 \tag{8}$$

where $n = \sum_k n_k$ and K is the number of classes. In the two-class classification case F-score is reduced to the t-score ($F = t^2$).

Predominant correlation proposed by Liu *et al.* [11] in their Fast Correlation-Based Filter (FCBF) compares relations between feature-class and feature-feature. First ranking using the SU coefficient Eq. 5 is performed, and the threshold coefficient determining the number of features left is fixed. In the second step each feature f_i is compared to all f_j lower in ranking, and if their mutual $SU(f_i, f_j)$ coefficient is larger then $SU(C, f_j)$ then f_j is considered redundant and removed.

ConnSF, selection method based on a consistency measure, has been proposed by Dash *et al.* [12]. This measure evaluates for a given feature subset the number of cases in which the same feature values are associated with different classes. More precisely, a subset of feature values that appears n times in the data, most often with the label of class c, has inconsistency $n - n(c)$. If all these cases are from the same class then $n = n(c)$ and inconsistency is zero. The total inconsistency count is the sum of all the inconsistency counts for all distinct patterns of a feature subset, and consistency is defined by the least inconsistency count. Application of this algorithm requires discrete values of the features.

2.2 Kolmogorov-Smirnov Test for Two Distributions

The Kolmogorov-Smirnov (K-S) test [8] is used to evaluate if two distributions are roughly equal and thus may be used as a test for feature redundancy. The K-S test consists of the following steps:

- Discretization process creates k clusters (vectors from roughly the same class), each typically covering similar range of values.
- A much larger number of independent observation $n_1, n_2 > 40$ are taken from the two distributions, measuring frequencies of different classes.
- Based on the frequency table the empirical cumulative distribution functions $F1_i$ and $F2_i$ for two sample populations are constructed.
- λ(K-S statistics) is proportional to the largest absolute difference of $|F1_i - F2_i|$:

$$\lambda = \sqrt{\frac{n_1 n_2}{n_1 + n_2}} \sup |F1_i - F2_i| \quad \text{for} \quad i = 1, 2, ..., k. \tag{9}$$

When $\lambda < \lambda_\alpha$ then the two distributions are equal, where α is the significance level and λ_α is the K-S statistics for α [13]. One of the features with distribution that are approximately equal is then redundant. In experiments described below all training samples $n_1 = n_2 = n$ were used.

2.3 Kolmogorov-Smirnov Correlation-Based Filter Approach

Kolmogorov-Smirnov test is a good basis for the Correlation-Based Selection algorithm (K-S CBS) for feature selection. This algorithm is sketched in Fig. 1. Feature ranking is performed first, requiring selection of the ranking index. F-score index Eq. 7 is used in all calculations here. The threshold for the number of features left for further analysis may be determined in a principal way using the frapper approach, that is evaluating the

---

Algorithm K-S CBS:
Relevance analysis
1. Order features according to the decreasing values of relevance indices creating $\mathcal{S}$ list.
Redundancy analysis
2. Initialize F_i to the first feature in the $\mathcal{S}$ list.
3. Use K-S test to find and remove from $\mathcal{S}$ all features for which F_i forms an approximate redundant cover $\mathcal{C}(F_i)$.
4. Move F_i to the set of selected features, take as F_i the next remaining feature in the list.
5. Repeat step 3 and 4 until the end of the $\mathcal{S}$ list.

Fig. 1. A two-step Kolmogorov-Smirnov Correlation Based Selection (K-S CBS) algorithm

quality of results as a function of the number of features. In the second step redundant features are removed using the K-S test. The optimal α significance level for feature removal may also be determined by crossvalidation.

This is of course quite generic algorithm and other ranking indices and tests for equality of distributions may be taken instead. Two parameters – the threshold for relevancy and the threshold for redundancy – are successively determined using crossvalidation, but in some cases there may be a clear change in the value of these parameters, helping to find their optimal values.

3   Empirical Study

To evaluate the usefulness of K-S CBS algorithm experiments on three gene expression datasets [5], [6] [7] have been performed. Datasets used here [1] are quite typical for this type of applications. A summary is presented in Table 1.

1. **Leukemia** data is divided into training set consists of 38 bone marrow samples (27 of the ALL and 11 of the AML type), using 7129 probes from 6817 human genes; 34 test samples are provided, with 20 ALL and 14 AML cases.
2. **Colon Tumor** contains 62 samples collected from colon cancer patients, with 40 biopsies from tumor areas (labelled as "negative") and 22 from healthy parts of the colons of the same patients. 2000 out of around 6500 genes were pre-selected, based on the confidence in the measured expression levels.
3. **Diffuse Large B-cell Lymphoma** [DLBCL] has measurements of gene expression data for two distinct types of diffuse large lymphoma B-cells (this is the most common subtype of non-Hodgkin's lymphoma). There are 47 samples, 24 of them are from "germinal centre B-like" group while 23 are from "activated B-like" group. Each sample is represented by 4026 genes.

Splitting such small data into training and test subsets does not make much sense. Results reported below for all data are from the leave-one-out (LOO) calculations, deterministic procedure that does not require averaging or calculation of variance.

---

[1] Downloaded from `http://sdmc.lit.org.sg/GEDatasets/Datasets.html`

Table 1. Summary of microarray dataset properties

Title	# Genes	# Samples	# Samples per class				Source
Colon cancer	2000	62	40	tumor	22	normal	Alon [5]
DLBCL	4026	47	24	GCB	23	AB	Alizadeh [6]
Leukemia	7129	72	47	ALL	25	AML	Golub [7]

The original gene expression data contain real numbers. To calculate mutual information probabilities Eq. (3, 4) are needed, therefore the data has been discretized. This also helps to reduce the amount of noise in the original observations and facilitates direct use of such predictive techniques as the Naive Bayesian Classifier (NBC). Although quite sophisticated methods of discretization exist, for comparison of information selection techniques simple discretization of gene expression levels into 3 intervals is used here. Using the variance σ and the mean μ for a given gene any value larger than $\mu + \frac{\sigma}{2}$ is transformed to $+1$, any value in the $[\mu - \frac{\sigma}{2}, \mu + \frac{\sigma}{2}]$ interval is transformed to 0, and any value smaller than $\mu - \frac{\sigma}{2}$ becomes -1. These three values correspond to the over-expressions, baseline, and under-expression of genes. Results obtained after such discretization are in some cases significantly improved and are given in parenthesis in the tables below.

For each data set K-S CBS algorithm using F-measure (results with SU coefficient are similar) in the filtering stage is compared with the three state-of-the-art feature selection algorithms: FCBF [11], CorrSF [9], ConnSF [12]. The number of features selected obviously depends on the parameters of the feature selection method. The authors of the FCBF algorithm recommend taking the relevance threshold corresponding to the $n \log n$ features, and treating as redundant features with larger SU index between features than between the classes. The CorrSF correlation coefficient Eq. 1 is used in a forward best-first search procedure with backtracking up to 5 times before search is terminated, and selecting only those features that have larger feature-class correlations than correlation to already selected features. For ConsSF the usual practice is followed, searching for the smallest subset with consistency equal to that of the full set of attributes. One could introduce additional parameters in FCBF, CorrSF and ConnSF to change the preference of the relevance vs. redundancy and optimize them in the same way, but we have not done so. For comparison the K-S CBS algorithm is used with $\alpha = 0.05$, representing quite typical value of confidence. This value can easily be optimized for individual classifiers in the frapper approach, therefore results for other values are provided.

Table 2. Number of features selected by each algorithm

Data	Number of features selected				
	Full set	FCBF	CorrSF	ConnSF	K-S CBS$_F$
Colon Cancer	2000	9	17	4	5
DLCBL	4026	33	18	3	16
Leukemia	7129	52	28	3	118

Table 3. Balanced accuracy from the LOO test for C4.5, NBC, 1NN and SVM classifier on features selected by four algorithms, results on discretized data in parenthesis

Method	C 4.5			
Data	All features	FCBF	CorrSF	ConnSF	K-S CBS$_{F,\alpha=0.05}$
Colon Cancer	72.05 (68.30)	81.36 (80.11)	77.84 (80.11)	78.07 (78.07)	73.30 (68.30)
DLCBL	89.40 (74.55)	82.77 (85.14)	72.28 (89.49)	87.14 (85.24)	80.80 (85.24)
Leukemia	73.23 (85.74)	86.68 (95.72)	79.49 (93.74)	96.94 (95.74)	86.55 (85.74)
Average	78.22 (76.20)	83.60 (86.99)	76.53 (87.78)	87.38 (86.35)	80.22 (79.76)
Method	NBC			
Data	All features	FCBF	CorrSF	ConnSF	K-S CBS$_{F,\alpha=0.05}$
Colon Cancer	57.84 (66.59)	85.91 (90.68)	84.43 (88.18)	74.77 (79.32)	78.64 (66.59)
DLCBL	97.92 (91.58)	100.0 (100.0)	100.0 (100.0)	91.49 (89.40)	97.92 (93.66)
Leukemia	100.00 (82.55)	96.94 (100.0)	98.94 (100.0)	86.94 (100.0)	98.00 (82.55)
Average	85.25 (80.24)	94.28 (96.89)	94.46 (96.06)	84.40 (89.57)	91.52 (80.93)
Method	1NN			
Data	All features	FCBF	CorrSF	ConnSF	K-S CBS$_{F,\alpha=0.05}$
Colon Cancer	73.07 (64.55)	82.39 (83.18)	83.41 (78.41)	79.09 (93.75)	74.55 (64.55)
DLCBL	76.27 (74.46)	100.0 (97.83)	100.0 (100.0)	93.66 (93.48)	93.66 (91.39)
Leukemia	84.81 (88.81)	96.94 (100.0)	93.87 (100.0)	94.81 (100.0)	92.94 (88.81)
Average	78.05 (75.94)	93.11 (93.67)	92.42 (92.80)	89.18 (95.74)	87.05 (81.58)
Method	SVM			
Data	All features	FCBF	CorrSF	ConnSF	K-S CBS$_{F,\alpha=0.05}$
Colon Cancer	80.11 (70.80)	84.89 (80.11)	87.16 (83.41)	74.77 (75.80)	82.61 (70.80)
DLCBL	93.66 (95.74)	100.0 (100.0)	100.0 (100.0)	91.58 (91.58)	95.83 (91.49)
Leukemia	98.00 (88.81)	98.00 (100.0)	96.94 (100.0)	85.87 (100.0)	98.00 (96.00)
Average	90.59 (85.12)	94.29 (93.37)	94.70 (94.47)	84.08 (89.13)	92.15 (86.09)

Features selected by each algorithm serve to calculate balanced accuracy using four popular classifiers, decision tree C4.5 (with default Weka parameters), Naive Bayes (with single Gaussian kernel, or discretized probabilities), nearest neighbor algorithm (single neighbor only) and linear SVM with $C = 1$ (using Ghostminer implementation[2]). Each of these classifiers is of quite different type and may be used on raw as well as on the discretized data.

The number of features selected by different algorithms is given in Table 2. K-S CBF selected rather small number of features except for the Leukemia data, where significantly larger number of features has been created. Even for $\alpha = 0.001$ the number of features is 47, which is relatively large. Unfortunately with the small number of samples in the microarray data a single error difference in the LOO test is translated to quite large 1.6% for colon, 2.1% for DLCBL and 1.4% for leukemia. Thus although percentages may clearly differ the number of errors may be similar.

First observation from results given in Table 3 is that feature selection has significant influence on the performance of classifiers. Improvements for C4.5 on Leukemia

---

[2] http://www.fqs.pl/ghostminer/

292   J. Biesiada and W. Duch

Table 4. LOO balanced accuracy for different significance levels α for all data set; $KSCBS_F$ on standarized data

α	0.001	0.01	0.05	0.1	0.15	0.2	0.25	0.3	0.35	0.4	0.45
Dataset	Colon cancer										
No. feat.	2	5	5	8	9	10	10	13	13	17	17
C4.5	77.61	80.34	73.30	77.84	66.25	70.80	70.80	74.09	74.09	69.32	69.32
NBC	82.61	67.95	78.64	74.89	79.89	82.16	82.16	78.64	78.64	81.93	81.93
1NN	78.64	75.34	74.55	72.61	72.05	71.82	71.82	71.82	71.82	76.82	76.82
SVM	72.50	72.50	82.61	81.36	81.36	81.36	81.36	80.34	80.34	84.89	84.89
Average	77.84	74.03	77.28	76.68	74.89	76.54	76.54	76.22	76.22	78.24	78.24
Dataset	DBCL										
No. feat.	7	13	16	22	22	30	43	43	43	63	63
C4.5	85.14	82.97	80.80	93.66	93.66	91.49	74.46	74.46	74.46	74.37	74.37
NBC	91.49	93.57	97.92	93.57	93.57	97.83	97.83	97.83	97.83	100.0	100.0
1NN	87.32	95.83	93.66	93.75	93.75	89.40	93.75	93.75	93.75	93.57	93.57
SVM	89.49	100.0	95.83	89.49	89.49	95.83	100.0	100.0	100.0	100.0	100.0
Average	88.36	93.09	92.05	92.62	92.62	93.64	91.51	91.51	91.51	91.99	91.99
Dataset	Leukemia										
No. feat.	47	75	118	167	207	268	268	331	331	456	456
C4.5	85.74	88.81	86.55	84.68	91.74	77.36	77.36	80.43	80.43	88.68	88.68
NBC	94.94	96.94	98.00	100.0	98.00	100.0	100.0	98.94	98.94	100.0	100.0
1NN	90.94	89.87	92.94	92.94	90.94	92.94	92.94	92.94	92.94	90.94	90.94
SVM	90.00	96.00	98.00	98.00	98.00	96.94	96.94	98.00	98.00	98.00	98.00
Average	90.41	92.91	93.87	93.91	95.17	91.81	91.81	92.58	92.58	94.41	94.41

exceed 20%, for NBC on colon cancer reach almost 30%, for 1NN on DLCBL almost 20% and for SVM on colon data over 7%. Discretization in most cases improves the results. For colon cancer SVM reaches the best result on all features (80.1%), and the highest accuracy on the 17 CorrSF selected features (87.2%), that also happens to be the largest subset. However, on the discretized data better results are achieved with Naive Bayes with 9 FCBF features (90.7%). For DLCBL with all features Naive Bayes reaches 97.9%, and 100% for both FCBF and CorrSF selections, with 1NN and SVM reaching also 100% on these features. For Leukemia again Naive Bayes is the winner, reaching 100% on all data, and for discretized data selected by FCBF, CorrSF and ConnSF achieving 100% balanced accuracy. K-S CBF always gives worse results on the discretized data, but on the raw data (K-S test is more appropriate for real-valued features) is not far behind.

It is clear that the default value for redundancy in K-S CBS is far from optimal; unfortunately Kolmogorov-Smirnov statistics can be used only to discover redundant features, but cannot be directly compared with relevance indices. In real applications estimation of optimal α using crossvalidation techniques for a given classifier will significantly improve results, as is evident from Table 4. Detailed analysis of the dependence of the number of features and balanced accuracy on α is presented in Table 4 starting from very small α.

With optimized α the best results with K-S CBS features are very similar to the best results of the other algorithms. For colon cancer SVM gives 84.9% on 17 features, which translates to 9 instead of 8 errors. For DBCL data SVM and Naive Bayes reach 100%, while for Leukemia 100% is also reached with Naive Bayes, although for somehow larger number of features. However, with such small statistics larger number of features is actually desirable to stabilize the expected profile. For example, with the original division between training and test data [7] a single gene gives 100% accuracy on the training set, but this does not mean that it is sufficient as it makes 3 errors on the test. It is much safer to use leave-one-out evaluation in this case.

4   Conclusions

Information filters may be realized in many ways [1]. They may help to reject some features, but the final selection should remove redundant features, not only to decrease dimensionality, but also to avoid problems that are associated with redundant features. Naive Bayes algorithm is clearly improved by removing redundancy, and the same is true for similarity-based approaches and SVM. Kolmogorov-Smirnov test for determination of redundant features requires only one parameter, the significance level, and is a well-justified statistical test, therefore it is an interesting choice for feature selection algorithms.

The K-S CBS algorithm presented here combines relevance indices (F-measure, Symmetrical Uncertainty Coefficient or other index) to rank and reduce the number of features, and uses Kolmogorov-Smirnov test to reduce the number of features further. It is computationally efficient and gives quite good results. Variants of this algorithm may identify approximate redundant covers $\mathcal{C}(f_i)$ for consecutive features f_i and leave in the $\mathcal{S}$ set only the one that gives best results (this will usually be the first one, with the highest ranking). Some ways of information aggregation could also be used, for example local PCA in the $\mathcal{C}(F_i)$ subspace. In this case the threshold for redundancy may be set to higher values, leaving fewer more stable features in the final set, and assuring that potentially useful information in features that were considered to be redundant is not lost. One additional problem that is evident in Table 4 and that frequently arises in feature selection for small microarray data, but may also appear with much larger data [3], is stability of results. Adding more features may degrade results instead of improving them. We had no space here to review literature results for microarray data (see comparison in [14] or results in [15]) but they are all unstable and do not significantly differ from our results given in Tables 3 and 4. The instability problem may be addressed using the frapper approach to select most stable (and possible non-redundant) subset of features in $O(m)$ steps, where m is the number of features left for ranking. This and other improvements are the subject of further investigation.

Acknowledgement. This work was financed by the Polish Committee for Scientific Research grant 2005-2007 to WD; JB has been supported by the Polish Fundation of Science, grant (2006-2009) No.: 6ZR9 2006 C/06742 and (2007-2010) No.: N N519 1506 33.

References

1. Duch, W.: Filter methods. In: [3], pp. 89–118 (2006)
2. Toussaint, G.T.: Note on optimal selection of independent binary-valued features for pattern recognition. IEEE Transactions on Information Theory 17, 618–618 (1971)
3. Guyon, I., Gunn, S., Nikravesh, M., Zadeh, L. (eds.): Feature extraction, foundations and applications. Physica Verlag, Springer, Heidelberg (2006)
4. Biesiada, J., Duch, W.: Feature Selection for High-Dimensional Data: A Kolmogorov-Smirnov Correlation-Based Filter Solution. In: Kurzynski, M., Puchala, E., Wozniak, M., Zolnierek, A. (eds.) Computer Recognition Systems. Proc. of the 4th International Conference on Computer Recognition Systems (CORES 2005). Advances in Soft Computing, vol. 9, pp. 95–104. Springer, Heidelberg (2005)
5. Alon, U., et al.: Broad Patterns of Gene Expression Revealed by Clustering Analysis of Tumor and Normal Colon Tissues Probed by Oligonucleotide Arrays. PNAS 96, 6745–6750 (1999)
6. Alizadeh, A.A., et al.: Distinct types of diffuse large B-cell lymphoma identified by gene expression profiling. Nature 403, 503–511 (2000)
7. Golub, T.R., et al.: Molecular Classification of Cancer: Class Discovery and Class Prediction by Gene Expression Monitoring. Science 286, 531–537 (1999)
8. Press, W.H., Teukolsky, S.A., Vetterling, W.T., Flannery, B.P.: Numerical recipes in C. The art of scientific computing. Cambridge University Press, Cambridge (1988)
9. Hall, M.A.: Correlation based feature selection for machine learning. PhD thesis, Dept. of Comp. Science, Univ. of Waikato, Hamilton, New Zealand (1999)
10. Peng, H., Long, F., Ding, C.: Feature selection based on mutual information: criteria of max-dependency, max-relevance, and min-redundancy. IEEE Transactions on Pattern Analysis and Machine Intelligence 27(8), 1226–1238 (2005)
11. Yu, L., Liu, H.: Feature selection for high-dimensional data: A fast correlation-based filter solution. In: Proceedings of the 12th International Conference on Machine Learning (ICML 2003), Washington, D.C., pp. 856–863. Morgan Kaufmann, San Francisco (2003)
12. Dash, M., Liu, H., Motoda, H.: Consistency based feature selection. In: Proc. 4th Pacific Asia Conference on Knowledge Discovery and Data Mining, pp. 98–109. Springer, Heidelberg (2000)
13. Evans, M., Hastings, N., Peacock, B.: Statistical Distributions. John Wiley & Sons, Chichester (2000)
14. Duch, W., Biesiada, J.: Margin-based feature selection filters for microarray gene expression data. International Journal of Information Technology and Intelligent Computing 1, 9–33 (2006)
15. Ding, C., Peng, H.: Minimum redundancy feature selection from microarray gene expression data. Journal of Bioinformatics and Computational Biology 3(2), 185–205 (2005)

Information Geometry and Information Theory in Machine Learning

Kazushi Ikeda[1] and Kazunori Iwata[2]

[1] Department of Systems Science, Kyoto University
Kyoto 606-8501 Japan
kazushi@i.kyoto-u.ac.jp
[2] Department of Intelligent Systems, Hiroshima City University
Hiroshima 731-3194 Japan
kiwata@hiroshima-cu.ac.jp

Abstract. Information geometry is a general framework of Riemannian manifolds with dual affine connections. Some manifolds (e.g. the manifold of an exponential family) have natural connections (e.g. e- and m-connections) with which the manifold is dually-flat. Conversely, a dually-flat structure can be introduced into a manifold from a potential function. This paper shows the case of quasi-additive algorithms as an example.

Information theory is another important tool in machine learning. Many of its applications consider information-theoretic quantities such as the entropy and the mutual information, but few fully recognize the underlying essence of them. The asymptotic equipartition property is one of the essence in information theory.

This paper gives an example of the property in a Markov decision process and shows how it is related to return maximization in reinforcement learning.

1 Introduction

Information geometry is a general framework of Riemannian manifolds with dual affine connections and was proposed by Amari [1] to give a clear view for the manifolds of statistical models. Since then, information geometry has widely been applied to other areas, such as statistical inference, information theory, neural networks, systems theory, mathematical programming, statistical physics, and stochastic reasoning [2], many of which are strongly related to machine learning community.

One example is that the Fisher information matrix appears as the Riemannian metric tensor of the statistical model in information geometry and another is that the Kullback-Leibler divergence and Hellinger distance are derived as the divergence defined for specific dual connections. Hence, if a study on machine learning considers the metric of a model or utilizes the mutual information, then it is based on information geometry in a sense, while there are a lot of more direct applications such as independent component analysis and semiparametric estimation. In this paper, we give another kind of applications of information geometry in Sec. 3.

M. Ishikawa et al. (Eds.): ICONIP 2007, Part II, LNCS 4985, pp. 295–304, 2008.

Another important tool in machine learning is information theory, which has much longer history than information geometry [3]. The asymptotic equipartition property (AEP) first stated by Shannon and developed through the method of types [3, Ch. 11] by Csiszár is based on a kind of the law of large numbers from the statistical viewpoint.

Although the AEP is an effective tool in analyzing learning algorithms, the importance of the AEP was not widely recognized in the machine learning community for a long time. However, some recent work utilizes the AEP for the analysis of learning algorithms such as genetic algorithms, since it holds in comprehensive stochastic processes related to machine learning. In this paper, we show that the AEP still holds in a Markov decision process (MDP) and discuss how it is related to return maximization in reinforcement learning (RL) in Sec. 5.

2   Preliminaries of Information Geometry

Information geometry discusses the properties of a manifold S, which is intuitively an n-dimensional differentiable subset of a Euclidean space with a coordinate system $\{\xi^i\}$ where ξ^i denotes the ith coordinate. Due to its smoothness, we can define the tangent space T_p at a point p in the manifold S as the space spanned by the tangent vectors $\{\partial_i \equiv \partial/\partial\xi^i\}$ of the coordinate curves, in other words, we locally linearize the manifold.

Since the tangent space T_p is a Euclidean space, an inner product can be defined as $g_{ij} \equiv \langle \partial_i, \partial_j \rangle$, where g_{ij} depends on the point $p \in S$ and it is called the Riemannian metric on S or simply the metric. Note that the metric is not naturally determined in general, the Fisher information matrix is a natural metric for the statistical manifold.

Since the tangent space T_p varies from point to point, we need to establish a linear mapping $\Pi_{p,p'} : T_p \to T_{p'}$ where p and p' are neighboring points and $\mathrm{d}\xi^i \equiv \xi^i(p') - \xi^i(p)$. Then, the difference between the vectors $\Pi_{p,p'}((\partial_j)_p)$ and $(\partial_j)_{p'}$ is a linear combination of $\{\mathrm{d}\xi^i\}$, that is,

$$\Pi_{p,p'}(\partial_j) = \partial_j' - \mathrm{d}\xi^i(\Gamma_{ij}^k)_p\partial_k', \tag{1}$$

where Γ_{ij}^k is the n^3 functions of p called the affine connection on S or simply the connection (Fig. 1). Using the connection of a manifold, any vector in T_p can be parallel-translated into another tangent space T_q along a curve connecting the two points p and q.

As well as the metric, the connection of a manifold can also be determined arbitrarily. However, if we require that the parallel translation of two vectors along a curve γ leaves their inner product unchanged, that is,

$$\langle \Pi_\gamma(D_1), \Pi_\gamma(D_2)\rangle_q = \langle D_1, D_2\rangle_p, \tag{2}$$

then the connection is uniquely determined that satisfies

$$\partial_k g_{ij} = \Gamma_{ki,j} + \Gamma_{kj,i} \tag{3}$$

$$\Gamma_{ij,k} \equiv \Gamma_{ij}^h g_{hk}, \tag{4}$$

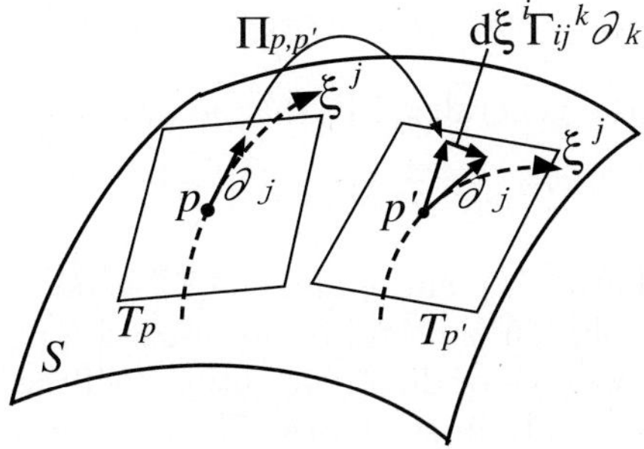

Fig. 1. Affine connection

which is called the Riemannian connection or the Levi-Civita connection with respect to g.

Information geometry introduces a pair of connections, called the dual connections, so that the inner product of two vectors is unchanged when one vector is parallel-translated with one connection and the other vector with the other connection, that is,

$$\langle D_1, D_2\rangle_p = \langle \Pi_\gamma(D_1), \Pi_\gamma^*(D_2)\rangle_q . \tag{5}$$

It is known that the dual connections Γ and Γ^* satisfy

$$\partial_k g_{ij} = \Gamma_{ki,j} + \Gamma_{kj,i}^*. \tag{6}$$

This means that the Riemann connection is a special case where the connection is self-dual.

If a manifold has a coordinate system satisfying $\Gamma_{ij}^k = 0$, the manifold is called to be flat and the coordinate system is called affine. We denote an affine coordinate system by $\{\theta^i\}$ in this paper. It is known that if a manifold is flat for a connection Γ, it is also flat for its dual connection Γ^*. However, $\{\theta^i\}$ is never affine in general and we need to introduce another affine coordinate system $\{\eta_i\}$. These two coordinate systems called the dual coordinate systems have the relationship

$$\eta_i = \partial_i \psi(\boldsymbol{\theta}) \equiv \frac{\partial \psi(\boldsymbol{\theta})}{\partial \theta^i}, \tag{7}$$

$$\theta^i = \partial^i \phi(\boldsymbol{\eta}) \equiv \frac{\partial \phi(\boldsymbol{\eta})}{\partial \eta_i}, \tag{8}$$

$$\psi(\boldsymbol{\theta}) + \phi(\boldsymbol{\eta}) - \theta^i \eta_i = 0 \tag{9}$$

where $\psi(\boldsymbol{\theta})$ and $\phi(\boldsymbol{\eta})$ are respectively convex potential functions of $\boldsymbol{\theta} \equiv (\theta^1, \ldots, \theta^n)$ and $\eta \equiv (\eta_1, \ldots, \eta_n)$. In short, $\boldsymbol{\eta}$ is the Legendre transform of $\boldsymbol{\theta}$ and vice versa. The divergence which expresses a kind of the distance from p to q has a similar form to (9),

$$D(p\|q) \equiv \psi(\boldsymbol{\theta}(p)) + \phi(\boldsymbol{\eta}(q)) - \theta^i(p)\eta_i(q) \geq 0. \tag{10}$$

The divergence holds the generalized Pythagorean relation

$$D(p\|r) = D(p\|q) + D(q\|r) \tag{11}$$

when the Γ-geodesic between p and q and the Γ^s-geodesic between q and r are orthogonal at q. This relation is useful in optimization problems.

The most popular example of dual connections will be the ones for the manifold of an exponential family in statistics. The e-connection and m-connection are defined as

$$\Gamma_{ij,k}^{(e)} \equiv E[(\partial_i\partial_j l_\theta)(\partial_k l_\theta)] \tag{12}$$

$$\Gamma_{ij,k}^{(m)} = E[(\partial_i\partial_j l_\theta + \partial_i l_\theta \partial_j l_\theta)(\partial_k l_\theta)] \tag{13}$$

where $l_\theta \equiv \log p(x;\theta)$ and θ^i's and η_i's are the canonical and expectation parameters, respectively. The Kullback-Leibler divergence is derived from these connections.

3   Dually-Flat Structure of Learning Machines

In the above, the dual connections of a manifold lead to the dually-flat structure with two potential functions. Conversely, a dually-flat structure can be derived from a coordinate system with a convex potential function as below.

Let S be an n-dimensional manifold with a coordinate system $\boldsymbol{\theta}$ and $\psi(\boldsymbol{\theta})$ a smooth convex function on S. Then, the dual coordinate system $\boldsymbol{\eta}$ is defined as

$$\eta_i(\boldsymbol{\theta}) \equiv \partial_i \psi(\boldsymbol{\theta}), \tag{14}$$

and $\boldsymbol{\eta}(\boldsymbol{\theta}) = \partial\psi(\boldsymbol{\theta})/\partial\boldsymbol{\theta}$, in short. From the convexity of $\psi(\boldsymbol{\theta})$, $\boldsymbol{\eta}$ is a one-to-one function of $\boldsymbol{\theta}$ and vice versa.

Let us define a function of $\boldsymbol{\eta}$ as

$$\phi(\boldsymbol{\eta}) \equiv \boldsymbol{\theta}(\boldsymbol{\eta}) \cdot \boldsymbol{\eta} - \psi(\boldsymbol{\theta}(\boldsymbol{\eta})), \tag{15}$$

where $\cdot$ is the canonical dot product and

$$\boldsymbol{\theta}(\boldsymbol{\eta}) \equiv \arg\max_{\theta^i} \left[\boldsymbol{\theta} \cdot \boldsymbol{\eta} - \psi(\boldsymbol{\theta})\right]. \tag{16}$$

It is easily shown $\partial^i \phi(\eta) = \theta^i$ and

$$\psi(\boldsymbol{\theta}) + \phi(\boldsymbol{\eta}) - \boldsymbol{\theta} \cdot \boldsymbol{\eta} = 0. \tag{17}$$

The divergence from P to Q is defined as

$$D(P\|Q) := \psi(\boldsymbol{\theta}_Q) + \phi(\boldsymbol{\eta}_P) - \boldsymbol{\theta}_Q \cdot \boldsymbol{\eta}_P, \tag{18}$$

which always takes a non-negative value and null if and only if $P = Q$, where $\boldsymbol{\theta}_P$ and $\boldsymbol{\theta}_Q$ respectively denote the $\boldsymbol{\theta}$-coordinates of two points $P \in S$ and $Q \in S$, and $\boldsymbol{\eta}_P$ and $\boldsymbol{\eta}_Q$ their $\boldsymbol{\eta}$-coordinates. Note that the divergence may be written as $D(\boldsymbol{\theta}_P, \boldsymbol{\theta}_Q)$ when we regard it as a function of $\boldsymbol{\theta}$-coordinates and $D(\boldsymbol{\eta}_P, \boldsymbol{\eta}_Q)$ when as a function of $\boldsymbol{\eta}$-coordinates.

Since the metric expresses the length of the infinitesimal segment, it is given by differentiating the divergence, that is,

$$G(\boldsymbol{\theta}) = [g_{ij}(\boldsymbol{\theta})] = \partial_i \partial_j \psi(\boldsymbol{\theta}) \tag{19}$$

$$H(\boldsymbol{\eta}) = [h^{ij}(\boldsymbol{\eta})] = \partial^i \partial^j \phi(\boldsymbol{\eta}) = G^{-1}(\boldsymbol{\theta}). \tag{20}$$

Since the dual connections and the geodesics for them are essentially equivalent, we determine the geodesics instead of explicitly defining the connections. Here, we assume that $\boldsymbol{\theta}$ is an affine coordinate system, that is, a geodesic for Γ is expressed as

$$\boldsymbol{\theta}(t) = \boldsymbol{c}t + \boldsymbol{b} \tag{21}$$

where $\boldsymbol{c}$ and $\boldsymbol{b}$ are constant vectors, and a geodesic for Γ^* is similarly expressed as

$$\boldsymbol{\eta}(t) = \boldsymbol{c}t + \boldsymbol{b}. \tag{22}$$

We apply the discussion above to the quasi-additive (QA) algorithms [4] according to [5]. The family of QA algorithms is a generalization of the perceptron learning for a linear dichotomy. It has two vectors, the parameter vector $\boldsymbol{\theta}$ to which a scaled input vector $\boldsymbol{x}$ is added and the weight vector $\boldsymbol{\eta}$ which is a nonlinear transform of $\boldsymbol{\theta}$ elementwise. More precisely,

$$\eta_i = f(\theta^i) \quad i = 1, \ldots, n, \tag{23}$$

where f is an monotonically increasing differentiable function. When f is an exponential function $\exp(\cdot)$, for instance, an addition to the parameter vector appears as a multiplication in the weight vector since

$$\eta_i^{(t)} = f(\theta^{(t)^i}) = f(\theta^{(t-1)^i} + x^{(t)^i}) = \eta_i^{(t-1)} \exp(x^{(t)^i}). \tag{24}$$

The output of the linear dichotomy is the sign $y \in \{\pm 1\}$ of the dot product with the weight vector $\boldsymbol{\eta}$ for an input vector $\boldsymbol{x}$, that is, $y = \mathrm{sgn}[\boldsymbol{\eta} \cdot \boldsymbol{x}] \in \{\pm 1\}$. In total, QA algorithms have a general form of

$$\dot{\boldsymbol{\theta}} = C(\boldsymbol{\eta}, \boldsymbol{x}, y) y \boldsymbol{x}, \qquad\qquad \boldsymbol{\eta} = f(\boldsymbol{\theta}). \tag{25}$$

Suppose that f satisfies $f(0) = 0$ and define a potential function

$$\psi(\boldsymbol{\theta}) = \sum_{i=1}^{n} g(\theta^i), \qquad\qquad g(s) = \int_0^s f(\sigma) d\sigma. \tag{26}$$

Then, we can introduce a dually-flat structure to QA algorithms from this potential function. In fact, the parameter vector $\boldsymbol{\theta}$ and the weight vector $\boldsymbol{\eta}$ of a QA algorithm are dual affine coordinate systems through the monotonically increasing function f as below:

$$\eta_i = \partial_i \psi(\boldsymbol{\theta}) = f(\theta^i), \quad g_{ij} = \partial_j \eta_i = f'(\theta^i)\delta_{ij} \tag{27}$$

$$\phi(\boldsymbol{\eta}) = \boldsymbol{\theta}^T \boldsymbol{\eta} - \psi(\boldsymbol{\theta}) = \sum_{i=1}^{n}\left[\theta^i f(\theta^i) - g(\theta^i)\right] = \sum_{i=1}^{n} h(f(\theta^i)) = \sum_{i=1}^{n} h(\eta_i), \tag{28}$$

$$\theta^i = \partial^i \phi(\boldsymbol{\eta}) = f^{-1}(\eta_i), \quad g^{ij} = \partial^j \theta^i = (f^{-1})'(\eta_i)\delta^{ij}, \tag{29}$$

where $'$ denotes the derivative and

$$h(s) = \int_0^s f^{-1}(\tau)\mathrm{d}\tau. \tag{30}$$

We can show that the QA algorithm is an approximate of the natural gradient descent method for the dually-flat structure derived from the potential (26). See [5] for details.

4　Preliminaries of Information Theory

Information theory gave answers to the two fundamental questions of the ultimate data compression and the ultimate data transmission in communication theory and has been applied to many other fields beyond the communication theory [3]. In this section, we introduce the so-called the asymptotic equipartition property (AEP) which is the analog of the low of large numbers.

The simplest version of the AEP is formalized in the following theorem.

Theorem 1 (AEP). *Let $p(x)$ be any probability density function defined over* $\mathcal{X}$. *If $X_1, X_2, \ldots$ are i.i.d. random variables drawn according to $p(x)$, then*

$$-\frac{1}{n}\log p(X_1, X_2, \ldots, X_n) \to H(p) \quad \text{in probability,} \tag{31}$$

as $n \to \infty$, where $H(p)$ denotes the entropy of $p(x)$.

The AEP yields the typical set of sequences in this i.i.d. case.

Definition 1 (Typical Set). *The typical set $A_\epsilon^{(n)}$ with respect to $p(x)$ is defined as the set of sequences $(x_1, x_2, \ldots, x_n)$ such that for any $\epsilon > 0$,*

$$\exp[-n(H(p) + \epsilon)] \le p(x_1, x_2, \ldots, x_n) \le \exp[-n(H(p) - \epsilon)]. \tag{32}$$

Theorem 2 (Asymptotic Properties).

1. *If $(x_1, x_2, \ldots, x_n) \in A_\epsilon^{(n)}$, then $H(p) - \epsilon \le (-\log p(x_1, x_2, \ldots, x_n))/n \le H(p) + \epsilon$.*
2. $\Pr(A_\epsilon^{(n)}) > 1 - \epsilon$ *for n sufficiently large.*

3. $|A_\epsilon^{(n)}| \leq \exp[n(H(p) + \epsilon)]$, *where $|A|$ is the number of elements in the set A.*
4. $|A_\epsilon^{(n)}| \geq (1 - \epsilon)\exp[n(H(p) - \epsilon)]$ *for n sufficiently large.*

These properties state that there exists the typical set of sequences with probability nearly one, that all the elements of the typical set are nearly equi-probable, and that the number of elements in the typical set is given by an exponential function of the entropy of the probability density function. This means that the number of elements in the typical set is quite small compared to the number of possible sequences. Hence, we can focus most of our attention on the elements in the typical set since the others appear with probability nearly zero.

The AEP still holds in a number of stationary ergodic processes related to machine learning. In fact, it holds in a Markov chain model formulated by genetic algorithms and this has been applied in [6, 7] for the analysis of genetic algorithms. In the next section, we show that the AEP holds in a Markov decision process (MDP). According to [8], we also discuss how this is related to return maximization in reinforcement learning (RL).

5   The AEP in Reinforcement Learning

In general, RL is formulated as a discrete-time piecewise stationary ergodic MDP with discrete state-actions. The elements of the MDP are described as follows: the sets of states, actions and rewards are denoted as $\mathcal{S} \equiv \{s_1, \ldots, s_I\}$, $\mathcal{A} \equiv \{a_1, \ldots, a_J\}$ and $\mathcal{R} \equiv \{r_1, \ldots, r_K\}$, respectively. Let $s(t)$, $a(t)$ and $r(t)$ denote the random variables of state, action and reward at time-step $t \in \{1, 2, \ldots\}$, defined over $\mathcal{S}$, $\mathcal{A}$ and $\mathcal{R}$, respectively. The policy matrix Γ^π of an agent and the state-transition matrix Γ^T of an environment are described as

$$\Gamma^\pi \equiv \begin{pmatrix} p_{11} & p_{12} & \cdots & p_{1J} \\ p_{21} & p_{22} & \cdots & p_{2J} \\ \vdots & \vdots & \ddots & \vdots \\ p_{I1} & p_{I2} & \cdots & p_{IJ} \end{pmatrix}, \quad \Gamma^\mathrm{T} \equiv \begin{pmatrix} p_{1111} & p_{1112} & \cdots & p_{111K} \\ p_{1211} & p_{1212} & \cdots & p_{121K} \\ \vdots & \vdots & \ddots & \vdots \\ p_{IJ11} & p_{IJ12} & \cdots & p_{IJIK} \end{pmatrix}, \quad (33)$$

respectively, where $p_{ij} \equiv \Pr(a(t) = a_j \mid s(t) = s_i)$ denotes the probability that the agent selects action $a_j \in \mathcal{A}$ in state $s_i \in \mathcal{S}$, and $p_{iji'k} \equiv \Pr(s(t + 1) = s_{i'}, r(t + 1) = r_k \mid s(t) = s_i, a(t) = a_j)$ denotes the probability that the agent receives scalar reward $r_k \in \mathcal{R}$ and observes subsequent state $s_{i'} \in \mathcal{S}$ of the environment when action $a_j \in \mathcal{A}$ is taken in state $s_i \in \mathcal{S}$. Let $\Gamma \equiv (\Gamma^\pi, \Gamma^\mathrm{T})$ for simplicity. Each of the initial state distribution in the environment is defined as $q_i \equiv \Pr(s(1) = s_i) > 0$ for any $s_i \in \mathcal{S}$. Note that the agent can determine the policy matrix Γ^π for action selection while it does not know the state-transition matrix Γ^T.

Suppose that the policy of the agent is improved sufficiently slowly such that the sequence of n time-steps, $x \equiv \{s(1), a(1), r(2), s(2), a(2), \ldots, r(n), s(n), a(n), r(n + 1)\}$, is drawn according to a stationary ergodic MDP described above. We let $r(n + 1) = r(1)$ for notational convenience, and hence the sequence is simply written as $x = \{s(t), a(t), r(t)\}_{t=1}^{n}$. As a result of actual trials by the agent, the empirical distributions $F_{\mathcal{S}}$, $F_{\mathcal{S}\mathcal{A}}$, Φ^{π} and Φ^{T} are uniquely obtained according to the observed sequence of x in the trials, where $F_{\mathcal{S}} \equiv \{f_i\}$ and $F_{\mathcal{S}\mathcal{A}} \equiv \{f_{ij}\}$ are the empirical state distribution and the empirical state-action distribution, respectively, where $f_i \equiv |\{t \in \{1, \ldots, n\} \,|\, s(t) = s_i \in \mathcal{S}\}|/n$ and $f_{ij} \equiv |\{t \in \{1, \ldots, n\} \,|\, s(t) = s_i \in \mathcal{S}, a(t) = a_j \in \mathcal{A}\}|/n$, and the empirical policy matrix Φ^{π} and the empirical state-transition matrix Φ^{T} are denoted as

$$\Phi^{\pi} \equiv \begin{pmatrix} g_{11} & g_{12} & \cdots & g_{1J} \\ g_{21} & g_{22} & \cdots & g_{2J} \\ \vdots & \vdots & \ddots & \vdots \\ g_{I1} & g_{I2} & \cdots & g_{IJ} \end{pmatrix}, \qquad \Phi^{\mathrm{T}} \equiv \begin{pmatrix} g_{1111} & g_{1112} & \cdots & g_{111IK} \\ g_{1211} & g_{1212} & \cdots & g_{121IK} \\ \vdots & \vdots & \ddots & \vdots \\ g_{IJ11} & g_{IJ12} & \cdots & g_{IJIK} \end{pmatrix}, \tag{34}$$

respectively. We need to consider Φ^{π}-shell and Φ^{T}-shell for more strict discussion. The following theorems are obtained from the AEP in the MDP.

Definition 2 (Typical Set). *The typical set $C_{\lambda_n}^{n}(\Gamma)$ in the MDP is defined as the set of sequences such that for any $\lambda_n > 0$, empirical distributions satisfy*

$$D(\Phi^{\pi}\|\Gamma^{\pi} \,|\, F_{\mathcal{S}}) + D(\Phi^{\mathrm{T}}\|\Gamma^{\mathrm{T}} \,|\, F_{\mathcal{S}\mathcal{A}}) \leq \lambda_n, \tag{35}$$

where $D(\Phi^{\pi}\|\Gamma^{\pi} \,|\, F_{\mathcal{S}})$ denotes the conditional divergence between the elements in Φ^{π} and Γ^{π} given $F_{\mathcal{S}}$.

Theorem 3 (Probability of Typical Set). *If $\lambda_n \to 0$ as $n \to \infty$ such that*

$$\lambda_n > \frac{(IJ + I^2 JK)\log(n+1) + \log I - \min p_{iji'k}}{n}, \tag{36}$$

there exists a sequence $\{\epsilon(\lambda_n)\}$ such that $\epsilon(\lambda_n) \to 0$, and $\Pr(C_{\lambda_n}^{n}(\Gamma)) = 1 - \epsilon(\lambda_n)$.

Theorem 4 (Equi-Probability of Elements). *If $x \in C_{\lambda_n}^{n}(\Gamma)$, then there exists a sequence $\{\rho_n\}$ such that $\rho_n \to 0$ as $n \to \infty$, and*

$$\frac{\min p_{iji'k}}{n} - \rho_n \leq -\frac{1}{n}\log \Pr(x) - \phi(\Gamma) \leq -\frac{\min q_i}{n} + \lambda_n + \rho_n, \tag{37}$$

where $\phi(\Gamma)$ is the stochastic complexity of the MDP, defined as

$$\phi(\Gamma) \equiv H(\Gamma^{\pi}|V) + H(\Gamma^{\mathrm{T}}|W), \tag{38}$$

where V and W are the limits of $F_{\mathcal{S}}$ and $F_{\mathcal{S}\mathcal{A}}$ with respect to n.

Theorem 5 (Typical Set Size). *There exist two sequences $\{\zeta_n\}$ and $\{\eta_n\}$ such that $\zeta_n \to 0$ and $\eta_n \to 0$ as $n \to \infty$, and*

$$\exp[n\{\phi(\Gamma) - \zeta_n\}] \leq |C_{\lambda_n}^{n}(\Gamma)| \leq \exp[n\{\phi(\Gamma) + \eta_n\}]. \tag{39}$$

Now let us consider how we can maximize the return in RL. In this paper, return maximization means maximizing the probability that the best sequences appear in trials. Since only the sequences in the typical set appear with probability nearly one, the typical set must be large enough such that it includes the best sequences. On the other hand, from the equi-probability of elements in the typical set, the size of the typical set should be minimized to increase the ratio of the best sequences to the elements in the typical set. This tradeoff is essentially identical to the exploration-exploitation dilemma widely recognized in RL. Because the size of the typical set is characterized by the stochastic complexity, and it is an important guide to solve the dilemma. For example, we can derive the dependency of the stochastic complexity on the learning parameter such as β in the softmax method and ϵ in the ϵ-greedy method, which gives some insight into an appropriate control of the parameter when the learning proceeds.

Information theory can also be applied to the multi-agent problem [9] which is the analog of the multi-terminal information theory. Let the sequence $\boldsymbol{x}_m$ of the m-th of M agents be $\{s_m(1), a_m(1), r_m(2), s_m(2), a_m(2), \ldots, r_m(n), s_m(n), a_m(n), r_m(n+1)\}$. The AEP still holds in an MDP in the multi-agent case, where p_{ij} and $p_{iji'k}$ in the elements of the matrices in (33) are extended to

$$p_{i_1\cdots i_M, j_1\cdots j_M} \equiv \Pr(\boldsymbol{a}(t) = \boldsymbol{a}_{j_1\cdots j_M} \mid \boldsymbol{s}(t) = \boldsymbol{s}_{i_1\cdots i_M}), \qquad (40)$$

$$p_{i_1\cdots i_M, j_1\cdots j_M, i'_1\cdots i'_M, k_1\cdots k_M} \equiv \Pr(\boldsymbol{s}(t+1) = \boldsymbol{s}_{i'_1\cdots i'_M}, \boldsymbol{r}(t+1) = \boldsymbol{r}_{k_1\cdots k_M}$$
$$\mid \boldsymbol{s}(t) = \boldsymbol{s}_{i_1\cdots i_M}, \boldsymbol{a}(t) = \boldsymbol{a}_{j_1\cdots j_M}), \qquad (41)$$

respectively, where $\boldsymbol{s}(t) \equiv (s_1(t), \ldots, s_M(t))$ and $\boldsymbol{s}_{i_1\cdots i_M} \equiv (s_{i_1}, \ldots, s_{i_M}) \in \mathcal{S}^M$. When the agents that exist in the same environment can communicate with each other, i.e., know their states and decide their actions together, the probability of their policy is expressed as (40). When each agent can know all of the other agents' states but cannot know how the others' actions are taken, $p_{i_1\cdots i_M, j_1\cdots j_M}$ in this case cannot take a general form but it is expanded as

$$p_{i_1\cdots i_M, j_1\cdots j_M} = \prod_{m=1}^{M} \Pr(a_m(t) = a_{j_m} \mid \boldsymbol{s}(t) = \boldsymbol{s}_{i_1\cdots i_M}). \qquad (42)$$

This visible case is more limited in the communication among the agents. When no agent can recognize any of the other agents' states nor actions, it is also

$$p_{i_1\cdots i_M, j_1\cdots j_M} = \prod_{m=1}^{M} \Pr(a_m(t) = a_{j_m} \mid s_m(t) = s_{i_m}). \qquad (43)$$

This blind case is much more limited than the visible case. The limitations in the communication increase the entropy $H(\Gamma^\pi|V)$ and make the performance of the agents worse. The multi-agent studies should take the limitations into account.

6   Conclusions

In this paper, we briefly introduced an essence of the information geometry, that is, the duality was shown to be one of the most important properties. When a manifold is dually-flat, the divergence is naturally derived. From a convex potential function, on the other hand, we can introduce a dually-flat structure to the space. One example on quasi-additive algorithms was given in Sec. 3.

Another important tool in machine learning is information theory. Although it has a wide diversity, we concentrate our attention on the asymptotic equipartition property (AEP), which is known as the law of large numbers in statistics. We showed that the AEP on the sequences generated from a Markov decision process using an example on the sequences in reinforcement learning (RL) in Sec. 5. This property should be taken into account in the analysis of algorithms since only the typical sequences appear with probability nearly one.

Information geometry and information theory are so powerful tools that there are a lot of fields to be applied in the future.

Acknowledgment

This study is supported in part by a Grant-in-Aid for Scientific Research (18300078, 18700157) from the Ministry of Education, Culture, Sports, Science and Technology of Japan.

References

1. Amari, S.I.: Differential-Geometrical Methods in Statistics. Lecture Notes in Statistics, vol. 28. Springer, Heidelberg (1985)
2. Amari, S.I., Nagaoka, H.: Methods of Information Geometry. Translations of Mathematical Monographs, vol. 191. AMS and Oxford Univ. Press, Oxford (2000)
3. Cover, T.M., Thomas, J.A.: Elements of Information Theory, 2nd edn. John Wiley and Sons, Inc., Hoboken (2006)
4. Grove, A.J., Littlestone, N., Schuurmans, D.: General convergence results for linear discriminant updates. Machine Learning 43(3), 173–210 (2001)
5. Ikeda, K.: Geometric properties of quasi-additive learning algorithms. IEICE Trans. Fundamentals E89-A(10), 2812–2817 (2006)
6. Suzuki, J.: A markov chain analysis on simple genetic algorithms. IEEE Trans. on Systems, Man and Cybernetics 25(4), 655–659 (1995)
7. Suzuki, J.: A further result on the markov chain model of genetic algorithms and its application to a simulated annealing-like strategy. IEEE Trans. on Systems, Man and Cybernetics, Part B, Cybernetics 28(1), 95–102 (1998)
8. Iwata, K., Ikeda, K., Sakai, H.: The asymptotic equipartition property in reinforcement learning and its relation to return maximization. Neural Networks 19(1), 62–75 (2006)
9. Iwata, K., Ikeda, K., Sakai, H.: A statistical property of multi-agent learning based on Markov decision process. IEEE Trans. on Neural Networks 17(4), 829–842 (2006)

Natural Conjugate Gradient
in Variational Inference

Antti Honkela, Matti Tornio, Tapani Raiko, and Juha Karhunen

Adaptive Informatics Research Centre, Helsinki University of Technology
P.O. Box 5400, FI-02015 TKK, Finland
{Antti.Honkela, Matti.Tornio, Tapani.Raiko, Juha.Karhunen}@tkk.fi
http://www.cis.hut.fi/projects/bayes/

Abstract. Variational methods for approximate inference in machine learning often adapt a parametric probability distribution to optimize a given objective function. This view is especially useful when applying variational Bayes (VB) to models outside the conjugate-exponential family. For them, variational Bayesian expectation maximization (VB EM) algorithms are not easily available, and gradient-based methods are often used as alternatives. Traditional natural gradient methods use the Riemannian structure (or geometry) of the predictive distribution to speed up maximum likelihood estimation. We propose using the geometry of the variational approximating distribution instead to speed up a conjugate gradient method for variational learning and inference. The computational overhead is small due to the simplicity of the approximating distribution. Experiments with real-world speech data show significant speedups over alternative learning algorithms.

1   Introduction

Variational Bayesian (VB) methods provide an efficient and often sufficiently accurate deterministic approximation to exact Bayesian learning [1]. Most work on variational methods has focused on the class of conjugate exponential models for which simple EM-like learning algorithms can be derived easily.

Nevertheless, there are many interesting more complicated models which are not in the conjugate exponential family. Similar variational approximations have been applied for many such models [2,3,4,5,6,7]. The approximating distribution $q(\boldsymbol{\theta}|\boldsymbol{\xi})$, where $\boldsymbol{\theta}$ includes both model parameters and latent variables, is often restricted to be Gaussian with a somehow restricted covariance. Values of the variational parameters $\boldsymbol{\xi}$ can be found by using a gradient-based optimization algorithm.

When applying a generic optimization algorithm for such problem, a lot of background information on the geometry of the problem is lost. The parameters $\boldsymbol{\xi}$ of $q(\boldsymbol{\theta}|\boldsymbol{\xi})$ can have different roles as location, shape, and scale parameters, and they can change the influence of other parameters. This implies that the geometry of the problem is in most cases not Euclidean.

Information geometry studies the Riemannian geometric structure of the manifold of probability distributions [8]. It has been applied to derive efficient natural

M. Ishikawa et al. (Eds.): ICONIP 2007, Part II, LNCS 4985, pp. 305–314, 2008.

gradient learning rules for maximum likelihood algorithms in independent component analysis (ICA) and multilayer perceptron (MLP) networks [9]. The approach has been used in several other problems as well, for example in analyzing the properties of an on-line variational Bayesian EM method [10].

In this paper we propose using the Riemannian structure of the distributions $q(\boldsymbol{\theta}|\boldsymbol{\xi})$ to derive more efficient algorithms for approximate inference and especially mean field type VB. This is in contrast with the traditional natural gradient learning [9] which uses the Riemannian structure of the predictive distribution $p(\boldsymbol{X}|\boldsymbol{\theta})$. The proposed method can be used to jointly optimize all the parameters $\boldsymbol{\xi}$ of the approximation $q(\boldsymbol{\theta}|\boldsymbol{\xi})$, or in conjunction with VB EM for some parameters. The method is especially useful for models that are not in the conjugate exponential family, such as nonlinear models [2,3,4,5,7] or non-conjugate variance models [6] that may not have a tractable exact VB EM algorithm.

2   Variational Bayes

Variational Bayesian learning [1,5] is based on approximating the posterior distribution $p(\boldsymbol{\theta}|\boldsymbol{X})$ with a tractable approximation $q(\boldsymbol{\theta}|\boldsymbol{\xi})$, where $\boldsymbol{X}$ is the data, $\boldsymbol{\theta}$ are the unknown variables (including both the parameters of the model and the latent variables), and $\boldsymbol{\xi}$ are the variational parameters of the approximation (such as the mean and the variance of a Gaussian variable). The approximation is fitted by maximizing a lower bound on marginal log-likelihood

$$\mathcal{B}(q(\boldsymbol{\theta}|\boldsymbol{\xi})) = \left\langle \log \frac{p(\boldsymbol{X},\boldsymbol{\theta})}{q(\boldsymbol{\theta}|\boldsymbol{\xi})} \right\rangle = \log p(\boldsymbol{X}) - D_{\mathrm{KL}}(q(\boldsymbol{\theta}|\boldsymbol{\xi})\|p(\boldsymbol{\theta}|\boldsymbol{X})), \qquad (1)$$

where $\langle\cdot\rangle$ denotes expectation over q. This is equivalent to minimizing the Kullback–Leibler divergence $D_{\mathrm{KL}}(q\|p)$ between q and p [1,5].

Finding the optimal approximation can be seen as an optimization problem, where the lower bound $\mathcal{B}(q(\boldsymbol{\theta}|\boldsymbol{\xi}))$ is maximized with respect to the variational parameters $\boldsymbol{\xi}$. This is often solved using a VB EM algorithm by updating sets of parameters alternatively while keeping the others fixed. Both VB-E and VB-M steps can implicitly optimally utilize the Riemannian structure of $q(\boldsymbol{\theta}|\boldsymbol{\xi})$ for conjugate exponential family models [10]. Nevertheless, the EM based methods are prone to slow convergence, especially under low noise, even though more elaborate optimization schemes can speed up their convergence somewhat.

The formulation of VB as an optimization problem allows applying generic optimization algorithms to maximize $\mathcal{B}(q(\boldsymbol{\theta}|\boldsymbol{\xi}))$, but this is rarely done in practice because the problems are quite high dimensional. Additionally other parameters may influence the effect of other parameters and the lack of this specific knowledge of the geometry of the problem can seriously hinder generic optimization tools.

Assuming the approximation $q(\boldsymbol{\theta}|\boldsymbol{\xi})$ is Gaussian, it is often enough to use generic optimization tools to update the mean of the distribution. This is because the negative entropy of a Gaussian $q(\boldsymbol{\theta}|\boldsymbol{\mu},\boldsymbol{\Sigma})$ with mean $\boldsymbol{\mu}$ and covariance $\boldsymbol{\Sigma}$ is $\langle \log q(\boldsymbol{\theta}|\boldsymbol{\xi})\rangle = -\frac{1}{2}\log\det(2\pi e\boldsymbol{\Sigma})$ and thus straightforward differentiation of Eq. (1) yields a fixed point update rule for the covariance

$$\boldsymbol{\Sigma}^{-1} = -2\nabla_{\boldsymbol{\Sigma}}\langle \log p(\boldsymbol{X},\boldsymbol{\theta})\rangle. \tag{2}$$

If the covariance is assumed diagonal, the same update rule applies for the diagonal terms.

3   Natural Gradient Learning for VB

Let $\mathcal{F}(\boldsymbol{\xi})$ be a scalar function defined on the manifold $S = \{\boldsymbol{\xi} \in \mathbf{R}^n\}$. If S is a Euclidean space and the coordinate system $\boldsymbol{\xi}$ is orthonormal, the direction of steepest ascent is given by the standard gradient $\nabla\mathcal{F}(\boldsymbol{\xi})$.

If the space S is a curved Riemannian manifold, the direction of steepest ascent is given by the natural gradient [9]

$$\tilde{\nabla}\mathcal{F}(\boldsymbol{\xi}) = \mathbf{G}^{-1}(\boldsymbol{\xi})\nabla\mathcal{F}(\boldsymbol{\xi}). \tag{3}$$

The $n \times n$ matrix $\mathbf{G}(\boldsymbol{\xi}) = (g_{ij}(\boldsymbol{\xi}))$ is called the Riemannian metric tensor and it may depend on the point of origin $\boldsymbol{\xi}$.

For the space of probability distributions $q(\boldsymbol{\theta}|\boldsymbol{\xi})$, the most common Riemannian metric tensor is given by the Fisher information [8]

$$I_{ij}(\boldsymbol{\xi}) = g_{ij}(\boldsymbol{\xi}) = E\left\{\frac{\partial \ln q(\boldsymbol{\theta}|\boldsymbol{\xi})}{\partial \xi_i}\frac{\partial \ln q(\boldsymbol{\theta}|\boldsymbol{\xi})}{\partial \xi_j}\right\} = E\left\{-\frac{\partial^2 \ln q(\boldsymbol{\theta}|\boldsymbol{\xi})}{\partial \xi_i \partial \xi_j}\right\}, \tag{4}$$

where the last equality is valid given certain regularity conditions [11].

3.1   Computing the Riemannian Metric Tensor

When applying natural gradients to approximate inference, the geometry is defined by the approximation $q(\boldsymbol{\theta}|\boldsymbol{\xi})$ and not the full model $p(\boldsymbol{X}|\boldsymbol{\theta})$ as usually. If the approximation $q(\boldsymbol{\theta}|\boldsymbol{\xi})$ is chosen such that disjoint groups of variables are independent, that is,

$$q(\boldsymbol{\theta}|\boldsymbol{\xi}) = \prod_i q_i(\boldsymbol{\theta}_i|\boldsymbol{\xi}_i), \tag{5}$$

the computation of the natural gradient is simplified as the Fisher information matrix becomes block-diagonal. The required matrix inversion can be performed very efficiently because

$$\mathrm{diag}(A_1,\ldots,A_n)^{-1} = \mathrm{diag}(A_1^{-1},\ldots,A_n^{-1}). \tag{6}$$

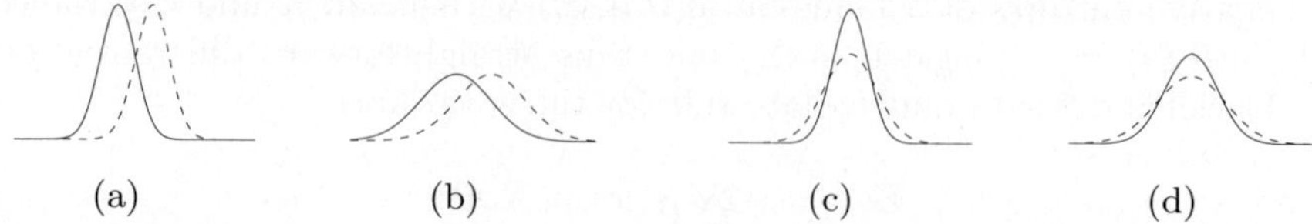

Fig. 1. The absolute change in the mean of the Gaussian in figures (a) and (b) and the absolute change in the variance of the Gaussian in figures (c) and (d) is the same. However, the relative effect is much larger when the variance is small as in figures (a) and (c) compared to the case when the variance is high as in figures (b) and (d) [12].

The dimensionality of the problem space is often so high that inverting the full matrix would not be feasible.

3.2 Gaussian Distribution

For the univariate Gaussian distribution parametrized by mean and variance $N(x;\ \mu, v)$, we have

$$\ln q(x|\mu, v) = -\frac{1}{2v}(x - \mu)^2 - \frac{1}{2}\ln(v) - \frac{1}{2}\ln(2\pi). \tag{7}$$

Furthermore,

$$E\left\{-\frac{\partial^2 \ln q(x|\mu, v)}{\partial\mu\partial\mu}\right\} = \frac{1}{v}, \tag{8}$$

$$E\left\{-\frac{\partial^2 \ln q(x|\mu, v)}{\partial v\partial\mu}\right\} = 0, \text{ and} \tag{9}$$

$$E\left\{-\frac{\partial^2 \ln q(x|\mu, v)}{\partial v\partial v}\right\} = \frac{1}{2v^2}. \tag{10}$$

The vanishing of the cross term between mean and variance further supports using the simpler fixed point rule (2) to update the variances.

In the case of univariate Gaussian distribution, natural gradient for the mean has a rather straightforward intuitive interpretation, which is illustrated in Figure 1 (left). Compared to conventional gradient, natural gradient compensates for the fact that changing the parameters of a Gaussian with small variance has much more pronounced effects than when the variance is large.

In case of multivariate Gaussian distribution, the elements of the Fisher information matrix corresponding to the mean are simply

$$E\left\{-\frac{\partial^2 \ln q(\mathbf{x}|\boldsymbol{\mu}, \boldsymbol{\Sigma})}{\partial\boldsymbol{\mu}^T\partial\boldsymbol{\mu}}\right\} = \boldsymbol{\Sigma}^{-1}. \tag{11}$$

Typically the covariance matrix $\boldsymbol{\Sigma}$ is assumed to have a simple structure (diagonal, diagonal+rank-k, simple Markov random field) that makes working with it very efficient.

4   Natural and Conjugate Gradient Methods

Many of the traditional optimization algorithms have their direct counterparts in Riemannian space. This paper concentrates on gradient based algorithms, in particular the generalized versions of gradient ascent and conjugate gradient method.

Gradient-based optimization algorithms in Euclidean space operate by deriving a search direction using the gradient at current search point and possibly other information. Then, either a fixed-length step is taken or a line search performed in this direction. The fixed step length can still be adjusted during learning.

When generalizing these methods to Riemannian space, the geometrically most natural approach would be to take the steps or perform the line search along geodesics, which are length-minimizing curves and hence Riemannian counterparts of straight lines. In practice this is rarely done because the mathematical forms of geodesics can be very complicated thus making operations with them computationally expensive. Euclidean straight lines are used instead of geodesics in this work as well.

4.1   Natural Gradient Ascent

The natural gradient learning algorithm is analogous to conventional gradient ascent algorithm and is given by the iteration

$$\boldsymbol{\xi}_k = \boldsymbol{\xi}_{k-1} + \gamma \tilde{\nabla}\mathcal{F}(\boldsymbol{\xi}_{k-1}), \tag{12}$$

where the step size γ can either be adjusted adaptively during learning [9] or computed for each iteration using e.g. line search. In general, the performance of natural gradient learning is superior to conventional gradient learning when the problem space is Riemannian; see [9].

4.2   Conjugate Gradient Methods and Riemannian Conjugate Gradient

For better performance it can be useful to combine natural gradient learning with some standard superlinear optimization algorithm. One such algorithm is the nonlinear conjugate gradient (CG) method [13]. The conjugate gradient method is a standard tool for solving high dimensional nonlinear optimization problems. During each iteration of the conjugate gradient method, a new search direction is generated by conjugation of the residuals from previous iterations. With this choice the search directions form a Krylov subspace and only the previous search direction and the current gradient are required for the conjugation process, making the algorithm efficient in both time and space complexity [13].

The extension of the conjugate gradient algorithm to Riemannian manifolds is done by replacing the gradient with the natural gradient. The resulting algorithm is known as the Riemannian conjugate gradient method [14,15]. In principle this extension is relatively simple, as it is sufficient that all the vector operations take into account the Riemannian nature of the problem space. Therefore, the line searches are performed along geodesic curves and the old gradient vectors $\tilde{\mathbf{g}}_{k-1}$ defined in a different tangent space are transformed to the tangent space at the origin of the new gradient by parallel transport along a geodesic [14].

4.3 Natural Conjugate Gradient

Like with natural gradient ascent, it is often necessary to make certain simplifying assumptions to keep the iteration simple and efficient. In this paper, the geodesic curves used in Riemannian conjugate gradient algorithm are approximated with (Euclidean) straight lines. This also means that parallel transport cannot be used, and vector operations between vectors from two different tangent spaces are performed in the Euclidean sense, i.e. assuming that the parallel transport between two points close to each other on the manifold can be approximated by the identity mapping. This approximative algorithm is called the natural conjugate gradient (NCG).

For small step sizes and geometries which are locally close to Euclidean these assumptions still retain many of the benefits of original algorithm while greatly simplifying the computations. Edelman et al. [15] showed that near the solution Riemannian conjugate gradient method differs from the flat space version of conjugate gradient only by third order terms, and therefore both algorithms converge quadratically near the optimum.

The search direction for the natural conjugate gradient method is given by

$$\mathbf{p}_k = \tilde{\mathbf{g}}_k + \beta \mathbf{p}_{k-1}, \tag{13}$$

and the Polak-Ribiére formula used to evaluate the coefficient β is given by

$$\beta = \frac{(\tilde{\mathbf{g}}_k - \tilde{\mathbf{g}}_{k-1}) \cdot \tilde{\mathbf{g}}_k}{\tilde{\mathbf{g}}_{k-1} \cdot \tilde{\mathbf{g}}_k}. \tag{14}$$

5 VB for Nonlinear State-Space Models

As a specific example, we consider the nonlinear state-space model (NSSM) introduced in [5]. The model is specified by the generative model

$$\mathbf{x}(t) = \mathbf{f}(\mathbf{s}(t), \boldsymbol{\theta}_{\mathbf{f}}) + \mathbf{n}(t) \tag{15}$$
$$\mathbf{s}(t) = \mathbf{s}(t-1) + \mathbf{g}(\mathbf{s}(t-1), \boldsymbol{\theta}_{\mathbf{g}}) + \mathbf{m}(t), \tag{16}$$

where t is time, $\mathbf{x}(t)$ are the observations, and $\mathbf{s}(t)$ are the hidden states. The observation mapping $\mathbf{f}$ and the dynamical mapping $\mathbf{g}$ are nonlinear and they are modeled with multilayer perceptron (MLP) networks. Observation noise $\mathbf{n}$

and process noise $\mathbf{m}$ are assumed Gaussian. The latent states $\mathbf{s}(t)$ are commonly denoted by $\boldsymbol{\theta}_S$. The model parameters include both the weights of the MLP networks and a number of hyperparameters. The posterior approximation of these parameters is a Gaussian with a diagonal covariance. The posterior approximation of the states $q(\boldsymbol{\theta}_S|\boldsymbol{\xi}_S)$ is a Gaussian Markov random field a correlation between the corresponding components of subsequent state vectors $s_j(t)$ and $s_j(t-1)$. This is a realistic minimum assumption for modeling the dependence of the state vectors $\mathbf{s}(t)$ and $\mathbf{s}(t-1)$ [5].

Because of the nonlinearities the model is not in the conjugate exponential family, and the standard VB learning methods are only applicable to hyperparameters and not the latent states or weights of the MLPs. The bound (1) can nevertheless be evaluated by linearizing the MLP networks $\mathbf{f}$ and $\mathbf{g}$ using the technique of [7]. This allows evaluating the gradient with respect to $\boldsymbol{\xi}_S$, $\boldsymbol{\xi}_\mathbf{f}$, and $\boldsymbol{\xi}_\mathbf{g}$ and using a gradient based optimizer to adapt the parameters. The natural gradient for the mean elements is given by

$$\tilde{\nabla}_{\boldsymbol{\mu}_q}\mathcal{F}(\boldsymbol{\xi}) = \boldsymbol{\Sigma}_q\nabla_{\boldsymbol{\mu}_q}\mathcal{F}(\boldsymbol{\xi}), \tag{17}$$

where $\boldsymbol{\mu}_q$ is the mean of the variational approximation $q(\boldsymbol{\theta}|\boldsymbol{\xi})$ and $\boldsymbol{\Sigma}_q$ is the corresponding covariance. The covariance of the model parameters is diagonal while the inverse covariance of the latent states $\mathbf{s}(t)$ is block-diagonal with tridiagonal blocks. This implies that all computations with these can be done in linear time with respect to the number of the parameters. The covariances were updated separately using a fixed-point update rule similar to (2) as described in [5].

6   Experiments

As an example, the method for learning nonlinear state-space models presented in Sec. 5 was applied to real world speech data. Experiments were made with different data sizes to study the performance differences between the algorithms. The data consisted of 21 dimensional mel frequency log power speech spectra of continuous human speech.

To study the performance differences between the natural conjugate gradient (NCG) method, standard natural gradient (NG) method, standard conjugate gradient (CG) method and the heuristic algorithm from [5], the algorithms were applied to different sized parts of the speech data set. Unfortunately a reasonable comparison with a VB EM algorithm was impossible because the E-step failed due to instability of the used Kalman filtering algorithm.

The size of the data subsets varied between 200 and 500 samples. A five dimensional state-space was used. The MLP networks for the observation and dynamical mapping had 20 hidden nodes. Four different initializations and two different segments of data of each size were used, resulting in eight repetitions for each algorithm and data size. The results for different data segments of the same size were pooled together as the convergence times were in general very similar. An iteration was assumed to have converged when $|\mathcal{B}^t - \mathcal{B}^{t-1}| < \varepsilon = (10^{-5}N/500)$

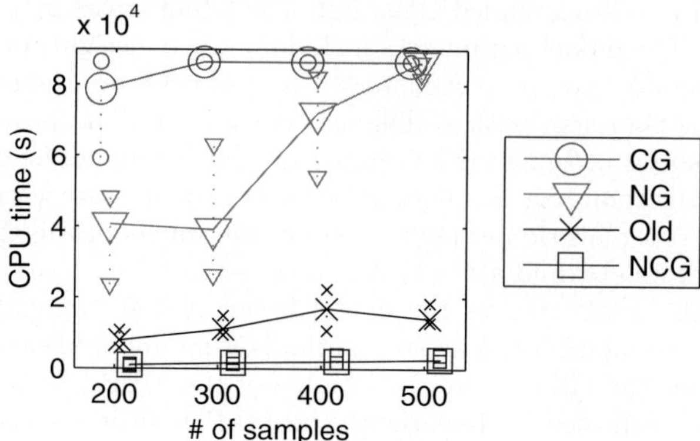

Fig. 2. Convergence speed of the natural conjugate gradient (NCG), the natural gradient (NG) and the conjugate gradient (CG) methods as well as the heuristic algorithm (Old) with different data sizes. The lines show median times with 25 % and 75 % quantiles shown by the smaller marks. The times were limited to at most 24 hours, which was reached by a number of simulations.

for 5 consecutive iterations, where $\mathcal{B}^t$ is the bound on marginal log-likelihood at iteration t and N is the size of the data set. Alternatively, the iteration was stopped after 24 hours even if it had not converged. Practically all the simulations converged to different local optima, but there were no statistically significant differences in the bound values corresponding to these optima (Wilcoxon rank-sum test, 5 % significance level). There were still some differences, and especially the NG algorithm with smaller data sizes often appeared to converge very early to an extremely poor solution. These were filtered by removing results where the attained bound value that was more than two NCG standard deviations worse than NCG average for the particular data set. The results of one run where the heuristic algorithm diverged were also discarded from the analysis.

The results can be seen in Figure 2. The plain CG and NG methods were clearly slower than others and the maximum runtime was reached by most CG and some NG runs. NCG was clearly the fastest algorithm with the heuristic method between these extremes.

As a more realistic example, a larger data set of 1000 samples was used to train a seven dimensional state-space model. In this experiment both MLP networks of the NSSM had 30 hidden nodes. The convergence criterion was $\varepsilon = 10^{-6}$ and the maximum runtime was 72 hours. The performances of the NCG, NG, CG methods and the heuristic algorithm were compared. The results can be seen in Figure 3. The results show the convergence for five different initializations with markers at the end showing when the convergence was reached.

NCG clearly outperformed the other algorithms in this experiment as well. In particular, both NG and CG hit the maximum runtime in every run, and especially CG was nowhere near convergence at this time. NCG also outperformed the heuristic algorithm [5] by a factor of more than 10.

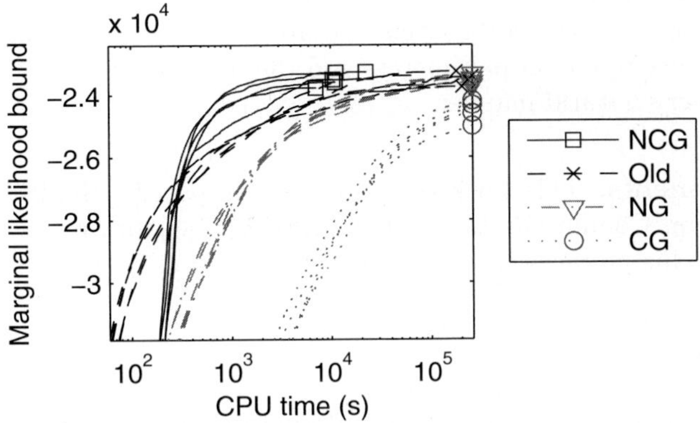

Fig. 3. Comparison of the performance of the natural conjugate gradient (NCG), the natural gradient (NG), the conjugate gradient (CG) methods and the heuristic algorithm with the full data set. Lower bound on marginal log-likelihood $\mathcal{B}$ is plotted against computation time using a logarithmic time scale. The tick marks show when simulations either converged or were terminated after 72 hours.

7   Discussion

In previous machine learning algorithms based on natural gradients [9], the aim has been to use maximum likelihood to directly update the model parameters $\boldsymbol{\theta}$ taking into account the geometry imposed by the predictive distribution for data $p(\boldsymbol{X}|\boldsymbol{\theta})$. The resulting geometry is often much more complicated as the effects of different parameters cannot be separated and the Fisher information matrix is relatively dense. In this paper, only the simpler geometry of the approximating distributions $q(\boldsymbol{\theta}|\boldsymbol{\xi})$ is used. Because the approximations are often chosen to minimize dependencies between different parameters $\boldsymbol{\theta}$, the resulting Fisher information matrix with respect to the variational parameters $\boldsymbol{\xi}$ will be mostly diagonal and hence easy to invert.

While taking into account the structure of the approximation, plain natural gradient in this case ignores the structure of the model and the global geometry of the parameters $\boldsymbol{\theta}$. This is to some extent addressed by using conjugate gradients, and even more sophisticated optimization methods such as quasi-Newton or even Gauss–Newton methods can be used if the size of the problem permits it.

While the natural conjugate gradient method has been formulated mainly for models outside the conjugate-exponential family, it can also be applied to conjugate-exponential models instead of the more common VB EM algorithms. In practice, simpler and more straightforward EM acceleration methods may still provide comparable results with less human effort.

The experiments in this paper show that using even a greatly simplified variant of the Riemannian conjugate gradient method for some variables is enough to acquire a large speedup. Considering univariate Gaussian distributions, the regular gradient is too strong for model variables with small posterior variance and too weak for variables with large posterior variance, as seen from Eqs. (8)–(10). The posterior variance of latent variables is often much larger than the posterior variance of model parameters and the natural gradient takes this into account in a very natural manner.

Acknowledgments. This work was supported in part by the IST Programme of the European Community, under the PASCAL Network of Excellence, IST-2002-506778. This publication only reflects the authors' views.

References

1. Bishop, C.: Pattern Recognition and Machince Learning. Springer, Heidelberg (2006)
2. Barber, D., Bishop, C.: Ensemble learning for multi-layer networks. In: Advances in Neural Information Processing Systems 10, pp. 395–401. The MIT Press, Cambridge (1998)
3. Seeger, M.: Bayesian model selection for support vector machines, Gaussian processes and other kernel classifiers. In: Advances in Neural Information Processing Systems 12, pp. 603–609. MIT Press, Cambridge (2000)
4. Lappalainen, H., Honkela, A.: Bayesian nonlinear independent component analysis by multi-layer perceptrons. In: Girolami, M. (ed.) Advances in Independent Component Analysis, pp. 93–121. Springer, Berlin (2000)
5. Valpola, H., Karhunen, J.: An unsupervised ensemble learning method for nonlinear dynamic state-space models. Neural Computation 14(11), 2647–2692 (2002)
6. Valpola, H., Harva, M., Karhunen, J.: Hierarchical models of variance sources. Signal Processing 84(2), 267–282 (2004)
7. Honkela, A., Valpola, H.: Unsupervised variational Bayesian learning of nonlinear models. In: Advances in Neural Information Processing Systems 17, pp. 593–600. MIT Press, Cambridge (2005)
8. Amari, S.: Differential-Geometrical Methods in Statistics. Lecture Notes in Statistics, vol. 28. Springer, Heidelberg (1985)
9. Amari, S.: Natural gradient works efficiently in learning. Neural Computation 10(2), 251–276 (1998)
10. Sato, M.: Online model selection based on the variational Bayes. Neural Computation 13(7), 1649–1681 (2001)
11. Murray, M.K., Rice, J.W.: Differential Geometry and Statistics. Chapman and Hall, Boca Raton (1993)
12. Valpola, H.: Bayesian Ensemble Learning for Nonlinear Factor Analysis. PhD thesis, Helsinki University of Technology, Espoo, Finland, Published in Acta Polytechnica Scandinavica, Mathematics and Computing Series No. 108 (2000)
13. Nocedal, J.: Theory of algorithms for unconstrained optimization. Acta Numerica 1, 199–242 (1991)
14. Smith, S.T.: Geometric Optimization Methods for Adaptive Filtering. PhD thesis, Harvard University, Cambridge, Massachusetts (1993)
15. Edelman, A., Arias, T.A., Smith, S.T.: The geometry of algorithms with orthogonality constraints. SIAM Journal on Matrix Analysis and Applications 20(2), 303–353 (1998)

A Robust ICA-Based Adaptive Filter Algorithm for System Identification Using Stochastic Information Gradient

Jun-Mei Yang and Hideaki Sakai

Graduate School of Informatics, Kyoto University,
Kyoto 606-8501, Japan

Abstract. This paper proposes a new adaptive filter algorithm for system identification by using an independent component analysis (ICA) technique, which separates the signal from noisy observation under the assumption that the signal and noise are independent. We first introduce an augmented state-space expression of the observed signal, representing the problem in terms of ICA. By using a nonparametric Parzen window density estimator and the stochastic information gradient, we derive an adaptive algorithm to separate the noise from the signal. The computational complexity of the proposed algorithm is compared with that of the standard NLMS algorithm. The local convergence is analyzed. Due to the additive noise is also on-line estimated during the iteration, the proposed algorithm shows excellent robustness. It can directly be applied to an acoustic echo canceller without any double-talk detector. Some simulation results are carried out to show the superiority of our ICA method to the conventional NLMS algorithm.

1   Introduction

Adaptive filter techniques have been applied to many system identification problems in communications and noise control [1][2]. The two most popular algorithms, i.e. LMS and RLS, are both based on the idea that the effect of additive observation noise is to be suppressed in the least square sense. But if the noise is non-Gaussian, the performances of the above algorithms degrade significantly. The other class of non-linear algorithms has been derived based on the robust estimation theory [3], but these algorithms are a little bit heuristic.

On the other hand, in recent years, independent component analysis (ICA) has been attracting much attention in many fields such as signal processing and machine learning [4]. However, in the adaptive filter area, there have been only a few papers which try to derive adaptive algorithms from the viewpoint of ICA. The authors in [5] tried to formulate the conventional system identification problem in the ICA context, but the proposed algorithm is nothing but the QR type RLS algorithm. In [6] a truly ICA type algorithm based on minimizing the mutual information has been derived for identification of multivariate autoregressive models. In [7], by combining the approaches in [5] and [6], we proposed

M. Ishikawa et al. (Eds.): ICONIP 2007, Part II, LNCS 4985, pp. 315–325, 2008.

a new adaptive algorithm for system identification using the technique of ICA. We try not to suppress the noise in the least mean square sense but to maximize the independence between the signal part and the noise. The usual mutual information is used to measure the independence and a nonlinear function concerning the probability density function (pdf) of the additive noise signal appears in the algorithm. Since this is unknown, it is fixed to some typical one, say, the hyperbolic tangent function as in many papers on the usual ICA. But this fixed function does not always fit to the changing situation and it is highly desirable to estimate the pdf directly by using some adaptive procedure. In this paper, on the basis of the framework in [7] we use the nonparametric Parzen window density estimator [8] and the stochastic information gradient (SIG) [9] to derive a new adaptive gradient descent algorithm for system identification. The organization of this paper is as follows: In Section 2 we introduce an augmented linear model representing the problem in the framework of ICA, and then propose a new adaptive algorithm in Section 3 by using the ICA technique. The computational complexity of the proposed algorithm is also compared with that of the standard NLMS algorithm. In Section 4, the local stability of the algorithm is analyzed and a step size condition is also derived. Section 5 shows that the new ICA-based method has an excellent robustness and can directly be applied to the acoustic echo canceller without the usage of double talk detector (DTD). Finally, some numerical simulations are demonstrated to show the superiority of our ICA-based method to the conventional NLMS algorithm.

2   Problem Formulation

We consider the problem of identifying a linear system described by

$$y(n) = \mathbf{h}^T \mathbf{x}(n), \tag{1}$$

where $\mathbf{h} = [h_0\ h_1 \cdots h_{m-1}]^T,$ $\mathbf{x}(n) = [x(n)\ x(n-1) \cdots x(n-m+1)]^T.$ $x(n)$ is the zero mean input signal. The measurement of the system output $y(n)$ is corrupted by additive noise $e(n)$, that is, $d(n) = y(n) + e(n)$. We assume the noise $e(n)$ is zero mean and statistically independent with the system input $\mathbf{x}(n)$. Statistical independence is a much stronger condition than uncorrelatedness. As a result, statistics of order higher than the second has to be considered for non-Gaussian signals.

We now introduce the following augmented linear model to formulate the problem of system identification in the frame work of ICA:

$$\begin{bmatrix} \mathbf{x}(n) \\ d(n) \end{bmatrix} = \begin{bmatrix} \mathbf{I} & \mathbf{0} \\ \mathbf{h}^T & 1 \end{bmatrix} \begin{bmatrix} \mathbf{x}(n) \\ e(n) \end{bmatrix}, \tag{2}$$

where $\mathbf{I}$ denotes the identity matrix. The noise signal $e(n)$, which is assumed to be independent of the input signal $\mathbf{x}(n)$, is expected to be separated from the observation signal. So we may consider the system identification problem as an

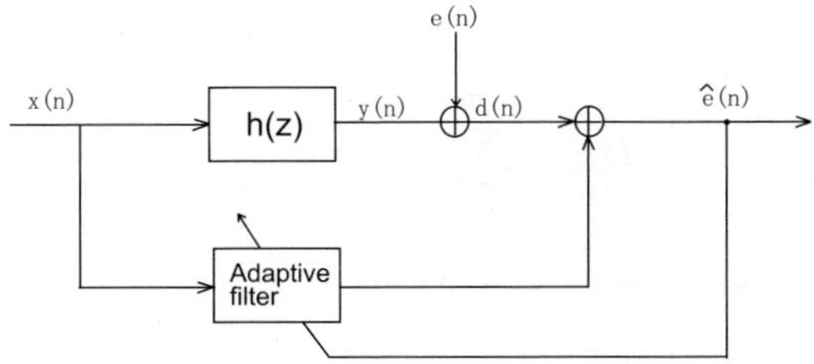

Fig. 1. General configuration of system identification

ICA problem, although the input signals $x(n-i), i = 0, 1, \cdots, m-1$ are heavily auto-correlated.

On the basis of model (2), we introduce the following system

$$\begin{bmatrix} \mathbf{x}(n) \\ \hat{e}(n) \end{bmatrix} = \hat{W} \begin{bmatrix} \mathbf{x}(n) \\ d(n) \end{bmatrix} \tag{3}$$

where

$$\hat{W} = \begin{bmatrix} \mathbf{I} & \mathbf{0} \\ \hat{\mathbf{w}}^T & a \end{bmatrix} \tag{4}$$

$$\hat{\mathbf{w}} = [\hat{w}_0 \ \hat{w}_1 \cdots \hat{w}_{m-1}]^T \tag{5}$$

$$\hat{e}(n) = \hat{\mathbf{w}}^T \mathbf{x}(n) + ad(n) \tag{6}$$

and a is a nonzero scalar quantity. In the usual adaptive filtering problem a is set to 1.

In the following, we will find a good estimate of the matrix $\hat{W}$ so that $\mathbf{x}(n)$ and $\hat{e}(n)$ are as independent as possible.

3   Derivation of the Proposed Algorithm

Mutual information is a natural measure of the dependence between random variables. It is always nonnegative, and zero if and only if the variables are statistically independent. It takes into account the whole dependence structure of the variables, and not just the covariance. Therefore it is a very natural way to estimate the independent components by finding a transform that minimizes the mutual information of their estimates.

The mutual information I between M (scalar) random variables, $\mathbf{y}_i, i = 1, \cdots, M$ is defined as follows:

$$I(y) = \int_{-\infty}^{\infty} p_{\mathbf{y}}(y) \log \frac{p_{\mathbf{y}}(y)}{\prod_{i=1}^{M} p_{\mathbf{y}_i}(y_i)} \, dy, \tag{7}$$

where $p_{\mathbf{y}}(y)$ denotes the joint pdf of $\mathbf{y} = (\mathbf{y}_1, \cdots, \mathbf{y}_M)$ and $p_{\mathbf{y}_i}(y_i)$ denotes the marginal pdf of $\mathbf{y}_i$ $(i = 1, \cdots, M)$. The mutual information defined in (7) can be formulated with the marginal and joint entropies:

$$I(y) = \sum_{i=1}^{M} H(y_i) - H(y) \tag{8}$$

where $H(\cdot)$ denotes the differential entropy

$$H(y) = -\int_{-\infty}^{\infty} p(y) \log p(y) \mathrm{d}y = E_p[-\log p(y)]. \tag{9}$$

On the basis of the definition of entropy in (9), for the invertible linear transformation (3), the output entropy can directly be computed from the input entropy:

$$H(\mathbf{x}, \hat{e}) = H(\mathbf{x}, d) + \log|\det \hat{W}| = H(\mathbf{x}, d) + \log|a|. \tag{10}$$

Hence, the cost function to be minimized is

$$I(\mathbf{x}, \hat{e}) = H(\mathbf{x}) + H(\hat{e}) - H(\mathbf{x}, \hat{e}) = H(\mathbf{x}) - H(\mathbf{x}, d) + H(\hat{e}) - \log|a|. \tag{11}$$

Note that the first two terms in (11) are both fixed quantities given the data of $\mathbf{x}(n)$ and $d(n)$. Hence, the cost function simply becomes

$$J = H(\hat{e}) - \log|a| = E_p[-\log p(\hat{e})] - \log|a|. \tag{12}$$

Since in realistic problems the analytical expression for the pdf is hardly ever known, a productive way is to nonparametrically estimate the density from the samples. That is where Parzen windowing comes into play. The Parzen window estimate of the probability distribution $\hat{p}_\mathbf{y}(y)$, of a random vector $\mathbf{y} \in \Re^M$ at a point y is defined as

$$\hat{p}_\mathbf{y}(\mathbf{y}) = \frac{1}{N} \sum_{i=1}^{N} \kappa_\sigma(\mathbf{y} - \mathbf{y}_i), \tag{13}$$

where the vectors $\mathbf{y}_i \in \Re^M$ are observations of the random vector, and $\kappa_\sigma(\cdot)$ is a kernel function, whose size is specified by the parameter σ. In general the kernel function itself should satisfy the properties of a pdf (i.e. $\kappa_\sigma(\mathbf{y}) > 0$ and $\int \kappa_\sigma(\mathbf{y})d\mathbf{y} = 1$). The Parzen windowing estimate in (13) is consistent under certain conditions [8]. Since we wish to make a local estimate of the pdf, the kernel function should be localized (i.e. unimodal, decaying to zero). If the estimator kernel function is also differentiable everywhere, the estimate will satisfy the properties of a pdf [8]. How to determine an optimal kernel choice is still an open question. A popular choice for $\kappa(\cdot)$ is the symmetric Gaussian kernel

$$\kappa_\sigma(\mathbf{x}) = G(\mathbf{x}, \sigma^2 \mathbf{I}) = \frac{1}{(2\pi)^{M/2}\sigma^M} \exp\left(-\frac{\mathbf{x}^T \mathbf{x}}{2\sigma^2}\right) \tag{14}$$

with the covariance matrix $\sigma^2 \mathbf{I}$ [10].

The estimator given by (13) uses a fixed window, which will lead to a batch algorithm. In a nonstationary environment, an online pdf estimate can be obtained using a sliding window of samples. Assuming a window length of L samples, one reasonable pdf estimate of $\hat{e}$ evaluated at $\hat{e}(n)$ is taken as

$$\hat{p}[\hat{e}(n)] = \frac{1}{L} \sum_{j=1}^{L} \kappa_\sigma\big(\hat{e}(n) - \hat{e}(n-j)\big). \tag{15}$$

Substitute the estimate in (15) for $\log p(\hat{e})$ in (12) and the cost function becomes

$$J \approx E\bigg[-\log\Big(\frac{1}{L}\sum_{j=1}^{L} \kappa_\sigma\big(\hat{e}(n) - \hat{e}(n-j)\big)\Big) - \log|a|\bigg] = E[\hat{J}] \tag{16}$$

We want to minimize the cost function J with respect to $\hat{\mathbf{w}}$ and a by using the standard steepest descent algorithm. Since the element of $\hat{W}$ in (4), we have

$$\frac{\partial J}{\partial \hat{W}} = \begin{bmatrix} \mathbf{0} & \mathbf{0} \\ E\big[\frac{\partial \hat{J}}{\partial \hat{\mathbf{w}}^T}\big] & E\big[\frac{\partial \hat{J}}{\partial a}\big] \end{bmatrix}. \tag{17}$$

But (16) contains the expectation operation, so we will derive the stochastic gradient for the cost function. As in the derivation of the LMS algorithm, instantaneous gradients are used by dropping the expectation in (17). Taking the derivatives of $\hat{J}$ with respect to $\hat{\mathbf{w}}$ and a, from (6) we get

$$\frac{\partial \hat{J}}{\partial \hat{\mathbf{w}}} = -\frac{\displaystyle\sum_{j=1}^{L} \kappa'_\sigma(\hat{e}(n) - \hat{e}(n-j))\mathbf{x}(n)}{\displaystyle\sum_{j=1}^{L} \kappa_\sigma(\hat{e}(n) - \hat{e}(n-j))}, \tag{18}$$

$$\frac{\partial \hat{J}}{\partial a} = -\frac{\displaystyle\sum_{j=1}^{L} \kappa'_\sigma(\hat{e}(n) - \hat{e}(n-j))d(n)}{\sum_{j=1}^{L} \kappa_\sigma(\hat{e}(n) - \hat{e}(n-j))} - \frac{1}{a}. \tag{19}$$

where $\kappa'_\sigma(\cdot)$ denotes the derivative of $\kappa_\sigma(\cdot)$. The overall update algorithm is then proposed as follows:

$$\hat{\mathbf{w}}(n+1) = \hat{\mathbf{w}}(n) - \mu_1 \frac{\partial \hat{J}}{\partial \hat{\mathbf{w}}}, \quad a(n+1) = a(n) - \mu_2 \frac{\partial \hat{J}}{\partial a} \tag{20}$$

where μ_1 and μ_2 are some small positive step sizes and

$$\hat{e}(n) = a(n)d(n) + \mathbf{x}^T(n)\hat{\mathbf{w}}(n). \tag{21}$$

The configuration of the new adaptive filter is shown in Fig.2.

The proposed algorithm (18)-(21) can be performed per iteration with $(2m + 3L)$ additions, $(2m + 4)$ multiplications, 2 divisions and $2L$ table look-ups for nonlinear functions $\kappa_\sigma(\cdot), \kappa'_\sigma(\cdot)$. The corresponding counts for the NLMS algorithm are $3m$ additions, $(3m + 1)$ multiplications and one division. As will be

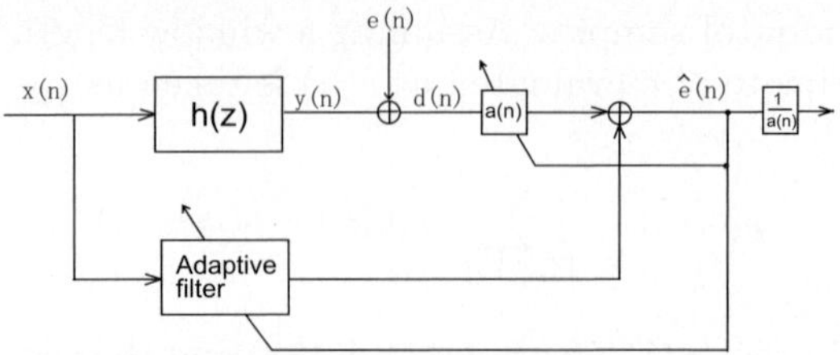

Fig. 2. Configuration of the new adaptive filter

seen from simulation results, we do not need to take the window width L large, so the computational complexity of our proposed algorithm is not much higher than that of the NLMS algorithm.

Remark 1. If we do not introduce the quantity a, the partial derivative in (19) with respect to a will be zero. Hence, the measurement $d(n)$ can not be explicitly used in the algorithm.

Remark 2. The stochastic gradients we derived in (18), (19) are different from those in [9]. The differences of samples $\mathbf{x}(n) - \mathbf{x}(n - j)$ and $d(n) - d(n - j)$ are used instead of the instantaneous samples $\mathbf{x}(n)$ and $d(n)$ in (18) and (19). In [9] the gradients are derived by assuming that $e(n), e(n - 1), \cdots, e(n - L)$ are produced by the same common weight $\mathbf{w}$. In our algorithm we think that $e(n - 1), \cdots, e(n - L)$ are already calculated fix quantities and only $e(n)$ is produced by the weight vector $\mathbf{w}$. This is reasonable, since the change of the weight vector $\mathbf{w}$ is slow and there will be a little difference between the two algorithms. Also by this simplification, the computational complexity is greatly reduced from $O(mL)$ to $O(m) + O(L)$.

4   Convergence Analysis

Let us first investigate the stationary point of the proposed ICA-based algorithm. By using the averaging method in [11], we consider the following averaged system corresponding to (20),

$$\hat{\mathbf{w}}(n + 1) = \hat{\mathbf{w}}(n) - \mu_1 E[\partial \hat{J}/\partial \hat{\mathbf{w}}], \quad a(n + 1) = a(n) - \mu_2 E[\partial \hat{J}/\partial a]. \tag{22}$$

The desired equilibrium point of (22) is

$$a(n) = a_0, \quad \hat{\mathbf{w}}(n) = -a_0 \mathbf{h}. \tag{23}$$

This is because at this point, from (1) and (21), we have

$$\hat{e}(n) = a_0 e(n), \tag{24}$$

and due to the assumption that $e(n)$ is zero mean and statistically independent with $\mathbf{x}(n)$, the expected value of the instantaneous gradient in (18) becomes zero, i.e.,

$$E\left[\frac{\partial \hat{J}}{\partial \hat{\mathbf{w}}}\right]\Bigg|_{(a_0,-a_0\mathbf{h})} = -E\left[\frac{\sum_{j=1}^{L} G'\big(a_0 e(n) - a_0 e(n-j), \sigma^2\big)\mathbf{x}(n)}{\sum_{i=1}^{L} G\big(a_0 e(n) - a_0 e(n-i), \sigma^2\big)}\right]$$

$$= -\sum_{j=1}^{L} E\left[\frac{G'\big(a_0 e(n) - a_0 e(n-j), \sigma^2\big)}{\sum_{i=1}^{L} G\big(a_0 e(n) - a_0 e(n-i), \sigma^2\big)}\right] \cdot E\big[\mathbf{x}(n)\big] = 0, \tag{25}$$

where a_0 is determined by

$$E[\partial \hat{J}/\partial a]\big|_{(a_0,-a_0\mathbf{h})} = 0. \tag{26}$$

In the following, we will analyze the local stability property of this nolinear algorithm near the equilibrium point. Letting

$$\hat{\mathbf{w}}(n) = -a_0\mathbf{h} + \Delta\hat{\mathbf{w}}(n), \;\; a(n) = a_0 + \Delta a(n),$$

from (21) we get

$$\hat{e}(n) = a_0 e(n) + \mathbf{x}^T(n)\Delta\hat{\mathbf{w}}(n) + d(n)\Delta a(n). \tag{27}$$

Assuming the Parzen window estimate in (15) is asymptotic to the pdf of $\hat{e}$, then

$$\partial\hat{J}/\partial\hat{\mathbf{w}} = \phi(\hat{e})\mathbf{x}(n), \;\; \partial\hat{J}/\partial a = \phi(\hat{e})d(n) - 1/a, \tag{28}$$

where the function $\phi(\cdot)$ is defined as

$$\phi(\hat{e}) = -p'(\hat{e})/p(\hat{e}). \tag{29}$$

From (25), we know $E\big[\phi\big(a_0 e(n)\big)e(n)\big] = 1/a_0$. Discarding the higher order terms, and noting the near-end signal $e(n)$ is zero mean and statistically independent with the transmitted input $\mathbf{x}(n)$, the averaged system can be linearized around the equilibrium point $(-a_0\mathbf{h}, \mathbf{w}_0)$ as follows:

$$\begin{bmatrix} \Delta\hat{\mathbf{w}}(n+1) \\ \Delta a(n+1) \end{bmatrix} = \left(I - \begin{bmatrix} \mu_1 & 0 \\ 0 & \mu_2 \end{bmatrix}\begin{bmatrix} A_{11} & A_{12} \\ A_{12}^T & A_{22} \end{bmatrix}\right)\begin{bmatrix} \Delta\hat{\mathbf{w}}(n) \\ \Delta a(n) \end{bmatrix}$$

$$= \left(I - \begin{bmatrix} \mu_1 & 0 \\ 0 & \mu_2 \end{bmatrix}\mathbf{A}\right)\begin{bmatrix} \Delta\hat{\mathbf{w}}(n) \\ \Delta a(n) \end{bmatrix} \tag{30}$$

where

$$A_{11} = E\big[\phi'(a_0 e(n))\big]R_{xx},$$
$$A_{12} = E\big[\phi'(a_0 e(n))\big]R_{xx}\mathbf{w}_0,$$
$$A_{22} = E\big[\phi'(a_0 e(n))(\mathbf{h}^T R_{xx}\mathbf{h} + e^2(n))\big] + 1/a_0^2.$$

The algorithm converges locally to its equilibrium $(-a_0\mathbf{h}, a_0)$ iff all the eigenvalues of the update matrix in (30) are strictly inside the unit circle. Let $\lambda_1 \geq \lambda_2 \geq \ldots \geq \lambda_{m+1}$ denote the eigenvalues of $\mathbf{A}$. It is easy and natural to use the same value for μ_1 and μ_2 in a real application. Hence, if $\mu_1 = \mu_2 = \mu$, the step size condition $0 < \mu < 2/\lambda_1$ is needed to ensure the proposed algorithm converges to its equilibrium point. Of course, this upper limit is an approximate one, since the averaging method assumes the slow adaptation limit $(\mu_1 \to 0, \mu_2 \to 0)$.

According to the above condition, the matrix $\mathbf{A}$ should be positive definite. It is easy to see, for any given near-end signal $e(n)$,

$$E[\phi'(a_0 e)] = \int \phi'(a_0 e) p_e(e) de = \int \phi'(\hat{e}) p(\hat{e}) d\hat{e} \tag{31}$$

$$= -\int p''(\hat{e}) d\hat{e} + \int \frac{(p'(\hat{e}))^2}{p(\hat{e})} d\hat{e} > 0 \tag{32}$$

The last inequality is valid because $\int p(\hat{e}) d\hat{e} \equiv 1$ and $\frac{(p'(\hat{e}))^2}{p(\hat{e})} > 0$. Then, it follows that both A_{11} and $A_{22} - A_{12}^T A_{11}^{-1} A_{12} \left(= E[\phi'(a_0 e) e^2] + \frac{1}{a_0^2} \right)$ are positive definite. As $\mathbf{A}$ is similar to the matrix

$$\begin{bmatrix} A_{11} & 0 \\ 0 & A_{22} - A_{12}^T A_{11}^{-1} A_{12} \end{bmatrix}, \tag{33}$$

hence $\mathbf{A}$ is positive definite.

5   Application to Acoustic Echo Cancellation

Figure 3 illustrates the general configuration of an acoustic echo canceller. Let $x(n)$ be the far-end signal going to the loudspeaker and $y(n)$ be the echo signal due to leakage from the loudspeaker to the microphone, which is heavily correlated with $x(n)$; $d(n)$ is the signal picked up by the microphone, which is always called the desired signal. Here the echo signal $y(n)$ and the near-end signal $e(n)$ are the independent sources to be separated from the microphone signal $d(n)$. We assume a linear echo

$$y(n) = \sum_{i=0}^{m-1} h_i x(n - i),$$

where the echo is a weighted sum of echo components $x(n-i), i = 0, 1, \cdots, m-1$. The echo components are delayed versions of the far-end signal and the microphone signal $d(n)$ is a sum of the near-end signal $e(n)$ and the echo $y(n)$.

In a common telephone call, double-talk is found to occur 20 percent of the time [12]. Double-talk is any period during a call when both the near-end signal and the far-end signal contain speech. The near-end signal is usually independent of the far-end signal and the echo signal. Also it may be of much larger amplitude than the echo, so during a double talk period, standard adaptive filtering schemes tend to get confused and cannot track the echo path properly. To solve this problem, a double talk detector (DTD) has been implemented to sense when the far-end speech is corrupted by the near-end speech. However,

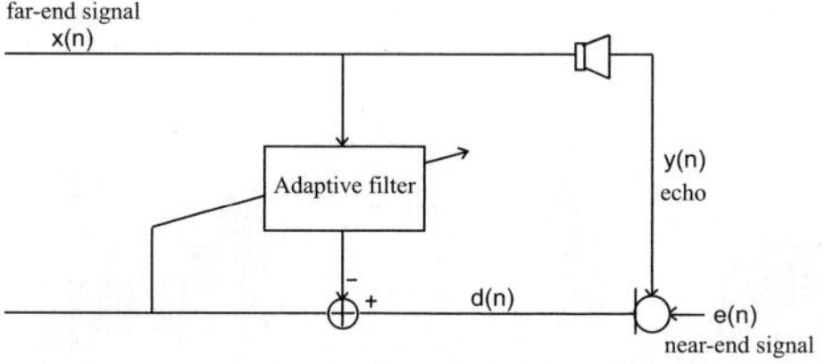

Fig. 3. General configuration of an acoustic echo canceller

during the time required by the DTD to detect double-talk, a few (e.g.,< 5) un-detected large amplitude samples perturb the echo path estimate considerably. It is an undisputable fact that all double-talk detectors have a probability of not detecting the double-talk. Once this happens, the echo canceller often diverges.

By treating the near-end signal as the additive noise, we get exactly the same mathematical formula as (2). From (21) we know that the near-end signal is also on-line estimated during the iteration. The estimation error is written as

$$e_{ICA}(n) = \frac{1}{a(n)}\hat{e}(n) - e(n) = \frac{1}{a(n)}[a(n)d(n) + \hat{\mathbf{w}}^T(n)\mathbf{x}(n)] - e(n)$$

$$= [\mathbf{h} + \frac{1}{a(n)}\hat{\mathbf{w}}(n)]^T\mathbf{x}(n). \tag{34}$$

It is not associated with any change in the near-end signal. Hence, the proposed ICA-based algorithm has an excellent robustness. It can directly be applied to the acoustic echo canceller without the usage of DTD.

6   Simulation Results

We simulate the performance of the acoustic echo canceller by using the proposed algorithm and the NLMS algorithm, respectively. The echo path consists of 1024 coefficients. We use a male speech as the far-end signal and another male speech as the near-end. Both of them have an 8kHz sampling rate. The near-end signal is added at the point of $N/2$. (N is the number of the samples). We simulated the echo canceller with different values of window length L and kernel size σ. It was found that the window length does not need to be very large and the kernel size could be chosen between 0.5 and 4. In the following simulations, we set $L = 50$, $\sigma = 2$ and the step sizes $\mu_1 = \mu_2 = 0.02$ were used for the proposed algorithm. For the simulation of the NLMS algorithm, the step size of 0.5 was used. We have selected the echo path coefficients as uniformly distributed random variables in the range of $[-1, 1]$ for each simulation run. The quantity $''error''$ is defined as the difference between the echo signal $y(n)$ and the reconstructed echo signal $d(n) - \hat{e}(n)/a(n)$. Figs. 4 and 5 plot the ensemble average of the MSE in dB over 100 simulation runs for the proposed algorithm and the NLMS algorithm, respectively. The simulation results show that the

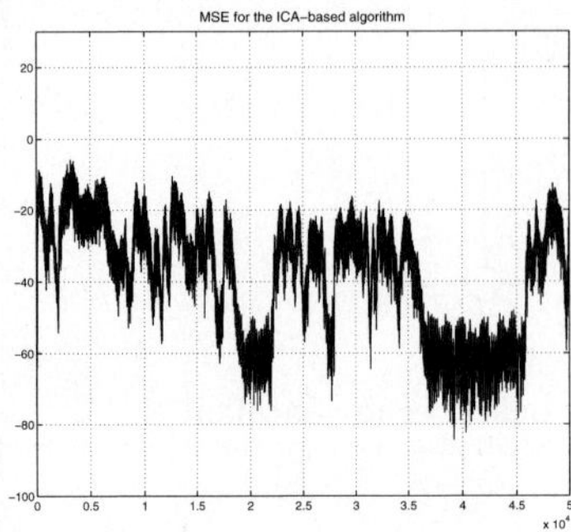

Fig. 4. The ensemble average of the MSE in dB over 100 simulation runs for the proposed algorithm

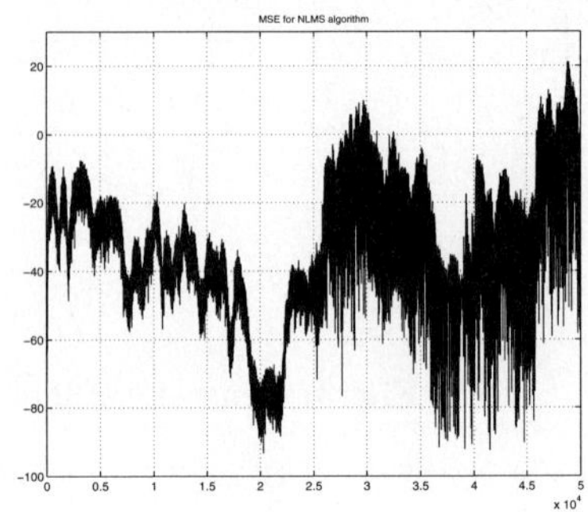

Fig. 5. The ensemble average of the MSE in dB over 100 simulation runs for the NLMS algorithm

NLMS algorithm gets confused when double talk occurs, however the proposed ICA-based algorithm works pretty well.

7 Conclusion

In this paper, by using a nonparamtric Parzen window density estimator and the stochastic information gradient, we have derived a new adaptive filter algorithm for system identification. The new algorithm is based on the idea of ICA. The local stability of the algorithm has also been analyzed. The proposed algorithm shows an excellent robustness. It can be applied to the acoustic echo canceller directly without using any DTD. Simulation results shows effectiveness of the proposed algorithm.

References

1. Haykin, S.: Adaptive Filter Theory, 4th edn. Prentice-Hall, Englewood Cliffs (2002)
2. Widrow, B., Stearns, S.D.: Adaptive Signal Processing. Prentice-Hall, Englewood Cliffs (1985)
3. Huber, P.J.: Robust Statistics. Wiley, New York (1981)
4. Hyvarinen, A., Karhunen, J., Oja, E.: Independent Component Analysis. Wiley, New York (2001)
5. Magadán, M., Niemistö, R., Ruotsalainen, U., Möttönen, J.: ICA for acoustic echo control. In: Proc. EUSIPCO, vol. I, pp. 503–506 (2002)
6. Nitta, M., Sugimoto, K., Satoh, A.: Blind system identification of autoregressive model using independent component analysis. Transactions of SICE 41(5), 444–451 (2005) (in Japanese)
7. Yang, J.M., Sakai, H.: A new adaptive filter algorithm for system identification using independent component analysis. In: Proceedings of the IEEE International Conference on Acoustics, Speech, and Signal Processing (ICASSP 2007), Honolulu, Hawaii, U.S.A., April 2007, vol. 3, pp. 1341–1344 (2007)

8. Parzen, E.: On estimation of a probability density function and mode. In: Time Series Analysis Papers, Holden-Day, Inc., CA (1967)
9. Erdogmus, D., Principe, J.C., Hild II, K.E.: On-line entropy manipulation: stochastic information gradient. IEEE Signal Processing Letters 10(8), 242–245 (2003)
10. Pricipe, J., Xu, D., Fisher, J.: Information theoretic learning. In: Haykin, S. (ed.) Unsupervised Adaptive Filtering, pp. 265–319. Wiley, New York (2000)
11. Solo, V., Kong, X.: Adaptive Signal Processing Algorithms: Stability and Performance. Prentice-Hall, Englewood Cliffs (1995)
12. Chao, J., Tsujii, S.: A stable and distortion-free echo and howling canceller. In: Proceedings of the IEEE International Conference on Acoustics, Speech, and Signal Processing (ICASSP 1988), pp. 1620–1623 (1988)

Component Reduction for Hierarchical Mixture Model Construction

Kumiko Maebashi, Nobuo Suematsu, and Akira Hayashi

Graduate School of Information Sciences,
Hiroshima City University, Hiroshima, 731-3194, Japan
bochin@robotics.im.hiroshima-cu.ac.jp,
{suematsu,akira}@hiroshima-cu.ac.jp

Abstract. The mixture modeling framework is widely used in many applications. In this paper, we propose a *component reduction* technique, that collapses a mixture model into a mixture with fewer components. For fitting a mixture model to data, the EM (Expectation-Maximization) algorithm is usually used. Our algorithm is derived by extending mixture model learning using the EM-algorithm.

In this extension, a difficulty arises from the fact that some crucial quantities cannot be evaluated analytically. We overcome this difficulty by introducing an effective approximation. The effectiveness of our algorithm is demonstrated by applying it to a simple synthetic component reduction task and a phoneme clustering problem.

1   Introduction

Component reduction is the task whereby a mixture model is collapsed into a mixture with fewer components. Since mixture models are used in a wide variety of applications, component reduction techniques are becoming more important. As an example, consider the case where data is compressed and represented in a mixture model and the original data is lost. We might use a component reduction technique to analyze this data further. Moreover, by iterating the component reduction, hierarchical mixture models can be constructed in a bottom-up manner. The hierarchical mixture model is a useful tool for analyzing data at various granularity levels[1].

Component reduction can be regarded as a task of fitting a mixture model to another mixture with more components. The EM-algorithm[2,3] is broadly applied to fit a mixture model to a set of data points[4]. We devise a component reduction algorithm by extending this application of the EM-algorithm to the case where a mixture model is fitted to another mixture with more components.

In deriving the algorithm, we first formulate the application of the EM-algorithm to component reduction. Although this formulation provides an EM-procedure, it cannot be performed in reality, because some quantities needed in the EM-procedure cannot be calculated analytically. Therefore, we propose an approximated version of the EM-procedure.

The organization of this paper is as follows. Section 2 provides the background and our motivation for this study. The EM-algorithm is described in Sect. 3.

M. Ishikawa et al. (Eds.): ICONIP 2007, Part II, LNCS 4985, pp. 326–335, 2008.

In Sect. 4, we formulate the application of the EM-algorithm to component reduction and obtain an EM-procedure. Thereafter, in Sect. 5, we derive an approximation of the EM-procedure. In Sect. 6, we apply our method and two related methods to synthetic data and a phoneme clustering problem.

2   Background and Motivation

The EM-algorithm alternates between performing an expectation step (E-step) and a maximization step (M-step). The assignment probabilities of the data points to the components of the mixture are calculated in the E-step. These probabilities determine the responsibilities of the components in representing the data points. In the M-step, each of the component parameters is updated so that its likelihood for the data points, weighted by the responsibilities, is maximized.

A straight-forward approach to component reduction is to generate samples from the given mixture model, and then to apply the EM-algorithm to these samples. This is, however, computationally inefficient.

By simply replacing "the data points" with "the components of the original mixture" in the above description, we can obtain the outline of a class of algorithms for fitting a mixture model to another mixture model. The existing component reduction algorithms[1,5] can be seen as members of this class.

The algorithm proposed in [1] uses the notion of virtual samples generated from the given mixture. In this algorithm, the assignment probabilities are calculated when the set of virtual samples drawn from a component of the given mixture model is assigned as a whole to the each component of the mixture model being fit. Therefore, the algorithm is regarded as soft clustering of components in the given mixture model.

In [5], another component reduction algorithm is proposed, although the authors considered the case where the component structure of the original model must be preserved. The algorithm assigns each component in the given mixture to one of the components in the fitted mixture, such that the KL-divergence between the mixture models is minimized. In other words, the algorithm involves hard clustering of components in the given mixture into groups corresponding to the components in the fitted mixture.

Since each of the components of the original mixture is spatially extended, unlike in the case of data points, the proper assignment probabilities of the original components to the components being fit should be position dependent. Any member of the aforementioned class of algorithms, such as the above two algorithms, does not take into account this fact adequately. To illustrate this problem, we consider a simple component reduction task shown in Fig. 1, in which we try to fit a two component mixture model to the three component mixture. When we consider the assignment of the original component in the middle, we should split it into two parts (illustrated by dashed lines) dependent on the spatial relationships of two components of the fitted mixture. Each of the two parts should then be incorporated into its corresponding component. However, such a splitting process cannot be realized by the algorithms belonging

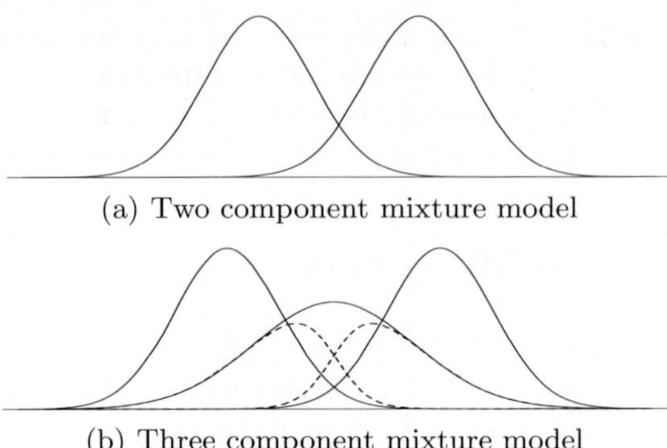

(a) Two component mixture model

(b) Three component mixture model

Fig. 1. An example of the fitting problem

to the above class. In this paper, we devise a component reduction algorithm which overcomes this limitation.

3   Fitting Mixture Models to Data

We devise a component reduction algorithm based on the application of the EM-algorithm for fitting mixture models to data. We review the application formulated by Dempster[2] here.

Let us consider approximating a data distribution with the mixture model,

$$f_\Theta(\boldsymbol{x}) = \sum_{j=1}^{C} \pi_j p(\boldsymbol{x}|\theta_j), \tag{1}$$

where C is the number of mixture components, $p(\boldsymbol{x}|\theta_j)$ is the probability density with parameter vector θ_j, π_j is a nonnegative quantity such that for $j = 1, \ldots, C$, $0 \leq \pi_j \leq 1$ and $\sum_{j=1}^{C} \pi_j = 1$, and $\Theta = \{\pi_1, \ldots, \pi_C, \theta_1, \ldots, \theta_C\}$ is the set of all the parameters in the mixture model.

Given a set of data points, $\mathcal{X} = \{\boldsymbol{x}_1, \ldots, \boldsymbol{x}_N\}$, when we apply the EM-algorithm, it is assumed that each data point $\boldsymbol{x}_i$ has been drawn from one of the components of the mixture model. Then, we introduce unobservable vectors $\boldsymbol{y}_i = (y_{i1}, \ldots, y_{iC})$ indicating the component from which $\boldsymbol{x}_i$ was drawn: where for every j, y_{ij} is 1 if $\boldsymbol{x}_i$ was drawn from the j-th component and 0 otherwise. Let $\mathcal{Y} = \{y_{ij}|i = 1, \ldots, N, j = 1, \ldots, C\}$. The log-likelihood of Θ for the complete data $(\mathcal{X}, \mathcal{Y})$ is given by

$$L(\Theta|\mathcal{X}, \mathcal{Y}) = \sum_{i=1}^{N} \sum_{j=1}^{C} y_{ij} \log\{\pi_j p(\boldsymbol{x}_i|\theta_j)\}. \tag{2}$$

Since $\mathcal{Y}$ is unobservable, we take the expectation of the log-likelihood with respect to $\mathcal{Y}$ under the given observed data $\mathcal{X}$ and the current estimate Θ'. The expected value of the log-likelihood is

$$Q(\Theta|\Theta') = E[L(\Theta|\mathcal{X}, \mathcal{Y}) \mid \mathcal{X}, \Theta'] = \sum_{i=1}^{N} \sum_{j=1}^{C} h_{ij} \log\{\pi_j p_j(\boldsymbol{x}_i|\theta_j)\}, \qquad (3)$$

where $h_{ij} = E[y_{ij} \mid \boldsymbol{x}_i, \Theta']$.

Starting with an initial guess $\Theta^{(0)}$, the EM-algorithm generates successive estimates, $\Theta^{(1)}, \Theta^{(2)}, \ldots$, by iterating the following E- and M-steps:

E-step: Compute $\{h_{ij}^{(t)}\}$, under current estimate $\Theta^{(t)}$.

M-step: Set $\Theta^{(t+1)} = \Theta$ which maximizes $Q(\Theta|\Theta^{(t)})$ given $\{h_{ij}^{(t)}\}$.

The iteration is terminated when the sequence of estimates converges.

4   Fitting Mixture Models to Another Mixture Model

In this section, we formulate a straight-forward application of the EM-algorithm for fitting mixture models to another mixture. We elucidate that it is difficult to perform the iterative procedure provided by the formulation because it requires the evaluation of integrals which cannot be solved analytically.

The task is described as fitting the U-component mixture model $f_{\Theta_U}(\boldsymbol{x})$ to the given L-component mixture model $f_{\Theta_L}(\boldsymbol{x})$, where $L > U$,

$$f_{\Theta_U}(\boldsymbol{x}) = \sum_{j=1}^{U} \pi_j^U p(\boldsymbol{x}|\theta_j^U), \qquad \text{and} \qquad f_{\Theta_L}(\boldsymbol{x}) = \sum_{i=1}^{L} \pi_i^L p(\boldsymbol{x}|\theta_i^L).$$

We now introduce a random vector $\boldsymbol{y} = (y_1, \ldots, y_U)$ corresponding to the unobservable vectors $\boldsymbol{y}_i$ in Sect. 3, where y_j are binary variables drawn according to the conditional probability distributions,

$$\Pr(y_j = 1|\boldsymbol{x}, \Theta_U) = \frac{\pi_j^U p(\boldsymbol{x}|\theta_j^U)}{\sum_{j'=1}^{U} \pi_{j'}^U p(\boldsymbol{x}|\theta_{j'}^U)}. \qquad (4)$$

Then, the log-likelihood of Θ_U for $(\boldsymbol{x}, \boldsymbol{y})$ is

$$L(\Theta_U|\boldsymbol{x}, \boldsymbol{y}) = \sum_{j=1}^{U} y_j \log\{\pi_j^U p(\boldsymbol{x}|\theta_j^U)\}, \qquad (5)$$

and the counterpart of $Q(\Theta|\Theta')$ in (3) is defined by taking the expectation of the log-likelihood with respect to $\boldsymbol{x}$ with distribution $f_{\Theta_L}(\boldsymbol{x})$ as

$$Q_{\text{hier}}(\Theta_U|\Theta_U') = E_{\boldsymbol{x}}\{E_{\boldsymbol{y}}\{L(\Theta_U|\boldsymbol{x}, \boldsymbol{y}) \mid \boldsymbol{x}, \Theta_U'\} \mid \Theta_L\},$$

$$= \sum_{j=1}^{U} \sum_{i=1}^{L} \pi_i^L \int p(\boldsymbol{x}|\theta_i^L) h_j(\boldsymbol{x}) \log\{\pi_j p(\boldsymbol{x}|\theta_j^U)\} d\boldsymbol{x}, \qquad (6)$$

where $h_j(\boldsymbol{x}) = \Pr(y_j = 1|\boldsymbol{x}, \Theta_U')$.

To derive an E-step and an M-step, we introduce another random vector $\boldsymbol{z} = (z_1, \ldots, z_L)$ which indicates the component of the original mixture model from which $\boldsymbol{x}$ is drawn, where z_i are binary variables whose (marginal) probability distributions are given by $\Pr(z_i = 1) = \pi_i^L$. Then, using Bayes' rule, we obtain the following relation:

$$\Pr(\boldsymbol{x}|z_i = 1, y_j = 1) = \frac{\Pr(y_j = 1|\boldsymbol{x}, z_i = 1)\Pr(\boldsymbol{x}|z_i = 1)}{\Pr(y_j = 1|z_i = 1)}. \tag{7}$$

From $\Pr(y_j = 1|\boldsymbol{x}, z_i = 1) = \Pr(y_j = 1|\boldsymbol{x}) = h_j(\boldsymbol{x})$ and $\Pr(\boldsymbol{x}|z_i = 1) = p(\boldsymbol{x}|\theta_i^L)$, by denoting $\Pr(\boldsymbol{x}|z_i = 1, y_j = 1)$ as $p(\boldsymbol{x}|i, j)$, (7) can be rewritten as

$$p(\boldsymbol{x}|i, j) = \frac{h_j(\boldsymbol{x})p(\boldsymbol{x}|\theta_i^L)}{h_{ij}}, \tag{8}$$

where $h_{ij} = \Pr(y_j = 1|z_i = 1)$. By substituting (8) into (6), we obtain

$$Q_{\text{hier}}(\Theta_U|\Theta_U') = \sum_{j=1}^{U} \sum_{i=1}^{L} \pi_i^L h_{ij} \int p(\boldsymbol{x}|i, j) \log\{\pi_j p(\boldsymbol{x}|\theta_j^U)\} d\boldsymbol{x}. \tag{9}$$

Although we cannot perform them in reality, we can define the E-step and the M-step simply based on (9) as follows:

E-step: Compute $\{p^{(t)}(\boldsymbol{x}|i, j)\}$ and $\{h_{ij}^{(t)}\}$ under current estimate $\Theta_U^{(t)}$.

M-step: Set $\Theta_U^{(t+1)} = \arg\max_{\Theta_U} Q_{\text{hier}}(\Theta_U|\Theta_U^{(t)})$ given $p^{(t)}(\boldsymbol{x}|i, j)$ and $h_{ij}^{(t)}$.

Since both of these steps involve integrals which cannot be evaluated analytically, we cannot carry them out (without numerical integrations).

5 Component Reduction Algorithm

From now on, we focus our discussion on Gaussian mixture models. Let, $p(\boldsymbol{x}|\theta_i^L)$ and $p(\boldsymbol{x}|\theta_j^U)$ be Gaussians where $\theta_i^L = (\boldsymbol{\mu}_i^L, \Sigma_i^L)$ and $\theta_j^U = (\boldsymbol{\mu}_j^U, \Sigma_j^U)$. Then, we introduce an approximation which enables us to perform the EM-procedure derived in Sect. 4.

5.1 Update Equations in the M-step

Without any approximation, the parameter set Θ_U which maximizes $Q_{\text{hier}}(\Theta_U|\Theta_U^{(t)})$ given $p^{(t)}(\boldsymbol{x}|i, j)$ and $h_{ij}^{(t)}$ is obtained by

$$\pi_j^U = \sum_{i=1}^{L} \pi_i^L h_{ij}^{(t)}, \quad \boldsymbol{\mu}_j^U = \frac{\sum_{i=1}^{L} \pi_i^L h_{ij}^{(t)} \boldsymbol{\mu}_{ij}^{(t)}}{\sum_{i=1}^{L} \pi_i^L h_{ij}^{(t)}},$$

$$\Sigma_j^U = \frac{\sum_{i=1}^{L} \pi_i^L h_{ij}^{(t)} \{\Sigma_{ij}^{(t)} + (\boldsymbol{\mu}_{ij}^{(t)} - \boldsymbol{\mu}_j^U)(\boldsymbol{\mu}_{ij}^{(t)} - \boldsymbol{\mu}_j^U)^{\mathrm{T}}\}}{\sum_{i=1}^{L} \pi_i^L h_{ij}^{(t)}}, \tag{10}$$

where for every i,j, $\boldsymbol{\mu}_{ij}^{(t)}$ and $\Sigma_{ij}^{(t)}$ are the mean vector and the covariance matrix, respectively, of $p^{(t)}(\boldsymbol{x}|i,j)$.

From (8), $p(\boldsymbol{x}|i,j) \propto h_j(\boldsymbol{x})p(\boldsymbol{x}|\theta_i^L)$ holds and we have the analytical forms of $h_j(\boldsymbol{x})$ and $p(\boldsymbol{x}|\theta_i^L)$. Let $q_{ij}(\boldsymbol{x}) = h_j(\boldsymbol{x})p(\boldsymbol{x}|\theta_i^L)$ for convenience. The difficulty stems from the fact that the integrals, $\int q_{ij}(\boldsymbol{x})d\boldsymbol{x}$, $\int \boldsymbol{x}q_{ij}(\boldsymbol{x})d\boldsymbol{x}$, and $\int \boldsymbol{x}\boldsymbol{x}^{\mathrm{T}}q_{ij}(\boldsymbol{x})d\boldsymbol{x}$, cannot be solved analytically. Therefore, we cannot calculate the means and covariances of $p(\boldsymbol{x}|i,j)$. So, we introduce an approximation of $p^{(t)}(\boldsymbol{x}|i,j)$ using a Gaussian distribution.

5.2   Approximation

Now, we are in a position to construct the Gaussian approximation of $p(\boldsymbol{x}|i,j)$, that is, to obtain $\hat{\boldsymbol{\mu}}_{ij}$ and $\hat{\Sigma}_{ij}$ such that $p(\boldsymbol{x}|i,j) \simeq N(\boldsymbol{x}|\hat{\boldsymbol{\mu}}_{ij}, \hat{\Sigma}_{ij})$, where $N(\boldsymbol{x}|\hat{\boldsymbol{\mu}}_{ij}, \hat{\Sigma}_{ij})$ is the Gaussian pdf. The mean and covariance are approximated as follows.

We set $\hat{\boldsymbol{\mu}}_{ij} = \arg\max_{\boldsymbol{x}} q_{ij}(\boldsymbol{x})$. While $\arg\max_{\boldsymbol{x}} q_{ij}(\boldsymbol{x})$ cannot be represented in analytical form, it can be obtained effectively from the solution of

$$\frac{\partial q_{ij}(\boldsymbol{x})}{\partial \boldsymbol{x}} = \boldsymbol{0}, \tag{11}$$

using the Newton-Raphson method starting from a carefully chosen point.

On the other hand, each $\hat{\Sigma}_{ij}$ is estimated using the relation

$$-\frac{1}{N(\boldsymbol{\mu}|\boldsymbol{\mu}, \Sigma)} \left. \frac{\partial^2 N(\boldsymbol{x}|\boldsymbol{\mu}, \Sigma)}{\partial \boldsymbol{x}^2} \right|_{\boldsymbol{x}=\boldsymbol{\mu}} = \Sigma^{-1}. \tag{12}$$

We are constructing an approximation of $p(\boldsymbol{x}|i,j)$ using the Gaussian distribution $N(\boldsymbol{x}|\hat{\boldsymbol{\mu}}_{ij}, \hat{\Sigma}_{ij})$, and hence a natural choice is

$$\hat{\Sigma}_{ij}^{-1} = -\frac{1}{p(\hat{\boldsymbol{\mu}}_{ij}|i,j)} \left. \frac{\partial^2 p(\boldsymbol{x}|i,j)}{\partial \boldsymbol{x}^2} \right|_{\boldsymbol{x}=\hat{\boldsymbol{\mu}}_{ij}} = -\frac{1}{q_{ij}(\hat{\boldsymbol{\mu}}_{ij})} \left. \frac{\partial^2 q_{ij}(\boldsymbol{x})}{\partial \boldsymbol{x}^2} \right|_{\boldsymbol{x}=\hat{\boldsymbol{\mu}}_{ij}}$$

$$= (\Sigma_i^L)^{-1} + (\Sigma_j^U)^{-1} - \sum_{j'=1}^{U} h_{j'}(\hat{\boldsymbol{\mu}}_{ij})(\Sigma_{j'}^U)^{-1}$$

$$+ \sum_{j'=1}^{U} h_{j'}(\hat{\boldsymbol{\mu}}_{ij})(\Sigma_{j'}^U)^{-1}(\hat{\boldsymbol{\mu}}_{ij} - \boldsymbol{\mu}_{j'}^U)(\hat{\boldsymbol{\mu}}_{ij} - \boldsymbol{\mu}_{j'}^U)^{\mathrm{T}}(\Sigma_{j'}^U)^{-1}$$

$$- \sum_{j'=1}^{U}\sum_{j''=1}^{U} h_{j'}(\hat{\boldsymbol{\mu}}_{ij})h_{j''}(\hat{\boldsymbol{\mu}}_{ij})(\Sigma_{j'}^U)^{-1}(\hat{\boldsymbol{\mu}}_{ij} - \boldsymbol{\mu}_{j'}^U)(\hat{\boldsymbol{\mu}}_{ij} - \boldsymbol{\mu}_{j''}^U)^{\mathrm{T}}(\Sigma_{j''}^U)^{-1}. \tag{13}$$

To complete the E-step, we also need to evaluate h_{ij}. From (8), we have

$$h_{ij} = \frac{h_j(\boldsymbol{x})p(\boldsymbol{x}|\theta_i^L)}{p(\boldsymbol{x}|i,j)}, \tag{14}$$

for any $\boldsymbol{x}$. With the approximation, $p(\boldsymbol{x}|i,j) \simeq N(\boldsymbol{x}|\hat{\boldsymbol{\mu}}_{ij}, \hat{\Sigma}_{ij})$, substituting $\boldsymbol{x} = \hat{\boldsymbol{\mu}}_{ij}$ yields the approximation of h_{ij},

$$\hat{h}_{ij} \propto \frac{h_j(\hat{\boldsymbol{\mu}}_{ij})p(\hat{\boldsymbol{\mu}}_{ij}|\theta_i^L)}{N(\hat{\boldsymbol{\mu}}_{ij}|\hat{\boldsymbol{\mu}}_{ij}, \hat{\Sigma}_{ij})}. \tag{15}$$

5.3   Approximated EM-Procedure

Here we summarize the EM-procedure with the approximation described in the previous subsection. Setting the number of components U, and starting from some initial estimate $\Theta_U^{(0)}$, the procedure iterates through the following E- and M-steps alternately:

E-step: Under the current estimate $\Theta_U^{(t)}$,
1. Set $\{\hat{\boldsymbol{\mu}}_{ij}^{(t)}\}$ by solving (11) using the Newton-Raphson method.
2. Calculate $\{\hat{\Sigma}_{ij}^{(t)}\}$ using (13).
3. Calculate $\{\hat{h}_{ij}^{(t)}\}$ using (15) and normalize them such that $\sum_{j=1}^{U} \hat{h}_{ij}^{(t)} = 1$.

M-step: Set $\Theta_U^{(t+1)} = \Theta_U$ where Θ_U is calculated by (10) with $\{\hat{\boldsymbol{\mu}}_{ij}^{(t)}\}$, $\{\hat{\Sigma}_{ij}^{(t)}\}$, and $\{\hat{h}_{ij}^{(t)}\}$.

After a number of iterations, some mixing rates of the components may converge to very small values. When this happens, the components with these small mixing rates are removed from the mixture model. As a result, the number of components can sometimes be less than U.

6   Experimental Results

To demonstrate the effectiveness of our algorithm, we conduct two experiments. For convenience, we refer to our algorithm as CREM (Component Reduction based on EM-algorithm) and the algorithms proposed by Vasconcelos and Lippman[1] and Goldberger and Roweis[5] are referred to as VL and GR, respectively.

6.1   Synthetic Data

This experiment is intended to verify the effectiveness of our algorithm in component reduction problems similar to the example described in Sect. 2. The experimental procedure is as follows.

1. Draw 500 data points from the 1-dimensional 2-component Gaussian mixture model

$$f_{\Theta_{true}}(x) = \frac{1}{2} \cdot N(x|-2,1) + \frac{1}{2} \cdot N(x|2,1). \tag{16}$$

Table 1. KL-divergence and log-likelihood for data

	$KL(f\Theta_L\|f\Theta_U)$	$KL(f\Theta_{EM}\|f\Theta_U)$	$KL(f\Theta_{true}\|f\Theta_U)$	LL
CREM	0.0120	0.0120	0.0179	-1030.7
GR	0.0347	0.0372	0.0444	-1039.8
VL	0.0780	0.0799	0.0823	-1057.5

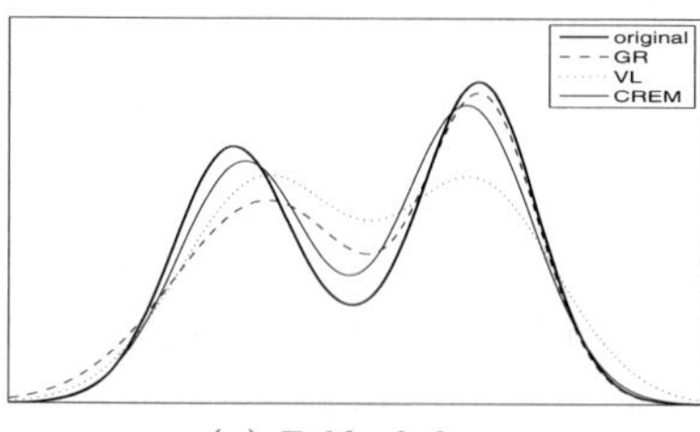

(a) Pdf of f_{Θ_U}

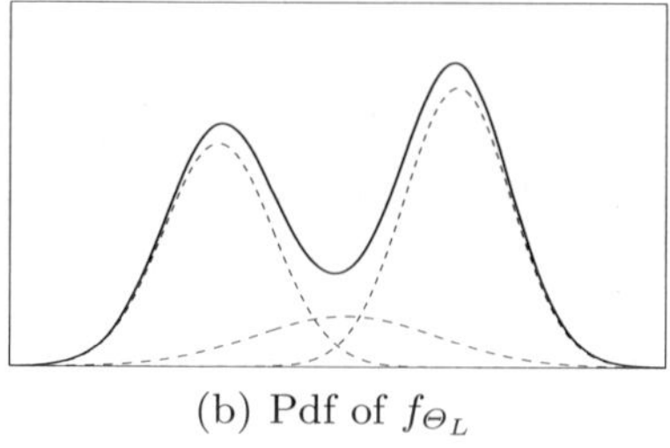

(b) Pdf of f_{Θ_L}

Fig. 2. Three and two component mixture model

Fig. 3. Structure of constructed hierarchical mixture models in the experiment

2. Learn a three component model using the standard EM-algorithm, starting from $f(x) = 1/3 \cdot N(x|-2,1) + 1/3 \cdot N(x|0,1) + 1/3 \cdot N(x|2,1)$.
3. Reduce the three-component model obtained in the previous step to a two component mixture using CREM, VL, GR and the standard EM, where the initial estimate is determined as

$$f_{\Theta_U}(x) = \pi_1^U \cdot collapsed[\frac{1}{\pi_1^U}\{\pi_1^L N(x|\mu_1,\sigma_1) + 0.5 \cdot \pi_2^L N(x|\mu_2,\sigma_2)\}]$$

$$+ \pi_2^U \cdot collapsed[\frac{1}{\pi_2^U}\{0.5 \cdot \pi_2^L N(x|\mu_2,\sigma_2) + \pi_3^L N(x|\mu_3,\sigma_3)\}], \quad (17)$$

where $\pi_1^U = \pi_1^L + \pi_2^L/2$, $\pi_2^U = \pi_2^L/2 + \pi_3^L$ and $collapsed[g]$ denotes the Gaussian which has the minimum KL-divergence from g.

The trial was repeated 100 times. We evaluate the results using the KL-divergence, calculated using numerical integration, and the log-likelihood for the generated data. Table 1 shows the averages taken over the 100 trials. The results for CREM show the best value of all the results. We show one of the results in Fig. 2. Fig. 2(a) is a plot of the pdfs obtained by GR, VL, and CREM for the original 3-component mixture shown in Fig. 2(b). We can see that the pdf obtained by CREM is closest to the original pdf.

6.2   TIMIT Phoneme Recognition

We apply the three algorithms to clustering the phoneme dataset described in
[6]. The dataset contains 5 phoneme classes of $4,509$ instances described by
log-periodograms of length 256. The dimension of the instances is reduced to
10 dimensions using PCA and 5-layered hierarchical mixture models are constructed according to the structure shown in Fig. 3. The bottom (zero'th) level
corresponds to $4,509$ data points.

In each trial of the three algorithms, a 50-component mixture model in the
first level is learned using the standard EM-algorithm. The second and higher
levels are obtained by applying each component reduction algorithm to the lower
levels. To compare these algorithms with the standard EM-algorithm, 20, 10, and
5-components mixtures are learned from the data points using the standard EM-
algorithm. Since all three algorithms depend on initial guesses $\Theta_U^{(0)}$, we ran the
trial 10 times. In the experiment, initial guesses $\Theta_U^{(0)}$ are obtained by picking
up the components of the U largest mixing rates from the L components of the
lower mixture. The terminal condition of our algorithm was empirically tuned
to ensure the convergence of the algorithm. As a result, in this experiment, the
EM-procedure was terminated when $\max_{i,j}(h_{ij}^{(t)} - h_{ij}^{(t-1)}) < 10^{-5}$.

We evaluate the clustering results in terms of NMI(normalized mutual infor-
mation)[7]. Let $\boldsymbol{\lambda}^{(c)}$ be the correct class labeling with 5 labels provided in the
dataset and $\boldsymbol{\lambda}^{(e)}$ be the cluster labeling with U labels representing a clustering
result. For every $n = 1, \ldots, 4059$, the estimated cluster label is defined by

$$\lambda_n^{(e)} = \underset{j}{\operatorname{argmax}}(\{\pi_j p(\boldsymbol{x}_n|\theta_j)|j = 1, \ldots, U\}). \tag{18}$$

The NMI ranges from 0 to 1, and a higher NMI indicates that the clustering is
more informative. For $\boldsymbol{\lambda}^{(c)}$ and $\boldsymbol{\lambda}^{(e)}$, the NMI is estimated by

$$\phi^{NMI}(\boldsymbol{\lambda}^{(e)}, \boldsymbol{\lambda}^{(c)}) = \frac{\sum_{h=1}^{5} \sum_{l=1}^{U} n_{h,l} \log \frac{n_{h,l} \cdot N}{n_h \cdot n_l}}{\sqrt{(\sum_{h=1}^{5} n_h \log \frac{n_h}{N}) \cdot (\sum_{l=1}^{U} n_l \log \frac{n_l}{N})}}, \tag{19}$$

where N is the number of samples, $n_{h,l}$ denotes the number of samples that have
a class label h according to $\boldsymbol{\lambda}^{(c)}$ as well as a cluster label l according to $\boldsymbol{\lambda}^{(e)}$,
$n_h = \sum_l n_{h,l}$, and $n_l = \sum_h n_{h,l}$.

Fig. 4 shows a boxplot of the NMI. Each box has horizontal lines at the lower
quartile, median, and upper quartile. Whiskers extend to the adjacent values
within 1.5 times the interquartile range from the ends of the box and $+$ signs
indicate outliers.

From Fig. 4, at the fourth level ($U = 5$), where mixture models have as many
components as the classes of the phoneme data, we confirm that CREM has an
advantage over GR and VL in terms of NMI. Moreover, CREM is comparable
to the standard EM directly applied to the data.

In viewing the results at the second and third levels, we cannot directly compare the results of VL with those of others. This is because the mixtures learned by VL always contained some almost identical components and hence the effective numbers of components were much fewer than the numbers intended. CREM appears to outperform VL and GR at all the levels. In addition, interestingly, we can see that CREM outperforms the standard EM in terms of NMI at the second and third levels. We conjecture that our algorithm is less likely to be trapped by low quality local minima thanks to the coarser descriptions of data. This is a highly preferable behavior for learning algorithms.

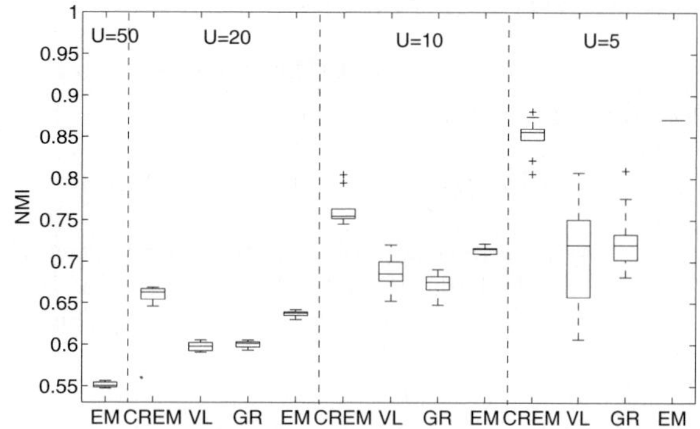

Fig. 4. Boxplot of the NMI for 10 trials

7   Conclusion

We have proposed a component reduction algorithm that does not suffer from the limitation of the existing algorithms proposed in [1,5]. Our algorithm was derived by applying the EM-algorithm to the component reduction problem and introducing an effective approximation to overcome the difficulty faced in carrying out the EM-algorithm.

Our algorithm and the two existing algorithms have been applied to a simple synthetic component reduction task and a phoneme clustering problem. The experimental results strongly support the effectiveness of our algorithm.

References

1. Vasconcelos, N., Lippman, A.: Learning mixture hierarchies. In: Kearns, M.J., Solla, S.A., Cohn, D. (eds.) Advances in Neural Information Processing Systems, vol. 11, pp. 606–612 (1999)
2. Dempster, A., Laird, N., Rubin, D.: Maximum likelihood from incomplete data via the em algorithm. Journal of the Royal Statistical Society B 39, 1–38 (1977)
3. McLachlan, G.J., Krishnan, T.: The EM Algorithm and Extensions. John Wiley and Sons Inc., Chichester (1997)
4. McLachlan, G., Peel, D.: Finite Mixture Models. John Wiley and Sons Inc., Chichester (2000)
5. Goldberger, J., Roweis, S.: Hierarchical clustering of a mixture model. In: Saul, L.K., Weiss, Y., Bottou, L. (eds.) Advances in Neural Information Processing Systems 17, pp. 505–512. MIT Press, Cambridge (2005)
6. Hastie, T., Tibshirani, R., Friedman, J.H.: The Elements of Statistical Learning: Data Mining, Inference, and Prediction. Springer, Heidelberg (2001)
7. Strehl, A., Ghosh, J.: Cluster ensembles - a knowledge reuse framework for combining multiple partitions. Machine Learning Research 3, 583–617 (2002)

Learning a Kernel Matrix for Time Series Data from DTW Distances

Hiroyuki Narita, Yasumasa Sawamura, and Akira Hayashi

Graduate School of Information Sciences, Hiroshima City University
3-4-1 Ozuka-Higashi, Asa-Minami-Ku, Hiroshima, 731-3194, Japan
narita@robotics.im.hiroshima-cu.ac.jp

Abstract. One of the advantages of the kernel methods is that they can deal with various kinds of objects, not necessarily vectorial data with a fixed number of attributes. In this paper, we develop kernels for time series data using dynamic time warping (DTW) distances. Since DTW distances are pseudo distances that do not satisfy the triangle inequality, a kernel matrix based on them is not positive semidefinite, in general. We use semidefinite programming (SDP) to guarantee the positive definiteness of a kernel matrix. We present neighborhood preserving embedding (NPE), an SDP formulation to obtain a kernel matrix that best preserves the local geometry of time series data. We also present an out-of-sample extension (OSE) for NPE. We use two applications, time series classification and time series embedding for similarity search to validate our approach.

1 Introduction

We have seen significant development of kernel methods for machine learning in the last decade [1]. Typical kernel method algorithms include support vector machines (SVMs) [2] for large margin classification, and kernel principal component analysis (KPCA) [3] for nonlinear dimensionality reduction. Symmetric positive semidefinite kernel functions that give similarity between objects, play a central role in kernel methods. One of the advantages of these kernel methods is that they can deal with various kinds of objects, not necessarily vectorial data with a fixed number of attributes. Such objects include strings, graphs, and weighted automata.

In this paper, we develop kernels for time series data using dynamic time warping (DTW) distances. Machine learning and data mining on time series data (also known as sequence data), such as speech, gesture, handwriting, and so on, has recently attracted more and more attention from the research community. The DTW distance is a frequently used dissimilarity measure for time series data [4]. Shimodaira et al. [5] proposed a dynamic time alignment kernel for voice recognition, and have reported better classification accuracy than HMMs when the number of training data is small. Bahlmann et al. [6] proposed the GDTW kernel, which substitutes the distance term in a Gaussian kernel with a DTW distance, and which achieves classification accuracy comparable with

M. Ishikawa et al. (Eds.): ICONIP 2007, Part II, LNCS 4985, pp. 336–345, 2008.
© Springer-Verlag Berlin Heidelberg 2008

that of HMMs for online handwritten characters. However, since DTW distances are pseudo distances that do not satisfy the triangle inequality, the previous approaches have failed to prove the positive semidefiniteness of the kernel matrix.

In order to guarantee the positive semidefiniteness of a kernel matrix, we use semidefinite programming (SDP) [7]. SDP has been used in machine learning to optimize a kernel matrix [8] for classification, and also to find low dimensional manifolds [9,10]. We present neighborhood preserving embedding (NPE), an SDP formulation, to obtain a kernel matrix that best preserves the local geometry of time series data in terms of the DTW distances. We also present an out-of-sample extension (OSE) for NPE.

We use two applications, time series classification [11] and time series embedding for similarity search [12], to validate our approach. In time series classification, the well known kernel trick is used to map time series data into a high dimensional feature space for linear separability and larger margin. On the other hand, in time series embedding for similarity search, a low dimensional feature space is sought for efficient multidimensional search. We present a suitable SDP formulation for the purpose.

The rest of this paper is organized as follows. In Section 2, we review DTW distances. In Section 3, we explain how to construct a kernel matrix from DTW distances using SDP. The resulting kernel matrix is used for large margin classification in Section 4. It is also used for low dimensional embedding via kernel PCA in Section 5. We conclude in Section 6.

2   Dynamic Time Warping(DTW)

A set of n time series data, $\mathcal{X} = \{X_1, \ldots, X_n\}$, is given, where X_i $(1 \leq i \leq n)$ is a sequence of feature vectors whose length is l_i $X_i = (\boldsymbol{x}_1^i, \ldots, \boldsymbol{x}_{l_i}^i)$. DTW finds the smallest distance, i.e., the maximal similarity, between the time series data through all nonlinear time warping that corresponds to a change in time scale [4]. In this paper, we use the DTW distances that are computed as follows, where $\| \cdot \|$ is the Euclidean norm.

1. Initial and boundary conditions.
    - start : $g(1, 1) = 0$
    - end $g(l_i, l_j)$
    - boundary $g(t_i, 0) = g(0, t_j) = \infty$
2. Repeat
    for $1 \leq t_i \leq l_i 1 \leq t_j \leq l_j$

$$g(t_i, t_j) = \min \begin{cases} g(t_i - 1, t_j) + \|\boldsymbol{x}_{t_i}^i - \boldsymbol{x}_{t_j}^j\|^2 \\ g(t_i - 1, t_j - 1) + 2\|\boldsymbol{x}_{t_i}^i - \boldsymbol{x}_{t_j}^j\|^2 \\ g(t_i, t_j - 1) + \|\boldsymbol{x}_{t_i}^i - \boldsymbol{x}_{t_j}^j\|^2 \end{cases} \tag{1}$$

3. Finish $d^2(X_i, X_j) = g(l_i, l_j)$

3   Learning a Kernel Matrix from DTW Distances

Let $\boldsymbol{\Phi}$ be a mapping from time series data into a feature space $\mathcal{F}$.

$$\text{mapping } \boldsymbol{\Phi} : \mathcal{X} \rightarrow \mathcal{F}$$
$$X_i \mapsto \boldsymbol{\Phi}(X_i)$$

In what follows, we write $\boldsymbol{K} \succeq 0$ as an abbreviation for $\boldsymbol{K}$ being a symmetric matrix that satisfies positive semidefiniteness. Our approach is to learn a kernel matrix $\boldsymbol{K} \succeq 0$, $\boldsymbol{K}(i,j) = \langle \boldsymbol{\Phi}(X_i), \boldsymbol{\Phi}(X_j) \rangle (1 \leq i, j \leq n)$ from DTW distances using the following well known relationship between distances and inner products.

$$d^2(X_i, X_j) = ||\boldsymbol{\Phi}(X_i) - \boldsymbol{\Phi}(X_j)||^2 = \langle \boldsymbol{\Phi}(X_i) - \boldsymbol{\Phi}(X_j), \boldsymbol{\Phi}(X_i) - \boldsymbol{\Phi}(X_j) \rangle$$
$$= \boldsymbol{K}(i,i) - \boldsymbol{K}(i,j) - \boldsymbol{K}(j,i) + \boldsymbol{K}(j,j)$$

3.1   Neighborhood Preserving Embedding (NPE)

DTW distances are pattern matching scores, so it is known that smaller distances are reliable, but larger distances are unreliable [11]. Therefore, it is expected that a mapping that pays attention only to neighborhood distances will have better results. Here we introduce Neighborhood Preserving Embedding (NPE), that learns a kernel matrix $\boldsymbol{K} \succeq 0$ that best preserves squared neighborhood distances. NPE entails the following procedure :

1. For a given n time series data $\{X_1, \ldots, X_n\}$, compute the DTW distance $\{d(X_i, X_j) | 1 \leq i, j \leq n\}$ between all data pairs.
2. Solve the following optimization problem by SDP [7].

$$\min_{\boldsymbol{K} \succeq 0} \sum_{i=1}^{n} \sum_{j : X_j \sim X_i} w_{ij} |d^2(X_i, X_j) - \langle \boldsymbol{B}_{ij}, \boldsymbol{K} \rangle| \qquad (2)$$

$$s.t. \sum_{i=1}^{n} \sum_{j=1}^{n} \boldsymbol{K}(i,j) = 0,$$

where "$X_j \sim X_i$" denotes that X_j is a neighbor of X_i and w_{ij} is a weight parameter. $\boldsymbol{B}_{ij}$ is a sparse $n \times n$ matrix used to compute square distances from $\boldsymbol{K}$, that is $\boldsymbol{B}_{ij}(i,i) = \boldsymbol{B}_{ij}(j,j) = 1, \boldsymbol{B}_{ij}(i,j) = \boldsymbol{B}_{ij}(j,i) = -1$ and all other elements are 0. Note that "$\langle \cdot, \cdot \rangle$" in Eq.(2) is an inner product operator between matrices.

$\sum_i \sum_j \boldsymbol{K}(i,j) = 0$ is the well known constraint for *centering* $\boldsymbol{K}$. Since $\sum_i \sum_j \boldsymbol{K}(i,j) = 0 \Leftrightarrow ||\sum_i \boldsymbol{\Phi}(X_i)||^2 = 0 \Leftrightarrow \sum_i \boldsymbol{\Phi}(X_i) = \boldsymbol{0}$ holds, the constraint causes the center of gravity of the feature vectors $\{\boldsymbol{\Phi}(X_i) | 1 \leq i \leq n\}$ to move to the origin. This is required in order to apply kernel PCA later for dimensionality reduction.

3. We eigen-decompose the kernel matrix K, that is optimized in step 2 above. The decomposed matrix is expressed as follows.

$$K = U\Lambda U^T, \tag{3}$$

where $\Lambda = \mathrm{diag}(\lambda_1, \ldots, \lambda_n), \lambda_1 \geq \ldots \geq \lambda_n \geq 0$ is a diagonal matrix of the eigenvalues, and $U = [e^1, \ldots, e^n]$ is a matrix of the eigenvectors.
Let us denote $\Phi(X_i)$ as Φ_i. Since $K = [\Phi_1\Phi_2, \ldots \Phi_n]^T[\Phi_1\Phi_2, \ldots \Phi_n]$ holds, Eq.(3) gives

$$[\Phi_1\Phi_2, \ldots \Phi_n] = \Lambda^{1/2}U^T \tag{4}$$

$$\Phi_i(k) = \sqrt{\lambda_k}e_k(i) \quad (1 \leq k \leq p) \quad \forall i \tag{5}$$

where $\Phi_i(k)$ is the kth entry of Φ_i, $e_k(i)$ is the ith entry of the kth eigenvector e_k, and p is the rank of K.

As for the neighborhood relationship, we have two choices. We define the ϵ-neighborhood relationship as $X_i \sim X_j \Leftrightarrow d(X_i, X_j) < \epsilon$. The symmetric k-nn neighborhood relationship is defined as $X_i \sim X_j \Leftrightarrow X_i \in knn(X_j) \vee X_j \in knn(X_i)$, where $knn(X_i)$ is the set of k nearest neighbors of X_i.

3.2 Out-of-Sample Extension (OSE)

Given additional time series data, X_{n+1}, it is natural to use NPE again to obtain an $(n+1) \times (n+1)$ kernel matrix K_{n+1}. However, this adds a heavy computational load. We therefore introduce Out-of-Sample Extension (OSE) to obtain a suboptimal kernel matrix $\tilde{K}_{n+1}$ by expanding the kernel matrix K_n that has already been computed by NPE. We define an extended kernel matrix $\tilde{K}_{n+1}$ as follows:

$$\tilde{K}_{n+1} = \begin{bmatrix} K_n & b \\ b^T & c \end{bmatrix} \succeq 0, \tag{6}$$

$$b = (\langle \Phi_1, \Phi_{n+1} \rangle, \langle \Phi_2, \Phi_{n+1} \rangle, \ldots, \langle \Phi_n, \Phi_{n+1} \rangle)^T \tag{7}$$

$$c = \langle \Phi_{n+1}, \Phi_{n+1} \rangle \tag{8}$$

Then, $\tilde{K}_{n+1}, b \in R^n$, and $c \in R$ are obtained by solving the following SDP.

$$\min_{\tilde{K}_{n+1} \succeq 0, b, c} \sum_{i: X_i \sim X_{n+1}} w_{i,n+1} |d^2(X_i, X_{n+1}) - \langle B_{i,n+1}, \tilde{K}_{n+1} \rangle| \tag{9}$$

$$s.t. \quad \tilde{K}_{n+1} = \begin{bmatrix} K_n & b \\ b^T & c \end{bmatrix}$$

Finally, we consider embedding the additional time series data, X_{n+1}, into the space in which $\{X_i | 1 \leq i \leq n\}$ are already embedded using Eq.(5). Let $\tilde{\Phi}_{n+1}$ be the projection of Φ_{n+1} into the space spanned by $\{\Phi_i | 1 \leq i \leq n\}$. Substituting Eq.(4) into Eq.(7) yields $(U\Lambda^{1/2})\tilde{\Phi}_{n+1} = b$. Hence, we obtain the following.

$$\tilde{\Phi}_{n+1} = (U\Lambda^{1/2})^\dagger b \tag{10}$$

$$\tilde{\Phi}_{n+1}(k) = \frac{1}{\sqrt{\lambda_k}}e_k^T b, \quad (1 \leq k \leq p) \tag{11}$$

where $(U\Lambda^{1/2})^\dagger$ is the pseudo inverse of $(U\Lambda^{1/2})$ and p is the rank of K_n.

4 Large Margin Classification

In this section, we classify time series data by SVM. We employ linear, polynomial, and RBF kernels.

$$\text{Linear kernel}: \boldsymbol{K}^{lin}(i,j) = \langle \boldsymbol{\Phi}_i, \boldsymbol{\Phi}_j \rangle$$

$$\text{Polynomial kernel}: \boldsymbol{K}^{pol}(i,j) = (1 + \langle \boldsymbol{\Phi}_i, \boldsymbol{\Phi}_j \rangle)^p$$

$$\text{RBF kernel}: \boldsymbol{K}^{rbf}(i,j) = exp(-||\boldsymbol{\Phi}_i - \boldsymbol{\Phi}_j||^2/2\gamma^2),$$

where $\boldsymbol{\Phi}_i$ $(1 \leq i \leq n+1)$ is the feature vector for X_i obtained by NPE and OSE using Eqs.(5) and (11) [1], and γ is the parameter for the RBF kernel. Note that since the linear kernels are positive semidefinite, the polynomial and RBF kernels are also positive semidefinite.

4.1 UNIPEN

The UNIPEN-DTW data[13] consists of DTW distance matrices that are based on the UNIPEN Train-R01/V07 online handwriting sequence dataset. The data contains 2 sets with 250 samples per set from 5 classes ('a' to 'e').

We conducted the multi class classification experiment in two settings.

- Transductive setting. (1) Both the training data and the test data are embedded by NPE. (2) The classifier is trained with the training data, and the test data is classified.
- Sequential setting. (1) The training data is embedded by NPE, and the classifier is trained. (2) Then, the test data, embedded by OSE, is classified.

To solve the SDP optimization problems in NPE and OSE, we use publicly available software SDPT3 [14]. We set the parameter $w_{ij} = 1$ for all i, j pairs and use a k-nn neighborhood, $k = 6$, for both NPE and OSE. Since the data has turned out to be linearly separable[2], we tested only hard margin SVMs, adjusting p for $\boldsymbol{K}^{pol}$ and γ for $\boldsymbol{K}^{rbf}$. We use *one-versus-the-rest* SVM as multiclass SVM.

We compare our results with those for the following *distance substitution*(DS) kernels [13].

$$\text{Linear distance kernel}: \boldsymbol{K}^{lin}_d(i,j) = \langle X_i, X_j \rangle_d$$

$$\text{Polynomial distance kernel}: \boldsymbol{K}^{pol}_d(i,j) = (1 + \gamma \langle X_i, X_j \rangle_d)^p$$

$$\text{RBF distance kernel}: \boldsymbol{K}^{rbf}_d(i,j) = exp(-d^2(X_i, X_j)/2\gamma^2),$$

where $\langle X_i, X_j \rangle_d = -1/2(d^2(X_i, X_j) - d^2(X_i, O) - d^2(X_j, O))$. O is the origin and was chosen as the point with the minimum squared distance sum relative to the other training data. Since DTW distances are pseudo distances, the distance

---

[1] In this section, we omit the tilde on top of $\tilde{\boldsymbol{\Phi}}_{n+1}$ to simplify the notation.

[2] Assuming $\boldsymbol{K}^{lin}$ is of full rank, its feature space dimension is n, the number of the training data. Hence, the VC dimension for $\boldsymbol{K}^{lin}$ is n+1.

Table 1. LOO-errors for UNIPEN. The error rates for NPD, CSE, RNE, 1-nn, and k-nn are from [13]. As for the k-nn classifier, the best k-nn are shown. Tra and Seq refer to the transductive and sequential settings, respectively. The order of $\boldsymbol{K}^{pol}$ is 3 for both datasets. The value of γ for $\boldsymbol{K}_d^{rbf}$ is 1.0 except for Tra in dataset #2, where it is 0.75.

dataset	$\boldsymbol{K}_d^{pol}$			$\boldsymbol{K}_d^{rbf}$			1-nn	k-nn	$\boldsymbol{K}^{lin}$		$\boldsymbol{K}^{pol}$		$\boldsymbol{K}^{rbf}$	
	NPD	CNE	RNE	NPD	CNE	RNE			Tra	Seq	Tra	Seq	Tra	Seq
#1	6.0	5.2	5.6	5.2	4.4	4.8	5.6	5.6	5.2	6.0	4.0	4.8	4.0	5.2
#2	7.6	6.8	6.4	6.0	6.0	5.6	7.2	6.4	6.8	6.0	6.0	4.8	6.4	5.2

substitution kernels are Not Positive semiDefinite (NPD) kernels. To transform NPD kernels to be positive semidefinite, two methods are provided. Cutting off Negative Eingenvalues (CNE) cuts off contributions corresponding to negative eigenvalues. Reflecting Negative Eingenvalues (RNE) reflects the negative eigenvalues by taking their absolute values. Note that CNE and RNE can be used only under the transductive setting.

The result is evaluated by leave-one-out (LOO) errors. See Table 1. In the transductive setting (Tra), our polynomial and RBF kernels, $\boldsymbol{K}^{pol}$ and $\boldsymbol{K}^{rbf}$, respectively, generally perform better for both datasets than CNE and RNE of the corresponding DS-kernels, $\boldsymbol{K}_d^{pol}$ and $\boldsymbol{K}_d^{rbf}$, respectively. The exception is that our rbf kernel has a larger error rate for the second dataset. In the sequential setting (Seq), our kernels always perform better than the corresponding NPD kernels. In addition, our kernels also perform better than 1-nn and k-nn classifiers. We are currently working hard to investigate the reason why all of our kernels perform better in the sequential setting (i.e., using NPE + OSE) than in the transductive setting (i.e., using only NPE) for the second dataset.

Table 2 shows how the size of k-nn neighborhoods influences the SVM classifications. Due to the relaiablility of smaller DTW distance, relatively small k values bring better results.

5   Low Dimensional Embedding for Similarity Search

In this section, we consider how to speed up a similarity search of time series data, when dissimilarity is defined in terms of DTW distances. Stated more

Table 2. LOO-errors for UNIPEM with k-nn neighborhoods ($6 \leq k \leq 250$). All errors are computed by linear SVM with NPE.

dataset	K^{lin}								
	k = 6	k = 8	k=12	k=15	k = 20	k = 50	k = 80	k = 150	k = 250
#1	5.2	5.6	4.8	6.8	14.8	14.8	11.6	19.6	16.0
#2	6.8	6.4	10.0	6.4	13.6	16.8	10.4	12.8	-

concretely, we consider the following problem. A set of n time series data (time series DB): $\mathcal{X} = \{X_1, \ldots, X_n\}$, is given. Given a query Q, another time series data, *quickly* find the k nearest neighbors of Q, i.e., find the k $X_i's$ with the smallest DTW distances.

5.1 Proposed Method

We adopt the approach of embedding time series data in a low dimensional Euclidean space with KPCA[3], and performing a multidimensional search. The time complexity of nearest neighbor search in the embedded space using the kd-tree is $O(\log n)$ [15], whereas that of the linear search is $O(n)$, where n is the number of data. In order to speed up the similarity search, the key issue is how to embed the data accurately (1) into a *low* dimensional space (2) from a *small* number of DTW distances.

Lower dimensional embedding is preferred because the complexity of the kd-tree search increases exponentially as the number of embedding dimensions p grows. For our purposes, we introduce NPE with regularization by adding a regularization term to the objective function in Eq. (2):

$$\min_{\boldsymbol{K} \succeq 0} \sum_{i} \sum_{j \in \boldsymbol{N}_i} w_{ij} |d^2(X_i, X_j) - \langle \boldsymbol{B}_{ij}, \boldsymbol{K} \rangle| + \eta \cdot \mathrm{tr}(\boldsymbol{K}), \qquad (12)$$

where $\mathrm{tr}(\boldsymbol{K})$ is the trace of $\boldsymbol{K}$ and η is a parameter to trade off the two terms in the objective function. It can be shown that $\mathrm{tr}(\boldsymbol{K}) = 1/(2n) \sum_i \sum_j ||\boldsymbol{\Phi}_i - \boldsymbol{\Phi}_j||^2$, i.e. $\mathrm{tr}(\boldsymbol{K})$ is proportional to the variance of data in the feature space. We promote low dimensional embedding by adjusting η.

To embed the data from a small number of DTW distances, we use OSE. We randomly select m ($m \ll n$) samples from n time series data in the DB, and apply NPE to m samples. The remaining non samples and the query are embedded by OSE using DTW distances to the m samples.

5.2 Experiment

The objective of this experiment is to evaluate the accuracy of low dimensional embedding using NPE and OSE. For two kinds of time series data (ASL [3] and ISOLET [4]), we compare our method with multidimensional scaling (MDS) [18]. We use the Nyström method [19] as an out-of-sample extension for MDS.

We adjust η in Eq. (2) so as to embed the data in a low dimensional space. Fig. 1 shows the eigenvalue distribution for ASL when η is changed.

For the task, we choose to search for 10 nearest neighbors (NNs) in the time series DB. We compute recall-precision (RP) curves for each embedding method.

---

[3] ASL is based on Australian sign Language data in the UCI KDD Archive [16]. The data consist of 95 signed words.

[4] ISOLET is a database of letters of the English alphabet spoken in isolation [17]. The database consists of 7800 spoken letters, two productions of each letter by 150 speakers.

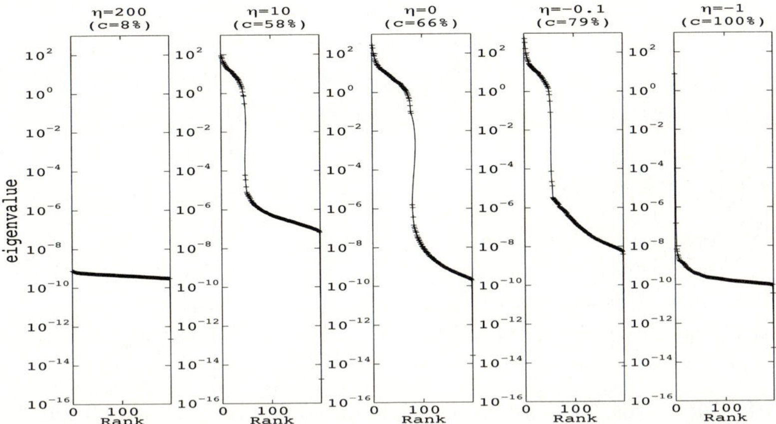

Fig. 1. The eigenvalue distribution of the kernel matrix for the ASL sample data. The *contribution rate* c under the embedding dimension p, $c = \sum_{i=1}^{p} \lambda_i / \sum_{j=1}^{m} tr(\boldsymbol{K})$ is also shown. As η decreases, big eigenvalues become dominant. Although, the rightmost image shows the highest contribution rate, the number of nonzero eigenvalues is only one, therefore the accuracy that preserves distances has been lost.

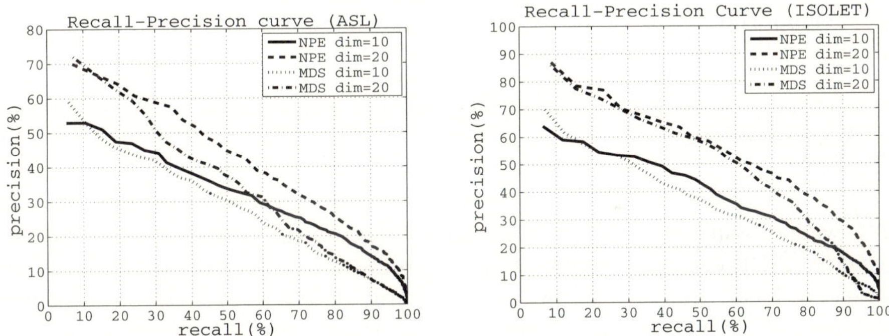

Fig. 2. RP curves for NPE and MDS. We set $w_{ij} = 1$ for all i,j pairs in Eqs. (12) and (9), used an ϵ neighborhood. The value of ϵ was selected so that each datum has at least 20 neighbors from the samples. DB size, $n = 3000$, and sample size, $m = 200$, the embedding dimension, $p = 10,20$. The average of 100 queries was taken. **(left)** ASL: We use as DB time series examples for 43 words, such as "change","deaf","glad","her", and "innocent", which have similar words. We use examples for "lose" and "love" as query time series. **(right)** ISOLET: We randomly selected data from the dataset and used thse as DB and as queries. The 28-dimensional feature vector consists of 14 MFCCs and their first-order time derivatives.

We view up to k ($k > 10$) NNs in the *embedded* space as retrieved (*positive*) results, and count how many of them are *true*, i.e., are within 10 NNs in terms of DTW distance.

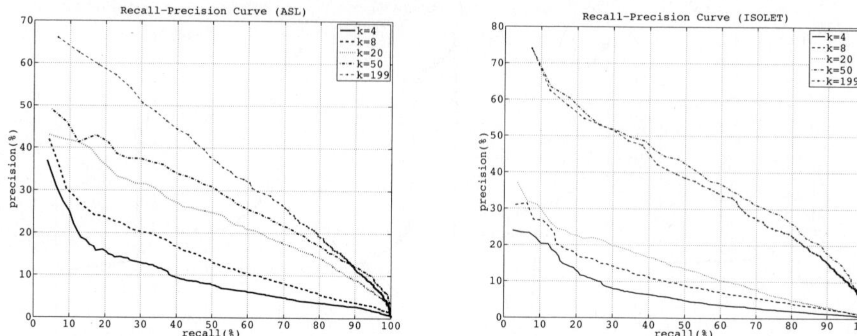

Fig. 3. RP Curves for NPE for k-nn neighborhoods where $k = 4$, 8, 20, 50, 199. $n = 3000$, $m = 200$, $p = 10$. The average of 100 queries. **(left)** ASL. **(right)** ISOLET.

Fig. 2 shows the RP curves for the ASL and ISOLET data. We see from the figure that NPE performs better than MDS. We attribute the reason to the fact that NPE constructs the kernel using only neighborhood distances, and it has no negative eigenvalues.

To examine the effect of the neighborhood size, we also experimented using k-nn neighborhoods for various k values. Fig. 3 shows the RP curves for the ASL and ISOLET. [5]

6   Conclusion

We have developed kernels for time series data from DTW distances. By using SDP, we can guarantee the positive definiteness of the kernel matrix. We have presented NPE, an SDP formulation to obtain a kernel matrix that best preserves the local geometry of time series data, together with its out-of-sample extension. We have shown two applications, time series classification and time series embedding for similarity search in order to validate our approach.

References

1. Shawe-Taylor, J., Cristianini, N.: Kernel Methods for Pattern Analysis. Cambridge University Press, Cambridge (2004)
2. Corres, C., Vapnik, V.: Support vector networks. Machine Learning 20, 273–297 (1995)
3. Schölkopf, B., Smola, A., Müller, K.: Nonlinear component analysis as a kernel eigenvalue problem. Neural Computation 10, 1299–1319 (1998)
4. Rabiner, L., Juang, B.: Fundamentals of Speech Recognition. Prentice-Hall, Englewood Cliffs (1993)

---

[5] Contrary to our expectation, larger neighborhood size generally leads to better results. It seems that low dimensional embedding is difficult with small neighborhood.

5. Shimodaira, H., Noma, K., Nakai, M., Sagayama, S.: Dynamic time-alignment kernel in support vector machine. In: Neural Information Processing Systems 14, pp. 921–928. MIT Press, Cambridge (2002)
6. Bahlmann, C., Haasdonk, B., Burkhardt, H.: On-line handwriting recognition with support vector machines-a kernel approach. In: Proc. 8th Int. W/S on Frontiers in Handwriting Recognition, pp. 49–54 (2002)
7. Vandenberghe, L., Boyd, S.: Semidefinite programming. SIAM Rev. 38(1), 49–95 (1996)
8. Lanckriet, G., Christianini, N., Barlett, P., Ghaoui, L., Jordan, M.: Learning the kernel matrix with semidifinite programming. Journal of Machine Learning Research 5, 27–72 (2004)
9. Weinberger, K.Q., Sha, F., Saul, L.K.: Learning a kernel matrix for nonlinear dimensionality reduction. In: Proc. 21st Int. Conf. on Machine Learning (ICML 2004), pp. 839–846 (2004)
10. Lu, F., Keles, S., Wright, S., Wahba, G.: Framework for kernel regularization with application to protein clustering. PNAS 102(35), 12332–12337 (2005)
11. Hayashi, A., Mizuhara, Y., Suematsu, N.: Embedding time series data for classification. In: Perner, P., Imiya, A. (eds.) MLDM 2005. LNCS (LNAI), vol. 3587, pp. 356–365. Springer, Heidelberg (2005)
12. Hayashi, A., Nisizaki, K., Suematsu, N.: Fast similarity search of time series data using the nystrom method. In: ICDM 2005 Workshop on Temporal Data Mining, pp. 157–164 (2005)
13. Haasdonk, B., Bahlmann, C.: Learning with distance substitution kernels. In: Rasmussen, C.E., Bülthoff, H.H., Schölkopf, B., Giese, M.A. (eds.) DAGM 2004. LNCS, vol. 3175, pp. 220–227. Springer, Heidelberg (2004)
14. Toh, K., Tütüncü, R., Todd, M.: Solving semidefinite-quadratic-linear programming using sdpt3. Mathematical Programming 95, 180–217 (2003)
15. Friedman, J., Bentley, J., Finkel, R.: An algorithm for finding the best matches in logarithmic expected time. ACM Trans. Mathematical Software 3(3), 209–226 (1977)
16. Kadous, W.: Australian sign language data in the uci kdd archive (1995), http://www.cse.unsw.edu.au/~waleed/tml/data/
17. Cole, R., Muthusamy, Y., Fanty, M.: The ISOLET spoken letter database. Technical Report CS/E 90-004 (1990)
18. Cox, T., Cox, M.: Multidimensional Scaling. Chapman and Hall, Boca Raton (2001)
19. Bengio, Y., Vincent, P., Paiement, J.: Learning eigenfunctions links spectral embedding and kernel pca. Neural Computation 16(10), 2197–2219 (2004)

Neural Network Method for Protein Structure Search Using Cell-Cell Adhesion

Cheng-Yuan Liou* and Cheng-Jung Ho

Department of Computer Science and Information Engineering
National Taiwan University
Republic of China
Supported by National Science Council
cyliou@csie.ntu.edu.tw

Abstract. We propose a neural network method for three dimensional protein structure search that utilizes the link relationships among features. This method is an offline index-based method which builds indices for protein structures in the database and the search is performed on the indices. We can easily extend this method to incoporate more physical properties of the protein structures since the structural information is preserved in the extracted features.

1 Introduction

Protein sequence and structure pattern analysis is a very important area of research in molecular biology. By analyzing and characterizing existing proteins, one can use the discovered relationship between structures and functions to predict the functions of newly discovered proteins. With proper matching and scoring algorithms, the structure or substructures of the new protein can be compared to the proteins in the database; the new protin can be assumed to have similar function as the highly similar proteins in the database. It is said that the proteins that are similar in structure have similar functions even if their amino acid sequences are not similar. Applying this idea in biomedical researches, we can find possible cures of a new virus from existing medicines. We search the virus database for similar protein structures to the new virus and check if the existing cures for the known viruses are effective against the new virus through more detailed examination. This method provides an efficient filter to identify the possible medicines from hundreds of thousands of possibilities. Figure 1 provides an illustration of this process.

2 Related Works

As the number of known protein structures increases (10213 in PDB as June 1999 to 44700 as July 2007), there is a need for efficient methods for describing and revealing common functionally important units in related structures.

---

* Correspondence author.

M. Ishikawa et al. (Eds.): ICONIP 2007, Part II, LNCS 4985, pp. 346–355, 2008.

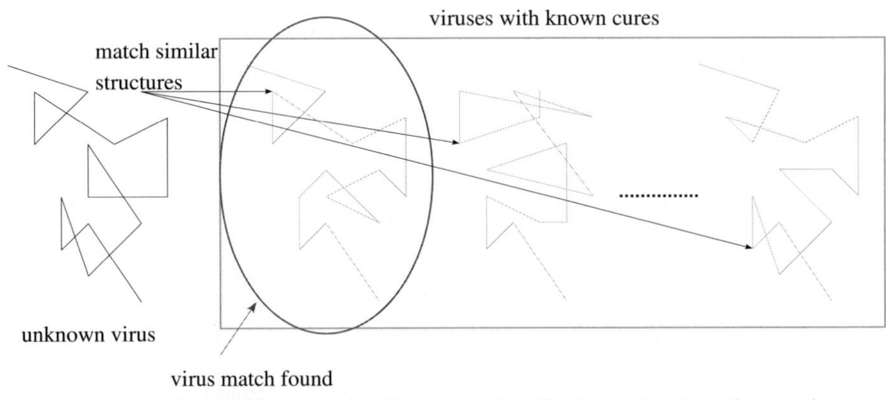

Fig. 1. Biomedical application of the CTCA method for protein structure matching. The medicine that is effective against a virus may be effective against another with similar structure. We can narrow down the area of search for effective medicines against an unknown virus efficiently using this method.

Multiple structure similarity search methods for protein database have been developed and can be classified into two types - comparison based and index based. There are many comparison based algorithms for protein structures and they are very accurate but those algorithms would take enormous time to query a large database. For comparison based methods, two structures must be aligned first then distance can be calculated. The root mean square deviation (RMSD) is a commonly used distance measure and there exists constant time algorithm to find the best alignement for minimal RMSD [7,1]. Related measures are designed for specific needs [5,4]. The index based methods are more efficient in searching the query but are less accurate than the first type of methods. Some methods modifies existing indexing techniques in other fields so that they can be used on the protein structures. For example, PSIST [3] and Geometric Suffix Tree [14] are both inspired by the suffix tree algorithm in string processing. The accuracy of protein structure matching is often measured by RMSD or sometimes by unit-vector root mean square deviation (URMSD). But to design an indexing structure that strictly considers RMSD or URMSD is thought to be too difficult.

3   The Method

Our method is an application of the handprinted Chinese character recognition method [11] that uses cell-to-cell adhesion (CTCA) property among extracted features. It is an efficient way of pattern matching[10,12] and the classifier can be prepared offline such that the memory and computing resource requirement is moderate even for a large database such as protein structures. Therefore we would like to apply it on the protein structure matching. However, the difference

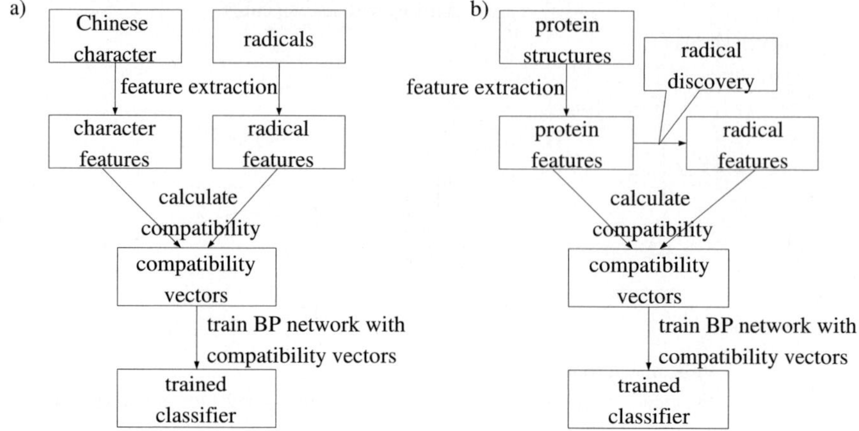

Fig. 2. a)Work flow of CTCA method for handprited Chinese character recognition.
b) Work flow of CTCA method for protein structure search.

between character pattern recognition and protein structure matching is more
than an increase in dimensionality of the dataset. We explain how the CTCA
method is modified to be applied on the protein structure matching in the following sections. The work flow of the original method and modified version are
illustrated in Figure 2.

3.1   Feature Extraction

A general method for describing the protein structure is using the center carbon
atom of each residue in the protein sequence to represent the position of the
residue. The residues of protein sequences are the amino acids and the center
carbon atom of the amino acid is referred as the C_α atom. The chain of C_α atoms
forms the backbone structure of proteins. We can observe a structure similar to
the bended ellipses in Chinese character patterns. A subsequence of three C_α
atoms forms a structure that can be represented by a bended ellipse.

Instead of the five dimensional feature in the original CTCA method, we use
four dimensional features here. The four dimensional feature is $[u, \phi\hat{x}, \phi\hat{y}, \phi\hat{z}]$
where u is the average length of two arms just like in the original CTCA method.
The definition of ϕ and $(\hat{x}, \hat{y}, \hat{z})$ are the same as the corresponding version in the
original CTCA with the only difference that the coordinate system is relative
to the previous feature. The reason why this approach is taken is to ensure
the features are invariant under rotation of the whole protein structure. The
template patterns, radical patterns and the unknown pattern now is written as:

$$S^i = \left\{ s_n^i | 1 \leq n \leq N^i \right\}, 1 \leq i \leq N \; where \quad s_n^i = \left[u_n^i, \phi_n^i \hat{x}_n^i, \phi_n^i \hat{x}_n^i, \phi_n^i \hat{z}_n^i \right]$$
$$R^j = \left\{ r_l^j | 1 \leq l \leq L^j \right\}, 1 \leq j \leq J \; where \quad r_l^j = \left[u_l^i, \phi_l^i \hat{x}_l^i, \phi_l^i \hat{x}_l^i, \phi_l^i \hat{z}_l^i \right]$$
$$H = \{ h_m | 1 \leq m \leq M \} \qquad where \; h_m = \left[u_m, \phi_m \hat{x}_m, \phi_m \hat{x}_m, \phi_m \hat{z}_m \right]$$

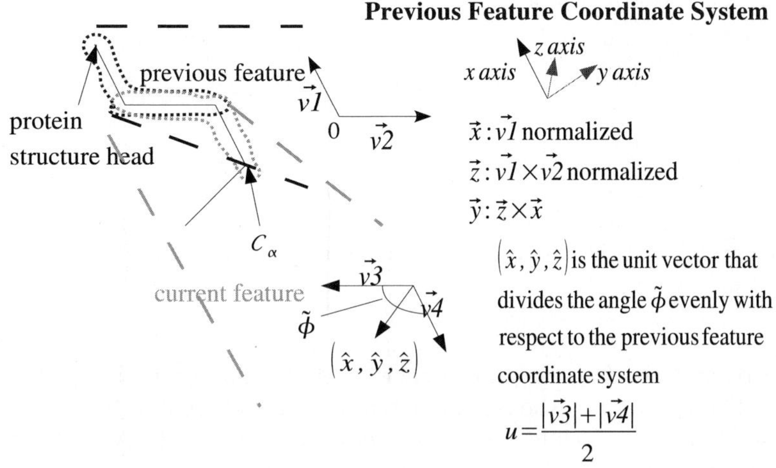

Fig. 3. 4D feature extraction from protein structure

Figure 3 illustrates the extraction of the four dimensional features.

The feature to feature (FTF) table that records the link information among features becomes a vector of length equal to the number of amino acids in the protein structure. In the vector, 0 means no link with previous feature and 1 means there exists a link with the previous feature.

3.2   Radical Discovery

The radicals used in the character recognition system are hand picked from the template characters but we can not do the same for protein structures. Hence we need a method that automatically extract the radicals out of the template patterns. We have chosen E. R. Caianiello's Procrustes algorithm [2] for this task. The algorithm was created to build an alphabet that under free concatenation and repetition of the symbols of the alphabet, the original text can be reconstructed unambiguously. Before explaining the Procrustes algorithm, we need to introduce a few terms. The first one is the alphabet and the hierarchy of alphabets. An alphabet is a set of letters or symbols and is denoted by $\Sigma = \{\sigma_k | 1 \leq k \leq K\}$ where σ_k are symbols of the alphabet and there are K of them. The hierarchy of alphabets is considered as $\Sigma^{(o)}$ where o denotes the level of the alphabet and $o = 0, 1, 2, \ldots$, up to a maximum level O. The Procrustes algorithm builds $\Sigma^{(o+1)}$ from $\Sigma^{(o)}$ and the text $\mathcal{T}$. The text $\mathcal{T}$ can be an article, a word or even other sequences of symbols and the $\Sigma^{(0)}$ is the set of basic unit of $\mathcal{T}$. The second term is the "free monoid" of an alphabet. The free monoid Σ^* of an alphabet is obtained by concatenating the symbols in the alphabet and the empty sequence $\emptyset$ in all possible ways, including repetitions. The symbols $\sigma_k^{(o+1)}$ of $\Sigma^{(o+1)}$ are required to stay in a one-to-one correspondence with a subset $s^{(h)}$ of

$\Sigma^{(o)*}$. In other words, the symbols in $\Sigma^{(o+1)}$ must be coded into words whose letters are the symbols $\sigma_k^{(o)}$ of $\Sigma^{(o)}$. Hence we have this relationship

$$\Sigma^{(o+1)} \subset \Sigma^{(o)*}$$

and of course

$$\Sigma^{(o+1)*} \subset \Sigma^{(o)*}$$

The last level $\Sigma^{(O)}$ is reached when the construction procedure yields

$$\Sigma^{(O)} \equiv \Sigma^{(O+1)} \equiv \Sigma^{(O+2)} \equiv \cdots$$

Also we require the free monoid of each level of alphabet to completely cover the text. The last term is the closed instantaneous code (CIC). In coding theory terms, an alphabet is a code and the symbols are code words. A CIC is a closed code under the left-cancellation operation and does not contain suffixes which have code words as prefixes. The following is an example of CIC:

$$a_1a_2a_3a_4;\ a_3a_4;\ a_3a_2;\ a_2;\ a_4$$

where a_i is the basic element.

The Procrustes algorithm is the procedure used to construct a higher level alphabet from a lower level alphabet, that is, how to build $\Sigma^{(o+1)}$ from $\Sigma^{(o)}$ and $\mathcal{T}$. In shorthand notation;

$$\Sigma^{(o)} \equiv A,\ \Sigma^{(o+1)} \equiv S$$

$$\sigma_i^{(o)} = a_i$$

$$s_i^{(o)} = s_i = a_{i_1}^{(o)} a_{i_2}^{(o)} \ldots a_{i_l}^{(o)}$$

where $s_i^{(o)}$ is a sequence of symbols in $\Sigma^{(o)}$ and its index i numbers all the possible sequences s_i of $A^* \equiv \Sigma^{(o)*}$. A sequence of length l is called a l-gram. The transition process from A to S is:

1. Find all digrams appear at least once in text $\mathcal{T}$ and denote the set as D, $D \subset A^2$.
2. Call x_i and y_j the first and second letter of a digram; therefore $x_i \equiv a_i$ and $y_j \equiv a_j$. Call the set of all x_i X and the set of all y_j Y. x_iy_j denotes any digram and a probability scheme associated with the space XY by means of the prescription

$$p(x_i, y_j) = \begin{cases} \frac{1}{N} & if\ x_iy_j \in D \\ 0 & if\ x_iy_j \notin D \end{cases}$$

where N is the number of digrams in set D. Notice the focus is on what digrams appear in the text, not the freqency they appear.

3. Denote the number of digrams in D having x_i as first symbol as h_i and the number of digrams in D having y_j as second symbol as k_j, the marginal probability that x_i and y_j occupies the first and second place in a digram is

$$p\left(x_i\right) = \sum_i p\left(x_i.y_j\right) = \frac{h_i}{N}$$

$$p\left(y_j\right) = \sum_j p\left(x_i, y_j\right) = \frac{k_j}{N}$$

We then find the conditional probabilities:

$$p\left(y_j|x_i\right) = \frac{p\left(x_i, y_j\right)}{p\left(x_i\right)} = \begin{cases} \frac{1}{h_i} & if\ x_i y_j \in D \\ 0 & if\ x_i y_j \notin D \end{cases}$$

$$p\left(x_i|y_j\right) = \frac{p\left(x_i, y_j\right)}{p\left(y_j\right)} = \begin{cases} \frac{1}{k_j} & if\ x_i y_j \in D \\ 0 & if\ x_i y_j \notin D \end{cases}$$

And the average information which is required to specify which symbol occupies the second place in a digram is:

$$H\left(Y\right) = -\sum_j p\left(y_j\right) \log p\left(y_j\right)$$

and the average information which is required for the same purpose when the first symbol of the digram is specified as x_i is:

$$H\left(Y|x_i\right) = -\sum_j p\left(y_j|x_i\right) \log p\left(y_j|x_i\right) = \log h_i$$

4. Now we choose a suitable criterion - a cut T such that $0 \leq T \leq H\left(Y\right)$ to split the alphabet A into two subsets:

$$A^{\geq} \equiv \{x_i \in A : H\left(Y|x_i\right) \geq T\}$$

$$A^{<} \equiv \{x_i \in A : H\left(Y|x_i\right) < T\}$$

Next, a new alphabet A_1 is formed by putting all elements in $A^{\geq}$ and the digrams in set D with the first symbol in set $A^{<}$. A_1 is the first provisional intermediate level and contains both monograms and digrams. The successive provisional intermediate levels are formed by iterating from step 1 again with the new set $D \supset A_1 A$. The new set D is formed by elements with x_i from A_1 and y_j from A. The iteration stops when $A^{<} = \emptyset$. In other words, no new provisional intermediate level can be constructed from the process since $A_n^{\geq} \equiv A_n$ and $A_m \equiv S$, which is an alphabet of higher level in the hierachy.

Through careful examination, an immediate defect of the Procrustes algorithm is found - the free monoid of S may not fully covers the text if the terminating character of the text is not included in the first $A^{\geq}$ set. One example is to use a single word "hello" as the text and start with the maximum cut possible. But simply include the last symbol of text in the $A^{\geq}$ of all provisional intermediate levels does not work because the a sequence s can still grow past an element in $A^{\geq}$ if the $H\left(Y|x_i\right) < T$ for $x_i = s$.

The solution for this problem comes from the observation of the $A_n^{\geq} \equiv S$ set in the last provisional intermediate level where $A_n^{<} = \varnothing$. As stated before, we can use the maximum possible T for all provisional intermediate levels. Therefore for all $s_i \in S$ $s_i = x_i \in A_n^{\geq}$, $H\left(Y|x_i\right) = T$ which means that for all s_i of length greater than one, the last symbol in the sequence is a monogram in S. To add this idea into the procedure, only step 4 needs to be modified as follows:

4. When building the first provisional intermediate level, this step stays the same. But for the following levels, the procedure to build A_{n+1} has changed to

$$A_n^{\geq} \equiv \left\{x_i^n = s_i^n = a_{i_1} a_{i_2} \ldots a_{i_l} \in A_n | a_{i_l} \in A_0^{\geq}\right\}$$

$$A_n^{<} \equiv \left\{x_i^n = s_i^n = a_{i_1} a_{i_2} \ldots a_{i_l} \in A_n | a_{i_l} \notin A_0^{\geq}\right\}$$

$$A_{n+1} \equiv A_n^{\geq} \cup \left\{x_i y_j \in D_n | x_i^n \in A_n^{<}\right\}$$

Also we only need to repeat step 1 and 4 for the rest of provisional intermediate levels since the probability calculations are no longer necessary.

One thing to notice is that before using the text $\mathcal{T}$ with $\Sigma^{(o)}$ to find $\Sigma^{(o+1)}$, we need to encode the text with the symbols in $\Sigma^{(o)}$ to ensure the correctness of the above procedures. We need to convert the extract features to character representation in order to use the Procrustes algorithm. The range of the four elements in the feature vector are divided into 5, 10, 10, 10 intervals respectively. If we denote the intervals each element is in as $int_0, int_1, int_2, int_3$, the character representation of the feature is an integer calculated by $int_0 \times 1000 + int_1 \times 100 + int_2 \times 10 + int_3$. Using the Procrustes algorithm, we find the radicals of each protein structure and the longest five radicals from each protein structure will be used in the compatibility computation.

3.3   Compatibility Computation

We employ the exact same compatibility computation process as the original CTCA method here. First a Hopfield network is used to find the optimal feature correspondences and the compatibility is calculated using the optimal correspondence. The energy of the Hopfield network that we want to minimize is defined as

$$E = \frac{A}{2} \sum_l \sum_{m1} \sum_{m_2 \neq m_1} V_{lm_1} V_{lm_2} + \frac{B}{2} \sum_m \sum_{l_1} \sum_{l_2 \neq l_1} V_{l_1 m} V_{l_2 m} + \frac{C}{2} \sum_l \left(\sum_m V_{lm} - 1\right)^2$$

$$-\frac{D}{2}\sum_{l}\sum_{l\neq l_1}\sum_{m}\sum_{m_1\neq m} D_2\left(r_l^j, r_{l_1}^j, h_m, h_{m_1}\right) V_{lm} V_{l_1 m_1}$$

and the network follows dynamic motion

$$\frac{\partial v_{lm}}{\partial t} = -\frac{v_{lm}}{\tau} - A\sum_{m_1\neq m} V_{lm_1} - B\sum_{l_1\neq l} V_{l_1 m} - C\left(\sum_{m} V_{lm} - 1\right)$$

$$+ D\sum_{l_1\neq l}\sum_{m_1\neq m} D_2\left(r_l^j, r_{l_1}^j, h_m, h_{m_1}\right) V_{l_1 m_1}$$

where τ is a constant. For each time step t, the new state of $V_{lm}^{(t)}$ is defined as

$$V_{lm}^{(t)} = \frac{1}{2}\left(1 + \tanh\left(\frac{v_{lm}^{(t)}}{v_0}\right)\right)$$

$$v_{lm}^{(t)} = v_{lm}^{(t-1)} + \frac{\partial v_{lm}^{(t-1)}}{\partial t}$$

D_2 in the above equation gives the compatibililty score between two pairs of features, one from each protein structure. The calculation for $D_2\left(r_l^j, r_{l_1}^j, h_m, h_{m_1}\right)$ is as follows

$$\begin{cases} \frac{\left(D_1\left(r_l^j, h_m\right) + D_1\left(r_{l_1}^j, h_{m_1}\right)\right)}{2} & if\ both\ pairs\ have\ link \\ -\mu & otherwise \end{cases}$$

where $D_1\left(r_l^j, h_m\right) = -\left\| r_l^j - h_m \right\|$. Here we pick the five longest radicals from each protein structure, whether they overlap each other or not. All the protein structures are then compared to each radical and the computed compatibility scores are stored in compatibility vectors.

3.4   Classification

Similarly, the classification step uses the compatibility vectors from previous step as the input and the corresponding protein structures as the output, a backpropagation network is trained as the classifier. The classification step is not modified from the original CTCA method.

4   Experiments

We set up an experiment using a subset of input data that T. Shibuya uses in his Geometric Suffix Tree [14] work in order to compare the performance between the Geometric Suffix Tree and our CTCA method. We divide the myoglobin

Table 1. The protein structure dataset we use in experiment. The names are the protein ID in PDB.

Subset #	Protein structures
1	1a6g, 1a6k, 1a6m, 1a6n, 1abs, 1ajg, 1ajh, 1zai, 1b0b, 1bje
2	1bvc, 1bvd, 1bz6, 1bzp, 1bzr, 1ch1, 1ch2, 1ch3, 1ch5, 1ch7
3	1ch9, 1cik, 1cio, 1co8, 1co9, 1cp0, 1cp5, 1cpw, 1cq2, 1dlw
4	1dm1, 1do1, 1do3, 1do4, 1do7, 1dti, 1dtm, 1duk, 1duo, 1dwr

Table 2. The parameter settings for CTCA protein structure search method in this experiment

Parameter	Value
A	500
B	500
C	$1000/\#$features in the radical
D	$500/80/\#$features in the radical$/\mu/2$
μ	4
ε	-1.0
v_0	0.02
v_{ij}	$\sum_i \sum_j V_{ij} = \#$features in the radical

dataset T. Shibuya uses into subsets of size 10 and use them as small databases for querying the structure. Table 1 lists the dataset we use in the experiment.

For the parameters, we use b=400 and d=5 for the Geometric Suffix Tree. For CTCA, the parameter values are listed in Table 2. Those parameter values are set by the rules given in previous work of using Hopfield network to solve optimization problems [6,13,11].

We use the same query structures as in the Geometric Suffix Tree paper [14]: 103m, amino acide 20-69 and 1f88, amino acid 20-69. Both Geometric Suffix Tree and our method finds nothing in subset 1 and 4. For subset 2, Geometric Suffix Tree finds 5 matches for 103m: 1ch1, 1ch2, 1ch3, 1ch5, 1ch7 and no match for 1f88. Our method finds 1 match for both 103m and 1f88 in 1bz6 chain C.

5 Conclusion

The new method we proposed fully utilizes the 3D geometry information of the protein structure. This is an advantage of our method over other methods since we can incorporate physical or chemical properties of the amino acides into the method to get more precise results. The other advantage of this method is that most of its work can be prepared offline, including the classifier. We only need to work with the unknown protein structure after the system has been built. However, this method also suffers from the same deficiency of other neural network methods in which the training time of the network is indefinite and computation cost grows more than linearly with the number of protein structures involved. The worst part is the Hopfield network designed to find the compatibility. Let the number of features in a radical be n and number of features in a protein strucuture be m. The Hopfield network's complexity is $O(n^2m^2 + n^2m + nm^2)$, which is going to be the system's bottleneck as the invovled radicals and protein structures are longer. This problem could be solved by picking shorter radicals with greater importance either by hand or statistical methods. But we still hope to make this method a generally applicable method with high level of automation[9,8] and least human interference possible. Our future work could be to improve the speed in the compatibility calculation step to make this system to be applicable to larger datasets.

References

1. Brown, N.P., Orengo, C.A., Taylor, W.R.: A protein structure comparison methodology. Computational Chemistry 20, 359–380 (1996)
2. Caianiel, E.R., Capocelli, R.M.: On form and language: The procrustes algorithm for feature extraction. Biological Cybernetics 8, 223–233 (1971)
3. Gao, F., Zaki, M.J.: Psist: Indexing protein structures using suffix trees. In: Proceedings of IEEE Computational Systems Bioinformatics Conference (CSB), pp. 212–222 (2005)
4. Godzik, A., Skolnick, J.: Flexible algorithm for direct multiple alignment of protein structures and sequences. Computer Applications in the Biosciences 10(6), 587–596 (1994)
5. Holm, L., Sander, C.: Protein structure comparison by alignment of distance matrices. Journal of Molecular Biology 233, 123–138 (1993)
6. Hopfield, J.J., Tank, D.W.: Neural computation of decisions in optimization problems. Biological Cybernetics 52, 141–152 (1985)
7. Kabsch, W.: A solution for the best rotation to relate two sets of vectors. Acta Crystallographica A32, 922–923 (1978)
8. Liou, C.-Y.: Backbone structure of hairy memory. In: Kollias, S., Stafylopatis, A., Duch, W., Oja, E. (eds.) ICANN 2006. LNCS, vol. 4132, pp. 688–697. Springer, Heidelberg (2006)
9. Liou, C.-Y., Lin, S.-L.: Finite memory loading in hairy neurons. Natural Computing 5(1), 15–42 (2006)
10. Liou, C.-Y., Yang, H.-C.: Handprinted character recognition based on spatial topology distance measurement. IEEE Transactions on Pattern Analysis and Machine Intelligence 18(9), 941–945 (1996)
11. Liou, C.-Y., Yang, H.-C.: Selective feature-to-feature adhesion for recognition of cursive handprinted characters. IEEE Transactions on Pattern Analysis and Machine Intelligence 21(2), 184–191 (1999)
12. Liou, C.-Y., Yang, H.-C.: Self-organization of high-order receptive fields in recognition of handprinted characters. In: ICONIP, Perth, Australia, November 1999, pp. 1161–1166 (1999)
13. Aiyer, M.N.S.V.B., Fallside, F.: A theoretical investigation into the performance of the hopfield model. IEEE Transactions on Neural Networks 1(2), 204–215 (1990)
14. Shibuya, T.: Geometric suffix tree: A new index structure for protein 3-d structures. In: Lewenstein, M., Valiente, G. (eds.) CPM 2006. LNCS, vol. 4009, pp. 84–93. Springer, Heidelberg (2006)

Unsupervised Anomaly Detection Using HDG-Clustering Algorithm

Cheng-Fa Tsai and Chia-Chen Yen

Department of Management Information Systems,
National Pingtung University of Science and Technology,
91201 Pingtung, Taiwan
{cftsai,m9556001}@mail.npust.edu.tw

Abstract. As intrusion posing a serious security threat in network environments, many network intrusion detection schemes have been proposed in recent years. Most such methods employ signature-based or data-mining based techniques that rely on labeled training data, but cannot detect new types of attacks. Anomaly detection techniques can be adopted to solve this problem with purely normal data. However, extracting these data is a very costly task. Unlike the approaches that rely on labeled data or purely normal data, unsupervised anomaly detection can discover "unseen" attacks by unlabeled data. This investigation presents a new mixed clustering algorithm named HDG-Clustering for unsupervised anomaly detection. The proposed algorithm is evaluated using the 1999 KDD Cup data set. Experimental results indicate that the proposed approach outperforms several existing techniques.

Keywords: data clustering, data mining, intrusion detection, anomaly detection, unsupervised anomaly detection.

1 Introduction

The growth of the Internet has led to increasing attention being paid to security research. Because an intrusion can result in severe damage to networks, robust and effective intrusion detection systems (IDS) need to be developed to protect systems from malicious action.

Many network intrusion detection approaches that have been presented recently. Signature-based methods are widely applied in intrusion detection systems. When the approaches first discover an attack action, the associated traffic pattern is labeled as a signature by human experts. Subsequently, those signature databases are adapted to identify malicious traffic. However, signature-based methods cannot detect new types of attacks.

Other schemes have been implemented by using machine learning algorithms or data mining techniques. These approaches can be classified as misuse detection and anomaly detection. In the former methods, the algorithm is trained with labeled training data, and constructs detection patterns automatically. The detection patterns are obviously similar to the signatures mentioned before. Nonetheless, these algorithms have the same difficulty as signature-based methods in detecting new types of attacks.

M. Ishikawa et al. (Eds.): ICONIP 2007, Part II, LNCS 4985, pp. 356–365, 2008.

In contrast, anomaly detection methods build patterns of normal action, and recognize deviations from these patterns. These approaches can detect new types of attacks, in accordance with the assumptions of [14]. However, they require a set of purely normal data, which is difficult to extract, which may not detect intrusion correctly if it contains traces of intrusions.

To circumvent these problems, this work proposes an unsupervised anomaly detection algorithm by hybridizing hierarchical, density-based and grid-based clustering approaches. Two assumptions regarding the data are revealed as follows:

Assumption 1. The majority of the network connections are from normal traffic. Only X% of traffic is malicious [14].

Assumption 2. The attack traffic is statistically different from normal traffic [14].

If one of these assumptions fails, then the accuracy of the algorithm is poor. For instance, if a similar number of intrusion actions to that of normal action occur, such Bandwidth DoS Attacks, then the intrusion is hard to detect [14]. To maximize the efficiency of the algorithm, this study only employed some of the 41 features, namely those recommended in [12], from the KDD Cup 1999 dataset. The entire detection process involves inputting a set of unlabelled data, and identifying anomalous actions mixed with the normal data. After finishing the identifying process, those labeled data can be adopted to train conventional anomaly detection and misuse detection algorithms.

In the simulation experiment, the proposed **HDG-Clustering** algorithm (**H**ierarchical, **D**ensity-based and **G**rid-based **Clustering**) was compared with those presented in [13], [11] and [14]. These previous approaches were also tested using the training and testing processes with KDD Cup 1999 dataset, which used widely in intrusion research area. As experiment results, the performance of the proposed approach outperforms that of existing techniques.

2   Related Works

Unsupervised anomaly detection approaches are increasingly being applied to network intrusion detection in security research because the approaches can be trained without labeled data. Portnoy proposed a method that automatically discovers both known and unseen intrusions [10]. The method applied a single-linkage clustering to distinguish between intrusion and normal actions. Eskin *et al.* demonstrated the effectiveness in intrusion detection of three algorithms, namely the fixed-width clustering algorithm, an optimized version of the k-nearest neighbor algorithm, and the one-class support vector machine algorithm [11]. Oldmeadow *et al.* developed a clustering-based scheme, and revealed that accuracy is improved when the clusters are adaptive to changing traffic patterns [13].

Data clustering in data mining is fundamental for numerous applications. Several data clustering algorithms have been presented in recent years, subsequently attracting strong attention [1]-[6]. Those approaches can be categorized as partitional, hierarchical, grid-based, density-based and mixed. The algorithms closely related to our investigation are described below.

Density-based clustering approaches measure the density of a region. DBSCAN is a first-density-detecting scheme, which depends on two arguments, namely *Eps* and *MinPts* [7]. *Eps* represents the radius of the search circle, and *MinPts* denotes a number of minimal neighbors in the search circle. These arguments are employed to examine the ε-neighbors contained in each object. By applying this expansion, DBSCAN can accurately recognize any arbitrary pattern and different size clusters, and filters noise.

Grid-based clustering approaches define clusters utilizing grid-cell structures. These approaches consider the grid-cell as a point to enhance the problem of time cost, and can therefore cluster all objects very quickly. CLIQUE integrates grid-based and density-based clustering methods [8]. CLIQUE initially generates a grid map from feature space. For each dimension, the algorithm identifies the high-density units by utilizing the priori approach. Although CLIQUE has a fast clustering time, its cluster boundaries are either horizontal or vertical, due to the nature of the rectangular grid.

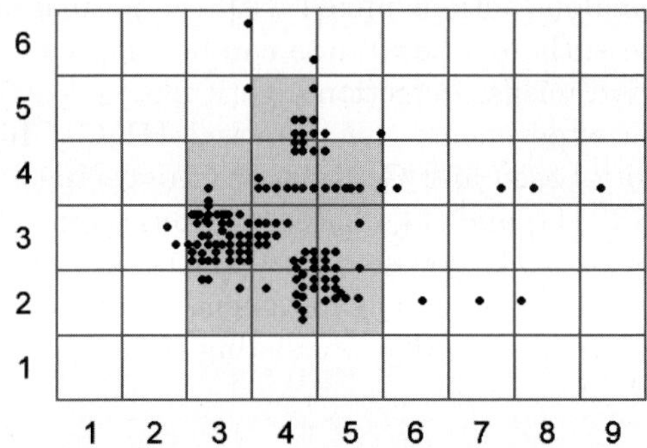

Fig. 1. In the structure of the 2-D cell map, the cells with dark colors are named populated cell

3 The Proposed Algorithm: HDG-Clustering

This section describes the proposed clustering concept, algorithm and its implemented steps in the algorithm step by step as follows:

The basic concept of the proposed clustering can be illustrated in terms of the following four parts.

(1) Feature space slicing and objects assigning: Reducing the number of searching spaces is the main idea of this step. The algorithm inputs the argument of cell's length, and splits the feature space into a cell set that forms a cell structure. Each object of the dataset is assigned to an appropriate cell. A cell is named populated cell if the number of objects in the cell is greater than the threshold Hd. Fig. 1 illustrates this concept.

A populated cell is called a density-tiptop if it has the maximum of objects among all cells. The density-tiptop is the initial point of the search space.

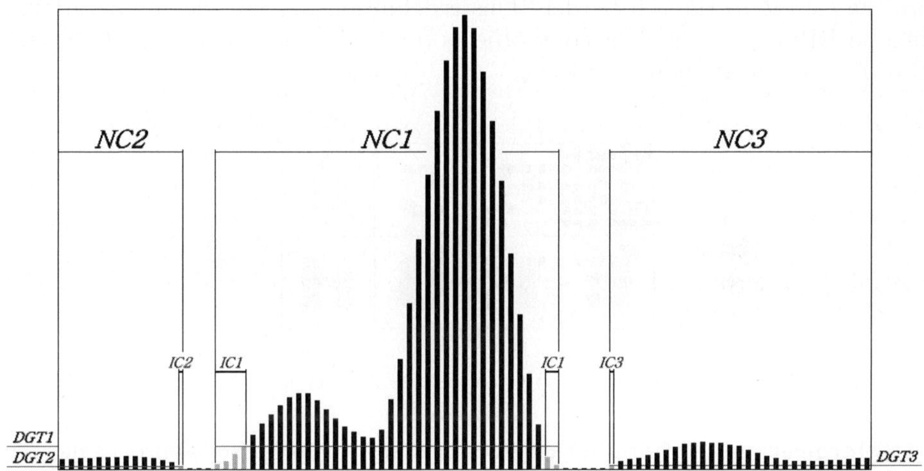

Fig. 2. Sample of Identification of main framework in 1-D feature space

(2) Identifying the main framework: This investigation adopts the dynamic-gradient-threshold as a measure of cell-density detecting preprocesses to discover the main framework of a cluster excluding the cluster edge. The dynamic-gradient-threshold is obtained as follows:

$$DGT = |Ci| * PSV \tag{1}$$

where $|Ci|$ indicates the number of object in cell Ci, and PSV denotes the percentage submontane value, which is the input argument. Fig. 2 depicts an example of the usage of dynamic-gradient-threshold. Every bar in Fig. 2 indicates the number of object in each cell. Since every bar within a cluster may be different, dynamic-gradient-threshold can dynamically determine the cell that would be treated as the main framework. Based on the **Assumption 1** stated above, a cluster such as $NC1$, $NC2$, or $NC3$ represents normal behavior. The areas between the clusters are deviations (noise) from the normal behavior. After computing the dynamic-gradient-threshold, such as $DGT1$, $DGT2$ and $DGT3$, for each normal behavior, the main framework can be identified and assigned directly to a cluster but excluding the areas (namely, cluster edges) representing the number of objects under dynamic-gradient-threshold, given as $IC1$, $IC2$ and

*IC*3. Subsequently, the edge detection method has to be utilized to detect those areas, as displayed on cells B, C, F and G of Fig. 3.

(3) Edge detection: The goal of this step is to detect accurately the edge of a cluster. A populated cell that does not belong to the main framework of the cluster may contain objects belonging to two different clusters, as described on cell B in Fig. 3. Core objects and border objects of the cluster and noise can be recognized by utilizing DBSCAN to perform detection on cells B, C, F and G of Fig. 3. Border objects are redefined as objects, generated by a DBSCAN run, that are the closest to the cell border. This redefinition reduces the computational time in DBSCAN. The light color objects (on the border) on cells B, C, F and G of Fig. 3 indicate border objects.

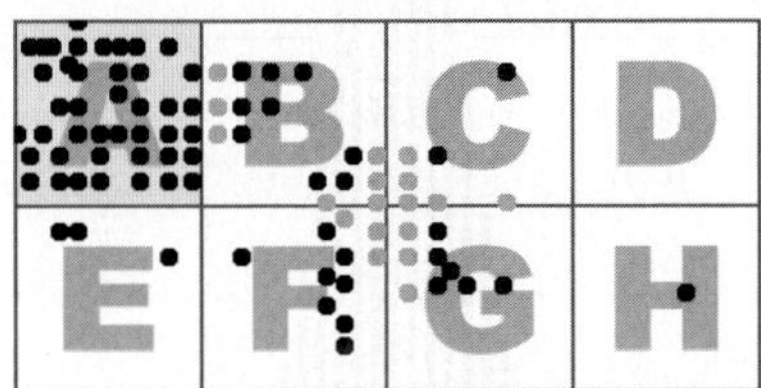

Fig. 3. Illustration of border objects for edge detection in 2-D feature space

(4) Merge stage: After the edge detection stage, the proposed approach merges the edge of the cluster with the main framework of the cluster, depending on which border object is closest to the main framework. The proposed algorithm repeats the process to recognize all clusters.

The HDG-Clustering algorithm can be described as follows:

```
HDG_Clustering(TrainingDataSets,Cl,PSV,Hd,Eps,MinPts)
  Initialization;
  createCellStructure(Cl);
  PopulCells = cacluateCellsInfo(TrainingDataSets,Hd);
  WHILE(TRUE) DO
    C = selectHighestDensityCell(PopulCells);
    IF C = NULL
      END ALGORITHM
    END IF
    DGT = calculateDynamicGradientThreshold(C,PSV);
    IF isDensityAboveSubmontane(C,DGT) == TRUE
      changeClusterId(C,ClusterId);
      searchNeighbors(C,DGT);
    ELSE
      Cs = BSCAN(C,Eps,MinPts);
      MPC = chooseMaxsizeSubcluster(Cs);
```

```
      changeClusterId(MPC,ClusterId);
      searchNeighbors(C,DGT);
    END IF-ELSE
    ClusterId++;
  END WHILE
END HDG_Clustering
```

`TrainingDataSets` represents an entire training dataset or a partial dataset. `Cl` denotes the length of a cell; `PSV` is the percentage submontane value, and `Hd` represents the threshold of the cell's density. `Eps` denotes a search radius, and `MinPts` is the smallest number of objects in the region. The proposed algorithm can be presented step by step below.

Step 1. Initialization of all arguments.
Step 2. `createCellStructure()` function generates the structure of the cell map, and assigns all objects to the appropriate cell.
Step 3. `cacluateCellsInfo()` function filters the cell that the density is below `Hd`, and returns the populated-cell-set `PopulCells`.
Step 4. Repeat the process by while loop.
Step 5. `selectHighestDensityCell()` function gets the density-tiptop from `PopulCells`, and returns to cell C.
Step 6. If cell `C` is null, then stop the algorithm.
Step 7. `calculateDynamicGradientThreshold()` function computes the dynamic-gradient-threshold and returns to DGT.
Step 8. If the density of cell `C` is above `DGT`, then assign cell `C` directly to a cluster, and continue searching neighbors by the `searchNeighbors()` function.
Step 9. Otherwise, the algorithm applies `DBSCAN` for the edge detection and returns a sub-cluster set to `Cs`.
Step 10. Assign a maximal-size sub-cluster `MPC` of `Cs` resulting from a `DBSCAN` run to a cluster utilizing the `changeClusterId()` function.
Step 11. The algorithm then searches the neighbors of the cell `C` with the `searchNeighbors()` function.

The neighbor searching process `searchNeighbors(Cell,DGT)` is as follows:

```
searchNeighbors(Cell,DGT)
  NeighborCells = selectNeighbors(Cell);
  WHILE NeighborCells.length() <> Empty DO
    CurrCell = selectHighestDensity(NeighborCells);
    IF isDensityAboveSubmontane(CurrCell,DGT) == TRUE
      changeClusterId(CurrCell,ClusterId);
      searchNeighbors(CurrCell,DGT);
    ELSE
      NCs = DBSCAN(CurrCell,Eps,MinPts);
      FOR i FROM 1 TO NCs.length() DO
```

```
        IF NCs.SubCluster(i).Borders.areNear(Cell) == TRUE
          changeClusterId(NCs.SubCluster(i),ClusterId);
        END IF
      END FOR
      searchNeighbors(CurrCell,DGT);
    END IF-ELSE
    NeighborCells.removeNeighbor(CurrCell);
  END WHILE
END searchNeighbors
```

The neighbor searching step `searchNeighbors(Cell,DGT)` can be described as follows:

Step 1. The `selectNeighbors()` function returns a set of neighbors `NeighborCells` located on neighborhood of the cell `Cell`.

Step 2. Continue the process until the neighbor set of the cell `Cell` is empty.

Step 3. `selectHighestDensity()` function returns the highest density cell among its neighbor set `NeighborCells` to cell `CurrCell`.

Step 4. As stated above, if the density of cell `CurrCell` is above `DGT`, then it is assigned directly to the same cluster as `Cell` by `changeClusterId()` function, and the neighbors searching continues by the `searchNeighbors()` function recursively.

Step 5. Otherwise, the HDG-Clustering algorithm applies `DBSCAN` for edge detection, and returns a sub-cluster set to `NCs`.

Step 6. Each sub-cluster of `NCs` is assigned to the same cluster as `Cell` if its border objects are close to the cell `Cell`.

Step 7. The algorithm then searches the neighbors of the cell `CurrCell` by the `searchNeighbors()` function recursively.

The process is repeated to merge the whole cluster.

4   Experiment and Analysis

The KDD Cup 1999 data mining competition data set (KDD Cup 1999) was widely adopted for training and testing in the evaluation stage. It originated from the 1998 DARPA Intrusion Detection Evaluation Program performed by MIT Lincoln Labs. The laboratory peppered those data with multiple attacks in a simulative military LAN. The training data set comprised 4.9 million records, and the testing data were composed of 311,029 connections. Notably, the testing data contained new types of abnormal behavior not present in the training data. Each connection included 41 features, including IP addresses, and a sequence of packets starting and ending at some defined times. Connections were labeled as either "normal" or "attack" type.

In the experiment, training data (around 10%) were regenerated from KDD data by filtering out most of the attacks to fit **Assumption 1**. The training

Table 1. Various parameter values used in HDG-Clustering algorithm for anomaly detection

Parameter	Value
Cl	0.135
PSV	0.025
Hd	123
Eps	0.015
MinPts	2

Table 2. Comparison of AUC for various anomaly detection methods

Algorithm	Area Under the Curve
pfMAFIA	0.867
Fixed-width Clustering	0.940
K-NN	0.895
SVM	0.949
Modified Clustering-TV	0.973
HDG-Clustering	0.976

data following filtering consisted of 98.5% normal instances and 1.5% attack instances, totaling 490,000 connections, and the testing data totaled around 61,515 connections, which had the same proportion of normal and attack instances. The parameter values used by HDG-Clustering algorithm are shown in Table 1. A set of clusters was obtained after the clustering phase was finished. The purpose of the proposed algorithm is to cluster the normal connections into several groups. Therefore, only the objects (connections or instances) that fell outside the boundary of the set of clusters were labeled as "anomalies". Subsequently, the testing data was employed in the same manner to measure the accuracy the proposed algorithm.

Two indicators, Detection Rate (DR) and False Positive Rate (FPR), were utilized to measure the performance of the proposed approach. The DR is given by the number of intrusion instances detected by the approach divided by the total number of intrusion instances in the data set; and the FPR is defined as the total number of normal that are incorrectly classified as intrusions divided by the total number of normal instances. The value of DR is generally expected to be high, while that of FPR is usually low.

The analytical results of the proposed **HDG-Clustering** algorithm revealed a trade-off between DR and FPR. Fig. 4 plots the ROC (Receiver Operator Characteristic) graphs of trade-offs from [11], [13] and [14] for comparison. To compare these well-known approaches (pfMAFIA, Fixed-width Clustering, K-NN, SVM, Modified Clustering-TV) accurately [11], [13], [14], the AUC (Area

Under the Curve), which indicates the area under the ROC curve, were applied to determine the performance value, and are shown in Table 2.

In the KDD Cup 1999 dataset, the distribution of the normal instances typically aggregated together, in contrast to that of the anomaly instances. Using these features, the proposed HDG-Clustering algorithm can first filter out the sparse anomaly instances by pruning the cells where the density is less than the threshold Hd. The normal instances can be directly aggregated with cell structure, rather than being partitioned. If some cell contains both normal and intrusion instances, then the segmentation between instances can be cleared by running DBSCAN.

Simulation results reveal that the proposed HDG-Clustering algorithm can achieve a high detection rate with a low false positive rate. Compared to other unsupervised anomaly detection approaches, the proposed method provides better performance over the KDD Cup 1999 dataset.

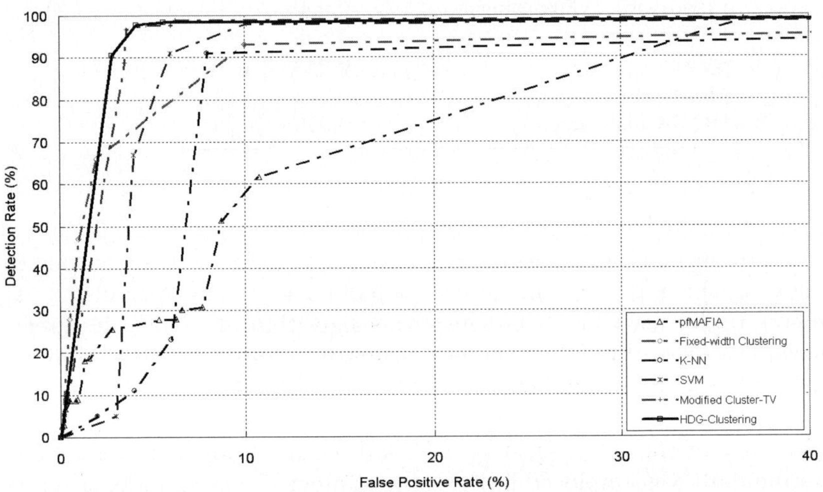

Fig. 4. Comparison of ROC curve for various anomaly detection methods

5   Conclusion

This paper develops a new mixed clustering algorithm called HDG-Clustering for unsupervised anomaly detection. The proposed algorithm can enhance the accuracy of the partitioning clustering approaches for intrusion detection. Additionally, the unlabeled data can be employed directly as training data without coding by human experts. Simulation results demonstrate that the proposed algorithm achieves a high detection rate with a low false positive rate. This feature may enable the proposed algorithm to detect both known and unseen intrusions.

Acknowledgments. The authors would like to thank the National Science Council of the Republic of China, Taiwan for financially supporting this research under Contract No. NSC 95-2221-E-020-036.

References

1. Tsai, C.F., Tsai, C.W., Wu, H.C., Yang, T.: ACODF: A Novel Data Clustering Approach for Data Mining in Large Databases. Journal of Systems and Software 73, 133–145 (2004)
2. Tsai, C.F., Liu, C.W.: KIDBSCAN: A New Efficient Data Clustering Algorithm for Data Mining in Large Databases. In: Rutkowski, L., Tadeusiewicz, R., Zadeh, L.A., Żurada, J.M. (eds.) ICAISC 2006. LNCS (LNAI), vol. 4029, pp. 702–711. Springer, Heidelberg (2006)
3. Tsai, C.F., Wu, H.C., Tsai, C.W.: A New Data Clustering Approach for Data Mining in Large Databases. In: The 6th IEEE International Symposium on Parallel Architectures, Algorithms, and Networks (ISPAN 2002), vol. 11 (2002)
4. Tsai, C.F., Chen, Z.C., Tsai, C.W.: MSGKA: An Efficient Clustering Algorithm for Large Databases. In: 2002 IEEE International Conference on Systems, Man, and Cybernetics, No. WA1D1, Tunisa (2002)
5. Tsai, C.F., Yang, T.: An Intuitional Data Clustering Algorithm for Data Mining in Large Databases. In: 2003 IEEE International Conference on Informatics, Cybernetics, and Systems, Taiwan, pp. 1487–1492 (2003)
6. Tsai, C.F., Yen, C.C.: ANGEL: A New Effective and Efficient Hybrid Clustering Technique for Large Databases. In: Zhou, Z.-H., Li, H., Yang, Q. (eds.) PAKDD 2007. LNCS (LNAI), vol. 4426, pp. 817–824. Springer, Heidelberg (2007)
7. Ester, M., Kriegel, H.P., Sander, J., Xu, X.: A Density-Based Algorithm for Discovering Clusters in Large Spatial Databases with Noise. In: Proceedings of the 2nd International Conference on Knowledge Discovery and Data Mining, pp. 226–231 (1996)
8. Agrawal, R., Gehrke, J., Gunopulos, D., Raghavan, P.: Automatic Subspace Clustering of High Dimensional Data for Data Mining Applications. In: Proceedings of the ACM SIGMOD International Conference on Management of Data, pp. 94–105. ACM Press, Seattle, Washington (1998)
9. KDD: The third international knowledge discovery and data mining tools competition dataset (KDD 1999 Cup), `http://kdd.ics.uci.edu/databases/kddcup99.html`
10. Portnoy, L., Eskin, E., Stolfo, S.: Intrusion detection with unlabeled data using clustering. In: Proceedings of ACM CSS Workshop on Data Mining Applied to Security (2001)
11. Eskin, E., Arnold, A., Prerau, M., Portnoy, L., Stolfo, S.: A geometric framework for unsupervised anomaly detection: Detecting intrusions in unlabeled data. In: Applications of Data Mining in Computer Security (2002)
12. Sung, A.H., Mukkamala, S.: Identify important features for intrusion detection using support vector machines and neural networks. In: Proceedings of the 2003 Symposium on Application and the Internet, pp. 209–216 (2003)
13. Oldmeadow, J., Ravinutala, S., Leckie, C.: Adaptive clustering for network intrusion detection. In: Proceedings of the Third International Pacific-Asia Conference on Knowledge Discovery and Data Mining (2004)
14. Leung, K., Leckie, C.: Unsupervised Anomaly Detection in Network Intrusion Detection Using Clusters. In: Australasian Computer Science Conference, Newcastle, NSW, Australia (2005)

A New Association Rule Mining Algorithm

B. Chandra and Gaurav

Indian Institute of Technology, Delhi
Hauz Khas, New Delhi, India 110 016
bchandra104@yahoo.co.in

Abstract. A new algorithm called STAG (Stacked Graph) for association rule mining has been proposed in this paper using graph theoretic approach. A structure is built by scanning the database only once or at most twice that can be queried for varying levels of minimum support to find frequent item sets. Incremental growth is possible as and when new transactions are added to the database making it suitable for mining data streams. Transaction scanning is independent of the order of items in a transaction. Performance of this algorithm has been compared with other existing algorithms using popular datasets like the mushroom dataset, chess and connect dataset of the UCI data repository. The algorithm excels in performance when the dataset is dense.

Keywords: Association rule mining, minimum support, frequent item set, undirected graph.

1 Introduction

The problem of association rule mining introduced by Agrawal et al. [2] aims at finding frequent item sets according to a user specified minimum support and the association rules according to a user specified minimum confidence. Finding frequent item sets is computationally more expensive than finding association rules. An efficient association rule mining algorithm is highly desired for finding frequent item sets. Apriori, AprioriTID and AprioriHybrid algorithms for association rule mining were developed by Agrawal et al. [3]. All these algorithms find frequent sets in a bottom-up fashion. A combinatorial explosion of item sets occurs when the minimum support is set low amounting to a high execution time. Pincer search algorithm developed by Lin et al. [4] is a 2-way algorithm that conducts a search in both bottom-up and top-down manner. An additional overhead of maintaining the maximal frequent candidate set and maximal frequent set is involved.

FP-Tree growth algorithm developed by J.Han et al. [5] compresses the database into a conditional pattern tree and mines frequent item sets separately. This algorithm incurs an additional cost by processing items in each transaction in the order of increasing support count and heavily uses memory when the dataset is large. Charu Agrawal et al. [1] gave a method for online mining by storing item sets satisfying a minimum support threshold in the form of a directed graph. The approach does not work if the user specified minimum support

M. Ishikawa et al. (Eds.): ICONIP 2007, Part II, LNCS 4985, pp. 366–375, 2008.

is less than the minimum support threshold. Zaki et al. [6] proposed an approach for finding frequent item sets using equivalence classes and hyper graph clique clustering. Hyper graph clique clustering produces more refined candidate sets as compared to equivalence class approach but identifying cliques in a graph is an NP-Complete problem.

The work presented in this paper is a new graph based approach (using one scan and two scans of the database) for finding frequent item sets in Market Basket Data (MBD). The best feature of one scan algorithm is that it requires only one scan of the database. The one scan algorithm aims at reducing the I/O drastically whereas the two scan algorithm reduces the computational time, run time storage and I/O at the same time. The efficiency of these algorithms have been compared with other existing association rule mining algorithms using popular datasets viz. mushroom, chess and connect datasets from the UCI data repository. It has been observed that this algorithm outperforms existing algorithms in dense datasets for lower minimum support.

2   ALGORITHM STAG

A new association rule mining algorithm, STAG (Stacked Graph) has been proposed, based on graph theoretic approach. Two issues have been addressed: the first one aiming at reducing the I/O drastically and the second one to bring a reduction in computational time, run time storage and I/O at the same time. This is achieved by one-scan STAG and two-scan STAG algorithm.

STAG overcomes the difficulty of answering a very low support online query by the user, if used for OLAP purposes. In comparison to disk based algorithms like Apriori, Pincer Search algorithm; it minimizes input-output operations by scanning a database only once or at most twice and the addition of new transactions does not require re-scanning of existing transactions. Some association rule mining algorithms require the items in a transaction to be lexicographically sorted or incorporate an additional step of sorting the items according to support value but there is no such imposition on items in STAG. The order of scanning of transactions is immaterial and the items need not be sorted (using support or lexicographically). The algorithm utilizes a depth first strategy to expand the search space of potential frequent item sets. The experiments with real life data show that it performs especially well in dense datasets i.e. datasets, which have a high average number of items per transaction. The transactions in a market basket data are scanned in their natural order but in the unlikely event of this order being disrupted, a sorting procedure on the numeric transaction identifiers can be incorporated. The algorithm consists of two steps: Building a graph structure (undirected weighted acyclic or cyclic graph with or without self loops) by scanning the transactions in the database and utilizing this structure in the second step to find frequent item sets, without scanning the database again.

2.1 Structure Building

Market basket data (MBD) is represented in the form of a graph denoted by $G(V,E)$ where V = vertex set and E = edge set. The vertex set V is defined as the set of all items occurring in the database i.e. If $I = \{i_1, i_2, \ldots i_n\}$ is the universe of items in a database where i_j is the jth item then $V = I$ and number of vertices, $|V| = n$. The structure building starts by creating a node labeled i, for all $i \in V$. An edge $X \to Y$, marked with the TID t is added to E if two items X and Y co-occur in transaction t. Such edges are called marked edges. Each transaction is scanned starting with the first item present in it and its occurrence with other items in the same transaction is considered to generate marked edges between the corresponding nodes. The structure building has been illustrated using market basket data [4] in horizontal format as shown in Table 1. The Boolean format is given in Table 2. The MBD consists of four transactions i.e. the set of transaction identifiers $T = \{1, 2, 3, 4\}$ and the universe of items, $I = \{1, 2, 3, 4, 5\}$. Considering $V = I$ and $|V| = 5$. For each item $i \in V$, the first step is to create a node labeled i. Figure 1 gives the algorithm for building

Table 1. Market basket data (MBD)

TID	Items
1	1 2 3 4 5
2	1 3
3	1 2
4	1 2 3 4

Table 2. Equivalent Boolean format of MBD

TID	Item1	Item2	Item3	Item4	Item5
1	1	1	1	1	1
2	1	0	1	0	0
3	1	1	0	0	0
4	1	1	1	1	0

the STAG structure. It assumes a Boolean horizontal format of the MBD. Function **BuildNode( )** creates the nodes of the structure by taking the vertex set as its argument. Function **MainFillStructure( )** creates the edges by considering the combinations of items present in the transaction and by passing them and the transaction identifier as parameters to function **AddToTransactionList( )**. $t(i)$ is a Boolean value indicating whether item i is present in transaction t or not. **Counter** $[i][j]$ gives the support of item i with item j and **TransactionList**$[i][j]$ gives the transaction identifiers common to items i and j. The structure is obtained as shown in Fig. 2.

```
BuildNode (VertexSet V)
    {
            for each item i ε V, create a node labeled i.
    }
MainFillStructure (Database D)
    {
      for each transaction t ε T
        for each item i in t such that t(i) = 1 and i = n-1
          for each item j such that t(j) = 1 and i = j = n
            AddToTransactionList(i, j, t)
    }
AddToTransactionList (item i, item j, TID t);
    {
        if item i = item j
            Counter[i] [i] ++
        else
            Counter[i] [j] ++ and Counter[j] [i] ++
            TransactionList[i] [j] = (TransactionList[i] [j]) ∪ t
    }
```

Fig. 1. STAG structure building algorithm

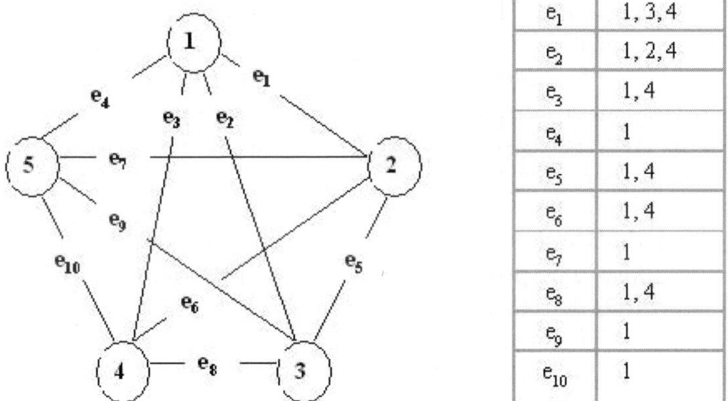

e_1	$1, 3, 4$
e_2	$1, 2, 4$
e_3	$1, 4$
e_4	1
e_5	$1, 4$
e_6	$1, 4$
e_7	1
e_8	$1, 4$
e_9	1
e_{10}	1

Fig. 2. Complete STAG structure

A transaction containing a single item does not contribute to the edge set. Such transactions produce self-loops in the graph structure and contribute only towards increasing the support count of an item.

The support count of an item can be found by taking the union of the list of transactions on the edges touching it and adding the transaction numbers contained in the self loop. For example the support count of item 1 is the union of $\{1, 3, 4\}$, $\{1, 2, 4\}$ $\{1, 4\}$ *and* $\{1\}$. The resulting set obtained has four transaction identifiers $\{1, 2, 3, 4\}$. Since item 1 has no self-loops, the final set has four TIDs, which is the support count of item 1. After building the complete structure we proceed to find the frequent item sets.

2.2   Finding Frequent Item Sets

The algorithm for finding frequent item sets is shown in Fig. 3. It uses a depth first traversal as opposed to a breadth first traversal (used by Apriori, Pincer search algorithm) to find frequent item sets. Stacks facilitate the depth first traversal by storing intermediate particulars like generating item, intersection lists and the large item sets. The following notation is being used in the algorithm. **item-set[item_num][gen_item][]** gives the frequent item set being generated by the item **item_num** using the generating item **gen_item**. IntersectList holds the transaction identifiers resulting from the intersection of transaction lists. The notation $n(x)$ where x is a set gives the number of elements in the set x e.g. **n(IntersectList)** gives the elements in the current intersection list. **minsupp** is the user defined minimum support. The three stacks **S1, S2 and S3** are used for storing the generating item, intersection list and frequent item set respectively. The function **ItemsetGeneration( )** starts by searching for an item i such that **counter**$[i][i]$ is greater than or equal to minsupp . The large item set being generated by item_num with item j is denoted by **item-set [item_num]** $[j]$ $[]$. While locating i and j the intersection list remains null (does not contain any transaction identifiers). Next search for an item $k > j$ such that k is not visited from j and n (TransactionList $[j]$ $[k]$ $\cap$ IntersectList) $\geq$ minsupp. If item k is added to the list of large item set it is termed as a "successful traversal". On a successful traversal (except to the nth item) it is required to store item j in a stack since there might be some item $l > k$ such that $\{i, j, l \ldots\}$ is also a large item set but $\{i, j, k, l \ldots\}$ is not. After scanning the last item , pop the particulars from the three stacks into the appropriate data structures, if the stacks are non-empty. The process is repeated with the popped items and stops when there is no item left to pop. After emptying the stacks, the item next to 'i' is considered. i.e. The algorithm finds an item p such that **counter** $[p]$ $[p]$ is greater than or equal to minsupp and sets i equal to p.

Working of the proposed algorithm has been illustrated on item1 using Fig. 2 and minsupp equal to two in Tables 3 to 6. The following notation is used: $X \to Y$ denotes an edge from item X to item Y, TL (Transaction List), IL (Intersection List), R (Result = TL $\cap$ IL), LI (Large item set), S1 (Stack for the generating item), S2 (Stack for the Intersection List) and S3 (Stack for the large item set). Start with item 1 which has a support of four.

Table 3.

$X \to Y$	TL	IL	R	L1	S1	S2	S3
$1 \to 2$	$\{1, 3, 4\}$	NULL	$\{1, 3, 4\}$	$\{1, 2\}$	NULL	NULL	NULL
$2 \to 3$	$\{1, 4\}$	$\{1, 3, 4\}$	$\{1, 4\}$	$\{1,2,3\}$	2	$\{1, 3, 4\}$	$\{1, 2\}$
$3 \to 4$	$\{1, 4\}$	$\{1, 4\}$	$\{1, 4\}$	$\{1, 2, 3, 4\}$	3	$\{1, 4\}$	$\{1,2,3\}$
$4 \to 5$	$\{1\}$	$\{1, 4\}$	$\{1\}$	$\{1, 2, 3, 4\}$	-same-	-same-	-same-

```
ItemsetGeneration (Counter, TransactionList, minsupp)
  {
    item_num = 1
    While (item_num ≤ n-1)
      {
        If counter [item_num] [item_num] = minsupp)
          {
              Find min j > item_num such that counter [item_num] [j] = minsupp && j
              not visited from item_num

              item-set [item_num] [j] [ ] = item_num ∪ j;
              IntersectList = TransactionList [item_num] [j]
              gen_item = j
Label 1:   While (j < n)
           Find min k > j such that
counter[j] [K] = minsupp && n (IntersectList ∩TransactionList[j] [K]) = minsupp && k ≤ n && k is not
visited from j
              If (k<n)
                Push (S1, gen_item)
                      Push (S2, IntersectList)
                Push (S3, itemset [item_num] [gen_item] [])
                IntersectList = IntersectList  ∩ TransactionList [j] [K]
              item-set [item_num] [gen_item] [] = Itemset [item_num] [gen_item] []∪K
                j = k
              }
          If (j = n or no k found)
            {
              if ( stack is nonempty)
                {
                    j = Pop (S1)
                    IntersectList = Pop (S 2)
                    Itemset [item_num] [gen_item] [ ] = Pop (S3)
                  Goto Label 1;
                }
              }
          Item_num++
        }
            large_itemset [item_num] [gen_item] [] = max (n (itemset [item_num] [gen_item] [ ] ))
    }
```

Fig. 3. Algorithm for finding frequent item sets

Since 5 is the last item, the process of popping the stacks begins.

Table 4.

$X \to Y$	TL	IL	R	L1	S1	S2	S3
$3 \to 5$	{1}	{1, 4}	{1}	{1,2,3}	2	{1, 3, 4}	{1, 2}

No other distinct frequent item set is found with item 3. Since item 5 is the last item the stacks are popped.

Table 5.

$X \to Y$	TL	IL	R	L1	S1	S2	S3
$2 \to 4$	{1, 4}	{1, 3, 4}	{1, 4}	{1, 2, 4}	2	{1, 3, 4}	{1, 2}
$4 \to 5$	{1}	{1, 4}	{1}	{1, 2, 4}	-same-	-same-	-same-

Since traversal from item 4 to 5 is successful, we again push item 2 in the stack S1.

Table 6.

$X \to Y$	TL	IL	R	L1	S1	S2	S3
$2 \to 5$	{1}	{1, 3, 4}	{1}	{1, 2}	NULL	NULL	NULL

The search tree induced by the above example is shown in the Fig. 4: The large item sets found till this point are $\{1, 2\}$, $\{1, 2, 4\}$ *and* $\{1, 2, 3, 4\}$. The algorithm further continues by considering the edge from item $1 \to 3$, $1 \to 4$ and $1 \to 5$. After fully inspecting item 1 the algorithm starts with edges starting with item 2. The largest frequent item set found with item 1 is a 4-item set viz. $\{1, 2, 3, 4\}$.

2.3 One-Scan and Two-Scan Strategies

The algorithm described is called one-scan algorithm since it makes only one pass over the database. One-scan does not take into account the *minsupp* for building the structure. It builds the structure first and then utilizes the *minsupp* for finding the frequent item sets. The elements of vertex set in one-scan is the same as the universe of items i.e. $V = I$ and $|V| = n$. In order to reduce the space and execution time further, we introduce a two-scan algorithm which makes two-passes over the database. The two-scan algorithm first identifies the items that satisfy the *minsupp* by counting the support of 1-item sets from the database (the first pass) and then uses only those items in the vertex set to build the structure. For the two-scan algorithm the vertex set $V \subseteq I$ and $|V| \leq n$. The

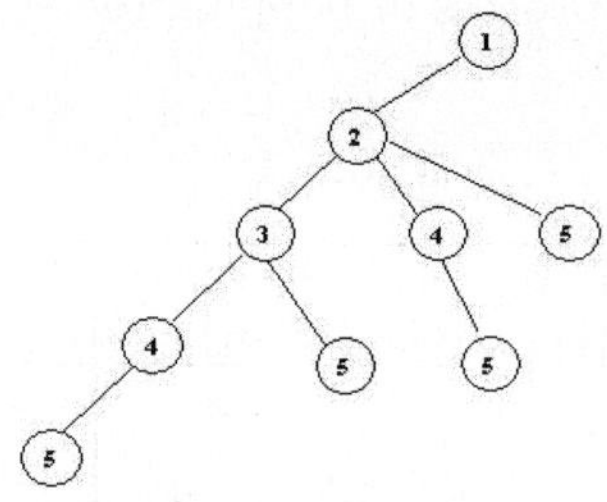

Fig. 4. Search Tree

second pass over the database is used to create the structure using the nodes obtained in the first pass. Hence the two-scan algorithm utilizes the *minsupp* to create the structure and builds a new structure for each different minimum support. Due to reduction in the number of nodes and associated overhead, it performs better than the one-scan algorithm in terms of computational time and run-time storage requirement. Figure 5 shows the structure of STAG using the two-scan strategy with minimum support equal to two.

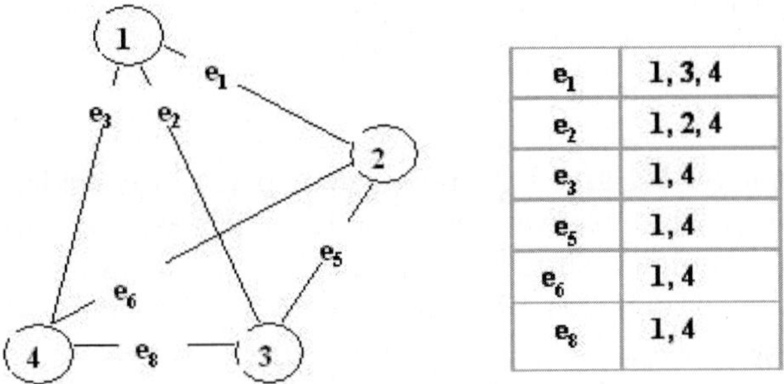

Fig. 5. STAG structure using two-scan strategy

2.4   Early Stopping Criterion for Intersection of Transaction Lists

This section deals with the early stopping criterion for intersection of transaction lists. Let $\{a_1, a_2, \ldots, a_M\}$ denote the current intersection list IL and $\{b_1, b_2, \ldots, b_N\}$ denote the transaction list of item j with item k TL$[j][k]$,β be the minimum support for $a_i < a_j$ and $b_i < b_j \forall\ i < j$.

In the process of finding the intersection of IL and TL$[j][k]$, let the number of common transactions found till the current point be C and the number of transaction identifiers in TL be N. Assume that C common transactions have been found after examining bt (the tth element in TL). The intersection process is stopped if $C + (N - t) < \beta$. This essentially means that if the sum of number of common transactions (C) found till the tth transaction and the transaction identifiers remaining in TL i.e. ($N-t$)) is less than minsupp there is no possibility of item k being added to the large item set generated by item i with j.

3   Results

The performance of STAG (one-scan and two-scan) was compared with Apriori, Pincer search and FP-Tree growth algorithm. Comparison of performance was made by finding frequent item sets on three popular datasets taken from the UCI data repository. All experiments were performed on a system having the following specifications: Speed: 2.66GHz, Pentium 4 Memory: 512MB RAM Operating system: Mandrake Linux 9.2

Table 7, 8 and 9 give the execution time for finding frequent item sets using various algorithms for Chess, Musroom and Connect dataset. In Table 7 and 9 * signifies that the execution time is more than one hour.

Chess Dataset: Total Transactions = 3196 Total Items = 75 All the other

Table 7.

Minsupp	1- Scan	2- Scan	FP-Growth	Apriori	Pincer Search
3000	1	0	0.24	*	*
2000	11	8	1.58	*	*
1000	26	26	136.17	*	*

algorithms except STAG and FP-Tree growth perform considerably slower on this dense dataset. The observations show the effectiveness of STAG in dense databases as the minimum support decreases.

Mushroom Dataset: Total Transactions = 8124 Total Items = 119 Mushroom

Table 8.

Minsupp	1- Scan	2- Scan	Apriori	Pincer Search	FP-Growth
7000	1	1	4	5	0.34
6000	0	0	5	5	0.35
5000	0	0	6	6	0.36
4000	1	1	13	14	0.43
3000	4	2	56	61	0.49
2000	9	6	361	376	0.59

data set is a sparse dataset with few items per transaction. The execution time of one-scan and two-scan show that they are faster than Apriori and Pincer search algorithm but not with respect to FP-tree growth. However in the case of dense datasets like Connect which is shown below, the one-scan and two scan algorithms outperform.

Connect Dataset: Total Transactions = 5000 Total Items = 127

Table 9.

Minsupp	1- Scan	2- Scan	FP-Growth	Apriori	Pincer Search
4000	43	38	10.88	*	*
3000	68	61	143.35	*	*

Connect dataset is more dense than the chess dataset and it is seen from Table one scan and two scan algorithms outperform Apriori and Pincer search algorithms and performs better than FP-Tree growth algorithm for lower minimum support.

4   Conclusion

A new algorithm STAG, for finding frequent item sets in market basket data has been proposed in this paper. The most redeeming feature of this algorithm is that it outperforms all other existing algorithms when the dataset is highly dense. The one-scan strategy scans the database only once but requires a greater amount of memory compared to two-scan strategy. The two-scan strategy performs better than one-scan with respect to computational time and memory. Both the strategies have no imposition on the order of scanning items within transactions or transactions in a database and require very low I/O. The execution time is low in dense datasets that makes them suitable for data mining applications in a memory constrained environment.

References

1. Aggarwal, C.C., Yu, P.S.: Online Generation of Association Rules. In: ICDE Conference (1998)
2. Agrawal, R., Imielinski, T., Srikant, R.: Mining associaton rules between sets of items in large databases. In: SIGMOD (May 1993)
3. Agrawal, R., Srikant, R.: Fast Algorithms for Mining Association Rules. In: Proc. of the 20th Int'l Conf. on Very Large Databases (VLDB 1994), Santiago, Chile (June 1994)
4. Lin, D., Kedem, Z.M.: Pincer-Search: A New Algorithm for Discovering the Maximum Frequent Set. In: Proc. of the Sixth European Conf. on Extending Database Technology (September 1997)
5. Han, J., Pei, J., Yin, Y.: Mining frequent Patterns without Candidate Generation. In: ACM-SIGMOD, Dallas (2000)
6. Zaki, M.J., Parthasarthy, S., Ogihara, M., Li, W.: New Algorithms for Fast Discovery of Association Rules. In: Proc. of the 3rd Int'l Conf. on KDD and Data Mining (KDD 1997), Newport Beach California (August 1997), http://kdd.ics.uci.edu/

A Multi-agent Architecture Based Cooperation and Intelligent Decision Making Method for Multirobot Systems

Tao Yang[1], Jia Ma[1], Zeng-Guang Hou[1], Gang Peng[2], and Min Tan[1]

[1] Key Laboratory of Complex Systems and Intelligence Science,
Institute of Automation, Chinese Academy of Sciences, Beijing 100080, China
{yangtao, jia.ma, zengguang.hou, min.tan}@ia.ac.cn
[2] Department of Control Science and Control Engineering,
Huazhong University of Science and Technology, Wuhan 430074, China
penggg@263.net

Abstract. The design of a hybrid multi-agent architecture is proposed for multirobot systems. Analysis of the architecture shows that it is suitable for multirobot systems dealing with changing environments. Meanwhile, it is capable of controlling a group of robots to accomplish multiple tasks simultaneously. Two associated issues about the architecture are cooperation between robots and intelligent decision making. Ability vector, cost function and reward function are used as criteria to describe and solve the role assignment problem in multirobot cooperation. A solution of information fusion based on RBF neural networks is applied to solve the reality problem in decision making of multirobot systems. And an experiment about robot soccer shooting is designed. The experimental results verify that the method can improve the whole decision system in accuracy.

1   Introduction

In many practical applications, a multirobot system is usually faster and more efficiently than a single powerful robot to accomplish complex or heavy tasks. The advantages of multirobot systems are as follows:

An overall task can be separated into several parts which can be executed simultaneously by a robot team. Multiple robots can accomplish performance benefits and are not spatially constrained as a single robot. Compared with developing a versatile robot, multirobot system is actually the combination of lots of robots with various simple functions. So building and using several simple robots can be easier, cheaper, more flexible and more fault tolerant than having a single powerful robot for each separate task [1].

Multirobot systems can improve performance and reliability; however, in multirobot systems the most challenging task is the coordination and cooperation of these robots to satisfactorily perform the overall mission [2]. Many researches have focused on this issue [3-5]. Among them, the method based on multi-agent system can give us a good way to solve the problem.

M. Ishikawa et al. (Eds.): ICONIP 2007, Part II, LNCS 4985, pp. 376–385, 2008.

The multi-agent system (MAS) is an emerging subfield of artificial intelligence (AI) and is one of the two sub-disciplines of distributed artificial intelligence (DAI) [6]. It tries to provide principles for construction of complex system, involving multiple agents and mechanisms for coordination of independent agents' behaviors [2].

An efficient intelligent control structure of MAS is the foundation for multi-robot systems to handle uncertainty and complexity and achieve the goal in the dynamic environments. The major structures proposed by many researches [7-9] can be categorized into two general types: hierarchical structures and behavioral structures.

In a hierarchical structure, information flows from sensors to high-level decision units in a fixed way, then the decision units send commands to low-level actuator units. Agents in this structure are cognitive, but the structure has poor flexibility. So it is difficult to adapt to modern robotic systems. In a behavioral structure, control problem is broken into behaviors without any central intelligent agent present [1]. So high-level decisions are usually difficult to achieve. A hybrid structure which combines hierarchical structure and behavioral structure can be designed to get rid of drawbacks associated with the above two and can help to develop practical and powerful multirobot systems.

From the standpoint of MAS, an individual robot with the abilities of domain knowledge, action selection and communication with others is considered an agent in multirobot systems. A system made up of this kind of robots can be treated as a MAS. Robot soccer system is a good example of multirobot systems. Soccer robots must work together (cooperation). They play the game in unpredictable conditions. Also they decide which actions to be selected in order to put the ball in opponent's goal. As what is mentioned above, the robot soccer system is always discussed as a test benchmark for MAS. In this paper, robot shooting decision is considered as a test bed for the hybrid MAS architecture.

This paper is organized as follows. Architecture of MAS is described in detail in Section 2. Section 3 presents function of cooperation module in this architecture. Function of another module, decision making module, is presented in Section 4. And a shooting decision in robot soccer system is designed to verify the effectiveness of the module. Concluding remarks are given in Section 5.

2   The Proposed Architecture

Fig. 1 shows the basic diagram of MAS architecture for multirobot systems. As mentioned in section 1, it is a hybrid architecture, including high-level deliberative agents and low-level reactive agents. What's more, in terms of [1], the agents in a MAS may have homogeneous or heterogeneous structures. To most multirobot systems, agents must have different goals, knowledge and actions, they receive different sensory inputs, meanwhile, they have to cooperate each other in order to accomplish some complex tasks. So the architecture must be heterogeneous, which is composed of various agents.

Agents are classified as three types: host agent, logic agent and physical agent in [10]. The classification meets the specification of real multirobot systems. The MAS architecture presented in this section also consists of master agent and real robot which is the combination of reasoning agent and actuator agent.

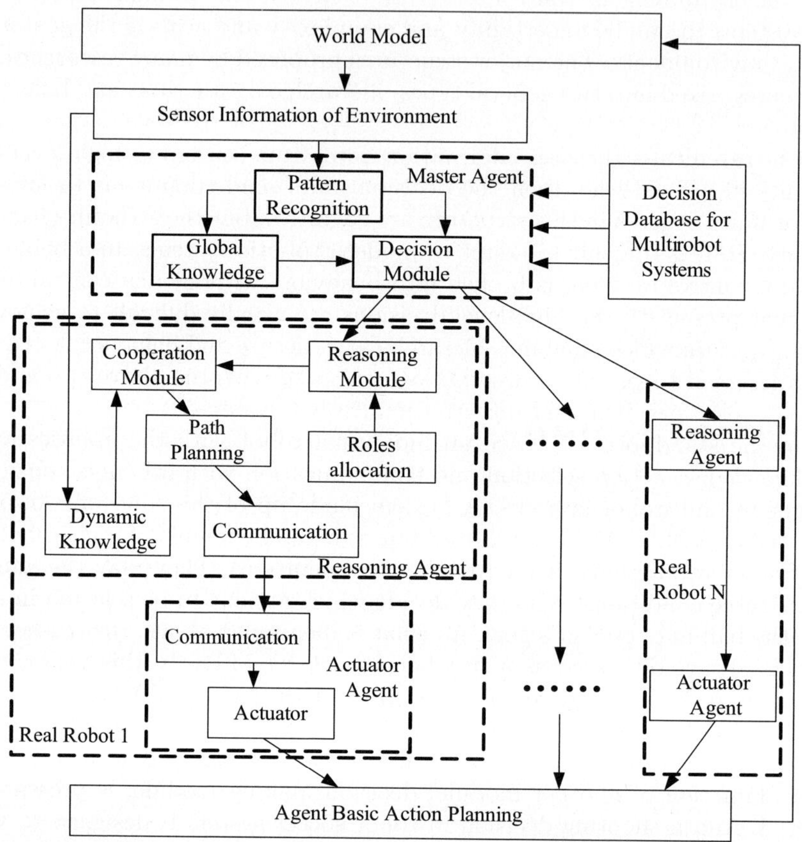

Fig. 1. A hybrid MAS architecture for multirobot systems

Master agent consists of strategies knowledge in global knowledge database, static knowledge and rational rules. Reasoning agent consists of dynamic knowledge database, reasoning and path planning. The components of dynamic knowledge include characteristics of robots and the objectives to be achieved. Each robot has its own reasoning agent, which can decide the path planning and share useful information with other robots. Actuator agent refers to mechanical and electrical devices of a robot. It can receive commands sent to the actuators of the robot and execute basic movement behaviors.

The architecture is a kind of reconstruction of multi-agent logic structure. It is not a straightforward compounding-form based on hierarchical and behavioral structures, but a joint intension framework of hierarchical reasoning and shared plan. The advantages are as follows:

(1) Robustness and fault tolerance. According to this architecture, breakdown of an individual robot will have little effect on the whole team, because of the existence of master agent; that is, the master agent has the ability to reallocate new roles to other reasoning agents and reconstruct team work.

(2) Real-time reactive ability. The architecture is a model based on knowledge and planning, which combines deliberative agents and reactive agents. On one hand, Agents behave more like they are thinking, by searching through a space of knowledge stored before, making a decision about action selection and predicting the effects of actions. On the other hand, Agents can simply retrieve present behaviors similar to reflexes without maintaining any rational reasoning. So multirobot systems based on this parallel distributed mechanism can fulfill the requirements of dynamic, complex and unpredictable environments.

(3) Flexibility. Agents with global or dynamic knowledge database can learn from experiences and learn from each other, so as to adapt themselves to dynamic environments. If a new agent can help to achieve the goal, it will be authorized to join the team by master agent. Accordingly the scale of teamwork can be enlarged.

(4) Simplification of reasoning process. Because it is not an efficient method to change strategies frequently for a certain task, design of master agents can be simplified. Reasoning agents become important parts of decision making system. The problem of collision between robots should be solved by means of negotiation. So the reasoning ability improves a lot.

As a result, the makeup of the hybrid architecture helps to coordinate planning activities with real-time reactive behaviors to deal with dynamic environments.

When the architecture is applied to real multirobot systems, there are several important functions that need to be performed. The associated issues are cooperation and intelligent decision making. Details of the two issues will be discussed in next two sections.

3   Role Assignment of Multirobot Systems

When multirobot systems accomplish a task by means of cooperation, how to assign roles of robots properly is a challenging problem. In order to implement team work, dynamic role assignment is acquired according to various robots' states.

Now, "ability vector" is introduced to describe whether a robot is able to accomplish its task. Generally speaking, a robot has various abilities including sensory and executive abilities. To a task, only when robots' abilities meet with it, can the objective be achieved.

"Ability set" C is defined, which is made up of unitary ability c_i , $1 \leq i \leq n$.

The ability T_j to accomplish a certain task is a linear combination of unitary ability c_i:

$$\hat{T}_j = \sum_{i=1}^{n} t_{ji} \cdot c_i, \quad j \in N, \quad t_{ji} \geq 0. \tag{1}$$

where t_{ji} is the weight value of c_i.

Correspondingly, R_j is used to describe the robot's ability.

$$R_j = \sum_{i=1}^{n} r_{ji} \cdot c_i, \quad j \in N, \quad r_{ji} \geq 0. \tag{2}$$

where r_{ji} is the weight value of c_i.

If the robot is competent for the task, $R_j \geq T_j$.

A task at different stages requires different abilities; that is, to fulfill the task, r_{ji} should change to correspond to the change of t_{ji}

Ability vector A_t is defined to describe various required abilities for the whole task.

$$A_t = \begin{pmatrix} t_{11} & t_{12} & \cdots & t_{1j} & \cdots & t_{1n} \\ t_{21} & t_{22} & \cdots & t_{2j} & \cdots & t_{2n} \\ \cdots & \cdots & \cdots & \cdots & \cdots & \cdots \\ t_{m1} & t_{m2} & \cdots & t_{mj} & \cdots & t_{mn} \end{pmatrix} \cdot \begin{pmatrix} c_1 \\ c_2 \\ \vdots \\ c_n \end{pmatrix} \tag{3}$$

where, $t_{ij} \geq 0$. When the task doesn't require the unitary ability c_i, $t_{ij} = 0$

And correspondingly, A_r describes various abilities of a robot to the task.

$$A_r = \begin{pmatrix} r_{11} & r_{12} & \cdots & r_{1j} & \cdots & r_{1n} \\ r_{21} & r_{22} & \cdots & r_{2j} & \cdots & r_{2n} \\ \cdots & \cdots & \cdots & \cdots & \cdots & \cdots \\ r_{m1} & r_{m2} & \cdots & r_{mj} & \cdots & r_{mn} \end{pmatrix} \cdot \begin{pmatrix} c_1 \\ c_2 \\ \vdots \\ c_n \end{pmatrix} \tag{4}$$

where, $r_{ij} \geq 0$. When the robot doesn't have the unitary ability c_i, $r_{ij} = 0$

So if a robot is fully qualified to the task, $A_r(i) \geq A_t(i)$, $\quad i = 1, \cdots, m$

Cost function $f(\text{cost})$ is defined to represent the cost with which a robot is capable of accomplishing a task, for example, spending a period of time and consuming a quantity of energy. After task accomplished, a robot will be rewarded. Reward function $f(\text{rewd})$ is defined to represent the reward. So according to equations (1)-(4), we can get the benefit from these two functions:

$$b_i = \begin{cases} f_i(\text{rewd}) - f_i(\text{cost}), & \text{if } A_r(i) \geq A_t(i) \text{ and } f_i(\text{rewd}) \geq f_i(\text{cost}) \\ 0 & \text{else} \end{cases} \tag{5}$$

By adopting this form of description, a robot's ability and a task can be described in detail. And the role assignment can be implemented in terms of maximizing the benefit, which is calculated by the specific design of cost function and reward function. Elements, for example, the distance from robot to ball and the distance between two robots, etc. have been taken into account for soccer robots cooperation in [11].

4   Intelligent Decision Making

In multirobot systems based on MAS, each robot is autonomous; that is, it can make decision independently by global or local information. But as what is mentioned in most robotics domains, sensors are noisy, action must be selected under time pressure. An effective decision making method is in great demand. As the tasks and environments become increasingly complex, decision making system can help a group of robots to coordinate their limited physical and computational resources effectively, and ensure that the robots will achieve their complex tasks in dynamic environments.

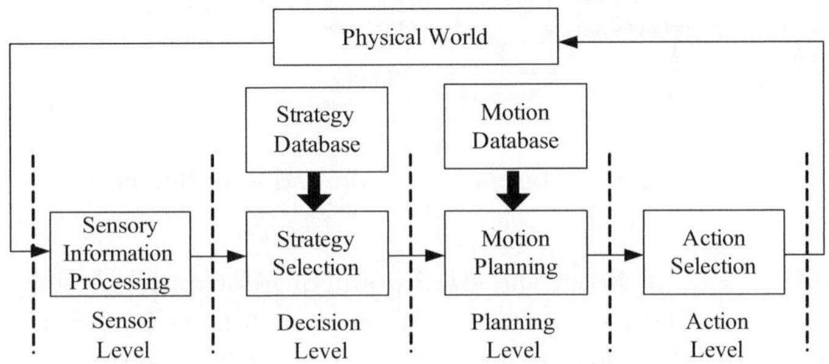

Fig. 2. A structure of decision making system

As what is mentioned in most researches, for example [12] [13], effective structures of decision making systems are almost all hierarchical. The structure of a decision making system is shown in Fig. 2, which consists of sensor level, decision level, planning level and action level. As a result, this hierarchical structure improves the efficiency and robustness of the robot decision.

Conventional decision algorithms always rely on the above decision structure presented in Fig. 2. While in most multirobot systems, reasoning methods often fail to handle large quantities of complex domains. Robots must have the abilities to learn from experiences as opposed to existing "If- Then" rules.

4.1   Information Fusion and Neural Networks

An information fusion decision method based on radial basis function neural networks (RBFNN) is proposed to solve the problem of learning from experiences. A typical example of multirobot systems, robot soccer, is used as test bed to verify the efficiency of the method.

Obviously, there are various sources of sensory information received by multirobot systems, for example ultra-sonic, laser-ranger, vision, etc. To robot soccer, raw information which can directly be obtained include coordinates of teammates, opponents (robots) and the ball; moving directions of robots; velocities of robots and the ball; predicted positions of robots; distances and angles between robots. Resources of information fusion made up of these data are the basis of next step decision.

Here a three-layered parallel information fusion structure is adopted for the decision system, which is proposed by Thomopoulos [14]. The parallel structure is constituted with sensor layer, reasoning layer and decision layer as is presented

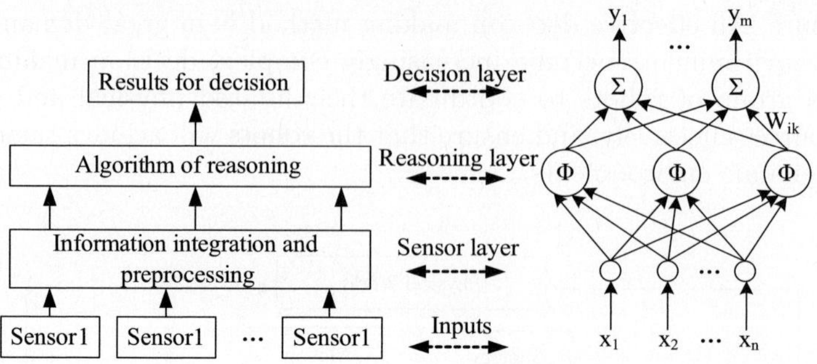

Fig. 3. A layered structure of information fusion and a feedforward neural networks

in the left side of Fig. 3. From the standpoint of information fusion and neural networks, the layered structure and function of each layer in information fusion totally correspond with those of neural networks. Fig. 3 shows the correspondence between information fusion structure and a feedforward neural networks with a single hidden layer.

An intelligent decision system in robot soccer usually involves huge state spaces, RBFNN poses as an attractive method for the task.

4.2   A Brief Introduction to RBFNN

The architecture of the RBFNN is presented in the right side of Fig. 3. The network contains a single hidden layer of neurons which are completely linked to input and output layers. The output of the RBFNN is calculated according to [15]:

$$y_i = f_i(x) = \sum_{k=1}^{N} w_{ik}\phi_k(x, c_k) = \sum_{k=1}^{N} w_{ik}\phi_k(\|x - c_k\|_2), \quad i = 1, 2, \cdots, m \quad (6)$$

where $x \in R^n$ is an input vector, $\phi_k(\cdot)$ is the activation function of hidden layer, $\|\cdot\|_2$ denotes the Euclidean norm, w_{ik} is the weight from the hidden layer to output layer, N is the number of neurons in hidden layer, and $c_k \in R^n$ is the radial basis function (RBF) center of neuron in the input vector space.

The form of activation function $\phi_k(\cdot)$ in the hidden layer is nonlinear function with radial symmetry. In practical applications, the most widely used RBF is the Gaussian kernel function as the functional form: $\phi(x) = \exp\left[-\dfrac{(x - c_k)^T(x - c_k)}{2\sigma^2}\right]$, where parameter σ is the radius that controls the "width" of RBF [15]. Detailed training algorithm for a RBFNN is also described in [15].

4.3   An Experiment in Robot Soccer System

In a robot soccer system, in order to win the game robots must ceaselessly make decisions, for example interception, obstacle avoidance, cooperation each other,

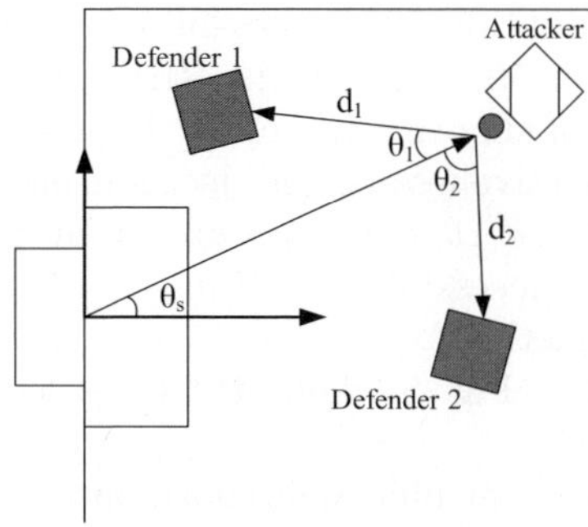

Fig. 4. Resources of information in robot soccer game

etc. Among them shooting is one of the important decisions. When an attacker is facing two defenders, an experiment about how to decide shooting angles is design to verify the effectiveness of the decision method mentioned above.

The following important information should be taken into account in the game. (1) Real-time data $\{x_i, y_i, \theta_i\}$, where (x_i, y_i) denote the current positions of robots and ball, θ_i denote the direction angle of robots. (2) Prediction data $\{x_i, y_i, \theta_i\}$, which represent the next positions and direction angles of robots and ball. (3) Command data $\{v_l, v_r, x, y, \theta\}$, v_l, v_r are the command of wheels' velocity, (x, y, θ) is the desired position and direction. Under the shooting condition, the data above should be preprocessed so as to be used to make decision.

The input vector to the network consists of four components $\langle d_1, \theta_{d1}, d_2, \theta_{d2} \rangle$ shown in Fig. 4. d_1, d_2 are distances between ball and two defenders respectively; θ_{d1}, θ_{d2} are angles between ball and two defenders respectively. The output to the network is θ_s, the desired angle of shooting.

Training set is necessary for the training of neural networks. A software "referee" manages the beginning and the end of training. Data for training are put into database respectively according to success and failure. Attacker is directed to shoot, while two defenders try to intercept the ball. Only if ball is put into the goal is the shooting successful and vice versa.

The position of attacker should be initialized stochastically, which is between 1 and 1.5 meters from goal. And two defenders are situated randomly between goal and attacker. The steps to be followed to obtain the training data are described below:

Step 1: Shooting angle is set to θ_s;

Step 2: Defenders rotate to face the ball if the distance between ball and goal is greater than 1 meter;

Step 3: If the distance between ball and goal is less than 1 meter, five components $\langle \theta_s, d_1, \theta_{d1}, d_2, \theta_{d2} \rangle$ are recorded and defenders rotate a random angle A between $-45°$ and $45°$;

Step 4: After Step 3, defenders try to intercept the ball;

Step 5: If shooting is successful (interception is failure), the experimental data will be sent to database, otherwise return to step 1.

The above method is to obtain 597 successful training data from 1000 experiments (the rate of success is 59.7%) then the RBFNN trained by these data can be used to make decision of shooting in online robot soccer games.

To demonstrate the effectiveness of the decision method based on RBFNN, several combinations of $\langle \theta_s, d_1, \theta_{d1}, d_2, \theta_{d2} \rangle$ are input to the trained networks. As a result, there are 224 successful scoring in 300 experiments, which is much better than conventional methods.

Illustrations are shown in Fig. 5 when attacker selects a successful shooting angle. Where,

(a) Defenders are in different phases of coordinate.

(b) Defenders are in the same phase of coordinate.

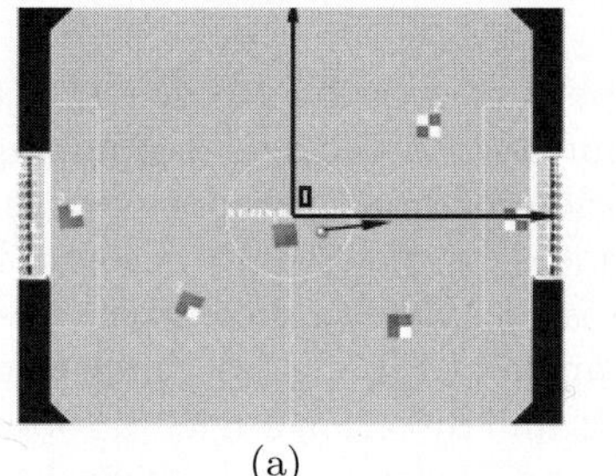 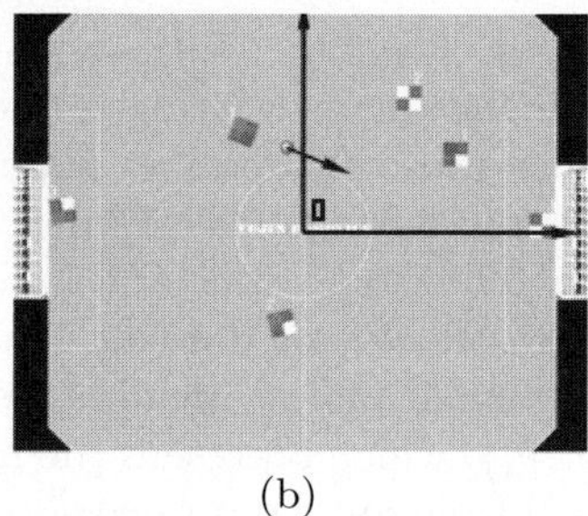

(a)   (b)

Fig. 5. Experimental results of soccer robot shooting decision

5   Conclusions and Future Work

A hybrid architecture of MAS, the role assignment method for cooperation and decision making based on RBFNN are proposed for multirobot systems. The architecture is composed of master agent and real robot that consists of reasoning agent and actuator agent. The favorable features of the architecture are as follows: **(1)** robustness and fault tolerance; **(2)** real-time reactive ability; **(3)** flexibility; **(4)** simplification of reasoning process. So the architecture, which is a combination of hierarchical and behavioral structures can meet the design specification of multirobot systems. Ability vector is used to describe the abilities of a robot and the abilities required for accomplishing a task. According to benefits calculated from reward function and cost function, role assignment can be implemented in an efficient way for cooperation between robots. Compared with conventional methods of decision making, a solution of decision based on RBFNN is more effective to improve the whole decision system. Results of shooting experiment in robot soccer game verify the efficiency and the effectiveness of the method.

The architecture and related issues are put forward to study the multirobot systems. In the opinion of the paper, the architecture should be further improved and be the basis for future research in the evaluation of multirobot systems.

References

1. Kim, J.H., Vadakkepat, P.: Multi-agent systems: a survey from the robot-soccer perspective. Intelligent Automation and Soft Computing 1, 3–17 (2000)
2. Zhu, A., Yang, S.X.: A som-based multi-agent architecture for multirobot systems. International Journal of Robotics and Automation 21, 92–99 (2006)
3. Parker, L.E., Emmons, B.A.: Cooperative multi-robot observation of multiple moving targets. In: Proceedings of the IEEE International Conference on Robotics and Automation, vol. 3, pp. 2082–2089 (1997)
4. Kube, C.R., Bonabeau, E.: Cooperative transport by ants and robots. Robotics and Autonomous Systems 30, 85–101 (2000)
5. Cao, Y., Fukunaga, A.S., Kahng, A.B.: Cooperative mobile robotics: Antecedents and Directions. Autonomous Robots 4, 1–23 (1997)
6. Stone, P., Veloso, M.: Multiagent systems: a survey from a machine learning perspective. Autonomous Robotics 8, 1–57 (2000)
7. Parker, L.E.: ALLIANCE: an architecture for fault tolerant multirobot cooperation. IEEE Transactions on Robotics and Automation 14, 220–240 (1998)
8. Yen, J., Yin, J.W., et al.: CAST: collaborative agents for simulating teamwork. In: The Seventeenth International Joint Conference on Artificial Intelligence, pp. 1135–1144 (2001)
9. Tambe, M.: Towards flexible teamwork. Journal of Artificial Intelligence Research 7, 83–124 (1997)
10. Tang, P., Yang, Y.M.: Study on multi-agent system and the structure of soccer game system. Journal of Guangdong University of Technology 18, 1–4 (2001)
11. Stone, P.: Layered learning in multi-agent systems. PhD. thesis. School of Computer Science Carnegie Mellon University Pittsburgh (1998)
12. Brumitt, B.L., Stentz, A.: Dynamic mission planning for multiple mobile robots. In: Proceedings of IEEE International Conference on Robotics and Automation, vol. 3, pp. 2396–2401 (1996)
13. Stone, P., Veloso, M.: Task decomposition, dynamic role assignment, and low bandwidth communication for real-time strategic teamwork. Artificial Intelligence 110, 241–273 (1999)
14. Thomopoulos, S.: Senor integration and data fusion. Journal of Robotic Systems 33, 337–372 (1990)
15. Ham, F.M., Kostanic, I.: Principles of neurocomputing for science and engineering. McGraw-Hill Science/Engineering/Math., pp. 140–162 (2000)

Hybrid Fuzzy Colour Processing and Learning

Daniel P. Playne, Vrushank D. Mehta,
Napoleon H. Reyes, and Andre L. C. Barczak

Massey University, Auckland, New Zealand
dan.p@dcmd.co.nz, v.mehta@direction.biz, n.h.reyes@massey.ac.nz,
a.l.barczak@massey.ac.nz

Abstract. We present a robust fuzzy colour processing system with automatic rule extraction and colour descriptors calibration for accurate colour object recognition and tracking in real-time. The system is anchored on the fusion of fuzzy colour contrast rules that operate on the red, green and blue channels independently and adaptively to compensate for the effects of glare, shadow, and illumination variations in an indoor environment. The system also utilises a pie-slice colour classification technique in a modified rg-chromaticity space. Now, colour operations can be defined linguistically to allow a vision system to discriminate between similarly coloured objects more effectively. The validity and generality of the proposed fuzzy colour processing system is analysed by examining the complete mapping of the fuzzy colour contrast rules for each target colour object under different illumination intensities with the presence of similarly coloured objects. The colour calibration algorithm is able to extract colour descriptors in a matter of seconds as compared to manual calibration usually taking hours to complete. Using the robot soccer environment as a test bed, the algorithm is able to calibrate colours with excellent accuracy.

Keywords. Computing with colours, fuzzy colour processing, computer vision, colour-object recognition.

1 Introduction

The process of characterizing a compendium of colours depicting an object in a dynamic environment for object recognition and tracking tasks needs to account for all confounding effects in the imaging system due to spatially varying illumination, presence of similarly coloured objects, lens focus, object rotation, shadows and sensitivities of the camera [1,2,3]. It is known that the colour descriptors transform non-linearly in the colour space due to these effects [1,2] and there are studies providing means of coping up with the problem [1,2,4,5,6,7]; however, the complexity of the calibration of the colour descriptors is proportional to the algorithms adaptability and robustness. In the human visual system, the qualities we assign to our perception of colour arise from our intuitive experience of colour. Colour perception underlies many complex processes that involve the photoreceptors in the retina as well as higher level processing mechanisms in the brain. Even to date, some of the intricacies in the mechanisms

M. Ishikawa et al. (Eds.): ICONIP 2007, Part II, LNCS 4985, pp. 386–395, 2008.
© Springer-Verlag Berlin Heidelberg 2008

involved still remain to be unveiled. Nonetheless, findings in neurophysiological researches suggest that contrast computation precedes segmentation [8], and that the human colour perception system possess the ability to recognize colours adaptively and consistently despite changes in the spectral illuminant [9,1]. In this research, we mimic to a minimal extent the contrast computation mechanisms by employing the fusion of fuzzy colour contrast operations on the colour channels adaptively. Fuzzy logic is the computational paradigm of choice in this work as it lends itself amenable to solving problems involving many ambiguities and noise in the sensory inputs [10]. In addition, the system allows for the ease of use of linguistic terms in defining the colour contrast operations for the target colours at hand. As compared to other knowledge-based fuzzy colour processing systems [11,12], the proposed approach focuses on employing fuzzy colour correction steps first prior to colour classification rather than merely fuzzifying the colour sensed values to account for ambiguities in the definition of colour descriptors. Previously, in [6], the fuzzy colour contrast fusion algorithm was tested for its applicability to work in different colour spaces. It was reported that the algorithm successfully improved the colour classification task in the YUV, HSI and rg-chromaticity colour spaces. However, there is one major drawback in the system described; that is, the fuzzy colour contrast rules as well as the colour descriptors used were all derived through rigorous manual calibration, usually taking several hours to complete, especially for a wide range of target colour objects. In this research we improved and extended fuzzy colour contrast fusion by incorporating colour learning algorithms that automatically resolve the issue of finding the best combination of fuzzy colour contrast rules and fine-tuning the colour descriptors. Results show that the rules and colour descriptors extracted automatically by the system is superior to manually derived ones, and calculated only at a fraction of time of manual calibration. Lastly, the robot soccer environment can provide the ultimate test bed for the proposed algorithms as the game requires object tracking in a span of less than 33 msec., in a dynamic and adversarial environment.

2   General System Architecture

The proposed fuzzy colour processing system is comprised of a myriad of novel algorithms that are combined together. The system architecture depicted in Fig. 1 is used for the automatic fine-tuning of the colour descriptors and for the generation, evaluation and discovery of the best combination of fuzzy colour contrast rules. Once all the rules and colour descriptors are extracted and refined, the system generates a look-up table of all possible colours that can be seen by the system (16.7 million pre-classified colours) for real-time colour object recognition and tracking. An overview of the functionalities of the main components and their interdependencies is discussed in this section while the next succeeding section zeroes-in on each of the components of the system, providing more details on them.

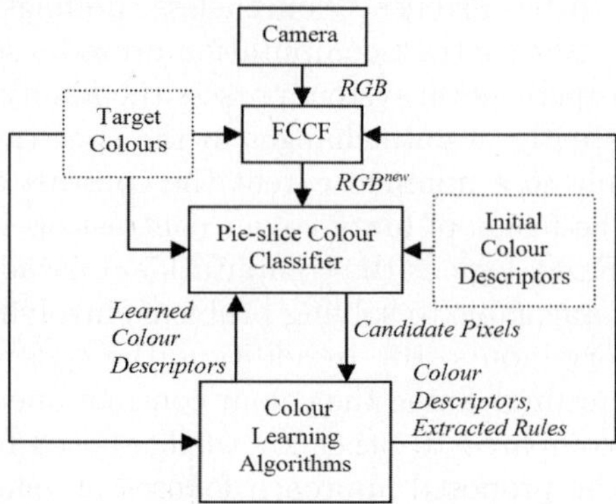

Fig. 1. General system architecture

At the top of the diagram (Fig. 1) is the camera component which returns the colour tri-stimulus in R, G and B values. The colour sensed values are then fed to the Fuzzy Colour Contrast Fusion (FCCF) algorithm which applies colour corrections on the colour tri-stimulus to allow for more accurate colour discrimination. FCCF however relies on the fuzzy colour rule-base and fine-tuned colour descriptors produced by the Colour Learning Algorithms, namely the Motion-based Predictive Colour Learning algorithm (MPCL) and the Colour Contrast Rule Extraction algorithm (CCRE). Lastly, the system employs the pie-slice colour classification technique which receives the corrected R, G, B values from the FCCF component and the refined colour descriptors from the Colour Learning Algorithms. The pie-slice colour classifier determines if the pixel being examined belongs to any of the target colour objects.

3   The Algorithms

3.1   Fuzzy Colour Contrast Fusion

It is adamant that the colours depicting an object must be adaptively corrected based on the relative illumination conditions of the environment they are exposed to. FCCF adaptively performs colour correction by either colour contrast enhancing or degrading the colour channels at different levels of intensity, prior to classifying the sensed colour tri-stimulus. For each target colour at hand (e.g. pink, orange), the RGB components will receive a unique set of fuzzy colour contrast operations.

Enhance or degrade operations are implemented via non-linear functions [3]. Figure 2 depicts the curve exhibiting the contrast enhance operator applied in different levels (1x, 2x, 3x, etc). The input signal can be any of the normalized RGB components within the range $[0, 1]$. In turn, the function amplifies input values greater than 0.5; and otherwise, attenuates it [10].

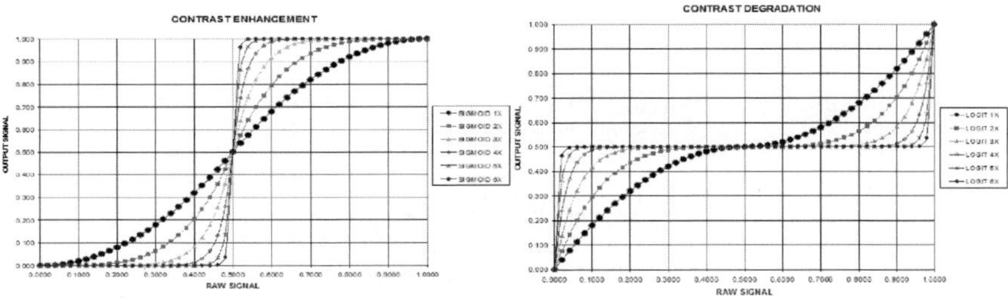

Fig. 2. On the left is the Contrast Enhance Operator, while on the right is the Contrast Degrade Operator

On the other hand, the contrast degrade operator performs the opposite fashion [1,6], as depicted in the curve in Fig. 2. It amplifies all signals less than 0.5; and otherwise, attenuates it. FCCF works on any desired colour space, provided that the colour pixels are expressed in terms of polar coordinates so that colour contrast rules can be applied selectively on colour pixels that fall within a pie-slice region classified as the general target colour region or colour contrast constraints [6].

3.2   rg Pie Slice Classifier

Colour recognition algorithms work by taking a single pixel and determining if it is of any of the colours specified by the current colour descriptors [5]. This classifier works in the rg-chromaticity colour space because it helps to reduce the effects of illumination intensity [1,6].The algorithm takes as input a pixel in RGB format and converts it into the rg colour space.

Once the pixel has been converted into rg-Hue and rg-Saturation [1,6], it can simply be checked to see if it is within the bounds of the colours as defined by the pie-sliced colour descriptors.

The algorithm does not have time to calculate the rg-hue and rg-saturation values for each pixel as the inverse tangent and square root calculations take too long, so look-up tables (LUT) were created to improve the performance. The program creates this LUT on initialization by calculating the rg-Hue and rg-Saturation values for every possible combination of RGB values. These look-up tables take several minutes to build at the beginning of the program but significantly speed up the classification process (< 33msec.) [7]. When a pixel is classified, the algorithm simply has to access the look-up table and the positions of the RGB values to discover the rg-Hue and rg-Saturation values.

3.3   Motion-Based Predictive Colour-Learning Algorithm (MPCL)

The colour discrimination ability of FCCF comes with a price. It requires a rich set of colour descriptors for each target colour, namely the boundaries for rg-Hue, rg-Saturation and contrast constraint angles, and a set of colour contrast

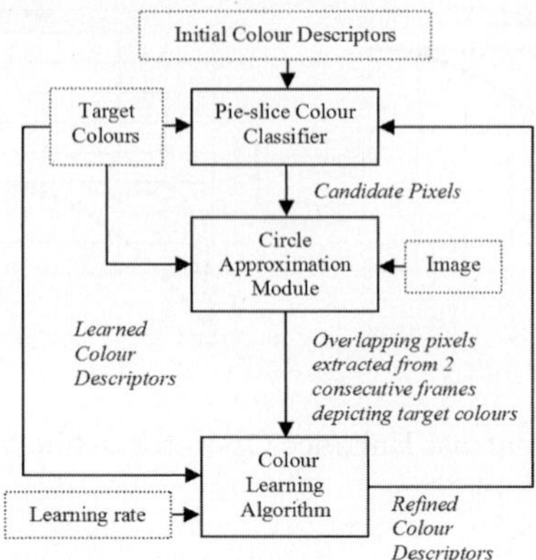

Fig. 3. The MPCL algorithm

rules. These parameters were previously extracted manually; involving an operator adjusting the values by hand until the results of the colour classification pinpoints the target colour unambiguously. However, hand calibration does not guarantee finding the optimal settings for the colour recognition system [4], and so this is the problem the MPCL algorithm is addressing. It automates the calibration process with superior calibration performance. In general, MPCL looks at two successive frames, extracting the best candidate pixels representing the object and fine-tuning the colour descriptors based on those pixels. For the purpose of easily finding the candidate pixels, a circularly shaped object was used during the calibration process. Nonetheless, after the system learns all the colour descriptors, the objects for tracking can come in any shape.

The series of steps for learning the colour descriptors are shown in Fig. 3. Initially, a broad set of colour descriptors is used by the pie-slice classifier to find the set of candidate pixels representing the target object. In turn, these pixels are fed into a circle approximation module that searches for the largest, most circular patch of colour present on the board. It calculates a formula approximating the circle by calculating the centre of the colour patch and averaging the extreme x and y values to approximate the radius of the circle. Two circle formulas will be generated for two consecutive images and the overlap of the two circles will be calculated. Once this overlap has been found the algorithm will find every pixel inside the area and filter them with the broad colour classifier to ensure that the approximated area does not include any non-colour pixels. Next, it takes all of the filtered pixels and record the extreme values for the rg-Hue and rg-Saturation values of the pixels to find the smallest possible pie-slice area that would classify every pixel inside the overlapping area. Once these extreme values have been calculated, the algorithm uses a moving average technique to adjust the actual colour descriptor parameters. The amount each set of extreme values affects the actual parameters depends on the learning rate.

Circle Generation The circle generated for each colour patch is generated by averaging the height and width of the circular patch from the centre of the circle. Once all of the pixels in the patch have been found, a centre of gravity equation is used to find the centre of the patch:

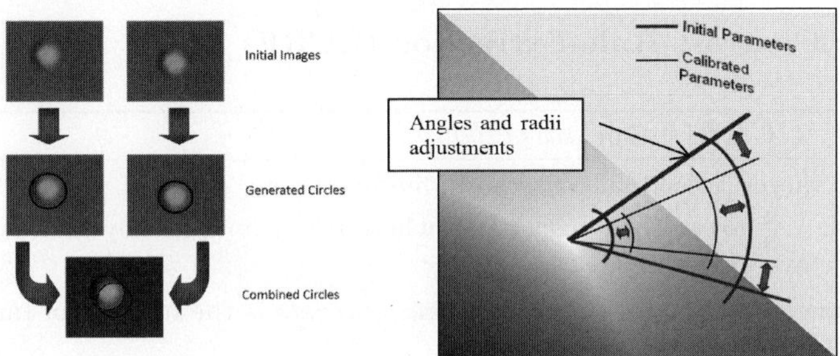

Fig. 4. On the left is the extracted object colour pixels from two consecutive frames. On the right is the calibration of colour descriptors.

$$x_{centre} = \sum_{i=0}^{n} x_i \qquad y_{centre} = \sum_{i=0}^{n} y_i \qquad (1)$$

Once the centre of the patch has been located, the height and width of the patch are found:

$$height = max(x_{centre}, y) \qquad width = max(x, y_{centre}) \qquad (2)$$

Then the radius is calculated with the following equation:

$$radius = \frac{height + width}{4} \qquad (3)$$

The centre and radius of the circle has now been found so the next part of the algorithm can run. The learning algorithm works on a moving average system combined with a decaying learning rate algorithm. The algorithm will run for a set number of iterations and keep moving average of the maximum and minimum rg-Hue and rg-Saturation:

$$rgHue_{max} = \frac{rgHue_{max}(i-1) + max(rgHue)}{i} \qquad (4)$$

$$rgHue_{min} = \frac{rgHue_{min}(i-1) + min(rgHue)}{i} \qquad (5)$$

$$rgSat_{max} = \frac{rgSat_{max}(i-1) + max(rgSat)}{i} \qquad (6)$$

$$rgSat_{min} = \frac{rgSat_{min}(i-1) + min(rgSat)}{i} \qquad (7)$$

The idea of the algorithm is to move a robot with a colour patch or roll a ball around the board to calibrate the colour. Because the object will move through all of the different illumination conditions, the algorithm will calibrate the colour classifier to work for the entire board, accounting for all possible illumination conditions.

3.4   Colour Contrast Rule Extraction (CCRE)

Algorithm 1. $CCRE(image, targetbounds)$

---

1. For each target object calculate an individual score: $score_i = \frac{hits_i}{area_i}$
    - if $hits_i < \frac{1}{n} \, area_i$ then $score_i = 0$; where $n = 4$ (empirically found)
2. Calculate average score:
    - $avescore = \frac{\sum_{i=1}^{ntargets} score_i}{ntargets}$;   where: $ntargets$ is the number of targets.
3. Calculate a general score:
    - $genscore = \frac{Totalhits}{Totalhits + Totalmisses}$
4. Final score:
    - $finalscore = (0.6 \, avescore) + (0.4 \, genscore)$
5. Adjust score to account for misclassifications:
    - $if(Totalhits > 0)$
    - $finalscore = finalscore - \left(\frac{Totalmisses}{Totalhits}\right)$

A colour contrast rule uniquely defines what combination of contrast operations and what levels of contrast operations will be applied to the red, green and blue channels. As indicated in Table 1, a light blue colour will receive a combination of contrast degrade, of level 1 on the red channel, contrast enhance, of level 1 on the green channel and no contrast operation on the blue channel. There are only 2 possible contrast operations: either to enhance or degrade. It is also possible that the colour channel does not require any contrast operation at all (i.e. no operation). Moreover, only 3 possible levels of contrast applications were considered (i.e. 1x, 2x, 3x). For example, a contrast level of three means that the contrast operator will be applied 3 times to the colour channel, using the output of each application as an input to the next. For each colour channel, there are 7 possible combinations of contrast operations: (enhance/degrade) - 3 possible levels each, no operation). Altogether, considering all 3 colour channels (RGB), there are 343 possible fuzzy colour contrast rules that can be applied for any target colour.

The algorithm hunts for the best rule by supplying the FCCF module with a generated colour contrast rule and using the pie-slice classifier for extracting the pixels representing the target colour object. It then counts the number of hits and misclassifications by examining the x and y-coordinates of those pixels if they fall within the actual boundaries of the target objects. Lastly, a formula for calculating the score for each rule is used:

The colour discrimination ability of FCCF comes with a price. It requires a rich set of colour descriptors for each target colour, namely the boundaries for rg-Hue, rg-Saturation and contrast constraint angles, and a set of colour contrast rules. These parameters were previously extracted manually; involving an operator adjusting the values by hand until the results of the colour classification pinpoints the target colour unambiguously. However, hand calibration does not guarantee finding the optimal settings for the colour recognition system [4], and so this is the problem the MPCL algorithm is addressing. It automates the calibration process with superior calibration performance

4   Experiments and Analysis

The MPCL has been tested on images of a circular colour patch in the centre of the board with promising results. MPCL was given a very broad set of parameters describing the colour and a series of images of this colour patch on the board. Several experiments using different coloured patches were run to make sure the algorithm works correctly with all kinds of colour classifier parameters. The algorithm was also tested by being set to calibrate one colour in the presence of other circular patches having relatively similar colours on the board.

The two images in Fig. 5 show a sample performance comparison results of the colour recognition algorithm using hand-calibrated settings and settings found by the MPCL algorithm. These images exhibit two circular colour patches, one orange and one green. The hand calibrated settings cause approximately 500 misclassifications whereas the MPCL algorithm settings cause 16 misclassifications. Fig. 6 shows an example of colour classification results for light blue targets. Details of classification results can be found in tables 1 and 2.

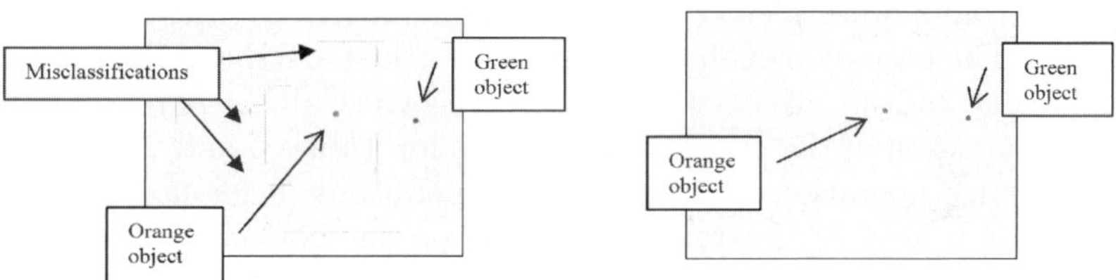

Fig. 5. MPCL results: on the left is the manual result. On the right is the system result.

Table 1. Manually derived colour contrast rules and their scores

Colour Name	Rank	Contrast Operation			Score	Hits	Misses
		R	G	B			
Yellow	0th	0	2	-2	0.48	2410	458
Green	8th	-1	2	-2	0.45	3252	608
Pink	4th	1	-1	0	0.59	1714	99
Purple	3rd	1	1	0	0.54	2629	320
Violet	0th	0	1	1	0.4	1873	415
LightBlue	15th	-1	1	0	0.63	2702	135

Table 2. System generated colour contrast rules and their scores

Colour Name	R	G	B	Score	Hits	Misses
Yellow	3	1	-2	0.65	2104	68
Green	0	-1	-3	0.55	3313	383
Pink	1	-1	0	0.59	1714	99
Purple	0	1	-3	0.57	2777	314
Violet	1	1	2	0.53	2535	497
LightBlue	0	3	1	0.67	2758	68

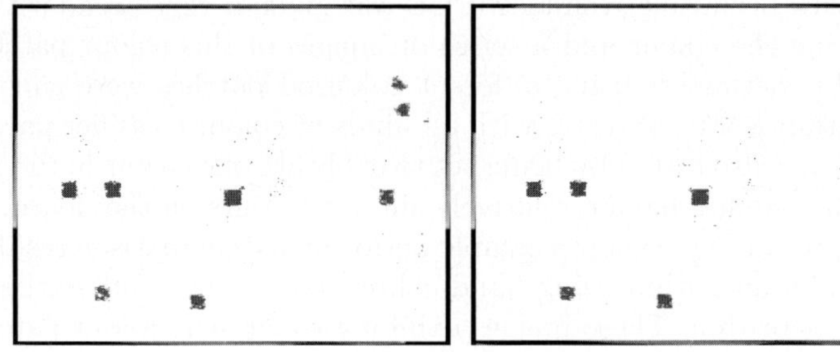

Fig. 6. Light blue targets: on the left is the result for the manual calibration, on the right is the result for the system calibration

Next, the CCRE was tested on 6 colours (i.e. pink, violet, etc.). Six colour patches per colour were placed at varying illumination intensities on the robot soccer field. The objective of the tests was to let the CCRE algorithm to extract the colour contrast rules that will accurately recognise all the patches simultaneously. The encoding of the contrast operations for Tables 1 and 2 are as follows: (+) for enhance operation, (-) for degrade operations, 0 for no operation and nonzero for any level of contrast application on the colour channel. It can be seen from Tables 1 and 2 that the system generated rules from CCRE always gives superior performance. The score and hits of the system rules were always greater than or equal to the manually generated ones. On the other hand, the misses could be greater sometimes, but we verified that such numbers never induce ambiguities during the object recognition task. Lastly, we used all the acquired colour descriptors and colour contrast rules to generate a look-up table (LUT) for real-time colour object recognition for the robot soccer game. The generated LUT guarantees that the robots can be recognised and tracked perfectly during the game without ambiguities in real-time.

5   Conclusions

We have successfully devised and tested a novel motion-based predictive colour learning algorithm (MPCL) and a colour contrast rule (CCRE) extraction algorithm that integrates with the Fuzzy Colour Contrast Fusion algorithm and pie-slice colour classifier. Results prove that the hybrid system is extremely faster and more accurate than hand-calibrated colour descriptors and colour contrast rules, while at the same time robust to changes in the illumination conditions. Lastly, by storing colour classification results in a look-up table, the hybrid vision system presented becomes very effective for the FIRA and Robocup real-time robot soccer vision systems.

References

1. Reyes, N.H.: Colour-Based Object Recognition Analysis and Application. PhD thesis, De La Salle University (2004)
2. Stonier, P.J.T.R.J., Wolfs, P.J.: Robustness of color detection for robot soccer. In: Seventh International Conference on Control, Automation, Robotics and Vision, ICARCV 2002, Singapore, pp. 1245–1249 (2002)
3. Reyes, N.H., Dadios, E.P.: Dynamic color object recognition. Journal of Advanced Computational Intelligence 8(1), 29–38 (2004)
4. Weiss, N., Jesse, N.: Towards local vision in centralized robot soccer leagues: A robust and flexible vision system also allowing varying degrees of robot autonomy. In: Proceedings of FIRA World Congress, Busan, FIRA (2004)
5. Klancar, G., Orqueda, O., Robust, D.M.R.K.: efficient vision for mobile robots control application to soccer robots. Electrotechnical Review 68(5), 305–312 (2001)
6. Reyes, N., Messom, C.: Identifying colour objects with fuzzy colour contrast fusion. In: 3rd International Conference on Computational Intelligence, Robotics and Autonomous Systems, and FIRA RoboWorld Congress, CIRAS 2005, Singapore (2005)
7. McNaughton, M., Zhang, H.: Color vision for robocup with fast lookup tables. In: 2003 IEEE International Conference on Robotics, Intelligent Systems and Signal Processing, Taipei, IEEE, Los Alamitos (2003)
8. Hurlbert, A., Wolf, K.: Color contrast: a contributory mechanism to color constancy. Progress in Brain Research 144, 147–160 (2004)
9. Funt, B., Barnard, K., Martin, L.: Is color constancy good enough? In: 5th European Conference on Computer Vision, pp. 445–459 (1998)
10. Ross, T.: Fuzzy Logic with Engineering Applications. McGraw-Hill, Inc., Singapore (1997)
11. Hildebrand, L., Fathi, M.: Knowledge-based fuzzy color processing. IEEE Trans. on Sys., Man. and Cybernectics-part C 34, 499–505 (2004)
12. Montecillo-Puente, F., Ayala-Ramirez, V., Perez-Garcia, A., Sanchez-Yanez, R.: Fuzzy color tracking for robotic tasks. In: IEEE International Conference on Systems, Man and Cybernetics, 2003, vol. 3, pp. 2769–2773 (2003)

Adaptive Face Recognition System Using Fast Incremental Principal Component Analysis

Seiichi Ozawa[1], Shaoning Pang[2], and Nikola Kasabov[2]

[1] Graduate School of Engineering, Kobe University
1-1 Rokko-dai, Nada-ku, Kobe 657-8501, Japan
ozawasei@kobe-u.ac.jp
[2] Knowledge Engineering & Discover Research Institute
Auckland University of Technology, Private Bag 92006,
Auckland 1020, New Zealand
shaoning.pang@aut.ac.nz, nik.kasabov@aut.ac.nz

Abstract. In this paper, a novel face recognition system is presented in which not only a classifier but also a feature space is learned incrementally to adapt to a chunk of incoming training samples. A distinctive feature of the proposed system is that the selection of useful features and the learning of an optimal decision boundary are conducted in an online fashion. In the proposed system, Chunk Incremental Principal Component Analysis (CIPCA) and Resource Allocating Network with Long-Term Memory are effectively combined. In the experiments, the proposed face recognition system is evaluated for a self-compiled face image database. The experimental results demonstrate that the test performance of the proposed system is consistently improved over the learning stages, and that the learning speed of a feature space is greatly enhanced by CIPCA.

1 Introduction

In general, the information processing in face recognition systems is composed of the two parts: feature selection and classifier. This means that when constructing an adaptive recognition system, we should consider two types of incremental learning: one is the incremental learning of a feature space and the other is that of a classifier. As for the feature selection, Hall and Martin [2] have proposed a method to update eigenvectors and eigenvalues in an incremental way called Incremental Principal Component Analysis (IPCA). Recently, to enhance the learning efficiency, we have proposed the two extended algorithms for the original IPCA. One is an extended IPCA in which the eigen-axis augmentation is carried out based on the accumulation ratio instead of the norm of a residue vector [5], and the other is Chunk IPCA in which a chunk of training samples are trained at a time [3]. On the other hand, we also have proposed an incremental learning algorithm for a neural classifier called Resource Allocating Neural Network with Long-Term Memory (RAN-LTM). As we have already presented in [4], IPCA and RAN-LTM are effectively combined to construct a powerful pattern recognition system.

M. Ishikawa et al. (Eds.): ICONIP 2007, Part II, LNCS 4985, pp. 396–405, 2008.

This paper is organized as follows. Section 2 gives a quick review on the two extended IPCA algorithms: IPCA Based on Accumulation Ratio and Chunk IPCA. Then, the face recognition system is briefly explained in Section 3. In Section 4, several experiments are conducted to evaluate the proposed face recognition system. Finally, Section 5 gives a brief summary of this work.

2 Incremental Principal Component Analysis (IPCA)

2.1 IPCA Based on Accumulation Ratio

Assume that N training samples $x_i \in \mathcal{R}^n$ $(i = 1, \cdots, N)$ have been presented so far, and an eigenspace model $\Omega = (\bar{x}, U_k, \Lambda_k, N)$, where $\bar{x} \in \mathcal{R}^n$ is a mean vector, U_k is an $n \times k$ matrix whose column vectors correspond to the eigenvectors, and Λ_k is a $k \times k$ matrix whose diagonal elements correspond to the eigenvalues. Here, k is the number of eigen-axes spanning the eigenspace (i.e., eigenspace dimensionality).

Now, assume that the $(N+1)$th training sample $y \in \mathcal{R}^n$ is given. The addition of this new sample will lead to the changes in both mean vector and covariance matrix; therefore, the eigenvectors and eigenvalues should also be updated. The new mean input vector $\bar{x}'$ is easily obtained as follows:

$$\bar{x}' = \frac{1}{N+1}(N\bar{x} + y) \ \in \mathcal{R}^n. \tag{1}$$

To update U_k and Λ_k, first we need to check if the eigenspace should be enlarged in terms of dimensionality. If almost all energy of the new sample is included in the current eigenspace, there is no need to increase the dimensionality. However, if a certain quantity of energy is included in the complementary eigenspace, the dimensional augmentation is needed, or crucial information on the new sample might be lost. In the original IPCA [2], the determination of the eigenspace augmentation is made based on the norm of the following residue vector $h \in \mathcal{R}^n$:

$$h = (y - \bar{x}) - U_k g \tag{2}$$

where $g = U_k^T(y - \bar{x})$, and T means the transpose of vectors and matrices. However, the threshold for the norm generally depends on datasets; therefore, we have proposed an extended IPCA algorithm [5] in which the accumulation ratio is used instead of the norm as a criterion to determine the dimensional augmentation.

In [5], we have shown that the accumulation ratio can be updated incrementally by

$$A'(U_k) = \frac{N(N+1)\sum_{i=1}^{k}\lambda_i + N\|U_k^T(y - \bar{x})\|^2}{N(N+1)\sum_{i=1}^{n}\lambda_i + N\|y - \bar{x}\|^2} \tag{3}$$

where λ_i is the ith eigenvalue corresponding to the ith diagonal element of Λ_k.

398   S. Ozawa, S. Pang, and N. Kasabov

Note that no past samples are necessary for the incremental update of $A'(\boldsymbol{U}_k)$.

It has been shown that the eigenvectors and eigenvalues are updated by solving the following intermediate eigenproblem [2]:

$$\left(\frac{N}{N+1} \begin{bmatrix} \boldsymbol{\Lambda}_k & \boldsymbol{0} \\ \boldsymbol{0}^T & 0 \end{bmatrix} + \frac{N}{(N+1)^2} \begin{bmatrix} \boldsymbol{g}\boldsymbol{g}^T & \gamma\boldsymbol{g} \\ \gamma\boldsymbol{g}^T & \gamma^2 \end{bmatrix} \right) \boldsymbol{R} = \boldsymbol{R}\boldsymbol{\Lambda}'_{k+1} \tag{4}$$

where $\gamma = \tilde{\boldsymbol{h}}^T(\boldsymbol{y} - \bar{\boldsymbol{x}})$, $\boldsymbol{R}$ is a $(k+1) \times (k+1)$ matrix whose column vectors correspond to the eigenvectors obtained from the above intermediate eigenproblem, $\boldsymbol{\Lambda}'_{k+1}$ is the new eigenvalue matrix, and $\boldsymbol{0}$ is a k-dimensional zero vector. Using the solution $\boldsymbol{R}$, the new $n \times (k+1)$ eigenvector matrix $\boldsymbol{U}'_{k+1}$ is calculated as follows:

$$\boldsymbol{U}'_{k+1} = [\boldsymbol{U}_k, \ \hat{\boldsymbol{h}}]\boldsymbol{R} \tag{5}$$

where

$$\hat{\boldsymbol{h}} = \begin{cases} \boldsymbol{h}/\|\boldsymbol{h}\| & \text{if } A(\boldsymbol{U}_k) < \theta \\ \boldsymbol{0} & \text{otherwise.} \end{cases} \tag{6}$$

Here, θ is a threshold value. Intuitively, $\boldsymbol{R}$ in Eq. (5) gives a rotation from old eigen-axes to new ones; hence, let us call $\boldsymbol{R}$ *rotation matrix* here.

2.2   Chunk IPCA

The IPCA in 2.1 is applied to one sample at a time, and the intermediate eigenproblem must be solved repeatedly for every training sample. Hence, the learning may get stuck in a deadlock if a large chunk of training samples is given to learn in a short period. To overcome this problem, the above IPCA is modified so that the eigenspace model Ω can be updated with any size of chunk training samples in a single operation. Let us call this extended algorithm 'Chunk IPCA (CIPCA)'.

Let us assume that N training samples $\boldsymbol{X} = \{\boldsymbol{x}_1, \cdots, \boldsymbol{x}_N\} \in \mathcal{R}^{n \times N}$ have been given so far and they were already discarded. Instead of keeping actual training samples, we preserve an eigenspace model $\Omega = (\bar{\boldsymbol{x}}, \boldsymbol{U}_k, \boldsymbol{\Lambda}_k, N)$. Now, assume that a chunk of L training samples $\boldsymbol{Y} = \{\boldsymbol{y}_1, \cdots, \boldsymbol{y}_L\} \in \mathcal{R}^{n \times L}$ are presented. Then, the mean vector $\bar{\boldsymbol{x}}'$ is easily updated as follows:

$$\bar{\boldsymbol{x}}' = \frac{1}{N+L}\left(\sum_{i=1}^{N} \boldsymbol{x}_i + \sum_{j=1}^{L} \boldsymbol{y}_j\right) = \frac{1}{N+L}(N\bar{\boldsymbol{x}} + L\bar{\boldsymbol{y}}). \tag{7}$$

To obtain the new eigenspace model, let us further assume that l eigen-axes must be augmented to avoid the serious loss of essential input information; that is, the eigenspace dimensions are increased by l. Let us denote the augmented eigen-axes as follows:

$$\boldsymbol{H} = [\boldsymbol{h}_1, \cdots, \boldsymbol{h}_l] \in \mathcal{R}^{n \times l}. \tag{8}$$

Then, the updated eigenvector matrix U'_{k+l} is represented by using the rotation matrix R and the current eigenvector matrix U_k as follows:

$$U'_{k+l} = [U_k, H]R. \tag{9}$$

A new eigenvalue problem to be solved is given by

$$\left(\frac{N}{N+L} \begin{bmatrix} \Lambda_k & 0 \\ 0^T & 0 \end{bmatrix} + \frac{NL^2}{(N+L)^3} \begin{bmatrix} \bar{g}\bar{g}^T & \bar{g}\bar{\gamma}^T \\ \bar{\gamma}\bar{g}^T & \bar{\gamma}\bar{\gamma}^T \end{bmatrix} + \frac{N^2}{(N+L)^3} \sum_{i=1}^{L} \begin{bmatrix} g'_i g'^T_i & g'_i \gamma'^T_i \\ \gamma'_i g'^T_i & \gamma'_i \gamma'^T_i \end{bmatrix} \right.$$

$$\left. + \frac{L(L+2N)}{(N+L)^3} \sum_{i=1}^{L} \begin{bmatrix} g''_i g''^T_i & g''_i \gamma''^T_i \\ \gamma''_i g''^T_i & \gamma''_i \gamma''^T_i \end{bmatrix} \right) R = R\Lambda'_{k+l} \tag{10}$$

where

$$\bar{g} = U_k^T(\bar{y} - \bar{x}), \ g'_i = U_k^T(y_i - \bar{x}), \ g''_i = U_k^T(y_i - \bar{y}),$$
$$\bar{\gamma} = H^T(\bar{y} - \bar{x}), \ \gamma'_i = H^T(y_i - \bar{x}), \ \gamma''_i = H^T(y_i - \bar{y}).$$

Solving this eigenproblem, a new rotation matrix R and the eigenvalue matrix Λ'_{k+l} are obtained. Then, the corresponding new eigenvector matrix U'_{k+l} is obtained by using Eq. (9).

In CIPCA, the number of augmented eigen-axes is also determined by finding a minimum k such that the accumulation ratio $A(U_k)$ satisfies the same condition described in 2.1. However, the update equation in Eq. (3) must be modified such that it can be updated with a chunk of training samples in one-pass [1]. This is given by

$$A'(U_k) = \frac{\sum_{i=1}^{k} \lambda_i + \frac{L}{N+L}\|\bar{g}\|^2 + \frac{1}{N}\sum_{j=1}^{L}\|g''_i\|^2}{\sum_{i=1}^{n} \lambda_i + \frac{L}{N+L}\|\bar{x} - \bar{y}\|^2 + \frac{1}{N}\sum_{j=1}^{L}\|y_j - \bar{y}\|^2}. \tag{11}$$

Finally, let us explain how to determined the augmented eigen-axes H in Eq. (8). In CIPCA, the number of augmented eigen-axes is not restricted to one. If the given L training samples are represented by $\tilde{L}$ linearly independent vectors, the maximum number of augmented eigen-axes is also $\tilde{L}$. However, the feature space spanned by all of the augmented eigen-axes is redundant in general; in addition, if the chunk size is large, the computation costs to solve the intermediate eigenproblem in Eq. (10) would be considerably expensive. Therefore, we should select informative eigen-axes from the $\tilde{L}$ eigen-axes efficiently. Since the number of eigen-axes to be augmented is varied from 0 to $\tilde{L}$, the number of possible combinations of eigen-axes is represented by $\sum_{i=0}^{\tilde{L}} {}_L C_i$. If the chunk size is large, the computation costs for finding an optimal set of augmented eigen-axes would be large. To avoid such an exhaustive search, we introduce a kind of greedy search based on the accumulation ratio.

To construct a compact feature space, we should find a smallest set H of augmented eigen-axes such that the eigenspace includes as much the energy of the given chunk data as possible. A straightforward way to find the set is to select an eigen-axis one by one, each of which gives a maximum accumulation ratio. The algorithm of the eigen-axis selection is summarized below.

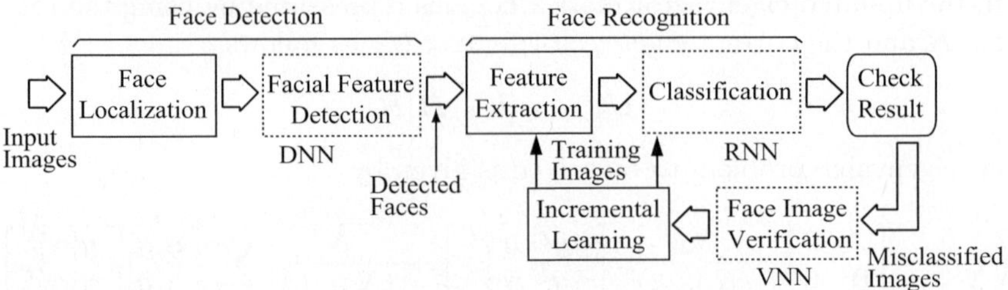

Fig. 1. The block diagram of information processing in the face recognition system. The block with a dotted line is implemented by a neural network.

[Selection of Eigen-axes in CIPCA]

Inputs: – Eigenspace model $\Omega = (\bar{x}, U_k, \Lambda_k, N)$.
   – A chunk of L training samples $Y = \{y^{(1)}, \cdots, y^{(L)}\}$.
   – Threshold θ of the accumulation ratio.
Do the following procedure:
   i) Set $H = \{\ \}$ and $l = 0$. Calculate the mean vector $\bar{y}$ of the given training samples Y.
   ii) Calculate the accumulation ratio $A'(U'_k)$ based on Eq. (3). If $A'(U'_k) > \theta$, terminate this algorithm.
   iii) Obtain the following residue vectors h_i $(i = 1, \cdots, L)$ for all of the given training samples $y^{(i)}$:

$$h_i = \frac{r_i}{\|r_i\|} \quad \text{where} \quad r_i = (y^{(i)} - \bar{x}) - [U_k, H][U_k, H]^T (y^{(i)} - \bar{x}).$$

   Define an index set $\mathcal{H}$ of h_i.
   iv) Find the following residue vector $h_{i'}$ which gives the maximum increment $\Delta \tilde{A}'_i$: $h_{i'} = \arg\max_{i \in \mathcal{H}} \Delta \tilde{A}'_i$ where

$$\Delta \tilde{A}'_i = \frac{L}{N + L}\{h_i^T(\bar{x} - \bar{y})\}^2 + \frac{1}{N}\sum_{j=1}^{L}\{h_i^T(y^{(j)} - \bar{y})\}^2.$$

   v) Add $h_{i'}$ to H (i.e., $H \leftarrow [H, h_{i'}]$), $l \leftarrow l + 1$, and remove i' from $\mathcal{H}$. If $\mathcal{H}$ is empty, terminate this algorithm.
   vi) Calculate the updated accumulation ratio $A'(U'_{k+l})$ based on Eq. (11). If $A'(U'_{k+l}) > \theta$, terminate this algorithm. Otherwise, go to Step iv).
Output: The optimal set of augmented eigen-axes $H = \{h_1, \cdots, h_l\}$.

3   Face Recognition System

Figure 1 shows the overall process in our face recognition system. As we can see from Fig. 1, the presented system mainly consists of the four parts: face detection, face recognition, face image verification, and incremental learning. See [4] for the further details of this system.

4   Performance Evaluation

4.1   Experimental Setup

To simulate real-life consecutive recognition and learning, 224 video clips are collected for 22 persons (19 males and 3 females) during about 11 months such that temporal changes in facial appearances are included. Seven people (5 males and 2 females) are chosen as registrants and the other people (14 males and a female) are non-registrants. The duration of each video clip is 5 - 15 (sec.). A video clip is given to the face detection part, and the detected face images are automatically forwarded to the face recognition part. The numbers of detected face images are summarized in Table 1. The three letters in Table 1 indicate the code of the 22 subjects in which M/F and R/U mean Male/Female and Registered/Unregistered, respectively; for example, the third registered male is coded as MR3.

Table 1. Two face datasets (Set A and Set B) for training and test. The three letters in the upper row mean the registrant code and the values in the second and third rows are the numbers of face images.

Set	MR1	FR1	MR2	MR3	FR2	MR4	MR5	FU1	MU1	MU2	MU3	MU4
A	351	254	364	381	241	400	186	133	181	294	110	103
B	170	220	297	671	297	241	359	126	228	292	80	233

Set	MU5	MU6	MU7	MU8	MU9	MU10	MU11	MU12	MU13	MU14	Total
A	170	186	174	33	79	15	75	17	10	9	3766
B	117	202	182	14	9	14	28	18	9	9	3816

To evaluate the recognition performance based on the two-fold cross-validation, the whole dataset is subdivided into two subsets: Set A and Set B. When Set A is used for learning RNN, Set B is used for testing the generalization performance, and vice versa. Note that since the incremental learning is applied only for misclassified face images, the recognition accuracy before the incremental learning is an important performance measure. Hence, there are at least two performance measures for the training dataset: one is the performance of RNN using a set of training samples given at each learning stage, and the other is the performance using all training datasets given so far after the incremental learning is carried out. In the following, let us call the former and latter datasets as *incremental dataset* and *training dataset*, respectively. Besides, let us call the performances over the incremental dataset and training dataset as *incremental performance* and *training performance*, respectively. We divide the whole dataset into 16 subsets, each of which corresponds to an incremental dataset. Table 2 shows the number of images included in the incremental datasets.

The size of an initial dataset can influence the test performance because different initial eigen-spaces are constructed. However, if the incremental learning is successfully carried out, the final performance should not depend on the size of the initial dataset. Hence, the three different series of incremental datasets

Table 2. Number of images included in the 16 incremental datasets

	1	2	3	4	5	6	7	8	9	10	11	12	13	14	15	16
Set A	220	232	304	205	228	272	239	258	212	233	290	212	257	188	199	217
Set B	288	204	269	246	273	270	240	281	205	249	194	241	214	226	210	206

Table 3. Three series of incremental datasets. The number in Table 3 corresponds to the tag number of the corresponding incremental dataset.

Stage	Init.	1	2	⋯	12	13	14	15
Case 1	1	2	3	⋯	13	14	15	16
Case 2	1, 2	3	4	⋯	14	15	16	—
Case 3	1, 2, 3	4	5	⋯	15	16	—	—

shown in Table 3 are defined to see the influence. Note that the number in Table 3 corresponds to the tag number (1-16) of the incremental dataset in Table 2. Hence, we can see that Case 1 has 15 learning stages and the number of images in the initial dataset is 220 for Set A and 288 for Set B, which correspond to 6.7% and 7.5% over the whole data. On the other hand, the sizes of the initial datasets in Case 2 and Case 3 are set to a larger value as compared with that in Case 1; while the numbers of learning stages are smaller than that in Case 1. Figure 2 shows the examples of detected face images for three registered persons at several learning stages.

When an initial dataset is trained in RNN, the number of hidden units is fixed with 50 in this experiment. The other parameters are set as follows: $\sigma^2 = 7$, $\varepsilon = 0.01$, and $\delta = 5$. The threshold θ of the accumulation ratio in IPCA is set to 0.9; thus, when the accumulation ratio is below 0.9, a new eigen-axis is augmented.

4.2 Experimental Results

Learning Time. Figure 3 shows the transition of learning time over 15 learning stages when the chunk size L is 10 in CIPCA. The curves of 'CIPCA' and 'IPCA' show the learning time for feature selection, while those of 'CIPCA+RAN-LTM'

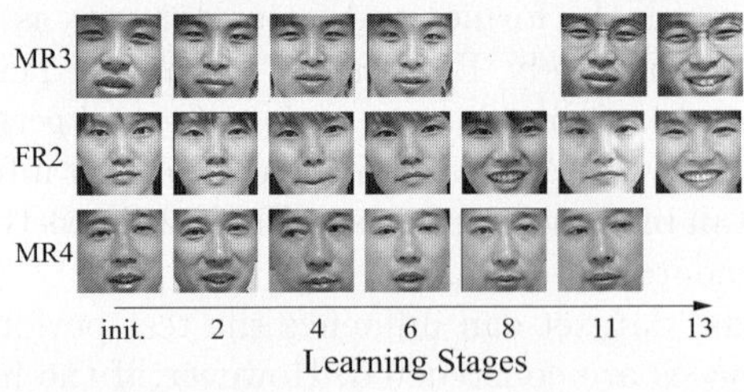

Fig. 2. Examples of face images trained at different learning stages

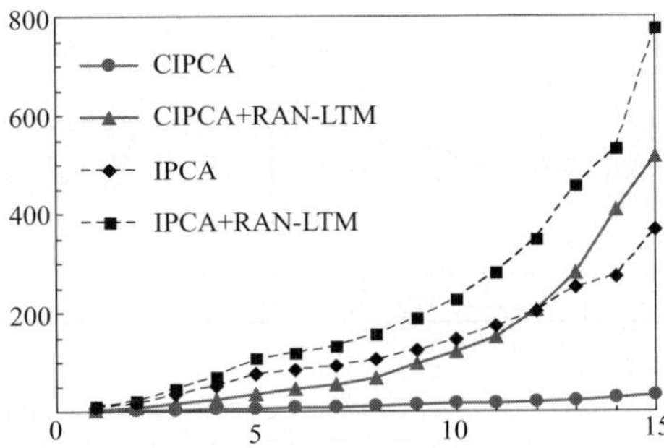

Fig. 3. Transition of learning time (sec.)

Table 4. Comparisons of Learning time and dimensions of feature vectors at the final learning stage. CIPCA(10), CIPCA(50), and CIPCA(100) stand for CIPCA in which the chunk sizes are set to 10, 50, and 100, respectively.

	IPCA	CIPCA(10)	CIPCA(50)	CIPCA(100)
Time (sec.)	376.2	45.6	22.5	18.1
Dimensions	178	167	186	192

and 'IPCA+RAN-LTM' mean the learning time for both feature selection and classifier. As you can see from the results, the learning time of feature selection by CIPCA is greatly reduced as compared with IPCA. This is also confirmed in Table 4.

The learning time of CIPCA decreases as the chunk size increases, and CIPCA is much faster than IPCA even though the feature dimensions at the final stage do not have large differences between IPCA and CIPCA. When the chunk size is 10, CIPCA is about 8 times faster than IPCA. The reason why the decreasing rate of the learning time becomes small for larger chunk size is that the time for finding eigen-axes dominates the total learning time [3].

Classification Accuracy. To evaluate the effectiveness of learning a feature space, the classification accuracy of RAN-LTM is examined when the following three eigen-space models are adopted: (1) static eigenspace model with PCA, (2) adaptive eigenspace model with the extended IPCA, and (3) adaptive eigenspace model with CIPCA. For notational simplicity, these three models are denoted by PCA, IPCA, and CIPCA, respectively.

Figures 4 (a)-(c) show the transition of recognition accuracy over 15 learning stages when the percentage of initial training data is (a) 6.7%, (b) 12.5%, and (c) 20%, respectively. As stated before, the size of an initial dataset can influence the recognition accuracy because different eigenspaces are constructed at the start point. As we can see from Figs. 4(a)-(c), the initial test performance at stage 0 is higher when the number of initial training data is larger; however, the test performance of IPCA and CIPCA is monotonously enhanced over the

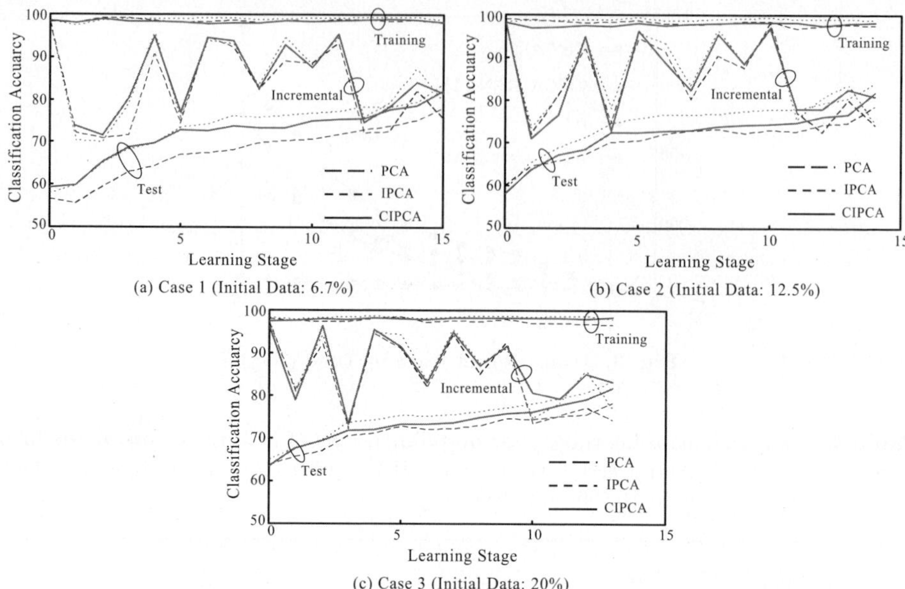

Fig. 4. Time courses of the recognition accuracy rate for three different datasets (incremental, training, test) over the learning stages when the percentages of initial training datasets are set to (a) 6.7%, (b) 12.5%, and (c) 20.0%

learning stages and it reaches almost the same accuracy regardless of the initial datasets. Considering that the total number of training data is the same among the three cases, we can say that all the information included in the training dataset is stably accumulated in RNN without serious forgetting. In addition, the test performance of RNN with IPCA and CIPCA has significant improvement against RNN with PCA although CIPCA has slightly lower performance than IPCA. This degradation originates from the approximation error of the eigenspace model with CIPCA. However, the above results still indicate that the reconstruction of RNN works well in accordance with the evolution of the eigenspace model, and that the incremental learning of a feature space is very effective to enhance the generalization performance of RNN.

Moreover, we can see that although the incremental performance is fluctuated, the training performance of RNN with IPCA and CIPCA changes very stably over the learning stages. On the other hand, the training performance of RNN with PCA rather drops down as the learning stage proceeds. Since the incremental performance is defined as a kind of test performance for the incoming training dataset, it is natural to be fluctuated. The important thing is that the misclassified images in the incremental dataset are trained stably without degrading the classification accuracy for the past training data.

From the above results, we can conclude that the proposed incremental learning scheme, in which the feature space and the classifier are simultaneously learned based on CIPCA and RAN-LTM, works quite well and the learning time is significantly reduced without serious performance degradation.

5   Conclusions

This paper presents a new approach to constructing adaptive face recognition systems in which a low-dimensional feature space and a classifier are incrementally learned in an online fashion. To learn a useful feature space incrementally, we adopt Chunk Incremental Principal Component Analysis (CIPCA) in which a chunk of given training samples are learned at a time to update an eigen-space model.

To evaluate the incremental learning properties, a self-compiled face image database is applied to the proposed model. In the experiments, we verify that the proposed incremental learning works well without serious forgetting and the test performance is improved as the incremental learning stages proceed. Furthermore, we also show that replacing the extended IPCA with CIPCA is very efficient in term of learning time; in fact, the learning speed of CIPCA was at least 8 times faster than IPCA.

Acknowledgment

The authors would like to thank Prof. Shigeo Abe for his useful discussions and comments, and would like to thank Mr. Michiro Hirai for his great devotion to the development of the face recognition system.

References

1. Kasabov, N.: Evolving Connectionist Systems: Methods and Applications in Bioinformatics, Brain Study and Intelligent Machines. Springer, Heidelberg (2002)
2. Hall, P., Martin, R.: Incremental Eigenanalysis for Classification. In: Proc. of British Machine Vision Conference, vol. 1, pp. 286–295 (1998)
3. Ozawa, S., Pang, S., Kasabov, N.: An Incremental Principal Component Analysis for Chunk Data. In: Proc. of FUZZ-IEEE, pp. 10493–10500 (2006)
4. Ozawa, S., Toh, S.L., Abe, S., Pang, S., Kasabov, N.: Incremental Learning of Feature Space and Classifier for Face Recognition. Neural Networks 18(5-6), 575–584 (2005)
5. Ozawa, S., Pang, S., Kasabov, N.: A Modified Incremental Principal Component Analysis for On-line Learning of Feature Space and Classifier. In: Zhang, C., W. Guesgen, H., Yeap, W.-K. (eds.) PRICAI 2004. LNCS (LNAI), vol. 3157, pp. 231–240. Springer, Heidelberg (2004)

Adaptive Spiking Neural Networks for Audiovisual Pattern Recognition

Simei Gomes Wysoski, Lubica Benuskova, and Nikola Kasabov

Knowledge Engineering and Discovery Research Institute
Auckland University of Technology, 581-585 Great South Rd, Auckland, New Zealand
http://www.kedri.info
{swysoski, lbenusko, nkasabov}@aut.ac.nz

Abstract. The paper describes the integration of brain-inspired systems to perform audiovisual pattern recognition tasks. Individual sensory pathways as well as the integrative modules are implemented using a fast version of spiking neurons grouped in evolving spiking neural network (ESNN) architectures capable of lifelong adaptation. We design a new crossmodal integration system, where individual modalities can influence others before individual decisions are made, fact that resembles some characteristics of the biological brains. The system is applied to the person authentication problem. Preliminary results show that the integrated system can improve the accuracy in many operation points as well as it enables a range of multi-criteria optimizations.

Keywords: Spiking Neural Networks, Multi-modal Information Processing, Face and Speaker Recognition, Visual and Auditory Integration.

1   Introduction

There is a strong experimental evidence that integration of sensory information occurs in the human brain [1][2][3][4] and a lot is known about the location in the brain where different modalities converge. In simple terms, the integration occurs in *supramodal* areas that contain neurons sensitive to more than one modality, i.e., neurons that process different types of information. Further, *crossmodal* coupling, which is related to the direct influence of one modality to areas that intrinsically belong to other modalities, is another integrative phenomenon noticed in behavioural observations and electrophysiological experiments (Figure 1).

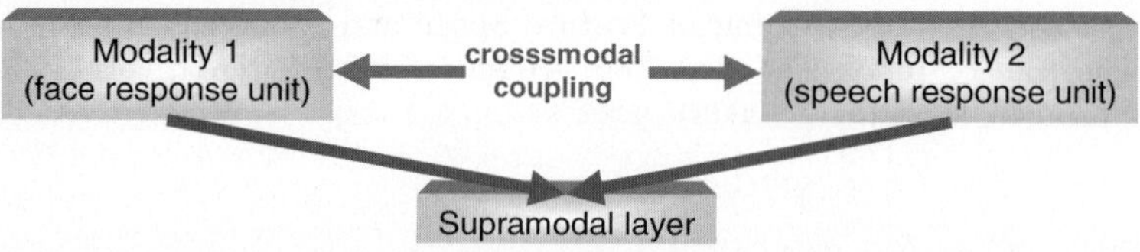

Fig. 1. Sensory integration. Supramodal region and the crossmodal coupling of modalities applied for audiovisual integration.

M. Ishikawa et al. (Eds.): ICONIP 2007, Part II, LNCS 4985, pp. 406–415, 2008.
© Springer-Verlag Berlin Heidelberg 2008

However, studies of neuronal mechanisms that underlie interaction among modalities at the level of single or ensemble of neural cells are still inconclusive. In this direction, computational models of interactions at a neuronal level inspired by perceptual studies can help to shed more light on the modular interdependences, and, in the same manner, the better understanding of these interactions can provide new insights to enhance performance of connectionist algorithms applied to pattern recognition. The latter is the immediate objective of our research.

The integration of modalities for the purpose of pattern recognition is often used in tasks that cannot be solved by a single system or can be facilitated by using more than one source (generally where there is unimodal ambiguity, unimodal lack of data and/or correlation among modes). Many works report significant performance improvement [5][6][7][8] as well as describe that the use of modularity results in systems easy to understand and modify. Added to that, modular approaches are known for contributing against modular damage and for facilitating training and the inclusion of prior knowledge [7].

In this work we consider some biological aspects that drive the integration of sensory modalities to present a system that integrates data from different sources for the purpose of pattern recognition. The processing of individual modalities is implemented using adaptive SNN. An integration procedure at the neuronal level is presented, which considers crossmodal interrelation among modalities, emulating what has been noticed in several biological experiments. In Section 2 we describe the architecture of the individual systems based on spiking neural networks as well as the integration procedure. Section 3 presents some computational simulations and shows preliminary results when the system is applied to the person authentication problem. A discussion on the main properties of the integrated system and future directions conclude the paper.

2   SNN-Based Multi-modal Pattern Recognition

Our approach of biologically inspired integration of modalities for pattern recognition uses the theory of spiking neural networks, where the individual modes and the integration procedure are implemented with spiking neurons. We are using a simplified version of an integrate-and-fire neuron. Neurons have a latency of firing that depends upon the order of spikes received and the connections' strengths. The postsynaptic potential (PSP) for a neuron i at time t is calculated as:

$$PSP(i,t) = \sum \mathrm{mod}^{\,order(j)}\, w_{j,i} \tag{1}$$

where $\mathrm{mod} \in (0,1)$ is the modulation factor, j is the index for the incoming connection and $w_{j,i}$ is the corresponding synaptic weight. When PSP reaches a given threshold (PSP_{Th}), an output spike is generated and the PSP level is reset. A detailed description of the dynamics of these neurons is given in [9].

Each individual modality has its own network of spiking neurons. In general, the output of each modality has neurons that, when issue output spikes, authenticate/not authenticate a class they represent.

Our approach for integrating modalities consists of attaching a new layer into the output of the individual modes. This layer (supramodal layer) represents the supramodal region and contains neurons that are sensitive to more than one modality [4]. In our implementation, the supramodal layer contains two spiking neurons for each class label. Each neuron representing class C in the supramodal layer has incoming excitatory connections from the output of class C neurons of each individual modality. The two neurons have the same dynamics, yet different PSP_{Th}. To one neuron, the PSP_{Th} is set in such a way that an output spike is generated after receiving incoming spike from any single modality (effectively it is a spike-based implementation of an OR gate). The other neuron has PSP_{Th} set so that incoming spikes from all individual modalities are necessary to trigger an output spike (AND gate). AND neuron maximizes the accuracy and OR neuron maximizes the recall.

In addition to the supramodal layer, a simple way to perform crossmodal coupling of modalities is designed. The crossmodal coupling is set as follows: when output neurons of an individual modality emit spikes, the spikes not only excite the neurons in the supramodal layer, but also excite/inhibit other modalities that still have ongoing processes. Effectively this excitation/inhibition influences the decision on other modalities, making it easier/more difficult to other modality to authenticate a pattern, respectively.

For the crossmodal coupling, differently from the supramodal layer connections that are only excitatory, both excitatory and inhibitory connections are implemented. Thus, class C output of one modality excites the class C neuronal maps in other modalities. On contrary, class $\hat{C}$ (not class C) output has in inhibitory effect on class C neuronal maps in other modalities.

In the following subsections we apply the supra/cross modal concepts to the case of audiovisual integration on person authentication problem based on face and speech information. A more detailed explanation of the implementation is also given.

2.1 Visual System Model

The visual system is modelled with a four-layer feedforward network of spiking neurons. In [10] a single frame configuration is presented, which is extended in [11] to integrate opinions over several frames to perform authentication. Figure 2 shows the network architecture used in this work that combines opinions of being/not being a desired face over several frames. Basically, the network receives in its input several frames that are processed in a frame-by-frame manner.

The first layer (L1) neurons represent the On and Off cells of retina, enhancing the high contrast parts of a given image (high-pass filter). Second layer (L2) is composed of orientation maps for each frequency scale, each one being selective to different directions. They are implemented using Gabor filters in eight directions (0°, 45°, 90°, 135°, 180°, 225°, 270°, and 315°) and two frequency scales. Maps in the third layer are trained to be sensitive to complex visual patterns (faces in our case study). In L3, neuronal maps are created or merged during learning in an adaptive on-line way. It is in L3, that neurons can receive crossmodal influences (multisensory neurons). Neurons in layer 4 (L4) accumulate opinions of being a certain class. If the opinions are able to trigger an L4 neuron to spike, the authentication is completed.

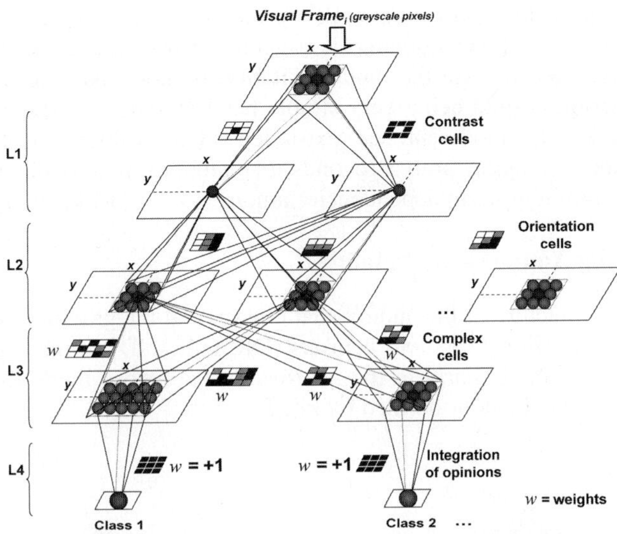

Fig. 2. Four layers adaptive spiking neural network (aSNN) architecture for visual pattern recognition. Neurons in L1 and L2 are sensitive to image contrast and orientations, respectively. L3 has the complex cells, trained to respond to specific patterns. It is in L3 that crossmodal coupling occurs. L4 accumulates opinions over different input excitations in time.

2.2 Auditory System Model

The auditory system is modelled with a two layers feedforward network of spiking neurons as proposed in our previous work [12]. In short, each speaker is represented by a set of prototype vectors that compute normalized similarity scores of MFCC (Mel Frequency Cepstrum Coefficients) features considering speaker and background models. The L1 neurons that define the prototypes of a given class can be also recipients of the crossmodal excitation/inhibition (multisensory neurons). The network architecture is illustrated in Figure 3.

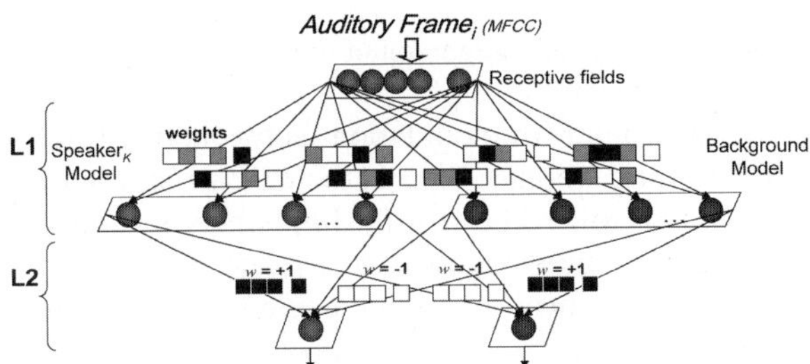

Fig. 3. Speaker authentication with spiking neural networks. L1 neurons with their respective connection weights implement the prototypes of a given class. L1 neurons also receive crossmodal excitation/inhibition. L2 accumulate binary opinions of being a claimant over several frames of speech signal.

There are two neurons in L2 for each speaker accumulating opinions over several frames of speech signals. One neuron is triggered if the speaker is authenticated and the other is triggered in case the input excitation is more likely to be a background model. This setup, despite being very simple has been proven efficient in traditional methods to tackle the short-sentence text-independent problem (typically comprised of input utterances ranging from 3 seconds to 1 minute), mainly due to the difficulty to extract and train long-term dependencies among frames [13][14][15].

2.3 Integrating Audiovisual Modalities

The detailed architecture of the audiovisual crossmodal integration is shown in Figure 4. In Figure 4 we can see the two neurons (OR and AND) in the supramodal layer. Each spiking neuron, similarly to the neurons that compose the SNNs of individual modalities, has the behaviour defined by Eq. 1.

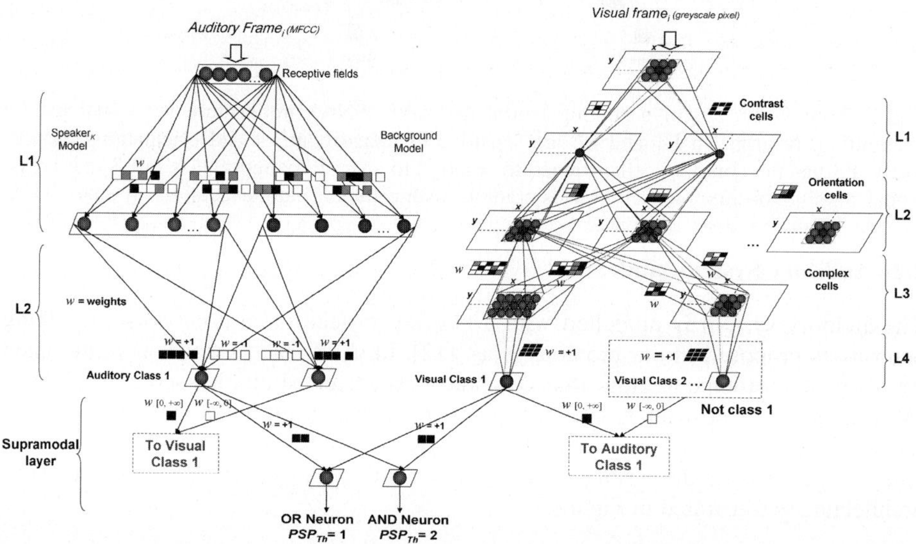

Fig. 4. Crossmodal integration of modalities using SNNs

Having supramodal neurons with modulation factor mod = 1 and setting all the incoming excitatory connection weights W to 1, the PSP_{Th} that implements the OR gate for two modalities is equal to 1. The neuron implementing the AND gate receives PSP_{Th} = 2. Notice that, it is only possible to set deterministically these parameters because of the properties of the neurons we are using (a neuron can spike only once at any stage of computation).

In this work we effectively model the crossmodal influence through the modification of PSP_{Th} in the layers responsible for decision making within each modality. More precisely, we modify the PSP_{Th} in layer 1 (L1) neurons in the auditory model (Section 2.2) and layer 3 (L3) neurons in the visual model (Section 2.1).

We use the following crossmodal parameters to denote the strength of the crossmodal influences: CM_{AVexc} (audio to video excitation), CM_{AVinh} (audio to video inhibition), CM_{VAexc} (video to audio excitation), CM_{VAinh} (video to audio inhibition), which are implemented with a proportional change in the usual PSP_{Th} values as:

$$PSP_{ThNew} = PSP_{ThOld}\,(1 + CM_{exc\,/\,inh})\tag{2}$$

where $CM_{exc/inh}$ is negative for crossmodal excitatory influence and positive for inhibitory influence. The crossmodal influence starts from the period one individual modality produces a result and lasts until all modalities finish processing.

Notice that, in the simplest case, setting crossmodal coupling to zero, we have effectively each modality processed separately, with a simple OR/AND fusion of opinions.

3 Experiments

We have implemented the integration of audiovisual modalities with a network of spiking neurons and used for evaluation the VidTimit dataset [6], which contains video and audio recordings of 43 persons. Our test setup deals specifically with the audiovisual person authentication problem. Thus, a person is authenticated based on spoken phrases and the corresponding facial information as the utterance is recorded (captured in frontal view).

In the following, we present the configuration details of each individual system as well as the parameters used in integration in our experiments:

Visual: Face detection was carried out with the Viola and Jones algorithm [16] implemented in the OpenCV [17]. Faces were converted into greyscale, normalized in size (height = 60 x width = 40), convolved with an elliptical mask, and encoded into spikes using rank order coding [18]. SNN does not require illumination normalization [8]. There are two scales of On/Off cells (4 L1 neuronal maps). In scale 1, the retina filters are implemented using a 3 x 3 Gaussian grid with $\sigma = 0.9$ and scale 2 uses a 5 x 5 grid with $\sigma = 1.5$. In L2, we have 8 different directions in each frequency scale with a total of 16 neuronal maps. The direction selective filters are implemented using Gabor functions with aspect ratio $\gamma = 0.5$ and phase offset $\varphi = \pi/2$. In scale 1 we use a 5 x 5 grid and wavelength $\lambda = 5$ and $\sigma = 2.5$ and in scale 2 a 7 x 7 grid with λ and σ set to 7 and 3.5, respectively. The modulation factor for the visual neurons was set to 0.995.

Auditory: Speech signals are sampled at 16 kHz, and features are extracted using standard MFCC with 19 MEL filter sub-bands ranging from 200 Hz to 7 kHz. Each MFCC feature is then encoded into spikes using rank order coding [18] with one receptive field neuron representing each coefficient. For each speaker model, we train a specific background model. For the sake of simplicity, we use the following procedure: the background model of a speaker i is trained using the same amount of utterances used to train the speaker model. The utterances are randomly chosen from the remaining training speakers. We have defined *a priori* the number of neurons in the auditory L1 neuronal maps for the speaker and background model (50 neurons each). The modulation factor for auditory neurons was set to 0.9.

Integration: The crossmodal parameters were set as: $CM_{AVexc} = CM_{VAexc} = 0.1$ and $CM_{AVinh} = CM_{VAinh} = 0$. We also present the results that do not consider the crossmodal coupling, i.e., $CM_{AVexc} = CM_{VAexc} = CM_{AVinh} = CM_{VAinh} = 0$.

The system is trained to authenticate 35 users using six utterances from each user for training. To train the visual part, only two frames from each user have been used, collected while uttering two distinct phrases from the same session.

For test, we use two phrases (each phrase corresponding to one sample) recorded in two different sessions. We have 35 users x 2 samples = 70 positive claims. Simulating impostors, we use two utterances of the eight remaining users that try to break into each of the 35 users' models, which give 560 false claims.

The test is carried out frame-by-frame keeping the time correspondence between speech and visual frames. However, to speed up the computational simulations, we downsampled the visual frames. Five visual frames per second have been used whereas the speech samples have rate at 50 frames per second (Figure 5). We noticed that it does not affect the performance of the system, as for period lower than 200 ms we could not notice substantial differences between one facial posture and another.

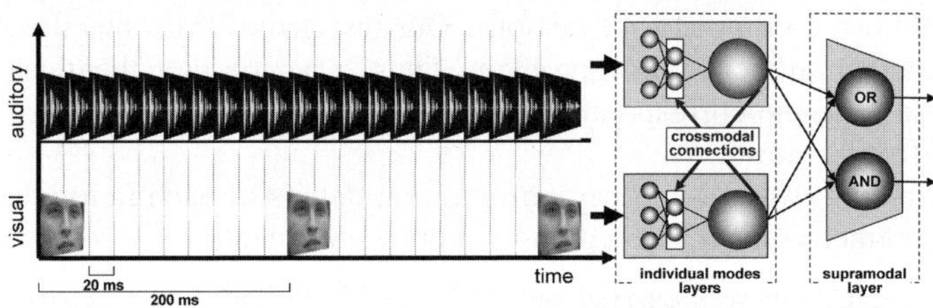

Fig. 5. Frame-based integration of modalities

The supramodal layer and the crossmodal coupling are updated when an individual modality outputs a spike, which may occur once in every frame. Here, we consider the same processing time for one frame regardless of the modality, although it is well known that auditory stimulus are processed faster than a visual stimulus (difference of approximately 40 to 60 ms [4]). In our experiments, for the speech mode, the number of opinions needed to validate a person is set proportionally to the size of a given utterance (we use 20% of the total number of frames in an utterance). For the visual mode, the number of opinions needed to authenticate a person is set to two (two frames).

Figure 6A shows the best performance obtained on each individual modality. While the best total error (TE) for the face authentication is 21%, the auditory authentication is TE $\approx$ 38% (varying values of L1 PSP_{Th} in the auditory system and L3 PSP_{Th} in the visual system).

Figure 6B shows the best performance of the system considering the integration held in the supramodal layer. First, we set the crossmodal coupling parameters to zero, simulating only the OR and AND integration of individual modalities done by the supramodal layer. Then, the crossmodal coupling was made active, setting $CM_{AVexc} = CM_{VAexc} = 0.1$ and $CM_{AVinh} = CM_{VAinh} = 0$. The same parameters of individual modalities are used in this experiment, i.e., auditory parameters (L1 PSP_{Th}) and visual parameters (L3 PSP_{Th}) ranging from [0.5, 0.9] and [0.1, 0.5], respectively. The x-axis represents different combination of L1 and L3 PSP_{Th} ordered according to the performance.

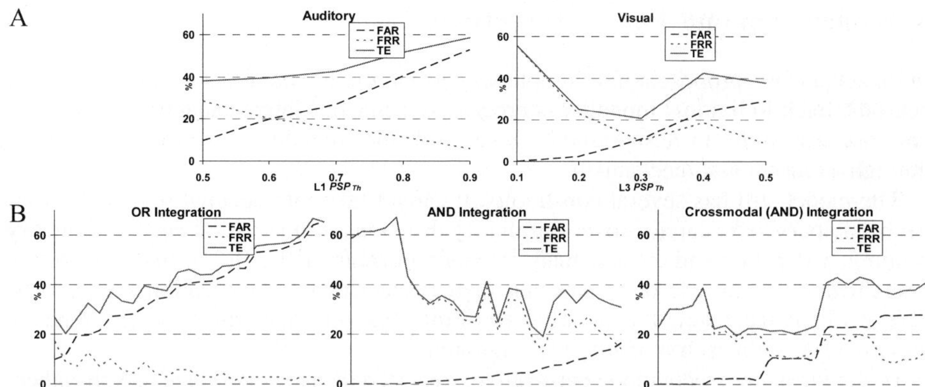

Fig. 6. A) Performance of individual modalities for different values of auditory (L1 PSP_{Th}) and visual parameters (L3 PSP_{Th}). On left: auditory system. On right: visual system. B) Performance of the OR and AND integration of modalities with a supramodal layer of spiking neurons (left and middle graphs, respectively). On right, when excitatory crossmodal influences were made active (for auditory L1 PSP_{Th} and L3 PSP_{Th} ranging from [0.5, 0.9] and [0.1, 0.5], respectively). FAR is the false acceptance rate, FRR is the false rejection rate and TE is the total error (FAR+FRR).

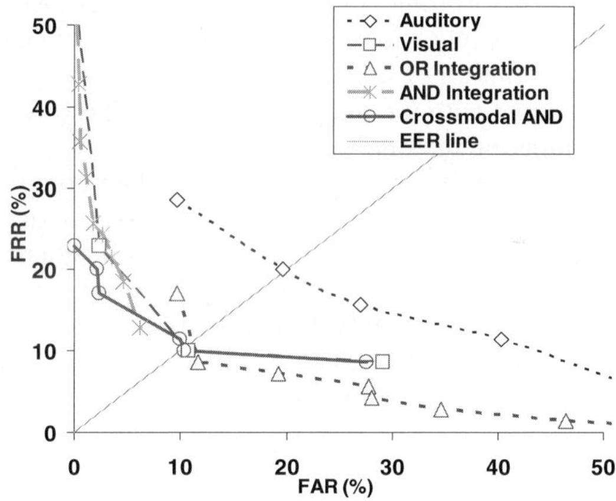

Fig. 7. Comparison between individual modes (auditory and visual) and the corresponding integration. Overall, the integration presents better performance than individual modes. OR, AND, Crossmodal AND alternates in the best position for different points of operation. EER is the equal error rate, where FAR = FRR.

Having in mind that the parameters have been optimized by hand, in Figure 7 we can see the potential advantages of the integration module. When the system needs to operate with low FAR levels (below 10%), AND and Crossmodal AND provide lower FRR than any singular modality. When the system requires operating with low FRR (below 10%), OR integration can be used instead, which gives lower FAR for the same FRR levels.

4   Conclusion and Future Directions

In this paper, we propose a new simple way to integrate modalities using fast spiking neurons. Each individual modality is processed using specialized adaptive SNNs. The integration is done in a supramodal layer and one modality can influence another through a crossmodal mechanism.

The model still has several constraints. It cannot take into account several biological behaviours, e.g., cannot cover familiarity decisions, semantic information, identity priming, and within and cross domain semantic priming [19][20][21]. In respect to the implementation, the use of frames and their respective synchronization seems to be very artificial, truncating the natural flow of information. In addition, the difference in processing time in each modality [4] is ignored.

Under the pattern recognition perspective, we tested the network on the person authentication problem. In preliminary experiments, we can clearly see that the integration of modes enhances the performance in several operation points of the system.

In [6], the integration of modalities was explored with the VidTimit dataset using a combination of mathematical and statistical methods. The auditory system alone, using MFCC features and GMM in a noise-free setup, reached TE (total error) = FAR (false acceptance rate) + FRR (false rejection rate) $\approx$ 22%. The visual system was reported to have TE $\approx$ 8% with features extracted using PCA (principal component analysis) and SVM (support vector machine) for classification. Several adaptive and non adaptive systems to perform integration have been tested, with the best performance obtained with a new approach that builds the decision boundaries for integration considering how the distribution of opinions are likely to change under noisy conditions. The accuracy obtained with the integration reached TE $\approx$ 6% using 35 users for training and 8 users simulating the impostors.

Despite some differences in our experiments setup when compared to [6], our preliminary results (Fig. 6) are clearly not as good. Nonetheless, to extract the best performance of the system and evaluate the crossmodal influence on pattern recognition, an optimization mechanism needs to be incorporated. As pointed out in [11], one of the promising properties of the computation with spiking neurons is that it enables the multi-criteria optimization of parameters according to accuracy, speed and energy efficiency. Since the integration uses spiking neurons, the optimization can be extended to cover the parameters used on integration as well (a good starting point to understand crossmodal learning can be found in [22][23]). Thus, the next step consists in investigating the gain in speed and performance with optimized parameters.

Acknowledgments

The work has been supported by the Tertiary Education Commission of New Zealand (S.G.W.) and by the NERF grant AUTX02001 funded by FRST (L.B., N.K.).

References

1. Calvert, G.A.: Crossmodal processing in the human brain: insights from functional neuro-imaging studies. Cerebral Cortex 11, 1110–1123 (2001)
2. von Kriegstein, K., Kleinschmidt, A., Sterzer, P., Giraud, A.: Interaction of face and voice areas during speaker recognition. Journal of Cognitive Neuroscience 17(3), 367–376 (2005)

3. von Kriegstein, K., Giraud, A.: Implicit multisensory associations influence voice recognition. Plos Biology 4(10), 1809–1820 (2006)

4. Stein, B.E., Meredith, M.A.: The merging of the senses. MIT Press, Cambridge (1993)

5. Sharkey, A.: Combining artificial neural nets: ensemble and modular multi-net systems. Springer, Heidelberg (1999)

6. Sanderson, C., Paliwal, K.K.: Identity verification using speech and face information. Digital Signal Processing 14, 449–480 (2004)

7. Ross, A., Jain, A.K.: Information fusion in biometrics. Pattern Recognition Letters 24(13), 2115–2125 (2003)

8. Kasabov, N., Postma, E., van den Herik, J.: AVIS: A connectionist-based framework for integrated auditory and visual information processing. Information Sciences 123, 127–148 (2000)

9. Delorme, A., Gautrais, J., van Rullen, R., Thorpe, S.: SpikeNet: a simulator for modeling large networks of integrate and fire neurons. Neurocomputing 26(27), 989–996 (1999)

10. Wysoski, S.G., Benuskova, L., Kasabov, N.: On-line learning with structural adaptation in a network of spiking neurons for visual pattern recognition. In: Kollias, S., Stafylopatis, A., Duch, W., Oja, E. (eds.) ICANN 2006. LNCS, vol. 4131, pp. 61–70. Springer, Heidelberg (2006)

11. Wysoski, S.G., Benuskova, L., Kasabov, N.: Fast and adaptive network of spiking neurons for multi-view visual pattern recognition. Neurocomputing (under review, 2007)

12. Wysoski, S.G., Benuskova, L., Kasabov, N.: Text-independent speaker authentication with spiking neural networks. In: de Sá, J.M., Alexandre, L.A., Duch, W., Mandic, D. (eds.) ICANN 2007. LNCS, vol. 4669, pp. 758–767. Springer, Heidelberg (2007)

13. Burileanu, C., Moraru, D., Bojan, L., Puchiu, M., Stan, A.: On performance improvement of a speaker verification system using vector quantization, cohorts and hybrid cohort-world models. International Journal of Speech Technology 5, 247–257 (2002)

14. Reynolds, D.A., Quatieri, T.F., Dunn, R.B.: Speaker verification using adapted Gaussian Mixture Models. Digital Signal Processing 10, 19–41 (2000)

15. Bimbot, F., et al.: A tutorial on text-independent speaker verification. EURASIP Journal on Applied Signal Processing 4, 430–451 (2004)

16. Viola, P., Jones, M.J.: Rapid object detection using a boosted cascade of simple features. Proc. IEEE CVPR 1, 511–518 (2001)

17. OpenCV - http://www.intel.com/technology/computing/opencv/

18. Delorme, A., Perrinet, L., Thorpe, S.: Networks of integrate-and-fire neurons using Rank Order Coding. Neurocomputing, 38–48 (2001)

19. Burton, A.M., Bruce, V., Johnston, R.A.: Understanding face recognition with an interactive activation model. British Journal of Psychology 81, 361–380 (1990)

20. Ellis, H.D., Jones, D.M., Mosdell, N.: Intra- and inter-modal repetition priming of familiar faces and voices. British Journal of Psycology 88, 143–156 (1997)

21. Ellis, A.W., Young, A.W., Hay, D.C.: Modelling the recognition of faces and words. In: Morris, P.E. (ed.) Modelling Cognition, Wiley, London (1987)

22. McIntosh, A.R., Cabeza, R.E., Lobaugh, N.J.: Analysis of neural interactions explains the activation of occipital cortex by an auditory stimulus. Journal of Neurophysiology 80, 2790–2796 (1998)

23. Gonzalo, D., Shallice, T., Dolan, R.: Time-dependent changes in learning audiovisual associations: a single-trial fMRI study. NeuroImage 11, 243–255 (2000)

Evolving Connectionist Systems for Adaptive Sport Coaching

Boris Bacic, Nikola Kasabov, Stephen MacDonell, and Shaoning Pang

Auckland University of Technology AUT, School of Computing and Mathematical Sciences,
Knowledge Engineering and Discovery Research Institute, KEDRI,
Private Bag 92006, Auckland 1142, New Zealand
{bbacic, nkasabov, smacdone, spang}@aut.ac.nz

Abstract. Contemporary computer assisted coaching software operates either on a particular sub-space of the wider problem or requires expert(s) to operate and provide explanations and recommendations. This paper introduces a novel motion data processing methodology oriented to the provision of future generation sports coaching software. The main focus of investigation is the development of techniques that facilitate processing automation, incremental learning from initially small data sets, and robustness of architecture with a degree of interpretation on individual sport performers' motion techniques. Findings from a case study using tennis motion data verify the prospect of building similar models and architectures for other sports or entertainment areas in which the aims are to improve human motion efficacy and to prevent injury. A central feature is the decoupling of the high-level analytical architecture from the low-level processing of motion data acquisition hardware, meaning that the system will continue to work with future motion acquisition devices.

Keywords: Classification, Coaching Rule, CREM, Coaching Scenario, ECOS, EFuNN, iB-fold, Feature Extraction, Local Personalised Global Knowledge Integration, Orchestration, Weighted Sum.

1 Introduction: Computer Assisted Sport Coaching

Contemporary computer assisted sport coaching software can be divided into two major categories:

1. Relatively expensive software and hardware solutions designed to be operated across domains by experts in the areas of Biomechanics or Physiotherapy [1, 2].
2. Specialised software for a particular sport's sub-domain that is affordable to the sport's enthusiasts and that does not need to be operated by a professional domain expert (although some initial and follow-up expert assistance may be recommended). In general, such solutions are *intended*[1] to provide feedback typically as an animated/video replay or as a report containing

---

[1] i.e. limited aspects of non-evolvable coaching compared to human coaching. It is also not intended to replace, but to complement human supervised coaching aspects.

M. Ishikawa et al. (Eds.): ICONIP 2007, Part II, LNCS 4985, pp. 416–425, 2008.
© Springer-Verlag Berlin Heidelberg 2008

measured values compared with 'optimal' biomechanical key values [3, 4]. In the case of entertainment applications (i.e. videogames and sport simulations) a player can interact with a virtual environment [5] using a motion sensitive input device such as the Wii controller (http://www.nintendo.com/overviewwii). Intended coaching may occur through repetitive interaction with the environment.

At present, commercial software development in this domain is restricted by the cost of 3D motion data acquisition relative to precision, accuracy, noise, sampling frequency and robustness to occasional data loss. Other restrictive and undesired factors that contribute to limited progress are: the degree of obtrusiveness, environmental and operational restrictions (e.g. autonomy of unsupervised operation, robustness to shock, vibration and ambient operating ranges), the often lengthy time required to set up the environment with initial settings, and the resulting extent of expert involvement. Examples of computational and operational limitations impeding the development, adoption and/or success of computer assisted coaching tools have also been discussed in [6].

In general, these limitations can be considered in terms of two major groupings:

1. The first category of drawbacks (of present sport coaching software) consists of excessive user operation/intervention, required sport domain knowledge, and the advanced nature of the computer equipment (e.g. motion data transfer, setting up recording environment, digitising and "slicing" video, annotations and measurements and measurements interpretation).

2. The second category of drawbacks relates to limitations in motion data processing e.g. lack of adaptability, inability to learn from data, and insufficient or limited results interpretations and personalisation.

A level of informed speculation (i.e. by extending Moore's Law) enables us to predict that near-future ICT technology for obtaining real-time, high precision motion data will be more ubiquitous and more affordable. The same level of speculation applied to Human Computer Interaction (HCI) devices suggests that it will soon be possible to provide multimedia-rich feedback to learners from systems that are capable of assessing human motion. Such predictions provide the necessary infrastructural support to underpin the feasibility of generic evolving computational models for assessing human motion as a separate layer from low-level motion data processing and HCI management layers.

2 Proposed Adaptive Coaching System

The initial stages of this study have been focused on scoping an appropriate experimental system design and choosing an initial case study in tennis.

2.1 Motivation for Adaptive Sports Coaching System

Bridging the interdisciplinary gap between Sport Biomechanics and the application area of Evolving Connectionist Systems (ECOS) [7], a novel coaching system based on a robust and adaptive software architecture should have the following capabilities:

- Adaptation to new playing motion data (e.g. swing techniques) that can be incrementally presented,
- Rule based knowledge interpretation from motion data, including knowledge insertion and extraction,
- Personalised (swing) technique assessment modelling and personalised coaching where new modules and connections can be introduced at any stage of the system's operation including adaptation to new (swing) rules and variables,
- Knowledge separation into Personalised, Global and Environmental levels (e.g. Coaching Scenarios (CS) and individual coaching approaches),
- Ability to work with initially small data sets, and with incomplete Global and Environmental knowledge,
- Supervised, Unsupervised, Incremental and On-line learning.

2.2 Evolving Coaching: An Adaptive Tennis Coaching System

In 'traditional' (i.e. human assisted) sport coaching, a coach can correct and potentially improve an observed learner's motion technique by communicating a set of relevant coaching rules combined with intervention instruction(s) to the learner. In the system proposed here, adherence or otherwise to each relevant coaching rule is observed and assessed individually in a Coaching Rule Evaluation Module (CREM), as shown in Fig. 1.

Section 2.4 further explains the Orchestration paradigm – as a set of individual CREMs collectively assessing human motion.

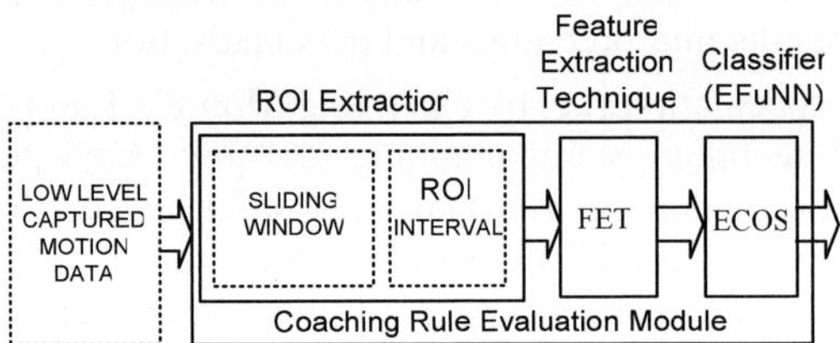

Fig. 1. CREM block diagram and stages of data processing. CREMs are responsible for classification of both temporal and spatial qualitative observations by a coach, although represented/expressed numerically. A process of transforming a temporal/spatial Region of Interest (ROI) to quantitative observations needed for machine learning classification is referred to here as Feature Extraction Technique (FET).

CREM motion data processing occurs in multiple stages:

1. The first stage of CREM processing involves the automated extraction of the Region of Interest (ROI). ROI automation in a stand-alone CREM (Fig. 1) would include the recognition of tennis shots and their ROI extraction from time series of 3D tennis data (section 3.1). A two-staged algorithm structure [8] allows hyper threading implementation for quick detection and ROI extraction.

2. In the Feature Extraction Technique (FET) stage, the system is responsible for mathematically transforming the ROI into a set of the most discriminative key

values representing each shot. Compared to human qualitative assessment of a shot, a coach would typically focus on constituent time sub-segments of the shot. Within each time sub-segment, the coach would analyse observed temporal (e.g. hip rotation leading shoulder turn) or spatial (e.g. swing width) key features to assess adherence to a particular coaching rule (or heuristic).

3. In the final stage, an ECOS classifier module is responsible for numerically assessing/evaluating adherence to a particular observed coaching rule. As the output of the last stage of CREM internal processing, an ECOS module provides the overall CREM output as and if required, to supply feedback to the learner and to augment the system's coaching knowledge (Fig. 5).

2.3   Evolving Fuzzy Neural Network Architecture (EFuNN)

ECOS has been developed to address several of the perceived disadvantages and limitations of traditional connectionist systems – by comparison, ECOS are resilient to over-training, they learn and adapt their structure quickly, and they are far more resistant to catastrophic forgetting [7]. Paradoxically, it is these very advantages that cause some of ECOS' disadvantages. Since they deal with new examples by adding nodes to their structure, they rapidly increase in size and can become unwieldy if no aggregation or pruning operations are applied. They also have some sensitivity to their parameters, which require constant adjustment for optimum performance.

An ECOS network always has at least one evolving layer, such as the middle layer shown in the Evolving Fuzzy Neural Network depicted in Fig. 2. This is the layer that will grow and adapt itself to the incoming data, and is the layer with which the learning algorithm is most concerned.

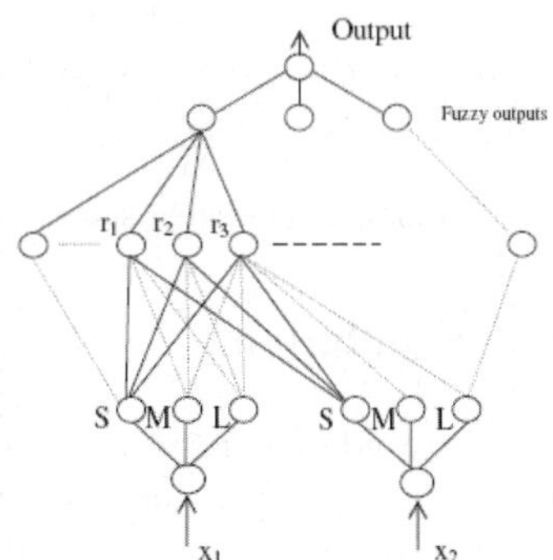

Fig. 2. EFuNN structure as an ECOS classifier with two inputs and one output ([9], p.677)

Although there are a growing number of ECOS implementations [7, 9, 10], that chosen here is a relatively simple solution. It would be an informative future exercise to assess which ECOS model works better for a particular CREM module. However, several have high-volume data requirements (in order to perform parameter optimisation) which could limit their viability in low-volume data applications.

A simple implementation of ECOS was achieved using EFuNN, Fig. 2, with its ability to work with initially small data sets and to extract knowledge as a set of fuzzy rules. Selecting the Membership Functions (MF) and their number in a given EFuNN would depend on the particular CREM task (e.g. if an expert would say "a player's wrist can be too far away from the body but never too close, when hitting …" then two MFs would be adequate for a CREM assessing swing width).

2.4 CREM Orchestration

To accommodate diversity in Coaching Scenarios (CS) and in human coaches' qualitative analyses, a method for their orchestration has been proposed, as depicted in Fig. 3, Proposed in [12], a weighted sum ECOS Architecture would support the implementation of Global, Local (i.e. Environmental – as CS and different coaching approaches) and Personalised modelling introduced in [9]. Each CREM uses its own features sub-set. Skill and Weights parameters (from Fig. 3) can also be stored in any of the Personalised, Environmental/CS or Global databases.

Automated shot extraction for each CREM is performed before the Rule Module Selector to avoid computational overlapping. Each selected CREM participating in the shot evaluation automatically extracts only the temporal sub set (sub event) needed for its own feature extraction.

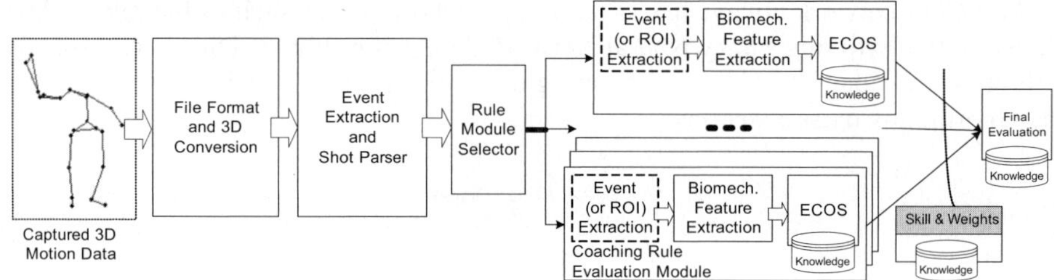

Fig. 3. CREM Orchestration and modular stages of data processing

3   Experimentation and Simulation

Aspects of experimental design are now addressed, followed by a description of the outcomes of different activities that led from ideas to specific results. Tennis data were recorded whereby an expert coach mimicked styles representative of beginner players. To ensure that data samples were sufficiently represented in typical swing style clusters, the expert's mimicking was verified by two independent coaching experts in two stages i.e. during the recording stage and later on, in a subsequent "blind review" manner examining only captured motion data in the from of an animated "stick model" (Fig. 4).

3.1 Motion Data Set Acquisition

The human motion dataset was recorded using 3D marker positions in a time series at a sampling frequency of 50HZ (or fps) and one millimetre resolution. To capture 3D motion using multi-camera infra-red (IR) recording technology in IR spectrum, a set of retro-reflective markers was attached to selected anatomical landmarks of the player's body. By defining the markers' topology a "stick model" was created to represent a human body. Animated visualization of the stick figure (Fig. 4) – approximating a human swinging a racquet – was sufficient for the expert coach to verify the mimicking process, to provide output labels for machine classification and to give qualitative analysis that influenced high level architecture design. The expert's involvement was also required in defining players' expected skill level relative to the operation of a set of CREM for a given Coaching Scenario (CS).

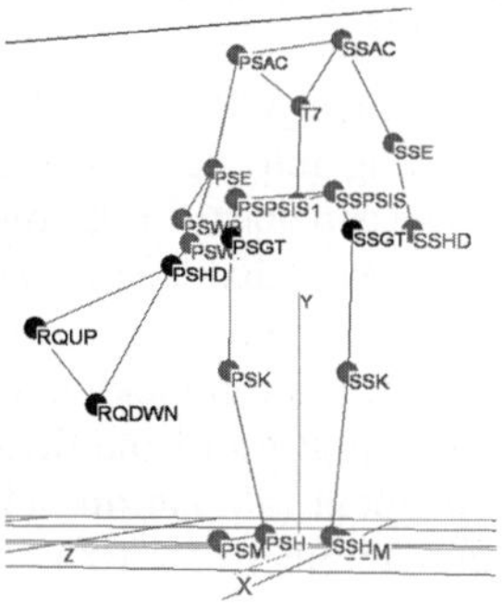

Fig. 4. A "stick figure" representing a tennis player holding a racquet

3.2 Processing and Validation

After qualitative analysis of critical key features on which a tennis coach would focus their attention, the first testable hypothesis was framed. This aimed to quantify the 'most critical' critical key features that could coarsely discriminate between tennis swings e.g. "good" or "bad" style for a forehand swing. A hypothesis asserting the correlation between motion of the racquet hitting surface (around the point of impact) and the player's body motion was chosen to be tested as the first and the strongest hypothesis for that purpose. The first prototype, constructed to enable the testing of the hypothesis (published in [11]), did not require adaptive learning. It was designed using a Radial basis function (RBF) neural network from the open source Netlab toolbox (http://www.ncrg.aston.ac.uk/netlab/down.php) and accompanying book [12].

The need for the experimental work to minimise generalisation error using a relatively small dataset (40 samples) in spite of potentially high dimensionality of the problem space demanded rigorous consideration in the following areas (see also Table 3):

1.   Choosing the validation method
2.   Exploring the benefits of expert cognitive pre-clustering
3.   Evolving architecture design.

Training and classification evaluation of the first experimental prototype was undertaken using the "leave-one-out" cross-validation method (Table 1).

Table 1. Leave-one-out cross-validation. To ensure that over-fitting was avoided, a sub-optimal model utilising 2 hidden neurons was tested and is included in the results. Due to incomplete time series markers position data, the original set of 19 extracted forehand shots was further reduced to 14.

	Number of Input Vectors	14
	Number of Cross-validations	20
Classification Accuracy	2 hidden neurons	66.4 [%]
	3 hidden neurons	99.9 [%]
	4 hidden neurons	99.9 [%]

During the design stages for subsequent CREMs, different validation methods were also considered and evaluated, taking into account the expert's familiarity with the data and probability for error. The stochastic relation between data and validation method error as incident prediction $P(C)$ has been investigated in [13]. The data set was pre-clustered into eight groups by the expert applying Gestalt observation model in biomechanics [1]. An erroneous validation incident example would occur where an entire cluster is allocated to the test portion of the dataset. The probabilistic formula (1) for single iteration data split incident calculation in hold-out validation method has been confirmed by comparing large number ($n \times 10^6$) of simulation results.

$$P(C) = \frac{\binom{j}{k}\binom{n-j}{m-k}}{\binom{n}{m}}.$$

(1)

Where:

$P(C)$ ... Probability of event C; defined as $P(k$ cluster samples in test dataset$)$

j ... size of observed cluster

k ... number of samples in test data from observed cluster

n ... size of the data sample

m ... size of the test dataset portion

To avoid $P(C)$ incidents further expert cognitive pre-clustering cross-validation algorithms (e.g. iB-fold [14], as modified leave-v-out) have been used.

3.3 Model Integration

The next stage of the research was focused on the automated extraction of the Region of Interest (ROI), including recognition of each tennis shot and its extraction from time series 3D data [8]. Compared to human expert shot extraction, the average prediction for the first frame number in the automated shot extraction was 0.789 frames slower; and for end swing the difference was -0.16 frames – i.e. predicting the end of swing was 3.2 ms earlier. The duration of a frame = 0.02 sec. Detailed results are given in Table 2.

By merging the outcome of both experimental studies into a single CREM prototype Fig. 1, the further CREMs were designed to operate as components of the integrated coaching system.

Table 2. Experimental results on automated Forehand ROI extraction compared to expert's manual ROI extraction. Number of extracted Forehand shots = 19.

	Duration [frames]	Start frame Delta	End frame Delta	Duration [frames]	Delta duration
Average	8.263	0.789	-0.16	7.316	0.947
Max	13	3	1	12	4
Min	5	0	-1	5	-1
Median	8	1	0	6	1
Range	8	3	2	7	5

3.4 Rule Extraction

The other CREMs were designed using ECOS, as per the overall architecture shown in Fig 1. By using EFuNN from Fig. 2, it was possible to extract knowledge as a set of fuzzy rules and apply further translation of that knowledge into a form closer to that provided by a human coach (rather than as a large number of rules that were potentially difficult to comprehend). To make effective use of these rules the coaching principle "less is more" was taken into account. The system was designed with the aim of reducing the rule set to key or high-priority issues – ideally in most CS a learner would address one improvement at a time.

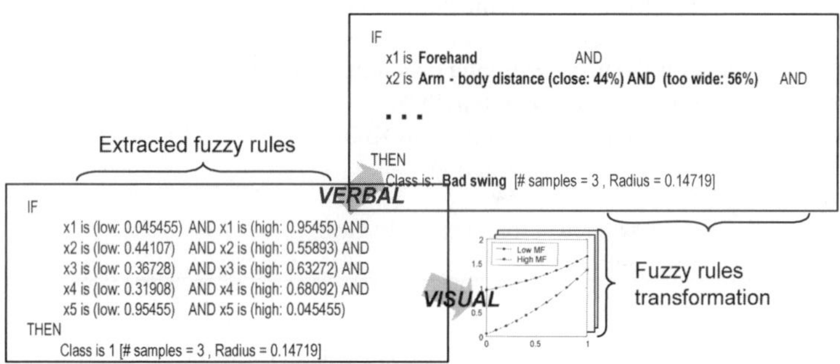

Fig. 5. CREM block diagram and stages of data processing. From human perspective a player can focus on individual improvement of particular coaching rule over a period of time.

4 Conclusions and Future Work

The methodology utilised in this work is shown in summary form in Table 3. Apart from contributing to the application area of ECOS and bridging the discipline with research in biomechanics, the methodology has parallels in diverse areas such as medicine and bioinformatics e.g. Inductive vs Transductive approach, Global, Local and Personal modelling in Bioinformatics [9] with CREM Orchestration. Similar to the approach shown in Table 3, another activity-driven approach was independently developed in the UK as the Standard Integrative Systems Biology Approach [15].

Table 3. Summary of main activities that have led from ideas to specific results

Step	Activity	Ideas and Opportunities	Outcome[2]
1.	Identify Sport Domain	Tennis, Golf	
2.a	Identify Key Factors – to evaluate human motion		
2.b	Identify and Develop Hypothesis	1st "Main" Hypothesis of "hitting surface"	Temporal and Spatial ROI and Coaching Rule(s)
3.a	Design Experiment	3D Stick data model. Biomechanics protocol.	
3.b	Collect Data		Sport motion data
4.	Generate Models	Automating swing extraction and classification. New FETs.	1st CREM using RBF, others using ECOS
5.	Evaluate Results	Modelling with initially small data set. Research rigour and re-evaluation. "Sub optimised" approach for "leave one out" (Table 1). Predicting validations incidents. Cognitive pre-clustering.	iB-fold [14], Prediction method for hold-out incidents. Evaluation of ECOS for the discovery of tennis coaching rules.
6.	Revise steps 2-5	Additional CREM. Experimental design focus.	Additional CREM. Automated ROI extraction
7.	Integrate Models – to explain high level system properties	CREM Orchestration Architectures. Personalisation.	Weighted Sum, GUI and User/Task Analysis [16]
8.	Identify Key Components of Integrated Models for Control and further directions	Evolving swing style and evolving coaching methods and hypothesis.	Global, Personal and Environmental/Coaching Scenario
9.	Revise and Modify Models – to be re-applied to the new sport domain	Learning and Knowledge Extraction	ECOS, ECM, EFuNN
10.	Repeat the above steps for new domain	From Tennis to Golf	

The modelling - follow up case study - of revisited models (step 9, Table 3) from tennis in the golf domain will soon be completed based on an already collected large data set of golf swings. Further advancement in presenting fuzzy rules to humans will promote applicative advancement in the area of neuro-fuzzy systems. In conclusion, for human motion applications, in spite of the constraints associated with state of the art technology of motion data acquisition (time consuming, labour intensive, expensive) the favourable experimental results to date give promise of an interesting and innovative future research area.

Acknowledgments. As the first author, I wish to express my appreciation to list of people who also inspired and offered their support: Dr. Zeke S. Chang, Prof. Patria Hume, Prof. Takeshi Yamakawa, Gordon Grimsey and Petar Bačić. Also I wish to acknowledge contributors' extended support and creating opportunities beyond PhD supervision. Tennis data was collected from "Peharec" Polyclinic for physical therapy and rehabilitation, Pula, Croatia. Golf data was collected from AUT Golf Driving Range. AUTEC ethics data collection approval, number 06/105.

References

1. Knudson, D.V., Morrison, C.S.: Qualitative Analysis of Human Movement. Human Kinetics, Champaign (2002)
2. SiliconCOACH PRO. SiliconCoach Ltd., Dunedin (2005)
3. SmartSwing. SmartSwing Inc., Austin (2005)
4. Leadbetter Interactive. Interactive Frontiers, New Hudson (2005)
5. Master Game List. Nintendo of America Inc., Redmond, WA, vol. 2007 (2007)
6. Bacic, B.: Bridging the Gap between Biomechanics and Artificial Intelligence. In: Schwameder, H., et al. (eds.) International Symposium on Biomechanics in Sports - ISBS 2006, Department of Sport Science and Kinesiology, vol. 1, pp. 371–374. University of Salzburg, Austria, Salzburg, Austria (2006)
7. Kasabov, N.K.: Evolving Connectionist Systems: Methods and Applications in Bioinformatics, Brain Study and Intelligent Machines. Springer, London (2002)
8. Bacic, B.: Towards a Neuro Fuzzy Tennis Coach: Automated Extraction of the Region of Interest (ROI). In: International Conference on Fuzzy Systems (FUZZ-IEEE) and International Joint Conference on Neural Networks (IJCNN), vol. 2, pp. 703–708. IEEE, Budapest, Hungary (2004)
9. Kasabov, N.: Global, Local and Personalised Modeling and Pattern Discovery in Bioinformatics: An Integrated Approach. Pattern Recognition Letters 28, 673–685 (2007)
10. Kasabov, N.: Adaptation and Interaction in Dynamical Systems: Modelling and Rule Discovery through Evolving Connectionist Systems. Applied Soft Computing 6, 307–322 (2006)
11. Bacic, B.: Automating Systems for Interpreting Biomechanical 3D Data Using ANN: A Case Study on Tennis. In: Kasabov, N., Chan, Z.S.H. (eds.) 3rd Conference on Neuro-Computing and Evolving Intelligence - NCEI 2003. Knowledge Engineering and Discovery Research Institute (KEDRI), Auckland, New Zealand, pp. 101–102 (2003)
12. Nabney, I.: Netlab: Algorithms for Pattern Recognition. Springer, London (2004)
13. Bačić, B.: Using Probability in Estimating the Size of a Test Data Sample. In: 6th International Conference on Hybrid Intelligent Systems (HIS 2006) and the 4th International Conference on Neuro Computing and Evolving Intelligence (NCEI 2006), Auckland, New Zealand, vol. 1, pp. 55–56 (2006)
14. Bacic, B.: A Novel Generic Cluster Based iB-fold Cross-validation, p. 6. Auckland University of Technology, Auckland (2005)
15. Narayanan, A.: Intelligent Bioinformatics and Cancer Systems Biology: The Computational Search for Killer Genes, p. 42. Auckland University of Technology, Auckland (2007)
16. Bacic, B.: Personalised Coaching System, p. 4. AUT, Auckland (2005)

A Novel Chaotic Neural Network for Function Optimization

Ting Zhou, Zhenhong Jia, and Xiuling Liu

College of Information science & engineering, Xinjiang University, Urumqi
830046, P.R. China
Corresponding author: Zhenhong Jia
jzhh@xju.edu.cn

Abstract. Chaotic neural networks have been proved to be powerful tools to solve the optimization problems. And the chaotic neural networks whose activation function is non-monotonous will be more effective than Chen's chaotic neural network in solving optimization problems, especially in searching global minima of continuous function and traveling salesman problems. In this paper, a novel chaotic neural network for function optimization is introduced. In contrast to the Chen's chaotic neural network, the activation function of the novel chaotic neural network is wavelet function and the different-parameters annealing function are adopted in different period, so it performs extremely better when compared to the convergence speed and the accuracy of the results. And two elaborate examples of function optimization are given to show its superiority. This chaotic neural network can be a new powerful approach to solving a class of function optimization problems.

Keywords: Chaotic neural network, Wavelet function, Annealing function, Function optimization.

1   Introduction

Neural networks have been shown to be powerful tools for solving optimization problems. The Hopfield neural network is proposed by Hopfield and Tank [1] and [2], has been extensively applied to many fields in the past years. Unfortunately, it was shown that the simple HNN often yields infeasible solutions for complicated optimization problems, such as TSP [3]. The main reason of this inefficiency is the structure of energy function in HNN, which has many local minima in which the network get stuck in one of them due to its strictly energy reducing behavior [4].

To overcome this difficulty, chaotic neural networks exploiting the rich behaviors of nonlinear dynamics have been developed as a new approach to extend the problem solving ability of standard HNN [5]-[7]. There have been much research interests and efforts in theory and applications of chaotic neural networks [8]-[10].

However, since CNN base on the periodic oscillations property of chaotic dynamics to search the optimal solution, the search time must be spent more than the HNN. There is a new trend in using improved simulated annealing mechanics to accelerate the convergence speed of CNN [11]-[13].

M. Ishikawa et al. (Eds.): ICONIP 2007, Part II, LNCS 4985, pp. 426–433, 2008.

Actually, some researchers have pointed out that the single neural unit can easily behave chaotic behavior if its activation function is non-monotonous [14]. And the reference [15] has presented that the effective activation function may adopt kinds of different forms, and should embody non-monotonous behavior. In many CNN model the activation functions almost adopt sigmoid function, theoretically speaking, they are not the basic function, so the ability of solving optimization problems is less effective than whose activation functions are composed of kinds of basic functions in chaotic neural networks [16]-[18].

We benefit from these ideas in our architecture. In this paper, we introduced a novel chaotic neural network to solve function optimization problems.

The organization of this paper is as follows: The WSAN model is formulated in Section 2. Afterward, the simulations of function optimization problems that show the superiority of our method are described in Section 3. Finally the conclusion will be presented in Section 4.

2   The Novel Chaotic Neural Network

In order to take advantage of the chaotic dynamics, convergent speed, and the activation function being wavelet function, the novel chaotic neural networks are defined as:

$$x_i(t) = exp(-(u \cdot y_i(t) \cdot (1+\eta(t)))^2 / 2) \cdot cos(5 \cdot u \cdot y(t) \cdot (1+\eta(t))) \quad (1)$$

$$y_i(t+1) = ky_i(t) + \alpha[\sum_j W_{ij}x_j + I_i] - z_i(t)(x_i(t)-I_0) . \quad (2)$$

$$z_i(t+1) = \begin{cases} (1-\beta_1)z_i(t), & if \ z_i(t) > z_i(0)/2 \\ (1-\beta_2)z_i(t), & if \ z_i(t) \le z_i(0)/2 \\ & and \ |x_i(t+1)-x_i(t)| > \delta \\ 0, & if \ z_i(t) \le z_i(0)/2 \\ & and \ |x_i(t+1)-x_i(t)| \le \delta \end{cases} \quad (3)$$

$$\eta_i(t+1) = \frac{\eta_i(t)}{ln[e+\lambda(1-\eta_i(t))]} . \quad (4)$$

where i is the index of neurons and n is the number of neurons, $x_i(t)$ the output of neuron i , $y_i(t)$ the internal state for neuron i , W_{ij} the connection weight from neuron j to neuron i , Ii the input bias of neuron i , α the positive scaling parameter for inputs, $k(0 \leq k \leq 1)$ the damping factor of the nerve membrane, $z_i(t)$ the self-feedback connection weight, $\beta_1, \beta_2 (0 \leq \beta_1 < \beta_2 \leq 1)$ are the simulated annealing parameter of $z_i(t)$, δ is a given positive constant which magnitude order is 10^{-3}., λ the damping factors of $\eta_i(t)$, I_0 the positive parameter.

In this model, the equation (1) is different from the activation function of conventional CNN, which is a wavelet function other than sigmoid function, so it has a better ability in local approaching [18]. The variable $z_i(t)$ corresponds to the temperature in the usual stochastic annealing process and the equation (3) [13] is an exponential cooling schedule for the annealing. Obviously, if the value of $z_i(t)$ tends towards zero with time evolution in the form of $z_i(t) = z_i(0)e^{-\beta t}$, the novel CNN converts into HNN. In this paper, we adopt a smaller value of $\beta(\beta_1)$ before the chaotic dynamics reach the steady period-doubling bifurcated points. Then, a larger value of $\beta(\beta_2)$ is used after the chaotic dynamics tend toward steady bifurcated points. In order to banish disturbance of the self-feedback connection, we subjectively put $z_i(t) = 0$ when the difference of $|x_i(t+1) - x_i(t)|$ is less than a given positive constant (δ).

3 Application to Continuous Function Optimization

In this section, we use this novel chaotic neural network to solve continuous function optimization problems. And two examples are presented to demonstrate the superiority of our method to other methods. When HNN model is applied to solve complicated optimization problems, its energy function is defined as:

$$E_{Hop}(t) = -\frac{1}{2}\sum_i \sum_{j \neq i} W_{ij} x_i(t) x_j(t) - \sum_i I_i x_i(t) + \frac{1}{\tau}\sum_i \int_0^{x_i(t)} f^{-1}(v)dv \qquad (5)$$

Without going further, we know that the stable points of the very high-gain, continuous deterministic Hopfield model corresponds to the stable points of the discrete stochastic Hopfield model with the following Lyapunov energy function [19]:

$$E_{Hop}(t) = -\frac{1}{2}\sum_i \sum_{j \neq i} W_{ij} x_i(t) x_j(t) - \sum_i I_i x_i(t) \ . \qquad (6)$$

Comparing (6) with the cost function of our method:

$$-\frac{\partial E}{\partial x_i} = -\frac{\partial f}{\partial x_i} = -\left(\sum_{j=1,j\neq i} W_{ij}x_j + I_i \right).$$

(7)

Where f is a function that needs to be calculated the global optimal solution.

Example 1: A classic nonlinear function optimization problem

$$min\ f_1(\ x_1, x_2\ ) = (\ x_1 - 0.7\ )^2 ((\ x_2 + 0.6\ )^2 + 0.1\ )$$
$$+(\ x_2 - 0.5\ )^2 ((\ x_1 + 0.4\ )^2 + 0.15\ )$$

(8)

The minimum value of this object function [equation (8)] is 0 and its responding point is (0.7, 0.5), and the total number of local optimal value is 3: (0.6, 0.4), (0.6, 0.5) and (0.7, 0.4).

The parameters are set as follows:

$$u = 2, k = 1, \alpha = 0.05, I_0 = 0.05, \beta_1 = 0.02, \beta_2 = 0.1, \lambda = 0.05, \delta = 0.001.$$

We adopt the same initial values of network in Reference [13]:

$$y(\ 0\ ) = [\ -0.283, -0.283\ ],\ z(\ 0\ ) = [\ 0.065, 0.065\ ],\ \eta(\ 0\ ) = [\ 0.05, 0.08\ ].$$

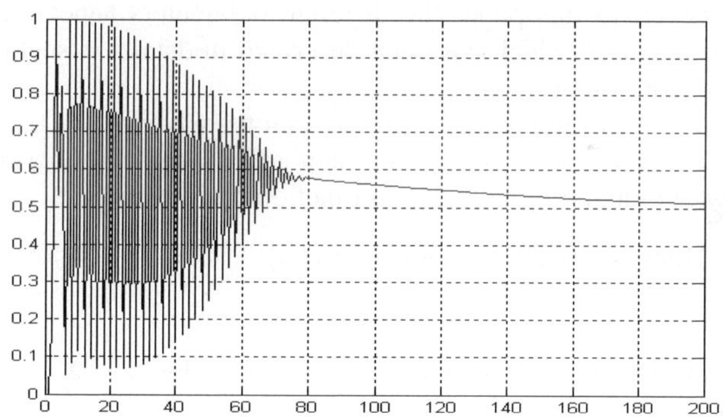

Fig. 1. The time evolution of x_2(t) in simulation of Chen's chaotic neural network

The CNN in figure 1, the activation function of neural unit is sigmoid function and the value of the simulated annealing parameter is only put a single value in the whole optimization procedure, so we can see that x_2(t) converges the global optimal value 0.5 more than 200 iterations. While in figure 2 x_2(t) reaches the global optimal value 0.5 only iterations 45.

In order to make it be understood much clearer, we divide the whole optimization procedure into two processes: the first process is based on the chaotic dynamics and

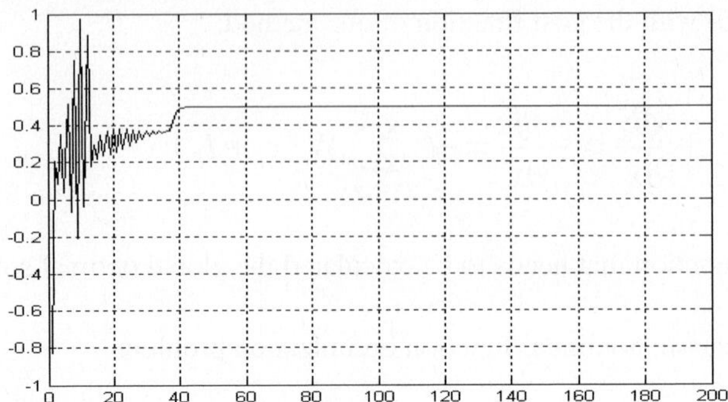

Fig. 2. The time evolution of x₂(t) in simulation of the novel chaotic neural network

the second process is based on the gradient decent dynamics. By transferring sigmoid function to wavelet function in the novel chaotic neural network model, it can accomplish the ergodic chaotic dynamics more quickly in the first process and arrive at the global optimal value round. The main reason is the activation function of neural unit is non-monotonous wavelet function, so it has a better ability in local approaching.

In the second process in figure 1 when x₂(t) tends toward to the global optimal value point 0.5, the value of the self-feedback connection weight remains very small. Moreover this small value continuously takes disturbance to the gradient convergent procedure. Therefore it leads to waste much more time to converge at the global optimal value. However, in this paper the different-parameters annealing function are adopted in different period which has been described in details in section 2, so it can overcome the above problems.

Compared figure 1 with figure 2, we can see that the CNN in this paper spends less time finding the global optimal value than Chen's CNN does. Furthermore it guarantees the accuracy of global optimal value to function optimization.

Example 2: Six-Hump Camel -Back Function [16]:

$$min\ f_2(x_1,x_2)=4x_1^2-2.1x_1^4+x_1^6/3+x_1x_2-4x_2^2+4x_2^4 \quad |x_i \le 1| \tag{9}$$

The minimal value of Equation (9) is −1.0316285, and its responding point is (0.08983, -0.7126) or (-0.08983, 0.7126).

We adopt our method to solve this function optimization problem, and we'll make a comparison with Reference [16] and [20] in Table 1. The parameters are set as follows:

$$u=0.05, k=1, \alpha=0.2, I_0=0.05, \lambda=0.3, \beta_1=0.015, \beta_2=0.1, \delta=0.001$$

The initial values of network are set as follows:

$$y(0)=[0.6,0.6], z(0)=[17.5,17.5], \eta(0)=[0.01,0.01]$$

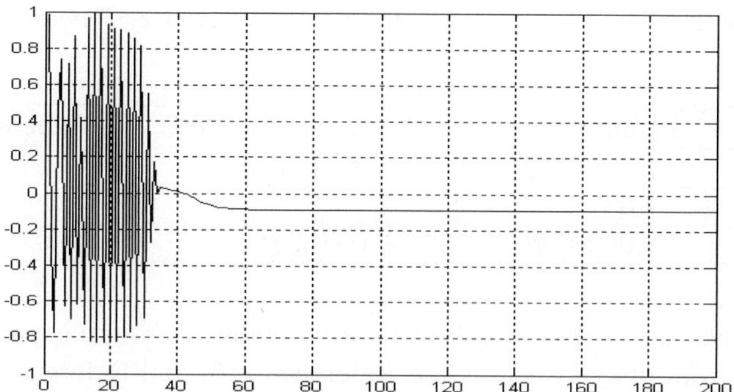

Fig. 3. The time evolution of $x_1(t)$ in simulation of function (9)

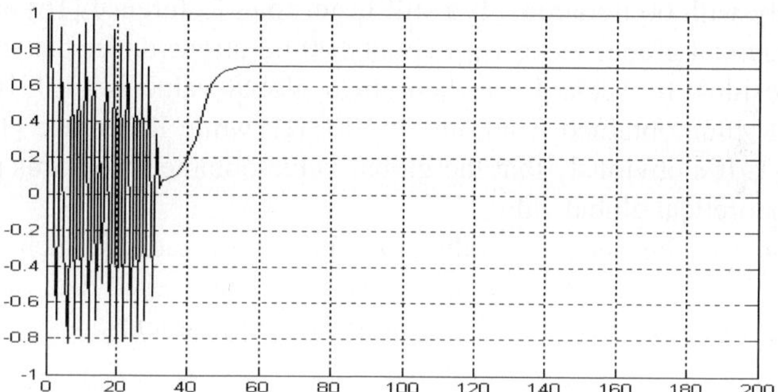

Fig. 4. The time evolution of $x_2(t)$ in simulation of function (9)

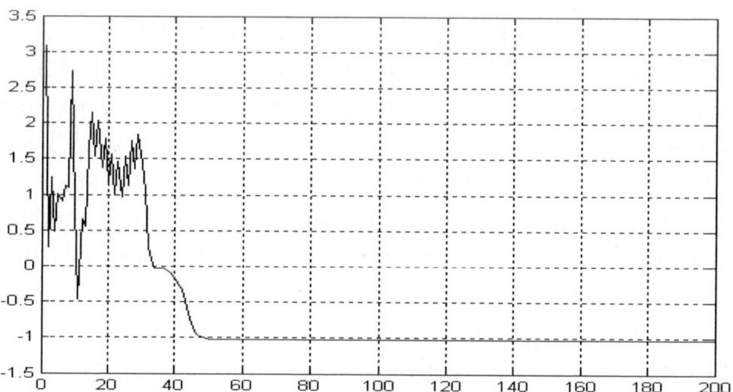

Fig. 5. The time evolution of energy function of (9)

The above figures suggest that a search of the global minima is through chaotic dynamics, the practical global minimal value of Equation (9) in Fig.5 is -1.0316 and its responding point of the simulation in Fig.5 is (-0.0898, 0.7127).

Analysis of the Simulation Results:

Table 1. Simulation results of equation (9) obtained from this paper, Reference [16] and Reference [20]

	f_2 (this paper)	f_2(Reference [16])	f_2 (Reference [20])
TGM	-1.0316285	-1.0316285	-1.0316285
PGM	-1.0316	-1	-1
ERR	-0.0000285	-0.0316285	-0.0316285

In Table 1, we compare the result of figure 5 obtained from this paper with the results obtained from others, such as the Reference [16] and Reference [20]. And the columns "TGM", "PGM" and "ERR" represent, respectively, theoretical global value, practical global value and error.

In figure 5, the energy function of Equation (9) in our paper reaches the global optimal value only with 60 iterations. It's still faster than Reference [16] and [20] which reached the practical global value with about 100 iterations under the same simulated parameters. Besides, In Table 1 the theoretical global value is −1.0316285, and the practice global value obtained from ours is −1.0316 while Reference [16] and Reference [20] are -1. It's obviously that the global value obtained from this paper is much closer to the theoretical global value.

And we also use this model to other function optimizations, such as the famous function called Rosenbrock function problem [21]. The overall data obtained proved this novel CNN to be effective in solving optimization problems.

4   Conclusion

In this paper, we introduced a novel chaotic neural network which activation function of neural unit is wavelet function and the different-parameters annealing function are adopted in the different period. In contrast to Chen's chaotic neural network, application of this model to continuous function optimization showed its superiority when compared to the convergence speed and the accuracy of the results. This model can be a new approach to solving a class of function optimization problems.

This paper has shown the potential of chaotic neural network model which activation function is composed of non-monotonic basic function for solving the optimization problems. From which has been shown that this neural techniques can find the global optimal value much faster and more accurate. And the model may also be well suited to solving the combinatorial optimization problems such as TSP and CAP, due to its inherently adaptive nature. Applications of the model for this purpose will be the subject of our future research.

Acknowledgements. This work was supported by Talent Supporting Project of Ministry of Education of the P.R.China (Grant number: NCET-05-0897) and Scientific Research Project for Universities in Xinjiang (Grant number: XJEDU2004E02 and XJEDU2006I10).

References

1. Hopfield, J.J., Tank, D.W.: Neural computation of decisions in optimization problems. Biological Cybernetics 52, 141–152 (1985)
2. Hopfield, J.: Neural networks and physical systems with emergent collective computational abilities. Proc. Natl. Acad. Sci. 79, 2554–2558 (1982)
3. Wilson, G.V., Pawley, G.S.: On the stability of the tap algorithm of hopfield and tank. Biol. Cybern. 58, 63–70 (1988)
4. Smith, K., Palaniswami, M., Krishnamoorthy, M.: Neural techniques for combinatorial optimization with applications. IEEE Trans. Neural Network 9(6), 1301–1318 (1998)
5. Yao, Y., Freeman, W.J.: Model of biological pattern recognition with spatially chaotic dynamics. Neural Networks 3, 156–170
6. Aihara, K., Takabe, T., Toyoda, M.: Chaotic neural networks. Phys. Lett. A 144(6,7), 333–340 (1999)
7. Chen, L.N., Aihara, K.: Chaotic simulated annealing by a neural network model with transient chaos. Neural Networks 8(6), 915–930 (1995)
8. Wang, L.: Oscillatory and chaotic dynamics in neural networks under varying operating conditions. IEEE Trans. Neural Networks 7, 1382–1388 (1996)
9. Tokuda, I., Aihara, K., Nagashima, T.: Adapitive annealing for chaotic optimization. Phys. Rev. E 58, 5157–5160 (1998)
10. Hirasawa, K., Murata, J., Hu, J., Jin, C.Z.: Chaos control on universal learning networks. IEEE Trans. Syst. Man, Cybern. C 30, 95–104 (2000)
11. Chuanquan, X., Chen, H.: Simulated annealing mechanics in chaotic neural networks. Jounal of Shanghai Jiaotong University 37(3), 36–39 (2003)
12. Zhou, C., Chen, T.: Chaotic annealing for optimization. Physical Review E 55(3), 2580–2587 (1997)
13. Bo, K., Xinyu, L., Bingchao, L.: Improved simulated annealing mechanics in transiently chaotic neural network. In: International conference on communications, Circuits and systems, vol. 2, pp. 1057–1060 (2004)
14. Potapove, A., Kali, M.: Robust chaos in neural networks. Physics Letters A 277(6), 310–322 (2000)
15. Shuai, J.W., Chen, Z.X., Liu, R.T.: Self-evolution neural model. Physics Letters A 221(5), 311–316 (1996)
16. Xu, Y.-q., Sun, M., Shen, J.-h.: Gauss wavelet chaotic neural networks. In: King, I., Wang, J., Chan, L.-W., Wang, D. (eds.) ICONIP 2006. LNCS, vol. 4232, pp. 467–476. Springer, Heidelberg (2006)
17. Xu, Y.-q., Sun, M., Shen, J.-h.: Shannon wavelet chaotic neural networks. In: Wang, T.-D., Li, X.-D., Chen, S.-H., Wang, X., Abbass, H.A., Iba, H., Chen, G.-L., Yao, X. (eds.) SEAL 2006. LNCS, vol. 4247, pp. 244–251. Springer, Heidelberg (2006)
18. Xu, Y.-q., Sun, M., Duan, G.-R.: Wavelet chaotic neural networks and their application to optimization problems. In: Adi, A., Stoutenburg, S., Tabet, S. (eds.) RuleML 2005. LNCS, vol. 3791, pp. 379–384. Springer, Heidelberg (2005)
19. Haykin, S.: Neural Networks: A Comprehensive Foundation, 2nd edn., pp. 680–696. Prentice Hall International, Englewood Cliffs (1999)
20. Yunyu, T., Xiangdong, L., Chunbo, X.: A novel neural network with transient chaos and its application in function optimization. Computer engineer and science 28(3), 116–118 (2006)
21. Yanchun, L., Chungang, C., Shoufan, L.: Optimization of Rosenbrock's function based on genetic algorithms. Journal of Sohare 8(9), 701–708 (1997)

Interpretable Piecewise Linear Classifier

Pitoyo Hartono

Department of Media Architecture,
Future University-Hakodate, Hakodate, Japan

Abstract. The objective of this study is to build a model of neural network classifier that is not only reliable but also, as opposed to most presently available neural networks, logically interpretable in a human-plausible manner. Presently, most of the studies of rule extraction from trained neural networks focus on extracting rule from existing neural network models that were designed without the consideration of rule extraction, hence after the training process they are meant to be used as a kind black box. Consequently, this makes rule extraction a hard task. In this study we construct a model of neural network ensemble with the consideration of rule extraction. The function of the ensemble can be easily interpreted to generate logical rules that are understandable to human. We believe that the interpretability of neural networks contributes to the improvement of the reliability and the usability of neural networks when applied critical real world problems.

1 Introduction

In the past decades, neural networks have been rigorously studied and applied in many fields. One of the most utilized models is Multilayered Perceptron (MLP) [1].The ability and flexibility of MLP to deal with vast kind of problems is the main reason for its unmatched success. Through the learning process, MLP is able to obtain knowledge to associate inputs and outputs, which is implicitly represented in the data set. However, in MLP this knowledge is represented as a set of connection weights values, which is not intuitively nor logically plausible (at least easily) for human. Hence, once trained, MLP is used as a kind of black box. Although, MLP is widely used for control, prediction, pattern recognition and so on, the lack of understanding in human side on the logical clarity on the decision making process inside MLP (and most of neural networks) is one of the drawback that hinders the usage of neural networks in more critical real world problems, for example problems that are crucial to human safety.

So far, several methods for extracting rules from a trained neural network were proposed [2,3,5]. The objective of most of these methods is to extract plausible rule from conventionally available neural networks, e.g. MLP. However, rule extractability is not considered in the design MLP, which naturally complicates the process of rule extraction. The nonlinearity of MLP complicates not only

M. Ishikawa et al. (Eds.): ICONIP 2007, Part II, LNCS 4985, pp. 434–443, 2008.

the rule extraction process but sometimes also reduces the plausibility of the extracted rules.

The objective of our study is to propose a neural network model which structure and behavior significantly simplifies the rule extraction process without compromising the performance. The model is based on the previously proposed ensemble model [9]. As opposed to previously proposed ensemble models [6,7,8] whose objectives are to achieve better generalization performances compared to singular neural network models, our main objective is to build an ensemble model which behavior can be easily interpreted to generate rules that are logically comprehensible for human. Although we do not focus on the improvement of the generalization performance, the performance of the proposed ensemble is assured to be at least competitive to that of MLP.

The proposed ensemble is composed of several linear perceptrons (member hereafter). It is also equipped with a competitive training mechanism, which automatically and efficiently decomposes a given learning space into several learning sub-spaces and assigns a sub-space to a member that can deal with it best. Consequently, because each member is a perceptron that can only learn to form a linear function, the ensemble decomposes an arbitrary learning problem into several manageable linear problems, thus realizing a piecewise-linear classifier. The linearity of each member significantly lessens the complexity of rule extraction process, and the structure of the ensemble also contributes to the simplicity, thus plausibility of the extracted rules.

In the experiment the behavior of the proposed model is illustrated using an artificial logic problem, while the efficiency is tested on several benchmark problems.

2   Ensemble of Linear Experts

The proposed Ensemble of Linear Experts (ELE) is composed of several linear perceptrons. Each perceptron (member) has an additional neuron in its output layer (shown as a black circle in Fig.1) called confidence neuron(CN). CN is connected to the input neurons in the same way as the ordinary output neurons. The difference between CN and the ordinary output neuron is that, for a given input, CN generates a value that indicates the "confidence" of the member with regards to its ordinary output. A high confidence value is an indication that the output of the member is highly reliable while a low confidence value is an indication of the opposite.

In the running process, an input to the ensemble is processed independently by all members, so each of them produces a confidence value and an output. The ensemble then selects a winner, which is a member with the highest confidence value and adopts the output of the winner as the final output while disregarding other members' outputs. Based on the members' confidence the ensemble also executes a competitive training mechanism that will be elaborated in the latter part of this section.

2.1   Structure and Behavior of ELE

The structure of ELE is illustrated in Fig.1. It is composed of several independent linear perceptrons [10]. The activation of the ordinary output neurons is as follows.

$$O_k^i(t) = f(I_k^i(t))$$

$$I_k^i(t) = \sum_{j=1}^{N_{in}} w_{jk}^i(t)x_j(t) + \theta_k^i(t) \tag{1}$$

$$f(x) = \frac{1}{1+e^{-x}}$$

In Eq. 1, $O_k^i(t)$, $I_k^i(t)$ and $\theta_k^i(t)$ are the output, potential and the threshold of the k-th output neuron in the i-th member at time t, respectively. w_{jk}^i is the connection weight from the j-th input neuron leading to the k-th output neuron in the i-th member, while N_{in} and $x_j(t)$ are the number of the input neurons and the value of j-th input, respectively.

Similarly, the activation of the confidence neuron in the i-th member, $O_c^i(t)$ is as follows.

$$O_c^i(t) = f(I_c^i(t))$$

$$I_c^i(t) = \sum_{j=1}^{N_{in}} v_j^i(t)x_j(t) + \theta_c^i(t) \tag{2}$$

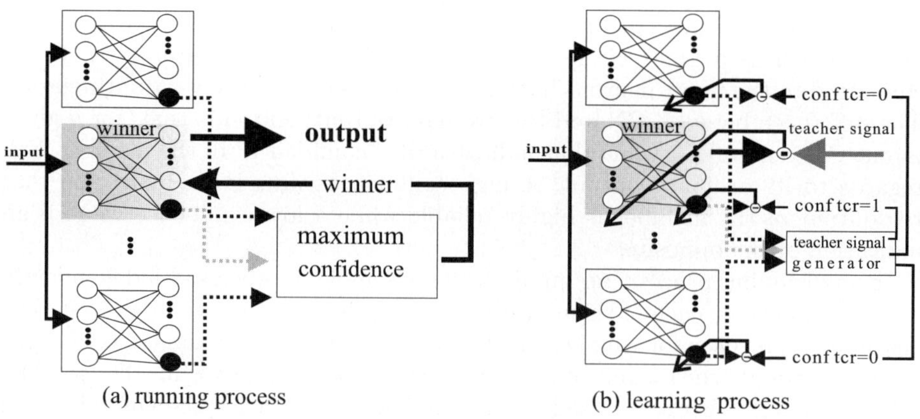

Fig. 1. Ensemble of Linear Experts

In Eq. 2, v_j^i and θ_c^i are the connection weights to from the j-th input neuron to the confidence neuron and the threshold of the confidence neuron in the i-th member, respectively.

The final output of ELE, $\mathbf{O}^{ens}$, given an input is formulated as follows, where the ensemble adopts the output of the winner and disregards others' outputs.

$$w = arg \max_i \{O_c^i(t)\} \tag{3}$$

$$\mathbf{O}^{ens}(t) = \mathbf{O}^w(t) \tag{4}$$

The running process of ELE is illustrated in Fig. 1 (a).

2.2   Competitive Learning of ELE

The competitive training of ELE is designed to enable the ensemble to decompose the learning space of a given problem into several sub-spaces and assign a sub-space to a member that is potentially the best to perform in that sub-space. Consequently, because each member is a linear perceptron, the ensemble behaves as a piecewise-linear classifier where a complex problem is efficiently decomposed into several more manageable linear sub-problems. The linearity of each of the member significantly simplifies the process for rule extraction.

In the training process, the ensemble chooses a winner in a similar manner as in the running process, and then calculates the performance of the winner, P^w as follows.

$$P^w(t) = 1 - E^w(t)$$

$$E^w = \frac{1}{N_{out}} \sum_{k=1}^{N_{out}} (O_k^w(t) - T_k(t))^2 \tag{5}$$

Where $T_k(t)$ is the teacher signal for the k-th output neuron at time t, and N_{out} is the number of the output neurons.

If the relative performance of the winner, R as shown in Eq.6 exceeds a threshold value, it is deemed to be potentially able to perform in the problem sub-space containing the given input, hence it is permitted to enhance its performance by applying Delta Rule to modify the connection weights leading to its ordinary output neurons as shown in Eq.7.

$$R(t) = \frac{P^w(t)}{\sum_{i=1}^{N} P^i(t)} \tag{6}$$

In Eq.6, N is the number of members.

$$\mathbf{W}^w(t+1) = \mathbf{W}^w(t) - \eta \frac{\partial E^{win}(t)}{\partial \mathbf{W}^w(t)} \tag{7}$$

In this equation, $\mathbf{W}^w$ is the weight vector of the winner and η is the learning rate.

In this case, consequently the confidence of the winner is enhanced by modifying the connection weight from input neurons to the confidence neuron, by setting the teacher for the confidence neuron, T_c, in Eq.8 as 1.

$$\mathbf{V}^w(t+1) = \mathbf{V}^w(t) - \eta\frac{\partial E^w(t)}{\partial \mathbf{V}^w(t)}$$

$$E_c^w(t) = (O^w - T_c)^2 \tag{8}$$

Furthermore, because the winner should dominate the rest of the members with regards to the given input, other members should suppress their confidence values by applying Eq. 8, by setting the teacher signal T_c to 0.

Oppositely, when the performance of the winner is below the threshold value, it is indication of the inability of the winner to perform, hence the winner should surrender the domination to other members. This is done by decreasing the confidence of the winner by setting the teacher signal for the confidence neuron of the winner to 0 and increasing the confidence values of the rest of the members by setting 1 as the teacher signals for their confidence neurons. Because, the confidence value and the actual performance have to be synchronized, in this case the losers are permitted to modify their weights leading to the ordinary output neurons according to Eq. 7.

The outline of the learning process is shown Fig.1(b) and Algorithm 1.

Algorithm 1. Competitive Learning Process of ELE

```
1: select a training example
2: run all members
3: select a winner
4: if performance(winner) ≥ threshold then
5:    train(winner)
6:    increase-confidence(winner)
7:    decrease-confidence(losers)
8: else
9:    decrease-confidence(winner)
10:   increase-confidence(losers)
11:   train(losers)
12: end if
```

The competitive learning process ensures the diversity of the members and at the same time guaranty the harmony between the confidence value and the actual performance of each member.

2.3   Rule Extraction from ELE

Because the activation of an output and a confidence neuron is sigmoidal and the neurons are trained to produce parity value of 0 or 1, we can assume that the following intermediate rule is true (by setting a very large slope for the sigmoid function).

$$I_c^i(t) = \sum_{j=1}^{N_{in}} v_j^i(t)x_j(t) + \theta_c^i(t) > 0 \Rightarrow i : winner \tag{9}$$

Simillarly, when the proposed ensemble is applied to 1-of-M classification problems, the ordinary output neurons are also trained to produce 0 or 1, hence the following intermediate rules are also true.

$$I_k^i(t) = \sum_{j=1}^{N_{in}} w_{jk}^i(t)x_j(t) + \theta_k^i(t) > 0 \Rightarrow O_k^i(t) = 1 \tag{10}$$

$$I_k^i(t) = \sum_{j=1}^{N_{in}} w_{jk}^i(t)x_j(t) + \theta_k^i(t) < 0 \Rightarrow O_k^i(t) = 0 \tag{11}$$

From these intermediate rules we can easily generate plausible $if-then$ rules by applying any of rule extraction algorithm proposed in [2,3,4]. However, for simplicity we apply a simple rule extraction method explained in [2], where the range of inputs is divided into three parts based on their values, namely small(s), medium(m) and large(l), which are then quantized to 0, 0.5 and 1, respectively, and adopts logical propositions that satisfy Equations 9, 10, 11 as the rules.

It is obvious that the each of the member represents rules that are valid in a particular sub-problem space (in which the member has the highest confidence), and the winner-takes-all selection based on the members' confidences acts as a kind of "meta rule", which is a rule to select a rule, because the selection winner selection mechanism can be translated into the following rule.

Algorithm 2. Meta Rule

---

    if winner = i **then**

        apply rule i

    end if

The rule expression of ELE increases the plausibility of the general rule that governs the learning space. Because instead of a single complicated rule set it offers more understandable several partial rules that we consider helpful for human in understanding the knowledge of a neural network. The high plausibility of the rule expression is possible because of the structure and the competitive training algorithm of ELE.

3   Experiments

To illustrate the characteristics, we apply ELE to XOR problem, which is a non-linear classification problem that naturally cannot be dealt with any linear

440   P. Hartono

classifier. Figure 2(a) shows the hyperspace of ELE with two members trained on this problem, in which areas that are classified as 1 are shown in black, areas that are classified as 0 are shown in white, and gray is for areas that are ambiguously classified in the vicinity of 0.5. For comparison Fig.2(b) shows the typical hyperspace of MLP. Figures 2 (c) and (d) show the hyperspace of member-1 and member-2 of ELE, respectively, where "low conf" indicates areas where the confidence of a member is lower than that of its counterpart. It is obvious that ELE decomposes this non-linear classification problem into two linear sub-problems and assigns each sub-problem to one of the member. After the learning process, the potentials of the confidence neurons of the members are as follows.

$$I_c^1 = -5.2x_1 + 0.3x_2 + 2.5$$
$$I_c^2 = 5.3x_1 - 0.2x_2 - 2.2 \tag{12}$$

From Eq. 12 it is clear that whenever $x_1 < medium$ then rule generated by member 1 is applied and rule generated by member 2 is otherwise applied.

Similarly, the potential of the output neurons of the members are as follows.

$$I_1^1 = -1.2x_1 + 4.9x_2 - 2.3$$
$$I_1^2 = 0.3x_1 + -5.0x_2 + 2.2 \tag{13}$$

From Eqs.12 and 13 the following rule can be extracted.

Algorithm 3. Extracted Rule: XOR

---

if $x_1 < medium$ **then**
   Apply **Rule 1**:
   if $x_2 > medium$ **then**
     classify as 1
   else
     classify as 0
   end if
else
   Apply **Rule 2**:
   if $x_2 < medium$ **then**
     classify as 1
   else
     classify as 0
   end if
end if

To test the efficiency of ELE, we apply ELE to several benchmark problems from UCI Repository [11]. The average generalization accuracies over 50 runs for each problem are listed in Table. 1. For comparison we also list the performances of MLP and Linear Perceptron. In every run, the number of learning

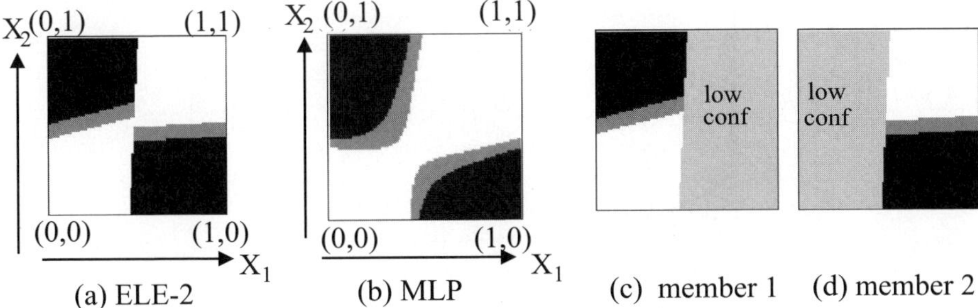

Fig. 2. Hyperspace (XOR)

Table 1. Generalization Accuracy (%)

	Perceptron	MLP	**ELE**
iris	72	100	**100**
cancer	97	97	**97**
liver	61	69	**70**
pima	75	76	**79**
balance	86	88	**88**
wine	90	97	**94**
ionos	91	94	**92**

iterations for the every classifier is the same. From Table 1, we can confirm that the performance of ELE over wide range of problems are competitive to the performance of MLP. In these experiments, the number of members in ELE is varied between 2 and 5, but we find that the difference in performance between ELEs with different number of members are not significant, because usually ELE is able to utilize a minimum number of members to deal with a given problem. The performance accuracies of ELE in Table 1 is the performance of the best ELE. For all the experiments, the learning rate η is set to 0.5, while the performance threshold, R is set to $\frac{1}{N}$, where N is the number of members.

To illustrate the characteristics of ELE, the learning process with regards to Iris Classification [12] problem is used as an example. This problem is a well known non-linear classification problem, where a four dimensional input (length and width of petal and sepal of an iris flower) has to be classified into one of the three classes of iris flower (setosa, versicolor and virginica). Figure 3(a) shows the learning curve of ELEs with two, three and four members, which clearly indicates that ELE can deal nicely with this non-linear problem. Figure 3(b) show the confidence of the winner during the training epoch. From Figures 3(a) and (b) we can draw a conclusion that the actual performance and the confidence of the winner are gradually synchronized by observing the fact that the decrease in the training error is always associated with the increase in the winner's confidence. Figure 3(c) shows the average of the losers' confidence. Figures 3(b) and (c) show that the increase of the winner's confidence is always associated with the decrease

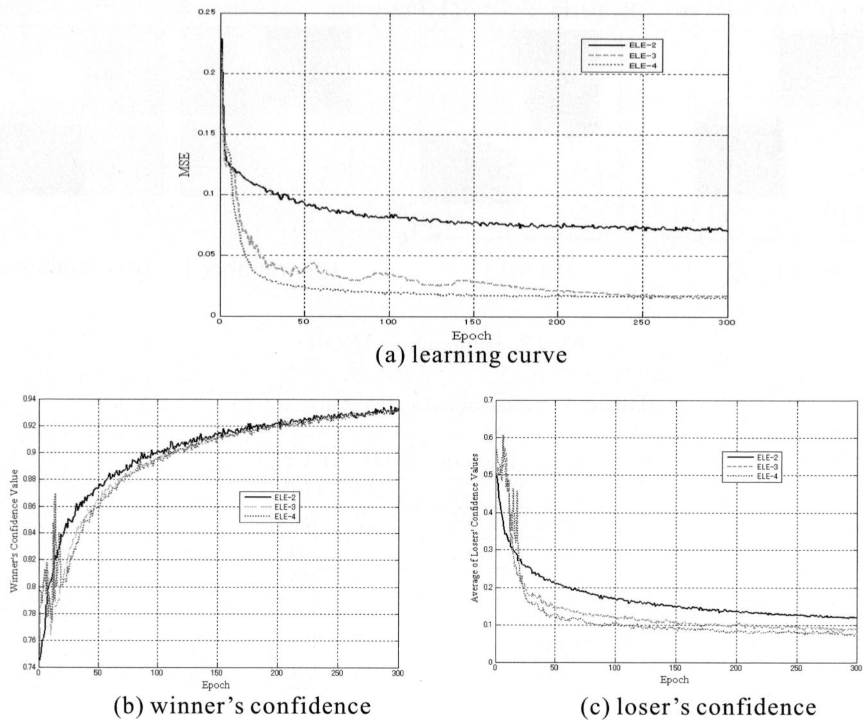

(a) learning curve

(b) winner's confidence   (c) loser's confidence

Fig. 3. Learning Characteristics (Iris)

in the losers' confidences, which indicates that ELE diversifies the expertise of its members over the progress of the learning process. For this problem, ELE is able to choose two of its members to perform the classification. If ELE has more than two members, then the rest of the members have very low confidences in the whole problem space, thus they do not contribute to the classification process. From the two members the following rules can be extracted.

Algorithm 4. Extracted Rule: Iris Classification

---

  if x_3 : *large* $\vee$ x_4 : *large* **then**
    Apply **Rule 2**:
    Classify as **Virginica**
  else
    Apply **Rule 1**:
    if x_3 : *small* $\wedge$ x_4 : *small* **then**
      Classify as **Setosa**
    else
      Classify as **Versicolor**
    end if
  end if

---

4   Conclusions

In this paper we propose a new of neural network ensemble model whose structure and learning algorithm support the extraction of plausible rules. The experiments confirm that the proposed ensemble acts as a piecewise linear classifier with a competitive accuracy compared with MLP and the generated rules are easily plausible for human. A thorough mathematical analysis of the behavior of ELE is one of the future plans of this research.

References

1. Rumelhart, D., McClelland, J.: Learning Internal Representation by Error Propagation. Parallel Distributed Processing I, 318–362 (1984)
2. Duch, W., Setiono, R., Zurada, J.: Computational Intelligence Methods for Rule-Based Data Understanding. Proceedings of The IEEE 92(5), 771–805 (2004)
3. Taha, A., Ghosh, J.: Symbolic Interpretation of Artificial Neural Networks. IEEE Trans. Knowledge and Data Engineering 11(3), 448–462 (1999)
4. Setiono, R.: Extracting M-of-N Rules from Trained Neural Networks. IEEE Trans. Neural Networks 11(2), 512–519 (2000)
5. Benitez, J.M., Castro, J.L., Requena, I.: Are Artificial Neural Networks Black Boxes? IEEE Trans. on Neural Networks 8(3), 1156–1164 (1997)
6. Jacobs, R., Jordan, M., Nowlan, S., Hinton, G.: Adaptive Mixture of Local Experts. Neural Computation 3, 79–87 (1991)
7. Freund, Y.: Boosting a Weak Learning Algorithm by Majority. Information and Computation 7 II, 256–285 (1995)
8. Hartono, P., Hashimoto, S.: Learning from Imperfect Data Applied Soft Computing Journal 7(1), 353–363 (2007)
9. Hartono, P., Hashimoto, S.: Analysis on the Performance of Ensemble of Perceptron. In: Proc. IJCNN 2006, pp. 10627–10632 (2006)
10. Widrow, B.: 30 Years of Adaptive Neural Networks: Perceptron, Madaline, and Backpropagation. Proceedings of IEEE 78(9), 1415–1441 (1990)
11. UCI Machine Learning Repository:
    http://www.ics.uci.edu/~mlearn/MLRepository.html
12. Fisher, R.: The Use of Multiple Measurements in Taxonomic Problems. Annual Eugenics 7(II), 179–188 (1936)

A Visualization of Genetic Algorithm Using the Pseudo-color

Shin-ichi Ito[1], Yasue Mitsukura[1], Hiroko Nakamura Miyamura[1],
Takafumi Saito[1], and Minoru Fukumi[2]

[1] Graduate School of Bio-Applications & Systems Engineering,
Tokyo University of Agriculture and Technology
2-24-16, Naka, Koganei, Tokyo, 184-8588, Japan
{ito_s,mitsu_e,miyamura,txsaito}@cc.tuat.ac.jp
[2] The University of Tokushima
2-1, Minami-Josanjima, Tokushima, 770-8506, Japan
fukumi@is.tokushima-u.ac.jp

Abstract. In this paper, we propose a visualization method to grasp the search process and results in the binary-coded genetic algorithm. The representation, the choices of operations, and the associated parameters can each make a major difference to the speed and the quality of the final result. These parameters are decided interactively and very difficult to disentangle their effects. Therefore, we focus on the chromosome structure, the fitness function, the objective function, the termination conditions, and the association among these parameters. We can indicate the most important or optimum parameters in visually. The proposed method is indicated all individuals of the current generation using the pseudo-color. The pixels related a gene of the chromosome are painted the red color when the gene of the chromosome represents '1', and the pixels related to one are painted the blue color when one represents '0'. Then the brightness of the chromosome changes by the fitness value, and the hue of the chromosome changes by the objective value. In order to show the effectiveness of the proposed method, we apply the proposed method to the zero-one knapsack problems.

Keywords: binary-coded genetic algorithm, zero-one knapsack problem, visualization, pseudo-color.

1 Introduction

It can be easy to quickly set up a genetic algorithm (GA), which is a search paradigm that applies ideas from evolutionary genetic operations (natural selection, crossover, mutation) in order to search an optimum solution or a quasi-optimal solution, but analyzing the results to discover whether or not the process is efficient or could be improved is often extremely difficult. The representation, the choices of operations, and the associated parameters can each make a major difference to the speed and the quality of the final result. These parameters are decided interactively and very difficult to disentangle their effects [1], because

M. Ishikawa et al. (Eds.): ICONIP 2007, Part II, LNCS 4985, pp. 444–452, 2008.

the user sets a chromosome structure of an individual, a fitness function, an objective function, genetic operation parameters, and the termination conditions.

Generally, the objective function and the fitness function are the same function, but there is the case that the objective function and the fitness function are the difference, because there is the case that the fitness function includes the user's knowledge gave as the penalty and has the multi-objective function. Furthermore, keeping a full record of everything that occurs during a GA run produces large quantities of data that can not be analyzed conveniently by hand. Ideally, the full recording data displays on only one-frame for carrying out the discussion of setting parameters and evaluating the fitness function and the penalty. We focus on the chromosome structure, the fitness function, the objective function, association among these parameters, and whether termination conditions have been satisfied. Then we indicate these on only one-frame. However, it is very difficult that the some parameters are indicated simultaneously. We proposed the visualization method to grasp the search process, the search result, and setting parameter associations. Then, the process of the genetic search of the GA can be visualized. We can indicate the most important or optimum parameters in visually. Therefore, we indicate all individuals' chromosomes of the current generation by using the pseudo-color; The pixels related a gene of the chromosome are painted the red color when the gene of the chromosome is '1', and the pixels related to one are painted the blue color when one is '0', the brightness of the chromosome changes by the fitness value, and the hue of the chromosome changes by the objective value. In order to show the effectiveness of the proposed method, we apply the proposed method to the zero-one knapsack problems (KP).

This paper is organized in the following manner. First, in the section 2, we introduce the zero-one knapsack problem. In the section 3, we explain the visualization method of GA based on the pseudo-color. In the section 4, we describe computer simulations applying the KP for showing the effectiveness of the proposed method. In the section 5, we discuss the proposed method and the computer simulation results. Finally, we indicate the conclusions and the feature works.

2   Knapsack Problem

The zero-one knapsack problems seek to place objects in a knapsack so as to maximum the total value of the objects without overfilling the knapsack. We are given n objects, each with a value v_i and weight w_i, and a knapsack with capacity C, and we seek a selection of objects for knapsack with maximum total value but with total weight no greater than C. That is, if n binary variables x_i indicate the inclusion ($x_i = 1$) or exclusion ($x_i = 0$) on each object. Formally, the KP can be stated as follows:

$$maximize \sum_{i=1}^{n} x_i v_i, \tag{1}$$

$$subject\ to \sum_{i=1}^{n} x_i w_i \leq C, \quad v_i \geq 0, \quad w_i \geq 0, \quad i = 1, ..., n.$$

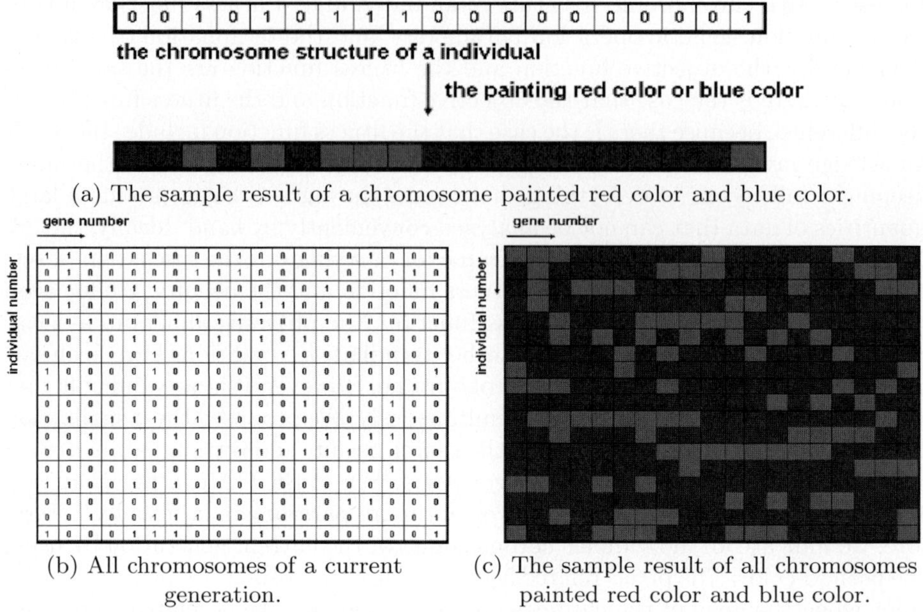

(a) The sample result of a chromosome painted red color and blue color.

(b) All chromosomes of a current generation.

(c) The sample result of all chromosomes painted red color and blue color.

Fig. 1. The chromosome structure and the sample result of the individual chromosomes of a current generation painted red color and blue color

3 Methods

3.1 Genetic Encoding

A simple genetic encoding scheme for the KP is as follows. Let each bit represent the inclusion or exclusion of one of the n objects from the knapsack. Note that it is possible to represent infeasible solutions by setting so many bits to '1' that the weight of the corresponding set of objects overflows the capacity of the knapsack.

3.2 Objective Function and Fitness Functions

The objective function is objective assessment (e.g., the recognition accuracy in the pattern classification problem, the total value in the KP). The fitness function is an evaluation function for searching the optimum solution or the quasi-optimum solution. Generally, the objective function and the fitness function are the same function. However there is the case that the objective function and the fitness function are the difference because there is the case that the fitness function includes the user's experimental knowledge and has some objective functions.

The objective function of the KP is shown Eq. (1). The case that the objective function (O) and the fitness function are the same function, the fitness function (F) is as follows:

$$maximize \ F = O = \sum_{i=1}^{n} x_i v_i, \tag{2}$$

$$subject \ to \ W = \sum_{i=1}^{n} x_i w_i \leq C, \quad v_i \geq 0, \quad w_i \geq 0, \quad i = 1, ..., n.$$

The case that the objective function and the fitness function are the difference, the fitness function has a penalty function as follows:

$$maximize \ F = \alpha O - \beta P, \tag{3}$$

$$subject \ to \ W = \sum_{i=1}^{n} x_i w_i \leq C, \quad v_i \geq 0, \quad w_i \geq 0, \quad i = 1, ..., n,$$

where α means the weight of the objective function, β means the weight of the penalty function (P). It is difficult that the user determines how to give the penalty and the weight value. Therefore the penalty is determined the user's knowledge and the weight value is determined experimentally. Then it is the difficult to evaluate the penalty, the weight value, and whether to search the optimum solution and/or the quasi-optimal solution.

3.3   Visualization of Genetic Algorithm

Keeping a full record of everything that occurs during a GA run produces large quantities of data that can not be analyzed conveniently by hand. Ideally, the full recording data displays on only one frame for carrying out the discussion of setting parameters of the GA and evaluating the fitness function and the penalty. We focus on the chromosome structure, the fitness function, the objective function, the association among these parameters, and whether to be satisfied the termination conditions, and then we indicate these on one-image. However, it is very difficult that the some parameters are indicated simultaneously. Therefore, we indicate all individuals' chromosomes of the current generation by using the pseudo-color. Then any generations indicate on only one-frame.

The method for visualization in the GA is as follows:

a) The image of $n * m$ is used when the length of chromosome is n and the number of the individual is m. A pixel of the image is related to a gene of the chromosome. The pixels related a gene of the chromosome are painted the red color when the gene of the chromosome is '1', and the pixels related to one are painted the blue color when one is '0' shown in Fig.1.

b) Fig.2 shows the sample result of the visualization using the pseudo-color. The brightness (range: $0 \leq Red_{brightness} \leq 40$, $120 \leq Blue_{brightness} \leq 160$) of the chromosome changes by the fitness value. Moreover the hue (range: $0 \leq Hue \leq 128$) of the chromosome changes by the objective value. In this paper, the range of the objective value and fitness value is 0.0 to 1.0 for having related the objective value and the fitness value to the brightness change and the hue change. We make the visualization image changed hue and brightness shown in Fig.2(b).

c) Any generations are indicated on one-frame shown in Fig.3.

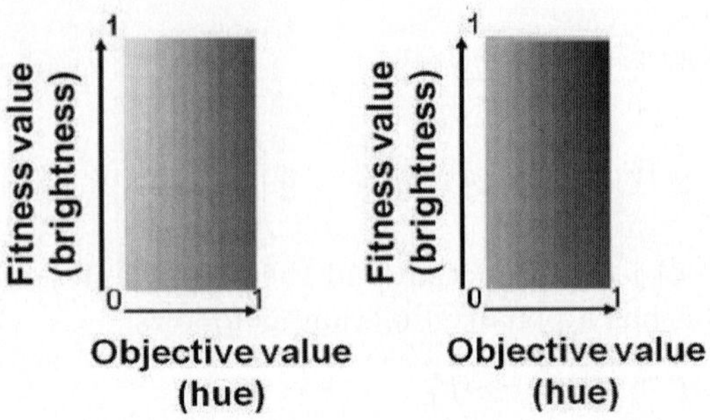

(a) The pseudo-color

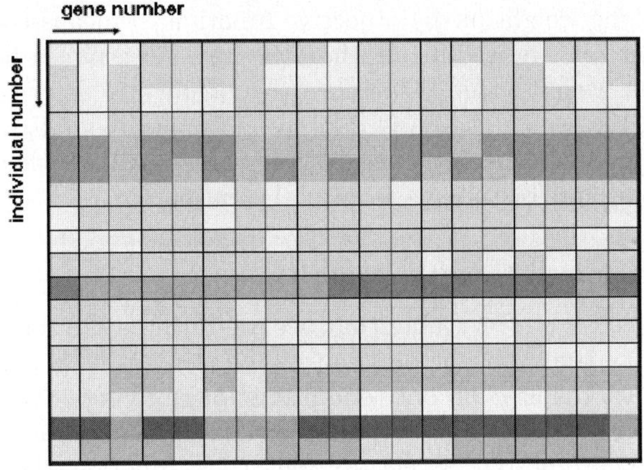

(b) All chromosomes of a current generation changed brightness and hue based on the objective value and fitness value

Fig. 2. The sample result of the visualization using the pseudo-color

4   Computer Simulations

In order to show the effectiveness of the proposed method, we solve the KP using three fitness functions (Eqs.(4)-(6)). The range of the fitness functions is from 0.0 to 1.0.

$$O = F_1 = \left(1.0 - \frac{T}{1.0 + \sum_{i=1}^{N} x_i v_i}\right)^3 \tag{4}$$

$$\textit{subject to}\ \ W = \sum_{i=1}^{n} x_i w_i \leq C, \qquad v_i \geq 0,\ \ w_i \geq 0,\ \ i = 1, ..., n$$

$$F_2 = \left(1.0 - \frac{T}{1.0 + \sum_{i=1}^{N} x_i v_i} - \frac{NumGene\text{‘}1'}{ChromoLen}\right)^3 \tag{5}$$

$$\textit{subject to}\ \ W = \sum_{i=1}^{n} x_i w_i \leq C, \qquad v_i \geq 0,\ \ w_i \geq 0,\ \ i = 1, ..., n$$

$$F_3 = \left(0.9 * \left(1.0 - \frac{T}{1.0 + \sum_{i=1}^{N} x_i v_i}\right) - 0.1 * \left(\frac{NumGene\text{‘}1'}{ChromoLen}\right)\right)^3 \tag{6}$$

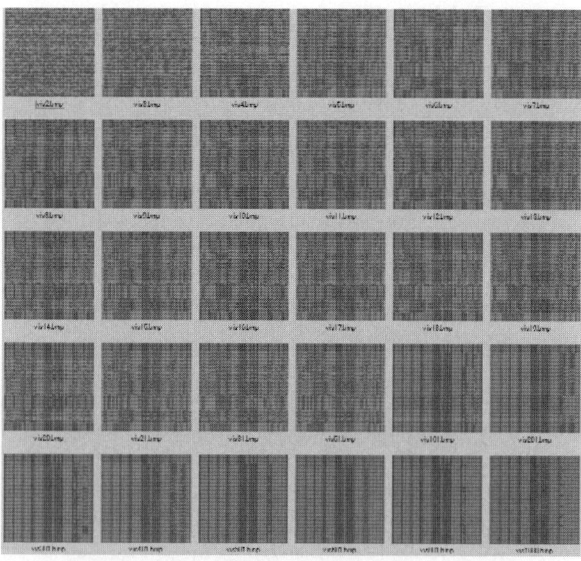

Fig. 3. The sample of the visualization frame indicated any generations

Table 1. The value and weight of the objects

object number	value	weight	object number	value	weight	object number	value	weight
(1)	1	24	(18)	9	6	(35)	15	24
(2)	14	21	(19)	18	0	(36)	13	28
(3)	4	29	(20)	4	13	(37)	15	1
(4)	13	19	(21)	14	26	(38)	16	19
(5)	10	2	(22)	3	11	(39)	5	23
(6)	6	1	(23)	7	5	(40)	3	27
(7)	13	9	(24)	12	26	(41)	17	25
(8)	16	17	(25)	5	29	(42)	19	2
(9)	19	11	(26)	15	22	(43)	0	16
(10)	19	13	(27)	19	4	(44)	13	3
(11)	19	26	(30)	11	27	(45)	2	13
(12)	3	10	(31)	14	27	(46)	6	23
(13)	0	1	(28)	14	4	(47)	12	25
(14)	9	11	(29)	10	23	(48)	0	19
(15)	4	5	(32)	4	3	(49)	9	2
(16)	8	18	(33)	6	5	(50)	12	6
(17)	0	0	(34)	10	25			

$$\text{subject to } \quad W = \sum_{i=1}^{n} x_i w_i \leq C, \quad v_i \geq 0, \quad w_i \geq 0, \quad i = 1, ..., n,$$

where O means the objective function, F_n means the fitness functions, $NumGene\text{‘}1\text{'}$ indicates the number of the gene that is '1' of an individual chromosome, $ChromoLen$ indicates the length of a chromosome.

Table 2. The parameters of the GA

The number of generations	1,000
The number of individuals	50
The length of chromosome	50
The rate of elite	0.1
The two-point crossover rate	0.8
The mutation rate	0.1

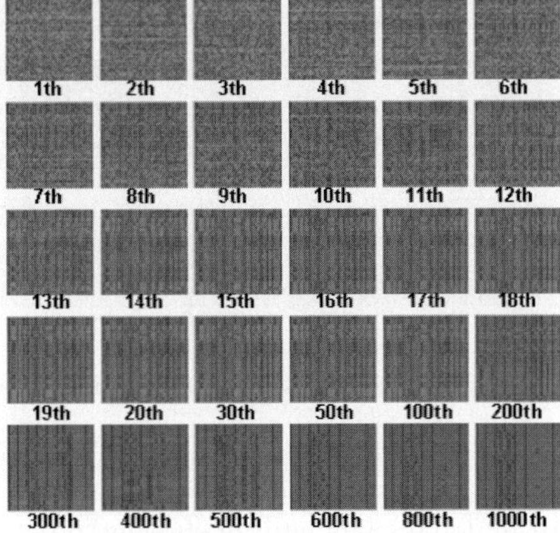

(a) The sample result of the case that the objective function and the fitness function
are the same function

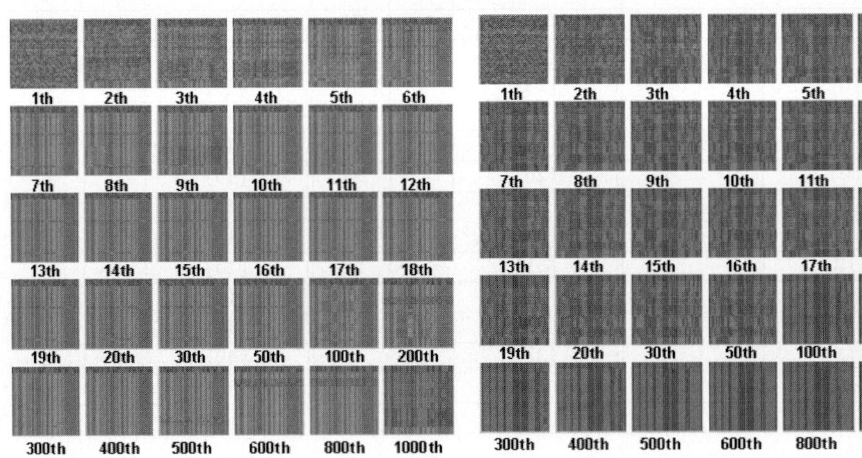

(b) The sample result of the case that the
fitness function included the penalty not
satisfied the user's desire

(c) The sample result of the case that the
fitness function included the penalty
satisfied the user's desire

Fig. 4. The sample of the simulation results

The genetic operations of the GA are the two-point crossover, the mutation, and the elite strategy. Table 1 shows the value and weight of the object of the KP, and Table 2 shows the parameters of the GA. The sample results of the computer simulation shown in Fig.4; (a) the case that the objective function and the fitness function (Eq.(4)) are the same function, (b) the case that the objective function and the fitness function are the difference and the fitness function (Eq.(5)) does not be given the penalty appropriate for being satisfied user's desire, (c) the case that the fitness function (Eq.(6)) is given the penalty appropriate for being satisfied user's desire. The generation number indicated the frame shown in Fig.4 is from 1 to 20, 30, 50, 100, 200, 300, 400, 500, 600, 800, and 1000.

5   Discussions

Based on the results shown in Fig.4, it is reasonable to support that it is understood intuitively that the chromosome structure, the fitness function, the objective function, association among these parameters on each generations. On the other hands, we think the validity of the fitness function is confirmed by seeing the colors of all generations and each generation, because if the colors are cloudy and light then the user knows the fitness function is not set appropriately shown in Fig.4(b) and if the colors are clear and dark then the user thinks the fitness function is set appropriately shown in Fig.4(c). Then we think the user is able to confirm whether to be satisfied the termination conditions set by the user, because if the termination conditions are satisfied then the color-gradation of all chromosomes on any generation is similar or same from top (individual number is 1) to bottom (individual number is 1000) shown in Fig.4(c). Moreover, if the color-gradation from top to bottom is not similar shown in Fig.4(b) then the user thinks that the termination conditions may be not able to be satisfied, because the color-gradation of the upper part and the low part is not similar for giving strongly the penalty of Eq.(5).

6   Conclusions and Future Works

We propose the method of the visualization in the search process and the search result of a binary-coded genetic algorithm. We focus on the chromosome structure, the fitness function, the objective function, association among these parameters, and whether to be satisfied the termination conditions. The proposed method makes the visualization image changed hue and brightness for showing the relationship among the chromosome structure, the fitness function, and the objective function. The chromosome of the individual having the most vivid color and the strongest contrast red color and blue color shows the highest fitness value and the optimum solution or the quasi-optimum solution. Furthermore, any generations are indicated on one-frame for showing the generation change that has the fitness value change, the objective value change, the searching condition of the optimum solution or the quasi-optimum solution, and whether to be satisfied the termination conditions. Finally, the performance of the proposed method was evaluated applying to the zero-one knapsack problem. It is understood intuitively that the proposed method shows the chromosome structure, the fitness function, the objective function, the association among these parameters, and whether to be satisfied the termination conditions.

We will involve efforts to improve the visualization techniques, except of using the pseudo-color, to further develop a real-coded genetic algorithm and an interaction genetic algorithm, to be used many users for evaluating the proposed method in the future works.

References

1. Hart, E., Ross, P.: Gavel-A New Tool for Genetic Algorithm Visualization. IEEE Transaction on Evolutionary Computation 5(4), 335–348 (2001)
2. Eick, S.G., Steffen, J.L., Summer, E.E.: Seesoft-A Tool for Visualization Line Oriented Software Statistics. IEEE Transaction on Software Engineering 18, 957–968 (1992)
3. Simoes, A., Costa, E.: An Evolutionary Approach to the Sero/One Knapsack Problem: Testing Ideas from Biology. In: Kurkova, V., Steele, N., Neruda, R., Karny, M. (eds.) Proceedings of the Fifth International Conference on Neural Networks and Genetic Algorithms (ICANNGA 2001), Prague, Czech Republic, April 22-25, pp. 236–239. Springer, Heidelberg (2001)
4. Jones, T.: Crossover, macromutation, and population-based search. In: Eshelman, L. (ed.) Proceedings of the 6th International Conference on Genetic Algorithms, pp. 73–80. Morgan Kaufmann, San Mateo (1995)
5. Shine, W., Eick, C.: Visualization the evolution of genetic algorithm search processes. In: Proceedings of 1997 IEEE International Conference on Evolutionary Computation, pp. 367–372. IEEE Press, Piscataway (1997)
6. Olsen, A.L.: Penalty Function and the Knapsack Problem. In: Fogel, D.B. (ed.) Proceedings of the 1st International Conference on Evolutionary Computation 1994, Orlando, FL, pp. 559–564 (1994)
7. Gordon, V., Bohm, A., Whitley, D.: A Note on the Performance of Genetic Algorithms on Zero-One Knapsack Problems. In: Proceedings of the 9th Symposium on Applied Computing (SAC 1994), Genetic Algorithms and Combinatorial Optimization, Phoenix, Az (1994)

A Novel Algorithm for Associative Classification

Gourab Kundu[1], Sirajum Munir[1], Md. Faizul Bari[1], Md. Monirul Islam[1,2,*],
and Kazuyuki Murase[2,3]

[1] Department of Computer Science and Engineering, Bangladesh University of
Engineering and Technology, Dhaka 1000, Bangladesh
[2] Department of Human and Artificial Intelligence Systems, Graduate School of
Engineering, University of Fukui, 3-9-1 Bunkyo, Fukui 910-8507, Japan
[3] Research and Education Program for Life Science, University of Fukui, 3-9-1
Bunkyo, Fukui 910-8507, Japan
`monirul@synapse.his.fukui-u.ac.jp`

Abstract. Associative classifiers have been the subject of intense research for the last few years. Experiments have shown that they generally
result in higher accuracy than decision tree classifiers. In this paper, we
introduce a novel algorithm for associative classification "**C**lassification
based on **A**ssociation **R**ules **G**enerated in a **B**idirectional **A**pporach"
(CARGBA). It generates rules in two steps. At first, it generates a set
of high confidence rules of smaller length with support pruning and then
augments this set with some high confidence rules of higher length with
support below minimum support. Experiments on 6 datasets show that
our approach achieves better accuracy than other state-of-the-art associative classification algorithms.

Keywords: Association rules, Data mining, Knowledge discovery, Classification, rule sorting.

1 Introduction

Building accurate classifiers is one of the essential tasks of data mining and
machine learning research. Given a set of training instances with known class
labels, classifiers aim to predict the target classes for a set of test instances for
which the class labels are not known. At first, a classification model is developed
from training data and then it is used to classify unseen instances. There are
various methods for building classifiers such as decision trees [1], naïve-Bayesian
methods [2], statistical approaches [3], support vector machines [4] etc.

In data mining, association rule mining algorithms are used to discover rules
which determine implication or correlation among co-occurring elements within
a dataset. Association rule mining algorithms try to answer questions such as
"if a customer purchases product A, how likely is he to purchase product B?"
or "What products will a customer buy if he buys products C and D?". The
actual task is to reduce a potentially huge amount of information into a small,
understandable set of statistically supported statements.

---

* The corresponding author.

M. Ishikawa et al. (Eds.): ICONIP 2007, Part II, LNCS 4985, pp. 453–459, 2008.

Recent works have proposed several techniques to generate high quality *class association rules* from the training data set to build a classifier, with specific thresholds for support and confidence. Such classifiers are CBA (Classification Based on Association) [5], CAEP (Classification based on Aggregating Emerging Patterns) [6] and CMAR (Classification based on Multiple Association Rules) [7]. These approaches have higher accuracy than decision tree classifier due to the fact that decision-tree classifier examines one variable at a time whereas association rules explore highly confident associations among multiple variables at a time. However, these approaches have a severe limitation. All associative classification algorithms use a support threshold to generate association rules. In that way some high quality rules that have higher confidence, but lower support will be missed. Actually the long and specific rules have low support and so they are mostly penalized. But a good classification rule set should contain general as well as specific rules. It should also contain exceptional rules to account for the exceptional instances.

This paper proposes a new algorithm for associative classifier, called CARGBA. It is essentially a bidirectional rule generation approach that generates crisp association rules. It not only tries to generalize the dataset but also tries to provide specific and exceptional rules to account for the specific characteristics and anomalies in the dataset. Although we generate these specific rules, the purpose of this rule generation is not knowledge extraction, rather the only purpose is using these rules for classification to obtain better accuracy. Experiments on 6 datasets show that CARGBA achieves better accuracy than other state-of-the-art associative classifiers.

The rest of the paper is organized as follows. Section 2 describes CARGBA in details. Section 3 presents our experimental results to compare with other state-of-the-art associative classifiers on accuracy. Finally, Section 4 concludes the paper with a brief summary and few remarks.

2 CARGBA

This section describes CARGBA algorithm in details. The algorithm has two main parts. The first part generates rules and it is called **CARGBA Rule Generator**. It generates rules in two steps. First, it generates all rules in Apriori [8] fashion. These rules are as general as possible. They have shorter length and so higher support and provide general knowledge about the training set. This step of our algorithm is similar to other state-of-the-art classification methods. In the second step, we generate rules that are as specific as possible. These rules have higher length and therefore lower support and thus they easily capture the specific characteristics about the data set. That is, if there is a classification pattern that exists over very few instances or there are instances that are exceptions to the general rule, then these instances will be covered by the specific rules. Since these instances are small in number, specific rules are produced without any support pruning. In short, our approach results in a better mixture of class association rules. All the rules generated by CARGBA rule generator will not be used in the classification. So, the second part builds a classifier with the essential rules and is called **CARGBA Classifier Builder**.

2.1   CARGBA Rule Generator

The key operation of CARGBA Rule Generator algorithm is to find some rules that have *confidence* above or equal to *SatisfactoryConfidence*. Let D be the dataset. Let I be the set of all items in D, and Z be the set of class labels. A rule is of the form: $<conditionset, z>$ which represents a rule: *conditionset* $\Rightarrow z$ where *conditionset* is a set of items, $z \in Z$ is a class label. The rule has *confidence* equal to $(ruleSupportCount\ /\ conditionSupportCount) * 100\%$ where, *conditionSupportCount* is the number of cases in D that contain *conditionset* and *ruleSupportCount* is the number of cases in D that contain *conditionSet* and are labeled with class z. The rule has *support* equal to $(rulesupCount\ /\ \|D\|) * 100\%$, where $\|D\|$ is the size of the dataset.

There are two major steps under CARGBA Rule Generator. The steps are summarized as follows:

1. $R_I = \{ 1\text{-}rules \}$;
2. Compute *confidence* of each *rule* of R_I;
3. $PR_I = \{ r \in R1 \mid confidence$ of $r >= SatisfactoryConfidence$
   and *support* of $r >= minSupport\}$;
4. **for** $(k = 2; R_{k-1} \neq \Phi$ **and** $k \leq l; k{+}{+})$ **do**
5. $R_k = \text{Apriori-Gen}(R_{k-1})$;
6.   Compute *support, confidence* of each *rule* of R_k
7. $PR_k = \{ r \in R_k \mid confidence$ of $r >= SatisfactoryConfidence\}$;
8. $R_k = \{ r \in R_k \mid support$ of $r >= minSupport\}$;
9. $PR_s = \cup_k PR_k$;

Fig. 1. The first step of CARGBA Rule Generator

Step 1 This step generates all the association rules of the form *1-rules* to *l-rules* that have *confidence* greater than or equal to *SatisfactoryConfidence* under support pruning where *k-rule* denotes a rule whose *conditionset* has k items and l is a parameter of the algorithm. This step is based on Apriori [8] algorithm for finding association rules. The corresponding algorithm is given in fig. 1. At each level of rule generation it prunes away the rules having *support* less than *minSupport*.

R_k denotes the set of *k-rules*. PR_k(Pruned R_k) denotes the set of *k-rules* that have *confidence* greater than or equal to *SatisfactoryConfidence*. *PRs*(Pruned Rules) denotes the set of all rules that have *confidence* greater than or equal to *SatisfactoryConfidence* and *support* greater than or equal to *minSupport*.

1. ruleList = Φ;
2. q = Φ;
3. **for** each record *rec* $\in$ training examples
4.   *r* = constructRule(*rec*);
5.   **if** (confidence of *r* $\geq$ *satisfactoryConfidence*
           and *r* $\notin$ ruleList)
6.   *ruleList = ruleList* $\cup$ *r*;
7.   enqueue (*q, r*);
8. **while** (*q* is not empty)
9.   *r* = dequeue(*q*);
10.   **for** each attribute $A \in r$
11.   *r2* = constructRule2(*A, r*);
12.   **if** (confidence of *r2* $\geq$ *satisfactoryConfidence*
              and *r2* $\notin$ ruleList **and** number of items
              at *conditionSet* of *r2* > *l*)
13.   *ruleList = ruleList* $\cup$ *r2*;
14.   enqueue(q, *r2*);

Fig. 2. The second step of CARGBA Rule Generator

Step 2 This step generates all the association rules of the form *(l+1)-rules* to *n-rules* that have *confidence* greater than or equal to *SatisfactoryConfidence* where n is the number of non-class attributes of the data set. This step is based on totally reverse manner of Apriori algorithm [8]. We call this algorithm the "Reverse Rule Generation Algorithm" and is given in figure 2.

ruleList is a list that contains the generated rules and *q* denotes a queue. *constructRule* function (line 4) constructs a rule *r* from a record *rec* in the training example. *constructRule* function also calculates the *confidence* of rule *r*. *constructRule2* function (line 11) constructs a rule *r2* from rule *r* by removing attribute *A. constructRule2* function also calculates the *confidence* of rule *r2*.

Finally, merging of rules generated from step 1 and 2 is done by:

$$PRs = PRs \bigcup ruleList;$$

2.2   CARGBA Classifier Builder

This section presents the CARGBA Classifier Builder algorithm. *PRs* contains a lot of rules generated by CARGBA Rule Generator. All these rules will not be used to classify test instances. In this step, we select a subset of the rules from *PRs* to cover the dataset. The selected rules are sorted in descending order of *confidence, support* and *rule length*. The classifier builder algorithm is given in figure 3.

1. *finalRuleSet* = Φ;
2. *dataSet* = **D**;
3. sort(*prRs*);
4. **for** each rule $r \in prRs$ **do**
5.   **if** r correctly classifies at least one training example $d \in dataset$ **then**
6.   remove d from *dataset*;
7.   insert r at the end of *finalRuleSet*;

Fig. 3. The CARGBA classifier builder

finalRuleSet is a list that will contain rules that will be used in the classifier. *sort* function (line 3) sorts *PRs* in descending order of *confidence, support* and rule length. Lines 4-7 take only those rules in the *finalRuleSet* which can correctly classify at least one training example. Note that the insertion in *finalRuleSet* ensures that all the rules of *finalRuleSet* will be sorted in descending order of *confidence, support* and *rule length*.

When a new test example is to be classified, the classifier classifies according to the first rule in the *finalRuleSet* that covers the test example. If all the rules of the classifier fail to cover the test example, then the test example will be classified to a *default* class i.e. the class with the maximum number of training examples associated with.

3   Experimental Studies

We have evaluated the accuracy of our algorithm on 6 datasets from UCI ML Repository [9]. The accuracy of each dataset is obtained by 10-fold cross-validations. We use C4.5's shuffle utility to shuffle the data sets. We have calculated the mean and variance of our accuracy based on several runs of our algorithm on each data set. On each run, we have randomly selected the training and test data. Discretization of continuous attributes is done using the same method used in CBA [5].

In the experiments, the parameters of the four methods are set as follows. All C4.5 [1] parameters are set to their default values. We test both C4.5 decision tree method and rule method. Since the rule method has better accuracy, we only present the accuracy for the rule method. For CBA [5], we set *support* threshold to 1% and *confidence* threshold to 50% and disable the limit on the number of rules. Other parameters remain default. For CMAR [7], the *support* and *confidence* thresholds are set as it is in CBA. The *database coverage* threshold is set to 4 and the *confidence difference* threshold is set to 20%. For CARGBA, we investigated parameter sensitivity in details and found that CARGBA is not too sensitive to any particular parameter. So we decided to go with the default parameter values used by other algorithms. Minsupport is set to 1%, *satisfactoryconfidence* is set to 50% and l is set to half of the number of attributes of the dataset. Maximum no. of rules in a level is set to 30,000 in CARGBA. We have performed pruning using correlation coefficient introduced in [10].

3.1   Results

In this section, we report our experimental results on comparing CARGBA against three other popular classification methods: C4.5 [1], CBA [5] and CMAR [7]. The experimental result is shown in Table 1. For CARGBA, we also present the variance of accuracies obtained for each data set.

Table 1. Comparison of C4.5, CBA, CMAR and CARGBA on accuracy

Dataset	C4.5	CBA	CMAR	CARGBA (Mean)	CARGBA (Variance)
pima	**75.5**	72.9	75.1	73.83	1.1
iris	95.3	94.7	94.0	**95.33**	0.8
heart	80.8	81.9	82.2	**82.22**	1.5
glass	68.7	**73.9**	70.1	73.83	0.7
tic-tac	99.4	**99.6**	99.2	**99.6**	0.3
diabetes	74.2	74.5	75.8	**76.17**	2.2
Average	82.32	82.92	82.73	**83.50**	

The won-loss-tied record of the CARGBA against C4.5 in term of accuracy is 4-1-1. The won-loss-tied record of the CARGBA against CBA and CMAR algorithms in term of accuracy are 4-1-1 and 4-1-1, respectively. The result shows that CARGBA outperforms CBA, C4.5 and CMAR in terms of average accuracy on 6 data sets.

4   Conclusion

Association rules generation algorithms that generate association rules based on Apriori algorithm with low support suffer from a limitation that they miss some high confidence rules with lower support. On the other hand, association rules generation algorithms that generate rules at a reverse order of Apriori algorithm without support pruning suffer from the limitation that the number of support less rules is very large in number and producing the general rules takes a lot of computational time. In this paper we have proposed a novel associative classi-fication method, CARGBA algorithm that overcomes the above two problems successfully. Our experiments on 6 databases in UCI machine learning database repository show that CARGBA is consistent, highly effective at classification of various kinds of databases and has better average classification accuracy in comparison with C4.5, CBA and CMAR.

Acknowledgement. MMI is currently a Visiting Associate Professor at University of Fukui supported by the Fellowship from Japanese Society for Promotion of Science (JSPS). This work was in part supported by grants to KM from JSPS, Yazaki Memorial Foundation for Science and Technology, and University of Fukui.

References

1. Quinlan, J.R.: C4.5: Programs for Machine Learning. Morgan Kaufmann, San Francisco (1993)
2. Duda, R., Hart, P.: Pattern Classification and Scene Analysis. John Wiley & Sons, Chichester (1973)
3. Lim, T.S., Loh, W.Y., Shih, Y.S.: A comparison of prediction accuracy, complexity, and training time of thirty-three old and new classification algorithms. Machine Learning 39 (2000)
4. Cristianini, N., Shawe-Taylor: An Introduction to Support Vector Machines. Cambridge University Press, Cambridge (2000)
5. Liu, B., Hsu, W., Ma, Y.: CBA: Integrating Classification and Association Rule Mining. In: KDD 1998, New York, NY (August 1998)
6. Dong, G., Zhang, X., Wong, L., Li, J.: Caep: Classification by Aggregating Emerging Patterns. In: Arikawa, S., Furukawa, K. (eds.) DS 1999. LNCS (LNAI), vol. 1721, Springer, Heidelberg (1999)
7. Li, W., Han, J., Pei, J.: CMAR: Accurate and efficient classification based on multiple class-association rules. In: ICDM 2001, San Jose, CA (November 2001)
8. Agrawal, R., Imielinski, T., Swami, A.: Mining Association Rules between Sets of Items in Large Databases. In: Proc. Of the SIGMOD, Washington, D.C., pp. 207–216 (1993)
9. Blake, C., Merz, C.: UCI repository of machine learning databases, `http://www.ics.uci.edu/~mlearn/MLRepository.html`
10. Antonie, M., Zaïane, O.R.: An Associative Classifier based on Positive and Negative Rules. In: DMKD 2004, Paris, France, June 13 (2004)

Solar Radiation Data Modeling with a Novel Surface Fitting Approach

Fatih Onur Hocaoğlu, Ömer Nezih Gerek, and Mehmet Kurban

Anadolu University, Dept. of Electrical and Electronics Eng., Eskisehir, Turkey
{fohocaoglu,ongerek,mkurban}@anadolu.edu.tr

Abstract. In this work one year hourly solar radiation data are analyzed and modeled. Using a 2-D surface fitting approach, a novel model is developed for the general behavior of the solar radiation. The mathematical formulation of the 2-D surface model is obtained. The accuracy of the analytical surface model is tested and compared with another surface model obtained from a feed-forward Neural Network(NN). Analytical surface model and NN surface model are compared in the sense of Root Mean Square Error (RMSE). It is obtained that the NN surface model gives more accurate results with smaller RMSE results. However, unlike the specificity of the NN surface model, the analytical surface model provides an intuitive and more generalized form that can be suitable for several other locations on earth.

1 Introduction

Solar radiation is the principal energy source for physical, biological and chemical processes. An accurate knowledge and an insightful model of the solar radiation data at a particular geographical location is of vital importance. Such knowledge is a pre-requisite for the simulation and design of solar energy systems. Architects, agriculturalists, air conditioning engineers and energy conscious designers of buildings also require such information. In many cases, the solar energy applications involve tilted surfaces. To compensate for the effect of radiation on tilted surfaces, knowledge of both diffusing and direct components of global radiation falling on a horizontal surface is required [1]. Menges et al. [2] reviewed and compared the available solar-radiation models for a region in detail. The majority of the models developed for the prediction of solar radiation are based on existing climatic-parameters, such as sunshine duration, cloud cover, relative humidity, and minimum and maximum temperatures [3,4,5]. Unfortunately, for many developing countries, solar-radiation measurements are not easily available because of the expensive measuring equipment and techniques required [6]. In this study, using a 2-D approach as mentioned in Section 2, a novel solar radiation model for one year solar radiation data that is acquired and collected between August 1, 2005 and July 30, 2006 in Iki Eylul campus of Anadolu University, is developed. The model is based on a surface fitting approach using the data rendered in 2-D. It is observed that hourly alteration of solar radiation

M. Ishikawa et al. (Eds.): ICONIP 2007, Part II, LNCS 4985, pp. 460–467, 2008.

data within a day has a Gaussian shaped function, hence the 2-D data along
the hour axes are fitted to Gaussian functions. Trust-region algorithm is used as
mentioned in Section 3 during calculating the parameters of Gaussian functions.
Also a NN model is developed for 2-D data as mentioned in Section 4. Finally
the models are compared in the sense of RMSE and the results are presented
in Section 5. The NNs provide a more "specific" model for the data, hence they
yield better prediction models. However, the 2-D surface model is more generic
and insightful. Therefore it can also be used as a global model for places with
similar yearly solar radiation conditions without utilizing data collection and
training.

2   Determination and Estimation of Surface Model Structure and Parameters

The first stage in data fitting is to determine a plausible model among known
mathematical models that characterizes the data accurately. After setting the
mathematical model, coefficients of the model must be estimated. Recently, a
novel 2-D interpretation approach that was developed by Hocaoğlu et al. [7]
indicated that "rendering" or "interpretation" of the data (i.e. transformation)
also proves to be critical even before proceeding to the modeling. In this approach
the solar radiation data in time series is rendered and presented in 2-D and it
is shown that the representation format has significant advantages over 1-D
time series approaches. In this work, starting from the mentioned 2-D rendered
representation, a novel surface model is proposed.

To determine the structure of the model for fitting to the data, transverse
sections are taken from the 2-D along the "hour" and the "day" axes as given
in Fig.1.

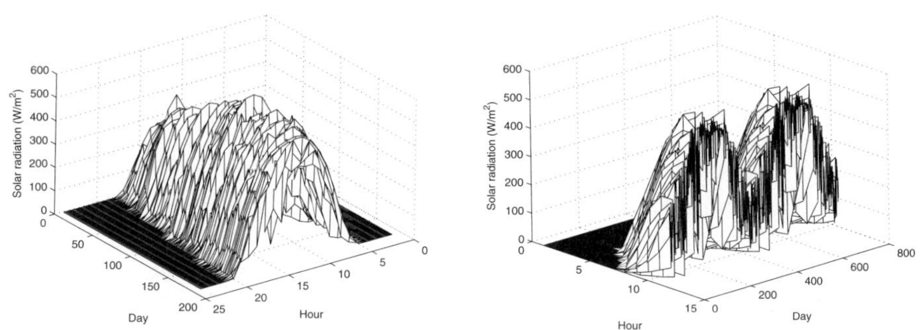

Fig. 1. Plots of cross sections along "hour" and "days" axes, respectively, for a two
year data

Examining Fig.1 it can be deduced that the cross section along the "hour"
axis is similar to a Gaussian function for all days. Conversely, the cross section

along the "days" axis exhibits an oscillatory behavior (seasons) that can be modeled with a sinusoidal function. The hourly variation function was chosen to be Gaussian due to its shape-wise resemblance and simple calculation, and the daily variation was chosen as a sinusoid due to its capability of physically explaining the seasonal variation phenomenon. Once the model of the data is determined, the fitting process must be applied. The result of the fitting process is an estimate of the "true" but unknown coefficients of the mathematical model. Method of least squares is the basic method that can be used for linear estimation. In this method, the sum of squared residuals is minimized. The residual for the ith data point is obtained as the difference between the actual value and the fitted value as given in equation 1.

$$e_i = y_i - \hat{y}_i \tag{1}$$

The summed square error (SSE), therefore, is given by equation 2

$$SSE = \sum_{i=1}^{n} e_i^2 = \sum_{i=1}^{n} (y_i - \hat{y}_i)^2, \tag{2}$$

where n is the number of data points included in the fit and SSE is the sum of squares error estimate. The supported types of least squares fitting include; Linear least squares, Weighted linear least squares, Robust least squares and Nonlinear least squares. Although linear least squares method can be used to fit a linear (polynomial) model to data, nonlinear functions such as Gaussians and sinusoids may not be suitable. In general, any surface model may be a nonlinear model which is defined in matrix form as in equation 3

$$y = f(X, \alpha) + \varepsilon, \tag{3}$$

where y is an n-by-1 vector of responses, f is a function of α and X, α is m-by-1 vector of coefficients. X is the n-by-m design matrix for the model. ε is an n-by-1 vector of errors. Obviously, nonlinear models are more difficult to fit than linear models because the coefficients cannot be estimated using simple matrix optimization techniques. Instead, an iterative approach is required that follows the following steps:

1. Start with an initial estimate for each coefficient. For some nonlinear models, a heuristic approach is provided that produces reasonable starting values. For other models, random values on the interval [0,1] are provided.
2. Produce the fitted curve for the current set of coefficients. The fitted response value y is given by equation 4
3. Adjust the coefficients and determine whether the fit improves.
4. Iterate the process by returning to step 2 until the fit reaches the specified convergence criteria.

$$\hat{y} = f(X, b) \tag{4}$$

The above iteration involves the calculation of the Jacobian of $f(X, b)$, which is defined as a matrix of partial derivatives taken with respect to the coefficients. The direction and magnitude of the adjustment in step-3 depend on the fitting algorithm.

There are several algorithms to find estimations of nonlinear model parameters. Around those, best knowns are trust-region and Levenberg-Marquardt algorithms. The Levenberg-Marquardt [8] algorithm has been used for many years and has proved to work most of the time for a wide range of linear and nonlinear models with relatively good initial values. On the other hand, trust-region algorithm [9] is specifically more powerful for solving difficult nonlinear problems, and it represents an improvement over the popular Levenberg-Marquardt algorithm. Therefore, trust-region method is used for obtaining the Gaussian parameters of surface functions in this study. The "days" axis is not optimized by any methods, because its behavior is analytically obtained using geographical facts such as its period being 365 days and its extrema corresponding to June 21 and Dec. 21.

3 NN Model for 2-D Data

To test and compare the accuracy of the 2-D model, a NN structure is also built. In this structure, the model does not yield a global, unified and analytical surface function. Instead, the result is a surface function that is more specifically trained to the available data. Although the analytical closed form is ambiguous, the NNs provide a dedicated and better surface model with less RMSE. Since the analytical surface model has two inputs (hour and day numbers) and one output (Solar radiation), the NN structure is constructed to be two input-one output. The input-output pairs are normalized as to fall in the range [-1,1]. It is obtained that using 5 neurons in the hidden layer is appropriate according to simulations. Due to its ability of fast convergence the Levenberg-Marquard learning algorithm is used in learning process of NN. The network is trained using 1 year solar radiation data and surface model of the data is obtained by this way. Both hidden and output layer's output from their net input are calculated using Tan-Sigmoid transfer function. The network is trained in 50 epochs. The results are obtained and compared with the global and analytical surface model in Section 4.

4 Numerical Results

The hourly solar radiation data along one day is considered as a Gaussian function as in equation 5

$$g(x) = ae^{-(x-b)^2/c^2} \tag{5}$$

where a is the height of the Gaussian peak, b is the position of the center of the peak and c is related to the full width at half maximum of the peak. Hourly radiation data are fitted to the Gaussian function for "all" days by determining

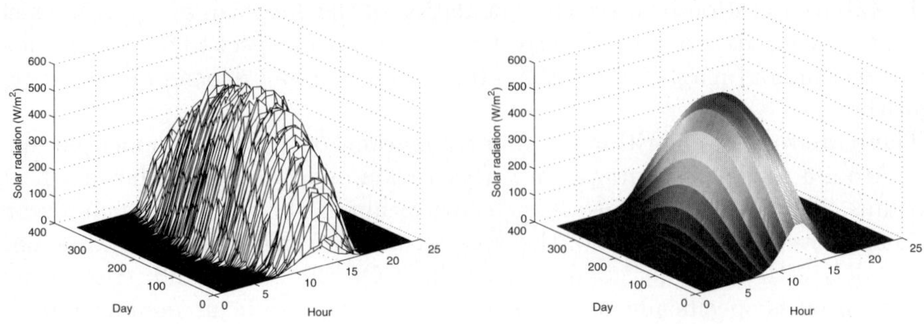

Fig. 2. 2-D plot of actual data and obtained analytical surface model

the Gaussian parameters a, b and c using the trust-region algorithm. Totally 365 parameter stes a ,b and c are obtained for one year of recorded data. Then to form the generic and global surface model of the data, variation of the parameter sets a ,b and c are explored along days. Since the daily behavior of the data is expected to have a sinusoidal form as explained in Section 2, the parameters a and c are modeled with sinusoidal functions with periods equal 365 days. For each Gaussian function the position of the center of the peak values should be around the 12.5 value which corresponds the center of the day time for whole year. As a result, the parameter b is judiciously taken to be 12.5. The other coefficients a and c are determined as sinusoidals in equations 6 and 7

$$a(day) = 364 \times \sin(2 \times pi \times day/720) + 162.1 \tag{6}$$

$$c(day) = 2.117 \times \sin(2 \times pi \times day/712) + 2.644 \tag{7}$$

Finally the analytical surface that models the data is obtained as given in equation 8.

$$Surface(day, hour) = a(day) \times e^{-((hour - 12.5)/c(day))^2} \tag{8}$$

As a visual comparison, the obtained surface model and 2-D plot of actual data are given in Fig.2. The error data calculated by subtracting actual data from the analytical surface model for each hour is given in Fig. 3.

The accuracy of the analytical surface model is tested and compared with surface function generated by NNs. A two input - one output feed forward neural network is built and given in Fig. 4.

To numerically compare the NN surface with the analytical surface model, the input-output pairs of network are chosen to be compatible with each other as hour - versus - day - versus - Solar radiation. For instance, if it is desired to find the estimation value of solar radiation at 50th day of the year, at 5 o clock, the inputs of the network are taken as (50,5) which also corresponds to the coordinates of the surface model. Various number of neurons are used in the

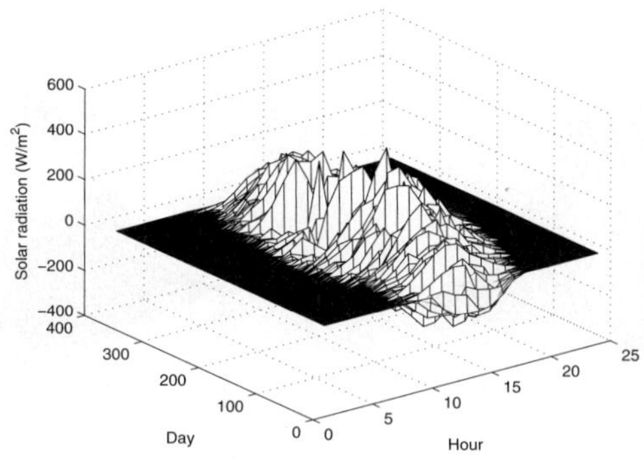

Fig. 3. Error surface of the model

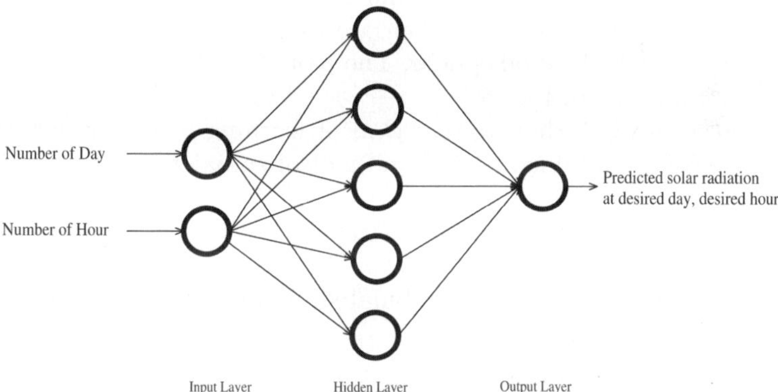

Fig. 4. The adopted NN structure

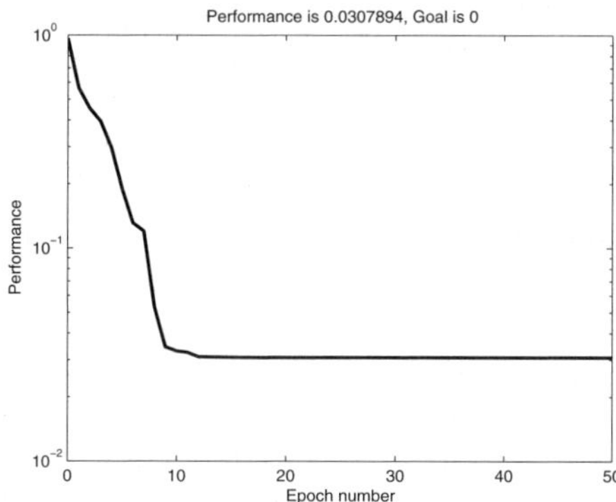

Fig. 5. Plot of performance versus epoch number

466   F.O. Hocaoğlu, Ö.N. Gerek, and M. Kurban

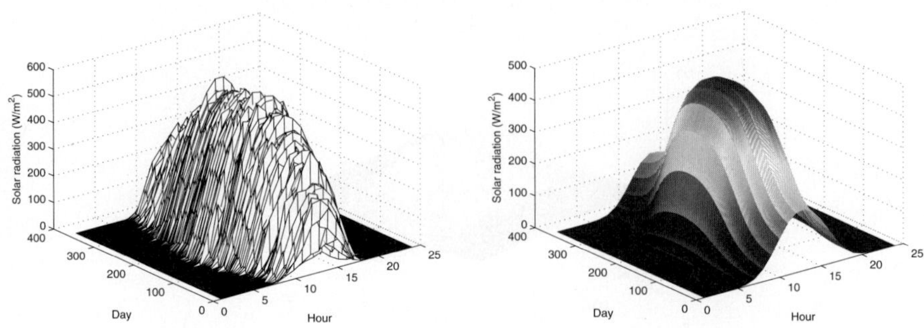

Fig. 6. 2-D plot of the solar radiation data, and the surface function obtained by NN

hidden layer to determine the optimal number of neurons and it is observed that using 5 neurons is experimentally appropriate to find more accurate prediction values. The network is trained 50 epochs. The plot of epoch number versus total RMS error is obtained as in Fig. 5.

It is obvious from Fig.5 that a great deal of learning is already achieved in 10 epochs. The surface obtained by NN and plot of actual 2-D data are given in Fig.6

The Correlation coefficient and RMSE values between actual and predicted values of solar radiation data obtained from both analytical surface model and the NN surface model are calculated, tabulated, and presented in Table I.

Table 1. RMSE values for proposed structures and Correlation coefficients between actual values and predicted values of solar radiation data

Model	RMSE	R
Analytical Surface Model	57.24	0.936
NN Surface Model	51.91	0.947

5   Conclusion

In this work, using the 2-D interpretation approach, surface models for solar radiation data are developed. The developed models have two inputs that are the number of days beginning from January 1 of the year and the number hours within the days. For these models, the hourly data variation within a day is fitted to Gaussian functions. The parameters of Gaussian functions are obtained for each day. In the analytical attempt of surface modeling, the behavior of the solar radiation data along the days corresponding to the same hour is observed to have a sinusoidal oscillation. Therefore, the parameters related with the height and width of the Gaussian are fitted to separate sinusoidal functions, and finally the analytical model of the surface is obtained. Alternatively, a NN structure is built with the same input-output data pairs in the 2-D form and a nonlinear and non-analytical surface model of whole data is obtained. Two models are compared using RMSE distortion relative to the original data. Due to its specificity, the NN model provides a more accurate surface model with less RMSE. On the other hand, the NN surface model is not analytical, and it cannot be generalized to other places. Conversely, the analytical surface model is very intuitive with simple seasonal parameters, and it provides a global view of the solar radiation phenomenon. Therefore, it can be easily adapted to other places in the world without a long data collection period.

Acknowledgements

The authors gratefully acknowledges the Anadolu University of Tecnology Research Fund for the financial support of this work through project 040258 and gratefully acknowledges to the Scientific and Technological Research Council of Turkey (TUBITAK) for the financial support of this work through project 107M212.

References

1. Muneer, T., Younes, S., Munawwar, S.: Discourses on solar radiation modeling. Renewable and Sustainable Energy Reviews 11, 551–602 (2007)
2. Menges, H.O., Ertekin, C., Sonmete, M.H.: Evaluation of global solar radiation models for Konya, Turkey. Energy Conversion and Management 47, 3149–3173 (2006)
3. Trabea, A.A., Shaltout, M.A.: Correlation of global solar-radiation with meteorological parameters over Egypt. Renew Energy 21, 297–308 (2000)
4. Badescu, V.: Correlations to estimate monthly mean daily solar global-irradiation: application to Romania. Energy 24, 883–893 (1999)
5. Hepbasli, A., Ulgen, K.: Prediction of solar-radiation parameters through the clearness index for Izmir, Turkey. Energy Source 24, 773–785 (2002)
6. Bulut, H., Büyükalaca, O.: Simple model for the generation of daily global solar-radiation data in Turkey. Applied Energy 84, 477–491 (2007)
7. Hocaoglu, F.O., Gerek, Ö.N., Kurban, M.: A Novel 2-D Model Approach for the Prediction of Hourly Solar Radiation. In: Sandoval, F., Prieto, A.G., Cabestany, J., Graña, M. (eds.) IWANN 2007. LNCS, vol. 4507, pp. 749–756. Springer, Heidelberg (2007)
8. Marquardt, D.: An Algorithm for Least Squares Estimation of Nonlinear Parameters. SIAM J. Appl. Math. 11, 431–441 (1963)
9. Branch, M.A., Coleman, T.F., Li, Y.: A Subspace, Interior, and Conjugate Gradient Method for Large-Scale Bound-Constrained Minimization Problems. SIAM Journal on Scientific Computing 21, 1–23 (1999)

Electricity Quality Control of an Independent Power System Based on Hybrid Intelligent Controller

Hee-Sang Ko[1], Min-Jae Kang[2], and Ho-Chan Kim[2]

[1] Wind Energy Research Center, Korea Institute of Energy Research, Daejeon, 305-343, Korea
hee-sang@ieee.org
[2] Faculty of Electrical and Electronic Engineering, Cheju National University, Jeju, 690-756, Korea
{minjk, hckim}@cheju.ac.kr

Abstract. Wind power generation is gaining popularity as the power industry in the world is moving toward more liberalized trade of energy along with public concerns of more environmentally friendly mode of electricity generation. The weakness of wind power generation is its dependence on nature—the power output varies in quite a wide range due to the change of wind speed, which is difficult to model and predict. The excess fluctuation of power output and voltages can influence negatively the quality of electricity in the distribution system connected to the wind power generation plant. In this paper, the authors propose an intelligent adaptive system to control the output of a wind power generation plant to maintain the quality of electricity in the distribution system. The target wind generator is a cost-effective induction generator, while the plant is equipped with a small capacity energy storage based on conventional batteries, heater load for co-generation and braking, and a voltage smoothing device such as a static Var compensator (SVC). Fuzzy logic controller provides a flexible controller covering a wide range of energy/voltage compensation. A neural network inverse model is designed to provide compensating control amount for a system. The system can be optimized to cope with the fluctuating market-based electricity price conditions to lower the cost of electricity consumption or to maximize the power sales opportunities from the wind generation plant.

1 Introduction

Autonomous renewable energy systems such as wind, solar, and micro-hydro require control methods to maintain stability due to the real time variation of input energy and load, while maximizing the use of the renewable resources.

Since the early eighties, wind-Diesel energy conversion system (WDECS) have been accepted and widely used as electricity generating systems for remote areas. In such cases, the WDECS serves an entire isolated load and is responsible for maintaining frequency and voltage stability. The main driving force in WDECS design was to secure both fuel saving and reliable power supply. Usually, Diesel

M. Ishikawa et al. (Eds.): ICONIP 2007, Part II, LNCS 4985, pp. 468–477, 2008.

generator installed capacity is sized to meet the peak power demand, but is used in practice to supply power only when the wind power output is insufficient to meet the load demand [1].

The random power disturbances at the output of wind-turbine generators can cause relatively large frequency and voltage fluctuations. In a large grid, these fluctuations can have a little effect on the overall quality of the delivered energy. However, with weak autonomous networks, these power fluctuations can have a marked effect, which must be eliminated regardless of the penetration rate [2,3]. Hence, the control of the voltage and frequency of a weak wind-Diesel system is considered more challenging than in large grids.

In this paper, fuzzy-neural hybrid controller is proposed and applied for pitch control of wind turbine. Fuzzy logic is applied for designing a feedback controller. Neural network inverse model is designed for a dynamic feed-forward controller. Therefore, fast damping from fuzzy controller and fast reference tracking can be accomplished.

2 System Description

Fig. 1 shows the prototype of a wind-diesel hybrid power system [3].

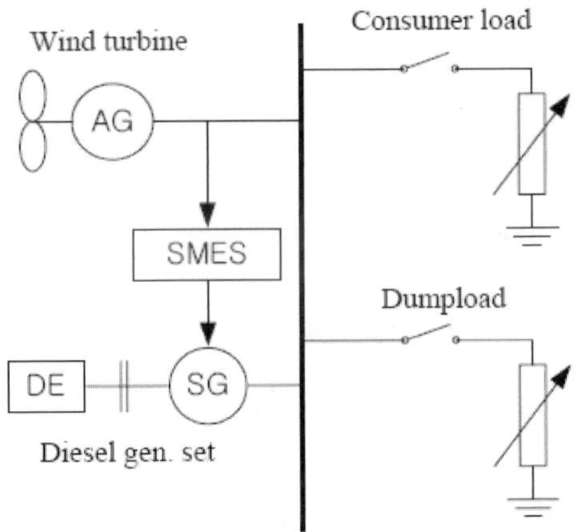

Fig. 1. The prototype of wind-diesel hybrid power system

Generator dynamics model consists of a synchronous machine driven by Diesel engine through flywheel and connected in parallel with an induction machine driven by a wind turbine.

Superconducting magnetic energy storage (SMES) [4] is a control unit for a synchronous machine. When there is a sudden rise in the demand of load, the stored energy is immediately released through power system. As the governor and pitch control mechanism start working to set the power system to the new operating condition, a SMES unit charges back to its initial value of current. In the case of sudden release of the loads, a SMES immediately gets charged towards its full value, thus absorbing some portion of the excess energy in the system, and as the system returns to its steady state, the excess energy absorbed is released and SMES current attains its normal value.

When wind power rises above the power set point and SMES unit is fully charged, the pitch control system begins operating to maintain an average power equal to the set point. The pitch control system consists of a power measurement transducer, a manual power set point control, a proportional plus integral feedback function, and hydraulic actuator, which varies the pitch of the blades. Variable pitch turbines operates efficiently over a wider range of wind speeds than fixed pitch machines. The study in this paper is focused on the designing of turbine blade pitch controller based on fuzzy logic and neural network.

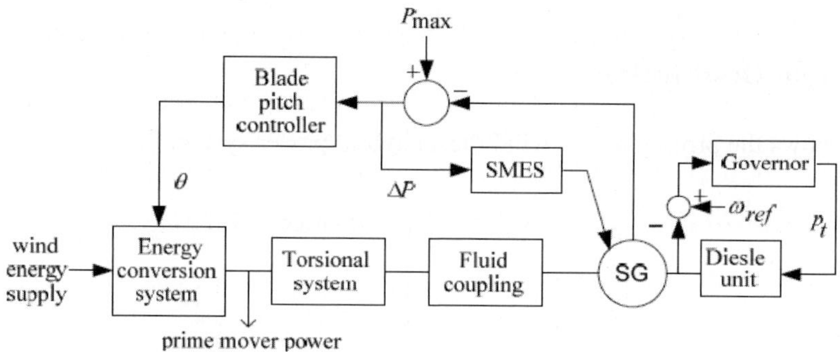

Fig. 2. The basic configuration of WDECS

3   Fuzzy-Neural Hybrid Control

3.1   Feedback Controller Based on Fuzzy Logic

Fuzzy control systems are rule-based systems in which a set of fuzzy rules represents a control decision mechanism to adjust the effects of certain system conditions. Fuzzy controller is based on the linguistic relationships or rules that define the control laws of a process between input and output [5,6]. This feature draws attention toward a fuzzy controller due to its nonlinear characteristics and no need for an accurate system modeling. The fuzzy controller consists of rule base, which represents a fuzzy logic quantification of the expert's linguistic description of how to achieve good control, fuzzification of actual input values, fuzzy inference, and defuzzification of fuzzy output.

In this paper, total of 121 rules are used for the power system under study. The general form of the fuzzy rule is given in the *if-then* form as follows:

$$\text{if } x(k) \text{ is } A \text{ and } \Delta x(k) \text{ is } B, \text{ then } y(k) \text{ is } C, \tag{1}$$

where $x, \Delta x$ are the input signals, y is controller output and A, B, C indicate the linguistic variables.

The linguistic values extracted from the experimental knowledge are NH (negative high), NL (negative large), NB (negative big), NM (negative medium), NS (negative small), ZE (zero), PS (positive small), PM (positive medium), PB (positive big), PL (positive large), PH (positive high).

In the power system under study, generator power deviation (ΔP) is chosen for the input of a fuzzy controller. The linguistic descriptions provide experimental expressions of the expert for a control decision-making process and each linguistic variable is represented as triangular membership functions shown in Fig. 3 and Fig. 4. In the fuzzy controller, the input normalization factors are chosen to represent the proper membership quantifications of linguistic values. In addition, normalization factors can be used to yield the desired response of the fuzzy controller. g_1, g_2 stand for a normalization factor for input of fuzzy controller and g_0 stands for a denormalization factor for output of fuzzy controller. Fig. 3 shows the membership function for error and change in error, Fig. 4 depicts the membership function for output.

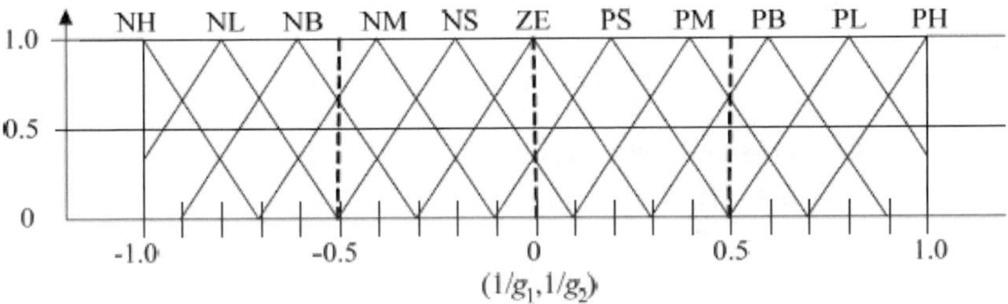

Fig. 3. Membership function of error and change in error

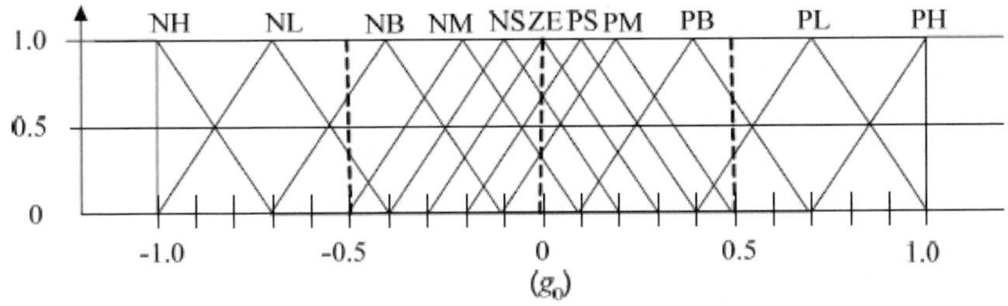

Fig. 4. Membership function of output

In Fig. 3 and Fig. 4, the membership functions are overlapped with each other to smooth a fuzzy system output and a fuzzy controller is designed to regulate a system smoothly when an error and a change in error are near zero. The rules are established to control transient stability problem for all possible cases. It is required to find the fuzzy region for the output for each rule. The centroid or the center of gravity defuzzification method [6] is used which calculates the most typical crisp value of the fuzzy set and "y is C" in (1) can be expressed by (2).

$$y = \frac{\sum_i \mu_A(y_i) \times y_i}{\sum_i \mu_A(y_i)} \tag{2}$$

where μ_A is a degree of membership function.

3.2 Feedforward Compensator Based on Neural Network Inverse Model

In [7], a two layer neural network is applied to obtain a dynamic feedforward compensator. In general, the output of a system can be described with a function or a mapping of the plant input-output history [7,8]. For a single-input single-output (SISO) discrete-time system, the mapping can be written in the form of a nonlinear function as follows:

$$y(k+1) = f(y(k), y(k-1),..., y(k-n), u(k), u(k-1),...,u(k-m)). \tag{3}$$

Solving for the control, (3) can be represented as following:

$$\begin{aligned} u(k) = g(y(k+1), y(k), y(k-1), y(k-2),..., y(k-n), \\ u(k-1), u(k-2), u(k-3),..., u(k-m)), \end{aligned} \tag{4}$$

which is a nonlinear inverse mapping of (3). The objective of the control problem is to find a control sequence, which will drive a system to an arbitrary reference trajectory. This can be achieved by replacing $y(k+1)$ in (4) with reference output y_{ref} or the temporary target $y_r(k+1)$ evaluated by

$$y_r(k+1) = y(k) + \alpha(y_{ref} - y(k)), \tag{5}$$

where α is the target ratio constant $(0 < \alpha \le 1)$. The value of α describes the rate with which the present output $y(k)$ approaches the reference output value, and thus has a positive value between 0 and 1.

In Fig. 5, the training mode is introduced, where Δ denotes the vector of delay sequence data. Fig. 6 shows the neural network inverse model (NNIM) in training mode. All activation functions in hidden layer are *tanh(x)* (described as f_j in Fig. 5) and the activation function in output layer is x (depicted as F_i in Fig. 6).

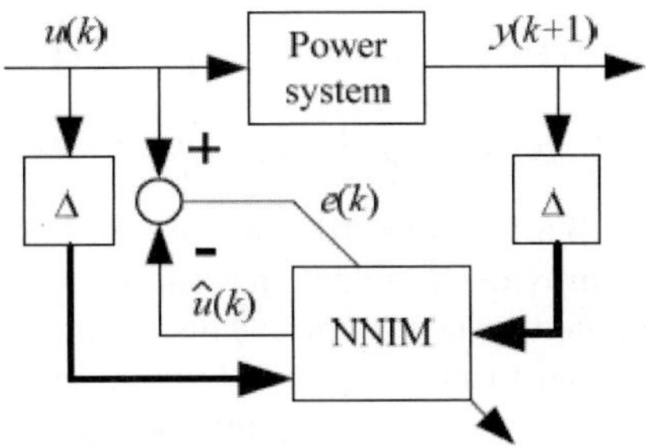

Fig. 5. Training mode of NNIM

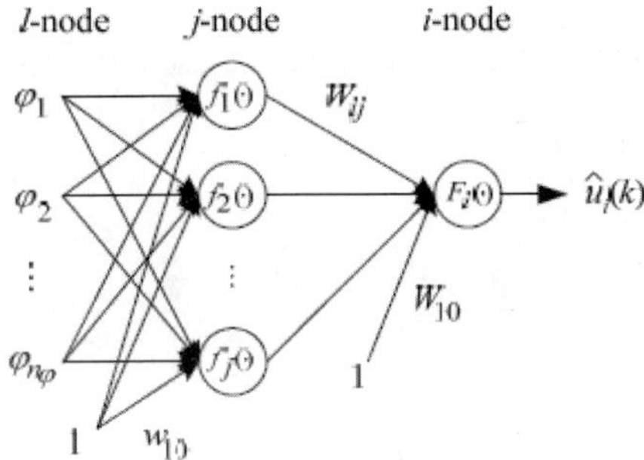

Fig. 6. Neural network inverse model (NNIM)

$$\hat{u}_i\,(k) = F_i\left[\sum_{j=1}^{n_h} W_{ij} f_j\left(\sum_{l=1}^{n_\varphi} w_{jl}\overline{\varphi} + w_{j0}\right) + W_{i0}\right],\tag{6}$$

where

$$\overline{\varphi} = [\,y(k+1),\,y(k),\ldots,\,y(k-n),u(k-1),\ldots,u(k-m)]^T$$
$$= [\varphi_1,\varphi_2,\varphi_3,\ldots,\varphi_{n_\varphi}]^T$$

$w_{jl}\quad$: weight between input and hidden layer,

n_h,n_φ : number of hidden neurons and external input,

$W_{ij}\quad$: weight between hidden and output layer.

The above NNIM is trained based on the input-output data described in Fig. 5. To train the neural network inverse model, Levenberg-Marquardt method is applied which is fast and robust [7,8]. The trained NNIM is used as a feedforward compensator.

The total control scheme is indicated in Fig. 7. Δ denote the vector of delay sequence data. The total control input is $u(k)=u_{fb}(k)+u_{ff}(k)$. $u_{fb}(k)$ is the output of fuzzy controller and the output of the feedforward controller, $u_{ff}(k)$ can be represented as following:

$$u_{ff}(k) = g(y_r(k+1), y_r(k), y_r(k-1),..., y_r(k-n),$$

$$u_{fb}(k-1), u_{fb}(k-2),..., u_{fb}(k-m)).$$

(7)

In Fig. 7, once a signal of a feedforward compensator is given into the control system, the fuzzy controller provides a signal that minimizes the inputs of controller, which contains a compensated system output. This control scheme can be a soft way of generating a control signal to minimize the tracking error and improve a system performance in the point of view of giving compensating signal in advance [9]. This implies the optimization of existing controller, which is the main purpose of a feedforward controller in a hybrid control scheme.

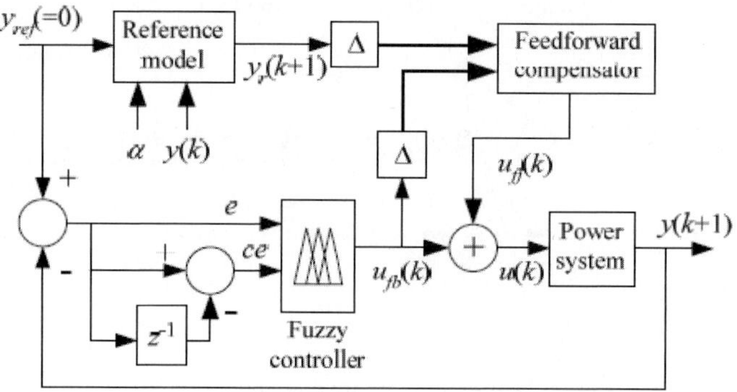

Fig. 7. The fuzzy-neural hybrid control

4   Simulation

First, a fuzzy controller is designed for a feedback controller and an NNIM is obtained for a feedforward compensator. In this paper, α is 0.1 and g_1, g_2, g_0 are 5, 50, and 5 by trial and error, respectively. Levenberg-Marquardt method is applied to train an NNIM. The sampling time is 0.01 sec. for the proposed control action.

The proposed fuzzy-neural hybrid controller (Fuzzy+NNIM) is tested in a wind-Diesel autonomous power system (WDAPS). Two cases are considered: first, the sudden step load increase of 0.01 [p.u.] and SMES is in discharging mode (rectifier) mode). Second, the SMES fully discharged and there is sudden step load increase. In this case, SMES is in recharging mode (inverter mode).

4.1   Case 1: A Sudden Step Load Increase

A load is suddenly increased by 0.01 [p.u.]. The SMES releases the charged current (2 p.u.). The governor and pitch mechanism start operating for charging current of SMES and damping of WDAPS. Fig. 8 shows improvement of the system frequency oscillations and power deviations.

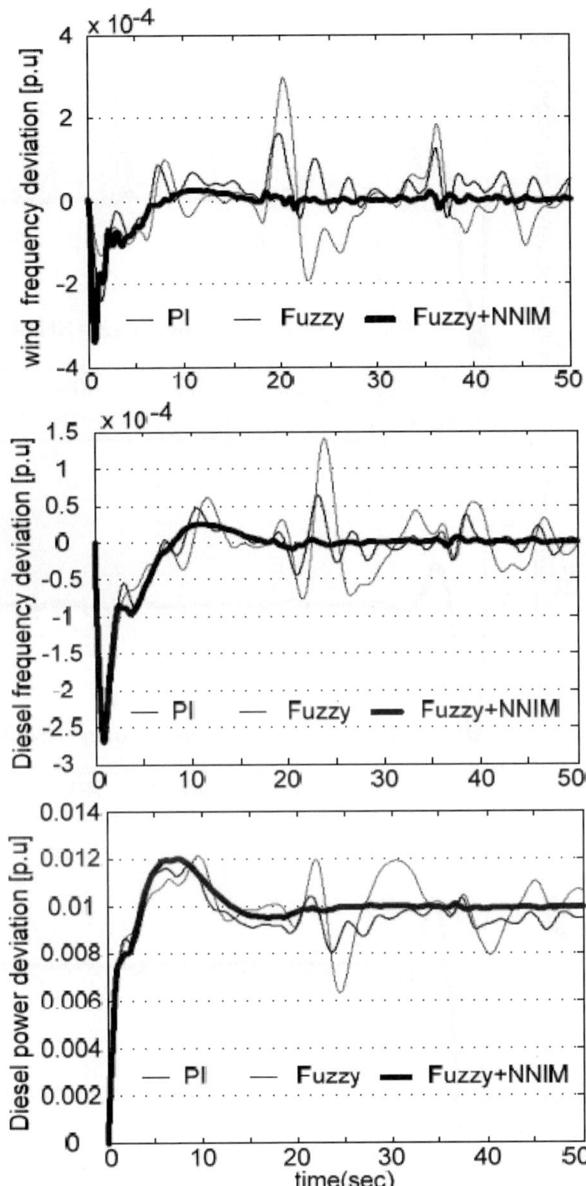

Fig. 8. Comparison of system response among PI, Fuzzy, and Fuzzy-NNIM

4.2   Case 2: Sudden Step Load Increase with Fully Discharged SMES

In this case, the SMES is fully discharged (0 p.u.). Then, the SMES needs to recharge current to set point (2 p.u.). The wind power generation from the wind turbine is assumed as not sufficient. Fig. 9 also shows that the Fuzzy-NNIM performance is much better than the PI and the Fuzzy controller.

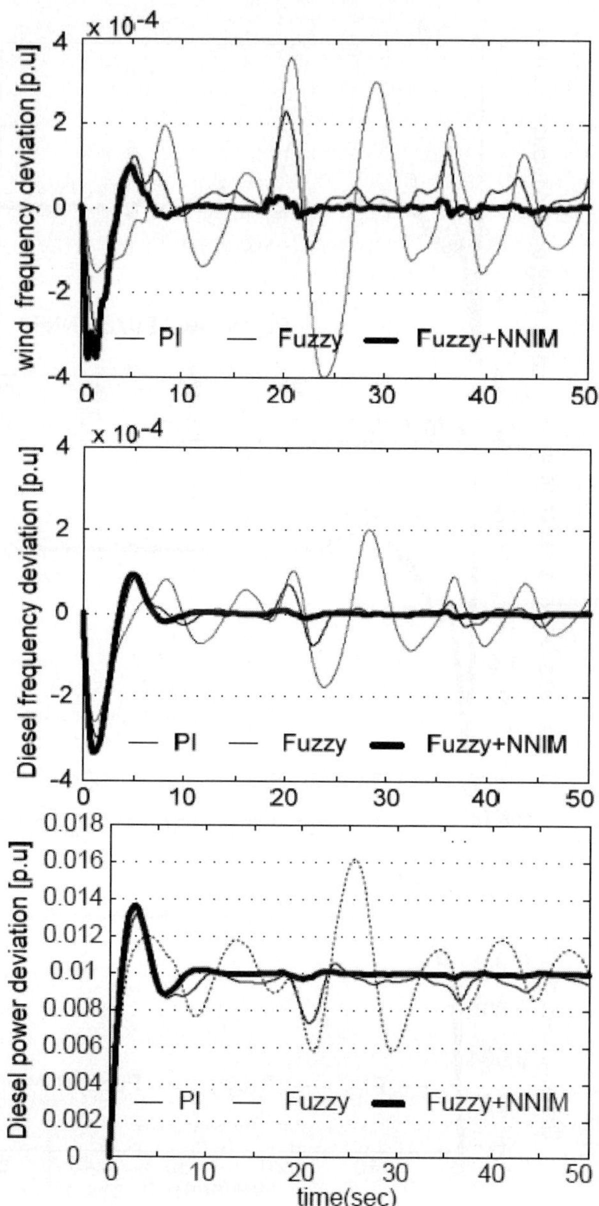

Fig. 9. Comparison of system response among PI, Fuzzy, and Fuzzy-NNIM

5   Conclusions

In this paper, the fuzzy-neural hybrid controller for electricity quality control of wind power generation plants is presented. The main idea of hybrid control is that the ynamic feedforward control can be used for improving the reference tracking while feedback is used for stabilizing the system and for suppressing disturbances. Feedforward controller is a neural network inverse model (NNIM), which is trained by Levenberg-Marquardt method and feedback controller is a fuzzy controller. The Fuzzy-NNIM was tested in a wind-Diesel autonomous power system and compared with the conventional PSS and the fuzzy controller. In all cases, the Fuzzy-NNIM out-performed the conventional PSS and the fuzzy controller. The Fuzzy-NNIM provides quite small frequency deviation and fuel saving of Diesel system. Thus, the usefulness of Fuzzy-NNIM based controller design is demonstrated.

Acknowledgement

The part of researchers participating in this study are supported by the grant from "the 2nd phase BK21 project".

References

1. Karaki, S.H., Chedid, R.B., Ramadan, R.: Probabilistic Production Costing of Diesel-Wind Energy Conversion Systems. IEEE Trans. on Energy Conversion 15, 284–289 (2000)
2. Pandiaraj, K., Taylor, P., Jenkins, N.: Distributed Load Control Autonomous Renewable Energy Systems. IEEE Trans. on Energy Conversion 16, 14–19 (2001)
3. Chedid, R.B., Karaki, S.H., Chadi, E.C.: Adaptive Fuzzy Control for Wind-Diesel Weak Power Systems. IEEE Trans. on Energy Conversion 15, 71–78 (2000)
4. Tripathy, S.C., Kalantar, M., Balasubramanian, R.: Dynamics and Stability of Wind and Diesel Turbine Generator with Superconducting Magnetic Energy Storage Unit on an Isolated Power System. IEEE Trans. on Energy Conversion 6, 579–585 (1991)
5. Passino, K.M.: Fuzzy Control: Theory and Applications. Addison Wesley Publishing, Reading (1997)
6. Yen, J., Langari, R.: Fuzzy Logic: Intelligence, Control, and Information. Prentice Hall, Englewood Cliffs (1999)
7. Haykin, S.: Neural Networks: A Comprehensive Foundation. Prentice Hall, New Jersey (1998)
8. Ng, G.W.: Application of Neural Networks to Adaptive Control of Nonlinear Systems. John Wiley and Sons Inc., Chichester (1997)
9. Madsen, P.P.: Neural Network for Optimization of Existing Control Systems. In: Proc. IEEE International Joint Conference on Neural Networks, Australia, pp. 1496–1501 (1995)

Enhancing Existing Stockmarket Trading Strategies Using Artificial Neural Networks: A Case Study

Bruce Vanstone and Gavin Finnie

Bond University
Gold Coast, Queensland, Australia
bruce_vanstone@bond.edu.au,
gavin_finnie@bond.edu.au

Abstract. Developing financially viable stockmarket trading systems is a difficult, yet reasonably well understood process. Once an initial trading system has been built, the desire usually turns to finding ways to improve the system. Typically, this is done by adding and subtracting if-then style rules, which act as filters to the initial buy/sell signal. Each time a new set of rules are added, the system is retested, and, dependant on the effect of the added rules, they may be included into the system. Naturally, this style of data snooping leads to a curve-fitting approach, and the resultant system may not continue to perform well out-of-sample. The authors promote a different approach, using artificial neural networks, and following their previously published methodology, they demonstrate their approach using an existing medium-term trading strategy as an example.

1 Introduction

There is a long established history of applying Artificial Neural Networks (ANNs) to financial data sets, with the hope of discovering financially viable trading rules. Despite the large amount of published work in this area, it is still difficult to answer the simple question, "Can ANNs be used to develop financially viable stockmarket trading systems?" Vanstone and Finnie [1] have provided an empirical methodology which demonstrates the steps required to create ANNs which allow us to answer this question.

In this paper, the authors demonstrate that the same methodology can be used to enhance already existing trading systems. This paper briefly reviews an existing medium-term long-only trading system, and then works through the authors methodology to create an ANN which will enhance this trading strategy.

The initial trading strategy and the ANN enhanced trading strategy are comprehensively benchmarked both in-sample and out-of-sample, and the superiority of the resulting ANN enhanced system is demonstrated. To prevent excessive duplication of effort, only the key points of the methodology outlined are repeated in this paper. The overall methodology is described in detail in 'An empirical methodology for developing stockmarket trading systems using artificial neural networks' by Vanstone and Finnie [1], and this methodology is referred to in this paper as 'the empirical methodology'.

M. Ishikawa et al. (Eds.): ICONIP 2007, Part II, LNCS 4985, pp. 478–487, 2008.

2 Review of Literature

There are two primary styles of stockmarket trader, namely Systems traders, and Discretionary traders. Systems traders use clearly defined rules to enter and exit positions, and to determine the amount of capital risked. The strategies created by systems traders can be rigorously tested, and clearly understood. The alternative, discretionary trading, is usually the eventual outcome of an individual's own experiences in trading. The rules used by discretionary traders are often difficult to describe precisely, and there is usually a large degree of intuition used. However, it is commonly accepted that discretionary traders produce better financial results [2].

For the purposes of this paper, it is appropriate to have a simple, clearly defined mathematical signal which allows us to enter or exit positions. This allows us to accurately benchmark and analyze systems.

This paper uses the GMMA as the signal generator. The GMMA is the Guppy Multiple Moving Average, as created and described by Daryl Guppy [3], a leading Australian trader. Readers should note that Guppy does not advocate the use of the GMMA indicator in isolation [4], rather it is appropriate as a guide. The GMMA is useful for this paper, as it is able to be implemented mechanically. In essence, any well defined signal generator could be used as the starting point for this paper.

The GMMA is defined as:

$$GMMA = \left(\left(\begin{array}{c} ema(3) + ema(5) \\ + ema(8) + ema(10) \\ + ema(12) + ema(15) \end{array} \right) - \left(\begin{array}{c} ema(30) + ema(35) \\ + ema(40) + ema(45) \\ + ema(50) + ema(60) \end{array} \right) \right) \tag{1}$$

Creation of the ANNs to enhance this strategy involves the selection of ANN inputs, outputs, and various architecture choices. The ANN inputs and outputs are selected as described in the authors PhD thesis [5], and, for the sake of brevity, are only briefly dealt with in this paper. Similarly, the choices of output and architecture are described in the empirical methodology paper. Again, these are only briefly dealt with here.

For each of the strategies created, an extensive in-sample and out-of-sample benchmarking process is used, which is described in the authors methodology paper.

3 Methodology

This paper uses data for the ASX200 constituents of the Australian stockmarket. Data for this study was sourced from Norgate Investor Services [6]. For the in-sample data (start of trading 1994 to end of trading 2003), delisted stocks were included. For the out-of-sample data (start of trading 2004 to end of trading 2006) delisted stocks were not included. The ASX200 constituents were chosen primarily for the following reasons:

1. The ASX200 represents the major component of the Australian market, and has a high liquidity – a major issue with previous published work is that it may tend to focus on micro-cap stocks, many of which do not have enough trading volume to allow positions to be taken, and many of which have excessive bid-ask spreads,
2. This data is representative of the data which a trader will use to develop his/her own systems, and is typical of the kind of data the system will be used in for out-of-sample trading

Software tools used in this paper include Wealth-Lab Developer, and Neuro-Lab, both products of Wealth-Lab Inc (now Fidelity) [7]. For the neural network part of this study, the data is divided into 2 portions: data from 1994 up to and including 2003 (in-sample) is used to predict known results for the out-of-sample period (from 2004 up to the end of 2006).   In this study, only ordinary shares are considered.

The development of an ANN to enhance the selected strategy is based on simple observation of the GMMA signals. Figure 1 show sample buy/sell signals using the points where the GMMA signal crosses above/below zero. One of the major problems of using the GMMA in isolation is the fact that it frequently whipsaws around the zero line, generating spurious buy/sell signals in quick succession.

One possible way of dealing with this problem is to introduce a threshold which the signal must exceed, rather than acquiring positions as the zero line is crossed. The method used in this paper, however, is to forecast which of the signals is most likely to result in a sustained price move. This approach has a major advantage over the threshold approach; namely, in a profitable position, the trader has entered earlier, and therefore, has an expectation of greater profit. By waiting for the threshold to be exceeded, the trader is late in entering the position, with subsequent decrease in profitability.

However, for the approach to work, the trader must have a good forecast of whether a position will be profitable or not. This is the ideal job for a neural network.

In figure 1 below, there are a cluster of trades taken between February 2007 and March 2007, each open for a very short period of time as the GMMA whipsaws around the zero line. Eventually, the security breaks out into a sustained up trend. What is required is an ANN which can provide a good quality short-term forecast of

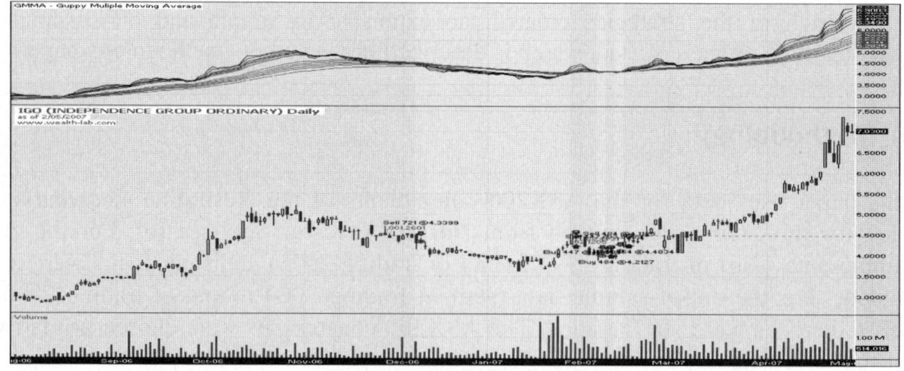

Fig. 1. GMMA signals

the return potential each time the zero line is crossed, to allow the trader to discard the signals which are more likely to become whipsaws, thus concentrating capital on those which are more likely to deliver quality returns.

The neural networks built in this study were designed to produce an output signal, whose strength was proportional to expected returns in the 20 day timeframe. In essence, the stronger the signal from the neural network, the greater the expectation of return. Signal strength was normalized between 0 and 100.

The ANNs contained 13 data inputs. These are the technical variables deemed as significant from the review of both academic and practitioner publications, and details of their function profiles are provided in the author's PhD thesis. The formulas used to compute these variables are standard within technical analysis, except for LPR and HPR, which are also defined in the authors PhD thesis. The actual variables used as inputs were:

1. EMA(close,3) / EMA(close,30)
2. RSI(3)
3. EMA(close,15) / EMA(close,60)
4. HPR
5. LPR
6. SMA(volume,3) / SMA(volume,15)
7. ATR(3) / ATR(15)
8. ADX(3)
9. ADX(15)
10.STOCHK(3)
11.STOCHK(15)
12.RSI(15)
13.MACD

The basic statistical characteristics of the in-sample data are provided below:

Table 1. Technical Variables: Statistical Properties

Variable	Min	Max	Mean	StdDev
1	0.85	2.04	1.04	0.06
2	0.84	1.91	1.04	0.06
3	0.07	1.00	0.89	0.13
4	0.02	1.00	0.72	0.17
5	0.01	1.67	0.99	0.32
6	0.00	3.71	1.00	0.30
7	3.59	100.00	53.44	19.54
8	6.05	99.71	25.13	10.77
9	0.00	100.00	54.56	36.62
10	0.00	100.00	65.02	27.73
11	0.43	100.00	58.08	24.99
12	32.70	98.03	58.64	8.46
13	-0.11	7.14	0.06	0.15

For completeness, the characteristics of the output target to be predicted, the 20 day return variable, are shown below. This target is the maximum percentage change in price over the next twenty days, computed for every element i in the input series as:

$$\left| \left(\frac{\left(highest(close_{i+20...i+1}) - close_i \right)}{close_i} \right) \times 100 \right| \qquad (2)$$

Effectively, this target allows the neural network to focus on the relationship between the input technical variables, and the expected forward price change.

Table 2. Target Variable: Statistical Properties

Variable	Min	Max	Mean	StdDev
Target	0.00	100.00	10.48	24.84

The calculation of the return variable allows the ANN to focus on the highest amount of change that occurs in the next 20 days, which may or may not be the 20-day forward return. For example, the price may spike up after 5 days, and then decrease again, in this case, the 5-day forward price would be used. Therefore, perhaps a better description of the output variable is that it is measuring the maximum amount of price change that occurs within the next 20 days.

As explained in the empirical methodology, a number of hidden node architectures need to be created, and each one benchmarked against the in-sample data.

The method used to determine the hidden number of nodes is described in the empirical methodology. After the initial number of hidden nodes is determined, the first ANN is created and benchmarked. The number of hidden nodes is increased by one for each new architecture created then created, until in-sample testing reveals which architecture has the most suitable in-sample metrics. A number of metrics are available for this purpose, in this paper, the architectures are benchmarked using the absolute profit per bar method. This method assumes unlimited capital, takes every trade signalled, and measures how much average profit is added by each trade over its lifetime. This figure is then refined to the amount of profit added by open trades on a daily basis. The empirical methodology uses the filter selectivity metric for longer-term systems, and Tharp's expectancy [8] for shorter term systems. This paper also introduces the idea of using absolute profit per bar for medium term systems.

4 Results

A total of 362 securities had trading data during the test period (the ASX200 including delisted stocks), from which 11,790 input rows were used for training. These were selected by sampling the available datasets, and selecting every 25th row as an input row.

Table 3 reports the profit per bar and average days held (per open trade) for the buy-and-hold naïve approach (1st row), the initial GMMA method (2nd row), and each of the in-sample ANN architectures created (subsequent rows). These figures include transaction costs of $20 each way and 5% slippage, and orders are implemented as day+1 market orders. There are no stops implemented in in-sample testing, as the

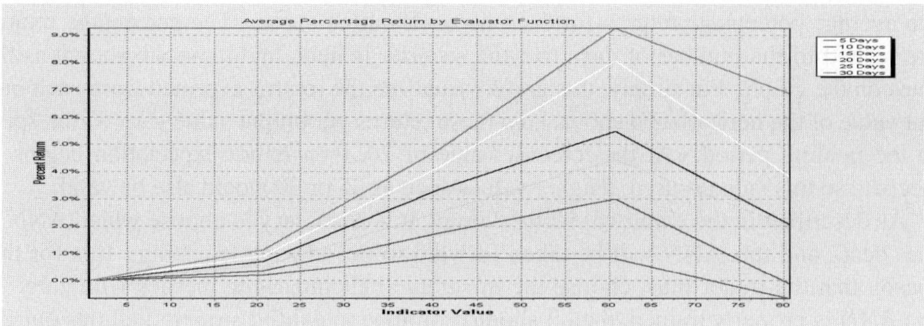

Fig. 2. In-sample ANN function profile

objective is not to produce a trading system (yet), but to measure the quality of the ANN produced. Later, when an architecture has been selected, stops can be determined using ATR or Sweeney's[9] MAE technique.

The most important parameter to be chosen for in-sample testing is the signal threshold, that is, what level of forecast strength is enough to encourage the trader to open a position. This is a figure which needs to be chosen with respect to the individuals own risk appetite, and trading requirements. A low threshold will generate many signals, whilst a higher threshold will generate fewer. Setting the threshold too high will mean that trades will be signalled only rarely, too low and the traders' capital will be quickly invested, removing the opportunity to take high forecast positions as and when they occur.

For this benchmarking, an in-sample threshold of 20 is used. This figure is chosen by visual inspection of the in-sample graph in Figure 2, which shows a breakdown of the output values of the first neural network architecture (scaled from 0 to 100) versus

Table 3. In Sample Characteristics

Strategy (In-Sample Data)	Avg. Profit / Day ($)	Avg. days held
Buy-and-hold naïve approach	1.89	2,528.00
GMMA alone	1.46	34.26
ANN – 6 hidden nodes + GMMA	4.30	55.73
ANN – 7 hidden nodes + GMMA	5.07	61.22
ANN – 8 hidden nodes + GMMA	8.07	47.16
ANN – 9 hidden nodes + GMMA	4.38	52.36

the average percentage returns for each network output value. The percentage returns are related to the number of days that the security is held, and these are shown as the lines on the graph. Put simply, this graph visualizes the returns expected from each output value of the network and shows how these returns per output value vary with respect to the holding period. At the forecast value of 20, then return expectation begins to steepen, so this value is used. Higher values such as 25 or 30 would also be valid.

As described in the empirical methodology, it is necessary to choose which ANN is the 'best', and this ANN will be taken forward to out-of-sample testing. It is for this reason that the trader must choose the in-sample benchmarking metrics with care. If the ANN is properly trained, then it should continue to exhibit similar qualities out-of-sample which it already displays in-sample.

From the above table, it is clear that ANN – 8 hidden nodes should be selected. It displays a number of desirable characteristics – it extracts the highest amount of profit per bar in the least amount of time. Note that this will not necessarily make it the best ANN for a trading system. Extracting good profits in a short time period is only a desirable trait if there are enough opportunities being presented to ensure the traders capital is working efficiently.

Therefore, it is also important to review the number of opportunities signalled over the 10-year in-sample period. This information is shown in **Table 4**.

Table 4. Number of Trades signalled

Strategy (In-Sample Data)	Number of trades signalled
Buy-and-hold naïve approach	**362**
GMMA alone	**10,545**
ANN – 6 hidden nodes + GMMA	**3,252**
ANN – 7 hidden nodes + GMMA	**2,446**
ANN – 8 hidden nodes + GMMA	**1,646**
ANN – 9 hidden nodes + GMMA	**4,282**

Here the trader must decide whether the number of trades signalled meets the required trading frequency. In this case, there are likely to be enough trades to keep an end-of-day trader fully invested.

This testing so far covered data unseen by the ANN, and is a valid indication of how the ANN can be expected to perform in the future. In effect, the in-sample metrics provide a framework of the trading model this ANN should produce.

Table 5 shows the effect of testing on the out-of-sample ASX200 data, which covers the period from the start of trading in 2004 to the end of trading in 2006. These figures include transaction costs and slippage, and orders are implemented as day+1 market orders.

This was a particularly strong bull period in the ASX200, hence the ANN figures are quite high. However, the strength of the bull market over the 2004 – 2006 period can also be seen in the buy-and-hold naïve approach.

Table 5. Out of Sample Performance

Strategy (Out-of-Sample Data)	Avg. Profit / Day ($)	Avg. days held
Buy-and-hold naïve approach	13.66	758.00
GMMA alone	4.91	37.37
ANN – 8 hidden nodes + GMMA	21.40	50.99

Although there appears a significant difference between the GMMA, and the ANN enhanced GMMA, it is important to quantify the differences statistically. The appropriate test to compare two distributions of this type is the ANOVA test (see supporting work in Vanstone [5]). The results for the ANOVA test are shown in **Table 6** below.

Table 6. Anova Comparison

ANOVA	GMMA	GMMA + 8 hidden nodes
Number of observations	2,284	151
Mean	183.61	1091.24
Std Dev	1265.30	3588.84
95% Confidence Internal of the mean – lower bound	131.69	514.46
95% Confidence Internal of the mean – upper bound	235.53	1,668.31

The figures above equate to an F-statistic of 50.81, (specifically, $F(1,2433) = 50.810$, $p=0.00$ ($p<0.05$)), which gives an extremely high level of significant difference between the two systems.

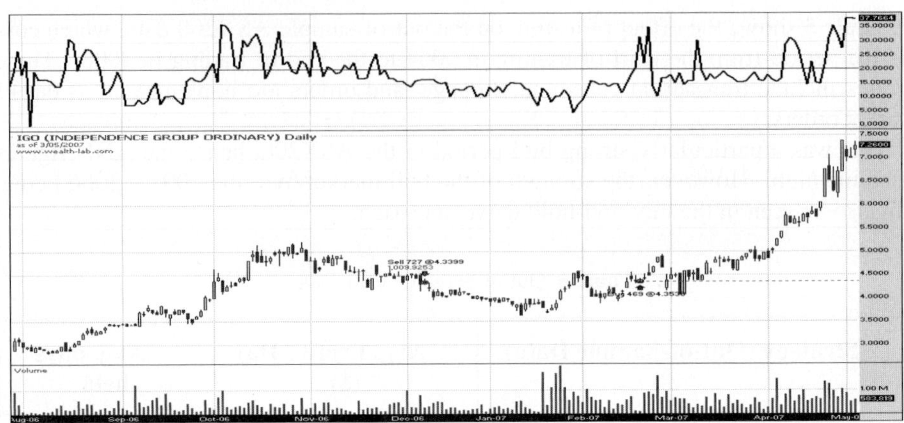

Fig. 3. GMMA signals filtered with ANN – 8 hidden nodes

5 Conclusions

The ANN out-of-sample performance is suitably close to the ANN in-sample performance, leading to the conclusion that the ANN is not curve fit, that is, it should continue to perform well into the future. The level of significance reported by the ANOVA test leads to the conclusion that the ANN filter is making a statistically significant improvement to the quality of the initial GMMA signals.

The trader now needs to make a decision as to whether this ANN should be implemented in real-life.

One of the main reasons for starting with an existing successful trading strategy is that it makes this decision much easier. If the trader is already using the signals from a system, and the ANN is used to filter these signals, then the trader is still only taking trades that would have been taken by the original system. The only difference in using the ANN enhanced system is that trades with low expected profitability should be skipped.

Often in trading, it is the psychological issues which undermine the traders success. By training ANNs to support existing systems, the trader can have additional confidence in the expected performance of the ANN.

Finally, Figure 3 shows the same security as Figure 1. The ANN has clearly met its purpose of reducing whipsaws considerably, which has resulted in the significant performance improvement shown in **Table 3** and **Table 5**.

Of course the result will not always be that all whipsaws are removed. Rather, only whipsaws which are predictable using the ANN inputs will be removed.

References

1. Vanstone, B., Finnie, G.: An Empirical Methodology for developing Stockmarket Trading Systems using Artficial Neural Networks (2007),
   http://epublications.bond.edu.au/infotech_pubs/21
2. Elder, A.: Entries & Exits: visits to sixteen trading rooms. John Wiley and Sons, Hoboken (2006)

3. Guppy, D.: Trend Trading. Wrightbooks, Milton (2004)
4. guppytraders.com. Guppy Multiple Moving Average,
   `http://www.guppytraders.com/gup329.shtml`
5. Vanstone, B.: Trading in the Australian stockmarket using artificial neural networks, Bond University (2006)
6. Norgate Premium Data (2004), `http://www.premiumdata.net`
7. Wealth-Lab (2005), `http://www.wealth-lab.com`
8. Tharp, V.K.: Trade your way to Financial Freedom. McGraw-Hill, NY (1998)
9. Sweeney, J.: Maximum Adverse Excursion: analyzing price fluctuations for trading management. J. Wiley, New York (1996)

Nonlinear Coordinate Unfolding Via Principal Curve Projections with Application to Nonlinear BSS

Deniz Erdogmus and Umut Ozertem

Department of CSEE, Oregon Health and Science University
Portland, Oregon, USA
`{deniz, ozertemu}@csee.ogi.edu`

Abstract. Nonlinear independent components analysis (NICA) is known to be an ill-posed problem when only the independence of the sources are sought. Additional constraints on the distribution of the sources or the structure of the mixing nonlinearity are imposed to achieve a solution that is unique in a suitable sense. In this paper, we present a technique that tackles nonlinear blind source separation (NBSS) as a nonlinear invertible coordinate unfolding problem utilizing a recently developed definition of maximum-likelihood principal curves. The proposition would be applicable most conveniently to independent unimodal source distributions with mixtures that have diminishing second order derivatives along the source axes. Application to multimodal sources would be possible with some modifications that are not discussed in this paper. The ill-posed nature of NBSS is also discussed from a differential geometric perspective in this context.

Keywords: Nonlinear independent component analysis, nonlinear blind source separation, principal curves and surfaces, manifold unfolding, nonlinear coordinate transformation.

1 Introduction

Nonlinear blind source separation (NBSS) is an ill-posed problem that requires various sources of a priori knowledge regarding the joint source distribution and topology of the mixing function. In a landmark paper [1] it has been shown that the square nonlinear independent component analysis (NICA) problem is ill-posed – that, without additional constraints it does not have a unique solution accepting the usual generalized scale and permutation ambiguities of ICA – and various conditions that would force the problem to have a unique solution have been proposed. Traditionally several methods, primarily based on parametric model fitting – especially neural networks of various forms – have been proposed in the literature, while minimizing the usual mutual information inspired independence or separation measures [2,3,4]. The general form of the NBSS problem is

$$\mathbf{x} = \mathbf{f}(\mathbf{s}) \tag{1}$$

where $\mathbf{f}: \Re^m \rightarrow \Re^n$ maps the source vector $\mathbf{s} \in \Re^m$ to the measured mixture vector $\mathbf{x} \in \Re^n$. In general, $\mathbf{f}$ is assumed to be a smooth function and $m=n$, since even in this case per

M. Ishikawa et al. (Eds.): ICONIP 2007, Part II, LNCS 4985, pp. 488–497, 2008.

existence theorems, there are infinitely many solutions to this ill-posed inverse estimation problem. In practice, unless further physical motivation is provided, there is no reason to be concerned about finding those solutions which correspond to noninvertible maps **f**. Therefore, limiting the search to the space of invertible **f** makes both theoretical and practical sense, especially since without additional domain information about the mechanisms that generate **x**, a noninvertible **f** would cause information loss that cannot be recovered. From this perspective, the additional uniqueness constraint of bounded source distributions could be viewed as a means of limiting the search to invertible **f**, whose domain becomes the finite support of the source density; while the extension of **f** to the whole real-valued vector space might not be invertible, the restriction to the support of $p(\mathbf{s})$, the source distribution could be.

An extensively studied invertible nonlinear mapping topology is the so-called post-nonlinear mixture model of the form $\mathbf{x} = \mathbf{g}(\mathbf{As})$, where **A** introduces an invertible (or full column rank if $n>m$) linear mixture and **g** is an invertible nonlinear map that acts elementwise (only monotonic scaling, not mixing further) on the mixed intermediate vector [4]. This problem is well defined and relatively straightforward extensions of traditional linear ICA techniques are able to cope with the specific mixture topology. An interesting contribution that focused on the overdetermined post-nonlinear mixture problem by exploiting the geodesic distances on nonlinear manifolds was made by Lee et al. [5]. Noticing that the monotonic nonlinearity simply acts as a local metric distortion independently on each coordinate axis, ideas from isometric dimensionality reduction and manifold learning were employed to *unwrap* the nonlinear mixture data manifold into the original source distribution space. Harmeling et al also followed a similar manifold unfolding approach using kernel techniques [6]. The current paper could be considered as an extension of these works focusing on square mixture scenarios where the intrinsic dimensionality of the mixture manifold is identical to that of the sources. The method would be immediately applicable to overdetermined situations where the data lies on a low dimensional manifold embedded in a higher dimensional Euclidean space – the principal coordinates proposed in the following would simply reduce to zeros for any additional dimensions outside the data manifold automatically.

The primary tool that will be exploited in this paper is a recently proposed definition of principal curves and surfaces that follow the maximum likelihood estimation principle, as opposed to the commonly employed conditional least-squares type principal curve/surface/manifold techniques. This new definition provides a well-defined principal manifold structure that underlies any multidimensional probability density function, leading to gradient ascent, mean-shift, or expectation maximization type algorithms for manifold learning.

2   Subspace Maximum Likelihood Principal Manifolds

Principal manifolds are underlying geometrical structures of probability distributions that manifest canonical solutions for denoising and dimensionality reduction. Traditionally, self-consistent principal surfaces defined by Hastie [7] and studied by various researchers [8-12] have relied on the conditional expectation and least-squares reconstruction error minimization approach due to the traditional appeal of second-order

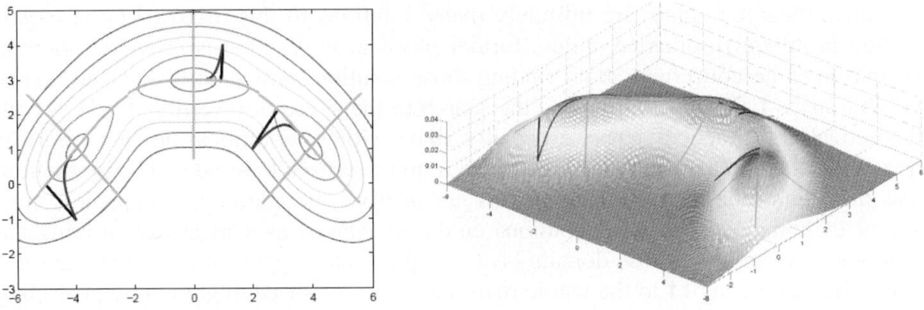

Fig. 1. The 1-dimensional principal manifolds (green) of a 2-dimensional 3-component Gaussian mixture model are shown. The regular gradient ascent trajectories (red) and subspace gradient ascent trajectories (blue) to identify local maxima and subspace local maxima starting from three illustrative points in the space are also shown to emphasize the difference between converging to the usual local maxima and projecting a point to the principal curve.

Table 1. Generalized local first and second order conditions for d-dimensional principal manifolds embedded in n-dimensions

x is a local max iff	**x** is in d-dim principal manifold iff
Gradient is zero	Gradient $\perp$ ($n\text{-}d$) eigenvectors of Hessian
Hessian eigenvalues < 0	Hessian eigenvalues of $\perp$ eigenvectors < 0

statistical optimality criteria and the uniqueness of the solution under the self-consistency conditions. This definition creates various practical difficulties for algorithmic solutions to identify such manifolds, besides the theoretical shortcoming that self-intersecting or nonsmooth manifolds are not acceptable in this framework. Recently, we have proposed a local subspace maxima approach to defining and identifying principal surfaces [13]. This new definition generalizes the usual first and second order derivative conditions to identify local maxima and provides a geometrically principled definition for identifying ridges of high probability density. For a mixture of three Gaussians in two dimensions, the principal curves and the subspace-gradient ascent trajectories are illustrated in Figure 1. We provide a summary comparison of the original local maxima identification conditions and the local principal manifold identification conditions in Table 1. These are the two local necessary and sufficient conditions for a point to belong to a principal manifold of specified dimension. For the following let $p(\mathbf{x})$ be the continuous and twice differentiable probability density function of the random vector of interest, $\mathbf{g}(\mathbf{x})$ its gradient-transpose, and $\mathbf{H}(\mathbf{x})$ its Hessian matrix evaluated at a particular point $\mathbf{x}$. Also let $\{\lambda_i(\mathbf{x}),\mathbf{q}_i(\mathbf{x})\}$, $i=1,\ldots,n$ be the eigendecomposition of the Hessian (the dependence of these on the evaluation point $\mathbf{x}$ will not be explicitly denoted in the following if clear from the context).

Definition 2.1. [13] A point $\mathbf{x}$ is an element of the d-dimensional principal set, denoted by P^d iff $\mathbf{g}(\mathbf{x})$ is orthogonal (null inner product) to at least $(n\text{-}d)$ eigenvectors of $\mathbf{H}(\mathbf{x})$ and $p(\mathbf{x})$ is a strict local maximum in the subspace spanned by these $(n\text{-}d)$ eigenvectors (eigenvalues corresponding to these eigenvectors are strictly less than zero).

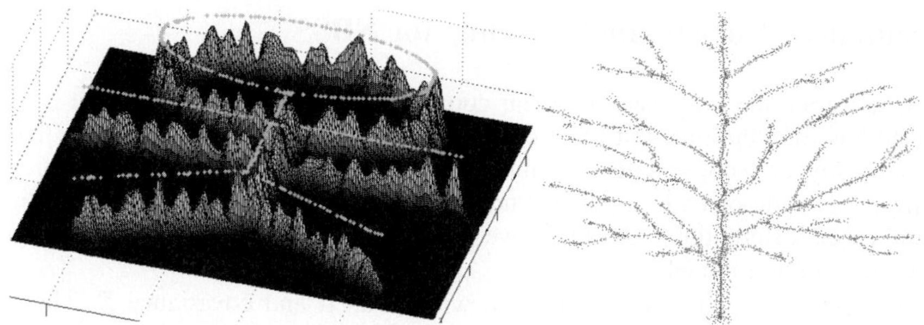

Fig. 2. The 1-dimensional principal manifolds of the diffused stickman distribution (green in left picture) and that of a diffused tree distribution (red in right picture), both identified using subspace mean-shift iterations

This definition states explicitly the conditions in Table 1 and lead to interesting properties regarding principal manifolds, such as the nonlinear deflation property ($P^d \subset P^{d+1}$) and local maxima being appointed as the 0-dimensional principal manifold. Consequently, principal curves pass through local maxima, principal 2-dimensional surfaces pass through principal curves, etc. Another natural consequence of this definition is the simple criterion for checking whether a point is on the principal curve or not. Specifically, the principal curves are characterized by points at which the gradient becomes an eigenvector of the Hessian (i.e., $\mathbf{Hg}=\lambda\mathbf{g}$) and all the other eigenvalues of $\mathbf{H}$ are negative. For iterative hill-climbing algorithms such as subspace gradient ascent or subspace mean-shift, this identity could be utilized to form a suitable stopping criterion to detect when the trajectory is in the vicinity of the principal curve.

The definition also highlights the potential complications that one might encounter in a general NBSS problem, such as self-intersecting, bifurcating, or looping principal curves. These occurrences are illustrated on two datasets in Figure 2, and are generally avoided by researchers addressing nonlinear coordinate unfolding problems. At this time, the only feasible approach to unify the local coordinate systems formed by each segment of a principal curve seems to utilize an atlas structure, stitching piecewise coordinate systems at boundaries. Limiting our discussion to simpler situations here the principal manifolds also form a global nonlinear coordinate frame at least in the domain defined by the bounded support of the source distribution, we can employ nonlinear manifold unfolding techniques and utilize geodesic or line-of-curvature based differential geometric measures of metrics to define an isometric nonlinear transformation of the mixture data into an Euclidean coordinate frame, in a manner similar to Lee et al [5] and Harmeling et al [6].

Specifically focusing on linear mixtures, it is straightforward to verify that the principal lines of a prewhitened mixture of independent sources with unimodal zero-mean densities coincide with the linear ICA solution. To see this one can check that after prewhitening only rotation remains, which does not change the geometric properties of the joint density of the sources, thus the structural principal lines defined via subspace maximum likelihood remains unchanged except for a coordinate rotation. For the special case of a jointly Gaussian density, this also means that the proposed subspace maximum likelihood nonlinear principal components coincide with the usual linear principal components.

3 Nonlinear Coordinate Unfolding for NBSS

We demonstrate the proposed nonlinear coordinate unfolding technique that is applicable to any distributions, but most conveniently employed for distributions that are symmetrically and unimodally distributed around a simple manifold structure that unwrap in a single piece to a global Euclidean frame. While the technique applies to general twice differentiable densities, we will illustrate a specific implementation for a Gaussian mixture model.

Consider a Gaussian data distribution with mean μ and covariance Σ. The logarithm of this density expressed as a quadratic form in δ, perturbation from a point $\mathbf{x}$, is obtained easily with some algebraic manipulation as

$$\log G(\mathbf{x}+\delta;\mu,\Sigma) = [\gamma_0 + \mu^T\Sigma^{-1}\mathbf{x} - \mathbf{x}^T\Sigma^{-1}\mathbf{x}/2] + [\mu^T\Sigma^{-1} - \mathbf{x}^T\Sigma^{-1}]\delta - \delta\Sigma^{-1}\delta/2 \quad (2)$$

for any perturbation δ from $\mathbf{x}$. Since the PCA projections of a data point from a joint Gaussian to a lower dimensional principal (linear) manifold follow trajectories along the eigenvectors of Σ^{-1}, we seek to create an analogy with this for projecting points drawn from arbitrary distributions to their corresponding nonlinear principal manifolds. For an arbitrary pdf $p(\mathbf{x})$, with gradient $\mathbf{g}$ and Hessian $\mathbf{H}$ at the point of interest (along a projection trajectory), we observe from Taylor's expension up to the quadratic term that

$$\log p(\mathbf{x}+\delta) \approx \log p + (\mathbf{g}/p)^T \delta + \delta^T [\mathbf{H}/p - (\mathbf{g}/p)(\mathbf{g}/p)^T]\delta/2 \quad (3)$$

where p, $\mathbf{g}$, $\mathbf{H}$ are all evaluated at $\mathbf{x}$. Equating terms in (2) and (3), we obtain that the local mean and the local covariance inverse of $p(\mathbf{x})$ is given by

$$\Sigma^{-1}(\mathbf{x}) \approx -\mathbf{H}(\mathbf{x})/p(\mathbf{x}) + (\mathbf{g}(\mathbf{x})/p(\mathbf{x}))(\mathbf{g}(\mathbf{x})/p(\mathbf{x}))^T]$$
$$\mu(\mathbf{x}) \approx \mathbf{x} + \Sigma(\mathbf{x})\mathbf{g}(\mathbf{x})/p(\mathbf{x}) \quad (4)$$

The GMM illustration in Fig. 1 is instructive to understand how one might use the principal curves as a means of measuring curvilinear local orthogonal coordinates. For simplicity of discussion let's focus on the 2-dimensional data case here. Specifically, at each local maximum, the principal curves form a locally Euclidean orthogonal coordinate frame (green). Starting from an arbitrary point $\mathbf{x}$, one can trace out subspace gradient ascent trajectories (blue) to project this point to the corresponding principal point. The subspace gradient ascent simply follows the eigenvector direction at the initial point $\mathbf{x}$ to which the projection of the gradient at $\mathbf{x}$ is maximum. The eigenvector of choice is the eigenvector of Σ^{-1} based on the discussion regarding analogies with Gaussian densities and linear PCA projections. The projection trajectory is simply traced out by solving the following differential equation

$$\dot{\mathbf{y}}(t) = \mathbf{q}_m(\mathbf{y}(t))\mathbf{q}_m^T(\mathbf{y}(t))\mathbf{g}(\mathbf{y}(t))$$
$$\text{where } m = \arg\min_i \|\dot{\mathbf{q}}_i(\mathbf{y}(t))\|, \quad \mathbf{y}(0) = \mathbf{x} \quad (5)$$

$$\text{and } \mathbf{q}_m(\mathbf{y}(0)) = \underset{\{\mathbf{q}_i(\mathbf{x})\}_{i=1,2}}{\arg\max} |\mathbf{g}^T(\mathbf{x})\mathbf{q}_i(\mathbf{x})|$$

Until the condition $\mathbf{Hg}=\lambda\mathbf{g}$ is satisfied (which is equivalently stated as $\Sigma^{-1}\mathbf{g}=\gamma\mathbf{g}$, since $\mathbf{g}$ is both an eigenvector of $\mathbf{H}$ and $\mathbf{gg}^{T}$). This differential equation solves for the trajectory initialized to $\mathbf{x}$ and tangent to the eigenvector $\Sigma^{-1}(\mathbf{x})$ that points towards the direction of maximal rate of increase of $p(\mathbf{x})$ among all orthogonal directions given by the candidate eigenvectors. The trajectory converges to a point $\mathbf{x}_p$ on the principal curve.[1] The length of the curvilinear trajectory from $\mathbf{x}$ to $\mathbf{x}_p$ can be appointed as the coordinate of $\mathbf{x}$ in the direction orthogonal to the principal curve. Taking an arbitrary reference point on the principal curve (which can now be traced by solving a differential equation that follows the eigenvector that is parallel to the gradient) as the origin (e.g., the local maximum in the middle of the three in Fig. 1), one could also measure the distance of $\mathbf{x}_p$ along the principal curve to this origin, yielding the second coordinate of $\mathbf{x}$ with respect to the global coordinate frame formed by the nonlinear principal curve. Note that these geometrically simple global curvilinear coordinates are only possible in a very limited set of scenarios and researchers have typically dealt with these simplified cases due to lack of an understanding of how to systematically globalize many piecewise local orthogonal curvilinear coordinate frames in challenging scenarios such as the stickman or the tree examples in Fig. 2.

Shortest Path Along the Principal Curve: For a given finite dataset drawn from a known or estimated density $p(\mathbf{x})$, once all data points are projected onto the principal curve using (5), the projections form a smooth one-dimensional manifold that could be approximated by a sparse connected graph such as a minimum spanning tree, k-nearest-neighbor graph, or an ε-ball graph. The *geodesic* distance between any two points on the graph could be determined with a shortest path algorithm, such as Dijkstra's greedy search [14]. A tempting idea is to employ sparse connected graph based approximations for approximately finding the projection lengths from $\mathbf{x}$ to $\mathbf{x}_p$, however this idea would not work on a graph formed by the original data points since not enough samples might lie sufficiently close to the sought principal curve. A possibility could be to iterate a small but sufficiently large number of additional points $\mathbf{z}$ using (5) to obtain $\mathbf{z}_p$ as a roughly uniform sample from the principal curve and include these in graph construction (i.e. union of $\mathbf{x}$ and $\mathbf{z}_p$), such that the distance from every data point $\mathbf{x}$ to every principal curve sample $\mathbf{z}_p$ can be approximated with a fast shortest path search method and te one that is closest (in a suitable sense) can be appointed as its projection. The graph formed only using the set $\mathbf{z}_p$ could then be utilized to find the second coordinate.

Gaussian Mixture Models for Nonlinear Coordinate Unfolding: Suppose that a set of independent and identically distributed (iid) samples are available: $\{\mathbf{x}_1,...,\mathbf{x}_N\}$. Assume that a Gaussian mixture model (GMM) fit in the form

$$p(\mathbf{x}) = \sum_m \alpha_m G(\mathbf{x};\mu_m,\Sigma_m) \tag{6}$$

---

[1] Convergence proof is relatively trivial. The pdf always increases since the derivative always points in a direction that has positive inner product with the gradient and when the trajectory reaches a point on the principal curve, the gradient becomes the eigenvector of $\Sigma^{-1}(\mathbf{y}(t))$ itself (but the one that is orthogonal to the trajectory), thus the stopping criterion is achieved.

is obtained using established density estimation techniques with proper attention paid to model order selection. The gradient and Hessian of this pdf estimate has a convenient self-similar form that facilitates algorithm design. Specifically, we have

$$\mathbf{g}(\mathbf{x}) = -\sum_m \alpha_m G(\mathbf{x}; \boldsymbol{\mu}_m, \boldsymbol{\Sigma}_m) \boldsymbol{\Sigma}_m^{-1}(\mathbf{x} - \boldsymbol{\mu}_m)$$
$$\mathbf{H}(\mathbf{x}) = \sum_m \alpha_m G(\mathbf{x}; \boldsymbol{\mu}_m, \boldsymbol{\Sigma}_m)[\boldsymbol{\Sigma}_m^{-1}(\mathbf{x} - \boldsymbol{\mu}_m)(\mathbf{x} - \boldsymbol{\mu}_m)^T \boldsymbol{\Sigma}_m^{-1} - \boldsymbol{\Sigma}_m^{-1}]$$

(7)

which leads to the expression

$$\boldsymbol{\Sigma}^{-1}(\mathbf{x}) = \sum_k w_k(\mathbf{x})\boldsymbol{\Sigma}_k^{-1} + \sum_k \sum_{l \neq k} w_k(\mathbf{x})w_l(\mathbf{x})\boldsymbol{\Sigma}_k^{-1}(\mathbf{x} - \boldsymbol{\mu}_k)(\mathbf{x} - \boldsymbol{\mu}_l)^T \boldsymbol{\Sigma}_l^{-1}$$

(8)

for the local covariance, where $w_k(\mathbf{x}) = \alpha_k G(\mathbf{x}; \boldsymbol{\mu}_k, \boldsymbol{\Sigma}_k) / p(\mathbf{x})$. Clearly, for points close to the mean of a particular Gaussian component with respect to the Mahalanobis distance involving the corresponding component covariance, the second term on the right hand side of (8) becomes negligible with respect to the first term, thus the local nonlinear coordinate frame approaches an orthogonal Euclidean frame centered at the local maximum, as expected. This observation provides a theoretical motivation for local PCA, which will also clearly fail in transient regions between components according to this theory.

Case Study with Periodic Sources: We demonstrate the nonlinear unfolding strategy on a case study that uses a 20-component GMM to approximate the density of a mixture that is obtained by spiral-wrapping of two sources with respective sinusoid and piecewise linear sources that are periodic with relatively prime frequencies (7Hz and

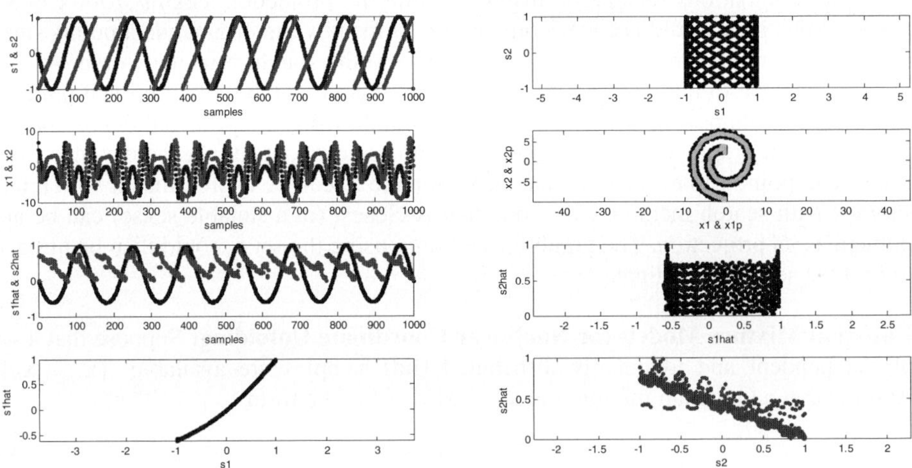

Fig. 3. Summary of coordinate unfolding results for the periodic sources. Rows from left to right: (1) Source signals versus time and the source distribution; (2) mixtures versus time and mixtures with respect to each other; (3) Unfolded sources versus time and the unfolded source distribution; (4) Estimated source 1 versus true source 1 and estimated source 2 versus true source 2 (ideally a monotonic curve is desired after correcting for permutation)

13Hz) respectively (see Fig. 3). Specifically, following example 5.3 of [6] (because it cannot be reduced to a post- or pre-nonlinear mixture problem) we had $s_1(t)=0.5\sin(14\pi t)$, $s_2(t)=\arctan(\sin(26\pi t)/\cos(26\pi t))/\pi$ and $z=6s_1+s_2+6$, $x_1=z\cos(3\pi s_1)$, $x_2=z\sin(3\pi s_1)$. Time index t is sampled in the interval [-0.5,0.5] at 1000Hz. The unfolding algorithm described above is employed. The mixture samples are projected onto their corresponding coordinate points along the principal curve using the differential equation in (5) using the GMM model as the basis for principal curve estimation. Once the principal curve projections are obtained, Dijkstra's algorithm is applied to the 1-ball neighborhood graph consisting of Euclidean distance between pairs connected according to the graph in order to get the relative coordinates along the principal curve. The results of this case study are presented in Fig. 3. Apart from some convergence-related noise and the expected nonlinear distortion of the source signals that cannot be recovered without source distribution information, the proposed technique is reasonably successful in identifying the original source signals. However, we note that this case study involves a nice global spiral principal curve that enables us to determine a global Euclidean unfolding solution that would be impossible otherwise.

Case Study with Random Sources: We present results with the same nonlinear mixture as in the previous case study, but replace the periodic (approximately) orthogonal sources with independent random sources that have Uniform (support [-1,1]) and Gaussian (0 mean, 0.2 standard deviation) distributions. The number of samples in this illustration is 1000. The procedure for identifying the unfolded coordinates is identical with the previous case study and the results are summarized in Fig. 4.

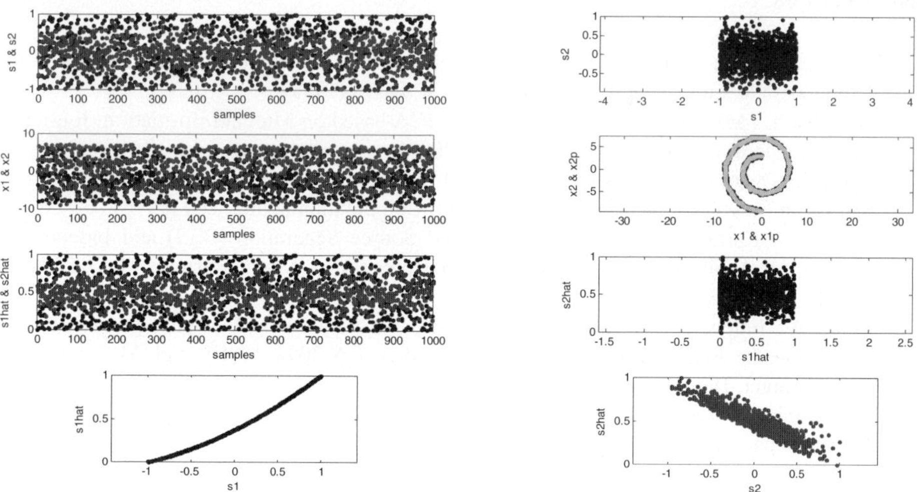

Fig. 4. Summary of coordinate unfolding results for the periodic sources. Rows from left to right: (1) Source signals versus time and the source distribution; (2) mixtures versus time and mixtures with respect to each other; (3) Unfolded sources versus time and the unfolded source distribution; (4) Estimated source 1 versus true source 1 and estimated source 2 versus true source 2 (ideally a monotonic curve is desired after correcting for permutation).

4 Conclusions

Nonlinear blind source separation is a challenging problem that has not yet been formulated satisfactorily to yield a unique well-defined solution. The literature on nonlinear independent components primarily focuses on the relatively trivial extension of linear ICA, referred to as postnonlinear mixture separation. More recent attempts to utilize ideas from manifold learning (for instance, isometric dimensionality reduction and kernel principal component analysis), have not clearly discussed the challenges involved in finding the intricate details of algorithms that will work in various scenarios – in fact there are many scenarios where nonlinear coordinate unfolding as proposed in such papers will not generalize to outside the limited set of geometries they consider. In this paper we aimed to achieve two goals: (i) point out some unmentioned caveats in nonlinear blind source separation using manifold learning (ii) present the application of a maximum likelihood type principal curve identification technique to the problem of coordinate unfolding in a differential geometric framework. Results obtained using a nonlinearity mixture used by researchers in another paper have shown that the unfolding technique is promising, the proposed principal curve coordinate system can recover sources under the assumption of unimodal variations around a global (in the support of source densities) curvilinear manifold.

Acknowledgments. This work is partially supported by NSF grants ECS-0524835, ECS-0622239, and IIS-0713690.

References

1. Hyvarinen, A., Pajunen, P.: Nonlinear Independent Component Analysis: Existence and Uniqueness Results. Neural Networks 12(3), 429–439 (1999)
2. Almeida, L.: MISEP – Linear and Nonlinear ICA based on Mutual Information. Journal of MachineLearning Research 4, 1297–1318 (2003)
3. Parra, L., Deco, G., Miesbach, S.: Statistical Independence and Novelty Detection with Information Preserving Nonlinear Maps. Neural Computation 8, 260–269 (1996)
4. Jutten, C., Karhunen, J.: Advances in Blind Source Separation (BSS) and Independent Component Analysis (ICA) for Nonlinear Mixtures. Int. J. Neural Systems 14(5), 267–292 (2004)
5. Lee, J.A., Jutten, C., Verleysen, M.: Nonlinear ICA by Using Isometric Dimensionality Reduction. In: Puntonet, C.G., Prieto, A.G. (eds.) ICA 2004. LNCS, vol. 3195, pp. 710–717. Springer, Heidelberg (2004)
6. Harmeling, S., Ziehe, A., Kawanabe, M., Muller, K.R.: Kernel Based Nonlinear Blind Source Separation. Neural Computation 15, 1089–1124 (2003)
7. Hastie, T., Stuetzle, W.: Principal Curves. Jour. Am. Statistical Assoc. 84(406), 502–516 (1989)
8. Tibshirani, R.: Principal Curves Revisited. Statistics and Computation 2, 183–190 (1992)
9. Sandilya, S., Kulkarni, S.R.: Principal Curves with Bounded Turn. IEEE Trans. on Information Theory 48(10), 2789–2793 (2002)
10. Kegl, B., Kryzak, A., Linder, T., Zeger, K.: Learning and Design of Principal Curves. IEEE Trans. on PAMI 22(3), 281–297 (2000)

11. Stanford, D.C., Raftery, A.E.: Finding Curvilinear Features in Spatial Point Patterns: Principal Curve Clustering with Noise. IEEE Trans. on PAMI 22(6), 601–609 (2000)
12. Chang, K., Grosh, J.: A Unified Model for Probabilistic Principal Surfaces. IEEE Trans. on PAMI 24(1), 59–74 (2002)
13. Erdogmus, D., Ozertem, U.: Self-Consistent Locally Defined Principal Curves. In: Proceedings of ICASSP 2007, vol. 2, pp. 549–552 (2007)
14. Cormen, T.H., Leiserson, C.E., Rivest, R.L., Stein, C.: Introduction to Algorithms, 2nd edn. MIT Press and McGraw-Hill (2001)

Blind Deconvolution of MIMO-IIR Systems: A Two-Stage EVA⋆

Mitsuru Kawamoto[1], Yujiro Inouye[2], and Kiyotaka Kohno[3]

[1] National Institute of Advanced Industrial Science and Technology (AIST),
Central 2, 1-1-1 Umezono, Tsukuba, Ibaraki 305-8568, Japan
[2] Department of Electronic and Control Systems Engineering, Shimane University,
1060 Nishikawatsu, Matsue, 690-8504, Japan
[3] Department of Electronic Control Engineering, Yonago National College of
Technology, 4448 Hikona, Yonago, Tottori 683-8502, Japan
m.kawamoto@aist.go.jp, inouye@riko.shimane-u.ac.jp, kohno@yonago-k.ac.jp

Abstract. This paper deals with a blind deconvolution (DB) problem for
multiple-input multiple-output infinite impulse response (MIMO-IIR) systems. To solve this problem, we propose an eigenvector algorithm (EVA).
In the proposed EVA, two kinds of EVAs are merged so as to give a good
performance: One is an EVA and the other is a Robust EVA (REVA) which
works with as little sensitive to Gaussian noise as possible. Owing to this
combination, two drawbacks of the conventional EVAs can be overcome.
Simulation results show the validity of the proposed EVA.

Keywords: Independent component analysis, Blind deconvolution,
Eigenvector algorithms, MIMO-IIR, Reference systems.

1   Introduction

This paper deals with a blind deconvolution (BD) problem for a multiple-input
and multiple-output (MIMO) infinite impulse response (IIR) systems. To solve
this problem, we use eigenvector algorithms (EVAs) [5,6,13]. The first proposal of
the EVA was done by Jelonnek et al. [5]. They have proposed the EVA for solving
blind equalization (BE) problems of single-input single-output (SISO) systems or
single-input multiple-output (SIMO) systems. In [13], several procedures for the
blind source separation (BSS) of instantaneous mixtures, using the generalized
eigenvalue decomposition (GEVD), have been introduced. Recently, the authors
have proposed the EVAs which can solve blind source separation (BSS) problems
in the case of MIMO static systems (instantaneous mixtures) [7,8]. Moreover,
based on the idea in [7], an EVA was derived for MIMO-IIR systems (convolutive
mixtures) [9].

In the EVAs in [7,8,9], an idea of using reference signals was adopted. Researches applying this idea to solving blind signal processing (BSP) problems,

---

⋆ Parts of the results in this paper were presented at IEEE Int. Conf. on Acoustics,
Speech and Signal Processing, April 2007.

M. Ishikawa et al. (Eds.): ICONIP 2007, Part II, LNCS 4985, pp. 498–508, 2008.

such as the BD, the BE, the BSS, and so on, have been made by Jelonnek et al. (e.g., [5]), Adib et al. (e.g., [1]), Rhioui et al. [14], and Castella, et al. [2]. Jelonnek et al. have shown in the single-input case that by the Lagrangian method, the maximization of a contrast function leads to a closed-form solution expressed as a generalized eigenvector problem, which is referred to as an eigenvector algorithm (EVA). Adib et al. have shown that the BSS for instantaneous mixtures can be achieved by maximizing a contrast function, but they have not proposed any algorithm for achieving this idea. Rhioui et al. [14] and Castella et al. [2] have proposed quadratic MIMO contrast functions for the BSS with convolutive mixtures, and have proposed an algorithm for extracting one source signal using a "fixed point"-like method. However, they have not presented a theoretical proof for the convergence of their proposed algorithm. In order to recover all source signals, in [14], the reference signals corresponding to the number of source signals which can be extracted were used, and in [2], a deflation approach was used, in which for each deflation, a different reference signal was used. The EVA in [9] can work so as to recover simultaneously all source signals using only one reference signal. However, the EVA has different performances for a different choice of the reference signal. Moreover, the conventional EVAs, e.g., [2,9], are sensitive to Gaussian noise.

In this paper, based on [8], we extend the EVA in [9] so as to work with as little influence of Gaussian noise as possible, which is referred to as a robust EVA (REVA). Then reference signals are chosen by utilizing the idea in [2], in order to overcome the drawback of the EVA in [9]. However this choice causes to use deflation methods. Since we want to show an algorithm without using the deflation method, then the following procedure is proposed as a two-stage EVA: 1) the EVA in [9] is executed with several iterations so that the solutions achieving the BD can be roughly found. As the next stage, 2) the REVA is executed using reference signals obtained by the scheme in [2], which are defined as appropriately chosen outputs of the deconvolvers with the filters obtained in Stage 1). Since the filters obtained in Stage 1) are linearly independent, the REVA with the reference signals based on the filters does not need deflation methods. Using this two-stage EVA, we try to overcome two drawbacks of the conventional EVAs, that is, the performances of the EVA are

   i) sensitive to Gaussian noise.
   ii) sensitive to choosing reference signals.

Simulation results show the validity of the proposed algorithm.

The present paper uses the following notation: Let Z denote the set of all integers. Let C denote the set of all complex numbers. Let C^n denote the set of all n-column vectors with complex components. Let $C^{m \times n}$ denote the set of all $m \times n$ matrices with complex components. The superscripts T, $*$, and H denote, respectively, the transpose, the complex conjugate, and the complex conjugate transpose (Hermitian) of a matrix. The symbols block-diag$\{\cdots\}$ and diag$\{\cdots\}$ denote respectively a block diagonal and a diagonal matrices with the

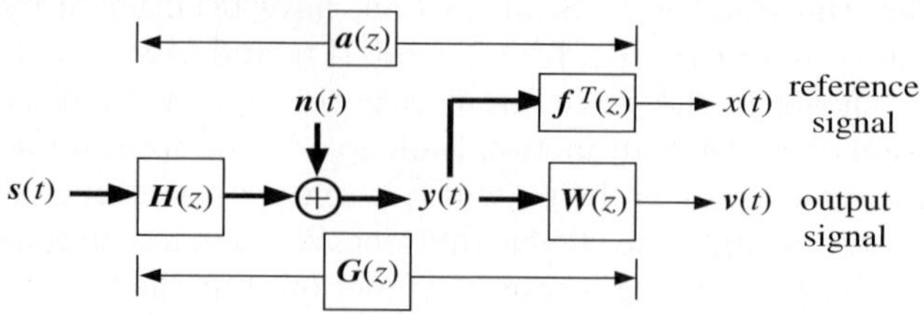

Fig. 1. The composite system of an unknown system and a deconvolver, and a reference system

block diagonal and the diagonal elements $\{\cdots\}$. The symbol $\mathrm{cum}\{x_1,x_2,x_3,x_4\}$ denotes the fourth-order cumulant of x_i's. Let $i = \overline{1,n}$ stand for $i = 1, 2, \cdots, n$.

2   Problem Formulation and Assumptions

We consider a MIMO system with n inputs and m outputs as described by

$$\boldsymbol{y}(t) = \sum_{k=-\infty}^{\infty} \boldsymbol{H}^{(k)}\boldsymbol{s}(t - k) + \boldsymbol{n}(t), \quad t \in Z, \tag{1}$$

where $\boldsymbol{s}(t)$ is an n-column vector of input (or source) signals, $\boldsymbol{y}(t)$ is an m-column vector of system outputs, $\boldsymbol{n}(t)$ is an m-column vector of Gaussian noises, and $\{\boldsymbol{H}^{(k)}\}$ is an $m \times n$ impulse response matrix sequence. The transfer function of the system is defined by $\boldsymbol{H}(z) = \sum_{k=-\infty}^{\infty} \boldsymbol{H}^{(k)} z^k, z \in C$.

To recover the source signals, we process the output signals by an $n \times m$ deconvolver (or equalizer) $\boldsymbol{W}(z)$ described by

$$\boldsymbol{v}(t) = \sum_{k=-\infty}^{\infty} \boldsymbol{W}^{(k)}\boldsymbol{y}(t - k) = \sum_{k=-\infty}^{\infty} \boldsymbol{G}^{(k)}\boldsymbol{s}(t - k) + \sum_{k=-\infty}^{\infty} \boldsymbol{W}^{(k)}\boldsymbol{n}(t - k), \tag{2}$$

where $\{\boldsymbol{G}^{(k)}\}$ is the impulse response matrix sequence of $\boldsymbol{G}(z) := \boldsymbol{W}(z)\boldsymbol{H}(z)$, which is defined by $\boldsymbol{G}(z) = \sum_{k=-\infty}^{\infty} \boldsymbol{G}^{(k)} z^k, z \in C$. The cascade connection of the unknown system and the deconvolver is illustrated in Fig. 1.

Here, we put the following assumptions on the system, the source signals, the deconvolver, and the noises.

A1) The transfer function $\boldsymbol{H}(z)$ is stable and has full column rank on the unit circle $|z| = 1$, where the assumption **A1)** implies that the unknown system has less inputs than outputs, i.e., $n \leq m$, and there exists a left stable inverse of the unknown system.

A2) The input sequence $\{\boldsymbol{s}(t)\}$ is a complex, zero-mean and non-Gaussian random vector process with element processes $\{s_i(t)\}$, $i = \overline{1,n}$ being mutually independent. Each element process $\{s_i(t)\}$ is an i.i.d. process with a variance $\sigma_{s_i}^2 \neq 0$ and a nonzero fourth-order cumulant $\gamma_i \neq 0$ defined as

$$\gamma_i = \mathrm{cum}\{s_i(t), s_i(t), s_i^*(t), s_i^*(t)\} \neq 0. \tag{3}$$

A3) The deconvolver $\boldsymbol{W}(z)$ is an FIR system of sufficient length L so that the truncation effect can be ignored.

A4) The noise sequence $\{\boldsymbol{n}(t)\}$ is a zero-mean, Gaussian vector stationary process whose component processes $\{n_j(t)\}$, $j = \overline{1,m}$ have nonzero variances $\sigma_{n_j}^2$, $j = \overline{1,m}$.

A5) The two vector sequences $\{\boldsymbol{n}(t)\}$ and $\{\boldsymbol{s}(t)\}$ are mutually statistically independent.

Under **A3)**, the impulse response $\{\boldsymbol{G}^{(k)}\}$ of the cascade system is given by

$$\boldsymbol{G}^{(k)} := \sum_{\tau=L_1}^{L_2} \boldsymbol{W}^{(\tau)} \boldsymbol{H}^{(k-\tau)}, \quad k \in Z, \tag{4}$$

where the length $L := L_2 - L_1 + 1$ is taken to be sufficiently large. In a vector form, (4) can be written as

$$\tilde{\boldsymbol{g}}_i = \tilde{\boldsymbol{H}} \tilde{\boldsymbol{w}}_i, \quad i = \overline{1,n}, \tag{5}$$

where $\tilde{\boldsymbol{g}}_i$ is the column vector consisting of the ith output impulse response of the cascade system defined by $\tilde{\boldsymbol{g}}_i := [\boldsymbol{g}_{i1}^T, \boldsymbol{g}_{i2}^T, \cdots, \boldsymbol{g}_{in}^T]^T$,

$$\boldsymbol{g}_{ij} := [\cdots, g_{ij}(-1), g_{ij}(0), g_{ij}(1), \cdots]^T, \quad j = \overline{1,n} \tag{6}$$

where $g_{ij}(k)$ is the (i,j)th element of matrix $\boldsymbol{G}^{(k)}$, and $\tilde{\boldsymbol{w}}_i$ is the mL-column vector consisting of the tap coefficients (corresponding to the ith output) of the deconvolver defined by $\tilde{\boldsymbol{w}}_i := \left[\boldsymbol{w}_{i1}^T, \boldsymbol{w}_{i2}^T, \cdots, \boldsymbol{w}_{im}^T\right]^T \in \boldsymbol{C}^{mL}$,

$$\boldsymbol{w}_{ij} := [w_{ij}(L_1), w_{ij}(L_1 + 1), \cdots, w_{ij}(L_2)]^T \in \boldsymbol{C}^L, \tag{7}$$

$j = \overline{1,m}$, where $w_{ij}(k)$ is the (i,j)th element of matrix $\boldsymbol{W}^{(k)}$, and $\tilde{\boldsymbol{H}}$ is the $n \times m$ block matrix whose (i,j)th block element $\boldsymbol{H}_{ij}$ is the matrix (of L columns and possibly infinite number of rows) with the (l,r)th element $[\boldsymbol{H}_{ij}]_{lr}$ defined by $[\boldsymbol{H}_{ij}]_{lr} := h_{ji}(l - r)$, $l = 0, \pm 1, \pm 2, \cdots$, $r = \overline{L_1, L_2}$, where $h_{ij}(k)$ is the (i,j)th element of the matrix $\boldsymbol{H}^{(k)}$.

In the multisystem blind deconvolution problem, we want to adjust $\tilde{\boldsymbol{w}}_i$'s ($i = \overline{1,n}$) so that

$$[\tilde{\boldsymbol{g}}_1, \cdots, \tilde{\boldsymbol{g}}_n] = \tilde{\boldsymbol{H}}[\tilde{\boldsymbol{w}}_1, \cdots, \tilde{\boldsymbol{w}}_n] = [\tilde{\boldsymbol{\delta}}_1, \cdots, \tilde{\boldsymbol{\delta}}_n]\boldsymbol{P}, \tag{8}$$

where $\boldsymbol{P}$ is an $n \times n$ permutation matrix, and $\tilde{\boldsymbol{\delta}}_i$ is the n-block column vector defined by $\tilde{\boldsymbol{\delta}}_i := [\boldsymbol{\delta}_{i1}^T, \boldsymbol{\delta}_{i2}^T, \dots, \boldsymbol{\delta}_{in}^T]^T$, $i = \overline{1,n}$, $\boldsymbol{\delta}_{ij} := \hat{\boldsymbol{\delta}}_i$, for $i = j$, otherwise $(\cdots, 0, 0, 0, \cdots)^T$. Here, $\hat{\boldsymbol{\delta}}_i$ is the column vector (of infinite elements) whose rth element $\hat{\delta}_i(r)$ is given by $\hat{\delta}_i(r) = d_i \delta(r - k_i)$, where $\delta(t)$ is the Kronecker delta function, d_i is a complex number standing for a scale change and a phase shift, and k_i is an integer standing for a time shift.

3 Eigenvector Algorithms (EVAs)

3.1 EVAs with Reference Signals

Jelonnek et al. [5] have shown in the single-input case that from the following problem, that is,

$$\text{Maximize } D_{v_i x} = \text{cum}\{v_i(t), v_i^*(t), x(t), x^*(t)\} \text{ under } \sigma_{v_i}^2 = \sigma_{s_{\rho_i}}^2, \tag{9}$$

a closed-form solution expressed as a generalized eigenvector problem can be led by the Lagrangian method, where $\sigma^2_{v_i}$ and $\sigma^2_{s_{\rho_i}}$ denote the variances of the output $v_i(t)$ and a source signal $s_{\rho_i}(t)$, respectively, and ρ_i is one of integers $\{1, 2, \cdots, n\}$ such that the set $\{\rho_1, \rho_2, \cdots, \rho_n\}$ is a permutation of the set $\{1, 2, \cdots, n\}$, $v_i(t)$ is the ith element of $\boldsymbol{v}(t)$ in (2), the reference signal $x(t)$ is given by $\boldsymbol{f}^T(z)\boldsymbol{y}(t)$ using an appropriate filter $\boldsymbol{f}(z)$ (see Fig. 1). The filter $\boldsymbol{f}(z)$ is called a *reference system*. Let $\boldsymbol{a}(z) := \boldsymbol{H}^T(z)\boldsymbol{f}(z) = [a_1(z), a_2(z), \cdots, a_n(z)]^T$, then $x(t)$ $= \boldsymbol{f}^T(z)\boldsymbol{H}(z)\boldsymbol{s}(t) = \boldsymbol{a}^T(z)\boldsymbol{s}(t)$. The element $a_i(z)$ of the filter $\boldsymbol{a}(z)$ is defined as $a_i(z) = \sum_{k=-\infty}^{\infty} a_i(k)z^k$ and the reference system $\boldsymbol{f}(z)$ is an m-column vector whose elements are $f_j(z) = \sum_{k=L_1}^{L_2} f_j(k)z^k$, $j = \overline{1, m}$.

In our case, $D_{v_i x}$ and $\sigma^2_{v_i}$ can be expressed in terms of the vector $\tilde{\boldsymbol{w}}_i$ as, respectively, $D_{v_i x} = \tilde{\boldsymbol{w}}_i^H \tilde{\boldsymbol{B}} \tilde{\boldsymbol{w}}_i$ and $\sigma^2_{v_i} = \tilde{\boldsymbol{w}}_i^H \tilde{\boldsymbol{R}} \tilde{\boldsymbol{w}}_i$, where $\tilde{\boldsymbol{B}}$ is the $m \times m$ block matrix whose (i, j)th block element $\boldsymbol{B}_{ij}$ is the matrix with the (l, r)th element $[\boldsymbol{B}_{ij}]_{lr}$ calculated by $\mathrm{cum}\{y_i^*(t - L_1 - l + 1), y_j(t - L_1 - r + 1), x^*(t), x(t)\}$ $(l, r = \overline{1, L})$ and $\tilde{\boldsymbol{R}} = E[\tilde{\boldsymbol{y}}^*(t)\tilde{\boldsymbol{y}}^T(t)]$ is the covariance matrix of m-block column vector $\tilde{\boldsymbol{y}}(t)$ defined by

$$\tilde{\boldsymbol{y}}(t) := \left[\boldsymbol{y}_1^T(t), \boldsymbol{y}_2^T(t), \cdots, \boldsymbol{y}_m^T(t)\right]^T \in \boldsymbol{C}^{mL}, \tag{10}$$

where $\boldsymbol{y}_j(t) := [y_j(t\text{-}L_1), y_j(t\text{-}L_1\text{-}1), \cdots, y_j(t\text{-}L_2)]^T \in \boldsymbol{C}^L$, $j = \overline{1, m}$. It follows from (10) that $\tilde{\boldsymbol{y}}(t)$ is expressed as $\tilde{\boldsymbol{y}}(t) = \boldsymbol{D}_c(z)\boldsymbol{y}(t)$, where $\boldsymbol{D}_c(z)$ is an $mL \times m$ converter (consisting of m identical delay chains each of which has L delay elements when $L_1 = 1$) defined by $\boldsymbol{D}_c(z) := \mathrm{block\text{-}diagonal}\{\boldsymbol{d}_c(z), \cdots, \boldsymbol{d}_c(z)\}$ with m diagonal block elements all being the same L-column vector $\boldsymbol{d}_c(z)$ defined by $\boldsymbol{d}_c(z) = [z^{L_1}, \cdots, z^{L_2}]^T$. Therefore, by the similar way to as in [5], the maximization of $|D_{v_i x}|$ under $\sigma^2_{v_i} = \sigma^2_{s_{\rho_i}}$ leads to the following generalized eigenvector problem;

$$\tilde{\boldsymbol{B}}\tilde{\boldsymbol{w}}_i = \lambda_i \tilde{\boldsymbol{R}}\tilde{\boldsymbol{w}}_i. \tag{11}$$

Moreover, Jelonnek et al. have shown in [5] that the eigenvector corresponding to the maximum magnitude eigenvalue of $\tilde{\boldsymbol{R}}^\dagger \tilde{\boldsymbol{B}}$ becomes the solution of the blind equalization problem, which is referred to as an *eigenvector algorithm* (EVA). It has been also shown in [9] that the BD for MIMO-IIR systems can be achieved

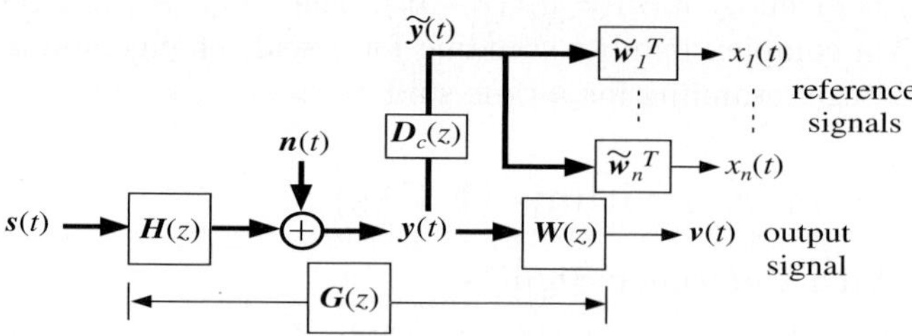

Fig. 2. The composite system of an unknown system and a deconvolver, and a reference system

with the eigenvectors of $\tilde{\boldsymbol{R}}^{\dagger}\tilde{\boldsymbol{B}}$, using only one reference signal. Note that since Jelonnek et al. have dealt with SISO-IIR systems or SIMO-IIR systems, the constructions of $\tilde{\boldsymbol{B}}$, $\tilde{\boldsymbol{w}}_i$, and $\tilde{\boldsymbol{R}}$ in (11) are different from those proposed in [5].

Castella et al. [2] have showed that from (9), a BD can be iteratively achieved by using $x_i(t) = \tilde{\boldsymbol{w}}_i\tilde{\boldsymbol{y}}(t)$ $(i = \overline{1,n})$ as reference signals (see Fig. 2), where the number of reference signals corresponds to the number of source signals and $\tilde{\boldsymbol{w}}_i$ is an eigenvector obtained by $\tilde{\boldsymbol{R}}^{\dagger}\tilde{\boldsymbol{B}}$ in the previous iteration. Then a deflation method was used to recover all source signals.

3.2   The Proposed EVA

In this paper, we want to avoid the conventional EVAs' drawbacks, that is, (a) they are sensitive to Gaussian noise and (b) difference performances are obtained for a different choice of the reference signal $x(t)$. In order to overcome (a), a matrix $\tilde{\boldsymbol{F}}$ is used instead of $\tilde{\boldsymbol{R}}$ in (11). This idea comes from [8]. Hence, (11) can be expressed as

$$\tilde{\boldsymbol{B}}\tilde{\boldsymbol{w}}_i = \lambda_i \tilde{\boldsymbol{F}}\tilde{\boldsymbol{w}}_i, \tag{12}$$

where $\tilde{\boldsymbol{F}}$ is a set of $m \times m$ block matrices $\boldsymbol{F}_{\boldsymbol{y},j,l}^{(4)}$, that is, $\sum_{j=1}^{m}\sum_{l=L_1}^{L_2}\boldsymbol{F}_{\boldsymbol{y},j,l}^{(4)}$, the elements of $\boldsymbol{F}_{\boldsymbol{y},j,l}^{(4)}$ are defined by fourth-order cumulants, that is,

$$\left[\boldsymbol{F}_{\boldsymbol{y},j,l}^{(4)}\right]_{[p,q]_{l_1 l_2}} = \mathrm{cum}\{y_q(t\text{-}L_1\text{-}l_2 + 1), y_p^*(t\text{-}L_1\text{-}l_1 + 1), y_j(t\text{-}l), y_j^*(t\text{-}l)\},$$

$$p, q, j = \overline{1,m}, \quad l_1, l_2 = \overline{1,L}, \quad l = \overline{L_1, L_2}, \tag{13}$$

Here the matrix $\tilde{\boldsymbol{B}}$ can be expressed as

$$\tilde{\boldsymbol{B}} = \tilde{\boldsymbol{H}}^{H}\tilde{\boldsymbol{\Lambda}}\tilde{\boldsymbol{H}}, \tag{14}$$

where $\tilde{\boldsymbol{\Lambda}}$ is the block diagonal matrix defined by

$$\tilde{\boldsymbol{\Lambda}} := \text{block-diag}\{\boldsymbol{\Lambda}_1, \boldsymbol{\Lambda}_2, \cdots, \boldsymbol{\Lambda}_n\}, \tag{15}$$

$$\boldsymbol{\Lambda}_i := \text{diag}\{\cdots, |a_i(-1)|^2\gamma_i, |a_i(0)|^2\gamma_i, |a_i(1)|^2\gamma_i, \cdots\}, \tag{16}$$

$i = \overline{1,n}$. It is shown by a simple calculation that $\tilde{\boldsymbol{F}}$ becomes

$$\tilde{\boldsymbol{F}} = \tilde{\boldsymbol{H}}^{H}\tilde{\boldsymbol{\Psi}}\tilde{\boldsymbol{H}}, \tag{17}$$

where $\tilde{\boldsymbol{\Psi}}$ is the diagonal matrix defined by

$$\tilde{\boldsymbol{\Psi}} := \text{block-diag}\{\boldsymbol{\Psi}_1, \boldsymbol{\Psi}_2, \cdots, \boldsymbol{\Psi}_n\}, \tag{18}$$

$$\boldsymbol{\Psi}_i := \text{diag}\{\cdots, \gamma_i\tilde{a}_i(\text{-}1), \gamma_i\tilde{a}_i(0), \gamma_i\tilde{a}_i(1), \cdots\}, i = \overline{1,n}, \tag{19}$$

$$\tilde{a}_i(k) := \sum_{j=1}^{m}\sum_{l=L_1}^{L_2}|h_{ji}(k-l)|^2, i = \overline{1,n}, k \in Z. \tag{20}$$

Let the eigenvalues of the diagonal matrix $\tilde{\boldsymbol{\Psi}}^{-1}\tilde{\boldsymbol{\Lambda}}$ be denoted by

$$\mu_i(k) := |a_i(k)|^2/\tilde{a}_i(k), \quad i = \overline{1,n}, \quad k \in Z. \tag{21}$$

We put the following assumption on the eigenvalues $\mu_i(k)'s$.

A6) All the eigenvalues $\mu_i(k)'s$ are distinct for $i = \overline{1,n}$ and $k \in Z$.

Then we can prove the following theorem.

Theorem 1. *Assume $L_1 = -\infty$ and $L_2 = \infty$, and suppose the following conditions holds true:*

T1) *All the eigenvalues $\mu_i(k)$'s are distinct for $i = \overline{1,n}$ and $k \in Z$.*
Then the n eigenvectors corresponding to n nonzero eigenvalues $\mu_i(k_i)$'s of $\tilde{\boldsymbol{F}}^{\dagger}\tilde{\boldsymbol{B}}$ become the vectors $\tilde{\boldsymbol{w}}_i$, $i = \overline{1,n}$, satisfying (8),

Outline of the proof: Based on (12), we consider the following eigenvector problem;

$$\tilde{\boldsymbol{F}}^{\dagger}\tilde{\boldsymbol{B}}\tilde{\boldsymbol{w}}_i = \lambda_i \tilde{\boldsymbol{w}}_i. \tag{22}$$

Then, from (14) and (17), (22) becomes

$$(\tilde{\boldsymbol{H}}^H \tilde{\boldsymbol{\Psi}}\tilde{\boldsymbol{H}})^{\dagger}\tilde{\boldsymbol{H}}^H \tilde{\boldsymbol{\Lambda}}\tilde{\boldsymbol{H}}\tilde{\boldsymbol{w}}_i = \lambda_i \tilde{\boldsymbol{w}}_i, \tag{23}$$

Under $L_1 = -\infty$ and $L_2 = \infty$, we have the following equations;

$$(\tilde{\boldsymbol{H}}^H \tilde{\boldsymbol{\Psi}}\tilde{\boldsymbol{H}})^{\dagger} = \tilde{\boldsymbol{H}}^{\dagger}\tilde{\boldsymbol{\Psi}}^{-1}\tilde{\boldsymbol{H}}^{H\dagger}, \quad \tilde{\boldsymbol{H}}^{H\dagger}\tilde{\boldsymbol{H}}^H = \boldsymbol{I}, \tag{24}$$

which are shown in [12] along with their proofs. Then it follows from (23) and (24);

$$\tilde{\boldsymbol{H}}^{\dagger}\tilde{\boldsymbol{\Psi}}^{-1}\tilde{\boldsymbol{\Lambda}}\tilde{\boldsymbol{H}}\tilde{\boldsymbol{w}}_i = \lambda_i \tilde{\boldsymbol{w}}_i. \tag{25}$$

Multiplying (25) by $\tilde{\boldsymbol{H}}$ from the left side and using (24), (25) becomes

$$\tilde{\boldsymbol{\Psi}}^{-1}\tilde{\boldsymbol{\Lambda}}\tilde{\boldsymbol{H}}\tilde{\boldsymbol{w}}_i = \lambda_i \tilde{\boldsymbol{H}}\tilde{\boldsymbol{w}}_i. \tag{26}$$

$\tilde{\boldsymbol{\Psi}}^{-1}\tilde{\boldsymbol{\Lambda}}$ is a diagonal matrix with diagonal elements $\mu_i(k)$, $i = \overline{1,n}$ and $k \in Z$, and thus (22) and (26) show that its diagonal elements $\mu_i(k)'s$ are eigenvalues of matrix $\tilde{\boldsymbol{F}}^{\dagger}\tilde{\boldsymbol{B}}$. Here we use the following fact;

$$\lim_{L \to \infty} (\text{rank } \tilde{\boldsymbol{F}})/L = n, \tag{27}$$

which is shown in [10] and its proof is found in [3]. Using this fact, the other remaining eigenvalues of $\tilde{\boldsymbol{F}}^{\dagger}\tilde{\boldsymbol{B}}$ are all zero. From the assumption **A6)**, the n nonzero eigenvalues $\mu_i(k) \neq 0$, $i = \overline{1,n}$, obtained by (26), that is, the n nonzero eigenvectors $\tilde{\boldsymbol{w}}_i$, $i = \overline{1,n}$, corresponding to n nonzero eigenvalues $\mu_i(k) \neq 0$, $i = \overline{1,n}$, obtained by (22) become n solutions of the vectors $\tilde{\boldsymbol{w}}_i$ satisfying (8).

Remark 1. Since the matrix $\tilde{\boldsymbol{F}}^{\dagger}\tilde{\boldsymbol{B}}$ consists of only fourth-order cumulants, the eigenvectors derived from the matrix can be obtained with as little influence of Gaussian noise as possible, which is referred as a *robust eigenvector algorithm* (REVA).

In order to overcome (b), because it is claimed in [2] that the best performance of the EVA can be obtained in the case where the recovered signals are used as the reference signals, we use $x_i(t) = \tilde{\boldsymbol{w}}_i\tilde{\boldsymbol{y}}(t)$ in Fig. 2 as the reference signals, where the number of the reference signals corresponds to the number of the source signals. However, the EVA using the reference signals needs deflation methods to recover all source signals (see [2]). On the contrary, we don't want to use deflation methods because the deflation is affected to the estimation errors and hence as the deflation process comes near to the final step, the accuracy of recovering source signals is getting worse. Therefore, the following two-stage EVA is proposed.

Stage 1) Roughly estimate the eigenvectors of $\tilde{\boldsymbol{R}}^{\dagger}\tilde{\boldsymbol{B}}$ with the reference signal $x(t)$ in (9)

In Stage 1), all the vectors $\tilde{\boldsymbol{w}}_i$ corresponding to (8) can be simultaneously obtained using only one reference signal $x(t)$ (see [9]). Since the estimate of $\tilde{\boldsymbol{R}}$ has a good accuracy with a few samples, compared with the estimate of $\tilde{\boldsymbol{F}}$, then first of all the eigenvectors are roughly estimated with $\tilde{\boldsymbol{R}}^{\dagger}\tilde{\boldsymbol{B}}$. However, the vectors obtained by $\tilde{\boldsymbol{R}}^{\dagger}\tilde{\boldsymbol{B}}$ are sensitive to Gaussian noise and their performances depend on reference signals (see Section 4). Then,

Stage 2) Estimate the eigenvectors of $\tilde{\boldsymbol{F}}^{\dagger}\tilde{\boldsymbol{B}}_i$ with the reference signals $x_i(t)$
$\tilde{\boldsymbol{w}}_i\tilde{\boldsymbol{y}}(t)$, $i = \overline{1, n}$,

where $\tilde{\boldsymbol{w}}_i$ $(i = \overline{1, n})$ are the eigenvectors obtained in Stage 1) and the matrix $\tilde{\boldsymbol{B}}$ obtained by using each $x_i(t)$ is denoted by $\tilde{\boldsymbol{B}}_i$.

Each eigenvector obtained in Stage 2) is the one corresponding to the absolute maximum eigenvalue $|\lambda_i|$ for each $\tilde{\boldsymbol{F}}^{\dagger}(t)\tilde{\boldsymbol{B}}_i(t)$. Although $x_i(t) = \tilde{\boldsymbol{w}}_i\tilde{\boldsymbol{y}}(t)$ $(i = \overline{1, n})$ are used as the reference signals (see Fig. 2), deflation methods are not needed to recover all source signals in this stage, because the vectors $\tilde{\boldsymbol{w}}_i$'s in $x_i(t)$'s, which are obtained in Stage 1), have been already linearly independent.

If the matrices of $\tilde{\boldsymbol{R}}$, $\tilde{\boldsymbol{F}}$, and $\tilde{\boldsymbol{B}}$ can be estimated with good accuracies, the two-stage algorithm can provide the solution in (8) with one iteration. In this paper, however, since we confine ourselves to implement their estimates iteratively, the procedure of the two-stage EVA is summarized as follows:

Choose an appropriate reference signal $x(t)$ and appropriate initial values of
$\tilde{\boldsymbol{w}}_i^{[1]}(0)$, $\tilde{\boldsymbol{w}}_i^{[2]}(0)$, $\tilde{\boldsymbol{R}}(0)$, $\tilde{\boldsymbol{F}}(0)$, $\tilde{\boldsymbol{B}}(0)$, $\tilde{\boldsymbol{B}}_i(0)$
for $t_l = 1 : t_{l_{all}}$
if $t_l < t_s$
for $t = t_d(t_l - 1)+1:t_d t_l$
Calculate $\tilde{\boldsymbol{R}}(t)$, $\tilde{\boldsymbol{F}}(t)$, and $\tilde{\boldsymbol{B}}(t)$ by their moving averages.
end
Calculate the eigenvectors $\tilde{\boldsymbol{w}}_i^{[1]}(t_l)$'s from $\tilde{\boldsymbol{R}}^{\dagger}(t)\tilde{\boldsymbol{B}}(t)$ (Stage 1)).
elseif $t_l \geq t_s$
if $t_l == t_s$, $\tilde{\boldsymbol{w}}_i^{[2]}(t_l - 1) = \tilde{\boldsymbol{w}}_i^{[1]}(t_s - 1)$
for $t = t_d(t_l - 1)+1:t_d t_l$
$x_i(t) = \tilde{\boldsymbol{w}}_i^{[2]T}(t_l - 1)\tilde{\boldsymbol{y}}_i(t)$
Calculate $\tilde{\boldsymbol{F}}(t)$ and $\tilde{\boldsymbol{B}}_i(t)$ by their moving averages.
end

Calculate the eigenvector $\tilde{\boldsymbol{w}}_i^{[2]}(t_l)$ associated with the absolute
maximum eigenvalue $|\lambda_i|$ from $\tilde{\boldsymbol{F}}^\dagger(t)\tilde{\boldsymbol{B}}_i(t)$, $i = \overline{1,n}$ (Stage 2)).
end
end

Here, $t_{l_{all}}$ denotes the total number of iterations and t_d denotes the number of data
samples for estimating the matrices $\tilde{\boldsymbol{R}}(t)$, $\tilde{\boldsymbol{F}}(t)$, $\tilde{\boldsymbol{B}}(t)$, and $\tilde{\boldsymbol{B}}_i(t)$. From a practical
viewpoint, it would be better to estimate the fourth-order cumulant matrix $\tilde{\boldsymbol{F}}(t)$
during $t_l = 1$ to $t_{l_{all}}$. $\tilde{\boldsymbol{w}}_i^{[1]}(t)$ and $\tilde{\boldsymbol{w}}_i^{[2]}(t)$ are the eigenvectors obtained for Stage 1)
and Stage 2), respectively. t_s denotes an arbitrary integer satisfying $2 < t_s < t_{l_{all}}$.
For $0 < t_l < t_s$ and $t_s \leq t_l \leq t_{l_{all}}$, the eigenvectors $\tilde{\boldsymbol{w}}_i^{[1]}(t_l)$'s and $\tilde{\boldsymbol{w}}_i^{[2]}(t_l)$'s are
iteratively calculated, respectively, according to Stage 1) and Stage 2).

4   Computer Simulations

To demonstrate the validity of the proposed algorithm, many computer simulations were conducted. Some results are shown in this section. The unknown
system $\boldsymbol{H}(z)$ was set to be the same system with two inputs and three outputs
as in [9]. The source signals $s_1(t)$ and $s_2(t)$ were a sub-Gaussian signal which
takes one of two values, -1 and 1 with equal probability $1/2$. The Gaussian
noises $n_j(t)$ with its variance $\sigma_{n_j}^2$ were included in the output $y_j(t)$ at various
SNR levels. The SNR was considered at the output of the system $\boldsymbol{H}(z)$. The parameters L_1 and L_2 in $\boldsymbol{W}(z)$ were set to be 0 and 11, respectively. As a measure
of performances, we used the *multichannel intersymbol interference* (M_{ISI})
[11], which was the average of 50 Monte Carlo runs. In each Monte Carlo run,
the number of iterations $t_{l_{all}}$ was set to be 10, the number of data samples t_d
was set to be 5,000, and the threshold t_s was set to be 6.

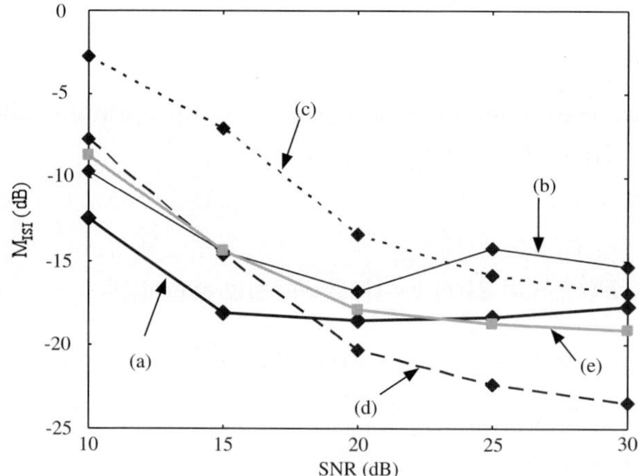

Fig. 3. The performances of the proposed algorithm and the conventional EVAs with
varying SNR levels, in the cases of 5,000 data samples

Fig. 3 shows the results of performances of the EVAs when the SNR levels were respectively taken to be 10 through 30 dB for every 5 dB. The line (a) represents the performance obtained by our proposed two-stage EVA, where in the EVA in the stage 1), $x(t) = f_2(2)y_2(t-2)$ was used as the reference signal and $f_2(2)$ was randomly chosen from a Gaussian distribution with zero mean and unit variance. The line (b) represents the performance obtained by only the REVA ($t_s = 1$), where the reference signal was given by the same equation as the line (a), but the parameter $f_2(2)$ was given by another Gaussian distribution with zero mean and unit variance. The lines (c) and (d) represent the performances obtained by only the EVA ($t_s = 11$) with respectively $x(t) = \sum_{i=1}^{3} f_i(2)y_i(t-2)$ and $f_2(2)y_2(t-2)$ as the reference signal. Finally, the line (e) represents the performance obtained by Castella et al. (CRMPA). From the line (b), the REVA has such a property that as the SNR level decreases, it can provide better performances than the EVA. That is, the REVA can work with as little influence of Gaussian noise as possible. However for the high SNR levels its performance is not so good compared with the EVA. From the lines (c) and (d), one can see that the EVA's performance depends on the choice of the reference signal. From the line (a), our proposed algorithm has such a property that as the SNR level decreases, it is more robust to Gaussian noise than the other algorithms, and for the high SNR levels, its performance is almost the same as the CRMPA. Therefore from all the results we conclude that our proposed algorithm can overcome the drawbacks of the conventional EVAs.

5   Conclusions

We have proposed a two-stage algorithm obtained by combining the EVA and the REVA for solving the BD problem. The proposed algorithm provides better performances than the conventional EVAs, because the proposed algorithm can overcome the drawbacks of the conventional EVAs, that is,

- The EVA is sensitive to Gaussian noise.
- The EVA depends on the selection of the reference signal.

Computer simulations have demonstrated the effectiveness of the proposed EVA.

Acknowledgments. This work is supported by the Research Projects, Grant-IN AIDs, No. 18500146[1] and No. 1850054[2] for Scientific Research of the JSPS.

References

1. Adib, A., et al.: Source separation contrasts using a reference signal. IEEE Signal Processing Letters 11(3), 312–315 (2004)
2. Castella, M., et al.: Quadratic Higher-Order Criteria for Iterative Blind Separation of a MIMO Convolutive Mixture of Sources. IEEE Trans. Signal Processing 55(1), 218–232 (2007)

3. Inouye, Y.: Autoregressive model fitting for multichannel time series of degenerate rank: Limit properties. IEEE Trans. Circuits and Systems 32(3), 252–259 (1985)
4. Inouye, Y., Tanebe, K.: Super-exponential algorithms for multichannel blind deconvolution. IEEE Trans. Sig. Proc. 48(3), 881–888 (2000)
5. Jelonnek, B., Kammeyer, K.D.: A closed-form solution to blind equalization. Signal Processing 36(3), 251–259 (1994)
6. Jelonnek, B., Boss, D., Kammeyer, K.D.: Generalized eigenvector algorithm for blind equalization. Signal Processing 61(3), 237–264 (1997)
7. Kawamoto, M., et al.: Eigenvector algorithms using reference signals. In: Proc. ICASSP 2006, May 2006, vol. V, pp. 841–844 (2006)
8. Kawamoto, M., et al.: Eigenvector algorithms using reference signals for blind source separation of instantaneous mixtures. In: Proc. of ISCAS 2006, May 2006, pp. 4191–4194 (2006)
9. Kawamoto, M., et al.: Eigenvector algorithms for blind deconvolution of MIMO-IIR systems. In: Proc. ISCAS 2007, May 2007, pp. 3490–3493 (2007)
10. Kohno, K., et al.: Adaptive super-exponential algorithms for blind deconvolution of MIMO systems. In: Proc. ISCAS 2004, May 2004, vol. V, pp. 680–683 (2004)
11. Kohno, K., et al.: Super-Exponential Methods Incorporated with Higher-Order Correlations for Deflationary Blind Equalization of MIMO Linear Systems. In: Proc. ICA 2004, pp. 685–693 (2004)
12. Kohno, K., et al.: Robust super-exponential methods for blind equalization of MIMO-IIR systems. In: Proc. ICASSP 2006, vol. V, pp. 661–664 (2006)
13. Parra, L., Sajda, P.: Blind source separation via generalized eigenvalue decomposition. Journal of Machine Learning (4), 1261–1269 (2003)
14. Rhioui, S., et al.: Quadratic MIMO contrast functions for blind source separation in a convolutive context. In: Proc. ICA 2006, pp. 230–237 (2006)

Blind Source Separation Coping with the Change of the Number of Sources

Masanori Ito[1], Noboru Ohnishi[1], Ali Mansour[2], and Mitsuru Kawamoto[3,4]

[1] Graduate School of Information Science, Nagoya University
Furo-cho, Chikusa-ku, Nagoya,464–8603 Japan
`ito-m@nagoya-u.jp`
[2] Lab. E^3I^2, ENSIETA, 29806 Brest cedex 09, France
[3] Advanced Industrial Science and Technology,
Central 2, 1-1-1 Umezono, Tsukuba, Ibaraki, 305–8568 Japan
[4] Bio-mimetic Control Research Center, RIKEN,
2271–120 Anagahora, Shimoshidami, Moriyama-ku, Nagoya, 463–0003 Japan

Abstract. This manuscript deals with the blind source separation problem with an instantaneous but dynamical mixture model. This study is limited to the case when the number of sources is time-variant. Theoretically, when new sources are detected, a new separating matrix should be estimated in order to extract all sources. However this effort implies an overwhelm computational cost. Our idea consists to use the previous separating matrix which was estimated before the appearance of the new sources. Owing to this point, the computational time and cost can be effectively reduced compared with the conventional separation scheme. Our new algorithm was corroborated with many simulations. Some results are given in the manuscript. The obtained and presented results clearly show that the proposed method outperformed the conventional method in processing time as well as in separation quality.

Keywords: blind source separation, time-variant system, dynamical instantaneous mixtures, independent component analysis.

1 Introduction

In the last decade, independent component analysis (ICA) has been greatly developed [1,2]. ICA is often used to solve blind source separation (BSS) problems, which means the estimation of original sources from their mixtures, using the only observed signals without any knowledge about the sources and the mixing process. Applying ICA algorithms the original sources can be estimated up to scaling and permutation factors.

A number of researchers have been struggling with BSS problems. However, most of the researches on BSS assume the time-invariant systems. The number of sources is a very important factor for BSS problems. However, most of the algorithms assumes that the number of sources is constant and known a priori. Ye et al. have proposed the BSS without knowing the number of sources [3]. But they

M. Ishikawa et al. (Eds.): ICONIP 2007, Part II, LNCS 4985, pp. 509–518, 2008.

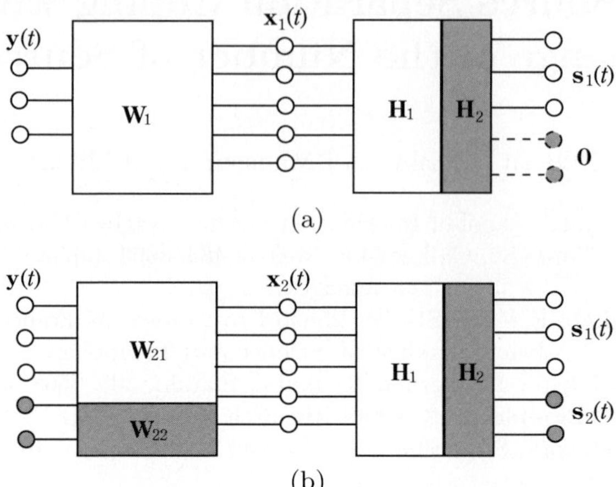

Fig. 1. Mixing and separating process. (a) The process before the appearance of $s_2(t)$. Only $s_1(t)$ exists. (b) The process after the appearance of $s_2(t)$.

have not considered the change of the number. For practical use, we need a solution of the BSS problems in time-variant systems, where the properties of the mixing process and sources may change. Some researchers have proposed methods to solve the blind separation of moving sources [4,5]. When source moves, the property of the mixing process varies, but the dimensions of the mixing matrix and the sources are constant. Therefore we deal with the case where the number of sources is not constant, that is, the dimensions of the mixing matrix and the sources are variable. Until now, such a problem has not been solved. In particular we consider the case that the number of sources increases because a decrease of sources does not affect the subsequent separation process.

In this manuscript, in order to solve the BSS problem with the change of the number of sources, the following conditions are assumed;

A1) The mixing process is invertible and instantaneous.
A2) There are no noise.
A3) The number of active sources is always known.
A4) The signals are real-valued.

Hereafter, the scheme of the separation coping with the case that new sources appear is proposed. Making use of the covariance matrix of the mixed signals, a new matrix which blocks undesired sources can be estimated. Through computer simulations, it is clarified that the proposed method can work efficiently.

2   Problem Formulation

It is supposed that n_1 sources initially exist for $t < T_0$ and at time $t = T_0$ new n_2 sources suddenly appear, i.e., $(n_1 + n_2)$ sources are active for the period $t \geq T_0$.

The former sources are denoted as $s_1(t)$, the latter source $s_2(t)$. We call $s_1(t)$ *initial* sources and $s_2(t)$ *additional* sources. We unite them into $s(t)$:

$$s(t) = \begin{bmatrix} s_1(t) \\ s_2(t) \end{bmatrix}. \tag{1}$$

Their mixtures are observed by multiple sensors whose number m is greater than or equal to that of whole sources $(n_1 + n_2)$. Mixed signals are denoted by $x_1(t)$ $(t < T_0)$ or $x_2(t)$ $(t \geq T_0)$. The initial mixed signals $x_1(t)$ can be expressed as follows (See Fig. 1 (a).):

$$x_1(t) = [H_1 \; H_2] \begin{bmatrix} s_1(t) \\ 0_{n_2} \end{bmatrix}. \tag{2}$$

$x_1(t)$ can be rewritten in another way:

$$x_1(t) = [H_1 \; O_{m \times n_2}] \begin{bmatrix} s_1(t) \\ s_2(t) \end{bmatrix}, \tag{3}$$

where H_1 and H_2 are $m \times n_1$ and $m \times n_2$ mixing matrices corresponding to sources $s_1(t)$ and $s_2(t)$, respectively. Matrices H_1 and $[H_1 \; H_2]$ are assumed to be column full rank. 0 and O are a zero vector and a zero matrix, and the subscript shows their dimensions. The above two equations are mathematically equivalent but physically different. In the former way it is supposed that additional sources emit no signals, while in the latter way, additional sources have no paths to sensors. In this research, the latter case of Eq. (3) is considered because of mathematical convenience. In order to achieve BSS for $x_1(t)$, an $n_1 \times m$ separating matrix W_1 is estimated and the separated signals $y_1(t)$ is written as

$$y_1(t) = W_1 x_1(t) = PD s_1(t), \tag{4}$$

where P is a permutation matrix and D is a diagonal matrix which results in a scaling factor. However, if $\hat{s}_1(t) = PD s_1(t)$ are considered as original sources, permutation and scaling ambiguity can be ignored.

After the appearance of new sources as shown in Fig. 1 (b), the mixed signals $x_2(t)$ are written as follows:

$$x_2(t) = [H_1 \; H_2] \begin{bmatrix} s_1(t) \\ s_2(t) \end{bmatrix}. \tag{5}$$

Then a new $(n_1 + n_2) \times m$ matrix $W_2 = \begin{bmatrix} W_{21} \\ W_{22} \end{bmatrix}$ should be estimated. The goal of the BSS problem is to obtain the original sources $s_1(t)$ and $s_2(t)$ by estimating a separating matrix using ICA.

3   Separation Scheme

3.1   Separation of Initial Sources

In the first stage, we estimate a separating matrix for initially existing sources applying ICA. Without loss of generality, let us define an ideal matrix W_1 which is represented without permutation and scaling ambiguity as follows:

$$W_1 = H_1^\dagger = (H_1^T H_1)^{-1} H_1^T, \tag{6}$$

where † denotes the pseudo inverse (Moore-Penrose generalized inverse) operation.

Because H_1 is unknown, W_1 should be estimated by applying some independent component analysis (ICA) algorithm to the mixed signal $x_1(t)$. Inversely using estimated W_1, H_1 can also be calculated as

$$H_1 = W_1^\dagger = W_1^T (W_1 W_1^T)^{-1}. \tag{7}$$

In this stage, we assume that we can estimate an ideal separating matrix, otherwise in the subsequent stage our method cannot avoid to fail the separation. Using the proposed method, the separation error in this stage affects the performance in the subsequent stage.

3.2 Separation After Sources Addition

When the appearance of the additional sources is detected, a new separating matrix should be calculated. As well as W_1 in (6), we can represent an ideal separating matrix $W_2 = \begin{bmatrix} W_{21} \\ W_{22} \end{bmatrix}$ as a function of H_1 and H_2:

$$W_2 = [H_1 \ H_2]^\dagger$$
$$= \begin{bmatrix} H_1^\dagger - H_1^\dagger H_2 \left(H_2^T (I_m - H_1 H_1^\dagger) H_2 \right)^{-1} H_2^T (I_m - H_1 H_1^\dagger) \\ \left(H_2^T (I_m - H_1 H_1^\dagger) H_2 \right)^{-1} H_2^T (I_m - H_1 H_1^\dagger) \end{bmatrix}, \tag{8}$$

where I denotes an identity matrix with a subscript of the dimension. Note that the matrix $(I_m - H_1 H_1^\dagger)$ is symmetric and idempotent, that is, $(I_m - H_1 H_1^\dagger)$ is the orthogonal projection [6]. In the rest of this paper, $(I_m - H_1 H_1^\dagger)$ is substituted with P_1. Then the above equation can be rewritten in short form:

$$W_2 = \begin{bmatrix} W_{21} \\ W_{22} \end{bmatrix} = \begin{bmatrix} H_1^\dagger \left(I_m - H_2 \{P_1 H_2\}^\dagger \right) \\ \{P_1 H_2\}^\dagger \end{bmatrix}$$
$$= \begin{bmatrix} H_1^\dagger (I_m - H_2 W_{22}) \\ \{P_1 H_2\}^\dagger \end{bmatrix}. \tag{9}$$

W_2 is also obtained by applying ICA to the mixed signal $x_2(t)$. However, we may suffer a computational load, because we have to estimate a big separating matrix of size $(n_1 + n_2) \times m$. The essence of our method is to reuse the estimated mixing matrix H_1 and to reduce the cost. Here, let us define a global matrix $G = \begin{bmatrix} W_{21} \\ W_{22} \end{bmatrix} [H_1 \ H_2]$, which is shown in Fig. 2. If the submatrices of the global matrix satisfy the following conditions:

$$W_{21} H_1 = I_{n_1}, \tag{10}$$
$$W_{21} H_2 = O_{n_1 \times n_2}, \tag{11}$$
$$W_{22} H_1 = O_{n_2 \times n_1}, \tag{12}$$
$$\tag{13}$$

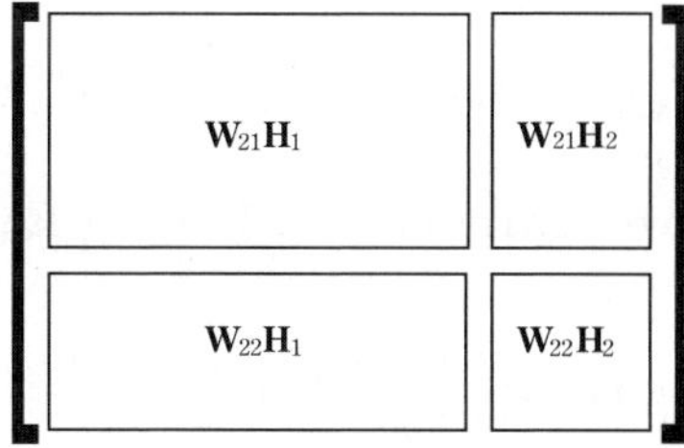

Fig. 2. Global matrix after the new sources appearance

the separation problem can be simplified, because we only have to solve the separation of the part $\boldsymbol{W}_{22}\boldsymbol{H}_2$. The proposed scheme to estimate $\boldsymbol{W}_2$ satisfying the above conditions is shown below.

Given $\boldsymbol{H}_2$, $\boldsymbol{W}_2$ in (8) can be estimated because $\boldsymbol{H}_1$ is known. However, there is no information about $\boldsymbol{H}_2$. Here, we substitute an arbitrary nonzero matrix $\boldsymbol{A}_2$ for $\boldsymbol{H}_2$ in $\boldsymbol{W}_2$ of Eq. (8) and we obtain

$$\tilde{\boldsymbol{W}}_2 = \begin{bmatrix} \tilde{\boldsymbol{W}}_{21} \\ \tilde{\boldsymbol{W}}_{22} \end{bmatrix} = \begin{bmatrix} \boldsymbol{H}_1^{\dagger} - \boldsymbol{H}_1^{\dagger}\boldsymbol{A}_2 \left(\boldsymbol{A}_2^T \boldsymbol{P}_1 \boldsymbol{A}_2 \right)^{-1} \boldsymbol{A}_2^T \boldsymbol{P}_1 \\ \left(\boldsymbol{A}_2^T \boldsymbol{P}_1 \boldsymbol{A}_2 \right)^{-1} \boldsymbol{A}_2^T \boldsymbol{P}_1 \end{bmatrix}. \tag{14}$$

Theorem 1. *For any matrix $\boldsymbol{A}_2$, the following equation is satisfied,*

$$\tilde{\boldsymbol{W}}_{22}\boldsymbol{H}_1 = \boldsymbol{O}_{n_2 \times n_1}. \tag{15}$$

$\tilde{\boldsymbol{W}}_{22}$ *works as a blocker [7] of $\boldsymbol{H}_1$ even if the mixing matrix $\boldsymbol{H}_2$ is unknown.*

Proof.

$$\begin{aligned} \boldsymbol{P}_1\boldsymbol{H}_1 &= (\boldsymbol{I}_m - \boldsymbol{H}_1\boldsymbol{H}_1^{\dagger})\boldsymbol{H}_1 \\ &= \boldsymbol{H}_1 - \boldsymbol{H}_1\boldsymbol{H}_1^{\dagger}\boldsymbol{H}_1 \\ &= \boldsymbol{H}_1 - \boldsymbol{H}_1 \\ &= \boldsymbol{O}_{m \times n_1}. \end{aligned} \tag{16}$$

Therefore $\tilde{\boldsymbol{W}}_{22}\boldsymbol{H}_1 = \left(\boldsymbol{A}_2^T \boldsymbol{P}_1 \boldsymbol{A}_2 \right)^{-1} \boldsymbol{A}_2^T \boldsymbol{P}_1 \boldsymbol{H}_1 = \boldsymbol{O}_{n_2 \times n_1}.$ □

Using Theorem 1, it is clear that $\tilde{\boldsymbol{W}}_{21}\boldsymbol{H}_1 = \boldsymbol{I}_{n_1}$.

Hereafter the method to estimated a separating matrix $\hat{\boldsymbol{W}}_{21}$, which satisfies $\hat{\boldsymbol{W}}_{21}\boldsymbol{H}_2 = \boldsymbol{O}_{n_1 \times M2}$, is shown. For the purpose, the following equation is calculated:

$$\tilde{\boldsymbol{A}}_2 = \boldsymbol{C}_{x_2}\tilde{\boldsymbol{W}}_{22}^T, \tag{17}$$

where $\boldsymbol{C}_{x_2}$ is the covariance matrix of $\boldsymbol{x}_2(t)$. The covariance matrix can be rewritten as

514   M. Ito et al.

$$C_{x_2} = [H_1 \ H_2] \, C_s \begin{bmatrix} H_1^T \\ H_2^T \end{bmatrix}, \tag{18}$$

where C_s is the covariance matrix of $s(t)$. Putting Eq. (18) into Eq. (17), we obtain

$$\begin{aligned}
\tilde{A}_2 &= [H_1 \ H_2] \, C_s \begin{bmatrix} H_1^T \\ H_2^T \end{bmatrix} \tilde{W}_{22}^T \\
&= [H_1 \ H_2] \begin{bmatrix} C_{s_1} & O_{n_1 \times n_2} \\ O_{n_2 \times n_1} & C_{s_2} \end{bmatrix} \begin{bmatrix} O_{n_1 \times n_2} \\ H_2^T \tilde{W}_{22}^T \end{bmatrix} \\
&= H_2 C_{s_2} H_2^T \tilde{W}_{22}^T,
\end{aligned} \tag{19}$$

where C_{s_1} and C_{s_2} are the covariance matrices of $s_1(t)$ and $s_2(t)$, respectively. For simplicity we replace $C_{s_2} H_2^T \tilde{W}_{22}^T$ by M. If $\det M \neq 0$, that is, $\det \tilde{W}_{22} H_2 \neq 0$, we substitute $\tilde{A}_2 = H_2 M$ for H_2 of Eq. (9) to get $\hat{W}_2 = \begin{bmatrix} \hat{W}_{21} \\ \hat{W}_{22} \end{bmatrix}$,

$$\hat{W}_2 = \begin{bmatrix} H_1^\dagger \left(I_m - H_2 M \{P_1 H_2 M\}^\dagger \right) \\ \{P_1 H_2 M\}^\dagger \end{bmatrix}. \tag{20}$$

Here, we notice the following attractive property.

Lemma 1. $\{P_1 H_2 M\}^\dagger$ *is a generalized inverse [8] of* $H_2 M$.

Proof. A generalized inverse of a matrix B, which is denoted as B^-, satisfies $B B^- B = B$. Thus $H_2 M \{P_1 H_2 M\}^\dagger H_2 M$ is calculated as follows:

$$\begin{aligned}
&H_2 M \{P_1 H_2 M\}^\dagger H_2 M \\
&= H_2 M \left\{ M^T H_2^T P_1 H_2 M \right\}^{-1} M^T H_2^T P_1 H_2 M \\
&= H_2 M.
\end{aligned} \tag{21}$$

Therefore $\{P_1 H_2 M\}^\dagger$ is a generalized inverse of $H_2 M$. $\qquad\square$

Then we have the following theorem.

Theorem 2. $\hat{W}_{21}$ *works as a blocker of* H_1, *i.e.,* $\hat{W}_{21} H_1 = O_{n_1 \times n_2}$.

Proof. Using Lemma 1, it is clear that $\hat{W}_{21}$ is a blocker of H_2;

$$\begin{aligned}
\hat{W}_{21} H_2 &= H_1^\dagger \left(I_m - H_2 M \{P_1 H_2 M\}^\dagger \right) H_2 \\
&= H_1^\dagger \left(H_2 - H_2 M \{P_1 H_2 M\}^\dagger H_2 M M^{-1} \right) \\
&= H_1^\dagger \left(H_2 - H_2 M M^{-1} \right) \\
&= O_{n_1 \times n_2}.
\end{aligned} \tag{22}$$

$\qquad\square$

Table 1. Summary of the proposed method

Step	Contents
1	Until $t < T_0$ given $\boldsymbol{x}_1(t)$, estimate $\boldsymbol{W}_1$ by ICA, and calculate $\boldsymbol{H}_1 = \boldsymbol{W}_1^\dagger$.
2	New sources appear at $t = T_0$.
3	Choose an arbitrary matrix $\boldsymbol{A}_2$ and calculate $\tilde{\boldsymbol{W}}_2$ in (14).
4	Calculate $\tilde{\boldsymbol{A}}_2 = \boldsymbol{C}_{x_2}\tilde{\boldsymbol{W}}_{22}^T$.
5	Substitute $\boldsymbol{H}_2$ with $\tilde{\boldsymbol{A}}_2$ and calculate $\hat{\boldsymbol{W}}_2$ in (20).
6	Apply ICA to $\tilde{\boldsymbol{x}}_2(t) = \hat{\boldsymbol{W}}_{22}\boldsymbol{H}_2\boldsymbol{s}_2(t)$.

Since $\hat{\boldsymbol{W}}_2$ has the same property as $\tilde{\boldsymbol{W}}_2$, $\hat{\boldsymbol{W}}_{21}$ and $\hat{\boldsymbol{W}}_{22}$ work as blockers of $\boldsymbol{H}_2$ and $\boldsymbol{H}_1$, respectively, so that the product of $\hat{\boldsymbol{W}}_2$ and $\boldsymbol{x}_2(t)$ is calculated as follows:

$$
\hat{\boldsymbol{W}}_2\boldsymbol{x}_2(t) = \begin{bmatrix} \hat{\boldsymbol{W}}_{21}\boldsymbol{H}_1 & \hat{\boldsymbol{W}}_{21}\boldsymbol{H}_2 \\ \hat{\boldsymbol{W}}_{22}\boldsymbol{H}_1 & \hat{\boldsymbol{W}}_{22}\boldsymbol{H}_2 \end{bmatrix} \begin{bmatrix} \boldsymbol{s}_1(t) \\ \boldsymbol{s}_2(t) \end{bmatrix}
$$

$$
= \begin{bmatrix} \boldsymbol{I}_{n_1} & \boldsymbol{O}_{n_1 \times n_2} \\ \boldsymbol{O}_{n_2 \times n_1} & \hat{\boldsymbol{W}}_{22}\boldsymbol{H}_2 \end{bmatrix} \begin{bmatrix} \boldsymbol{s}_1(t) \\ \boldsymbol{s}_2(t) \end{bmatrix}
$$

$$
= \begin{bmatrix} \boldsymbol{s}_1(t) \\ \tilde{\boldsymbol{x}}_2(t) \end{bmatrix}. \tag{23}
$$

As a result, the BSS problem of $\tilde{\boldsymbol{x}}_2(t) = \hat{\boldsymbol{W}}_{22}\boldsymbol{H}_2\boldsymbol{s}_2(t)$ has only to be solved. Our method avoids to calculate the whole separating matrix $\boldsymbol{W}_2$ by ICA. It implies a low computational cost. The proposed method is summarized in Table 1.

4   Simulation

For the sake of clarity of the proposed method, BSS computational simulations were conducted on a PC (Core2 Duo E4300, 1.0GB RAM) using FastICA algorithm [9] implemented on MATLAB. Speech signals were used as source signals. The number of initial sources n_1 was four and the number of additional sources n_2 was varied from one to three. The number of sensors m was seven and the mixed signals were generated through a mixing matrix. The coefficients of the mixing matrix were set randomly. We measured the processing time and the separation performance in order to evaluate the proposed method and the conventional method, which estimates a new separating matrix without any initialization. As a performance measure, signal to interference ratio (SIR) was calculated as follows:

$$
\text{SIR} = \frac{1}{n_1 + n_2} \sum_{i=1}^{n_1+n_2} 10 \log_{10} \frac{\sum_t y_{i,s_j}^2(t)}{\sum_{k \neq j} \sum_t y_{i,s_k}^2(t)}, \tag{24}
$$

where $y_{i,s_j}(t)$ and $y_{i,s_k}(t)$ are ith separated signals which are contributed by a certain source $s_j(t)$ and an interfering source $s_k(t)$, respectively. The results of 100 trials are shown. Fig. 3 (a) illustrates the processing time varying the number of the new sources. It is clear that the processing time using the proposed

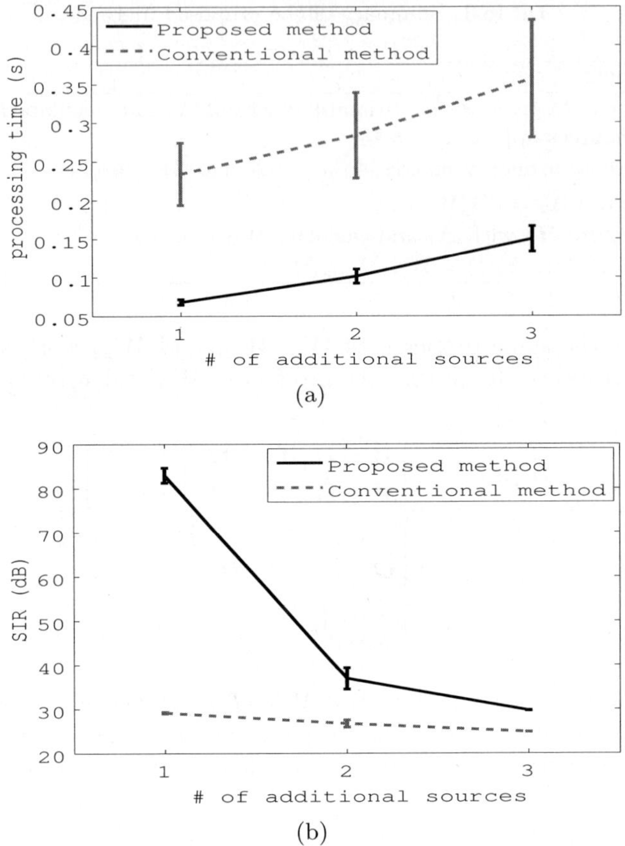

Fig. 3. The performance of the proposed method and the conventional method varying the number of additional sources. (a) The averaged processing time with standard deviation. (b) The averaged SIR with standard deviation.

method is significantly smaller than the conventional one. Our concern lies in the fact to estimate as $n_2 \times n_2$ separating matrix, instead of the conventional method that estimates $(n_1 + n_2) \times m$ separating matrix. Fig. 3 (b) depicts the separation performance. It is shown that our method outperforms the conventional method since the blockers work efficiently. Furthermore the conventional method caused permutation problems due to re-estimation of the separating matrix. The output channels of initial sources were different from those obtained by initial matrix, while using the proposed method the initial sources $s_1(t)$ are given in the same order despite the appearance of new sources.

5   Discussion

The problem of detecting the number of active sources is very important for BSS and have been discussed by many authors [10,11,12]. Although some problems need to be solved, for instance when we have additional sources that appear after estimation of the separating matrix. In this research we proposed a new method that is based on the number of souces known a priori and the number of the dominant eigenvalues of the covariance matrix that can be solved straightforward using the well known FastICA algorithm. The highlight in this problem is to determine the sources dimension that is not solved easily by any BSS algorithm.

Until now we discussed the separation in the case when new sources appear. In addidion, the separation with a disappearance can be solved by a simple procedure based on the columns of the mixing matrix. Moreover, if a disappearance is detected the output energy become zero, which make the algorithm identify the vanished sources. Consequently, the corresponding columns of the vanished sources are removed from the mixing matrix, which was estimated before the disappearance, resulting in a new mixing matrix. Finally a new separating matrix is given as a pseudo inverse of the mixing matrix.

6 Conclusion and Future Works

In this manuscript we have proposed a scheme to separate mixed signals in the situation of new sources appearing. Utilizing the covariance matrix of the mixed signals, blockers of the initial sources and the additional sources can be obtained. As a result, blind separation of the new sources is only needed. Thus the computational load can be reduced compared with the conventional method. Through a computer simulation validity of the proposed method is shown.

Assuming that the matrix $M = C_{s_2} H_2^T \tilde{W}_{22}^T$ is nonsingular, namely $\tilde{W}_{22} H_2$ is also regular. To obtain $\tilde{W}_{22}$ an arbitrary matrix A_2 is used, further investigation about the way of choosing A_2 is needed such that $\tilde{W}_{22} H_2 = \{P_1 A_2\}^\dagger H_2$ is full rank.

The next goal is the extension of the proposed method to convolutive mixture to achieve blind separation of audio signals.

References

1. Hyvärinen, A., Karhunen, J., Oja, E.: Independent Component Analysis. John Wiley & Sons, Inc., Chichester (2001)
2. Lee, T.W.: Independent Component Analysis. Kluwer Academic Publishers, Dordrecht (1998)
3. Ye, J.M., Zhu, X.L., Zhang, X.D.: Adaptive blind separation with an unknown number of sources. Neural Computation 16, 1641–1660 (2004)
4. Ito, M., Takeuchi, Y., Matsumoto, T., Kudo, H., Kawamoto, M., Mukai, T., Ohnishi, N.: Moving-source separation using directional microphones. In: Proceedings of the 2nd International Symposium on Signal Processing and Information Technology, pp. 523–526 (2002)
5. Mukai, R., Sawada, H., Araki, S., Makino, S.: Blind source separation for moving speech signals using blockwise ica and residual crosstalk subtraction. IEICE Trans. Fundamentals E87-A(8), 1941–1948 (2004)
6. Golub, G.H., Van Loan, C.F.: Matrix Computaions, 3rd edn. Johns Hopkins (1996)

7. Inouye, Y., Liu, R.W.: A system-theoretic foundation for blind equalization of an fir mimo channel system. IEEE Trans. Circuits and Systems I: Fundamental Theory and Applications 49(4), 425–436 (2002)
8. Rao, C.R., Mitra, S.K.: Generalized Inverse of Matrices and its Applications. John Wiley & Sons, Chichester (1971)
9. Hyvärinen, A.: Fast and robust fixed-point algorithms for independent component analysis. IEEE Trans. on Neural Networks 10(3), 626–634 (1999)
10. Wax, M., Kailath, T.: Detection of signals by information theoretic criteria. IEEE Trans. Acoustics, Speech and Signal Processing 33, 387–392 (1985)
11. Sawada, H., Mukai, R., Araki, S., Makino, S.: Estimating the number of sources using independent component analysis. Acoustical Science and Technology 26(5), 450–452 (2005)
12. Olsson, R.K., Hansen, L.K.: Estimating the number of sources in a noisy convolutive mixture using bic. In: Proceedings of the 5th International Conference on Independent Component Analysis and Blind Signal Separation, pp. 618–625 (2004)

Blind Image Separation Using Nonnegative Matrix Factorization with Gibbs Smoothing

Rafal Zdunek* and Andrzej Cichocki**

RIKEN Brain Science Institute, Wako-shi, Saitama, Japan
zdunek@brain.riken.jp

Abstract. Nonnegative Matrix Factorization (NMF) has already found many applications in image processing and data analysis, including classification, clustering, feature extraction, pattern recognition, and blind image separation. In the paper, we extend the selected NMF algorithms by taking into account local smoothness properties of source images. Our modifications are related with incorporation of the Gibbs prior, which is well-known in many tomographic image reconstruction applications, to a underlying blind image separation model. The numerical results demonstrate the improved performance of the proposed methods in comparison to the standard NMF algorithms.

1 Introduction

Nonnegative Matrix Factorization (NMF) [1] attempts to recover hidden nonnegative structures or patterns from usually redundant data. This technique has been successfully applied in many applications, e.g. in data analysis (pattern recognition, segmentation, clustering, dimensionality reduction) [1, 2, 3, 4, 5, 6, 7, 8, 9, 10, 11, 12], signal and image processing (blind source separation, spectra recovering) [13, 14], language modeling, text analysis [15, 16], music transcription [4, 17], or neuro-biology (gene separation, EEG signal analysis) [18, 19, 20].

NMF decomposes the data matrix $\boldsymbol{Y} = [y_{ik}] \in \mathbb{R}^{I \times K}$ as a product of two nonnegative matrices $\boldsymbol{A} = [a_{ij}] \in \mathbb{R}^{I \times J}$ and $\boldsymbol{X} = [x_{jk}] \in \mathbb{R}^{J \times K}$, i.e.

$$\boldsymbol{Y} = \boldsymbol{AX}, \tag{1}$$

where $\forall i, j, k : a_{ij} \geq 0, \ x_{jk} \geq 0$.

Depending on an application, the hidden components may have different interpretation. For example, Lee and Seung in [1] introduced NMF as a method to decompose an image (face) into parts-based representations (parts reminiscent of features such as lips, eyes, nose, etc.). In NMF with application to Blind Source Separation (BSS) [21], the matrix $\boldsymbol{Y}$ represents the observed mixed (superposed)

---

* Dr. R. Zdunek is also with Institute of Telecommunications, Teleinformatics and Acoustics, Wroclaw University of Technology, Poland.

** Dr. A. Cichocki is also with Systems Research Institute (SRI), Polish Academy of Science (PAN), Warsaw University of Technology, Dept. of EE, Warsaw, Poland.

M. Ishikawa et al. (Eds.): ICONIP 2007, Part II, LNCS 4985, pp. 519–528, 2008.

images, A is a mixing operator, and X is a matrix of true source images. Each row of Y or X is a 1D image representation, where I is a number of observed mixed images and J is a number of hidden (source) components. The 1D representation of a 2D image $\tilde{X} = [\tilde{x}_{mn}] \in \mathbb{R}^{M \times N}$ is obtained as lexicographical ordering of the pixels, i.e. $\tilde{x} = [\tilde{x}_{11}, \tilde{x}_{12}, \ldots, \tilde{x}_{1N}, \tilde{x}_{21}, \ldots, \tilde{x}_{MN}]^T \in \mathbb{R}^{MN}$. The index k denotes the pixel's position in a 1D image representation, and K is a total number of pixels. In BSS, we usually have $K >> I \geq J$, and J is known or can be relatively easily estimated using SVD.

Our objective is to estimate the mixing matrix A and sources X subject to nonnegativity constraints of all the entries, given Y and possibly the prior knowledge on the nature of the true images to be estimated or on a statistical distribution of noisy disturbances.

The basic approach to NMF is the alternating minimization of the specific cost function $D(Y \| AX)$ that measures the distance between Y and AX. Lee and Seung [1] were the first who proposed two types of NMF algorithms. One minimizes the Euclidean distance, which is optimal for a Gaussian distributed additive noise, and the other for minimization of the Kullback-Leibler divergence, which is suitable for a Poisson distributed noise. The NMF algorithms that are optimal for many other distribution of additive noise can be found, e.g. in [22, 21, 23].

Unfortunately, the alternating minimization does not provide a unique solution, and often some additional constraints must be imposed to select a solution that is close to the true one. For example, finding such $P > 0$ for which $P^{-1} > 0$, we have: $AX = (AP^{-1})(PX) = \tilde{A}\tilde{X} = Y$, where $A \neq \tilde{A}$ and $X \neq \tilde{X}$. Obviously, P could be any permutation matrix. Also, the alternating minimization is not convex with respect to both sets of the arguments $\{A, X\}$, even though the cost function is expressed by a quadratic function. To relax the ambiguity and non-convexity effects, the common approach is to incorporate some penalty terms to the cost function, which adequately regularizes the solution or restricts a set of all admissible solutions. Such regularization has been widely discussed in the literature with respect to various criteria for selection of the desired solution. The penalty terms can enforce sparsity, smoothness, continuity, closure, unimodality, orthogonality, or local rank-selectivity. A widely-used approach in many NMF applications is to apply sparsity constraints [24, 22, 25, 26, 27].

In the paper, we apply the penalty term that enforces local smoothness in the estimated 2D images. This case may take place in many BSS applications with locally smooth features. This paper is motivated by the preliminary results obtained in [28], where we have proposed the NMF algorithm for blind separation of locally smooth nonnegative signals.

The penalty term, which we use in the paper, is motivated by the Markov Random Field (MRF) models that are widely applied in image reconstruction. Such models, which are often expressed by the Gibbs prior, determine local roughness (smoothness) in the analyzed image with consideration of pair-wise interactions among adjacent pixels in a given neighborhood of a singe pixel. Thus, a total smoothness in an image can be expressed by a joint Gibbs distribution with a nonlinear energy function. In our approach, we use the Green's function for measuring strength of the pair-wise pixel interactions. Using a Bayesian framework, we get the Gibbs regularized Euclidean cost function that is minimized with a gradient descent alternating minimization technique subject to nonnegativity constrains that can be imposed in many ways. One of them is achieved with standard multiplicative updates that were used, e.g. by Lee and Seung [1]. Another approach is to apply the projected Alternating Least Squares (ALS) algorithms [27], which are generally more efficient to NMF problems than standard multiplicative algorithms.

2   Gibbs Regularized Algorithms

Since in practice a Gaussian noise occurs the most often in BSS applications, we restrict our considerations only to the following joint multivariate normal likelihood model:

$$p(\boldsymbol{Y}|\boldsymbol{X}) \propto \exp\left\{-\frac{1}{2}\operatorname{tr}\{(\boldsymbol{Y} - \boldsymbol{AX})^T \boldsymbol{\Sigma}^{-1}(\boldsymbol{Y} - \boldsymbol{AX})\}\right\}, \qquad (2)$$

where each sample $\boldsymbol{n}_k$ from the residual (noise) matrix $\boldsymbol{N} = \boldsymbol{Y} - \boldsymbol{AX} = [\boldsymbol{n}_1, \ldots, \boldsymbol{n}_K]$ is assumed to follow the same statistics with the covariance matrix $\boldsymbol{\Sigma}$.

Let us assume the prior information on total smoothness of the estimated images is given by the following Gibbs distribution

$$p(\boldsymbol{X}) = \frac{1}{Z}\exp\left\{-\alpha U(\boldsymbol{X})\right\}, \qquad (3)$$

where Z is a partition function, α is a regularization parameter, and $U(\boldsymbol{X})$ is a total energy function that measures the total roughness in the object of interest. The function $U(\boldsymbol{X})$ is often formulated with respect to the Markov Random Field (MRF) model that is commonly used in image reconstruction to enforce local smoothing.

The prior can be incorporated into the likelihood function with the Bayesian framework:

$$p(\boldsymbol{X}|\boldsymbol{Y}) = \frac{p(\boldsymbol{Y}|\boldsymbol{X})p(\boldsymbol{X})}{p(\boldsymbol{Y})}, \qquad (4)$$

where $p(\boldsymbol{Y})$ is a marginal likelihood function. Thus the Gibbs regularized Euclidean cost function can be expressed in the form:

$$\Psi = -2\ln p(\boldsymbol{X}|\boldsymbol{Y}) = ||\boldsymbol{Y} - \boldsymbol{AX}||_F^2 + 2\alpha U(\boldsymbol{X}) + c, \qquad (5)$$

where c is a constant.

The stationary points of Ψ can be derived from the gradients of Ψ with respect to $\boldsymbol{X}$ and $\boldsymbol{A}$. Thus:

$$\nabla_X \Psi = 2\boldsymbol{A}^T(\boldsymbol{AX} - \boldsymbol{Y}) + 2\alpha \nabla_X U(\boldsymbol{X}) \equiv 0, \qquad (6)$$

$$\nabla_A \Psi = (\boldsymbol{AX} - \boldsymbol{Y})\boldsymbol{X}^T \equiv 0. \qquad (7)$$

2.1 NMF Algorithms

From (6)–(7), we have:

$$\frac{[\boldsymbol{A}^T\boldsymbol{Y} - \alpha\nabla_X U(\boldsymbol{X})]_{jk}}{[\boldsymbol{A}^T\boldsymbol{A}\boldsymbol{X}]_{jk}} = 1, \quad \frac{[\boldsymbol{Y}\boldsymbol{X}^T]_{ij}}{[\boldsymbol{A}\boldsymbol{X}\boldsymbol{X}^T]_{ij}} = 1. \tag{8}$$

Using multiplicative updates, we get the Gibbs regularized multiplicative NMF algorithm:

$$x_{jk} \leftarrow x_{jk} \frac{\left[[\boldsymbol{A}^T\boldsymbol{Y}]_{jk} - \alpha[\nabla_X U(\boldsymbol{X})]_{jk}\right]_\varepsilon}{[\boldsymbol{A}^T\boldsymbol{A}\boldsymbol{X}]_{jk}}, \tag{9}$$

$$a_{ij} \leftarrow a_{ij} \frac{[\boldsymbol{Y}\boldsymbol{X}^T]_{ij}}{[\boldsymbol{A}\boldsymbol{X}\boldsymbol{X}^T]_{ij}}, \quad a_{ij} \leftarrow \frac{a_{ij}}{\sum_{j=1}^J a_{ij}}, \tag{10}$$

where $[x]_\varepsilon = \max\{\varepsilon, x\}$ is a nonlinear operator for projection onto a positive orthant (subspace $\mathbb{R}_+$) with small ε (*eps*). Typically, $\varepsilon = 10^{-16}$. The normalization in (10) additionally constrains the basis vectors to a unit l_1-norm, which relaxes the intrinsic scaling ambiguity in NMF.

It is easy to notice that for $\alpha = 0$ in (9), the updating rules (9)–(10) simplify to the standard Lee-Seung algorithm that minimizes the Euclidean distance (Frobenius norm).

The algorithm (9)–(10) can also be improved by replacing the step (10) with a more exact updating rule. It is well-known that multiplicative algorithms are slowly-convergent, and the system of linear equations to be solved in the step (10) is highly over-determined. Hence, the update (10) can be successfully replaced with the projected Moore-Penrose pseudo-inverse [27] or the quasi-Newton approach [26]. For simplicity, we consider only the former approach, thus from (7) we have

$$\boldsymbol{A} \leftarrow \left[\boldsymbol{Y}\boldsymbol{X}^T(\boldsymbol{X}\boldsymbol{X}^T)\right]_\varepsilon. \tag{11}$$

2.2 Markov Random Field Model

MRF models have been widely applied in many image reconstruction applications, especially in tomographic imaging. In our application, MRF models motives the definition of the total energy function in the Gibbs prior (3). Thus

$$U(\boldsymbol{X}) = \sum_{j=1}^J \sum_{k=1}^K \sum_{l\in S_k} w_{kl}\psi\left(x_{jk} - x_{jl}, \delta\right), \tag{12}$$

where S_k is a set of pixels in the neighborhood of the k-th pixel, w_{kl} is a weighting factor, δ is a scaling factor, and $\psi(\xi, \delta)$ is some potential function of ξ, which can take various forms. Exemplary potential functions are listed in Table 1.

Since the Green's function [34] satisfies all the properties mentioned in [35], i.e. it is nonnegative, even, 0 at $\xi = 0$, strictly increasing for $\xi > 0$, unbounded,

Table 1. Potential functions

Author(s) (Name)	Reference	Functions: $V(\xi, \delta)$
(Gaussian)		$\left(\dfrac{\xi}{\delta}\right)^2$
Besag (Laplacian)	[29]	$\left\lvert\dfrac{\xi}{\delta}\right\rvert$
Hebert and Leahy	[30]	$\delta \log\left[1 + (\frac{\xi}{\delta})^2\right]$
Geman and McClure	[31]	$\dfrac{16}{3\sqrt{3}}\dfrac{(\xi/\delta)^2}{(1 + (\xi/\delta)^2)}$
Geman and Reynolds	[32]	$\dfrac{\lvert\xi/\delta\rvert}{1 + \lvert\xi/\delta\rvert}$
Stevenson and Delp (Hubert)	[33]	$\min\{\lvert\frac{\xi}{\delta}\rvert^2, 2\lvert\frac{\xi}{\delta}\rvert - 1\}$
Green	[34]	$\delta \log[\cosh(\xi/\delta)]$

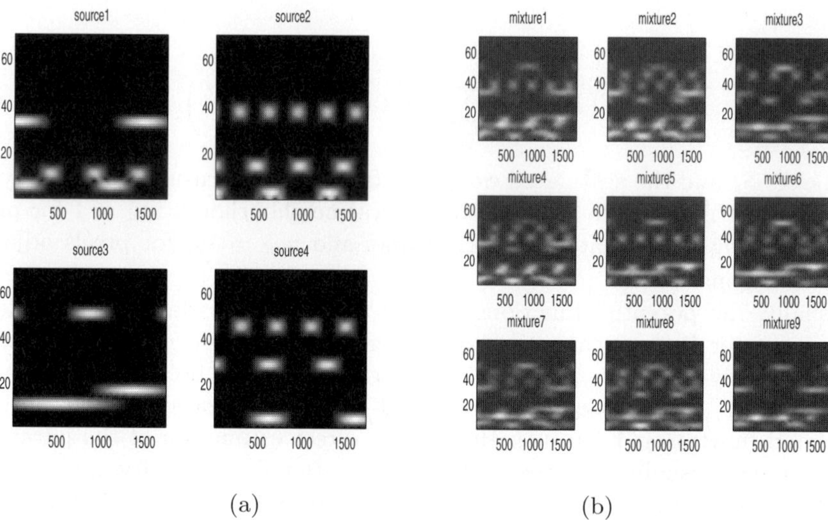

Fig. 1. (a) Original 4 smooth source images; (b) Observed 9 very noisy mixed images with $SNR = 10[\text{dB}]$)

convex, and has bounded first-derivative, we decided to select this function to our tests. Thus

$$\psi(\xi, \delta) = \delta \log[\cosh(\xi/\delta)], \tag{13}$$

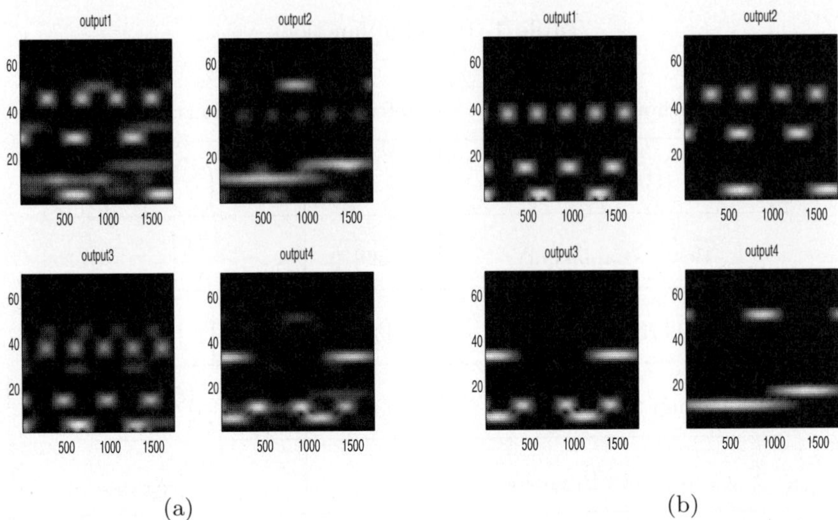

(a)   (b)

Fig. 2. Estimated sources with: (a) standard multiplicative (Lee-Seung) NMF algorithm (9)–(10) at $\alpha = 0$ ($SIR_X = 7.1, 11.7, 12.6, 13.1$[dB], $SIR_A = 12.3, 7.6, 14.8, 13.3$[dB] respectively); (b) Gibbs regularized algorithm given by (9)–(10) with parameters $\alpha = 0.2$ and $\delta = 10^{-3}$ ($SIR_X = 18.5, 18.3, 17.9, 18$[dB], $SIR_A = 29.6, 39.7, 27.4, 31.2$[dB], respectively)

which leads to

$$[\nabla_X U(\boldsymbol{X})]_{jk} = \sum_{l \in S_k} w_{kl} \tanh\left(\frac{x_{jk} - x_{jl}}{\delta}\right). \tag{14}$$

The set S_k and the associated weighting factors w_{kl} are usually defined by the MRF model. Taking into account the nearest neighborhood, $w_{kl} = 1$ for pixels adjacent along a horizontal or vertical line, and $w_{kl} = \frac{1}{\sqrt{2}}$ for pixels adjacent along a diagonal line.

Usually, the potential functions in (12) are parameter-dependent. At least, one parameter (in our case, the parameter δ) must be set up in advance, or simultaneously with the estimation. Generally, this can be regarded as a hyperparameter, and consequently estimated with maximization of the marginal likelihood function $p(\boldsymbol{Y})$ in (4). However, a direct estimation of the parameter from the data usually involves a high computational complexity, and it is not absolutely needed if we operate on one class of data for which preliminary simulations can be performed. We notice that for our class of data, the parameter has a very slight impact on the estimation in quite a wide range of its values. Thus, we set $\delta = 10^{-3}$ in all the tests in the paper.

3   Numerical Tests

The proposed algorithms have been extensively tested for various sets of the parameters (α and δ), and the algorithms are compared with the standard NMF

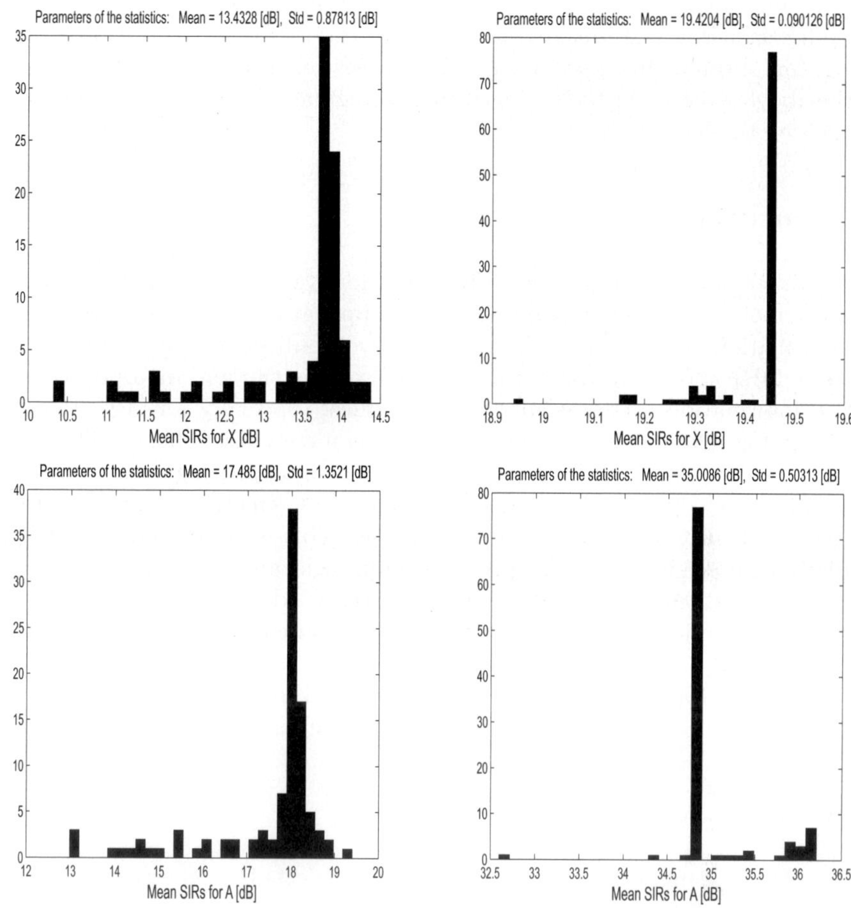

Fig. 3. Histograms from 100 mean-SIR samples generated with the following algorithms: (left) standard multiplicative (Lee-Seung) NMF algorithm; (right) Gibbs regularized algorithm; (top) estimation of X (sources); (bottom) estimation of columns in mixing matrix A

algorithm. For the numerical tests we have used the benchmark of 4 smooth original images (Fig. 1(a)) which are mixed with the dense random mixing matrix $A \in \mathbb{R}^{9 \times 4}$ uniformly distributed (cond(A) = 4.11). The mixtures are then corrupted with the Gaussian noise of $SNR = 10[\mathrm{dB}]$. Fig. 1(b) presents the noisy mixed images. The estimated images with the standard Lee-Seung algorithm (the updates (9)–(10) at $\alpha = 0$) are shown in Fig. 2(a). The results obtained with the improved Gibbs regularized NMF algorithm given by (9)–(10) are illustrated in Fig. 2(b) for $\alpha = 0.2$. The updating process for each algorithm has been terminated after 1000 alternating steps. The estimations are also quantitatively assessed with the standard Signal-to-Interference Ratio (SNR).

The same algorithms are also tested with the Monte Carlo (MC) analysis where for each run the initial conditions are randomly set. Fig. 3 presents the histograms obtained from 100 mean-SIR samples generated with the MC analysis for the above-mentioned NMF algorithms: unregularized version (left) and Gibbs regularized version (right).

4   Conclusions

In the paper, we derived the new algorithm for NMF, which may be useful for estimation of locally smooth images in BSS applications. The algorithm exploits the information on pair-wise interactions between adjacent pixels, which is motivated by MRF models in tomographic image reconstruction. Incorporating such a prior information to the NMF updating rules (especially for X) is also very profitable for relaxing NMF ambiguity and non-convexity effects. The numerical results demonstrate the robustness of the proposed algorithm, especially for highly noisy data. The algorithm is much less sensitive to initialization in comparison to the standard NMF algorithms. This is confirmed with the MC simulations shown in Fig. 3. The proposed approach can be further extended with additional constraints or different updating rules. Also, another extension may concern the application of data-driven hyperparameter estimation techniques, especially for the regularization parameter.

The proposed algorithm has been implemented in Matlab Toolbox for Nonnegative Matrix Factorization: NMFLAB for Signal and Image Processing [36].

References

1. Lee, D.D., Seung, H.S.: Learning the parts of objects by nonnegative matrix factorization. Nature 401, 788–791 (1999)
2. Guillamet, D., Vitrià, J., Schiele, B.: Introducing a weighted nonnegative matrix factorization for image classification. Pattern Recognition Letters 24, 2447–2454 (2003)
3. Ahn, J.H., Kim, S., Oh, J.H., Choi, S.: Multiple nonnegative-matrix factorization of dynamic PET images. In: ACCV, p. 5 (2004)
4. Lee, J.S., Lee, D.D., Choi, S., Lee, D.S.: Application of nonnegative matrix factorization to dynamic positron emission tomography. In: 3rd International Conference on Independent Component Analysis and Blind Signal Separation, San Diego, CA, pp. 556–562 (2001)
5. Li, H., Adali, T., Wang, W., D.E.: Non-negative matrix factorization with orthogonality constraints for chemical agent detection in Raman spectra. In: IEEE Workshop on Machine Learning for Signal Processing, Mystic, USA (2005)
6. Carmona-Saez, P., Pascual-Marqui, R.D., Tirado, F., Carazo, J.M., Pascual-Montano, A.: Biclustering of gene expression data by non-smooth non-negative matrix factorization. BMC Bioinformatics 7 (2006)
7. Pascual-Montano, A., Carazo, J.M., Kochi, K., Lehmean, D., Pacual-Marqui, R.: Nonsmooth nonnegative matrix factorization (nsNMF). IEEE Trans. Pattern Analysis and Machine Intelligence 28, 403–415 (2006)

8. Shahnaz, F., Berry, M., Pauca, P., Plemmons, R.: Document clustering using non-negative matrix factorization. Journal on Information Processing and Management 42, 373–386 (2006)

9. Okun, O., Priisalu, H.: Fast nonnegative matrix factorization and its application for protein fold recognition. EURASIP Journal on Applied Signal Processing Article ID 71817, 8 (2006)

10. Wang, Y., Jia, Y., Hu, C., Turk, M.: Non-negative matrix factorization framework for face recognition. International Journal of Pattern Recognition and Artificial Intelligence 19, 495–511 (2005)

11. Liu, W., Zheng, N.: Non-negative matrix factorization based methods for object recognition. Pattern Recognition Letters 25, 893–897 (2004)

12. Spratling, M.W.: Learning image components for object recognition. Journal of Machine Learning Research 7, 793–815 (2006)

13. Sajda, P., Du, S., Brown, T.R., Shungu, R.S.D.C., Mao, X., Parra, L.C.: Nonnegative matrix factorization for rapid recovery of constituent spectra in magnetic resonance chemical shift imaging of the brain. IEEE Trans. Medical Imaging 23, 1453–1465 (2004)

14. Cichocki, A., Zdunek, R., Amari, S.: New algorithms for non-negative matrix factorization in applications to blind source separation. In: Proc. IEEE International Conference on Acoustics, Speech, and Signal Processing, ICASSP2006, Toulouse, France, pp. 621–624 (2006)

15. Dhillon, I.S., Modha, D.M.: Concept decompositions for large sparse text data using clustering. Machine Learning J. 42, 143–175 (2001)

16. Berry, M., Browne, M., Langville, A., Pauca, P., Plemmons, R.: Algorithms and applications for approximate nonnegative matrix factorization. Computational Statistics and Data Analysis 52, 55–173 (2007)

17. Cho, Y.C., Choi, S.: Nonnegative features of spectro-temporal sounds for classification. Pattern Recognition Letters 26, 1327–1336 (2005)

18. Brunet, J.P., Tamayo, P., Golub, T.R., Mesirov, J.P.: Metagenes and molecular pattern discovery using matrix factorization. In: PNAS, vol. 101, pp. 4164–4169 (2000)

19. Rao, N., Shepherd, S.J., Yao, D.: Extracting characteristic patterns from genome – wide expression data by non-negative matrix factorization. In: Proc. of the 2004 IEEE Computational Systems Bioinformatics Conference (CSB 2004), Stanford, CA (2004)

20. Rutkowski, T.M., Zdunek, R., Cichocki, A.: Multichannel EEG brain activity pattern analysis in time-frequency domain with nonnegative matrix factorization support. International Congress Series 8611, 266–269 (2007)

21. Cichocki, A., Zdunek, R., Amari, S.: Csiszar's divergences for non-negative matrix factorization: Family of new algorithms. In: Rosca, J.P., Erdogmus, D., Príncipe, J.C., Haykin, S. (eds.) ICA 2006. LNCS, vol. 3889, pp. 32–39. Springer, Heidelberg (2006)

22. Dhillon, I., Sra, S.: Generalized nonnegative matrix approximations with Bregman divergences. In: Neural Information Proc. Systems, Vancouver, Canada, pp. 283–290 (2005)

23. Kompass, R.: A generalized divergence measure for nonnegative matrix factorization. Neural Computation 19, 780–791 (2006)

24. Hoyer, P.O.: Non-negative matrix factorization with sparseness constraints. Journal of Machine Learning Research 5, 1457–1469 (2004)

25. Kreutz-Delgado, K., Murray, J.F., Rao, B.D., Engan, K., Lee, T.W., Sejnowski, T.J.: Dictionary learning algorithms for sparse representation. Neural Computation 15, 349–396 (2003)
26. Zdunek, R., Cichocki, A.: Nonnegative matrix factorization with constrained second-order optimization. Signal Processing 87, 1904–1916 (2007)
27. Cichocki, A., Zdunek, R.: Regularized alternating least squares algorithms for nonnegative matrix/tensor factorizations. In: Liu, D., Fei, S., Hou, Z., Zhang, H., Sun, C. (eds.) ISNN 2007. LNCS, vol. 4493, pp. 793–802. Springer, Heidelberg (2007)
28. Zdunek, R., Cichocki, A.: Gibbs regularized nonnegative matrix factorization for blind separation of locally smooth signals. In: 15th IEEE International Workshop on Nonlinear Dynamics of Electronic Systems (NDES 2007), Tokushima, Japan, pp. 317–320 (2007)
29. Besag, J.: Toward Bayesian image analysis. J. Appl. Stat. 16, 395–407 (1989)
30. Hebert, T., Leahy, R.: A generalized EM algorithm for 3-D Bayesian reconstruction from Poisson data using Gibbs priors. IEEE Transactions on Medical Imaging 8, 194–202 (1989)
31. Geman, S., McClure, D.: Statistical methods for tomographic image reconstruction. Bull. Int. Stat. Inst. LII-4, 5–21 (1987)
32. Geman, S., Reynolds, G.: Constrained parameters and the recovery of discontinuities. IEEE Trans. Pattern Anal. Machine Intell. 14, 367–383 (1992)
33. Stevenson, R., Delp, E.: Fitting curves with discontinuities. In: Proc. 1-st Int. Workshop on Robust Computer Vision, Seattle, Wash., USA (1990)
34. Green, P.J.: Bayesian reconstruction from emission tomography data using a modified EM algorithm. IEEE Trans. Medical Imaging 9, 84–93 (1990)
35. Lange, K., Carson, R.: EM reconstruction algorithms for emission and transmission tomography. J. Comp. Assisted Tomo. 8, 306–316 (1984)
36. Cichocki, A., Zdunek, R.: NMFLAB for Signal and Image Processing. Technical report, Laboratory for Advanced Brain Signal Processing, BSI, RIKEN, Saitama, Japan (2006)

Diagnosis of Lung Nodule Using Independent Component Analysis in Computerized Tomography Images

Cristiane C.S. da Silva, Daniel Duarte Costa, Aristófanes Corrêa Silva, and Allan Kardec Barros

Federal University of Maranhão - UFMA
Av. dos Portugueses, SN, Campus do Bacanga, Bacanga
65085-580, São Luís, MA, Brazil
cristianecristina@yahoo.com.br,
danieldc82@gmail.com,
ari@dee.ufma.br,
akbarros@ieee.org

Abstract. This paper analyzes the application of Independent Component Analysis to the characterization of lung nodules as malignant or benign in computerized tomography images. The characterization method is based on a process that verifies which combination of measures, from the proposed measures, has been best able to discriminate between the benign and malignant nodules using Support Vector Machine. In order to verify this application we also describe tests that were carried out using a sample of 38 nodules: 29 benign and 9 malignant. The methodology reaches 100% of Specificity, 98.34% of Sensitivity and 96.66% of accuracy. Thus, preliminary results of this approach are very promising in contributing to pulmonary nodules diagnosis, but it will be necessary to test it in larger series and to make associations with other quantitative imaging methods in order to improve global performance.

Keywords: Lung Nodule Diagnosis, Independent Component Analysis, Support Vector Machine, Texture Analisys.

1 Introduction

Lung cancer is a serious problem of public health in Europe, United States and many other countries around the world because it is becoming the cancer mortality leader for men and women . The disease is also known as one of the shortest survival among other malignancies [1]. The main problem of the solitary pulmonary nodule is the identification of its nature. Sometimes this is possible only with radiological findings that allow diagnosis of benignity like total, central, lamellar or popcorn calcification and high fat contents (hamartoma).

In spite of the gold standard diagnosis be the histological examination - normally obtained by invasive procedures - image methods and in special computerized tomography (CT) can aid diagnostic process in analyzing nodule's

M. Ishikawa et al. (Eds.): ICONIP 2007, Part II, LNCS 4985, pp. 529–538, 2008.

attributes [2]. Radiologic characteristics of benignity are well known and based in calcification or fat texture patterns which change the mean radiologic density out of range from soft tissues. Malignity doesn't have similar texture criteria and the diagnosis is normally suggested by a irregular shape associated to some clinical data, like tobacco's load. Recently, there is a renewed attention to quantify wash-in and washout after contrast injection to obtain a nodule characterization [3]. Unfortunately, small diameters and allergic reactions are limiting factors of these techniques. Even the most modern metabolic image method in clinical use that is the Positron Emission Tomography (PET) superposed to helical CT examination (PET - CT) with images acquisitions before and after 18-fluoro-deoxyglucose intravenous administration, also has important limitations represented by false positivity of some inflammatory processes and false negativity of small or indolent cancers [4], [5], [6].

Computer-Aided Diagnosis (CAD) systems have been developed to assist radiologists and other specialized physicians in the diagnostic setting like early detection of lung cancer in radiographs and CT images. These systems can provide a second opinion and will may be used as a first stage of radiologic interpretation in near future [7], [8]. On the other hands, there are numerous reports of qualitative morphologic CT data in medical literature, but there are relatively few reports of quantitative CT data and it seems that, in general, they are underutilized.

Some authors have been hypothesized that quantitative CT data derived from geometric and texture parameters may contribute to differential diagnosis between benign and malignant solitary pulmonary nodules, even without contrast utilization. McNitt-Gray et al. [9], [10] extracted measurements from nodule's shape, attenuation coefficient, attenuation distribution and texture. Kawata et al. [11] presented a method to characterize the internal structure of 3-D nodules using computerized tomography images' shape index and density to locally represent each voxel. Hadjiisk et al. [12] developed linear discriminant classifier to extract and analyze features from corresponding malignant and benign lung nodules on temporal pairs of CT scans.Marten and Engelke [13] give an overview of current CAD in lung nodule detection and volumetry and discuss their relative merits and limitations. Reeves et al. [14] presented methods for measuring the change in nodule size from two computed tomography image scans recorded at different times. Suzuki et al. developed a computer-aided diagnostic (CAD) scheme for distinction between benign and malignant nodules in LDCT scans by use of a massive training artificial neural network (MTANN). Silva et al. [15], [16] showed that geostatiscal functions as semivariogram, covariogram, correlogram and madogram or some indices of spatial autocorrelation as Moran's Index and Geary's Coefficient, supply good results to discriminate malignant from benign nodules.

Independent Component Analysis (ICA)is a widely used technique for audio, electrocardiogram, electromagnetic encephalogram signal processing. Campos et al. [17] applied ICA to extract texture features of digital mammographies, classifying those mammographies in benign, malignant and normal using

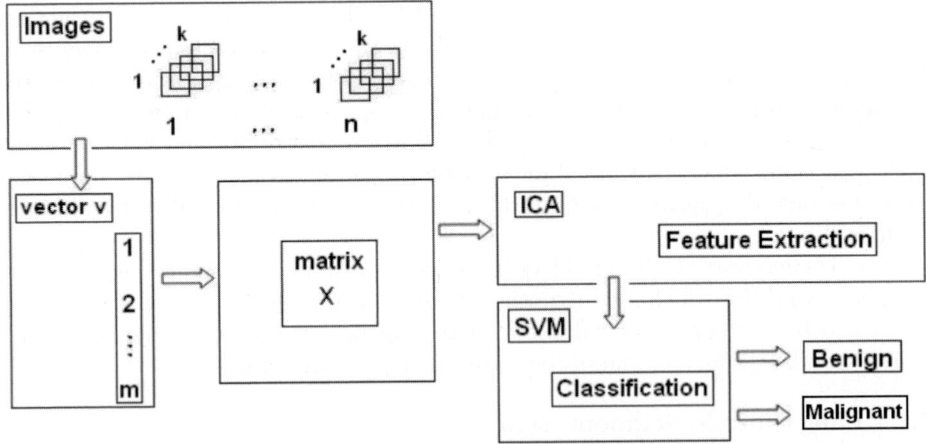

Fig. 1. The *Images* block presents the images of n segmented nodules of the k slices; the *vector* block consists in the storage k slices of the m voxels for each nodule in a column vector **v**. Next the **v** vector is rotated to a square matrix X. At the *ICA* block occurs the statistics characteristics extractions of the image using *ICA*. The *SVM* block makes the final diagnostic decision using *SVM*.

Neural Networks (Multilayered). The method obtained an average success rate of 97.83%, with 97.5% of specificity and 98% of sensitivity. Christoyianni et al [18] compared three : Gray Level Histogram Moments (GLHM), Spacial Gray Level Dependence Matrix (SGLD) and ICA, to extract significant characteristics from each image and, next, classify them using an ANN. According to the authors, ICA obtained the best performance, with 88% success when discriminating between normal and abnormal mammogram and 79.31% when discriminating normal, benign and malignant.

This work intends to apply Independent Component Analysis to three-dimensional pulmonary nodules imaged by CT. The main contribution and objective consist in observing the discriminatory power of this new method to reach distinction between benign and malignant nodules.

2   Methods

The diagram of the proposed method is showed in Figure 1. We describe below in details each block.

2.1   Image Acquisition

The images herein used were provided by the Fernandes Figueira Institute and the Pedro Ernesto University Hospital - both from Rio de Janeiro city - for a project of CAD tools development. They were obtained from different real patients, providing a total of 38 nodules (29 benign and 9 malignant).

The images were acquired with a Helical GE Pro Speed tomography under the following conditions: tube voltage 120 kVp, tube current 100 mA, image size 512×512 pixels, voxel size 0.67 × 0.67 × 1.0 mm. The images were quantized in 12 bits and stored in the DICOM format [19].

It is important to stand out that the CT exam was performed with no contrast injection, which may be clinically used in order to increase the diagnosis readiness but also carries some morbidity and occasional mortality by allergic complications.

It is also necessary to highlight that the nodules were previously diagnosed by physicians and that the final diagnosis of benignity or malignancy was posteriorly confirmed by histopathological exam of the surgical specimen or by radiologic 3-year stability, which explains the reduced size of our sample.

2.2   Lung Nodule Segmentation

In most cases, lung nodules are easy to be visually detected by physicians, since their shape and location are different from other lung structures. However, the nodule's voxel density is similar to that of other structures, such as blood vessels, which makes makes difficult any kind of automatic computer detection.

This happens especially when a nodule is adjacent to the pleura. For these reasons, we have used the 3D region-growing algorithm with voxel aggregation [20], which provides physicians greater interactivity and control over the segmentation and determination of required parameters (thresholds, initial and final slice, and seed).

A semi-automatic process of segmentation was performed using a Pulmonary Nodule Analysis System [21] called Bebúi. In this, beyond the 3D region-growing algorithm with voxel aggregation, two resources help and provide greater control in the segmentation procedure: the barrier and the eraser. The barrier is a cylinder placed around the nodule by the user with the purpose of restricting the region of interest and stopping the segmentation by voxel aggregation from invading other lung structures. The eraser is a resource of the system that allows physicians to erase undesired structures, either before or after segmentation, in order to avoid and correct segmentation errors [21].

2.3   Nodules Textural Characterization by ICA

Texture represents tonal variations in the spatial domain and determines the overall visual smoothness or coarseness of image features. It reveals important information about the structural arrangements of the objects in the image and their relationship to the environment. Consequently, texture analysis provides important discriminatory characteristics related to variability patterns of digital classifications.

Texture processing algorithms are usually divided into three major categories: structural, spectral and statistical [22]. Structural methods consider textures as repetitions of basic primitive patterns with a certain placement rule [23]. Spectral methods are based on the Fourier transform, analyzing the power spectrum [23]. The third and most important group in texture analysis is that of statistical methods, which are mainly based on statistical parameters such as the Spatial Gray Level Dependence Method-SGLDM, Gray Level Difference Method-GLDM, Gray Level Run Length Matrices-GLRLM [24], [25], [26].

In practice, some of the most usual terms used by interpreters to describe textures, such as smoothness or coarseness, bear a strong degree of subjectivity and do not always have a precise physical meaning. Analysts are capable of visually extracting textural information from images, but it is not easy for them to establish an objective model to describe this intuitive concept. For this reason, it has been necessary to develop quantitative approaches to obtain texture descriptors. Thus, in a statistical context, textures can be described in terms of an important conceptual component associated to pixels (or other units), their spatial association. This component is frequently analyzed at the global level by quantifying the aggregation or dispersion of the element in study [27].

In this work, the texture analysis is done by quantifying the spatial association between individual voxel values from the nodule image by applying the local form of the Independent Component Analysis (ICA) - which will be discussed in the following subsection.

Independent Component Analysis (ICA). Let us observe n linear mixtures $x_1, .., x_n$ of n independent components [28], such that:

$$x_j = a_{j1}s_1 + a_{j2}s_2 + ... + a_{jn}s_n \qquad j = 1, ..., n \qquad (1)$$

and that each mixture x_j, as well as each independent component s_i be a random variable, and a_j the coefficients (weights) of the linear mixture. For convenience, we will use the vectorial notation instead of the sum. In this way, we can re-write the Equation 1 as follows:

$$X = As \qquad (2)$$

The objective of this techniques is to recover the fonts through x_j, with no information about the proprieties of A. The statistic model is defined by Equation 2 is called Independent Component Analysis. This model describes the observed data by the mixture process of the s_i independent components, that can not be observed directly. It is necessary to estimate s_i and the mixture matrix A, which is also unknown, because the only vector observed is the vector x_j. The most used algorithm to estimate theses base functions from the mixture matrix is the FastICA.

FastICA Algorithm. The data matrix X is considered to be a linear combination of non-Gaussian (independent) components i.e., $X = A.\ S$ where columns of S contain the independent components and A is a linear mixing matrix. In short ICA attempts to un-mix the data by estimating an un-mixing matrix W, where $X.W = S$. Under this generative model of ICA, the measured X will tend to be more Gaussian than the source components S. Thus, in order to extract the independent components we search for an un-mixing matrix W that maximizes the non-gaussianity of the sources. In FastICA, non-gaussianity is measured using approximations to negentropy (J) which is more robust than kurtosis based measures and fast to compute [29]. The approximation takes the form

$$J_{G(y)} = |E_y\{G(y)\} - E_v\{G(v)\}|^P \tag{3}$$

where v is a standartized Gaussian randon variable, y is assumed to be normalized to unit variance, and the exponent is $p = 1.2$ typically.

2.4 Support Vector Machine

The Support Vector Machine (SVM) introduced by V. Vapnik in 1995 is a method to estimate the function classifying the data into two classes [30]. The basic idea of SVM is to construct a hyperplane as the decision surface in such a way that the margin of separation between positive and negative examples is maximized. The SVM term come from the fact that the points in the training set which are closest to the decision surface are called support vectors. SVM achieves this by the structural risk minimization principle that is based on the fact that the error rate of a learning machine on the test data is bounded by the sum of the training-error rate and a term that depends on the Vapnik-Chervonenkis (VC) dimension.

The process starts with a training set of points $x_i \in \Re^n, i = 1, 2, \cdots, l$ where each point x_i belongs to one of two classes identified by the label $y_i \in \{-1, 1\}$. The goal of maximum margin classification is to separate the two classes by a hyperplane such that the distance to the support vectors is maximized. The construction can be tinkled as follow: each point x in the input space is mapped to a point $z = \Phi(x)$ of a higher dimensional space, called the feature space, where the data are linearly separated by a hyperplane. The nature of data determines how the method proceeds. There is data that are linearly separable, nonlinearly separable and with impossible separation. This last case be still traced by the SVM. The key property in this construction is that we can write our decision function using a kernel function $K(x, y)$ which is given by the function $\Phi(x)$ that map the input space into the feature space. Such decision surface has the equation:

$$f(x) = \sum_{i=1}^{l} \alpha_i y_i K(x, x_i) + b \tag{4}$$

where $K(x, x_i) = \Phi(x).\Phi(x_i)$, and the coefficients α_i and the b are the solutions of a convex quadratic programming problem, namely

$$\begin{aligned} \min_{w,b,\xi} \quad & \tfrac{1}{2}w^T \cdot w + C \sum_{i=1}^{l} \xi_i \\ \text{subject to} \quad & y_i \left[w^T \cdot \phi(x_i) + b\right] \geq 1 - \xi_i \\ & \xi_i \geq 0. \end{aligned} \tag{5}$$

where $C > 0$ is a parameter to be chosen by the user, which corresponds to the strength of the penality errors and the ξ_i's are slack variables that penalize training errors.

Classification of a new data point x is performed by computing the sign of the right side of Equation 4. An important family of kernel functions is the Radial

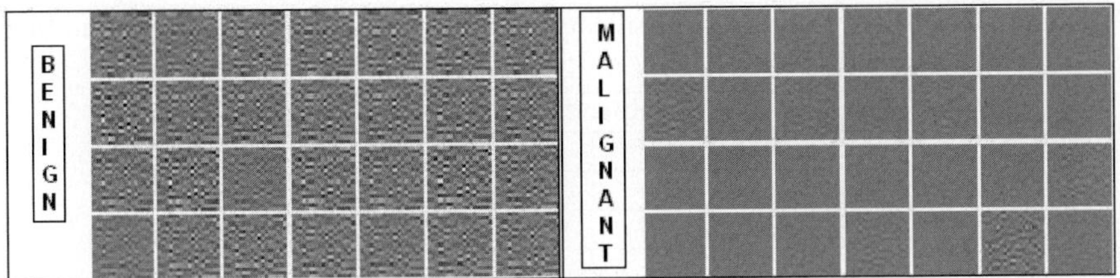

Fig. 2. Sample of base-images got from benign and malignant tissues

Basis Function, more commonly used for pattern recognition problems, which has been used in this paper, and is defined by:

$$K(x,y) = e^{-\gamma \|x-y\|^2} \tag{6}$$

where $\gamma > 0$ is a parameter that also is defined by the user.

2.5   Validation of the Classification Methods

In order to evaluate the classifier in respect to its differentiation ability, we have analyzed its sensitivity, specificity and accuracy. Sensitivity is defined by $TP/(TP + FN)$, specificity is defined by $TN/(TN + FP)$, and accuracy is defined by $(TP + TN)/(TP + TN + FP + FN)$, where TP is true-positive, TN is true-negative, FN is false-negative, and FP is false-positive. Herein, true-positive means Benign samples were correctly classified as Benign. The meaning of the others are analogous.

3   Results

As the size and the amount of slices used at each tomography are different, we store the voxels values of all slices in two unidimensional vectors v_1 and v_2, where v_1 e v_2 represents the benign and malignant cases respectively. Next, as the amount of (voxels) elements of vector v_1 is less than the (voxels) elements of vector v_2, where 21273 is the number of elements in v_1 and as the small square valor of 21273 is 145, we made v_1 and v_2 squared matrices with 145 dimension. These matrices represents the mixture matrix Equation 2, where each sample represents one line of matrix X and each collum corresponds to one weight status of the base function, thus, an input parameter of SVM. The algorithm used to make the extraction of the parameters through ICA was the FastICA.

Figure 2 shows 28 base images using the 145 base functions of the malignant and benign samples. It can be observed clearly the difference between the base images of each class.

As to apply the SVM classification technique, we use the libSVM [31] library, in which the chosen Kernel function was the Radial Basis Function (RBF). The best estimated values for the parameters (C e and γ) of the Kernel function

Table 1. Results of the SVM classification of the n benign or malignant nodules

Sensitivity (%)	Specificity (%)	accuracy (%)
100	100	100
98.6111	100	99.3103
98.6111	100	99.3103
95.8333	100	97.931
90.2778	100	95.1724
94.4444	100	97.2414
93.0556	100	96.5517
100	100	100
100	100	100
95.8333	100	97.931
96.6667	**100**	**98.3448**

were **2** and **0.001220703125** respectively. Table 1 shows the best results for classification between Benign and Malign ones. We performed 10 interactions with all 145 components, with 73 for training and 72 for tests randomly got. The last line of the Table 1 shows the average found between, sensitivity, specificity and accuracy, respectively.

4   Conclusion

This paper has presented Independent Component Analysis with the purpose of characterizing lung nodules as malignant or benign. The measures extracted from ICA were analyzed and had great discriminatory power, using SVM in order to make the classification. The methodology reaches 100% of Specificity, 98.34% of Sensitivity and 96.66% of accuracy. This numbers were obtained without contrast injection which has been clinically used to increase specificity and sensitivity but also carries some morbidity and mortality by allergic complications.

The number of studied nodules in our data set is too small to state definitive conclusions, but the preliminary results of this work are very encouraging, demonstrating that a SVM classifier using ICA to three-dimension sample data, can contribute to discriminate benign from malignant lung nodules on CT images.

In addition, due to the relatively small size of the existing CT lung nodule databases and the various CT imaging acquisition protocols, it is difficult to compare the diagnosis performance between the developed algorithms and others proposed in the literature.

References

1. Tarantino, A.B.: 38. In: Nódulo Solitário Do Pulmão, 4th edn., pp. 733–753. Guanabara Koogan, Rio de Janeiro (1997)
2. Ost, D., Fein, A.M., Feinsilver, S.H.: The solitary pulmonary nodule. N. Engl. J. Med. 25, 2535–2542 (2003)

3. Jeong, Y., Lee, K., Jeong, S., Chung, M., Shim, S., Kim, H., Kwon, O., Kim, S.: Solitary pulmonary nodule: characterization with combine wash-in and washout features of dynamic multidector row CT. Radiology 2, 675–683 (2005)
4. Gould, M.K.: Cost-effectiveness of alternative management strategies for patients with solitary pulmonary nodules. Ann. Intern. Med. 9, 724–735 (2003)
5. Pepe, G., Rosseti, C., Sironi, S., Landoni, G., Gianoli, L., Pastorino, U., Zannini, P., Mezzetti, M., Grimaldi, A., Galli, L., Messa, C., Fazio, F.: Patients with known or suspected lung cancer: evaluation of clinical management changes due to 18 F - deoxyglucose positron emission tomography (18 F - FDG PET) study. Nucl. Med. Commun. 9, 831–837 (2005)
6. Armato III, S.G., Giger, M.L., Moran, C.J., Blackburn, J.T., Doi, K., MacMahon, H.: Computerized detection of pulmonary nodules on CT scans. Radiographics 19, 1303–1311 (1999)
7. Kim, D.: Pulmonary nodule detection using chest ct images. Acta Radiologica, 252–257 (2003)
8. Delegacz, A., Lo, S., Choi, J., Xei, H., Freedman, M., Mun, S.: Three-dimensional visualization system as an aid for lung cancer diagnosis. In: SPIE Proc. Med., vol. 3976 (2000)
9. McNitt-Gray, M.F., Hart, E.M., Wyckoff, N., Sayre, J.W., Goldin, J.G., Aberle, D.R.: A pattern classification approach to characterizing solitary pulmonary nodules imaged on high resolution CT: Preliminary results. Medical Physics 26, 880–888 (1999)
10. McNitt-Gray, M.F., Hart, E.M., Wyckoff, N., Sayre, J.W., Goldin, J.G., Aberle, D.R.: The effects of co-occurrence matrix based texture parameters on the classification of solitary pulmonary nodules imaged on computed tomography. Computerized Medical Imaging and Graphics 23, 339–348 (1999)
11. Kawata, Y., Niki, N., Ohmatsu, H., Kusumoto, M., Kakinuma, R., Mori, K., Nishiyama, H., Eguchi, K., Kaneko, M., Moriyama, N.: Computer aided differential diagnosis of pulmonary nodules using curvature based analysis. In: IEEE Transactions on Nuclear Science, vol. 2, pp. 470–475. IEEE Computer Society Press, Los Alamitos (1999)
12. Hadjiiski, L., Way, T.W., Sahiner, B., Chan, H.P., Cascade, P., Bogot, N., Kazerooni, E., Zhou, C.: Computer-aided diagnosis for interval change analysis of lung nodule features in serial CT examinations. In: Giger, M.L., Karssemeijer, N. (eds.) Proceedings of the SPIE, the Society of Photo-Optical Instrumentation Engineers (SPIE) Conference, vol. 6514, p. 651411 (2007)
13. Marten, K., Engelke, C.: Computer-aided detection and automated ct volumetry of pulmonary nodules. Eur. Radiol. 17, 888–901 (2007)
14. Reeves, A., Chan, A., Yankelevitz, D., Henschke, C., Kressler, B., Kostis, W.: On measuring the change in size of pulmonary nodules. MedImg 25, 435–450 (2006)
15. Silva, A.C., Carvalho, P.C.P., Gattass, M.: Analysis of spatial variability using geostatistical functions for diagnosis of lung nodule in computerized tomography images. Pattern Analysis & Applications 7, 227–234 (2004)
16. Silva, A.C., da Silva, E.C., de Paiva, A.C., Nunes., R.A.: Diagnosis of lung nodule using Moran's Index and Geary's Coefficient in computerized tomography images. Pattern Analysis and Applications (submitted, 2005)
17. Campos, L.F.A., Silva, A.C., Barros, A.K.: Independent component analysis and neural networks applied for classification of malign, benign and normal tissue in digital mammography. In: Fifth International Workshop on Biosignal Interpretation, vol. 1, pp. 85–88 (2005)

18. Christoyianni, I., Koutras, A., Kokkinahis: Computer aided diagnosis of breast cancer in digitized mammograms. Comp. Med. Imag. e Graph 26, 309–319 (2002)
19. Clunie, D.A.: DICOM Structered Reporting. PixelMed Publishing, Pennsylvania (2000)
20. Nikolaidis, N., Pitas, I.: 3-D Image Processing Algorithms. John Wiley, New York (2001)
21. Silva, A.C., Carvalho, P.C.P.: Sistema de análise de nódulo pulmonar. In: Workshop de Informática aplicada a Saúde, Itajai, Universidade de Itajai, Itajai, Universidade de Itajai (2002), http://www.cbcomp.univali.br/pdf/2002/wsp035.pdf
22. Gonzalez, R.C., Woods, R.E.: Digital Image Processing, 3rd edn. Addison-Wesley, Reading (1992)
23. Meyer-Baese, A.: Pattern Recognition for Medical Imaging. Elsevier, Amsterdam (2003)
24. Kovalev, V.A., Kruggel, F., Gertz, H.J., Cramon, D.Y.V.: Three-dimensional texture analysis of MRI brain datasets. IEEE Transactions on Medical Imaging 20, 424–433 (2001)
25. Li, X.: Texture analysis for optical coherence tomography image. Master's thesis, The University of Arizona (2001)
26. Mudigonda, N.R., Rangayyan, R.M., Desautels, J.E.L.: Gradient and texture analysis for the classification of mammographic masses. IEEE Transactions on Medical Imaging 19, 1032–1043 (2000)
27. Scheuerell, M.D.: Quantifying aggregation and association in three dimensional landscapes. Ecology 85, 2332–2340 (2004)
28. Hyvarinen, A., Karhunen, J., Oja, E.: Independent component analysis. J. Wiley, Chichester (2001)
29. Marchini, J., Heaton, C., Ripley, B.: Fastica algorithms to perform ica and projection pursuit (2004), http://www.stats.ox.ac.uk/~marchini/#software
30. Burges, C.J.C.: A Tutorial on Support Vector Machines for Pattern Recognition. Kluwer Academic Publishers, Dordrecht (1998)
31. Hsu, C.W., Chang, C.C., C.-J., L.: A practical guide to support vector classification (2006), http://www.csie.ntu.edu.tw/~cjlin/papers/guide/guide.pdf

A Knowledge Processing Neural Network Based on Automatic Concept Hierarchization

Masahiro Saito and Masafumi Hagiwara

Keio University, 3-14-1 Hiyoshi, Kohoku-ku, Yokohama, 223-8522, Japan

Abstract. In this paper, we propose a knowledge processing neural network which is capable of inductive and deductive inference. The proposed network looks up relations between words in a concept dictionary and co-occurrence dictionary. First, the proposed network divides sentences into the subject words and the other words. Then these words are input into two-layer network. Second, hierarchical structure is composed using concept dictionary. Third, the network induces general knowledge from individual knowledge. We added a function to respond to questions in natural language with "Yes/No/I don't know" in order to confirm the validity of proposed network by evaluating the quantity of correct answers.

1   Intoroduction

Interface of a person and a computer becomes more and more important in these days. A command-line and graphic user interface have been generally used widely. However, we have to learn the usage. A natural language is one of the most natural methods when human communicates with others. Therefore, computer interface by natural language might be the best.

Studies on a natural language have been performed by various methods by such a point of view [1]-[9]. The method of knowledge processing is one of the most important issues when we process a natural language with a computer. There are two approaches in established researches for this problem. One approach is top-down knowledge processing using dictionaries [1]-[3], and the another approach is bottom-up knowledge processing such as a method using neural networks [4]-[6]. Top-down knowledge processing can perform high level inference such as inductive or deductive. However it is difficult to cope with unknown situation. In contrast, knowledge processing of bottom-up can acquire knowledge by learning. Although bottom-up knowledge processing has learning ability, high level inference is difficult.

In this paper, we propose a new neural network to make hierarchical structure by using an EDR electronic dictionary [12]. The proposed network can perform inductive inference and the deductive inference while getting knowledge by learning. Section 2 explains the process of constructing neural networks. Inference mechanism in the proposed network is explained in section 3. Evaluation experiments and the results are shown in section 4 and we conclude the paper in section 5.

M. Ishikawa et al. (Eds.): ICONIP 2007, Part II, LNCS 4985, pp. 539–548, 2008.

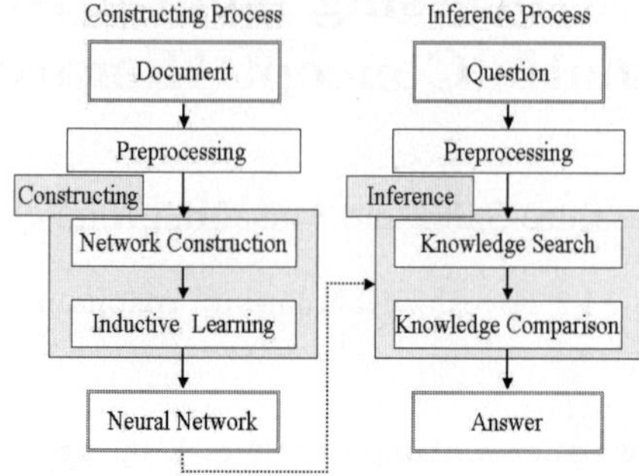

Fig. 1. Flow of the proposed network

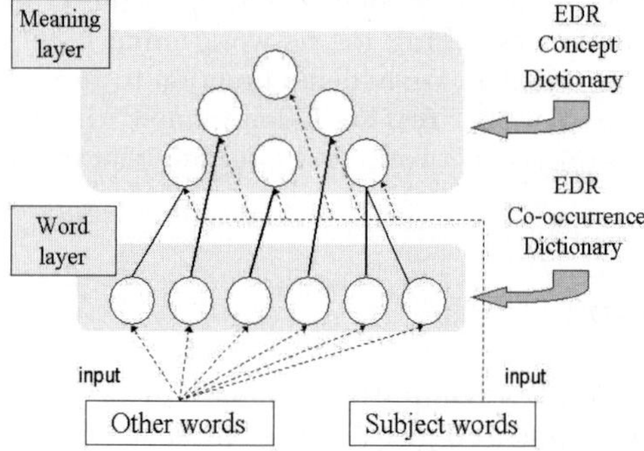

Fig. 2. The proposed network

2   The Proposed Network

In this section, the proposed network is explained.

2.1   Summary of the Proposed Network

The proposed network obtains knowledge from documents of natural language. And the neural network is constructed to perform high level inference using EDR electronic dictionary. Fig.1 shows flow of the proposed network. The proposed network consists of two processes. First process is a network construction process from learning documents. Second process is inference process.

In the network construction process, the neural network is constructed by extracting knowledge from learning documents. Fig.2 shows this network. The proposed neural network consists of two layers: the meaning layer and the word layer. In the meaning layer, hierarchical structure is constructed by an EDR dictionary. In the word layer, a code vector is set to each neuron. This code vector is mapped onto a two-dimensional Self-Organized Feature Map [9]. An EDR

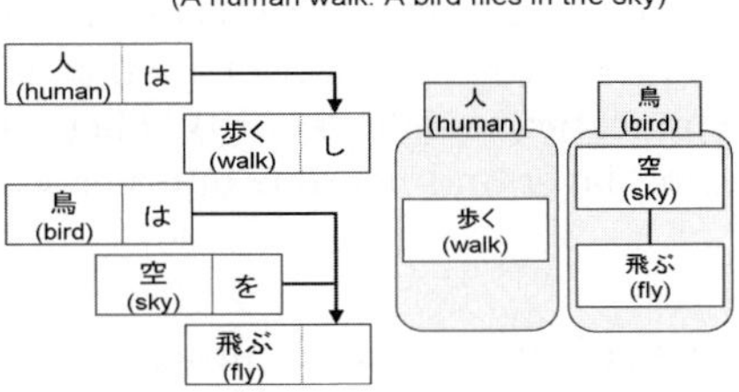

Fig. 3. Result of CaboCha analysis

Co-occurrence Dictionary is employed for this mapping. Furthermore, inductive knowledge extraction is performed with hierarchical structure of the meaning layer. In the inference process, inference is carried out for a question sentence of natural language using the network.

2.2   Preprocessing

In the preprocessing, input document of a natural language is divided into the subject words and the other words using CaboCha. CaboCha is Japanese syntax analyzer [11]. An example of result of CaboCha analysis is shown in Fig.3. Fig.3 is the result of analysis that " 人は歩くし、鳥は空を飛ぶ。" (”A human walks. A bird flis in the sky.”) was analyzed by CaboCha. The word which has a particle ‘ は ’ , ‘ が ’ , ‘ も ’ is considered as subject. This is a particular processing for Japanese. By this processing, ”人” (”a human”) and ”鳥” (a bierd) are considered as subject. The word that the subject affects is considered to be a predicate. ”歩く” (walks) and ”飛ぶ” (flies) , are considered as predicate. Next, subject and the other words are classified into groups based on dependency to the predicate. At first a word concerning to a predicate belongs to each group. A word to concerning to the word belonging to a group next is put in a group. Groups are made by repeating this process.

In Fig.3, words are classified in two groups of dependency to show predicate ”歩く” (walk) next.

$$歩く \text{ (walk)}$$
$$空 \text{ (sky)} \rightarrow 飛ぶ \text{ (fly)}$$

It is able to get knowledge from a complicated sentence by grouping. In addition, the group having ”ない” with the predicate is considered to be a negation sentence.

2.3   Network Construction

In the proposed network, each neuron corresponds to one word in the learning documents. Hierarchical structure of neurons is made using EDR Concept Dictionary in the meaning layer. And code vectors are mapped onto a two-dimensional neural sheet using EDR Co-occurrence Dictionary. The indicative knowledge extraction is performed. The proposed network is constructed by these processes.

Word input. Neuros of the subjects created by preprocessing and each neuron of other words are connected. These connections differ depending on affirmative sentences or in negation sentences. Connection weight is 1.0 if the sentence is affirmative, otherwise connection weight is -1.0. Then neurons of the subjects are input into the meaning layer and neurons of other words are input into the word layer.

Hierarchization of meaning layer. Neurons in the meaning layer are arranged in hierarchy using hyperonym-hyponym relations searched from a concept dictionary. At first, the upper concept represented in a neuron in the meaning layer is searched in the concept dictionary. Then the nearest concept is allotted as a new neuron and is connected to the neuron in the meaning layer.

This operation is performed to a broader term input as neuron. In this way, hierarchical structure is constructed based on upper-lower relation of concepts.

Code vector of neuron of word layer. A code vector is set to each neuron of the word layer. This code vector is onto a two-dimensional neural sheet. It is expressed by degree of similarity between word distance of code vectors. Distance of code vectors are determined based on their similarity using EDR Co-occurrence Dictionary. The learning algorithm is based on Kohonen's Self-Organizing Feature Map [9] At first, random value is given to each code vector. Code vectors of neurons are moved with information of EDR Co-occurrence Dictionary. If neuron i and neuron j are co-occurring, the code vector of neuron j is learned as follows.

$$\boldsymbol{p}_j = \boldsymbol{p}_j + k\sigma(t_c)(\boldsymbol{p}_i - \boldsymbol{p}_j) \tag{1}$$

In this equation, $\boldsymbol{p}_j$ is the code vector of neuron j, $\boldsymbol{p}_i$ is the code vector of neuron i, k is co-occurring frequency, t_c is the number of learning times for approaching.

If neuron i and neuron j are not co-occurring, neuron j is learned as follows.

$$\boldsymbol{p}_j = \boldsymbol{p}_j - k\sigma(t_a)(\boldsymbol{p}_i - \boldsymbol{p}_j) \tag{2}$$

In this equation, t_a is the number of times that network operates. And $\sigma(t)$ is a function to decrease according to increase of t. $\sigma(t)$ is shown as follows.

$$\sigma(t) = \frac{1}{t} exp \frac{|\boldsymbol{p}_i - \boldsymbol{p}_j|^2}{(\frac{2}{R})^{\frac{1}{t}}} \tag{3}$$

R is the parameter to determine the initial value of movement distance.

Inductive knowledge extraction. In inductive knowledge extraction, general knowledge is extracted from individual knowledge. Knowledge extraction is performed with the propagation of an activation level and firing of neuron. An activation level is the energy that neuron has. The neuron exceeds the threshold level fires.

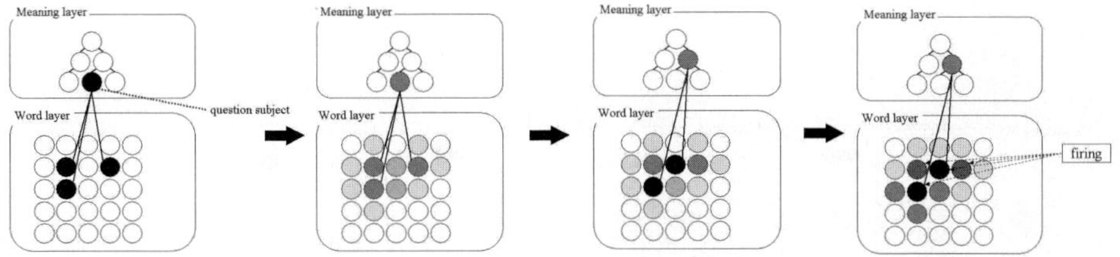

Fig. 4. Activation level propagate between two layers

An initial value of activation level z_{init} is propagated from plural neuron of the meaning layer to the word layer. Fig.4 shows this propagation. An activation level that propagates to neuron of the word layer is shown in the next equation.

$$z_i = w z_{init} \tag{4}$$

z_i is activation level of neuron i, w is connection weight, and z_{init} is initial value of activation level. This propagation is performed in every group. When an activation level of neuron satisfied the next equation, the neuron in word layer fires.

$$z_i > K \tag{5}$$

K is parameter called generalized co-occurrence number. The neurons which fired are connected to meaning layer's neuron. Connected neuron in meaning layer is hyperonym conncept of neurons which were given initial activation level. The knowledge that has an exception is hard to fire. By this process, proposed network can extract knowledge inductively.

3 Inference

As in the learning process, a question sentence in natural language is pre-processed. Next, the neuron having a word same as the subject is searched from the meaning layer. And initial activation level z_{init} is given. This activation level is propagated to meaning layer through connections. The equation of this propagation is shown in equation 4. The activation level that is propagated to the word layer is propagated other neighbor neurons in the word layer. Fig.5 shows this propagation. An activation level to be propagated is strengthened in inverse proportion to distance between the neurons. Activation level from neuron i to neuron j is expressed in the next equation.

$$z_{ji} = \frac{a Z_i}{|\boldsymbol{p}_i - \boldsymbol{p}_j|} \tag{6}$$

z_i is activation level of neuron i, and a is parameter which decides strength of propagation. If there are n neurons propagate to neuron j, total activation level of neuron j is shown in the next equation.

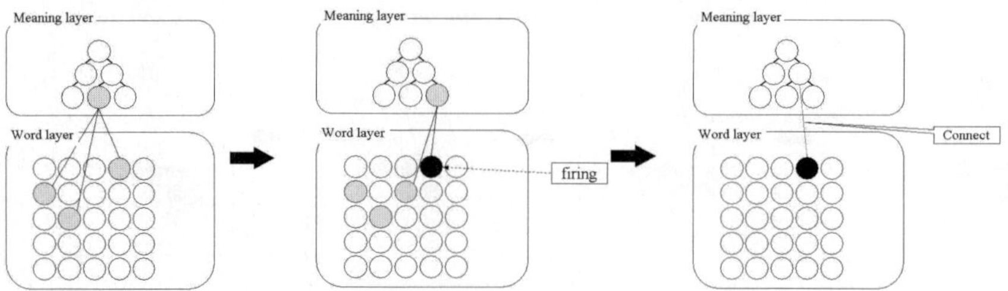

Fig. 5. Activation level propagate in the word layer

$$Z_j = \sum_{k}^{n} z_{jk} \tag{7}$$

If z_j satisfies the next expression, neuron j fires.

$$|Z_j| > W_{min} \tag{8}$$

W_{min} is the parameter called fire level. Words except for the subject word in a question sentence are compared with the words of the neurons that firing. If all neurons of question sentence's words are fired, network considers knowledge is found. At the same time activation level is propagated to the hyperonym concept. The deductive inference is enabled by this processing. This example is shown in 4.1. If a neuron having the subject of a question sentence was not discovered in the meaning layer, the hyperonym is examined by concept dictionary. And an initial level of activation level is given. By this process, network can answer the question of a negation sentence.

4   Experiment

We evaluated the proposed network by experiments. The proposed network outputs three kinds of answers "Yes/No/I don't know". The condition that each answer appears is shown as follows.

- Yes
  All of the neurons having a word except the subject of a question sentence catches fire. If activation level is plus, this answer is appeared.
- No
  All of the neurons having a word except for the subject of a question sentence catches fire. If activation level is minus, this answer is appeared.
- I don't know
  If neither condition mentioned above is satisfied, this answer is appeared.

Table 1 shows a specific example. In this specific example, the learning document is "鳥は飛ぶ" (A bird flys).

Table 1. Example answer

Question sentence	Firing neuron	System answer
鳥は飛ぶか (Does a bierd fly?)	"飛ぶ" (fly) Positive	Yes
鳥は飛ばないか (Does a bird not fly?)	"飛ぶ" (fly) Negative	No
飛ぶは鳥か (Is fly a bird?)	No	I don't know

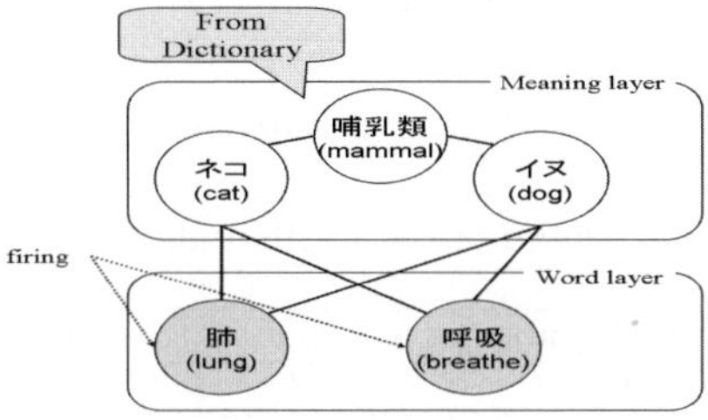

Fig. 6. Setting hyperonym

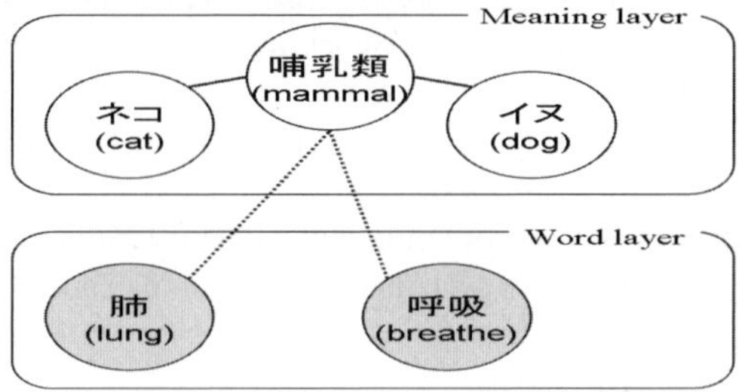

Fig. 7. Connect neurons

4.1 An Experiment of a Network

We tested learning and inference algorithm of the proposed network by experiments. In this experiment, the learning document is "ネコは肺で呼吸する。 イヌも肺で呼吸する。" (A cat breathes in lungs. A dog breathes in lungs too).

State of inductive knowledge extraction The network looked for hyperonym from concept dictionary. Because the hyperonym of "ネコ" (cat) and "イヌ" (dog) is "哺乳類" (mammal), the network sets a neuron "哺乳類" to network. This state is shown in Fig.6. And the network performs inductive knowledge extraction. By this process, the network connects the neuron "哺乳類" (mammal) between neurons of "肺" (lung) and "呼吸" (breathe). This state is shown in Fig.7.

State of deductive inference After inductive knowledge extraction, we input question sentence "クジラは肺で呼吸するか。" (Does whale breathe in lungs?)

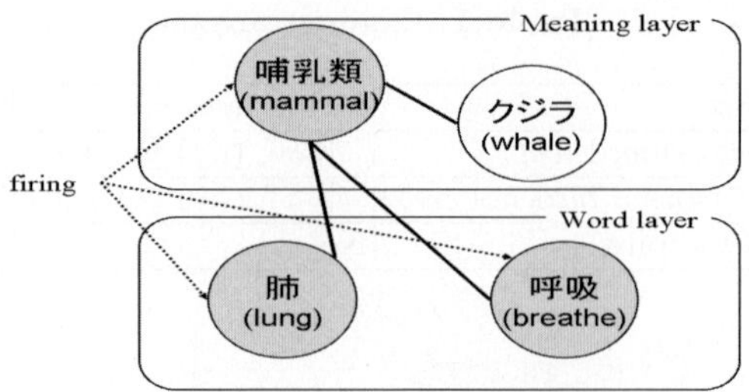

Fig. 8. Deductive inference

Table 2. Detail of the learning documents

	Number of word	Number of subject
Document1	604	82
Document2	1368	159

to the network. The network looked for the neuron having the word "クジラ" (whale) from the meaning layer. In this experiment, the neuron having the word "クジラ" (whale) does not exist. The network looked for the "クジラ" hyperonym that is "哺乳類" (mammal) from concept dictionary. The network found the neuron having "哺乳類" (mammal) in the meaning layer. The neuron having "哺乳類" (mammal) is connected "肺" (lung) and "呼吸" (breathe) in the word layer. The activation level was propagated to these neurons. So the network answered "Yes". A state of this inference is shown in Fig.8.

4.2 Experimental Condition

In the experiment, we prepared two learning documents. These learning documents obtained from textbook of junior high school [14] and Wikipedia [13]. These documents are described by close grammar. The detail of two learning documents are shown in Table 2. From these learning documents, we carried out two experiments. We input an existing sentence into the learning document as a question sentence by experiment 1 and confirmed remembrance rate. We input question sentences of a field same as the learning documents by experiment 2. In these experiments, input question sentences were only simple ones. The parameters that we used in an experiment are shown in Table 3.

4.3 Result of Experiments

The results of experiments are shown in Table 4.

Input question sentences and the network's answers are shown in experiment 1 in Table 5. Equal data in experiment 2 is shown in Table 6.

From the experimental result, it is considered that proposed network learns knowledge from a document of a natural language. The proposed network can perform the inductive inference and the deductive inference.

Table 3. Parameter of experiments

Initial activation level Z_{init}	1.0
Generalize co-occurrence number K	5.0
Movement distance R	5.0
Fire level W_{min}	0.6
Strength of propagation at experiment 1 a	0.01
Strength of propagation at experiment 2 a	0.001

Table 4. Result

	Percentage correct experiment 1	Percentage correct experiment 2
Document1	88.0	75.0
Document2	90.0	77.8

Table 5. Sample question in experiment1

Question sentence	Network answer	Correct answer
魚はうろこに覆われているか。 (Is a fish covered with a scale?)	Yes	Yes
哺乳類は肺で呼吸するか。 (Does mammal breathe in lungs?)	Yes	Yes
惑星は光輝くか。 (Does a planet shine?)	No	No
月は衛星か。 (Is the moon a satellite?)	Yes	Yes

Table 6. Sample question in experiment2

Question sentence	Network answer	Correct answer
動物は呼吸಴をするか。 (Does an animal breathe in lungs?)	Yes	Yes
爬虫類は卵を産むか。 (Do reptiles lay an egg?)	I don't know	Yes
空は鳥を飛ぶか。 (Do sky fly in a bird?)	I don't know	I don't know
衛星は天体か。 (Is a satellite an astronomical object?)	Yes	I don't know

5   Conclusion

In this paper, we proposed a knowledge processing neural network which is capable of inductive and deductive inference. The proposed network constructs a hierarchical structure from the input sentences and performs inference. One of the distinctive features of the proposed network is usage of electronic dictionary. The network can find and use information that is not contained in the learning sentences. We performed an evaluation experiment. As a result, it is confirmed that proposed network can perform the inductive inference and apriority for an unlearned question.

References

1. Schank, R.C.: Conceptual Dependency A theory of natural language understanding. Cognitive Psychology, 552–631 (1972)
2. Minsky, M.: A Framework for Representing Knowledge. The Psychology of Computer vision, 211–277 (1975)
3. Kenji, W., Tetsuzo, U., Tomoo, I.: A Sentence-Structure Collation System for EDR Japanese Corpus. The IEICE Transactions on Informaton and Systems, 139–149 (2001)
4. Atsushi, T., Anzai, Y.: Natural Language Processing System Based on Connectionist Models. Journal of Information Processing, 202–210 (1987)
5. Takashi, O.: Rule based nature of infant word learning behavior. Journal of Japanese Cognitive Science Society, 223–235 (2000)
6. Kai, S., Masafumi, H.: A proposal of 3-dimensional self organizing memory and its application to knowledge extraction from natural language, IEICE technical report Neurocomputing, 59–64 (2006)
7. d'Avila Garcez, S., Luis, C.L., Dov, M.G.: A Connectionist Inductive Learning System for Modal Logic Programming. In: IEEE International Conference on Neural Information Processing ICONIP 2002 (2002)
8. Makoto, N.: Natural Language Procecing, Iwanamishoten (1996)
9. Masatoshi, S.: Intoroduction of Neuro Computing, Morikitashuppan (1999)
10. Bernhard, G., Rudolf, W.: Formal Concept Analysis. Springer, Heidelberg (2004)
11. Rabinowitz: Yet Another Japanese Dependency Structure Analyzer, Nara Institute of Science and Technology (2001)
12. EDR Electoronic Dictionary, National Institute of Information and Communications Technology
13. http://ja.wikipedia.org
14. Noboru, M., Sadanori, O.: New Science, Tokyoshoseki (2006)

Classification Using Multi-valued Pulse Coupled Neural Network

Xiaodong Gu

Department of Electronic Engineering, Fudan University, Shanghai 200433, China
guxiaodong@263.net, xdgu@fudan.edu.cn

Abstract. This paper introduces how to use multi-valued PCNN (Pulse Coupled Neural Network) proposed in this paper to do classification. 2-dimensional data can be projected onto two-dimensional PCNN locally laterally linked. Different pulse waves generated by training data label different regions corresponding to different classes. The same pulse wave labels the region corresponding to the same class. Meeting of different pulse waves obtains the separatrixes of different classes. In order to differentiate different pulse waves, outputs of neurons in PCNN should be multi-valued. We call networks composed of these neurons multi-valued PCNNs. The number of classes determines the number of output value of each neuron. N-valued PCNN can be used to classify N-1 different classes. Experimental results of the 2-dimensional salmon-weever classification show that the correct recognition rate of test set is 98.11% (3477/3544) when training samples are only 10% of all samples.

Keywords: PCNN (Pulse Coupled Neural Network); Multi-valued PCNN; Pulse waves; Classification.

1 Introduction

Assigning labels to data based on their features is the function of the classifier. In this paper, we use pulse-spreading of multi-valued PCNN (Pulse Coupled Neural Network) that we proposed based on conventional binary PCNN to assign labels. In 1990, Eckhorn introduced the linking network [1] exhibiting synchronous pulse bursts in the cat or the monkey visual cortex [2]–[4]. It is a model pulse-emitting and spatio-temporal coding. Introducing the linking strength to the linking model obtains binary PCNN [5], which retains the main characteristics of the linking network.

Binary PCNN has been applied in many fields, such as image processing, object detection, optimization [6]-[18]. Almost all existing applications of binary PCNN are based on its pulse-spreading characteristic. Using this pulse-spreading characteristic can extend binary PCNN's applications conveniently. The output of each neuron in binary PCNN is binary. In this paper multi-valued PCNN, consisting of neurons with multi-valued outputs, is introduced, and pulse-spreading of multi-valued PCNN is used in classification. Pulses generated by conventional binary PCNN have the same amplitude value so that using them cannot label different classes. So pulses generated by conventional binary PCNN cannot be used to do classification. If amplitudes of pulses are multi-valued, multi-valued amplitudes can be used to label different

M. Ishikawa et al. (Eds.): ICONIP 2007, Part II, LNCS 4985, pp. 549–558, 2008.

classes. Therefore, in this paper we introduce multi-valued PCNN to do classification. In classification based on multi-valued PCNN, different values of pulse amplitudes are used to differentiate different pulse waves that label different classes. In classification, firstly 2-dimensional training data are projected onto 2-dimensional multi-valued PCNN locally laterally linked. Then we make neurons that correspond to training data of different classes emit different-valued pulses. These pulses spread over the network in parallel like the flood, and the same-valued pulses generate the same-valued pulse waves. The training data in the same class produce same-valued pulses so as to generate the same-valued pulse waves. Same-valued pulse waves label their spreading-over regions as the same class. In this paper, in order to classify N different classes, the output of each neuron should be $(N+1)$–valued. In training of classification, when different pulse waves corresponding to different classes meet, the separatrixes of different classes are obtained. In test, test data are projected onto the network and they are assigned labels of the regions that training data have already labeled. In this paper, we address this approach in 2-dimensional space.

In Section 2, multi-valued PCNN for classification is described. In Section 3, classification based on multi-valued PCNN is introduced. In Section 4, computer simulations of 2-class and 2-dimensional classification based on 3-valued PCNN, and experimental results of the practical application of 3-valued PCNN to salmon-weever classification are shown, followed by computer simulations of 3-class and 2- dimensional classification based on 4-valued PCNN. Conclusions are obtained in Session 5.

2 Multi-valued PCNN

Fig.1 illustrates a simplified neuron j in multi-valued PCNN in classification in this paper. It consists of three parts: the receptive field, the modulation field, and the multi-valued pulse generator. Its output is multi-valued, not binary, which is different from that in binary PCNN.

Eq. (1) to Eq.(5) describe this neuron. Neuron j has two channels (F channel and L channel). F channel is feeding input ($F_j(t)$); and L channel is linking input ($L_j(t)$).In Fig.1, I_j is an input signal from the external source, and only inputs to F channel of j (see (1)). In classification, if neuron j is projected onto a training sample, I_j equals to

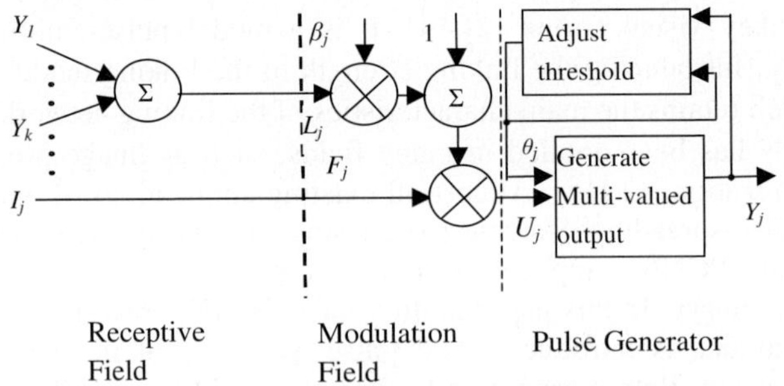

Fig. 1. A simplified neuron j in multi-valued PCNN in this paper

the value corresponding to this training sample's class label. If neuron j is not projected onto a training sample, I_j equals to a smaller value. $Y_1(t),...,Y_k(t)...$, multi-valued output signals of neurons connected with j , are also input signals of neuron j, and only input to L channel of j. Y_j (t) is the output signal of neuron j. In (2), $N(j)$ is the neighbor field of neuron j and j may belong or not belong to $N(j)$. In this paper, j does not belong to $N(j)$. $L_j(t)$ is added a constant positive bias firstly. Then it is multiplied by $F_j(t)$ and the bias is taken to be unity (see Eq. (3)). In Eq. (3), β_j is the linking strength. The total internal activity $U_j(t)$ is the result of modulation and it inputs to the multi-valued pulse generator. If $U_j(t)$ is greater than the threshold $\theta_j(t)$, the neuron output $Y_j(t)$ equals to a value determined by $(U_j(t)-\theta_j(t))$. Then $Y_j(t)$ feedbacks to make $\theta_j(t)$ rise over $U_j(t)$ immediately so that $Y_j(t)$ turns into 0. Therefore, when $U_j(t)$ is greater than $\theta_j(t)$, neuron j outputs a multi-valued pulse.

Eq.(4) shows the 3-valued output case. In Eq.(4), C_1, C_2 and b_1, are constants, and according to the algorithm in this paper, we can assign them suitable values easily. 3-valued PCNN composed of 3-valued neurons can be used to classify 2 different classes. N-valued PCNN composed of N-valued neurons can be used to classify N-1 different classes. In conventional binary PCNN neuron, if U_j (t) is greater $\theta_j(t)$, Y_j (t) equals to 1; else equals to 0. It is the main difference between multi-valued PCNN in this paper and conventional binary PCNN that whether the output of each neuron is multi-valued. If neuron j outputs a multi-valued pulse (namely Y_j is more than 0), we call neuron j firing. In Eq.(5), V_j^T and α_j^T are the amplitude gain and the time constant of the threshold adjuster. Solving Eq.(5), the lower limit of integration is just before the last firing. When neuron j fires, its threshold increases to constant V_j^T fast, and the threshold value is independent of the threshold value at the time just before firing. Then $\theta_j(t)$ descends with time increasing.

$$F_j(t) = I_j \tag{1}$$

$$L_j(t) = \sum_{k \in N(j)} Y_k(t) \tag{2}$$

$$U_j(t) = F_j(t)[1 + \beta_j L_j(t)] \tag{3}$$

$$Y_j(t) = \begin{cases} C_2 & , \quad b_1 \leq U_j(t) - \theta_j(t) \quad , firing \\ C_1 & ,0 < U_j(t) - \theta_j(t) < b_1 \quad , firing \\ 0 & , \quad U_j(t) - \theta_j(t) \leq 0 \ , non-firing \end{cases} \tag{4}$$

$$\frac{d\theta_j(t)}{dt} = -\alpha_j^T + V_j^T Y_j(t) \tag{5}$$

In 2-dimensional classification, multi-valued PCNN is a single layer 2-dimensional array of laterally linked neurons and one of those neurons is illustrated in Fig.2. All neurons are identical. Each neuron is connected with neurons by its L channel in its 4-neighbor field (See Fig.2). In 2-dimensional classification each datum corresponds

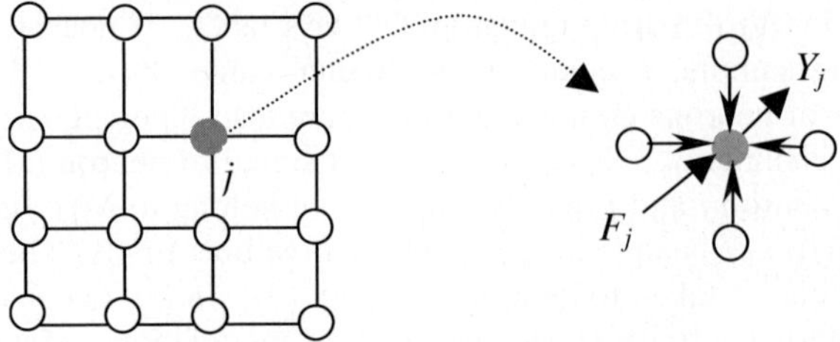

Fig. 2. The connection mode of each neuron in multi-valued PCNN for 2-dimensional classification

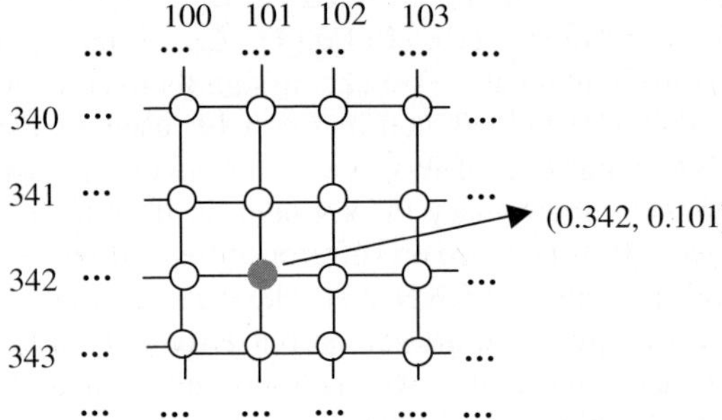

Fig. 3. The neuron in the 342nd row and the 101st column corresponds to the 2-dimensional data sample (0.342, 0.101)

to a neuron in 2-dimensional PCNN. A 2-dimensional PCNN likes a coordinate plane and neurons in different locations can denote different data. In this paper, 2-dimensional data are normalized in [0.001,1.000], and the effective value is millesimal (0.001), and the size of PCNN is 1000*1000 (the number of neurons is million). For example, if a data sample is (0.342, 0.101), it is projected onto neuron (342, 101) in multi-valued PCNN (see Fig.3). Namely the neuron in the 342nd row and the 101st column corresponds to the datum (0.342, 0.101).

In training, if a neuron is projected onto a training sample, the F channel of this neuron receives the value 'l' corresponding to this sample's class label, namely $F_j(t) = I_j = l$; if a neuron is not projected onto a training sample, the feeding input ($F_j(t)$) equals to an other value smaller than those corresponding to class labels. These values can not equals to 0, or pulses cannot spread over the network. For 2-class classification, $F_j(t) = I_j, I_j \in \{l_1, l_2, l_3\}$, l_1, l_2, l_3 are constants corresponding to non-training-sample, the training sample of class I, and the training sample of class II respectively. We can assign l_1, l_2, l_3 suitable values easily based on the algorithm in this paper. In Section 4, the parameter values of multi-valued PCNN in our experiments are shown. After training, each neuron is assigned a label. In test, test samples are projected onto multi-valued PCNN labeled, and labels of test samples equal to those of corresponding neurons.

3   Classification Using Multi-valued PCNN

Pulse-spreading of binary PCNN has been efficiently used in image processing and optimization.   For example, we have used binary PCNN in image thinning [10]. In thinning, skeletons are obtained when pulse waves meet. In training in classification in this paper, first data are projected onto multi-valued PCNN. More corresponding details have been shown in Section 2. Next, multi-valued pulse-waves generated by training samples label all regions, and separatrixes are obtained when different pulse waves meet. In thinning based on binary PCNN, pulse waves are identical. In classification based on multi-valued PCNN, pulse waves are not identical, and multi-valued PCNN is used to generate different pulse waves to label different classes. N-valued PCNN can be used to differentiate N-1 different classes. For example, 4-valued PCNN can be used to differentiate 3different classes.

In training in classification, neurons corresponding to training data samples fire to produce pulses to excite neurons not projected onto training data samples to generate multi-valued pulse-waves to spread over the network in parallel. Setting enough large threshold amplitude gain (V_j^T make each neuron fire only once. Output values of firing neurons captured by different pulse-waves are different. The output value of the firing neuron labels this neuron. When all neurons have fired, the training finishes. After training, each neuron is assigned a class label. In test, test data samples are projected onto labeled PCNN, and their labels are those of corresponding neurons. Now, we describe the multi-valued PCNN classification algorithm. Firstly we introduce the symbols in the following algorithm. $\mathbf{F}$ is a feeding input matrix. In training, if a neuron is projected onto a training sample, the corresponding element in $\mathbf{F}$ equals to the value corresponding to the class label of this training sample. $\mathbf{L}$ is a linking input matrix, where $\mathbf{L} = \mathbf{Y} \otimes \mathbf{K}$, where $\mathbf{Y}$ is a multi-valued output matrix, and '$\otimes$' indicates two-dimensional convolution, and $\mathbf{K}$ is a 3*3 kernel,

$$\mathbf{K} = \begin{bmatrix} 0 & 1 & 0 \\ 1 & 0 & 1 \\ 0 & 1 & 0 \end{bmatrix}.$$

This $\mathbf{K}$ corresponds to the connection mode of 4-neighbor field. Because in this paper each neuron's 4-neighbor field does not include itself, the center element of $\mathbf{K}$ equals to 0. $\mathbf{U}$ is an internal activity matrix and $\mathbf{\Theta}$ is a threshold matrix. $\mathbf{Lab}$, a label matrix, saves the training result, namely the segmentation result of the classification space. $\mathbf{F}$, $\mathbf{L}$, $\mathbf{U}$, $\mathbf{Y}$, $\mathbf{\Theta}$, and $\mathbf{Lab}$ have the same dimensions (1000*1000). β is the linking strength and each neuron has the same β. $Height$ (1000) and $Width$(1000) are the height and the width of 2-dimensional multi-valued PCNN.

The training process of multi-valued PCNN classification algorithm for 2-dimensional data is described below.

1) 2-dimensional training samples are projected onto 2-dimensional multi-valued PCNN.
2) $\mathbf{L} = \mathbf{0}.\mathbf{U} = \mathbf{0}.\ \mathbf{Y} = \mathbf{0}.\ \beta=1$. Initialize $\mathbf{F}$, $\mathbf{\Theta}$ and other parameters.
3) Calculate $\mathbf{L}$,$\mathbf{U}$,$\mathbf{Y}$ in order.

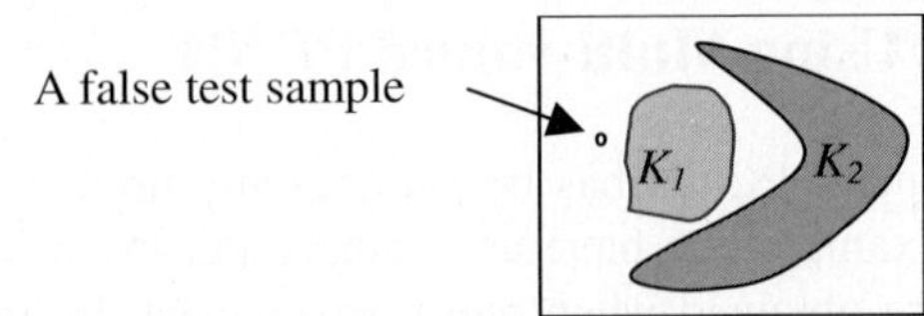

Fig. 4. In this 2-class (K_1 and K_2) classification space, all data distribute in shadows. A false test sample out of shadows is not rejected and still assigned the label corresponding to class K_1, by using multi-valued PCNN classification algorithm.

4) If $\mathbf{Y}(i,j) > 0$, record the corresponding class label to $\mathbf{Lab}(i,j)$ and increase $\Theta(i,j)$ to a enough large value so that the corresponding neuron will not fire again. ($i=1,\ldots,Height$; $j=1,\ldots Width$)

5) If all neurons have fired, end; else go back to 3)

In test, projecting test samples onto $\mathbf{Lab}$ obtains test results quickly. Pulse-spreading is only used in training and not be used in test. Using $\mathbf{Lab}$ can be easy to obtain separatrixes too. In 2-dimensional classification, separatrixes are 2-dimensional curves. In this algorithm, any test sample is assigned a class label and a false test sample not belonging to any existing class is also assigned a label. For example (see Fig.4), in a 2-class (K_1 and K_2) classification space, all data (the training and the test data) distribute in part regions of the whole classification space and these distribution regions (namely data sets) are described by shadows in Fig.4. In Fig.4, a false test sample out of shadows appears, and it is incorrectly assigned the class label corresponding to class K_1 although it neither belongs to class K_1 nor belongs to class K_2. In order to reject false test samples, in training we can finish the training before all neurons fire by controlling the spreading distances of pulse waves. However, in this situation, the gaps might appear in shadows in Fig.4. If correct test samples falls into these gaps, they will not be assigned class labels and rejected incorrectly. In this paper, training does not finish until all neurons have fired. Therefore, at last any test sample is assigned a label. The parameter values of multi-valued PCNN in our experiments are shown in Section 4.

4   Experimental Results and Discussions

4.1   Computer Simulations of 2-class and 2-dimensional Classification Based on 3-valued PCNN and the Practical Salmon-weever Classification

In computer simulations of 2-class and 2-dimensional classification based on 3-valued PCNN, we used 50 data sets, one of which is shown in Fig.5 (a). For each data set, data are normalized in [0.001,1.000] and the effective value is millesimal (0.001), and the size of PCNN is 1000*1000 (the number of neurons is 1 million). For each data set, we have randomized 10% of all samples as training ones, and used residuary samples as test ones. The mean correct recognition rate of test set is 97.77% and that of training set is 100%.

In initialization of the feeding input matrix $\mathbf{F}$ for 2-class and 2-dimensional classification, if a element corresponds a training sample, its value is 2 for class I and 10 for class II; if a element does not correspond to a training sample, its value is 1. Namely, $F_j(t) = I_j, I_j \in \{1,2,10\}$. At the beginning, each element of threshold matrix Θ equals to 1.5. When a neuron fires, increase its threshold to an enough large value (1000) so that it will not fire again. Each neuron's linking strength (β) is 1. Eq.(6) is the output function of each neuron. According to the algorithm, it is easy to choosethe parameters of the neuron.

$$Y_j(t) = \begin{cases} 10 & , \quad 8.5 \leq U_j(t) - \theta_j(t) \quad , firing \\ 2 & ,0 < U_j(t) - \theta_j(t) < 8.5 \quad , firing \\ 0 & , \quad U_j(t) - \theta_j(t) \leq 0 \ , non-firing \end{cases} \tag{6}$$

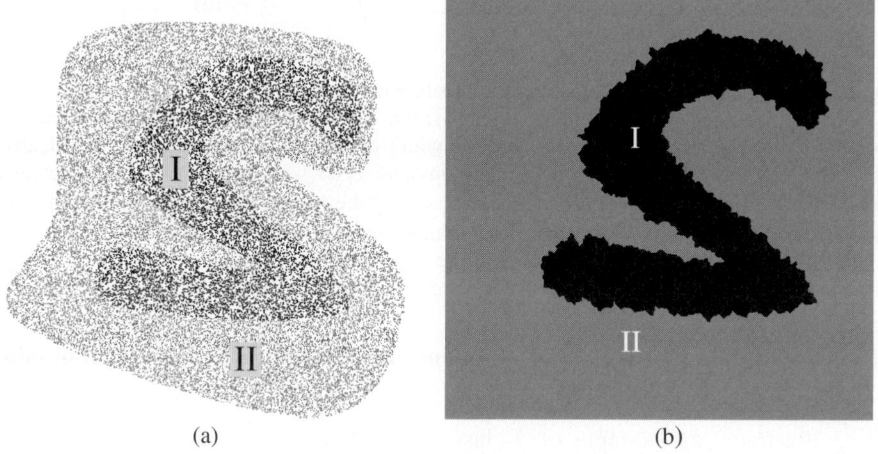

Fig. 5. (a) A data set among 50 data sets in computer simulations of 2-class and 2-dimensional classification based on 3-valued PCNN. There are 36587 samples in this set. (b) The training results based on 10% of all samples in (a). The training samples are randomizedïïIn (b), the black region corresponds to class I and the grey region corresponds to class II. In test, each test sample is assigned the class label according to which region it is projected onto.

In the practical application, we used 3-valued PCNN to classify 2 different kinds of fish (salmons and weevers). In general, weever is lighter than salmon and its width is also some different from salmon's width, so the mean lightness and the width of the fish were used as 2 features in classification. The range of the width (12cm-25cm) is normalized in [0.001,1.000]. The mean lightness (0-255) is also normalized in [0.001,1.000]. After normalization, a sample can be projected onto a neuron in 3-valued PCNN (1000*1000). In this salmon-weever classification, there are 2135 salmons and 1703 weevers (see Fig.6(a)). We randomized 394 ones, 10% of all samples, as training ones, and used residuary 3544 samples as test ones. In the test set, 3477 test samples are assigned correct labels and 67 test samples are labeled wrong labels. The correct recognition rate of test set is 98.11% (3477/3544).

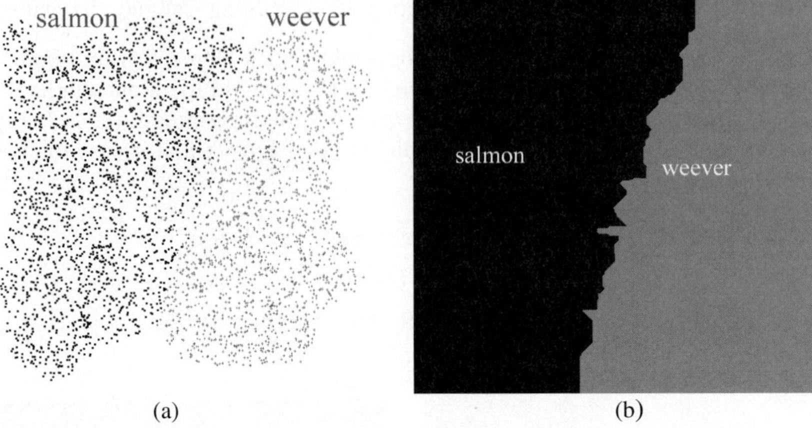

Fig. 6. A practical 2-class and 2-dimentional salmon-weever classification based on 3-valued PCNN. The 2-dimensional feature vector is (*width, lightness*). The mean lightness increases from the left to the right horizontally, and the width increases from the top down vertically in (a) or (b). (a) All 3938 samples (2135 salmons and 1703 weevers). (b) The training results based on 394 samples, 10% of all samples in (a) and the training samples are randomizediïln (b), the black region corresponds to class salmon and the grey region corresponds to class weever. In test, each test sample is assigned the class label according to which region it is projected onto, and the correct recognition rate of residuary test samples is 98.11%.

4.2   An Example of 3-class and 2-dimensional Classification Based on 4-valued PCNN

Fig. 7 illustrates an example of 3-class and 2-dimensional classification using 4-valued PCNN. In this example data are also normalized in [0.001,1.000], and the effective value is also millesimal (0.001), and the size of PCNN is also1000*1000. In initialization of the feeding input matrix **F**, if a element corresponds a training sample, its value is 2 for class I, 10 for class II, and 50 for class III; if a element does not correspond to a training sample, its value is 1. $F_j(t) = I_j, I_j \in \{1,2,10,50\}$. At the beginning, each element of threshold matrix Θ equals to 1.5. When a neuron fires, increase its threshold to an enough large value (20000) so that it will not fire again. Each neuron's linking strength (β) is 1. Eq. (7) is the output function of each neuron for this 3-class and 2-dimensional classification. This output function is 4-valued.

$$Y_j(t) = \begin{cases} 50, & 48.5 \le U_j(t) - \theta_j(t), & , firing \\ 10, & 8.5 \le U_j(t) - \theta_j(t) < 48.5 & , firing \\ 2, & 0 < U_j(t) - \theta_j(t) < 8.5 & , firing \\ 0, & U_j(t) - \theta_j(t) \le 0 & , non-firing \end{cases} \qquad (7)$$

This method also can be extended to 3-dimensional classification. In 3-dimensional classification, separatrixes are 3-dimensional hood faces. If we want to extend this

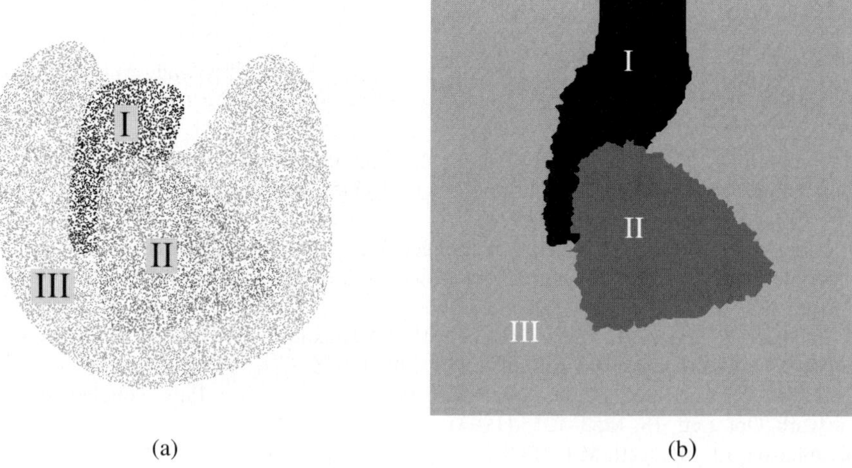

(a)   (b)

Fig. 7. An example of 3-class and 2-dimensional classification. (a) All 28684 samples in the data set (class I, class II, and class III). (b) The training result based on random 10% of all samples in (a). In (b) the black region corresponds to class I, and the dark grey region corresponds to class II, and the light grey region corresponds to class III. In test, each test sample is assigned the label according to which region it is projected onto and the correct recognition rate of residuary test samples is 99.23%.

method to k-dimensional classification ($k>3$, $k\in Z$), in simulations we may connect neurons based on indexes of multi-arrays where they are stored. However, it is very complex to do so, and pulse-spreading phenomena are not so obvious as in 2 or 3-dimensional classification.

5   Conclusions

Pulse-spreading of binary PCNN can be extended to multi-valued PCNN, and   multi-valued pulse waves of multi-valued PCNN can be applied in classification. In multi-valued PCNN classification, data samples are projected onto multi-valued PCNN, and different multi-valued pulse waves label different classes in parallel. Meeting of different multi-valued pulse waves obtains the separatrixes of different classes. N-valued output can be used to classify N-1 different classes. In this paper, we address this method in 2-dimensional classification. Experimental results of 2-dimensional classification show that multi-valued PCNN in this paper can efficiently do classification even the training samples are only 10% of all samples. In the salmon-weever classification, the correct recognition rate of test set is 98.11% (3477/3544) when training samples are only 10% of all samples. Next we will use more practical data to test this method further and try to extend this method to higher dimensional space.

Acknowledgments. This work was supported by National Natural Science Foundation of China (No. 60671062 and 60571052) and National Basic Research Program of China (2005CB724303).

References

1. Eckhorn, R., Reitboeck, H.J., Arndt, M., et al.: Feature Linking via Synchronization among Distributed Assemblies: Simulation of Results from Cat Cortex. Neural Computation 2, 293–307 (1990)
2. Eckhorn, R., Bauer, R., Jordan, W., et al.: Coherent oscillations: a mechanism of feature linking in the visual cortex? Multiple electrode and correlation analyses in the cat. Biological Cybernetics 60, 121–130 (1988)
3. Gray, C.M., Konig, P., Engel, A.K., Singer, W.: Oscillatory responses in cat visual cortex exhibitioner-columnar synchronization which reflects global stimulus properties. Nature 338, 334–337 (1989)
4. Eckhorn, R., Frien, A., Bauer, R., et al.: High frequency oscillations in primary visual cortex of awake monkey. NeuroRep. 4, 243–246 (1993)
5. Johnson, J.L., Ritter, D.: Observation of Periodic Waves in a Pulse-coupled Neural Network. Opt. Lett. 18, 1253–1255 (1993)
6. Johnson, J.L., Padgett, M.L.: PCNN Models and Applications. IEEE Trans. on Neural Networks 10, 480–498 (1999)
7. Kuntimad, G., Ranganath, H.S.: Perfect Image Segmentation Using Pulse Coupled Neural Networks. IEEE Trans. on Neural Networks 10, 591–598 (1999)
8. Broussard, R.P., Rogers, S.K., Oxley, M.E., Tarr, G.L.: Physiologically Motivated Image Fusion for Object Detection using a Pulse Coupled Neural Network. IEEE Trans. on Neural Networks 10, 554–563 (1999)
9. Kinser, J.M.: Foveation by a Pulse-Coupled Neural Network. IEEE Trans. on Neural Networks 10, 621–625 (1999)
10. Gu, X.D., Yu, D.H., Zhang, L.M.: Image Thinning Using Pulse Coupled Neural Network. Pattern Recognition Letters 25, 1075–1084 (2004)
11. Gu, X.D., Yu, D.H., Zhang, L.M.: Image Shadow Removal Using Pulse Coupled Neural Network. IEEE Trans. on Neural Networks 16, 692–698 (2005)
12. Caulfield, H.J., Kinser, J.M.: Finding Shortest Path in the Shortest Time Using PCNN's. IEEE Trans. on Neural Networks 10, 604–606 (1999)
13. Gu, X.D., Guo, S.D., Yu, D.H.: A New Approach for Automated Image Segmentation Based on Unit-linking PCNN. In: Proceedings in IEEE International Conference on Machine learning and Cybernetics, Beijing, China, pp. 175–178 (2002)
14. Gu, X.D.: A New Approach to Image Authentication Using Local Image Icon of Unit-linking PCNN. In: Proceedings in Int. Joint Conf. Neural Networks, Vancouver, Canada, pp. 2015–2020 (2006)
15. Gu, X.D., Zhang, L.M., Yu, D.H.: General Design Approach to Unit-linking PCNN for Image Processing. In: Proceedings in Int. Joint Conf. Neural Networks, Montreal, Canada, pp. 1836–1841 (2005)
16. Gu, X.D., Zhang, L.M.: Global Icons and Local Icons of Images based Unit-linking PCNN and their Application to Robot Navigation. In: Wang, J., Liao, X.-F., Yi, Z. (eds.) ISNN 2005. LNCS, vol. 3497, pp. 836–841. Springer, Heidelberg (2005)
17. Gu, X.D.: Research on Pulse Coupled Neural Network and its Applications. Ph.D. dissertation, Peking University (2003)
18. Gu, X.D.: Research on several Theoretical and Applied Aspects on Unit-linking Pulse Coupled Neural Network. Post-doctoral research report, Fudan University (2005)

Detection for Pickup Errors by Artificial Neural Networks

Hirotake Esaki, Taizo Umezaki, and Tetsumi Horikoshi

Graduate School of Engineering, Nagoya Institute of Technology,
Gokiso-cho, Showa-ku, Nagoya 466-8555, Japan
`hi.esaki@ume.mta.nitech.ac.jp`

Abstract. Taping machines, chip mounters and surface mount device (SMD) inspection systems use image processing techniques for the positioning of SMDs. The improvement of the production quality as well as the productivity is strongly requested in these systems. The image processing system in these systems have inspection functions to improve production quality. Generally, images of the part being picked up by the nozzle are acquired in a horizontal direction, and pickup errors are detected by processing these images. The aim of this paper is to develop a system for detecting pickup errors by processing images of parts acquired from the bottom. By using our proposed method, the detection rate of pickup errors is 99.3%.

Keywords: SMT, vision, discriminant analysis, neural networks.

1 Introduction

The improvement of the electronic equipment in recent years is remarkable. As the miniaturization, weight reduction and increased functionality of the electronic equipment, such as digital cameras, notebook computers, and cellular phones advances, the technology in taping machines used to inset surface mount devices (SMDs) into the tape, in chip mounters used to place SMDs onto printed circuit boards (PCBs), and in SMD inspection systems, advances, too. In these systems, highly accurate positioning and inspection of SMDs are indispensable, and these are achieved by image processing techniques.

The improvement of the production quality as well as the productivity is strongly requested in these systems. The image processing system in these systems has inspection functions to improve production quality.

In chip mounters, SMDs are picked up by the nozzle during placement onto the PCB. When extremely small parts, for example rectangular chips, are picked up from a feeder by the nozzle, pickup errors such as the part being picked up diagonally or sideways may occur. Fig. 1a shows an example of the part being picked up normally, and Fig. 1b-1d show examples of pickup errors. Placing these parts may result in production of defective PCBs or nozzle damage. Therefore, it is important to detect these errors.

M. Ishikawa et al. (Eds.): ICONIP 2007, Part II, LNCS 4985, pp. 559–568, 2008.

There are many proposed methods to detect these errors. One of the typical systems of these methods is shown in Fig. 2. In this system, images of the part being picked up by the nozzle are acquired in a horizontal direction, and pickup errors are detected by processing these images. Therefore, it is necessary to install an additional camera, light source and background. This result in a cost increases and extra installation space is also required.

Generally, in chip mounters, SMDs are picked up from a feeder by the nozzle, and carried into the field of view of the camera. The image is then acquired from the bottom of the part, and the position and the angle of the part is detected by the image processing techniques. Next, the location of the part is corrected by detection result, and the part is placed onto the PCB. If it is possible to detect pickup errors by using the image acquired from the bottom of the part, pickup error detection becomes possible without installing an additional detection device.

The aim of this paper is to develop a system for detecting pickup errors by processing part images acquired from the bottom for positioning. By using this system, it is possible to implement a function to detect pickup errors without the need to install a separate device on the chip mounter for detecting pickup errors. In this paper, the detection methods by linear discriminant, by neural networks and by subspace method were compared and examined.

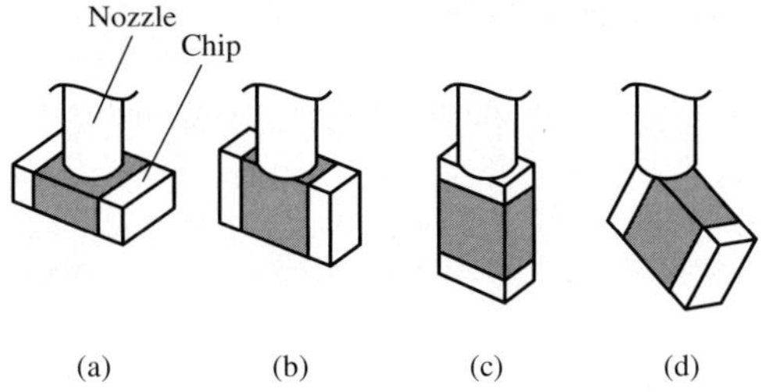

Fig. 1. Examples of Part Being Picked Up

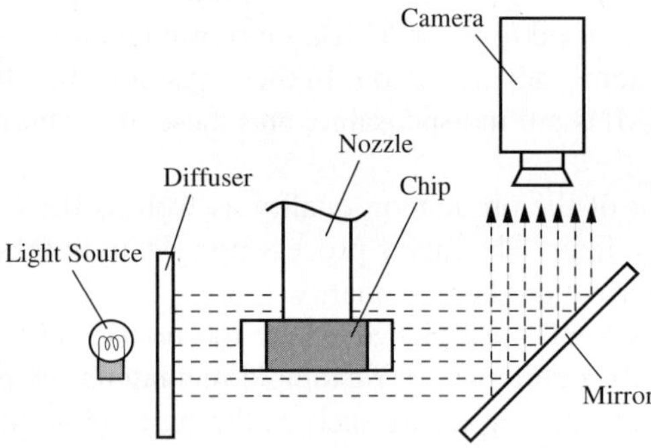

Fig. 2. Typical System Components

2 Applicable Parts

Pickup errors occur easily when the size of the part is small. Therefore, applicable parts for this system are extremely small rectangular chip parts (0.6x0.3 mm) where pickup errors occur easily most. Fig. 3a shows image of the part being picked up correctly, and Fig. 3b-3d shows images of pickup errors. The image is 256 gray level, and 32 by 24 pixels in size.

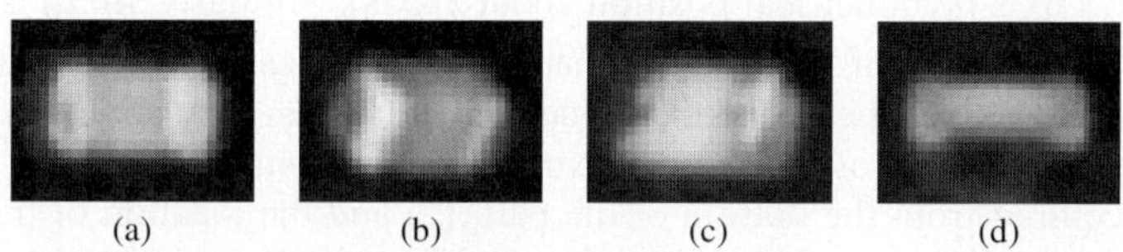

(a)   (b)   (c)   (d)

Fig. 3. Examples of Part Image

3 Detection by Linear Discriminant Method

First of all, the detection method by Fisher's linear discriminant method using the features extracted from the image acquired from the bottom of parts is examined.

3.1 Features

When the images of the part being picked up normally are compared to the pickup error images, the external shape of the part, especially the shape outside of the electrode is different. Therefore, it seems that pickup errors can be detected by extracting the feature that is the shape outside of the electrode, and using Fisher's linear discriminant method.

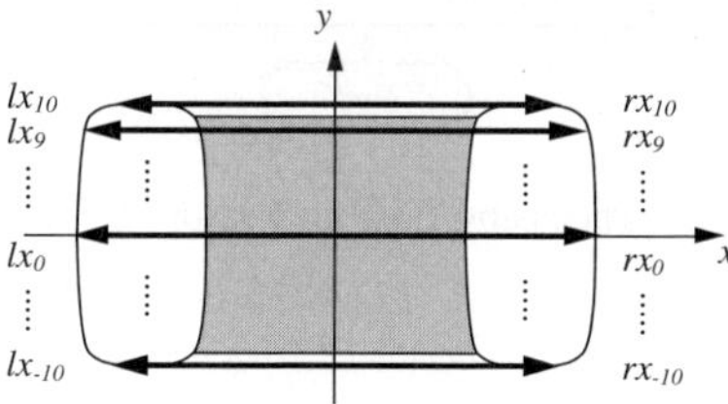

Fig. 4. Extracted Features

Fig. 4 shows the extracted features. lx_n (n=-10, -9, ..., 10) is the distance between center axis (y axis) of the part and the edge of left electrode of the part, and rx_n (n=-10, -9, ..., 10) is the distance between center axis (y axis) and the edge of right electrode of the part.

In addition, the features shown in the following are calculated.

$$dlx_n = \mid lx_n - lx_{-n} \mid . \quad (n=1, 2, \ldots, 10) \qquad (1)$$

$$drx_n = \mid rx_n - rx_{-n} \mid . \quad (n=1, 2, \ldots, 10) \qquad (2)$$

$$dlrx_n = \mid lx_n - rx_n \mid . \quad (n=-10, -9, \ldots, 10) \qquad (3)$$

dlx_n and drx_n are the absolute values of the difference of the distance that is at both sides of the x axis (symmetrical position about x axis). Similarly, $dlrx_n$ is the absolute value of the difference of the distance that is at both sides of the y axis (symmetrical position about y axis). The above-mentioned 83 features in total are extracted.

The processing flow of the feature extraction is shown in Fig. 5. At first, (1) the image is acquired from the bottom of the part, (2) and the location of the part is corrected by the detected position and angle. (3) Next, the image of the part is clipped. (4) Next, the electrode of the part and the background is separated. This is executed by calculating the histogram of the image and calculating the threshold to binarize by the Ootsu binarization method, and binarizing the image. (5) Finally, the distances between the center axes of the parts and the edge of the electrode are extracted as features.

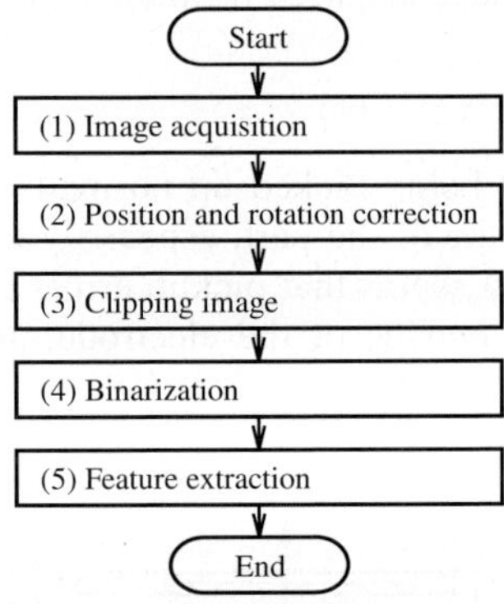

Fig. 5. Processing Flow of Feature Extraction

3.2 Experimental Result

Using above-mentioned features, the detection experiment was performed. The experimental result is shown in Fig. 6 and Table 1. The classification error rate is about 6.9%.

Fig. 7 shows the examples of the classification error images. The part side appears very dark in many of the classification error images, and the gray value at this point is below the threshold. Therefore, the difference of the shape outside of the part cannot be extracted, and it causes the classification error. It is necessary to extract the feature to which the part side with a low gray value can be extracted to classify parts correctly in such images.

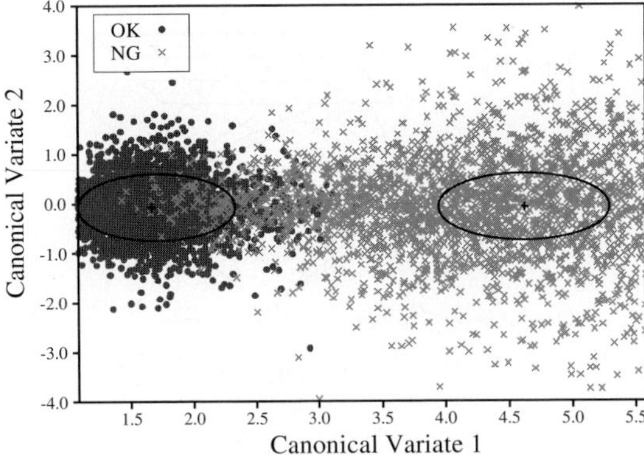

Fig. 6. Feature Space

Table 1. Experimental Result (Fisher's linear discriminant method)

	Recognition Results	
	Correct	Error
Correct	3643	2
Error	473	2765

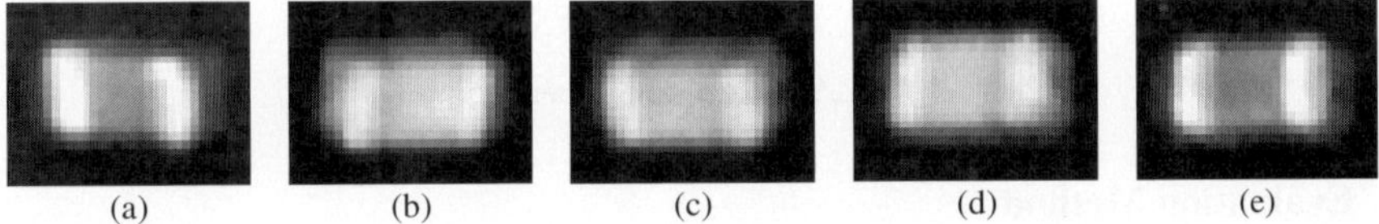

(a)   (b)   (c)   (d)   (e)

Fig. 7. Examples of Classification Error Images

4 Detection by Neural Networks

Next, the detection method by neural networks that use the gray value of each pixel of the image acquired from the bottom of parts as input is examined.

4.1 Structure of Neural Networks

Fig. 8 shows the structure of three-layer neural networks used for the pickup error detection. The size of input layer is 32 x 24 pixels, the hidden layer is 128 units, and the output layer is 1 unit. If the output is more than the threshold, it is recognized that the part is picked up normally. The back propagation algorithm is used for learning three-layer neural networks.

4.2 Learning Method

Fig. 9 shows the learning method. One teacher data is used for learning continuously N times. And then, the next teacher data is used. In this research, N=10 is used. Moreover, the sequence of the teacher data is replaced at random at each learning.

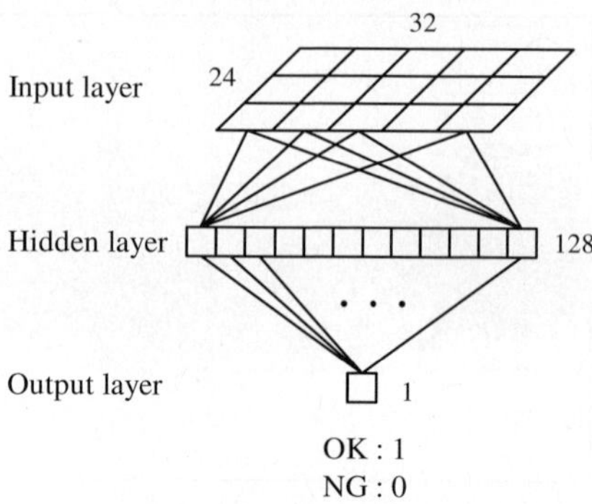

Fig. 8. Three-layer Neural Networks

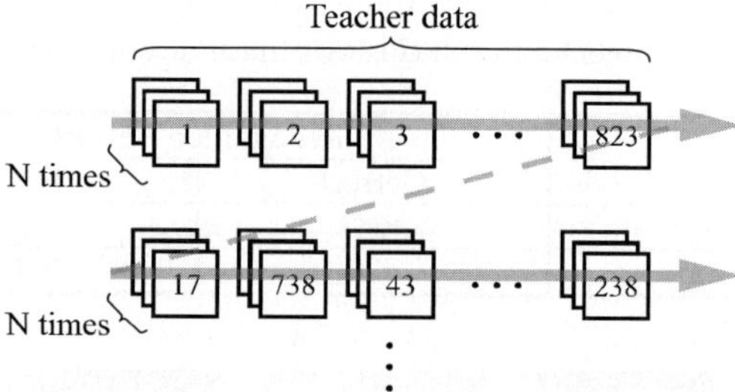

Fig. 9. Learning Sequence

4.3   Evaluation Method

Performance evaluation of neural networks is performed by classifying test data and comparing the average classification error rate. The average classification error rate is calculated as follows. At first, the cumulative relative frequency of the output value of normal data and the cumulative relative frequency of the output value of error data is

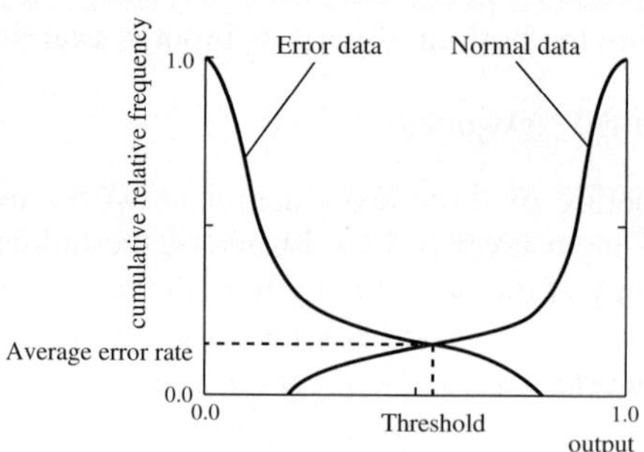

Fig. 10. Average Classification Error Rate

calculated separately. Next, the output value where each cumulative relative frequency is the same value is selected as a threshold. If it does so, the error rate of normal data becomes equal to the error rate of error data. The error rate in this case is the average classification error rate (Fig. 10).

4.4 Evaluation Experiment (1)

The evaluation experiment was performed by training neural networks with the teacher data by the above-mentioned method, and classifying the test data. 3597 normal images and 6208 error images (9805 images in total) were prepared. 411 normal images and 412 error images were chosen from these images at random, and they were used for training neural networks as teacher data. The rest of these images were used for performance evaluation experiment.

Fig. 11 shows the average classification error rate at each learning count, and the experimental result by neural networks trained 3000 times is shown in Table 2. As a result, detection rate is about 99.3% (error rate is 0.7%).

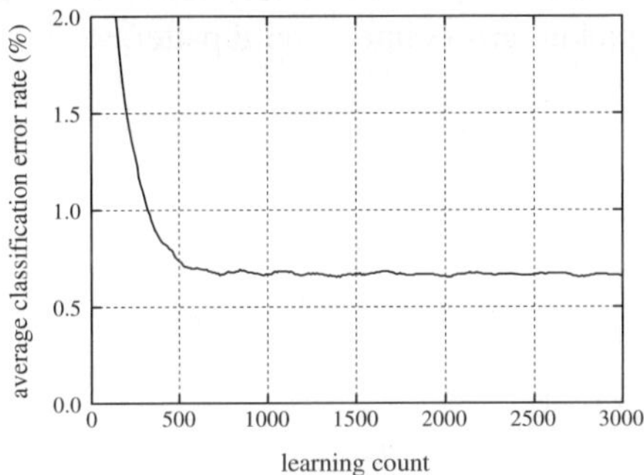

Fig. 11. Average Classification Error Rate at Each Learning Count

Table 2. Experimental Result (Neural Networks)

	Recognition Results	
	Correct	Error
Correct	3274	6
Error	114	5848

4.5 Increasing Number of Output

By observing pickup error images, it is found that there are three patterns in pickup errors. Fig. 12b-12d shows the example of pickup error patterns. Therefore, neural networks whose output layer is 4 units (1 normal pattern and 3 error patterns) are examined. The parts are classified to the class with the largest output value. The learning method is similar to the above-mentioned method.

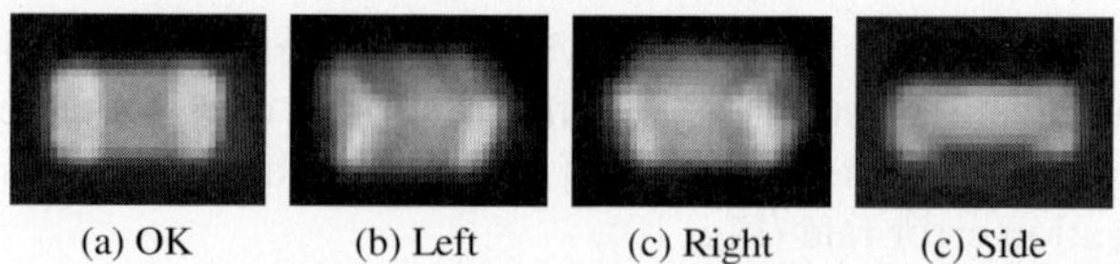

<table>
<tr><td>(a) OK</td><td>(b) Left</td><td>(c) Right</td><td>(c) Side</td></tr>
</table>

Fig. 12. Examples of Pickup Pattern

4.6 Evaluation Experiment (2)

The evaluation experiment was performed using 4-output neural networks.

3657 normal images, 3300 right diagonal images, 3371 left diagonal images and 44 sideways images (10372 images in total) were prepared. The teacher data was chosen from these images at random, and they were used for training neural networks. The rest of these images were used for performance evaluation experiment.

Fig. 13 shows the average classification error rate at each learning count, and the experimental result by neural networks trained 3000 times is shown in Table 3. As a result, detection rate is about 99.7% (error rate is 0.3%). The detection rate is improved by dividing the pickup errors into several patterns.

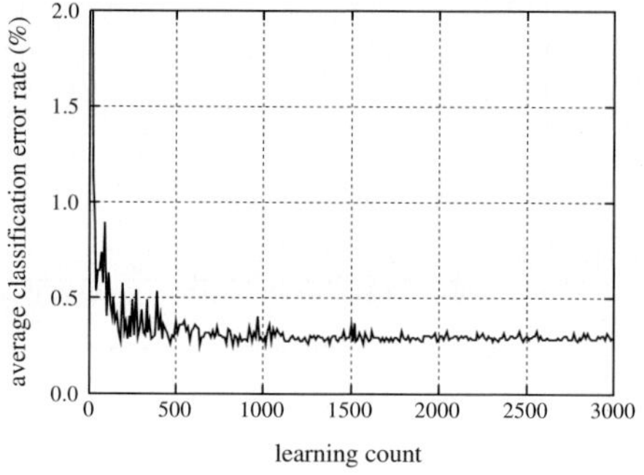

Fig. 13. Average Classification Error Rate at Each Learning Count

Table 3. Experimental Result (4-Output Neural Networks)

	Recognition Results	
	Correct	Error
Correct	3253	14
Error	12	5874

5 Detection by Subspace Method

Finally, the detection method by the subspace method that is the method often used for the pattern recognition is examined.

5.1 CLAFIC Method

There are various methods in the subspace method. In this paper, the CLAFIC method that is a traditional subspace method is used.

In the CLAFIC method, the similarity $S_i(x)$ between feature vector x and class w_i is defined as

$$S_i(x) = \left\| P_i x \right\|^2 .$$
$$= x^t P_i x .$$
$$= \sum_{j=1}^{d_i} (x^t u_{ij})^2 . \tag{4}$$

Where P_i is an orthogonal projection matrix, and u_{ij} is an orthonormal vector.

u_{ij} $(j = 1, 2, ..., d_i)$ is given as jth eigenvector of autocorrelation matrix R_i of class w_i.

The number of eigenvectors d_i is decided depending on the cumulative proportion. The cumulative proportion $a(d_i)$ is given as

$$a(d_i) = \frac{\sum_{j=1}^{d_i} \lambda_{ij}}{\sum_{j=1}^{d} \lambda_{ij}} . \tag{5}$$

Where λ_{ij} is jth eigenvalue of class w_i. In this paper, cumulative proportion 99% was used.

The similarity for each class is calculated, and the part is classified into the class with the largest similarity.

5.2 Evaluation Experiment

The evaluation experiment was performed using the above-mentioned method.

The teacher data and the test data are the same as used in the 4-output neural networks method. The part is classified into 4 classes, that is, "Normal", "Left diagonal", "Right diagonal", and "Sideways".

The experimental result by CLAFIC method is shown in Table 4. As a result, detection rate is about 96.5% (error rate is 3.5%). The detection rate by the CLAFIC method that uses linear subspace is lower than that by the neural networks.

Table 4. Experimental Result (CLAFIC)

	Recognition Results	
	Correct	Error
Correct	2960	320
Error	7	5955

6 Conclusion

Currently, pickup errors are detected using the image that is acquired in a horizontal direction. In this paper, we examined several detection methods that use the image acquired from the bottom of the part for positioning.

First of all, the detection method by Fisher's linear discriminant method using the features extracted from the image is examined. As a result, detection rate is about 93.1%. In this method, it is found that the part side appears very dark in some error images and it causes classification errors.

Next, we examined the detection method by neural networks that use the gray value of each pixel of the image as input. As a result, detection rate is about 99.3%, and the detection rate is improved. It seems that the part whose side appears dark is classified correctly by using each pixel value of the image.

Moreover, we examined the detection method by 4-output neural networks. As a result, detection rate is about 99.7%, and the detection rate is further improved. The detection rate is improved by dividing the pickup errors into several patterns.

Finally, we examined the detection method by the subspace method that uses the gray value of each pixel of the image as features. The detection rate by the CLAFIC method is lower than that by the neural networks. The nonlinearity of the neural networks works effectively in this case.

The occurrence probability of pickup errors is very low. Therefore, the detection rate of 99.7% obtained in this research is useful enough for practical use. We will examine other method to further improve detection rate in the future.

References

1. Rumellhart, D.E., McClelland, J.L., PDP Research Group: Parallel Distributed Processiong, vol. 1. The MIT Press, London (1986)
2. Lippmann, R.P.: An Introduction to Computer with Neural Nets. IEEE ASSP Magazine (April 1987)
3. Duda, R.O., Hart, P.E., Stork, D.G.: Pattern Classification. John Wiley & Sons, Chichester (2000)
4. Kurita, T.: A Study on Applications of Statistical Methods to Flexible Information Processing, National Institute of Advanced Industrial Science and Technology (1993)
5. McLachlan, G.J.: Discriminant Analysis and Statistical Pattern Recognition. Wiley, Chichester (1992)

SOM-Based Continuous Category Learning for Age Classification by Facial Images

Koichi Ikuta[1], Hiroshi Kage[1], Kazuhiko Sumi[1], Ken-ichi Tanaka[1], and Kazuo Kyuma[2]

[1] Advanced Technology R&D Center, Mitsubishi Electric Corporation,
8-1-1 Tsukagushi Honmachi, Amagasaki,
Hyogo, 661-8661, Japan
`Ikuta.Koichi@ak.MitsubishiElectric.co.jp`
[2] Corporate Research & Development Group, Mitsubishi Electric Corporation,
2-7-3 Marunouchi, Chiyoda Ward, Tokyo, 100-8310, Japan

Abstract. In machine learning for person identification from facial images, feature sets are assigned into discrete categories. The age classification task, however, cannot be solved in the same way because the age-related face features go through gradual, or rather continuous, changes over the ages. From the machine learning viewpoint, age groups in terms of face images do not have clear borders, and it can be said that they can form 'continuous category'. Therefore we think that we should add the continuousness of face features to the learning process for enhancing the performance of age estimation. In this paper, we propose a model of age classification using one dimensional Self-Organizing Map, which can train the classifiers without preparing complete age information and reinforce the classifier's performance. We show the effectiveness of our model and compare the performance to that of using discrete category machine learning. In conclusions, we clarify our future directions.

Keywords: Self-Organizing map, facial image recognition, continuous category, personal identification.

1 Introduction

Recently cameras have been all around us, ranging from mobile phone to automatic recognition system. In terms of visual surveillance, the study of face recognition technology attracts attention from not only academic, but also industrial fields. The demand of this technology will lead to the improvement of the credibility of security systems for the purpose of preventing crime and terrorism. Another aspect of face recognition technology is to estimate personal attributes, and applicable algorithms to estimate gender or age from faces have been studied [1]. This technology will lead to practical applications such as market research and video surveillance. As an example of market research application, the algorithm can be applied to the system that controls advertisement timely depending on gender and age of people looking at advertising displays. Moreover, as an assistant application for video surveillance, the system can automatically browse by focusing on gender and age as key features. It will dramatically reduce the total amount

M. Ishikawa et al. (Eds.): ICONIP 2007, Part II, LNCS 4985, pp. 569–576, 2008.

of time and cost. In the current status, however, the technology has many problems to realize a commercial system mainly in terms of the algorithm performance. Here we would like to emphasize that age estimation from faces is quite different from personal identification or gender classification. Gender and age are personal facial attributes, but gender classification task is basically similar to personal identification in terms of machine learning. Because gender classification has two discrete categories, men or women. The same goes for the case of personal identification, identical or non-identical. Personal identification by faces actually have challenging problems from the practical viewpoint, but the framework of learning is very simple. But age classification task cannot be solved in the same way because the age-related face features go through gradual, or rather continuous, changes over the ages. Therefore age groups in terms of face images do not have clear borders, and it can be said that they can form 'continuous category'. Therefore we think that we should add the continuousness of face features to the learning process. For this reason, we considered applying one dimensional Self-Organizing Map (hereafter SOM) to the problem of age estimation. The algorithm is capable of dealing with such one-dimensional topology of the feature space. In this paper, we introduce a age estimation framework with one dimensional SOM. We tested our method by computer simulation and show the effectiveness quantitatively. The remainder of this paper is organized as follows. In Section 2, we explain the differences between age and gender classification. In Section 3, we describe our algorithm for age classification. In Section4, we show the experimental results and comparative studies. In Section 4, we refer to the future works by summarizing this paper.

2   Differences Between Age and Gender Classifications

As mentioned in the previous section, gender and age classification tasks are different in terms of category learning. Gender classification is a similar task to personal identification because both tasks are two-category problems, while age classification does not have discrete categories because relevant facial features have gradual changes over the ages. We developed gender classification algorithm based on Ada-boost. Our gender classification algorithm has a single classifier, which is designed to have positive response to female facial images and negative response to male ones. According to our evaluation results, the recognition rate was 89% for male and 93% for female. Now we describe why such a discrete classification method will be inappropriate for age classification. Before training face images as discrete categories, we should assign each training image into a relevant category. Now we assume that two age categories of 10's and 20's to build up a classifier to discriminate these two categories. Then a face image at the age of 19 and that at the age of 20 will be assigned to different categories, even if those facial features will be close together in the feature space. Therefore there is a possibility that the resulting age classification task will have bad performances. Based on this consideration, we introduce one-dimensional SOM to maintain neighbourhood information between face images in the feature space.

3   Age Classification as a Continuous Category

3.1   Feature Extraction

3.1.1   Filter Region

Before classifying face images in terms of their ages, the system should extract various features and build up the feature space. In the literature of age discrimination of faces, effective methods have been developed in computer graphics or related research fields, where it has been known that specific facial regions have dominant factors on facial aging. The changes of the factors are due to flabbiness of the muscle with age. Based on this knowledge, we set up the feature extraction to estimate facial ages.

Fig.1 specifically shows facial regions essential to feature extraction in our framework. There are four regions: (a) region including cheeks, (b) region including mouth and jaw, (c) eye region, and (d) nasal region. These positions are fixed, but coefficients sets of the filters placed inside each region are determined by filter learning.

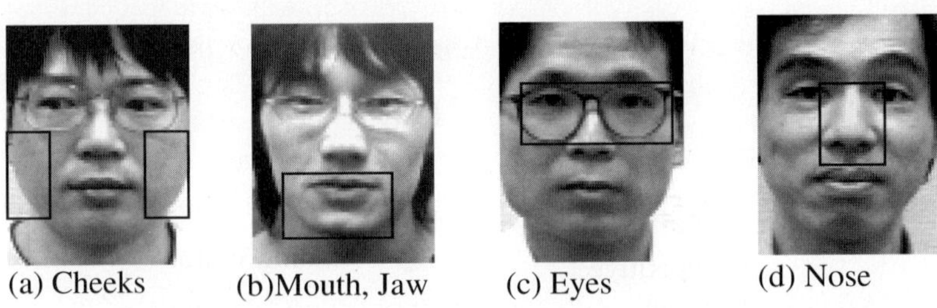

Fig. 1. This figure shows the facial regions for the feature extract filters

3.1.2   Filter Learning

The 2-dimensional coefficients of filters are generated by the learning. The filter learning is independently done every feature regions. The learning rule of each region is the same. In our construction, we use 3 filters for each region, each of which corresponds to the specific age (20's, 30's, 40's) and is composed from training data by the learning. Here we consider the case of one region. We show the equations for filter learning rule below.

$$c = \arg\min_{i}\|m_i - x\| \tag{1}$$

where x is the vector of training image region corresponding to the region of the filter i. i denotes the filter index, which corresponds specific generation (0 for 20's, 1 for 30's, 2 for 40's). x is not the raw value of image region, but processed in the way that DC (direct current) components are removed by subtracting the average value of the image area. m_i is the vector of the filter i. The filter c is selected as the winner, which has the minimum distance to the vector x. The learning rule of the filter is below.

572   K. Ikuta et al.

$$m_i(t+1) = m_i(t) + h_{ci}(t)[x(t) - m_i(t)] \qquad (2)$$

where $h_{ci}(t)$ is a neighborhood function for competitive and cooperative learning between filters. The filters close to the winner is also trained toward the direction vector x. The filters distant from the winner are trained toward the opposite direction vector x. Fig.2 shows the work of the rule. While this rule keeps the continuousness of the filters close to neighboring generation, the rule prevents the concentration of filters to the small feature area.

In general, it will be easiest to construct the feature vector from the pixel values, but the feature space will be affected by the change of illuminating condition or face pose. Therefore we decided that the feature vector should be constructed by the above filtering method.

$$\begin{aligned}
&h_{ci}(t){=}\varepsilon \quad (i{=}c), \\
&h_{ci}(t){=}\varepsilon/2 \quad (|c{-}i|{=}1), \\
&h_{ci}(t){=}{-}\varepsilon/2 \quad (|c{-}i|{=}2)
\end{aligned} \qquad (3)$$

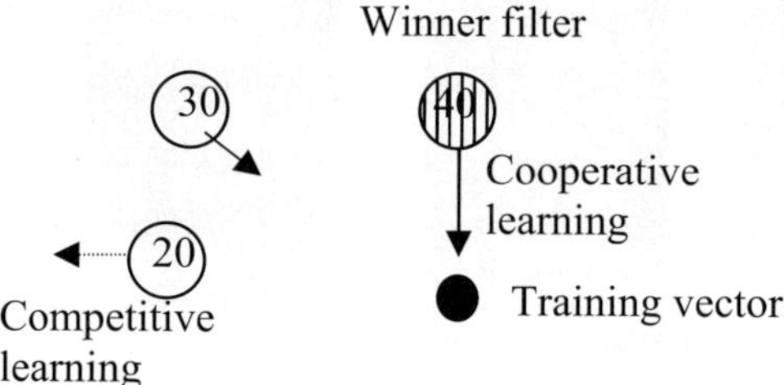

Fig. 2. The filters are updated by competitive learning and cooperative learning. The *30's filter* is updated for the direction to the *training vector* and the *20's filter* moves away from the training vector, when the *winner filter 40's* learning proceed.

3.2 One-Dimensional SOM

SOM is a machine learning method based on unsupervised and competitive learning proposed by Kohonen[2]. SOM can be regarded as a data mining method to compress extremely high dimensional data to lower (usually one or two) dimensional one, which fits well to the original training data structure. From the viewpoint of age classification, it is desirable that one-dimensional data structure will be extracted from higher dimensional face data. In our SOM-based learning algorithm, we assumed a one-dimensional chain structure composed of several classifiers each of which is placed arbitrary and regarded as a reference vector in the feature space. These classifiers are updated by the unsupervised learning. We call the classifier as the UnSupervised Learning classifier (USL classifier).

Here we explain how the learning algorithm works. Let y and n_i $(i{=}1,2,...)$ represent a feature vector corresponding to a face image and reference vectors. Then the closest reference vector to y in the feature space, denoted as n_d, is called a winner vector. The suffix d is formulated as follows:

$$d = \arg\min_i \|n_i - y\| \tag{4}$$

The learning process for reference vectors $\mathbf{n}_i$ proceeds by the following formula:

$$n_i(t+1) = n_i(t) + J_{di}(t)[y(t) - n_i(t)] \tag{5}$$

The above process proceeds only for neighboring reference vectors, and $J_{di}(t)$ indicates neighborhood function, which has a monotonically decreasing profile along the distance. The neighboring function can be described using Gaussian function as follows:

$$J_{di} = \alpha \exp\left(-\frac{\|r_d - r_i\|^2}{2\delta^2}\right) \tag{6}$$

where r indicates the distance of the reference vector from the winner vector n_d.

3.3 Supervised Learning of Age

We introduce Supervised Learning classifiers (SL classifier) on the one-dimensional SOM adding to the Unsupervised Learning classifiers (USL classifier) described above. The SL classifiers has specific age index. The face image feature is high dimensional and the one-dimensional SOM has high degree of freedom to move in the feature space. Therefore, the one-dimensional SOM may be trained along the direction of unexpected feature but the age feature. The SL classifiers are arranged among the USL classifiers on the one-dimensional SOM and works as pins fix the specific points of string of SOM chain. We show the equation of learning of the SL classifier below.

$$n_i(t+1) = n_i(t) + \alpha[y(t) - n_i(t)] \tag{7}$$

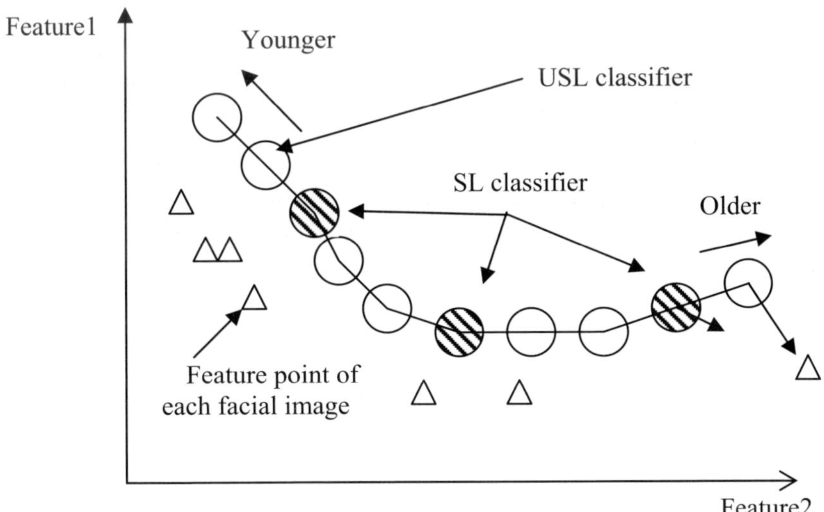

Fig. 3. This depicts the structure of the one-dimensional SOM. *USL classifiers* and *SL classifiers* are assigned on the chain of one-dimensional *SOM* along the axis of age.

The rule of the learning is basically the same to the rule for the USL classifier. The SL classifier is only updated by the learning when the facial data with corresponding age index is given. For example, the SL classifier with 25 age index is only updated by a facial image with 25 age index. Note that the USL classifiers close to the SL classifiers is also updated by equation (5), when the SL classifier is updated.

4   Experimental Results and Comparative Studies

We verified performance of our model mentioned above by computer simulation. We also evaluated the age classification model which is based on Ada-boost for comparing to our model's performance. The performance was compared under the task for classifying 3 categories (20's, 30's, 40's age).

4.1   General Settings

Facial images for training and classifying are 36x45 pixels, 256 gray level images. The facial images are taken as the front view image and under proper illumination and without specific expression. All the facial image data is previously processed in condition of face clipped image with regulated tone level.

The number of facial images for training data is 400 pictures; the number of images for verifying classification is 120. The images for verification consist of 60 images for each class (20's, 30's, 40's age). Each image has one of the 3 types of age index (20's, 30's, 40's age). The ratio of male and female is unfortunately not balanced, because we gather up the data from the facial images of our working place members.

4.2   DC Classifier Model

We make the simple model based on the person identification technology to compare with our model. We call the model for comparison as Discrete Category classifier model (DC classifier model), because the model is made based on the classification method suitable for the discrete category.

The DC classifier model has 3 classifiers, each of them is for 20's, 30's, 40's age category. Each of classifiers is trained to have positive response to corresponding category's facial image, the training is the supervised learning with age index of each facial image by Ada-boost algorithm.

4.3   Proposed Model

Our proposed model has 15 classifiers on a one-dimensional SOM. Only 3 of classifiers are SL classifiers, which are trained with age index. The rest 27 of the classifiers are USL classifiers, which are trained without age index. We assign numbers to the classifiers in the order of age from youngest to oldest. Then the USL classifiers are No.3, No.8, and No.13. Each of classifiers roughly corresponds to the center of 20's, 30's, 40's age, respectively.

In this model, we use the filters set for 3 generations. Filter set for each generation has 4 types of area filters depicted in Fig .1. Therefore the dimension of the feature space is 12.Only 50 images of training data set are used for the supervised learning with age index for SL classifier. The rest 350 facial images for training are used for the unsupervised learning for USL classifier.

4.4 Classification Performance Verification

We used 180 facial images to verify the performance of the both model. The test images consists of 60 image sets for each 20's, 30's, 40's age. We counted outputs of the facial images to make the age classification performance table. In DC classifier model, we counted each classifier as corresponding age class.

In our proposed model, we take a classifier with minimum output, we counted classifier 1-5 as 20's age, 6-10 as 30's age, 11-15 as 40's age. Table1 shows the age classification performance table of our proposed model and DC classifier model.

Table 1. This table shows the performance result of Age Classification performance table of the Proposed model and the DC classifier model

	Proposed model			DC classifier model		
	20's classified	30's classified	40's classified	20's classified	30's classified	40's classified
20's data	(47/60) 78.3%	(11/60)	(2/60)	(42/60) 70.0%	(12/60)	(6/60)
30's data	(13/60)	(32/60) 53.3%	(15/60)	(20/60)	(19/60) 31.7%	(21/60)
40's data	(4/60)	(18/60)	(38/60) 63.3%	(10/60)	(15/60)	(35/60) 58.3%

5 Summary and Conclusions

In this paper, we described our age classification model. Our model use one-dimensional SOM for learning the seriality of the age features. This learning algorithm can makes each age identifier arrange along the order of age. Besides, this learning can be processed without age information of each facial image. This is also the important merit of this algorithm. Because, recently management of personal information becomes so strict that it becomes difficult to gather up facial images with personal data for the system development. We tested our algorithm by computer simulations and showed higher performance than that of age classification algorithm to which we applied Ada-boost base algorithm.

In current stage, our algorithm was only evaluated with the condition that all the facial data was taken as the front view and under proper illumination and without specific expression. Related to face identification, when operating the system in real situations, there should be many problems brought by illumination variation, face tilt and facial expression.

The feature extraction filters are trained and set fix before the system use. However, the variation of face depends on the country. We plan to introduce the algorithm of filter reconstruction with the feedback signal of the classification results [3].

As personal attribution, ethnic group category has also continuous structure the same as age category. However, it is thought that features are not distributed on one-dimensional plane like age, but higher dimensional plane. As future work, we will apply to this higher dimensional feature structure problem based on the SOM approach.

References

1. Ueki, Hayashida, K., Kobayashi, T.: Subspace-based age-group classification using facial images under various lighting conditions. In: 7th International Conference on Automatic Face and Gesture Recognition, 2006, pp. 10–12 (2006)
2. Kohonen, T.: Self-Organizing Maps, 3rd edn. Springer, Berlin (2001)
3. Ikuta, K., Tanaka, H., Tanaka, K., Kyuma, K.: Learning algorithm by reinforcement signals for the automatic recognition. In: Proc. IEEE SMC 2004, The Netherlands, Hague, pp. 4844–4848 (2004)

A Complete Hardware Implementation of an Integrated Sound Localization and Classification System Based on Spiking Neural Networks

Mauricio Kugler, Kaname Iwasa, Victor Alberto Parcianello Benso, Susumu Kuroyanagi, and Akira Iwata

Department of Computer Science and Engineering
Nagoya Institute of Technology
Showa-ku, Gokiso-cho, 466-8555, Nagoya, Japan
mauricio@kugler.com, {kaname,benso}@mars.elcom.nitech.ac.jp,
{bw,iwata}@nitech.ac.jp

Abstract. Several applications would emerge from the development of artificial systems able to accurately localize and identify sound sources. This paper proposes an integrated sound localization and classification system based on the human auditory system and a respective compact hardware implementation. The proposed models are based on spiking neurons, which are suitable for processing time series data, like sound signals, and can be easily implemented in hardware. The system uses two microphones, extracting the time difference between the two channels with a chain of coincidence detection spiking neurons. A spiking neural networks process the time-delay pattern, giving a single directional output. Simultaneously, an independent spiking neural network process the spectral information of on audio channel in order to classify the source. Experimental results show that a the proposed system could successfully locate and identify several sound sources in real time with high accuracy.

1 Introduction

In recent years, sound localization and spacial hearing have been extensively studied. Many works aims to model biological hearing systems, while others try to reproduce their basic functionality with artificial systems. However, the development of a consistent and robust artificial hearing system remains a challenge. Nevertheless, several practical implementations have been proposed, the majority of them based on the estimation of the time-delay between the signals from one or more pairs of microphones.

Several authors proposed methods for time-delay estimation based on variations of the the Generalized Cross-Correlation technique [1]. Although mathematically consistent and achieving good performance, those methods presents complex implementations and have no relation with the true biological hearing systems. More recently, several biologically inspired sound localization approaches based on spiking neural networks have emerged. Those methods have

M. Ishikawa et al. (Eds.): ICONIP 2007, Part II, LNCS 4985, pp. 577–587, 2008.

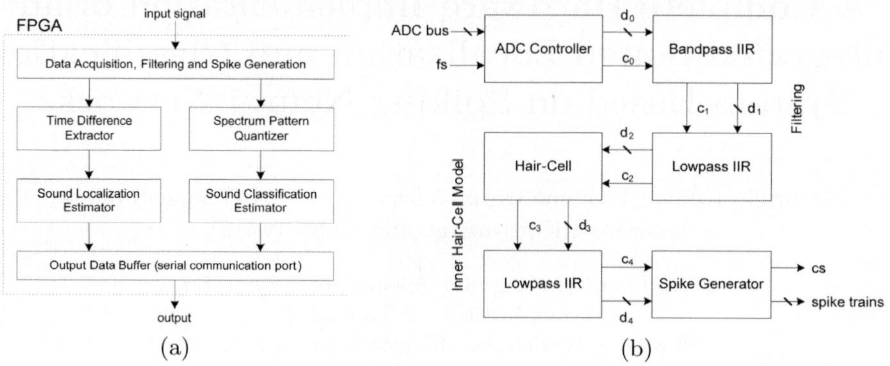

Fig. 1. Block diagrams of (a) main sound localization and classification system (b) filtering and spike generation stage (d_n: 32-bit bus signals, c_n: control signals)

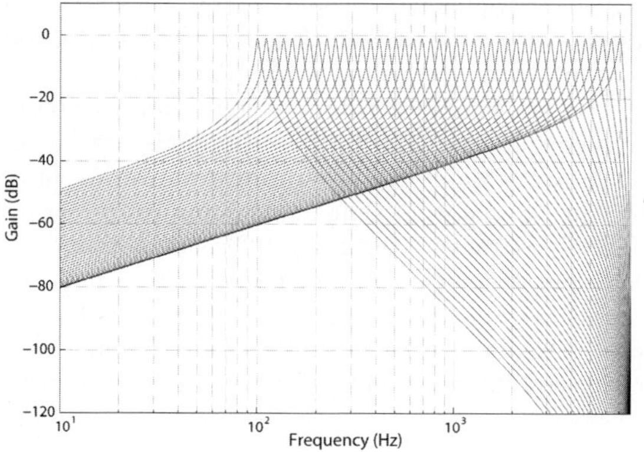

Fig. 2. IIR bandpass filter bank frequency response

the advantages of naturally dealing with temporal data and presenting a simple implementation in hardware [2].

Kuroyanagi and Iwata [3] proposed a spiking neural model for detecting the localization of a sound source based on the inter-aural time difference (ITD) and the inter-aural level difference (ILD). This model was further extended by the addition of a competitive learning spiking neural network [4] in order to combine the output of the ITD extractors of all frequency channels [5]. Schauer and Paschke [6] proposed a similar structure, except for the use of a Winner-Take-All (WTA) spiking neuron structure for combining the several frequency channels outputs. Later, the model was extended for a 360° localization model by using a special microphone arrangement [7]. They also presented a partial hardware implementation of their system [8].

In contrast to sound localization, systems capable of identifying the nature of non-speech sound sources were not deeply explored. Some authors study the application of speech-recognition techniques [9], while others attempt to divide

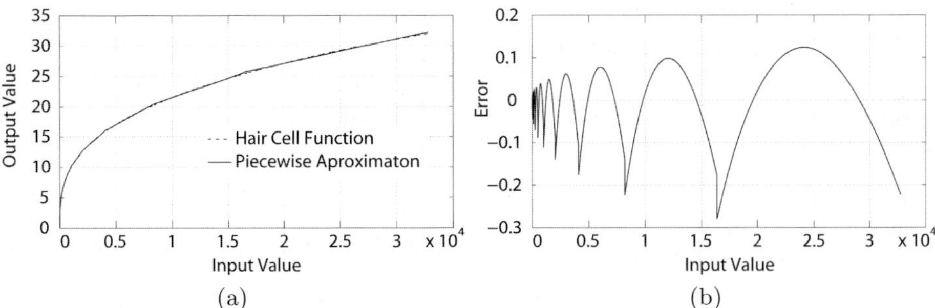

Fig. 3. Piecewise function of the Hair Cell model and the approximation error

all possibly mixed sound sources and apply independent techniques for each kind of signal [10]. Sakaguchi, Kuroyanagi and Iwata [11] proposed a sound classification system based on the human auditory model, using spiking neural networks for identifying six different sound sources.

From all the works described above, the models proposed in [3,4,5,11] have several advantages. The models are purely based on spiking neurons, making its hardware implementation very efficient. They also presents several common components, reducing the model's complexity while keeping the system generic and extendable. Based on these models and on a preliminary hardware implementation presented in [12], this paper proposes an integrated solution for sound localization and classification using only spiking neurons based components (except the filtering and spike generation stage), fully implemented in an FPGA device.

2   Proposed Model

The proposed system consists on the implementation of a sound localization and classification system in a portable hardware suitable for real-time applications. The system is able to localize a sound source using the signal from two microphones, as well as classify the source in one of the predefined types.

The block diagram of the proposed model's main structure is show in Fig. 1(a). The system is divided in two branches, sound localization and sound recognition. Both of them use input data from the filtering and spike generation stage, which detailed diagram is shown in Fig. 1(b). The following section describe each block in details.

2.1   Filtering and Spike Generation

All circuits described in this section were implemented using single precision floating point numerical representation. The filtering stage is composed by 43 filters for the left channel (used for localization and recognition) and 15 filters for the right channel (used only for localization). Each filter block implements a second order Infinite Impulse Response (IIR) elliptical filter with unitary gain on the center frequency or pass band. A cascade of a bandpass and a low-pass

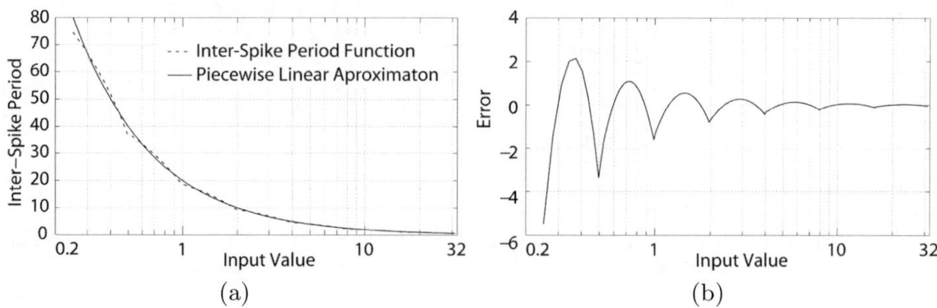

(a)   (b)

Fig. 4. Piecewise functions of the Spike Generator model and the approximation error

produces an approximation for the cochlea's frequency response. The total gain of all the filters is shown in Fig. 2. Equation (1) shows the basic equation of the used filters:

$$y_0 = (b_0 x_0 + b_1 x_1 + b_2 x_2) - (a_1 y_1 + a_2 y_2) \tag{1}$$

where x_n and y_n correspond, respectively, to the input sample on the instant of time n, or $x(t-n)$ and the output of the filter on the instant of time n, or $y(t-n)$, and a_n, b_n are the filter coefficients.

The filters were implemented in a pipeline structure, in which all the multiplications are made in parallel, followed by three levels of additions and subtractions. The input and output values are stored and delayed by shift registers, avoiding the use of RAM memories with complex addressing logic. Due to restrictions of the architecture of the used FPGA and to simplify the circuit, the pipeline calculates 64 filters outputs at each cycle, 6 of them being ignored on this implementation. Thus, a new sample can be processed 64 clocks after the previous sample was received.

The output of the filters are then transformed by a non-linear function corresponding to the inner hair-cells of the hearing system. The hair-cells function is shown in equation 2:

$$f(x) = \begin{cases} x^{\frac{1}{3}} & x \geq 0 \\ \frac{1}{4} x^{\frac{1}{3}} & x < 0 \end{cases} \tag{2}$$

The implementation of a true exponential function in hardware is very complex. Instead, this paper proposes the use of a piecewise linear approximation for implementing this function. Usually, this would require several comparisons for determining which linear function should be used for a certain value. Instead of determining the range by the total value (what would require 32-bits comparisons), the ranges for the linear functions were determined by the exponent of the input value, represented by the first 8 bits after the sinal bit in a single-precision floating point. From the maximal range of the input signal and desired precision, only exponents from -16 to +15 were used. This requires 5 exponent bits plus the signal bit, resulting in 64 different pairs of coefficients. The required multiplication and addition were also constructed using a pipeline structure of 16 stages.

Figure 3(a) shows the true hair cell function and the piecewise approximation. The approximation error is shown in Fig. 3(b). The different scales on the graphics shows that the error is negligible. The result from the hair-cell block is applied in a second order IIR Butterworth 400 Hz low-pass filter, which structure is identical to the filters described above.

The same piecewise linear approximation approach was used for the spikes generation. Equation 3 is used for calculating the inter-spike period T:

$$T = K \frac{x_{max} - x_{min}}{x - m_{min}} \tag{3}$$

where x is the input value, x_{max} and x_{min} are limiting factors for the value of x and K is a constant. From the resulting range of the hair-cell function (-8 to +32) and the minimal possible interval between spikes (determined by the sampling frequency), only exponents from -2 to +5 were used. The true function and the piecewise approximation are shown in Fig. 4(a) and the associated error in Fig. 4(b). After the period is calculated, the equivalent integer value it is compared with the correspondent timer and, if it overflows the calculated period, a spike is generated on the respective channel.

2.2   Spiking Neuron Model

The spiking neuron model used in this research is based on the standard integrate-and-fire (I&F) model [2]. A block diagram of the FPGA implementation of this model is shown in Fig. 5. As the input signals are pulse trains, their weighted sum can be implemented with AND circuits, which outputs are then added and the result compared with the threshold. The neuron's output $u(t)$ of the used spiking neuron model is:

$$u(t) = H\left(\sum_{k=1}^{n} p_k(t) - \theta\right) \qquad p_k(t) = e^{-\Delta t/\tau} p_k(t - \Delta t) \tag{4}$$

where $H(\cdot)$ is the unit step function, θ is the threshold and $p_k(t)$ is the membrane potential of the kth input. The model also has a refractory period t_r, during which the neuron is unable to fire, independently of the membrane potential.

The time constant decaying is achieved by a bit shift and a complement operation, subtracting a fraction of the former inner potential. Ideally, all local membrane potential units should contain the decaying operator. However, on this research, for the sake of simplicity, only the inner potential unit contains that operator, as the time constant is the same for all local membrane potentials.

2.3   Time-Difference Extractor

Each spike train generated at each frequency channel is inputted in an independent Time Difference Extractor (TDE). The structure of the extractor is based on Jeffress's model [13]. The left and right signals are inputted in opposed sides of the extractor, and the pulses are sequentially shifted at each clock cycle. When a neuron receives two simultaneous spikes, it fires. The position of

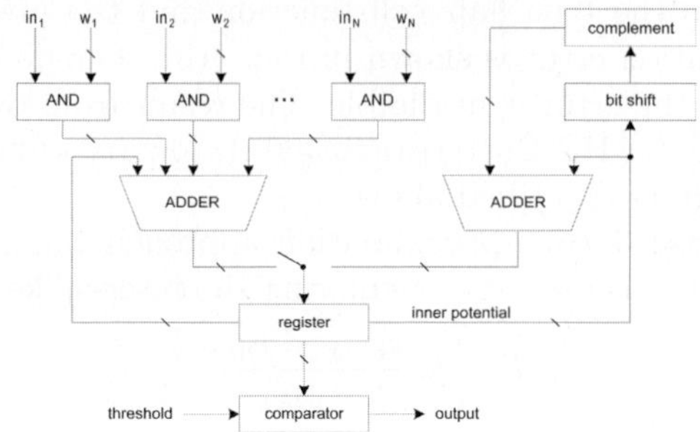

Fig. 5. Hardware implementation of the spiking neuron model

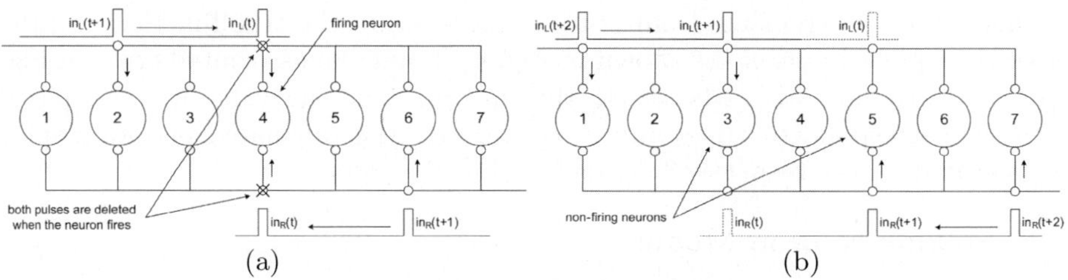

(a)   (b)

Fig. 6. Time difference extractor and the spike deletion algorithm in the instants of time (a) t and (b) $t + 1$

the firing neuron on the chain determines the time difference. The TDE's basic diagram is shown in Fig. 6(a).

This work uses an improved version of the model, initially proposed in [12]. Each neuron fires only when both input's potentials reach the threshold θ_{TDE}. Also, when a neuron fires, the two input spikes are deleted, preventing several false detections due to the matching of pulses of different cycles, as shown in Fig. 6(b). The spiking neurons on the TDE uses 8-bit fixed-point numerical representation.

2.4   Competitive Learning Network

The Sound Recognition Estimator, the Spectrum Pattern Quantizer and the Sound Recognition Estimator are based on the Competitive Learning Network using Pulsed Neurons (CONP) proposed in [4]. The CONP is a single layer spiking neural network trained primarily by unsupervised learning (but also supporting supervised learning). In order to have just one neuron firing at a time, the CONP model presents two types of control. The non-firing and multi-firing detection neurons fire respectively in case of no firing or multiple firing neurons, increasing or decreasing the inner potential of the neurons. This is also equivalent of changing the firing threshold. Another mechanism only enables the neuron to fire when the input spike train has a sufficiently high input potential (potential without weighting). The FPGA implementation of CONP, previously presented

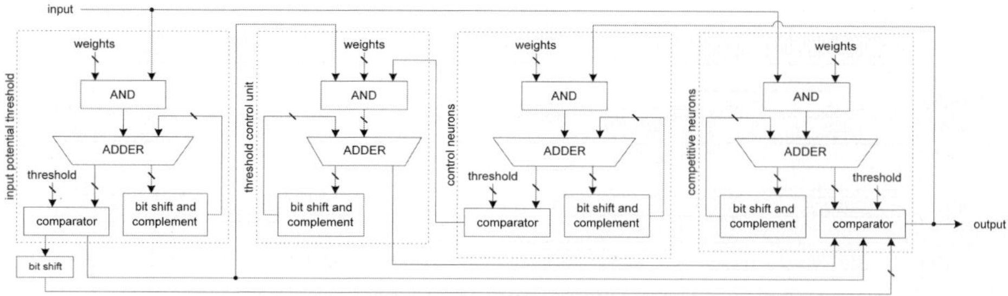

Fig. 7. FPGA implementation of the CONP model

Fig. 8. Proposed system's FPGA board

in [12], is shown in Fig. 7. The CONP implementation uses 32-bit fixed-point numerical representation for the spiking neurons weights and potentials.

A single neuron circuit can be used for calculating the input potential, as the time decays and weights are constant. The input potential is then used for calculating the new threshold. The control neurons also do not act directly on the inner potentials, but instead are sent to the threshold control unit, which calculate the change on the threshold. The final equation for the spiking neuron then becomes:

$$u\left(t\right) = H\left(\sum_{k=1}^{n} p_k\left(t\right) - \theta - \theta_{nfd}\left(t\right) - \theta_{mfd}\left(t\right) - \theta_{in}\left(t\right)\right)\tag{5}$$

where $\theta_{nfd}\left(t\right)$, $\theta_{mfd}\left(t\right)$ and $\theta_{in}\left(t\right)$ are, respectively, the no-firing detection threshold, the multi-firing detection threshold and the inner-potential threshold.

2.5 Proposed Models FPGA Board

In order to attend the performance requirements of the presented implementation and allow future extensions, a custom 10x7cm hardware platform, shown in Fig. 8, was developed. The core of the system is a state of the art FPGA device, an Altera Stratix II EPS260F484C4, containing 48352 ALUTs (Adaptive Look-Up

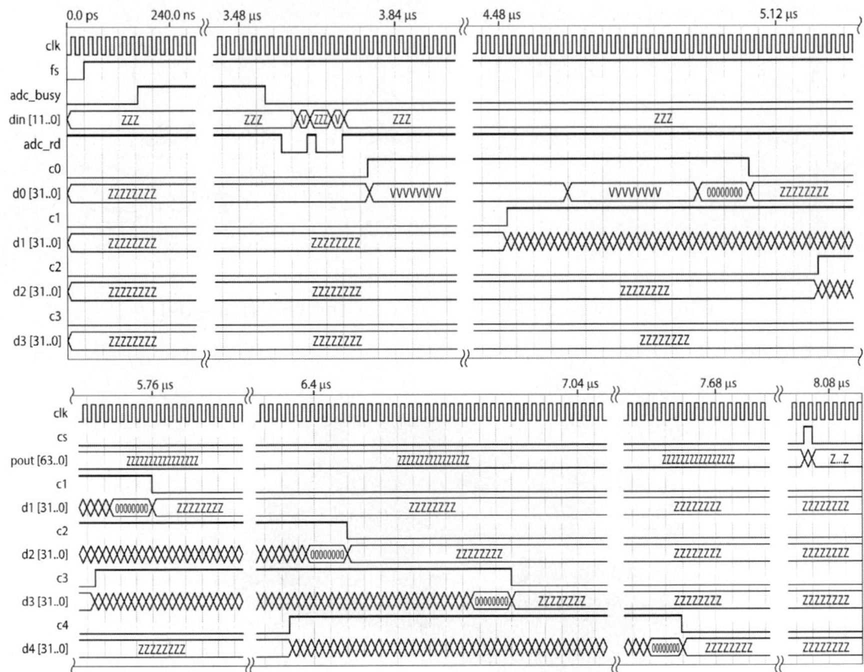

Fig. 9. Timing for data acquisition, filtering and spike generation

Table) and 288 9-bit DSP block elements. The audio sampling interface is based in a AD7864, providing analog-to-digital conversion rate up to 520kSPS with 12 bits of resolution on 4 simultaneous channels. This, in addition to a serial interface and a couple of LEDs and switches, makes the board a general purpose development platform for audio based applications.

3   Experimental Results

Figure 9 provides the timing for the digital signal processing blocks. The signal names corresponds to the diagram in Fig. 1(b). The process is triggered by a rising edge on the sampling frequency clock signal *fs*. After the ADC reads the left and right channels values, the pipeline process starts. All the processing for a single sample takes $4.24\mu s$ at 50MHz, enabling real time processing for standard audio sampling frequencies.

Six sound signals were used on the localization and classification experiments: "Alarm Bell", "Interphone", "Phone Ring", "FM Noise", "Kettle" and "Human Voice". The experimental sounds were recoded in an semi-anechoic chamber and a Neumann KU100 Dummy Head was used as a microphone. The sound source was moved circularly from 90° left to 90° right in relation to the dummy head, 1m away from it. The test results (calculated from the number of correct firings in a fixed direction sound signal) correspond to the average of three different

Table 1. Recognition rates (%) for the FPGA sound localization

True Location	Recognized Source Location: (-) left, (+) right													
	FM Noise							Alarm Bell						
	-90°	-60°	-30°	0°	+30°	+60°	+90°	-90°	-60°	-30°	0°	+30°	+60°	+90°
-90°	**98.3**	0.4	0.3	0.3	0.3	0.2	0.2	**61.3**	15.5	8.9	3.5	4.6	3.0	3.1
-60°	0.4	**98.1**	0.3	0.3	0.3	0.3	0.3	19.7	**47.6**	7.1	2.0	14.4	5.2	4.1
-30°	0.3	0.3	**98.4**	0.3	0.3	0.2	0.2	10.6	4.0	**69.8**	1.7	2.6	8.0	3.3
0°	0.3	0.2	0.3	**98.6**	0.2	0.2	0.2	3.9	2.6	2.2	**80.9**	1.4	3.8	5.2
+30°	0.2	0.2	0.2	0.3	**98.5**	0.3	0.3	4.4	9.9	3.0	1.6	**56.9**	5.4	18.9
+60°	0.3	0.3	0.3	0.3	0.3	**98.2**	0.3	4.8	6.3	13.5	3.7	6.1	**46.7**	18.9
+90°	0.2	0.2	0.3	0.3	0.3	0.3	**98.4**	2.1	3.2	5.9	2.6	8.3	10.9	**66.9**

Table 2. Recognition rates (%) for the FPGA sound classification

True Sound Source	Recognized Sound Source					
	Alarm Bell	Interphone	Kettle	Phone Ring	Voice	FM Noise
Alarm Bell	**99.5**	0.0	0.0	0.4	0.0	0.1
Interphone	0.0	**96.9**	0.0	0.3	1.5	1.3
Kettle	0.0	0.0	**99.5**	0.5	0.0	0.0
Phone Ring	0.4	0.3	0.5	**99.0**	0.5	0.2
Voice	0.0	1.5	0.0	0.0	**98.8**	0.2
FM Noise	0.1	1.3	0.0	1.0	0.0	**99.0**

test signals independent of the training signal. As each channel's time difference extractor uses only one frequency band and the time difference for each frequency is the same for a fix direction, only the "FM Noise" data was used for training the sound localization estimator. As it contains a wide spectrum, all other sound sources could be correctly located.

Table 1 shows the sound localization results for the "FM Noise" and "Alarm Bell" signals. While the "FM Noise" signal presents a high accuracy for all directions, the "Alarm Bell" sound does not present similar performance. One reason form this is the majority of high frequency components on this signal spectrum, which cannot be efficiently located due to the small wave length in comparison to the microphones' distance [7]. Nevertheless, when taking averaged firing rates in short intervals, it always correspond to the correct direction, confirming the efficiency of the proposed FPGA implementation on locating the sound source.

The results for the sound classification experiments are shown in Table 2. All the sound sources could be accurately identified in all cases. The slightly lower value of the "Interphone" reflects the problem of short duration sounds or sound signals composed by different sequential sounds (e.g. door bells).

Table 3 shows the processing time and logic utilization of each of the circuit blocks shown in Fig. 1. The CPU processing time corresponds to a software simulation running in a Pentium IV 3.8GHz with 2GB of RAM. The logic utilization values do not include the external interfaces (ADC and serial port).

Table 3. Processing time for a 10 seconds sound signal and FPGA logic utilization

Component	Processing Time		Logic Utilization		
	CPU(s)	FPGA(s)	ALUTs	Memory Bits	DSP blocks
Filtering & Spike Generation	11.61	0.68	10564	71528	136
Time Difference Extractor	41.25	0.84	14025	-	-
Sound Localization Estimator	8.61	0.88	10011	-	-
Frequencial Pattern Quantizer	2.31	0.73	4594	-	-
Sound Recognition Estimator	1.66	0.64	1570	-	-
Total	65.44	1.78	40764	71528	136

4   Conclusion

This paper proposes an integrated sound localization and classification system and a respective compact hardware implementation. Such kind of system can be the core of several applications, including support and safety devices. The proposed system can successfully localize and classify several sound sources, without requiring any external processing.

Future works also include the optimization of the FPGA code in order to use smaller devices, by converting the spiking neural network to a serial-processing architecture. Moreover, a 360° localization system and an extension for classifying multiple simultaneous sound sources are already being developed.

References

1. Knapp, C.H., Carter, G.C.: The generalized correlation method for estimation of time delay. IEEE Transactions on Acoustics, Speech, and Signal Processing 24(4), 320–327 (1976)
2. Maass, W., Bishop, C.M.: Pulsed Neural Networks. MIT Press, Cambridge (2001)
3. Kuroyanagi, S., Iwata, A.: Auditory pulse neural network model to extract the inter-aural time and level difference for sound localization. IEICE Transactions on Information and Systems - Special Issue on Neurocomputing E77-D(4), 466–474 (1994)
4. Kuroyanagi, S., Iwata, A.: A competitive learning pulsed neural network for temporal signals. In: Lee, S.Y., Yao, X. (eds.) Proceedings of the 9th International Conference on Neural Information Processing (ICONIP 2002), Singapore, vol. 1, pp. 348–352 (2002)
5. Kuroyanagi, S., Hirata, K., Iwata, A.: A competition learning rule for the pulsed neuron model. Technical Report NC2001-210, Nagoya Institute of Technology, pp. 113–120 (2002)
6. Schauer, C., Paschke, P.: A spike-based model of binaural sound localization. International Journal of Neural Systems 9(5), 447–452 (1999)
7. Schauer, C., Gross, H.M.: Model and application of a binaural 360° sound localization system. In: Proceedings of the International Joint Conference on Neural Networks, Washington, vol. 2, pp. 1132–1137. IEEE Computer Society, Los Alamitos (2001)

8. Ponca, M., Schauer, C.: Fpga implementation of a spike-based sound localization system. In: Proceedings of the 5th International Conference on Artificial Neural Networks and Genetic Algorithms, Prague, pp. 22–25 (2001)
9. Cowling, M., Sitte, R., Wysocki, T.: Analysis of speech recognition techniques for use in a non-speech sound recognition system. In: Proceedings of the 6th International Symposium on Digital Signal Processing for Communication System, Manly, TITR, pp. 16–20 (2002)
10. Turk, O., Sayli, O., Dutagaci, H., Arslan, L.M.: A sound source classification system based on subband processing. In: Hansen, J.H.L., Pellom, B. (eds.) Proceedings of the 7th International Conference on Spoken Language Processing, Denver, pp. 641–644 (2002)
11. Sakaguchi, S., Kuroyanagi, S., Iwata, A.: Sound discrimination system for environment acquisition. Technical Report NC99-70, Nagoya Institute of Technology, pp. 61–68 (1999)
12. Iwasa, K., Kugler, M., Kuroyanagi, S., Iwata, A.: A sound localization and recognition system using pulsed neural networks on FPGA. In: Proceedings of the 20th International Joint Conference on Neural Networks, Orlando, pp. 1252–1257. IEEE Computer Society, Los Alamitos (2007)
13. Jeffress, L.A.: A place theory of sound localization. Journal of Comparative and Physiological Psychology 41, 35–39 (1948)

Binarizing Training Samples with Multi-threshold for Viola-Jones Face Detector

Hiroaki Inayoshi and Takio Kurita

Neuroscience Research Institute,
Nat. Inst. of Advanced Industrial Science and Technology (AIST), 305-8568, Japan

Abstract. We propose an alternative method to Viola-Jones face-detector: in learning stage, we replace each of the gray-scale training images with multiple binary images using multi-threshold; and in detection stage, we use a binarized input-image instead of a gray-scale one. We call this method "TMBMT" (Training by Multiple Binarized samples using Multi-Threshold). Using face images of 1040 individuals from the CAS-PEAL face database, we show that proposed face-detector improves the conventional Viola-Jones facedetectors in terms of numbers of both missed-faces and false-alarms. We also discuss (hypothetical) reasons for the improved performance with (partially) supporting evidence: (1) binarization leads to sharpening of feature distribution; (2) use of multi-threshold leads to better selection of feature location. We speculate these two reasons explain the improved performance.

1   Introduction

Face detection is a useful component in visual surveillance systems. It could be used either as a component for privacy protection (by blocking the detected facial area) or as a pre-processor for "face hallucination" which synthesizes a high-resolution face image from an input low resolution image [1]. Face detection has many applications and although recent research have demonstrated excellent results, it is not yet a solved problem. (For review, see [2]) After Viola and Jones have proposed a rapid object detection method based on a boosted cascade of rectangular feature classifiers [3], face-detectors using their method became popular because of their speed and robustness. In this paper, we propose to replace each of gray-scale training images with 'its binarized images using multiple thresholds' for Viola-Jones face-detector and to replace gray-scale input image with a binarized one in detection process. We call our method "TMBMT" (Training by Multiple Binarized samples using Multi-Threshold).

The rest of the paper is organized as follows: In section 2, Viola-Jones Face Detector is briefly described followed by the proposed method in section 3. Experiments and results are presented in section 4, and we discuss the hypothetical reasons for improvement in section 5.

M. Ishikawa et al. (Eds.): ICONIP 2007, Part II, LNCS 4985, pp. 588–597, 2008.

2   Viola-Jones Face Detector (VJFD)

As depicted in Fig.1, the VJFD is composed of a cascade of nodes (circles in Fig.1) each of which decides whether detection window contains a single face or not. Cascade of nodes means the following: once rejected as non-face the detection window does not go to the next node and that when passing all nodes the detection window is regarded as containing a face. Each of the nodes consists of weak classifiers and the output of a single node is determined by the voting of weak classifiers. Each weak classifier decides its vote based on a rectangle-feature value (Fig.1 bottom) which is computed as the difference between averages of pixel values in white area and black area. The decision functions of weak classifiers (i.e. sizes and locations of rectangle features, etc) are learned from training samples in a process called boosting.

We can draw an analogy between the VJFD and the neural systems: Each rectangle feature would correspond to a receptive field of a neuron and voting among weak classifiers corresponds to integration of multiple inputs in a neuron (although the weights are fixed after learning).

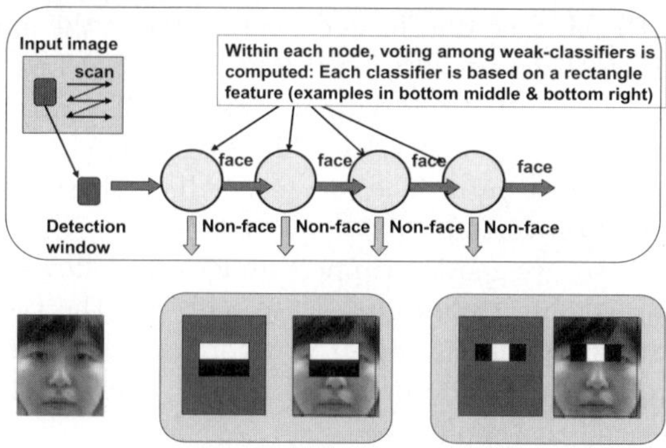

Fig. 1.   Cascade structure in Viola-Jones Face-Detector (top) and examples of rectangle-features (bottom)

3   Proposed Method

The proposed method is depicted in Fig.2. It makes the following replacements upon the conventional method: in learning stage, each of the gray-scale training images is replaced by multiple binary images using multi-thresholds; and in detection stage, a binarized input-image is used instead of a conventional gray-scale one.

We introduced the binarization hoping that it would enhance the distinction between facial-parts (such as eyes, mouth, to be black) and non-facial-parts (to be white). Multi-thresholding is also introduced expecting that distinction between invariant part and variant part could be learned.

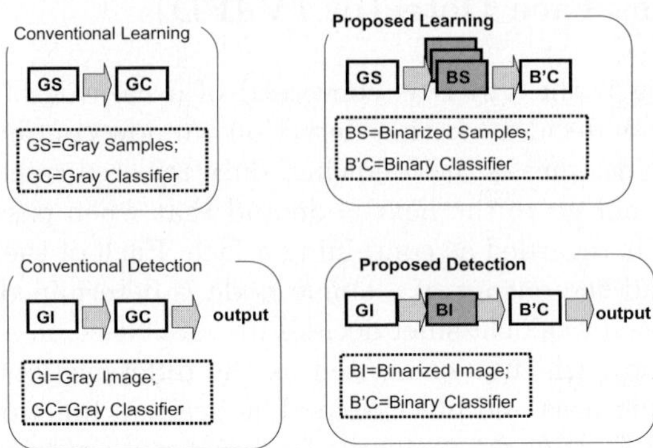

Fig. 2. Conventional (left) vs Proposed (right) methods

4   Experiments

4.1   Dataset and Training-vs-Detection Settings

We used the CAS-PEAL face database collected under the sponsor of the Chinese National Hi-Tech Program and ISVISION Tech. Co. Ltd [4]. The database contains 99,594 images of 1040 individuals (595 males and 445 females) with varying Pose, Expression, Accessory, and Lighting (PEAL). In our experiment, we used a subset of 1040 frontal face images. (All of these uncroppped images are used in face detection tests.)

For training purpose, we made cropped images as follows: For each of 1040 frontal face images, (letting the origin as the center of the two eyes, and $2w$ as the horizontal width between the eyes) we cropped $2w$ to the both right and left, $2w$ to the top, and $3w$ to the bottom from the center. All of these cropped images are then resized to 40x50 pixels.

As binarization methods, we adopted the following three methods: (1) Otsu's method [5], which operates directly on the gray level histogram and finds the threshold as a point that maximizes the between-class (black vs white) variance; (2) fixed thresholds of {80, 90, 100, 110}; and (3) percentile of black-pixels in hair-excluded area (15, 20, 25 %).

We made 100 trials, each of which used different random combination of 100 (out of 1040) cropped images as positive training samples. In each trial, we trained the following fourteen face detectors (using the same 100 positive samples):

- # 1: a detector trained with 100 gray-scale images (i.e. conventional);
- # 2: (single threshold) a detector trained with 100 binarized images using "Otsu-method";
- # 3,4,5: (single threshold) detectors each trained with 100 binarized images using percentile values of 15,20,25, respectively;
- # 6,7,8,9: (single threshold) detectors each trained with 100 binarized images using fixed threshold values of 80,90,100,110, respectively;

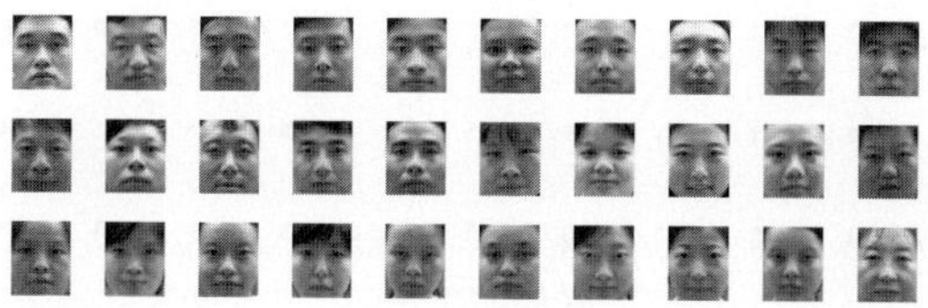

Fig. 3. Samples of cropped grayscale image from CAS-PEAL

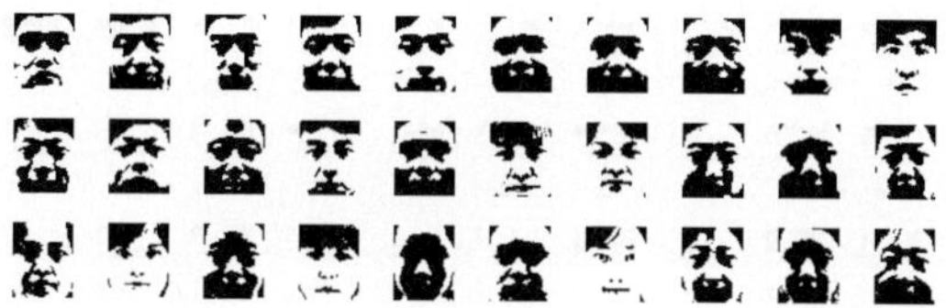

Fig. 4. Binarized samples for Fig.3 using Otsu's method [5]

- # 10: (multiple thresholds) a detector trained with 500 (= 100 images * 5 thresholds-per-image) binarized images using "Otsu-method" and fixed threshold values of 80,90,100,110.
- # 11: (multiple thresholds) a detector trained with 400 (= 100 images * 4 thresholds-per-image) binarized images using "Otsu-method" and percentile values of 15,20,25.
- # 12: (multiple thresholds) a detector trained with 400 (= 100 images * 4 thresholds-per-image) binarized images using fixed threshold values of 80,90,100,110.
- # 13: (multiple thresholds) a detector trained with 300 (= 100 images * 3 thresholds-per-image) binarized images using percentile values of 15,20,25.
- # 14: a detector trained with 500 gray-scale images (i.e. five times redundant images, for control purpose);

As negative samples for training, we used 2000 natural scene images around a campus from [6]. Binarized version of these images are made using Otsu's method. (The same negative set is applied to the above detectors 2 to 13.)

More specifically, we run "opencv-haartrainig" from OpenCV with the following options: "-nonsym -w 40 -h 50 -npos 1000 -nneg 2000".

Figs 3 to 6 show samples of grayscale cropped images (Fig.3), binarized images using Otsu's method, (Fig.4), fixed threshold (Fig.5), and percentile (Fig.6),

After training, we run detection experiment for all of the 1040 uncropped images with the following six detection conditions:

- (1): grayscale input image (i.e. conventional);
- (2) to (6): binarized input image using fixed threshold values of 70, 80, 90, 100, and 110, respectively;

Fig. 5. Binarized samples for Fig.3 using fixed threshold of 90

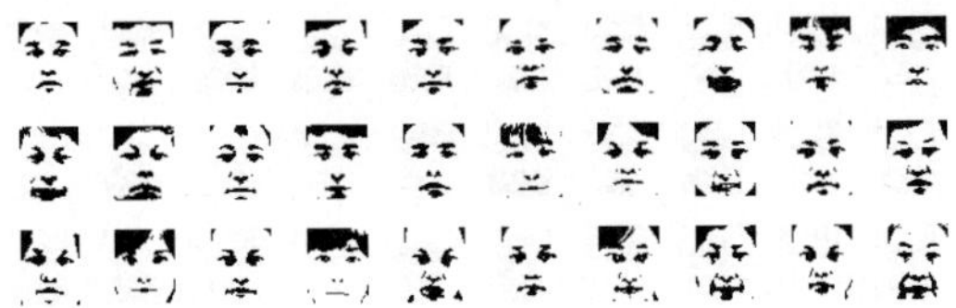

Fig. 6. Binarized samples for Fig.3 using percentile of 20 %

4.2   Results

Tables 1-4 show the number of missed faces and false alarms for 14 detectors (with 6 detection settings each). Scores of the conventional method and best scores of proposed method are in bold. Detector #12 with binarization thresholds of either 80 or 90 performed best, beating the conventional one (in terms of the average or median numbers of both missed faces and false alarms). As an example of a learned detector by proposed method, Fig.7 shows rectangle features used accumulated images of consecutive rectangle features.

Proposed face-detector improves the conventional Viola-Jones face-detectors in terms of numbers of both missed-faces and false-alarms.

5   Discussion

In this section, we discuss the reason why proposed method improves conventional one. First, as a thought experiment, consider two feature distributions as shown in Fig.8(left). Suppose these two distributions for target (face) class have the same mean, but different variances. Then, assuming the same distribution for non-target class, classification boundary of feature A would be A_0 and that of feature B would be B_0. But since overlapping area between two classes is wider in feature A than in feature B, the probability of classification errors (i.e. misses and false alarms) is higher in feature A than in feature B. Therefore in general, assuming anything else being equal, we can expect less classification errors by the sharpening of feature distributions.

Next, consider the effect of binarization on feature output. Fig.9 shows two example distributions of two rectangle feature outputs. This is a piece of evidence that binarization can sharpen distributions of rectangle feature outputs.

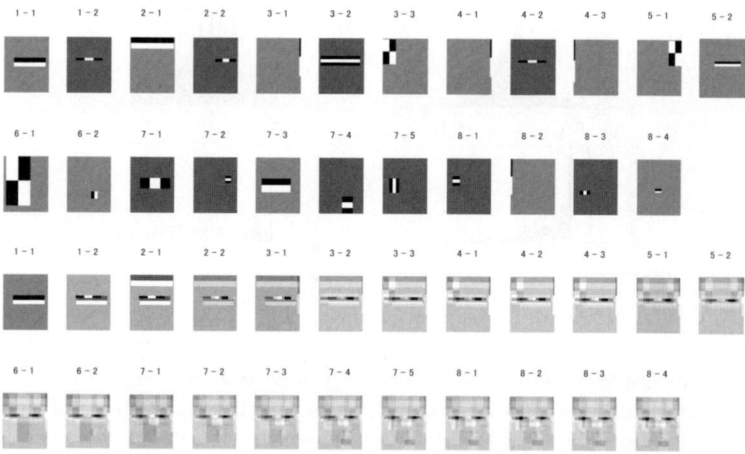

Fig. 7. Example of a learned detector by proposed method. Top two rows show rectangle features used and bottom two rows show accumulated images of consecutive rectangle features.

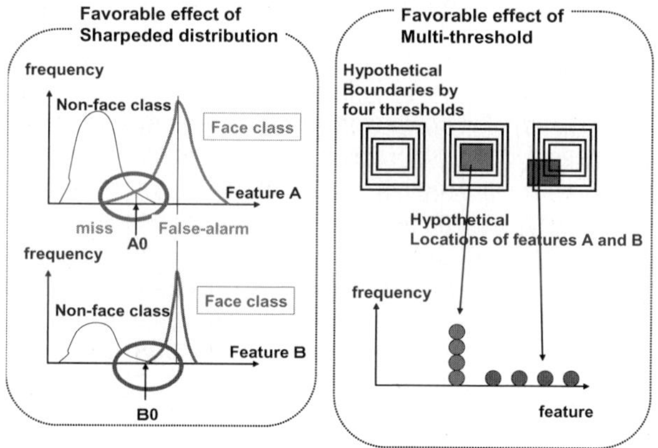

Fig. 8. Effect of sharpened distribution on classification errors (left) and Effect of multi-threshold on selection of feature location (right)

Finally, consider the effect of the use of multi-threshold on selection of feature location. As shown in top-left of Fig.8(right), assume (hypothetical) four binarization boundaries by four thresholds and also assume two locations of rectangle features (top-center and top-right). While in top-center case, the outputs of the rectangle feature for four binarized images could be the same, but in top-right case, they are different as depicted in the bottom of the figure. Therefore, if the location of a feature is "good" (as in top-right case) then we can expect more sharp distribution (bottom-left) than that from "bad" location (as in top-right).

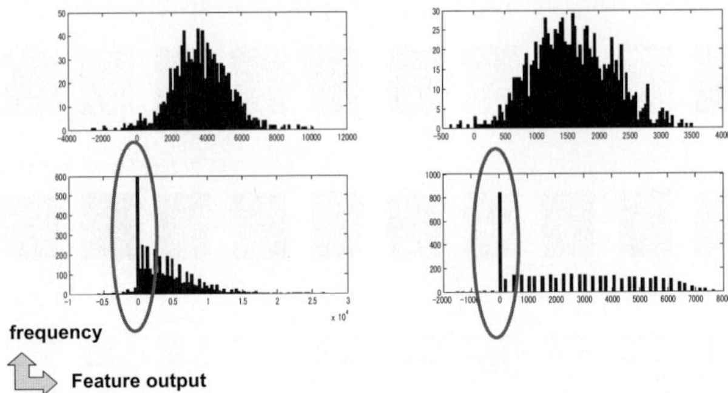

Fig. 9. Two example distributions of two rectangle feature outputs (left and right) showing the effect of binarization (bottom). Each top shows histogram of each feature output on 1040 **gray-scale** cropped face images and each bottom shows histogram of each feature output on 4160 **binarized** images of above using four thresholds.

Table 1. Missed faces out of 1040 individuals (average of 100 trials)

training \ detection	gray	bin70	bin80	bin90	bin100	bin110
# 1 (gray)	**33.95**	571.5	525.34	490.46	459.04	426.38
# 2 (otsu)	34.26	182.1	113.62	72.14	52.81	49.39
# 3 (ptile15)	63.33	485.17	396.08	319.67	260.78	222.44
# 4 (ptile20)	77.15	235.51	183.26	154.95	146.77	151.9
# 5 (ptile25)	79.79	745.73	662.43	575.67	487.37	400.68
# 6 (fix80)	180.3	32.29	35.52	49.23	74.49	114.1
# 7 (fix90)	109.34	38.3	32.31	36.37	50.81	78.95
# 8 (fix100)	66.96	49.1	35.59	33.23	40.09	60.24
# 9 (fix110)	38.22	99.68	65.42	45.63	39.99	46.77
# 10	160.63	29.72	22.01	19.93	23.94	36.1
# 11	33.23	211.87	138.29	87.45	62.08	58.74
# 12	97.53	22.33	**17.86**	**17.58**	24.72	40.95
# 13	76.86	344.71	253.75	185.17	146.04	132.72
# 14	33.31	520.53	473.51	441.85	414.6	387.19

In summary, we speculate the following two reasons for the improvement: (1) binarization leads to sharpening of feature distribution; (2) use of multi-threshold leads to better selection of feature location.

As additional comments on the use of multi-threshold, we point out the following: In our previous work [7], we showed some examples in which "virtual increase of the number of samples" is possible by adding noises along the directions of principal axes in sample distribution. By using the multi-threshold, we obtain "virtual increase of the number of samples" which is common to the above work. Another comment is that Bowyer et al [8] argue that in face recognition task multisample improves the recognition performance. Our work shows it is also true in face detection task.

Table 2. Missed faces out of 1040 individuals (median of 100 trials)

training \ detection	gray	bin70	bin80	bin90	bin100	bin110
# 1 (gray)	**28**	557	515.5	487.5	457.5	427
# 2 (otsu)	12	152	94	62.5	47	45
# 3 (ptile15)	51	518	404	327	255	217
# 4 (ptile20)	70	183	132.5	123.5	130	146.5
# 5 (ptile25)	63.5	787.5	703.5	586	457	367
# 6 (fix80)	90.5	27	30	44.5	70	109
# 7 (fix90)	52.5	31	25.5	33	47	74.5
# 8 (fix100)	29	42	31.5	28	37	56
# 9 (fix110)	17	81.5	51.5	38	35	40
# 10	23.5	23	17.5	17	21	34
# 11	9.5	191	118	73	53	53
# 12	22.5	19	**15**	**16**	22	37
# 13	36	332	230	171.5	133	118.5
# 14	31.5	514	453	416.5	383	360

Table 3. False-alarms for 1040 individuals (average of 100 trials)

training \ detection	gray	bin70	bin80	bin90	bin100	bin110
# 1 (gray)	**391.12**	185.24	186.22	176.19	176.19	176.19
# 2 (otsu)	317.78	211.3	227.98	236.52	236.52	236.52
# 3 (ptile15)	493.37	244.36	262.9	271.12	271.12	271.12
# 4 (ptile20)	394.46	313.03	320.86	313.66	313.66	313.66
# 5 (ptile25)	536.78	184.66	201.6	213.3	213.3	213.3
# 6 (fix80)	205.92	545.06	526.25	478.25	478.25	478.25
# 7 (fix90)	244.78	361.5	365.68	352.56	352.56	352.56
# 8 (fix100)	248.78	289.83	304.14	304.37	304.37	304.37
# 9 (fix110)	304.56	327.57	345.01	347.47	347.47	347.47
# 10	136.74	434.77	446.24	445.66	445.66	445.66
# 11	302.37	212.38	233.74	247.02	247.02	247.02
# 12	139.98	362.81	**367.29**	**361.34**	361.34	361.34
# 13	393.72	277.59	289.12	278.15	278.15	278.15
# 14	343.77	151.63	145.78	128.09	128.09	128.09

6   Concluding Remarks

An alternative method to Viola-Jones face-detectors that utilizes binarization with multi-threshold is proposed. Experimental results, using the CAS-PEAL face database (images of 1040 individuals), show that proposed method improves the performance of face-detection (in terms of the numbers of missed-faces and those of false-alarms) upon conventional method. Finally, two hypothetical reasons for improvement are discussed.

Table 4. False-alarms for 1040 individuals (median of 100 trials)

training \ detection	gray	bin70	bin80	bin90	bin100	bin110
# 1 (gray)	**345.5**	139	144	136.5	136.5	136.5
# 2 (otsu)	264.5	121.5	144	155.5	155.5	155.5
# 3 (ptile15)	464	156.5	195	207	207	207
# 4 (ptile20)	360	220	233	232.5	232.5	232.5
# 5 (ptile25)	475	105	113.5	136	136	136
# 6 (fix80)	164	432	399	358	358	358
# 7 (fix90)	215	293.5	289.5	295.5	295.5	295.5
# 8 (fix100)	195.5	185	206	203.5	203.5	203.5
# 9 (fix110)	251	226	240.5	248	248	248
# 10	109.5	261	277.5	270.5	270.5	270.5
# 11	219.5	134.5	148	156.5	156.5	156.5
# 12	100.5	266	**275**	**284**	284	284
# 13	357	227.5	237	231	231	231
# 14	316.5	114.5	105.5	103	103	103

One of the important messages of this paper is, as depicted in Fig.8, sharpening of feature distribution could expectably result in improved classification.

As a final remark, we should point out that like our use of multiple thresholds seeking invariant regions, MSER (Maximally Stable Extremal Region) detector [9] seeks stable regions in a image against change of binarization threshold. (In comparison study of six affine covariant region detectors [10], the MSER detector exhibited the best performance.)

References

1. Liu, C., Shum, H.Y., Freeman, W.T.: Face hallucination: theory and practice. International Journal of Computer Vision (IJCV) 75(1), 115–134 (2007)
2. Yang, M.H., Kriegman, D., Ahuja, N.: Detecting Faces in Images: A Survey. IEEE Transactions on Pattern Analysis and Machine Intelligence 24(1), 34–58 (2002)
3. Viola, P., Jones, M.J.: Robust Real-Time Face Detection. IJCV(57) (2), 137–154 (2004)
4. Gao, W., Cao, B., Shan, S., Zhou, D., Zhang, X., Zhao D.: The CAS-PEAL Large-Scale Chinese Face Database and Evaluation Protocols, Technical Report No. JDL_TR_04_FR_001, Joint Research & Development Laboratory, CAS (2004)
5. Otsu, N.: A Threshold Selection Method from Grey-Level Histograms. SMC(9) (1), 62–66 (1979)
6. van Hateren, J.H., van der Schaaf, A.: Independent component filters of natural images compared with simple cells in primary visual cortex. Proc. R. Soc. Lond. B 265, 359–366 (1998), http://hlab.phys.rug.nl/imlib/index.html
7. Inayoshi, H., Kurita, T.: Improved generalization by adding both auto-association and hidden-layer-noise to neural-network-based-classifiers. In: Proceedings of 2005 IEEE International Workshop on Machine Learning For Signal Processing, pp. 141–146 (2005)

8. Bowyer, K.W., Chang, K.I., Flynn, P.J., Chen, X.: Face Recognition Using 2-D, 3-D, and Infrared: Is Multimodal Better Than Multisample? Proceedings of the IEEE 94(11), 2000–2012 (2006)
9. Matas, J., Chum, O., Urban, M., Pajdla, T.: Robust wide baseline stereo from maximally stable extremal regions. In: BMVC-2002, pp. 384–393 (2002)
10. Mikolajczyk, K., Tuytelaars, T., Schmid, C., Zisserman, A., Matas, J., Schaffalitzky, F., Kadir, T., Van Gool, L.: A comparison of affine region detectors. IJCV 65(1/2), 43–72 (2005)

Selection of Histograms of Oriented Gradients Features for Pedestrian Detection

Takuya Kobayashi[1], Akinori Hidaka[1], and Takio Kurita[2]

[1] University of Tsukuba,
Tennoudai 1-1-1, Tsukuba, Ibaraki, 305-8577 Japan
{taku-kobayashi,hidaka.akinori}@aist.go.jp
[2] Institute of Advanced Industrial Science and Technology (AIST),
Neuroscience Research Institute,
Umezono 1-1-1, Tsukuba, Ibaraki, 305-5868, Japan
takio-kurita@aist.go.jp

Abstract. Histograms of Oriented Gradients (HOG) is one of the well-known features for object recognition. HOG features are calculated by taking orientation histograms of edge intensity in a local region. N.Dalal *et al.* proposed an object detection algorithm in which HOG features were extracted from all locations of a dense grid on a image region and the combined features are classified by using linear Support Vector Machine (SVM). In this paper, we employ HOG features extracted from all locations of a grid on the image as candidates of the feature vectors. Principal Component Analysis (PCA) is applied to these HOG feature vectors to obtain the score (PCA-HOG) vectors. Then a proper subset of PCA-HOG feature vectors is selected by using Stepwise Forward Selection (SFS) algorithm or Stepwise Backward Selection (SBS) algorithm to improve the generalization performance. The selected PCA-HOG feature vectors are used as an input of linear SVM to classify the given input into pedestrian/non-pedestrian. The improvement of the recognition rates are confirmed through experiments using MIT pedestrian dataset.

1 Introduction

Pedestrian detection in images could be used in video surveillance systems and driver assistance systems. It is more challenging than detecting other object such as faces and cars because appearance of people has lots of fluctuations such as clothing, pose, or illumination.

So far, many algorithms for pedestrian detection have been proposed. For a practical real-time pedestrian detection system, Gavrila [9] employed hierarchical template matching to find pedestrian candidates from incoming images. His method provide multiple templates and they are matched by using Chamfer distance. Papageorgiou *et al.* [7] proposed a pedestrian detection algorithm based on a polynomial SVM using Haar wavelets as input features. Mohan *et al.* [6] extended this algorithm by combining the results of the component detectors. Nishida *et al.* [8] automated the selection process of the components by using

M. Ishikawa et al. (Eds.): ICONIP 2007, Part II, LNCS 4985, pp. 598–607, 2008.

AdaBoost. These researches show that the selection of the components and the combination of them are important to get a good pedestrian detector.

Recently many local descriptors are proposed for object recognition and image retrieval. Mikolajczyk *et al.* [11] compared the performance of the several local descriptors and showed that the best matching results were obtained by the Scale Invariant Feature Transform (SIFT) descriptor [2].

Dalal *et al.* [1] proposed a human detection algorithm using histograms of oriented gradients (HOG) which are similar with the features used in the SIFT descriptor. HOG features are calculated by taking orientation histograms of edge intensity in a local region. They are designed by imitating the visual information processing in the brain and have robustness for local changes of appearances, and position. Dalal *et al.* extracted the HOG features from all locations of a dense grid on a image region and the combined features are classified by using linear SVM. They showed that the grids of HOG descriptors significantly outer-performed existing feature sets for human detection. Ke *et al.* [12] applied Principal Components Analysis (PCA) to reduce the dimensionality of the feature vectors and tested them in an image retrieval application.

On the other hand, Kurita *et al.* [13] showed that the performance of face detection could be improved by selecting a subset of local Gabor features. Viola *et al.* [10] selected Haar-like local features using AdaBoost. These studies show the importance of the selection of a proper subset of the local features in image recognition.

In this paper, we employ HOG features extracted from all locations of a grid on the image as candidates of the feature vectors. Principal Component Analysis (PCA) is applied to the HOG feature vectors to obtain the score vectors. This process reduces the dimensionality of the feature vectors. We call the score vectors PCA-HOG feature vectors. Then a proper subset of PCA-HOG feature vectors is selected by using Stepwise Forward Selection (SFS) algorithm or Stepwise Backward Selection (SBS) algorithm to improve the generalization performance. The selected PCA-HOG feature vectors are used as the input of the linear SVM to classify the given input into pedestrian/non-pedestrian. The improvement of the recognition rates are confirmed through experiments using MIT pedestrian dataset.

In the next section, the proposed algorithm is shown. Then the experimental results are described in section 3. The conclusion and the future works are given in section 4.

2   Feature Selection for Pedestrian Detection

In the works by Dalal *et al.* [1], the HOG features are extracted from all points on a dense grid. In this paper we use the grids of HOG features as the primitive features because they significantly outer perform existing feature sets for human detection as shown in [1]. To improve the recognition performance and reduce the computation cost, we also apply PCA to the HOG features. In this paper, we call them PCA-HOG features.

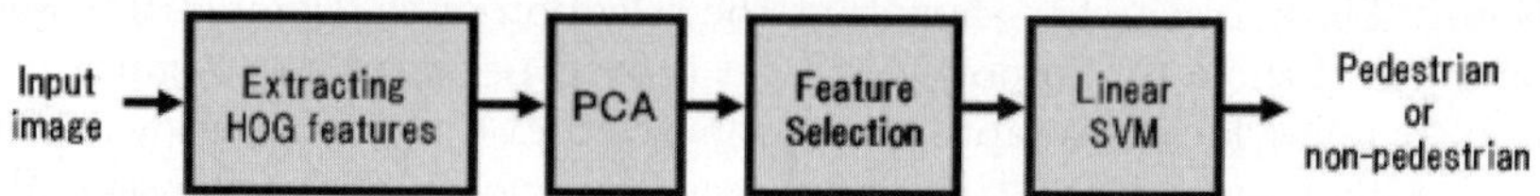

Fig. 1. The overview of our pedestrian detection algorithm. The HOG features are extracted from all locations in an image grid. Then PCA is applied to the extracted HOG features to reduce the dimensionality (PCA-HOG features). A proper subset of these PCA-HOG features are selected to improve the generalization. The selected PCA-HOG features are used as an input vector of the linear SVM.

It is well known that feature selection is effective for pattern classification as shown in [14]. It is expected that the recognition performance can be further improved by selecting a proper subset of the PCA-HOG features because some local regions are irrelevant to pedestrian detection. For example, textures in clothes are not relevant to person detection. Then the selected PCA-HOG features are used as an input vector of linear SVM for person/non-person classification. The overview of our pedestrian detection algorithm is shown in Fig.1.

2.1   Histograms of Oriented Gradients (HOG) Features

Local object appearance and shape can often be characterized rather well by the distribution of local intensity gradients or edge derection. HOG features are calculated by taking orientation histograms of edge intensity in local region. HOG features are used in the SIFT descriptor proposed by Lowe [2]. Mikolajczyk *et al.* reported in [11] that the best matching results were obtained by the SIFT descriptor.

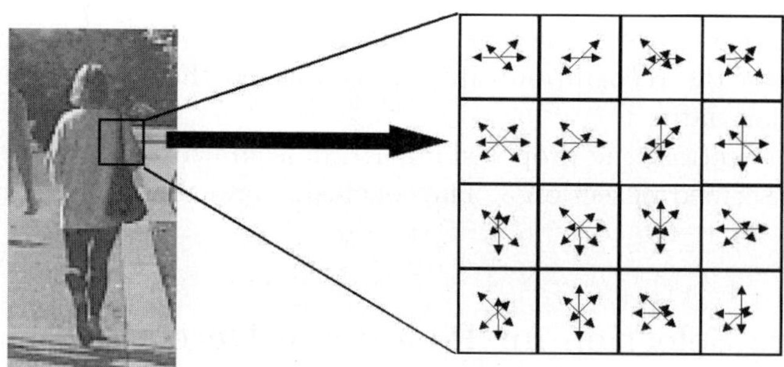

Fig. 2. Extraction Process of HOG features. The HOG features are extracted from local regions with 16×16 pixels. Histograms of edge gradients with 8 orientations are calculated from each of 4×4 local cells. The edge gradients and orientations are obtained by applying Sobel filters. Thus the total number of HOG features becomes $128 = 8 \times (4 \times 4)$.

In this paper, we extract HOG features from 16×16 local regions as shown in Fig.2. At first, edge gradients and orientations are calculated at each pixel in this local region. Sobel filters are used to obtain the edge gradients and orientations. The gradient magnitude $m(x, y)$ and orientation $\theta(x, y)$ are calculated using the x- and y-directional gradients $dx(x, y)$ and $dy(x, y)$ computed by Sobel filter as

$$m(x, y) = \sqrt{dx(x, y)^2 + dy(x, y)^2}$$

$$\theta(x, y) = \begin{cases} \tan^{-1}\left(\frac{dy(x,y)}{dx(x,y)}\right) - \pi & \text{if } dx(x, y) < 0 \text{ and } dy(x, y) < 0 \\ \tan^{-1}\left(\frac{dy(x,y)}{dx(x,y)}\right) + \pi & \text{if } dx(x, y) < 0 \text{ and } dy(x, y) > 0 \\ \tan^{-1}\left(\frac{dy(x,y)}{dx(x,y)}\right) & \text{otherwise} \end{cases} \quad (1)$$

This local region is divided into small spatial area called "cell". The size of the cell is 4×4 pixels. Histograms of edge gradients with 8 orientations are calculated from each of the local cells. Then the total number of HOG features becomes $128 = 8 \times (4 \times 4)$ and they constitute a HOG feature vector. To avoid sudden changes in the descriptor with small changes in the position of the window, and to give less emphasis to gradients that are far from the center of the descriptor, a Gaussian weighting function with σ equal to one half the width of the descriptor window is used to assign a weight to the magnitude of each pixel.

A HOG feature vector represents local shape of an object, having edge information at plural cells. In flatter regions like a ground or a wall of a building, the histogram of the oriented gradients has flatter distribution. On the other hand, in the border between an object and background, one of the elements in the histogram has a large value and it indicates the direction of the edge. Although the images are normalized to position and scale, the positions of important features will not be registered with same grid positions. It is known that HOG features are robust to the local geometric and photometric transformations. If the translations or rotations of the object are much smaller than the local spatial bin size, their effect is small.

Dalal *et al.* [1] extracted a set of HOG feature vectors from all locations in an image grid and are used for classification. In this paper, we extract the HOG features from all locations on a 6×14 grid of a given input image with 56×120 pixels as shown in Fig.3 (a).

2.2 Principal Component Analysis of HOG (PCA-HOG) Features

The total number of features becomes over ten thousands when the HOG features extracted from all locations on the grid. These features are probably too many and are redundant. Ke *et al.* [12] applied Principal Components Analysis (PCA) to reduce the dimensionality of the feature vectors. In this paper, we utilize this idea but we have to take the properties of HOG features into account. The HOG features extracted from regions without edges are not effective for classification because they are based on the information on edges. We have to gather training samples for PCA from effective regions. To select such regions, we use Difference

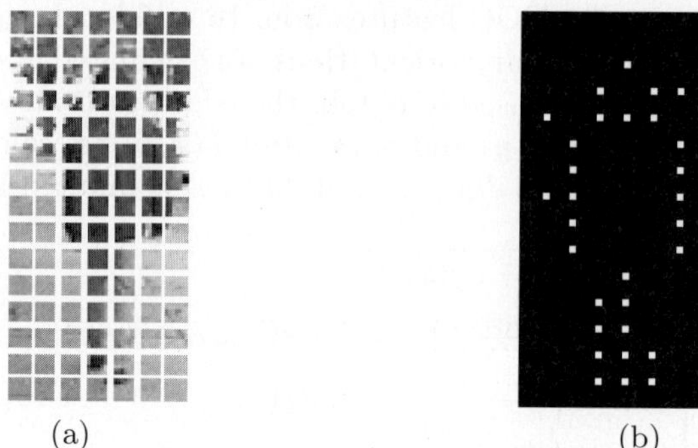

(a)   (b)

Fig. 3. (a) HOG features are extracted from all locations on a 6 × 14 grid of a given input image with 56 × 120 pixels. (b) Selected points for PCA.

of Gaussian (DOG). In the SIFT descriptor, the DOG filter is used to detect the key-points for image matching [2]. DOG can be define as the difference of two images smoothed with different Gaussian filters as

$$D(x, y, \sigma) = (G(x, y, k\sigma) - G(x, y, \sigma)) * I(x, y), \tag{2}$$

where $I(x, y)$ is an input image and

$$G(x, y, \sigma) = \frac{1}{2\pi\sigma^2} \exp\left(-\frac{(x^2 + y^2)}{2\sigma^2}\right). \tag{3}$$

The absolute value of outputs of the DOG filter became large at the point with large variations. This means that DOG filter has the effect to emphasize the contrast. When we select points from a pedestrian image whose absolute value of DOG filter is greater than a threshold, a silhouette of the human appears as shown Fig.3 (b). The HOG features of the selected points are used as the training samples for PCA.

PCA is one of the well known techniques for dimensionality reduction. It has been applied to several computer vision problems. PCA can be defined as the orthogonal projection of the data onto a lower dimensional linear subspace, known as the principal subspace, such that the variance of the projected samples is maximized. Equivalently, it can be defined as the liner projection that minimizes the mean squared distance between the data points and their projections.

Let $\{x_i | i = 1, \ldots, N\}$ be a set of M-dimensional vectors. This is a given training samples for PCA. Then the principal scores are defined by using the projection matrix U as

$$y = U^T(x_i - \bar{x}) \tag{4}$$

where the mean vector of the training samples are defined as $\bar{x} = \frac{1}{N}\sum_{i=1}^{N} x_i$. The optimum projection matrix U is obtained by solving the eigen equations of the covariance matrix Σ

$$\Sigma U = U \Lambda, \quad (UU^T = I) \tag{5}$$

where the covariance matrix Σ is defined as

$$\Sigma = \frac{1}{N} \sum_{n=1}^{N} (\boldsymbol{x}_i - \bar{\boldsymbol{x}})(\boldsymbol{x}_i - \bar{\boldsymbol{x}})^T. \tag{6}$$

After the training of PCA, we can compute PCA scores for any HOG features by using the equation (4). We call this new features PCA-HOG features.

To determine the number of principal components, we use the rate of cumulative contribution. In the following experiments, we use the principal scores whose cumulative contribution is less than 90%.

2.3   Selection of PCA-HOG Features

It is well known that the selection of a proper subset of the features can improve the recognition performance in pattern recognition. Kurita *et al.* [13] showed that the performance of face detection could be improved by selecting a subset of local Gabor features. Viola *et al.* [10] selected Haar-like local features using AdaBoost. These studies show the importance of the selections of local features in image recognition. In this paper, we select a subset of locations on a 6×14 grid and PCA-HOG features extracted on the subset of the locations are used as input of the SVM classifier. To evaluate the goodness of the subset, a set of sample images of pedestrians and non-pedestrians is prepared. The goodness of the subset is evaluated by the recognition rate to this evaluation samples.

To find the optimal subset we have to evaluate the all possible combinations of $M = 84 = 6 \times 14$ locations on the grid. But it is not feasible because the number of combinations becomes 2^M. Several sub-optimal methods have been proposed. Two of the simplest methods are Stepwise Forward Selection (SFS) and Stepwise Backward Selection (SBS). SFS starts from the subset with the empty set and repeatedly adds the best feature vector in terms of the goodness of the subset. On the other hand, SBS starts from the set with all feature vectors and repeatedly removes the most unnecessary feature vector in terms of the goodness of the subset.

Let $\{\boldsymbol{y}_i | i = 1, \dots, M\}$ be a set of PCA-HOG features extracted from all M locations on the grid. In SFS algorithm, the feature vector F is initialized as empty set $F^{(0)} = \emptyset$. Then the best feature vector $\boldsymbol{y}^*$ is searched in terms of the goodness of the subset of feature vectors $F^{(k-1)} + \boldsymbol{y}^*$. The selected feature vector is added to the feature vector as $F^{(k)} = F^{(k-1)} + \boldsymbol{y}^*$. This process is repeated until all feature vectors are included in the feature vector F. Similarly in SBS algorithm, the feature vector F is initialized as $F^{(0)} = \{\boldsymbol{y}_i | i = 1, \dots, M\}$. Then the best feature vector $\boldsymbol{y}^*$ is searched in terms of the goodness of the subset of feature vectors $F^{(k-1)} - \boldsymbol{y}^*$. The selected feature vector is removed from the feature vector as $F^{(k)} = F^{(k-1)} - \boldsymbol{y}^*$. This process is repeated until no vector is left in the set F.

2.4 Linear SVM Classifier

In the human detection algorithm proposed by Dalal *et al.* [1], the HOG features are extracted from all locations of a dense grid and the combined features are classified by linear Support Vector Machine (SVM). They showed that this HOG features significantly outer-performed existing feature sets for human detection. In this paper, we also use the linear SVM because the dimension of the selected PCA-HOG features is enough high.

SVMs were proposed by Vapnik [5] and have yielded excellent results in various data classification tasks. Let $\{\boldsymbol{f}_i, t_i\}_{i=1}^N$ ($\boldsymbol{f}_i \in R^D, t_i \in \{-1, 1\}$) be the given training samples in D-dimensional feature space. The classification function is given as

$$z = \operatorname{sign}(\boldsymbol{w}^T \boldsymbol{f}_i - h) \tag{7}$$

where $\boldsymbol{w}$ and h are the parameters of the model. For the case of soft-margin SVM, the optimal parameters are obtained by minimizing

$$L(\boldsymbol{w}, \boldsymbol{\xi}) = \frac{1}{2}||\boldsymbol{w}||^2 + C\sum_{i=1}^N \xi_i \tag{8}$$

under the constraints

$$\xi_i \geq 0, \ t_i(\boldsymbol{w}^T \boldsymbol{f}_i - h) \geq 1 - \xi_i \ (i = 1, \ldots, N) \tag{9}$$

where $\xi_i(\geq 0)$ is the error of the i-th sample measured from the separating hyperplane and C is the hyper-parameter which controls the weight between the errors and the margin. The dual problem of Eq.(8) is obtained by introducing Lagrange multipliers $\boldsymbol{\alpha} = (\alpha_1, \ldots, \alpha_N), \alpha_k \geq 0$ as

$$L_D(\boldsymbol{\alpha}) = \sum_{i=1}^N \alpha_i - \frac{1}{2} \sum_{i,j=1}^N \alpha_i \alpha_j t_i t_j \boldsymbol{f}_i^T \boldsymbol{f}_j \tag{10}$$

under the constraints

$$\sum_{i=1}^N \alpha_i t_i = 0, \ \ 0 \leq \alpha_i \ (i = 1, \ldots, N). \tag{11}$$

By solving Eq.(10), the optimum function is obtained as

$$z = \operatorname{sign}(\sum_{i \in S} \alpha_i^* t_i \boldsymbol{f}_i^T \boldsymbol{f} - h^*) \tag{12}$$

where S is the set of support vectors.

To get a good classifier, we have to search the best hyper-parameter C. The cross-validation is used to measure the goodness of the linear SVM classifier.

3 Experiments

The proposed algorithm was evaluated by using MIT CBCL pedestrian database which contains 924 images of pedestrians in city scenes [18]. It contains only front or back views with relatively limited range of poses and the position and the hight of human in the image are almost adjusted. The size of the image is 64 × 128 pixels. These images were used for positive samples in the following experiments. The negative samples were originally collected from images of sky, mountain, airplane, building, etc. The number of negative images is 2000. From these images, 800 pedestrian images and 1600 negative samples were used as training samples to determine the parameters of the linear SVM. The remaining 100 pedestrian images and 200 negative samples were used as test samples to evaluate the recognition performance of the constructed classifier. When we implemented Dalal algorithm using that dataset, the recognition rate for test dataset is 98.3%. We applied PCA and feature selection to improve its result.

PCA-HOG feature vectors were extracted from all locations of the grid for each training sample. Then subsets of PCA-HOG feature vectors were selected by using SFS or SBS algorithms. The selected feature vectors were used as input of the linear SVM. The goodness of the selected subsets were evaluated by cross

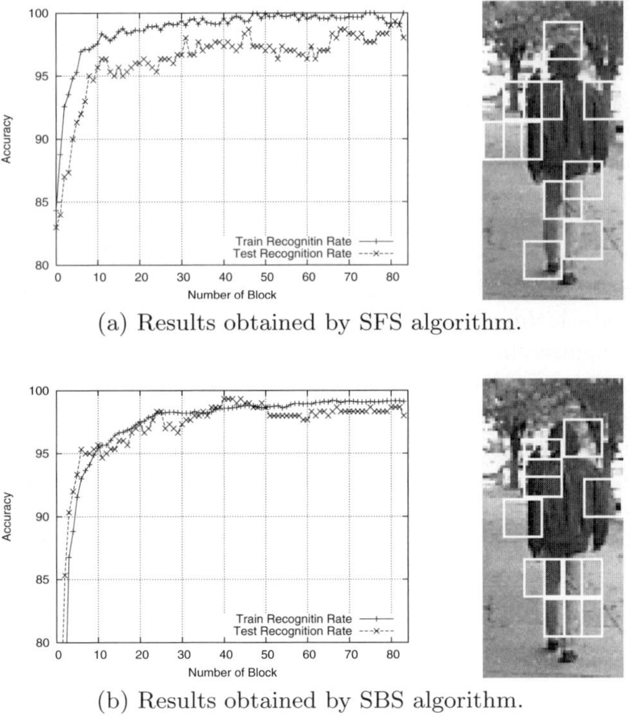

(a) Results obtained by SFS algorithm.

(b) Results obtained by SBS algorithm.

Fig. 4. Experimental results on feature selecting. The left graphs show the relation between the recognition rates and the number of selected PCA-HOG feature vectors. The Right images represent locations of the selected features.

Fig. 5. Examples of pedestrian detection. In upper image pedestrians are correctly detected. Lower images show example of false detection.

validation. Also we evaluated the recognition rates of the constructed classifier using test samples.

The left graphs of Fig.4 show the relation between the recognition rates and the number of selected PCA-HOG feature vectors. The graph in Fig.4 (a) was obtained by using SFS algorithm. Similarly SBS algorithm was used to obtain the graph in Fig.4 (b).

When we used SFS algorithm, the best recognition rate 99.3 % for test dataset was obtained at 82 PCA-HOG feature vectors. This is 1.3% better than the recognition rate obtained by using all 84 feature vectors. When SFS and SBS algorithms were compared, SBS algorithm gave better results. The best recognition rate 99.3 % was obtained at 41 PCA-HOG feature vectors. This means that we can reduce the number of features less than half.

The white squares in the right images of Fig4 show the 10 locations of the selected feature vectors by using SFS or SBS. It is noticed that the proposed algorithm succeeded to select some of reasonable regions such as the head, the shoulder, the leg, the arms, etc.Again SBS algorithm seems give better results.

Finally we applied to proposed algorithm to detect pedestrians in images of INRIA person dataset [1]. The final detector for this experiment was produced to retrain using an augmented dataset (initial 2400 sample + 1161 false positive samples). The results are shown in Fig5.

4   Conclusion

We evaluated the effect of the selection of PCA-HOG feature vectors for pedestrian detection.As a result, we could reduce the number of features less than half without lowering the performance.

References

1. Dalal, N., Triggs, B.: Histograms of Oriented Gradients for Human Detection. In: IEEE Conference on Computer Vision and Pattern Recognition (CVPR) (2005)
2. Lowe, D.G.: Distinctive Image Features from Scale-Invariant Keypoints. IJCV 60(2), 91–110 (2004)
3. Swain, M.J., Ballard, D.H.: Color Indexing. Int'l j. Computer Vision 7(1), 11–32 (1991)
4. Daugman, J.: Entropy reduction and decorrelation in visual coding by oriented neural receptive fields. Trans. on Biomedical Engineering 36(1), 107–114 (1989)
5. Vapnik, V.N.: Statistical Learning Theory. John Wiley and Sons, Chichester (1998)
6. Mohan, A., Papageorgiou, C., Poggio, T.: Example-Based Object Detection in Images by Components. PAMI 23(4), 349–361 (2001)
7. Papageorgiou, C., Oren, M., Poggio, T.: A General Framework for Object Detection. In: Proc. Int'l Conf. Computer Vision (January 1998)
8. Nishida, K., Kurita, T.: Boosting Soft-Margin SVM with Feature Selection for Pedestrian Detection. In: Proc. of International Workshop on Multiple Classifier Systems, vol. 13, pp. 22–31 (2005)
9. Gavrila, D.M.: Pedestrian Detection form a Moving Vehicle. In: Vernon, D. (ed.) ECCV 2000. LNCS, vol. 1843, pp. 37–49. Springer, Heidelberg (2000)
10. Viola, P., Jones, M.J., Snow, D.: Detecting pedestrians using patterns of motion and appearance. In: Proc of the 9th International Conf. of Computer Vision, Nice, vol. 1, pp. 734–741 (2003)
11. Mikolajczyk, K., Schmid, C.: A performance evaluation of local descriptors. In: Proc. of Computer Vision and Pattern Recognition (2003)
12. Ke, Y., Sukthankar, R.: PCA-SIFT: A more distinctive representation for local image descriptors. In: Proc. of Computer Vision and Pattern Recognition, Washington, pp. 66–75 (2004)
13. Kurita, T., Hotta, K., Mishima, T.: Feature ordering by cross validation for face detection. In: Proc. of IAPR Workshop on Machine Vision Applications, The University of Tokyo, Japan, November 28-30, pp. 211–214 (2000)
14. Tanaka, K., Kurita, T., Meyer, F., Berthouze, L., Kawabe, T.: Stepwise feature selection by cross validation for EEG-based Brain Computer Interface. In: Proc. of Inter. Joint Conf. on Neural Networks, Vancouver, July 16-21, pp. 9422–9427 (2006)
15. Wu, B., Nevatia, R.: Detection of Multiple, Partially Occluded Humans in a Single Image by Bayesian Combination of Edgelet Part Detectors
16. Zhu, Q., Avidan, S., Yeh, M.-C., Cheng, K.-T.: Fast Human Detection Using a Cascade of Histograms of Oriented Gradients. In: CVPR 2006 (2006)
17. Viola, P., Jones, M.: Rapid object detection using a boosted cascade of simple features. In: Conference on Computer Vision and Pattern Recognition (CVPR) (2001)
18. MIT CBCL: http://cbcl.mit.edu/software-datasets/PedestrianData.html

Relevance Optimization in Image Database Using Feature Space Preference Mapping and Particle Swarm Optimization

Mayuko Okayama[1], Nozomi Oka[1], and Keisuke Kameyama[2]

[1] Department of Risk Engineering,
Graduate School of Systems and Information Engineering,
University of Tsukuba
[2] Department of Computer Science,
Graduate School of Systems and Information Engineering,
University of Tsukuba,
1-1-1 Tennodai, Tsukuba, Ibaraki 305-8573, Japan
`Keisuke.Kameyama@cs.tsukuba.ac.jp`

Abstract. Two methods for retrieval relevance optimization using the user's feedback is proposed for a content-based image retrieval (CBIR) system. First, the feature space used in database image clustering for coarse classification is transferred to a *preference feature space* according to the user's feedback by a map generated by supervised training, thereby enabling to collect user-preferred images in the matching candidates. Second, the parameters in the fine-matching relaxation operation is optimized according to the user's evaluation of the retrieved image ranking using Particle Swarm Optimization. In the experiments, it is shown that the retrieval rankings are improved suiting the user's preference when feature space mapping and parameter optimization are used.

Keywords: Content-Based Image Retrieval (CBIR), database indexing, Relaxation Matching, Optimal Linear Map, Particle Swarm Optimization.

1   Introduction

Content-Based Image Retrieval (CBIR) is a method that enables image relevance evaluation and retrieval using the image information themselves, thus avoiding the labor of manual attributing. Among the features commonly used for relevance evaluation are, color, texture, shape and their spatial relations within the images. Various approaches for CBIR have been reported in the literature, based on various retrieval methods and similarity metrics using single or composite features. Among the systems developed in the CBIR research are, TRADEMARK, ART MUSEUM [1], QBIC [2], Photobook [3] and Viper [4]. Image database with CBIR capability can be used in various fields such as designing and automated visual surveillance.

Among the issues residing in CBIR implementation is utilization of the user's relevance feedback. Since the relevance preference can vary user by user, it is

M. Ishikawa et al. (Eds.): ICONIP 2007, Part II, LNCS 4985, pp. 608–617, 2008.

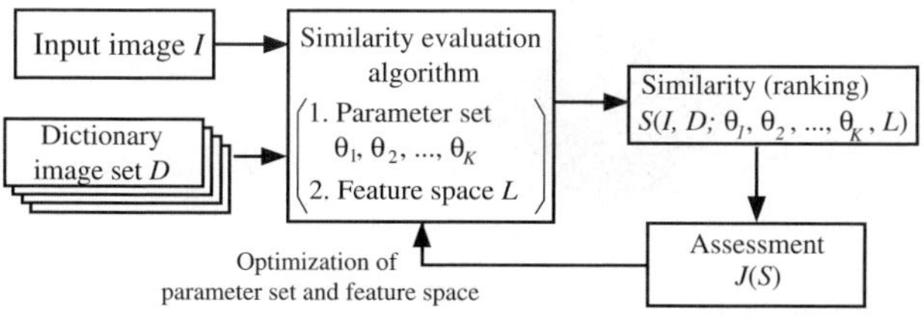

Fig. 1. The scheme for optimizing the parameters and the feature space mapping in the image similarity evaluation algorithm

important that the system can cope with varying subjective scores of the retrieved images for further refinement.

In this work, first, we show that the user's preference can be reflected to the eventual search by mapping the feature space to a *preference feature space*. The mapping will be determined by supervised learning of the user's relevance feedback. Second, we focus on tuning the parameters in the matching algorithms. The parameters do affect the retrieval results (rankings), however, direct connection between the results and the parameter values are uncertain. In this work, we propose to use Particle Swarm Optimization in parameter optimization according to the user's feedback. Progress over the preliminary work [5] include experiments ascertaining the successful adaptation to the users' different relevance feedback. Overall, the aim is to adapt the similarity evaluation according to the user's various preferences in the retrieved image rankings. The process of image retrieval and the user's relevance feedback is shown in Fig. 1.

The remaining of this paper is organized as follows. In Sec. 2, the CBIR system to which the proposed idea was implemented, is explained. In Sec. 3, parameter optimization using PSO and the method for preference-mapping the feature space will be introduced. The effectiveness of the proposed method will be evaluated in Sec. 4, and Sec. 5 ends the paper with concluding remarks.

2   CBIR System Using Contour Information and Two-Stage Matching

In this section, a binary image similarity evaluation method based on piecewise modeling of contours and two-stage matching [6] [7] will be reviewed.

2.1   Modeling

The CBIR database used for implementing the proposed idea will deal with binary images as shown in Fig. 2. The extracted contours in the image will be modeled by piecewise function approximation using the elementary function types of straight line, arc and quadratic curve (Fig. 2(b)). Each such contour segment will be a component of the image.

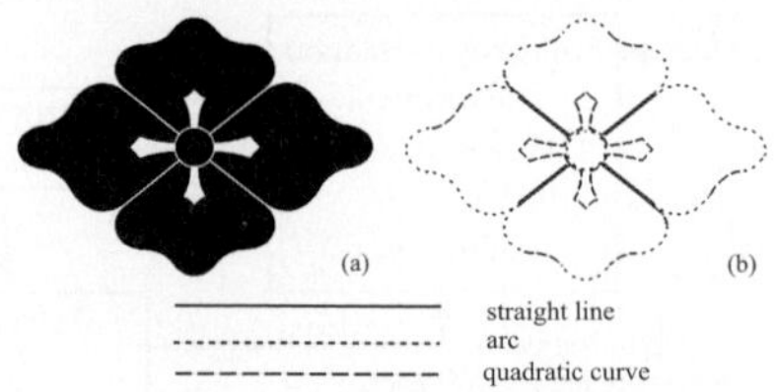

Fig. 2. An example of a contour-modeled kamon image

2.2   Clustering in Feature Space

The modeled images in the database will be mapped on feature space L as vectors. The image vectors will be clustered into several subsets among which one of them will be used for the detailed matching with the query image.

Here, histograms of contour segment lengths for three types of contours (straight line, arc and quadratic curve) will be concatenated to make a feature vector for each image. Each element will represent the sum length of the segments having particular type and length range. The feature dimension will be $dim(L) = 3B$, where B is the number of segment length bins in each of the three histograms.

For unsupervised clustering, SR-tree [8] used for efficient hierarchical indexing will be used in space L. In the SR-tree, one leaf structure will represent a subset of database images.

2.3   Matching

Detailed matching between the query image and the selected database subset will be done by relaxation matching. Relaxation matching [9] is a method for optimizing the assignments of the elements of the *label set* to elements of another set called the *object set*.

In image similarity evaluation, the query and dictionary images are both modeled by a common process. The two images make a set of N objects and a set of M labels. The assignment of the labels to object i will be expressed in a vector of assignment probabilities as, $\boldsymbol{p}_i = [p_{i1}, ..., p_{iM}]^T \in \boldsymbol{R}^M$, where "$T$" denotes the transpose. A set of $\boldsymbol{p}_i$ for all the N objects will make the *state vector* $\boldsymbol{p} = [\boldsymbol{p}_1, \ldots, \boldsymbol{p}_N]^T \in \boldsymbol{R}^{MN}$, which represents the object labeling in the image-to-image matching.

For updating and optimizing the state $\boldsymbol{p}$, a symmetric matrix $R = [r_{ij}(k,l)] \in \boldsymbol{R}^{MN \times MN}$ is defined. An element $r_{ij}(k,l)$ is called the compatibility coefficient, and is calculated reflecting the compatibility of two label assignments, k to i and l to j, respectively.

The state vector will be updated according to,

$$\boldsymbol{p}(t+1) = \boldsymbol{f}(\boldsymbol{p}(t), \boldsymbol{q}(t)) = [f_{11}, \ldots, f_{NM}]^T, \tag{1}$$

$$f_{ik} = q_{ik}p_{ik} \Big/ \sum_{k'=1}^{M} q_{ik'}p_{ik'}, \tag{2}$$

and

$$\boldsymbol{q}(t) = R\boldsymbol{p}(t), \tag{3}$$

where t denotes the time. For a symmetric R, a function defined as,

$$-A(\boldsymbol{p}(t)) = -\boldsymbol{p}(t)^{T}R\boldsymbol{p}(t), \tag{4}$$

decreases by the iterative transition of $\boldsymbol{p}$ until one of the local minima of $-A(\boldsymbol{p})$ is reached [10]. The value of function $A(\boldsymbol{p})$ can be a measure of the total consistency of the label assignments, namely the distance between the two images.

2.4   Matching Parameters

In the actual implementation of relaxation matching process, eight parameters are involved, and each one of them will affect the calculated similarity of query and database images. Here only the roles of the parameters will be introduced. Please refer to [5] for the details.

- C_1, C_2 : controlling the initial object-label matching candidate filtering.
- W_1, C_3 : controlling the initial assignment probability.
- W_2,W_3, C_4, C_5 : used in the calculation of compatibility coefficient $r_{ij}(k,l)$.

2.5   Aim of This Work

The retrieved images and their similarity ranking will be determined by the coarse classification and the detailed matching evaluated by Eq. (4). In our implementation, this process is a function of the selection of the features of feature space L and parameters $\{C_1, C_2, C_3, C_4, C_5, W_1, W_2, W_3\}$. This work aims to construct a framework utilizing the user's non-unique evaluation of the initial retrieval result to tune the feature space and the parameter values according to each user's needs.

3   Relevance Optimization Using Retrieval Ranking Feedback

3.1   Utilization of Preference Feature Space L_p

In transferring the feature space, the user is asked to choose the preferred images (class 0) and unpreferred images (class 1) after the initial retrieval. This feedback of P preferences will provide a training set of P input-output vector pairs, consisting of the feature vector $x_i \in L$ and class unit vector $u_i \in \{[0\ 1]^{T}, [1\ 0]^{T}\}$. An Optimal Linear Map [11]

$$MX = M[x_1\ x_2 \dots x_P] = [u_1\ u_2 \dots u_P] = U \tag{5}$$

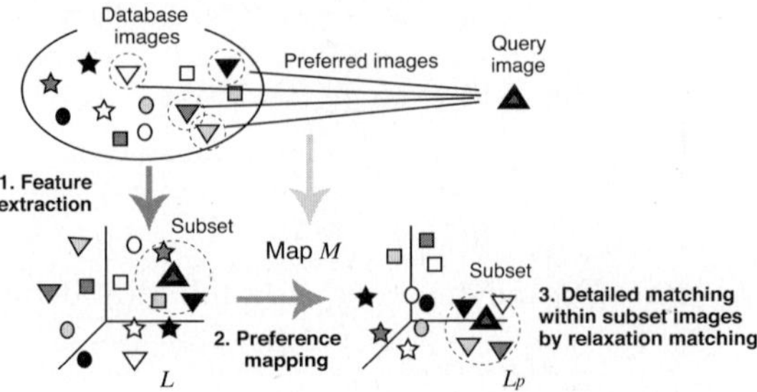

Fig. 3. Matching in mapped space L_p according to the user's relevance feedback

will be sought by way of minimum-norm approximation

$$M = UX^{\dagger} \tag{6}$$

where $X^{\dagger}$ is the pseudoinverse of X. Then map M will be used to map the images in feature space L to L_p, and coarse classification defining the image subset will be done on L_p as shown in Fig. 3.

3.2   Parameter Optimization Using PSO

On optimizing the parameters, an evaluation score function J will be used. However, in our method of image component matching and similarity evaluation, the relation between the parameters and the score J can be highly nonlinear. Therefore, conventional optimization methods based on the gradient of J are not feasible. In such cases, multiple local evaluations of J can serve as a quasi-gradient information. By considering this problem-specific condition, we chose the Particle Swarm Optimization [12] for optimizing the parameters.

PSO employs a parallel search of multiple (H) points (swarm), each of which are changed along a smooth trajectory within the search space.

Each search point is called the *particle*. The i-th particle holds its current coordinate in the search space $\boldsymbol{x}_i(t)$ and its moving velocity $\boldsymbol{v}_i(t)$. The fitness of $\boldsymbol{x}_i(t)$ is evaluated by an oracle(J). Each particle has a memory of its maximally evaluated coordinate so far ($\boldsymbol{p}_i$). Also the best coordinate in the swarm so far $\boldsymbol{g}$ is shared by all the particles.

The updating rule of the particle's coordinate and velocity is,

$$\boldsymbol{x}_i(t+1) = \boldsymbol{x}_i(t) + \boldsymbol{v}_i(t+1), \tag{7}$$

$$\boldsymbol{v}_i(t+1) = \boldsymbol{v}_i(t) + \lambda_1(\boldsymbol{p}_i - \boldsymbol{x}_i(t)) + \lambda_2(\boldsymbol{g} - \boldsymbol{x}_i(t)). \tag{8}$$

where λ_1 and λ_2 are given parameters. At each generation, vectors $\boldsymbol{p}_i$ ($i = 1, \ldots, H$) and $\boldsymbol{g}$ will be updated as necessary.

Upon optimizing the parameters in the similarity evaluation between two images, the particles move and search in a K-dimensional search space spanned by the parameters $(\theta_1, \theta_2, \ldots, \theta_K)$. The oracle is the image similarity evaluation

Table 1. Retrieval results for various dimensions of feature space, each for before and after preference mapping. The images chosen to be preferred and unpreferred by the user are displayed with white and black backgrounds, respectively.

	Matching conditions (time : s)	Query image	Retrieved image similarity ranking (Ranks 1 - 10)									
			1	2	3	4	5	6	7	8	9	10
(a)	Before mapping dim(L) = 18 (25.297)											
(b)	After mapping dim(L_p) = 2 (6.844)											
(c)	Before mapping dim(L) = 24 (29.344)											
(d)	After mapping dim(L_p) = 2 (9.484)											
(e)	Before mapping dim(L) = 30 (31.563)											
(f)	After mapping dim(L_p) = 2 (12.375)											

algorithm and the scoring function J which evaluates the fitness of the current parameter set $\boldsymbol{x}_i(t) = (\theta_{i1}(t), \theta_{i2}(t), \ldots, \theta_{iK}(t))$. At each timestep, all the particles will be evaluated by retrieval and evaluation. Then the positions (parameter settings) of the particles will be modified according to Eqs. (7) and (8). This cycle will take place for a certain number of generations (G), and a parameter set corresponding to the final $\boldsymbol{g}$ will be used as the optimal parameter setting.

4   Experimental Results

Preference Mapping Using Relevance Feedback. An example of the retrieved images before and after preference mapping are shown in Table 1. Initial feature space L for different histogram bin numbers ($3B = 18, 24, 30$) were tried for a set of 1000 Japanese family crest (Kamon) images. After initial retrieval, the user chose 5 preferred and unpreferred images each from the 20 highly ranked images as the user's relevance feedback (only top 10 shown in Table 1). It is seen that after mapping the preferred images appear at higher ranks where the unpreferred images are suppressed.

Table 2 show another result for a different query image. For the preference map however, the estimated map M from the previous experiment was used, thereby providing a test case. No significant differences are observed for 18 and 24 dimension cases. However for 30 dimension cases, the previous preference towards a dense flower pattern in a thick circular rim is reflected in the top four retrievals after mapping.

Table 2. Retrieval results using a test query image for various dimensions of feature space, each before and after preference mapping

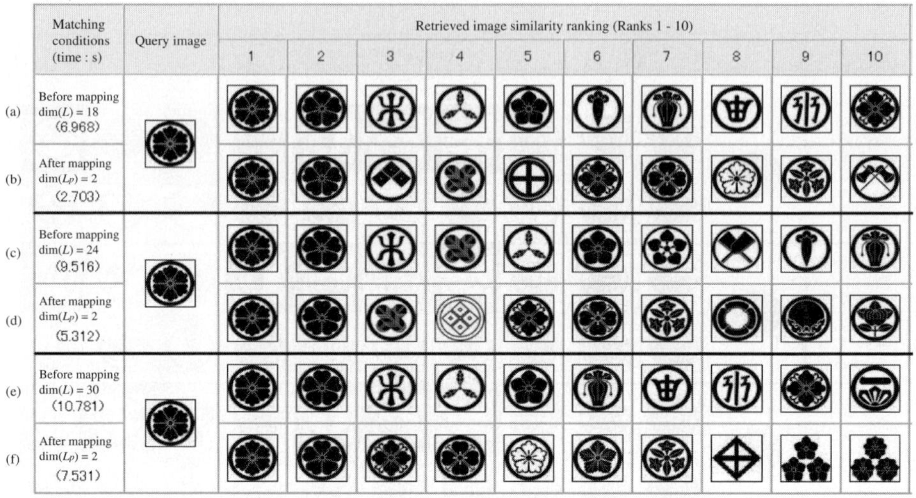

	Matching conditions (time : s)	Query image	Retrieved image similarity ranking (Ranks 1 - 10)									
			1	2	3	4	5	6	7	8	9	10
(a)	Before mapping $\dim(L) = 18$ (6.968)											
(b)	After mapping $\dim(L_P) = 2$ (2.703)											
(c)	Before mapping $\dim(L) = 24$ (9.516)											
(d)	After mapping $\dim(L_P) = 2$ (5.312)											
(e)	Before mapping $\dim(L) = 30$ (10.781)											
(f)	After mapping $\dim(L_P) = 2$ (7.531)											

Parameter Optimization Using PSO. The proposed optimization of eight parameters in Sec. 2 was tried using an image collection consisting of five groups of six subjectively similar images shown in Table 3. The five images in Set 1 were used as query images in turn. For each query, all the 30 images were sorted according to the similarity to the query image. Assuming that the query belongs to Group i, the ranking was assessed by the sum of the ranks of the images in the same Group i as J_i. Thus the lower the J_i the better the result. These scores were summed for all the five groups as, $J = \sum_{i=1}^{5} J_i$, and was used as the score of the current parameter setting. The minimum (best) score was $(0 + 1 + 2 + 3 + 4 + 5) \times 5 = 75$ when the in-group images rank the top six similarities for all five queries.

Maximum generation (G) of PSO was set to 300, and maximum iteration of the relaxation operation for image pair matching was set to 5. Parameters λ_1 and λ_2 were uniform random numbers in $[0, 2]$ generated every generation, and maximum particle speed was set to 0.05.

Parameter values before and after optimization are compared in Table 4. In Table 5, retrieved similar image rankings using the parameter sets before and after optimization are shown. It clearly shows the improvement of the rankings as more subjectively similar images are ranked higher after optimization. The query image for Table 5 is included in the image set of Table 3, however, it was not included in Set 1 used for query in the PSO process. Improvement is also clear by the change in the retrieval score J_5 which decreased from 43 to 16.

Parameter Optimization for Different Criteria. Next, the parameters were optimized for two different criteria, namely to prefer rotated or scaled images

Table 3. Database images used in the experiment. The 30 images were divided to subjectively similar 5 groups of 6 images.

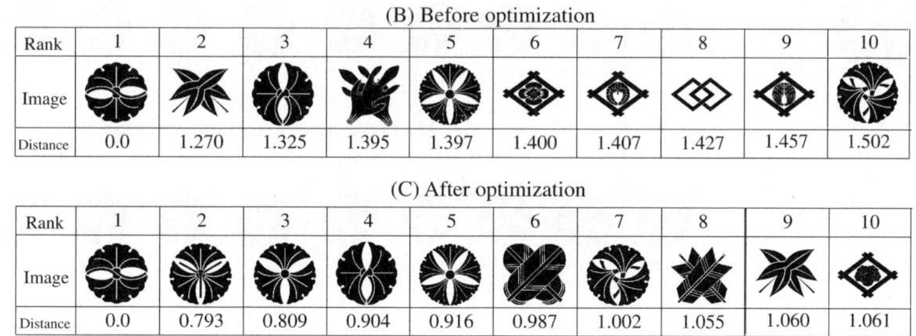

Table 4. The eight parameters, before and after optimization

Parameter	C_1	C_2	C_3	C_4	C_5	W_1	W_2	W_3
Initial value (empirical)	0.1	15	0.1	0.5	0.5	0.1	0.05	0.01
Optimized (300 generation)	1.835	3	0.815	1.691	1.964	0.004	0.227	0.696

Table 5. Retrieved images ranked according to their similarity to the query image (A), which was included in the set of Table 3. Rankings are shown for (B) before parameter optimization ($J_5 = 43$) and, (C) after optimization ($J_5 = 16$).

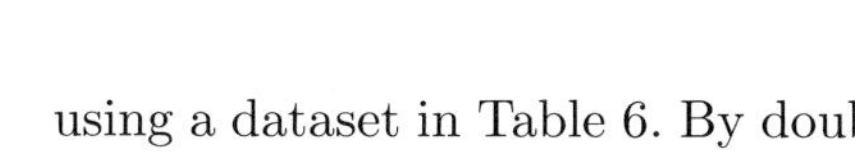

(B) Before optimization

Rank	1	2	3	4	5	6	7	8	9	10
Distance	0.0	1.270	1.325	1.395	1.397	1.400	1.407	1.427	1.457	1.502

(C) After optimization

Rank	1	2	3	4	5	6	7	8	9	10
Distance	0.0	0.793	0.809	0.904	0.916	0.987	1.002	1.055	1.060	1.061

(A) Query

using a dataset in Table 6. By doubling the weights in the scoring function J for the unpreferred types of variations of the query image, it is seen in Table 7 that the preferences are reflected to the rankings after each optimization.

Table 6. Rotated and scaled variations of images in Group 5 in Table 3. The image with "*" was used as a query upon optimization.

	Group1	Group2	Group3	Group4	Group5	Group6
Set1 (standard)						
Set2 (rot. 5 deg.)						
Set3 (rot. 5 deg.)						
Set4 (scale 95%)						
Set5 (scale 105%)						

Table 7. Retrieval for the query image used in optimization (A). (B) Before optimization (rated $J = 25$ and $J = 20$ for scaling and rotation preferring criteria, respectively). (C) After optimization preferring scaling ($J = 13$). (D) Same for rotation ($J = 14$). Legends "O", "R1", "R2", "S1", "S2" denote the original, 5 deg. rotated, -5 deg. rotated, 95% scaled and 105% scaled images, respectively.

(B) Before optimization

Rank	1	2	3	4	5	6	7	8	9	10
Image	O	R1	S1	R2					S2	
Distance	0.0	0.817	0.888	0.981	0.9901	0.9906	1.071	1.073	1.075	1.081

(A) Query

(C) After optimization (scaling preferred)

Rank	1	2	3	4	5	6	7	8	9	10
Image	O	S1	R1	S2	R2					
Distance	0.0	0.522	0.638	0.850	0.856	0.916	0.917	0.924	0.938	0.940

(D) After optimization (rotation preferred)

Rank	1	2	3	4	5	6	7	8	9	10
Image	O	R1	R2	S1	S2					
Distance	0.0	1.079	1.216	1.243	1.409	1.438	1.489	1.494	1.507	1.526

5   Conclusion

Two methods for retrieval relevance optimization by user's feedback was proposed for a content-based image retrieval (CBIR) system. The feature space used for coarse classification was transferred to a *preference feature space* according to the user's feedback. A similar attempt to deform the feature space appears in [1]. It is clear that the idea can be extended to using nonlinear mappings by neural networks, etc.

Also, the parameters in the fine-matching relaxation operation was optimized according to the users' evaluation of the retrieved image ranking using Particle Swarm Optimization. It was shown in the experiments that the retrieval rankings are improved suiting the user's preference when feature space mapping and parameter optimization were used.

References

1. Kato, T., Kurita, T., Shimogaki, H.: Intelligent visual interaction with image database systems - toward the multimedia personal interface. Journal of Information Processing 41(2), 134–143 (1991)
2. Niblack, W., Barber, R., Equitz, W., Flickner, M.D., Glasman, E.H., Petkovic, D., Yanker, P., Faloutsos, C., Taubin, G.: QBIC project: querying images by content, using color, texture, and shape. In: SPIE Proceedings, vol. 1908, pp. 173–187 (1993)
3. Pentland, A., Picard, R.W., Sclaroff, S.: Photobook: Tools for content-based manipulation of image databases. International Journal of Computer Vision 18(3), 233–254 (1996)
4. Squire, D.M., Müller, W., Müller, H., Pun, T.: Content-based query of image databases: inspirations from text retrieval. Pattern Recognition Letters 21, 1193–1198 (2000)
5. Kameyama, K., Oka, N., Toraichi, K.: Optimal parameter selection in image similarity evaluation algorithms using particle swarm optimization. In: Proceedings of IEEE Congress of Evolutionary Computation, World Congress of Computational Intelligence 2006, pp. 3824–3831 (2006)
6. Yamamoto, K.: Recognition of handprinted kanji characters by relaxation matching. IECE Trans. J65-D(9), 1167–1174 (1982)
7. Kwan, P.W.H., Kameyama, K., Toraichi, K.: Trademark retrieval by relaxation matching on fluency function approximated image contours. In: Proceedings of IEEE Pacific Rim Conference on Communication, Computer and Signal Processing, pp. 255–258 (2001)
8. Katayama, N., Satoh, S.: The SR-tree: An index structure for high-dimensional nearest neighbor queries. In: Proceedings of the 1997 ACM SIGMOD International Conference on Management of Data, pp. 369–380 (1997)
9. Rosenfeld, A., Hummel, R.A., Zucker, S.W.: Scene labeling by relaxation operations. IEEE Trans. Sys., Man and Cybern. SMC-6(6), 420–433 (1976)
10. Pelillo, M.: On the dynamics of relaxation labeling processes. In: Proc. IEEE Int'l. Conf. on Neural Networks, vol. 2, pp. 1006–1011 (1994)
11. Kohonen, T.: Self-Organizing Maps, 3rd edn. Springer, Heidelberg (2006)
12. Kennedy, J., Eberhart, R.C.: Particle swarm optimization. In: Proceedings of IEEE International Conference on Neural Networks, pp. 1942–1948 (1995)

3-D Shape Reconstruction from Stereovision Data Using Object-Consisted Markov Random Field Model

Hotaka Takizawa

University of Tsukuba, 1-1-1 Tennodai, Tsukuba, 305-8573, Japan
`takizawa@cs.tsukuba.ac.jp`

Abstract. In the present paper, we propose a method for reconstructing the shapes of block-like objects from stereovision data. Flat surfaces and ridge lines are represented by three-dimensional (3-D) discrete object models. Interrelations between the object models are formulated by use of the framework of a 3-D Markov Random Field (MRF) model. The shape reconstruction is accomplished by searching for the most likely state of the MRF model. The searching is performed by the Markov Chain Monte Carlo (MCMC) method. An experimental result is shown for real stereo data.

Keywords: 3-D Shape reconstruction, Stereovision, Object models, Markov Random Field model, Markov Chain Monte Carlo.

1 Introduction

Shape reconstruction from stereovision data is one of the most important topics in computer vision. It can provide effective clues for solving problems in, for example, object recognition, scene description, and scene interpretation. As such, extensive research has been dedicated to shape reconstruction from stereo data.

In a number of studies such as [1,2,3,4], shape reconstruction is accomplished by representing object surfaces by use of primitive models, such as triangles, that are generated so as to interpolate points in stereo data. These studies, however, do not have a mechanism to represent other parts of objects such as ridge lines. Although a ridge line should be represented as the line of intersection of two plane surfaces, it is rounded off by unnecessarily inserted triangles. In addition, they do not pay attention to the noises of stereo data, that often make the surfaces rugged. For more faithful shape reconstruction, ridge lines should be modeled explicitly, and the models should be smoothly connected to each other as well as being properly fitted to the points in stereo data.

In this paper, we propose a method for reconstructing the surfaces and ridge lines of 3-D objects from stereovision data considering a tradeoff between the smooth connection and proper fitting. Here, we suppose that a 3-D object is composed of simple parts, which are locally interrelated with each other. The object parts are represented by primitive models, and their interrelations are formulated by a MRF[5] model that is extended so as to have the primitive models as elements of the random field.

M. Ishikawa et al. (Eds.): ICONIP 2007, Part II, LNCS 4985, pp. 618–627, 2008.

Figure 1 illustrates the overview of the proposed method. First, a pair of stereo images of a target object in a scene is obtained by a stereo camera system. Next, the 3-D positions of *edges* are calculated by applying an edge-based stereo matching method to the stereo images. A rectangular solid is settled so as to include the edges, and is divided into $M(= M_1 \times M_2 \times M_3)$ rectangular solids that are sufficiently smaller than the object. The large rectangular solid and the smaller rectangular solids are called the volume of interest (VOI) and *cells*, respectively. Four types of 3-D discrete object model, *solid, hollow, surface* and *roof*, are generated in each cell. Each object model is represented by several parameters such as positions and directions. The object models in the cells are combined with one another, and the likelihood of the appearance of the object model combination is defined through an MRF posterior energy function. To search for the most likely state of the models, the MCMC method is applied to the energy function. The most likely state provides the faithful reconstruction of the object.

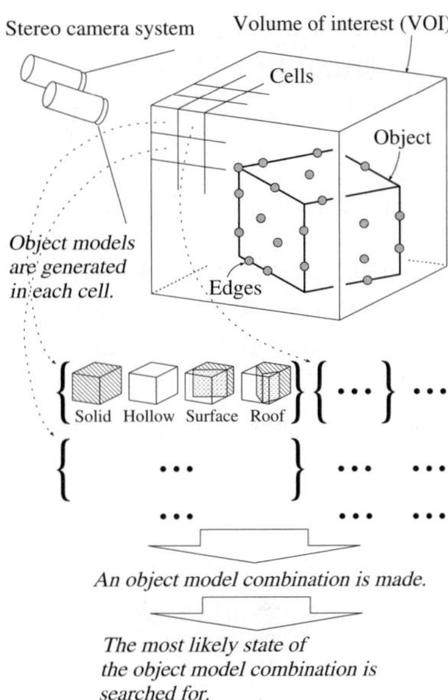

Fig. 1. Overview of the proposed method

2 Object Models

The following four types of object model are used in the proposed method:

Solid: A solid model represents that a cell is completely included in the space occupied by an object.

Hollow: A hollow model represents that a cell is completely excluded from an object.

Surface: A surface model represents that a piecewise plane surface of an object intersects a cell. Figure 2(a) illustrates an example of a surface model. Let Q_s denote a cell at site s. A surface model in Q_s is represented by a control point on the surface $\boldsymbol{b}_s^{SF} = (x_s^{SF}, y_s^{SF}, z_s^{SF})^T$, and a normal vector $\boldsymbol{n}_s^{SF}$. The normal vector is set from inside to outside, and is represented by two angles, as follows:

$$\boldsymbol{n}_s^{SF} = \boldsymbol{n}_s^{SF}(\phi_s^{SF}, \psi_s^{SF}), \tag{1}$$

where ϕ_s^{SF} and ψ_s^{SF} are the azimuth and zenith angles in the global coordinate system, respectively.

Roof: A roof model represents that two piecewise plane surfaces intersect in a line in a cell. In this paper, orthogonally intersecting surfaces are modeled. Figure 2(b) illustrates two surfaces, $x \geq 0, y = 0$ and $x = 0, y \geq 0$, that intersect in a line, $x = y = 0$, at the right angle. We use these surfaces as the standard type of a roof model. The standard roof model is represented by a control point $\boldsymbol{b}^{RF} = (0,0,0)^T$, a normal vector $\boldsymbol{n}^{RF} = \left(-\dfrac{1}{\sqrt{2}}, -\dfrac{1}{\sqrt{2}}, 0\right)^T$ from inside to outside, and the direction vector of the ridge line $\boldsymbol{d}^{RF} = (0,0,1)^T$. A roof model in a cell Q_s is generated by rotating and translating the standard roof model. The control point $\boldsymbol{b}_s^{RF}$, normal vector $\boldsymbol{n}_s^{RF}$ and direction vector $\boldsymbol{d}_s^{RF}$ of the roof model is obtained by

$$\boldsymbol{b}_s^{RF} = \boldsymbol{b}^{RF} + \boldsymbol{t}_s^{RF}, \qquad \boldsymbol{n}_s^{RF} = R_s^{RF}\boldsymbol{n}^{RF}, \qquad \boldsymbol{d}_s^{RF} = R_s^{RF}\boldsymbol{d}^{RF}, \qquad (2)$$

where

$$\boldsymbol{t}_s^{RF} = (x_s^{RF}, y_s^{RF}, z_s^{RF})^T \quad and \quad R_s^{RF} = R_s^{RF}(\theta_s^{RF}, \phi_s^{RF}, \psi_s^{RF}) \qquad (3)$$

are a translation vector and rotation matrix, respectively.

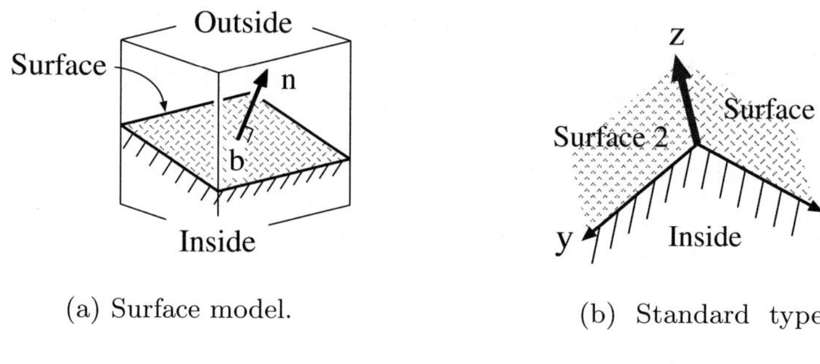

(a) Surface model.

(b) Standard type

of a roof model.

Fig. 2. Object models

2.1   Presence of Object Models

We introduce another type of parameter, namely *presence*, which represents explicitly the appearance or disappearance of object models in a cell. Let $p_s(SL)$, $p_s(HL)$, $p_s(SF)$ and $p_s(RF)$ denote the presence of solid, hollow, surface and roof models, respectively, in a cell Q_s. The presence values vary between 1 and 0, which correspond to the complete appearance and disappearance, respectively, and satisfy

$$\sum_{o_s \in \{SL, HL, SF, RF\}} p_s(o_s) = 1 \qquad (4)$$

to represent the exclusive appearance of object models in one cell. To satisfy Eq.(4), four additional variables $\check{p}_s(o_s)$ ($o_s \in \{SL, HL, SF, RF\}$) are introduced that can independently vary between a constant value $\check{P} > 0$ and 0. Each presence value is represented by

$$p_s(o_s) = \frac{\check{p}_s(o_s)}{\displaystyle\sum_{o_s} \check{p}_s(o_s)}. \tag{5}$$

3 Evaluation of Interrelations Between Adjoining Object Models

Six cells adjoining a central cell in Figure 3 are defined to be its neighborhood. The 6-neighborhood system provides the ten different types of pair of adjoining object models, as listed in Table 1. Some of these pairs are consistent, others are not. Our previous work[6] described the consistency of the pairs indicated by from 1 to 6 in Table 1. In this section, the consistency of the other pairs are defined.

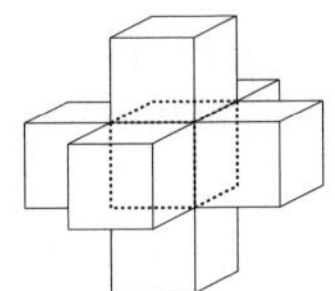

Fig. 3. 6 neighborhood system

Table 1. Ten types of pairs of adjoining object models

	Solid	Hollow	Surface	Roof
Solid	1	3	4	7
Hollow	3	2	5	8
Surface	4	5	6	9
Roof	7	8	9	10

Let $Q_{t \in N(s)}$ denote an adjoining cell of Q_s in the 6-neighborhood system $N(\cdot)$, and $h(o_s, o_t)$ denote the level of consistency of two adjoining object models: $o_s \in \{SL, HL, SF, RF\}$ in a cell Q_s and $o_t \in \{SL, HL, SF, RF\}$ in an adjoining cell $Q_{t \in N(s)}$. $h(o_s, o_t)$ is defined in the following range:

$$OK \leq h(o_s, o_t) \leq NG, \tag{6}$$

where OK denotes that the pair is consistent and NG denotes that the pair is inconsistent.

3.1 Roof and Solid

The consistency level of this pair varies depending on the parameter values of the roof model. We define the consistency level based on the volume of the inconsistent region in the same way as the pair of surface and solid models in [6]. The consistency level is formulated by

$$h(RF, SL) = (1 - r^{p7}) \cdot OK + r^{p7} \cdot NG, \tag{7}$$

where r^{p7} is the ratio of the volume of the inconsistent region to that of the entire solid cell.

3.2 Roof and Hollow

The consistency level of this pair is defined in the same way as that of the pair of roof and solid models.

3.3 Roof and Surface

Figure 4(a) illustrates roof and surface models that adjoin each other. If the ridge line of the roof model is formed by the surface model, the ridge line should be on the surface model. It is evaluated by

$$h_1^{p9} = \left(\theta(\boldsymbol{b}_{st}, \boldsymbol{n}_t) - \frac{\pi}{2}\right)^2 \quad and \quad h_2^{p9} = \left(\theta(\boldsymbol{d}_s, \boldsymbol{n}_t) - \frac{\pi}{2}\right)^2, \tag{8}$$

where $\boldsymbol{b}_{st}$ is a vector from $\boldsymbol{b}_s$ to $\boldsymbol{b}_t$, and $\theta(\boldsymbol{x}_1, \boldsymbol{x}_2)$ is the angle between $\boldsymbol{x}_1$ and $\boldsymbol{x}_2$.

Since it is supposed that two surfaces forming a ridge line intersect orthogonally, the angle between the normal vector of the roof model and that of the surface model should be the 45 degree. The angle is evaluated by

$$h_3^{p9} = \left(\theta(\boldsymbol{n}_s, \boldsymbol{n}_t) - \frac{\pi}{4}\right)^2. \tag{9}$$

Using these preliminary evaluation values, the consistency level of the pair is defined by

$$h(RF, SF) = (1 - r^{p9}) \cdot OK + r^{p9} \cdot NG, \tag{10}$$

$$where \quad r^{p9} = \frac{\alpha^{p9} \cdot h_1^{p9} + \beta^{p9} \cdot h_2^{p9} + \gamma^{p9} \cdot h_3^{p9}}{\alpha^{p9} \cdot \left(\frac{\pi}{2}\right)^2 + \beta^{p9} \cdot \left(\frac{\pi}{2}\right)^2 + \gamma^{p9} \cdot \left(\frac{3\pi}{4}\right)^2}. \tag{11}$$

The α^{p9}, β^{p9} and γ^{p9} are weight coefficients.

3.4 Roof and Roof

Two adjoining ridge lines should connect smoothly. It is evaluated by

$$h_1^{p10} = (\theta(\boldsymbol{b}_{\overline{st}}, \boldsymbol{d}_s))^2, \quad h_2^{p10} = (\theta(\boldsymbol{b}_{\overline{st}}, \boldsymbol{d}_t))^2, \quad h_3^{p10} = (\theta(\boldsymbol{n}_s, \boldsymbol{n}_t))^2, \tag{12}$$

where $\boldsymbol{b}_{\overline{st}}$ is a line segment from $\boldsymbol{b}_s$ to $\boldsymbol{b}_t$ (see Figure 4(b)).

The consistency level of the pair is defined by

$$h(RF, SF) = (1 - r^{p10}) \cdot OK + r^{p10} \cdot NG, \tag{13}$$

$$where \quad r^{p10} = \frac{\alpha^{p10} \cdot h_1^{p10} + \beta^{p10} \cdot h_2^{p10} + \gamma^{p10} \cdot h_3^{p10}}{\alpha^{p10} \cdot \left(\frac{\pi}{2}\right)^2 + \beta^{p10} \cdot \left(\frac{\pi}{2}\right)^2 + \gamma^{p10} \cdot \pi^2}. \tag{14}$$

The α^{p10}, β^{p10} and γ^{p10} are weight coefficients.

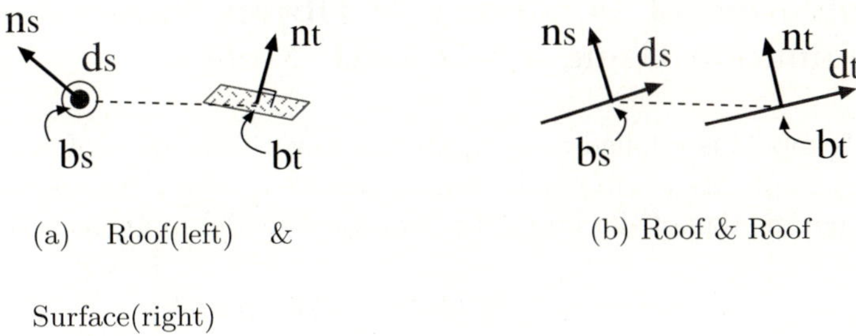

Fig. 4. Pairs of adjoining object models

4   Observation Model

The degree of fitness of a point to a surface is often measured by the Euclidean distance between the point and the surface. The proposed method also uses the Euclidean distance to evaluate the fitness of an edge to a surface model. Let $e = \{e^{(1)}, e^{(2)}, ..., e^{(I)}\}$ denote a set of edges obtained by the stereo camera system. The fitness of an edge $e^{(i)}$ to a surface model is defined by

$$f(e^{(i)}, SF) = \left(d(e^{(i)}, SF) \right)^2 , \tag{15}$$

where $d(e, SF)$ is the Euclidean distance from the edge to a surface model.

The fitness of an edge to a roof model is defined by

$$f(e^{(i)}, RF) = \left(\min \left(d(e^{(i)}, RF_1), d(e^{(i)}, RF_2) \right) \right)^2 , \tag{16}$$

where RF_1 and RF_2 are the two surfaces of the roof model.

The method should also define the fitness functions of an edge to solid and hollow models. An edge might fall into a solid or hollow cell when its position cannot be correctly determined due to some errors occurred in a stereo matching process. Such an isolated edge would originate from an object surface in another cell. We cannot obtain a distance between the edge and the object surface because we cannot determine beforehand which cell provides the isolated edge. Therefore, we use another metric for an isolated edge in a cell. Suppose that there is a surface piece in its peripheral cell. The distance between the edge and the surface becomes smaller as the distance between the edge and the centroid of the cell including the edge becomes larger. There is a relationship between these distances. We use, as an approximation, the latter distance instead of the former distance. The fitness of an isolated edge $e^{(i)}$ to an object model $o \in \{SL, HL\}$ is evaluated by

$$f(e^{(i)}, o) = \left(\frac{l_{diag}}{2} - d\left(e^{(i)}, c(e^{(i)}) \right) \right)^2 , \tag{17}$$

where l_{diag} and $c(e)$ is the diagonal length and the centroid of the cell of the edge e, respectively.

5 Formulation of Possibility of Object Model Combination Using a 3-D MRF Model

The MRF[5] model is applied to compute the most likely state of object models in the $M_1 \times M_2 \times M_3 \ (= M)$ cells. Let ω_s denote a vector that is composed of the fifteen parameters of the four types of object model in Q_s as follows:

$$
\begin{aligned}
\omega_s = \Big(\ & \check{p}_s(SL), \check{p}_s(HL), \check{p}_s(SF), \check{p}_s(RF), \\
& x_s^{SF}, y_s^{SF}, z_s^{SF}, \phi_s^{SF}, \psi_s^{SF}, \\
& x_s^{RF}, y_s^{RF}, z_s^{RF}, \theta_s^{RF}, \phi_s^{RF}, \psi_s^{RF} \Big),
\end{aligned}
\tag{18}
$$

and let $\boldsymbol{\omega} \in \Omega$ denote a set of ω_ss as follows:

$$
\boldsymbol{\omega} = \{\omega_1, \omega_2, ..., \omega_M\}.
\tag{19}
$$

The posterior energy function for the MRF model is defined by

$$
U(\boldsymbol{\omega} \in \Omega | e) = \sum_{c \in C} V_c(\boldsymbol{\omega}) - \lambda \cdot L(e|\boldsymbol{\omega}),
\tag{20}
$$

where C is a set of cliques of adjoining object models in the MRF model, and $V_c(\boldsymbol{\omega})$ measures the potential (energy) of a clique c under parameters $\boldsymbol{\omega}$, $L(e|\boldsymbol{\omega})$ is the likelihood that the edges e originate from the object models of the parameters $\boldsymbol{\omega}$, and λ is a constant weighting coefficient.

The definitions of the clique potential and the edge likelihood are described below.

5.1 Clique Potential

For efficiency concerns, the proposed method considers only 1-clique and 2-clique (in other words, $V_c(\boldsymbol{\omega}) = 0$, $|c| > 2$).

A 1-clique consists of a single object model (i.e. $c = \{o_s\}$), and its potential is defined by

$$
V_1(\omega_s) = - \sum_{o_s \in \{SL, HL, SF, RF\}} p_s(o_s) \log p_s(o_s).
\tag{21}
$$

The potential is made a formula same as the information entropy. The $V_1(\omega_s)$ decreases as the uncertainty of the object presence is reduced, and should be minimal if the object is uniquely determined in a cell.

A 2-clique consists of two adjoining object models (i.e. $c = \{o_s, o_{t \in N(s)}\}$), and its potential is defined by

$$
V_2(\omega_s, \omega_{t \in N(s)}) = V_2'(\omega_s, \omega_t) + V_2''(\omega_s, \omega_t),
\tag{22}
$$

where

$$V_2'(\omega_s, \omega_t) = \sum_{o_s, o_t \in \{SL, HL, SF, RF\}} p_s(o_s) \cdot p_t(o_t) \cdot h(o_s, o_t), \qquad (23)$$

$$V_2''(\omega_s, \omega_t) = \sum_{o_s, o_t \in \{SF, RF\}} V_{LG}(|\boldsymbol{b}_{\overrightarrow{st}}|). \qquad (24)$$

The V_2' is the mean consistency level of the object models o_s and o_t in the 2-clique. The $V_{LG}(r)$ is the Lennard-Jones potential function that is defined by

$$V_{LG}(r) = C_{LG} \left(\left(\frac{\sigma_{LG}}{r} \right)^{n_{LG}} - \left(\frac{\sigma_{LG}}{r} \right)^{m_{LG}} \right), \qquad (25)$$

where C_{LG} and σ_{LG} are coefficients. $n_{LG}, m_{LG} \in \mathbb{Z}$ and $n_{LG} > m_{LG} > 0$. In the atomic physics, the Lennard-Jones potential function is used to model a force between atoms. If atoms get too near to each other, a strong repulsive force acts on them. On the other hand, if the atoms leave, an attractive force acts on them. In this method, the potential function is used to keep the distance between the control points of surface and roof models adequate. The too-short distance makes V_2' unstable because V_2' includes $|\boldsymbol{s}_{st}|$ implicitly. The too-large distance would let reconstructed surfaces and ridge lines get loose.

5.2   Edge Likelihood

The likelihood of the edges $\boldsymbol{e}$ is defined by

$$L(\boldsymbol{e}|\boldsymbol{\omega}) = -\frac{1}{I} \sum_i \sum_{o_{s(i)} \in \{SL, HL, SF, RF\}} p_s(o_{s(i)}) \cdot f(e_s^{(i)}, o_{s(i)}), \qquad (26)$$

where $e_s^{(i)}$ is an edge in $Q_{s(i)}$. Eq.(26) represents a mean fitness value weighted by $p_s(o_{s(i)})$.

6   Searching Strategy

The most likely state of $\boldsymbol{\omega}$ in Eq.(20) is defined by

$$\boldsymbol{\omega}^* = \int_{\boldsymbol{\omega} \in \Omega} \boldsymbol{\omega} \cdot \frac{\exp\left(-U(\boldsymbol{\omega}|\boldsymbol{e})\right)}{Z} d\boldsymbol{\omega}, \qquad (27)$$

where Z is a normalizing constant. The $\boldsymbol{\omega}^*$ is obtained by applying the MCMC method[7] to Eq.(27).

7   Experimental Result

Figure 5(a) and (b) show a pair of stereo images of a scene that includes a box. Figure 5(c) shows depth data obtained from the stereo images. Figure 5(d)

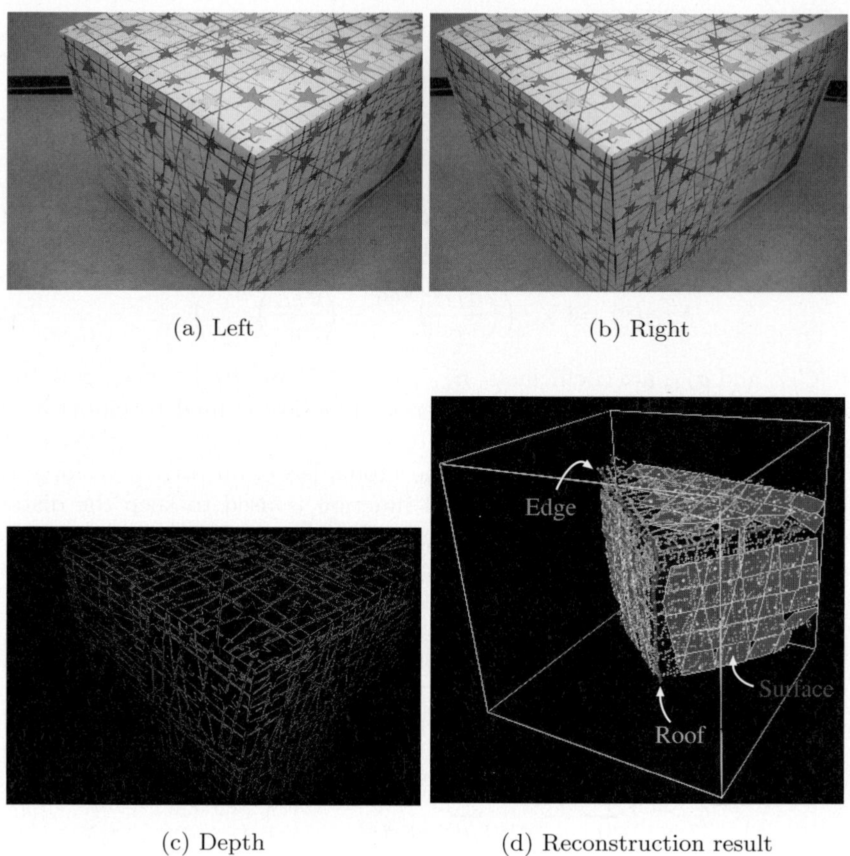

(a) Left   (b) Right

(c) Depth   (d) Reconstruction result

Fig. 5. Stereo images, its depth data (the depth is coded in gray values) and reconstruction result

shows the side view of the result of shape reconstruction. The small points, squares and pipes represent edges, surface models and ridge lines of roof models. For the scene, $9 \times 9 \times 9$ cells are used. The calculation time is about two hours.

The three flat surfaces and three ridge lines of the box are almost faithfully reconstructed by a set of surface and roof models, respectively.

8   Conclusion

This paper has described a novel method for reconstructing the shapes of block-like objects from stereovision data. Flat surfaces and ridge lines are represented by 3-D discrete object models, such as surface and roof models. The interrelations between the object models are formulated by use of the framework of a 3-D

MRF that is composed of the object models. The shape reconstruction is accomplished by searching for the most likely state of the MRF model, and the searching is performed by the MCMC method. An experimental result is shown for real stereo data. The result has proved that the proposed method is effective in reconstructing the shapes of artificial objects.

Currently the application area of the proposed method is limited to the reconstruction of angulated objects. One of our future works is to extend the application area to more natural objects by the use of, for example, curved surface models.

References

1. Grimson, W.: From Images to Surfaces, A Computational Study of the Human Early Visual System. MIT Press, Cambridge (1981)
2. Floriani, L., Puppo, E.: Constrained Delaunay Triangulation for Multiresolution Surface Description. In: Proc. International Conference on Pattern Recognition 1988, pp. 566–569 (1988)
3. Faugeras, O.D., Bras-Mehlman, E., Boissonnat, J.D.: Representing Stereo Data with the Delaunay Triangulation. Artificial Intelligence 44, 41–87 (1990)
4. Taylor, C.J.: Surface Reconstruction from Feature Based Stereo. In: Proceedings of the 9th IEEE International Conference on Computer Vision, pp. 184–190 (2003)
5. Geman, S., Geman, D.: Stochastic Relaxation, Gibbs Distribution, and the Bayesian Restoration of Images. IEEE Trans. on Pattern Analysis and Machine Intelligence(PAMI) PAMI-6(6), 721–742 (1984)
6. Takizawa, H., Yamamoto, S.: Surface Reconstruction from Stereo Data using a Three-dimensional Markov Random Field Model. IEICE Transactions on Information and Systems E89-D(7), 2028–2035 (2006)
7. Winkler, G.: Image Analysis, Random Fields and Markov Chain Monte Carlo Methods. Springer, Heidelberg (2006)

Application of the Unusual Motion Detection Using CHLAC to the Video Surveillance

Kenji Iwata, Yutaka Satoh, Takumi Kobayashi, Ikushi Yoda, and Nobuyuki Otsu

National Institute of Advanced Industrial Science and Technology (AIST)
AIST Tsukuba Central 2, 1-1-1, Umezono, Tsukuba, Ibaraki, 305-8568, Japan

Abstract. Cubic Higher-Order Local Auto-Correlation (CHLAC) is feature vector that simultaneously represent motion and shape. The system learns a sample set of "usual motion" to create a "usual subspace" with PCA. Feature vectors are then similarly extracted from unknown input data, and accurate detection of "unusual motion" is achieved by measuring the deviation from the usual subspace. Therefore, by defining unusual motion as "motion that is outside the usual motion," this method can detect unusual motion without an actual model of unusual motion, which differs depending on the situation, and furthermore, is difficult to define. This paper reports on the fast CHLAC that we have developed, so that these capabilities of CHLAC can be put to practical use as an unusual motion detection system that operates in real time. This paper also demonstrated the effectiveness of this method through example tests, conducted using real images both indoors and outdoors.

Key words: Surveillance, Motion Analysis, CHLAC, PCA, SIMD.

1 Introduction

The recent rise in concerns over security has led to the deployment of a large number of surveillance cameras in a variety of locations. However, cost inhibits the constant human monitoring of all the images, and so often these images are simply recorded and used for verification after a crime or incident has occurred. Centralized control enables security staff in large facilities to monitor the images from many cameras in real time. But, it is difficult for people to pay constant attention to a large number of images. Hence, there is a strong demand for the development of a system that can automatically detect unusual motion from surveillance camera images. If unusual motion is automatically detected, then we could find unusual activity in real time in more places, and surveillance cameras could provide more active security rather than being limited to the conventional use of verification after an incident has occurred.

Research into the analysis of human actions is underway in order to achieve such a system [1]. This kind of research is generally based on a method whereby the image of a person is segmented from the background image, and actions are identified by using a model or from a history of those actions. For example, Aoki et al. detected unusual situations by locating the position of the person and then studying behavioral patterns of daily activity using HMM (Hidden Markov Model) [2]. However, in such

M. Ishikawa et al. (Eds.): ICONIP 2007, Part II, LNCS 4985, pp. 628–636, 2008.

methods, the segmentation quality of the person greatly influences the performance of the overall system. Generally speaking, the segmentation of people's images is easily affected by changes in lighting, and so it is particularly difficult to attain stable operation in an outdoor environment.

On the other hand, this problem does not occur in the approach where changes are detected directly from the images because segmentation of the subject is not required [3] [4]. Therefore, it can be used universally without restricting the subject, for example, to humans. However, these methods depend on the subject's position within the image, and the motion information is not actively used. Optical-flow-based motion detection [5] is well suited when vigorous movements are to be recognized as unusual, because it is hard to distinguish slight movements. Therefore, methods using feature values that simultaneously treat motion and shape equally have been proposed. One such method is MHI (Motion History Image) [6], in which the history of the changes in shape is expressed as images. Another method, which was developed by the authors of this paper, uses Cubic Higher-order Local Auto-Correlation (CHLAC) features [7]. CHLAC is an extension of HLAC [9] to a three-dimensional system, and exhibits superior performance in distinguishing human gaits using discriminant analysis. Recognition of unusual motion from an image is achieved by defining unusual motion as a deviation from usual motion, and then detecting movements that do not fall under the learned usual motion [8]. The high processing cost of conventional CHLAC, however, has made it difficult to use in real time.

This paper focuses on a study of a high-speed implementation method, which is necessary for the commercialization of CHLAC as an unusual motion detection system that operates in real time. To increase speed, real-time processing was made possible on a processing system of the notebook PC level by using SIMD (Single Instruction, Multiple Data) to batch-process multiple pixels in accordance with the CHLAC displacement patterns. This paper also demonstrated the effectiveness of this method through example tests, conducted using real images both indoors and outdoors.

2   Cubic Higher-Order Local Auto Correlation

2.1   Outline of CHLAC

HLAC [9] is based on general image recognition features, and is widely used in two-dimensional pattern recognition. The N-dimensional autocorrelation function can be formularized as follows.

$$x(a_1,\cdots,a_N) = \int I(r)I(r+a_1)\cdots I(r+a_N)dr \tag{1}$$

where I is the image, and the variable vector r and the N displacement vectors a_i ($i=1,...,N$) are two-dimensional vectors that have image coordinates x, y. The number of displacement vector combinations is equal to the number of dimensions of the feature vector. If we use 3×3 local regions, where $N=0$, 1, 2, then we get a 35-dimensional feature vector for a grayscale image. With a binary-format image, coincident displacement vectors can be eliminated because they are equivalent, and so we are left with the 25 displacement vector combinations.

CHLAC [7] is HLAC expanded into a three-dimensional system by the addition of the time axis. The formularization is just about the same as in Eqn. (1), with I as the time-series image, and variable vector r and the displacement vectors a_i expanded to three-dimensional vectors by the addition of time (t) to the coordinates (x, y). The number of displacement vector combinations corresponds to the number of dimensions of the feature vector, just as it did with HLAC. CHLAC with 3×3×3 local regions and N=0, 1, 2 gives 275 dimensional vectors on a grayscale image, which would be 251 dimensional vectors when applied to a binary-format image, after redundancies have been eliminated.

Shift-invariance and frame-additivity hold true in both HLAC and CHLAC. Shift invariance is the property whereby the same feature vectors are obtained wherever the subject is in the image. Because the feature vectors are independent of the subject's location in the image, segmentation or position matching is unnecessary. Frame-additivity is the property whereby the overall feature vector for multiple subjects is equal to the sum of the feature vectors for each subject. This means that the pattern recognition for multiple subjects can be handled by the same process as pattern recognition for a single subject. These properties are also important in achieving parallel processing to increase the speed, as described in the following section.

2.2 Fast CHLAC Through SIMD

Figure 1 depicts the CHLAC extraction method. The gray elements in the displacement patterns in this figure represent the displacement vectors. This pattern is applied to the time-series image, and the product of the pixel values corresponding to the elements shown in gray is calculated. The same is done for all the frames in a certain time range T, and the results are summed to get a total. The feature vectors are obtained by performing this process with all the displacement patterns. An actual example is shown in Fig. 2. The displacement pattern in Fig. 2 (a) is first applied to the upper left of the image shown in Fig. 2 (b), and A2*B2*C1 is calculated. Next, the displacement pattern is shifted one pixel to the right, and A3*B3*C2 is calculated. This procedure is repeated over the entire image, and all of the totals are calculated. The method for the calculations corresponding to the other displacement patterns is identical.

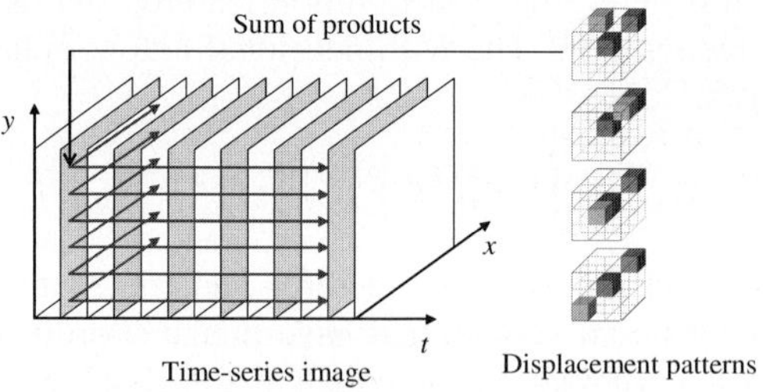

Fig. 1. The CHLAC extraction method

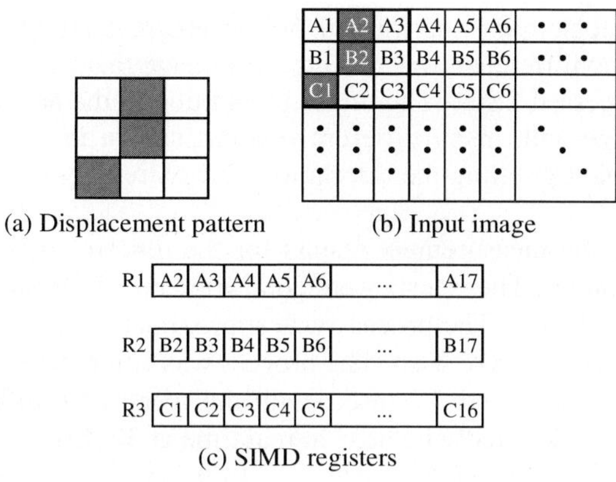

(a) Displacement pattern   (b) Input image

(c) SIMD registers

Fig. 2. Process of CHLAC using SIMD

CHLAC for a binary-format image results in a 251-dimensonal vector, and so the extraction process involves the product and sum being calculated 738 times per pixel. If we take a QVGA (320×240) image as an example, CHLAC extraction would require an enormous 57 million product and sum calculations per frame. This could not be done in real time (at 30 or more frames per second) using ordinary instruction sets on current PCs.

Therefore, we investigated parallel processing by exploiting the frame additivity property of CHLAC. Parallelization methods include hardware implementation or methods involving PC-clusters, but these run into cost and equipment size problems. Consequently, in order to increase the speed at low cost, we used SIMD instructions to parallelize the process by using an ordinary PC alone. The SIMD instruction set, which is incorporated in the majority of current CPUs, allows a process to be performed on elements in a data set in parallel by using a single instruction.

SIMD uses registers that can hold a set of data. The values corresponding to the HLAC/CHLAC displacement pattern are loaded into the elements of the registers R1, R2 and R3, as shown in Fig. 2, with pixel data for consecutive pixels in the x-direction of a general image held in consecutive memory locations. Once the leading values A2, B2, and C1 are ready, the values for the adjacent pixels are collected and loaded into the registers. Because SIMD calculations are performed on the elements in the vertical direction, multiple products can be found at once. If 128-bit registers are used with an 8-bit format input image, then 16 pixels can be handled in parallel and so the number of times the process needs to be repeated is reduced to 1/16.

SIMD instructions are employed in the majority of AMD and Intel processors, but we implemented the CHLAC extraction process using the MMX and SSE2/SSE3 instruction sets incorporated into the Intel x86 processor. MMX uses 64-bit registers, whereas SSE uses 128-bit registers. The processing times were measured by using each of these. In these tests, a 320×240 image size was used, and a hand waved in front of a camera was filmed. The inter-frame time differential was binarized by using a fixed threshold value.

Because no calculation is performed by the HLAC/CHLAC extraction processes for pixels where no difference was detected, an image that show fewer differentials in the pixels are processed faster. Therefore, in addition to the normal example shown in Fig. 3(a), an image with many different regions, shown in Fig. 3(b), was used as a worst-case example by setting the threshold value extremely low to measure the processing time.

Table 1 shows the measurement results for the time required for CHLAC extraction using three frames. These tests were conducted on a PC that had a Pentium D 840 (3.2 GHz) running Linux. The process was approximately nine times faster when the SSE2/SSE3 instructions were used. The process was completed in 0.12 msec. with the normal difference image and 2.2 msec. with the worst-case image; the results show this process could undoubtedly be used in real time at 30 fps.

(a) Normal threshold   (b) Lower threshold

Fig. 3. Test images for the benchmark of CHLAC

Table 1. Result of benchmarks

	Normal threshold	Lower theshold
SIMD is not used	1.33 msec	20.05 msec
64bit SIMD(MMX)	0.34 msec	6.02 msec
128bit SIMD(SSE2/SSE3)	0.16 msec	2.2 msec

3 Detection of Unusual Motion

An anomaly is defined as a deviation from normal circumstances (i.e., usual motion). Because this definition makes it unnecessary for the discriminator to learn samples of unusual motion, it is exceedingly practical in application. The reason for this is that large amounts of sample data on normal circumstances can be obtained simply by deploying the camera, whereas it would be difficult to obtain a large sample of data on the many conceivable unusual situations.

Here, a subspace method is applied to the 251-dimensional CHLAC feature vectors corresponding to an image with an inter-frame time differential that is binarized using a threshold process. A linear subspace, called the "usual subspace," is generated using the CHLAC feature vectors obtained from the learning data which is usual motion. The usual subspace is spanned by the principle vectors obtained by PCA of the learned samples. The eigenvalues, $\lambda_1,\cdots,\lambda_M$ and eigenvectors $u_1,\cdots,u_M$ are obtained from the variance-covariance matrix of the M-dimensional feature vectors of the training set $x=x_i,\cdots,x_M,$, and then the cumulative contribution rate η_K is calculated.

$$\eta_K = \frac{\sum_{i=1}^{K} \lambda_i}{\sum_{i=1}^{M} \lambda_i} \tag{2}$$

The usual subspace is taken to be the subspace spanned by the eigenvectors $u_1,...,u_K$, where the number of dimensions is the value of K at which the contribution rate η_K reaches a threshold, U . If usual motion is used as test data, then its feature vectors will lie within the usual subspace. If the motion is unusual, then the feature vectors will deviate from the usual subspace. The degree of deviation used is the subspace distance $d_\perp$, found by mapping the input vector onto the ortho-component subspace.

$$d_\perp = \left\| P_\perp x \right\| \tag{3}$$

where $P_\perp$ is the projection onto the ortho-component subspace. This value $d_\perp$, an indicator of whether or not the motion is unusual, is defined as the deviation value.

This definition of the deviation value also makes use of CHLAC frame-additivity. (8). For example, even if there are a number of people in the image, if they are all moving normally (e.g., walking), then the vector will be in the usual subspace because the sum of the vectors in this subspace will lie in the same subspace, and so a deviation value will not occur. However, if any one of these people moves in an unusual fashion, then the vector will deviate from the subspace, and a deviation value will be detected.

The deviation value threshold R can be determined from the variance in the usual-motion data during the learning period. The standard deviation σ_K of the deviation values, $d_\perp$, can be obtained using the eigenvalues, as follows:

$$\sigma_\perp^2 = \sum_{i=K+1}^{M} \lambda_i \tag{4}$$

$$R = n\sigma_\perp \tag{5}$$

where n is a coefficient. Statistically, 99.7% of usual motion will lie within the threshold if $n=3$, so this value was used as the standard.

4   Experiments

4.1   Experiments in an Indoor Experiment

Unusual motion detection tests were conducted in an indoor environment, using a scene in which a locker was opened and closed. A training set comprising approximately 1000 frames of the locker being opened and closed in a normal manner, as shown in Fig. 4, was used for learning a usual motion. The experimental data was shot at a rate of 30 frames per second of size 320 × 240 pixels using a DV

(a) frame in   (b) opening and shutting   (c) frame out

Fig. 4. Example of usual motions

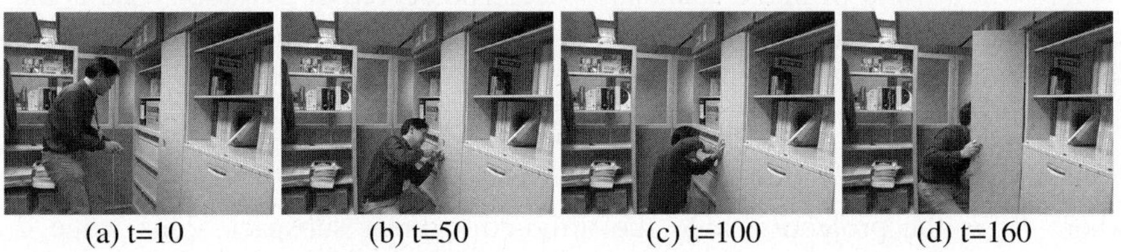

(a) t=10   (b) t=50   (c) t=100   (d) t=160

Fig. 5. Example of unusual motions

camera. For the unusual motion test data, the movement of someone trying to break open the locker, as shown in Fig. 5, was used.

The change over time of the subspace distance to the experiment data is shown in Fig. 6. Time t (frame number) is on the horizontal axis, and the subspace distance divided by the standard deviation ($d_{\perp}/\sigma_K$) is on the vertical axis. The parameter values were as follows: displacement pattern width $\Delta x=3$, $\Delta y=3$, $\Delta t=1$; time integral range $T=30$ (1 sec); and cumulative contribution rate threshold $U=0.999$. These parameters were set using a comparative test. The usual subspace had six dimensions with these parameter values. The usual motions all lay within the deviation value of $3\sigma_K$, and so they were not detected as anomalies. On the other hand, it can be seen that unusual motion had subspace distance of considerably over $3\sigma_K$.

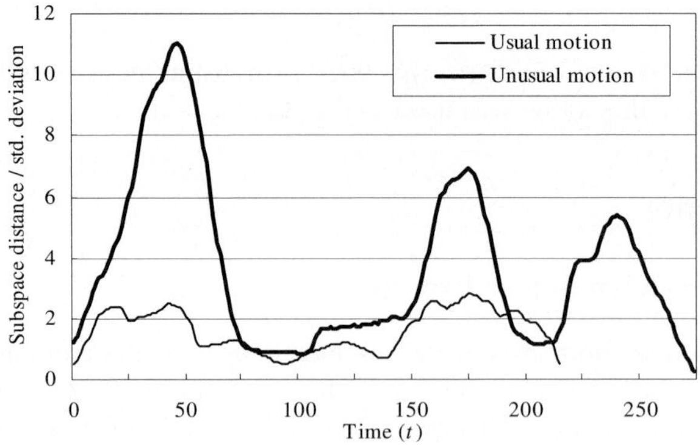

Fig. 6. The change over time of the subspace distance

4.2   Experiments in an Outdoor Experiment

Anomaly detection tests were then conducted outside in an environment greatly different from that indoors. The data used in the tests, together with the binarized images, is shown in Fig. 7. Many pixels showing differences are evident due to the wind blowing the leaves and branches of the trees. This creates major problems in methods that rely on segmentation. In the method described in this paper, the entire motion is learned as usual motion, without separating the differences due to the swaying of the trees and the differences due to the person walking.

For the normal motion in these tests, a training set of around 3000 frames of an image of people walking along the street at the back of the image while the wind was blowing the trees was used. The parameters were set using a comparative test. The

(a) Usual motion (sway of trees by the wind, and walking people)

(b) Unusual motion (invading in the hedge)

Fig. 7. Example of experimental data at outside

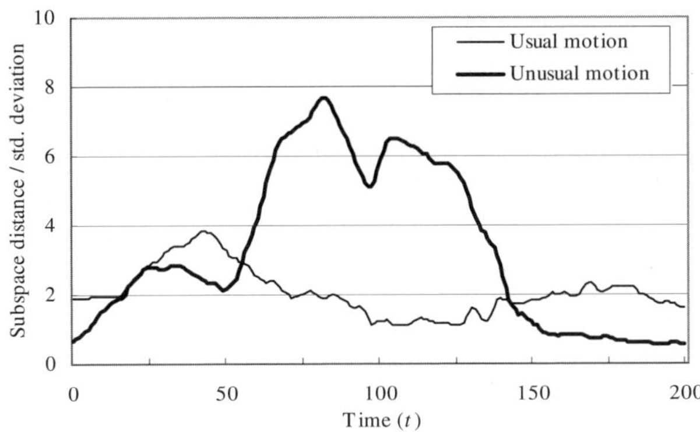

Fig. 8. Subspace distance at outside environment

unusual motion test data used was a recording of someone at the front of the image climbing over a fence.

Figure 8 shows the anomaly detection results. Figure 7(a) shows a scene from the usual motion test data, which includes a number of elements such as several pedestrians and swaying trees. However, since these elements were already learned as usual motion, the deviation values remain small for the usual motion in Fig. 8, due to the frame-additivity of the feature vectors. Meanwhile, Fig. 7(b) shows a scene from the unusual motion test data, and it can be seen from the unusual motion graph in Fig. 14 that significant subspace distance are detected.

5 Conclusion

A fast method using CHLAC for unusual motion detection from time-series image has been described. This method is very versatile since it defines unusual motion in terms of the degree of deviation from usual subspace, obviating the need for segmentation or models. This paper described a high-speed method using SIMD to enable the practical application of an unusual motion detection system running in real time. This paper also demonstrated the effectiveness of this method through example tests, conducted using real images both indoors and outdoors.

As further study, we would like to investigate the automation of the setting of the parameters, and online training using incremental PCA.

References

[1] Haritaoglu, I., Harwood, D., Davis, L.S.: W4: Who? When? Where? What? A real time system for detecting and tracking people. In: Proc. FG 1998, pp. 222–227 (1998)
[2] Aoki, S., Onishi, M., Kojima, A., Fukunaga, K.: Learning and Recognizing Behavioral Patterns Using Position and Posture of Human. In: Proc. of IEEE Conference on Cybernetics and Intelligent Systems, December 2004, pp. 1299–1302 (2004)
[3] Zelnik-Manor, L., Irani, M.: Event-Based Analysis of Video. In: Proc. CVPR 2001, vol. 2, pp. 123–130 (2001)
[4] Zhong, H., Shi, J., Visontai, M.: Detecting Unusual Activity in Video. In: Proc. CVPR 2004, vol. 2, pp. 819–826 (2004)
[5] Lucas, B., Kanade, T.: An Iterative Image Registration Technique with an Application to Stereo Vision. In: Proc. IJCAI 1981, April 1981, pp. 674–679 (1981)
[6] Bobick, A.F., Davis, J.W.: The Recognition of Human Movement Using Temporal Templates. IEEE Trans. PAMI 23(3) (2001)
[7] Kobayashi, T., Otsu, N.: Action and Simultaneous Multiple Persons Identification Using Cubic Higher-order Local Auto-Correlation. In: Proc. ICPR 2004 (2004)
[8] Nanri, T., Otsu, N.: Unsupervised Abnormality Detection in Video Surveillance. In: Proc. MVA 2005, pp. 574–577 (2005)
[9] Otsu, N., Kurita, T.: A new scheme for practical flexible and intelligent vision systems. In: Proceedings of IAPR Workshop on Computer Vision, pp. 431–435 (1988)

Bio-Inspired Functional Asymmetry Camera System

Yoshiki Yamaguchi[1], Noriyuki Aibe[1], Moritoshi Yasunaga[1],
Yorihisa Yamamoto[2], Takaaki Awano[3], and Ikuo Yoshihara[4]

[1] Graduate School of Systems and Information Engineering, University of Tsukuba,
1-1-1 Ten-no-dai Tsukuba Ibaraki, 305-8573, Japan
{yoshiki, susu@islab, yasunaga@}cs.tsukuba.ac.jp
http://www.islab.cs.tsukuba.ac.jp
[2] Yamamoto System Design Inc., 3481 Oozone Tsukuba Ibaraki, 300-3253, Japan
yori@edonagasaki.ne.jp
[3] Bethel Inc., 3-11 Aragane Ishioka Ibaraki, 315-0021, Japan
http://www.bethel.co.jp
t-awano@mail.bethel.co.jp
[4] Faculty of Engineering, University of Miyazaki,
1-1 Gakuen Kibanadai Nishi Miyazaki Miyazaki, 889-2192 Japan
yoshiha@cs.miyazaki-u.ac.jp
http://w1.cs.miyazaki-u.ac.jp

Abstract. Robust tracking is the key subject to real target-tracking-cameras. In this article, we present a filtering method that can achieve the robust tracking under noisy environment. We have also developed an asymmetry camera system. The system consists of double lens modules to mimic the eye's function of watching and tracking the target with seeing the whole image concurrently. In this article, we also explain the design of the newly developed camera system and demonstrate its performance in the task of tracking a target fish among multiple fish in an aquarium.

Keywords: object tracking, moving object detection, background subtraction, electromagnetic servomechanism.

1 Introduction

Evil crimes (terrorism, abduction, public nuisance), troubles (traffic accident, explosion at a factory), and environmental affairs (hazardous substance pollution) have risen distinctly in recent years. It has become a huge issue in the world, and many researchers and organizations carry out research and development for a secure and safe society(S. C. Wong (2005); I. Matthews (2004); L. J. Latecki (2006); F. Porikli (2006); M. J. Black (1995); R. Oi (2003); S. Khan (2001)). Towards the realization of surveillant infrastructure for a secure and safe society, we focus on a surveillance camera system.

The requirements of surveillance camera systems can be classified into four main groups: range of surveillance, sufficient resolution to realize objects, crippling suspicious behavior, and keep a watch on the actions. The first two groups are relevant to human visual field because human can catch a scent of danger with one's own

M. Ishikawa et al. (Eds.): ICONIP 2007, Part II, LNCS 4985, pp. 637–646, 2008.

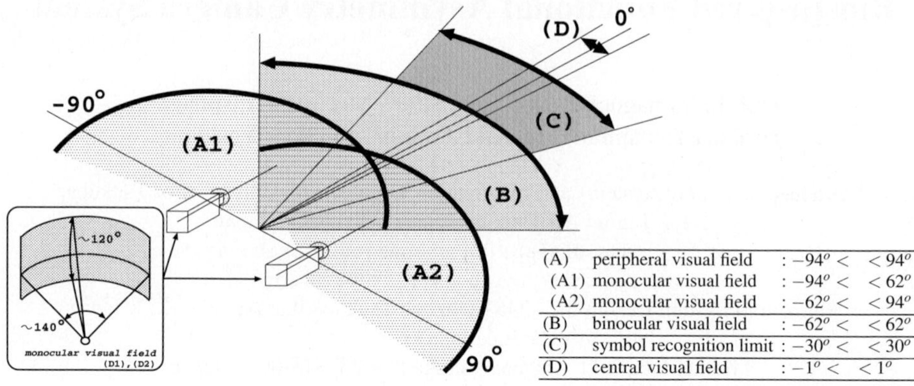

(A)	peripheral visual field	: $-94^o <$	$< 94^o$
(A1)	monocular visual field	: $-94^o <$	$< 62^o$
(A2)	monocular visual field	: $-62^o <$	$< 94^o$
(B)	binocular visual field	: $-62^o <$	$< 62^o$
(C)	symbol recognition limit	: $-30^o <$	$< 30^o$
(D)	central visual field	: $-1^o <$	$< 1^o$

Fig. 1. The area of a scene that can be seen at the same time

eyes on surrounding circumstances, and therefore the first point of that we should discuss is the development of a bio-inspired system that mimics the functions of a human eye. The next group is a computational technique of how the system detects specific objects. It is interesting to follow up bio-inspired smart detection algorithms further, but the point is different from our current focus that is the development of a primitive camera system. Therefore, assume that the input images are incoming signals, a simple filtering approach is used to detect and clip specified objects. The other is a driving ability of the tracking camera. Most of the off-the shelf tracking camera system adopts motors and gears for the driving system. In addition, Yorick(P. M. Sharkey (1993)), TRICLOPS(A. J. Wavering (1995)), ESCHeR(Y. Kuniyoshi (1995)), the KTH head(K. Pahlavan (1996)) are designed to control the camera direction by motors. It is easy to implement and control but the traction makes the initial velocity of the reaction reduce. Consequently, we developed a novel tracking camera with electrical-magnetic driving module.

This article is organized as follows. Section 2 discussed the issues regarding human visual field and the functions. Section 3 describes our proposed algorithm for target detection and clipping the image. Section 4 described our system and discusses the experiment, and finally Section 5 concludes this article.

2   Bio-Inspired Asymmetry Camera System

In the beginning, we will examine about the function of human visual field for realizing a surveillance camera system. The visual field shows the area of a scene that can be seen at the same time(K. Yokomizo (1987)).

In Figure 1, (A) is called *peripheral visual field* which is the combination of *monocular visual fields* (A1) and (A2). In general, each *monocular visual field* is a quadrangular pyramid whose horizontal and vertical angles are about 120 and 140 degrees, respectively. (B) is *binocular visual field*. It is only an overlapping field of (A) and (B); we can only capture the scene and not recognize the details. We can distinguish the image pattern when an object should be placed in (C). It means that our image recognition works in the range of (C). (D) is *central visual field* and we can discriminate an object.

To mimic human eyes, one of advenced approaches has been proposed the binocular system with Fish-Eye lenses(T. Kurita (2000)). It is an attractive approach as a monitoring system within doors but it can not be used for our target application such as illegal dumping detection system. The coverage of our application is too large to watch with one single camera. In the open air, some approaches has also been proposed(C. Stauffer (1999)) but the system can watch within narrow limits. In general, the visual field of proposed and off-the-shelf systems is narrower than 90 degrees and its limitation causes a serious problem in a practical application standpoint.

Accordingly, we propose an asymmetry camera system; one wide-angle camera covers larger than (B) and observe roughly, and the other camera, namely telephoto camera, captures a target image which is enough magnified for its recognition.

3 Frame Subtraction

3.1 Moving Object Detection

For target tracking, we will begin our discussion by considering the moving object detection. It is a fundamental problem of target tracking and recognition in a real environment, and therefore a considerable number of researches have been conducted on video sequences(G. Kuhne (2001); K. Kitai (1997); M. Takatoo (1997); S. Nagaya (1996)).

One of approaches is to get the difference between a current input frame at time t_n $(c(t_n))$, and a specified background image $(bg())$; the subtraction Δ is denoted as

$$\Delta = |\, c(t_n) - bg \,| \tag{1}$$

and then the X-Y coordinate of each point is calculated as follows.

$$\Delta(t_n, I, j) = |\, p(t_n, I, j) - bg(I, j) \,| \, \{I = 1, 2, \cdots, x \, ; \ \ j = 1, 2, \cdots, y\} \tag{2}$$

The character I and j respectively indicate integer values of vertical and horizontal coordinates in a frame $c(t_n)$, and $p(t_n, I, j)$ expresses the central value of each discrete point (I, j) at time t_n.

This is a naive approach intended as to implement on an embedded system because most of computations is represented as simple numerical functions such as subtractions. However, in practical use, it is necessary to address

- illumination
  - gradual changes(e.g. race of the sun)
  - sudden changes(e.g. clouds, street lamp)
- flickering (e.g. murmuration, flag, windmill)
- excess detection (e.g. caused by headlight)

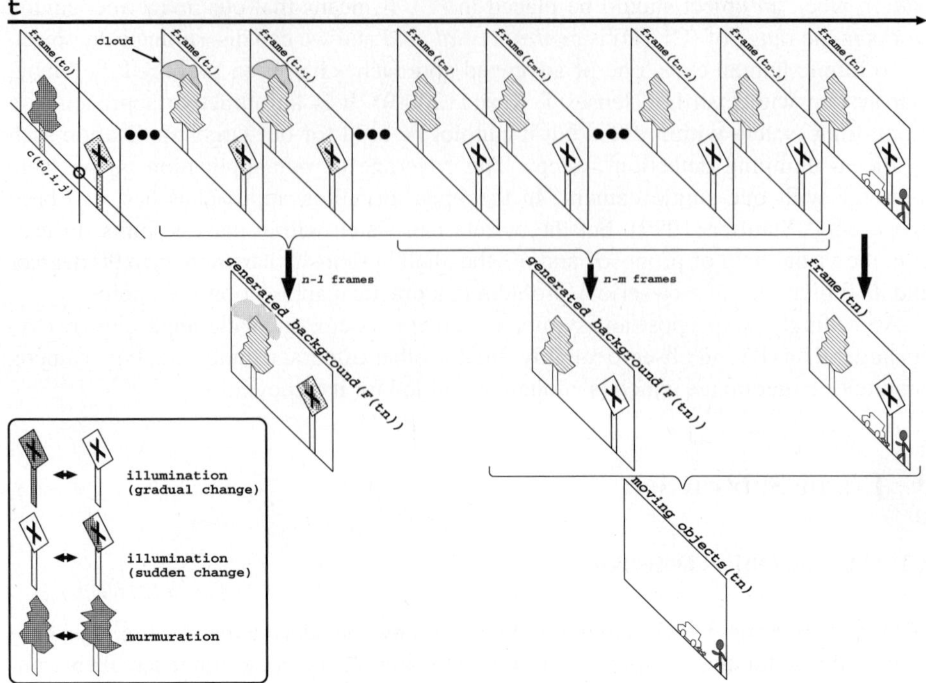

Fig. 2. The overview of background generation and moving object clipping

3.2   Real-Time Background Generation

In response to dynamic changes as identified in Sec.3.1, an adaptive method that generates a background image in real time is proposed(G. Kuhne (2001); K. Kitai (1997); M. Takatoo (1997); S. Nagaya (1996)). The image is generated among $n - m$ frames as shown in Fig.2 and denoted as

$$bg(t_n) = F\left(c(t_k)\right)$$

$$= \sum_{k=m}^{n-1} g(t_k)c(t_k) \tag{3}$$

In general, the function $F()$ returns a central value of each point on $n - m$ frames, such as an arithmetic mean or a median. The $g()$ is a weighting factor regarding time series and this model can be ascribe to a low-pass filter. The generated background is modified promptly to dynamic changes and can reduce noises as a low pass filter. But, another problems arise: how many frames are used for generating a background image and how often the image should be updated.

3.3   Proposed Approach for Real-Time Background Generation

It is good for the noise tolerance $bg()$ to apply a median value to a central value. However, it is clear that the real-time background generation requires large computational

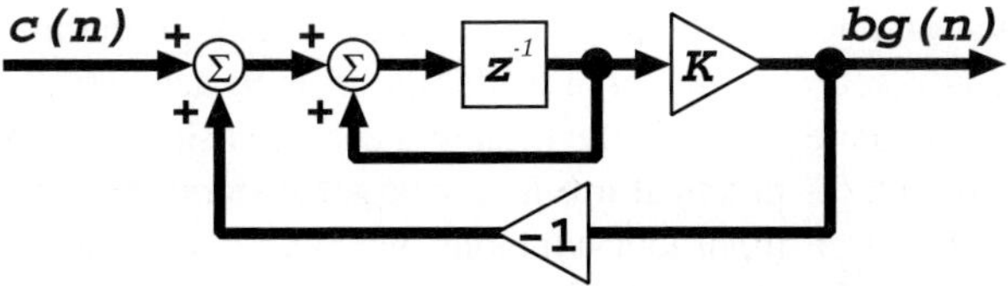

Fig. 3. Control function for real-time background generation

cost; the system should have arithmetic capacity in frame rate and large memory resources whose size is bigger than the summation size of $n - m$ frames. We have proposed an approach to satisfy in both image updates at frame rate and a reduction of the computational effort in consideration of discussion of sec.3.2. The block diagram is shown in Fig.3 and denoted as

$$bg(t_{n+1}) = Kc(t_n) + (1 - K)bg(t_n)$$

$$= \sum_{k=m}^{n} K(1 - K)^{n-k}c(t_k) + (1 - K)^{n-m+1}bg(t_m) \qquad (4)$$

Under the assumption that m, $c(t_{k<0})$, and $bg(t_{k<0})$ are 0, eq.(3) and eq.(4) are equivalent. To understand properties of our model, the following eq.(5) represents the transfer function G(z) of eq.4, namely the z transformation of $g(t_n)$.

$$G(z) = \frac{Kz}{z - 1 + K} \qquad (5)$$

It is clear that our model is one of Infinite Impulse Response (IIR) filter and we recognized from eq.5 that the function G(z) can provides a low pass filter.

3.4 Hardware Implementation

Our target is the development of a stationary surveillance camera system and there are many requested specifications such as electrical power saving, small size, realization of fast object tracking, covering a wide range and low price. Consequently, our proposed approach should be customized for implementing to small circuits on an embedded system and the detailed diagram is depicted in Fig.4.

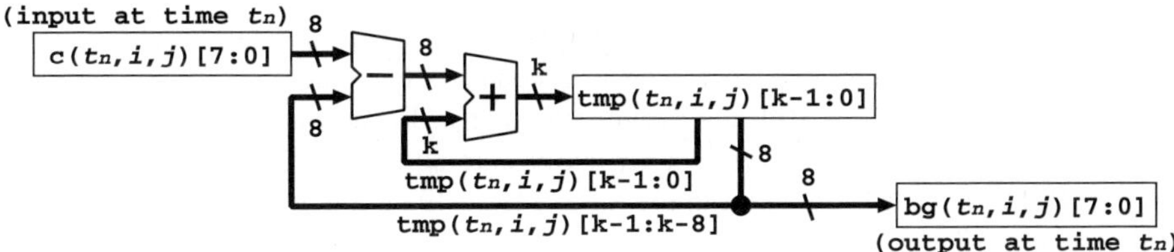

Fig. 4. Low pass filter unit

Its implementation allows the system to generate a background image in real time and reduces circuit resources compared to the naive approach. The k means the data width to store intermediate results in the filter and each box shows the register in Fig.4. It is very small enough for practical use in our target system; the circuit is composed of 16 registers and 24 four-input look-up tables when $k = 16$ in case to use an FPGA as an embedded device. In addition, k also means a time parameter for the background generation and corresponds with K in eqs.(4) and (5). The conversion equation is written as $K = \frac{1}{2^k}$.

3.5   Band-Pass Tracking Method

The background generation is liken to a low pass filter, as stated above. The larger the $k(= n - m)$ is, the stronger the influence of the past frames is. We are here concerned with everything a human does and therefore limit the discussion to the object detection of human movement. The velocity of human action is up to 10 m/sec; it is the upper threshold of our considerable range. Therefore, our system has two regulatory function; one $(k = n - l)$ works for the background generation and the other $(k = n - m)$ works for disregarding high-speed movement in Fig.2. The subtraction of them results the clipping image of moving objects which we should consider. Thus, the band-pass filter for human movement is realized and we can save hardware resources for real-time image recognition.

4   System Development

4.1   Overall System Configuration

The overall system configuration and the outline of the target tracking process are shown in Fig.5 and Fig.6 respectively. The system comprises a fixed wide-angle camera and a telephoto camera that can be panned and tilted by electromagnetic actuators.

In our approach, first the panoramic image input from the wide-angle camera passes through an NTSC decoder into the FPGA (Fig.5 ①). The results of the image processing are passed through the NTSC encoder and can be observed on a video monitor. Second the FPGA proceeds to template matching (Fig.5 ②) and obtains the target position from the panoramic image (Fig.5 ③). The position is fed to a D/A converter and power amplifier to control the pan-tilt direction so as to orient the telephoto camera toward the target (Fig.5 ④). The image data from the telephoto camera goes directly to a video monitor to display the magnified image of the target (Fig.5 ⑤).

During the A/D conversion process in the NTSC decoder, the panoramic image is pre-processed before template matching is executed. The image is sampled digitally from 768×494 pixels to 100×72 segments in size. Each segment is also digitized or, quantified to binary data. The size reduction rate and the quantization rate are not fixed to 100×72 and 1 bit. (We can use up to 719×494 and 24-bit color quantization in this system.) Those values can be changed and implemented by easy reconfiguration directly onto the FPGA.

We applied the system to the task of tracking a target fish among multiple fish in an aquarium. The target is identified from the panoramic image and tracked as a magnified

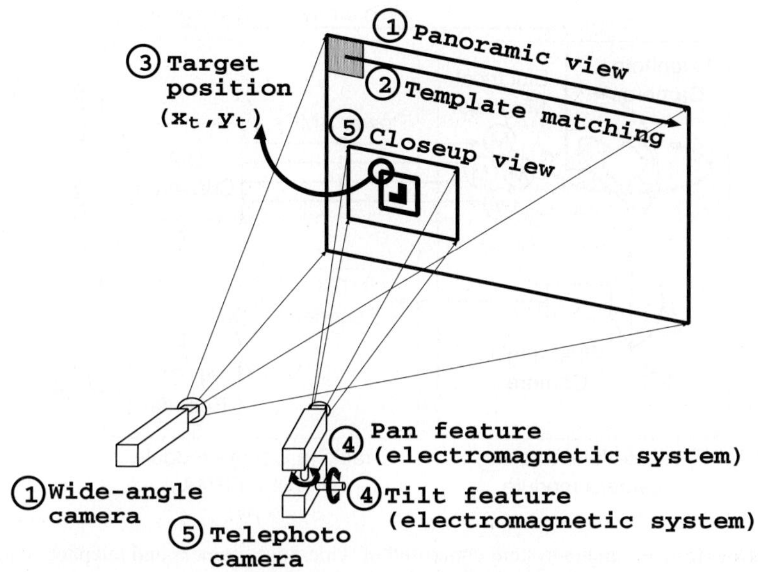

Fig. 5. General picture of target-tracking process

image by the telephoto-lens module (Fig. 9). We also developed a network interface to connect the camera system with the Internet to broadcast the live images widely. This kind of tropical fish observation system is capable of stable, long-term tracking of complex target motion verifies the practicality of this tracking algorithm.

A magnified image of the target fish tracked with the pan-tilt telephoto-lens module is shown in Fig. 11; the panoramic image of the entire aquarium is shown in Fig. 10. The target fish in the full aquarium image is magnified by a factor of three so that its face and fins can be clearly observed. The target fish was tracked successfully, even when multiple fish were present. Observers could watch the target fish clearly, seeing the entire aquarium. We are now planning to apply this double-lens tracking camera to actual surveillance applications.

4.2 Proposed Tracking Camera

A photograph of the double-lens tracking camera prototype is presented in Fig. 7 (The circuit board mounted with the FPGA for controlling the camera is not included.). Whole images are captured through the wide-angle lens module (the small module in the figure) in the beginning, and the captured images are processed in an FPGA. The target position is detected immediately and fed back to the telephoto-lens module that is mounted on a pan-tilt mechanism (the large module in the figure). The double-lens tracking camera does not closely resemble the eye in appearance, but it provides the same function as the eye does inexpensively. The image sensor is an inexpensive commercially-available product. We fabricated only the telephoto-lens mount.

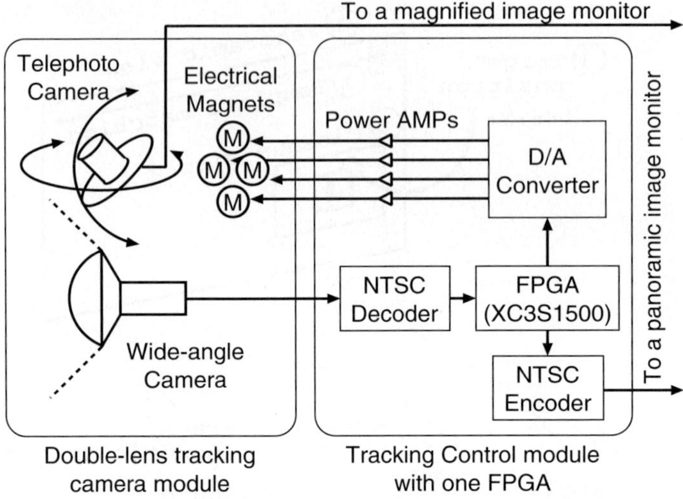

Fig. 6. Double-lens camera system composed of wide-angle camera and telephoto camera

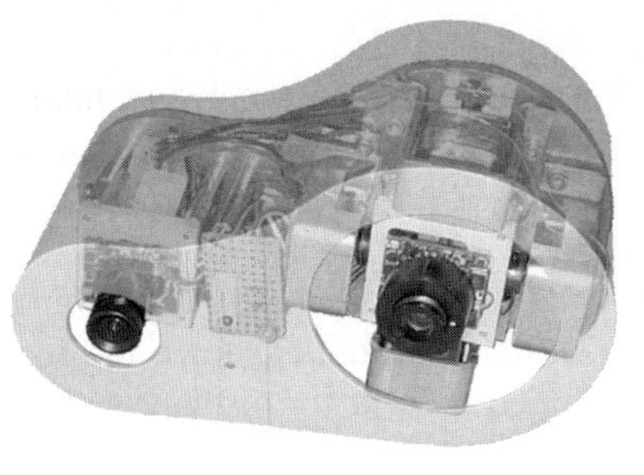

Fig. 7. Double-lens tracking camera

Fig. 8. Tracking camera control board

We also developed a new magnet-based pan-tilt drive to replace the traditional servo-motor drive (M. Yasunaga (2007)). The new drive enables the lens module to move at least three times as fast as the conventional one. The servo-motor drive has mechanical parts as well as magnetic parts. Those additional parts impede high-speed rotation and make it difficult to reduce the overall size. The magnet-based pan-tilt drive eliminates the troublesome mechanical parts. In the newly developed magnet-based drive, the lens module is directly driven to move in the pan and tilt directions. The lens module has four magnets placed at right angles to each other. An electromagnet is placed opposite the four magnets and driving forces are generated and controlled by the amplitude and the direction of the current applied to the electromagnet. This design allows panning

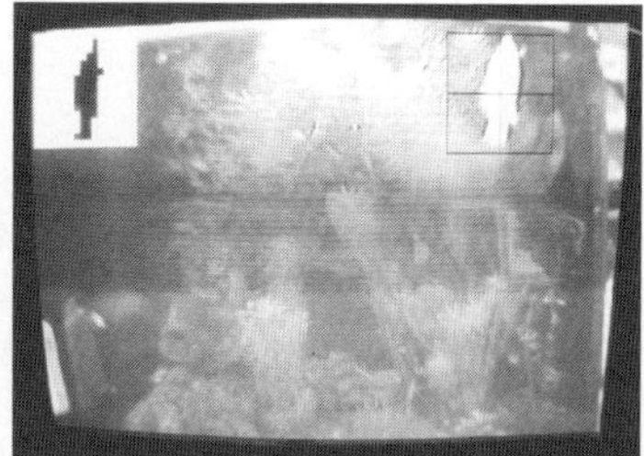

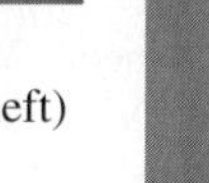

Fig. 9. Experimental circumstance, fish tracking (left)

Fig. 10. Wide-angle camera's image (top-right)

Fig. 11. Telephoto camera's image (bottom-right)

and tilting movements that are about three times as fast as the conventional direct-drive mechanism. In addition, the size is reduced to less than 1/2 that of the conventional design. The four electromagnets are also controlled by the FPGA that performs the image processing as described in the previous section.

5   Conclusion

We have proposed a filtering method and developed tracking camera system that employs real-time template updating. The camera consists of two lens modules. One provides a panoramic image of the tracked target and the other provides a telephoto image. A magnet-based pan-tilt drive was also developed for high-speed tracking. A prototype of the camera was developed and it showed the desired performance in a fish-tracking application. The demonstration can be viewed at the URL: "http://bicam.islab.cs.tsukuba.ac.jp/".

Acknowledgements

The research and development reported in this paper was supported in part by the MEXT 2006 and 2007 Cooperation of Innovative Technology and Advanced Research in Evolutional Areas and the 2006 grant of Japan Society for Promotion of Science (No. 16360197).

Reference

Wong, S.C., et al.: Towerd a reconfigurable tracking system. In: Int. Conf. on Field Programmable Logic and Applications, pp. 456–462 (2005)

Matthews, I., et al.: The Template Update Problem. IEEE Trans. on Pattern Analysis and Machine Intelligence 26(6), 810–815 (2004)

Latecki, L.J., Miezianko, R.: Object Tracking with Dynamic Template Update and Occlusion Detec. In: IEEE 18th Int. Conf. on Pattern Recognition, pp. 556–560 (2006)

Porikli, F.: Achieving real-time object detection and tracking under extreme conditions. J. Real-Time Image Proc. 1, 33–40 (2006)

Black, M.J., Yacoob, Y.: Tracking and recognizing rigid and non-rigid facial motions using local parametric models of image motion. In: IEEE Fifth Int. Conf. on Comp. Vision, pp. 374–381 (1995)

Oi, R., et al.: A Solid-State, Simultaneous Wide Angle-Detailed View Surveillance Camera. In: Int. W. on Vision, Modeling, and Visualization, pp. 19–21 (2003)

Khan, S., et al.: Human Tracking in Multiple Cameras. In: The Eighth IEEE Int. Conf. on Comp. Vision (2001)

Sharkey, P.M., et al.: A modular head/eye platform for real-time reactive vision. Mechatoronics 3(4), 517–535 (1993)

Wavering, A.J., et al.: High-performace tracking with triclops. In: 2nd Asian Conf. on Comp. Vision, vol. 1, pp. 171–180 (1995)

Kuniyoshi, Y., et al.: Active stereo vision system with foveated wide angle lenses. In: 2nd Asian Conf. on Comp. Vision, vol. 1, pp. 359–363 (1995)

Pahlavan, K., et al.: Dynamic fixation and active perception. Int. J. of Comp. Vision 17, 113–135 (1996)

Yokomizo, K., Komatsubara, A.: Human Factors for engineer. Japan Publication Service (1987)

Kurita, T., Shimai, H., Baba, Y., Mishima, T.: Gaze control on virtual active vision system with binocular fish-eye lenses. In: IEEE Int. Conf. on Systems, Man & Cybernetics, pp. 1644–1649 (2000)

Stauffer, C., Grimson, W.E.L.: Adaptive background mixture models for real-time tracking. In: IEEE Int. Conf. on Comp. Vision and Pattern Recognition, pp. 246–252 (1999)

Kühne, G., et al.: Motion-based segmentation and contour-based classification of video objects. In: 9th ACM Int. Conf. on Multimedia, pp. 41–50 (2001)

Kitai, K.: Automatic Tracking System of Pedestrians using Image Processing Method. J. Archit. Plann. Environ. Eng. (493), 195–200 (1997)

Takatoo, M., et al.: Vehicles Extraction Using Spatial Defferentiation and Subtraction. IEICE J 80 D-II(11), 2976–2985 (1997)

Nagaya, S., et al.: Moving Object Detection by Time-Correlation-Based Background Judgement Method. IEICE J 79 D-II(4), 568–576 (1996)

Yasunaga, M., et al.: A Reconfigurable-VLSI-based Double-lens Tracking-camera. In: Int. Symp. on Artificial Life and Robotics, pp. 665–668 (2007)

Making a Robot Dance to Music Using Chaotic Itinerancy in a Network of FitzHugh-Nagumo Neurons

Jean-Julien Aucouturier, Yuta Ogai, and Takashi Ikegami

Department of General Systems Studies
Graduate School of Arts and Sciences, The University of Tokyo
3-8-1 Komaba, Meguro-ku, Tokyo 153-8902, Japan
aucouturier@gmail.com, {yuta,ikeg}@sacral.c.u-tokyo.ac.jp

Abstract. We propose a technique to make a robot execute free and solitary dance movements on music, in a manner which simulates the dynamic alternations between synchronisation and autonomy typically observed in human behaviour. In contrast with previous approaches, we preprogram neither the dance patterns nor their alternation, but rather build in basic dynamics in the robot, and let the behaviour emerge in a seemingly autonomous manner. The robot motor commands are generated in real-time by converting the output of a neural network processing a sequence of pulses corresponding to the beats of the music being danced to. The spiking behaviour of individual neurons is controlled by a biologically-inspired model (FitzHugh-Nagumo). Under appropriate parameters, the network generates chaotic itinerant behaviour among low-dimensional local attractors. A robot controlled this way exhibits a variety of motion styles, some being periodic and strongly coupled to the musical rhythm and others being more independent, as well as spontaneous jumps from one style of motion to the next. The resulting behaviour is completely deterministic (as the solution of a non-linear dynamical system), adaptive to the music being played, and believed to be an interesting compromise between synchronisation and autonomy.

1   Introduction

Music makes people want to move - either in imagination or actually, as in dance. Quantitative psychological investigations reveal that humans associate gestural movements to music with remarkable consistency. When asked to translate music into free drawings, listeners systematically associate sound patterns composed of a percussive onset followed by a long decay with strokes composed of a steep slope followed by a long descent [Godoy et al., 2006]. Clarinetists are found to often perform semi-unconscious bell shape movements with the tip of their instrument, which boundaries correspond to those of musical phrases, and which amplitudes are dynamically modulated with the music's rhythmic and metric interpretation [Wanderley et al., 2005].

M. Ishikawa et al. (Eds.): ICONIP 2007, Part II, LNCS 4985, pp. 647–656, 2008.
© Springer-Verlag Berlin Heidelberg 2008

However, the same studies often reveal (or concede) that such directly interpretable mappings from sound to movement are not always predictable, and often found to vary within a given task. Movements without any clear correspondance with music are often performed in alternation with more interpretable gestures. Some types of clarinetists movements occur throughout an entire performance regardless of the change in character of the associated music. Even cyclic movements such as regular weight transfer between forward and back may not be synchronized with the piece's rhythm, or depend on extrinsic physiological constraints (such as breathing rate). More generally, musicians and dancers exhibit an intriguingly fluid use of gestural patterns, "continuous but not repetitive" [Wanderley et al., 2005], with successive and seemingly unpredictable switches of attachement and detachement to the auditory stimulus.

Designing entertainment systems that exhibit such dynamic compromise between short-term synchronisation and long-term autonomous behaviour is key to maintain an interesting relationship between a human and an artificial agent in the long-term [Pachet, 2004]. However, this remains largely unaddressed in the recent academic and industrial efforts to design dancing robots. One common strategy is to design manually a number of dance presets (i.e. a fixed sequence of motor commands), which are then rendered to a given piece of music by adapting the execution speed of the sequence to the musical tempo (automatically extracted from the audio signal) [Goto, 2001]. The approach has merits, notably a convincing effect of synchronisation, but typically fails at sustaining long-term interest, since the dance repertoire of the robotic is rapidly exhausted and frequent patterns begin to reoccur without any variation. A more evolved approach relies on building imitative behaviour in the robot, which uses typically vision sensors to reproduce movements taught by a human [Nakazawa et al., 2002]. Behavioral studies [Michalowski et al., 2007] show that even passive rhythmic imitation by a robot can generate interesting patterns of interactions with human users (teaching, turn-taking, etc.). However, programming robots to initiate such interactions modes autonomously is still in the domain of speculation. Taking inspiration from the physiology of mirror neurons, [Tanaka and Suzuki, 2004] propose e.g. to use a learning model (Recurrent Neural Network with Parametric Biase) to switch between movement patterns dynamically stored in memory. Finally, richer interaction is often believed to come from physical contact between dance partners, and some recent research addresses the difficult motor control of a robot dancer's haptic interaction with a human [Kosuge et al., 2003].

In this work, we propose a technique to make a robot execute free and solitary dance movements on music, in a manner which simulates the dynamic alternations between attachement/detachment typically observed in human behaviour. In contrast with previous approaches, we preprogram neither the dance patterns nor their alternation, but rather build in basic dynamics in the robot, and let the behaviour emerge in a seemingly autonomous manner. To this aim, we make use a special type of chaotic dynamics, namely chaotic itinerancy (CI). CI is a relatively common feature in high-dimensional chaotic systems, which shows itinerant behaviour among low-dimensional local attractors

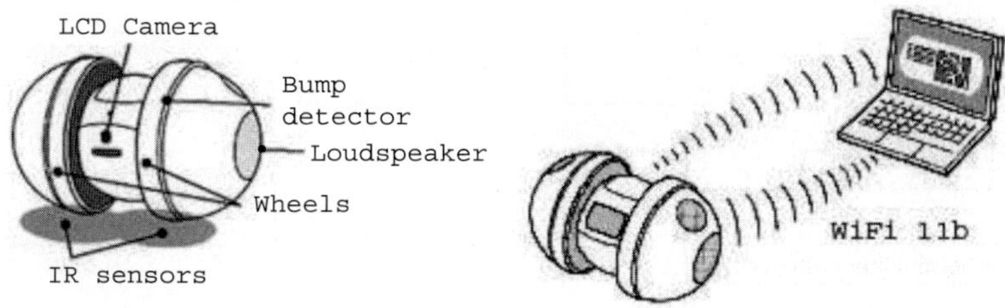

Fig. 1. Our robotic platform, the MIURO manufactured by ZMP Inc, is a two-wheeled musical player equipped with an IPod mp3 player interface and a set of loudspeakers. Wheel velocities can be controlled in real-time through wireless communication with a computer. *(Illustration courtesy of ZMP Inc.)*

through higher-dimensional chaos [Ikeda et al., 1989, Kaneko and Tsuda, 2003]. Recently, CI was proposed to model many exploratory behaviours in living systems, such as insect flight trajectory [Takahashi et al., 2007], neurodynamics in the rat olfactory system [Kay, 2003], or attachment/detachment mechanisms in conscious states [Ikegami, 2007]. In each of these domains, CI appears as an elegant model to describe seemingly spontaneous switches between exploratory/motion styles, with alternations between local periodic patters and global exploratory wanderings.

Here, we generate CI with a dynamical system composed of a network of artificial spiking neurons, each controlled by a biologically-inspired model (FitzHugh-Nagumo (FHN)). FHN neurons are connected to one another randomly with time delays[1]. We showed in a recent experiment [Ikegami, 2007] that such an architecture could generate CI when sensorimotor coupling exists (i.e. when the network outputs influences its input) - a situation we specifically call "embodied chaotic itinerancy" (ECI). In the present paper, we show that this still holds without any coupling, i.e. when the network is fed with a sequence of pulses corresponding to the beats of the music being danced to, and its output is converted to motor command in real-time. We find that chaotic itinerancy in the network output can be converted to control a robot to a variety of motion styles, some being periodic and strongly coupled to the musical rhythm and others being more independent, as well as spontaneous jumps from one style of motion to the next. The resulting behaviour is completely deterministic (as the solution of a non-linear dynamical system), adaptive to the music being played, and believed to be an interesting compromise between synchronisation and autonomy.

We demonstrate the system using a relatively simple vehicle-like robot, the MIURO manufactured by ZMP Inc. [2] (Figure 1). Note that the dance movements performed by the robot are two-dimensional trajectories controlled with

---

[1] Note that this involves no learning: we only use the network to specify a non-linear dynamical system, using fine-tuned parameters.

[2] ZMP Inc., 10F Aobadai Hills 4-7-7 Aobadai, Meguro Ward Tokyo, Japan. Miuro Homepage: http://miuro.com. ZMP Official Homepage http://www.zmp.co.jp

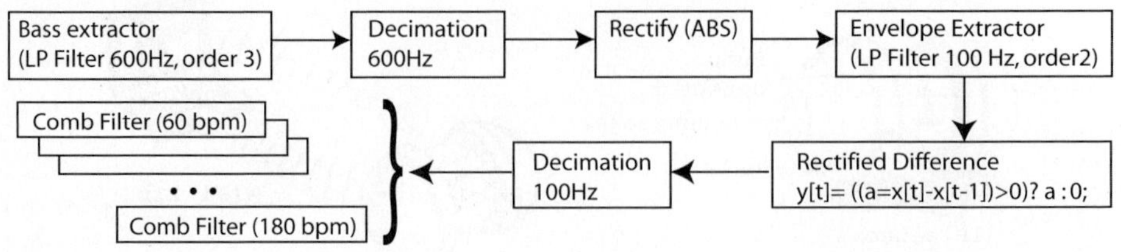

Fig. 2. Block diagram of the beat-tracking algorithm used to send pulses to the neural network in real-time correspondence with the music

wheel speed, therefore well below the complexity and expressivity aimed at other proposals closer to human kinesiology [Tanaka and Suzuki, 2004].

Finally, note also that this work is not the first to propose to use chaotic dynamics to simulate dance movements. Most notably, [Bradley and Stuart, 1998] exploit the ever-changing trajectories of symbolic states around a common attractor (R'ossler) to generate variations on ballet choreographic movements. Chaos is used to explore the compromise between novelty and consistency: chaotic dependency on initial conditions guarantees that each variation is different from the original, while the attractor structure maintains consistency between the two. In contrast, in the current paper, we use chaos to compromise between attachement and detachment to the auditory stimulus, in order to simulate autonomous dance movements to music.

2   System Description

2.1   Audio Analysis

The audio front-end for our system is responsible for sending pulses to the neural network, in real-time correspondence with the beats of the music being danced to. We use a stripped-down implementation of the beat-tracking algorithm introduced in [Scheirer, 1998]. Figure 2 shows a block diagram of the algorithm. Buffers of audio are sent to the algorithm at regular time intervals (typically 5 ms, see Section 3). Each buffer of audio is processed by successively filtering out all frequencies above 600Hz, then extracting the amplitude envelope by a succession of drastic decimations and low-pass filtering. The signal is then fed to a filterbank of comb-shaped filters (or resonators), each tuned to a specific tempo (from 60 to 180 beat-per-minutes). The output of a comb filter of period T is given by:

$$y(t) = \alpha y(t - T) + (1 - \alpha)x(t) \tag{1}$$

where $x(t)$ is the input signal of the filter, and $|\alpha| < 1$ is a gain factor regulating the respective importance of novelty vs memory (here we put $\alpha = 0.9$). Each resonator has an output buffer of the last T samples $y(t)$ in the past.

After each processed buffer, the algorithm selects the resonator which output has the highest energy (this gives the current tempo), finds the position of the latest maximum in the resonator's output buffer (this gives the position of the latest beat), and if this position if different from that of the previous beat (i.e. this is a *new* beat), sends an impulse to the neural network with fixed width (typically 50ms) and a height proportional to the beat's amplitude (computed as the root-mean-square of the original audio signal in a 50 ms window around the beat position, normalized in $[0, 1]$).

The system is not tuned for consistency: nothing is done to prevent switches between locally optimal solutions. Musical passages with ambiguous or complex rhythm typically generate rapid switches between correlated bpm estimates (e.g. with integer ratio), which are then processed by the network to result in greater complexity than with more stable rhythms. Note that an abundant literature exists to extract robust tempo and beat estimates which prevent such switches, should it be needed (see e.g. [Gouyon et al., 2006] for a recent review).

2.2   FitzHugh-Nagumo Neuron

The FitzHugh-Nagumo (FHN) model is a simplification of the Hodgkin-Huxley model describing the depolarization of a neural membrane in a squid axon [Fitzhugh, 1961]. Each neuron is a coupled system of a fast variable u responsible for the excitation of membrane potential and a slow variable ω controlling its refractory state:

$$\frac{du}{dt} = c(u - \frac{u^3}{3} - \omega + I(t)) \tag{2}$$

$$\frac{d\omega}{dt} = a + u - b\omega \tag{3}$$

where $I(t)$ is an input signal (in our case a pulse train), and we take $a = 0.7$, $b = 0.8$ and $c = 10$. The neuron is said to overshoot (or generate a spike) when its output u reaches above 0. In this work, we integrate the $\{\frac{du}{dt}, \frac{d\omega}{dt}\}$ system with 4th-order Runge-Kutta [Press et al., 1986] from some initial conditions $u_0 = -1.2$, $\omega_0 = -0.62$.

The dynamic properties (attractor, bifurcations) of the FHN equations have been studied intensively (see e.g. the review by [Kostova et al., 2004]). It is known for instance that the membrane spiking behaviour is well controlled by the periodicity of the input spike train $I(t)$. Figure 3 shows the joint histogram of the inter-spike intervals (counted in numbers of Runge-Kutta update steps) in the input and output spike trains of a FHN neuron. It appears that for large ranges of input periods, the output spike train enters a rational-ratio entrained periodic state. However, chaotic and non periodic responses also occur for certain input periods. Finally, fast input spikes (with periods smaller than 100 steps) do not generate any spike in output, as the neuron is caught in permanent refractory state.

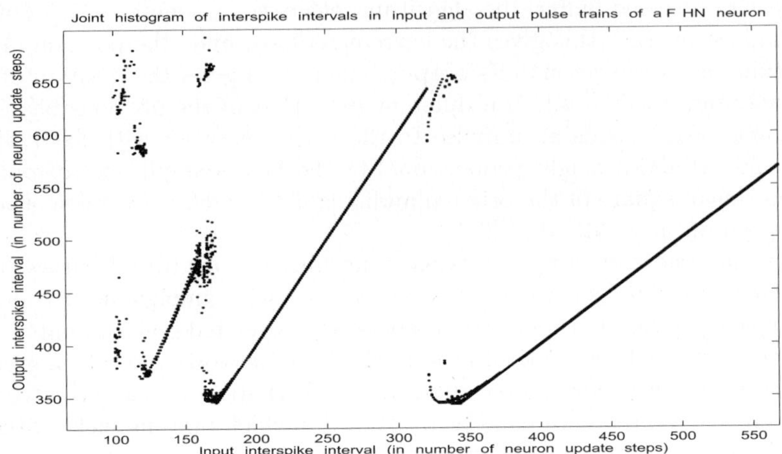

Fig. 3. Joint histogram of the inter-spike intervals (counted in numbers of Runge-Kutta update steps) in the input and output spike trains of a FHN neuron. Output periods are measured over 100 periods of the input train, for each input period.

2.3   Network Architecture

The robot is equipped with a sparse network of FHN neurons, randomly connected with a probability $p_c = 0.2$. Neurons are connected to one another with time-delayed connections of two types "fast" $\Delta_f = 100$ and "slow" $\Delta_s = 300$, decided randomly upon initialisation with probability $p_{fast} = 0.6$. When a neuron overshoots ($u > 0$), a pulse (with a given width W_p and height H_p) is transmitted to the neurons to which it is connected, with the appropriate time delay. Coincident pulses at a recipient neuron are not integrated, and equivalent to a single pulse. In the experiments reported here, we use 12 neurons divided into 3 groups:

- 4 *sensory* neurons which all receive the same input $I(t)$ from the audio analyser, namely a pulse train with local periodicity corresponding to the local musical tempo, width $W_p^{sens} = 10$ and height H_p^{sens} corresponding to the audio signal's energy around the beat.
- 4 *internal* neurons, which generate pulses with $W_p^{int} = 10$ and $H_p^{int} = 0.7$
- 4 *motor* neurons, which generate pulses with $W_p^{mot} = 300$ and $H_p^{mot} = 0.7$.

All neurons are equipped with FHN dynamics, integrated with Runge-kutta as described above.

2.4   Motor Output

Finally, the motor neurons collaborate to constitute the motor commands (left and right wheel velocities) sent to the robot

$$V_L(t) = \tanh\left(h_1(t) + h_2(t)\right) \tag{4}$$

$$V_R(t) = \tanh\left(h_3(t) + h_4(t)\right) \tag{5}$$

where $h_i(t)$ is a test function holding on the output *spike train* (and not output *variable u*) of the ith motor neuron, returning 1 if a spike is active at time t (i.e. was generated within W_p time steps in the past), else 0. Note that the time scale corresponding to iterator t needn't be the same time scale as the network time scale: one may downsample the motor output spike train before computing the motor commands (see Section 3).

Finally, the trajectory of the robot can be simulated on computer using the following approximations:

$$\frac{dx}{dt} = g_1(V_L(t) + V_R(t))\cos\theta(t) \tag{6}$$

$$\frac{dy}{dt} = g_1(V_L(t) + V_R(t))\sin\theta(t) \tag{7}$$

$$\frac{d\theta}{dt} = g_2(V_L(t) - V_R(t)) \tag{8}$$

where x, y is the space displacement vector and θ the heading direction. We use $g_1 = 50$ and $g_2 = 10$.

3   The 3-Time-Scale Problem

Information in the network, from the input beat pulse to the output of the motor neurons can be processed at different time scales, upon which hold the following constraints:

1. As seen in Figure 3, input pulse trains with periods smaller than 100 neuron time steps do not generate pulses in output (due to the slow refractory dynamics of the FHN neurons). Typical beats in music occur every 500-1000ms (i.e. 60 to 120 beats-per-minute). Neurons should therefore update faster than every 5-10ms (we call this time scale *network time scale* (NTS), and take it equal to 5 ms)
2. Because of hardware limitations, it is generally impossible to update the speed of a robot at a rate faster than a few tens of milliseconds. The practical limitation we observed for our specific platform (Miuro) was 100ms. We call this time scale the *robot time scale* (RTS).
3. Also from Figure 3, output pulses, generated when neurons overshoot, are sent with period roughly equivalent to the neurons' input, i.e. at longest 500-1000ms. The width of such output pulses W_p^{mot} should therefore be smaller than a few 1000ms, else they would concatenate to continuous output, and command the robot to a straight line. We take here $W_p^{mot} = 100$ NTS steps (i.e. 500 ms).

It follows that, if equ. 4-5 are processed at the RTS, output pulses are downsampled from W_p^{mot} NTS steps down to $\frac{W_p^{mot} NTS}{RTS}$ steps, which is in the order of 1-5. This turns out to be too crude, especially since we are interested in chaotic

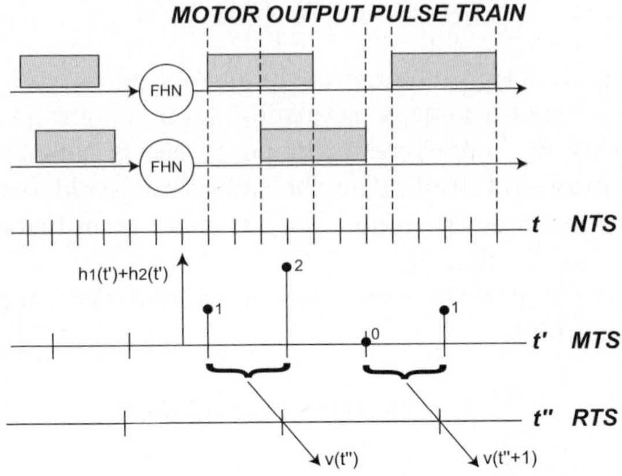

Fig. 4. Converting the network's chaotic dynamics into suitable motor commands of
the robot requires 3 simultaneous time scales. Output pulse train of the motor neurons
are generated at NTS (e.g. 5ms), sampled at MTS (e.g. 30ms), and the corresponding
speeds interpolated and sent to the robot at RTS (100ms).

dynamics resulting in fine overlaps between pulses. Therefore, the activation of
the robot (under the RTS constraints) using chaotic dynamics at a time scale
NTS constrained both by the dynamics of the FHN neurons and the typical time
scale of the environment (music) requires the introduction of a third, intermediary time scale (the *motor time scale* MTS), at which to sample the output
pulse train of the motor neurons. Figure 4 illustrates this 3-time-scale process:
Motor output pulses are generated by updating the network at NTS. Pulses are
sampled to generate a new set of wheel velocities at MTS. Then velocities are interpolated (averaged) over the RTS period, and sent to the robot's. MTS should
be intermediary between NTS and RTS:

- If MTS is too close to RTS, we downsample the output pulses too much, and
  lose most of the chaotic dynamics happening at NTS.
- If MTS is too close to NTS, we interpolate among too many consecutive
  velocity vectors, and smooth the resulting trajectory too much.

4   Results and Experiments

Figure 5 shows successive steps of a simulation of the robot trajectory (using
eq. 6-8), for a given music piece. The orbit shows typical chaotic itinerancy
behaviour, with locally quasi-periodic trails in attractors of various shapes, and
abrupt transitions from one attractor to the next through higher-dimensional
chaos. We observe that different songs generate different types of orbits and
styles of motion. Fine variations of time scales create considerable variation of
the robot motor behaviour, with disappearance of CI for limit values.

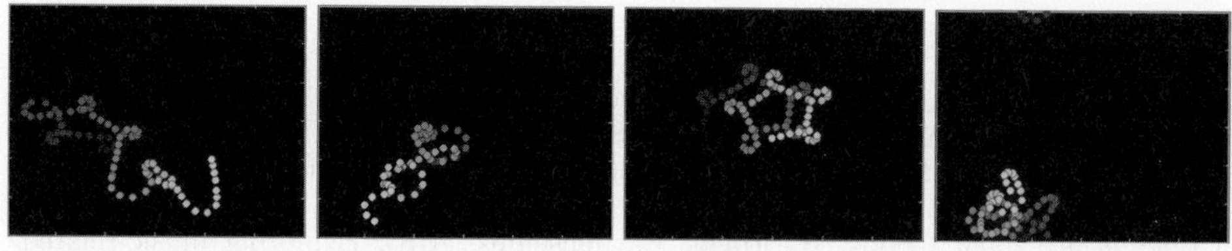

Fig. 5. Simulation of the robot trajectory in the (x,y) plane for a given music piece. Each figure is an overlay of 100 successive robot time steps. Time scales were chosen as NTS = 5ms, MTS = 30ms, RTS = 100ms. Successive figures correspond to different stages of the simulation (every 25 sec.). The trail shows typical chaotic itinerancy behaviour.

Transitions from one attractor to the next are generally triggered by sudden changes of periodicity in the network input (which in turn often correspond to changes of rhythm in the music). Thanks to fast signalling from sensory to motor neurons, quasi-periodic motion generated by most of the attractors tends to happen with a period correlated to the input bpm.

For more information, please refer to the online supplemental material[3], which includes animations of simulated orbits synchronized to music, as well as some parameter effects.

The system was demonstrated in public in Apple Store Ginza, Tokyo, Japan on May 31st, 2007 using the MIURO platform manufactured by ZMP Inc. (Figure 1) See supplemental material for details about the implementation and a video footage of the demonstration.

5   Conclusion

When excited with a pulse train corresponding to beats in a musical signal, a network of FitzHugh-Nagumo neurons is able to generate chaotic itinerancy dynamics. Using a 3-time-scale architecture, the output of the network can be converted to motor commands able to drive the trajectory of a robot in real-time. The resulting dance alternates in a seemingly autonomous manner between a variety of motion styles, some being periodic and strongly coupled to the musical rhythm and others being more independent. This illustrates that interesting compromises between synchronisation and autonomy can emerge from appropriate non-linear dynamics, without requiring patterns and their alternations to be programmed a priori.

Acknowledgements

This work was partially supported by the European Community project ECAgent (IST-1940) and a Postdoctoral Fellowship of the Japanese Society for the Promotion of Science. The authors thank the ZMP team for their willingness for collaboration and the technical help provided with robot miuro.

---

[3] http://www.jj-aucouturier.info/docs/miuro

References

[Bradley and Stuart, 1998] Bradley, E., Stuart, J.: Using chaos to generate variations on movement sequences. Chaos 8, 800–807 (1998)

[Fitzhugh, 1961] Fitzhugh, R.: Impulses and psychologial states in theoretical models of nerve membrane. BioPhys. Journal 1(1), 445–466 (1961)

[Godoy et al., 2006] Godoy, R., Haga, E., Jensenius, A.R.: Exploring music-related gestures by sound-tracing. - a preliminary study. In: 2nd ConGAS International Symposium on Gesture Interfaces for Multimedia Systems, Leeds (UK) (2006)

[Goto, 2001] Goto, M.: An audio-based real-time beat tracking system for music with or without drum-sounds. Journal of New Music Research 30(2), 159–171 (2001)

[Gouyon et al., 2006] Gouyon, F., Klapuri, A., Dixon, S., Alonso, M., Tzanetakis, G., Uhle, C., Cano, P.: An experimental comparison of audio tempo induction algorithms. IEEE Transactions on Audio, Speech and Language Processing 14(5), 1832–1844 (2006)

[Ikeda et al., 1989] Ikeda, K., Otsuka, K., Matsumoto, K.: Maxwell bloch turbulence. Prog. Theor. Phys (supplement) 99, 295–324 (1989)

[Ikegami, 2007] Ikegami, T.: Simulating active perception and mental imagery with embodied chaotic itinerancy. Journal of Consciousness Studies 14(7), 111–125 (2007)

[Kaneko and Tsuda, 2003] Kaneko, K., Tsuda, I.: Chaotic itinerancy. Chaos 13(3), 926–936 (2003)

[Kay, 2003] Kay, L.: A challenge to chaotic itinerancy from brain dynamics. Chaos 13(3), 1057–1066 (2003)

[Kostova et al., 2004] Kostova, T., Ravindran, R., Schonbek, M.: Fitzhugh nagumo revisited: Types of bifurcations, periodical forcing and stability regions by a lyapunov functional. International Journal of Bifurcation and Chaos 14(3), 913–925 (2004)

[Kosuge et al., 2003] Kosuge, K., Hayashi, T., Hirata, Y., Tobiyama, R.: Dance partner robot -ms dancerr-. In: Proceedings of the IEEE/RSJ International Conference on Intelligent Robots and Systems (2003)

[Michalowski et al., 2007] Michalowski, M.P., Sabanovic, S., Kozima, H.: A dancing robot for rhythmic social interaction. In: Proceedings of HRI (2007)

[Nakazawa et al., 2002] Nakazawa, A., Nakaoka, S., Ikeuchi, K.: Imitating human dance motions through motion structure analysis. In: Proceedings of International Conference on Intelligent Robots and Systems (2002)

[Pachet, 2004] Pachet, F.: On the Design of Flow Machines. In: The Future of Learning, IOS Press, Amsterdam (2004)

[Press et al., 1986] Press, W., Flannery, B., Teukolsky, S., Vetterling, W.: Numerical Recipes, The Art of Scientific Computing. Cambridge University Press, Cambridge (1986)

[Scheirer, 1998] Scheirer, E.: Tempo and beat analysis of acoustic musical signals. Journal of the Acoustic Society of America 103(1), 588–601 (1998)

[Takahashi et al., 2007] Takahashi, H., Horibe, N., Ikegami, T., Shimada, M.: Analyzing house fly's exploration behavior with ar methods. Journal of the Japanese Phycis Society (submitted, 2007)

[Tanaka and Suzuki, 2004] Tanaka, F., Suzuki, H.: Dance interaction with qrio: A case study for non-boring interaction by using an entrainment ensemble model. In: Proceedings of the 2004 IEEE International Workshop on Robot and Human Interactive Communication (2004)

[Wanderley et al., 2005] Wanderley, M.M., Vines, B., Middleton, N., McKay, C., Hatch, W.: The musical significance of clarinetists' ancillary gestures: An exploration of the field. Journal of New Music Research 34(1), 97–113 (2005)

Interactive Clothes Design Support System

Yuki Ogata[1] and Takehisa Onisawa[2]

[1] Onisawa Lab., Graduate School of Systems and Information Engineering, Univ.of Tsukuba
1-1-1, Tennodai, Tsukuba, 305-8573 Japan
`sabukiti@fhuman.esys.tsukuba.ac.jp`
[2] Graduate School of Systems and Information Engineering, University of Tsukuba
1-1-1, Tennodai, Tsukuba, 305-8573 Japan
`onisawa@iit.tsukuba.ac.jp`

Abstract. This paper proposes a clothes design support system. Interactive Genetic Algorithms are applied to the support system in order to reflect users's Kansei to clothes design. The system presents several designed clothes candidates to a user and a user evaluates them. According to user's evaluation, the system gives genetic algorithms (GA) operations, selection, crossover and mutations, to clothes candidates. Repeating the procedures, presentation, evaluation and GA operations, satisfying clothes are obtained. Subjects experiments are performed to verify usefulness of the presented system.

Keywords: Clothes design, interactive genetic algorithms, soft computing, human Kansei and subjectivity.

1 Introduction

It is said that clothes have three roles, (1) protection of a body, (2) expression of sociality and/or an age, i.e., expression of trend, and (3) self-expression [1]. Especially, self-expression means that clothes express individuality of a person wearing them. Obviously, we have recently opportunities to wear not only branded clothes but also originally designed ones, and express ourselves by wearing them. Therefore, especially demand of originally designed clothes of our own becomes high, and there appear many web sites undertaking to design original clothes or performing T-shirt design contests which many laypersons participate in easily [2]. That is, we individuals have many opportunities to design clothes by ourselves.

However, since technical knowledge is needed for clothes design, the design is very hard for laypersons. Although studies on design support system with a computer appear recently so that even laypersons can design clothes [3], [4], these studies are about fashion coordinates, i.e., about fashion design of clothes parts combination or clothes parts colors combination. Furthermore, although three kinds of factors, shape, color, material, are very important for clothes design, there is few study considering these three factors [1].

This paper aims at proposing a clothes design system considering the factors by which even laypersons can design clothes reflecting their own Kansei [5] with interaction between the system and them. Interactive Genetic Algorithms (IGA) [6], [7] are applied to the interaction part of the presented system. As for applications of IGA to design related systems, for example, references [3], [4], [8], [9] get good results. In IGA a user evaluates designed candidates based on user's own Kansei, and according to user's evaluation the system modifies the candidates. Repeating the procedures, presentation of candidates,

M. Ishikawa et al. (Eds.): ICONIP 2007, Part II, LNCS 4985, pp. 657–665, 2008.

their evaluations and modifications, satisfying candidates, i.e., satisfying designed outputs, are finally obtained. Therefore, even a lay user, who has little technical knowledge on clothes design and has difficulty in realizing design image such as drawing design pictures, can design clothes reflecting user's Kansei by only evaluating candidates. Furthermore, since the system presents many types of clothes candidates, the presented system helps a user to get unexpected design candidates.

The organization of the paper is as follows. Chapter 2 explains system outline. Chapter 3 describes subjects experiments using the presented system and shows experimental results. Chapter 4 describes conclusions of the paper.

2 System Outline

2.1 Design Object

This paper deals with design of a jacket, which is hard for a lay user since jacket shapes are various and many, where not only the combination of a body part, a collar

Table 1. Parameters of Jacket Parts

Body	X_b, Y_b	Coordinates of 6 feature points P_b's
Collar	X_c, Y_c	Coordinates of 4 feature points P_c's
	h_c	Collar height
Sleeve	X_s, Y_s	Coordinates of 3 feature points P_s's
Pocket	X_p, Y_p	Coordinates of feature point P_p
	h_p, w_p	Pocket height and pocket width
Material	T	Texture number of material and pattern
Color	C	Color Number

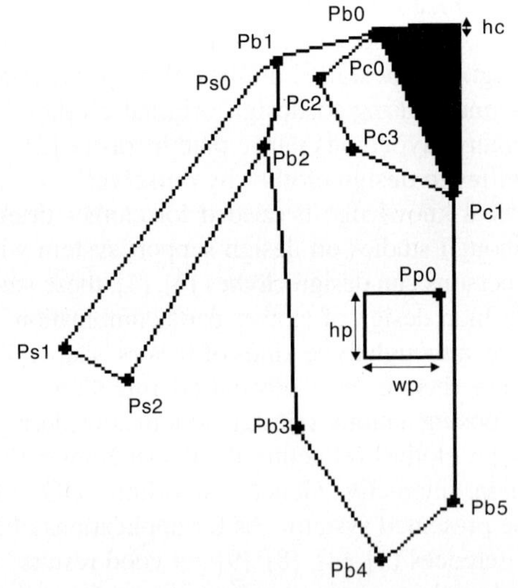

Fig. 1. Parameters of Jacket Parts

part, a sleeve part, pockets, material and color of a jacket but also original design of these parts is considered in this paper. The parameter of each part point of a jacket is expressed by x coordinate and y coordinate as shown in Table 1, where coordinates values of each point are expressed by integer values, and a jacket is expressed by the connection of these points as shown in Fig.1. As for material, quality property and pattern are dealt with by texture in this paper.

2.2 Flow of Design

Fig. 2 shows the system outline. The jacket design flow is as follows.

(1) A user starts jacket design having an image of designed jackets. The system generates jacket candidates by the random combination of each part of a jacket, i.e., a body, a collar, a sleeve, pockets, material and color of a jacket, and presents them a user as initial candidates.

(2) A user subjectively evaluates jackets presented in procedure (1) based on his/her own image of jackets. A user also chooses the most favorite jacket among presented jackets.

(3) The system modifies jackets according to user's evaluations using Genetic Algorithms (GA) operations.

(4) The system presents a user designed jacket candidates again.

(5) Repeating procedures (2), (3) and (4), i.e., evaluations, modifications and presentations, with interaction between a user and the system, the system designs jackets that satisfy a user. When a user is satisfied some designed jacket, design procedures are finished and satisfying jackets are obtained reflecting user's Kansei and subjective evaluation.

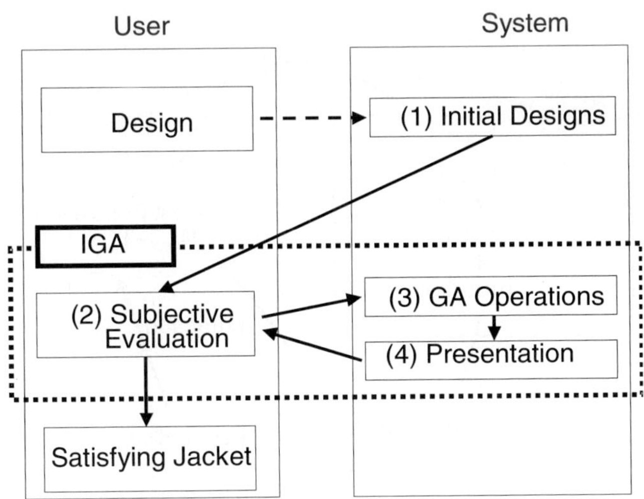

Fig. 2. System Outline

2.3 GA Operations

Fig. 3 shows the flow of GA operations in the presented system. GA parameters in this paper are as follows. N: the number of individuals in an individual pool, N_{user}: the number of individuals presented to a user, N_{elite}: the number of elites, N_{PC}: the number of parent candidate individuals, T: the maximum number of repeating generations, P_c: probability of crossover, ε : expansion rate, P_m: probability of mutation.

2.3.1 User Evaluation

A user evaluates N_{user} presented designed jacket candidates with 5-point scale subjectively whether they fit user's image of jackets or not. +2: very good, +1: good, 0: neutral, -1: bad, -2: very bad. An individual, which is chosen as the most favorite among presented jacket candidates, is dealt as an elite. The elite candidates have evaluation value +3.

2.3.2 Decision of Parents (Selection)

Parent candidates at the next generation are selected according to user's evaluation for individuals at the current generation. In this paper the roulette selection strategy is used at the selection. That is, the higher evaluation individuals have, the more the number of copied individuals at the next generation is, and the lower evaluation individuals have, the less the number of copied individuals at the next generation is. Let the evaluation of an individual i (i=1, 2, ..., N_{user}) be v(i). As for an individual i (v(i)+3) individuals are copied as the parent candidate at the next generation. As for an elite individual, its evaluation is considered as +3. Therefore, 6 elite individuals are copied at the next generation. If the number of copied parent candidates at the next generation is less than N_{PC}, the remainder of parent candidates is supplemented from the individual pool at random.

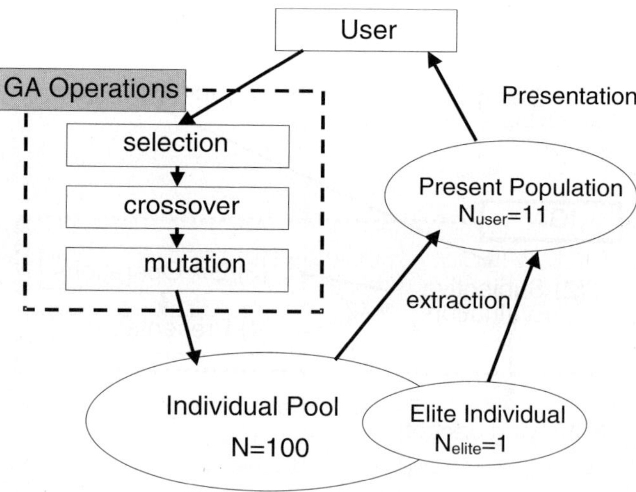

Fig. 3. Flow of GA Operations

2.3.3 Crossover

Two individuals are chosen at random from N_{PC} individuals and they are crossovered. A simplex crossover [10] is used in this paper. Let parameters of parents A and B, a parameter of a new individual C, the parameter expressing the dividing point between parents A and B and the expansion rate be $P_{parent\ A}$, $P_{parent\ B}$, $P_{individual\ C}$, $x\ (0 \leq x \leq 1)$ and ε, respectively. $P_{individual\ C}$ is obtained by Eq. (1).

$$P_{individual\ C} = (1 + \varepsilon) \times \{P_{parent\ A} \times x + P_{parent\ B} \times (1-x)\} \tag{1}$$

The number of individuals, which are generated newly by the crossover, is $N \times Pc$.

2.3.4 Mutation

After the crossover, individuals are mutated at probability P_m. The parameter of an individual is changed at random as the mutation in this paper. The number of individuals, which are generated newly by the mutation, is $N \times P_c \times P_m$.

2.3.5 Presentation to User

The individual pool at the next generation consists of N individuals which are $N \times P_c$ individuals obtained by crossover/mutation and $N-N \times P_c$ individuals copied at random from the individual pool at the current generation. (N_{user} -1) individuals are chosen at random from N individuals in the individual pool. N_{user} individuals including elite individuals are presented a user again and a user evaluates them.

3   Subjects Experiments

Subjects experiments are performed in order to verify whether subjects without knowledge on clothes design can design jackets reflecting their own Kansei and subjectivity using the presented system or not. In the experiments subjects design jackets having images of a good jacket. Parameter values are fixed as follows. N=100, N_{user} =11, N_{elite}=1, N_{PC}=56, T=15, P_c=0.8, ε =0, P_m=0.2.

3.1   Clothes Design and Questionnaire

Each subject designs jackets from the 1st generation to the 15th one using a user interface of the presented system. Fig. 4 shows a user interface for evaluation, and also shows initial individuals at the 1st generation, where it is assumed that the initial individuals and the individual group for GA operations at the 1st generation are all the same in order to confirm diversity of designed jackets. The interface has several kinds of buttons for subjects evaluations; a button for an overall subjective evaluation of presented jackets with 5-point scale evaluation, a button for best evaluation among presented jackets and buttons for partial evaluations, i.e., for evaluations of jacket parts, where in this paper only overall evaluation buttons and a best evaluation button are used. Subjects evaluate 11 presented jackets, where an elite individual, i.e., a jacket with the best evaluation at the current generation, is presented at the left-upper side of the interface.

After the design of jackets subjects are asked to answer questionnaire as shown in Table 2. Subjects answer 10 questionnaires with 5-point scale and give some

Table 2. Questionnaire

No.	Questionnaire
1	A human interface is simple to understand.
2	A human interface is simple to use.
3	Satisfying jackets are obtained.
4	Satisfying jacket shapes are obtained.
5	Satisfying jacket colors are obtained.
6	Satisfying jacket materials are obtained.
7	New image of jacket is obtained watching presented jackets.
8	You can design jackets by yourself without the system.
9	Your evaluation is reflected on jacket design.
10	It takes short time to design satisfied jackets.

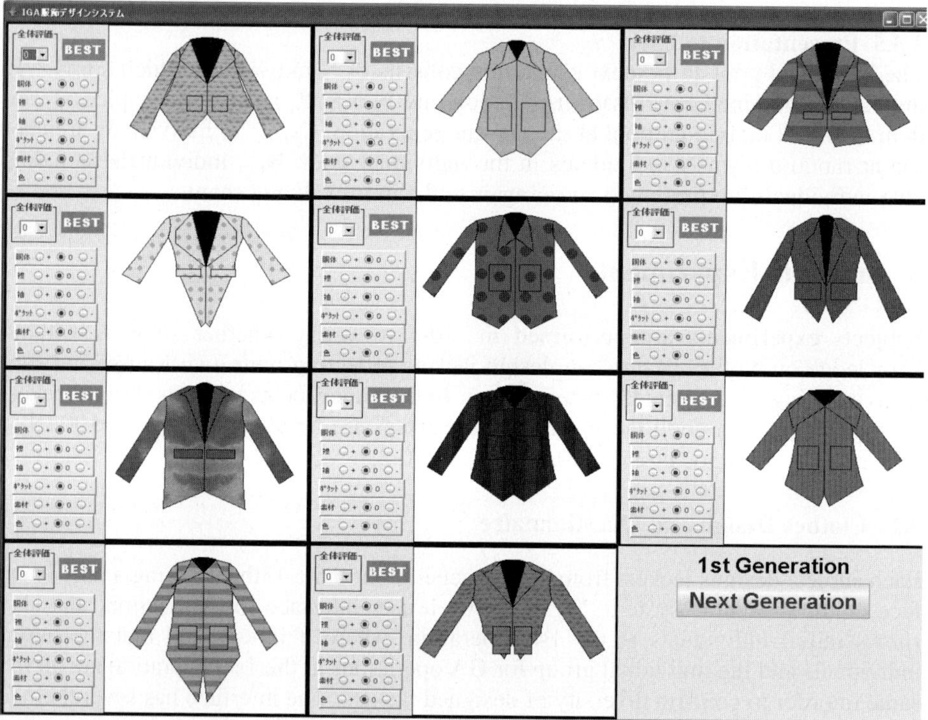

Fig. 4. User Interface for Subjective Evaluation and Initial Individuals

comments if any. +2: I think so very much, +1: I think so, 0: neutral, -1: I don't think so, -2: I don't think so very much. Subjects also evaluate elite individuals, i.e., jackets with the best evaluation at each generation, absolutely with 7-point scale, where jackets are presented at random so that subjects don't know which generation presented jackets are obtained. +3: satisfied very much, +2: satisfied, +1: satisfied a little, 0: neutral, -1: satisfied little, -2: unsatisfied, -3: unsatisfied very much. This last evaluation shows whether subject's satisfaction degrees become high or not as generations progress.

3.2 Experimental Results and Remarks

In this section the presented system is discussed from the following three points of view, quetionnnaire results, diversity of designed jackets and satisfation degree at each generation.

3.2.1 Questionnaire Results

Table 3 shows questionnaire results. From the questionnaire results of numbers 1 and 2, it is found that the human interface of the presented system is estimated to be simple to use. The questionnaire results from numbers 3 to 7, i.e., the average evaluation over 1 for each evaluation item, show that subjects can design and obtain jackets with high satisfaction degree using the presented system. Especially, the questionnaire results of number 8 show that subjects cannot design jackets without any design support systems. That is, even if subjects cannot design jackets without any design support systems, they can design and obtain satisfying jackets using the presented system. Therefore, the presented system is useful for users who have not knowledge on clothes design.

Table 3. Questionnaire Results

No.	Subjects							Average
	A	B	C	D	E	F	G	Degrees
1	2	2	1	2	2	1	2	1.71
2	2	2	1	2	0	0	1	1.14
3	2	1	2	2	1	2	2	1.71
4	2	2	2	2	2	1	2	1.86
5	2	0	2	2	-1	2	1	1.14
6	2	2	2	2	2	1	1	1.71
7	2	1	2	2	1	2	2	1.71
8	-2	0	0	-2	-2	0	-2	-1.14
9	0	2	1	1	2	1	2	1.29
10	0	2	0	2	1	2	2	1.29

3.2.2 Diversity of Designed Jackets

Fig. 5 shows some examples of jackets obtained at the 15th generation by subjects. Although they have image of a good jacket and start with same initial individuals, i.e., same jackets, various types of jackets are obtained. It is found that subjects design and obtain jackets reflecting their Kansei and image of a good jacket, and that the presented system is useful.

Fig. 5. Some Examples of Jackets Obtained by Subjects

3.2.3 Change of Satisfaction Degrees

Fig. 6 shows the average of satisfaction degrees among subejcts at every generation and its standard deviation. This figure shows that the satisfaction degree becomes high as generations progress. And in the questionnaire some subjects answer that they can design and obtain satsifying jackets using the presented system. From the experimental results it is found that the present system is useful for subjects without knowledge on clothes design .

However, the average of satisfaction degrees is saturated with at the 5th or 6th generation. Although some subjects have comments that they can obtain satisfying jackets design around this generation, there is a possibility that individuals with local minimum are obtained. Therefore, it is necessary to consider design procedures furthermore.

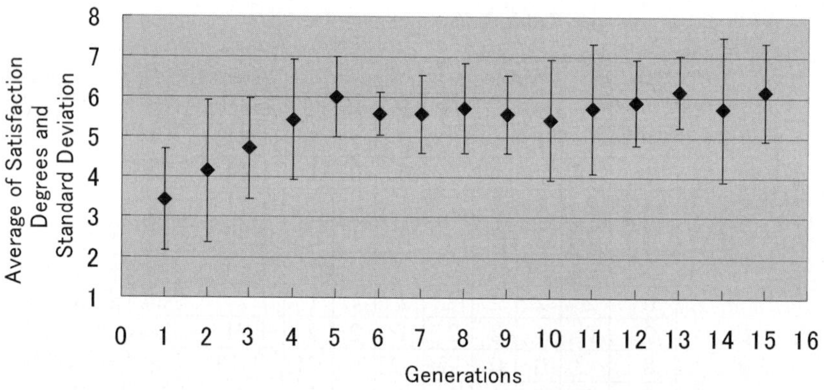

Fig. 6. Average of Satisfaction Degrees among Subjects and Its Standard Deviation

3.3 Future Works

Almost all subjects have comments that at earlier generations they have rough design plans. For example, they evaluate jackets shapes and colors roughly at the ealier generations, and then they evaluate jackets parts in detail. However, the presented system deals with only overall evaluation of designed jackets and does not consider the partial evaluation of a jacket. Partial evaluation and partial design of a jacket are necessary for reflecting subject's Kansei and subjectiviry, and for more satisfied designed jackets.

In this paper only two dimesional design drawings of jacksts are dealt with. However, for realization of actual clothes design three dimensional design drawings are necessary. Body size information on a user is also necessary for better clothes design fitting user's body.

4   Conclusions

In this paper the clothes design system interacting a user is considered. Interactive GAs are applied to the interaction clothes design system. A user evaluates presented designed jackets and according to user's evaluations jackets are modified and finally satisfied jackets reflecting user's satisfaction are obtained. In order to verify the usefulness of the present system subjects experiments are performed and experimental results are discussed.

As future works partial evaluation and partial design sould be considered. And for actual clothes design three dimensional design drawing and body size information of a user are needed.

References

1. Bunka Fashion College (ed.): Specialty Course of Clothes-related (9) Clothes Design, Bunka Publishing Bereau (2005)
2. Uniqlo Creative Award (2007): `http://www.uniqlo.jp/creative/`
3. Kim, H.-S., Cho, S.-B.: Application of interactive genetic algorithm to fashion design. Engineering Applications of Artificial Intelligence 13(6), 635–644 (2000)
4. Tanaka, M., Ohsaki, M., Hayashibe, K.: Development and Evaluatiom of an IEC-based Fashion Coordinate System. In: Proc. of 18th Fuzzy Systems Symposium, pp. 207–210 (2002)
5. Nagamachi, M.: Kansei Engineering and Comfort –Preface. International Journal of Industrial Ergonomics 19(1), 79–80 (1987)
6. Kitano, H. (ed.): Genetic Algorithms 4, Sangyo Tosho (2000)
7. Takagi, H.: Interactive Evolutionary Computation: Fusion of the Capabilities of EC Optimization abd Human Evaluation. Proc. Of IEEE 89(9), 1275–1296 (2001)
8. Yamada, M., Onisawa, T.: Logo Drawing System Applying Interactive Genetic Algorithms. In: Proc. of the 2006 IEEE International Conference on Information Reuse and Integration, pp. 238–243 (2006)
9. Kagawa, T., Nishino, H., Utsumiya, K.: A Design Support Method Using Interactive Evolutionary Computation. In: Proc. of IPSJ Kyusyu Chapter Symposium 2004, vol. (A5-2) (2004)
10. Higuchi, T., Tsutsui, S., Yamamura, M.: Simplex Crossover for Real-coded Genetic Algolithms. In: Proc. of Transactions of the Japanese Society for Artificial Intelligence, vol. 16, pp. 146–155 (2001)

Neural Network for Modeling Esthetic Selection

Tamás (Tom) Domonkos Gedeon

Department of Computer Science
Australian National University
Acton ACT 0200 Australia
tom@cs.anu.edu

Abstract. Some real world problems require significant human interaction for labeling the data, which is very expensive. Worse, in some cases, the exercise of human judgement is inherently subjective and contextual, and so the entire labeling must be done in one session, which may be too long. Our domain is the automatic generation of Mondrian-like images with an interactive interface for the user to select images. We use back-propagation neural networks to learn an approximation of a viewer's aesthetic using 2 category labelled data (images liked/disliked). We construct a data set for training in a sequential fashion related to the interactive art appreciation task, and produce an output profile which well approximates a regression task, even trained on classification data. Analysis of the learned network produces some surprises, with the discovery of some input contributions which are unexpected to the user.

Keywords: Neural networks, back-propagation, training set, incremental learning, artistic esthetic, art, Mondrian.

1 Introduction

We briefly introduce the work of the artist Piet Mondrian, discuss the computer generation and evaluation of art, propose our approach for almost real time learning and construction of a training set, describe our results and come to some conclusions.

1.1 Mondrian

Pieter Cornelis (Piet) Mondriaan, after 1912 Mondrian, (pronounced: Pete Mon-dree-on, IPA: [pit 'm_nd_i_n]) (b. Amersfoort, Netherlands, March 7, 1872 — d. New York City, February 1, 1944) was a Dutch painter.

He was an important contributor to the De Stijl art movement and group, which was founded by Theo van Doesburg. Despite being well-known, often-parodied and even trivialized, Mondriaan's paintings exhibit a complexity that belies their apparent simplicity. He is best known for his non-representational paintings that he called "compositions", consisting of rectangular forms of red, yellow, blue, white or black, separated by thick, black rectilinear lines. They are the result of a stylistic evolution that occurred over the course of nearly 30 years and continued beyond that point to the end of his life. [1].

M. Ishikawa et al. (Eds.): ICONIP 2007, Part II, LNCS 4985, pp. 666–674, 2008.

An example of one of Mondrian's abstract compositions is shown below:

Fig. 1. Composition of Red, Blue and Yellow

There have been multiple attempts to perform mathematical analyses [2, 3] of the compositions by Piet Mondrian. None of them are successful in giving a convincing result revealing the "hidden math" within Mondrian's painting [1].

Hill [2] used "number math" for measuring the grid size, analysing the ratio between grids, and so on. One example of the conclusions reached is that some of Mondrian's compositions are triple connected, in that you can not separate the graph into two without cutting at least three lines. This applies to about half of Mondrian's work in the period 1918 – 1938.

More success was achieved by Reynolds [3] using "structural analysis" based on graph theory, which is consistent for many Mondrian works, though certainly not all.

1.2 Mondrian's Esthetic Choices

Mondrian's artistic role in esthetic choices in his compositions is still debated. Lee (2001) found that art students could not correctly identify genuine Mondrian compositions. Contrarily, McManus [4] found that the majority of subjects could distinguish between original and modified Mondrian compositions. Wolach [5] found that subjects could distinguish (preferred) Mondrian line spacings from divergent spacings. If subjects could select divergently spaced pictures that they preferred, then the preference for Mondrian spacings vanished. That is, Mondrian was good at producing compositions which appeal to many/most people, but compositions which appeal to any one person will be perceived as positively as Mondrian's by that person.

It appears then that while Mondrian could design his compositions to appeal to some communal esthetic appreciation. Where participant selection is possible, some individual esthetic appreciation is felt, which for an individual is as strong as the communal esthetic, since the preference for original Mondrian (spacings) vanish.

Our approach is to construct Mondrian-like images for individual users which they find esthetically pleasing. Our technique is described in the next sub-section.

Computer Generation of Art. We construct Mondrian-like images using a number of parameters describing a possible image. These parameters are chosen by a random process initially. Subsequently, we use an evolutionary algorithm to improve the images for each user [6].

In De Stijl, only vertical lines and horizontal lines are allowed in the graph, and all lines (almost always) terminate on other lines or the edge of the painting. The rectangle is also a basic element of Neo-Plasticism, but from a programming viewpoint, rectangles are a 'by-product' of horizontal and vertical lines. Thus a Mondrian-like graph could be deemed a collection of horizontal and vertical lines.

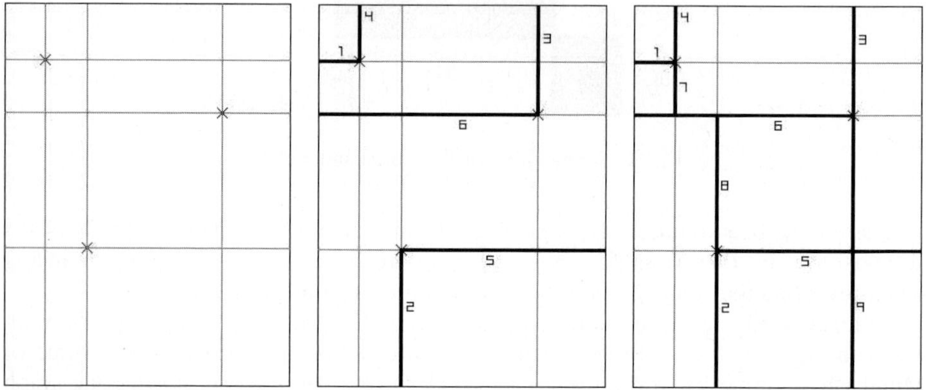

Fig. 2. Random initial points generated on a given canvas (x's on left), with imaginary lines drawn crossing the initial points (left). Draw lines emitted from each point in numbered sequence (middle). Skeleton complete (right). The final step is to randomly fill some rectangles with colour, being red, yellow, or blue (not shown above).

Clearly there are many potential choices here. How many initial points do we generate? How close may they be to each other? How far apart? How close to the edges can they get? And so on. We can deduce many properties which often hold for Mondrian's own compositions. We have already mentioned his spacing of lines.

Taylor [7] analysed the positions of 170 lines featured in 22 paintings, and found that Mondrian was twice as likely to position a line close to the canvas edge as he was to position it near the canvas centre. As we are interested in the development of individual esthetic choices, and we know [5] that the ability to chose can swamp the effect of Mondrian's own choices, we do not impose such conditions on our generation process.

In the centre of Figure 2 (above), we show a partially completed skeleton. The drawing of lines is probability based, so the same initial points can lead to different final images. Once all the lines are generated a remediation stage adds lines to eliminate remaining right angles, note this was unnecessary in the example above.

User's individual esthetic choices. To demonstrate briefly that individual esthetic choices lead to easily discernible differences in images, we provide the following examples for 4 subjects from our previous work [6].

In this paper we will concentrate on one subject as we will learn a single esthetic.

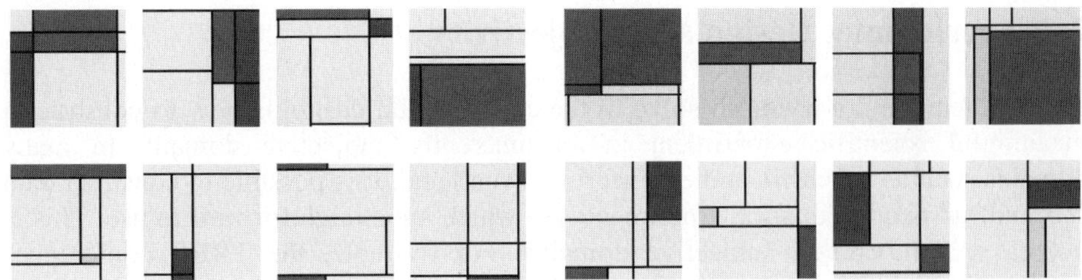

Fig. 3. Selected output for subjects (top left then right, bottom left then right) Z, P, J, T

Clearly, for Z's esthetic red and blue are present, and mostly touching along a rectangular edge (top left 4 images). Subject P seems to prefer 2 colours, particularly including blue, which usually touch, and extend across at least one of the horizontal or vertical dimensions (top right 4 images). Subject J clearly prefers small blocks of colours very close to the edges (bottom left 4 images). Finally, Subject T seems to prefer 'medium sized' blocks of colour separated by some space (bottom right 4 images). Subjects T and J were the authors of our previous work [6]. Subject T in the previous experiment will continue as the single subject for the experiments reported in this paper. This introduces an element of subjectivity which is considered in §2.

Computer Evaluation of Art. It has variously been suggested that it is worthwhile to consider trying to calculate the esthetic worth of images [8, 9].

We do not try to calculate the esthetic worth of images explicitly, rather we use neural network models to predict user preference. Hence the neural network weights arguably encode a representation of a user's esthetic preference.

Based on our previous work [6], we had some notions of the ways individual user esthetic preferences can vary. This was used to augment our search of the literature and wide internet browsing to identify image components which are likely to be significant. For example, line spacing [e.g., 5] has been extensively studied in Mondrian's work. It is also reported that Mondrian would sometimes spend days to decide on the placement of a single line. We generate Mondrian-like images from a vector based model, hence we have access to the exact point and line positionings at that stage, and hence the rectangles, and also their colours.

Table 1. Pre-processed vector image features

parameters	Description of image feature(s) encoded by parameters
1, 2	Number of lines in image; Sum of their lengths
3, 4, 5	Number of lines spanning entire image: horiz., vert. or in total
6, 7, 9, 10	Biggest/smallest distance between horizontal/vertical lines
8, 11	Length of smallest distance between lines vertically/horizontally
12, 13	Smallest/biggest distance between lines either horiz. or vert.
14, 15	Smallest horiz./vert. distance to and edge
16, 17, 18. 19	Proportion of image which is red/yellow/blue/coloured
20, 21, 22, 23, 24	Min distance between r&y/r&b/y&b/2 cols/2 cols Manhattan dist.
25, 26	Length 2 colours touch; Longest contiguous coloured areas.
27, 28	Longest parallel non-touching coloured areas; Distance between them.

2 Experimental Design and Subjectivity

The problem we are trying to solve in the experimental design is how to construct a meaningful scientific experiment in an inherently subjective domain. In many domains such as scientific and engineering, even legal, it is possible to construct data sets and run neural network experiments [9] which are straightforward to use. This is not easy in inherently subjective domains. For example, the TREC conferences provide some very large information retrieval data sets, which in essence assume that the overall ratings of search results are comparable from one expert to the next. This is likely to be a valid assumption in that domain. The equivalent in the generative art domain would be an average of the esthetic appreciation of the general population. One could argue that this is exactly what Mondrian has done in his compositions. But as we defined our focus earlier, with an emphasis on individual esthetic preference, it is not suitable for us here.

Our process using our evolutionary algorithm tool is that the user is presented with a number of generations of computer constructed Mondrian-like images at a time. The user is encouraged to indicate some active preference for, or dislike of, some images. While it is possible to rate every image, typically users will only select images for rating which they actively like or dislike. The first generation is completely at random, while subsequent generations use the rating information to improve images for that user. Ideally, the typical generation size would be 20, however the paucity of information available in that setting means improvement of images is small and likely indirectly reflects the esthetic preferences of the programmer (subject J in our previous work) implemented via the initial probabilistic settings the code uses. That is, the program clearly 'worked' when the images improved over time. This is based on observations from subject T. Note that the probabilistic settings are significant, because for a process to be seen to be generating art rather than 'just' images, some degree of randomness is probably essential [10], at least in so far as to ensure that the "result must not be precisely predictable" [11]. That is, some degree of surprise.

Hence our attempt to use neural networks to learn the user esthetic model. Neural local search methods require less training data than evolutionary global search, so the notion is to use the scarce data we have and train neural networks which can then act as the evaluation function for the evolutionary algorithm generating new images.

2.1 Experiment 1 – A Traditional Neural Network Data Set

In our first experiment, we use some labelled data to construct a training set of 100 patterns, being encodings of 50 images the user liked, and 50 images the user disliked. The test set of 44 patterns is similarly divided between liked/disliked image representations. This data set (training and test set) is based on an extremely long series of sessions viewing some 3,000 Mondrian-like images. This was impossible to get most users to commit to, hence this paper discusses the results on subject T only from our previous experiment.

Note that multiple subjects would only demonstrate that we can learn the esthetic preference for more than one person, as most of the inherent subjectivity would remain in the selection of liked/disliked images. Further, the elephant in the room would remain. The design of the experiment is not really independent of the measures used and subjects available. There is some tension here, which is usually expressed in the neural network community by the use of multiple test sets.

There is a training set to use to train a network, another set to decide when to stop training and another set ("which is not seen at all by the network") to actually calculate the usefulness of the network. The 2nd and 3rd sets are called test and validation sets, but some authors do train-validate-test while others do train-test-validate (the sequence we prefer). Arguably, the use of a 3rd set is to prevent cheating.

A set of 1,000 Mondrian-like images was classified by subject T into like/unsure/dislike groups. This classification was used to calculate the mean square error as well as classification error. For neural network predictions in the range 0.4 images was classified by subject T into like/unsure/dislike groups. This classification was used to calculate the mean square error as well as classification error. For neural network predictions in the range $0.4 \leq p \leq 0.6$ where the label was 0.5, we record a correct classification (into the implicit 'unsure' category), while predictions above/below this are correct if the label is 1/0 respectively. The number of patters in each classification is as follows: yes 87, maybe 803, no 310.

2.2   Experiment 2 – Sequentially Trained Neural Networks

In experiment 1, we constructed a traditional type training and test set. In experiment 2, we follow a path more appropriate to the problem, following the sequence of presentation of results from a generation of Mondrian-like images to a user (again, for comparison, subject T), and so on.

The experiment was as follows. The user was presented with a sequence of 20 Mondrian-like images, from which the expectation was that 1 would be selected as liked, and one disliked. This sequence repeated in the first phase until 20 liked and 20 disliked images were collected. (For data set purposes, any episodes in which more or less liked/disliked images were collected are resorted so that it appears as if there is a guaranteed liked and disliked image in each cycle of presentations.)

For this phase all images are generated randomly. The 40 labelled images are used to construct the initial training set with 28 training and 12 test patterns, being alternating liked and disliked patterns. These sets are used to train neural networks (or varying topology described below), which are then used to select the next images to be presented in the next phase, with 10 of the images selected evenly distributed from the neural network results suggesting the user will like these, 2 dislike, and 8 at random. For reproducibility purposes, 1,000 images are constructed, and ranked by the trained neural network. Hence the "8 at random" represents about 1 in 4 of the remaining images once the liked and disliked are included.

For data set purposes, an entire phase of presentations of 20 images at a time is done before any further training, though otherwise we could use each extra image to retrain a neural net while the user is looking at the next set on screen. From the 20 liked and 20 disliked images collected, the training and test sets are increased in size, with 20 more training patterns and 20 more test patterns, again alternating liked and disliked patterns. A new network with the same topology is trained each time, with the previous learned weights ignored, to eliminate any extra effect of the initial set.

This overall process is repeated 4 times. Finally, the same 1,000 Mondrian-like images are used as the validation set as used in experiment 1.

3 Results

The results presented in this section are the validation results on a set of 1,000 Mondrian-like images (being their representation as described previously) which were fully classified by subject T into yes/maybe or unsure/no categories, which are represented by 1/0.5/0 values. These are used normally for mean squared error (MSE) calculations, and used to determine the number of correct classifications in §2.1.

Table 2. Performance of 3 trials, 2 neural network topologies for experiment 1, and one for 2

Expt 1, 28 x 5 x 1 net	Expt 1, 28 x 50 x 10 x 1 net	Expt 2, 28 x 5 x 1 net
TSS = 189.1	TSS = 190.3	TSS = 109.1
		START Train: 28 Test: 12
		THEN Train: 48 Test: 32
		THEN Train: 68 Test: 52
		THEN Train: 88 Test: 72
Train: 100 Test: 44	Train: 100 Test: 44	FINAL Train: 108 Test: 92

In experiment 1, two different initial topologies were used. The results were essentially identical, hence the simpler topology was used for experiment 2. Clearly, our experiment 2 performs significantly better than experiment 1. The number of training patterns is quite similar, though the test patterns are approximately double. While the number of test patterns is, we believe, of limited significance, we will test this in the future. In experiment 2, the correct classifications are 94%. This is a very high degree of prediction. At this point it is appropriate to remind the reader that there is significant subjectivity involved with the use of a single subject, and that being subject T, however there seems little reason to believe this would affect the success or otherwise of experiment 1 versus experiment 2.

Our view is that the difference in performance is due to much of the final data sets in Experiment 2 being in some sense related to and fine tuning the neural network representation of the user's esthetic preference, rather than 'randomly' adding to a training set in a very complex space. (Subject T has reported that during the extensive interaction with our Mondrian-like images, his perception of what he likes/dislikes has changed and evolved, and that there were images he liked "notwithstanding he should not like them"! We interpret this statement to mean that the images were ones that did not match his own view of the "kinds of images" he liked.) That is, if we consider the training set in experiment 1 being similar to experiment 2, then the training set in experiment 1 is like the initial training set of experiment 1 with 72 randomly chosen additions, while the training set of experiment 2 has the addition of 80 increasingly well chosen additions.

The difference between experiments 1 and 2 are very clearly illustrated in plotting the predicted values for patterns in the validation set.

The difference between prediction profiles is profound. Clearly the difference is significant, in that in experiment 1 the results are to produce classifications which are

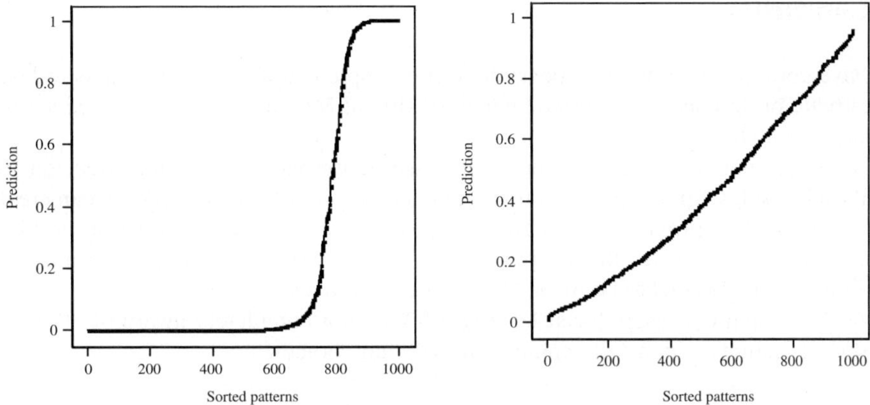

Fig. 4. Predicted output for each validation pattern, for subject T (experiment 1 on left, 2 right)

yes/no with a small transition, whereas in experiment 2 the results are a smooth transition from no via maybe/unsure to yes. The plots in the left and right of Figure 4 above are similar to what one would expect for a classification and a regression problem respectively. This suggests a possible explanation, in that the sequential, and contextual, construction of the training set has created (effectively) a regression style training set for a classification problem.

Significance of input parameters. We analysed the weight matrix (of experiment 2) to determine the significance of each of the input parameters [8]. The most significant were 19 9 24 22 17 15 20 25, in decreasing order of significance, representing approximately 10% down to 5% contribution each and overall accounting for over 50% of the contributions of the input to the hidden layer.

There are some surprises here. Parameter 19 is the proportion of coloured area is not surprising. Parameter 9 is the biggest vertical distance between lines. None of the rest of the related group (6 7 9 10) are similarly significant, with 7 (smallest horizontal distance between lines) having 1/2 the contribution while being double or more the contribution of the remaining parameters in that group. Parameter 24 is the Manhattan distance between 2 colours, and has double the contribution of Euclidean distance in parameter 23. Possibly this is due to the rectilinear nature of Mondrian's De Stijl compositions (the parameter was introduced to investigate whether different distance metrics make a difference, the result suggests further investigation).

Parameters 22, 20 and 17 were particularly surprising, being the distance between yellow and blue, distance between yellow and red, and proportion yellow. In none of our observations in this experiment or the prior work we reported [6] did we notice any relation or pattern in the esthetic choices of subject T which relate to yellow. This suggests that our technique is able to identify relationships which are not consciously available to users (or at least not available to subject T).

4 Conclusion

We have demonstrated that it is possible to use simple neural network models to learn the esthetic preferences of a subject when looking at Mondrian-like images generated by our computational process.

We found that the process of data set construction has a profound effect on the results achieved, with a hypothesis that an appropriate construction process can create a data set which approximates a regression problem even on a classification problem base. This would have huge significance as it would allow probabilistic or possibilistic conclusions to be made from categorical data.

We also found that users (or at least user T) are not completely aware of all of the significant features which can explain some of their choices.

References

1. Wikipedia, entries on de stijl, Piet Mondrian, http://www.wikipedia.com
2. Hill, A.: Art and Mathesis: Mondrian's Structures. Leonardo I, 233–234 (1968)
3. Reynolds, D.: Symbolist Aesthetics And Early Abstract Art, Cambridge UP, page 260 (1995)
4. McManus, I.C., Cheema, B., Stoker, J.: The aesthetics of composition: A study of Mondrian. Empirical Studies of the Arts 11(2), 83–94 (1993)
5. Wolach, A.H.: Line spacing in Mondrian paintings and computer-generated modifications. Journal of General Psychology (July 2005)
6. Gedeon, T.D., Shen, J.Y.: Making art using evolutionary algorithms and artificial AI. In: Proceedings BOOM 2007, p. 6 (2007)
7. Taylor, R.P.: Fractal expressionism-where art meets science, Art and Complexity. Elsevier Press, Amsterdam (2003)
8. Gedeon, T.D.: Data Mining of Inputs: Analysing Magnitude and Functional Measures. International Journal of Neural Systems 8(2), 209–218 (1997)
9. Brown, W.M., Gedeon, T.D., Groves, D.I.: Use of noise to augment training data to compensate for lack of deposit examples in training a neural network for mineral potential mapping. Natural Resources Research 12(2), 141–151 (2003)
10. Granger, M.J., Mazlack, L.J.: Representing Aesthetic Judgments. In: Proceedings of the International Conference on Cybernetics and Society, pp. 16–20 (1981)
11. Maiocchi, R.: Can you make a computer understand and produce art? AI & Society 5, 183–201 (1991)

Adaptive Computer Game System Using Artificial Neural Networks

Kok Wai Wong

School of Information Technology
Murdoch University
South St, Murdoch
Western Australia 6155
k.wong@murdoch.edu.au

Abstract. In this paper, we examine the use of Artificial Neural Networks (ANNs) for designing an adaptive computer game system. This adaptive computer game system will enhance the game play experience of a player by adopting the concept of player centred game design. In this paper, the ANN is used to handle the dynamic difficulty level adjustment for each individual player. The difficulty level for each player can be customised using the proposed method, thus allowing game player to have a more personalised game play experience.

Keywords: We would like to encourage you to list your keywords in this section.

1   Introduction

The entertainment computing and game industry have experienced exponential growth over the last few years and have attracted many researchers recently as well. This area of the entertainment industry has become a highly competitive area. While in the past, excellent graphics were enough to increase the likelihood of success for a game, in the present climate a high standard of graphics is assumed or expected. Rapid advances in technology and computer science are producing games which are increasingly entertaining and impressive. In the past, computer games were very simple programs; graphics were limited to basic angular shapes, two dimensional and only black and white in colour. From such humble beginnings, computer games have since developed into highly exciting multi-media experiences, rich in visual and audio content. Recently, it can observe a shift to focus on the game design for individual player. The shift of this focus is similar to the customer relationship management (CRM), the term used in business world for a while. However, in game design, it is know as player centred design.

Player centred game design could be defined as the approach that aims to improve the game design and development from the individual players' perspective. A benefit of taking a player centred design approach is that it should ideally result in enhanced game play experiences for players regardless of gender, age or experience [1]. With the advancement of intelligent technique, adaptive game system could be one of the solutions for producing a player centred game [1]. Adaptive game system performs

M. Ishikawa et al. (Eds.): ICONIP 2007, Part II, LNCS 4985, pp. 675–682, 2008.

this customisation for each player using a method for creating dynamic heuristic models of player types. This method adjusts and adapts itself over time based on input and measurement from the individual players. Once such a model is developed it can then be used to perform dynamic difficulty level adjustment, to adapt game player's preference playing style, and to assist game player during game play. The main objective of all these is to maintain the interest level of each individual game player.

In this paper, we will only examine the adaptive difficulty level adjustment using Artificial Neural Networks.

2 Level of Difficulty

In games development, level editing is a challenging task. A level is normally referred to a separate area in the game's virtual world, sometimes also known as a stage, course or map. In most of the modern games, it is typically representing a specific location such as a building or a city. Level design is consider more towards the art than it is a science. The level designer needs artistic skills and know-how as well as extensive technical knowledge to perform the tasks.

Besides focusing on the artistic side of the level design as mentioned above, another area which is known in early days for level design is the "level of difficulty". This is still an important area in level design for games, as this has direct effect on the game play experiences that engage and motivate the game players. If the games are too easy, the players may feel bored. If it is too difficult, the players may feel frustrated. Of course, most games allow players to adjust the difficulty level like setting to "beginner", "average" and "advance", however, the experience is static and in the worse case, the "beginner" or "advance" settings are subjective to individual and predictable. Will you play a game if you are "killed" in less than 30 second of the game play all the time? [1] has also stated *"Every player is different; each has a different preference for the pace and style of gameplay within a game, and the range of game playing capabilities between players can vary widely. Even players with a similar level of game playing ability will often find separate aspects of a game to be more difficult to them individually, and the techniques that each player focuses on to complete the various challenges a game offers can also be very different. This is at the core of our reasoning that adaptive game technology can have an important role to play in next-generation games."*

Dynamic Difficulty Adjustment (DDA) system can be used to improve these game play experience by providing some flexibilities [2,3]. However, DDA system is not easy to achieve and few commercial developers have implemented and delivered them. There are two broad approaches used by commercial systems. The first is to perform the task manually, where designer annotate the difficulty design. Secondly, designer uses a combination of data mining and off-line analysis [4].

3 Adaptive Game System

In this paper, we have utilised ANN specifically BPNN (Backpropagation Neural Network) as software agent for each player to provide an intelligent personalised difficulty adjustment system. As each player will be presented with their own BPNN agents, thus personalisation can be obtained. With the use of these intelligent agents, the difficulty level presented to each player may be slightly different; i.e. the "beginner" or "advance" settings for player A may not be the same as the setting for player B. BPNN [5] is the most widely used ANN and that is why it is used to create the intelligent adaptive level adjustment system. Back propagation is a systematic method for training multilayer ANN. It has been implemented and applied successfully to various problems.

When designing game using AI, the purpose is to enhance game play experience but at the same time keeping the AI processing power to the minimum when the game is running [6]. This could be one of the main reasons why BPNN is not popular as one of the AI technique used in games, due to the complexity for training a BPNN. However, in this paper, we will examine how BPNN can be used in game and how it can enhance the player's experience by assisting the difficulty level design.

Before designing the difficulty level using BPNN, we will first need to create a data warehouse that contains all possible outcome behaviours of the AI in the game. For example, an AI plane trying to bomb the player's targets in game, we will need to record all the possible input parameters like the height, speed and direction of the plane, as well as the wind direction and speed of all the successful hits into the data warehouse. We will also need to include records for unsuccessful hits into the data warehouse as well.

Let us assume for discussion purposes that the training data warehouse has been created based on the following. Figure 1 shows the design of the training data warehouse. There are two parts. The first part will contain all recorded data inclusive of successful and unsuccessful hits made by the AI plane on the player's targets. In the second part, there are a total of 18 databases that contains samples for accuracies range from 5% to 95% AI opponent's accuracy with a step of 5%. This set of data samples are formed by the data extracted from the first part of the data warehouse which contains information of successful and unsuccessful hits made by the AI plane on the player's targets. When creating the individual database within the data warehouse, the proportional of the hit and missed data are used to create those databases. The total number of data used in each database is 500. For example, for the training

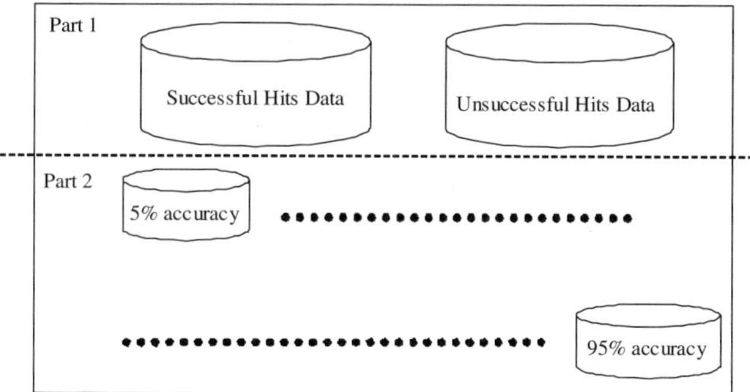

Fig. 1. The design of the training data warehouse

database used to train a BPNN which exhibit the behaviour of 5% accuracy, it will contain a total of 25 hit data and 475 missed data.

With these records, BPNNs can be trained to learn the association between the inputs and the outputs. After which, each corresponding BPNN will be saved in the database that contains individual content database based on the difficulty level inferred by the trained BPNN. As BPNN used back propagation to continuing adjust the weights in order to "learn", it is a long and time consuming iterative process. This is the main reason why it is not used for most real time and online application. In this paper, we proposed the design of the BPNN difficulty level system offline. That is the reason why we will pre-train all networks (the designing stage of the game), and store it in a database.

For the prediction of the BPNN, it is only one pass. The prediction phase is simple and not as time consuming as compared to the training phase. Once the weight parameters of the BPNN are loaded before the game start, it will require minimum computation when the game is being played. This design arrangement could provide the usability of BPNN as an intelligent agent for the games.

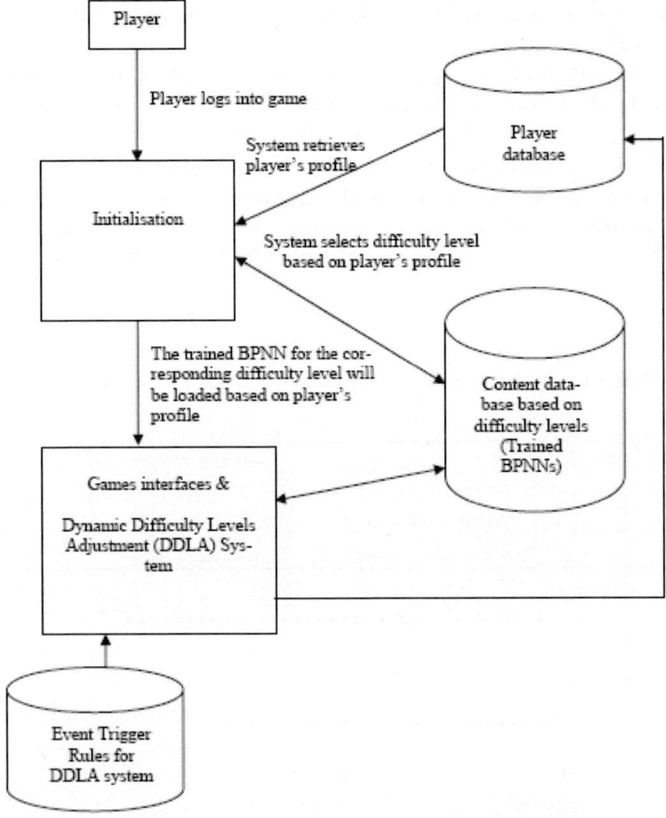

Fig. 2. Adaptive Difficulty Level Adjustment

Figure 2 shows the framework for the adaptive difficulty level adjustment system. When a player logs in and selects dynamic difficulty level adjustment setting when starting the game, the player will be loaded with their personalized difficulty levels. For discussion purpose in this paper, we use "easy", "normal" and "difficult" for the levels. If the player logs into the game for the first time, the default difficulty levels setting will be loaded. In this case, the default "Easy" setting will be set as when the AI opponent's accuracy is 20%, "normal" as 50%, and "difficult" as 95%. If the player has played the game before, the previous difficulty level before they ended the last session of the game play will be saved into the "student database", see Figure 2.

The adaptive system relies on the events trigger system, a.k.a the DDLA system in Figure 2 The trigger events could trigger the system to select a more difficult or easier level from the "Content database". This is determined by the predefined parameters store in the "Event Trigger Rules" database in Figure 2. One of the triggering rules could be "If the health of the player is low, and the play time for this level is short then select one level down". In this case, if the level is easy and set to 20%, it will go to the "Content database" and load the BPNN that can exhibit the 15% accuracies into the game interface. In this case, the difficulty level is dynamically adjusted and hopefully with the reduced difficulty level, the player can manage the game play better.

With the DDLA system, there will be some delay when the game wants to swap the BPNNs in and out of the game interface. The designer could design such that when the game need to do the swapping, a piece of low resolution movie is played. Alternatively, the designer could also just maintain the screen with some static objects and remove the dynamic AI objects until the swapping has finished. With this DDLA system, it could also manage the time game player spend on the game. If it is realized that the play time is too long, the difficulty level could increase slightly to shorten the time of the game play.

4 Simulation

A simple game is created for the purpose of the simulation. This game simulates a military warplane on a bombing run. The human player (and the computer opponent) will take turns in assuming control of a military aircraft, which will fly in at random altitudes above ground, and at random speeds. The plane will carry a bomb, and the objective of this game (for both the human and computer player) is to drop the bomb onto a target tank which appears on the ground. See Figure 3 for an example of the game caputure.

Separate scores are kept for both the human and computer player, and the respective scores are incremented every time when either of the players has a successful hit on the target tanks. The plane's velocities and altitudes above ground will also be shown, as well as the distance from the tank where the bomb was released. The 2 players will take turns to try and destroy the tank with their planes.

Every time when the player starts the games, he/she will be asked to identify himself/herself. After which, the player can select from the three settings available; namely "easy", "normal" and "difficult". After this, the personalised ANN agent designated to serve the respective player will be loaded and used to determine the difficulty level.

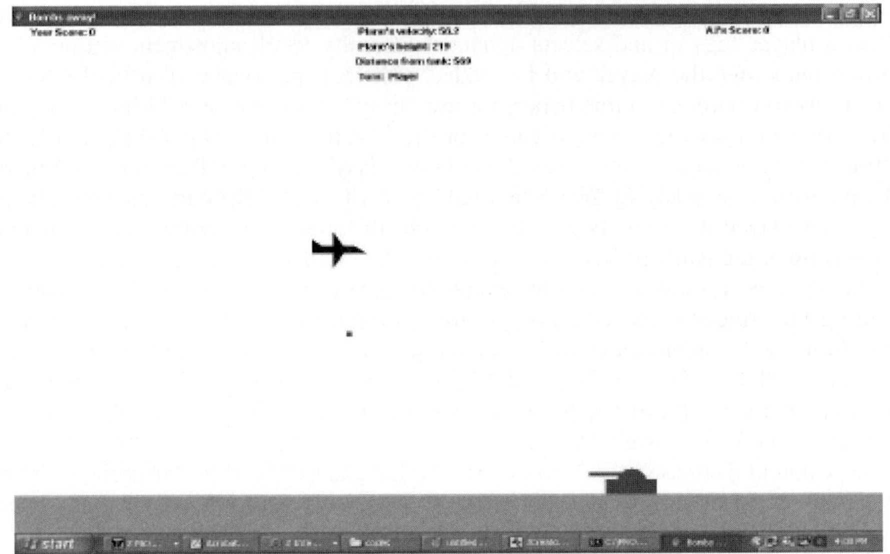

Fig. 3. Example of the game screen

By default, and when the player first encountered the personalised ANN agent, the difficulty level is set as follows. "Easy" setting will be set as when the computer opponent's accuracy is 20%, "normal" as 50%, and "difficult" as 95%.

For the ease of testing, we started off with only 2 inputs to the BPNN, which is the scaled vertical displacement between the plane and the target tank, and the scaled velocity of the plane. There is only one output from the intelligent personalised ANN agent, which is a ratio used to multiply with the full range of the horizontal distance between the plane and the target tank. The result will give the actual distance from the target tank, within which to release the bomb.

Before the intelligent ANN agent can be used, we need to create a pool of databases that contains samples of various accuracies. We have a total of 18 databases that contains samples for accuracies range from 5% to 95% with a step of 5%. This set of data samples are recorded instances of successful and unsuccessful hits made by the plane on the target tank.

In creating the database, one can try to hard code the hit rate using formulas based on ballistic trajectories. See Figure 4 for a suggestion of some parameters.

As we want to eliminate the interference of human and to provide flexibilities in future to incorporate additional input parameters into the agent, we have used a sample collection simulation program to generate the different databases. The simulation basically performs random searches for the correct distance to release the bomb. This is performed as follows. For a given speed and height of the plane, the simulation program randomly select the distance between the plane and the tank, within which the bomb is released. Regardless whether the bomb hit the tank, the speed and height of the plane will be recorded. The distance from the tank where the bomb was

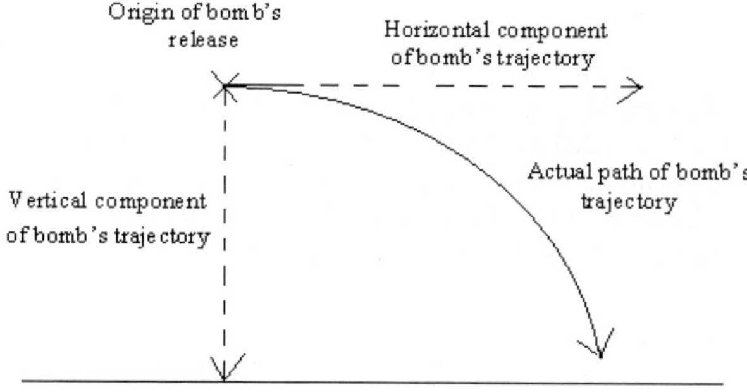

Fig. 4. Parameters used for calculations

released will also be recorded. When collecting data, no visual and sound need to be presented, the process can be speed up to be in line with the processor speed, instead of game play timing.

When creating the individual accuracies databases, the proportional of the hit and miss data are used to create that database. The total number of data used in each database is 500.

With these records, the BPNN agent will be trained to learn the association between the inputs and the outputs. When training is completed, the neural network should be able to accurately judge for itself, given a random speed and height of the plane, when to release the bomb to score a successful hit on the tank.

After the first run of the game, if the DDLA feels that even at easy level, it is still too difficult for the player to hit the tanker, swapping of database can be activated. The DDLA may lower the "easy" level to 15%. After which, the personalised ANN agent will present the behavior of a slightly worse skill player. The process continues until DDLA thinks that the player can effectively play the game. If in the later stage, the player has learned the skill, the DDLA will automatically load the appropriate percentage until a present threshold for that "easy" level. When the threshold has reached, the player will be advanced to the next level, i.e. "normal".

5 Conclusions

In this paper, we have investigated the use of AI specifically using BPNN as a software agent to create new and personalised game play experience for gamer players. The objective is to provide an adaptive computer game system which can facilitate player centred game design. The adaptive computer game system in this paper only focuses on creating personalised difficulty levels, thus with the view that not all game players will agree on the generic difficulty levels created by the game programmers or designers. We have also presented a model of organising the data warehouses and an algorithm in order to take care of the disadvantages of using BPNN for real time games due to the complexity of training.

References

1. Charles, D., McNeill, M., McAlister, M., Black, M., Moore, A., Stringer, K., Kücklich, J., Kerr, A.: Player-Centred Game Design: Player Modelling and Adaptive Digital Games. In: Proceedings of DiGRA 2005 Conference: Changing Views - Worlds in Play (2005)
2. Hunicke, R., Chapman, V.: AI for Dynamic Difficulty Adjustment in Games. In: Proceedings of Challenges in GameAI workshop, 19th National Conference on Artificial Intelligence (2004)
3. Wong, K.W., Fung, C.C., Depickere, A., Rai, S.: Static and Dynamic Difficulty Level Design for Edutainment Game Using Artificial Neural Networks. In: Proceedings of Edutainment 2006: International Conference on E-learning and Games, Hangzhou, China, April 2006, pp. 463–472 (2006)
4. Kennerly, D.: Better Game Design through Data Mining. Gamasutra.com (2003), http://www.gamasutra.com/features/20030815/kennerly_01.shtml
5. Rumelhart, D.E., Hinton, G.E., Williams, R.J.: Learning Interval Representation by Error Propagation. Parallel Distributed Processing 1, 318–362 (1986)
6. Wright, I., Marshall, J.: More AI in Less Processor Time: 'Egocentric' AI. Gamasutra.com (2000), http://www.gamasutra.com/features/20000619/wright_pfv.htm

Manifold Construction by Local Neighborhood Preservation

Cheng-Yuan Liou* and Wei-Chen Cheng

Department of Computer Science and Information Engineering
National Taiwan University
Republic of China
Supported by National Science Council
cyliou@csie.ntu.edu.tw

Abstract. This work presents a neighborhood preservation method to construct the latent manifold. This manifold preserves the relative Euclidean distances among neighboring data points. Its computation cost is close to the linear algorithm and its performance in preserving the local relationships is promising when we compared it with the methods, LLE and Isomap.

1   Background

Dimension reduction in manifold space can eliminate many difficult noises in a large dataset and configure meaningful relationships among data points. Foundations for data manifold have been set down for factorial components [5], oblique transformations [6], ICA [16], generalized adalines [17]. They have been successfully applied in various temporal data analyses [18]. Principle Component Analysis and Multidimensional Scaling (MDS) [15] are two linear models that have been developed for such reduction. Many nonlinear reduction algorithms [4][9][8][3][2] have been developed with varying degrees of success. The Isomap [14][1] extends MDS by using geodesic distance to learn the nonlinear manifold. The Locally Linear Embedding (LLE) [10] computes certain linear coefficients to maintain the local geometric properties in the manifold. Both Isomap and LLE have distinguished performance. Isomap has been extended to find intrinsic curvature manifold [12], such as a fishbowl dataset. In this paper, we present a fast learning algorithm to construct the manifold.

2   Method

2.1   Problem Description

Suppose there are P data points in a D-dimensional space, $X = \{\mathbf{x}^j, j = 1, ..., P\}$. Each point is a D-dimensional column vector, $\mathbf{x}^j \in R^D$. Let $Y = \{\mathbf{y}^j, j = 1, ..., P\}$

---

* Corresponding author.

M. Ishikawa et al. (Eds.): ICONIP 2007, Part II, LNCS 4985, pp. 683–692, 2008.
© Springer-Verlag Berlin Heidelberg 2008

be their corresponding points in the M-dimensional manifold space, where $\mathbf{y}^j$ is the corresponding point of $\mathbf{x}^j$. $\mathbf{y}^j$ is a M-dimensional column vector, $\mathbf{y}^j \in R^M$. Let $U_{k_p}(\mathbf{x}^p)$ contains the collection of all k_p neighbors of the data point $\mathbf{x}^p$. $U_{k_p}(\mathbf{x}^p)$ should be determined in advance for all data points in X. The relative distance between any two points should be calculated, that is $\{\|\mathbf{x}^i - \mathbf{x}^j\|, i, j = 1, ., P\}$. Any point, $\mathbf{x}^m$, with less value $\|\mathbf{x}^m - \mathbf{x}^p\|$ will be taken as the neighbor of $\mathbf{x}^p$ and included in the collection $U_{k_p}(\mathbf{x}^p)$. The latent relationship in X may be simple, that is $D > M$. Consider the following objective function [7],

$$E = \frac{1}{4} \sum_p \sum_{\mathbf{y}^m \in U_{k_p}(\mathbf{x}^P)} \left(\|\mathbf{y}^p - \mathbf{y}^m\|^2 - \|\mathbf{x}^p - \mathbf{x}^m\|^2 \right)^2, \tag{1}$$

where $\|\mathbf{u} - \mathbf{v}\|$ is the Euclidean distance between two vectors $\mathbf{u}$ and $\mathbf{v}$, that is

$$\|\mathbf{u} - \mathbf{v}\| = \left(\sum_i (u_i - v_i)^2 \right)^{\frac{1}{2}}. \tag{2}$$

Each manifold point, $\mathbf{y}^p$, will be forced to maintain the same distance relationship, $\|\mathbf{x}^p - \mathbf{x}^m\|^2$, in the M-dimensional space when the value E of the objective function (1) is reduced. It is cost to minimize E (1) using any relaxation methods. We present an iteration method to decrease E efficiently.

2.2   The Iterative Method

Using the known positions of neighbors in the M space to locate the position of a new point, $\mathbf{y}^p$, is a maneuver way. After the position of this new point is decided, it can be used to locate the output of its neighbors. The main algorithm is as follows:

Algorithm

1. Construct the neighbor collection, $V(m)$, for each point $\mathbf{x}^m$ where $V(m) = \{\mathbf{x}^p | \mathbf{x}^m \in U_{k_p}(\mathbf{x}^p)\}$.
   Point $\mathbf{x}^m$ has a connection to point $\mathbf{x}^p$ if $\mathbf{x}^m$ is one of k_p neighbors of $\mathbf{x}^p$. Neighbors can be prepared in advance by the measure of Euclidean distance but not limited to it.

2. Initialize a waiting-queue as a priority queue, a point's priority depends on how many among the k_p neighbors of the point have been determined.
   Initially, none of the point has its corresponding point. Let X^m be the collection of all points that have their corresponding points in Y and X^c be the collection that contains those points that have no corresponding point determined yet. X^m is empty initially and X^c contains the all data points. X^m and X^c contain all points, $X^m \cup X^c = X$. A point with more number of computed neighbors in X^m has stronger supports, hence has higher priority. When we dequeue, we pick the point with the highest priority. If there is more than one point with the same highest priority, we randomly pick one among them.

3. Randomly pick one point $\mathbf{x}^s$ from input space and set it to be at the origin of the M-dimensional manifold space, that is, $\mathbf{y}^s = \mathbf{0}$. Then add all elements in $V(\mathbf{x}^s)$ into the waiting-queue.

   The algorithm starts from point $\mathbf{x}^s$ and computes its neighbors' corresponding points iteratively. Now X^m contains only one element $\mathbf{x}^s$ and X^c contains the rest $P-1$ points. Set iteration number $t=1$.

4. Dequeue a point $\mathbf{x}^p$ from the waiting-queue and pick one of its neighbor point $\mathbf{x}^q$, $\mathbf{x}^q \in X^c$ and $\mathbf{x}^q \in V(\mathbf{x}^q)$, into waiting-queue if q is not in the waiting-queue yet.

   For convenience, we define a collection $U_{k_p}^t(\mathbf{y}^p)$, that contains k_p^t computed neighbor points of $\mathbf{y}^p$ among X^m. k_p^t is a pre-defined parameter. Therefore the number of total points in current collection $U_{k_p}^t(\mathbf{y}^p)$ is k_p^t. If we know that the size of X^m is less than k_p^t, then $U_{k_p}^t(\mathbf{y}^p)$ may contain all points of X^m.

5. Retrieve the corresponding points in $U_{k_p}^t(\mathbf{y}^p)$.

   Their vector representations are $\{\mathbf{y}^i, \mathbf{y}^i \in U_{k_p}^t(\mathbf{y}^p)\}$.

6. Determine $\mathbf{y}^p$ by minimizing the objective function (3) using the neighbors in $U_{k_p}^t(\mathbf{y}^p)$. $\mathbf{y}^p$ is the corresponding point of $\mathbf{x}^p$ in the M-dimensional manifold space.

   For the point $\mathbf{x}^p$, we use the following objective function

$$E^p = \frac{1}{4} \sum_{\mathbf{y}^p \in U_{k_p}^t(\mathbf{y}^p)} \left(\|\mathbf{y}^p - \mathbf{y}^q\|^2 - \|\mathbf{x}^p - \mathbf{x}^q\|^2 \right)^2 , \tag{3}$$

   where $\mathbf{y}^p$ and $\mathbf{y}^q$ are the corresponding points of $\mathbf{x}^p$ and $\mathbf{x}^q$ respectively. $\mathbf{y}^p$ is the desired variable. After $\mathbf{y}^p$ has been determined, point $\mathbf{x}^p$ is added to X^m, and X^c removes the point $\mathbf{x}^p$ from its collection. Set the iteration number $t=t+1$.

7. If there are more elements in the waiting-queue, repeat from step 4.

The time complexity of this algorithm is roughly the total number of all relative distances, that is, $O\left(DP^2\right)$, plus the number of neighbors of each point, $O\left(k_p P^2\right)$. When the dimension D is huge, D will be a dominate factor. Note that the time complexity of calculating all corresponding points is $O\left(cP\right)$ where c is the time complexity required for calculating one corresponding point.

   In Step 6 of the algorithm, the gradient $\frac{\partial E^p}{\partial \mathbf{y}^p}$ is

$$\frac{\partial E^p}{\partial \mathbf{y}^p} = \left(\mathbf{y}^p \mathbf{1}^T - \mathbf{B}\right)\mathbf{e} . \tag{4}$$

In the above equation, the error vector $\mathbf{e}$ is

$$\mathbf{e} = diag\left(\left(\mathbf{y}^p \mathbf{1}^T - \mathbf{B}\right)^T \left(\mathbf{y}^p \mathbf{1}^T - \mathbf{B}\right)\right) - \mathbf{d} . \tag{5}$$

The rectangular matrix $\mathbf{B}$ contains all computed neighbors $\{\mathbf{y}^i, \mathbf{y}^i \in U_{k_p}^t(\mathbf{y}^p)\}$ in its columns, that is, $\mathbf{B} = \left[.., \mathbf{y}^i, ..,\right]$. $\mathbf{B}$ is a M by k_p^t matrix. The unit column vector, $\mathbf{1}$, is $\mathbf{1} = [1, \ldots, 1]^T$. $\mathbf{1}$ is an M by 1 vector. T means transpose. The column vector $\mathbf{d}$ contains the element $d_q = \|\mathbf{x}^p - \mathbf{x}^q\|^2$ in its qth entry, $\mathbf{d} = [.., d_q, ..]^T$. $\mathbf{d}$ is a k_p^t by 1 vector. Note that $\mathbf{y}^q \in U_{k_p}^t(\mathbf{y}^p)$. Note that E^p has a compact form, $E^p = \frac{1}{4}\mathbf{e}^T\mathbf{e}$.

Following the descent direction of this gradient to decrease E^p, $\mathbf{y}^p$ is trained by the following equation.

$$\mathbf{y}^p \longleftarrow \mathbf{y}^p - \eta\frac{\partial E^p}{\partial \mathbf{y}^p}, \tag{6}$$

where η is the training rate. Usually this gradient descent method converges slowly. We use the Gauss-Newton method to update $\mathbf{y}^p$ to improve its training speed.

2.3 Gauss-Newton Method

Let t represent the number of updating iterations. Since $\mathbf{e}$ is a function of $\mathbf{y}^p$, we linearize the dependence of $\mathbf{e}(t)$ on $\mathbf{y}^p$ by writing

$$\mathbf{e}'(t, \mathbf{y}^p) = \mathbf{e}(t) + \mathbf{J}(t)(\mathbf{y}^p - \mathbf{y}^p(t)). \tag{7}$$

$\mathbf{J}(t)$ is an $k_p^t - \mathrm{by} - M$ Jacobian matrix of $\mathbf{e}$,

$$\mathbf{J}(t) = \begin{bmatrix} \frac{\partial e_1}{\partial y_1^p} & \cdots & \frac{\partial e_1}{\partial y_M^p} \\ \vdots & \ddots & \vdots \\ \frac{\partial e_{k_p^t}}{\partial y_1^p} & \cdots & \frac{\partial e_{k_p^t}}{\partial y_M^p} \end{bmatrix} = 2\left[\mathbf{y}^p\mathbf{1}^T - \mathbf{B}\right]^T. \tag{8}$$

The square of Euclidean norm of $\mathbf{e}'(t, \mathbf{y}^p)$ is

$$\frac{1}{2}\|\mathbf{e}'(t, \mathbf{y}^p)\|^2 = \frac{1}{2}\mathbf{e}^T(t)\mathbf{e}(t) + \mathbf{e}^T(t)\mathbf{J}(t)(\mathbf{y}^p - \mathbf{y}^p(t)) \tag{9}$$

$$+ \frac{1}{2}(\mathbf{y}^p - \mathbf{y}^p(t))^T\mathbf{J}^T(t)\mathbf{J}(t)(\mathbf{y}^p - \mathbf{y}^p(t)).$$

Then we differentiate (9) with respect to $\mathbf{y}^p(t)$ and set it to 0,

$$\mathbf{J}^T(t)\mathbf{e}(t) + \mathbf{J}^T(t)\mathbf{J}(t)(\mathbf{y}^p - \mathbf{y}^p(t)) = 0. \tag{10}$$

Solve the above equation and get

$$\mathbf{y}^p(t+1) = \mathbf{y}^p(t) - \left(\mathbf{J}(t)^T\mathbf{J}(t)\right)^{-1}\mathbf{J}(t)^T\mathbf{e}(t). \tag{11}$$

In order to calculate the inverse of $\mathbf{J}(t)^T\mathbf{J}(t)$ in each iteration t, the rank has to be M. To prevent insufficient rank, we add $\delta\mathbf{I}$ to $\mathbf{J}(t)^T\mathbf{J}(t)$ to get a modified method. Rewrite (11) as

$$\mathbf{y}^p(t+1) = \mathbf{y}^p(t) - \left(\mathbf{J}(t)^T\mathbf{J}(t) + \delta\mathbf{I}\right)^{-1}\mathbf{J}(t)^T\mathbf{e}(t), \tag{12}$$

where $\mathbf{I}$ is the identity matrix, δ is a small positive constant chosen to conform the rule such that $\mathbf{J}(t)^T\mathbf{J}(t) + \delta\mathbf{I}$ must be positive definite. In the case of dimension

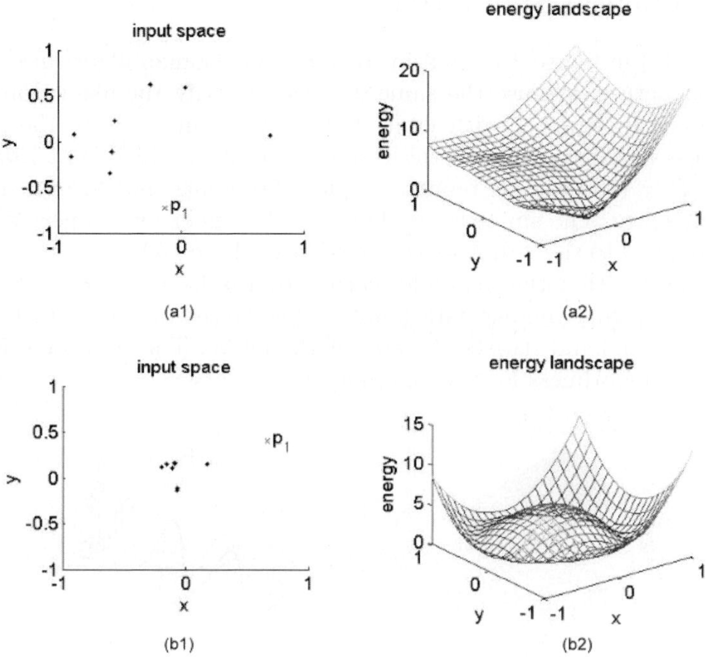

Fig. 1. The points are plotted in the xy plane at z=0. Black dots are the 8 neighbors and cross sign denotes $\mathbf{x}^p$. (a1) Neighbors surround $\mathbf{x}^p$ sparsely. (a2) There is only one minimum in this situation. (b1) Neighbors are close to each other and $\mathbf{x}^p$ is far away from the neighbors. (b2) It forms a circular valley, but there is only one minimum.

reduction, M is always small. Due to local distance preservation, k_p^t is usually small too. Therefore, $\left(\mathbf{J}\left(t\right)^T \mathbf{J}\left(t\right)\right)^{-1}$ in (12) only requires the calculation for a M−by−M matrix. The cost for updating is

$$c = \#iteration \times O\left(M^3 + M^2 k_p^t\right),$$

where M^3 is the time complexity for inverse matrix and $M^2 k_p^t$ is the time complexity for matrix multiplication.

2.4   Examples on Local Surfaces of E^p

Figure 1 shows two examples of energy landscapes of $E^p(3)$. The eight black dots are the computed neighbors contained in the current collection $U_{k_p}^t\left(\mathbf{x}^p\right)$. $\mathbf{x}^p$ is labeled by a cross sign. In this figure, $D = 3$, $M = 2$ and $k_p^t = 8$. The error surfaces E^p are not very complex and suitable for the method. When the algorithm falls into a local minimum, one may reset the initial value of $\mathbf{y}^p$ in Step 6. We can easily find a better updation through few resets.

3   Experimental Simulation

The dataset [13] in figure 2 is used in to show that Isomap algorithm can learn the global structure. We use the same dataset to verify the algorithm and the result is shown in figure 2 with lable 'LDP'. We compare it to the result by LLE, which is at lower left, and the result by Isomap, which is at lower right. Among the $P = 1500$ sample points, we pick 100 points that form a sine curve in the 3-dim space. The sin curve is shown in the upper left corner. When this dataset is mapped to the 2-dim space, we connect those 100 points that form the sine curve. We see that the manifold learned by the Isomap does not maintain the local relationships among data points. This causes the curve to be jagged. LLE on the other hand, twists the size of the curve. The proposed algorithm maintains the smoothness locally and globally.

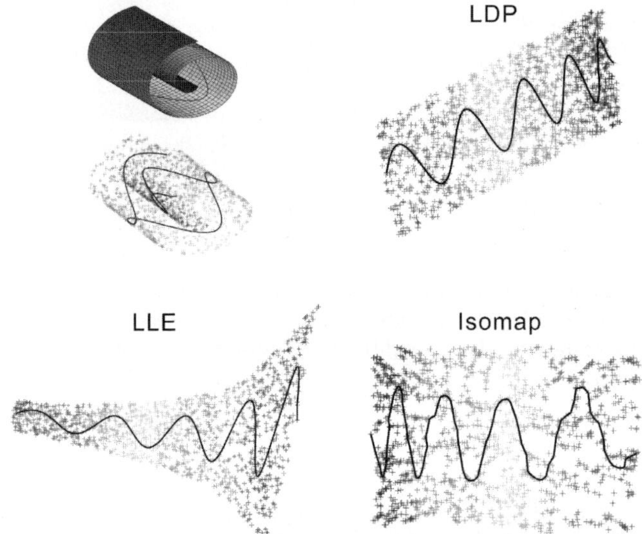

Fig. 2. 3D dataset sampled from 2D manifold. Input data has 1500 points in total. The LDP image shows the latent manifold found by proposed algorithm with $k_p = k_p^t = 10$. The proposed algorithm preserves the local relative relationships in the original space and correctly recovers the hidden variable within the dataset. The color shows the correspondence of data points in the input space and the output space. We set $k = 7$ for Isomap and $k = 12$ for LLE.

Figure 3 shows the execution times of LDP and LLE. The program code of LLE is obtained from [19] and that of Isomap is obtained from [20]. All three methods are coded in MATLAB. The execution time of Isomap is much more than the other two, so we don't include it in this figure. From this figure, we see that proposed algorithm has speed comparable to LLE.

Another experiment is that we rotate a 3D model in two axes and randomly sample 400 images of $51 \times 81 = 4131$ pixels with Azimuth $-20° \sim 20°$ and

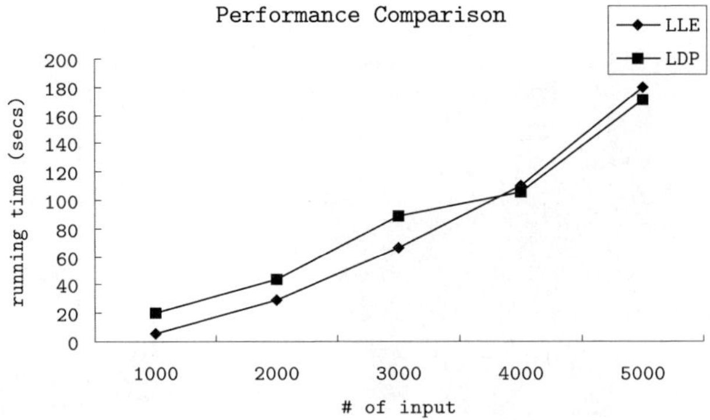

Fig. 3. Execution time of LDP and LLE. Data are ten times averages of algorithm execution.

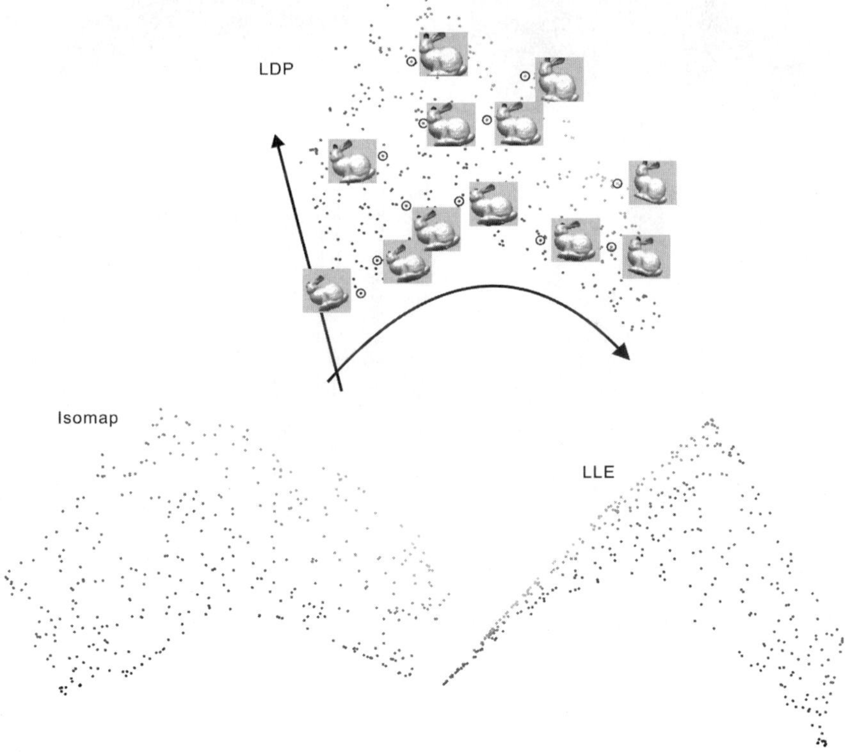

Fig. 4. Map 4131 dimensions to two dimensions. The curved horizontal axis corresponds to azimuth and the straight vertical axis is elevation. Color represents the rotation angle. The closer the color is to green, the larger the azimuth. We use $k = 15$ for Isomap and LLE and $k_p = k_p^t = 15$ for LDP.

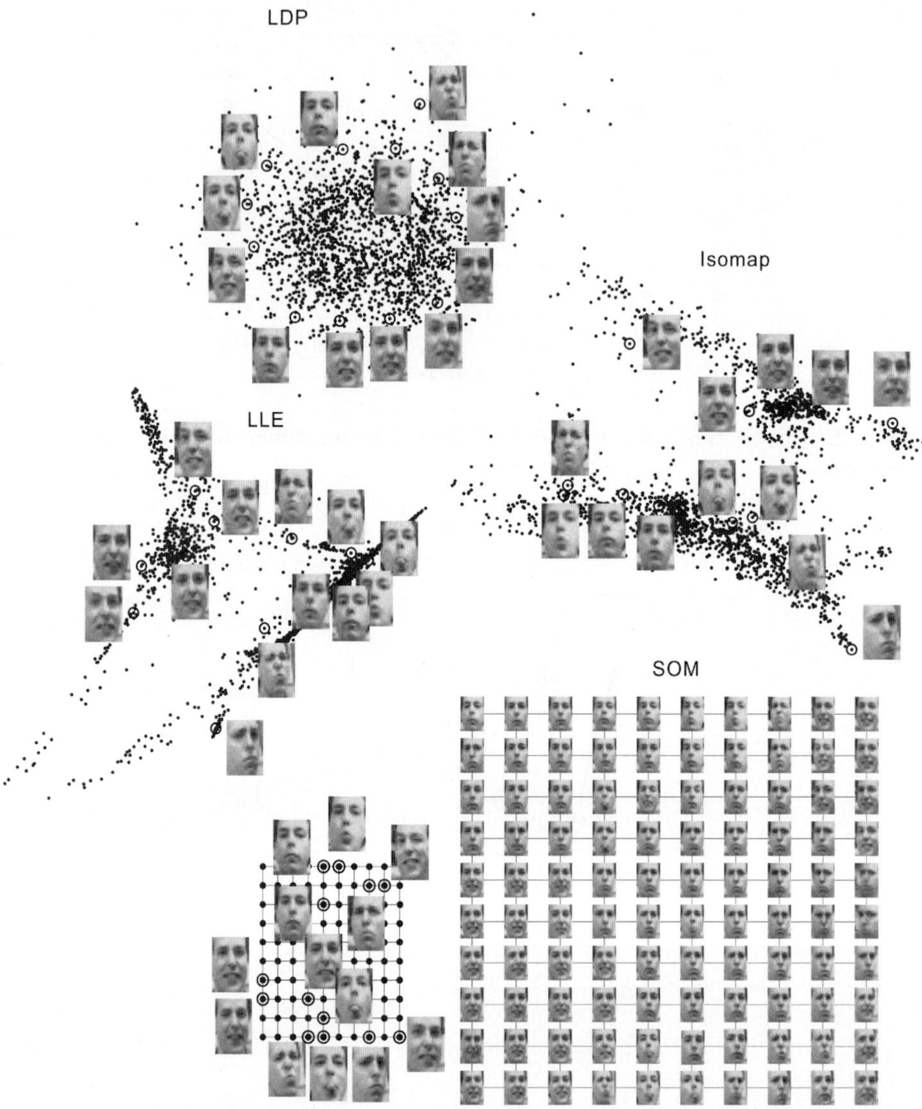

Fig. 5. The result of four algorithms which map facial expression images from 560 dimensions to two dimensional space. Thirteen randomly selected images are illustrated in two dimensional space for each algorithm. After training by SOM[4], images which are represented by neurons are shown in the grid form at the right hand side and those thirteen images next to the activated neurons are at the left hand side.

Elevation $-20° \sim 0°$. The result is shown in figure 4. The algorithm finds the two dimensional relationship from the $D = 4131$ dimensions. This can be used to model the motion of the object without any segmentation work. When we compare the algorithm with Isomap and LLE, we see that the result is similar to Isomap but the performance is much better.

In the last experiment, we test the algorithm on real face data. The data are facial expression images in [10]. We exam four algorithms on this dataset which contains 1965 images and includes smile, sad, comical facial expression. We briefly describe the basic parameters setting of those algorithms. The program of SOM randomly select 400 images for training from the whole dataset at the beginning of each epoch. There are totally 1000 epochs and the effective region of the neighborhood function shrinks linearly. We set $k = 12$ for LLE, $k = 16$ for Isomap, and $k_p = k_p^t = 30$ for LDP. We map those images to two dimensional space to see and to compare the result which is shown in figure 5. The mapping shows the distance relation of different facial expression.

4   Summary

To operate Isomap, one needs to calculate the shortest path, which has $O\left(P^3\right)$ time complexity. Execution time increases proportional to the cube of data size, which is unattractive for large scale data. A research has been done in [11] showing that LLE needs to solve a very large $P \times P$ eigen decomposition problem. The time complexity for solving this problem with brutal force is $O\left(MP^2\right)$.

When the input dimensionality is high, LLE takes most of time to find the neighbors in which the time complexity is $O\left(DP^2\right)$.

LDP's time complexity is dominated by neighbor lookup, which is $O\left(DP^2\right)$. Calculating the corresponding point has time complexity $O((M^3+M^2k)P)$. Cost of LDP is usually dominated by the square of input data size. There are some more improvements to be done such as solving the unstable property, the different results caused by different initial points and the occasional folding problem. We know that Isomap and LLE have been applied in many fields, such as identification of facial expression and representation of semantic space. Our method can find the most appropriate global structure and maintain local structure. In computer vision, LDP does not need segmentation and edge detection to find the 2D parameters of object movement from a series of images.

References

1. Balasubramanian, M., Schwartz, E.L.: The Isomap Algorithm and Topological Stability. Science 295, 5552 (2002)
2. Belkin, M., Niyogi, P.: Laplacian Eigenmaps for Dimensionality Reduction and Data Representation. Neural Computation 6, 1373–1396 (2003)
3. Bishop, C.M., Svensen, M., Williams, C.K.I.: GTM: The Generative Topographic Mapping. NCRG/96/015 (1997)
4. Kohonen, T.: Self-Organization and Associative Memory, 2nd edn., pp. 119–157. Springer, Berlin (1988)

5. Liou, C.Y., Musicus, B.R.: Separable cross-entropy approach to power spectrum estimation. IEEE Transactions on Acoustics, Speech and Signal Processing 38, 105–113 (1990)
6. Liou, C.Y., Musicus, B.R.: Cross entropy approximation of structured covariance matrices. arXiv (2006),
   http://arxiv.org/PS_cache/cs/pdf/0608/0608121v1.pdf
7. Liou, C.Y., Chen, H.T., Huang, J.C.: Separation of internal representations of the hidden layer. In: Proceedings of the International Computer Symposium, ICS, Workshop on Artificial Intelligence, Chiayi, Taiwan, December 6-8, pp. 26–34 (2000)
8. Liou, C.Y., Tai, W.P.: Conformal Self-Organization for Continuity on a Feature Map. Neural Networks 12, 893–905 (1999)
9. Liou, C.Y., Tai, W.P.: Conformality in the Self-Organization Network. Artificial Intelligence 116, 265–286 (2000)
10. Roweis, S.T., Saul, L.K.: Nonlinear Dimensionality Reduction by Locally Linear Embedding. Science 290, 2323–2326 (2000)
11. Saul, L., Roweis, S.: Think Globally, Fit Locally: Unsupervised Learning of Low Dimensional Manifolds. Journal of Machine Learning Research 4, 119–155 (2003)
12. Silva, V., Tenenbaum, J.B.: Unsupervised Learning of Curved Manifolds. In: Nonlinear Estimation and Classification, Springer, New York (2002)
13. Tenenbaum, J.: Advances in Neural Information Processing 10. In: Jordan, M., Kearns, M., Solla, S. (eds.), pp. 682–688. MIT Press, Cambridge (1998)
14. Tenenbaum, J., Silva, V., Langford, J.C.: A Global Geometric Framework for Nonlinear Dimensionality Reduction. Science 290, 2319–2323 (2000)
15. Torgerson, W.S.: Multidimensional Scaling, I: Theory and Method. Psychometrika 17, 401–419 (1952)
16. Wu, J.M., Chiu, S.J.: Independent component analysis using Potts models. IEEE Transactions on Neural Networks 12, 202–212 (2001)
17. Wu, J.M., Lin, Z.H., Hsu, P.H.: Function approximation using generalized adalines. IEEE Transactions on Neural Networks 17, 541–558 (2006)
18. Wu, J.M., Lu, C.Y., Liou, C.Y.: Independent component analysis of correlated neuronal responses in area MT. In: International Conference on Neural Information Processing, ICONIP, pp. 639–642 (2005)
19. http://www.cs.toronto.edu/~roweis/lle/
20. http://isomap.stanford.edu/

Nonparametric Time-Varying Phasor Estimation Using Neural Networks

Jaco Jordaan, Anton van Wyk, and Ben van Wyk

Tshwane University of Technology
Staatsartillerie Road, Pretoria, 0001, South Africa
{jordaan.jaco, mavanwyk, vanwykb}@gmail.com

Abstract. A new approach to nonparametric signal modelling techniques for tracking time-varying phasors of voltage and current in power systems is investigated. A first order polynomial is used to approximate these signals locally on a sliding window of fixed length. Non-quadratic methods to fit the linear function to the data, give superior performance over least squares methods in terms of accuracy. But these non-quadratic methods are iterative procedures and are much slower than the least squares method. A neural network is then used to model the non-quadratic methods. Once the neural network is trained, it is much faster than the least squares and the non-quadratic methods. The paper concludes with the presentation of the representative testing results.

1 Introduction

An important component for power system protection and control is the estimation of the magnitude, phase and frequency of voltage and current waveforms as they vary over time. The presence of noise and interference in the recorded waveforms are complicating efforts to estimate these values. Interference may be in the form of harmonics of the system fundamental frequency, or of inter-harmonics.

For algorithms belonging to the class of parametric estimation algorithms, the approach is to assume that the signal model is a pre-specified function, which is valid on a selected fixed data window size. One of the most common parametric approaches in designing frequency estimation algorithms is based on projecting the signal on a set of orthogonal basis functions. If these basis functions are trigonometric functions, then the outcome is the Discrete Fourier Transform (DFT) based method [1]. These basis functions are designed for the fundamental frequency and harmonics of that frequency and this causes the method to be inaccurate in practice when the fundamental frequency changes. Other classes of algorithms are: fitting the signal samples with a non-linear signal model [2] and Newton based iteration algorithms [3]. These algorithms could be computationally intensive, which makes implementation difficult.

Instead of using parametric algorithms, we could use nonparametric algorithms. The estimation is then done without reference to a specific signal model [4,5]. It could be done with a fixed or with the use of a variable window size

M. Ishikawa et al. (Eds.): ICONIP 2007, Part II, LNCS 4985, pp. 693–702, 2008.

[6], or with a variable sampling interval [7]. Another class of algorithms [1,8] is based on a transformation that divides the input voltage signals into two orthogonal components: the real and imaginary parts of the complex voltage signal. This signal is then shifted down (demodulated) with the angle representing the fundamental frequency. The demodulation is done to remove the fundamental frequency from the signal. The demodulated signal represents the deviation from the fundamental frequency. The frequency is then estimated from the instantaneous phase angle of this demodulated complex signal.

In the section 2, we use a first order Taylor polynomial model to model the demodulated signal's amplitude or phase angle. To fit the polynomial, we apply the Least Squares (LS) method and a non-quadratic method, the Quadratic-Squares-Root (QSR) method, on a central window. This means that the sample we want to estimate (smooth) is in the middle of the window. Results from [9] show that if there are outliers in the data, the QSR method will detect them, and downweight them, whereas the LS method will use the bad data just as it is. This could severely affect the accuracy of the predicted voltage waveform parameters.

The computational time of the QSR method is much longer than that of the LS method. In section 2.3 we propose the use of neural networks to model the QSR fitting of the data. Once the network is trained, the computational speed to obtain the waveform parameters is much faster than that of the QSR method. Results obtained in testing the algorithms are presented in section 3. The paper ends with a conclusion.

2   Proposed Technique

2.1   Time Varying Phasor

The Root Mean Square (RMS) value and phase angle of either the voltage or current complex phasor could be used in the calculations. We shall use the voltage in our derivations. Working with voltage sample k, we could use samples of a three-phase voltage set $(v_a(k),\ v_b(k),\ v_c(k))$ to estimate the instantaneous phase angle or magnitude. First, the orthogonal components $v_d(k)$ and $v_q(k)$ of a complex voltage signal are obtained through the Park transformation:

$$\begin{bmatrix} v_d(k) \\ v_q(k) \end{bmatrix} = \sqrt{\frac{2}{3}} \begin{bmatrix} 1 & -\frac{1}{2} & -\frac{1}{2} \\ 0 & \frac{\sqrt{3}}{2} & -\frac{\sqrt{3}}{2} \end{bmatrix} \begin{bmatrix} v_a(k) \\ v_b(k) \\ v_c(k) \end{bmatrix} \tag{1}$$

The complex voltage signal $v_d(k) + jv_q(k)$ could be represented as the sum of time-varying harmonics:

$$v_d(k) + jv_q(k) = \sqrt{3} \sum_{i \geq 0} \underline{v}_i(k) e^{jki\theta_0}, \tag{2}$$

where $\theta_0 = \omega_0 T$ is the sampling angle (digital frequency), T is the sampling interval, and $\omega_0 = 2\pi f_0$ is the nominal fundamental frequency. Next, the complex voltage signal is shifted down (demodulated) in the frequency domain to the angle value that corresponds to the nominal fundamental frequency:

$$v_m(k) = \frac{1}{\sqrt{3}} \left(v_d(k) + j v_q(k) \right) e^{-jk\theta_0}$$

$$= \underline{v}_1(k) + \sum_{i \geq 0, i \neq 1} \underline{v}_i(k) e^{jk(i-1)\theta_0}. \tag{3}$$

Finally, the time-varying RMS value and phase angle of the complex phasor $\underline{v}_m(k) = v_m(k) e^{j\phi_m(k)}$ are:

$$v_m(k) = \frac{1}{\sqrt{3}} \left| \left(v_d(k) + j v_q(k) \right) e^{-jk\theta_0} \right|, \tag{4}$$

$$\phi_m(k) = \arg \left(\frac{1}{\sqrt{3}} \left(v_d(k) + j v_q(k) \right) e^{-jk\theta_0} \right). \tag{5}$$

Note that the voltage phasor (3) consists of the slow time-varying component (positive sequence) , and the rest are fast time-varying oscillatory signals.

The frequency could be calculated by taking the derivative of the phase angle, but this leads to the amplification of noise, and therefore additional filtering is required to smooth the estimates. Alternatively, the frequency can be calculated by approximating the phase angle signal with a first order polynomial model and then take the first order coefficient as a frequency estimate.

In the next section we could model either the magnitude (4) or the phase angle (5).

2.2 First Order Polynomial Approximation

Weighted Least Squares. From a total of N available voltage samples, we are working with a window of $2w_n + 1$ samples, where the sample to be estimated is sample number $w_n + 1$, which is the sample in the middle of the interval. Let this data sample to be smoothed have index $k = 0$. The index k only refers to the samples in the window, and not to the whole data set. The window is slided over the data, and a new local polynomial approximation (LPA) model is fitted for each window. The LPA filtering of data was made popular by Savitsky and Golay [10,11]. Assume the data points are sampled with a sampling period of T seconds. In continuous time (without sampling) a simple first order power series of polynomial basis functions is given by

$$f(t) = c_0 + c_1 t, \tag{6}$$

and the sampled version of (6) would be

$$f(k) = c_0 + c_1 k T. \tag{7}$$

To solve for coefficients c_0 and c_1, we use the least-squares criterion, which defines the following objective function:

$$J = \sum_{k=-w_n}^{w_n} (y_k - f(k))^2, \tag{8}$$

where y_k is the k-th sample of either the magnitude (4) or the phase angle (5) and $f(k)$ is the estimated value of y_k. The objective function could be minimised by setting its gradient equal to zero:

$$\frac{\partial J}{\partial c_i} = 0, \; i = 0, 1. \tag{9}$$

This leads to a set of equations in the unknown coefficients c_i. Solving the least squares problem, we obtain the coefficients $\mathbf{c} = \begin{bmatrix} c_0 & c_1 \end{bmatrix}^T$ as:

$$\mathbf{c} = \begin{bmatrix} \displaystyle\sum_{k=-w_n}^{w_n} \frac{1}{2w_n+1} y_k \\ \displaystyle\frac{1}{T} \sum_{k=-w_n}^{w_n} \frac{3k}{w_n(w_n+1)(2w_n+1)} y_k \end{bmatrix} \tag{10}$$

Quadratic-Squares-Root (QSR). The least-squares criterion is the best in the maximum-likelihood sense when the errors are Gaussian. But it does not exhibit the inherent capability of filtering bad data. The use of non-quadratic criteria could be used as a means of automatically rejecting faulty data, and still provide good parameter estimates. These non-quadratic methods are iterative, and during the solution steps certain measurements which have larger residuals than a predefined break-even point β, are downweighted. The objective function of the robust criterium QSR is a function of residuals, where the residuals are defined as [12]:

$$r_k = y_k - f(k), \tag{11}$$

$$E_s = \underset{k}{median} \; |r_k|, \tag{12}$$

$$r_{s_k} = \frac{r_k}{E_s}, \tag{13}$$

where the residual r_k is the difference between the k-th measurement y_k and the computed value $f(k)$ of the corresponding measured quantity, r_{s_k} is the standardised residual and E_s is a scaling factor whose purpose is to implement robust scaling of the standardised residual.

Finally the non-quadratic objective function is defined as follows

$$J = \rho(r_{s_1}) + \rho(r_{s_2}) + \cdots + \rho\left(r_{s_{\widetilde{N}}}\right) \tag{14}$$

where $\rho(r_{s_k})$ is the non-quadratic function

$$\rho(r_{s_k}) = \begin{cases} \dfrac{r_{s_k}^2}{2} & |r_{s_k}| \leq \beta \\ 2\beta^{\frac{3}{2}}\sqrt{|r_{s_k}|} - \frac{3}{2}\beta^2 & |r_{s_k}| > \beta \end{cases}, \tag{15}$$

and $\widetilde{N} = 2w_n + 1$ is the number of data samples in the current window. To solve the parameters c_i of eq. (7), apply eq. (9) to eq. (14). The resulting set of equations should be solved to find parameters c_i.

As already mentioned, the non-quadratic methods are iterative. An iterative procedure could be used and better iterates of vector $\mathbf{c}$ could be calculated by

$$\mathbf{c}_{j+1} = \mathbf{c}_j + \boldsymbol{\Delta}\mathbf{c}_j, \tag{16}$$

where $\boldsymbol{\Delta}\mathbf{c}_j = [\Delta c_0^{(j)} \quad \Delta c_1^{(j)}]^T$ is used to update $\mathbf{c}_j$ at the j-th iteration. The expressions for the update $\boldsymbol{\Delta}\mathbf{c}_j$ is given by [9]

$$\boldsymbol{\Delta}\mathbf{c} = \begin{bmatrix} \displaystyle\sum_{k=-w_n}^{w_n} h_0\left(w_n, f_i, k\right)\sqrt{q_k}r_k \\[2em] \dfrac{1}{T}\displaystyle\sum_{k=-w_n}^{w_n} h_1\left(w_n, f_i, k\right)\sqrt{q_k}r_k \end{bmatrix}, \tag{17}$$

$$h_0 = \frac{2w_n^3 + 3w_n^2 + w_n +}{4w_n^4 + 8w_n^3 + 5w_n^2 + w_n + 6f_2w_n + 3f_2 +} \cdots$$
$$\frac{3f_2 - 3f_1 k}{2f_0w_n^3 + 3f_0w_n^2 + f_0w_n + 3f_0f_2 - 3f_1^2}, \tag{18}$$

$$h_1 = 3\frac{2kw_n - f_1 +}{4w_n^4 + 8w_n^3 + 5w_n^2 + w_n + 6f_2w_n + 3f_2 +} \cdots$$
$$\frac{k + f_0 k}{2f_0w_n^3 + 3f_0w_n^2 + f_0w_n + 3f_0f_2 - 3f_1^2}, \tag{19}$$

$$q_k = \begin{cases} 1 & |r_{s_k}| \le \beta \\ \beta^{\frac{3}{2}}\dfrac{1}{|r_{s_k}|\sqrt{|r_{s_k}|}} & |r_{s_k}| > \beta \end{cases}, \tag{20}$$

$$f_i = \sum_{k \in \widetilde{\beta}} k^i \alpha_k, \quad i = 0, 1, 2, \tag{21}$$

$\widetilde{\beta}$ is the set of indices that represent all the scaled residuals larger than β, and α_k is a function of the scaled residuals larger than β:

$$\alpha_k = \sqrt{\frac{\beta^{\frac{3}{2}}}{|r_{s_k}|\sqrt{|r_{s_k}|}} - 1} \tag{22}$$

2.3   Neural Network

An artificial neural network (ANN) [13] is a system composed of many simple processing elements operating in parallel whose function is determined by network structure, connection strengths and the processing performed at computing elements or nodes. Artificial neural networks generally consist of three layers: input, hidden and output. Each layer consists of one or more nodes. The inputs to each node in input and hidden layers are multiplied with proper weights and summed together. The weighted composite sum is passed through a proper transfer function whose output is the network output. Typical transfer functions are Sigmoid and Hyperbolic Tangent. For an example of a neural network, see Fig. 1.

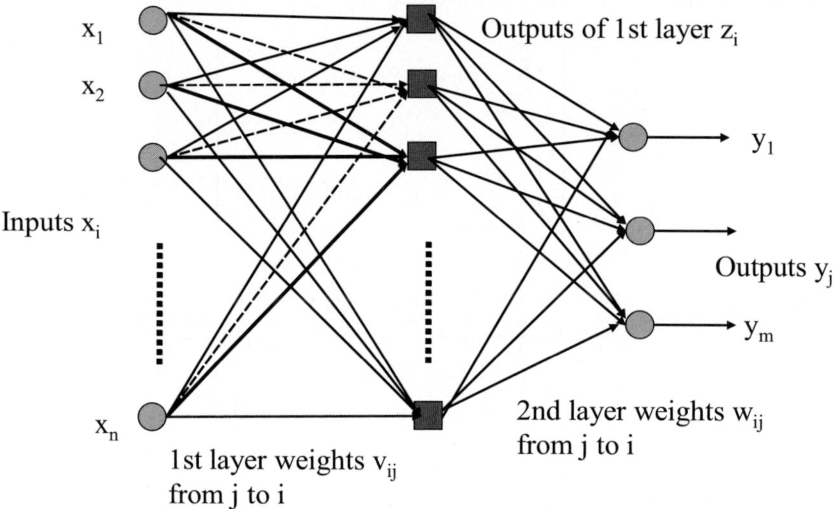

Fig. 1. Artificial Neural Network (borrowed from [14])

A neural network could be used to predict the coefficients of the linear polynomial. The input data will then be the $2w_n + 1$ samples in the current data window and the output will be c_0 and c_1, the two coefficients of the linear polynomial in eq. (7). Thus, the input is a $(2w_n + 1)$ - dimensional vector and the output is a two-dimensional vector.

3   Numerical Results

For this experiment we used a Back-propagation Multi-layer Perceptron neural network with one hidden layer containing 34 nodes. The MATLAB Neural Network toolbox [15] was used for implementation. To evaluate the performance of the different networks, we define two performance indices, the Mean Absolute Prediction Error (MAPE):

$$MAPE = \frac{1}{N} \sum_{i=1}^{N} |t_i - p_i| , \tag{23}$$

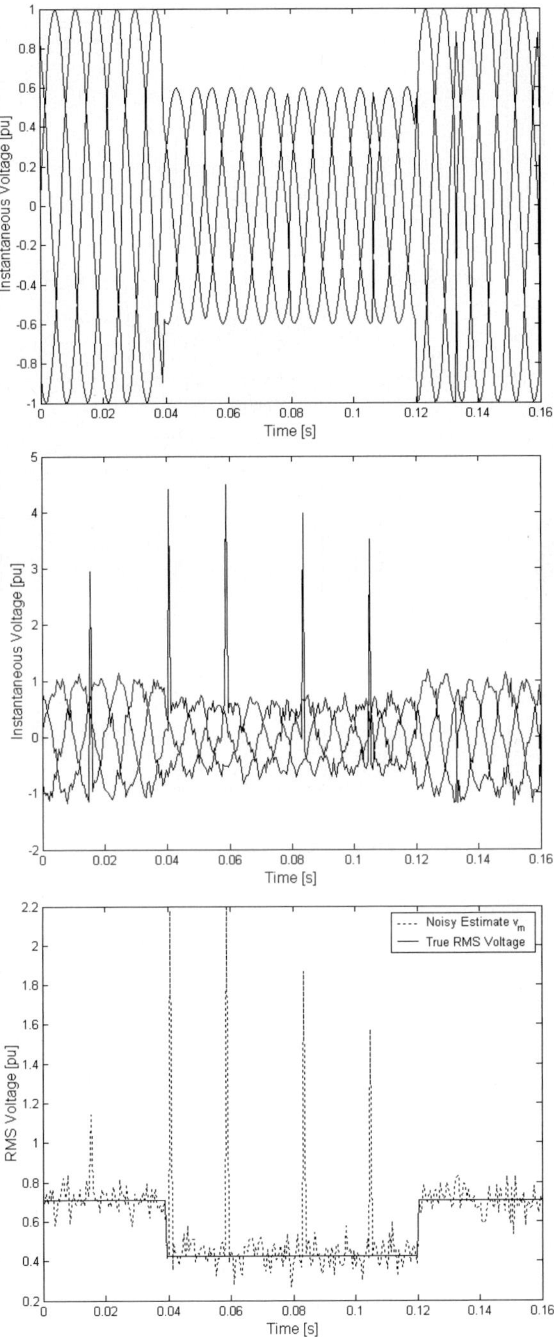

Fig. 2. Three-phase signals with and without noise and harmonics during voltage drop conditions. True RMS and noisy estimate using equation (4).

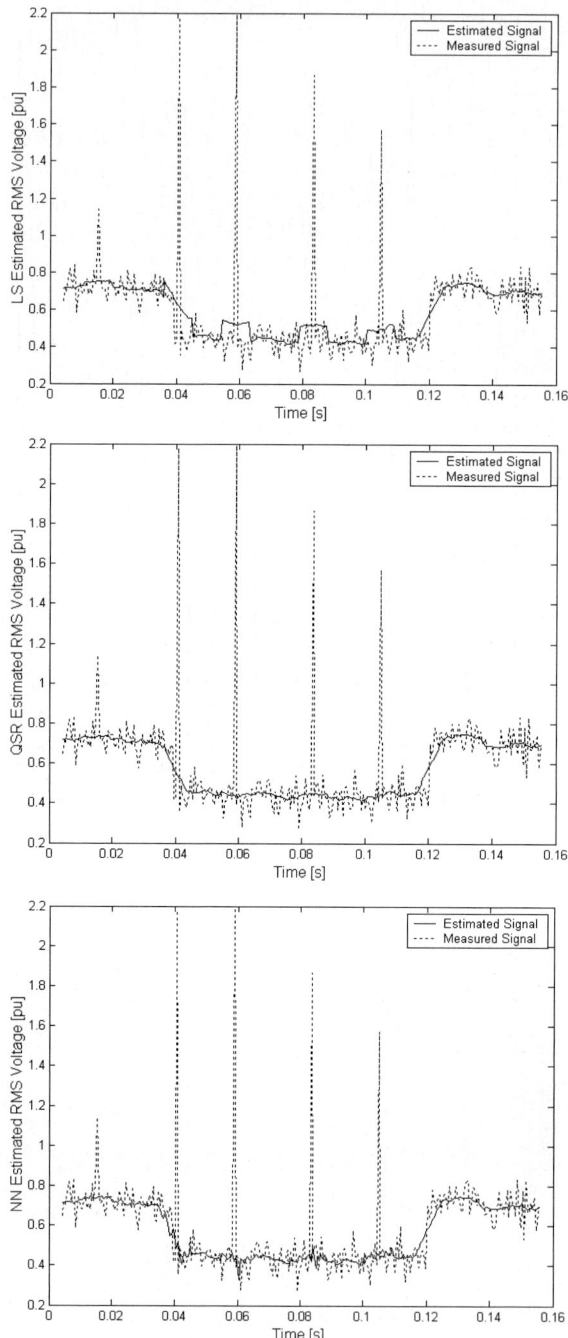

Fig. 3. Noisy RMS and the estimated RMS value using the Neural Network, LS and QSR methods

and the Median Absolute Prediction Error (MeAPE), which is the median of the absolute prediction error $|\mathbf{t} - \mathbf{p}|$, where t_i is the i-th sample of the vector $\mathbf{t}$ of true values of the voltage amplitude (or phase angle), p_i is the i-th predicted value, and N is the total number of predicted samples.

A voltage drop shown in Figure 2 can occur in power systems due to faults and switching operations. Figure 2 also shows the three-phase voltage signals corrupted with voltage spikes and normally distributed noise with zero mean and standard deviation equal to 10%. This figure also shows the true RMS value and noisy estimate using equation (4). The sampling frequency of the voltage drop scenario is 1869.2 Hz, the number of samples used are 300 and the window length parameter is $w_n = 8$. This implies that the ANN input signal has a dimension of 17. For this scenario we will demonstrate the methods on the RMS value of the voltage. The methods could also be used to estimate the phase angle, from which the frequency could be calculated.

The results of the RMS voltage estimation using the neural network, LS and QSR methods are presented in Figure 3. Table 1 shows the overall performance of the three methods. The time shown in this table is the total time to calculate the two polynomial coefficients for all the data windows as the window is sliding over the data set of 300 samples. From this figure and table it can be seen that the neural network is able to model the QSR method, which is able to downweight the outliers in the samples. But most importantly the neural network's computational time is much less than that of the QSR and LS methods. Although the the LS method is much faster than the QSR method, it tends to follow the outliers. The neural network seems to be a good replacement for the QSR method.

Table 1. Performance summaries

Method	MAPE [pu]	MeAPE [pu]	Time [s]
WLS	0.0399	0.0229	0.859
QSR	0.0238	0.0190	2.063
ANN	0.0244	0.0178	0.016

4   Conclusion

In this paper we have presented a robust local linear approximation technique for tracking time-varying phasors in power systems. This technique belongs to the class of nonparametric statistical methods where a linear model is fitted on a sliding central window by making use of the QSR or LS objective functions. It is shown that the QSR method is quite slow compared to the LS method. The disadvantage of the LS methods is that it tends to follow the outliers in the data, whereas the QSR method is able to downweight these outliers in the data and produce better results than the LS method. We proposed the use of neural networks to replace the QSR method. The neural network is trained as such that it tries to produce the same results as the QSR method. Once the neural network is trained, it is shown that the neural network is much faster to calculate the polynomial coefficients than the QSR and LS methods. It gives results comparable to that of the QSR method, and it gives much more accurate results than the LS method. Especially for real time implementation by power utilities the neural network model has a clear advantage over the LS and QSR models in terms of execution speed.

References

1. Begovic, M., et al.: Frequency tracking in power networks in the presence of harmonics. IEEE Transactions on Power Delivery 8, 480–486 (1993)
2. Sachdev, M., Giray, M.: A least squares technique for determining power system frequency. IEEE Transactions on PAS (1985)
3. Terzija, V.V., Djurić, M.B., Kovačević, B.D.: Voltage phasor and local system frequency estimation using Newton type algorithm. IEEE Transactions on Power Delivery 9, 1368–1374 (1994)
4. Terzija, V.V., Djurić, M.B., Kovačević, B.D.: A new self-tuning algorithm for the frequency estimation of distorted signals. IEEE Transactions on Power Delivery 10, 1779–1785 (1995)
5. Sidhu, T.S., Sachdev, M.S.: An iterative technique for fast and accurate measurement of power system frequency. IEEE Transactions on Power Delivery 13, 109–115 (1998)
6. Hart, D., et al.: A new frequency tracking and phasor estimation algorithm for generator protection. IEEE Transactions on Power Delivery 12, 1064–1073 (1997)
7. Benmouyal, G.: An adaptive sampling interval generator for digital relaying. IEEE Transactions on Power Delivery 4, 1602–1609 (1989)
8. Akke, M.: Frequency estimation by demodulation of two complex signals. IEEE Transactions on Power Delivery 12, 157–163 (1997)
9. Jordaan, J.A., van Wyk, M.A.: Nonparametric Time-Varying Phasor Estimation using Non-Quadratic Criterium. In: The Sixth IASTED International Conference on Modelling, Simulation, and Optimization, Gaborone, Botswana (2006)
10. Gorry, P.A.: General Least-Squares Smoothing and Differentiation by the Convolution (Savitzky-Golay) Method. Analytical Chemistry 62, 570–573 (1990)
11. Bialkowski, S.E.: Generalized Digital Smoothing Filters Made Easy by Matrix Calculations. Analytical Chemistry 61, 1308–1310 (1989)
12. Pires, R.C., Costa, A.S., Mili, L.: Iteratively Reweighted Least-Squares State Estimation Through Givens Rotations. IEEE Transactions on Power Systems 14, 1499–1506 (1999)
13. Bishop, C.M.: Neural Networks for Pattern Recognition, 1st edn. Clarendon Press, Oxford (1997)
14. Multi-Layer Perceptron (MLP), Neural Networks Lectures 5+6 (2007), http://www.cogs.susx.ac.uk/users/andrewop/Courses/NN/NNs5_6_MLP.ppt
15. Mathworks: MATLAB Documentation - Neural Network Toolbox. Version 6.5.0.180913a Release 13 edn. Mathworks Inc., Natick, MA (2002)

A New Approach for Next Day Load Forecasting Integrating Artificial Neural Network Model with Weighted Frequency Bin Blocks

M. Kurban and U. Basaran Filik

Anadolu University, Dept. of Electrical and Electronics Eng., Eskisehir, Turkey
{mkurban, ubasaran}@anadolu.edu.tr

Abstract. In this study, a new method is developed for the next day load forecasting integrating Artificial Neural Network(ANN) model with Weighted Frequency Bin Blocks (WFBB). After the WFBB is applied to all data, the results obtained from this analysis are used as the inputs in the ANN structure. However, the conventional ANN structure is also used for the next day load forecasting. The forecasting results obtained from ANN structure and the hybrid model are compared in the sense of root mean square error (RMSE). It is observed that the performance and the RMSE values for the hybrid model,the ANN model with WFBB, are smaller than the values for the conventional ANN structure. Furthermore, the new hybrid model forecasts better than the conventional ANN structure. The suitability of the proposed approach is illustrated through an application to actual load data taken from the Turkish Electric Power Company in 2002.

1   Introduction

Load forecasting is important in power system planning and operation. The main problem of the planning is the demand knowledge in the future. Basic operating functions such as hydrothermal unit commitment, economic dispatch, fuel scheduling and unit maintenance can be performed efficiently with an accurate forecast [1]. A wide variety of models have been proposed in the last decades owing to the importance of load forecasting, such as regression-based methods [2-3], Box Jenkins model [4], exponential smoothing [5], and Kalman filters [6]. However, these methods can not represent the complex nonlinear relationships [7]. Also, these methods have higher load forecasting errors in some particular time zones. The computational intelligence techniques have been developed to overcome these problems [8-13].

Many studies on the load forecasting have been made to improve the prediction accuracy using various conventional methods, such as deterministic, stochastic, knowledge based, and ANN methods. ANN methods have two advantages: one is capability of approximating any nonlinear function and the other is model determination through the learning process. The objective of this study is to develop a new method using the hybrid model which is a combination of WFBB

M. Ishikawa et al. (Eds.): ICONIP 2007, Part II, LNCS 4985, pp. 703–712, 2008.

and ANN training by Feed Forward Back Propagation (FFBP) algorithm for the next day load forecasting. The previous two-day values are used for predicting the next day values.

This paper introduces a new aprroach for next day load forecasting integrating ANN model with WFBB. First, ANN models and adaptive filters with WFBB are explained briefly in Section 2 and 3, respectively. In Section 4, next day load forecasting integrating ANN with WFBB is discussed giving the sample block diagram. Applications and simulations for next day load forecasting using the conventional ANN and the proposed approach are given in Section 5. The results that are obtained from both methods are presented.

2   Artificial Neural Network Models

An ANN operates by creating connections between many different processing elements, each analogous to a single neuron in a biological brain. Each neuron takes many input signals, then, based on an internal weighting system, produces a single output signal that's typically sent as input to another neuron. The neurons are tightly interconnected and organized into different layers. The input layer receives the input, the output layer produces the final output. A neural network is massively parallel-distributed processor made up of simple processing unit called neuron, which has a natural propensity for storing experimental knowledge and making it available for use. A back-propagation ANN, conversely, is trained by humans to perform specific tasks. During the training period, the teacher evaluates whether the ANN's output is correct. If it's correct, the neural weightings that produced that output are reinforced; if the output is incorrect, those weightings responsible are diminished. This type is most often used for cognitive research and for problem-solving applications. Feedback networks can have signals travelling in both directions by introducing loops in the network [14].

The main advantages of the ANN are:

1. Adaptive learning: An ability to learn how to do tasks based on the data given for training or initial experience.
2. Self-Organisation: An ANN can create its own organisation or representation of the information it receives during learning time.
3. Real Time Operation: ANN computations may be carried out in parallel, and special hardware devices are being designed and manifactured which take advantage of this capability.
4. Fault Tolerance via Redundant Information Coding: Partial destruction of a network leads to the corresponding degradation of performance. However, some network capabilites may be retained even with major network damage.

An ANN is configured for a specific application, such as pattern recognition or data classification, through a learning process. In order to train an ANN to perform some task, the weights of each unit are adjusted in such a way that the error between the desired output and the actual output is reduced.

3   Adaptive Filters with WFBB

Adaptive filters are the most efficient solutions for the filtering, smoothing, and prediction problems that the input signal's characteristics are not available. In most of the applications like system identification, equalization,and noise canceling, the input signal's characteristics is not available [15]. An adaptive filter is used in applications that require differing filter characteristics in response to variable signal conditions. Adaptive filters are typically used when noise occurs in the same band as the signal, or when the noise band is unknown or varies over time.

Block implementation of a Finite Impulse Response (FIR) filter allows parallel processing. Digital Signal Processing (DSP) processors are better suited to frame-based processing. By assembling the samples into blocks, the algorithm can take advantage of DSP hardware features such as Direct Memory Access (DMA) and caching to improve effective throughput. If the memory is accessed for each sample, this will slow down the processor speed. But if the memory is accessed for a block of data, DMA will increase processing speed. Fig.1 shows a schematic block diagram of processing system. A general block diagram of adaptive filter structure is given in Fig. 2 [16].

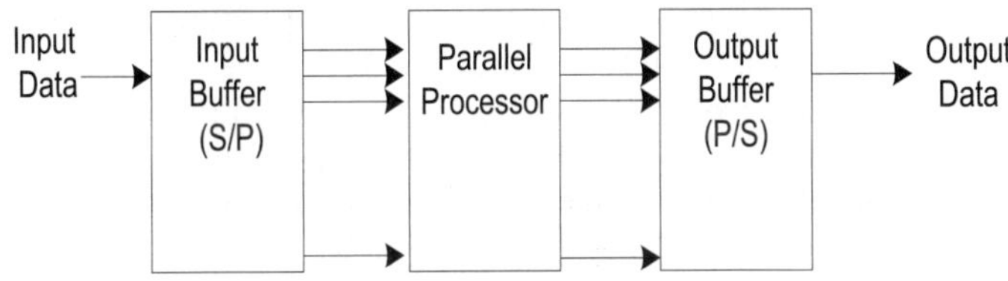

Fig. 1. Block diagram of processing system

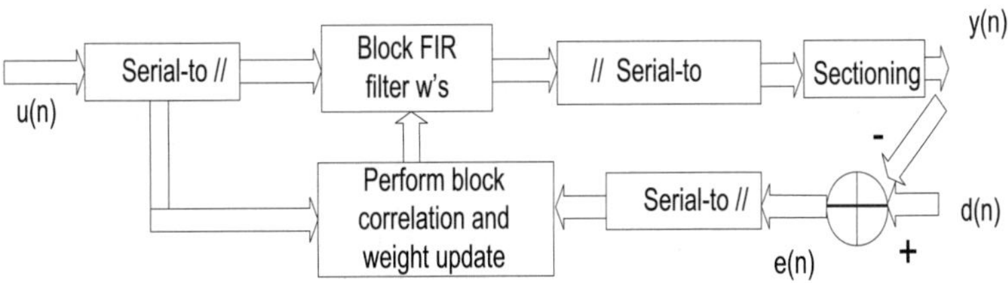

Fig. 2. General block diagram of adaptive filter structure[d(n) : desired signal, e(n) : error signal, y(n): output signal vector, u(n) : input signal vector, sectioned into L-point blocks]

In the adaptive filter, the frequency-domain error vector e_k in the kth block is given by[17]

$$e_k = d_k - \mathcal{P}_{0,L}(X_k P_{M,0} w_k) \tag{1}$$

where d_k is and w_k are the (Nx1) desired response and filter weight vectors, respectively, both in the frequency domain , and X_k is an (NxN) dioganal elementsare the transformed input data. In equation 1, the two (NxN) matrices $\mathcal{P}_{0,L}$ and $\mathcal{P}_{M,0}$ realize the sectioning procedures needed for computing the filter output and adjusting the filter weights, respectively. They are defined as

$$\mathcal{P}_{0,L} \triangleq F \begin{bmatrix} 0 & 0 \\ 0 & I_L \end{bmatrix} F^{-1} \tag{2}$$

and

$$\mathcal{P}_{M,0} \triangleq F \begin{bmatrix} I_M & 0 \\ 0 & 0 \end{bmatrix} F^{-1} \tag{3}$$

where F is the (NxN) discrete Fourier transform matrix, I_L and I_M denote (LxL) and (MxM) identity matrices, respectively, and 0 is a zero matrix. As a performance criterion in adjusting filter weights, the frequency-weighted block least mean square $\epsilon^f w$ is defined by

$$\epsilon^{fw} = E[e_k^* \Gamma e_k] \tag{4}$$

where the asterisk and E[.]denote complex conjugate transpose of a matrix and statistical expectation, respectively. In equation 4, Γ is an (NxN) dioganal matrix whose dioganal elements are of a nonnegative values and their relative magnitudes, represent the relative signifiance of each frequency component. Following the same aproach used for the least mean square adaptive filter we can have from equation 1 and equation 4 a gradient of the frequency-weighted block least mean square with respect to w_k as [18]

$$\nabla \epsilon^{fw}(w_k) = \frac{\partial \epsilon^{fw}}{\partial w_k} = -2E[P_M, X_k^* P_{0,L} \Gamma e_k] \tag{5}$$

Thus, using an instanteneously estimated gradient , we obtain from equation 5 an WFBB least mean square weight adjustment algorithm as the following:

$$w_{k+1} = w_k + \mu \mathcal{P}_{M,0} X_k^* P_{0,L} \Gamma e_k \tag{6}$$

where μ is a convergence factor controlling the convergence behaviour of the algorithm of equation 6 can be realized alternatively as

$$w_{k+1} = \mathcal{P}_{M,0}(w_k + \mu X_k^* P_{0,L} \Gamma e_k) \tag{7}$$

It is noted here that, when Γ is an identity matrix, the WFBB least mean square algorithm becomes identical to the the WFBB least mean square algorithm since $\mathcal{P}_{0,L} e_k = e_k$. Also, it is noted that, when L is sufficiently larger than M, $\mathcal{P}_{O,L}$ can be approximated as an identity matrix. In that case, one can eliminate the Fast Fourier Transform (FFT) and inverse Fast Fourier Transform (IFFT) operations that are needed just after the freguency weighting operation in the requency-weighted block least mean square adaptive filter [19].

4   Next Day Load Forecasting Integrating ANN with WFBB

The next day load forecasting is basically aimed at predicting system load with a leading time of one hour to day, which is necessary for adequate scheduling and operation of power systems. The next day load forecasting traditionally has been an essential component of Energy Management Systems (EMS) [20-22], as it provides the input data for load flow and contingency analysis. ANN-based methods are a good choice to study the next day load forecasting problem, as these techniques are characterized by not requiring explicit models to represent the complex relationship between the load and the factors that determine it.

The hybrid method of ANN model with WFBB is divided six steps:
1) FFT algorithm is applied to all given data.
2) All data found from step 1 is arranged according to the magnitude of frequency values.
3) The results of the step 2 are multiplied by appropriate weighted values. Higher frequency values of the FFT signal are multiplied lower weihgted values.
4) IFFT algorithm is applied to the results of the step 3.
5) The results of the IFFT algorithm are used for the input of the ANN Structure.
6) The outputs of ANN structure are next day load forecasting values.

The sample diagram of ANN model with WFBB for next day load forecesting is given in Fig. 3.

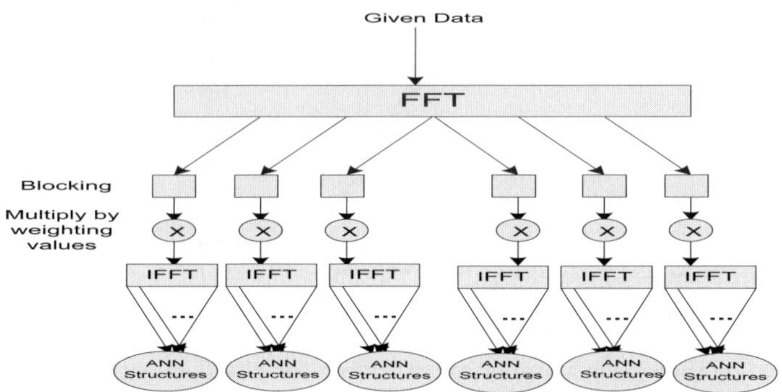

Fig. 3. Sample diagram of the ANN model with WFBB

5   Applications and Simulations

In this study, the performances of the conventional ANN structure and the ANN model with WFBB are tested separately. FFBP is used in both ANN structure and the hybrid model. The daily data composed some periodicities which are similar from one day to the other. But some unexpected events such as holidays, failures on power plants,and weather condition changing effect the load values.

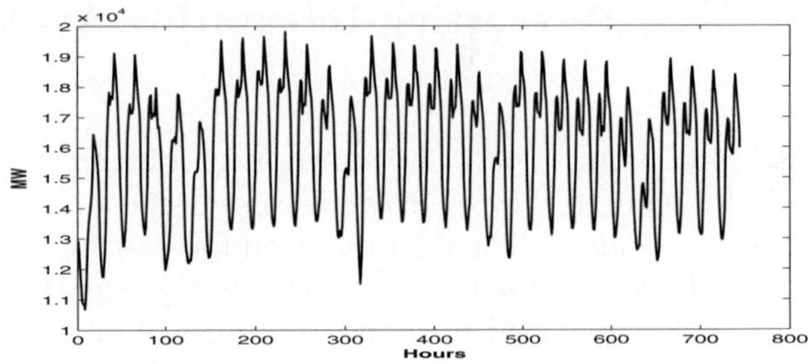

Fig. 4. The hourly load values for January

In this model based on the parametric methods, it is assumed that the data sequence is stationary. The hourly load values for January is given in Fig. 4.

The conventional ANN and the hybrid method(ANN with WFBB)are used for predicting the next day load values based on the previous two-day values, respectively. The conventional ANN structure has 2 layers. First layer and output layer are composed of 48 and of 24 neurons, respectively. The size of the input and output vector are 48x10 and 24x10 in this structure,respectively. ANN is trained 15 epochs. The curve of the epoch number and training for the conventional ANN structure with FFBP is shown in Fig. 5. Error curve is shown in Fig. 6.

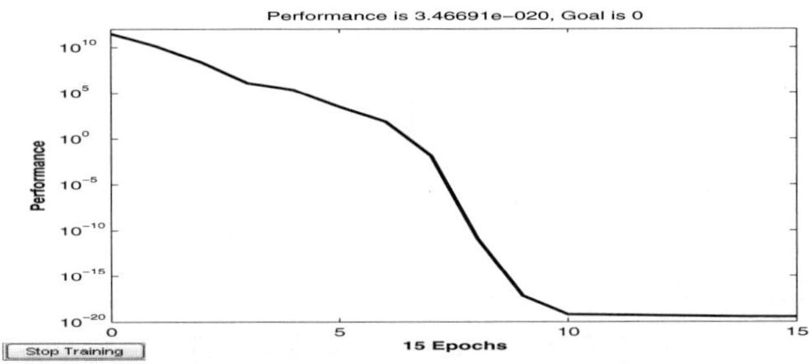

Fig. 5. Curve of the epoch number and training for the conventional ANN structure with FFBP

The FFT algorithm is applied to all given data for the integrating ANN with WFBB method. The FFT structure of this data is given in Fig. 7. Frequency response of the training set is also given in Fig. 8.

The results of the IFFT algorithm are used for the input of the ANN structure, this structure has 2 layers. First layer and output layer are composed of 48 and 24 neurons, respectively. In this cases, the sizes of the input and output vectors are 48x10 and 24x10, respectively. ANN training is finished at the end of 16 epochs. The curve of the epoch number and training for the FFBP structure for ANN model with WFBB is shown in Fig. 9. Error curve is shown in Fig. 10.

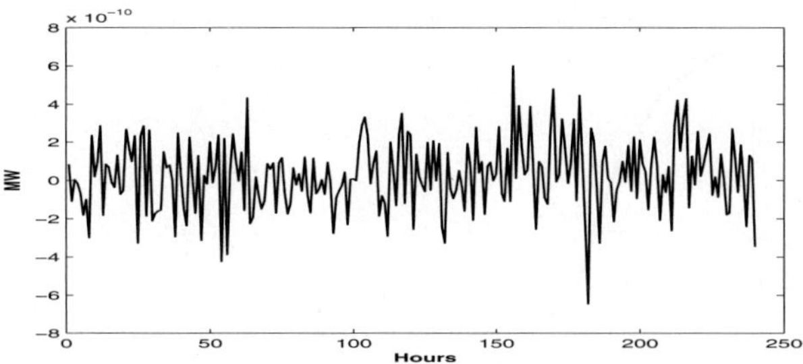

Fig. 6. Error curve for the ANN structure

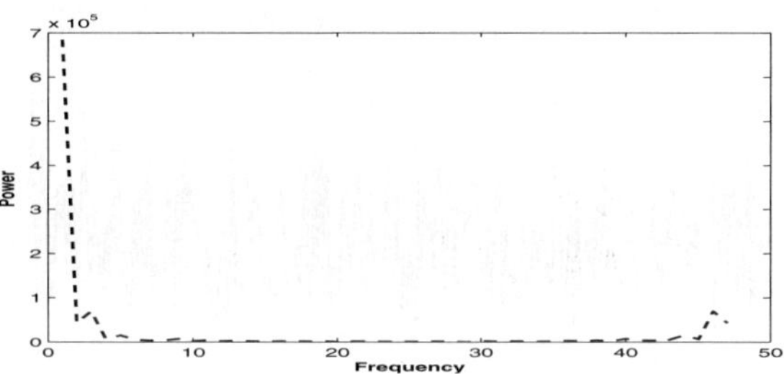

Fig. 7. FFT structure of the data

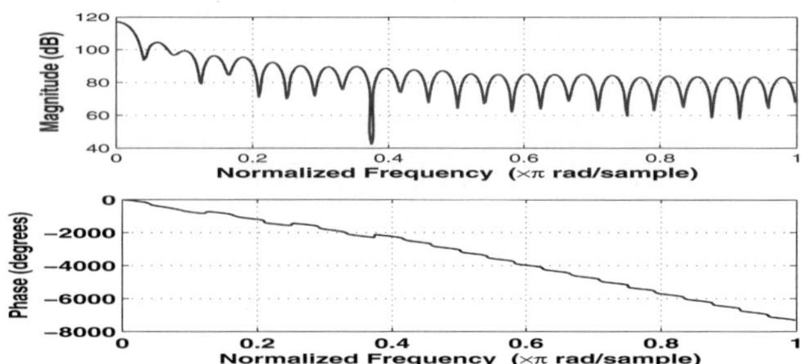

Fig. 8. The frequency response for the training data

RMSE is calculated by following formula;

$$RMSE = [(1/N) \sum_{i=1}^{N} (x_i - xpredict_i)^2]^{1/2} \qquad (8)$$

where N: Data number, x_i= Actual value, $xpredict_i$ = Predicted value

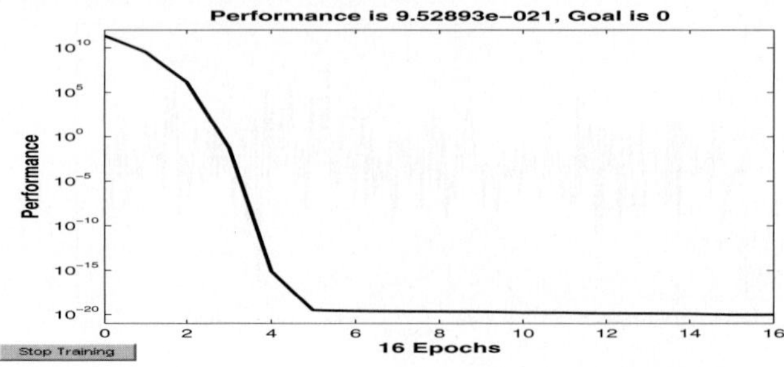

Fig. 9. Curve of the epoch number and training for ANN model with WFBB

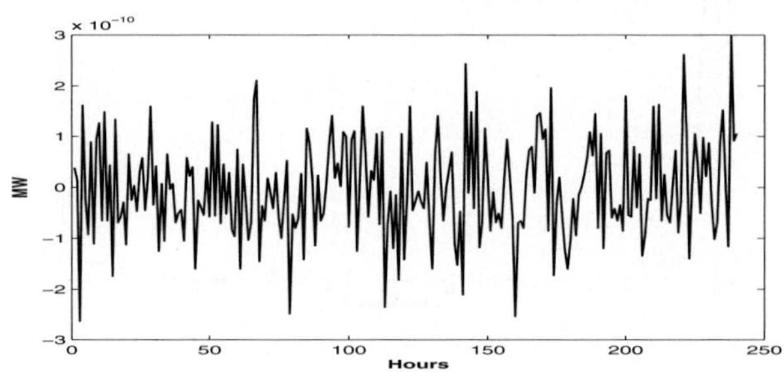

Fig. 10. Error curve for the ANN model with WFBB

Table 1. RMSE values of the methods

Method	RMSE values
Conventional ANN	2.8845e-009
ANN model with WFBB	1.5123e-009

Performance and RMSE values of both methods are given in Table 1.

6   Conclusion

A new method using the hybrid model, the ANN with WFBB, for the next day load forecasting is applied to actual load data taken from the Turkish Electric Power Company in 2002. Also, the conventional ANN Structure is applied to the given data for forecasting. The ANN structure used in this study has 2 layers. First and output layers are composed of 48 and 24 neurons, respectively. The performances of the ANN structure and the hybrid model are tested separately. As seen the results in Table 1, the performance and the RMSE values for the hybrid model are smaller than the values for the conventional ANN structure. Then, the new hybrid model forecasts better than the conventional ANN structure.

References

1. Kim, K., Youn, H.S., Kang, Y.C.: Short-Term Load Forecasting for Special Days in Anomalous Load Conditions Using Neural Networks and Fuzzy Inference Method. IEEE Transactions on Power Systems 15, 559–565 (2000)
2. Asbury, C.: Weather Load Model for Electric Demand Energy Forecasting. IEEE Transactions on Power Apparatus and Systems PAS-94, 1111–1116 (1975)
3. Papalexopoulos, A.D., Hesterberg, T.C.: A Regression Based Approach to Short-Term System Load Forecasting. In: Proceedings of PICA Conference, pp. 414–423 (1989)
4. Hill, T., O'connor, M., Remus, W.: Neural Networks Models for Time Series Forecasts. Management Sciences, 1082–1092 (1996)
5. Huang, H., Hwang, R., Hsieh, J.: A New Artificial Intelligent Peak Power Load Forecaster Based on Non-Fixed Neural Networks. E. Power Energy Systems, 245–250 (2002)
6. Irisarri, G.D., Widergren, S.E., Yehsakul, P.D.: On-Line Load Forecasting for Energy Control Center. Application IEEE Transactions on Power Apparatus and Systems (1982)
7. Christiaanse, W.R.: Short-Term Load Forecasting Using General Exponential Smoothing. IEEE Transactions on Power Apparatus and Systems PAS-90, 900–911 (1971)
8. Lamedica, R., et al.: A Neural Network Based Technique for Short-Term Forecasting of Anomalous Load Periods. IEEE Transactions on Power Systems 11, 1749–1756 (1996)
9. Mori, H., Yuihara, A.: Deterministic Annealing Clustering For Annbased Short-Term Load Forecasting. IEEE Transactions on Power Systems 16(3), 545–551 (2001)
10. Senjyu, T., Takara, H., Funabashi, T.: One-Hour-Ahead Load Forecasting Using Neural Network. IEEE Transactions on Power Systems 17, 113–118 (2002)
11. Song, K.B., Baek, Y.S., Hong, D.H., Jang, G.S.: Short-Term Load Forecasting for the Holidays Using Fuzzy Linear Regression Method. IEEE Transactions on Power Systems 20, 96–101 (2005)
12. Basaran Filik, U., Kurban, M.: A New Approach for the Short-Term Load Forecasting with Autoregressive and Artificial Neural Network Models. International Journal of Computational Intelligence Research 3, 66–71 (2007)
13. Park, H.S., Mun, K.J., Kim, H.S., Hwang, G.H., Lee, H.S., Park, J.H.: Application of Neural Networks to Short-Term Load Forecasting Using Electrical Load Pattern. IEEE Transactions on Power Systems 48A, 8–13 (1999)
14. Chauhan, B.K., Sharma, A., Hanmandlu, M.: Neuro Fuzzy Approach Based Short Term Electric Load Forecasting. In: IEEE/PES Transmission and Distribution Conference & Exhibition: Asia and Pacific Dalian, China (2005)
15. Farhang-Boroujeny, B., Chan, K.S.: Analysis of the Frequency-Domain Block LMS Algorithm. IEEE Transactions on Signal Processing 48, 2332–2342 (2000)
16. Haykin, S.: Adaptive Filter Theory. Prentice-Hall International Inc., USA (1996)
17. Mansour, D., Gray Jr., A.H.: Performance Charaterictics of the Unconstrained Frequency-Domain Adaptive Filter. In: IEEE Int. Symp. on Circuits and Systems (1982)
18. Lee, J.C., Un, C.K.: Performances of Time and Frequency Domain Block LMS Adaptive Digital Filters. IEEE Trans.Acoust Speech Signal Process, 499–510 (1986)

19. Lee, J.C., Un, C.K., Cho, D.H.: A Frequency-Weihgted Block LMS Algorithm and Its Application to Speech Processing. Proceedings of the IEEE 73, 1137–1138 (1985)
20. Papalexopoulos, A.D., Hao, S., Peng, T.M.: An Implementation of a Neural Network Based Load Forecasting Model for the EMS. IEEE Trans. Power Systems 9, 1956–1962 (1994)
21. Chen, H.: A Practical On-line Predicting System for Short- Term Load. East China Electric Power 24 (1996)
22. Chen, H.: An Implementation of Power System Short-Term Load Forecasting. In: Power System Automation, China (1997)

Distribution Feeder Phase Balancing Using Newton-Raphson Algorithm-Based Controlled Active Filter

M.W. Siti, D.V. Nicolae, J.A. Jordaan, and A.A. Jimoh

Graduate School of Electrical and Electronic Engineers, Tshwane University of Technology
Private Bag X07, 0116, Pretoria North, South Africa
willysiti@yahoo.com, danaurel@yebo.co.za,
jordaan.jaco@gmail.com, jimohaa@tut.ac.za

Abstract. The distribution system problems, such as planning, loss minimization, and energy restoration, usually involve the phase balancing or network reconfiguration procedures. The determination of an optimal phase balance is, in general, a combinatorial optimization problem. This paper proposes a novel reconfiguration of the phase balancing using the active power filter control and the combinatorial optimization-based Newton-Raphson algorithm to solve the unbalance problem. By utilizing the load switches as state variable, a constant Jacobian matrix can be obtained. The model developed in this paper uses combinatorial optimization techniques to translate the change values (kVA) into a number of load points and then selects the specific load points. It also performs the inter-changing of the load points between the releasing and the receiving phases in an optimal fashion. Application results balancing a distribution feeder network in South Africa for domestic loads are presented in this paper.

1 Introduction

The distribution system will typically have a great deal of single–phase loads connected to them. Therefore distribution systems are inherently unbalanced. The load is also very dynamic and varies with time; these factors contribute to increase difficulties in controlling the distribution voltage within certain limits. In addition to this most of the time the phases are unequally loaded and they produce undesired negative and zero sequence currents. The negative sequence will cause excessive heating in machines, saturation of the transformers and ripple in rectifiers [1, 2], Phase balancing is very important and usable operation to reduce distribution feeder losses and improve system security.

In South Africa, to reduce the unbalance current in a feeder the connection phases of some feeders are changed manually after some field measurement and software analysis. Although in some cases this process can improve the phase current unbalance, this strategy is more time-consuming and erroneous, but it is important to balance the three phase voltages. The conventional solution using a passive compensator has been used as a solution to solve voltage unbalance [1], but this presents several disadvantages namely resonance can occur because of the interaction between the compensator and the load, with unpredictable results. To cope with these disadvantages, recent efforts have been concentrated in the development of active filters [2, 3].

M. Ishikawa et al. (Eds.): ICONIP 2007, Part II, LNCS 4985, pp. 713–720, 2008.

Using three-legged power converters to deal with the unbalanced load and source has been addressed in [3]. By engaging a feed forward control, the negative–sequence component caused by an unbalanced source/load can be cancelled out so that the input power becomes constant and the DC link voltage is free of low frequencies, even harmonic ripples. However, a three-legged power converter is incapable of dealing with zero sequence unbalance. To solve the problem, normally split DC link capacitors are used. The zero-sequence current path is provided by connecting the neutral point to the middle point of the two DC link capacitors [3]. The drawback of this model is that excessively large DC link capacitors are needed; therefore the cost is high for high voltage applications. In [2] they propose the four-legged inverter. In a three-phase wire system there is always difficulties to reduce the zero sequence current. In this paper, the active filter combined with the Newtown-Raphson method (NR) will be applied to achieve the balance.

In section 2, 3 and 4 the proposed model and Newton-Raphson based controller is introduced. Section 5 shows some results and the paper ends with conclusions.

2 Proposed Model

In general, distribution loads show different characteristics according to their corresponding distribution lines and line sections. Therefore, load levels for each time period can be regarded as non-identical. In the case of a distribution system with some overloaded and some lightly loaded branches, there is the need to balance the system such that the loads are rearranged. The maximum load current, which the feeder conductor can take, may be considered as the reference. Nevertheless, the rearranging of loads must be such that a certain predefined objective is satisfied. In this case, the objective is to ensure the network has minimum real power loss.

In [4] is presented an artificial neural network algorithm (ANN) applied for a small distribution feeder with six loads. Some results of ANN load balancing for 15 consumers are presented in Table 1. The table shows the current after load balancing in each of the three phases (for three different test cases), as well as the largest difference between the three phase currents. As can be seen from Table 1, after applying ANN there still is an unbalance. In this paper, which is a continuation of [4], a further effort is proposed to optimally balance the feeder by means of an active power filter (APF) working in an unbalanced system.

Table 1. Balanced phase currents of the ann

	1ST Data Set	2ND Data Set	3RD Data Set
I_{ph1} (A)	270.9	175.5	299.6
I_{ph2} (A)	304.1	245.2	227.4
I_{ph3} (A)	307.3	213.9	266.9
$\Delta I_{ph\text{-}max}$ (A)	**36.4**	**69.7**	**72.2**

In general, an active power filter is a device that cancels harmonic current from the non-linear loads and compensates reactive power. In the configuration shown in Fig. 1, The APF is connected in parallel to the load in order to compensate the remaining unbalance after applying the neural network algorithm. The control of this APF is based on the Newton-Raphson method. Thus, after the minimization of the unbalance, the efficiency of the distribution transformer will be improved.

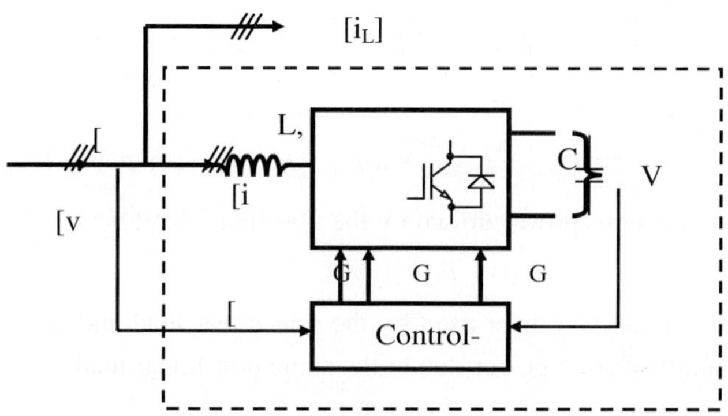

Fig. 1. Active power filter in parallel with a partially balanced feeder

3 Power Balance Principle

This analysis is intended to clarify the power exchange between the supply, non-linear load (which could be in the form of reactive power, harmonics or unbalance) and the converter while it performs simultaneous functions of unity power factor rectification – as the main function, reactive power compensation, harmonic compensation (active power filter) and unbalancing correction. Throughout the analysis the AC bus will be considered to be infinite and no voltage distortion is taking place. Neglecting the losses of the bridge converter (**H** topology), the relation between the instantaneous powers delivered by the supply (p_s), the instantaneous power drawn by the non-linear load (p_L) and the switching-mode converter (p_c) can be written as:

$$p_s = p_L + p_c \tag{1}$$

The parameters of the supply are:

$$\left[v_s\right]^T = \sqrt{2}\times V_s \sin\left[\omega t - \frac{2\pi}{3}(i-1)\right] \tag{2}$$

with $i = 1,2,3$ and t meaning vector transpose,

$$\left[i_s\right]^T = \sqrt{2}\times I_s \sin\left[\omega t - \frac{2\pi}{3}(i-1)\right] \tag{3}$$

with $i = 1,2,3$ and where V_s and I_s are the rms value of the supply voltage and current respectively.

$$\left[i_L\right]^T = \sum_{h=1}^{\infty} \sqrt{2} \times I_L \sin\left[h \times\left(\omega t - \frac{2\pi}{3}(i-1)\right) - \varphi_h\right] \tag{4}$$

$$p_L = \left[v_s\right]^T \cdot \left[i_L\right] = 3 \cdot V_s \cdot I_{L1} \cdot \cos\varphi_1 + \sum_{h=2}^{\infty} P_{3h} \cdot \cos\left(3h\omega t - \varphi_{3h}\right) \tag{5}$$

where:

$$P_{3h} = 3V_s \sqrt{I_{L(3h-1)}^2 + I_{L(3h+1)}^2 + 2I_{L(3h-1)}I_{L(3h+1)}\cos\left(\varphi_{3h+1} - \varphi_{3h-1}\right)} \tag{6}$$

and

$$\tan\varphi_{3h} = \left(I_{L(3h+1)}\sin\varphi_{3h+1} + I_{L(3h-1)}\sin\varphi_{3h-1}\right) / \left(I_{L(3h+1)}\cos\varphi_{3h+1} + I_{L(3h-1)}\cos\varphi_{3h-1}\right) \tag{7}$$

The instantaneous power drawn by the non-linear load is:

$$p_L(t) = P_L + \tilde{p}_L(t) \tag{8}$$

where P_L is the active power used by the non-linear load and $\tilde{p}_L(t)$ is the instantaneous fluctuant/distortion power due to the same non-linear load.

$$P_L = 3 \cdot V_s \cdot I_{L1} \cdot \cos\varphi_1 \tag{9}$$

After compensation the instantaneous power delivered by the supply is:

$$p_s = \left[v_s\right]^T \cdot \left[i_s\right] = P_s = 3 \times V_s \times I_s \tag{10}$$

where P_s is the dc component of $p_s(t)$ and represents the active power delivered by the supply.

The instantaneous power transferred through the active converter is:

$$p_c(t) = p_L(t) - P_s + P_o = P_L - P_s + \tilde{p}_L(t) = P_c + \tilde{p}_c(t) \tag{11}$$

where P_o is the active power delivered to dc bus.

$$\text{But: } P_c = P_L - P_s + P_o \tag{12}$$

Therefore:
$$\tilde{p}_c(t) = \tilde{p}_L(t) \tag{13}$$

In steady state, the fluctuating power $\tilde{p}_c(t)$ at the output of the active converter compensates the fluctuating power of the non-linear load which could be in the form of reactive power, harmonics or unbalance. Equation (12) expresses the active power exchange between the supply, non-linear load and active converter. If the losses in the *H* converter are neglected, then the fluctuating power $\tilde{p}_c(t)$ is converted into the ripple voltage $\tilde{v}_o(t)$ across the condenser. When a transient change in the active power demanded by the load occurs, the storage element (C) should be capable of compensating this unbalance. This results in a variation of the dc bus voltage. If the active power delivered by the source was inferior to the load demand ($P_c > 0$), then the average (V_o) voltage across the capacitor decreases. If the load demands less active power ($P_s < 0$), then V_o increases. The variation of the dc bus is compensated for by the voltage regulator.

4 Control System

For this application of the APF, the control system is shown in Fig. 2. The switching matrix, which is used in the control system, is computed using the Newton-Raphson algorithm, which is presented next. For the mentioned system, we propose, in this paper, an active power filter balancing technique along with a combinatorial optimization oriented Newton system for implementing the load change decision.

With reference to Fig. 2, I_{si} represents the source current that should be minimized

$$I_{si} = I_{Fi} + \frac{V_{Li} - V_{ref}}{Z_{Li}} \tag{14}$$

with $i = 1, 2, 3$.

Where I_{Fi} is the active power filter current, V_{Li} represents the voltage across each load and Z_{Li} is the impedance of each load.

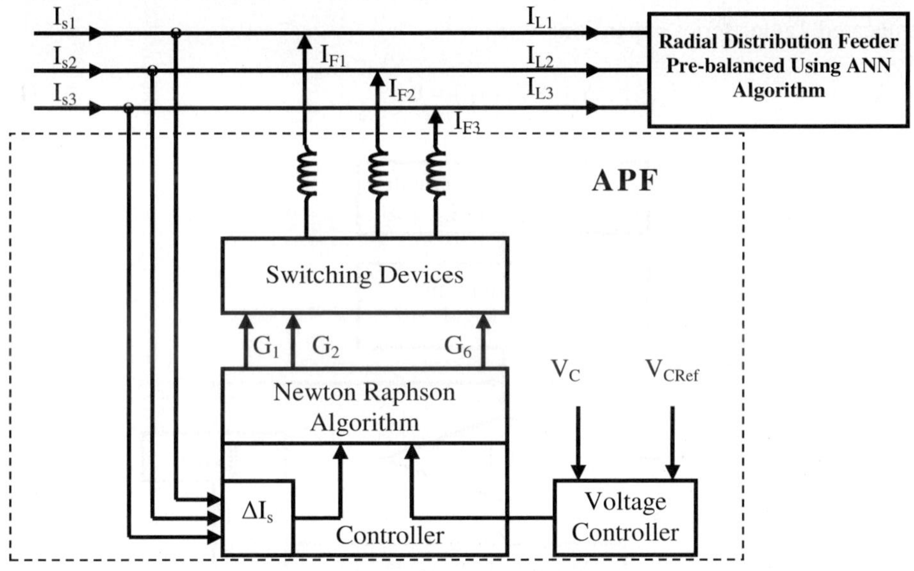

Fig. 2. Control system

Therefore, the objective of this new algorithm is to minimize the difference of the amplitude of the phase currents I_{si}.

$$\text{Minimize} \begin{vmatrix} I_{s1} - I_{s2} \\ I_{s2} - I_{s3} \\ I_{s1} - I_{s3} \end{vmatrix} \tag{15}$$

The Least Squares objective function proposed for this study is:

$$J = (I_{s1} - I_{s2})^2 + (I_{s1} - I_{s2})^2 + (I_{s1} - I_{s2})^2 \qquad (16)$$

When the objective function (16) is minimized, the power losses in the system will also be reduced. This procedure results in a non-linear system of equations that will be solved using Newton-Raphson. To solve the minimization problem, the gradient of the least square objective function J as defined in (16), can be expressed in terms of x, where $x = [sw_1, sw_2, ..., sw_6]$ is the vector of the APF switches. Then the gradient J_x should be equal to zero.

$$J_x = \left[\frac{\partial J}{\partial sw_1}, \frac{\partial J}{\partial sw_2}, ..., \frac{\partial J}{\partial sw_6} \right] = 0 \qquad (17)$$

Equation (17) is a system of non linear equations. To solve the system of non linear equations, the system should be linearized around some working points x_k by using a truncated Taylor series expansion:

$$J_{xx}(x_k)\Delta_{xk} + J_x(x_k) = \mathbf{0}, \qquad (18)$$

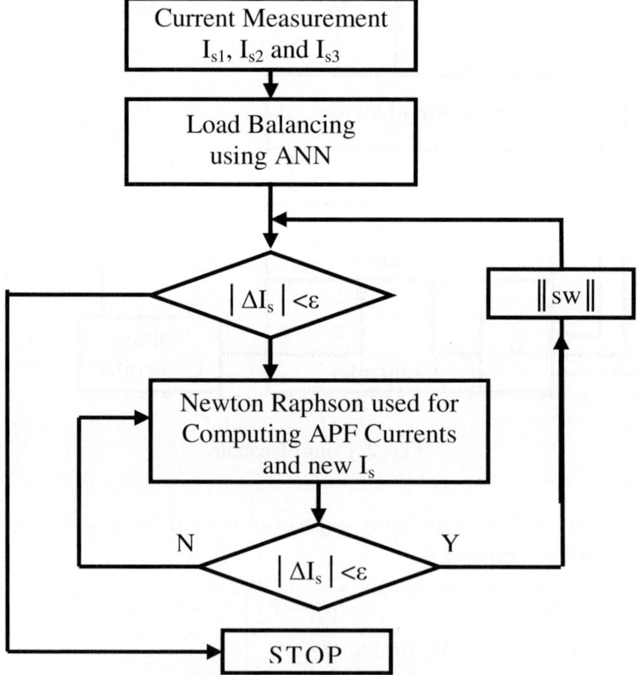

Fig. 3. Flow chart

where $J_{xx}(x_k)$ is the 6×6 Hessian matrix, containing the second order derivatives of the objective function J evaluated at point x_k, and $J_x(x_k)$ is the gradient of J evaluated at point x_k. The correction vector Δx_k can then be calculated by solving the following system of linear equations:

$$J_{xx}(x_k)\Delta_{xk} = -J_x(x_k) \tag{19}$$

The initial value for the parameter vector x_k is arbitrary chosen and then an iterative procedure is used to obtain a better value of the parameter vector.

$$x_{k+1} = x_k + \Delta_{xk} \tag{22}$$

Fig. 3 shows the flow chart of the control process.

5 Test Results

In order to illustrate the proposed balancing method, the group currents "data1" from Table 1 has been chosen. Fig. 4 shows the currents (I_{s1}, I_{s2}, I_{s3} in Fig. 2) after applying the artificial neural network algorithm.

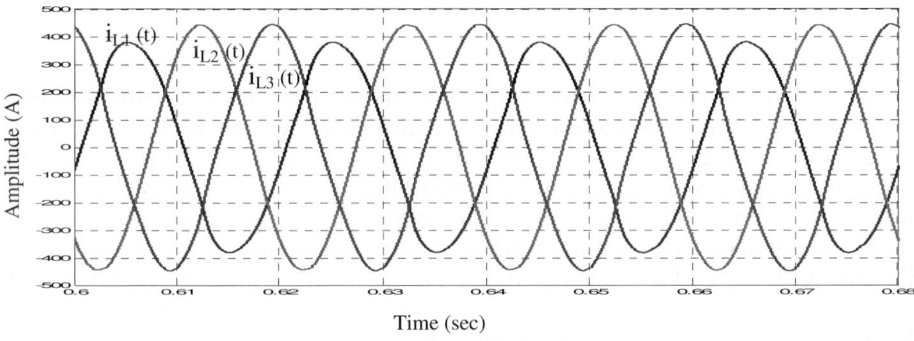

Fig. 4. Feeder currents partially balanced by ANN

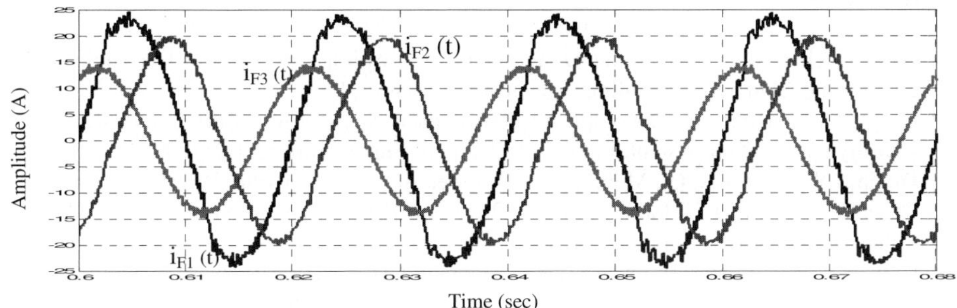

Fig. 5. Active power filter currents

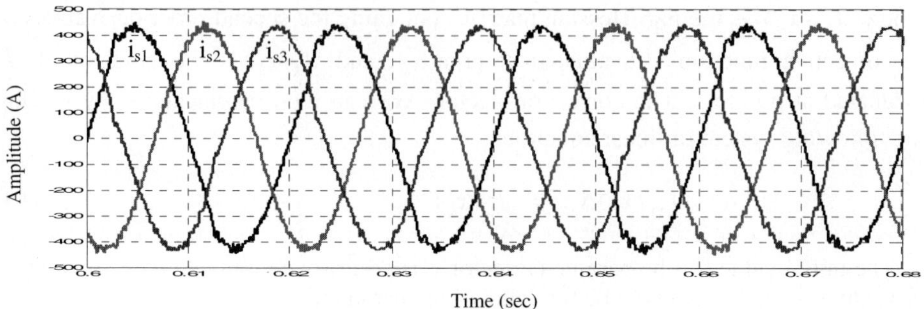

Fig. 6. Balanced feeder currents

Fig. 5 shows the filter currents (I_{F1}, I_{F2}, I_{F3} in Fig. 2) produced by the active power filter using the Newton-Raphson method to control the switching devices. Fig. 6 shows the result of active power filter distribution feeder balancing (phase currents I_{L1}, I_{L2}, I_{L3} in Fig. 2).

From Fig. 4 – Fig. 6 it can be seen how the APF is injecting current from the partially ANN balanced system to correct any small scale unbalances that may still be in the system.

6 Conclusions

The use of a power electronic active power filter in conjunction with an artificial neural network for optimally mitigating unbalance in a distribution network feeder has been proposed and demonstrated. An analysis intended to clarify the power exchange between the supply, non-linear load and the converter while it performs simultaneous functions of unity power factor rectification – as the main function reactive power compensation, harmonic compensation (active power filter) and unbalancing correction has been presented. The switches of the APF are controlled for optimal phase unbalancing mitigation by using a Newton-Raphson algorithm to iteratively solve an optimization problem, which results are then used to control the voltage and current controller of the converter. The proposed method was implemented for a practical case with a satisfactory result.

References

[1] McGranaghan, M.: Active Filter Design and Specification for control of Harmonics in Industrial and Commercial Facilities, Electrotek Concepts, Inc.
[2] Chaghi, A., Guettafi, A., Benoidjit, A.: Four Legged Active Power filter Compensation For a Utility Distribution System. Journal of Electrical Engineering 55(1-2) (2004)
[3] Dixon, J.W., Venegas, G., Moran, L.A.: A series Active Power filter Based on a sinusoidal Current- Controlled Voltage – Source Inverter. IEEE Transaction on Industrial Electronic 44(5) (October 1997)
[4] Ukil, Siti, M., Jordaan, J.: Feeder Load Balancing Using Neural Network. In: International Symposium on Neural Networks (ISNN 2006) held in Chengdu, China, May 28-31 (2006)

The Use of Support Vector Machine for Phase Balancing in the Distribution Feeder

M.W. Siti, A.A. Jimoh, J.A. Jordaan, and D.V. Nicolae

Graduate School of Electrical and Electronic Engineers, Tshwane University of Technology
Private Bag X07, 0116, Pretoria North, South Africa
willysiti@yahoo.com, jimohaa@tut.ac.za, jordaan.jaco@gmail.com,
danaurel@yebo.co.za

Abstract. Phase voltage and current unbalances in power system distribution networks are major factors leading to extra losses, communication interference, equipment overloading, and malfunctioning of the protective relay, which consequently results in service quality and operation efficiency being reduced. As a better alternative to the traditional practices of manual trial and error, and the contemporary solution technique of network reconfiguration or load rearrangement, this paper investigates and proposes a novel method that is based on the use of the historical data and artificial intelligence for eliminating or minimizing phase unbalance problems. The proposed method is based on support vector machine.

Keywords: Feeder load balancing; Support vector Machine.

1 Introduction

The distribution system technology has changed drastically, both qualitatively and quantitatively. This may be adduced to the fact that with increase in technological development, the dependence on electric power supply has increased considerably. Consequently, while demand has increased, the need for a steady power supply with minimum power interruptions and fast fault restoration has also increased. To meet these demands, automation of the power distribution system needs to be widely adopted. All switches and circuit-breakers involved in the controlled networks are equipped with facilities for remote operation. The control interface equipments must withstand extreme climatic conditions. Also, control equipments at each location must have a dependable power source. To cope with the complexity of the distribution system, the latest computer, communication, and power electronics equipment in distribution technologies are needed to be employed. The distribution automation can be defined as an integrated system concept. It includes control, monitoring and some times, decision to alter any kind of loads. The automatic distribution system provides directions for automatic re-closing of the switches and remote monitoring of the loads contributing towards phase balancing.

The phase voltage and current unbalances are major factors leading to extra losses, communication interference, equipment overloading and malfunctioning of the protective relay which consequently results into service quality and operation efficiency being reduced [2]. Phase unbalance is also manifested in increased complex power unbalance, increased power loss, enhanced voltage drop, and increased neutral current.

M. Ishikawa et al. (Eds.): ICONIP 2007, Part II, LNCS 4985, pp. 721–729, 2008.

Traditionally, to reduce the unbalance current in a feeder the connection phases of some feeders are changed manually after some field measurement and software analysis. Although in some cases this process can improve the phase current unbalance, this strategy is more time-consuming and erroneous. In this paper, we propose the use of support vector machine based load balancing as novel procedures to perform the feeder phase balancing.

In most of the cases, the phase voltage and current unbalances can be greatly improved by suitably arranging the connection phases between the distribution transformers and a primary feeder. It is also possible to advance the phase current unbalances in every feeder segment by means of changing the connection phases [1]. The phase voltage unbalances along a feeder can also be improved in common cases by system reconfiguration, which involves the rearrangement of loads or transfer of load from heavily loaded area to the less loaded.

In the modern power distribution systems, the sectionalizing switches and the tie switches for feeder reconfiguration are extensively used [2]. The authors in [3] presented the way to control the tie switches using heuristic combinatorial optimization-based method. The only disadvantage with the tie-switch control is that, in most of the cases, it makes the current and the voltage unbalances worse. Some of the references [5, 6, 7, 8, 9] presented the use of the neural networks to find the optimum switching option of the loads among the different phases. On the basis of these results, other networks identify the radial topology satisfying the optimal condition.

In all these the phase balancing problem is mathematically formulated and then solved. The results are therefore used to initiate certain actions to eliminate or minimize the problem. With artificial intelligence it is wondered if there cannot be a simpler, more straightforward, better, and faster method. It is possible to use historical data with a more intelligent method to arrive at actions that minimize and eliminate the phase unbalance. This will not require solving a more complex problem as an intermediate step. In this paper, therefore, such a novel method is proposed by the use of support vector machine based phase balancing as procedure to perform the feeder load/phase balancing.

2   Problem Description and Mathematical Formulation

In South Africa a distribution feeder is usually a three-phase, four-wire system. It can be a radial or open loop structure. The size of the conductor for the entire line of the feeder is the same. These feeders consist of a mixture of loads, e.g. residential, commercial, industrial, etc. Single-phase loads are fed by single-phase two-wire service, while three-phase loads are fed by three-phase four-wire ($3\phi 4$) service. The behavior of the load pattern (daily) depends on the function of time and the type of customers. The resulting power system voltages at the distribution end and the points of utilization can be unbalanced due to several reasons. The reasons include the following: unequal voltages magnitude at the fundamental system frequency (under voltage and over voltages); fundamental phase angle deviation; asymmetrical transformer winding impedances [9], etc. A major cause of this unbalance is uneven distribution of single-phase loads that can be continually changing across a three-phase power system due to use. Normally the consumption of consumers connected to a feeder fluctuates, thus leading to the fluctuation of the total load connected to each phase of the feeder. This in turn implies that the degree of unbalance keeps varying. The worse the degree of unbalance the higher the voltage drop and the less reliable the feeder is.

The phase voltage and current unbalances are major factors leading to extra losses, communication interference, equipment overloading and malfunctioning of the protective relay which consequently results into service quality and operation efficiency being reduced [2]. Phase unbalance is also manifested in increased complex power unbalance, increased power loss, enhanced voltage drop, and increased neutral current.

Traditionally, to reduce the degree of the phase current unbalance, thus avoiding the malfunctioning of the protective relay and unintentional service discontinuity, the connection phases of some critical distribution transformers are usually changed manually following many field measurements and analysis. In some cases, this process certainly improves the phase voltage and currents unbalances. However, considerable time must be spent to achieve an acceptable result. In addition, the balancing status of the system, most of the time, lasts only for a short time, sometimes even only an hour. This consequence is expected because the time varying characteristic of the load is usually not considered in detail in the trial and error approach.

In general, distribution loads show different characteristics according to their corresponding distribution lines and line sections. Therefore, at the load levels, each time period can be regarded as non-identical. In the case of a distribution system, with some overloaded and some lightly loaded branches, there is the need to reconfigure the system such that loads are transferred from heavily loaded to less loaded feeders. Here the maximum load current the feeder conductor may be taken as the reference [4]. Nonetheless, the transfer of load must be such that a certain predefined objective is satisfied. The objective function can normally be defined using the property or characteristic of the problem to be solved. In this case, the objective can for example be for the ensuing network to have minimum real power loss, minimum complex power unbalance (TCPU), minimum voltage drop, minimum neutral point current (NC), or it could be to optimize the unbalance factors, or it could be weighted combination of all these.

Consequently, phase balancing may be redefined as the rearrangement of the network such as to minimize any either the total real power losses (TPL) arising from line branches, the total complex power unbalance, or total voltage drop (AVD), or the neutral point current, or the unbalance factors, or the combination of all these [8].

$$f = TCPU + TPL + AVD + NC. \tag{1}$$

Mathematically, the total complex power unbalance, may according to [2] be expressed as:

$$TCPU = \sum_{j=1}^{m} \left| V_j \times I_j^* \right|, \tag{2}$$

in which, m is the total number of feeder segments of the object feeder, V_j and I_j are the voltage and current of each segment respectively. *TCPU* can be applied to evaluate the complex power unbalance of a feeder because a lower *TCPU* means a better load balance. *TCPU = 0* Indicates the complex power at every feeder segment along the feeder is balanced.

Decreasing system loss and improving system operation efficiency are usually the major objectives of a power utility. Hence minimization of line losses is also the objective function where the total power loss may be expressed as

$$TPL = \sum_{j=1}^{m}\sum_{p=1}^{3}\left(I_j^p\right)^2 \cdot r_j^p \,, \tag{3}$$

where I_j^p and r_j^p are the current and resistance of phase p of the j-th feeder segment, respectively.

Better load balance will regularly depreciate the voltage drop. Reducing the voltage drop and compressing the voltage spread are also important objectives to be achieved by distribution engineers. The average voltage drop can be evaluated as follows.

$$AVD = \frac{1}{n}\sum_{k=1}^{n} I^P \cdot Z_k \,, \tag{4}$$

where n is the total number of load points of the feeder.

The total current unbalance factors for zero and negative sequence labeled TCU_0 and TCU_2 are defined as follows:

$$TCU_0 = \sqrt{\frac{1}{n}\sum_{k=1}^{n}\left(I_{0,k}\right)^2} \tag{5}$$

$$TCU_2 = \sqrt{\frac{1}{n}\sum_{k=1}^{n}\left(I_{2,k}\right)^2} \tag{6}$$

The Neutral Current: keeping the neutral current flowing from the common point in the wye-connection windings of the main transformer to the ground, under a specified level, is very important to avoid malfunction of the zero sequence relay. The neutral current is the summation of the three phase currents of the transformer

$$NC = \sum_{p=1}^{3} I^p \,, \tag{7}$$

in which the I^p represents the total phase current of the main transformer that feeds the consumer feeders, and NC is the neutral current of the main transformer.

In the proposed radial distribution system, the consumers should be connected to a phase via a selector switch as shown in Fig. 1.

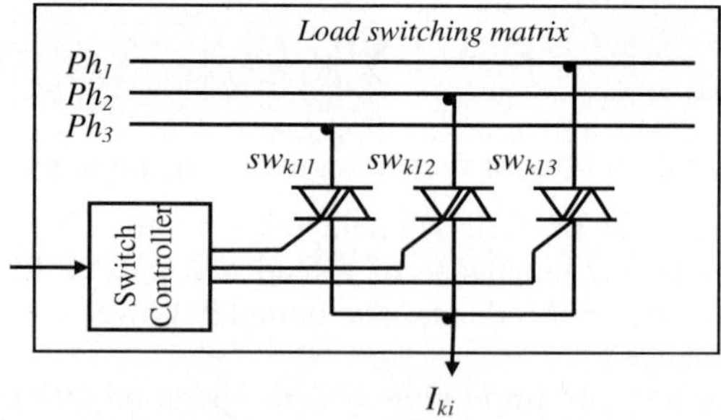

Fig. 1. Switch selector

Given the topology of the selector switch, the phase current could be written as:

$$\mathbf{I}_{ph1k} = \sum_{i=1}^{3} sw_{k1i}\mathbf{I}_{ki}^{p} + \mathbf{I}_{ph1(k-1)}^{p}, \tag{8}$$

$$\mathbf{I}_{ph2k} = \sum_{i=1}^{3} sw_{k2i}\mathbf{I}_{ki}^{p} + \mathbf{I}_{ph2(k-1)}, \tag{9}$$

$$\mathbf{I}_{ph3k} = \sum_{i=1}^{3} sw_{k3i}\mathbf{I}_{ki} + \mathbf{I}_{ph3(k-1)}, \tag{10}$$

where $\mathbf{I}_{ph1k}$, $\mathbf{I}_{ph2k}$ and $\mathbf{I}_{ph3k}$ represent the currents (phasors) per phase (1, 2 & 3) after the k –th point of connection, $sw_{k11},\ldots,sw_{k33}$ are different switches (the value of '1' means the switch is closed and '0' means it is open). Following the constraint of allowing only one breaker in each of the equations (2) – (4) to be closed, we can write the following set of modified constraints:

$$\sum_{i=1}^{3} sw_{k1i} - 1 = 0 \tag{11}$$

$$\sum_{i=1}^{3} sw_{k2i} - 1 = 0 \tag{12}$$

$$\sum_{i=1}^{3} sw_{k3i} - 1 = 0. \tag{13}$$

3 Support Vector Machine

The Support Vector Machine (SVM) is a training algorithm for learning classification and regression rules from data. The general problem with machine learning is to search, usually very large, space of potential hypotheses to determine the one that will best fit the set of data and any prior knowledge. When the data is labelled the problem is one of supervised learning in that the true answer is known for a given set of data. If the labels are categorical the problem is one of classification. When the data is unlabeled the problem is one of unsupervised learning and the aim is to categorise the data into groups with similar properties and distinct from other groups of data. The result of the learning process is known as an approximating function or alternatively as a hypothesis [9, 10].

SVMs were first introduced by Vapnik in the 1960's for classification. SVMs arose from statistical learning theory where you only solve the problem at hand without solving a more complex problem as an intermediate step. Here we focus on SVMs for regression with n inputs and n outputs. The application of the Support Vector regression (SVR) is done by the introduction of an alternative loss function. The loss function must be modified to include a distance measure. To address the issue of the loss functions Vapnik Proposed the insensitive loss function [11], which will be applied in this paper with the support vector machine, controlling the sequence of the different switches at the consumer loads for the reduction of the current and to achieve a phase balancing. The inputs to the support vector machine are load currents at each of the consumers and the outputs indicate to which phase each load should be connected, where L_{loads} represent the input data and C_{sw} the output of the support vector machine.

$$L_{laods} = \begin{bmatrix} I_{L1} \\ \vdots \\ I_{Lj} \end{bmatrix} \quad \text{and} \quad C_{sw} = \begin{bmatrix} C_{L1} \\ \vdots \\ C_{Lj} \end{bmatrix} \tag{14}$$

The output of the network is in the range $\{1, 2, 3\}$ for each load, i.e., which switch (to the specific phase) should be closed for that specific load.

3.1 Training Data

We have used the support vector machine operation for real data for 45 loads. The real data set consisted of unbalanced load data from a South African city. The test data set had average load current values per consumer in a specific locality of the city for the different times of each day in a month. We randomly selected 45 consumers as our test data for each specific time, and we tested our result on 300 data sets each of 45 loads. We consider the loads to be equally distributed per phase, i.e., we assume 15 loads to be connected per phase. So, the problem is to find the optimum sets of n loads, with *minimum* differences among the individual sums of the three sets.

The optimal regression function is given by the minimum of the functional.

$$\Phi(w, \xi) = \frac{1}{2}\|w\|^2 + C\sum_i \left(\xi_i^- + \xi_i^+\right), \tag{15}$$

where C is a pre-specified value, ξ_i^-, ξ_i^+ are slack variables representing upper lower constraints on the switch sequence Φ.

A non-linear model is usually required to adequately model data. In the same manner as the non-SVR approach, mapping can be used to map the data into a high dimensional feature space where linear regression is performed. The kernel approach is again employed to address the curse of dimensionality.

The above-mentioned support vector machine is then trained using the real unbalanced load as the input vector, and the output switching sequences as the target vector. Then, the network is tested with different unbalanced load data set. The output was the optimal switching sequences of $\{1, 2, 3\}$ for the three-phases as explained above.

4 Simulation Results

The algorithm was tested on real data, received from local electricity supply. The test data set had average load current values per consumer in a specific locality of the city. Randomly 45 consumers have been selected as a case study. The load currents were

Table 1. 45 LOADS APPLICATION

	Unbalanced		Balanced	
		Switch	ANN	SVR
I_1(A)	40.16	1	1	1
I_2(A)	92.61	2	2	1
I_3(A)	90.77	3	3	2
I_4(A)	40.61	1	1	3
I_5(A)	88.47	2	3	2
I_6(A)	5.73	3	1	3
I_7(A)	34.93	1	3	1
I_8(A)	80.50	2	1	2
I_9(A)	0.97	3	2	3
I_{10}(A)	13.75	1	1	1
I_{11}(A)	20.07	2	3	3
I_{12}(A)	19.67	3	2	3
I_{13}(A)	59.77	1	3	2
I_{14}(A)	26.94	2	2	1
I_{15}(A)	19.68	3	2	2
I_{16}(A)	1.51	1	1	3
I_{17}(A)	73.93	2	2	3
I_{18}(A)	44.06	3	3	2
I_{19}(A)	92.24	1	1	3
I_{20}(A)	46.13	2	1	3
I_{21}(A)	41.44	3	2	2
I_{22}(A)	83.77	1	3	1
I_{23}(A)	51.99	2	1	3
I_{24}(A)	20.06	3	3	1
I_{25}(A)	66.54	1	2	3
I_{26}(A)	82.97	2	2	2
I_{27}(A)	1.94	3	3	3
I_{28}(A)	67.44	1	1	1
I_{29}(A)	37.56	2	1	2
I_{30}(A)	82.34	3	1	1
I_{31}(A)	94.06	1	1	3
I_{32}(A)	22.88	2	2	3
I_{33}(A)	60.07	3	1	2
I_{34}(A)	48.11	1	3	1
I_{35}(A)	88.23	2	1	2
I_{36}(A)	75.44	3	1	1
I_{37}(A)	45.19	1	2	1
I_{38}(A)	1.83	2	3	2
I_{39}(A)	81.31	3	2	3
I_{40}(A)	60.92	1	1	2
I_{41}(A)	78.40	2	3	3
I_{42}(A)	91.25	3	2	1
I_{43}(A)	73.08	1	2	1
I_{44}(A)	17.45	2	2	2
I_{45}(A)	44.02	3	1	3
I_{ph1}(A)	-	822.1	746.1	783.7
I_{ph2}(A)	-	809.9	778.5	773.1
I_{ph3}(A)	-	678.8	788.1	762.7
$\Delta I_{ph\text{-}max}$(A)	-	143.3	42	21
T_c(sec)	-	-	0.2	0.07

measured at 20:00 (peak load), when most consumers are in their houses and most of the equipments used in domestic sector are on.

The results are as presented in Table 1. In the first column the load values are shown. In the second column switch positions for the unbalanced case are shown, where '1' ('2' or '3') means the load is currently connected to phase 1 (phase 2 or phase 3). In the last two columns the SVR and neural network (ANN) results are shown. This is the output of the SVM and ANN for the new switch positions to obtain a balancing of the phase currents. The last five rows in Table 1 show the total phase current for each phase $(I_{ph1}(A), I_{ph2}(A), I_{ph3}(A))$, the maximum difference between the phase currents (phase unbalance $\Delta I_{ph\text{-}max}(A)$) and the computational time $(T_C(sec))$ to do the load balancing. From these results it is seen that the SVR gives better results than the ANN in terms of the load balancing since it has a much smaller unbalance in the phase currents. Also the computational time of the SVM is less than that of the ANN.

5   Conclusion

Phase and load balancing are important complements to network and feeder reconfiguration. In distribution automation these problems have to be continuously solved simultaneously to guarantee optimal performance of a distribution network. In this paper the phase balancing problem at the distribution transformers in a radial structure, and the load balancing along a LV feeder have been formulated as current balancing optimization problems with due consideration for the various constraints using the SVR models. The SVR model achieved a good load balancing result.

References

[1] Civanlar, S., Grainger, J.J.: Distribution feeder reconfiguration for loss reduction. IEEE Trans. PWRD-3, 127–1223 (1998)

[2] Chen, T.H., Cherng, J.T.: Optimal Phase Arrangement of Distribution Transformers Connected to a Primary Feeder for System Unbalance Improvement and Loss Reduction Using Generic Algorithm. IEEE Trans. Power Systems 15(3) (August 2000)

[3] Baran, M.E., Wu, F.F.: Network Reconfiguration in distribution Systems for Loss Reduction and Load balancing. IEEE Trans. Power Delivery 7(2) (April 1989)

[4] Siti, M.,, A.: Load Balancing in distribution feeder Through Reconfiguration. In: IECON 2005, Raleigh, North Caroline, November 6-12 (2005)

[5] Siti, M.,, A.: Reconfiguration circuit loss minimization through feeder reconfiguration. In: Proc. SAUPEC Conf., Stellnbosch, South Africa (2004)

[6] Ukil,, Siti, M., Jordaan, J.: Feeder Load Balancing Using Neural Network. In: International Symposium on Neural Networks (ISNN 2006) held in Chengdu, China, May 28-31 (2006)

[7] Yang, X., Carull, S.P., Miu, K.: Reconfiguration Distribution Automation and Control Laboratory: Multiphase Radial Power Flow Experiment. IEEE Trans. on Power Systems 20(3) (August 2005)

[8] Chen, T.-H., Cherng, J.-T.: Optimal Phase Arrangement of Distribution Transformers Connected to a Primary Feeder for System Unbalance Improvement and Loss Reduction Using a Genetic Algorithm. IEEE Transactions on Power Systems 15(3), 994–1000 (2000)

[9] von Jouanne, A., Basudeb,: Assessment of Voltage Unbalance. IEEE Trans. On Power Systems 15(3) (August 2000)

[10] Gunn, S.R.: Support Vector Machines for classification and regression, Technical report May 10 (1998)

[11] Pelckmans, K., Suykens, J.A.K., Van Gestel, T., De Brabanter, J., Lukas, L., Hamers, B., De Moor, B., Vandewalle, J.: LS-SVMLab Toolbox User's Guide version 1.5, Catholic University Leuven (February 2003)

Energy Dissipation Effect on a Quantum Neural Network

Mitsunaga Kinjo[1], Shigeo Sato[2], and Koji Nakajima[2]

[1] University of the Ryukyus, Dept. of Electrical and Electronic Eng.,
Nishihara 903-0213, Japan
mitsu@eee.u-ryukyu.ac.jp
[2] Tohoku University, Research Institute of Electrical Communication,
Sendai 980-8577, Japan

Abstract. A quantum neural network based on the adiabatic quantum computation is one of candidates to overcome the difficulty for developing a quantum computation algorithm. Furthermore, by applying energy dissipation to the adiabatic quantum computation, an application of the quantum neural network is expanded. In this paper, we discuss effect which arises from the utilization of energy dissipation on a quantum neural network. Preliminary results which have been shown by numerical simulations indicate an availability of the energy dissipation for the quantum neural network.

1 Introduction

Computational power utilizing quantum states have attracted much research interests since superposition of quantum states can achieve highly parallel computation. Many quantum computation algorithms utilizing quantum mechanical behavior have been proposed [1]. However, the scope in which these algorithms are applied has been limited to specific problems such as factorization and database search [2,3]. The adiabatic quantum computation (AQC), which is one of approaches to overcome this difficulty, has been proposed by Farhi et al. [4] If one could know an appropriate Hamiltonian for a target problem, a quantum system composed of qubits to solve the problem could be implemented. The adiabatic change of a Hamiltonian leads a quantum state to a final state, in which one can find a solution. Therefore, if a Hamiltonian for an arbitrary problem is given, one can utilize a quantum computational power though some restrictions such as no energy degeneration and no level crossing are imposed [5].

To construct "partially" general purpose quantum computation, we have proposed neuromorphic quantum computation [6,7,8] based on the analogy between a Hopfield neural network (HNN) [9] and a qubit network. By regarding synaptic couplings as interactions between qubits, a quantum neural network (QNN) is constructed. Therefore, qubit interactions converted from synaptic couplings obtained for a HNN enable us to solve combinatorial optimization problems with a quantum system. Since a cost function must be expressed in a quadratic form as

M. Ishikawa et al. (Eds.): ICONIP 2007, Part II, LNCS 4985, pp. 730–737, 2008.

same manner in a HNN, this method is not applicable to an arbitrary problem. But it can be applied to wider range of problems.

However, these AQC can not be applied to a quantum system with degenerated states during the evolution of a Hamiltonian because of no guarantee according to the adiabatic theorem [5]. Therefore, we have proposed an application of energy dissipation to the AQC in order to remove the above restriction [8]. In this paper, we study details of energy dissipation effect on the QNN. First, we discuss the energy relation between a HNN and a QNN. Next, we focus on energy dissipation.

2 Quantum Neural Network

A HNN which is a full-connection neural network is composed of neurons with symmetrical synaptic connections [9]. The synaptic weights w_{ij}s for a combinatorial optimization problem are given by comparing the cost function and the energy E of a HNN. In a QNN, such a neuron is regard as a basic information unit of a quantum computer (qubit), and a synaptic connection corresponds to a qubit interaction. A qubit is expressed as a quantum superposition of the logical 0 and 1, and coherently interacts with other qubits. A quantum algorithm in the QNN is executed by utilizing the interactions. In the following section, the AQC, which is one of the quantum algorithms, is introduced briefly, and we explain a design method of a Hamiltonian for the AQC.

2.1 Adiabatic Quantum Computation

The adiabatic Hamiltonian evolution according to the AQC [4] is given as

$$H(t) = \left(1 - \frac{t_{\mathrm{AQC}}}{T}\right) H_I + \frac{t_{\mathrm{AQC}}}{T} H_F, \tag{1}$$

where H_I and H_F are the initial and final Hamiltonians, respectively. H_I is chosen so that its ground state is given by the superposition of all states as

$$|\psi(0)\rangle = \frac{1}{\sqrt{2^N}} \sum_{m=0}^{2^N - 1} |m\rangle, \tag{2}$$

where N is the number of qubits and $|m\rangle$ indicates the mth eigenvector. H_F is chosen so that assignments of its ground state satisfies a solution for a target problem. We assume that a quantum system starts at $t_{\mathrm{AQC}} = 0$ in the ground state of H_I, so that all possible candidates are set in the initial state $|\psi(0)\rangle$ as shown in Eq. (2). T denotes the period in which the Hamiltonian evolves and the quantum state changes, and we can control the speed of such changes to be suitable for finding an optimal solution among all candidates set in $|\psi(0)\rangle$. If a sufficiently large T is chosen, the evolution becomes adiabatic. The adiabatic theorem says that the quantum state will remain close to each ground state [5]. Therefore, the optimal solution can be found as the final state $|\psi(T)\rangle$.

Table 1. Relation between a qubit and a neuron

Hamiltonian	$\begin{pmatrix} E & 0 & 0 & A \\ 0 & E & 0 & 0 \\ 0 & 0 & E & 0 \\ A & 0 & 0 & E \end{pmatrix}$	$\begin{pmatrix} E & 0 & 0 & 0 \\ 0 & E & A & 0 \\ 0 & A & E & 0 \\ 0 & 0 & 0 & E \end{pmatrix}$
Ground State	$\lvert0\rangle\lvert0\rangle - \lvert1\rangle\lvert1\rangle$	$\lvert0\rangle\lvert1\rangle - \lvert1\rangle\lvert0\rangle$
Measured States	$\lvert0\rangle\lvert0\rangle$ or $\lvert1\rangle\lvert1\rangle$	$\lvert0\rangle\lvert1\rangle$ or $\lvert1\rangle\lvert0\rangle$
Interaction	excitatory	inhibitory
Neuron States	(-1 -1) or (1 1)	(-1 1) or (1 -1)
Synaptic Weights	$w_{12} > 0$	$w_{12} < 0$

2.2   Hamiltonian Synthesis Based on Interaction Between Neurons

Supporse we have a two-qubit system and use the rather simplified nonrealistic Hamiltonian as shown in Table 1 than the Hamiltonian of two spin-$\frac{1}{2}$ particles. This is because we try to find fundamental possibility of quantum learning in this study. $E(\geq 0)$ and A denote the magnitude of diagonal and non-diagonal elements, respectively. Please note that A corresponds to the magnitude of interaction between two states. If neuron states -1 and 1 correspond to $\lvert0\rangle$ and $\lvert1\rangle$, respectively, we can design a Hamiltonian with excitatory or inhibitory interaction between two qubits according to the relations shown in Table 1.

Here we define the final Hamiltonian for a N-qubit system as given by the following equation,

$$H_F \equiv E \cdot I + \sum_{ij,i\neq j}^{N} \left\{ H_{ij}(w_{ij})^{\dagger} + H_{ij}(w_{ij}) \right\}, \tag{3}$$

where E denotes energies of all independent states when qubits have no interaction, I denotes the $2^N \times 2^N$ identity matrix, w_{ij} denotes the synaptic weight from jth neuron to ith neuron, and $H_{ij}(w_{ij})$ denotes interaction between qubits as follows,

$$H_{ij}(w_{ij}) = \begin{cases} \lvert w_{ij} \rvert a_i a_j & w_{ij} > 0 \\ \lvert w_{ij} \rvert a_i^{\dagger} a_j & w_{ij} \leq 0 \end{cases}, \tag{4}$$

where a_i and $a_i^{\dagger}$ denote the annihilation-like and creation-like operators related to ith qubit. For more precisely, the operator a for one qubit is given as,

$$a = \begin{pmatrix} 0 & 0 \\ 1 & 0 \end{pmatrix}. \tag{5}$$

For example, suppose the symmetric synaptic weights given as,

$$W = \begin{pmatrix} 0 & -1 & 1 \\ -1 & 0 & -1 \\ 1 & -1 & 0 \end{pmatrix}. \tag{6}$$

Then H_F is given by Eq.(3) as follows,

$$
\begin{aligned}
H_F &= E \cdot I + \left\{ H_{21}(-1)^\dagger + H_{21}(-1) \right\} + \left\{ H_{31}(1)^\dagger + H_{31}(1) \right\} \\
&\quad + \left\{ H_{32}(-1)^\dagger + H_{32}(-1) \right\} \\
&= E \cdot I - \left\{ (I \otimes a^\dagger \otimes a)^\dagger + I \otimes a^\dagger \otimes a \right\} + \left\{ (a \otimes I \otimes a)^\dagger + a \otimes I \otimes a \right\} \\
&\quad - \left\{ (a^\dagger \otimes a \otimes I)^\dagger + a^\dagger \otimes a \otimes I \right\} \\
&= \begin{pmatrix}
E & 0 & 0 & 0 & 0 & 1 & 0 & 0 \\
0 & E & -1 & 0 & 0 & 0 & 0 & 0 \\
0 & -1 & E & 0 & -1 & 0 & 0 & 1 \\
0 & 0 & 0 & E & 0 & -1 & 0 & 0 \\
0 & 0 & -1 & 0 & E & 0 & 0 & 0 \\
1 & 0 & 0 & -1 & 0 & E & -1 & 0 \\
0 & 0 & 0 & 0 & 0 & -1 & E & 0 \\
0 & 0 & 1 & 0 & 0 & 0 & 0 & E
\end{pmatrix} .
\end{aligned}
\tag{7}
$$

Here we consider the simplest case $E = 1$, because the magnitude of E is not important in this study.

3   Energy Dissipation Effect on a QNN

In the previous section, the method for implementing the QNN has been shown. Now we focus on energy dissipation with the QNN. Quantum device is always affected by external noise, and quantum coherence disappears gradually as time goes. It is basic requirement that quantum coherence is kept during operation for a conventional quantum computation algorithm. The same holds for using the AQC. However, such decoherence is worth for the AQC eventually. This is because the successful execution of a AQC is not guaranteed for a quantum system with degenerated states during the evolution of a Hamiltonian, and then decoherence can be helpful for the state transition from a degenerated state to a lower energy state. Thus, we evaluate performance enhancement of a AQC after introducing decoherence. We suppose a quantum system obeying Boltzmann distribution as the simplest case and use Monte Carlo method in numerical simulations. The decoherence effect is incorporated as fluctuation of a Hamiltonian. An amplitude of the fluctuation is set to λ. A parameter $\beta = 1/k_B T_s$ of Boltzmann distribution, where k_B and T_s are Boltzmann factor and temperature, respectively, has same amplitude as $1/\lambda$. The proposed algorithm has two time constants for system and Hamiltonian evolutions. The former is sufficientry small compared to the later following the requirement of adiabatic evolution.

In order to understand the basic behavior of the QNN with energy dissipation, we suppose a simplest case where $H_I = H_F$ and $|\psi(0)\rangle \neq$ the ground state. Figure 1 shows an algorithm for the AQC in the proposed situation. At first, the initial state $|\psi(0)\rangle$ is set to a proper state. Next, the state evolves from $|\psi(t_{AQC})\rangle$ to $|\psi(t_{AQC}+1)\rangle$ adiabatically, and the energy $E(t_{AQC}+1)$ is calculated. Then, ΔH_k which is introduced in order to simulate energy dissipation is generated

1. Generate the initial state $|\psi(0)\rangle$
2. for $0 \leq t_{AQC} \leq T$
3. $|\psi(t_{AQC} + 1)\rangle := \exp\{-i \cdot \tau \cdot H_F\}|\psi(t_{AQC})\rangle$
4. $E(t_{AQC} + 1) := \langle\psi(t_{AQC} + 1)|H_F|\psi(t_{AQC} + 1)\rangle$
5.   for $1 \leq k \leq k_{max}$
6.   Generate ΔH_k at random
7. $|\psi_k(t_{AQC} + 1)\rangle := \exp\{-i \cdot \tau \cdot (H_F + \Delta H_k)\}|\psi(t_{AQC})\rangle$
8. $E_k(t_{AQC} + 1) := \langle\psi_k(t_{AQC} + 1)|H_F|\psi_k(t_{AQC} + 1)\rangle$
9.   Calculate Boltzmann distribution,
$$Z := \sum_k \exp\{-\beta \cdot (E_k(t_{AQC} + 1) - E(t_{AQC} + 1))\},$$
$$P(k) := \tfrac{1}{Z} \exp\{-\beta \cdot (E_k(t_{AQC} + 1) - E(t_{AQC} + 1))\}$$
10.   Pick a state $|\psi_j(t_{AQC} + 1)\rangle$ from among k_{max} states according to $P(k)$
11. $|\psi(t_{AQC} + 1)\rangle := |\psi_j(t_{AQC} + 1)\rangle$
12. Observe the final state $|\psi(T)\rangle$

Fig. 1. Algorithm for adiabatic evolution with energy dissipation

at random ($(\Delta h_{ij})_k \in \Delta H_k, \ -\lambda \leq (\Delta h_{ij})_k \leq \lambda$). $|\psi_k(t_{AQC} + 1)\rangle$ evolves from $|\psi(t_{AQC})\rangle$ depending on $H_F + \Delta H_k$. We calculate a probability $P(k)$ for $|\psi_k(t_{AQC} + 1)\rangle$ based on Boltzmann distribution. We pick a state $|\psi_j(t_{AQC} + 1)\rangle$ from among k_{max} states according to $P(k)$ and thus get $|\psi(t_{AQC} + 1)\rangle = |\psi_j(t_{AQC}+1)\rangle$. Repeating the procedure T times results in $|\psi(T)\rangle = |\psi_{0_F}\rangle$ where $|\psi_{0_F}\rangle$ is the ground state of H_F. Finally we get a result for a target problem by observing the system. Let us show the state change of the QNN with interactions converted from a HNN which has the synaptic weights as given by the following equation,

$$W = \begin{pmatrix} 0 & -1 & 0 & -1 \\ -1 & 0 & -1 & 0 \\ 0 & -1 & 0 & -1 \\ -1 & 0 & -1 & 0 \end{pmatrix}. \tag{8}$$

The final Hamiltonian is obtained automatically according to Eq.(3). The energy of the QNN changes as shown in Fig. 2. In this case, $\tau = 10000$ and $|\psi(0)\rangle$ is set to a superpositional state between the first excited state and the second excited state. It can be seen the energy is dissipated as time goes and have the almost same energy of the ground state after evolution. And the energy of the QNN with large λ changes early. Furthermore, all changes stagnate at close to the first excited energy E_1 on the way to the ground energy. Please note that the energy doesn't reach the ground energy exactly with any λ since the finite error rises from the fluctuation of a Hamiltonian in this simulation. Next, we consider another case where $H_I = H_F$ and $|\psi(0)\rangle =$ the ground state to investigate the finite error. The energy of the QNN changes as shown in Fig. 3. All changes start from the ground energy in this case. It can be seen the energy fluctuates because of the fluctuation of a Hamiltonian. And the fluctuation increases with increasing λ.

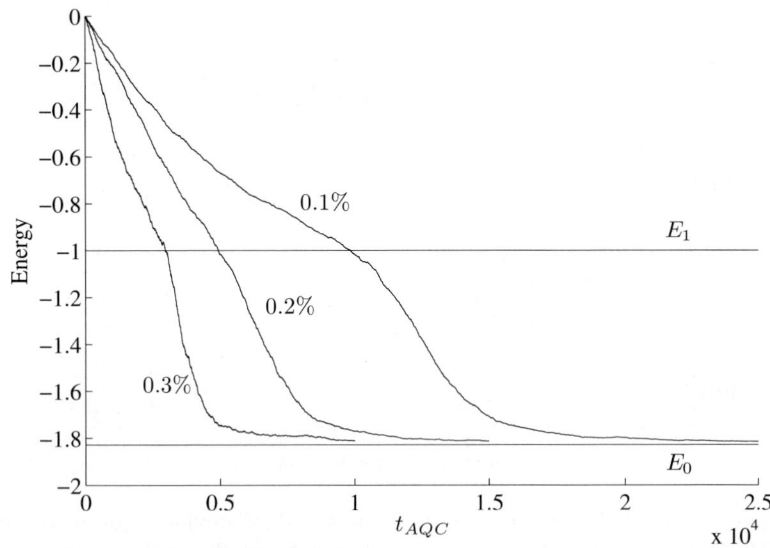

Fig. 2. Energy changes with H_F given as Eq. (3) and Eq. (8) by using adiabatic evolution with 0.1%, 0.2%, and 0.3% energy dissipation rate. The straight lines denote energy levels. E_0 and E_1 denote the ground and the first excited energy, respectively.

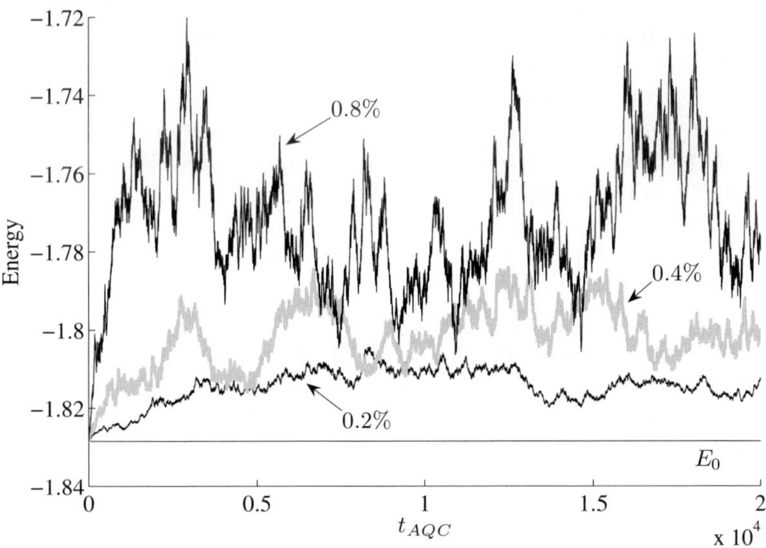

Fig. 3. Energy changes by using adiabatic evolution with 0.2%, 0.4%, and 0.8% energy dissipation rate. The straight line denotes the ground energy E_0.

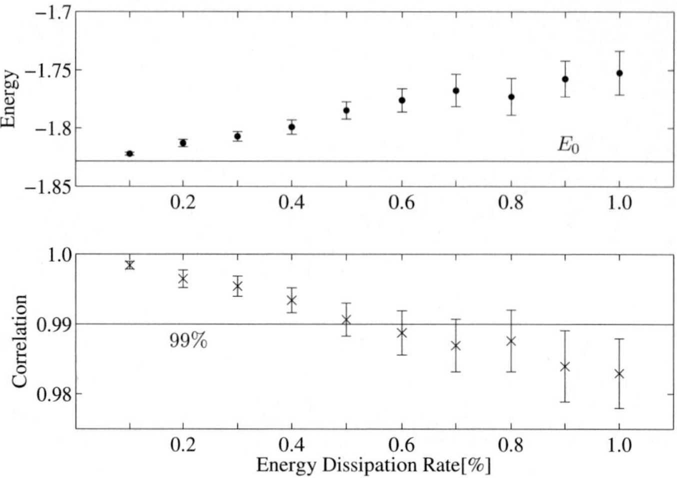

Fig. 4. Upper figure shows the average and the standard deviation of energy of the QNN as a function of energy dissipation rate. Lower figure shows the average and the standard deviation of correlation between the ground state of H_F and the final state of the QNN as a function of energy dissipation rate. The straight line denotes 99%.

In order to study an influence of the fluctuation upon the final state after evolution, we show energy and correlation between the ground state of H_F and the final state as a function of λ as shown in Fig. 4. The gap between the ground energy E_0 and the average of energy of the QNN after evolution become wide with increasing λ. It can also be seen the correlation decreases with increasing λ. Naturally, the decrease in the correlation cause the decrease in the measurement probability of the desired state. If 1% as a maximum of error is allowed, we can not use $\lambda \geq 0.5\%$ in this case.

4   Discussion

Here, we discuss about energy dissipation effect. The AQC can not be applied to a quantum system with degenerated states during the evolution of a Hamiltonian because of no guarantee according to the adiabatic theorem [5]. However, by the energy dissipation effect, any state of such system will reach close to the ground state of H_F with enough time. Thus, the AQC with energy dissipation can be applied to such system. Nevertheless a less energy dissipation rate requires great time and a more one requires the decrease in the successful probability. The rate must be set to an appropriate rate for a target problem. The best solution of the difficulty is to control the rate properly like simulated annealing.

Annealing methods are used in many optimization methods including artificial neural networks in order that the state of a target system is not trapped at local minima. The advantage of the proposed method in comparison with such system is that the traps which originate from classical dynamics can be eliminated by incorporating quantum dynamics. However, the probability observed for the desired state is still small because the ground state includes the undesired states. A study on some other procedure in order to improve the probability is future work.

Additionally, its physical implementation is easy since the H_F is realized only by the interactions between qubits. Spin qubits are the most likely candidates for implementing the proposed algorithm [10].

5   Conclusion

We sutdy energy dissipation effect on a quantum neural network. Results from numerical simulations show that we must adjust energy dissipation rate to an appropriate rate for a target problem. A study on some other procedure like simulated annealing in order to improve the probability observed for the desired state is future work.

Acknowledgements

This work was supported in part by the Grant-in-Aid for Scientific Research by the Ministry of Education, Culture, Sports, Science, and Technology of Japan.

References

1. Nielsen, M.A., Chuang, I.L.: Quantum Computation and Quantum Information. Cambridge University Press, Cambridge (2000)
2. Shor, P.W.: Polynomial-time algorithm for prime factorization and discrete logarithms on a quantum computer. SIAM J. Comput. 26, 1484–1509 (1997)
3. Grover, L.K.: A fast quantum mechanical algorithm for database search. In: Proc. Twenty-Eighth Annual ACM Symp. on the Theory of Computing, pp. 212–219 (1996)
4. Farhi, E., Goldstone, J., Gutmann, S., Lapan, J., Lundgren, A., Preda, D.: A quantum adiabatic evolution algorithm applied to random instances of an np-complete problem. Science 292, 472–475 (2001)
5. Messiah, A.: Quantum Mechanics. Dover, New York (1999)
6. Sato, S., Kinjo, M., Nakajima, K.: An approach for quantum computing using adiabatic evolution algorithm. Jpn. J. Appl. Phys. 42, 7169–7173 (2003)
7. Kinjo, M., Sato, S., Nakajima, K.: Artificial Neural Networks and Neural Information Processing. In: Kaynak, O., Alpaydin, E., Oja, E., Xu, L. (eds.), pp. 951–958. Springer, Heidelberg (2003)
8. Kinjo, M., Sato, S., Nakamiya, Y., Nakajima, K.: Neuromorphic quantum computation with energy dissipation. Physical Review A 72, 052328 (2005)
9. Tank, D.W., Hopfield, J.J.: Simple neural optimization networks: An a/d converter, signal decision circuit, and a linear programming circuit. IEEE Trans. Circuits Syst. 36, 533–541 (1986)
10. Nakamiya, Y., Kinjo, M., Takahashi, O., Sato, S., Nakajima, K.: Quantum Neural Network Composed of Kane's Qubits. Jpn. J. Appl. Phys. 45, 8030–8034 (2006)

Learning and Memorizing Models of Logical Theories in a Hybrid Learning Device

Helmar Gust, Kai-Uwe Kühnberger, and Peter Geibel

Institute of Cognitive Science, University of Osnabrück
D-49076 Osnabrück, Germany

Abstract. Although there are several attempts to resolve the obvious tension between neural network learning and symbolic reasoning devices, no generally acceptable resolution of this problem is available. In this paper, we propose a hybrid neuro-symbolic architecture that bridges this gap (in one direction), first, by translating a first-order input into a variable-free topos representation and second, by learning models of logical theories on the neural level by equations induced by this topos. As a side-effect of this approach the network memorizes a whole model of the training input and allows to build the core of a framework for integrated cognition.

1 Introduction

There is an obvious gap between symbolic and subsymbolic representations. Whereas symbolic approaches have been successfully applied for modeling higher cognitive abilities (such as reasoning, theorem proving, planning, or problem solving), subsymbolic approaches have been proven to be extremely successful in domains often connected to lower cognitive abilities (such as learning from noisy data, controlling real-world robots, or detecting visual patterns). From a methodological perspective major differences between symbolic and subsymbolic approaches concern the recursion principle, compositionality, and the representation of complex data structures: for example, on the symbolic level, the recursion principle ensures that the formalism is productive and allows very compact representations. Both, recursion and compositionality is not available in the standard theory of neural networks.

There are certain attempts to resolve the gap between symbolic and subsymbolic computations. With respect to representing complex data structures with neural means, sign propagation [8], tensor product representations [13], or holographic reduced representations [9] are examples for such approaches. Unfortunately, these theories do not fully solve the problem or have certain principal flaws: sign propagation lacks the ability of learning, and tensor product representations result in an exponentially increasing number of elements to represent variable bindings, only to mention some of the problems. Furthermore, researchers tried to solve the so-called inference problem, namely the specification of the neural correlate for symbolic inferences. An example to solve this problem

M. Ishikawa et al. (Eds.): ICONIP 2007, Part II, LNCS 4985, pp. 738–748, 2008.

is theoretically described in [7], where a logical deduction operator is approximated by a neural network and the generated fixed point provides the semantics of a logical theory. [1] is a further development of this theory by providing some preliminary evaluation results for covered logic programs. Another approach is [6], where category theoretic methods are assigned to neural constructions. In [2], tractable fragments of predicate logic are learned by connectionist networks. In [4] and [5], a procedure is proposed how to translate predicate logic into a variable-free logic that can be used as input for a neural network.[1] The aim of the present paper is to provide a theory for a neural memory module that is able to learn a model of first-order logic in the spirit of [4]. The present approach should be distinguished from soft computing techniques, such as fuzzy neural networks. The research question is how we can bridge the gap between symbolic theories and subsymbolic approaches by neuro-symbolic integration for memorizing facts implicitly coded by the weights of a network.

The paper is structured as follows: Section 2 sketches the idea of using Topos theory as a semi-symbolic level for generating the input for a neural network (as was preliminary described in [4]). Section 3 describes the architecture of the system and a programming language fragment. Section 4 discusses the learning of the neural network. In Section 5, we propose a neuro-symbolic architecture and Section 6 concludes the paper.

2   Topos Theory as the Semi-symbolic Level

2.1   Basic Topos Theory

The paradigmatic example of a topos $\mathcal{T}$ is the category of sets and functions $\mathcal{SET}$, i.e. a category having nice properties.[2] The central properties of a topos are (a) all finite diagrams have limits, (b) exponents exist, and (c) there is a subobject classifier. Consequently a topos has an initial object i, a terminal object $!$, a truth-value object Ω, and finite products and coproducts.

We list the fundamental constructions of a topos: first, we have product arrows (denoted by $g \times f$) given by the adjointness condition $\frac{g:c \rightarrow a, f:c \rightarrow b}{g \times f:c \rightarrow a \times b}$, such that $\pi_1 \circ g \times f = g$ and $\pi_2 \circ g \times f = f$ (where π_i are the corresponding projections). Product constructions in $\mathcal{SET}$ correspond to Cartesian products $a \times b$ of given sets a and b together with the projection functions π_1 and π_2. Second, there are coproduct arrows (denoted by $\langle g, f \rangle$) given by $\frac{g:a \rightarrow c, f:b \rightarrow c}{\langle g,f \rangle:a+b \rightarrow c}$, such that $\langle g, f \rangle \circ j_1 = g$ and $\langle g, f \rangle \circ j_2 = f$ (where j_i are the corresponding injections). In $\mathcal{SET}$, a coproduct $a + b$ corresponds to the disjoint union of two sets a and b together with left and right injections j_l and j_r. Third, there are exponents (denoted by

---

[1] All the mentioned approaches try to model predicate logical reasoning on a neural basis. Although it may be the case that many computational problems can be reduced to a "propositional version" of logic, some complex problems of theorem proving require necessarily full first-order logic. Additionally the neural modeling of predicate logic is important from the perspective of basic research.

[2] Due to space limitations the interested reader is referred to [3] for more information.

740   H. Gust, K.-U. Kühnberger, and P. Geibel

$exp(f))$ given by $\frac{f:c\times a\to b}{exp_{\pi_1}(f):c\to b^a}$. Exponents in $\mathcal{SET}$ are set theoretic exponents a^b. The subobject classifier generalizes the concept of subsets in $\mathcal{SET}$ and can be used to characterize the interpretation of a predicate. Finally, the truth-value object in $\mathcal{SET}$ corresponds to a two-element set.

2.2   Translating Logic into Topos Theory

The basic idea of the present approach is to translate a first-order logical input into a homogeneous representation in topos theory (semi-symbolic level) and to use equations generated by structural properties of the topos to train a neural network. We give some examples of the translation of logic into a topos: the interpretation of an n-ary predicate p maps an n-tuple of individuals to a truth value. In a topos, this corresponds to an arrow $[p] : u^n \longrightarrow \Omega$, where u denotes an object representing the universe. For an n-ary function symbol f we get $[f] : u^n \longrightarrow u$ and for a constant c we get $[c] : ! \longrightarrow u$.

Logical expressions are composed by basic operators like $\wedge$, $\vee$, or $\neg$. Just to mention an example, a conjunction maps products of truth values to truth values, i.e. a conjunction in a topos is of type $\Omega \times \Omega \longrightarrow \Omega$. The corresponding equation of the commuting diagram specifying conjunction is: $[\wedge] \circ (true \times true) = true \circ !$, i.e. the diagonal arrow $true \times true$ concatenated with $[\wedge]$ is equal to the $true$ arrow mapping the terminal object ! to the truth-value object Ω.[3]

The topos representation of quantified formulas is slightly more complicated in comparison to the mentioned logical connectives. We exemplify existential quantification intuitively without going into details.[4] Consider the logical formula $\exists y_2 : \phi(y_2, y_1)$. Since ϕ is a 2-ary predicate the interpretation of ϕ in a topos is an arrow $[\phi] : u \times u \longrightarrow \Omega$. The interpretation of the quantified formula refers to a 1-ary predicate $\lambda y_1.\exists y_2 : \phi(y_2, y_1)$. Variables do no longer occur in the interpretation of formulas. The *information* they code in the classical case is covered in the domains of the predicates. Therefore, we get:

$$[\phi(y_2, y_1)] = [\phi] : u \times u \longrightarrow \Omega$$
$$[\exists y_2 : \phi(y_2, y_1)] = \exists \pi_2 : [\phi(y_2, y_1)] = \exists \pi_2 : [\phi]$$

With these prerequisites we are able to translate an arbitrary FOL formula A into an arrow $[A]$ in a topos. The constructions used for the translation process introduce commuting triangles in the topos (i.e. equations of the form $h = f \circ g$). In order to code a given first-order axiom system, we introduce for every axiom A the equation $[A] = true$. Clearly, the translation process introduces many additional equations originating from the constructions. Equations are constraints for an interpretation of the FOL theory T, i.e. $[.] : \mathcal{L} \longrightarrow \mathcal{T}$ corresponds to a model of T, if it obeys all constraints from translating the axioms. Proving a query Q means checking whether $[Q] = true$ holds in all models.

---

[3] Abusing notation, we use ! for both, the terminal object and the terminal arrow.

[4] Compare [5] for a detailed description of the construction including the necessary commuting diagrams.

Table 1. The specification of language $\mathcal{L}_T$ encoding topos entities

$\mathcal{L}_T$	Intended Interpretation
!	Terminal object !
@	Truth value objects Ω
u	The universe U
t	Truth value *true*
f	Truth value *false*
Y x Z	Product object of Y and Z
y x z	Product arrow of y and z
!	Terminal arrows
f: Y --> Z	Definition of an arrow
y o z	Composition of arrows y and z

3   The Implementation of the System

3.1   Architecture

In order to solve the problem of representing logical heterogeneous data structures with neural networks, it is necessary to code the meaning of logical expressions in a homogeneous way. Section 2 sketches a possibility to achieve a suitable translation. Now we describe how this translation can be implemented for a neural learning device.

(i) Input data is given by a set of logical formulas (axioms and queries) in a first-order logical language $\mathcal{L}$.

(ii) This set of formulas is translated into (variable-free) objects and arrows of a topos as described in Section 2.

(iii) A PROLOG program generates equations in normal form $f \circ g = h$ identifying new arrows in the topos due to topos constructions like limits, exponentiation etc. We developed a simple topos language $\mathcal{L}_T$ to code objects and arrows for processability by the program components (cf. Subsection 3.2).

(iv) These equations are used as input for the training of a neural network (compare Section 4).

3.2   A Programming Language Fragment for Topos Constructions

Table 1 summarizes the coding of topos entities in $\mathcal{L}_T$ of some important constructions concerning objects and arrows. By using a macro mechanism defined in $\mathcal{L}_T$ it is possible to code compactly complex equations. Derived objects and arrows, e.g. identities and products, are recognized by the PROLOG program and the corresponding defining equations are automatically generated.

The operator and the variable concept of PROLOG provide powerful tools for defining macros for compact and readable translations: for all logical connectives there are corresponding macros which then expand to the spelled-out categorical constructions. The first part of Table 2 (lines 1 to 4) specifies the relevant macros.

Table 2. Relevant macros used in $\mathcal{L}_T$ (first 4 lines) and example code of objects and arrows (lines 5 to 18)

```
define X and Y :: (and) o (X,Y).
define X or Y   :: (or)  o (X,Y).
define X -> Y   :: (->)  o (X,Y).
define X ==> Y :: (->)  o (X x Y) = t.

!.                      # the terminal object
@.                      # the truthvalue object
! x ! = !.
u.                      # the universe
static  t:: ! --> @, # true
static  f:: ! --> @. # false
not:: @       --> @,   # negation
->:: @ x @ --> @.   # implication
not t = f,
not f = t,
-> o t x t = t,
-> o t x f = f,
-> o f x t = t,
-> o f x f = t.
```

The macros **not**, **and**, **or**, **->** are categorical counterparts of the logical connectives $\neg, \wedge, \vee, \rightarrow$, respectively. The macro **not** expands a predicate P to its negation. Binary connectives (**and**, **or**, **->**) translate a pair of predicates to the product predicate. The macro **==>** expands to an equation defining the universal closure of an implication, where premise and consequence have identical arguments.

The introduced constructions need to be specified with respect to their semantics. Some examples of how certain logical properties of objects and arrows of the topos can be coded in $\mathcal{L}_T$ are mentioned (cf. Table 2, lines 5–18). The terminal object, the truth-value object, and the universe are specified as ordinary objects in the topos. The modifier **static** for truth values is interpreted by the network program to keep representations fixed. The logical connectives are introduced as arrows mapping truth values or pairs of truth values to truth values. The defining equations realize the corresponding truth tables.

4   Learning Models by a Network

4.1   Network Topology

Contrary to the standard approach to use neural networks as universal function approximators [11], we will use neural networks to approximate the composition process (and thereby the behavior) of functions and predicates. More precisely, not the structural properties of these entities will be represented, rather the behavior in the composition process is modeled. This means that representations of arrows need to be learned.

Figure 1 depicts the structure of the neural network that is used to model the composition process of evaluating terms and formulas. Each arrow and object

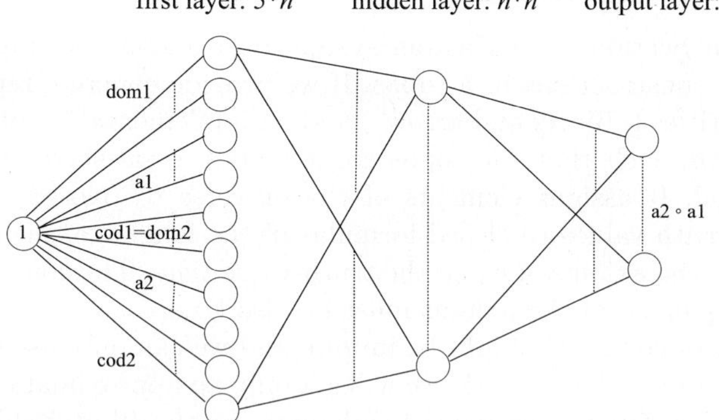

Fig. 1. The structure of the neural network that is used to learn the composition of first-order formulas

in the topos is represented as a point in the n-dimensional real-valued unit cube together with pointers to the respective domain and codomain. The input of the network is represented by weights from the initial node with activation 1. This allows to backpropagate errors to the representation of the inputs. The input represents the two arrows that need to be composed: the domain of the first arrow, the representation of the first arrow, the codomain of the first arrow (which must be equal to the domain of the second arrow), the representation of the second arrow, and the codomain of the second arrow. These requirements lead to a net with $5 \cdot n$ many input values (compare the first layer in Figure 1). In practice, we use $h \cdot n$ many nodes for the hidden layer, where h is a parameter. For simple examples a value of $h = 2$ works well. The output of the network is the representation of the composed arrow.

The overall idea of the approach is to transform an interpretation function I of classical logic into a function $I' : \mathcal{R}^m \to \mathcal{R}^n$ to make it appropriate as input for a neural network. In order to enable the system to learn inferences, some arrows have static representations. These representations correspond directly to truth values:[5]

- The truth value $true$: $(1.0, 0.0, 0.0, \ldots, 0.0)$
- The truth value $false$: $(0.0, 1.0, 0.0, \ldots, 0.0)$

Notice that the truth value $true$ and the truth value $false$ are maximally distinct in the first two dimensions. All other objects and arrows are initialized with the value $(0.5, 0.5, 0.5, \ldots, 0.5)$.[6]

---

[5] The choice of the particular values for $true$ and $false$ are motivated by the usage of a simple projection to a two-dimensional plane for visualizing the results. The actual values used in the applications (cf. Subsection 4.3) are 0.999954 and 0.000046.

[6] The actual value used in applications is 0.622459.

4.2   Approximating Models

As described in Section 2 each axiom system of a first-order language can be translated into constructions in a topos. If we provide concrete representations of the topos entities (objects and arrows) and an implementation of the concatenation operation, such that the topos constraints are satisfied, such a system realizes a model: It assigns elements of the universe to (closed) terms of the language and truth values to closed formulas of the language, such that the interpretations of the axioms $\mathcal{A}$ equal the truth-value *true*. The constraints ensure that the consequences of the axioms must be also true.

Since the set of equations might be infinite and we can only use finitely many equations for training the network, we will get only an approximation of a model. The quality of the approximation depends first, on the (finite) subset of equations chosen for training and second, on the error of the network, especially how errors propagate when the concatenation operation needs to be iterated. We minimize the first problem by avoiding universal constructions (particularly pullbacks, equalizers, and exponents) and try to keep products small. Because pullbacks and equalizers are involved in certain constructions, it is not possible to eliminate universal constructions completely. Nevertheless it should be possible to approximate a model in a sense that the approximation coincides with a proper model on a "relevant" set of formulas. Relevance is clearly hard to characterize, but as a first idea we can say that all formulas can be learned to be *true* that can be derived with n applications of an appropriate deduction operator $\mathcal{D}$. Concerning the second issue (error propagation), currently we do not have estimations about error propagation. The training of the networks minimizes the average error over the test equations. A possibility to estimate the quality of the result is to look at the maximal error. If the maximal error does not converge, it cannot be expected that the net will provide good results.

4.3   Example Applications

We applied the presented approach to rather simple learning problems, e.g. where the task was to learn the transitivity of implications [4]. We tested the system also on more complex problems (benchmark problems of symbolic theorem provers). Due to space limitations we cannot give a detailed description of these experiments here. The interested reader is referred to the forthcoming [5] for more information concerning complex problems. To get a flavor of complex learning tasks, consider the famous steamroller problem (benchmark problem for symbolic theorem provers [14]). Here is a natural language description of the steamroller:

> Wolves, foxes, birds, caterpillars, and snails are animals, and there exist some of each of them. Also there are some grains, and grains are plants. Every animal either likes to eat all plants or all animals much smaller than itself that like to eat some plants. Caterpillars and snails are much smaller than birds, which are much smaller than foxes, which in turn are much smaller than wolves. Wolves do not like to eat foxes or grains, while birds like to eat caterpillars, but not snails. Caterpillars and snails like to eat some plants. Prove: There is an animal that likes to eat a grain eating animal.

Table 3. Results of a test run of the steamroller problem focusing on queries concerning the underlying ontology and the *much-smaller* relation

```
Equation:                    error:       representation of composition:
animal o gr  = t     0.523919  0.096594   0.406415   0.015048   0.257761
plant  o gr  = t     0.227860  0.651427   0.042832   0.489557   0.304671
animal o sn  = t     0.072986  0.622445   0.022519   0.020093   0.050558
animal o ca  = t     0.090758  0.588392   0.032222   0.036294   0.098955
animal o bi  = t     0.076140  0.614318   0.035708   0.021240   0.042989
animal o fo  = t     0.080184  0.602162   0.025493   0.013849   0.035990
animal o wo  = t     0.101175  0.553314   0.039884   0.012865   0.033384

Equation:                         error:       representation of composition:
much_smaller o wo x ca  = t     0.062300  0.705555  0.169615  0.020756  0.093564
much_smaller o wo x bi  = t     0.043545  0.736651  0.113148  0.016931  0.068486
much_smaller o ca x wo  = t     0.001257  0.988095  0.003977  0.039950  0.027726
much_smaller o bi x wo  = t     0.001088  0.992163  0.002388  0.036556  0.027928
```

A straightforward logical representation of the given theory yields 27 clauses (containing also non-Horn clauses). Using a many-sorted logic we can reduce the total number of clauses to 12, which also include non-Horn clauses. We just mention the learning of the underlying ontology and the *much-smaller* relation as depicted in Table 3. The depicted equations correspond to queries. The network learned the underlying ontology of the steamroller problem. Although the significance of the classification could be better, the system classified *wolf, fox* etc. as *animal* and *grain* as *plant*. Furthermore the *much-smaller* relation was successfully learned.

5   A Neuro-symbolic Architecture for Learning and Memory

In order to develop a theory of integrated cognition, research is often confronted with a trade-off between robust connectionist systems and exact symbolic approaches. Whereas neural systems often show a robust behavior and seem to be appropriate for many learning tasks, they lack the precision of symbolic approaches and have problems to model higher cognitive abilities. On the other hand, symbolic models have problems in time-critical situations, they are usually less robust and do not seem to be appropriate for lower cognitive abilities. We think that a promising step towards a theory of integrated cognition is the development of hybrid neuro-symbolic architectures. Only in this case it is possible to benefit from the advantages of both approaches. We sketch in the following some ideas for such an integration with respect to learning and memory.

The main idea of the proposed neuro-symbolic integration is the introduction of a semi-symbolic level, namely the coding of logic in a topos. It should be mentioned that the representation of first-order logic in a topos is not a one-to-one translation of the logical formulas into objects and arrows: some logical subexpressions have no explicit topos representation (e.g. quantifiers and variables do not correspond to any arrows in the topos) and there are a lot of arrows in the topos constructions that do not correspond to logical (sub)formulas.

Figure 2 depicts the overall architecture of the system including memory aspects. On the symbolic level (input level) a finite set of first-order formulas specify a logical theory T. Background knowledge is initially not coded in this

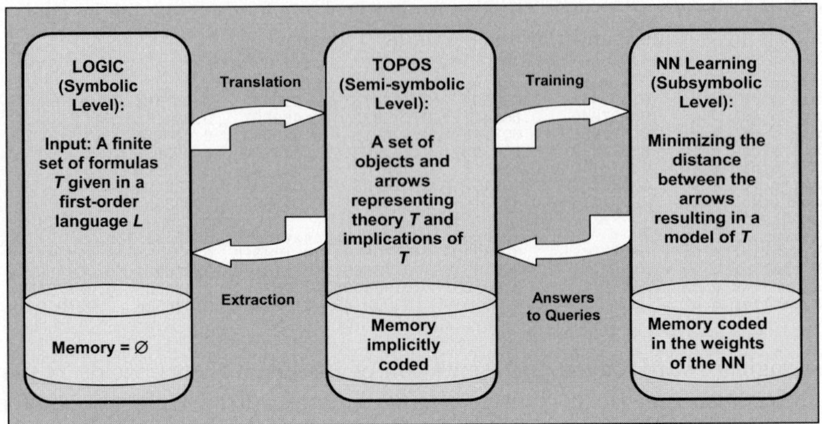

Fig. 2. A hybrid architecture for neuro-symbolic integration

module. The translation of logical formulas into a topos representation yields a set of objects and arrows that induce a memory M of T in terms of commuting diagrams. M is only implicitly coded due to the fact that knowledge is coded in topos constructions. Nevertheless these constructions can be used to extract knowledge and to translate it back to the logical level, thanks to the usage of macros in coding categorical constructions.

It is important to notice that learning a model $\mathcal{M}$ of T by the neural network induces a memory in terms of the trained weights of the neural network. Memory modules in cognitive architectures, as well as knowledge bases for technical applications are often confronted with problems like the profusion of knowledge and the trade-off between the size of explicitly coded knowledge and the formalization of axioms that can be used to deduce relevant facts about the environment on-the-fly. The neural coding of memory has the advantage that the an approximation of all possible facts that can be deduced from given axioms are learned and are immediately available given appropriate queries.

Currently we are not able to extract knowledge directly from the neural correlate, but it is possible to extract knowledge implicitly by querying the network. By re-translating the answers of the network to the logical level, memory can be expanded on the topos level or on the logical level. The added-value of the proposed architecture can be summarized as follows:

- The architecture is robust, because the trained neural network can answer queries even though noise might be contained in the training data.
- Even in time-critical situations the proposed framework is able to react and to provide relevant information.
- The architecture gives a first idea how an interaction between a symbolic level and a sub-symbolic level of computation can be achieved.
- The architecture is cognitively more plausible than pure symbolic or sub-symbolic approaches.

We think that a major advantage of the present architecture is the learning of *models* instead of focusing on deductions: from a cognitive perspective model-based reasoning seems to be more adequate than inference-based reasoning.

6   Conclusions

In this paper, an approach of learning first-order theories with neural networks was proposed. The system allows to learn rather complex logical theories and store models of the respective theories. This enables the network to represent not only the logical input, but furthermore to represent an approximation of all consequences of the given axioms. We think that this type of a neuro-symbolic architecture is a promising approach for neuro-symbolic integration tasks and has a strong advantages for memory modules in comparison to classical symbolic knowledge bases. Future research concerns a further development of the system with respect to theoretical and practical aspects, as well as a thorough evaluation.

References

1. Bader, S., Hitzler, P., Hölldobler, S., Witzel, A.: A Fully Connectionist Model Generator for Covered First-Order Logic Programs. In: Proceedings of the Twentieth International Joint Conference on Artificial Intelligence, pp. 666–671 (2007)
2. D'Avila Garcez, A., Broda, K., Gabbay, D.: Neural-Symbolic Learning Systems: Foundations and Applications. Springer, Heidelberg (2002)
3. Goldblatt, R.: Topoi: The Categorial Analysis of Logic. Studies in Logic and the Foundations of Mathematics. North-Holland, Amsterdam (1979)
4. Gust, H., Kühnberger, K.-U.: Learning Symbolic Inferences with Neural Networks. In: Bara, B., Barsalou, L., Bucciarelli, M. (eds.) CogSci 2005, XXVII Annual Conference of the Cognitive Science Society, pp. 875–880. Lawrence Erlbaum, Mahwah (2005)
5. Gust, H., Kühnberger, K.-U., Geibel, P.: Learning Models of Predicate Logical Theories with Neural Networks based on Topos Theory. In: Hitzler, P., Hammer, B. (eds.) Perspectives of Neuro-Symbolic Integration. LNCS, Springer, Heidelberg (in press)
6. Healy, M., Caudell, T.: Neural Networks, Knowledge and Cognition: A Mathematical Semantic Model Based upon Category Theory. University of New Mexico (2004), EECE-TR-04-020
7. Hitzler, P., Hölldobler, S., Seda, A.: Logic Programs and Connectionist Networks. Journal of Applied Logic 2(3), 245–272 (2004)
8. Lange, T., Dyer, M.G.: High-Level Inferencing in a Connectionist Network. Technical report UCLA-AI-89-12 (1989)
9. Plate, T.: Distributed Representations and Nested Compositional Structure. PhD thesis, University of Toronto (1994)
10. Pollack, J.: Recursive Distributed Representations. Artificial Intelligence 46(1), 77–105 (1990)
11. Rojas, R.: Neural Networks – A Systematic Introduction. Springer, New York (1996)

12. Shastri, L., Ajjanagadde, V.: From Simple Associations to Systematic Reasoning: A Connectionist Representation of Rules, Variables and Dynamic Bindings Using Temporal Synchrony. Behavioral and Brain Sciences 16, 417–494 (1990)
13. Smolenski, P.: Tensor Product Variable Binding and the Representation of Symbolic Structures in Connectionist Systems. Artificial Intelligence 46(1–2), 159–216 (1996)
14. Walter, C.: A Mechanical Solution of Schubert's Steamroller by Many-Sorted Resolution. Artificial Intelligence 1985, 217–224 (1985)

Mixtures of Experts: As an Attempt to Integrate the Dual Route Cascaded and the Triangle Models for Reading English Words

Shin-ichi Asakawa

Centre for Information Sciences,
Tokyo Womens' Christian University,
2-6-1 Zempukuji, Suginami, Tokyo 1678585, Japan
asakawa@twcu.ac.jp*

Abstract. An implementation of neural network models for reading English words aloud is proposed. Since 1989, there has been existing a debate in neuropsycholgy and cognitive science about the models of reading. One is the Dual Route Cascaded model, another is the Triangle model. Since there exist arbitrary variables in both models, it was difficult to decide which model would be appropriate to explain the data from psychological experiments and neuropsychological evidence. Therefore, in order to provide a solution of this debate, an attempt to integrate both models was attempted. By introducing the Mixtures of Experts Network model, a solution to overcome the arbitrariness of both models could be given. The Mixtures of Experts Network model could include both models as a special case. From the Mixtures of Experts network's point of view, the difference between the Dual Route Cascaded model and the Triangle model would be considered as a quantitative difference of the dispersion parameters.

Keywords: Mixtures of Experts, Dual Route Cascaded Model, Triangle Model, Reading English words aloud.

1 Introduction

We discuss here an implementation of neural network models for reading English words aloud. Neuropsychologists and speech therapists, who have to take care of dyslexic patients, ask for neural network modelers to develop an efficient model to explain the performance of the language abilities of their patients. Among models proposed previously, two models have been considered as important, the Dual Route Cascaded (DRC)[1–3] and the Triangle model[9, 10]. Although these models can describe dyslexic symptoms, some problems remains still unsolved. We can point out several problems; the arbitrariness of the blending parameter, the existence of the lookup table, and the problem of division of labor. Therefore, nobody could judge which model is able to give a better description. The debate between them still continues, no consensus has not hitherto been reached. In this

---

* Special thanks to Eddy.

M. Ishikawa et al. (Eds.): ICONIP 2007, Part II, LNCS 4985, pp. 749–758, 2008.
© Springer-Verlag Berlin Heidelberg 2008

paper, we tried to elucidate the features of the DRC and the Triangle model. This paper will show that these models can be regarded as just a special case of the more general model, the Mixtures of Experts (ME) model originally proposed by Jordan and Jacobs [5, 6]. This paper will also prove that the qualitative differences between the DRC and the Triangle models could be integrated as the quantitative difference in terms of the dispersion parameter in the ME.

This paper is organized as follows: Section 2 will try make terminology clear to prompt understanding the neuropsychological symptoms of reading disorders and related neural network models. Section 3, will introduce the two major models: the Dual Route Cascaded and the Triangle models, and will clarify problems to be solved. Section 4 will introduce the Mixture of Experts model in order to integrate the Dual Route Cascaded and the Triangle model. In section 5, focuses on attempts to confirm the validity of the Mixture of Experts model by numerical experiment. Section 6, will wrap things up with a discussion and some conclusions.

2   Terminology

Here, we will try to make some terms clear: the distinction between regular words and exception words, and between consistent words and inconsistent words. Regular words are the words which is in accordance with the Grapheme–to–Pronunciation–Corresponding (GPC) rule. Irregular words are the ones that the pronunciation of the words is not accordance with the GPC rules, for example "yacht". With regard to consistency, since the words like "hint", "mint", "saint", and "lint" share the same pronunciation /int/, they are consistent words. But the word "pint" is inconsistent, because it does not share the pronunciation /páint/. Consistent words have many neighbor words like "hint" and "mint" and inconsistent words have few neighbors like "yacht". Exception words, as the definition per se., are inconsistent (Glushko, 1979, p.676). Therefore, the concept "regular–irregular" and the concept "consistent–inconsistent" are not independent.

The surface dyslexic patients can read regular words and non words, but they cannot read exception words, especially low frequency non words. On the contrary, the symptom of phonological dyslexia is described as that the phonological dyslexic patients can read real words but they cannot read non words.

3   The DRC and the Triangle Models

3.1   The DRC Model

The DRC model has one to one corresponding between orthographic and phonological lexicons. All the real words have been registered into the orthographic and the phonological lexicons in advance. And each orthographic lexicon has a connection to the corresponding unit in the phonological lexicon[3]. Coltheart and his colleagues employed 7981 real words, which means there were 7981 entries, which can be regarded as a lookup table) in the orthographic and the phonological lexicons. This path way from orthography to phonology is called a lexical route. On the other hand, non-words and pseudo words can be read via GPC route. The GPC route was consisted of general rules so that it can translate given words to sound. The GPC rule are not always perfect since English as a orthographic language has many exception words, but almost all non–words can be pronounced by the GPC route. Real words might be read through the lexical route, because there are entries in the lookup table. However, since non–words and pseudo words do not have any entries in the lookup table, these words would be pronounced through the GPC route.

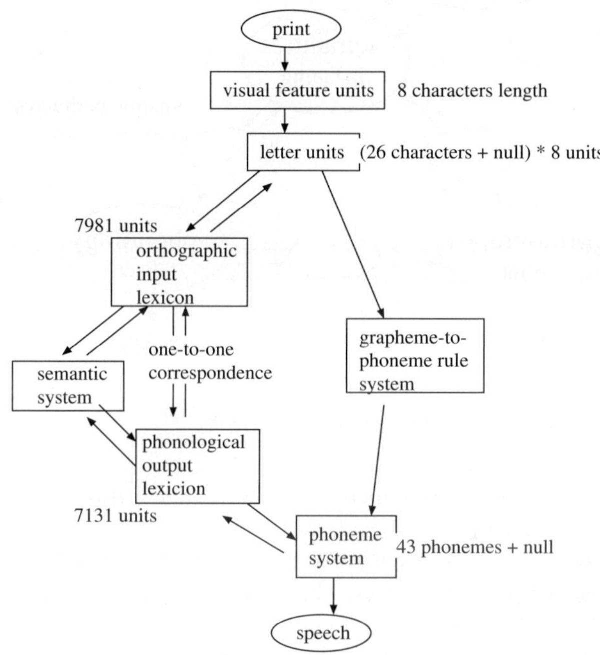

Fig. 1. The DRC model

In the original DRC model, a discrete switch was postulated to decide which route have to be adopted when we read a word. If there is an entry in the lookup table, then the word is pronounced via the lexical route. However, in the latest version of the DRC (Coltheart et al.,2001), a parameter was introduced in order to merge the outputs from two routes. Here, we can point out the problem how we can adjust the value of this parameter by hand.

3.2   The Triangle Model

In the framework of the Triangle model, on the contrary, dyslexic symptoms can be explained as follows. The surface dyslexia might be caused by the lesion in a single route (Plaut et al[8], simulation 4). The letters in the orthography can be pronounced both the direct route and the indirect route via semantics. The pronunciations are affected both routes. In the direct route, regular words and high frequency exception words will be learned, exception words with low frequency need a support of semantics. The degree of dependency on the semantics is called the "division of labor".

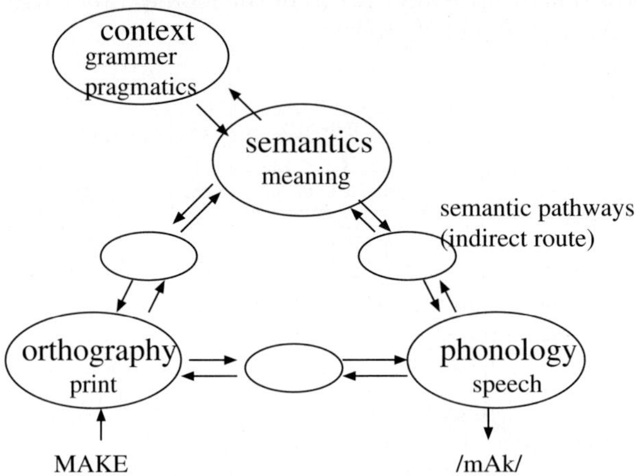

Fig. 2. The Triangle model

Suppose we can extent the concept of the lexical route in the DRC model such that the lexical route can deal with not only the words which it could recognize, but also it can deal with the words which the GPC route could not deal with. Then we can regard that there are no difference between the DRC and the Triangle models, because we cannot point out through which route the word was pronounced. The point is that the DRC model has an arbitrariness to decide the parameter to blend the lexical and the GPC route. Also in the Triangle model, as O'Reilly and Munakata[7, p.322] pointed out as follows: "Note that PMSP (Triangle model) did not actually simulate the full set of pathways. Instead, they simulated the effect of a semantic pathway by providing partial correct input to the appropriate phonological representation during training of their direct pathway model, and then removed these inputs to simulate semantic damage (p.322)"

The Triangle model has an arbitrariness to the degree of contribution of the semantic system. As discussed above, the model should be sufficient to cover all the dyslexic symptoms for reading English words aloud so that how it deals with the problem of blending between the outputs of the lexical and the GPC route in the DRC model. In other words, how it can implement the division of labor problem in the Triangle model.

4   Introduction of the Mixtures of Experts Model

In this paper, we propose to introduce the Mixtures of Experts model[5, 6] so that we can let the model learn the GPC rules and classify regular and exception words automatically at the same time. Also, it could become a model which can suggest a solution for the problem of the division of labor if it can learn to classify distinction with regular words and exception words automatically. The ME can learn both the GPC rules and an automatic classification of the lexicons simultaneously. Mixtures of Experts (ME) model has been applied to many problems such as the problem of control of robot arms[6], the problem of character recognition and its location[5]. However, no attempts to apply the ME model as a psychological model of reading English words aloud has not been done. The ME is a technique to solve a complicated problem so that it divides the input space into a set of regions and fits simple surfaces to the data that fall in these regions. The division of input space into a set of regions and the rule of the regions were called "divide and conquer" strategy, which would take effectively in many cases. The regions have "soft" boundaries, meaning that data points may lie simultaneously in multiple regions. This "soft" boundaries seems to be roughly "fusion parameter" between the lexical route and the GPC route in the DRC model, or the solution of the "division of labor" problem in the Triangle model, because the boundaries between regions are themselves simple parameterized surfaces that are adjusted by the learning algorithm.

If we trained one large hierarchal neural network by the back propagation algorithm for the data comprising the problems that we can divide into small tasks, then we would observe that learning became slow and we would get only poor generalization because of interference among tasks to be solved. If we know in advance that training data set can be divided into some small regions, then we can apply expert networks to the divided regions by some kinds of gating mechanisms. This kind of strategy would lead us to let each small expert network do effective learning. Learning in the ME stands for letting the gating networks discover ways of the division of input space and let the experts find out the most suitable output for the data belonging to each divided region. The ME model is a kind of supervised learning algorithms. The ME consists of experts networks and gating networks. The gating networks are used to divide problem space, and each expert network is a comparatively simple network producing an output in divided regions. The ME is able to divide problem space automatically and the ME is also able to allocate expert networks for suitable spaces which gating network divided. A two level of the ME architecture is shown in Figure 1. The original Mixtures of experts allows hierarchical multi tree structures more than two layers, but for the sake of our purpose, a two layers' architecture is sufficient here.

4.1   The Dispersion Parameter, and the Dirac's Delta Function

We can formulate the probability of an output y_i of the ith expert network as a conditional probability in which the value is in accordance with a density

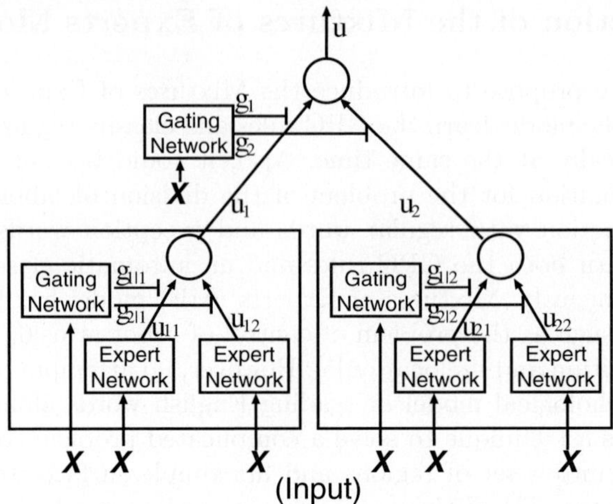

Fig. 3. A two–level mixtures of experts. Each expert network is a simple feed forward network. All the experts are given the same input and have the same number of output units. The gating networks are also feed forward networks and were given the same inputs as the inputs of the experts. The symbol g in the figure is an output (as a probability) of a gating network, and the sum of the values of all the gs is 1.0. The symbol u is the output of an expert. The outputs of experts is the mixtures of weighted sum of variables.

function with parameter $\boldsymbol{\theta}_i$ as follows:

$$P_i\left(\boldsymbol{y}_i | \boldsymbol{x}, \boldsymbol{\theta}_i\right) = \frac{1}{\left(2\pi\sigma_i^2\right)^{n/2}} e^{-\left(1/2\sigma_i^2\right)\left(\boldsymbol{y}-\boldsymbol{\mu}_i\right)^T\left(\boldsymbol{y}_i-\boldsymbol{\mu}_i\right)} \ . \tag{1}$$

where $\boldsymbol{\theta}_i$ is a parameter vector which determine the density function. If P_i is in accordance with a multi dimensional normal distribution, and its covariance matrix is given as $\sigma^2 \boldsymbol{I}$, where $\boldsymbol{I}$ is a n dimensional unitary matrix, then we can get the final probability of the output vector $\boldsymbol{y}$:

$$P\left(\boldsymbol{y} | \boldsymbol{x}, \boldsymbol{\theta}\right) = \frac{1}{\left(2\pi\sigma_i^2\right)^{n/2}} \sum_i g_i e^{-\left(1/2\sigma_i^2\right)\left(\boldsymbol{y}-\boldsymbol{\mu}_i\right)^T\left(\boldsymbol{y}-\boldsymbol{\mu}_i\right)} \ . \tag{2}$$

where we postulate that g is known in advance as a producing from a Gaussian density function. We can regard that the dispersion parameter σ_i^2 determines a radius of a hyper sphere. At the limitation $\sigma^2 \to 0$, it tends to the Dirac's delta function. The Dirac's delta function is a function which satisfy:

$$\int_{-\infty}^{\infty} \delta(x)\, dx = 1 \ , \tag{3}$$

and,

$$\begin{cases} \delta(x) = \infty, \text{when } x = 0, \\ \delta(x) = 0, \text{otherwise} \end{cases} \tag{4}$$

The function $\delta(x)$ is 0 everywhere except for the point $x = 0$. The value of the $\delta(x)$ at the point of $x = 0$ is ∞, and the value of the integral which the interval contains $x = 0$ is 1. There are several definitions of the Dirac's delta function. As one of them, there exists a definition in the limitation as we approximate $\sigma^2 \to 0$ in the normal distribution, where σ^2 is a variance of the normal distribution.

4.2   An Explanation of Reading English Words in the ME

The DRC model has two routes, the lexical route and the GPC route. The Triangle model has also two routes, the direct route and the indirect route. The meanings, the purposes, the processes, and the mechanisms of the two routes in both models are different. However, whatever the names these routes are, and whatever these routes' implementations are, we might have to postulate at least two routes in order to explain the data from dyslexic patients (surface and phonological dyslexia). The ME is able to have more than two routes, or expert networks, and is able to have gating networks. We could consider that the gating networks in the ME might be regarded as a solution of the blending parameter in the DRC model, or a solution of the arbitrariness in the Triangle model. In the limitation of $\sigma^2 \to 0$, the output of the gating network is the Dirac's delta function, which means that the expert network controlled the expert network become to respond the only one input vector $\boldsymbol{x}$, or the only one word. This word might be special, an exception word or a low frequency inconsistent words. On the contrary, when we set the value of σ^2 greater, then the expert network controlled by this gating network can deal with many similar words. This network might have to read regular words or consistent words.

One of the main points in this paper is that the ME can learn the dispersion parameter automatically, in which we do not need to look for a high dimensional parameter space. Also, we do not need to prepare an arbitrary input like the equation which was adopted Plaut et al.(p.96, eq. 16). Therefore, introducing the ME, we can implement that the gating networks which would become to respond the word 'pint' only, but it would not respond other neighbor words like 'hint', 'mint', 'print', 'lint' and so on. We would be able to have the model in which the high dimensional space consist of many monosyllabic English words and the model could divide this space according to the regularity and irregularity of the words in this corpus. Also we can regard that when the small value of σ^2, almost 0, it can be identified the same as the lookup table in the DRC model, because these networks could respond the only one word in the corpus. On the other hand, when the dispersion parameter σ^2 is large, the expert network controlled by this gating network can be regarded as an implementation of the GPC rule, because this network could read many words. In addition, the gating networks force their expert networks to learn words shared the same pronunciations, and in other case the gating networks force their expert networks to learn words with specific pronunciations. In this way, the ME model could explain the frequency effect as well. Thus, we can consider that the ME model is possible model to explain both the lookup table and the division of labor simultaneously.

5   Numerical Experiment

All the 2998 words which Plaut et al.[8] adopted were used in our experiment[1] . We set the learning coefficient 0.01. All the initial values of connection weights were randomized with uniform random numbers $[-0.1, 0.1]$ The criterion to complete the learning were set the mean squared error as below 0.1. Almost every trial, the iterations were within 20–50 times, and we could get the almost the same results. Plaut et al.[8] checked the generalization ability of their Triangle model by applying the non words list in Glushko[4]. They asserted the validity the Triangle model to compare the result of the model and the data of human subjects. If the ME proposed in this paper showed the same performance as the human subjects, then it might be possible to claim that the ME is one of the candidates models to solve the problems of the way of implementation. This way of implementation is not clear in both the DRC and the Triangle models. Then, we presented the Glushko's non words list to the ME after learning completed, then compared the results with others. The ratios of percent correct are shown in Table1. The results of the human subjects and the Triangle model in the figure are from Plaut et al.(1996) simulation 1, p.69, Table 3.

Table 1. The results of the generalization test of the non words list(Glushko,1979)(%)

	consistent	inconsistent
human	93.8	78.3
Triangle	97.7	72.1
ME	93.0	69.7
bp3(100 hidden units,MSE=0.03)	90.7	53.5
bp3(100 hidden units,MSE=0.05)	95.3	58.1
bp3(30 hidden units,MSE=0.05)	88.4	58.1

For the sake of comparison, the normal back propagation methods were applied with 100 and 30 hidden units and the convergence criteria of the mean square error (MSE) 0.03 and 0.05. All the results of the back propagations are worse in the inconsistent words than other results of human, the Triangle, and the ME. In case of the 100 hidden units and 0.03 MSE, which means the most strict convergence criterion, the performance was the worst of all. This might imply that when we employ a large network to learn the complicated task which

---

[1] All the data we used here was obtained from the URL `http://www.cnbc.cmu.edu/~Plaut/`. Also we obtained the Glushko's non–word list for the generalization experiment from the same URL. Thus, all the data we used in this paper were exactly the same as Plaut et al.(1996).

can be divided into some regions, it is difficult for the model to extract the statistical characteristics included in the training data. It can be regarded to confirm the findings by Jordan and Jacobs(1994) that we would have poor generalization abilities when we trained large networks to learn complicated problems. It should be considered to employ the "divide and conquer" strategy in such a case.

6   Discussion

As mentioned, the DRC model requires humans to look for the best point of the blending parameter between the lexical and the GPC routes in the high dimensional space. Also, the Triangle has not implemented the division of labor yet. Therefore, these models might not be able to give any substance solutions for simulating dyslexic symptoms even when these models are well mimic human behavior. For the sake of discussion about merits and demerits of the models, we must consider not only the task performances, but also the real nature behind the models. In addition to this point, we should take into consideration about the possibilities of implementations for models as well.

If we could consider that there are expert networks specialized to process exception words, roughly corresponds to the lexical route in the DRC model, and where there exists localized division of regions, roughly corresponds to the division of labor, it might be possible to solve the problems of arbitrariness of both models. In this point of view, when we take into consideration of the limitation the dispersion parameter $\sigma^2 \to 0$, the region divided by this parameter can be identified the lookup table in the DRC model. That is, from the point of the ME model's prospects, we could reinterpret the difference between the DRC model and the Triangle model without discrepancy. Not only the problem of the lookup table and the blending parameter between the lexical route and the GPC route, but also the problem of the division of labor and the arbitrariness of the degree of contribution of semantic pathways, we can provide an unified description.

There is no essential difference between the DRC and the Triangle model in this meaning. In different words, the qualitative difference between the two model can be described as the quantitative difference of the dispersion parameters. It could be considered that the DRC and the Triangle model are particular cases of more general and comprehensive model. When we introduce the ME model as a model of reading English words aloud, it is possible to explain the difficult problem to tune the best point in high dimensional parameter space, and to formulate the arbitrary problem remained unsolved.

Numerous articles have cited the works of Plaut et al.[8] and Coltheart et al.[3]. Thus, it is obvious that both the models are the most valuable model for reading English words and its impairments. On the other hand, in this paper we showed an only one result shown in Table1. Therefore, it is difficult to insist that the ME is superior to previous two models. Not so much as saying so, this model still can be uncompleted. A number of points remain unclear. However, this model might be considered to formalize clearly the problems remained to be unclear in the previous models. Rather than closing the debate between two models, it might be worth attempting to integrate both of them.

References

1. Coltheart, M., Curtis, B., Atkins, P., Haller, M.: Models of reading aloud: Dual-route and parallel-distriputed-processing approaches. Psychological Review 100(4), 589–608 (1993)
2. Coltheart, M., Rastle, K.: Serial processing in reading aloud: Evidence for dual-route models of reading. Journal of Experimental Psychology: Human Perception and Performance 20, 1197–1211 (1994)
3. Coltheart, M., Rastle, K., Perry, C., Langdon, R., Ziegler, J.: Drc: A dual route cascaded model of visual word recognition and reading aloud. Psychological Review 108, 204–256 (2001)
4. Glushko, R.J.: The organization and activation of orthographic knowledge in reading aloud. Journal of Experimental Psyhology: Human Perception and Performance 5, 674–691 (1979)
5. Jacobs, R.A., Jordan, M.I., Nowlan, S.J., Hinton, G.E.: Adaptive mixtures of local experts. Neural Computation 3, 79–87 (1991)
6. Jordan, M.I., Jacobs, R.A.: Hierarchical mixtures of experts and the em algorithm. Neural Computation 6, 181–214 (1994)
7. O'Reilly, R.C., Munakata, Y.: Computational Explorations in Cognitive Neuroscience: Understanding in mind by simulating the brain. MIT Press, Cambridge (2000)
8. Plaut, D.C., McClelland, J.L., Seidenberg, M.S., Patterson, K.: Understanding normal and impaired word reading: Computational principles in quasi-regular domains. Psychological Review 103, 56–115 (1996)
9. Seidenberg, M.S., McClelland, J.L.: A distributed, developmetal model of word recognition and naming. Psychological Review 96(4), 523–568 (1989)
10. Seidenberg, M.S., Petersen, A., Plaut, D.C., MacDonald, M.C.: Pseudohomophone effects and models of word recognition. Journal of Experimental Psychology: Learning, Memory, and Cognition 22(1), 48–62 (1996)

A Multilayered Scheme of Bidirectional Associative Memory for Multistable Perception

Teijiro Isokawa[1], Haruhiko Nishimura[2],
Naotake Kamiura[1], and Nobuyuki Matsui[1]

[1] Division of Computer Engineering, Graduate School of Engineering,
University of Hyogo, 2167 Shosha, Himeji, 671-2280, Japan.
[2] Graduate School of Applied Informatics, University of Hyogo,
1-3-3, Chuo-ku, Kobe, 650-0044, Japan

Abstract. Multistable perception phenomena in seeing ambiguous figures have been observed and their distribution curves of alternation durations are well-known as the Gamma distribution through psychophysical experiments. It is important and interesting to investigate its describable model for clarifying brain functions. In this paper, we propose a model based on the multilayered bidirectional associative memories and report good simulation results on the distribution of alternation durations.

1   Introduction

Multistable perception is a perception in which two (or more) interpretations of the same ambiguous image alternate spontaneously while an observer looks at them. Three kinds of this phenomenon, figure-ground, perspective (depth), and semantic ambiguities are well known (As an overview, for example, see[1,2]). In this circumstance the external stimulus is kept constant, but perception undergoes involuntary and random-like change. The measurements have been quantified in psychophysical experiments and it has become evident that the frequency of the time intervals spent on each percept is approximately Gamma distributed[3,4,5,6]. Moreover, a new finding was recently reported that a shape-defining parameter of Gamma distribution fitted to time intervals data takes a quantal and natural number[5].

Figure-ground reversal is an automatic process which happens even if there is no premise knowledge about the object form. However, perspective and semantic ones are processes depending on conceptual knowledge. This indicates a possibility that each perceptual conflict happens similarly in the individual (different) place within the large region from the initial vision process to the higher cognitive reasoning process. Therefore, existence of some neural mechanism common to all is suggested.

Several models of neural networks concerning the multistable perception have been proposed, such as synergetic computer[7], chaotic neural network[8], and stochastic resonance[9].

In this work, we propose a perception model of ambiguous patterns based on the multilayered bidirectional associative memory. This model has two main

M. Ishikawa et al. (Eds.): ICONIP 2007, Part II, LNCS 4985, pp. 759–768, 2008.

features, one of which is a bottom-up and top-down information (signal) flow between the lower layers and higher ones by expansion of the bidirectional associative memory scheme[10]. The other is a checking process of the conformity of the bidirectional signals. These features are consistent with the brain mechanisms [11,12]. According to the input signal from the lower level, the higher level feeds back a suitable candidate among the stored templates to the lower level. If the lower area cannot get a good match, the process starts over again and lasts until a suitable interpretation is found. We demonstrate temporal behaviors of the system under this framework through computer simulations and investigate the perceptual dominance time structures in order to check the agreement with psychophysical experiments.

2   Multistable Perception and Brain Mechanism

2.1   Multistable Perception

Multistable perception (or so-called perceptual alternation) is a phenomenon occurred in our brains, in which there are plural candidates of interpretation whereas retinal input is not changed and only one interpretation of them arises in our brains at a time. Interpretations are autonomously exchanged over time and the timing of exchanges is known to be random. This phenomenon usually occurs when we see ambiguous figures, such as the Necker-cube in Fig. 1. We have two interpretations on this cube. From psychophysical experiments, the distribution of the perceptual durations can be obtained. It is known that this distribution follows well the Gamma distribution [3,4,5,6] defined by

$$f(x) = \frac{1}{a^b \Gamma(b)} x^{b-1} \exp(-x/a). \tag{1}$$

We show a typical example of the distribution of the perceptual duration in seeing Necker-cube and its corresponding Gamma distribution in Fig. 2.

2.2   Brain Mechanisms for Multistable Perception

The mechanism for multistable perceptions should be functional in the wide range of cerebral cortex beyond primary visual cortex, since there exist several levels (kinds) of multistable perceptions, such as figure-ground, perspective, and semantic ambiguities. The cortico-cortical fibers connect among areas on the cortex and their circuitry is uniform over it, regardless of their functions or locations [13]. Information processing in the neocortex is performed by the interactions among areas through these cortico-cortical fibers. This type of interactions between higher-order and lower-order cortex areas would contribute to the recognition of an object.

Higher-order cortex receives signals from lower-order cortex, and based on these signals it retrieves the pattern that is most feasible for them from stored templates and transmits this pattern as a feedback to lower-order cortex. An interpretation for the object is achieved by making a match of information between

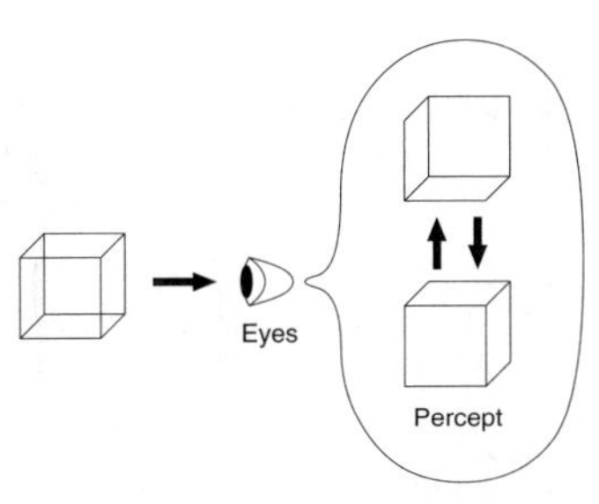
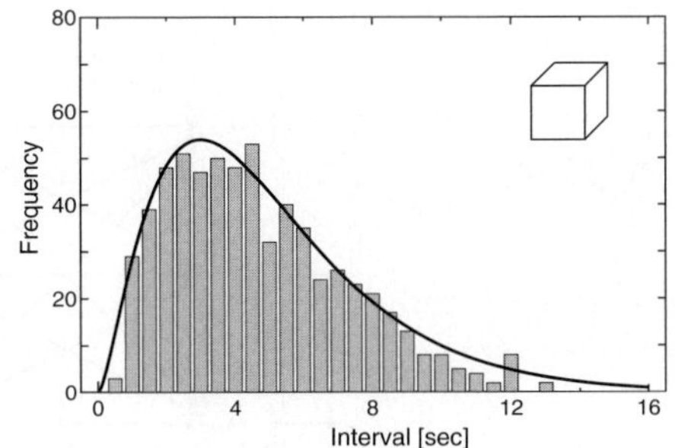

Fig. 1. Multistable perception in looking at Necker cube

Fig. 2. Frequency distribution of the perceptual duration of the Necker cube for a subject (From Ref.[5])

the higher and lower cortex. Ping-pong style of matching process based on inter-actions in the brain is expected to serve as a candidate for the general (common) neural mechanism of multistable perception. The brain mechanism proposed by Körner and Matsumoto [11], in which the top-down prediction from inferotempo-ral cortex confronts with the bottom-up recognition from primary visual cortex, corresponds to this matching process. This matching process is also consistent with the recognition network scheme of feature integration in visual processing by Treisman [12] in cognitive science.

3   Multilayered Bidirectional Associative Memory

3.1   Bidirectional Associative Memory (BAM) Network

Bidirectional Associative Memory (BAM) network is a kind of associative mem-ory with capability of retrieving input patterns from target patterns, as well as retrieving target patterns from input patterns[10].

First we recapitulate the structure and mechanism of BAM network. Figure 3 shows the structure of BAM network. It consists of two layers of neurons, U-layer ($\{u_i\}$) and V-layer ($\{v_j\}$), connected with each other. The connection weight from the i-th neuron in U-layer to the j-th neuron in V-layer is calculated by Hebbian learning as

$$w_{ij} = \sum_{q=1}^{Q} \xi_i^q \cdot \zeta_j^q \tag{2}$$

where ξ_i^q and ζ_j^q are the pattern states of the i-th and the j-th neurons in U-layer and V-layer, for the q-th pair of stored patterns respectively, and Q is the number of stored patterns. The weights from V-layer to U-layer are given as the transverse to Eq. (2), thus the matrix of weights from V-layer to U-layer is

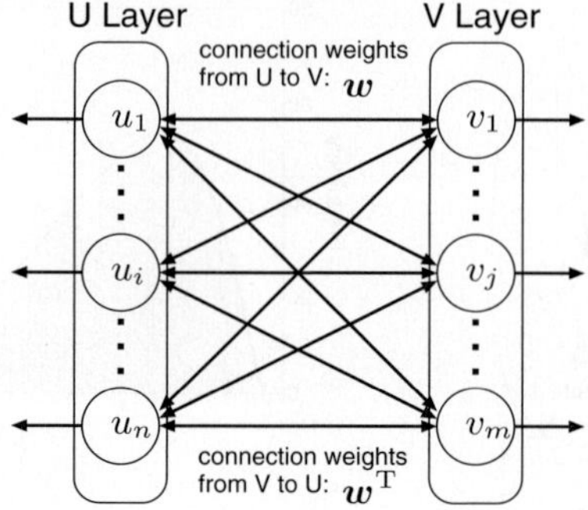

Fig. 3. The structure of the Bidirectional Associative Memory (BAM) network

represented as $\boldsymbol{w}^{\mathrm{T}}$ when $\boldsymbol{w}$ is the weight matrix from U-layer to V-layer. The state of a neuron in BAM is updated as follows:

$$x_i = \sum_{j=1}^{m} w_{ji} v_j(t), \quad u_i(t+1) = \begin{cases} 1 & \text{if } x_i > 0 \\ u_i(t) & \text{if } x_i = 0 \\ -1 & \text{if } x_i < 0 \end{cases},$$

$$y_j = \sum_{i=1}^{n} w_{ij} u_i(t), \quad v_j(t+1) = \begin{cases} 1 & \text{if } y_j > 0 \\ v_i(t) & \text{if } y_j = 0 \\ -1 & \text{if } y_j < 0 \end{cases}$$

where m and n are the numbers of neurons in V-layer and U-layer, respectively. The outputs of neurons in U-layer are input to those in V-layer through weight $\boldsymbol{w}$ and the outputs in V-layer make feedback to U-layer through $\boldsymbol{w}^{\mathrm{T}}$, so the information flows between these layers repeatedly.

The energy function of BAM network is defined as

$$E(t) = -\frac{1}{2} \sum_{i=1}^{n} \sum_{j=1}^{m} w_{ij} u_i(t) v_j(t). \tag{3}$$

This value decreases monotonically whenever the state of a neuron is updated and converges to one of local minima in the landscape of energy function, as in Hopfield network. The neuron states of these local minima are stored patterns, thus this network has a capability of retrieving stored patterns from incomplete input pattern in either U-layer or V-layer.

3.2 Multilayered BAM (MBAM) Network

In this paper, we introduce a Multilayered BAM (MBAM) network, which allows more layers in BAM network. Figure 4 shows the structure of MBAM network where the information flows from the lowest layer to the highest layer and vice versa. The lowest layer of the network corresponds to visual receptor that accepts

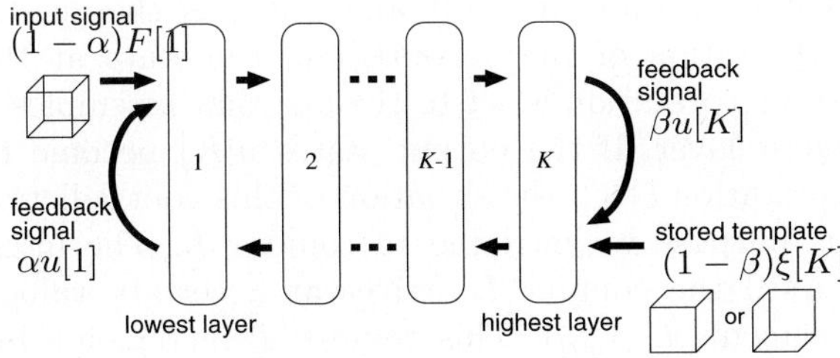

Fig. 4. The structure of the multilayered BAM network for multistable perception

ambiguous inputs from outside and the highest layer exhibits interpretations for the input signals.

The connection weight between the i-th neuron in the k-th layer and the j-th neuron in the $(k+1)$-th layer, $w[k]_{ij}$, is defined as

$$w[k]_{ij} = \sum_{q=1}^{Q} \xi[k]_i^q \cdot \xi[k+1]_j^q. \tag{4}$$

where $\xi[k]_i^q$ is the pattern state of the i-th neuron in the k-th layer, given the q-th pattern.

We introduce stochastic processes in updating the state of a neuron. The state of the i-th neuron in the $(k+1)$-th layer, $u[k+1]_i$, is updated by

$$u[k+1]_i = \begin{cases} f(x[k]_i) & \text{(with probability of } p = g(x[k]_i)) \\ -f(x[k]_i) & \text{(with probability of } 1-p) \end{cases} \tag{5}$$

where

$$f(x[k]_i) = \tanh(x[k]_i/\epsilon), \quad g(x[k]_i) = \frac{1}{1+\exp(-|x[k]_i|/T)},$$

$$x[k]_i = \frac{1}{m}\sum_{j=1}^{m} w[k]_{ji} \cdot u[k]_j.$$

ϵ is a slope parameter of the sigmoid function and T is a temperature of the stochastic process.

At the lowest layer and the highest layer of the network, the ambiguous input and the candidate of interpretations are dealt with by

$$u[1]_i(t+1) = \alpha u[1]_i(t) + (1-\alpha)F[1]_i, \tag{6}$$

$$u[K]_i(t+1) = \beta u[K]_i(t) + (1-\beta)\xi[K]_i^q, \tag{7}$$

respectively, where α and β are loop-input rates in the lowest layer and the highest layer respectively. $F[1]$ represents ambiguous input signal, which has an intermediate state between $\xi[1]^1$ and $\xi[1]^2$ (in the case of two patterns). In

Eq. (7), which interpretation of $\xi[K]^1$ and $\xi[K]^2$ is chosen depends on both the current interpretation of the network and the state at the highest layer $u[K]$. The initial interpretation is set to the one that resembles the first output state at the highest layer. If the output states $u[K]$ become to contradict to the chosen interpretation $\xi[K]$, the situation of this contradiction is allowed for a while. For this purpose we introduce a counter L. The interpretation $\xi[K]$ is not changed until the counter L arrives at a certain value (called upper-bound of disagreement, $L_{\text{u-bnd}}$). This counter L increments by one whenever the interpretation and the neuron states $u[K]$ in the highest layer are different.

For the evaluation of the resemblance between output states $u[K]$ and the interpretation $\xi[K]$, we introduce an overlap value $M(t)$ as

$$M(t) = \frac{1}{N}\left(\sum_{i=1}^{N} u[K]_i(t) \cdot \xi[K]_i^1\right) \tag{8}$$

where N is the number of neurons in the highest(K-th) layer.

For the computer simulation in this work we take two patterns for the stored templates for all layers. Those for the k-th layer are represented by

$$\begin{aligned}
\xi[k]^1 &= \{\quad 1, \cdots, 1 \quad -1, \cdots, -1 \,\}, \\
\xi[k]^2 &= \{\, -1, \cdots, -1 \quad 1, \cdots, 1 \quad \},
\end{aligned}$$

where the same number of 1's and -1's are contained.

4   Simulation Results

4.1   Experimental Setup

We explore the behaviors of our MBAM network by the computer simulations. An MBAM network with 4 layers each of which has 4 neurons, i.e., 4-4-4-4 network, is used. We employ $\epsilon = 10^{-10}$ (the sigmoid function corresponds to sign function in effect) and $T = 0.1$ in Eq.(5) in the simulations.

As an ambiguous pattern, the input pattern $F[1]$ at the lowest layer is always kept to be the intermediate pattern between the two stored templates, i.e., $F[1] = \{1, 1, 1, 1\}$. The initial interpretation at the highest layer of the network is determined following the information flow from the lower layers. The interpretation is changed to another one when the number of disagreements L at the highest layer reaches the upper-bound of disagreements $L_{\text{u-bnd}}$, and then new duration of the changed interpretation starts. The number of disagreements L is incremented by one when $|M(t)| < 0.5$ and is reset to zero when new duration starts. MBAM network is updated until acquiring 2,500 durations of the interpretation for the template #1 ($\xi[K]^1$).

We introduce the Kolmogorov-Smirnov one-sample test [14] with 0.05 of significant level ($p < 0.05$) for checking whether durations of interpretation (perceptual durations) follow the Gamma distribution or not. The parameters of Gamma distribution in Eq. (1), a and b, are estimated by

$$a = \sigma^2/\mu, \quad b = \mu/a,$$

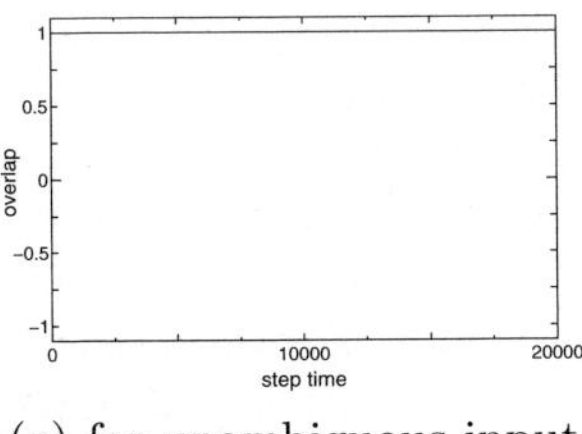

(a) for unambiguous input

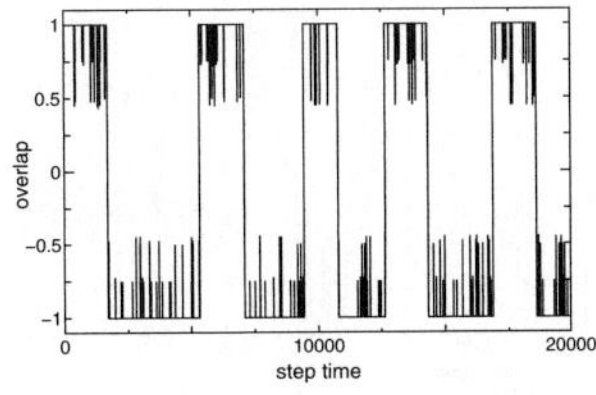

(b) for ambiguous input

Fig. 5. The transitions of overlap $M(t)$ in the cases of applying (a) an unambiguous pattern and (b) an ambiguous pattern as the input, where $\alpha = 0.1$, $\beta = 0.1$, $L_{\text{u-bnd}} = 20$

where σ and μ are the standard deviation and the mean of the duration data, respectively. The test statistic is the maximum difference between the empirical duration data and the theoretical Gamma distribution:

$$D_n = \max_x |F(x) - S_n(x)| \tag{9}$$

where $F(x)$ and $S_n(x)$ are cumulative frequency functions of the Gamma distribution and the duration data, respectively, and n is the number of duration data ($n = 2500$ in this work). The critical value associated with 0.05 of significant level, $D_n^{0.05}$, is given by

$$D_n^{0.05} = 1.358/\sqrt{n}.$$

If $D_n < D_n^{0.05}$, the duration data is regarded as following the given Gamma distribution. We can also check whether the duration data obeys normal distribution in the same way.

4.2   Temporal Behavior of MBAM Network

In this section, we show examples of temporal behaviors of our network as the transition of the overlap value $M(t)$ (Eq. (8)) at the highest layer that corresponds to which of patterns is recognized in our network.

We first consider the case of applying $F[1] = \xi[K]^1$, i.e., the input stimulus is not ambiguous. This is for confirming that alternation between the stored templates does not occur in our network when an unambiguous stimulus is input to the network, as usually done in our brains. The parameters in the network are taken to $\alpha = 0.1$, $\beta = 0.1$, and $L_{\text{u-bnd}} = 20$. Figure 5(a) shows the overlap $M(t)$ in this case, in which $M(t)$ stays at 1 in all step time, i.e., the network always recognizes the input pattern $\xi[K]^1$ as it is. We then change the input stimulus into ambiguous one, $F[1] = \{1, 1, 1, 1\}$, with the same setting of parameters as the above simulation, and show the transition of $M(t)$ in Fig. 5(b). In this case, the $M(t)$ changes over time and the obtained durations staying at the points $M(t) = 1.0$ ($\xi[K]^1$ is recognized) and $M(t) = -1.0$ ($\xi[K]^2$ is recognized) appear to have different time interval one another.

We next investigate the effects of the parameters, α and β, to the behaviors of the network. Examples of the behaviors are shown in Fig. 6 in which α is

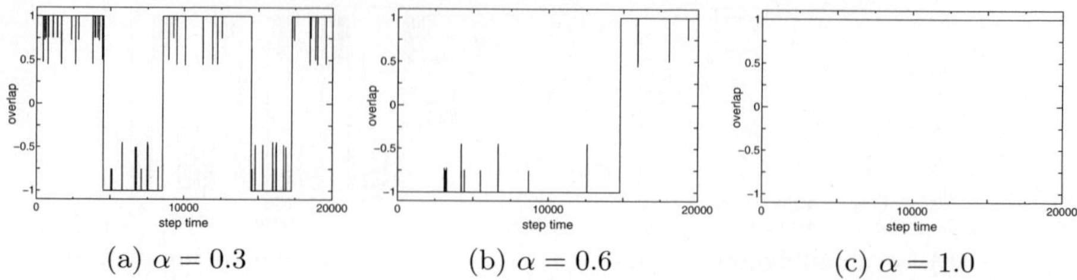

(a) $\alpha = 0.3$ (b) $\alpha = 0.6$ (c) $\alpha = 1.0$

Fig. 6. The temporal behavior of the network with the parameter $\beta = 0.1$ and $\alpha = 0.3, 0.6$ and 1.0

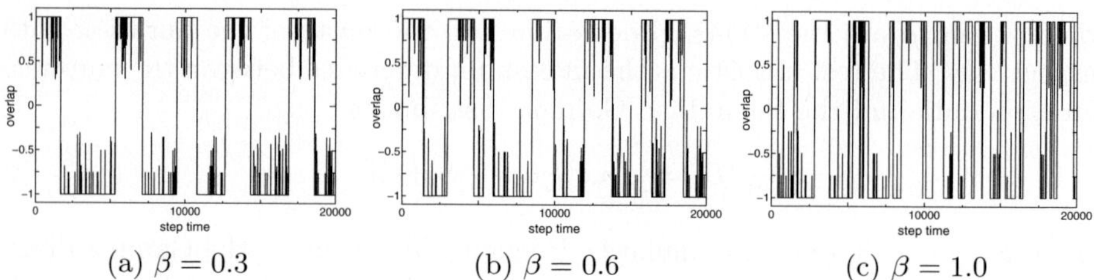

(a) $\beta = 0.3$ (b) $\beta = 0.6$ (c) $\beta = 1.0$

Fig. 7. The temporal behavior of the network with the parameter $\alpha = 0.1$ and $\beta = 0.3, 0.6$ and 1.0

changed to 0.3, 0.6 and 1.0. As defined in Eq. (6), this parameter represents the degree of input signal $(1 - \alpha)F[1]$ and feedback signal $\alpha u[1]$ to the lowest layer, and as α increases, the network tends to ignore input signal $F[1]$. When $\alpha = 1.0$, it corresponds to the situation that the network has no $F[1]$, thus the perception never changes (Fig. 6(c)), and when α decreases, the frequency of the alternation increases (Figs. 6(a) and 6(b)). Similarly, we examine the behavioral changes with respect to the parameter β, which represents the degree of input stored template $(1 - \beta)\xi[K]$ and feedback signal $\beta u[K]$ to the highest layer controlling the perceptual effectiveness. Figure 7 shows examples of behaviors in the case of $\beta = 0.3, 0.6$ and 1.0. In the case of $\beta = 1.0$, the perception in the network is completely determined by the thermal noise T, so the alternation often occurs over time.

4.3   Evaluation of Distributions for Duration Data

From the (empirical) duration data of our network, the candidate values of parameters in Gamma distribution and normal distribution can be estimated. Figure 8(a) shows an example of the distribution of the (empirical) duration data with its candidate (theoretical) Gamma and normal distributions, where the parameters of the network are set to $\alpha = 0.1$, $\beta = 0.1$ and $L_{\text{u-bnd}} = 20$. In this case, the

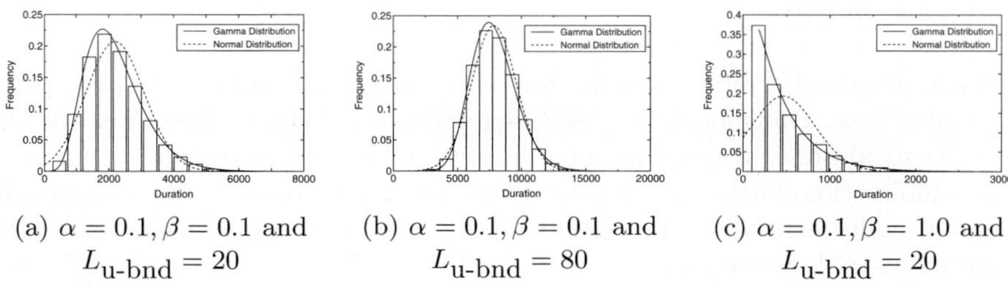

(a) $\alpha = 0.1, \beta = 0.1$ and $L_{\text{u-bnd}} = 20$

(b) $\alpha = 0.1, \beta = 0.1$ and $L_{\text{u-bnd}} = 80$

(c) $\alpha = 0.1, \beta = 1.0$ and $L_{\text{u-bnd}} = 20$

Fig. 8. Frequency distributions of the duration data and their candidate Gamma and normal distributions

Table 1. The number of acceptance ($D_n < D_n^{0.05}$) out of 10 trials by the K-S one-sample test for Gamma (without brackets) and normal (with brackets) distributions

$L_{\text{u-bnd}}$	10	20	30	40	50	60	70	80	90	100
0.1	8 (0)	9 (0)	9 (0)	10 (0)	10 (1)	10 (1)	10 (0)	10 (3)	10 (1)	10 (6)
β 0.2	6 (0)	10 (0)	10 (0)	10 (0)	10 (0)	10 (2)	10 (1)	10 (3)	10 (3)	10 (6)
0.3	9 (0)	8 (0)	9 (0)	10 (0)	9 (1)	10 (0)	10 (0)	10 (3)	10 (2)	10 (4)

distribution of the duration data follows the Gamma distribution rather than the normal distribution. The distributions in the case of $L_{\text{u-bnd}} = 80$ are also shown in Fig. 8(b). The duration distribution looks like following the Gamma distribution as well as the normal distribution. This seems to be because the influence of the thermal noise becomes greater on the alternation due to the increase of $L_{\text{u-bnd}}$. When the alternations occur more frequently, as shown in Fig. 8(c) where the parameter β is set to 1.0, the duration does not follow both the Gamma distribution expected by the psychophysical experiments and the normal distribution. It rather fits the exponential-like distribution.

To evaluate whether the duration data from our network follow the Gamma distribution or normal distribution more quantitatively, we perform the Kolmogorov-Smirnov (K-S) one-sample test for the duration data. We prepare 10 trial sets of duration data, each of which has different initial states of neurons under the thermal noise $T = 0.1$. 10 sets of the duration data are obtained through simulations in the conditions of $\alpha = 0.1$, $\beta = 0.1, 0.2$ and 0.3, $L_{\text{u-bnd}} = 10, 20, \cdots, 100$, and the K-S one-sample test is performed for each set of the duration data. Table 1 shows the number of acceptance ($D_n < D_n^{0.05}$) by the K-S one-sample test for Gamma and normal distributions. In this table, the number without (or with) brackets represents the number of acceptance for Gamma (or normal) distribution. The duration data fit Gamma distributions in almost all cases of the parameter combinations for β and $L_{\text{u-bnd}}$. It is also shown that the duration data tend to fit the normal distribution as well as Gamma distribution when $L_{\text{u-bnd}}$ takes larger values. As stated regarding Fig. 8(b), this is due to the increase of the influence of the thermal noise.

5 Conclusion

We have proposed a model scheme for representing the multistable perception in visual system. Our model can describe interactions between the lower and the higher cortical areas in brain by introducing a multilayered associative memory and its bidirectional information flow. From the simulation results, the durations from our model well follow the Gamma distribution that is one of characteristics in the multistable perception.

In the future research, we further explore the relations and validation of our scheme with the cortical architecture and brain-like computation, and view the difference with the previously proposed models [7,8,9]. It is also interesting to investigate the relevance of the discreteness for a shape-defining paratemer in the Gamma disctribution[5] on our scheme.

References

1. Attneave, F.: Multistability in perception. Scientific American 225, 62–71 (1971)
2. Kruse, P., Stadler, M. (eds.): Ambiguity in Mind and Nature: Multistable Cognitive Phenomena. Springer, Heidelberg (1995)
3. Borsellino, A., Marco, A.D., Allazatta, A., Rinsei, S., Bartolini, B.: Reversal time distribution in the perception of visual ambiguous stimuli. Kybernetik 10, 139–144 (1972)
4. Borsellino, A., Carlini, F., Riani, M., Tuccio, M.T., Marco, A.D., Penengo, P., Trabucco, A.: Effects of visual angle on perspective reversal for ambiguous patterns. Perception 11, 263–273 (1982)
5. Murata, T., Matsui, N., Miyamoto, S., Kakita, Y., Yanagida, T.: Discrete stochastic process underlying perceptual rivalry. NeuroReport 14(10), 1347–1352 (2003)
6. Zhou, Y.H., Gao, J.B., White, K.D., Merk, I., Yao, K.: Perceptual dominance time distributions in multistable visual perception. Biological Cybernetics 90(4), 256–263 (2004)
7. Haken, H.: Principles of Brain Functioning. Springer-Verlag, Berlin, Heidelberg (1996)
8. Nagao, N., Nishimura, H., Matsui, N.: A Neural Chaos Model of Multistable Perception. Neural Processing Letters 12(3), 267–276 (2000)
9. Riani, M., Simonotto, E.: Stochastic Resonance in the Perceptual Interpretation of Ambiguous Figures: A Neural Network Model. Physical Review Letter 72, 3120–3123 (1994)
10. Kosko, B.: Bidirectional Associative Memory. IEEE Transaction on System, Man, and Cybernetics 18(1), 49–60 (1988)
11. Körner, E., Matsumoto, G.: Cortical Architecture and Self-Referential Control for Brain-like Processing in Artificial Neural Systems. IEEE Engineering in Medicine and Biology Magazine 21(5), 121–133 (2002)
12. Treisman, A.: Features and objects in visual processing. Scientific American 254(11), 114–125 (1986)
13. Mumford, D.: On the computational architecture of the neocortex ii.the role of cortico-cortical loops. Biological Cybernetics 66, 241–251 (1992)
14. Siegel, S.: Non-parametric statistics for the behavioral sciences. McGrow-Hill, New York (1956)

Text Categorization with Semantic Commonsense Knowledge: First Results

Pawel Majewski and Julian Szymański

Gdańsk University of Technology,
Narutowicza 11/12, 80-952 Gdańsk, Poland
{pawel.majewski, julian.szymanski}@eti.pg.gda.pl

Abstract. Most text categorization research exploit bag-of-words text representation. However, such representation makes it very hard to capture semantic similarity between text documents that share very little or even no vocabulary. In this paper we present preliminary results obtained with a novel approach that combines well established kernel text classifiers with external contextual commonsense knowledge. We propose a method for computing semantic similarity between words as a result of diffusion process in ConceptNet semantic space. Evaluation on a Reuters dataset show an improvement in precision of classification.

1 Introduction

Text is the primal medium of representing and distributing information, while categorization is one of the basic methods of organizing textual data. Research on this topic have been dominated with machine learning approach and a predominant number of recent papers focus on kernel methods [1]. In most of works, text was represented with a Vector Space Model (a.k.a. bag-of-words), and similarity between two pieces of text computed as a function of words shared by the two. This assumption, however, makes it very hard to capture any semantic relation between text documents that share very little or even no vocabulary. This issue was addressed with both statistical and algebraic tools [2]. On the other hand, there is a long history of works, getting back to 1960s [3], that incorporate hierarchical semantic networks as sources of external knowledge. More recent works of this group concentrate on WordNet [4] as a primal source of information on relations between words (e.g. [5][6]). In this paper, however, we exploit common-sense knowledge base ConceptNet [7] which has some attractive properties that might be useful in some text categorization problems. Additionally, we propose a method for computing semantic similarity between words that is backed by the common-sense relations graph. The similarity is expressed as a result of diffusion process. Proposed kernel function is later evaluated in a text categorization problem.

This paper is organized as follows. In the next section we briefly describe linear kernels for text classification problems. The third section discusses semantic proximity of words. Fourth section describes ConceptNet and points out properties of the semantic graph's structure that had significant influence on design of

M. Ishikawa et al. (Eds.): ICONIP 2007, Part II, LNCS 4985, pp. 769–778, 2008.

the diffusion function presented in the following section. In fifth section we describe in details our diffusion algorithm. Results of experimental evaluation are presented in sixth section. Finally, we conclude and give an outlook for future works in the last section.

2   Linear Kernels for Text

Simple linear kernels perform very well in text categorization problems [1]. They implement an IR-developed Vector Space Model (VSM) which embeds a piece of text d into a space where each dimension corresponds to one of N words in dictionary $\mathcal{D}$. With this mapping $\phi(d)$, order in which words appear in text is neglected. Similarity between two pieces of text, $d_1, d_2 \in Docs$, is computed as a dot product of their embeddings,

$$\kappa(d_1, d_2) = \langle \phi(d_1), \phi(d_2) \rangle = \boldsymbol{d}_1 \boldsymbol{d}_2^T.$$

The more words documents have in common, the more similar they are.

Due to simplistic assumption, however, linear kernels are not able to capture any semantic similarity between text documents that share very little, or even no, vocabulary. This problem can be addressed by incorporating additional relations between words [8] [9]. *Semantic linear kernels* [10] implement this extension, and introduce additional information on words similarity. They are defined as,

$$\kappa_s(d_1, d_2) = \langle \phi_s(d_1), \phi_s(d_2) \rangle = \phi(d_1) \boldsymbol{S} \boldsymbol{S}^T \phi(d_2)^T. \tag{1}$$

where $\boldsymbol{S}$ is a *semantic matrix*. The $\boldsymbol{S}$ matrix could be any $N \times k$ matrix with all positive entries that captures semantic similarity between words. If k is equal to N, the semantic matrix can be regarded as a word-to-word similarity matrix. Indeed, the s_{ij} entry would express semantic similarity between i-th and j-th words in a dictionary. When k is smaller then N, this leads to some dimensionality reduction step, so that subsequent computations are performed in this k-dimensional, reduced space.

3   Semantic Proximity of Words

Proximity is usually defined as an inverse of a distance function, $\Delta : \mathcal{D} \times \mathcal{D} \to \mathbb{R}$ (e.g. [6]). Two objects are given a large proximity value if they are in a close distance. If they are the same, proximity is equal to 1. With help of a distance function, proximity is given as

$$p(u, v) = \begin{cases} inv(\Delta(u, v) + 1) \iff \Delta(u, v) \neq \infty, \\ 0 \qquad\qquad\qquad \iff \Delta(u, v) = \infty, \end{cases} \tag{2}$$

where $inv : [1, \infty) \to [0, 1]$ is some monotonically decreasing function, e.g. $1/x$ or $\exp(-x)$. The definition above could be generalized to functions expressing desired relations between words without explicit use of a distance. Since, the semantic matrix S in (1) could be any positive matrix, the only requirement for the proximity function $p : \mathcal{D} \times \mathcal{D} \rightarrow [0,1]$ is to express intuitive relatedness of word meanings with a positive value.

To construct proximity matrix as in (1) we need

 - source of information on relations between words,
 - method for computing proximity and relevance of words.

In most approaches the training data itself is used to extract relations between words, with common co-occurrence being the most frequent indicator of their relatedness. On the other hand there are relatively few works that involve external sources of information on relations between words (e.g. [5], [6]). Depending on the representation of external knowledge various methods of semantic proximity computation are adopted. For structured representations, usually graphs, diffusion methods can be applied [2] [11].

In this paper we investigate application of external data and a novel method of proximity computation. In two subsequent sections we discuss in details the source of relations on words proximity and propose a diffusion algorithm.

4   ConceptNet as a Source of Information on Relations Between Words

First, we should decide what properties a good source of information on words relations should possess? There are some conflicting requirements to be met. Since we are analyzing general text classification problem the ideal knowledge base should include vocabulary covering wide scope of topics. Moreover, it should incorporate tricky relations clear to humans but hard to discover in an automatic way. At the same time, the source should be specific enough to include sophisticated vocabulary that turns out to make the most discriminative features in categorization problems. In fact, there are only very few publicly available sources of structured information that could be used for this purpose.

The best known and used in predominant number of works is WordNet [4]. This hand-crafted lexical database system consist of well structured information organized within part of speech groups. WordNet's recent version lacks, however, relations between these groups. For instance, it does not provide obvious information that a "dog" "barks", but comes with a detailed mammals taxonomy. For context aware processing such information are of a little value, though. Additionally WordNet requires an disambiguation step to map analyzed words to senses.

We argue that for classification problem, information on contextual rather than structural relations is of greater need. ConceptNet [7], made publicly available recently, is a semantic network designed for commonsense contextual reasoning. It was automatically built from a collection of 700,000 sentences, a corpus being a result of collaboration of some 14,000 people. It provides commonsense contextual associations not offered by any other knowledge base. However, automation of its construction as well as distributed collaboration attribute to errors and imprecision of the relations, comparing to fine and clean WordNet. Nevertheless, ConceptNet brings a lot of useful common-sense knowledge. For instance, it lacks any information on mammals taxonomy that WordNet provides, but comes with an obvious hint that "dog" is a "pet".

ConceptNet is organized as a massive directed and labelled graph. It is made of about 300,000 vertexes and about 1.5 million edges, corresponding to words or phrases, and relations between them, respectively. Most vertexes represent common actions or chores given as phrases, e.g. "drive a car" or "buy food". There are approx. 260,000 vertexes of this type. The remaining nodes correspond to single words (including stopwords). There are also six types of relations (or edges) between vertexes. The largest connected component encompasses almost the whole ConceptNet graph. Its structure is also a bit bushy, with a group of highly connected nodes, and "person" being the most connected, having in-degree of about 30,000 and outdegree of over 50,000. There are over 86,000 leaf nodes and approximately 25,000 root nodes (nodes that have no incoming edges). An average degree of a node is 4.69.

5   Evaluation of Semantic Proximity in Semantic Graph

Having the structure of ConceptNet in mind, we propose an alternative proximity function defined on graph vertexes. General idea of the algorithm is also in-line with classic psycholinguistic theory of spreading activation in semantic memory [12]. We have chosen the following objectives for its construction:

- proximity decreases with number of visited nodes,
- vertexes connected directly or through some niche links are in a short distance, hence they are proximate,
- connections going through highly connected nodes increase ambiguity, therefore proximity should be inversely proportional to number of nodes that could be visited within given number of steps,
- computational complexity should be low.

An algorithm constructed according to these rules is presented in the following.

Outline of the Algorithm Here we propose an algorithm that computes proximity of words basing on a graph structure. It should be noted that this procedure is not symmetric, i.e. $p(t_1, t_2)$ does not necessarily have to be equal to $p(t_2, t_1)$, depending on structure of a semantic graph.

Our procedure is based on an assumption that the proximity is proportional to amount of some virtual substance that reaches the destination node v as a result of injection to node u, followed by diffusion through graph edges. The diffusion process is governed according to the following simple rules,

1. at every node the stream splits into smaller flows proportional to number of edges going out from the node,

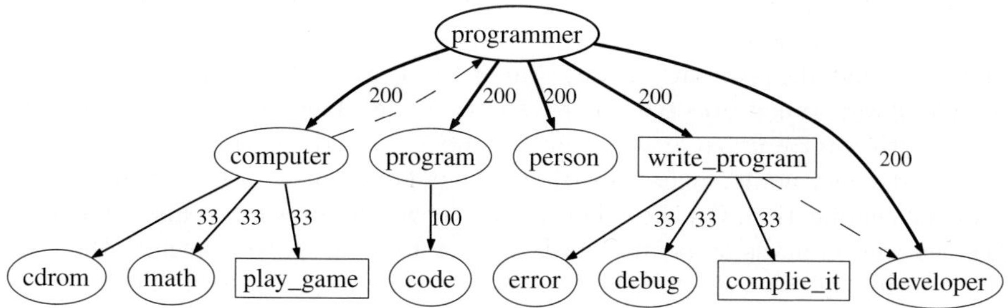

Fig. 1. A fragment of ConceptNet graph; rounded nodes correspond to single words and rectangular nodes represent phrases, all types of relations were collapsed into a single one

2. at every junction (node), a fraction ϱ of the substance sinks in and does not go any further,
3. if some edge points to a node that has been visited before, we assume that the node is saturated and can not take in any more substance.

The process continues until all reachable nodes "get wet".

Description. After this somewhat informal introduction, we will discuss the algorithm in details and give relationale for particular design choices that justify our approach. We will use ConceptNet's fragment given in Fig. 1 as an illustration. As an example we compute proximity of the **programmer** node to the rest of the nodes. In the kick off step, the **programmer** has been injected with 2,000 units of some fluid.

The first rule of the diffusion process assures that proximity of a node to its direct neighbors is proportional to number of neighbors. Consequently, highly connected nodes are given some penalty. On the other hand, if there are very few outlinks, they are considered much more informative. The **programmer** (see Fig. 1) has five adjacent nodes, therefore each of them is flooded with one fifth of the amount of the substance available to **programmer**. The purpose of this rule is to diminish proximity of nodes reachable through some highly connected nodes. For instance, ConceptNet's "person" is connected to about 50,000 other nodes. Clearly, any association going through this node can not be considered informative or unique. This rule assures that any connection going through the "person" node will yield very low proximity to the source.

The second rule of the diffusion process was introduced to decrease proximity with number of intermediate nodes required to reach the destination node. Since with every junction risk of drifting off the topic increases, this rule requires paths connecting proximate nodes to be as short as possible. In our example, at every intermediate node half of the substance is retained (ϱ is equal to 0.5), and only the other half diffuses further through edges. If this rule was omitted **programmer** would be equally related to **program** and **code**. While in our example this turns out to be quite accurate, such relation does not hold in general.

The purpose of the third rule is to assure monotonicy of the function with increasing length of a path connecting some nodes. By saturating a node we make sure that its proximity always takes fixed value that is smaller than the amount of substance injected to the source node. This rule also assures that the algorithm terminates after a finite number of steps. If this rule were to be suspended, every node reachable with more than one walk would be boosted with every such connection. On the other hand, the saturation rule seems to be in line with the way humans associate words — our first guesses are usually the most accurate. In Fig. 1 edges pointing to saturated nodes are dashed. They are not taken into account when a degree of a node is computed. For instance, `computer` has four outgoing edges. However, since an edge pointing back to `programmer` is neglected, the effective degree of `computer` is decreased to three.

There is one more point to be discussed about the algorithm. We have not decided yet on the order in which nodes and edges are visited during diffusion process. We propose to process a graph in order of node's proximity values. This process imitates a tide surging in a pipe system — the strongest wave goes furthest. To implement this flow we pick nodes in order of their proximity — proximate vertexes go first. If some nodes are equally proximate, then the degree decides and nodes having lower number of outgoing edges are given a privilege. However, if there is more than one node of the same degree, a conflict arises. We show how to resolve it in the next paragraph.

Conflicts Resolution. As we have said the vertexes are picked in order of their proximity to the source node. A problem arises when there is more than one equally proximate vertex. In fact this is the situation that always occurs immediately after the initial step of the algorithm, because the kick-off injection is always split equally between nodes adjacent to the source. We have chosen degree of a node as the second criterion — the lower the better. However, what to do when the rules above are not conclusive and there is still more than one possibility?

To solve this problem we propose to process all conflicting nodes in a single step. As a 'single step' we understand that nodes adjacent to the conflicting vertexes are not saturated until the last of them is processed. The order in which nodes are processed might change proximity results only if it affects effective degrees of nodes. It will not happen if the saturation is postponed. There are two cases to be analyzed — when conflicting vertexes share no adjacent nodes and the other situation when there are some shared adjacent nodes.

Clearly, if there are no shared adjacent nodes the effective degree of any of conflicting nodes will not be affected by any other. Therefore, all nodes adjacent to S yield equal proximity of $\frac{p'\varrho}{d}$.

In the other case, there are some nodes that share adjacent nodes. Now by applying the normal processing routine that involves immediate saturation to some node, we would decrease the effective degree of some of the remaining nodes. Although, if saturation of edges is postponed until the last of the conflicting nodes is processed, effective degree of any node will not be changed. Hence, the order in which the nodes are picked does not matter and all adjacent nodes are given equal proximity value of $\frac{p'\varrho}{d}$.

A way in which node are processed resemble Dijkstra SP-algorithm. The main difference are changed criteria used for picking a next node. Moreover, the purpose is quite opposite — the algorithm is used not to compute SP-distances but to assign values to nodes.

Running Time. Running time of a single diffusion operation using a standard binary heap as a backing data structure is $O((|V| + |E|)log|V|)$, where $|V|$ and $|E|$ are numbers of vertexes and edges of ConceptNet graph, respectively. Since, to construct complete proximity matrix we require results of diffusion operations for all words in the graph, total running time rises to $O(W(|V| + |E|)log|V|)$, where W is number of words. However, since word nodes make a small fraction of of the whole ConceptNet graph and most of nodes correspond to phrases, $W << |V|$.

6   Experiments

Here we want to investigate how does the algorithm presented above perform in practice and how does it compare to established text classifiers. In our preliminary experimental works we intended to answer the following questions:

(Q1) Do ConceptNet and the diffusion algorithm described above improve classification performance?

(Q2) Are there any cases where they can decrease performance? Why?

(Q3) What is the influence of diffusion parameter ϱ?

In order to answer the questions we conducted a series of experiments using a standard benchmark for text classification problems: the Reuters-21578 "ModApte split". We experimented only on ten most frequent categories, i.e. `acquisition`, `corn`, `crude`, `earn`, `grain`, `interest`, `money-fx`, `ship`, `trade` and `wheat`.

6.1   Preprocessing

ConceptNet as it comes is a bit noisy. For propose of our experiments we cleaned it a little. At first, all redundant entries were removed. Subsequently, all entries containing digits and self-loops were deleted. Afterwords we extracted the largest connected component of the graph and removed other nodes. Remaining nodes were then indexed in a dictionary and divided into three groups — words, phrases and junk words. By a phrase we considered a string with white spaces. There were 260,954 nodes of this type. Words were stemmed with a Lovins stemmer [13] and ones sharing a common stem were collapsed down into a single node. As junk words we considered stopwords found on Weka [14] stoplist and words with stems shorter than four letters. There were 1,638 such words. The junk words were retained to keep connectivity of the graph. After the filtering procedure there were 20,227 words left that we consider features.

Documents of the Reuters corpus were indexed using two separated dictionaries. The first dictionary was built in a usual way from all words that occurred in the training set. The other dictionary was constructed from ConceptNet's feature words. We also removed terms that occurred in the training set less than three times. Documents indexed with these dictionares made two experimental data sets, $\mathbf{D}$ and $\mathbf{D}_{CN}$, respectively. Subsequently, all vectors were normalized with L_1-norm.

6.2 Comparative Evaluation

In order to answer questions Q1 and Q2 we experimentally compared SVM classifiers built on diffusion proximity kernels and standard linear kernels. Experiments were conducted on $\mathbf{D}_{CN}$ and $\mathbf{D}$ datasets, while the latter was used as a baseline. In all experiments SVMs' C parameter was set to 1 and diffusion parameter ϱ to 0.5. Results obtained with a 10-fold cross-validation are given in Table 1.

The proposed kernels improved precision while decreasing recall of the classifiers. For 5 out of 10 classes precision increased even over results obtained with a full vectors (L-$\mathbf{D}$ column). However, for 4 classes (marked with a "-") our method could not recognize any positive sample, and simply degradated to a majority voter. Moreover, the increase in precision came at a price of lower recall for classes that were learned correctly. Relatively high recall was reported only for acq and earn classes. We suspect that introduction of relations between words brought in with ConceptNet allowed for disambiguation of words, and as a result improved precision of categorization. However, they also reduced the influence of individual words that were allowed to play a discriminative role in linear kernels. Low recall may also be due to a weak fitting between the ConceptNet's and Reuters' vocabulary. The latter uses rather formal and precise style, while the former is organized around informal activities. We expect our algorithm to work much better in more casual text categorization tasks which are planned in near future.

Table 1. Results of experimental evaluation. Columns: L-$\mathbf{D}$ — linear kernel and $\mathbf{D}$ dataset; L-$\mathbf{D}_{CN}$ — linear kernel and $\mathbf{D}_{CN}$ dataset; DD-$\mathbf{D}_{CN}$ — diffusion kernel and $\mathbf{D}_{CN}$ dataset.

Class	Precision			Recall			F_1		
	L-$\mathbf{D}$	L-$\mathbf{D}_{CN}$	DD-$\mathbf{D}_{CN}$	L-$\mathbf{D}$	L-$\mathbf{D}_{CN}$	DD-$\mathbf{D}_{CN}$	L-$\mathbf{D}$	L-$\mathbf{D}_{CN}$	DD-$\mathbf{D}_{CN}$
acq	0.954	0.903	0.943	0.946	0.905	0.740	0.950	0.904	0.829
corn	0.097	0.089	-	0.099	0.110	-	0.098	0.098	-
crude	0.848	0.841	-	0.776	0.630	-	0.810	0.720	-
earn	0.981	0.959	0.984	0.974	0.935	0.819	0.978	0.947	0.894
grain	0.303	0.315	0.366	0.127	0.150	0.025	0.179	0.204	0.047
interest	0.678	0.649	0.944	0.553	0.400	0.049	0.609	0.495	0.094
money-fx	0.707	0.672	0.719	0.745	0.687	0.143	0.725	0.679	0.239
ship	0.650	0.689	-	0.484	0.461	-	0.555	0.553	-
trade	0.854	0.810	1.000	0.826	0.724	0.057	0.840	0.764	0.107
wheat	0.086	0.033	-	0.103	0.004	-	0.094	0.008	-

6.3   Diffusion Parameter ϱ

For $\varrho = 1$ the diffusion kernel coincides with a standard linear kernel and the diffusion process is not performed at all. At the other extreme, when $\varrho = 0$, the distribution of the substance depends only on the structure of the graph. To examine influence of the parameter ϱ on classification performance we conducted a series of experiments in a whole domain of the parameter, $\varrho \in [0, 1]$, with a 0.05 step. Results for selected classes obtained with 10-fold cross-validation for C set to 1 are presented in Fig. 2. The plots are rather flat with very small differences

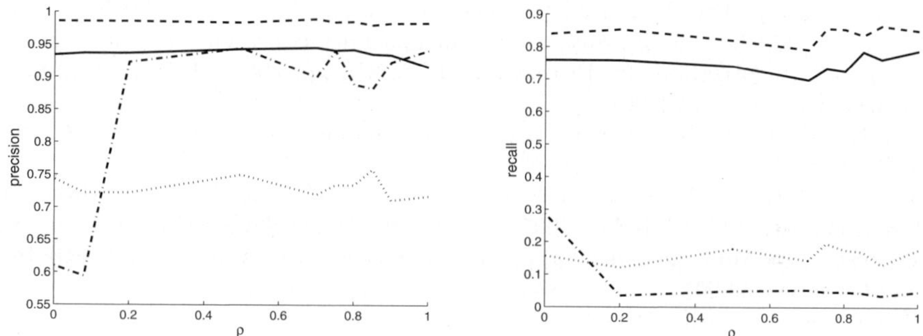

Fig. 2. Precision (left) and recall (right) of classifier in function of ϱ; Classes: `acq` (solid line), `earn` (dashed line), `interest` (dash-dotted line), `money` (dotted line)

in a whole range of the parameter with larger fluctuations at the extremes. This indicates that the influence of the diffusion parameter ϱ is limited and the proximity of words comes mostly from the structure of ConceptNet graph. Therefore, for practical usage ϱ could be set any value within its domain and does not introduce much additional burden to a learning task.

7   Conclusions

In this paper we presented preliminary results obtained with a method that combined kernel text classifiers with contextual commonsense knowledge brought by ConceptNet. Experimental evaluation have shown that contextual relations contained within ConceptNet allowed for increased precision. This came, however, at a price of lower recall. This might be due to limitations of the semantic space. In future, we plan to address this problem by extanding semantic space by combining ConceptNet, WordNet and Microsoft Mindnet [15] into a single graph.

Acknowledgments. This work was supported by KBN grants 3 T11C 047 29 and N516 035 31/3499.

References

1. Joachims, T.: Learning to Classify Text Using Support Vector Machines: Methods, Theory and Algorithms. Kluwer Academic Publishers, Dordrecht (2002)
2. Kandola, J., Shawe-Taylor, J., Cristianini, N.: Learning semantic similarity. In: NIPS 15, pp. 657–664. MIT Press, Cambridge (2003)
3. Collins, A., Quillian, M.: Retrieval from semantic memory. Journal of Verbal Learning and Verbal Behavior 8, 240–247 (1969)
4. Miller, G., Beckwith, R., Fellbaum, C., Gross, D., Miller, K.: WordNet: An on-line lexical database. International Journal of Lexicography 3, 235–312 (1990)
5. Basili, R., Cammisa, M., Moschitti, A., Rome, I.: A Semantic Kernel to Classify Texts with Very Few Training Examples. Informatica 30, 163–172 (2006)
6. Siolas, G., dAlché Buc, F.: Support Vector Machines Based on a Semantic Kernel for Text Categorization. In: Proceeding of IJCNN, pp. 205–209. IEEE Computer Society, Washington (2000)
7. Liu, H., Singh, P.: Conceptnet – a practical commonsense reasoning tool-kit. BT Technology Journal 22, 211–226 (2004)
8. Jiang, F., Littman, M.L.: Approximate dimension equalization in vector-based information retrieval. In: ICML 2000: Proceedings of the Seventeenth International Conference on Machine Learning, pp. 423–430. Morgan Kaufmann Publishers Inc., San Francisco (2000)
9. Wong, S.K.M., Ziarko, W., Wong, P.C.N.: Generalized vector spaces model in information retrieval. In: SIGIR 1985: Proceedings of the 8th annual international ACM SIGIR conference on Research and development in information retrieval, pp. 18–25. ACM Press, New York (1985)
10. Shawe-Taylor, J., Cristianini, N.: Kernel Methods for Pattern Analysis. Cambridge University Press, Cambridge (2004)
11. Kondor, R.I., Lafferty, J.: Diffusion kernels on graphs and other discrete structures. In: Proceedings of MGTS at ECML/PKDD, pp. 315–322 (2002)
12. Collins, A., Loftus, E.: A spreading-activation theory of semantic processing. Psychological Review 82(6), 407–428 (1975)
13. Lovins, J.: Development of a stemming algorithm. Mechanical Translation and Computational Linguistics 11, 22–31 (1968)
14. Witten, I., Frank, E., Trigg, L., Hall, M., Holmes, G., Cunningham, S.: Weka: Practical Machine Learning Tools and Techniques with Java Implementations. Department of Computer Science. University of Waikato. New Zealand
15. Vanderwende, L., Kacmarcik, G., Suzuki, H., Menezes, A.: Mindnet: an automatically-created lexical resource. In: Proceedings of HLT/EMNLP on Interactive Demonstrations, Morristown, NJ, USA, Association for Computational Linguistics, pp. 8–9 (2005)

Classification of Documents Based on the Structure of Their DOM Trees

Peter Geibel[1], Olga Pustylnikov[2], Alexander Mehler[2],
Helmar Gust[1], and Kai-Uwe Kühnberger[1]

[1] University of Osnabrück, Institute of Cognitive Science, AI Group, Germany
{pgeibel,hgust,kkuehnbe}@uos.de
[2] University of Bielefeld, Text Technology Group, Germany
{Alexander.Mehler,Olga.Pustylnikov}@uni-bielefeld.de

Abstract. In this paper, we discuss kernels that can be applied for the classification of XML documents based on their DOM trees. DOM trees are ordered trees in which every node might be labeled by a vector of attributes including its XML tag and the textual content. We describe five new kernels suitable for such structures: a kernel based on predefined structural features, a tree kernel derived from the well-known parse tree kernel, the set tree kernel that allows permutations of children, the string tree kernel being an extension of the so-called partial tree kernel, and the soft tree kernel as a more efficient alternative. We evaluate the kernels experimentally on a corpus containing the DOM trees of newspaper articles and on the well-known SUSANNE corpus.

1 Introduction

In recent years, text mining has become one of the main application fields of machine learning methods [1]. One of the main problems considered is the classification of documents. Classes can, for instance, be "ham" and "spam" in the case of email classification, which can often be accomplished successfully based on the occurring words only. In the emerging new field of so-called web corpora, however, one is interested in more complex concepts, as for instance, the genre or type of a document [2,3]. For determining the genre of a text, not only the occurring words play a role, but it is to a large extend determined by its visual and organizational structure. In this article, we will also investigate the computer linguistic question to which extend the type can be learned based on structural properties *only*. In particular, we will consider the structure based classification of XML documents based on their DOM trees (Document Object Model) using the SVM [4].

Methods like the SVM can be applied to non-vectorial data like sequences, trees, and graphs by defining an appropriate kernel for the data at hand [5,6]. An example of a kernel for structures is the *parse tree kernel* [7,8], which is applicable to parse trees of sentences. In contrast to parse trees, in which the grammar rule applied to a non-terminal determines number, type and sequence of the children, structural parts of a text represented by its DOM tree might

M. Ishikawa et al. (Eds.): ICONIP 2007, Part II, LNCS 4985, pp. 779–788, 2008.

have been deleted, permuted or inserted compared to a similar text. This higher flexibility should be taken into account by the similarity measure represented by the tree kernel, because otherwise the kernel value for similar documents might be unreasonably small.

In this paper, we extend previous work on tree kernels suitable for XML data in several respects. Our extensions are based on an extension of the parse tree kernel to trees not generated by a grammar, which will be called *simple tree kernel* (SimTK) in the following. Based on the SimTK, we derive new kernels that are useful in the context of HTML and XML documents. The *"left-aligned" tree kernel* (LeftTK) is a straightforward generalization of the SimTK to DOM trees. The LeftTK relies on a feature space spanned by so-called left-aligned subtrees. In contrast to the LeftTK, *set tree kernel* (SetTK) allows permutations of child subtrees in order to model document similarity more appropriately, but can still be computed relatively efficiently.

Since it can be shown that the introduced kernels are convolution kernels [9], we can suggest a method for including node properties in a natural way by combining the respective tree kernel with suitable kernels operating on node properties. Based on this technique, the *soft tree kernel* (SoftTK) combines the set tree kernel with a "fuzzified" comparison of child positions in order to account for the ordering of subtrees to some extend while at the same time still allowing permutations of subtrees.

Both Kashima and Konayagi [10] and Moschitti [11] presented kernels for trees called labeled ordered tree kernel and partial tree kernel, respectively. Both kernels are based on the idea of employing a string kernel for the sequence of children of a tree node. We present a (slight) extension of this idea allowing for the inclusion of complex node properties: the *string tree kernel* (StringTK) is derived from a combination of the simple tree kernel with a standard string kernel (cp. [12]).

In contrast to the mentioned tree kernels, we also consider a method for describing the trees using predefined features resulting in a flat representation that can be combined with standard kernels, e.g., polynomial or RBF. This methods will be called Quantitative Structure Analysis (QSA).

The rest of this paper is structured as follows. After a short definition of trees and various kinds of subtrees in Section 2, we will describe the parse tree kernel, and afterwards the simple tree kernel. The new kernels are defined in section 3, followed by an experimental evaluation in section 4. The conclusions can be found in section 5.

2   The Parse Tree Kernel

In the following, we consider labeled, ordered, rooted trees whose nodes $v \in V$ are labeled by a function $\alpha : V \longrightarrow \Sigma$, where Σ is a set of node labels. The elements of Σ can be thought of as tuples describing the XML tag and attributes of a non-leaf node in the DOM tree. Leaves are usually labeled with words or parts of texts. We will incorporate node information by using a kernel k^{Σ} operating on pairs of node labels, i.e., on tags, attributes, and/or texts. Two trees T and T' are called isomorphic if there is a bijective mapping of the nodes that respects the structure of the edges, the labellings specified by α and α', and the ordering of child nodes.

Collins and Duffy [7] defined a tree kernel for parse trees of natural language sentences (see also [8]), in which non-leaf nodes are labeled with the non-terminal of the node, and leaves with single words. The production applied to a non-leaf node determines the number, type, and ordering of the child nodes.

Collins and Duffy showed that, for two trees T and T', the kernel value $k(T, T')$ can be computed efficiently by determining the number of possible *mappings* of isomorphic partial parse trees (excluding such consisting of a single node only). Partial parse trees correspond to incomplete parse trees, in which leaves might be labeled with non-terminals. The function $\Delta(v, v')$ is defined as the number of isomorphic mappings of partial parse trees rooted in two nodes v and v', respectively. Collins and Duffy stated in their article the fact that k can be expressed as

$$k(T, T') = \sum_{v \in V, v' \in V'} \Delta(v, v') \,. \tag{1}$$

The Δ-function can be computed recursively by setting $\Delta(v, v') = 0$ for *any* words and if the productions applied in v and v' are different. If the productions in v and v' are identical and both nodes are pre-terminals, we set $\Delta(v, v') = 1$. Pre-terminals are non-terminals occuring directly before leaves corresponding to words. Identical productions in pre-terminals imply identical words. For other non-terminals with identical productions, Collins and Duffy use the recursive definition

$$\Delta(v, v') = \prod_{i=1}^{n(v)} (1 + \Delta(v_i, v_i')) \,, \tag{2}$$

where v_i is the i-th child of v, and v_i' is the i-th child of v'. $n(v)$ denotes the number of children of v (here corresponding to that of v'). It is possible to weight deeper trees using a multiplier $\lambda \geq 0$.

We can both simplify and generalize parse tree kernels to arbitrary labeled, ordered trees using the following definition. The simple tree kernel (SimTK) is based on (1) with a modified Δ defined as $\Delta_{\mathrm{SimTK}}(v, v') = \lambda \cdot k^\Sigma(\alpha(v), \alpha'(v'))$ if there are either no children, or the number of children differs. For non-leaves with the same number of children $n(v)$, we set

$$\Delta_{\mathrm{SimTK}}(v, v') = \lambda \cdot k^\Sigma(\alpha(v), \alpha'(v'))(1 + \prod_{i=1}^{n(v)} \Delta_{\mathrm{SimTK}}(v_i, v_i')) \,. \tag{3}$$

Compared to the recursion of the parse tree kernel in (2), the number "1" now appears in front of the product because we no longer exclude pattern trees consisting of a single node only.

It can be shown that the parse tree kernels and the SimTK are so-called convolution kernels that have been introduced by Haussler [9]. The proof of this property is a bit tricky, because the definitions of the kernel for leaves and non-leaves have to be collapsed into a single definition. The proof is based on induction on the structural complexity of the trees involved.

It follows from the proof that it is possible to just multiply with $k^{\Sigma}(\alpha(v), \alpha'(v'))$, which is difficult to see from a feature space interpretation. Kashima and Konayagi [10], for instance, present a technique for including node attributes that involves computations of $\sum_a k^{\Sigma}(\alpha(v), a)k^{\Sigma}(a, \alpha'(v'))$ where a ranges over all possible nodes label. This is obviously only possible if Σ is finite. In this respect, our tree kernels extend previous approaches.

3   Kernels for DOM Trees

We will describe the tree kernels tailored for XML documents in the following. We usually only give the case that the kernel is applied to a pair of trees, where at least one is not a leaf. The case of two leaves is identical to the definition given above. The approach we present first, however, is not a tree kernel in the above sense, but describes a tree by a set of pre-defined features.

3.1   Quantitative Structure Analysis (QSA)

The general idea behind this approach is to utilize quantitative indicators of text structure in order to thematically discriminate input texts. This approach is based on the correlation hypothesis of Biber [13] who argues that situation types vary by their linguistic instances. In the experiments described in section 4, we will test how far we can reach when identifying the genre of input texts by looking only at their expression plane.

Given a corpus of texts for which structural information is available in terms of their *logical document structure*[1], we represent each text as a vector of structure features (e.g., by the their mean sentence length) and apply SVM-based supervised learning in order to classify the texts subsequently.[2] Thus, we represent any input text as a *bag-of-features* where each vector is composed of features of various levels:

Structure Level. S is the set of constituent types of logical document structure as, e.g., sentence, paragraph, phrase. Every structure type $s_i \in S$ is then represented in terms of quantitative characteristics of its tree structure [15].

Features. Each input structure level $s_i \in S$ is described with respect to a set of features F_j. F_j may represent, for example, the *complexity* (i.e., the number of immediate daughter elements) of or the *length* (i.e., the number of leafs dominated by) a corresponding instance of s_i. For any input text x and

---

[1] In this study we use a 10 years newspaper corpus of *Süddeutsche Zeitung* (SZ) with logical document structure assigned in a preliminary step using the TextMiner system [14].

[2] For calculating the input features, we assume that a DOM-tree is the underlying text representation model which consists of nested paragraphs, sentences, phrases etc.

some feature F_j, this gives a separate vector whose coefficients represent the instances of s_i ordered according to their presence in input text x. Next, these vectors are mapped onto single numbers per feature F_j.

Feature Characteristics. This is done by means of some parameters of location or statistical spread. In order to compute these parameters the input vectors are conceived as feature value distributions. For each input text and a given set of features $\{F_j\}$ this gives a separate feature value vector which is finally input to text categorization — cf. Pustylnikov [16] for a detailed description of this approach.

Next we use the feature vectors to categorize all instances of the 31 categories of the SZ. As can be seen in the experiments section, we get promising results in terms of F-score when categorizing the input documents using structural features only.[3]

3.2   The Left-Aligned Tree Kernel (LeftTK)

The LeftTK is relatively straightforward extension of the SimTK defined in section 3. Its basic idea is to compare just as many children as possible using the given order $\leq$ on the child nodes if the number of children differs. If we choose k^Σ as the identity (matching) kernel we can arrive at a feature space interpretation by allowing arbitrary trees t in the sequence of pattern trees. For defining the feature value $\phi_t(T)$, a feature tree t is allowed to be a general subtree of a tree T, with the restriction that only the rightmost children of a node may be missing (possibly all), i.e., the subtree is left-aligned.

Note that when comparing two trees T and T', we have two take into account shorter prefixes of the child tree sequences of two nodes v and v' as well. This is done by redefining the recursive part of the Δ-function (3) by

$$\Delta(v, v') = \lambda \cdot k^\Sigma(\alpha(v), \alpha'(v'))\Big(1 + \sum_{k=1}^{\min(n(v),n'(v'))} \prod_{i=1}^{k} \Delta(v_i, v_i')\Big). \qquad (4)$$

Note that this way trees occurring more to the left have a higher influence on the kernel value than trees that occur more to the right.

The *complexity* of evaluating LeftTK (and SimTK) for two trees is $O(|V| \cdot |V'| \cdot \min(b, b'))$, where V and V' are the node sets of the two trees, b is the maximum branching factor of T, and b' the one of T'. The remaining kernels to be defined in the following all have a complexity of $O(|V| \cdot |V'| \cdot \min(b, b')^2 \cdot C)$, with a factor $C = 1$ for the SetTK and the SoftTK, and $C = L$ for the string tree kernel ($L = $ max. length of substrings).

3.3   The Set Tree Kernel (SetTK)

The DOM tree kernel defined in the previous section does not allow the child trees of v and v' to be permuted without a high loss in similarity as measured by

---

the kernel value $k(T, T')$. This behavior can be improved, however, by considering the child tree sequences as *sets* and applying a so-called set kernel to them, which is also an instance of the convolution kernel. The corresponding definition of Δ is obtained as

$$\Delta(v, v') = \lambda \cdot k^{\Sigma}(\alpha(v), \alpha'(v'))\Big(1 + \sum_{i=1}^{n(v)} \sum_{i'=1}^{n'(v')} \Delta(v_i, v'_{i'})\Big), \tag{5}$$

i.e., all possible pairwise combinations of child trees are considered.

When looking for a suitable feature space in the case $\lambda = 1$ and $k^{\Sigma} = k^{id}$ (identity kernel), we find that the definition in (5) corresponds to considering *paths* from the root to the leaves. This is a well-known technique for characterizing labeled graphs (see, e.g., [17]), which can also be applied to trees.

Since the pairwise comparison in (5) is ignorant of the order of the child trees in the child sequences of v and v', we cannot distinguish the trees that differ only in the ordering of the children using label sequences alone. This can, however, be achieved with the kernel defined in the following section.

3.4   The Soft Tree Kernel (SoftTK)

The basic idea of the soft tree kernel is to take the position of a node in the child sequence into account. The position $\mu(v_i) = i$ of some child of a node v can be used as an attribute of the respective node. When comparing two positions we are interested in their distance. This suggests to use of the RBF kernel defined as $k_{\gamma}(x, y) = e^{-\gamma(x-y)^2}$ for node positions x and y. The maximum value is attained for $x = y$. γ is a parameter to be set by the user. It determines how different the positions are allowed to be. We can state the recursive part of the definition of the soft tree kernel as

$$\Delta(v, v') = \lambda \cdot k^{\Sigma}(\alpha(v), \alpha'(v')) \cdot k_{\gamma}(\mu(v), \mu'(v')) \cdot \Big(1 + \sum_{i=1}^{n(v)} \sum_{i'=1}^{n'(v')} \Delta(v_i, v'_{i'})\Big).$$

In the definition, we assume a canonical labeling of the children of a node, i.e. $\mu(v_j) = j$ and $\mu'(v'_j) = j$ for any children v_j and v'_j in the trees. The position of the root node is defined as 1. Giving a feature space interpretation in terms of pattern trees is again difficult, because of the use of k^{Σ} and k_{γ}. The string tree kernel defined in the next section provides an alternative method for taking into account the ordering of the children of a node.

3.5   The String Tree Kernel

Kashima and Koyanagi [10] and Alessandro Moschitti [11] describe extensions of the parse tree kernel, the latter of which is called the partial tree kernel. The partial tree kernel is based on a string kernel, i.e., one considers common subsequences of the two child tree sequences with gaps allowed. For the experiments, we used a slight extension of the partial tree kernel that is based on a different computation of the string kernel (based on [12]) and includes node attributes. Moreover, we do not consider all subsequences, but allow the user to specify a maximum length in order to limit computational complexity. We leave out the details for reasons of space.

4   Experiments

In order to validate our approach, we applied the different kernels to a small training set with three classes and 10 examples in each class, resulting in 30 artificial trees. The classes have been defined as follows:

1. The class 1 examples all have a left-aligned subtree of the form $g(a, b(e), c)$. A typical instance is $f(h(m, c), g(a, b(e), c), g(m, n, m))$.
2. The class 2 examples all have a general subtree of the form $g(c, b, e(a))$, where gaps are allowed but the ordering of the subtrees c, b and $e(a)$ has to be preserved. A typical example is $f(h(g(n, c, b, n, e(a))), h(m, b, h(a, n)))$.
3. The class 3 examples contain subtrees of the form $g(c, b, a(e))$, where the child trees c, b and $a(e)$ are allowed to occur reordered and gaps might have been inserted, too. A typical instance would be $f(g(b, h(m), c, h(n), a(b, e, a)))$.

We compared the four kernels LeftTK, SetTK, SoftTK, and StringTK with the baseline approach of classifying the trees according to the occuring tags (TagTK). In contrast to QSA, TagTK does only look at the occurring tags. The optimal F-measures for the different approaches and the three classes can be found in Table 1.

The implementations of SoftTK and StringTK perform best on our small dataset: they achieve an F-measure of 1.00 for each class. As an advantage of the SetTK, however, it can be computed much more efficiently than the StringTK. SetTK performs a bit worse for class 1 with an F-measure of 0.952. The LeftTK, our simplest approach, performed the worst for classes 2 and 3 – even worse than the default approach given by TagTK. It seems to be useful for only class 1, which is defined by a certain left-aligned subtree. It should be noted that LeftTK can be computed more efficiently than SetTK, SoftTK, and StringTK, because the complexity only depends linearly on the maximum branching factor of the trees.

The picture looks quite different, if we apply the techniques to the corpus described in Section 3.1. For applying the tree kernels, we had to downsample

Table 1. F-Measures

	Class 1	Class 2	Class 3
TagTK	0.727	0.6	0.736
LeftTK	0.909	0.363	0.44
SetTK	0.952	1.00	1.00
SoftTK	0.952	1.00	1.00
StringTK	1.00	1.00	1.00

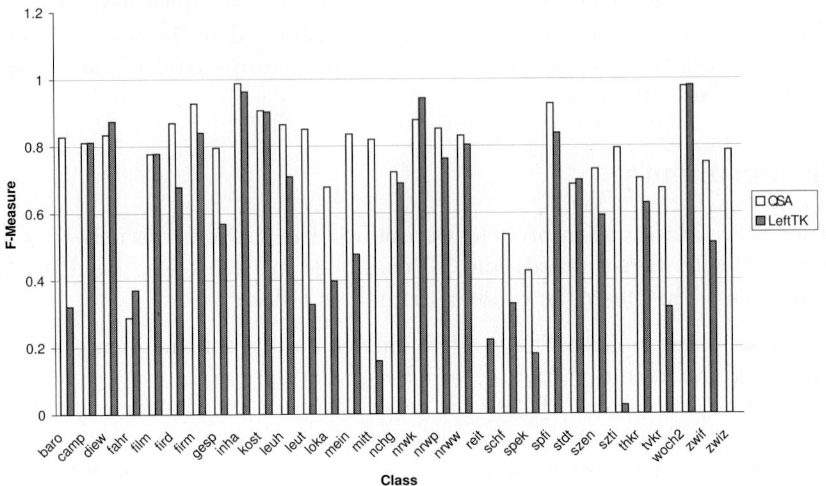

Fig. 1. Categorization experiment with 31 rubrics of the SZ ordered alphabetically: optimal F-measures (cross validation) for the binary classification problems (class vs. rest)

the dataset originally containing about 35000 examples, resulting in a set with 6250 examples. Still, we were not able to apply the StringTK, and SetTK and SoftTK yielded bad results. Among the tree kernels, now the LeftTK performed best. QSA, however, could be applied to the whole dataset.

Fig. 1 presents the results of the experiment for QSA and LeftTK. Every category is identified by a short-cut representing a rubric (e.g. `woch2` = *'Wochenchronik'* 'chronicle of the weak' etc.). The corresponding F-Score values demonstrate the separability of most of the categories. LeftTK performs better for six classes, QSA performs better for 20 classes, and the performance is almost identical for four classes. This, to some extend, confirms results also found in other areas that generic structure-based methods often perform worse than feature-based methods with hand-crafted structural attributes. Note that LeftTK had to operate on a down-sampled dataset and fewer parameter combinations could be tried, too.

The SUSANNE Corpus [18] consists of 64 files which are annotated version of texts from the Brown corpus, each of which contains more than 2000 words. Sixteen texts are drawn from each of the following genre categories: A (press reportage), G (belles lettres, biography, memoirs), J (learned, mainly scientific and technical, writing), and N (adventure and Western fiction). Because we are interested in the structure based classification, we removed all information on specific words and kept only a simplified version of the parsed text and sentence structure, with tags like N (noun phrase), V (verb phrase), etc., in which the

Table 2. Results for Susanne Corpus: F-Measures

Cat.	LeftTK	-N	SetTK	-N	SoftTK	-N	StringTK	-N	QSA
A	0.538	0.4	0.97	0.968	1.0	1.0	1.0	1.0	1.0
G	0.405	0.367	0.733	0.89	0.733	0.89	0.687	0.727	0.86
J	0.688	NAN	0.903	0.903	0.903	0.953	0.8	0.903	0.97
N	0.4	NAN	0.97	1.0	0.97	1.0	0.967	0.967	1.0

specific tag Y was used to denote the occurrence of **some** word. Interestingly enough, we could still obtain very good classification results, see Table 2.

In Table 2, the estimated optimal F-measure for the four categories are shown (using the leave-one-out method). For every type of kernel (see above), we considered the original definition and the normalized version given. Note that for large values of γ, SoftTK shows the same results like SetTK.

It can be seen, that the classes A, J, N can be learned quite well with any of the approaches, except LeftTK. For class G, however, normalized SetTK and (normalized) SoftTK perform best. QSA performs best for class J.

5   Conclusions

In this paper, we described several new (kernel) methods for trees: QSA, which is based on vectors of structural features, the LeftTK which is a straightforward extensions of the parse tree kernel to XML documents; the set tree kernel, which in contrast to the LeftTK, allows the permutation of children; the soft tree kernel, which is an extension of the set tree kernel, that employs a soft comparison of node positions and therefore favors trees with more similar orderings of child sequences; and, last, the so-called string-tree kernel, which extends the partial tree kernel by Moschitti [11] and the labeled ordered tree kernel by Kashima and Konayagi [10]. We presented a new, straightforward method for including node properties via sub-kernels.

The most important result in terms of computational linguistics is that, seemingly, the type of a text can often be determined based on structural features only. The evaluation moreover showed that complexity is a critical issue, particularly for large corpora containing complex trees. In particular, the string tree kernel could not be applied to the newspaper corpus. Although we did not perform experiments with the labeled ordered tree kernel and the partial tree kernel, we assume problems for these kernels, too, because they perform a similar recursive computation.

Related to the complexity issues, we could only do a limited parameter search for the newspaper corpus. We varied λ in the interval $[0.0; 2.0]$, with best results usually for λ between 0.2 and 0.7. For the StringTK, we set the maximum string length, L, to 3, and the gap penalty ρ to 0.9. Future work will comprise more extensive experiments, and the reduction of the complexity of the tree kernels (if possible).

Acknowledgments. We thank Alessandro Moschitti (University of Rome) for helpful discussions. We thank Sebastian Herold for performing parts of the experiments.

References

1. Feldmann, R., Sanger, J.: The Text Mining Handbook: Advanced Approaches in Analyzing Unstructured Data. Cambridge University Press, Cambridge (2006)
2. Mehler, A., Gleim, R., Dehmer, M.: Towards structure-sensitive hypertext categorization. In: Spiliopoulou, M., Kruse, R., Borgelt, C., Nürnberger, A., Gaul, W. (eds.) Proc. of the 29th Ann. Conf. of the German Class. Soc., Springer, Heidelberg (2005)
3. Mehler, A., Geibel, P., Gleim, R., Pustylnikov, S.H.O., Jain, B.J.: Learning text types solely by structural differentiae, vol. 1. Publications of the Institute of Cognitive Science (PICS), Osnabrück (January 2007)
4. Vapnik, V.N.: The Nature of Statistical Learning Theory. Springer, Heidelberg (1995)
5. Gärtner, T.: A survey of kernels for structured data. SIGKDD Explorations 5(2), 49–58 (2003)
6. Geibel, P., Jain, B.J., Wysotzki, F.: Combining recurrent neural networks and support vector machines for structural pattern recognition. Neurocomputing 64, 63–105 (2005)
7. Collins, M., Duffy, N.: Convolution kernels for natural language. In: NIPS, pp. 625–632 (2001)
8. Moschitti, A.: A study on convolution kernels for shallow statistic parsing. In: ACL, pp. 335–342 (2004)
9. Haussler, D.: Convolution Kernels on Discrete Structure. Technical Report UCSC-CRL-99-10, University of California at Santa Cruz, Santa Cruz, CA, USA (1999)
10. Kashima, H., Koyanagi, T.: Kernels for semi-structured data. In: Proc. ICML, pp. 291–298 (2002)
11. Moschitti, A.: Efficient convolution kernels for dependency and constituent syntactic trees. In: Fürnkranz, J., Scheffer, T., Spiliopoulou, M. (eds.) ECML 2006. LNCS (LNAI), vol. 4212, pp. 318–329. Springer, Heidelberg (2006)
12. Lodhi, H., Saunders, C., Shawe-Taylor, J., Cristianini, N., Watkins, C.J.C.H.: Text classification using string kernels. JMLR 2, 419–444 (2002)
13. Biber, D.: Dimensions of Register Variation. A Cross-Linguistic Comparison. Cambridge University Press, Cambridge (1995)
14. Mehler, A.: Hierarchical orderings of textual units. In: Proceedings of the 19th International Conference on Computational Linguistics (COLING 2002), pp. 646–652. Morgan Kaufmann, San Francisco (2002)
15. Köhler, R.: Syntactic Structures: Properties and Interrelations. Journal of Quantitative Linguistics, 46–47 (1999)
16. Pustylnikov, O.: Guessing Text Type by Structure. In: Proceedings of the ESSLLI Student Session 2007 (to appear, 2007)
17. Geibel, P., Wysotzki, F.: Learning relational concepts with decision trees. In: Saitta, L. (ed.) Machine Learning: Proceedings of the Thirteenth International Conference, pp. 166–174. Morgan Kaufmann Publishers, San Francisco (1996)
18. Sampson, G.: English for the Computer: The Susanne Corpus and Analytic Scheme: SUSANNE Corpus and Analytic Scheme. Clarendon Press (1995)

Perfect Population Classification on Hapmap Data with a Small Number of SNPs

Nina Zhou[1] and Lipo Wang[2]

[1] College of Information Engineering, Xiangtan University,
Xiangtan, Hunan, China
[2] Nanyang Technological University
Block S1, 50 Nanyang Avenue, Singapore 639798

Abstract. The single nucleotide polymorphisms (SNPs) are believed to determine human differences and, to some degree, provide biomedical researchers a possibility of predicting risks of some diseases and explaining patients' different responses to drug regimens. With the availability of millions of SNPs in the Hapmap Project, although large amount of information about SNPs is available, the tremendous size also causes a major challenge for research on SNPs. Inspired from the recent research work on population classification by Park et al (2006), we attempt to find as few SNPs as possible from the original nearly 4 millions SNPs to classify the 3 populations in the Hapmap genotype data. In this paper, we propose to first use a modified t-test measure to rank SNPs, and then combine the ranking result with a classifier, e.g., the support vector machine, to find the optimal SNP subset. Compared with Park et al's result, our proposed method is more efficient in ranking features and classifying the three populations, i.e., we obtained perfect classification using only 11 SNPs in comparison with 82 SNPs used by Park et al.

1 Background

A single nucleotide polymorphism (SNP, pronounced as "snip") is a small genetic variation occurring within a person's DNA sequence. For example, when the DNA sequence $AAAT\underline{C}CGG$ is changed to $AAAT\underline{T}CGG$, the variation, i.e., the replacement of the single nucleotide C by the single nucleotide T, is called an SNP variation. SNPs are the most common type of genetic variations in the human genome, very stable from generation to generation [4] and are believed to determine the human difference between any two unrelated individuals, e.g., different physical traits, different predispositions to diseases, and different responses to medicine. Therefore, SNPs can be effective biological markers for scientists to diagnose disease and track population ancestry.

Much research work on SNPs has already been explored, such as searching for genetic regions associated with complex diseases [8, 17], summarizing and analyzing SNPs for cost-effective genotyping [1, 7, 32]. These work can be categorized into association studies on SNPs. Usually association studies are based on the fact that SNPs in close proximity on the same chromosome are often correlated, which is measured by 'linkage disequilibrium' (LD) [2]. Therefore, the

M. Ishikawa et al. (Eds.): ICONIP 2007, Part II, LNCS 4985, pp. 789–797, 2008.
© Springer-Verlag Berlin Heidelberg 2008

correlation between SNPs is always used to selecting the optimal subset of SNPs (also referred as the tagging SNPs). For example, Bafna et al. [1] and Hall et al. [7] searched for the SNPs with predictive power and determined neighborhoods for those predictive SNPs based on the correlation between SNPs. Then Bafna et al. [1] and Hall et al. [7] proposed the notion of informativeness, which measures how well a single SNP or a set of SNPs predict another single SNP or another set of SNPs within the neighborhoods. Finally, based on the informativeness measure, Bafna et al. [1] and Hall et al. [7] optimally selected the most informative subset of SNPs (tag SNPs) with the minimum size. Eran et al. [8] proposed a prediction accuracy measure to measure how well the value of an SNP is predicted by the values of only two closest tag SNPs, and utilized dynamic programming to find the set of tag SNPs which had the maximum prediction accuracy. For quickly finding a small number of tag SNPs, Eran et al. [8] also utilized the random sampling algorithm to randomly generate some sets of tag SNPs and find the set of tag SNPs with the maximum prediction accuracy. Phuong et al. [17] proposed to select tag SNPs by discarding redundant features, which was based on the method of feature selection using feature similarity (FSFS) [15]. Phuong et al. [17] first grouped features into clusters in which each feature is similar by the linkage disequilibrium (LD) measure γ^2 [18] and then choose one feature from each cluster as the representation of the cluster.

Other research such as tracking population history also has been developed, which is categorized into population studies on SNPs. For example, Rosenberg et al. [19] proposed to select genetic markers with highest informativeness for inference of individual ancestry. In 2005, Rosenberg proposed to select informative marker panels for population assignment. He used genotypes from eight species, i.e., carp, cat, chicken etc., as the experiment data, and compared five proposed multivariate algorithms to select efficient marker panels. All the five approaches are based on a performance function, which is used to measure the probability of correctly assigning individuals to its populations. The probability is the optimal rate of correct assignment (ORCA) in [19]. Although this algorithm is approximately a performance function, he pointed out that the algorithm can not be realistically realized if some terms in the ORCA are large. With the development of the Hapmap Project (www.hapmap.org), Park et al [16] proposed a different way to select informative SNPs to classify the three populations, i.e., Utah residents with ancestry from Northern and Western Europe (CEU), Yoruban in Ibadan, Nigeria in West Africa (YRI), and Han Chinese in Beijing together with Japanese in Tokyo (CHB+JPT). They proposed to adopt the nearest shrunken centroid method (NSCM) to rank SNPs for each class. That is, each SNP has three ranking scores for three populations. If the three scores of one SNP have great variance, this SNP will have great power for classifying the three populations. Or otherwise. In this way, they obtain the result of using the top 82 SNPs from nearly 4 millions SNPs to completely classify the three populations.

Inspired from the research work by Park et al (2006), we attempt to find as few SNPs as possible from the original nearly 4 millions SNPs to classify the 3 populations in the Hapmap genotype data. In this paper, we propose to firstly rank SNPs according to a feature importance ranking measure, i.e., a modified t-test, where the higher the ranking value, the stronger the corresponding classification power. Secondly, from the ranking list, we randomly choose different numbers of top ranked SNPs, e.g., 2, 5, 7, 10 and so on, test them through a classifier, e.g., the support vector machine (SVM) [25, 26] and determine the SNP subset which has the smaller size and highest classification accuracy.

2   Methods

In many existed feature selection algorithms, feature ranking is often used to show which input features are more important [6, 28] so as to improve the efficiency of feature selection process, especially when a great number of features are involved. Therefore, feature ranking is used in our experiment to determine each feature's classification power. In this paper, we will adopt a t-test ranking measure modified from [3, 23, 27].

2.1   Modified T-test

The t-test, also called as the student t-test [3], is originally used to evaluate whether the means of two classes are statistically different from each other by calculating a ratio between the difference of two class means and variability of the two classes. It was adopted by [11, 21] to rank features (genes) for microarray data and for mass spectrometry data [31, 13]. We notice that the original t-test is only limited to 2-class problems. In order to extend the original t-test to multi-class problems, Tibshirani et al. [23] developed the nearest shrunken centroid method, i.e., calculating a t-statistic value (1) for each gene of each class. This t-statistic value measured the difference between the mean of one class and the mean of all the classes. The difference is standardized by the within-class standard deviation.

$$t_{ic} = \frac{\overline{x}_{ic} - \overline{x}_i}{M_c \cdot (S_i + S_0)} \tag{1}$$

$$S_i^2 = \frac{1}{N - C} \sum_{c=1}^{C} \sum_{j \in c} (x_{ij} - \overline{x}_{ic})^2 \tag{2}$$

$$M_c = \sqrt{1/n_c + 1/N} \tag{3}$$

Here t_{ic} denotes the t-statistics value for the i-th feature of the c-th class. $\overline{x}_{ic}$ denotes the i-th feature's mean value in the c-th class and $\overline{x}_i$ indicates the i-th feature's mean value for all classes. x_{ij} represents the i-th feature of the j-th sample. N is the total number of all the samples for all the C classes and n_c is the number of samples for the c-th class. S_i is the within-class standard deviation and S_0 is set to be the median value of S_i for all the features. This t-statistic value of [23] measured the deviation between each class and the mean of all classes and was used to constitute a classifier. The authors did not refer to using the t-statistic of each class to rank features for all the classes. In the following work [27], Wang et al. extended the t-statistic algorithm to rank features for all the classes. That is, the t-score (t-statistic value) of feature i is calculated as the greatest t-score for all classes:

$$t_i = max \left\{ \frac{|\overline{x}_{ic} - \overline{x}_i|}{M_c S_i}, c = 1, 2, ...C \right\} \tag{4}$$

However, (4) still can not be used to deal with our data. It is because of the non-numerical type. For example, if two alleles for one SNP are A and T, its feature values are expressed as AA, AT and TT. If representing them simply by three numerical values, e.g., 1, 2 and 3, and making the calculation according to (4), it will be meaningless. We proposed to use vectors to represent different feature values and thereby obtained the modified t-test (5), which can deal with our problem. In the following, we generalized the t-score of each feature in 3 steps:

1. Suppose the feature set is $F = (f_1, ..., f_i, ..., f_g)$, and feature i has m_i different nominal values represented as $f_i = (x_i^{(1)}, x_i^{(2)}, ..., x_i^{(m_i)})$
2. Transform each nominal feature value into a vector with the dimension m_i, i.e., $x_i^{(1)} \Rightarrow \boldsymbol{X}_i^{(1)} = \{0, ..., 0, 1\}$, $x_i^{(2)} \Rightarrow \boldsymbol{X}_i^{(2)} = \{0, ..., 1, 0\}$, ..., $x_i^{(m_i)} \Rightarrow \boldsymbol{X}_i^{(m_i)} = \{1, ..., 0, 0\}$.
3. Replace all the numerical features in (1) and (2) with the format of vectors (see (5) and (6)).

$$t_i = max \left\{ \frac{|\boldsymbol{X}_{ic} - \boldsymbol{X}_i|}{M_c S_i}, c = 1, 2, ..., C \right\} \tag{5}$$

$\overline{\boldsymbol{X}}_{ic}$ and $\overline{\boldsymbol{X}}_i$ are two row vectors indicating the i-th SNP's mean status in the c-th class and mean status for all the classes. $|\overline{\boldsymbol{X}}_{ic} - \overline{\boldsymbol{X}}_i|$ denotes the Euclidean distance of the two vectors.

$$S_i^2 = \frac{1}{N - C} \sum_{c=1}^{C} \sum_{j \in c} (\boldsymbol{X}_{ij} - \overline{\boldsymbol{X}}_{ic})(\boldsymbol{X}_{ij} - \overline{\boldsymbol{X}}_{ic})^T \tag{6}$$

Here $\boldsymbol{X}_{ij}$ is a row vector denoting the i-th SNP in the j-th class. $(\boldsymbol{X}_{ij} - \overline{\boldsymbol{X}}_{ic})(\boldsymbol{X}_{ij} - \overline{\boldsymbol{X}}_{ic})^T$ is a scalar.

The ranking rule is: the greater the t-scores, the more relevant the features.

2.2 The Classifier

The classifier in our experiment will be used twice. In the first time, we will use a classifier to test different feature subsets, formed from the ranking list with top ranking values, and determine a candidate feature subset. In the second time, we again need to test different feature subsets generated from the candidate feature subset, and find the optimal feature subset, i.e., the one with the best classification accuracy and minimum size. Considering the importance of the classifier, we would like to choose the support vector machine (SVM) [25] as the classifier because of its very good performance, such as effectively avoiding overfitting and accomodating large feature spaces, and successfully used in bioinformatics [14, 27]. Since Hsu et al. [9] indicated that RBF kernel is generally a first choice and Keerthi et al. [12] showed that the linear kernel is special case of the RBF kernel, we choose the RBF kernel for the SVM in our experiment. During the classification process, the kernel parameter γ and the penal parameter ν [9] are determined through a double cross-validation method [5]. For example, for a 10-fold cross validation method, we first separate the original samples into 10 equal subsets, each time having one subset as the testing set, and the other nine subsets as the training set. Then for the training set, we use the 10-fold cross validation one more time.

3   Experiments and Discussion

3.1   Experimental Data and Its Preprocessing

The genotype data is downloaded from the the directory of (/Index of/genotypes/ latest_ncbi_build36/rs_strand/non-redundant) on the website (http://www. hapmap.org/genotypes/), which contains data files with genotypes submitted by HapMap genotyping centers to the HapMap Data Coordination Center (DCC) to date. From the column 12 to the last column, data files provide observed genotypes of samples (one genotype per column) with sample identifiers in column headers (Coriell catalog numbers, example: NA10847) and duplicate samples having .dup suffix. The genotypes are provided for each chromosome of each population, i.e., chromosomes 1-22, chromosome X and Y, and four populations: CEU, YRI, JPT and HCB. Here CEU represents Utah residents with ancestry from northern and western Europe. YRI represents Yoruba individuals from Ibadan and Nigeria. Each of the two populations has 90 reference individuals (samples) which are comprised of 30 father-mother-offspring trios. JPT represents Japanese individuals from Tokyo, and HCB means Han Chinese individuals from Beijing. Each of these two populations has 45 samples and the individuals in each of the populations are unrelated. For efficient experiments, we remove the children samples from the CEU and YRI populations to make sure all the samples involved in the experiment are unrelated. Thus the total number of samples used in our experiment is 210. Usually the JPT and CHB can be classified as one population (denoted as JPT+CHB) because of their similar DNA sequence. In this paper, we will carry out two respective classifications on the original 4 populations and the 3 populations, i.e., CEU, YRI, JPT+CHB.

Combining all the features together from the 24 chromosomes (Chromosome 1, 2, ..., 22, X and Y), we have nearly 4 million SNPs involved in the experiment. SNPs are usually expressed as strings of two or more alleles, e.g., *AT* or *ATCG*. SNPs with two alleles are called as bi-allelic SNPs and SNPs with 3 or 4 alleles are called as multi-allelic SNPs. If the alleles consisting of one SNP are the same, e.g., AA or TT, this type of SNPs are called homozygous. Or they are called as hyterozygous, e.g., AT. Although some locus show us there may be 3 or 4 alleles at those positions, e.g., 4 alleles $A/T/C/G$ at one SNP position, their real feature values consist of only two alleles, e.g., A/T. These are the error descriptions existed in the data and have already been announced in the website. Therefore, all data samples are strings of bi-allelic SNPs. Besides, we notice some features have unknown value for some samples. In this case, instead of removing those features from our experiment, we will replace them according to the rule adopted by Park et al [16] in their experiment. That is, we replace the missing value with the major allele of each population class. After this preprocessing, we need to transform the nominal features into vectors as the modified t-test algorithm required. For example, according to description of the generalized steps, AA is represented by $\{0, 0, 1\}$, TT is represented by $\{0, 1, 0\}$, and AT is represented by $\{1, 0, 0\}$. The three bits of vectors represent three different features (SNPs). Therefore, the calculation between them will not lose the information of the three different feature values.

3.2   Implementation

After using the modified t-test ranking measure, we have two experiments to conduct, i.e., classification on 3 populations and 4 populations, respectively. From the 210 samples, we randomly choose 40 samples from YRI and CEU, respectively, and 30 samples from JPT and CHB, respectively, as the training set. The 70 samples left are used as the testing set.

We first rank the SNPs of 24 chromosomes, respectively. Then from the 23 ranking lists (except chromosome Y which only has 49 SNPs) we choose their top 100 SNPs to form a new feature subset with 2300 features together with the 49 features form Chromosome Y. According to their ranking scores, we re-rank them again. In this way, we greatly reduce the number of features involved in the experiment. Furthermore, this will not lead to loss of important information and instead will facilitate to improve the efficiency of the experiment.

3.3   Results and Discussions

In Table 1, we provide the ranking result from the modified t-test ranking measure. It includes four types of information. The first column (Ranking NO.) means the ranking order of top 11 features corresponding to their ranking scores. The second column lists the 11 features' names and the third column (Chromosome) provides the location of each SNP. The fourth and fifth column list the ranking score of each SNP, respectively for 3-population and 4-population problem. Although the ranking list for 3 populations is the same as the one for 4 populations, ranking values are different for the two conditions. Based on the ranking list in Table 1, we combine different number of features (see Table 2), i.e., 2, 5, 7, 10, 11 and 20, and input them into the classifier, respectively. From Table 2, we find out that 3 populations are completely classified (100% accuracy) when the top 11 features are input. While using the same 11 features to classify the 4 populations, we obtain the accuracy 78.57% (55/70), in which 55

Table 1. Top 11 features' ranking list for the modified t-test ranking measure. SNP names by boldface indicate that those SNPs' combination leads to best classification.

Ranking No.	Name of SNPs	Chromosome	Ranking value for 3 populations	Ranking value for 4 populations
1	**rs11499**	chr3	9.6017	9.5666
2	rs5825	chr4	8.1264	8.1022
3	rs4143483	chr4	7.2546	7.2281
4	rs1299386	chr7	7.2546	7.2281
5	rs1813166	chr7	6.7457	6.7210
6	rs2040513	chr7	6.7457	6.7210
7	rs4131595	chr7	6.7457	6.7210
8	**rs289632**	chr8	6.5661	6.5421
9	rs1785847	chr18	6.5661	6.5421
10	rs2474273	chrX	6.5661	6.5421
11	**rs4120141**	chrX	6.4379	6.4144

Table 2. Classification accuracy for different feature subsets formed from the ranking list in Table 1. The number of SNPs that leads to the best classification is indicated by boldface.

Number of features	Accuracy for 3 populations	Accuracy for 4 populations
2	70% (49/70)	55.71% (39/70)
5	70% (49/70)	55.71% (39/70)
7	70% (49/70)	57.14% (40/70)
10	98.57% (69/70)	57.14% (40/70)
11	100% (70/70)	78.57% (55/70)
20	100% (70/70)	78.57% (55/70)

of 70 testing samples are correctly classified. It means that CEU and YRI are completely recognized and JPT and CHB are recognized as the third class.

4   Conclusion

In this paper, we proposed a modified t-test ranking measure to rank a large amount of SNPs. This measure is able to deal with data with nominal features in the form of vectors, which is the major superiority over the original t-test ranking measure. Besides, we adopted the F-statistics ranking measure [24] on the genotype data and compared the results with those obtained from the modified t-test ranking measure. The comparisons showed that the modified t-test ranking measure is comparable with the F-statistics ranking measure. However, due to space limitation, we will not present the comparisons in this paper. After obtaining the ranked features, we utilize a classifier to determine an optimal feature subset, which has the minimum size but leads to the highest classification accuracy. The final results show that the modified t-test ranking method is efficient on determining the importance of the SNPs. Compared to the classification method of Park et al[16], we obtained better result, i.e., perfect classification of the 3 populations using only 11 SNPs, compared to 82 SNPs used in [16].

References

[1] Bafna, V., Halldorsson, B., Schwartz, R., Clark, A., Istrail, S.: Haplotypes and Informative SNP selection: Don't block out information. In: Proc. of RECOMB, pp. 19–27 (2003)

[2] Celedon, J.C.: Candidate genes, SNPs, Haplotypes and linkage disequilibrium. Powerpoint presentation (2004), `http://innateimmunity.net/files/CANDGENES/siframes.html`

[3] Devore, J., Peck, R.: Statistics:the exploration and analysis of data, 3rd edn. Duxbury Press, Pacific Grove (1997)

[4] Duerinck, K.F.: (2001), `http://www.duerinck.com/snp.html`

[5] Francois, R., Langrognet, F.: Double Cross Validation for Model Based Classification, User (2006), `http://www.r-project.org/user-2006/Abstracts/Francois+Langrognet.pdf`

[6] Guyon, I., Elisseeff, A.: An Introduction to Variable and Feature Selection. Journal of Machine Learning Research 3, 1157–1182 (2003)

[7] Halldrsson, B., Bafna, V., Lippert, R., Schwartz, R., de la Vega, F., Clark, A., Istrail, S.: Optimal haplotype blockfree selection of tagging snps for genome-wide association studies. Genome research 14, 1633–1640 (2004)

[8] Halperin, E., Kimmel, G., Shamir, R.: Tag SNP selection in genotype data for maximizig SNP prediction accuracy. Bioinformatics 199, 195–203 (2005)

[9] Hsu, C.W., Chang, C.C., Lin, C.J.: A practical guide to support vector classification. Technical report, Department of Computer Science and Information Engineering, National Taiwan University, Taipei (2003)

[10] Human genome project information (2006), `http://www.ornl.gov/sci/techresources/Human_Genome/faq/snps.html`

[11] Jaeger, J., Sengupta, R., Ruzzo, W.L.: Improved Gene Selection For Classification Of Microarrays. Pac. Symp. Biocomput., 53–64 (2003)

[12] Keerthi, S.S., Lin, C.-J.: Asymptotic behaviors of support vector machines with Gaussian kernel. Neural Computation 15, 1667–1689 (2003)

[13] Levner, I.: Feature selection and nearest centroid classification for protein mass spectrometry. BMC Bioinformatics 6, 68 (2005)

[14] Liu, B., Wan, C.R., Wang, L.P.: An efficient semi-unsupervised gene selection method via spectral biclustering. IEEE Trans. on Nano-Bioscience 5, 110–114 (2006)

[15] Mitra, Pabitra, Murthy, C.A., Pal, S.K.: Unsupervised feature selection using feature similarity. IEEE trans. on Pattern analysis and machine intelligence 3, 301–312 (2002)

[16] Park, J.S., Hwang, S.H., Lee, Y.S., Kim, S.C.: SNP@Ethnos: a database of ethnically variant single-nucleotide polymorphisms. Nucleic Acids Research 0, D1–D5 (2006)

[17] Phuong, T.M., Lin, Z., Altman, R.B.: Choosing SNPs using Feature Selection. In: Proc IEEE Comput Syst Bioinform Conf. 2005 (CSB 2005), pp. 301–309 (2005)

[18] Pritchard, J.K., Przeworski, M.: Linkage disequilibrium in humans: models and data. Am. J. Hum. Genet. 69, 1–14 (2001)

[19] Rosenberg, N.A., et al.: Informativeness of genetic markers for inference of ancestry. Am. J. Hum. Genet. 73, 1402–1422 (2003)

[20] Rosenberg, N.A.: Algorithms for selecting informative marker panels for population assignment. Journal of computational biology 9, 1183–1201 (2005)

[21] Su, Y., Murali, T.M., Pavlovic, V., Schaffer, M., Kasif, S.: RankGene: Identifcation of Diagnostic Genes Based on Expression Data. Bioinformatics 19, 1578–1579 (2003)

[22] The International HapMap Consortium: The international Hapmap Project. Nature 426, 789–796 (2003), www.hapmap.org/genotypes

[23] Tibshirani, R., Hastie, T., Narasimhan, B., Chu, G.: Diagnosis of multiple cancer types by shrunken centroids of gene expression. PNAS 99, 6567–6572 (2002)

[24] Trochim, W.M.: The Research Methods Knowledge Base, 2nd edn. Atomic Dog Publishing (2004), http://www.socialresearchmethods.net/kb/

[25] Vapnik, V.: Statistical learning theory. Wiley, NewYork (1998)

[26] Wang, L.P.: Support Vector Machines: Theory and Applications. Springer, Heidelberg (2005)

[27] Wang, L.P., Chu, F., Xie, W.: Accurate cancer classification using expressions of very few genes. IEEE Transactions on Bioinformatics and Computational Biology 4, 40–53 (2007)

[28] Wang, L.P., Fu, X.J.: Data Mining with Computational Intelligence. Springer, Berlin (2005)

[29] Welch, B.L.: The generalizaition of student's problem when several different population are involved. Biomethika 34, 28–35 (1947)

[30] Wright, S.: The interpretation of population structure by F-statistics with special regard to systems of mating. Evolution 19, 395–420 (1965)

[31] Wu, B., Abbott, T., Fishman, D., McMurray, W., Mor, G., Stone, K., Ward, D., Williams, K., Zhao, H.: Comparison of statistical methods for classifcation of ovarian cancer using mass spectrometry data. BioInformatics 19, 1636–1643 (2003)

[32] Zhen, L., Altman, R.B.: Finding Haplotype Tagging SNPs by Use of Principle Components Analysis. Am. J. Hum. Genet. 75, 850–861 (2004)

Automatic Factorization of Biological Signals Measured by Fluorescence Correlation Spectroscopy Using Non-negative Matrix Factorization

Kenji Watanabe[1] and Takio Kurita[2]

[1] Department of Computer Science, Graduate School of Systems and Informatoin Engineering, University of Tsukuba,
1-1-1 Tennodai, Tsukuba-shi, Ibaraki-ken, 305-8577 Japan
[2] National Institute of Advanced Industrial Science and Technology (AIST),
AIST Central 2, 1-1-1 Umezono, Tsukuba-shi, Ibaraki-ken, 305-8568 Japan
{kenji-watanabe, takio-kurita}@aist.go.jp

Abstract. We proposed automatic factorization method of biological signals measured by Fluorescence Correlation Spectroscopy (FCS). Since the signals are composed from several positive components, the signals are decomposed by using the idea of Non-negative matrix factorization (NMF). Each component is represented by model functions and the signals are factorized as the non-negative sum of the model functions. Analytical accuracy of our proposed method was verified by using biological data that were measured by FCS. The experimental results showed that our method could automatically factorize the signals and the obtained components were similar with the ones obtained manually.

Keywords: Signal processing, NMF, Pattern recognition, Protein dynamics.

1   Introduction

Factorization of time series signals is very important in biological researches, such as spike analysis in brain science [1] and analysis of the protein dynamics in molecular biology [2], [3]. Especially, in the field of molecular biology, Fluorescence Correlation Spectroscopy (FCS) [4], [5], [6] begins to be often used to measure and analyze the protein dynamics in living cell [2], [3]. Such analysis of time series signals would be more important in the future. However, the current methods of time series analysis are not efficient because each sample is fitted as a linear combination of the model functions and the parameters of model functions are plotted to find the frequent components. In addition, there is a possibility to have danger that the subjectivity of researchers is included in the results obtained by the current methods because the examination of analytical results and judgments of re-analysis are decided manually. To improve the current methods, a model function [7] or an approximation method [8] has been modified. But these modifications were not sufficient because the researchers in this field want to know what components are included in the set of signals and the statistical analysis of the large amount of samples is required to estimate the components. In molecular biology, the components are manually found through statistical investigation.

M. Ishikawa et al. (Eds.): ICONIP 2007, Part II, LNCS 4985, pp. 798–806, 2008.

Automatic signal factorization has been examined in a lot of fields, for example, factor analysis, independent component analysis (ICA) [9], [10], non-negative matrix factorization (NMF) [11], [12]. Especially, NMF is probably effective for the factorization of non-negative energy distribution such as a molecular dynamics in thermal equilibrium. On the other hand, ICA is not suitable for this application because the independency is not guaranteed.

In this paper, we proposed a factorization method of biological signals measured by FCS in which the idea of NMF is used to decompose the signals into several positive components. Each component is represented by model functions derived by considering its physical phenomena and is fitted by the nonlinear least squares method. By using NMF approach, we can directly find the components included in the autocorrelation functions from the all samples.

To verify the effectiveness of our method, we applied the proposed method to the signals obtained by FCS.

2 Method

In FCS, autocorrelation function (ACF) was extracted from time series signals measured from a living cell and they are represented as a feature vector. ACF may include several components related with different origins. Usually a set of feature vectors is obtained by measuring ACF from different cells in the same situation. The set of feature vectors is represented as a matrix. To analyze the protein dynamics of such cells, we have to decompose the matrix into the components (the basis vectors). The basis vectors can be modeled by the probability density function of Boltzmann distribution law. Usually they are modeled by fitting a model function using the nonlinear least squares method. Since both the ACFs and the basis vectors are non-negative, we have to decompose the matrix with the non-negative coefficients.

Non-negative matrix factorization (NMF) [11], [12] was proposed to decompose a given non-negative matrix into a non-negative basis matrix and a coefficient matrix. We combine this non-negative decomposition with the nonlinear least squares fitting of model function. Once the basis vectors are modeled by the model function, we can estimate the diffusion time of each component and the component ratios from the estimated probability densities. For example, the diffusion time corresponding to a basis vector can be calculated from the probability density function estimated for the basis vector considering its Boltzmann distribution.

2.1 Fluorescence Correlation Spectroscopy

FCS is one of the techniques to measure the fluorescence intensity fluctuations caused by fluorescent probe movement of free diffusion and to deduce diffusion times and existence ratios of fluorescent probes from autocorrelation function (ACF) calculated from the fluorescence intensity fluctuations. ACF is defined as follow:

$$G(\tau) = \frac{\langle \mathbf{I}_t \mathbf{I}_{t+\tau} \rangle}{\langle I \rangle^2} \tag{1}$$

where $\mathbf{I}_t$ is the signal intensity in time t. Diffusion time τ is defined as $\tau = \Delta t$. $\langle I \rangle^2$ is square of the averaged signal intensity.

Since ACF may include several components related with different origins, usually the obtained ACFs are fitted by one-, two-, or three-component model as follows:

$$G(\tau) = 1 + \frac{1}{N}\sum_i F_i \left(1 + \frac{\tau}{\tau_i}\right)^{-1}\left(1 + \frac{\tau}{s^2\tau_i}\right)^{-1/2} \tag{2}$$

where F_i and τ_i are the fraction and diffusion time of component i, respectively, N is the number of fluorescence molecules in the detection volume element defined by $s = z_0 / w_0$, radius w_0 and length $2z_0$. The correlation amplitude of the function (y intercept, the value of $G(0)$) is determined by the reciprocal of the number of fluorescence molecules in detection volume. ACF of rhodamine 6G (Rh6G) solution were measured for 30s five times at 10s interval, then the diffusion time (τ_{Rh6G}) and s were obtained by one-component fitting of the measured ACF in each sample.

Usually ACFs are obtained from different cells in the same situation and the statistical properties are investigated.

2.2 Signal Factorization

To analyze the protein dynamics of many cells, we have to decompose the matrix of ACFs into the components (the basis vectors). Since both the ACFs and the basis vectors are non-negative, we have to decompose the matrix with the non-negative coefficients.

Non-negative matrix factorization (NMF) [11], [12] was proposed to decompose a given non-negative matrix into a non-negative basis matrix and a coefficient matrix. We combine this non-negative decomposition with the nonlinear least squares fitting of model function.

NMF decomposes the given $n \times m$ input matrix V into a $n \times r$ basis matrix W and an $r \times m$ coefficient matrix as follow:

$$V \approx WH \tag{3}$$

This means that WH is an approximation of the matrix V.

NMF uses the objective function that is the divergence of V from WH as the measure of the cost for factorization. The objective function in NMF is given as follow:

$$D(V \parallel WH) = \sum_{ij}\left(V_{ij}\log\frac{V_{ij}}{(WH)_{ij}} - V_{ij} + (WH)_{ij}\right) \tag{4}$$

From this objective function (4), we can derive multiplicative update rules in NMF as follow:

$$W_{ia} \leftarrow W_{ia} \sum_{\mu} \frac{V_{i\mu}}{(WH)_{i\mu}} H_{a\mu} \tag{5}$$

$$W_{ia} \leftarrow \frac{W_{ia}}{\sum_{j} W_{ja}} \tag{6}$$

$$H_{a\mu} \leftarrow H_{a\mu} \sum_{i} W_{ia} \frac{V_{i\mu}}{(WH)_{i\mu}} \tag{7}$$

The proof of these objective function and multiplicative update rules are shown in [12]. Initial values of W are usually randomly assigned. In the following experiments, all random values were generated using Mersenne Twister algorithm (mt19937ar.c).

There is no guarantee to reflect a physical phenomenon in the basis matrix computed using NMF.

In FCS, generally ACF are fitted by using equation (2). But molecular dynamics in thermal equilibrium follows Boltzmann distribution law. An exponential function that is represented as like Boltzmann distribution is often used in spectroscopy but the exponential function is uncommonly used to the analysis of FCS [8]. To modify the original NMF, the probability density functions of Boltzmann distribution law are fitted to the basis vectors w_r by using the nonlinear least square method. The probability density function of Boltzmann distribution law is given as follow:

$$w_r = A\,exp\left(-\frac{\tau}{\tau_r}\right) \tag{8}$$

where A is amplitude and τ_r is the diffusion time of w_r. This fitting process is repeated at each iteration of the NMF update.

3   Experiments and Results

We applied the proposed method to two kinds of FCS data that were measured from the fluorescent molecule in water solution and the functional protein in living cell. In water solution data, the fluorescent fluctuations of Rh6G were used as a standard sample. In living cell data, we used Signal transducers and activators of transcription 3 (STAT3). The fluorescent fluctuations of functional protein were fused to the enhanced green fluorescence protein (EGFP). STAT3 has been shown to play pivotal roles in the cytokine signaling pathway, and also in regulating cell growth and differentiation. STAT3 is activated by stimulation with interleukin-6 (IL-6) which is a multifunctional cytokine. Molecular weight of STAT3 changes from monomer to dimer after IL-6 stimulation. In this paper, we used STAT3 measurement data in the nucleus before and after IL-6 stimulation because its diffusion time is expected to change into slow diffuse.

3.1 Results for Rh6G Data

We applied the proposed automatic factorization method to the 54 samples of Rh6G data that were measured on a 10^{-7} M concentrated solution. The $\mathbf{142 \times 54}$ input matrix V was obtained by using these 54 samples. The number of basis vector must be one because Rh6G has only one component. The proposed method was applied to this data. The approximation of V by $\mathbf{wh}^T$, the products of the basis vector $\mathbf{w}$ and the coefficients of each sample $\mathbf{h}$, is shown in Fig. 1. Here the basis vector $\mathbf{w}$ was approximated by fitting the model function shown in equation (8). This suggests that our proposed method gives a good fitting except in slow diffusion times.

Table 1 shows that the diffusion times of Rh6G that were estimated manually and by our proposed method. The manually estimated diffusion time was 24.9 μ s when it was calculated as the average of the 54 samples. The standard deviation of this diffusion

Table 1. Estimated Diffusion time of Rh6G

Using method	Diffusion time / μ s (ratio / %)
Manually estimated	24.9 (100)
Proposed method	39.0 (100)

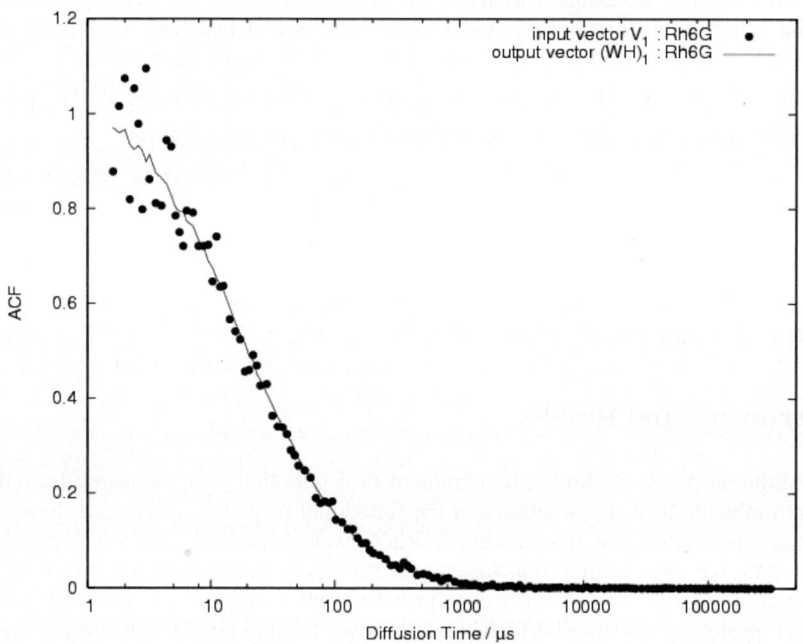

Fig. 1. Automatic factorization of Rh6G data measured by FCS. FCS measurements were carried out in water solution. The closed circles show the samples measured by FCS and the line is the result of approximation.

time was 11.5. The diffusion time estimated by fitting the model function to the basis vector $\mathbf{W}$ was $39.0\,\mu$ s. We can say that the estimated diffusion time seems biologically valid.

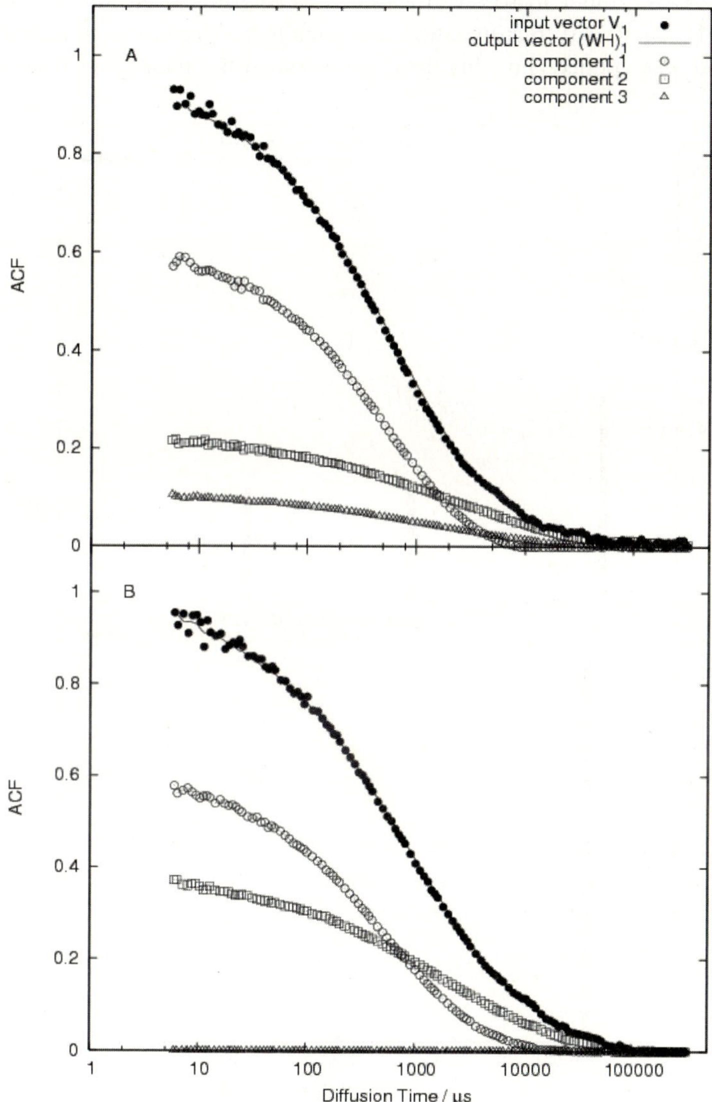

Fig. 2. Automatic factorization of STAT3-GFP measured by FCS before and after IL-6 stimulation. FCS measurements were carried out for STAT3-GFP in the nucleus of living cell. Normalized ACF before and after IL-6 stimulation is shown A and B, respectively. The closed circles show the samples measured by FCS (A, B). Line is the result of the approximation by NMF-based automatic factorization (A, B). The open circles, squares and triangles are the estimated basis of each diffusion component 1, 2 and 3, respectively (A, B).

3.2 Results for STAT3 Data

STAT3 was fused to EGFP (STAT3-GFP) and the 47 samples and the 43 samples before and after IL-6 stimulation were measured by using FCS [2]. Thus, we can obtain the 124×47 input matrix V for before IL-6 stimulation and the 127×43 input matrix V for after IL-6 stimulation. For each input matrix the proposed factorization method was applied. For this data, we assumed the number of basis vectors,

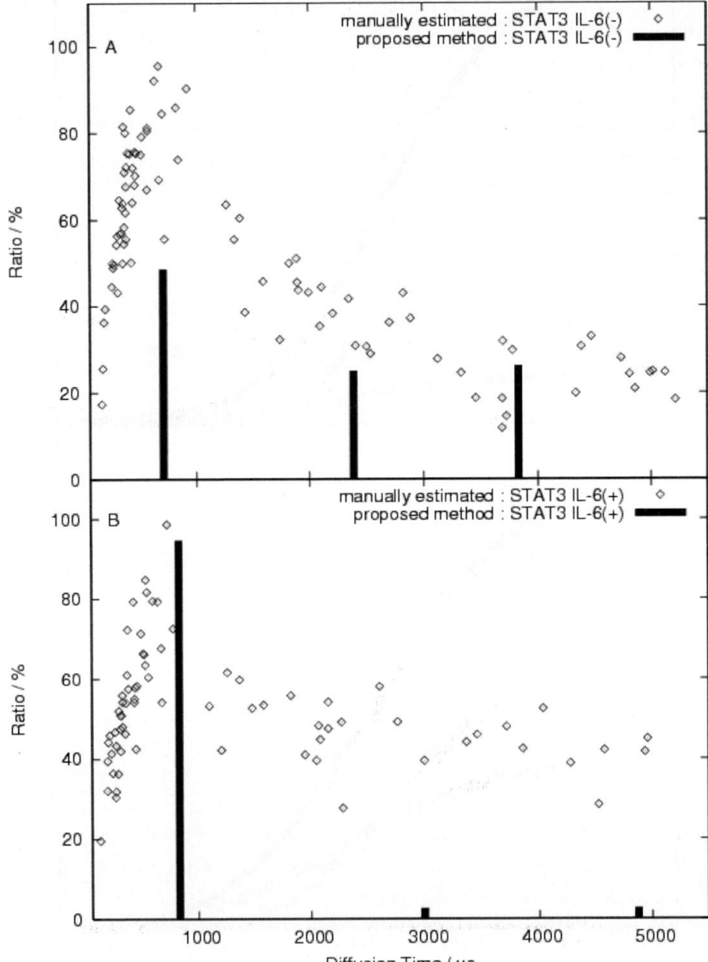

Fig. 3. The distribution of the diffusion times of STAT3-GFP measured by FCS in the nucleus of living cell before and after IL-6 stimulation is shown A and B, respectively. The manually estimated diffusion times of each measurement are shown in the scatter plots of open diamonds. Bars shows the diffusion times calculated from the estimated basis vectors by the proposed method.

namely rank of the NMF, was at most three because STAT3 in the nucleus of living cell is inhibited free diffusion and exists as the monomeric form or the dimeric form before and after IL-6 stimulation, respectively.

The results of automatic factorization for STAT3-GFP measured by FCS before and after IL-6 stimulation were shown Fig. 2. Fig.2 A and B show the results for before IL-6 stimulation and after IL-6 stimulation, respectively. The closed circles show the samples measured by FCS. Line is the result of the approximation by NMF-based automatic factorization. The open circles, squares and triangles are the estimated basis of each diffusion component 1, 2 and 3, respectively. These results are reasonable because the number of samples with faster diffusion times increase after the stimulation.

The distribution of the diffusion times of STAT3-GFP measured by FCS in the nucleus of living cell before and after IL-6 stimulation is shown in A and B of Fig. 3, respectively. The manually estimated diffusion times of each measurement are shown in the scatter plots of open diamonds. Bars shows the diffusion times calculated from the estimated basis vectors by the proposed method. The distribution of the diffusion times and the existence ratios are shown in Fig. 3. The diffusion time of the main component obtained by the automatic factorization is 702.1 μ s (48.7%) and the other components are 3830.5 μ s (26.3%) and 2385.8 μ s (25.1%) as shown in Fig. 3 A. On the other hand, the diffusion time of the main component for after stimulation is 831.4 μ s (94.7%) and the other components are 4876.4 μ s (2.70%) and 2994.4 μ s (2.63%) as shown in Fig. 3 B. The diffusion time of the main component increased after IL-6 stimulation. This reflects the physical phenomenon that changes from the monomeric form to the dimeric form. These results show the validity of the proposed method.

4   Discussion

The proposed method gave the similar tendency with the previous biological theory. In General, the current biological theory about the state of STAT3 in the nucleus is as follow. Before IL-6 stimulation, the main component of STAT3 exists as monomer and the sub components exist as lower movements. However, after IL-6 stimulation, a main component of STAT3 exists as dimer. Such a biological theory was confirmed by using classical biological experimental methods in dead cell and was also verified by using FCS in living cell [2].

In our experimental results, the different diffusion time of the main components were estimated by using our proposed factorization method before and after IL-6 stimulation. The results of the main components are probably STAT3 monomer and dimer. The other diffusion times of the sub components were over 2000 μ s before IL-6 stimulation. These results of sub components may be inhibited by the free diffuse of STAT3. These results have the similar tendency of the biological theory. The proposed method can also give the same results with the ordinal method in FCS data analysis (Fig 3). Even if our proposed method could not obtain the results of completely same tendency, it may be caused for a spectroscopy problem such as the effect of triplet state. This problem can be solved by changing the model function to another.

In ordinal FCS data analysis, the diffusion times and the existence ratios are estimated by fitting the equation (2) to each measurement sample. When we need a statistics that reflects the physical phenomena measured by FCS, we have to manually analyze the diffusion times. In this manual treatment of the data, there is a possibility to have danger that the subjectivity of researchers is included. The manual analysis requires a great labor because the analysis has to perform for each sample. However, the proposed method makes automatic statistical analysis of all samples possible. From these reasons, the proposed method is useful.

For future works, we have to modify NMF to introduce the probability density function of Boltzmann distribution law to the multiplicative update rules. This modified NMF will be verified by using the simple simulation data that is generated by the model function. Also we have to select the number of basis vectors automatically. We will try to use model selection techniques. Thereafter we have to confirm the effectiveness of the proposed method by applying to other biological data sets.

References

1. Hochberg, L.R., Serruya, M.D., Friehs, G.M., Mukand, J.A., Saleh, M., Caplan, A.H., Branner, A., Chen, D., Penn, R.D., Donoghue, J.P.: Neuronal ensemble control of prosthetic devices by a human with tetraplegia. Nature 442, 164–171 (2006)
2. Watanabe, K., Saito, K., Kinjo, M., Matsuda, T., Tamura, M., Kon, S., Miyazaki, T., Uede, T.: Molecular dynamics of STAT3 on IL-6 signaling pathway in living cells. Biochem. Biophys. Res. Commun. 324, 1264–1273 (2004)
3. Kitamura, A., Kubota, H., Pack, C.-G., Matsumoto, G., Hirayama, S., Takahashi, Y., Kimura, H., Kinjo, M., Morimoto, R.I., Nagata, K.: Cytosolic chaperonin prevents polyglutamine toxicity with altering the aggregation state. Nature Cell. Biol. 8, 1163–1170 (2006)
4. Ehrenberg, M., Rigler, R.: Rotational brownian motion and fluorescence intensify fluctuations. Chem. Phys. 4, 390–401 (1974)
5. Elson, E.L., Magde, D.: Fluorescence correlation spectroscopy. I. Conceptual basis and theory. Biopolymers 13, 1–27 (1974)
6. Koppel, D.E.: Statistical accuracy in fluorescence correlation spectroscopy. Phys. Rev. A 10, 1938–1945 (1974)
7. Rao, R., Langoju, R., Golsch, M., Rigler, P., Serov, A., Lasser, T.: Stochastic Approach to Data Analysis in Fluorescence Correlation Spectroscopy. J. Phys. Chem. A 110, 10674–10682 (2006)
8. Kim, H.D., Nienhaus, G.U., Ha, T., Orr, J.W., Williamson, J.R., Chu, S.: Mg2+-dependent conformational change of RNA studied by fluorescence correlation and FRET on immobilized single molecules. Proc. Natl. Acad. Sci. USA 99, 4284–4289 (2002)
9. Comon, P.: Independent component analysis, A new concept? Signal Processing 36, 287–314 (1994)
10. Delorme, A., Sejnowski, T., Makeig, S.: Enhanced detection of artifacts in EEG data using higher-order statistics and independent component analysis. NeuroImage 34, 1443–1449 (2007)
11. Lee, D.D., Seung, H.S.: Learning the parts of objects by non-negative matrix factorization. Nature 401, 788–791 (1999)
12. Lee, D.D., Seung, H.S.: Algorithms for Non-negative Matrix Factorization. Adv. Neural Info. Proc. Syst. 13, 556–562 (2001)

Controller Design Method of Gene Networks by Network Learning and Its Performance Evaluation

Yoshihiro Mori, Yasuaki Kuroe, and Takehiro Mori

Kyoto Institute of Technology, Kyoto 606-8585, Japan

Abstract. Investigating gene regulatory networks is important to understand mechanism of cellular functions. Recently, construction of gene networks having desired functions is of interest to many researchers because it is a complementary approach to understanding gene regulatory networks, and it could be the first step to control living cells. A synthesis method of gene networks based on given gene expression pattern sequences by network learning was already proposed. The objective of the paper is to apply the synthesis method to a controller design problem and to evaluate performance of the method. Some numerical experiments are given to evaluate the performance of the proposed method.

1 Introduction

Recently there have been increasing research interests in synthesizing gene networks and several studies have been done [1,2,3,4,5]. Those studies were motivated two ways. One is that the construction of gene networks having desired properties is a complementary approach to investigating mechanism and functions of gene networks. The other is that the construction of gene networks could be the first step to the control problem of living cells. In [1,2], gene networks are synthesized such that their time responses have desired properties. In [3,4,5], the gene network synthesis problem is formulated in a way that desired properties are given by desired expression pattern sequences, and methods to synthesize a model of gene network such that the expression pattern changes of the gene network become equal to given desired ones are proposed. In [5], we proposed a synthesis method based on network learning, which can be applied to more general gene network models than those considered in [3,4].

In this paper, we discuss the controller design problem of gene networks. The problem is: given gene expression pattern sequence and a gene network as a controlled object, design a controller gene network such that the expression pattern changes of the controlled network become equal to given desired ones. In [4], a controller design method which introduces additional variables to the synthesis method in [3] is proposed. In [5], it is shown that the synthesis method proposed in the literature is applicable to the controller design problem. The objective of this paper is to apply the proposed synthesis method in [5] to the controller design problem and to evaluate its performance. We show that controllers can be

M. Ishikawa et al. (Eds.): ICONIP 2007, Part II, LNCS 4985, pp. 807–816, 2008.

designed by modifying the synthesis method in [5]. The controller design problem can be reduced to the learning problem of a class of Recurrent Higher-Order Neural Networks(RHONNs) if the model of the target gene network is given by the piecewise linear network model. It is shown that the proposed method makes it possible to solve several controller design problems through numerical experiments.

2   Problem Statement

The piecewise linear network is a model which is widely used for analysis of gene networks[6]. In this paper, we consider more general model which is given by the following differential equations.

$$\dot{x}_i(t) = g_i(x_i(t)) + f_i(w_{i1}, w_{i2}, \ldots, w_{im_i}, y_1(t), y_2(t), \ldots, y_n(t)), \tag{1}$$

$$y_i(t) = H(x_i(t)), \quad i = 1, 2, \ldots, n \tag{2}$$

where

$$H(x_i) = \begin{cases} 1 & \text{if} \quad x_i \geq 0, \\ 0 & \text{if} \quad x_i < 0, \end{cases} \tag{3}$$

n is the number of genes, $x_i(t)$ is normalized expression quantity of ith gene, $y_i(t) \in \{0, 1\}$ is a binary variable describing the expression of the ith gene, that is, $y_i(t) = 1$ if the ith gene is expressed, $y_i(t) = 0$ if it is not, $f_i(\cdot) : \{0, 1\}^n \to R$ is a nonlinear function which describes an interaction among genes, w_{ij}, $j = 1, 2, \ldots, m_i$ are parameters of f_i, m_i is the number of them and $g_i(\cdot) : R \to R$ is a nonlinear function representing the degradation on ith gene. In what follows, this model is represented in the vector form:

$$\dot{x}(t) = g(x(t)) + f(w, y(t)), \quad y(t) = H(x(t)), \tag{4}$$

where $x = [x_1, x_2, \ldots, x_n]^T$, $y = [y_1, y_2, \ldots, y_n]^T$, $g = [g_1, g_2, \ldots, g_n]^T$, $f = [f_1, f_2, \ldots, f_n]^T$, $H(x) = [H(x_1), H(x_2), \ldots, H(x_n)]^T$, $w = [w_1, w_2, \ldots, w_n]^T$ and $w_i = [w_{i1}, w_{i2}, \ldots, w_{im_i}]^T$. The binary vector y is called an expression pattern.

In (4), $y(t)$ changes if a sign of elements of $x(t)$ changes. We describe a change of expression pattern $y(t)$ by $\hat{y} \to \bar{y}$, that is, $\hat{y} \to \bar{y}$ means that the expression pattern $y(t)$ changes from $\hat{y}$ to $\bar{y}$ at some time and if there exists an initial value $x(0)$ of $x(t)$ such that $y(t)$ changes as an expression pattern sequence: $y^{(0)} \to y^{(1)} \to \cdots \to y^{(p)}$, where p is the length of the sequence, we say that a gene network (4) has the expression pattern sequence.

We discuss the following controller design problem. Let a gene network (4) be a controlled object. The problem is designing a controller gene network so that the controlled objective gene network has a desired expression pattern sequence. Let a controller gene network be described by

$$\dot{x}_{ci}(t) = g_{ci}(x_{ci}(t)) + f_{ci}(w_{ci1}, w_{ci2}, \ldots, w_{cim_i}, y_{c1}(t), y_{c2}(t), \ldots, y_{cn_c}(t)), \tag{5}$$

$$y_{ci}(t) = H(x_{ci}(t)), \quad i = 1, 2, \ldots, n_c \tag{6}$$

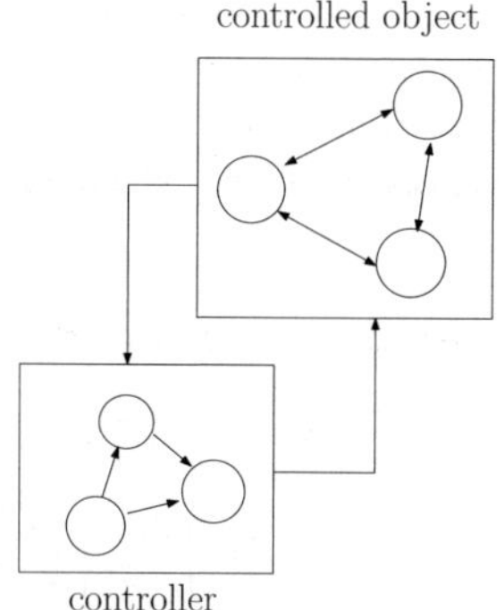

Fig. 1. A gene network consisting of a controller and an objective gene network

or in the vector form

$$\dot{x}_c(t) = g_c(x_c(t)) + f_c(w_c, y_c(t)), \quad y_c(t) = H(x_c(t)) \tag{7}$$

where the symbols with subscript c correspond to those without subscript c in (4). There are interactions among genes of the objective gene network (4) and those of the controller gene network (7). Fig. 1 is a schematic of the whole gene network. The whole gene network consisting of an objective gene network (4) and a controller gene network (7) is described by the following equations.

$$\dot{\hat{x}}(t) = \begin{bmatrix} \dot{x}(t) \\ \dot{x}_c(t) \end{bmatrix} = \begin{bmatrix} g(x(t)) + f(w, y(t)) + \hat{f}(\hat{w}, y(t), y_c(t)) \\ g_c(x_c(t)) + f_c(w_c, y_c(t)) + \hat{f}_c(\hat{w}_c, y(t), y_c(t)) \end{bmatrix} \tag{8}$$

$$\hat{y}(t) = \begin{bmatrix} y(t) \\ y_c(t) \end{bmatrix} = \begin{bmatrix} H(x(t)) \\ H(x_c(t)) \end{bmatrix} \tag{9}$$

where $\hat{f}(y(t), y_c(t))$ and $\hat{f}_c(y(t), y_c(t))$ are the interaction functions, $\hat{w} = [\hat{w}_1, \hat{w}_2, \ldots, \hat{w}_n]^T$, $\hat{w}_i = [\hat{w}_{i1}, \hat{w}_{i2}, \ldots, \hat{w}_{i\hat{m}_i}]^T$, $\hat{w}_c = [\hat{w}_{c1}, \hat{w}_{c2}, \ldots, \hat{w}_{cn_c}]^T$, $\hat{w}_{ci} = [\hat{w}_{ci1}, \hat{w}_{ci2}, \ldots, \hat{w}_{ci\hat{m}_{ci}}]^T$, $\hat{w}_{ij}$, $j = 1, 2, \ldots, \hat{m}_i$ and $\hat{w}_{cij}$, $j = 1, 2, \ldots, \hat{m}_{ci}$ are parameters of $\hat{f}_i$ and $\hat{f}_{ci}$, respectively. In this paper, we suppose that $g_i(\cdot)(g_{ci}(\cdot))$ has the inverse function $g_i^{-1}(g_{ci}^{-1})$.

Let the desired expression pattern sequence for the objective gene network (4) be given as:

$$y^{*(0)} \to \cdots \to y^{*(r)} \to \cdots \to y^{*(p)}. \tag{10}$$

We assume that $||y^{*(r+1)} - y^{*(r)}||_2^2 = 1$, for $r = 0, 1, \ldots, p$ where $||x||_2 = \sqrt{\sum_{i=1}^n x_i^2}$ for $x \in R^n$. This assumption is natural because it rarely happens that the signs of the multiple expression quantities of x change at the same time. The controller design problem is:

Problem. *For a given expression pattern sequence (10) and an objective gene network (4), determine the interactions $\hat{f}$, f_c and $\hat{f}_c$ of the network (8), (9), that is, determine $\hat{w}$, w_c and $\hat{w}_c$ such that an expression pattern sequence of the objective network (4) in the gene network (8), (9) becomes equal to the given sequence (10).*

For an expression pattern $\hat{y}^*$, let define a region $\Omega(\hat{y}^*)$ and $\hat{e}(\hat{y}^*)$ as follows.

$$\Omega(\hat{y}^*) := \{\hat{x} = [x^T, x_c^T]^T \in R^{n+n_c} | y^* = H(x), y_c^* = H(x_c)\}, \tag{11}$$

$$\hat{e}(\hat{y}^*) := \begin{bmatrix} e(y^*, y_c^*) \\ e_c(y^*, y_c^*) \end{bmatrix} = \begin{bmatrix} g^{-1}(-f(y^*) - \hat{f}(y^*, y_c^*)) \\ g_c^{-1}(-f_c(y_c^*) - \hat{f}_c(y^*, y_c^*)) \end{bmatrix} \tag{12}$$

where $\hat{y}^* = [y^{*T}, y_c^{*T}]^T$. $\Omega(\hat{y}^*)$ describes the region of state space in which the expression pattern $\hat{y}(t)$ of the gene network (8), (9) is equal to $\hat{y}^*$.

Now, we make the following assumption. Note that several models proposed so far satisfy this assumption.

Assumption. *Let $\hat{x}(t)$ be any trajectory of the network (8), (9) starting from $\hat{x}(0)$, $\hat{x}(0) \in \Omega(\hat{y}^*)$. If there exists $\bar{y}$ such that $\hat{e}(\hat{y}^*) \in \Omega(\bar{y})$, $\|\hat{y}^* - \bar{y}\|_2^2 = 1$ and $\hat{y}_i^* \neq \bar{y}_i$ for some i, then there exists $t_1 > 0$ such that $\hat{x}_i(t_1) = 0$ and $\hat{x}_j(t) \neq 0$ for any t, $0 \leq t \leq t_1$ and any $j \neq i$.*

3   Controller Design Method

In [5], we proposed a synthesis method of gene networks by network learning. In this section, we show that the controller design problem can be formulated as a network learning problem and a controller gene network can be designed by modifying the synthesis method in [5].

3.1   Problem Formulation as Optimization Problem

Let a desired expression pattern sequence for the whole gene network (8), (9) be given $\hat{y}^{*(0)} \to \cdots \to \hat{y}^{*(r)} \to \cdots \to \hat{y}^{*(p)}$. From [5], we can show that under the Assumption, the expression pattern of gene network (8), (9) changes from $\hat{y}^{*(r)}$ to $\hat{y}^{*(r+1)}$, $\forall r$, if the parameters w, $\hat{w}$, w_c and $\hat{w}_c$ satisfy the constraints :

$$\hat{y}^{*(r+1)} = H(\hat{e}(\hat{y}^{*(r)})), \quad r = 0, 1, \cdots, p-1. \tag{13}$$

Unlike the synthesis problem, $y^{*(r)}$, $r = 0, 1, \ldots, p$ are not given in the controller design problem, that is, no desired expression pattern sequence is given for the expression pattern vector of the controller network, and the parameters w of the objective gene network are given. Hence, the problem is to define parameters $\hat{w}$, w_c and $\hat{w}_c$ satisfying the constraints :

$$y^{*(r)} = H(e(y^{*(r)}, y_c^{*(r)})), \quad r = 0, 1, \cdots, p-1, \tag{14}$$

where $y_c^{*(r)} = H(e_c(y^{*(r-1)}, y_c^{*(r-1)}))$ for some $y_c^{*(0)}$.

The set of parameters $\hat{w}$, w_c and $\hat{w}_c$ satisfying constraints (14) can not be uniquely determined. Therefore, the controller design problem is reduced to an optimization problem of the parameters whose constraints are given in (14):

$$\min_{\hat{w},w_c,\hat{w}_c,y_c^{*(0)}} J \quad \text{s.t.} \quad y^{*(r+1)} = H(e(y^{*(r)}, y_c^{*(r)})), \quad r = 0, 1, \cdots, p-1, \quad (15)$$

where J is a cost function depending on $\hat{w}$, w_c and $\hat{w}_c$, which represents a measure of the complexity of the network. In this paper, we choose the l^1 norm of the parameter vector, that is, $J = \sum |\hat{w}_{ij}| + \sum |w_{cij}| + \sum |\hat{w}_{cij}|$, which could bring that the number of nonzero elements of an optimal solution $\hat{w}^*$, w_c^* and $\hat{w}_c^*$ is smaller. In [7], it is shown that in the learning problem of neural networks, the choice of l^1 norm of the parameter vector as the cost function $J = \sum |w_{ij}|$ brings the smaller number of non zero elements of the parameter vector than that of Euclidean norm $J = \|w_{ij}\|_2$. The number of nonzero elements of the parameters is related to the number of interactions among the genes. Hence, a simpler gene network can be obtained with smaller number of interactions by the choice of the cost function.

3.2   Learning Method for Controller Design

To solve the optimization problem (15), we introduce a discrete-time network described by

$$x_i[k+1] = g_i^{-1}(-f_i(w_i, y[k]) - \hat{f}_i(\hat{w}_i, y[k], y_c[k])), \tag{16}$$

$$x_{cj}[k+1] = g_{cj}^{-1}(-f_{cj}(w_{cj}, y_c[k]) - \hat{f}_{cj}(\hat{w}_{cj}, y[k], y_c[k])), \tag{17}$$

$$y_i[k] = H(x_i[k]), \tag{18}$$

$$y_{cj}[k] = H(x_{cj}[k]), \quad i = 1, 2, \ldots, n, \quad j = 1, 2, \ldots, n_c \tag{19}$$

or

$$\hat{x}[k+1] = \hat{g}^{-1}(w, \hat{w}, w_c, \hat{w}_c, y[k], y_c[k]), \quad \hat{y}[k] = H(\hat{x}[k]), \tag{20}$$

in the vector form where $\hat{x} = [x^T, x_c^T]^T$, $\hat{y} = [y^T, y_c^T]^T$, $g^{-1} = [g^{-1T}, g_c^{-1T}]^T$. Let $y[k, \hat{x}[0]]$, $y_c[k, \hat{x}[0]]$ be outputs of the discrete-time network (20), where $\hat{x}[0] = [x[0]^T, x_c[0]^T]^T$ with $x[0]$ and $x_c[0]$ being the initial values of the state $x[k]$ and $x_c[k]$, respectively. Note that $y_c[0]$ depends on $x_c[0]$ and that the constraint conditions in (15) can be satisfied if $y[k, \hat{x}[0]] = y^{*(k)}$. This implies that the controller design problem can be reduced to the learning problem of the discrete-time network (20) as follows:

$$\min_{\hat{w},w_c,\hat{w}_c,x_c[0]} \hat{J} = J_1 + \beta J, \tag{21}$$

where β is a weighting coefficient, $J_1 = \frac{1}{2}\sum_{k=1}^{p} \|y[k, \hat{x}[0]] - y^{*(k)}\|_2^2$, $x[0] \in \Omega(y^{*(0)})$. Note that $y[k, \hat{x}[0]] = y^{*(k)}$ if we achieve $J_1 = 0$ for some $x_c[0]$.

The problem (21) can be solved by the gradient based method if the step function $H(\cdot)$ is replaced by a smooth function $S(\cdot)$ which can closely approximate $H(\cdot)$. The learning algorithm is given as follows.

Step 1. Choose initial values of $\hat{w}$, w_c, $\hat{w}_c$ and $x_c[0]$ as $\hat{w}^{(0)}$, $w_c^{(0)}$, $\hat{w}_c^{(0)}$ and $x_c^{(0)}[0]$. Set an initial state of x as $x[0] \in \Omega(y^{*(0)})$. Solve the discrete-time network (20) and obtain $y[k, \hat{x}^{(0)}[0]]$, $k = 1, 2, \cdots, p$ where $\hat{x}^{(0)}[0] = [x[0]^T, x_c^{(0)}[0]^T]^T$. Then calculate $\hat{J}^{(0)}$ by using them. Set $\alpha = 0$.

Step 2. Compute the gradient $\partial \hat{J}/\partial \hat{w}_{ij}$, $\partial \hat{J}/\partial w_{cij}$, $\partial \hat{j}/\partial \hat{w}_{cij}$ and $\partial \hat{J}/\partial x_{ci}[0]$. Set $\alpha = \alpha + 1$.

Step 3. Update $\hat{w}$, w_c, $\hat{w}_c$ and $x_c[0]$: $\hat{w}^{(\alpha)}$, $w_c^{(\alpha)}$, $\hat{w}_c^{(\alpha)}$ and $x_c^{(\alpha)}[0]$ by a gradient based method. Solve the discrete-time network (20) and obtain $y[k, \hat{x}^{(\alpha)}[0]]$, $k = 1, 2, \cdots, p$ where $\hat{x}^{(\alpha)}[0] = [x[0]^T, x_c^{(\alpha)}[0]^T]^T$. Update $\hat{J} : \hat{J}^{(\alpha)}$.

Step 4. If $|\hat{J}^{(\alpha)} - \hat{J}^{(\alpha-1)}|$ is small enough, stop, else go to Step 2.

Note that the algorithm to compute gradient $\partial J/\partial \hat{w}_{ij}$, $\partial J/\partial w_{cij}$, $\partial J/\partial \hat{w}_{cij}$ and $\partial J/\partial x_{ci}[0]$ can be obtained based on the sensitivity analysis method by using adjoint equations or sensitivity equations. In addition, given several desired expression pattern sequences, the proposed design method can design a controller gene network having them by slight modification.

3.3 Controller Design Method for Piecewise Linear Network Model

In this section, we show that the controller design problem is reduced to a learning problem of a class of RHONNs if the model of the target gene network is given by the piecewise linear network model[6] with some class of interaction functions. The piecewise linear network is one of well known models of gene networks:

$$\dot{x}_i(t) = -d_i x_i(t) + f_i(w_i, y(t)), \quad y_i(t) = H(x_i(t)), \tag{22}$$

or in the vector form

$$\dot{x}(t) = Dx(t) + f(w, y(t)), \quad y(t) = H(x(t)), \tag{23}$$

where $D = \mathrm{diag}(-d_1, -d_2, \ldots, -d_n)$, $d_i > 0$. This model satisfies the Assumption[5]. The following function f_i

$$f_i(a_i, y) = a^{(i)} + \sum_{j=1}^{n} a_j^{(i)} y_j + \sum_{j=1}^{n-1} \sum_{k=j+1}^{n} a_{jk}^{(i)} y_j y_k + \cdots + a_{12\cdots n}^{(i)} y_1 \cdots y_n, \tag{24}$$

is one of representatives of the interaction functions, where a_i is parameter of f_i. In the numerical experiments, we use this function as the interaction function. In this case, the problem can be reduced to a learning problem of RHONN as follows.

The controller gene network is given by

$$\dot{x}_c(t) = D_c x_c(t) + f_c(w_c, y_c(t)), \quad y_c(t) = H(x_c(t)), \tag{25}$$

where $D_c = \mathrm{diag}(-d_{c1}, -d_{c2}, \ldots, -d_{cn})$, $d_{ci} > 0$. The whole gene network consisting of these gene networks is given by

$$\dot{x}(t) = Dx(t) + f(w, y(t)) + \hat{f}(\hat{w}, y(t), y_c(t)), \tag{26}$$

$$\dot{x}_c(t) = D_c x_c(t) + f_c(w_c, y_c(t)) + \hat{f}_c(\hat{w}_c, y(t), y_c(t)), \tag{27}$$

$$y(t) = H(x(t)), \quad y_c(t) = H(x_c(t)), \tag{28}$$

or in the vector form

$$\dot{\hat{x}}(t) = \hat{D}\hat{x}(t) + W z(\hat{y}(t)), \quad \hat{y}(t) = H(\hat{x}(t)), \tag{29}$$

where $\hat{D} = \mathrm{diag}(-d_1, -d_2, \ldots, -d_n, -d_{c1}, -d_{c2}, \ldots, -d_{cn_c})$, $\hat{x} = [x^T, x_c^T]^T$, $\hat{y} = [y^T, y_c^T]^T$, $z = [z_1, z_2, \ldots, z_m]^T$, $z_1(\hat{y}) = 1$, $z_2(\hat{y}) = \hat{y}_1$, $z_3(\hat{y}) = \hat{y}_2, \ldots, z_{n+n_c+1}(\hat{y}) = \hat{y}_{n+n_c}$, $z_{n+n_c+2}(\hat{y}) = \hat{y}_1\hat{y}_2, \ldots, z_m(\hat{y}) = \hat{y}_1\hat{y}_2 \ldots \hat{y}_{n+n_c}$, $W = \{w_{ij}\}$, $w_{ij} = \hat{a}_j^{(i)}$, $\hat{a}_j^{(i)}$ is a parameter of f, $\hat{f}$, f_c or $\hat{f}_c$. Now, we get a discrete-time network

$$\hat{x}[k + 1] = \hat{W} z(\hat{y}[k]), \quad \hat{y}[k] = H(\hat{x}[k]), \tag{30}$$

where $\hat{W} = -\hat{D}^{-1}W$. This network can be considered as a discrete-time RHONN where $\hat{x}$ is membrane potentials of neurons, $\hat{W}$ is weight matrix, $\hat{y}$ is the output of the neural network. [8] proposed a method for calculating the gradients of J_1 and derived an efficient learning algorithm by introducing adjoint network for RHONNs. The controller design problem can be solved by using the learning algorithm.

4   Controller Design Experiments

We show numerical experiments to evaluate the performance of the proposed method. We use the piecewise linear networks (29) for numerical experiments. For a smooth function $S(\cdot)$, which approximates the step function $H(\cdot)$, we use the sigmoidal function $S(x) = 1/(1+\exp(-5x))$ in these experiments. We assume that the parameter d_{ci} of controller genes are given as $d_{ci} = 1$ for $i = 1, 2, \ldots, n_c$.

4.1   Numerical Experiment 1

In this numerical experiment, a controller gene network consisting of one gene is designed so that the objective gene network has a desired cyclic expression pattern sequence. Desired expression pattern sequence is a cyclic sequence:

$$(0,0,0,0)^T \rightarrow (0,0,0,1)^T \rightarrow (0,0,1,1)^T \rightarrow (0,1,1,1)^T \rightarrow (1,1,1,1)^T$$
$$\rightarrow (1,1,1,0)^T \rightarrow (1,1,0,0)^T \rightarrow (1,0,0,0)^T \rightarrow (0,0,0,0)^T. \tag{31}$$

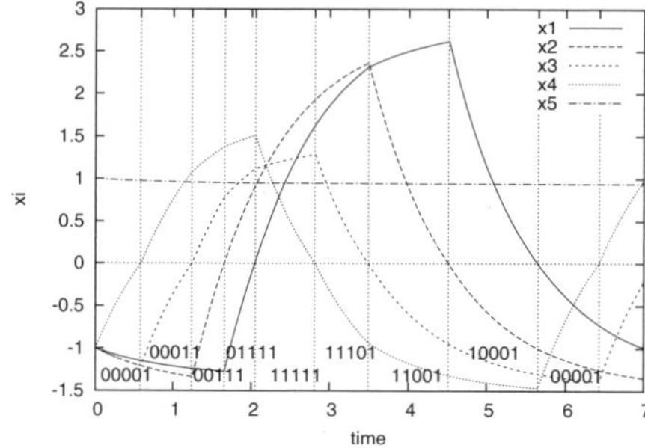

Fig. 2. Simulation result of the obtained gene network : example 1

The given objective gene network consists of four genes and the network doesn't have the desired expression pattern (31). We set the weight β of the objective function $\hat{J}$ as $\beta = 0.0001$.

An example of simulation results of the gene network obtained by the proposed design method is shown in Fig. 2, in which the initial values of x is $x(0) = [-1.0, -1.0, -1.0, -1.0, 1.0]^T$. The binary numbers placed at the bottom of Fig. 2 represent expression patterns of the gene network. It can be seen that the obtained gene network model has the desired expression pattern sequence (31).

4.2   Numerical Experiment 2

In this numerical experiment, the objective of control is stabilizing a cyclic expression pattern sequence of the controller network. The controlled gene network being same as the network in experiment 1 and the desired expression pattern sequence (31) are given. Let a controller gene network consist of one gene. In this experiment, a desired property is stability of the expression pattern sequence (31), that is, the objective gene network (4) has the cyclic expression pattern (31) and for any initial state $x(0)$ of $x(t)$, there exists $\hat{t} > 0$ such that $x(\hat{t}) \in \Omega(y^{*(r)})$ for some r where $y^{*(r)}$ is an expression pattern in (31). The number of controller gene is one and then the whole gene network consists of five genes. We design a controller gene network so that the controlled network has the expression pattern sequence (31) and

$$(0, 1, 0, 0) \rightarrow (0, 1, 0, 1)^T \rightarrow (1, 1, 0, 1)^T \rightarrow (1, 0, 0, 1)^T \rightarrow (1, 0, 1, 1)^T$$
$$\rightarrow (1, 0, 1, 0)^T \rightarrow (0, 0, 1, 0)^T \rightarrow (0, 1, 1, 0)^T \rightarrow (0, 1, 1, 1)^T. \tag{32}$$

in order to stabilize (31). Note that the two sequences (31) and (32) consist of all $16(= 2^4)$ different patterns of the 4 bit binary vector $y(t)$ and the last pattern of the sequence (32) is the fourth pattern of the sequence (31). Hence, if the controlled network has these sequences, the controller network can bring the stability of the cyclic sequence (31). We set the weight β of the objective function $\hat{J}$ as $\beta = 0.00001$.

An example of simulation results of the gene network obtained by the proposed method is shown in Fig. 3, in which the initial values of x are $x(0) = [-1.0, 1.0, -1.0, 1.0, 1.0]^T$. It can be seen that the obtained gene network model has the desired expression pattern sequences (31), (32). We can see that a stability condition of the cyclic sequence (31) is satisfied with the obtained parameters of the whole network. Hence we can conclude that the target gene network has a stable cyclic expression pattern sequence (31).

4.3   Numerical Experiment 3

In the above numerical experiments, controller gene networks consist of a gene. In this numerical experiment, a controller consists of two genes and three desired expression pattern sequences are given. The objective is to stabilize a given desired cyclic expression pattern sequence. Let an controlled gene network

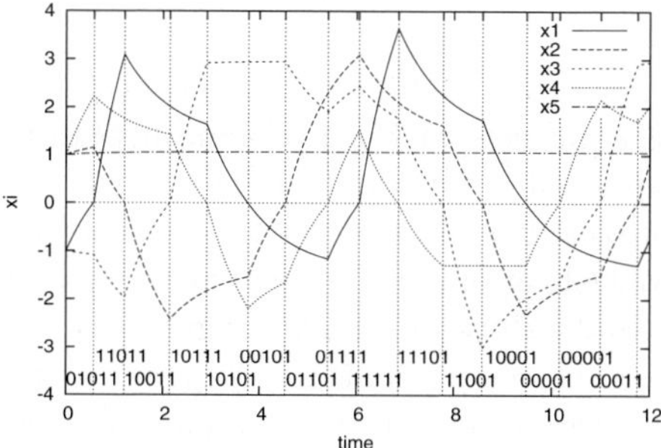

Fig. 3. Simulation result of the obtained gene network : example 2

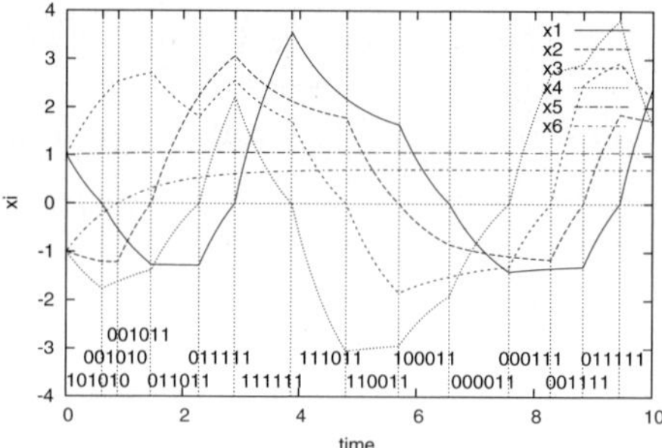

Fig. 4. Simulation result of the obtained gene network : example 3

consisting of four genes be given and desired cyclic expression pattern sequences be as (31). We choose two expression pattern sequences in order to stabilize (31):

$$(0,1,0,0)^T \to (0,1,0,1)^T \to (1,1,0,1)^T \to (1,0,0,1)^T \to (1,0,1,1)^T$$
$$\to (1,1,1,1)^T, \tag{33}$$
$$(1,0,1,0)^T \to (0,0,1,0)^T \to (0,1,1,0)^T \to (0,1,1,1)^T. \tag{34}$$

We set the weight β of the objective function $\hat{J}$ as $\beta = 0.00001$.

An example of simulation results of the gene network obtained by the proposed method is shown in Fig. 4, in which the initial values of x are $x(0) = [1.0, -1.0, 1.0. - 1.0, 1, 0]^T$. It can be seen that the obtained gene network model has the desired expression pattern sequences (31) and the expression pattern sequence (33). We also observed that the obtained gene network has the expression pattern sequence (34). It can be seen that a stability condition of the cyclic sequence (31) is satisfied with the obtained parameters of the whole network. Hence, we can conclude that the target gene network has a stable cyclic expression pattern sequence (31).

5   Conclusion

In this paper, we discussed the controller design problem of gene network models. We showed that a synthesis method of gene networks by network learning proposed [5] can be applied to the controller design problem by some modification. We derived constraint conditions with respect to the parameters of the whole gene network consisting of an objective network and a controller network and with respect to initial values of controller genes so that the controlled gene network possesses given expression pattern sequences. Then, the problem was formulated as a parameter optimization problem. We proposed a method for solving these parameter optimization problems by network learning. The proposed method can be applied to more general gene network models because of the generality of the learning method. In the numerical experiments, the controller design problem of piecewise linear network models was considered. With this model, we showed that the problem is reduced to a learning method of some class of higher-order neural networks. These numerical experiments showed that the proposed method can solve several controller design problem.

References

1. Elowitz, M.B., Leibler, S.: A synthetic oscillatory network of transcriptional regulators. Nature 403, 335–338 (2000)
2. Hasty, J., Isaacs, F.: Designer gene networks: Towards fundamental cellular control. Chaos 11(1), 207–220 (2001)
3. Ichinose, N., Aihara, K.: A gene network model and its design. In: The 15th Work shop on Circuit and Systems, pp. 589–593 (2002) (in Japanese)
4. Nakayama, H., Tanaka, H., Ushio, T.: The formulation of the control of an expression pattern in a gene network by propositional calculus. Journal of Theoretical Biology 240(3), 443–450 (2006)
5. Mori, Y., Kuroe, Y., Mori, T.: A synthesis method of gene networks based on gene expression by network learning. In: Proc. of SICE-ICASE International Joint Conference, pp. 4545–4550 (2006)
6. Glass, L.: Classification of biological networks by their qualitative dynamics. Journal of Theoretical Biology 54, 85–107 (1975)
7. Ishikawa, M.: Structural learning with forgetting. Neural Networks 9(3), 509–521 (1996)
8. Kuroe, Y., Ikeda, H., Mori, T.: Identification of nonlinear dynamical systems by recurrent high-order neural networks. In: Proc. of IEEE Int. Conf. on Syst. Man Cybern., vol. 1, pp. 70–75 (1997)

Quantitative Morphodynamic Analysis of Time-Lapse Imaging by Edge Evolution Tracking

Yuki Tsukada, Yuichi Sakumura, and Shin Ishii

Nara Institute of Science and Technology, Takayamacho 8916-5 Ikoma Nara, Japan

Abstract. To perform morphodynamic profiling from time lapse images of neurite outgrowth, we developed an edge evolution tracking (EET) algorithm, by which cell boundary movements including an arbitrary complex boundary transition are quantified. This algorithm enables us to estimate temporal evolution of cellular edge, and thus to trace the transition of any objective edge movements. We show advantages of EET by comparing it with the other two methods on an artificial data set that imitates neural outgrowth. We also demonstrate the usefulness of our EET by applying it to a data set of time-lapse imaging of neural outgrowth. The results show verification of quantitative profiling for arbitrary complex cell boundary movements.

1   Introduction

During the formation of neural circuits, neurons exhibit highly dynamic morphological changes to construct precise wiring. For instance, stop and branch behaviors, or stop and go behaviors of the thalamic axons have been examined by former time-lapse studies [9,11]. Thus, neurons show typical morphological changes in the various developmental stages and such character is thought to be important for precise construction of the neuronal network [5]. In different morphological stages, molecular mechanisms such as the regulation of cytoskeletal reorganization and focal adhesion dynamics are orchestrated differently [4]. Such dynamic orchestration is hard to understand because of the difficulty in describing dynamic behaviors of cell morphology, although the role of each molecule in each mechanism is being elucidated.

To understand dynamic molecular functions in neural development, it is necessary to elucidate the dynamics of morphology which is a biologically significant readout of intracellular molecular information processing. Progress in live cell imaging technology shed light on understanding of dynamic property of the cell biology as illustrated by the time-lapse studies of thalamic axons. In comparison with such imaging technologies, software algorithms to analyze live cell images have not been fully developed, and most of the studies to compare cell images depend on visual inspection for biological phenomena. Among the algorithms currently used for quantification of morphodynamic properties, one computes the differences in cell areas between two sequential images to identify total protrusion and retraction areas [7]. Although this approach easily extracts global

M. Ishikawa et al. (Eds.): ICONIP 2007, Part II, LNCS 4985, pp. 817–826, 2008.

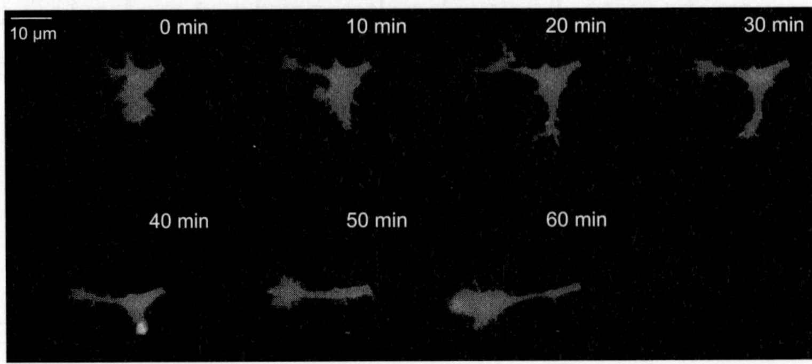

Fig. 1. Time lapse images of neurite outgrowth in PC12 cell. Each image was obtained by segmentation of original images to emphasize the neurites.

morphodynamic features, it is not enough to track continuous changes of local areas. Another way is to use kymograph, a popular method to analyze time lapse data; a kymograph gives a graphical representation of one-dimensional intensity distribution over time in which a spatial axis represents time. While kymograph is able to trace spatial intensity over time, it requires manual procedures to specify a narrow region of interest, suggesting a risk to contain ambiguity when selecting the orientation of the region of interest [10]. To quantify precise morphodynamic property of an entire cell, one has to evaluate dynamics by unbiased measurement of the whole object alnog time course. In addition, computer-based automatic methods are essential for high-throughput quantification of time lapse images.

Polar coordinate representation of cellular edges has been used for cell spreading assays of relatively non-movable cells [2,6]. This representation is an extension of kymograph so as to deal with entire cell edges. Although cellular edges in a circular shape can be traced by this method, it is difficult to define an appropriate polar origin for neural protrusion that changes its shape drastically. Machacek and Danuser pointed out this coordinate-associated problem and proposed a framework for tracking arbitrary and complex movements of cell boundary by level set method employing virtual edge markers [8]. While the marker-based tracking system can successively profile cell edges that move actively, it still remains difficulty to deal with persistently protruding edges as seen in neurite outgrowth, because of possible decrease in number of markers during development. The fixed number of markers restricts sampling points, which could cause biases in sampling if the density of markers varies. In the case of neurite outgrowth, the consecutively protruding edges and branching of neurites alter the initial uniform distribution of markers drastically. Thus, the marker-based tracking with a fixed number of markers is not suitable for the data containing continuous protrusion like neurite growth.

In this article, we propose a method to quantify morphodynamic properties of neurite outgrowth by tracking the edge evolution and the difference in areas surrounded by the traced edges. The goal of this study is to quantify spatio-temporal protrusion and retraction in the cellular local space. Especially, we focus on the consistency of tracking edges because of the interest in the transition of edge evolution. We evaluated the utility of our algorithm by comparing with the existing methods on an artificial data set that imitates neural outgrowth. We also discuss possible application of our method to images of protein activity of a living cell.

2   Methods

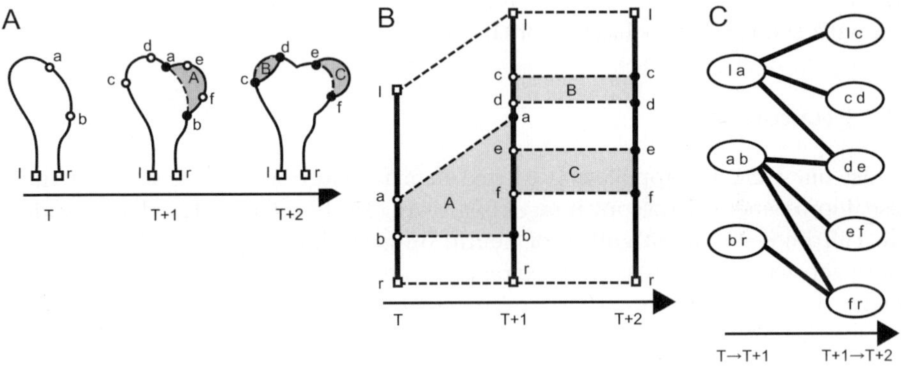

Fig. 2. Schematic view of edge evolution tracking: (A) Traced edge, anchor points a-f and subtracted areas A-C during the period from T to $T+2$. l and r denote terminals of the trace. (B) Mapping of edge profiling. All characters correspond to those in (A). (C) Diagram of edge lineage corresponding to (A) and (B). Each node corresponds to the subdivided edge in (A).

2.1   Edge Evolution Profiling

Given a sequence of cell boundaries and area differences extracted from time-lapse series of cell images, we mapped the edge evolution according to the following procedure.

At time T, the cell edge was traced and labeled corresponding to the adjacent area difference with $T+1$ (see Fig. 2A. In this case, the region between the open circles a and b is labeled). Filled circles a and b at $T+1$ correspond respectively to the open circles a and b at T. They denote the boundaries of different transitions, and we therefore call them "anchor points". Similarly, the anchor points c-f were marked, and the subdivided region on the edge was labeled at time $T+1$. In addition, the area difference A was evaluated. The retracting area B at $T+2$ was also identified. l and r in Fig. 2A denote the terminals of the traced edge.

Fig. 2B exhibits mapping of the subdivided edges, whose transitions and area differences are extracted in Fig. 2A. All characters correspond to those in Fig. 2A. The vertical axis stands for the position on the traced edge and the square regions such as A, B and C are labeled according to the detection of area difference. Matched anchor points, such as the pair of the open circle a at T and the filled circle a at $T+1$ are connected in Fig. 2B. These connected anchor points indicate the spatially corresponding regions during the time lapse from T to $T+1$. We can thus trace the corresponding region along the time course by connecting the anchor points. The connected boundary regions construct a tree structure like the evolutionary lineage. Fig. 2C illustrates the tree structure corresponding to Fig. 2A and Fig. 2B. The connected nodes represent the evolution of the edges along time course. This is the algorithm of edge evolution tracking (EET) we propose. Although thresholding parameters for cell boundaries affect to the EET profile, results of EET are basically determined uniquely from the data sets. Thus, if appropriate parameters are determined, EET results are robust even with the random behaviors of the cell.

2.2   Preprocessing

To test our EET for application to real neurite outgrowth data, we used time-lapse fluorescence microscopy images of growing PC12 cells. PC12 cells are widely used cell lines for investigation of neural outgrowth or cell polarization. First, a data set was preprocessed for extracting cell boundaries. The subdivided cell images that included growth cone-like structures at the tip of neurites were used for further analysis. To emphasize cell edges, the images were filtered with an unsharp mask (implemented by image processing software MetaMorph by Universal Imaging, Sunnyvale, CA) executed by subtracting the scaled low-pass filtered image from the original image. After the filtering, the inside and outside cell regions were segmented by the global threshold determined on the first frame. The cell boundary was obtained as the directory extracted from the thresholded images. Typically, the extracted cell boundaries were distorted when edge extraction was applied to thresholded regions with one-pixel width, such as thin spikes. To avoid this, each pixel in the thresholded images was divided into subpixels. We did not apply smoothing filtering such as spline functions because our data contained steep edges with filopodium-like thin structures and the spline fitting often spoils such steep structures.

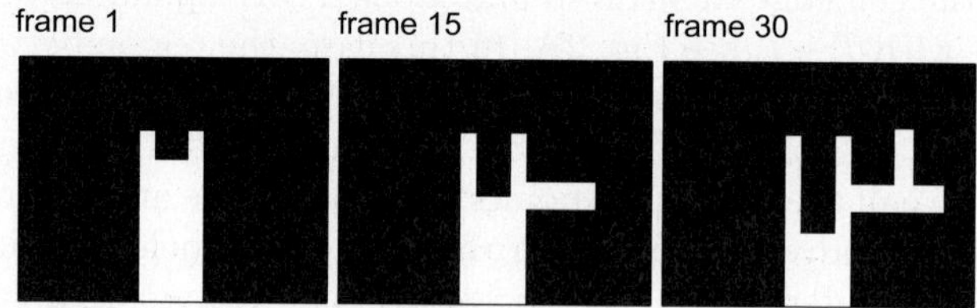

Fig. 3. The snapshots of the artificial data set. The object is colored white.

3   Results

3.1   Validation of EET by Artificial Data

To test the performance of our EET, an artificial data set was constructed as
to imitate the neural outgrowth. Continuous extension and retraction of neurite
outgrowth including formation of branches were indicated as 30 planes of binary
images of 312×312 pixels. The size of each increased and decreased area of the
object is constant throughout the data set. Fig. 3 shows the first, 15th and 30th
frames.

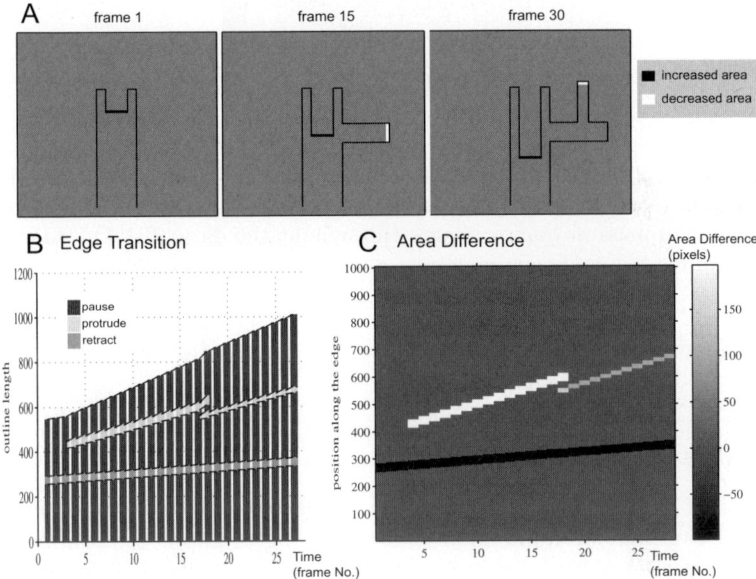

Fig. 4. Profiling of artificial data set by edge evolution tracking: (A) The snapshots of
the traced edges and the identified area differences. (B) The edge transition map. (C)
The area difference map corresponding to (B).

The results of application of EET to this data set are shown in Fig. 4. Fig.
4A shows the traced boundary edges, and the increased and decreased areas at
the first, 15 and 30th frames. Fig. 4B shows the edge transition map similar to
Fig. 2B. In Fig. 4B, the persistently protrusive and retracting regions of the data
are displayed as the connected regions in the same color. Fig. 4C represents the
area difference map corresponding to the transition map in Fig. 4B. Note that
the continued region in the same color in Fig. 4C means the persistent increase
or decrease of area. We evaluated the region consistency in Fig. 4B and the value

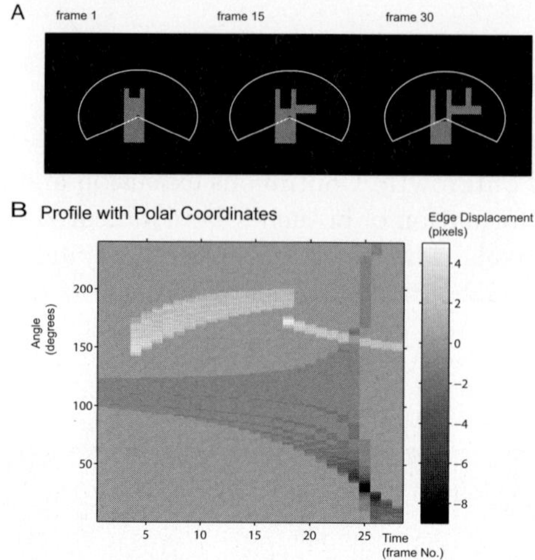

Fig. 5. Profiling of artificial data with polar coordinates: (A) The snapshots of the profiled regions. Note that the position of the polar orientation is determined by the average center of mass in binary images throughout the data. (B) The edge displacement map as position and time matrix.

of area changes in Fig. 4. The quantity of edge transition was profiled in spite of complicated morphological changes.

3.2   Profiling by Comparative Methods

Profiling with Polar Coordinates: For the purpose of examining the performance of our EET method, we implemented two existing methods of profiling morphodynamic properties of living cells. One is kymographic approach using polar coordinates [2,6]. The average center of mass in binary images of the data set was used as the origin of the coordinate axis. Then, according to the fixed polar coordinate, edge displacement of radial direction was measured along the time course.

Results of the polar coordinate profiling to the same data set used in the previous section are shown in Fig. 5. Fig. 5A shows the profiled regions of the first, 15th and 30th frames. White sectors denote the origins of polar coordinates and the range of profiled areas. Fig. 5B shows the edge displacement map as position (angle) and time (frame number) matrix. As expected, the edge displacement values of extending and retracting regions were distorted, as expressed with color gradations in the matrix which was due to the inconsistency in the coordinate system. Similarly, each width of the extending or retracting regions was distorted. Most critically, the output map contained overlapping retraction and protrusion areas around 150 degree at frame 24.

Profiling by Marker Tracking: Another method is marker-based tracking proposed by Machacek and Danuser [8]. This method assigns virtual markers along the cell boundary and traces the marker displacements between sequential images.

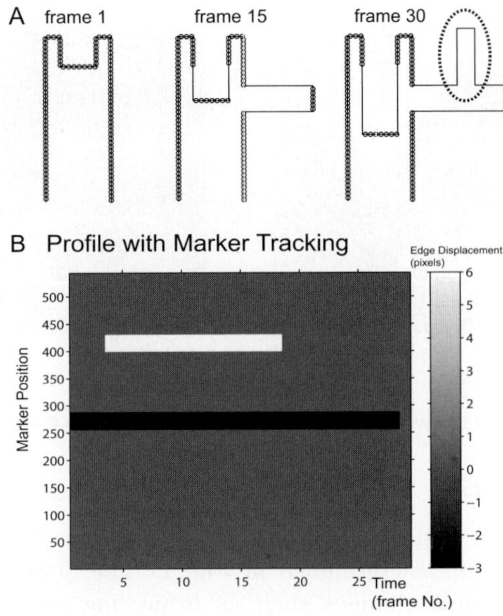

Fig. 6. Profiling of artificial data by marker tracking: (A) The snapshots of the detected boundaries and distribution of the markers. (B) The edge displacement map obtained by the marker tracking method.

Markers are reassigned to the point on the edge of the next frame which is an intersection point of the perpendicular line to the former edge and the next edge.

The results obtained by applying the implemented marker tracking method to the data set used in the previous section are shown in Fig. 6. Fig. 6A shows the representative markers of the first, 15th and 30th frames with each edge boundary. Since the edge displacement was defined as a path-length of virtual markers that traversed perpendicularly to the cell membrane, the density of the markers varied as the profiling advanced. In this benchmark test, uniformly assigned markers at the first frame were re-distributed in a non-uniform manner with time, as shown in Fig. 6A. This marker density disruption was discussed by Machacek and Dunser, and they effectively prevented topological violation by using the level set method [8]. The alteration of the marker density could be prevented if the speed coefficients were appropriately chosen in the level set method, but the fixed number of virtual markers would still restrict the sampling of new marker positions. As a result, the markers missed the second branching region completely as shown by the dotted ellipse in Fig. 6A. Therefore, the map of edge displacement shows only two continuous regions, even though the regions show precise values of edge displacement (Fig. 6B). The lack of sampling points as seen in this case is critical for analysis of branching or persistently protruding objects like growing neurites.

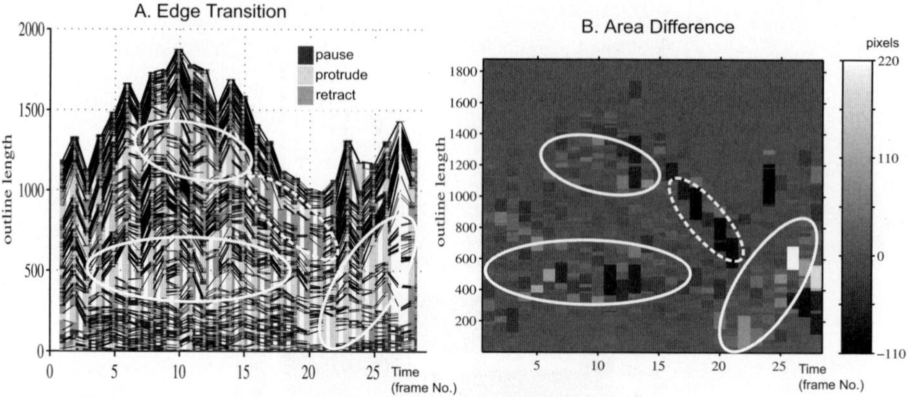

Fig. 7. EET Profiling of the time lapse imaging of the neurite outgrowth shown in Fig. 1.

3.3   Edge Evolution Tracking for Neurite Outgrowth

To demonstrate the performance, our EET was next applied to the time lapse images of neurite outgrowth shown in Fig. 1. The neurite outgrowth involves complex morphological changes such as branching and persistent protrusion or retraction. Such complexity makes it hard for us to quantify neurite movement. The data set consisted of 30 frames of 2-min time lapse fluorescent microscopy images. After boundary extraction by preprocessing, edge transitions were mapped as shown in Fig. 7A. The white solid ellipses show persistently protrusive regions, in which subdivided regions are mainly labeled as "protrude". The area denoted by solid ellipses corresponded to the formation of neurites in the original images. On the other hand, the white dash ellipse shows such a persistently retracted region to correspond to the disappearance of axonal regions in the original images. By referring to area differences with the corresponding boundary region, the EET program outputs the area difference map as shown in Fig. 7B. Persistently protruding and retracting regions are also marked by white ellipses as in the edge transition map. These profiling results show that EET successfully quantified the edge transitions and local area differences along the whole cell boundary of the target neurite. As shown in Fig. 2C, the edge evolution lineage can be described as a tree structure (result not shown). Therefore, we can trace the edge evolutional dynamics of any region at any time by referring to the tree expression of the mapping. Although we have to compare the existing methods with EET in the case of real data sets same as have been done in the case of the artificial data set, it needs much work to compare arbitrary complex profile like Fig. 7. Thus, it should be elucidated in another paper.

4   Discussion

We demonstrated the effectiveness of our EET method to quantify live cell imaging data of neural outgrowth. For closer investigation, EET was able to address the persistency and lineage of edge protrusion or retraction, indicating the method should be efficient to examine time windows of a particular event. This is an important feature for investigation of neural development because activation or inhibition of specific molecules often causes changes of the morphology with delays. In addition, the effect of activation or inhibition is not as simple as just to promote the edge evolution, but may often change the duration or effect of morphological change. EET is useful to investigate the statistics of the change in morphology during an observation period. One example of concrete application of EET is the combination with fluorescent resonance energy transfer (FRET) which monitors spatio-temporal activities of proteins [1]. By defining the local activity along cell boundaries, EET can be used for comparing edge evolution dynamics and local molecular activities.

Compared to the other methods, EET is different in its sampling strategy. As shown in the results on the artificial data set, the fixed number of sampling and the coordinates are disadvantageous in the case of profiling branching movements or highly complex morphodynamic objects. To overcome the problems, it is necessary to introduce an insertion and deletion strategy of virtual markers. The problem of inserting sampling points is similar to the problem of control point insertion in spline fitting with active contour [3]. In addition, marker-based edge tracking method requires the consistency among markers even with the marker insertion during a certain time course. Our EET does not suffer from such problems stemming from fixed sampling, but faces the modifiable area unit problem (MAUP), which frequently occurs in studies of geographical information systems (GIS). However, the problem could be solved if the data extracted by EET are normalized by edge length or classified based on area sizes. This will be our future work.

5   Conclusions

We proposed the EET method for quantitative analysis of cell edge morphodynamics. The effectiveness of our method was shown by applying it to the real images of neurite outgrowth. Furthermore, we demonstrated the validity of this method by using the artificial data set that imitated time-lapse imaging of developing neurites. The problem associated with fixed sampling remains as the future study.

Acknowledgements

We thank Drs. M. Matsuda, T. Nakamura, and K. Aoki in Kyoto University for providing neurite outgrowth images and making helpful discussion.

References

1. Aoki, K., Nakamura, T., Matsuda, M.: Spatio-temporal Regulation of Rac1 and Cdc42 Activity during Nerve Growth Factor-induced Neurite Outgrowth in PC12 Cells. J. Biol. Chem. 279(1), 713–719 (2004)
2. Betz, T., Lim, D., et al.: Neuronal Growth: a Bistable A Stochastic Process. Phys. Rev. Lett. 96(9), 098103 (2006)

3. Cham, T., Cipolla, R.: Automated B-Spline Curve Representation Incorporating MDL and Error-Minimizing Control Point Insertion Strategies. IEEE Trans. on Pattern Analysis and Machine Intelligence 21(1), 49–53 (1999)
4. Dent, E.W., Gertler, F.B.: Cytoskeletal Dynamics and Transport in Growth Cone Motility and Axon Guidance. Neuron. 40(2), 209–227 (2003)
5. Dotti, C.G., Sullivan, C.A., et al.: The Establishment of Polarity by Hippocampal Neurons in Culture. J. Neurosci. 8(4), 1454–1468 (1988)
6. Dubin-Thaler, B.J., Giannone, G., Döbereiner, H., Sheetz, M.P.: Nanometer Analysis of Cell Spreading on Matrix-Coated Surfaces Reveals Two Distinct Cell States and STEPs. Biophys. J. 86(3), 1794–1806 (2004)
7. Dunn, G.A., Zicha, D.: Dynamics of Fibroblast Spreading. J. Cell. Sci. 108, 1239–1249 (1995)
8. Machacek, M., Danuser, G.: Morphodynamic Profiling of Protrusion Phenotypes. Biophys. J. 90(4), 1439–1452 (2006)
9. Skaliora, I., Adams, R., Blakemore, C.: Morphology and Growth Patterns of Developing Thalamocortical Axons. J. Neurosci. 20(10), 3650–3662 (2000)
10. Woo, S., Gomez, M.T.: Rac1 and RhoA Promote Neurite Outgrowth through Formation and Stabilization of Growth Cone Point Contacts. J. Neurosci. 26(5), 1418–1428 (2006)
11. Yamamoto, N., Higashi, S., Toyama, K.: Stop and Branch Behaviors of Geniculocortical Axons: A Time-Lapse Study in Organotypic Cocultures. J. Neurosci. 17(10), 3653–3663 (1997)

Incorporating Domain Knowledge into a Min-Max Modular Support Vector Machine for Protein Subcellular Localization

Yang Yang[1] and Bao-Liang Lu[1,2,⋆]

[1] Department of Computer Science and Engineering, Shanghai Jiao Tong University
[2] Laboratory for Computational Biology, Shanghai Center for Systems Biomedicine
800 Dong Chuan Rd., Shanghai 200240, China
{alayman, bllu}@sjtu.edu.cn

Abstract. As biological sequences and various annotation data grow rapidly in public databases, the classification problems become larger and more complicated. New classifier designs are necessitated. Besides, how to incorporate some explicit domain knowledge into learning methods is also a big issue. In this paper, we adopt a modular classifier, min-max modular support vector machine (M^3-SVM) to solve protein subcellular localization problem, and use the domain knowledge of taxonomy information to guide the task decomposition. Experimental results show that M^3-SVM can maintain the overall accuracy and improve location average accuracy compared with traditional SVMs. The taxonomy decomposition is superior to other decomposition methods on a majority of the classes. The results also demonstrate a speedup on training time of M^3-SVM compared with traditional SVMs.

1   Introduction

The rapid progress of biotechnology led to a significant growth of biological information and data. Due to computational intensity of traditional methods or memory capacity, huge data sets cannot be handled by traditional methods. In such cases, "divide and conquer" is a natural way to solve the problem. Till now, many algorithms and techniques have been developed to complement existing machine learning methods for handling large data sets. For instance, support vector machines (SVMs), the state-of-the-art classifier, also suffer from the complexity of their training algorithm. A few methods for implementing SVM training in a parallel way have been developed [1,2]. They generally follow into two trends according to different layers where the partition is conducted. The first trend divides original data set to subsets, assembles them to a certain number of subproblems, learns the subproblems respectively and combines them to get the solution to the original problem [1]. The second trend splits major computation body of the learning method to submodules, assigns them to distributed processors and combines the result on each processor for a final output [2], such as the parallel implementation of the sequential minimal optimization (SMO) algorithm [3] which is widely used in training of SVMs.

⋆ To whom correspondence should be addressed. This work was supported by the National Natural Science Foundation of China under the grant NSFC 60473040.

M. Ishikawa et al. (Eds.): ICONIP 2007, Part II, LNCS 4985, pp. 827–836, 2008.
© Springer-Verlag Berlin Heidelberg 2008

The min-max modular support vector machine (M^3-SVM)[4] belongs to the former type. It uses min-max modular (M^3) network [5] to organize multiple SVMs, each of which is trained on a subset of the original data set. In this work, we adopt M^3-SVMs to solve the protein subcellular localization problem, which is an important issue in computational biology since the location of a protein in a cell is very important for understanding its function. A lot of machine learning methods have been used to predict the subcellular locations based on protein sequences, such as Mahalanobis distance [6], neural network, hidden Markov model, and support vector machines [7]. However, as new protein sequences and all kinds of annotations grow rapidly in the public databases, the deluge of information makes the problem more complicated. Traditional methods can not address it efficiently when size of data set and dimensionality increase significantly. In this work, we use M^3-SVM to solve the problem in a modular manner.

On the other hand, since much more helpful information and knowledge have been available in public databases, they can be built into computational models to yield more precise solutions. Thus our aim is to incorporate domain knowledge into modular classifiers to make the "divide and conquer" more effective. Here, we propose a new method integrating the domain knowledge, taxonomy information of proteins' source organism, into min-max modular classifiers. This new ensemble classifier can predict proteins from various species. The proposed method was tested on the well-studied data set collected by Park and Kanehisa [8]. The results show that M^3-SVM can maintain the overall accuracy and improve location average accuracy compared with traditional SVMs. The new decomposition method is superior to the existing decomposition methods on classification for a majority of the locations. In addition, M^3-SVM spends less time on training than SVMs even in sequential running, and has an expansibility for adding new training data into the model without retraining the former data.

2   Min-Max Modular Network

M^3-SVM [4] has been shown to be an efficient classifier, especially in solving large-scale and complex multi-class pattern classification problems. It divides a complex classification problem into small independent two-class classification problems, and then integrates these modules to get a final solution to the original problem according to two module combination rules, namely minimization and maximization principles. For solving a large-scale and complex multi-class problem, M^3 method consists of three main steps: a) Decompose the original problem into a number of two-class problems; b) Further decompose the two-class problems which are difficult to learn into a number of relatively balanced two-class subproblems as small as needed. All the two-class subproblems can be learned parallelly; c) Combine all the trained submodules into a hierarchical, parallel, and modular pattern classifier.

2.1   Decomposition of K-Class Problem

Given a K-class problem $\mathcal{T}$, the training set is described as follows:

$$\mathcal{T} = \{(X_l, Y_l)\}_{l=1}^{L}, \tag{1}$$

where $X_l \in \mathbb{R}^n$ is the lth sample in the training set, Y_l is the label of X_l, and L denotes the number of samples in the training set.

We use the one-versus-one strategy to decompose the original problem $\mathcal{T}$ into $K(K-1)/2$ two-class problems. The training set of subproblem T_{ij}, consisting of samples from class C_i and class C_j, is defined as,

$$\mathcal{T}_{ij} = \{(X_l^{(i)}, +1)\}_{l=1}^{L_i} \bigcup \{(X_l^{(j)}, -1)\}_{l=1}^{L_j} \tag{2}$$
$$i = 1, \cdots, K \text{ and } j = i+1, \cdots, K$$

where $X_l^{(i)}$ and $X_l^{(j)}$ are the training samples belonging to class C_i and class C_j, respectively.

2.2 Further Decomposition of Two-Class Problem

Now we have $K(K-1)/2$ two-class problems. All of them can be solved by traditional learning methods, such as neural networks or support vector machines. Here we adopt SVMs for their excellent performance in two-class classification.

Although each of the two-class subproblems is smaller than the original K-class problem, this partition may not be adequate for parallel computation and fast learning because some of the two-class subproblems might 1) fall into a "load imbalance" situation; 2) still be too large for learning; 3) have great disparity between the amount of respective samples, i.e., imbalanced data set. Therefore, M^3 model further divides all the large and imbalanced two-class subproblems into relatively smaller and more balanced two-class subproblems by using a *part-versus-part* task decomposition strategy [4].

Suppose the training input data sets for class C_i and C_j are respectively divided into a certain number of subsets. The two-class problem $\mathcal{T}_{ij}$ can be divided into a series of two-class subproblems, $\mathcal{T}_{ij}^{(u,v)}$, and their training data sets are defined as follows:

$$\mathcal{T}_{ij}^{(u,v)} = \{(X_l^{iu}, +1)\}_{l=1}^{L_i^{(u)}} \bigcup \{(X_l^{jv}, -1)\}_{l=1}^{L_j^{(v)}}, \tag{3}$$

where X_l^{iu} and X_l^{iv} are the input vectors belonging to the uth subset of class C_i and the vth subset of class C_j, respectively.

Now, the original problem has been divided into a series of smaller and more balanced subproblems. In the learning phase, each of these subproblems can be trained by SVMs. In the classification phase, the outputs of these trained SVMs are integrated by two combination principles, namely the minimization principle and the maximization principle [5], to produce a solution to the original problem.

2.3 Network Structure

All the subproblems decomposed in both sections 2.1 and 2.2 are organized by min-max networks. And the predicted label for an unknown sample is determined by the integrated result of the network.

The network structure for each two-class problem is shown in Fig. 1. Taking $\mathcal{T}_{ij}$ as an example, the positive class C_i and negative class C_j are decomposed into p and q subsets respectively, thus there are totally p MIN units and one MAX unit. The MIN

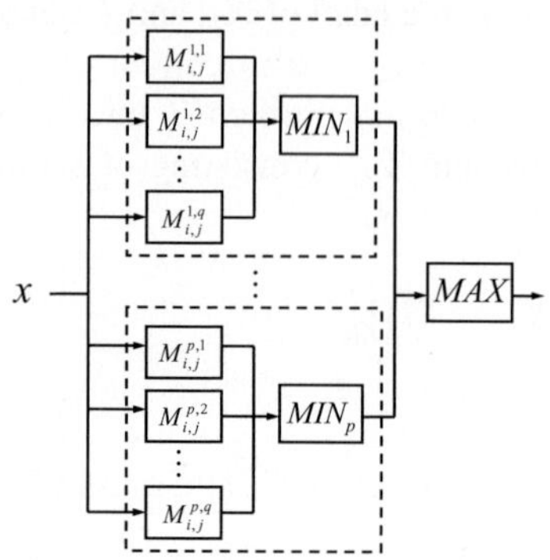

Fig. 1. Structure of min-max modular network for a two-class problem which is divided into $p \times q$ two-class subproblems

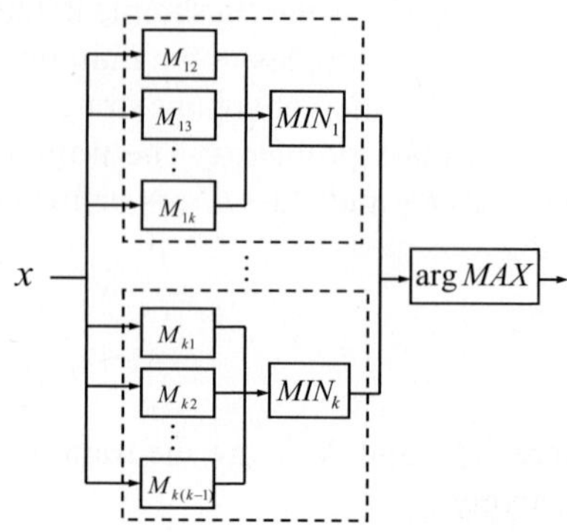

Fig. 2. Structure of min-max modular network for a K-class problem

and MAX units output the minimal and maximum values of their multiple inputs, respectively. The output of each module in the network could be either continuous value or bool value. When the module M_{ij} classifies an unknown sample x, the module could output 1 denoting that x is recognized as in class C_i, or output 0 for C_j.

All of the two-class problems are combined using MIN units as shown in Fig. 2. Suppose the original problem has K class labels, thus there are totally K MIN units. To decide the label of a test sample, the outputs of all MIN units will be compared according to *argMax* operation, i.e., the sample will be assigned to the class C_i if the ith MIN unit outputs the maximum value.

3 Task Decomposition Method

Task decomposition is a key issue for modular algorithms. Appropriate decomposition strategy can simplify the decision boundary, thus improve generalization ability and save learning time at the same time. Fig. 3 depicts the effect of different decomposition methods on the decision boundary of M^3-SVM. This is a simple two-class problem. Each class distributes in a half-circle area. And the two classes twist together.

Fig. 4 exhibits the corresponding subsets divided randomly and by the lines parallel to the diagonal, respectively. Boundaries in Figs. 3(b) and (c) are obtained using the

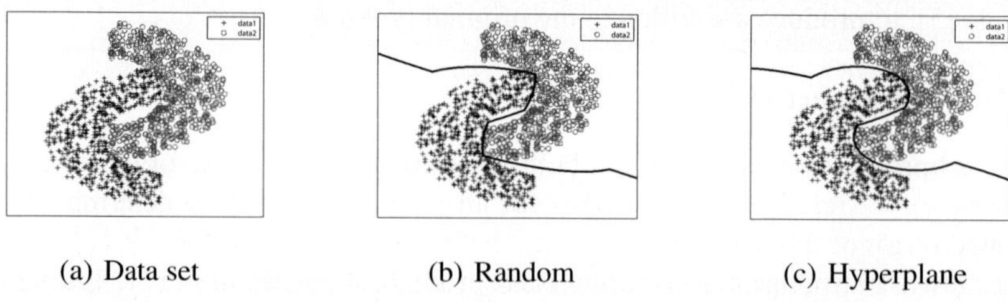

(a) Data set   (b) Random   (c) Hyperplane

Fig. 3. Classification boundary of M^3-SVM with different task decomposition methods

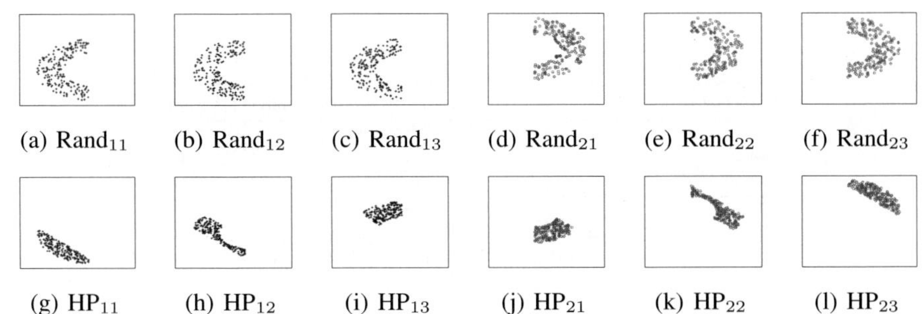

<table>
<tr><td>(a) Rand$_{11}$</td><td>(b) Rand$_{12}$</td><td>(c) Rand$_{13}$</td><td>(d) Rand$_{21}$</td><td>(e) Rand$_{22}$</td><td>(f) Rand$_{23}$</td></tr>
<tr><td>(g) HP$_{11}$</td><td>(h) HP$_{12}$</td><td>(i) HP$_{13}$</td><td>(j) HP$_{21}$</td><td>(k) HP$_{22}$</td><td>(l) HP$_{23}$</td></tr>
</table>

Fig. 4. Subsets of the two classes decomposed by random decomposition and hyperplane decomposition respectively. Rand$_{ij}$ stands for the jth subset of class i decomposed randomly. HP $_{ij}$ stands for the jth subset of class i decomposed by hyperplanes.

same classifier settings (RBF kernel with $\gamma=1$ and $C=1$). The latter one shows a more similar shape with the data distribution. However, it is hard to tell which decomposition method is better, especially when the data distribution is unknown to us.

Random partition is the most simple and straightforward way. Given a specific module size, when we choose samples randomly from the training set to form a submodule, the samples may have no distribution relationship with each other. In such cases, although the subproblem has a reduced data size, it is still hard to solve, and has complex decision boundary apt to overfitting. Since the overall classification capability lies on the performance of all the submodules, the poor generalized sub-boundary would degrade prediction accuracy of the whole system. Therefore, the random partition can not obtain a stable performance.

Several decomposition strategies have also been developed for M^3 model [4,9,10]. All these methods aim to utilize the geographical distribution characteristics of data points in the high-dimension space. However, in most real applications, data distribution is unknown and complicated. The most effective way is to use prior knowledge. What kind of prior knowledge could be built into the model? Considering proteins from the same organism share some similar characteristics, we cluster protein sequences based on the distance on taxonomy tree thus decompose the training set to modules.

To get taxonomic information, we searched the OC (Organism Classification) lines in SWISS-PROT [11], where the hierarchical classification is listed top-down. The most general groups, including archaea, bacteria, eukaryota and viruses, are given first. For example, the OC line of a human sequence is as follows:

"OC Eukaryota; Metazoa; Chordata; Craniata; Vertebrata; Euteleostomi;
OC Mammalia; Eutheria; Euarchontoglires; Primates; Catarrhini; Hominidae;
OC Homo."

Fig. 5 shows four top layers of the corresponding taxonomy tree. The proteins whose source organisms are close to each other in a taxonomy tree will be clustered together. The clustering process starts from the leaf node of the tree in a "bottom up" way. Distance between two proteins in the training set is the distance between their species nodes in the taxonomy tree. Proteins belonging to the same leaf node are certainly in a cluster. At the beginning, each leaf node in the tree is a cluster. We define the distance between

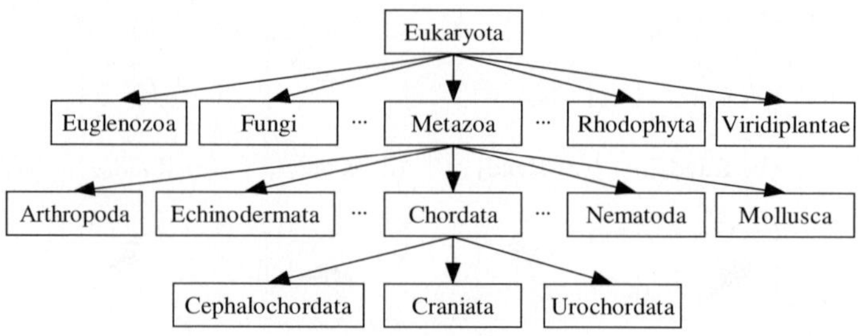

Fig. 5. A partial taxonomy tree

two nodes is the distance from the nodes to their nearest common ancestor node. Then the nodes near to each other are merged together to get a new bigger cluster. The nearest common ancestor node of all the cluster members stands for the new cluster. The clusters merge iteratively. A cluster will stop merging with others when its size reaches the designated size of a subset in the modules of M^3-SVM.

4   Experimental Results

4.1   Dataset and Experimental Settings

We conducted experiments on the data set published by Park and Kanehisa[8]. There are 7579 protein sequences in total (sequence homology less than 80%), located in 12 subcellular Locations. This data set includes merely mono-label data and gets rid of the protein sequences with multiple or amphibolous location description. There are totally 707 species identification, covering three major groups: archaea, eukaryota and viruses.

We use the sequence-based features, amino acid composition and residue pair composition, to be feature vectors feeding the classifier. They convert a protein sequence S to a vector of 20 and 400 dimensions respectively, each dimension recording the occurrence frequency of an amino acid or residue pair in the protein sequence.

Here we chose LibSVM version 2.6 [12] as the base classifiers. We experimented polynomial, sigmoid and RBF kernels and observed that RBF kernel has the best classification accuracy. The experimental results reported in the following sections are all obtained with the best kernel parameter γ and penalty parameter C from a grid search procedure for both traditional SVMs and M^3-SVM. All experiments were performed on a Pentium 4 double CPU(2.8GHz) PC with 2GB RAM.

To compare the results with Park and Kanehisa [8], we used the same accuracy measurement, total accuracy (TA) and location accuracy (LA), and the same cross-validation folds. TA is the overall success rate, and LA is the average location accuracy.

4.2   Results and Discussions

Fig. 6 depicts TA (the upper two lines) and LA (the lower two lines) of the two classifiers using amino acid composition as features. Random and taxonomy decomposition methods are compared under different module sizes of 2000, 1000, 500, 200 and 100,

Table 1. Accuracies(%) of traditional SVMs and M^3-SVM

Location	SVM	M^3-SVM					
		R_{2000}	R_{1000}	T_{2000}	T_{1000}	H_{2000}	H_{1000}
Chloroplast(671)	67.0	66.7	**68.2**	66.0	67.8	65.7	66.2
Cytoplasmic(1241)	70.0	**71.0**	66.7	70.5	66.9	69.9	70.2
Cytoskeleton(40)	30.8	23.3	35.5	28.3	**45.5**	30.8	27.9
Endoplasmic reticulum(114)	50.8	46.5	48.3	53.5	**56.1**	51.7	50.9
Extracellular(861)	76.5	78.2	77.6	77.2	**80.1**	77.2	77.4
Golgi apparatus(47)	10.7	6.2	12.4	10.9	**23.6**	12.9	12.9
Lysosomal(93)	53.6	52.5	55.7	56.8	**58.9**	54.7	**58.9**
Mitochondrial(727)	52.4	57.2	59.7	57.5	**62.2**	54.0	55.4
Nuclear(1932)	87.1	82.8	84.4	85.0	84.0	**87.4**	86.5
Peroxisomal(125)	22.4	18.3	21.5	21.4	**24.8**	24.0	22.4
Plasma membrane(1674)	90.1	**91.8**	87.0	91.3	88.7	90.3	90.0
Vacuolar(54)	26.0	20.4	22.2	**35.6**	**35.6**	33.8	30.2
Total accuracy	75.4	75.2	74.4	**75.9**	75.7	75.8	75.7
Location accuracy	53.1	51.2	53.3	54.5	**57.9**	54.3	54.1

respectively. The module size is actually an upper bound of the total number of training data in each module. It can be observed that as the number of modules increases, i.e., size of modules reduces, the overall success rate of M^3-SVM drops, while location average goes up. That is because the big classes, which take an overwhelming portion, are sacrificed to improve the prediction accuracy of small classes. M^3-SVM(R) drops faster on TA and increases slower on LA than M^3-SVM(T).

Table 1 lists the classification accuracies for each location and overall accuracies for the four methods: traditional SVMs, M^3-SVM(R), M^3-SVM(T) and M^3-SVM(H)(R, T, H stand for random, taxonomy and hyperplane decomposition, respectively). Here two kinds of module size (2000 and 1000) are examined. Feature vectors are amino acid pair composition. Hyperplane decomposition uses a group of parallel hyperplanes to partition data into subsets. The normal vector of the hyperplane used in M^3-SVM(H) is $[1, 1, ..., 1]_{400}$. All the accuracies are the average of 5-fold cross-validation.

The experimental results show that M^3-SVM with taxonomy decomposition gains both the highest LA and TA. Especially, it has a remarkable improvement on average location accuracy. The prediction accuracy of cytoskeleton and Golgi apparatus improves more than 10% when the module size was set to 1000. M^3-SVM (T) wins on 8 locations among the four methods, and is better than SVMs on 9 locations. The other 3 locations, Cytoplasmic, nuclear and plasma membrane, are all big classes which take up about 64% of the whole data set. SVMs obtain relatively low accuracies on small classes, such as cytoskeleton and Golgi apparatus (more than 10% lower than M^3-SVM(T)).

In general, decomposition based on taxonomy has better performance than random and hyperplane method on classification results on both two module sizes. Actually, the data distribution of many real world applications is usually very complex. In such cases, domain knowledge may supply useful hints for problem decomposition. Efficient

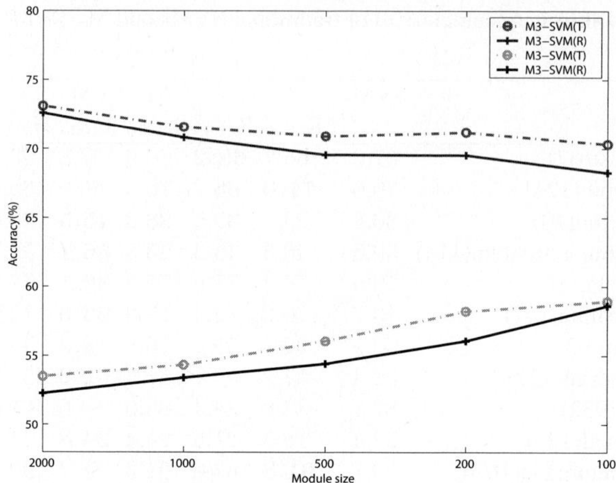

Fig. 6. Accuracies of M^3-SVM(T) and M^3-SVM(R). The upper two lines denote total accuracy and the lower two denote location accuracy.

Table 2. Training time of M^3-SVM with different decomposition methods

	SVM	M^3-SVM					
		R_{2000}	R_{1000}	T_{2000}	T_{1000}	H_{2000}	H_{1000}
Training time in series (sec)	288	259	264	251	236	237	216
Maximum module training time (sec)	21	11	6	11	6	10	5

decomposition method can maintain the generalization ability and improve the performance of M^3-SVM.

In addition, table 2 exhibits a comparison on training time between traditional SVMs and M^3-SVM with different decomposition methods under two module sizes. Two kinds of time were recorded. One is the training time of the classifier running all modules in series. The other is the longest training time among all the modules. Because for parallel learning, the training time depends on the module which costs the longest time. As for SVMs, a module means a two-class problem decomposed by one-vs-one strategy. We can observe that M^3-SVM achieves a speedup on training time even in sequential running.

5   Comparison with Other Methods

SVMs have been demonstrated as powerful tools in predicting subcellular locations [7,8]. Using the same feature vectors of amino acid pair composition, M^3-SVM(T) has improvements of 4.8% and 0.5% on location accuracy and total accuracy, respectively, compared with SVMs with one-vs-one strategy. A speedup of M^3-SVM can be also observed even when running all modules in sequential. And to SVMs with one-vs-rest strategy reported in [8], M^3-SVM(T) gains advantages on more than half of the

Table 3. Comparison between M^3-SVM and SVMs when add new training data

	SVM	M^3-SVM
Total accuracy (%)	73.37	73.44
Location accuracy (%)	49.28	51.98
Extra time cost (in series) (sec)	257	28

locations, and has 1.1% improvement on location accuracy while maintain an equal total accuracy.

A system built by Pierleoni *et al.* [13], the BaCeILo, also focuses on the imbalance problem in protein subcellular localization. They avoid the bias on majority classes by shifting the classification hyperplane to the direction that can benefit for classification on the small classes. The shift distance is the optimum value searching through cross-validation on the validation set. It depends on data distribution of the training data. The distance should be searched again once data set changes. On the contrast, M^3-SVM with taxonomy decomposition has easier implementation for users. The taxonomy information is known for all the training data, and users only need to assign a module size. As more and more protein location information becomes available, the M^3 network can add in new modules simply by connecting them with previous modules with MIN and MAX operation when new training data come.

To illustrate, we did an experiment studying the effect of adding some extra proteins. We took four of the five folds divided by [8] as training set and the rest one for test. 537 extracellular proteins were newly added into the training set, none of which is in the original data set, while test set remains the same. As for M^3-SVM, when we set the module size as 2000, for the original data set, three classes (Cytoplasmic, nuclear and plasma membrane) are split into two subsets respectively. And the newly added 537 extracellular proteins constitute a new subset, which brings additional 14 modules. We use $[1, 2, ..., 12]$ to denote the labels of 12 locations, especially, 5 for extracellular proteins. The new subset is the second set of extracellular class. The new modules are: $M_{1,5}^{1,2}, M_{2,5}^{1,2}, M_{2,5}^{2,2}, M_{3,5}^{1,2}, M_{4,5}^{1,2}, M_{5,6}^{2,1}, M_{5,7}^{2,1}, M_{5,8}^{2,1}, M_{5,9}^{2,1}, M_{5,9}^{2,2}, M_{5,10}^{2,1}, M_{5,11}^{2,1}, M_{5,11}^{2,2}, M_{5,12}^{2,1}$. Here $M_{i,j}^{u,v}$ stands for the module constituted by the uth subset of class C_i and vth subset of class C_j. Table 3 shows the classification accuracy in test data and the time needed to train classifiers. Extra time is spent on retraining the whole data set for SVMs, and on training the 14 new modules for M^3-SVM.

6   Conclusions and Future Work

This paper focuses on incorporating domain knowledge into a modular classifier to solve complex biological problems. We have used the M^3-SVM classifier to predict protein subcellular location, and proposed a new decomposition method based on taxonomic classification information to improve the performance. M^3 model has simple combination principles and can be implemented easily in practice. Module decomposition is especially important for the modular classifier. Using random decomposition, the global topology information of the data would lose during the decomposition process. Taking into account the taxonomy information, we merged predictors specific to certain subgroup in the taxonomy tree, such as animals, plants or fungi, into a unified framework. The ensemble predictor can discriminate a wide range of subcellular compartments and supply useful hints for biologists to determine the locations.

The experimental results show the effectiveness of the proposed decomposition method, and demonstrate that the M^3-SVM classifier is very competent in solving such an imbalance problem. The proposed method is not limited to deal with protein subcellular localization problem. It is also suited to solve other problems with respect to the classification of protein sequences.

As a future work, we will consider using other feature extraction methods combined with M^3-SVM to give more precise predictions. We believe that it will have far more advantages when solving new classification tasks with much higher feature space and massive data sets.

References

1. Collobert, R., Bengio, S., Bengio, Y.: A parallel mixture of SVMs for very large scale problems (2002)
2. Cao, L.J., Keerthi, S.S., Ong, C.J., Zhang, J.Q., Periyathamby, U., Fu, X.J., Lee, H.P.: Parallel sequential minimal optimization for the training of support vector machines. IEEE Trans Neural Network 2006, 1039–1049 (2004)
3. Platt, J.C.: Fast training of support vector machines using sequential minimal optimization. Advances in kernel methods: support vector learning table of contents, 185–208 (1999)
4. Lu, B.L., Wang, K.A., Utiyama, M., Isahara, H.: A part-versus-part method for massively parallel training of support vector machines. In: Proceedings of IEEE International Joint Conference on Neural Networks, vol. 1, pp. 735–740 (2004)
5. Lu, B.L., Ito, M.: Task decomposition and module combination based on class relations: a modular neural network for pattern classification. IEEE Transactions on Neural Networks 10(5), 1244–1256 (1999)
6. Cedano, J., Aloy, P., Perez-Pons, J.A., Querol, E.: Relation between amino acid composition and cellular location of proteins. Journal of Molecular Biology 266(3), 594–600 (1997)
7. Hua, S., Sun, Z.: Support vector machine approach for protein subcellular localization prediction. Bioinformatics 17(8), 721–728 (2001)
8. Park, K.J., Kanehisa, M.: Prediction of protein subcellular locations by support vector machines using compositions of amino acids and amino acid pairs. Bioinformatics 19(13), 1656–1663 (2003)
9. Liu, F.Y., Wu, K., Zhao, H., Lu, B.L.: Fast text categorization with a min-max modular support vector machine. In: Proceedings of IEEE International Joint Conference on Neural Networks, pp. 570–575 (2005)
10. Wen, Y.M., Lu, B.L., Zhao, H.: Equal clustering makes min-max modular support vector machine more efficient. In: Proceedings of the 12th International Conference on Neural Information Processing, pp. 77–82 (2006)
11. Boeckmann, B., Bairoch, A., Apweiler, R., Blatter, M., Estreicher, A., Gasteiger, E., Martin, M., Michoud, K., O'Donovan, C., Phan, I., et al.: The SWISS-PROT protein knowledgebase and its supplement TrEMBL in 2003. Nucleic Acids Research 31(1), 365–370 (2003)
12. Chang, C., Lin, C.: LIBSVM: a library for support vector machines. Software 80, 604–611 (2001), http://www.csie.ntu.edu.tw/cjlin/libsvm
13. Pierleoni, A., Martelli, P.L., Fariselli, P., Casadio, R.: BaCelLo: a balanced subcellular localization predictor. Bioinformatics 22(14), 408–416 (2006)

Fuzzy *K*-Nearest Neighbor Classifier to Predict Protein Solvent Accessibility

Jyh-Yeong Chang, Jia-Jie Shyu, and Yi-Xiang Shi

Department of Electrical and Control Engineering
National Chiao Tung University
1001 Ta Hsueh Road, Hsinchu, Taiwan 300, R.O.C
jychang@mail.nctu.edu.tw

Abstract. The prediction of protein solvent accessibility is an intermediate step for predicting the tertiary structure of proteins. Knowledge of solvent accessibility has proved useful for identifying protein function, sequence motifs, and domains. Using a position-specific scoring matrix (PSSM) generated from PSI-BLAST in this paper, we develop the modified fuzzy *k*-nearest neighbor method to predict the protein relative solvent accessibility. By modifying the membership functions of the fuzzy *k*-nearest neighbor method by Sim *et al.* [1], has recently been applied to protein solvent accessibility prediction with excellent results. Our modified fuzzy *k*-nearest neighbor method is applied on the three-state, E, I, and B, and two-state, E, and B, relative solvent accessibility predictions, and its prediction accuracy compares favorly with those by the fuzzy *k*-NN and other approaches.

1   Introduction

The solvent accessibility of amino acid residues plays an important role in tertiary structure prediction, especially in the absence of significant sequence similarity of a query protein to those with known structures. The prediction of solvent accessibility is less accurate than secondary structure prediction in spite of improvements in recent researches. Predicting the three-dimensional (3D) structure of a protein from its sequence is an important issue because the gap between the enormous number of protein sequences and the number of experimentally determined structures has increased [2], [3]. However, the prediction of the complete 3D structure of a protein is still a big challenge, especially in the case where there is no significant sequence similarity of a query protein to those with known structures. The prediction of solvent accessibility and secondary structure has been studied as an intermediate step for predicting the tertiary structure of proteins, and the development of knowledge-based approaches has helped to solve these problems [4]–[8].

Secondary structures and solvent accessibilities of amino acid residues give a useful insight into the structure and function of a protein [8]–[11]. In particular, the knowledge of solvent accessibility has assisted alignments in regions of remote sequence identity for threading [2], [12]. However, in contrast to the secondary structure, there is no widely accepted criterion for classifying the experimentally determined solvent accessibility into a finite number of discrete states such as *buried*,

M. Ishikawa et al. (Eds.): ICONIP 2007, Part II, LNCS 4985, pp. 837–845, 2008.
© Springer-Verlag Berlin Heidelberg 2008

intermediate and *exposed* states. Also, the prediction accuracies of solvent accessibilities are lower than those for secondary structure prediction, since the solvent accessibility is less conserved than secondary structure [2], although there has been some progress recently.

The prediction of solvent accessibility, as well as that of the secondary structure, is a typical pattern classification problem. The first step for solving such a problem is the feature extraction, where the important features of the data are extracted and expressed as a set of numbers, called feature vectors. The performance of the pattern classifier depends crucially on the judicious choice of the feature vectors. In the case of the solvent accessibility prediction, using evolutionary information such as multiple sequence alignment and position-specific scoring matrix generally has given good prediction results [13], [14]. Once an appropriate feature vector has been chosen, a classification algorithm is used to partition the feature space into disjoint regions with decision boundaries. The decision boundaries are determined using feature vectors of a reference sample with known classes, which are also called the reference dataset or training set. The class of a query data is then assigned depending on the region it belongs to.

Various classification algorithms have been developed. Bayesian statistics is a parametric method where the functional form of the probability density is assumed for each class, and its parameters are estimated from the reference data. In nonparametric methods, no specific functional form for the probability density is assumed. There are various nonparametric methods such as, for example, neural networks, support vector machines and nearest neighbor methods. In the neural network methods, the decision boundaries are set up before the prediction using a training set. Support vector machines are similar to neural networks in that the decision boundaries are determined before the prediction, but in contrast to neural network methods where the overall error function between the predicted and observed class for the training set is minimized, the margin in the boundary is maximized.

In the k-nearest neighbor methods, the decision boundaries are determined implicitly during the prediction, where the prediction is performed by assigning the query data the class most matched among the k-nearest reference data. The standard k-nearest neighbor rule is to place equal weights on the k-nearest reference data for determining the class of the query, but a more general rule is to use weights proportional to a certain power of distance. Also, by assigning the fuzzy membership to the query data instead of a definite class, one can estimate the confidence level of the prediction. The method employing these more general rules is called the fuzzy k-nearest neighbor methods [15].

The k-nearest neighbor method has been frequently used for the classification of biological and medical data, and despite its simplicity, the performances are competitive compared to many other methods. However, the k-nearest neighbor method has few been applied for predicting solvent accessibility, although it has been used to predict protein secondary structure. In this paper, we apply the modified fuzzy k-nearest neighbor method to the prediction of solvent accessibility where PSI-BLAST [16] profiles are used as the feature vectors. We obtain relatively high accuracy on various benchmark tests.

2   Protein Relative Solvent Accessibility Prediction

2.1   The Definition of Solvent Accessibility

Amino acid relative solvent accessibility is the degree to which a residue in a protein is accessible to a solvent module. The relative solvent accessibility can be calculated by the formula as follows:

$$RelAcc(\%) = \frac{100 \times Acc}{MaxAcc(\%)} \tag{1}$$

where *Acc* is the solvent accessible surface area of the residue observed in the 3D structure, given in Angstrom units, calculated from coordinates by the dictionary of protein secondary structure (DSSP) program. *MaxAcc* is the maximum value of solvent accessible surface area of each kind of residue for a Gly-X-Gly extended tripeptide conformation [2].

RelAcc can hence adopt values between 0% and 100%, with 0% corresponding to a fully buried and 100% to a fully accessible residue, respectively. Different arbitrary threshold values of relative solvent accessibility are chosen to define categories: buried and exposed, or ternary categories: buried, intermediate, or exposed. The precise choice of the threshold is not well defined.

We used two kind of class definitions: (1) buried (B) and exposed (E); and (2) buried (B), intermediate (I), and exposed (E). For the two-state, B and E definition, we chose various thresholds of the relative solvent accessibility such as 25%, 16%, 9%, 5%, and 0%. For the three-state, B, I, and E, description of relative solvent accessibility, one set of thresholds that we selected is the same as those in Rost and Sander [2]:

Buried (B): *RelAcc* < 9%

Intermediate (I): 9% ≤ *RelAcc* < 36%

Exposed (E): *RelAcc* ≥ 36%

2.2   Fuzzy *k*-Nearest Neighbor Method

The present analysis used the classical local coding scheme of the protein sequences with a sliding window. PSI-BLAST matrix with n rows and 20 columns can be defined for single sequence with n residues. Each residue is represented using 20 components in a vector, based on the PSSM. Then, each input vector has $20 \times w$ components, where w is a sliding window size.

In Sim's work [1], they constructed a window of size 15 centered on a target residue [6], and use the profile that falls within this window, a 15×20 matrix, as a feature vector. Then, the distance between two feature vectors A and B is defined as

$$D_{AB} = \sum_{i,j} W_i \left| P_{ij}^{(A)} - P_{ij}^{(B)} \right| \tag{2}$$

where $P_{ij}^{(A)}$ ($i = 1, 2, \ldots, 15; j = 1, 2, \ldots, 20$) is a component of the feature vector A, and W_i is a weight parameter. Since it is expected that the profile elements for residues nearer to the target residue to be more important in determining the local environment of the target residue, weights W_i are set to $W_i = (8 - |8 - i|)^2$.

They applied the fuzzy k-nearest neighbor method to the solvent accessibility prediction. In the fuzzy k-nearest neighbor method, the fuzzy class membership $u_i(x)$ to the class i is assigned to the query data x according to the following equation:

$$u_i(x) = \frac{\sum_{j=1}^{k} u_i(x^{(j)}) D_j^{-2/(m-1)}}{\sum_{j=1}^{k} D_j^{-2/(m-1)}}, \quad i = 1, 2, \ldots, c, \tag{3}$$

where m is a fuzzy strength parameter, which determines how heavily the distance is weighted when calculating each neighbor's contribution to the membership value, k is the number of nearest neighbors, and c is the number of classes. Also, D_j is the distance between the feature vector of the query data x and the feature vector of its jth nearest reference data $x^{(j)}$, and $u_i(x^{(j)})$ is the membership value of $x^{(j)}$ to the ith class, which is 1 if $x^{(j)}$ belongs to the ith class, and 0 otherwise. The advantage of the fuzzy k-nearest neighbor algorithm over the standard k-nearest neighbor method is quite clear. Modulating the i-th neighbor's fuzzy class membership $u_i(x)$ through its percentile distance to the query residue can be considered as the estimate of the probability that the query data belongs to class i, and provides us with more information than a definite prediction of the class for the query data. Moreover, the reference samples which are closer to the query data are given more weight, and an optimal value of m can be chosen along with that for k, in contrast to the standard k-nearest neighbor method with a fixed value of $2/(m-1) = 0$. In fact, the optimal value of k and m are found from the leave-one-out cross-validation procedure, and the resulting value for $2/(m-1)$ is indeed nonzero.

We adopt the optimal values of m and k in [1], which are $(m, k) = (1.33, 65)$ for the 3-state prediction (for both 9% and 36% thresholds) and $(m, k) = (1.50, 40)$, $(1.25, 75)$, $(1.29, 65)$ and $(1.33, 65)$ for the 2-state predictions (for 0, 5, 16, and 25% thresholds, respectively). Moreover, we use $(m, k) = (1.27, 70)$ for the 9% threshold, whose prediction accuracy is slightly higher than other (m, k) values.

2.3 Modified Fuzzy k-Nearest Neighbor Method

In Sec. 2.2 above, we can see $u_i(x^{(j)})$ is defined as the membership value of $x^{(j)}$ to the i-th class, which is 1 if $x^{(j)}$ belongs to the i-th class, and 0 otherwise. Here, we modify the definition of $u_i(x^{(j)})$ in Eq. (3). It is expected that a neighbor residue close to the threshold *RelAcc* chosen is not as decisive in determining query values as a neighbor residue far from the residue's *RelAcc* state. For the two-state model for accessibility, we have to choose a threshold to distinguish the two states (Buried and Exposed). If we choose a value *Th* (must fall between 0 and 1) as our threshold, the residues where *Relacc* values range from 0 to *Th* will be classified to the buried state, and others (from *Th* to 1) will be classified to the exposed state.

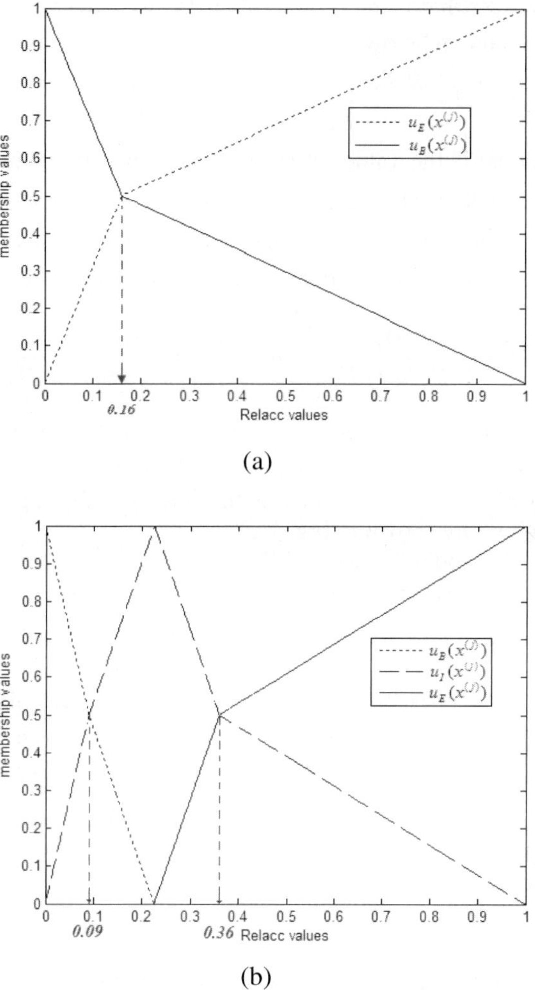

Fig. 1. The 2-state and 3-state membership functions. (a) The 2-state membership functions with *Th* = 16%. (b) The 3-state membership functions with *Ths* = 9% and 36%.

It is known that 0 is the minimum for *RelAcc* value, and 1 is the maximum. That means 0 is the most buried point and 1 is the most exposed one. For each residue of a protein sequence, we can calculate a "buried distance, D_B" which represents the "distance" from present residue to 0 and a "exposed distance, D_E" which represents the "distance" from present residue to 1. If the *RelAcc* value of a residue is smaller than *Th*, then we calculate its D_B and D_E values by the following equations:

$$D_B = \frac{RelAcc}{Th}, \qquad D_E = 1 + \frac{Th - RelAcc}{Th}. \tag{4}$$

In contrast, if the *RelAcc* value is larger than *Th*, we calculate the D_B and D_E values by the equation shown below:

$$D_B = 1 + \frac{RelAcc - Th}{1 - Th}, \quad D_E = \frac{1 - RelAcc}{1 - Th} \tag{5}$$

In both conditions, if the value of D_B is larger, then the "buried degree" of this residue should be small. That is, D_B is inversely proportional to the "buried degree." Similarly, D_E value is also inversely proportional to the "exposed degree." With this concept in mind, we can use D_B and D_E to calculate membership values $u_i(x^{(j)})$:

$$u_E(x^{(j)}) = \frac{1/D_E}{1/D_E + 1/D_B}, \quad u_B(x^{(j)}) = \frac{1/D_B}{1/D_E + 1/D_B}. \tag{6}$$

Obviously, if we let $u_B(x^{(j)}) = u_E(x^{(j)}) = 0.5$ in both conditions (buried an exposed) to calculate *RelAcc* value, then we will obtain that *RelAcc* = *Th*. That means the membership values of both classes at the threshold *Th* are 50%. The two-state membership functions are shown in Fig. 1(a).

For the three-state model for accessibility, we know that the boundaries are 0 and 9% for the buried state, 9% and 36% for the intermediate state, 36% and 100% for the exposed state, so the center value of the intermediate class, $\frac{0.09 + 0.36}{2}$, is 0.225.

$u_B(x^{(j)})$ is set to zero when the *RelAcc* value of a residue is greater than 0.225, so we can calculate $u_I(x^{(j)})$ and $u_E(x^{(j)})$ by two-class method given above. In the same manner, we set the $u_E(x^{(j)})$ to zero when *RelAcc* value is smaller than 0.225, and we can calculate $u_I(x^{(j)})$ and $u_B(x^{(j)})$ as above. The three-state membership functions are shown in Fig. 1(b).

2.4 Data Set

The data set contains 126 nonhomologous globular protein chains used in the experiment of Rost and Sander [2], referred to as the RS126 set, was utilized to evaluate the accuracy of the classifiers. The RS126 dataset contains 23606 residues, and the proteins in this set have less than 25% pairwise sequence identity for lengths greater than 80 residues. Fuzzy *k*-nearest neighbor approaches were implemented with multiple sequence alignments, and tested on the dataset using a seven-fold cross validation technique to estimate the prediction accuracy. With seven-fold cross validation, approximately six-seventh of the RS126 dataset was selected for training and, after training, the left one-seventh of the dataset was used for testing.

3 Performance Measures

In this work, two measures are used to evaluate the performance of prediction methods. One is the accuracy, the percentage of correctly classified residues, and the other is the Matthew's correlation coefficients (MCC). These measures can be calculated by the following equations:

$$\text{accuracy} = \frac{\sum_{i}^{c} p_i}{N},$$

(7)

$$\text{MCC}_i = \frac{p_i n_i - o_i u_i}{\sqrt{(p_i + o_i)(p_i + u_i)(n_i + o_i)(n_i + u_i)}},$$

(8)

where N is the total number of residues, and c is the class number. Also, p_i, n_i, o_i, and u_i are the number of true positives, true negatives, false positives and false negatives for class i, respectively. The MCCs have the same value for the two classes in the case of the 2-state prediction, i.e. $\text{MCC}_B = \text{MCC}_E$.

4   Results

Fuzzy *k*-nearest neighbor approaches are applied on three-state, E, I, and B, and two-state, E and B, relative solvent accessibility predictions. On the RS126 data set processed by ourselves, fuzzy *k*-nearest neighbor approach [1] led to the overall prediction accuracy 58.14% for the three-state prediction with respect to thresholds: 9% and 36%; and 87.93%, 79.18%, 77.59%, 75.35%, 73.49% for the two-state prediction with the thresholds of 0%, 5%, 9%, 16%, and 25%, respectively.

Modified fuzzy *k*-nearest neighbor approach gave the overall prediction accuracy 58.57% for the three-state prediction with respect to the following two thresholds chosen: 9% and 36%; and 87.93%, 79.84%, 77.76%, 76.34%, 75.26% for the two-state prediction with the chosen thresholds of 0%, 5%, 9%, 16%, and 25%, respectively.

The MCCs of fuzzy *k*-NN and modified fuzzy *k*-NN approaches on the RS126 data set is shown in Table 1. In the two-state model, we only show the 16% threshold case. The performance comparison of our fuzzy *k*-NN approach and modified fuzzy *k*-NN approach to other methods is shown in Table 2.

Sim *et al.* [1] has led to slightly better prediction accuracies than other methods by fuzzy *k*-nearest neighbor method using PSI-BLAST profiles on the RS126 data set

Table 1. Matthew's Correlation Coefficients of the two approaches on RS126

3-state (9%; 36%)			
method \ MCC	MCC_E	MCC_I	MCC_B
Fuzzy *k*-NN	0.439	0.133	0.499
Modified fuzzy *k*-NN	0.432	0.163	0.485

2-state (16%)	
method \ MCC	$\text{MCC}_E = \text{MCC}_B$
Fuzzy *k*-NN	0.492
Modified fuzzy *k*-NN	0.514

produced by them. In [1], they reported 63.8% for the three-state prediction with respect to thresholds of 9% and 36%; 87.2%, 82.2%, 79.0%, and 78.3% for the two-state predictions with the thresholds of 0%, 5%, 16%, and 25%, respectively. Using the same method and best parameter settings on our produced RS126 data set, we just obtained 58.1% for the three-state prediction; 87.9%, 79.2%, 75.4%, and 73.5% for the two-state predictions with the thresholds of 0%, 5%, 16%, and 25%, respectively.

Table 2. Comparison of performance of modified fuzzy k-NN approach with other methods in RSA prediction on the RS126 data set with PSSMs generated by PSI-BLAST

| | | | | | | accuracy: % |
method \ thresholds	3-state (9% ; 36%)	2-state (0%)	2-state (5%)	2-state (9%)	2-state (16%)	2-state (25%)
Modified fuzzy k-NN (on our dataset)	58.6	87.9	79.8	77.8	76.3	75.3
Fuzzy k-NN (on our dataset)	58.1	87.9	79.2	77.6	75.4	73.5
Fuzzy k-NN (on their dataset [1])	63.8	87.2	82.2	—	79.0	78.3
PHDacc	57.5	86.0	—	74.6	75.0	—
SVMpsi	59.6	86.2	79.8	—	77.8	76.8
Two-Stage SVMpsi	—	90.2	83.5	81.3	79.4	—

Fuzzy k-NN (Sim, Kim and Lee, 2005) used fuzzy k-nearest neighbor method [1].
PHDacc (Rost and Sander, 1994) used neural networks [2].
SVMpsi (Kim and Park, 2004) was based on support vector machine [17].
Two-Stage SVMpsi (Nguyen and Rajapakse, 2005) used a two-stage SVM approach [18].

5   Conclusion and Discussion

Using PSI-BLAST profiles as feature vectors, we have proposed in this paper modified fuzzy k-nearest neighbor approach to predict relative solvent accessibility of RS126 data set.

In the future study, we can apply dimensionality reduction technique to reflect the structure existent in the data set. Then we can find more reliable distance metrics faithfully from PSSM table to improve the classification accuracy of our fuzzy k-NN method. Besides, we can apply our method on a larger data set, like CB513. Protein data set growth can give an indirect advantage to our method. Our modified fuzzy k-NN approach can be selected as a promising approach for various protein applications.

Acknowledgement

This research was supported in part by the National Science Council under grant NSC 95-2752-E-009-011-PAE, the program for promoting university academic excellence, by the Ministry of Economic Affairs under grant 95-EC-17-A-02-S1-032, and by the National Science Council under Grant NSC95-2221-E-009-212, Taiwan, R.O.C.

References

1. Sim, J., Kim, S.Y., Lee, J.: Prediction of protein solvent accessibility using fuzzy k-nearest neighbor method. Bioinformatics 21, 2844–2849 (2005)
2. Rost, B., Sander, C.: Conservation and prediction of solvent accessibility in protein families. Proteins 20, 216–226 (1994)
3. Thompson, M.J., Goldstein, R.A.: Predicting solvent accessibility: higher accuracy using Bayesian statistics and optimized residue substitution classes. Proteins 25, 38–47 (1996)
4. Cuff, J.A., Barton, G.J.: Application of multiple sequence alignment profiles to improve protein secondary structure prediction. Proteins 40, 502–511 (2000)
5. Frishman, D., Argos, P.: Seventy-five percent accuracy in protein secondary structure prediction. Proteins 27, 329–335 (1997)
6. Jones, D.T.: Protein secondary structure prediction based on position specific scoring matrices. J. Mol. Biol. 292, 195–202 (1999)
7. Przybylski, D., Rost, B.: Alignments grow, secondary structure prediction improves. Proteins 46, 197–205 (2002)
8. Wohlfahrt, G., et al.: Positioning of anchor groups in protein loop prediction: the importance of solvent accessibility and secondary structure elements. Proteins 47, 370–378 (2002)
9. Eyal, E., et al.: Importance of solvent accessibility and contact surfaces in modeling side-chain conformations in proteins. J. Comput. Chem. 25, 712–724 (2004)
10. Russell, S.J., et al.: Stability of cyclic beta-hairpins: asymmetric contributions from side chains of a hydrogen-bonded cross-strand residue pair. J. Am. Chem. Soc. 125, 388–395 (2003)
11. Totrov, M.: Accurate and efficient generalized born model based on solvent accessibility: derivation and application for LogP octanol/water prediction and flexiblepeptide docking. J. Comput. Chem. 25, 609–619 (2004)
12. Rost, B., et al.: Protein fold recognition by prediction-based threading. J. Mol. Biol. 270, 471–480 (1997)
13. Gianese, G., et al.: Improvement in prediction of solvent accessibility by probability profiles. Protein Eng. 16, 987–992 (2003)
14. Pei, J., Grishin, N.V.: Combining evolutionary and structural information for local protein structure prediction. Proteins 56, 782–794 (2004)
15. Keller, J.M., et al.: A fuzzy k-nearest neighbor algorithm. IEE Trans. Syst. Man Cybern. 15, 580–585 (1985)
16. Altschul, S.F., et al.: Gapped BLAST and PSI-BLAST: a new generation of protein database search programs. Nucleic Acids Res 25, 3389–3402 (1997)
17. Kim, H., Park, H.: Prediction of protein relative solvent accessibility with support vector machines and long-range interaction 3D local descriptor. Proteins 54, 557–562 (2004)
18. Nguyen, M.N., Rajapakse, J.C.: Prediction of protein relative solvent accessibility with a two-stage SVM approach. Proteins 59, 30–37 (2005)
19. Rost, B., Sander, C.: Prediction of protein secondary structure at better than 70% accuracy. J. Mol. Biol. 232, 584–599 (1993)

Ontology-Based Framework for Personalized Diagnosis and Prognosis of Cancer Based on Gene Expression Data

Yingjie Hu and Nikola Kasabov

Knowledge Engineering and Discovery Research Institute,
Auckland University of Technology, Auckland, New Zealand
{rhu, nkasabov}@aut.ac.nz

Abstract. This paper presents an ontology-based framework for personalized cancer decision support system based on gene expression data. This framework integrates the ontology and personalized cancer predictions using a variety of machine learning models. A case study is proposed for demonstrating the personalized cancer diagnosis and prognosis on two benchmark cancer gene data. Different methods based on global, local and personalized modeling, including Multi Linear Regression (MLR), Support Vector Machine (SVM), K-Nearest Neighbor (KNN), Evolving Classifier Function (ECF), weighted distance weighted variables K-nearest neighbor method (WWKNN) and a transductive neuro-fuzzy inference system with weighted data normalization (TWNFI) are investigated. The development platform is general that can use multimodal information for personalized prediction and new knowledge creation within an evolving ontology framework.

Keywords: Ontology, cancer, gene, global, local, personalized modeling, neural network, WWKNN, TWNFI.

1 Introduction

One fundamental task in bioinformatics research is to analyze vast amount of gene expression data and thereby to create intelligent system for knowledge discovery. Owing to the ability to profile differential gene expression, gene expression profiling with DNA microarray has provided a revolutionary approach to study the pathology of cancer.

A substantial number of methods and models for cancer diagnosis and risk management have been so far proposed, in which impressive results have been reported in the experiments [1-4]. However, many proposed models do not have the ability to provide reliable and precise information to the patients who require individual therapy schemes. Personalized modeling has been reported efficient for clinical and medical applications of learning systems, because its focus is not on the model, but on the individual sample [5, 6]. Thus, to solve the cancer heterogeneity issue, the implementation of personalized modeling can be an appropriate solution for properly diagnosing cancers and predicting clinical outcomes for cancer patients [6, 7]. Several local and personalized models have been developed and patented by KEDRI, such as Evolving Connectionist Systems (ECOS) [8], weighted distance weighted variables

M. Ishikawa et al. (Eds.): ICONIP 2007, Part II, LNCS 4985, pp. 846–855, 2008.

K-nearest neighbor method (WWKNN) [9] and a transductive neuro-fuzzy inference system with weighted data normalization (TWNFI) [6].

As the quantity of findings in cancer research based on gene expression data grows, there is an increasing need to collect and retrieve the discovered information and knowledge from a variety of sources. Cancer research using gene data analysis is still difficult and expensive to fulfill in terms of financial cost, patients' privacy right and intellectual property right [10, 11]. Meanwhile, the advances in cancer research have created a large amount of data and insight, which require a sophisticated management system to store and share existing information and knowledge.

Ontology is used here for constructing a framework to represent the knowledge discovery in the domain of cancer diagnosis and prognosis. Ontology provides a new way to collect knowledge in some domains of interest which can be shared and exchanged by researchers [12]. Ontology development is an iterative process in which iterative constructing will exit all through the lifecycle of ontology, which makes it very appropriate to support the sharing and reusing formal represented knowledge for cancer gene data analysis.

There are two main contributions of this paper. First, it presents a comparative analysis of different modeling approaches on two benchmark caner gene expression datasets. The emphasis of this comparison is on the knowledge that these models facilitate to discover from data rather than on the prediction accuracy obtained from computational intelligent models. Second, this paper introduces an integrated ontology-based framework with personalized modeling for cancer diagnosis and prognosis using gene expression data. The rest of this paper is organized as follows: Section 2 presents a case study in which global, local and personalized models, including Multi Linear Regression (MLR), K-Nearest Neighbor (KNN), Support Vector Machine (SVM), Evolving Classifier Function (ECF) [13], WWKNN and TWNFI are applied on two cancer data for classification. Section 3 gives an introduction to the ontology system that will be used to incorporate the personalized models for cancer diagnosis and prognosis based on gene expression data analysis. Also, the prototype of this ontology-based framework is described. Finally, the conclusion is presented based on the experimental results and the future research direction is discussed as well.

2   Case Study - Personalized Modeling for Cancer Diagnosis and Prognosis Based on Gene Expression Data

Gene expression data is defined as the data containing a group of samples in which a pattern of expression of massive genes is collected. Gene microarray is one of the most common technologies for gene expression data analysis, and is able to identify certain genes that are differently expressed among different states. Gene expression data has been widely used in cancer diagnosis and prognosis for distinguishing patients tissue samples.

2.1   Data

Here, we present a case study to demonstrate the personalized modeling for cancer diagnosis based on gene expression level data. Two published benchmark cancer gene datasets – (i) the diffuse large B-cell lymphoma (DLBCL) datasets for classifying different types of lymphoma presented by Shipp *et al.* [14], has 58 DLBCL samples versus 19 Follicular lymphoma (FL) samples, and each sample containing 6,817 genes, and (ii) the central nervous system (CNS) cancer data proposed by Pomeroy *et al.*[15]. This data contains 60 samples, 39 are survivors and 21 are failures. Survivors represent the patients who are alive after the treatment while the failures are those who succumb to the CNS cancer. Each sample is represented by 7,129 genes.

The two datasets are used in two separate experiments in this case study. DLBCL data is used for the comparison experiment based on five different models. A subset derived from DLBCL (56 samples with 11 genes and the international prognostic index (IPI)) and CNS data are used to investigate WWKNN and TWNFI for personalized gene data analysis.

2.2 Global, Local and Personalized Models

The objective of the first experiment is to investigate the global, local and personalized models for lymphoma classification. As we discussed in introduction section, cancer is a very complex disease which needs individual (personalized) treatment. Having extracted knowledge form established models, a personalized treatment strategy can be attempted targeting the informative genes and important clinical variables for each patient.

Six models - MLR, KNN, SVM, ECF - a local modeling derived from ECOS [8] based on fuzzy neural network, WWKNN and TWNFI - two newly developed personalized models are applied on cancer data analysis experiment. The algorithm of ECF has been well described in [8, 9]. To discuss the details of ECF model is beyond the scope of this paper, but in general ECF is a simple version of the evolving connectionist system that evolves its structure and functionality from incoming information through a continuous, self-optimized, adaptive and interactive way.

2.3 Personalized Models: WWKNN and TWNFI

WWKNN is a newly developed personalized model by KEDRI. The main idea behind WWKNN algorithm is: the K nearest neighbor vectors are weighted based on their distance to the new vector, and also the contribution of each variable is weighted according to their importance within the local area where the new vector belongs [9]. It is assumed that the different variables have different importance to classify samples into different classes when the variables are ranked in terms of their discriminative power of class samples over the whole V-dimensional space. Therefore, the variables probably have different ranking scores if the discriminative power of the same variables is measured for a sub-space (local space) of the problem space.

In WWKNN algorithm, the Euclidean distance d_j between a new vector x_i and a neighbor x_j is calculated as follows:

$$d_j = \sqrt{\sum_{l=1}^{k} c_{i,l}(x_{i,l} - x_{j,l})^2} \tag{1}$$

where: $c_{i,l}$ is the coefficient weighing x_l in relation with its neighborhood of x_i, and k is the number of the nearest neighbors. The coefficient $c_{i,l}$ can be calculated by

Signal-to-Noise-Ratio (SNR) function that ranks each variable across all vectors in the neighborhood set D_i:

$$\mathbf{c}_{i,l} = (c_{i,1}, c_{i,2}, \ldots, c_{i,k})\tag{2}$$

$$c_{i,l} = \frac{S_l}{\sum S_l}, \quad l = 1, 2, \ldots, k, \text{ where:}\tag{3}$$

$$S_l = \frac{\left|\overline{x}_l^{class1} - \overline{x}_l^{class2}\right|}{\sigma_l^{class1} + \sigma_l^{class2}}\tag{4}$$

where $\overline{x}_l^{class1}$ and σ_l^{class1} represent the mean value and the standard deviation of vector x_l for all vectors in D_i belonging to class 1 respectively.

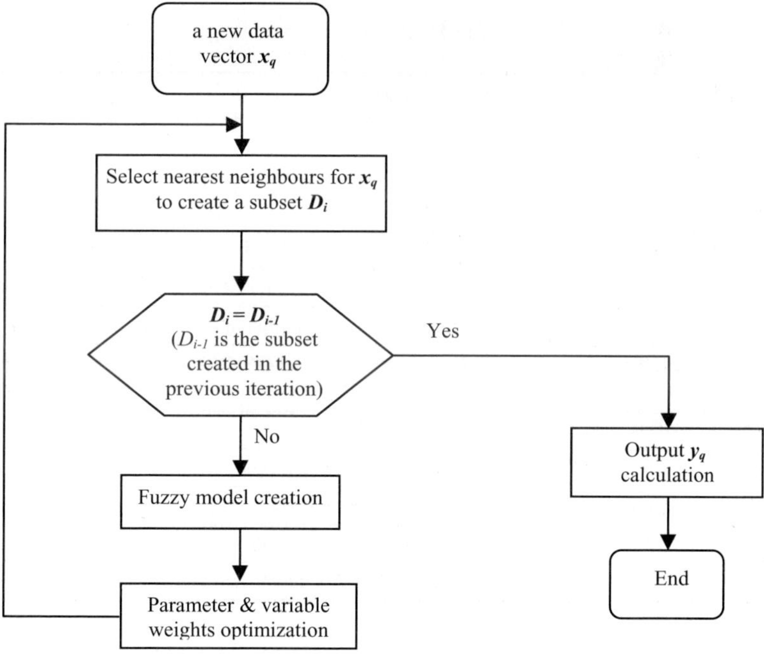

Fig. 1. A brief black diagram of TWNFI model, where x_q is the input new data vector while y_q is the responding output vector (adapted from Song [10])

Comparing to other variants of classical KNN method, the new point in WWKNN is the new distance measure: all variables are weighted according to their importance as discriminating factors in the neighborhood area (personalized sub-space) D_i.

TWNFI is a more sophisticated algorithm based on personalized modeling. The detailed description of the algorithm of TWNFI can be found in [6]. For simplicity, a brief block diagram of TWNFI algorithm is demonstrated in Fig. 1. In TWNFI model, the nearest neighbors regarding the new data vector is measured through a weighted normalized Euclidean distance. A steepest descent learning algorithm is applied for optimizing the parameters of the fuzzy membership functions. In this paper, Gaussian fuzzy membership function is adopted to extract fuzzy rules.

2.4 Experimental Results and Discussion

Each of the models used in our experiments is validated through leave-one-out cross validation (LOOCV). We started our experiment with 12 selected genes based on their SNR ranking scores, and then applied different classifier models on the lymphoma data with these selected genes. The 12 genes selected in our experiment can be found in the list of 50 biomarker genes reported by Shipp, *et al.* [14] for distinguishing two types of lymphoma: DLBCL and FL. Table 1 lists these 12 genes with their biological information. The classification accuracy obtained by different models is listed in table 2, in which k is the number of neighbors used in KNN algorithm.

Table 1. 12 selected genes

Distinction	Gene	Description
DLBCL	HG1980-HT2023_at	Tubulin, Beta 2
DLBCL	M14328_s_at	ENO1 Enolase 1, (alpha)
DLBCL	X56494_at	PKM2 Pyruvate kinase, muscle
DLBCL	X02152_at	LDHA Lactate dehydrogenase A
DLBCL	M57710_at	LGALS3 Lectin, galactoside-binding, soluble, 3 (galectin 3)
DLBCL	L17131_rna1_at	High mobility group protein (HMG-I(Y)) gene exons 1-8
DLBCL	J03909_at	GAMMA-INTERFERON-INDUCIBLE PROTEIN IP-30 PRECURSOR
DLBCL	HG417-HT417_s_at	Cathepsin B
DLBCL	HG2279-HT2375_at	Triosephosphate Isomerase
DLBCL	M63138_at	CTSD Cathepsin D (lysosomal aspartyl protease)
DLBCL	D82348_at	5-aminoimidazole-4-carboxamide-1-beta-D-ribonucleoti de
DLBCL	M22382_at	HSPD1 Heat shock 60 kD protein 1 (chaperonin)

Table 2. Experiment results obtained from five models on Shipp's data with 12 genes

Model	MLR	KNN	SVM	ECF	WWKNN ($k = 15$)
Number of Selected genes	12	12	12	12	12
Overall Accuracy (%)	84.42	81.8	84.42	85.71	87.01

The best classification accuracy (87.01%) achieved on Shipp's data is from personalized WWKNN model - 67 out 77 samples are successfully classified. The local model – ECF performs better than other models (MLR, KNN, SVM). In the experiment, WWKNN is found that its performance is sensitive to the selection of some parameters, *e.g.* the number of the nearest neighbors (k). In Shipp's work, the best accuracy they achieved is 92.2% using a weighted voting algorithm with 30 selected genes based on cross-validation testing, which is better than the result from our WWKNN model.

This lymphoma dataset has been extensively studied, and many models and approaches have been developed for its classification task. However, most of the papers are focused on the performance in terms of computational accuracy. Currently, it is generally agreed that no model or approach can always perform well on different gene expression data for cancer diagnosis and prognosis. In many cases, the performance of prediction can not be the only factor to judge whether a model is superb than others. Other factors, such as the consistency of prediction performance, and reproducibility of the experimental results should be taken into account [16].

Additionally, out aim is to use personalized models to analyze individual cancer data sample. To investigate the personalized modeling, we have applied two models, WWKNN and TWNFI on two data: one is the subset Shipp's DLBCL data which contains 56 samples with 11 selected genes and the international prognostic index (IPI), and the other is Pomeroy's CNS cancer data.

In this experiment, 12 genes are selected from CNS data using SNR method. The experimental results are summarized in Table 3. TWNFI slightly outperforms WWKNN in terms of the classification accuracy, because TWNFI has employed a more sophisticated algorithm to optimize the classifier during the learning process.

Table 3. Experiment results from TWNFI and WWKNN on two cancer data

Data Model	Overall accuracy (class 1, class 2 accuracy) (%)	
	DLBCL (56 samples) data	**CNS** data
TWNFI	**83.9** (93.3, 73.1)	**83.3** (76.2, 87.2)
WWKNN	**83.9** (83.3, 84.6)	**78.3** (76.2, 79.5)

For the personalized data analysis, a data sample is randomly selected from the two above data respectively in this experiment. TWNFI and WWKNN models are capable of discovering certain important information and knowledge specialized for the individual testing sample. An example for personalized data analysis is demonstrated in table 4.

Table 4. An example for personalized data analysis using WWKNN on CNS data

Sample 9		Sample 32	
Gene ID	Importance (weighted value)	Gene ID	Importance (weighted value)
2695	1.000	5812	1.000
1352	0.5495	2196	0.9058
3320	0.4480	**2032**	0.8813
327	0.4470	**2695**	0.6978
2032	0.1594	348	0.4812
1478	0.1515	**3320**	0.3723

It is shown in table 4 that the contribution of each gene to sample 9 and 32 of CNS cancer data is significantly different. Gene 2695 is the most important gene for sample 9, while it is the 4th important for sample 32 in terms of cancer data classification. For DLBCL data, we have obtained similar results in which the importance of genes is computed. Here we only propose table 4 based on the result from CNS data for demonstration due to the limitation of paper length.

TWNFI - another personalized model can also discover the information for individual cancer data analysis. The importance of each gene for sample 40 calculated in TWNFI model on CNS data is summarized in table 5. Additionally, using the fuzzy membership function implemented in TWNFI model, fuzzy rules can be extracted, e.g. if {Gene(L13923) is about(0.10); Gene(S76475) is about(0.20); Gene(D29956) is about(0.17); Gene(D28124) is about(0.40); Gene(U08998) is about(0.77); Gene(M73547) is about(0.23)… then y = 1.95.
where y represents the output value of the class responding to the input new data.

Table 5. An example for personalized data sample analysis using TWNFI on CNS data

Sample 40	
Gene ID	Importance (Weight)
L13923	0.9687
S76475	0.9736
D29956	**0.9815**
D28124	0.9714
U08998	0.9334
M73547	0.9562

We have so far presented the classification results obtained by global, local and personalized models. In this paper, we are more interested in what information and knowledge can be discovered from these models and whether the knowledge can be reused for cancer diagnosis rather than simply measuring the classification accuracy. One of our findings is the 12 selected genes are common to the most important genes reported by other published paper, which means these genes can probably be further studied to evaluate whether they are contributive to other cancer diagnosis and prognosis. With two personalized models - WWKNN and TWNFI, we can obtain the important information that is specialized for an individual new data sample, which is appropriate for complex cancer diagnosis and prognosis.

3   An Ontology-Based Framework for Personalized Cancer Diagnosis

There have been several attempts to use ontology for cancer research. The National Cancer Institute Thesaurus (NCIT) is a biomedical ontology that provides consistent, unambiguous definitions for concepts and terminologies in cancer research domain [17]. NCI is also linked to other internal or external information resources, such as caCore, caBIO and Gene Ontology (GO). In the study proposed by Dameron *et al.*

[18], ontology has been demonstrated that it is capable of automatically analyzing the grading of lung cancer.

An ontology for gene expression data analysis used for assisting personalized cancer diagnosis and risk measurement is currently progressing in KEDRI. The cancer diagnosis and prognosis ontology will help scientists in providing the relationships, either evidential or predicted, among genes; therefore, scientists can target their research appropriately. The other benefit is to avoid repeatedly re-discovering any relationships that have been already made by other researchers.

The main advantage of this system is the evolving ontology and the use of machine learning module. This module will have a personalized modeling system, which has been demonstrated to be efficient for clinical and medical applications of learning systems. Ultimately, the results of the personalized modeling will be used to evolve the ontology in such a way that it will be able to find any emerging patterns, as well as strengthening the existing ones.

The cancer diagnosis and prognosis ontology can also be a sophisticated platform to store, manage, and to share the large amount of data and insight collected from the last two decades of advances in cancer research. Moreover, with such a system, the disparate datasets and distinct computational models for cancer research can be integrated. Furthermore, such data can serve as a good base for our machine learning module to make its predictions and analysis.

Our target is to create a methodology for an ontology-based decision support development framework and populate it with gene expression and other relevant data to cancer disease. This platform will bring ontology knowledge repository methods and systems, machine learning techniques to facilitate sophisticated adaptive data and information storage, retrieval, modeling and knowledge discovery together. Fig.2 demonstrates a general and brief framework that allows for adaptation of existing knowledge base from new data sources and through entering results from machine learning and reasoning models. This type of ontology-based system can be developed for cancer diagnosis and risk assessment on genomic scale and multiple types of cancer.

The design of modeling construction is briefly outlined as follows:

The Ontology-based personalized framework for cancer diagnosis and prognosis is a generic framework that consists of two main parts: an ontology-based system and a machine learning system (see Fig. 2). Protégé will be used for constructing and maintaining an ontology-based knowledge system.

For the presented case study, all the information and discovery from the cancer data can be stored in this ontology-based framework, which will be easily retrieved by

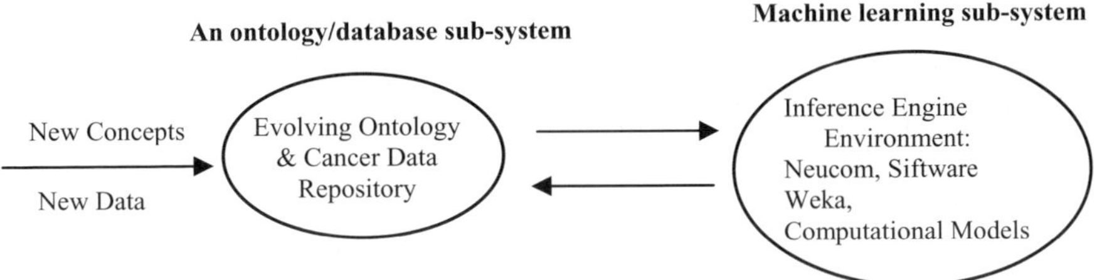

Fig. 2. The ontology-based framework for personalized cancer diagnosis and prognosis

other researchers. And also, the framework is able to be self-learned and consequently extracts certain hidden information and knowledge from the existed information inside the framework. The development of the framework for integrating computational intelligent models is in the progress.

4 Conclusions

This paper presents an ontology based framework for personalized cancer diagnosis and prognosis using gene expression data. Global, local and personalized models, including MLR, KNN, SVM, ECF, WWKNN and TWNFI are applied on two benchmark datasets for cancer classification. In our comparative analysis experiment, the personalized model WWKNN outperforms the local model ECF and global model MLR under the same condition in terms of classification performance over Shipp's lymphoma data. The more important finding in our work is using two personalized models – TWNFI and WWKNN, we can discover the information specialized for individual new data sample. Our experiment shows that the personalized modeling may be a more appropriate approach for analyzing difficult cancer gene expression data (the data is difficult to analyze through traditional computational models, due to its complex interactions among massive genes).

The prototype of ontology based framework integrating the models for cancer diagnosis and prognosis has been introduced in this paper. A variety of approaches for cancer diagnosis and prognosis can be integrated into this type of framework. Further development of the framework and models is in progress. The future directions include the analysis on different cancer gene expression data with different computation intelligent models and approaches, the ontology based framework construction and the creation of cancer knowledge base.

References

1. Alizadeh, A.A., Eisen, M., Davis, R., Ma, C., et al.: Distinct types of diffuse large B-cell lymphoma identified by gene expression profiling. Nature 403, 503–511 (2000)
2. Golub, T.R., Slonim, D.K., Tamayo, P., Huard, C., Gaasenbeek, M., Mersirov, J.P., Coller, H., Loh, M.L., Downing, J.R., Caligiuri, M.A., Bloomfield, C.D., Lander, E.S.: Molecular classification of cancer: class discovery and class prediction by gene expression monitoring. Science 286, 531–537 (1999)
3. van't Veer, L., Dai, H., van de Vijver, M.J., Hc, Y.D., Hart, A.A., et al.: Gene expression profiling predicts clinical outcome of breast cancer. Nature 415, 530–536 (2002)
4. Cho, H.S., Kim, T.S., Wee, J.W., Jeon, S.M., Lee, C.H.: cDNA Microarray Data Based Classification of Cancers Using Neural Networks and Genetic Algorithms. Nanotech 1, 28–31 (2003)
5. Nevins, J.R., Huang, E.S., Dressman, H., Pittman, J., Huang, A.T., West, M.: Towards integrated clinico-genomic models for personalized medicine: combining gene expression signatures and clinical factors in breast cancer outcomes prediction. Human Molecular Genetics 12, R153–R157 (2003)
6. Song, Q., Kasabov, N.: TWNFI - a transductive neuro-fuzzy inference system with weighted data normalization for personalized modeling. Neural Networks 19, 1556–1591 (2006)

7. Kasabov, N., Pang, S.: Transductive support vector machines and applications in bioinformatics for promoter recognition. Neural Inform. Process. – Lett. Rev. 3(2), 31–38 (2004)
8. Kasabov, N.: Evolving Connectionist Systems. In: Methods and Applications in Bioinformatics, Brain Study and Intelligent Machines, Springer, London (2002)
9. Kasabov, N.: Global, local and personalised modeling and pattern discovery in bioinformatics: An integrated approach. Pattern Recognition Letters 28, 673–685 (2007)
10. Hermida, L., Schaad, O., Demougin, P., Descombes, P., Primig, M.: MIMAS: an innovative tool for network-based high density oligonucleotide microarray data management and annotation. BMC Bioinformatics 7 (2006)
11. Shippy, R., Fulmer-Smentek, S., Jensen, R.V., Jones, W.D., Wolber, P.K., Johnson, C.D., Pine6, P.S., et al.: Using RNA sample titrations to assess microarray platform performance and normalization techniques. Nature Biotechnology 24, 1123–1131 (2006)
12. Noy, N.F., McGuinness, D.L.: Ontology Development 101: A Guide to Creating Your First Ontology. Standford Knowledge Systems Laboratory (2001)
13. Kasabov, N.: Evolving fuzzy neural networks for supervised/unsupervised online knowledge-based learning. IEEE Transactions on Systems, Man and Cybernetics 31, 902–918 (2001)
14. Shipp, M.A., Ross, K.N., Tamayo, P., Weng, A.P., Kutok, J.L., Aguiar, R.C.T., Gaasenbeek, M., Angelo, M., et al.: Diffuse Large B-Cell Lymphoma Outcome Prediction by Gene Expression Profiling and Supervised Machine Learning. Nature Medicine 8, 68–74 (2002)
15. Pomeroy, S., Tamayo, P., et al.: Prediction of central nervous system embryonal tumour outcome based on gene expression. Nature 415(6870), 436–442 (2002)
16. Pang, S., Havukala, I., Hu, Y., Kasabov, N.: Classification Consistency Analysis for Bootstrapping Gene Selection. Neural Computing and Applications (2007)
17. Ceusters, W., Smith, B., Goldberg, L.: A Terminological and Ontological Analysis of the NCI Thesaurus. Methods of Information in Medicine 44, 498–507 (2005)
18. Dameron, O., Roques, E., Rubin, D., Marquet, G., Burgun, A.: Grading lung tumors using OWL-DL based reasoning. In: 9th International Protégé Conference (2006)

Ensemble Neural Networks with Novel Gene-Subsets for Multiclass Cancer Classification

Jin-Hyuk Hong and Sung-Bae Cho

Dept. of Computer Science, Yonsei University
134 Sinchon-dong, Sudaemoon-ku
Seoul 120-749, Korea
hjinh@sclab.yonsei.ac.kr, sbcho@cs.yonsei.ac.kr

Abstract. Multiclass gene selection and classification of cancer are rapidly gaining attention in recent years, while conventional rank-based gene selection methods depend on predefined ideal marker genes that basically devised for binary classification. In this paper, we propose a novel gene selection method based on a gene's local class discriminability, which does not require any ideal marker genes for multiclass classification. An ensemble classifier with multiple NNs is trained with the gene subsets. The Global Cancer Map (GCM) cancer dataset is used to verify the proposed method for comparisons with the conventional approaches.

1 Introduction

Gene expression measured by the microarray technology is useful for cancer diagnosis. Since it produces large volume of gene expression profiles, selecting a small number of relevant genes is essential for accurate classification [1]. There are two major gene selection approaches: filter and wrapper. The former selects genes according to their ranks individually measured by certain criteria, while the latter selects genes according to their classification performance measured by collaborating with a classifier. Even though the wrapper approach has a greater potential for measuring the relationship among genes and classifiers or applying to multiclass cancer classification, it requires many training samples to correctly measure the classification performance as well as a great cost of computation [1,2]. On the contrary, the filter approach, often called rank-based gene selection approach, finds appropriate genes with a relatively small cost.

As multiclass cancer classification is rapidly gaining attention recently, various methods have been proposed in the literature [3,4,5]. However, most of them rely upon conventional rank-based gene selection schemes basically devised for binary classification. Moreover, because they usually find out most similar genes to an ideal marker gene set with a strict form, some informative genes for multiclass classification are often missed out due to their dissimilarity to the ideal marker gene [6].

This paper proposes ensemble neural networks with a novel gene selection method for multiclass cancer classification. Without any ideal marker genes, the proposed method segments a gene into several regions and measures their discriminability on class according to the frequency of training samples on the regions. After selecting

M. Ishikawa et al. (Eds.): ICONIP 2007, Part II, LNCS 4985, pp. 856–865, 2008.

informative genes, multiple neural networks are learned with the different size of training sets for maintaining the diversity among base classifiers. The proposed ensemble classifier produces a final result by combining the outputs of multiple neural networks with the majority voting scheme. The proposed method has been validated on the GCM cancer dataset, a representative multiclass gene expression dataset.

2   Background

2.1   Multiclass Cancer Classification Based on Gene expression

Multiclass cancer classification concerns the data consisting of more than two classes. Let $S = \{(x_1,y_1), .., (x_n,y_n)\}$ be a set of n training samples where $x_i \in X$ is the input of the ith sample and $y_i \in Y = \{1,2,\ldots, k\}$ is its multiclass label. Many recent works have been actively investigated to find a function $F: X \rightarrow Y$ which maps an instance x into a label $F(x)$ as shown in Table 1. They can be roughly divided into direct and indirect approaches. Direct methods formulate a classification algorithm for multiclass problems such as regression, decision trees, kNN (k nearest neighborhoods classifier) and NB (naïve Bayes classifier) [2,5,6,10,14], while indirect methods decompose multiclass problems into binary ones according to schemes such as one-versus-rest, pairwise and error-correcting output codes, and solve the binary problems with a binary classification algorithm such as SVMs (support vector machines) [4,5,7,11,12].

Table 1. Related works on multiclass cancer classification

Researcher	Gene selection	Classification	Data
Ramaswamy (2001) [7]	-	SVM	GCM
Yeang (2001) [5]	*SN*	kNN, WV, SVM	GCM
Deutsch (2003) [2]	EA	kNN	DLBCL, GCM
Hsu (2003) [8]	Neighborhood analysis	Dynamic SOM	Leukemia cancer data
Lee (2003) [3]	BSS/WSS	Multicategory SVM	Leukemia data, SRBCT
Ooi (2003) [9]	GA	Maximum likelihood	GCM, NCI60
Li (2004) [4]	*IG, TR, GI, SM, MM, SV*, t-statistics	SVM, NB, kNN	Leukemia cancer data, GCM, SRBCT, NCI60
Zhou (2004) [10]	Gibbs sampling, MCMC	Logistic regression	Breast cancer data, SRBCT, leukemia data
Liu (2005) [11]	GA	SVM	NCI60, Brown dataset
Statnikov (2005) [12]	*BW, SN*, one-way ANOVA	SVM, kNN, NNs, Multicategory SVM	GCM, brain, leukemia, lung cancer data, SRBCT
Tan (2005) [13]	k-TSP		Leukemia, breast, lung, cancer dataset, DLBCL, GCM, SRBCT
Wang (2005) [6]	Relief-F, *IG*, x^2-statistics	kNN, SVM, C4.5, NB	Leukemia cancer data
Yeung (2005) [14]	BSS/WSS, BMA	Logistic regression	Leukemia data, hereditary breast cancer data
Hong (2006) [15]	*PC*	SVM, NB	GCM
Zhang (2006) [16]	Point biserial correlation coefficients	Linear regression	Breast cancer data

2.2 Rank-Based Gene Selection

Conventional rank-based gene selection selects genes by measuring the similarity with a predefined ideal marker gene [17]. At first, it has to decompose a multiclass problem into multiple pairs of binary class problems for multiclass classification, usually using the one-versus-rest scheme. Assume the class label $y_i \in Y = \{1, 2, \ldots, m\}$, where m is the number of classes. Given n training samples, we can define ideal marker genes $K = \{K_1^{+}, K_1^{-}, K_2^{+}, K_2^{-}, \ldots, K_m^{+}, K_m^{-}\}$, represented as strings of n real values where $j = 1, 2, \ldots, m$ as follows:

$$
\begin{aligned}
&\text{Ideal marker gene } K_j^{+} : (k_j^{1}, k_j^{2}, \ldots, k_j^{n}) \\
&\qquad \left\{ \begin{array}{ll} k_j^{i} = 1, & \text{if } y_i = j, \\ k_j^{i} = 0, & \text{if } y_i \mathrel{!}= j. \end{array} \right. \\
&\text{Ideal marker gene } K_j^{-} : (k_j^{1}, k_j^{2}, \ldots, k_j^{n}) \\
&\qquad \left\{ \begin{array}{ll} k_j^{i} = 0, & \text{if } y_i = j, \\ k_j^{i} = 1, & \text{if } y_i \mathrel{!}= j. \end{array} \right.
\end{aligned}
\tag{1}
$$

The ith gene of training samples, g_i, can be expressed as

$$
g_i = (e_1^{i}, e_2^{i}, \ldots, e_n^{i}),
\tag{2}
$$

where e_j^{i} is the expression level of the ith gene of the jth training sample.

The similarity of g_i and an ideal marker gene of K is calculated by using similarity measures such as Pearson correlation (PC), Spearman correlation (SC), Euclidean distance (ED), cosine coefficient (CC), information gain (IG), mutual information (MI) and signal to noise ratio (SN) as shown in Table 2. The most similar s genes are selected for each ideal marker gene, and finally $s \times 2m$ genes are used for multiclass classification.

Table 2. Mathematical formula for similarity measures of g_i and g_{ideal}

$$
PC(g_i, g_{ideal}) = \frac{\sum g_i g_{ideal} - \dfrac{\sum g_i \sum g_{ideal}}{N}}{\sqrt{\left(\sum g_i^2 - \dfrac{(\sum g_i)^2}{N}\right)\left(\sum g_{ideal}^2 - \dfrac{(\sum g_{ideal})^2}{N}\right)}}
$$

$$
SC(g_i, g_{ideal}) = 1 - \frac{6 \sum (D_g - D_{ideal})^2}{N(N^2 - 1)}, \qquad (D_g \text{ and } D_{ideal} \text{ are the rank matrices of } g_i \text{ and } g_{ideal})
$$

$$
ED(g_i, g_{ideal}) = \sqrt{\sum (g_i - g_{ideal})^2}
$$

$$
CC(g_i, g_{ideal}) = \frac{\sum g_i g_{ideal}}{\sqrt{\sum g_i^2 \sum g_{ideal}^2}}
$$

$$
IG(g_i, c_j) = P(g_i \mid c_j) \log \frac{P(g_i \mid c_j)}{P(c_j) \cdot P(g_i)} + P(\bar{g}_i \mid c_j) \log \frac{P(\bar{g}_i \mid c_j)}{P(c_j) \cdot P(\bar{g}_i)}, \qquad (c_j \text{ signifies the } j^{\text{th}} \text{ class})
$$

$$
MI(g_i, c_j) = \log \frac{P(g_i, c_j)}{P(c_j) \cdot P(g_i)}
$$

$$
SN(g_i) = \frac{\mu_{c1}(g_i) - \mu_{c0}(g_i)}{\sigma_{c1}(g_i) + \sigma_{c0}(g_i)}
$$

3   Proposed Method for Multiclass Cancer Classification

3.1   Overview

The proposed method consists of two parts: Gene selection and ensemble classifier as shown in Fig. 1. Informative gene selection includes four steps such as (1) preprocessing, (2) calculating class discriminability, (3) ranking genes, and (4) constructing gene subsets. Multiple gene subsets are constructed according to genes' ranks, and classifiers are trained with the corresponding gene subsets as shown in Fig. 1. Genes holding a high rank might be included in training more classifiers, while others have a less opportunity to join in learning classifiers. Finally, a combining module is accompanied to combine the outputs of these classifiers.

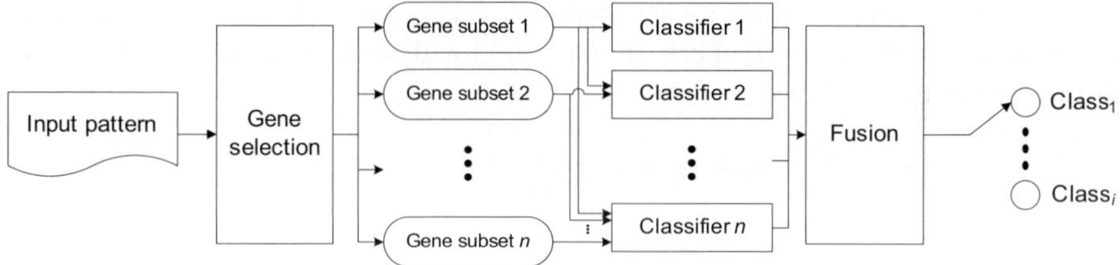

Fig. 1. The overview of the proposed method

3.2   Multiclass Gene Selection

Different from conventional rank-based methods, the proposed gene selection method ranks genes without any ideal marker genes. It measures the usefulness in multiclass classification by directly analyzing genes. After normalizing gene expression levels from 0 to 1, the proposed method sectionalizes the expression level of a gene into several discrete regions according to its distribution on training samples. Given m (# of classes) and d (# of discrete regions, 5 in this paper), it plots the ith gene, g_i, with respect to the class as follows:

$$g_i = \begin{bmatrix} f_1^1 & f_1^2 & \cdots & f_1^m \\ f_2^1 & f_2^2 & \cdots & f_2^m \\ \vdots & \vdots & \ddots & \vdots \\ f_d^1 & f_d^2 & \cdots & f_d^m \end{bmatrix}, \tag{3}$$

where f_j^i is the frequency of training samples whose class label is i and expression level is subject to the jth discrete region. Then, the proposed method calculates class discriminability (*CD*) and region intensity (*RI*), defined respectively as follows:

$$CD(g_i) = \begin{bmatrix} cd_1^1 & cd_1^2 & \dots & cd_1^m \\ cd_2^1 & cd_2^2 & \dots & cd_2^m \\ \vdots & \vdots & \ddots & \vdots \\ cd_d^1 & cd_d^2 & \dots & cd_d^m \end{bmatrix}, \quad RI(g_i) = \begin{bmatrix} ri_1^1 & ri_1^2 & \dots & ri_1^m \\ ri_2^1 & ri_2^2 & \dots & ri_2^m \\ \vdots & \vdots & \ddots & \vdots \\ ri_d^1 & ri_d^2 & \dots & ri_d^m \end{bmatrix}, \tag{4}$$

$$cd_j^i = \frac{f_j^i}{\sum_{k=1}^{m} f_j^k}, \quad ri_j^i = \frac{f_j^i}{\sum_{k=1}^{d} f_k^i}.$$

Large cd means that the region is discriminable for class and large ri signifies that samples are concentrated in the region, so discrete regions of large cd and large ri are informative. In order to find informative genes for multiclass classification, we define $m+1$ kinds of goodness values for g_i: goodness values for each class (c_i) and a goodness value for total classes (t). They are measured with respect to CD, RI and a simple entropy function as follows:

$$c_i = \sum_{j=1}^{d} (E(cd_j^i) \times ri_j^i), \quad t = \sum_{i=1}^{m} c_i,$$

$$E(x) = \begin{cases} 1 - m \times x, & if\ x < \dfrac{1}{m} \\[2ex] -\dfrac{1}{m-1} + \dfrac{m-1}{m} \times x, & if\ x \geq \dfrac{1}{m}. \end{cases} \tag{5}$$

After calculating the goodness values of all genes, the proposed method produces order tables $O = \{o_1, o_2, \dots, o_{m+1}\}$ by sorting genes according to each goodness value. Finally, the rank of genes R is calculated as shown in Fig. 2.

```
gene = 0;
for (i=0; i<m; i++) {              // m: the number of classes
    cDiscriminability = 0.0f;
    for (j=0; j<g; j++) {          // g: the number of genes
        if (cDiscriminability > a)  // a: a threshold for class discriminability
            break;
        R[gene++] = o_{i+1}[j];
        cDiscriminability += c^j_i;  // c^j_i: goodness value of j^th gene for i^th class
}}
for (i=0; gene<g; gene++, i++)
    R[gene++] = o_{m+1}[i];
```

Fig. 2. Pseudo code of the gene ranking algorithm

In order to include discriminable genes for each class as initial seeds, it first ranks genes whose goodness values for each class (c_i) are large. And then, it ranks the other genes according to the goodness value for total classes (t), which can be useful for multiclass classification.

3.3   Ensemble NNs with Multiple Training Sets

As classifiers are often highly parametric and only a few samples of many genes for each class are available, it is apt to be overfit both the classifiers and the gene selection procedures [12]. Therefore, the proposed method combines multiple neural networks trained with different training sets to improve the generalization capability of classification. Multiple training sets for the ensemble classifier are constructed by the algorithm as shown in Fig. 3. By incrementally differentiating genes, multiple diverse and accurate neural networks can be obtained.

```
for (i=0; i<k; i++)               // k: the number of training sets
   for (j=0; j<n; j++)            // n: the number of training samples
      for (l=0; l< a +k × b; l++)  // a, b: parameters for determining the number
      of
         TrainingSet_i[j][l] = R[l];   //        genes (in this paper, a: 400, b: 100)
```

Fig. 3. Pseudo code for constructing training sets for the ensemble classifier

Since base classifiers trained for each gene subsets produce their own outputs, the final answer can be judged by a combining module. Majority voting, used for the combining module in this paper, is a simple ensemble method that selects the class most favored by the base classifiers. It does not require any kind of prior knowledge and complex computation. Where c_i is the output of the ith classifier (i=1,..., m), and $s_i(x)$ is 1 if the output of the classifier x is i otherwise 0, majority voting is defined as follows:

$$c_{ensemble} = \arg\max_{1 \leq i \leq m}\left\{ \sum_{j=1}^{k} s_i(c_j) \right\}. \tag{6}$$

4   Experimental Results

4.1   Experimental Environment

We have verified the proposed method with the GCM cancer dataset consisting of 144 training samples and 54 test samples with 16,063 gene expression levels, which is a popular multiclass cancer dataset [7]. There are 14 different tumor categories including breast adenocarcinoma, prostate, lung adenocarcinoma, colorectal adenocarcinoma, lymphoma, bladder, melanoma, uterine adenocarcinoma, leukemia, renal cell carcinoma, pancreatic adenocarcinoma, ovarian adenocarcinoma, pleural mesothelioma, and central nervous system. Since the dataset provides only a few samples with lots of features, it is a challenging task for many machine learning researchers to construct a competitive classifier.

Both of Ramaswamy *et al.*[7] and Yeang *et al.*[5] produced an accuracy of 78% by using OVR SVMs, while Li *et al.* yielded an accuracy of 63.3% [4]. Statnikov *et al.* obtained an accuracy of 76.6% for an extended GCM cancer dataset that includes 308 samples of 26 categories [12]. Most of them divided the data as 144 training samples and 54 test samples like the initial setting of Ramaswamy *et al.*, which we also follow.

For gene selection, we set $a=400$, $b=100$ and discrete size $d=5$, respectively. Six gene subsets from the training samples are constructed for six base classifiers. For classification, a 3-layered multilayer perceptron is used as a base classifier with 10 hidden nodes, 14 output nodes, 0.05 learning rate and 0.7 momentum.

4.2   Results and Analysis

As shown in Fig. 4 (k_i^+: positive ideal vector for i^{th} class, k_i^-: negative ideal vector for i^{th} class), the proposed method selects more informative genes rather than a conventional method for the multiclass problem. The conventional rank-based gene selection often commits to select a peculiar gene with which only few training samples of a target class can be correctly classified. Moreover, many genes are duplicative selected even for different ideal marker genes. On the other hand, the proposed method selects the genes of various characteristics, since it does not rely on any ideal marker genes.

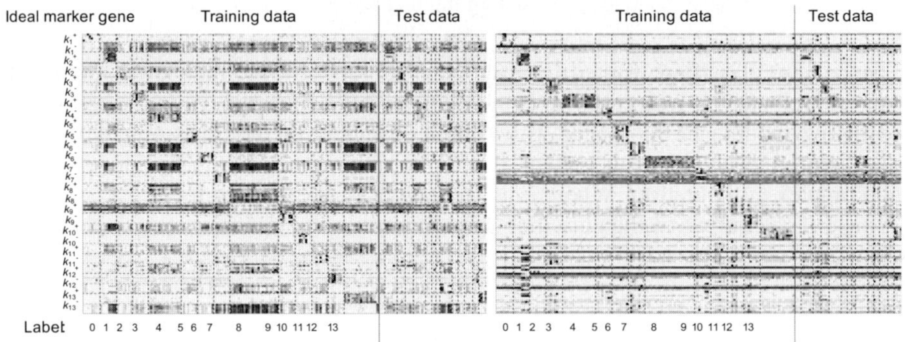

Fig. 4. Gene analysis (left: rank-based gene selection (*PC*), right: Proposed method)

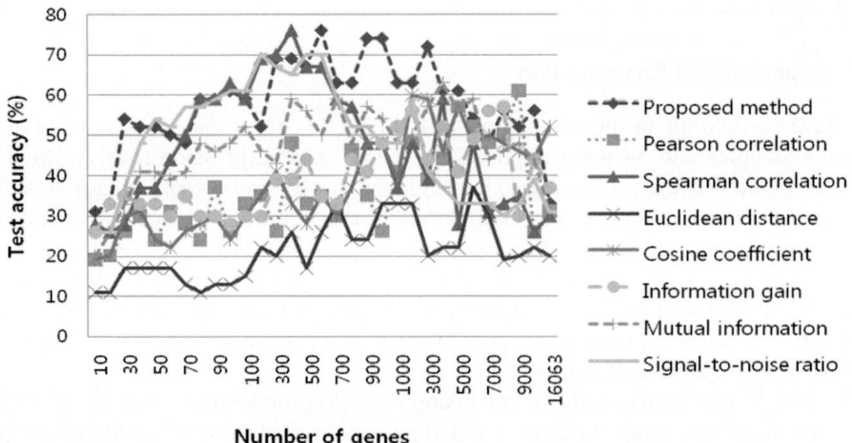

Fig. 5. Test accuracy according to the number of genes used

It is difficult to find the optimal number of genes, so many practical solutions are usually based on experience or some heuristics. A set of experiments are conducted by varying the number of genes selected to investigate the effects of the number of genes using single NNs. As shown in Fig. 5, when the number of genes selected is near hundreds, most cases show the good performance. As can be seen, there is much decrease of accuracy with all genes, since it includes lots of unrelated genes to cancer classification. This also verifies the usefulness of feature selection. The proposed method is superior to the others in most cases, especially when using hundreds of high rank genes.

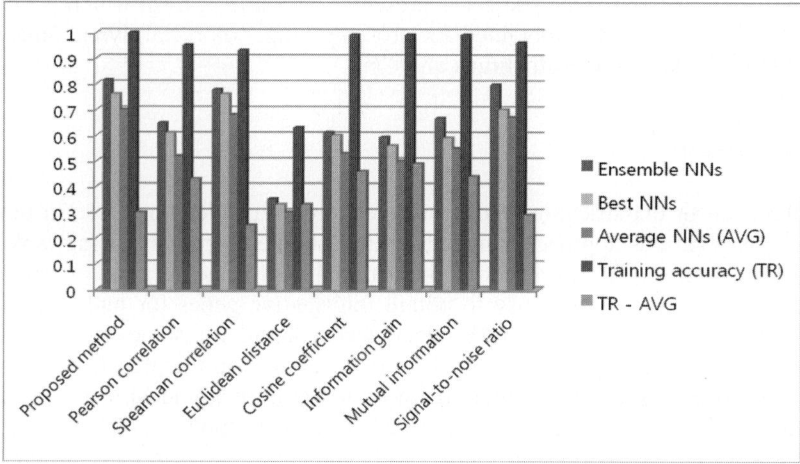

Fig. 6. Comparion with conventional approaches

Table 3. Confusion matrix (0:Breast, 1:Prostate, 2:Lung, 3:Colorectal, 4:Lymphoma, 5:Bladder, 6:Melanoma, 7:Uterus_Adeno, 8:Leukemia, 9:Renal, 10:Pancreas, 11:Ovary, 12:Mesothelioma, 13:CNS)

		Classifying label														
	%	0	1	2	3	4	5	6	7	8	9	10	11	12	13	n
	0	25					25					25	25			4
	1		83										17			6
	2			100												4
	3				100											4
	4					100										6
	5		33				67									3
True	6							100								2
class	7								100							2
	8									100						6
	9						33		33		34					3
	10				33							67				3
	11							25				25	50			4
	12													100		3
	13														100	4
	n	1	6	4	5	6	3	3	3	6	1	3	2	3	4	54

Fig. 6 shows the competitive performance of the proposed method for the test samples against conventional rank-based gene selection methods. In all cases, ensemble NNs obtained higher accuracy than single NNs. This signifies that ensembling can improve the generalization capability of the classifier, especially for NNs that are apt to be overfit. The proposed gene selection method obtains higher test accuracy with comparison of conventional methods including *PC, SC, ED, CC, IG, MI* and *SN*. Moreover, the proposed method shows good generalization capability by producing lower *TR-AVG. PC, CC, IG* and *MI* yield higher training accuracy but they fail to obtain higher test accuracy, while *SC* and *SN* do not get relatively high training accuracy but they show higher test accuracy.

A confusion matrix for the test set is presented in Table 3, from which we can see that high accuracy has been obtained for prostate, lung, colorectal, lymphoma, melanoma, uterus, leukemia, mesothelioma and CNS.

5   Conclusion

Multiclass cancer classification and gene selection are challenging tasks in bioinformatics, where various approaches have been investigated especially using rank-based gene selection methods. Since many conventional approaches depend on predefined ideal marker genes, it is not easy to obtain informative genes for multiclass cancer classification. Moreover, they often select genes biased for some specific training samples so as to fail to get the generalization capability. In this paper, we have proposed a novel gene selection method that does not require any ideal marker genes for multiclass classification, and an ensemble classifier with multiple NNs trained using multiple gene subsets. A popular multiclass benchmark dataset in bioinformatics, the GCM cancer dataset, has been used to verify the proposed method with better performance than conventional approaches. As the future work, we will apply the proposed method with other popular benchmark datasets of multiclass.

Acknowledgement

This work was supported by the Korea Science and Engineering Foundation (KOSEF) through the Biometrics Engineering Research Center (BERC) at Yonsei University.

References

[1] Hong, J.-H., Cho, S.-B.: Efficient huge-scale feature selection with speciated genetic algorithm. Pattern Recognition Letter 27(2), 143–150 (2006)

[2] Deutsch, J.: Evolutionary algorithms for finding optimal gene sets in microarray prediction. Bioinformatics 19(1), 45–52 (2003)

[3] Lee, Y., Lee, C.-K.: Classification of multiple cancer types by multicategory support vector machines using gene expression data. Bioinformatics 19(9), 1132–1139 (2003)

[4] Li, T., Zhang, C., Ogihara, M.: A comparative study of feature selection and multiclass classification methods for tissue classification based on gene expression. Bioinformatics 20(15), 2429–2437 (2004)

[5] Yeang, C.-H., Ramaswamy, S., Tamayo, P., Mukherjee, S., Rifkin, R., Angelo, M., Reich, M., Lander, E., Mesirov, J., Golub, T.: Molecular classification of multiple tumor types. Bioinformatics 17(1), 316–322 (2001)

[6] Wang, Y., Makedon, F., Ford, J., Pearlman, J.: HykGene: A hybrid approach for selecting marker genes for phenotype classification using microarray gene expression data. Bioinformatics 21(8), 1530–1537 (2005)

[7] Ramaswamy, S., Tamayo, P., Rifkin, R., Mukherjee, S., Yeang, C., Angelo, M., Ladd, C., Reich, M., Latulippe, E., Mesirov, J., Poggio, T., Gerald, W., Loda, M., Lander, E., Golub, T.: Multiclass cancer diagnosis using tumor gene expression signatures. Proc. National Academy of Science 98(26), 15149–15154 (2001)

[8] Hsu, A., Tang, S.-L., Halgamuge, S.: An unsupervised hierarchical dynamic self-organized approach to cancer class discovery and marker gene identification in microarray data. Bioinformatics 19(16), 2131–2140 (2003)

[9] Ooi, C., Tan, P.: Genetic algorithms applied to multi-class prediction for the analysis of gene expression data. Bioinformatics 19(1), 37–44 (2003)

[10] Zhou, X., Liu, K.-Y., Wong, S.: Cancer classification and prediction using logistic regression with Bayesian gene selection. J. Biomedical Informatics 37(4), 249–259 (2004)

[11] Liu, J., Cutler, G., Li, W., Pan, Z., Peng, S., Hoey, T., Chen, L., Ling, X.: Multiclass cancer classification and biomarker discovery using GA-based algorithms. Bioinformatics 21(11), 2691–2697 (2005)

[12] Statnikov, A., Aliferis, C., Tsamardinos, L., Hardin, D., Levy, S.: A comprehensive evaluation of multicategory classification methods for microarray gene expression cancer diagnosis. Bioinformatics 21(5), 631–643 (2005)

[13] Tan, A., Naiman, D., Xu, L., Winslow, R., Geman, D.: Simple decision rules for classifying human cancers from gene expression profiles. Bioinformatics 21(20), 3896–3904 (2005)

[14] Yeung, K.-Y., Bumgarner, R., Raftery, A.: Bayesian model averaging: Development of an improved multi-class, gene selection and classification tool for microarray data. Bioinformatics 21(10), 2394–2402 (2005)

[15] Hong, J.-H., Cho, S.-B.: Multi-class cancer classification with OVR-support vector machines selected by naive Bayes classifier. In: King, I., Wang, J., Chan, L.-W., Wang, D. (eds.) ICONIP 2006. LNCS, vol. 4234, pp. 155–164. Springer, Heidelberg (2006)

[16] Zhang, W., Rekaya, R., Bertrand, K.: A method for predicting disease subtypes in presence of misclassification among training samples using gene expression: Application to human breast cancer. Bioinformatics 22(3), 317–325 (2006)

[17] Cho, S.-B., Ryu, J.-W.: Classifying gene expression data of cancer using classifier ensemble with mutually exclusive features. Proceedings of the IEEE 90(11), 1744–1753 (2002)

Identification of Different Sets of Biomarkers for Diagnostic Classification of Cancers

Yu-Shuen Tsai[1], I-Fang Chung[1], Chin-Teng Lin[2], and Nikhil Ranjan Pal[3]

[1] Institute of Biomedical Informatics, National Yang-Ming University, Taipei, Taiwan
[2] Department of Electrical and Control Engineering, Department of Computer Science, and Brain Research Center, National Chiao-Tung University, Hsinchu, Taiwan
[3] Electronics and Communication Sciences Unit, Indian Statistical Institute, Kolkata, India
g39528010@ym.edu.tw, ifchung@ym.edu.tw, ctlin@mail.nctu.edu.tw,
nikhil@isical.ac.in

Abstract. Accurate diagnosis of neuroblastoma, non-Hodgkin lymphoma, rhabdomyosarcoma, and Ewing sarcoma, is often difficult because these cancers appear similar in routine histology. Finding a few useful biomarkers (not all related genes) that can discriminate between the subgroups will help designing better diagnostic systems. In an earlier study we reported a set of seven genes having excellent discrimination power. In this investigation we extend that study and find other *distinct* sets of genes with strong class specific signatures. This is achieved analyzing the correlation between genes. This led us to find another set of seven genes with better discriminating power. Our original gene selection method used a neural network whose output may significantly depend on initialization of the network, network size as well as the training data set. To address these issues we propose a scheme based on re-sampling. This method can also reduce the effect wide variation in number of data points in the training set from different classes. This method led us to find a set of five genes with good discriminating power. The genes identified by the proposed methods have roles in cancer biology.

Keywords: Biomarker, Gene expression, Neural networks.

1 Introduction

Microarray data are being extensively used in identifying markers for different stages of cancers, for analysis of survival of cancer patients as well as for categorization of cancers into different diagnostic subgroups, which may appear similar in routine histology [3, 5, 7, 8]. Success in any one of these areas heavily depends on identification of discriminating biomarkers for the groups of cancers under consideration. Consequently many attempts have been made to identify useful genes for categorization of subgroups and for designing diagnostic prediction systems. In this investigation we consider the problem of identification of biomarkers for designing diagnostic prediction/classification systems for a group of four types of childhood cancers, collectively known as *small round blue cell tumors* (SRBCTs). This is the third most frequently occurring group of childhood cancers. This group consists of neuroblastoma (NB),

M. Ishikawa et al. (Eds.): ICONIP 2007, Part II, LNCS 4985, pp. 866–875, 2008.

Burkitt lymphomas (BL), rhabdomyosarcoma (RMS), and Ewing sarcoma (EWS). In routine histology these groups often look similar and may lead to misdiagnosis. Correct identification of these subgroups is very important because the treatment options and monitoring of the responses depend on the group.

This being such an important problem, many authors have tried to find biomarkers for these four categories. For these different types of tools such as neural networks (NNs), support vector machines (SVMs) and nearest neighbor rules have been used [2, 4, 5, 6, 8]. Most of these methods ignore the interaction between the tool and genes and look at the utility of each gene separately and hence may fail to account for the nonlinear interaction between genes. In order to find a small set of genes taking into account the possible nonlinear interaction between tools, genes and the problem at hand we have used an online feature selection method based on neural networks. The set of genes selected by the NN is then further reduced using non-Euclidean relational clustering methods [6]. This method could find seven genes with excellent class-specific signatures. In this paper we discuss some of the important issues relating to the method in [6] and propose some solutions. Moreover, using the set of seven genes reported in [6] we could find other sets of genes with better or comparable discriminating power.

2 Materials and Methods

In this study, we use the SRBCT dataset [5] as our test platform. This is a cDNA microarray dataset containing 63 samples from 4 classes: 23 Ewing sarcomas (EWS), 8 Burkitt lymphomas (BL), 12 neuroblastomas (NB), and 20 rhabdomyosarcomas (RMS). We use these 63 samples as training data. In addition, an independent dataset with 20 samples (6 EWS, 3 BL, 6 NB, and 5 RMS) is used in the blind test. Each sample is represented by 2308 genes. Both datasets are available at http://research. nhgri.nih.gov/microarray/Supplement/

In [6] we first used an online feature selection (OFS) method as described in Section 2.1 for selecting 20 genes based on gate opening values. Then the OFS net is applied on the selected genes to pick up a set of 10 genes with adequate discriminating power. With a view to removing redundant/correlated genes, the non-Euclidean relational c-means clustering algorithm was used to finally find a set of seven genes: {FGFR4, AF1Q, NAB2, CDH2, EHD1, LSP1, FVT1}[6].

2.1 Online Feature Selection (OFS) Method

The OFS network is a modified form of MLP for simultaneous gene selection and designing of the diagnostic system [6]. The idea is not to allow unimportant or bad genes to get into the network and thus eliminate the effect of those genes. We realize this equipping each input node (hence each gene/feature) with a tuneable gate. For *important* genes we want to open the associated gates completely while for an *unimportant* gene the gate should be closed tightly. Each gate is modeled using a gate (or modulator) function that is associated with each input node. The product of the input (gene expression values) and the gate function value is taken as the modulated output which is then passed to the next layer. The gate function should produce a value of 1 or nearly 1 for discriminatory genes while for not-so-important genes, the desired values of gate functions should be near 0. Here we have used the sigmoidal function, $F(\gamma) = \dfrac{1}{1 + e^{-\gamma}}$, although many other choices are possible. If x is the input value to a node then $xF(\gamma)$ is the output from that node. The training begins with all gates *almost closed* (i.e. as if no gene is discriminatory) and then opens the gates as required during the training.

Suppose, q = number of hidden nodes, μ = learning rate for the parameters of the attenuator functions, η = learning rate for the connection weights (typically $\eta < \mu$), $w_{ij}^{hi}(t)$ = weight connecting j-th node of the input layer to the i-th node of the hidden layer for the t-th iteration, $w_{ij}^{oh}(t)$ = weight connecting j-th node of the hidden layer to the i-th node of the output layer for the t-th iteration, δ_i = error term for the i-th node of the hidden layer (we consider single hidden layer), and $F'(\gamma_j)$ = derivative of F with respect to tuneable parameter γ at γ_j. The learning rule for connection weights remains the same as in case of an ordinary MLP for all layers except for $w_{ij}^{hi}(t)$. The update rule for $w_{ij}^{hi}(t)$ and γ_j are:

$$w_{ij}^{hi}(t+1) = w_{ij}^{hi}(t) - \eta x_j \delta_i F(\gamma_j(t)) \qquad (1)$$

$$\gamma_j(t+1) = \gamma_j(t) + \mu x_j F'(\gamma_j(t)) \sum_{i=1}^{q} w_{ij}^{hi} \delta_i \qquad (2)$$

For all genes we initialize γ_j so that when the training starts $F(\gamma_j)$ is nearly zero and thus no gene enters the network. As the gradient descent learning proceeds, gates for the features/genes that can reduce the error faster are opened relatively faster. The parameters of the gate functions and the connection weights are learnt together. Note that, we do not need to continue the training till termination; the training can be stopped when the error reduces to a reasonable value. At the end of the training we select useful genes based on the gate opening values. A good attribute of the OFS scheme is that it can take into account possible subtle nonlinear interactions between genes. Consequently, it can identify a small and better subset of genes.

2.2   Some Issues Relating to the OFS Method

Since the OFS training settles at a local minimum, different runs of the OFS network may lead to different subsets of useful genes because of different initializations. Each of these sets could be equally effective. Since we are using the online learning philosophy, the final gene set may also depend on the order of feed of the data. The network may pick up a set of genes and there could be another set of equally effective correlated genes. Typically, the dimension of expression data is very high but the number of training samples available is quite small. Moreover, often the number of samples from different classes could be widely different making the training more biased to the classes having higher representations in the training set. Here we shall try to address all these issues.

First, we shall check whether there exist any set of genes that is strongly correlated with set of seven genes that we found earlier [6]. If yes, how good is the performance of these new sets of genes in diagnosis? In order to reduce the effect of initializations, we shall repeat the experiment many times with a fixed architecture. Then to reduce the effect of variations in sample sizes of different classes, we shall use a re-sampling scheme and suggest a simple scheme to aggregate the results of different runs of the OFS network.

2.3 Correlation Based Method

Based on the 7 genes reported in our previous work [6], we perform the following experiments. First, among the 7 genes we want to check if there are some highly correlated genes. Table 1 depicts the Peason's Correlation coefficients for the seven genes. Table 1 reveals that only three different pairs of genes have high correlation (in bold face) of > 0.5. This implies that for three of the classes we have two genes each while for one class (BL) there is only gene EHD1 characterizing that class. A scatterplot of EHD1 (not shown here) reveals that it has a strong BL specific signature.

Second, for each of the original 7 genes, in all of the 2308 genes we look for five genes (in total 5×7=35 genes in the list) possessing the highest correlation value with that original gene (Table 2). Note that in Table 2 some genes appear more than once. For example, in Table 2 the gene with Image ID 789253 appears twice in column 2 and column 3. Here we make two assumptions: (1) we do not want to find any newly selected gene being the same with the original 7 genes. (2) we do not want any gene to appear in more than one list of seven genes. Thus to satisfy (1) and (2) we remove any gene from the original set and we also remove any other gene that appears more than once. For example, the gene 789253 appears twice and we replace the gene 789253 in column 3, row 4 by the next correlated gene in the same row, i.e., by the gene 809494. In this way, we get three distinct sets of genes, each having seven members as shown in Table 3. Table 3 also lists the correlation values. We name these sets as **New Set 1 – New Set 3**. Thus each column of Table 3 gives a set of seven genes for the SRBCT groups and each such set is expected to have a good discriminating power.

2.4 Method Based on Re-sampling and Aggregation of Gating Values

In most gene expression data sets, the distribution of samples in different classes is often far from uniform. For example, in the SRBCT datasets, the numbers of training samples in different classes are 23 (EWS), 8 (BL), 12 (NB), and 20 (RMS). Obviously, since almost all supervised biomarker identification methods rely on the training error and that being dependent on the number of samples in each class, the gene set identified by such methods may not pick enough markers for the class having the least number of representations. This is found to be true even in case of our OFS based method – this does not of course mean that it will not pick up any good gene for the least represented class. In order to guard against such a problem, typically in re-sampling approaches [1] samples of same size as that of the training set are generated with replacement. Although this may account for the effect of limited sample size, this will not minimize the bias that we have explained. Hence we proceed as follows. Let n_i, $i=1,...,c$, be the number of training samples in the ith class. Let $n_k=\min\{n_i, i=1,...,c\}$, then we re-sample with replacement to pick from each class n_k number of samples. With each such re-sampled data we train an OFS network. The process is repeated a large number of times. In every run, r, of OFS, we get a set of gate opening values as $g_{r,i}$, $i=1,...,n$; $r=1,...,T$; where T (here T=50) is the total number of OFS runs. Now we compute the average gate opening values over the T runs and use that to select the genes for further analysis.

Table 1. Correlation coefficients between the seven genes reported in [6]

		Image IDs						
		325182	784224	745019	143306	814260	812105	770868
	325182	1.00	-0.19	-0.20	-0.05	-0.26	**0.73**	-0.20
	784224		1.00	0.01	**0.57**	-0.36	-0.20	-0.20
Image	745019			1.00	-0.24	-0.23	-0.27	-0.19
IDs	143306				1.00	-0.32	-0.09	-0.14
	814260					1.00	-0.29	**0.50**
	812105						1.00	-0.32
	770868							1.00

Table 2. Top five correlated genes among all of 2308 genes for the seven genes reported in [6]

Image IDs	Image IDs with Pearson's R values				
	Top 1	Top 2	Top 3	Top 4	Top 5
325182	629896/0.76	812105/0.73	308231/0.61	134748/0.60	878652/0.59
784224	789253/0.78	796258/0.75	142134/0.75	839552/0.68	246035/0.68
745019	236282/0.78	767183/0.74	624360/0.71	814526/0.70	1469292/0.69
143306	207274/0.73	789253/0.67	809494/0.67	755975/0.66	296448/0.61
814260	770394/0.78	866702/0.72	298231/0.69	1473131/0.67	767345/0.67
812105	878280/0.78	81518/0.76	786084/0.74	949934/0.73	325182/0.73
770868	1435862/0.67	787857/0.66	30473/0.66	1374571/0.64	740554/0.63

Table 3. Three new datasets with the highest correlation to the original seven genes

Image IDs of original genes	Image IDs with Pearson's R values					
	New Set 1		New Set 2		New Set 3	
325182	629896	0.76	308231	0.73	134748	0.61
784224	789253	0.78	796258	0.75	142134	0.75
745019	236282	0.78	767183	0.74	624360	0.71
143306	207274	0.73	809494	0.67	755975	0.66
814260	770394	0.78	866702	0.72	298231	0.69
812105	878280	0.78	81518	0.76	786084	0.74
770868	1435862	0.67	787857	0.66	30473	0.66

3 Results

First we present the results obtained using the correlation analysis. For example, in Table 2, the gene 325182 has a very high correlation with genes 629896, 812105, 308231, 134748, and 878652, the gene 629896 has the highest correlation, while 878652 has the least correlation. These genes are listed in the first row of the Table 2. Thus each row of the Table lists five genes that are correlated with the corresponding gene in the original list shown in the first column. Since in the original list there are some correlated genes (more than one gene with class specific signature for a particular class), some genes may appear in more than one column of the list. Here if a gene is selected as a correlated gene with any one of the original set of seven genes, then that gene is excluded for further consideration so that each set of seven genes is distinct. This of course, will exclude any set of genes consisting of members from different groups that may have better discriminating power than any of the four sets. The three sets of genes along with the original set are displayed in Table 3.

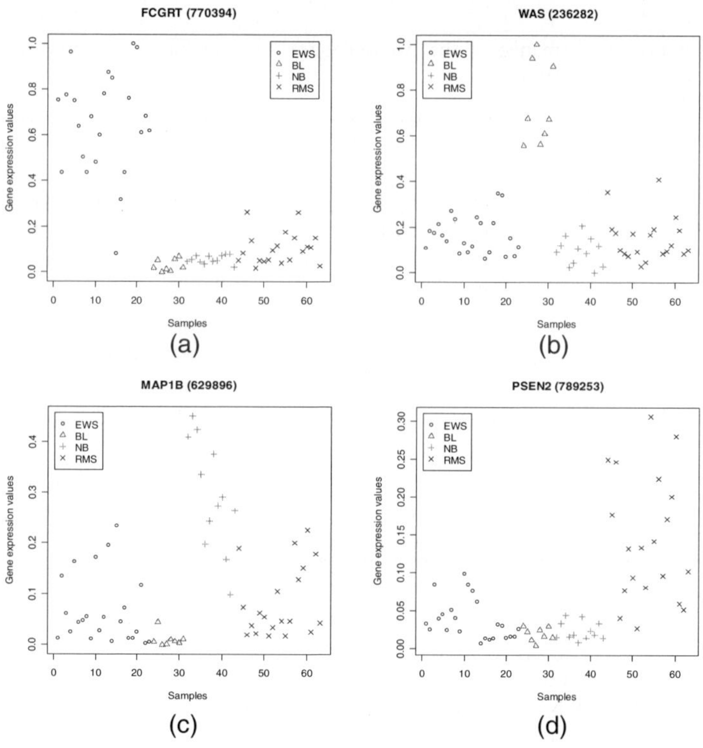

Fig. 1. Scatterplots of 4 genes in the New Set 1. (a) Gene FCGRT (770394) shows a specific signature for class EWS; (b) Gene WAS (236282) shows a specific signature for class BL; (c) Gene MAP1B (629896) shows a specific signature for class NB; (d) Gene PSEN2 (789253) shows a specific signature for class RMS.

In order to examine, how good each of these new sets with respect to the original set, we made 100 runs of the multi-layer perceptron (MLP) neural network (with 5 hidden nodes) in the Matlab environment. If the training error is reduced to zero, then only the associated network is applied on the test data set. The experiments are repeated with different choices of the learning parameters also. Table 4 summarizes the average performance of the network using different sets of genes. The *average* performance on the original set and the New Set 1 (which has the strongest correlation with the original set) are quite good and very comparable. The description of these genes is included in Table 5. Although, the *average* performance for the New Set 1 is slightly better than that of the original set, the worst performance of the net with the original set is quite better than the New Set 1. This establishes the fact that there exists several sets of equally good genes.

In addition, we further check if these 7 genes in the New Set 1 have been reported by other researches and observe the characteristics of these genes. First, all of these 7 genes in the New Set 1 have been reported in previous studies [2, 4, 5, 8]. However,

Table 4. Prediction performance of the original gene set and three new sets of genes with multi-layer perceptron (MLP) networks

Gene set	Mu	Accuracies in test set			Accuracies of each group			
		Max.	Mean	Min.	EWS	BL	NB	RMS
Original Set	0.3	1.00	0.91	0.75	0.89	0.89	1.00	0.82
	0.2	0.95	0.90	0.75	0.88	0.91	0.99	0.82
	0.1	0.95	0.91	0.80	0.89	0.88	1.00	0.82
New Set1	0.3	1.00	0.92	0.75	0.83	0.99	0.96	0.95
	0.2	0.95	0.92	0.65	0.82	1.00	0.97	0.95
	0.1	1.00	0.93	0.70	0.83	0.99	0.96	0.96
New Set 2	0.3	0.80	0.74	0.60	0.94	0.80	0.29	1.00
	0.2	0.80	0.76	0.55	0.92	0.87	0.33	1.00
	0.1	0.80	0.75	0.60	0.92	0.85	0.32	1.00
New Set 3	0.3	0.65	0.57	0.45	0.63	0.94	0.24	0.68
	0.2	0.80	0.57	0.40	0.68	0.95	0.23	0.64
	0.1	0.65	0.56	0.40	0.65	0.93	0.20	0.65

Table 5. Description of the seven genes in the New Set 1

Image IDs	Gene Name	Description
629896	MAP1B [4][5]	Microtubule-associated protein 1B
789253	PSEN2 [8]	Presenilin 2 (Alzheimer disease 4)
236282	WAS [4]	Wiskott-Aldrich syndrome (ecezema-thrombocytopenia)
207274	IGF2 [4][5][8]	Insulin-like growth factor 2 (somatomedin a)
770394	FCGRT [2][5][8]	Fc fragment of IgG, receptor, transporter, alpha
878280	CRMP1 [2][5]	Collapsin response mediator protein 1
1435862	CD99 [2][5][8]	MIC2 surface antigen (CD99)

Table 6. Top 20 genes with the highest average gate-opening values (GOV)

Image IDs	Description	Average GOV
770394	Fc fragment of IgG, receptor, transporter, alpha	0.4805
486110	profilin 2	0.3279
236282	Wiskott-Aldrich syndrome (ecezema-thrombocytopenia)	0.1420
142134	ESTs	0.1333
784224*	fibroblast growth factor receptor 4	0.1106
789204	translocation protein 1	0.1100
767183	hematopoietic cell-specific Lyn substrate 1	0.1070
878652	postmeiotic segregation increased 2-like 12	0.0966
1435862	MIC2 surface antigen (CD99)	0.0962
839552	nuclear receptor coactivator 1	0.0944
325182*	cadherin 2, N-cadherin (neuronal)	0.0898
220096		0.0869
823886	Smooth muscle myosin heavy chain isoform SMemb [human, umbilical cord, fetal aorta, mRNA Partial, 971 nt]	0.0805
812965	v-myc avian myelocytomatosis viral oncogene homolog	0.0802
193913	v-yes-1 Yamaguchi sarcoma viral related oncogene homolog	0.0800
770059	heparan sulfate proteoglycan 2 (perlecan)	0.0778
183337	major histocompatibility complex, class II, DM alpha	0.0760
134748	glycine cleavage system protein H (aminomethyl carrier)	0.0734
81518	apelin; peptide ligand for APJ receptor	0.0719
814526	ESTs	0.0692

Table 7. Prediction performance of the top genes (selected by the OFS network) with MLP networks

Gene sets	mu	Accuracies in test set			Accuracies of each group			
		Max.	Mean	Min.	EWS	BL	NB	RMS
Top 7	0.3	0.75	0.63	0.50	0.81	0.83	0.18	0.82
Top 10	0.3	0.70	0.80	0.55	0.83	0.96	0.36	0.79
Top 14	0.3	0.90	0.78	0.45	0.80	0.94	0.66	0.79
Top 19	0.3	0.90	0.71	0.55	0.83	0.96	0.42	0.79

Table 8. Prediction performance of the top one/two genes selected for each class with MLP networks

Gene sets	Mu	Accuracies in test set			Accuracies of each group			
		Max.	Mean	Min.	EWS	BL	NB	RMS
Top 1 gene for each class	0.3	0.90	0.84	0.70	0.61	0.87	0.99	0.91
	0.2	0.95	0.85	0.65	0.61	0.89	0.99	0.94
	0.1	0.95	0.83	0.70	0.61	0.82	0.99	0.91
Top 2 genes for each class	0.3	0.90	0.86	0.75	0.84	0.99	0.86	0.79
	0.2	0.90	0.85	0.70	0.84	1.00	0.82	0.80
	0.1	0.95	0.85	0.70	0.83	0.98	0.86	0.79

Table 9. The list of the final five genes

Image IDs	Gene Name	Average GOV.	Class
770394	FCGRT [2][5][8]	0.4805 (top1)	EWS
236282	WAS [4]	0.1420 (top3)	BL
784224*	FGFR4 [2][4][5][6]	0.1106 (top5)	RMS
1435862	CD99 [2][5][8]	0.0962 (top9)	EWS
325182*	CDH2 [2][5][6]	0.0869 (top11)	NB

*, common genes with the original set of seven genes

two of these genes (PSEN2 and WAS) are reported only once (Table 5). From OMIM (Online Mendelian Inheritance in Man, NCBI), we find that defects in PSEN2 are the cause of Alzheimer disease type4 and WAS is the cause of Wiskott-Aldrich syndrome (also known as eczema-thrombocytopenia-immunodeficiency syndrome). Although these two genes are not studied in the context of cancer biology, a search in GEO profile (Gene Expression Omnibus, NCBI) shows some interesting phenomena. For examples, PSEN2 is found to be upregulated in RMS but downregulated in several tumors, including EWS cases (GPL1977). And this dataset (GPL1977) also shows upregulation of WAS in several tumors (including both RMS and EWS cases), but downregulation in Gastrointestinal Stromal tumor. Hence, not only these genes have strong class specific signatures, but also are likely to play important roles in tumor/cancer biology. Figure 1 depicts scatterplots of four genes from the New Set 1. Figure 1 clearly reveals that the genes FCGRT (770394), WAS (236282), MAP1B (629896), and PSEN2 (789253) have very strong EWS, BL, NB, RMS class specific signatures, respectively.

Next we describe the results with the re-sampling based method. Table 6 lists the top 20 genes along with the average gate opening values. It may be noted that only 2 of the original seven genes appear in the list of 20 (marked by asterisk). Inspection of the scatterplots (not shown here) of the 20 genes suggests that among these 20 genes there are 2 genes with class specific signature for EWS, 3 for RMS, 3 for BL, and 3 for NB groups. Table 7 displays the average prediction accuracies using the top 7 (gate opening > 0.1), 10 (gate opening > 0.09), 14 (gate opening > 0.08), and 19 (gate opening > 0.07) genes in the list of 20 genes (Table 6). Table 7 shows that increasing the number of genes beyond 10 makes the average performance poorer. This poor performance could be because of interaction between genes. So we experiment with just four genes (one gene for each class) and eight genes (two genes for each class) and Table 8 shows that with four genes the average performance of the classifiers is better than the results reported in Table 7. Moreover, increasing the number of genes to 8 improves the overall average prediction accuracies marginally but the performance for the EWS class improves significantly. This motivated us to use two genes for the EWS class and one gene each for the remaining classes leading to five genes as shown in Table 9. Average prediction accuracies with these are about 90% which is better than the results reported in Table 7 and Table 8. Note that these five genes are important discriminators for these four childhood cancers because four of the five are reported by several authors as important (Table 9), while the remaining one, WAS, is also found important in [4].

4 Conclusions

In an earlier study [6] we identified seven good biomarkers for the SRBCT group of cancers. The method in [6] used a modified form of the multilayer neural network and consequently different trials of the network may lead to different sets of genes. Moreover, usually expression data are in very high dimension with very few samples from each class. Often the number of samples from different classes may vary significantly making the neural network outcome biased to one or more classes. Here first using correlation analysis we have found other distinct sets of seven markers with almost equal or marginally better performance compared to the original set of seven genes. To address the other issues we have proposed a re-sampling based method. Although we have used a simple aggregation scheme for the gate opening values, this opens up possibilities of developing other, perhaps more useful, aggregation schemes. In this investigation we identified a set of five genes with quite good prediction accuracies. However, such a small set of genes has practically no redundancy and consequently diagnostic systems designed using so few genes may fail with minor error in the test data.

References

1. Efron, B., Tibshirani, R.J.: An Introduction to the Bootstrap. Chapman and Hall, Boca Raton (1993)
2. Fu, L.M., Fu-Liu, C.S.: Evaluation of Gene Importance in Microarray Data Based upon Probability of Selection. BMC Bioinformatics 6, 67 (2005)
3. Golub, T.R., Slonim, D.K., Tamayo, P., Huard, C., Gaasenbeek, M., Mesirov, J.P., Coller, H., Loh, M.L., Downing, J.R., Caligiuri, M.A., Bloomfield, C.D., Lander, E.S.: Molecular Classification of Cancer: Class Discovery and Class Prediction by Gene Expression Monitoring. Science 286, 531–537 (1999)
4. Hong, H., Tong, W., Perkins, R., Fang, H., Xie, Q., Shi, L.: Multiclass Decision Forest – A Novel Pattern Recognition Method for Multiclass Classification in Microarray Data Analysis. DNA and Cell Biology 23(10), 685–694 (2004)
5. Khan, J., Wei, J.S., Ringner, M., Saal, L.H., Ladanyi, M., Westermann, F., Berthold, F., Schwab, M., Antonescu, C.R., Peterson, C., Meltzer, P.S.: Classification and Diagnostic Prediction of Cancers Using Gene Expression Profiling and Artificial Neural Networks. Nature Medicine 7, 673–679 (2001)
6. Pal, N.R., Aguan, K., Sharma, A., Amari, S.I.: Discovering Biomarkers from Gene Expression Data for Predicting Cancer Subgroups Using Neural Networks and Relational Fuzzy Clustering. BMC Bioinformatics 8, 5 (2007)
7. Pomeroy, S.L., Tamayo, P., Gaasenbeek, M., Sturla, L.M., Angelo, M., McLaughlin, M.E., Kim, J.Y., Goumnerova, L.C., Black, P.M., Lau, C., Allen, J.C., Zagzag, D., Olson, J.M., Curran, T., Wetmore, C., Biegel, J.A., Poggio, T., Mukherjee, S., Rifkin, R., Califano, A., Stolovitzky, G., Louis, D.N., Mesirov, J.P., Lander, E.S., Golub, T.R.: Prediction of Central Nervous System Embryonal Tumour Outcome Based on Gene Expression. Nature 415, 436–442 (2002)
8. Tibshirani, R., Hastie, T., Narasimhan, B., Chu, G.: Diagnosis of Multiple Cancer Types by Shrunken Centroids of Gene Expression. Proc. Natl. Acad. Sci. 99(10), 6567–6572 (2002)

Model Screening: How to Choose the Best Fitting Regression Model?

Stefan W. Roeder[1], Matthias Richter[1], and Olf Herbarth[1,2]

[1] UFZ – Centre for Environmental Research Leipzig-Halle Ltd.,
Department Human Exposure Research/Epidemiology,
D - 04318 Leipzig, Germany
{stefan.roeder, matthias.richter, olf.herbarth}@ufz.de
[2] University of Leipzig, Faculty of Medicine,
D - 04103 Leipzig, Germany

Abstract. The problem space in epidemiological research is characterized by large datasets with many variables as candidates for logistic regression model building. Out of these variables the variable combinations which form a sufficient logistic regression model have to be selected. Usually methods like stepwise logistic regres`sion apply.

These methods deliver suboptimal results in most cases, because they cannot screen the entire problem space which is formed by different variable combinations with their resulting case set. Screening the entire problem space causes an enormous effort in computing power. Furthermore the resulting models have to be judged. This paper describes an approach for calculating the complete problem space using a computer grid as well as quality indicators for judgement of every particular model in order to find the best fitting models.

We are using this system for epidemiological studies addressing specific problems in human epidemiology.

Keywords: model screening, logistic regression, computer grid.

1 Introduction

Building of logistic regression models requires the screening of many potential models for finding a plausible solution. Use of step forward/step backward methods [6] is the state-of-the-art method for investigation of these variable combinations. Combinatorial explosion leads to a high number of possible models. Therefore we looked for a solution which enables us to calculate quality indicators for these models in order to select the models with highest quality.

This paper introduces a method for calculation and quality criteria for selection of best regression models in epidemiological studies using a computer grid.

Investigation in genetic epidemiology requires dealing with a large number of variables. These variables are combined with each other and regression models are built. The objective is to find sufficient models in problem space. Subset selection is also possible.

If these requirements should be achieved, a large number of potential models are resulting. All these models have to be calculated for selection of sufficient models.

M. Ishikawa et al. (Eds.): ICONIP 2007, Part II, LNCS 4985, pp. 876–883, 2008.

"The required computational resources are often not available at the labs that carry out such studies. This, and the need to integrate inherently distributed systems into workflows, has made it necessary to investigate Grid solutions ..." [1, p. 1023].

"The key concept [of grid computing] is the ability to negotiate resource-sharing arrangements among a set of participating parties (providers and customers) and then to use the resulting resource pool for some purpose." [3]

Many approaches to implement grid systems exist. The complexity of them is adequate to the addressed problem (e.g. GriPhyN [4], EU Data Grid [2]). The subject of our system was as low complexity as possible.

2 Material and Methods

The problem space is defined by a set of possible logistic regression models consisting of varying subsets of variables.

Every combination represents a complete model defined by a dependent variable, an independent variable, a set of confounder variables, a set of selection conditions based on selection variables, and their respective values.

If multiple independent variables are under consideration, investigators can handle them by multiplying them. The resulting product is considered as sole independent variable in further steps.

The question is: "How to find sufficient models?" A widely used approach, if the outcome variable is dichotomous, is stepwise logistic regression (see section 2.2).

2.1 Logistic Regression Model

A logistic regression model is defined on base of a linear regression model. In contrast to linear regression, the probability of a dichotomous dependent variable is predicted. To describe this probability, logit transformation is used.

It's a matter of common knowledge, that each logistic regression model can be described with the following equation [6].

$$p(DV) = e^{a+\sum_{1}^{n} x_n * IV_n} \tag{1}$$

The regression equation is formed by a dependent variable (DV) on the left side and a set of independent variables (IV) and confounders on the right side of the equation. The logit transformation is carried out, in order to the exponentiation of the Euler number e with the term of linear regression.

2.2 Stepwise Logistic Regression

The background of model screening for logistic regression models lies in stepwise logistic regression.

This procedure starts with an initial model (which can include all selected variables, or only the constant term ("a" in equation 1)). By means of stepwise inclusion or exclusion of independent variables new models are constructed and the quality indicator (significance level of each independent variable; see section 2.4) is measured.

This quality indictor serves as entry or removal criterion for the variable under consideration in the current step. The process terminates if no further stepping is possible (i.e. all possible combinations are calculated) or a defined number of steps is reached.

If the interactions between independent variables and dependent variable are not well understood, then the use of stepwise regression is a good idea [6]. In this case, stepwise regression can act as a hypothesis generating method and deliver a subset of possibly good models.

Besides the number of models formed by complete enumeration of all possible variable combinations, additional methods are used to improve the specificity of the resulting models, such as stratification [5, p. 244]. Stratification is desirable, because each stratum can cause completely different models. On the other hand, stratification reduces the number of cases. In extreme situations, the maximum likelihood algorithm behind logistic regression does not converge. In this case, there is no analyzable result for the model. Inclusion of stratification into the consideration process causes an increase in the number of possible combinations.

If the number of possible variable combinations exceeds a certain limit, stepwise regression is no longer suitable, because it covers only a subset of combinations. The tremendous number of possible models leads to the use of a grid architecture ([8], [9]) for calculating the quality indicators for these models. Our approach enables us to calculate the complete problem space for a given set of variables.

2.3 Handling of Missing Values

Missing cases occur in most scientific data sets. Possible causes are: measurement equipment was out of order, sample material was lost or sample concentration was below detection limit.

For handling of missing cases two methods are in use: casewise deletion if a missing case occurs and replacement of missing values by a substitute.

For substitute replacement this substitute usually is the average of the values of the remaining cases in this variable. The number of cases remains the original one. Therefore different models with this method for handling of missings are comparable.

For casewise deletion this comparability is not given. If the initial dataset contains many missing values in the variables under consideration and these missing values occur not in the same cases, casewise deletion yields a different set of cases for every variable combination. This causes the problem that different models are not directly comparable, because each model consists of different cases.

In our approach we calculate both models: The one with missing values replaced by average value and the one with casewise deletion of missing values. The quality indicators of both variants are stored for later analysis.

2.4 Quality Indicators for Potential Models

Usually, model quality is measured as significance level of the main independent variable of the logistic regression model. This is adequate if model calculation comprises only a few models.

If there are many different models, the researcher has to decide which models are worth further investigation. For this reason, a quality indicator for ranking the results is needed.

Besides the significance level of the main independent variable some other parameters of each model can serve as quality estimator:

- size of the confidence interval;

Confidence interval size depends on the number of cases in the respective model. Higher case counts yield to smaller confidence intervals, which are favourable.

- number of significant independent variables;

Comparison of a large number of different models requires information on the number of significant independent variables. Models with the highest number of significant variables are worth further investigation.

- number of confounding variables;

The number of confounding variables is determined by the current variable combination. Sometimes a fixed set of counfounders is desirable, but a different set of confounders leads to higher model quality. In such cases the investigator can use this quality criterion to decide for the variable set, which better fits its needs.

- number of cases;

Number of cases is determined by the chosen method for missing handling. If casewise deletion of missings was chosen, then most variable combinations lead to different number of cases. If missings were replaced by mean or any other value, all variable combinations have the same case count. Usually higher case count describes the better model, but restrictions from the casewise deletion of missings apply.

- significance level of the constant term;

Usually the significance level of the constant term ("a" in equation 1) is an indicator for hidden effects. This means if there are effects in the model, which are not described by the included variables. So better models do have an insignificant constant term.

- hit rate (divided into 0 and 1);

The hit rate is calculated by comparing the predicted output of the regression model with the measured outcome in real life. It is the fraction of correct predicted cases, separately calculated for outcome=0 and outcome=1. This separation is needed, because in many cases there are only a few cases with outcome=1. If one calculates the overall hit rate in such a case it is very easy to achieve a high value. This high value is misleading to a good model, because it is very easy to gain a high hit rate if most outcomes are zero. The few but important cases with outcome=1 are then ignored.

All models with at least a feasible result are marked with a flag as possibly good model. Out of the top N of possibly good models, the sufficient models are manually selected. N is selected by the investigator needs.

Each quality criterion is stored in a separate database field. Thus, it is possible to apply different weights for each criterion into an overall weighting.

Sometimes there are no models which fit the desired quality criteria. In such cases the investigator is able to lower the limit for model inclusion into possible good models by changing the inclusion criteria to a least stringent condition. Typically those models are no longer significant, but in some cases they can reveal a trend.

2.5 Definition of Combinatorial Packages

The whole set of possible models for a given dependent variable with their assigned independent variables, confounders and selection criteria is called combinatorial package. The following figure shows an example:

Dependent Variable	Independent Variables	Selection Condition	Result
423	469	smoking=1	0,51
423	470	smoking=1	0,03
423	469 470	smoking=1	0,82
423	469	infection=1	0,9
423	469 470	infection=1	0,04

Fig. 1. Combinatorial package (fragment)

The number of models to be built depends on the number of independent variables assigned to a dependent variable as well as on the number of different values stored in each independent variable. If a selection variable is used, the problem space is increased by another dimension.

2.6 Model Processing

Combinatorial packages are calculated using a computer grid system. The database process of the problem task database (see **Fig. 2**) is running as a central instance on a dedicated machine.

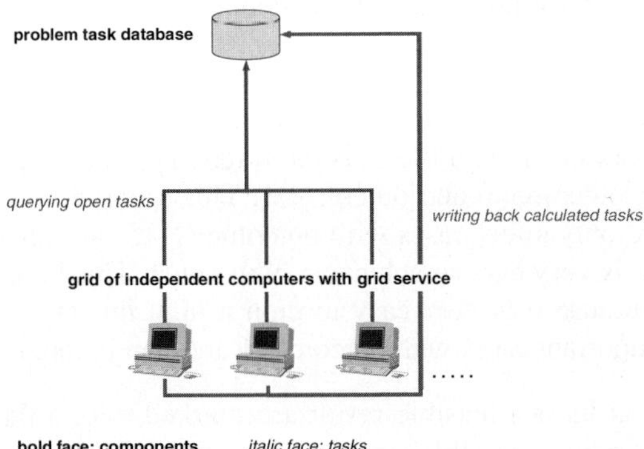

Fig. 2. System architecture

Clients make their requests for pending combinatorial packages directly to the database. There is a controlling of combinatorial packages in progress using a simple flag mechanism. New attempts to get combinatorial packages are restricted by "checkedOut=0 AND calculated=0". The client sets the "checkedout"-flag at the moment it gets the package for calculation. After writing the result, this flag is set back and the "calculated"-flag is set. Using this simple method we ensure, that no combinatorial package is left out and no package is calculated twice (except for cross verification purposes).

A typical run follows these steps:

1. selection and preprocessing the data;
2. definition of dependent variable;
3. definition of independent variables;
4. definition of adjustment variables;
5. definition of selection variables;
6. generating of potential models;
7. calculation of quality indicators for potential models;
8. review of models with high quality indicators;
9. selection of real good models.

Step 7 is the most time consuming step and therefore done by a computer grid. The result after step 8 is a set of selected models with a high quality indicator. These models are to be considered for further investigation and explanation.

2.7   Partitioning of Problem Space

For parallel calculation, the problem space is subdivided into several partitions. Each partition consists of several models to analyze and is calculated on another machine of the computer grid.

It is possible to assign different priority states for each analysis (see section 0). This enables us to process high priority packages faster than others.

The number of models in a partition depends on grid size, size of problem space and on connection speed between the grid computers.

A large grid requires small partitions for better distribution, whereas a slow grid uses large partitions for less communication overhead. If the problem space is large, small partitions for faster processing through more clients are recommended.

Depending on the current workload of the grid nodes and on the priority level of pending combinatorial packages, the combinatorial packages are distributed over the grid. Low workload of a node results in a higher number of assigned packages. High priority level leads to urgent calculation throughout the grid.

2.8   Error Handling

Sometimes a model does not converge and there are no estimates for quality parameters. These models are marked as calculated with errors. So investigators can easy identify them.

Error handling is necessary on two levels: First level errors are communication errors. These are not critical, because the calculation results are not affected. In case of a communication error the client waits a randomly chosen time span before its try to reconnect.

Second level errors are calculation errors. They occur if the maximum likelihood algorithm did not converge. In this case there is no model for the given variable combination. A recalculation is not necessary. If there were other errors, the affected model has to be recalculated. The related combinatorial package is rescheduled for recalculation on another machine.

Using this method we ensure, that errors are not misleadingly accepted as correct results. As an additional precaution a subset of already calculated models can be rescheduled for calculating [7, p. 587].

2.9 Data Structure

The grid is working on top of the data structure shown in **Fig. 3**. Central ancestor is the table "analysis". Each definition of a combinatorial package (see 2.5) is represented by a record in this table. Each package is represented by an identifier, which is used to assign the corresponding models from table "combinations". The "priority" attribute is used to set a execution priority for each analysis.

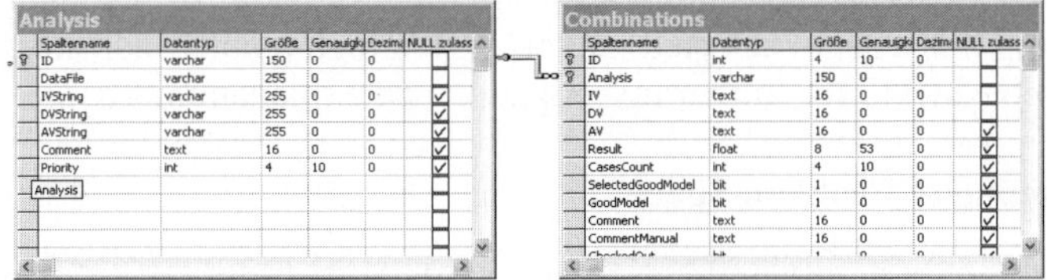

Fig. 3. Data structure of potential models

Adjacent to this table the detail table "combinations" is attached: It is responsible for storing of distinct models with their variables, selection conditions and calculation results.

The table "combinations" holds information about the quality indicators (see section 2.4) of the model and the selection as sufficient model. If required, the user can write down comments for every model.

Ranking of models is done by selecting the models according to the chosen combination of quality criteria.

3 Conclusion

Using the described approach, we are able to calculate the complete enumeration of possible models under consideration. The described quality criteria allow selection of best fitting models for further investigation.

Many calculated models in genetic epidemiology gave us the insight that we were unable to find most significant models using classic step forward/step backward calculations.

The shown approach enables us to generate logistic regression models using the following advantages:

-    easier and faster calculation and selection of logistic regression models for a given problem space;
-    cross validation of real data using variable descriptions;

- we are able to ensure that no other logistic regression models from the problem space than the selected sufficient models have significant results;
- ranking of calculated models by using the described quality indicators.

References

[1] Dubitzky, W., Mccourt, D., Galushka, M., Romberg, M., Schuller, B.: Grid-Enabled Data Warehousing For Molecular Engineering. Parallel Computing 30, 1019–1035 (2004)
[2] Eu Data Grid (05-22-2007),
    `http://eu-datagrid.web.cern.ch/eu-datagrid/`
[3] Foster, I.: What Is The Grid? A Three Point Checklist Global Grid Forum (05-15-2007),
    `http://www-fp.mcs.anl.gov/~foster/articles/whatisthegrid.pdf`
[4] Grid Physics Network (05-22-2007), `http://www.griphyn.org/`
[5] Harrell, F.E.: Regression Modeling Strategies. Springer, New York (2001)
[6] Hosmer, D.W., And Lemeshow, S.: Applied Logistic Regression, 2nd edn. Wiley, New York (2000)
[7] Myers, D.S., And Cummings, M.P.: Necessity Is The Mother Of Invention: A Simple Grid Computing System Using Commodity Tools. J. Parallel Distrib. Comput. 63, 578–589 (2003)
[8] The Globus Toolkit (05-25-2007), `http://www.globus.org`
[9] The Unicore Project (05-25-2007), `http://unicore.sourceforge.net`

Japanese Neuroinformatics Node and Platforms

Shiro Usui[1], Teiichi Furuichi[1], Hiroyoshi Miyakawa[2], Hidetoshi Ikeno[3],
Soichi Nagao[1], Toshio Iijima[4], Yoshimi Kamiyama[5],
Tadashi Isa[6], Ryoji Suzuki[7], and Hiroshi Ishikane[1]

[1] RIKEN Brain Science Institute
[2] Tokyo University of Pharmacy and Life Sciences
[3] School of Human Science and Environment, University of Hyogo
[4] Graduate School of Life Sciences, Tohoku University
[5] Information Science and Technology, Aichi Prefectural University
[6] National Institute for Physiological Sciences
[7] Kanazawa Institute of Technology

Abstract. Neuroinformatics is a new discipline which combines neuroscience with information technology. The Japan-Node of INCF was established at NIJC of RIKEN Brain Science Institute to address the task of integrating outstanding neuroscience researches in Japan. Each platform subcommittee from selected research areas develops a platform on the base-platform XooNIps. NIJC operates the J-Node portal to make platform resources open accessible in public. We introduce our concepts and the scheme of J-Node including nine platforms.

Keywords: Neuroinformatics, INCF, J-Node, XooNIps.

1 Introduction

The task of understanding the human brain is subject to tight focus and specialization in neuroscience. This fragmentation necessitated the synthesis and integration of research resources combined with information science and technology, which converged to the new discipline, neuroinformatics (NI), with the intra/international organized framework. INCF (International Neuroinformatics Coordinating Facility)[1] was established to facilitate the development of neuroinformatics. The Japan Node (J-Node), among the thirteen National Nodes of INCF, aims to improve the utility and availability of the vast quantities of high quality data, models, and tools developed by brain and neuroscience researchers in Japan. We introduce the nine platforms (PFs) in Section 2, which are or will be accessible through J-Node[2] .

The available resources of J-Node are hosted by NIJC (Neuroinformatics Japan Center) of RIKEN Brain Science Institute (BSI). NIJC provides the NI base platform XooNIps [3] developed by NI-Team at RIKEN BSI for these

---

[1] http://www.incf.org/
[2] http://www.neuroinf.jp/
[3] http://xoonips.sourceforge.jp/

M. Ishikawa et al. (Eds.): ICONIP 2007, Part II, LNCS 4985, pp. 884–894, 2008.

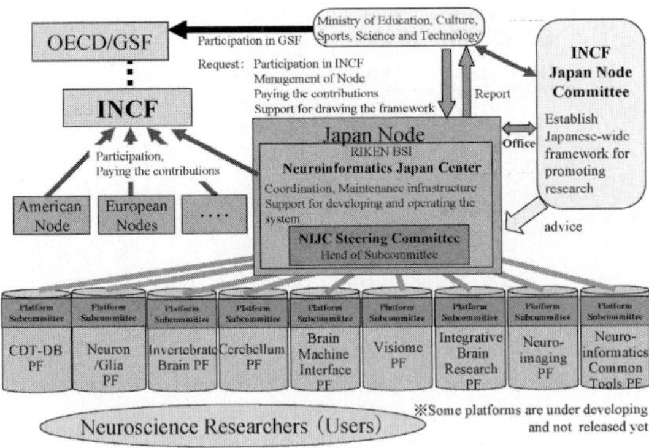

Fig. 1. Japan-Node scheme with INCF

databases and is designing the NI infrastructure in Japan. It also facilitates the cooperation and distribution of information stored in those databases (fig.1).

2 Overview of the INCF J-Node Platforms

2.1 Cerebellar Development Transcriptome Database

The brain is the ultimate genetic system to which a large number of genes are devoted. In the post-genomic sequencing era, it is now possible to analyze brain development and function at a whole genomic level. To elucidate the genetic basis for mouse cerebellar development, as a model system, we plan to analyze all of the transcriptional events (i.e., the transcriptome) responsible for developmental stages. Informatics provides a powerful means for sharing and mining data as well as systematizing data. We then developed the Cerebellar Development Transcriptome Database (CDT-DB) by combining the large datasets of the expression profile information and the relevant bioinformatics (fig.2). As a result, the combining genome-wide neuroscience research and informatics research not only allows us to delineate the complex genetic mechanisms underpinning cerebellar development but also provides a tool for sharing and mining of our large datasets. [1] (http://www.cdtdb.brain.riken.jp/)

[PF MEMBERS: Teiichi Furuich, Akira Sato[1], Noriyuki Morita[2], Tetsushi Sadakata[3], and Yo Shinoda[3]. ([1]RIKEN GSC, [2]Mimasaka University, [3]RIKEN BSI)]

2.2 Neuron-Glia PF: Neuroinformatics at the Cellular and Local Network Level

A brain is a highly complex and dynamical system composed of neuronal and glial cells. To understand how brains work, we need to understand how these cells and the networks of these cells work. At the cellular level and local network level, an immense number of experimental findings have been accumulated in the last

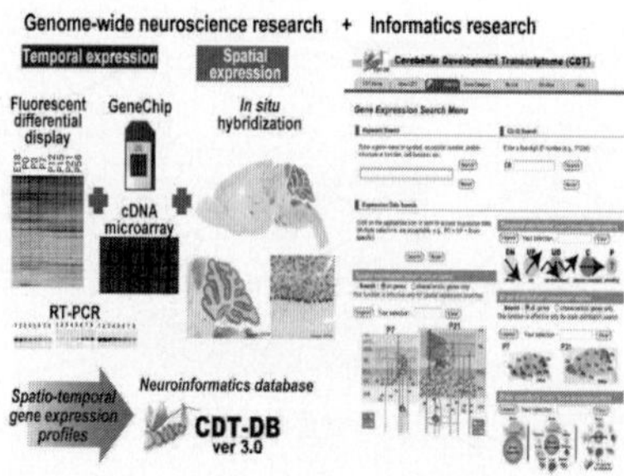

Fig. 2. CDT-DB

few decades. With regard to the basic principle on neural information processing, however, we have not achieved much during the last 100 years since Cajal's neuron doctrine. To go forward, we need to share newly accumulated knowledge and new ideas, and integrate them. To do so, we proposed to give mathematical model descriptions of new findings and ideas, and built an platform, an infrastructure on which we can share models and data. Model description would not only help sharing findings, but would help intense collaboration of experimental and theoretical researchers, which will be a hatchery for novel pictures of neuronal information processing.

This platform makes use of the base platform XooNIps. Registered users are allowed to submit computational models, experimental data, tools, notes etc to the platform. Editorial board would check submitted contents, and if the contents meet criteria, they will be made public. Submission of models and data suitable for collaboration of experimental and theoretical researchers, and those obtained by collaborations of experimental and theoretical researchers are en couraged. Registered users can set up groups in which group members can share contents only among groups without making them public. This functionality helps collaboration of researchers.

As shown in Fig.3 and 4 for examples, the change in membrane potential of CA1 pyramidal neurons due to applied extra-cellular electric field was measured by use of fast voltage-imaging technique. Compartmental models with simple and realistic morphology were used to analyze the data.

[PF MEMBERS: Hiroyoshi Miyakawa, Toru Aonishi[1], Kiyohisa Natsume[2], Haruo Kasai[3] and Ryuichi Shigemoto[4]. ([1]Tokyo Institute of Technology, [2]Kyusyu Institute of Technology, [3]University of Tokyo, [4]RIKEN BSI)]

2.3   Invertebrate Brain PF

We are currently constructing a websites, Invertebrate Brain PF (IVB-PF), for sharing such resources as the physiological and behavioral data from insects and other invertebrate animals. The platform was developed based on a Content Management System (CMS), XOOPS (The eXtensible Object Oriented Portal System). It is a widely used, open source CMS, coded in PHP. XOOPS can be run on many operating systems under Apache for WWW server, MySQL for

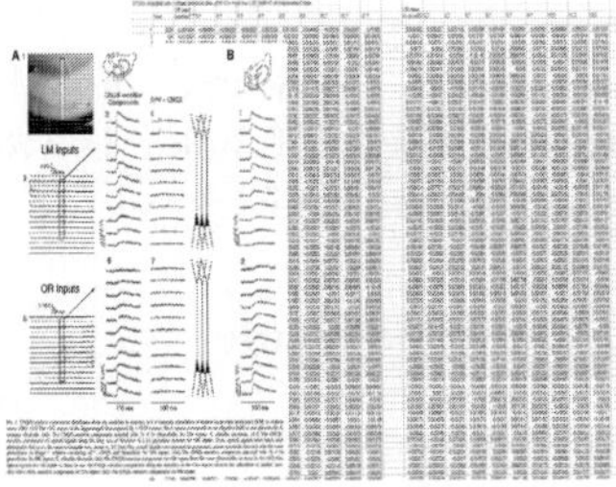

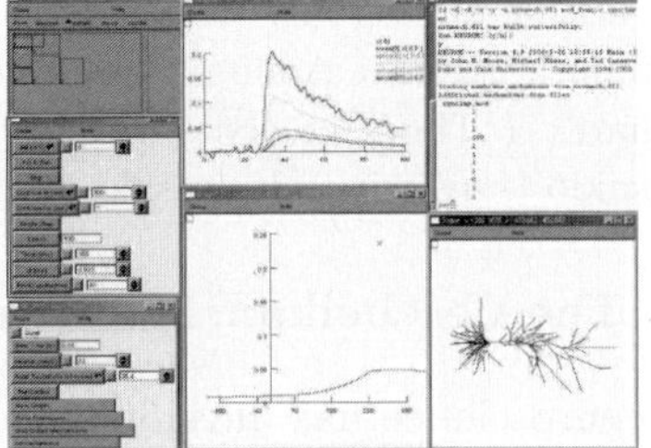

Fig. 3. Experimental data used for a figure in a published article

Fig. 4. A simulation used for an analysis reported in a published article

database and PHP for script language. Many valuable functions for managing portal site, such as scheduler and message board, are available as open source modules on the Internet. In the site, the XooNIps module manages user accounts because the original XOOPS user accounting system was not sufficient for the site's operational policy (more information about the user was required by the site). Our originally developed modules, CosmoDB and PubMedPDF, manage the contents of the site. For example, Invertebrate Brain Gallery, which is a collection of images of nervous systems in various invertebrates, is constructed and managed by the CosmoDB module. Literary information about invertebrate behavior and physiology is collecting and managing by the PubMedPDF module. Original image data of invertebrate neurons, for example, interneuron of antennal lobe of moth brain, are collected on the site.

In our platform project, a laboratory based database system, XAMPP/XLP, is also developed to manage and share the research resource inside the laboratory. XAMPP is an integrated server package of Apache, mySQL, PHP and Perl. It can easily run on various operating system, Windows, Linux and so on. Our package is provided with CosmoDB and PubMedPDF with XAMPP. Application software in collaboration with this database package is also developed and distributed on our site. It is a software for automatic registration of sequence of images, which is scanned by Laser Scanning Microscope. It could be very useful for experimentalists because they wouldn't need to consider data transformation and management. In near feature, we will provide data transfer functions from XAMPP/XLP database to the IVB-PF. It would be very important to integrate and publish various contents on the platform. XML based descriptions, such as NeuroML, will be applied to use as a common language to connect between private and public database systems.

It must be important for the research in the various dimension to be provided convenient server environment in order to collect high-standard research results in the field of invertebrate science. We believe that the aggregation and sharing of research resources can accelerate the progress of science. Improvement of these database tools and applications in the neuroscience fields can become cornerstone for research undertaken with information technologies. [2] (http://platform.invbrain.neuroinf.jp/)

[PF MEMBERS: Ryohei Kanzaki[1], Hidetoshi Ikeno, Nobuyuki Matsui[2], Makoto Mizunami[3], Hitoshi Aonuma[4], Masakazu Takahata[4], Kouji Yasuyama[5], and Fumio Yokohari[6]. ([1]The University of Tokyo, [2]University of Hyogo, [3]Tohoku University, [4]Hokkaido University, [5]Kawasaki Medical University, [6]Fukuoka University)]

2.4   The Cerebellum: Its Structure and Functional Role

The neuroscience has developed dramatically since 1960s, when the microelectrodes technique became widely utilized to investigate the mystery of the brain. The cerebellum has attracted the interests of researchers both in the experimental and theoretical studies for more than 5 decades, because of its unique structure and roles in motor learning. The Marr-Albus-Ito theory on the cerebellar computational rule, and the discovery of plasticity of long-term depression (LTD) at the parallel fiber-Purkinje cell synapses gave a large impact on many researchers studying the cerebellum. Here, we open a new website for the cerebellum research to widely distribute the knowledge to the general audience in order to promote further progress on the cerebellar research.

Our Cerebellum PF is a database / repository of the all kinds of information on the cerebellum. The platform will provide mini-reviews on a history of the cerebellar research and the basic concepts of the cerebellar structure and function, references and images, experimental data for the modeling, source codes of neural network models, and other tools for the study of the cerebellum. The platform users can download and use its contents freely. They can also upload and open their own contents on the platform by a simple procedure with the approval of the platform committee. Especially we will focus on the two important cerebellum-dependent experimental paradigms, i.e., adaptation of the eye movements and eyeblink conditioning. One can easily simulate the changes of dynamics of the cerebellar circuits during the vestibule-ocular reflex (VOR) adaptation, and eyeblink conditioning, and also can modify the network structure or cell parameters to add new features on her/his own computers for further investigation, using source codes written on MATLAB Simulink, GENESIS, NEURON, and C. For beginners of the cerebellum research, the cerebellar platform will thus provide software and tools that assist their researches. Selected references would be informative and useful to catch the general view of the cerebellum. The cerebellum PF also targets graduate / undergraduate students, and any new comers to the field, to help them by providing good educational materials and advice. These materials may be used in lectures and seminars to assist students in learning about the cerebellum and to have fun in them.

We propose that many people with various different viewpoints join the platform, and increase and polish its contents. This platform will become more attractive if more contents are available, and more discussion on them is promoted. We are looking for people who contribute their cerebellum-related contents to the platform. We expect that the functions of the cerebellum from the motor learning to cognitive functions will be further clarified from a wide range of viewpoints, including neurobiology and computational engineering through this platform.

[PF MEMBERS: Soichi Nagao, Yutaka Hirata[1], Tadashi Yamazaki[2], and Kenji Yamamoto[3]. ([1]Chubu University, [2]RIKEN BSI, [3]National Institute for Radiological Sciences)]

2.5 Brain-Machine Interface PF

The brain-machine interface (BMI) is the interface in which mechanical devices provide sensory input to the brain, or are controlled by the motor output signals recorded in the brain. Modern attempts have been driven by concrete technological and clinical goals. The most advanced of these has brought the perception of sound to thousands of deaf individuals by means of electrodes implanted in the cochlea. Similar trials are underway to provide images to the visual cortex via video cameras or artificial retina, and to allow the brain of paralyzed patients to re-establish control of the external environment by extracted control signals either from surface electroencephalographic (EEG) signals or from electrodes implanted in the cerebral cortex. Due to recent breakthroughs in device technology and implantation techniques, a basic framework is now sufficiently developed to allow design of systems level interface strategies producing robust, scalable BMIs that adapt quickly to optimize information transfer at the interface. Although the evolution of BMI is likely to remain driven by important clinical and practical goals, it will also offer a unique family of tools for challenging some of the most fundamental ideas of modern neuroscience. In fact, research on BMI can be successful to the extent that we understand how sensory-motor transformations are learned and encoded by the nervous system.

BMI-PF is a database of BMI researches covering the research fields of neuroscience, computational theory, robotics etc., which allows all registered users to share experimental data, mathematical models and tools for various researches about BMI. The aim of this platform is to provide organically linked information about BMI to researchers of the field inside and outside the country and support researches to develop their study or understand about BMI. By using a clickable map of research sites about BMI, users can figure out trends of BMI studies around the world. Main contents of BMI-PF are as follows: **1) Physiology;** This content include physiological data, such as brain activity, muscle activity and motion picture of experiments. For example, movies file which includes an image of an arm movement of a monkey and simultaneously recorded unit activity of M1 neurons is available. **2) Computer theory;** this content is about theoretical approach to the brain activity. Computer programs for simulation of motion of arms are available. In addition, programs involving a development of an artificial arm using myoelectric signals or an interface of flexible robot control will be published. **3) Robotics;** this content is about the control engineering based on experimental data of brain activity and muscle activity. Experimental data, programs, and motion pictures are available. **4) Document search;** users can search for papers about BMI or involved studies. Each paper has original tags, for example, recording method and subject, for easy searching. **5) The future of BMI;** in this content, users can have access to the information concern of the future investigation of BMI. Registered users can also propose their vision.

6) Research Sites; registered users can search for research institutes investigating BMI from the world map. At present, Japan, North America and Europe are covered. Contact address and URL of websites of each research institute are available. (http://platform.bmi.neuroinf.jp/)

[PF MEMBERS: Toshio Iijima, Takahiro Ishikawa[1], Ken-ichiro Tsutsui[1], Yasuharu Koike[2], Yoshio Sakurai[3], and Hajime Mushiake[4]. ([1]Tohoku University, [2]Tokyo Technology University, [3]Kyoto University, [4]Tohoku University School of Medicine)]

2.6   Visiome PF

Vision science increasingly uses computational tools to assist in the exploration and interpretation of complex visual functions and phenomena. There is a critical need for a database where published data can be archived so that they can be accessed, uploaded, downloaded, and tested. Visiome PF is being developed to answer this need as a web-based database system with a variety of digital research resources in vision science.

Visiome PF has been designed to be a site with reusable digital resources [3]. The platform system has been developing with a base platform system, XooNIps and accessible at J-Node. At the left block on the top page is Index Tree section which allows navigation by item type such as mathematical model, experimental data, visual stimulus and analytical tool. For example, clicking "Model" generates lists of all available models in the central block. These lists contain links to information pages that describe individual items and allow users to download items that are of interest. At the right block of the welcome page is "XooNIps Login". Many of the items may be browsed and downloaded as a guest user. However, other items may require a registered user status for downloading. Contributing new items also requires a user account.

Visiome PF has 9 basic items, Binder, Model, Data, Simulus, Tool, Presentation, Paper, Book and URL. Since reproducibility is a key principle of the scientific method, it is essential that published results be testable by other researchers using the same methods. However, for example, most modeling articles do not contain enough information that is necessary for readers to be able to resimulate and verify the results due to lack of initial conditions, incorrect parameter values and so on. Visiome PF has been designed to make the items reusable. The platform accepts archive files (in zip, lzh or other compression formats) including any formats of model, data or stimulus with files of explanatory figures, program sources, readme and other related files. The information in the readme file includes a concise statement of the purpose of the item and how to use the files in the archive. Visiome Binder is a virtual binder and makes collections of any registered items organized and packaged as a single item. It is useful for providing suggestive reading list for students, a collection of models and data with a particular interest, a collection of educative movies in vision science and so on.

Visiome PF is still evolving, so there are several issues to be solved. One of important issues is an incentive for submitting the works to Visiome PF. The ranking function has been implemented in XooNIps and the ranking in Visiome

PF is displayed at the top page. We still need to improve the functions of Visiome PF to make it useful to the vision science community. (http://platform.visiome. neuroinf.jp/)

[PF MEMBERS: Yoshimi Kamiyama, Shigeki Nakauchi[1], and Shin'ya Nishida[2]. ([1]Toyohashi University of Technology, [2]NTT Communication Science Laboratories)]

2.7   Integrative Brain Research Project Database

The Integrative Brain Research Project (IBR) is the project supported by a Grant-in-Aid for Scientific Research on Priority Areas from the Ministry of Education, Culture, Sports, Science and Technology (MEXT) of Japan. It was initiated in the FY 2005 and will continue until the FY 2009. The whole budget size is about 2.3 billion JPY. The whole group is composed of 5 subgroups, (1) Integrative brain research, headed by Dr. Jun Tanji of Tamagawa University, (2) System study on higher-order brain functions, headed Dr. Minoru Kimura of Kyoto Prefectural Medical University, (3) Elucidation of neural network function in the brain headed by Dr. Masanobu Kano of Osaka University, (4) Molecular Brain Sciences headed by Dr. Masayoshi Mishina of Tokyo University, and (5) Research on pathomechanisms of brain disorders, headed by Dr. Nobuyuki Nukina of RIKEN Brain Science Institute. The whole group is comprised of about 300 principal investigators, and their work field ranges from molecular neuroscience, cellular neuroscience to systems neuroscience, non-invasive human brain imaging and computational neuroscience. A major concept of composing such a large research group is to facilitate interdisciplinary research by encouraging interaction and communication between neuroscientists with different disciplines inside the group. To facilitate the interaction and communication between the PIs and collaborators belonging to this project, the website of this project was opened to public [4] , which includes announcement of various activities and is also linked to social networking site (SNS) of neuroscientists. The project has started to construct the database of the scientific outcome of the researches conducted by members of the group. The database committee of the project is planning to construct two different ways of database. One is the topdown type of the database. For this, the database committee will collect the outcome of the research of individual PIs and will publish these research outcomes on IBR-PF of NIJC. In addition, the project constructed the personal information of neuroscientists. The researchers database is comprised of information of neuroscientists, mainly PIs of the project and their collaborators, including their research topics, scientific interest and publication lists. Another type of the database is the bottom-up type. We are inviting the members of the project to construct the database which will be useful for other members of the project. One of the database that has already launched is the mouse behavioral phenotype database constructed by Dr. Tsuyoshi Miyakawa of Kyoto University, who has just promoted to a professor of Fujita Health Science University. Dr. Miyakawa and his colleagues are working on the test battery of mouse behaviors. Behavioral phenotypes of various mouse

---

[4] http://www.togo-nou.nips.ac.jp/

lines are now available on this database. The database committee will support such self-initiated idea of database construction. The committee is hoping that the activity of SNS will facilitate such proposals. Although the activity of the project will finish in 5 years, the content will be maintained and updated by the IBR-PF committee afterwards.

[AUTHOR:Tadashi Isa]

2.8   Neuroimaging PF: NIMG-PF

Introduction: We organized NIMG-PF committee with 18 members of Japanese research sites as an activity of NIJC at RIKEN, and are constructing a database of neuroimaging, i.e., non-invasive measurements of brain functions. It will be open in this year.

NIMG-PF contents: It is desirable to collect the contents which lack in the existing databases and are useful for beginners as well as specialists of neuroimaging. We NIMG-PF committee members are registering the following contents related to various neuroimaging technologies such as MRI, MEG, EEG, PET, and NIRS, and their integrations:

- Bibliographies of major and recent research papers
- Tutorial materials such as measuring technologies, standard protocols for measurement and analysis, and sample data
- Software contents such as visualization of brain images, models, and tools
- Experimental data for papers such as raw data, stimulus data, and programs / scripts
- Related information and links

NIMG-PF system designs: We are constructing NIMG-PF based on XooNIps operated by RIKEN NIJC. Users can search and view contents by selecting either of indices, items, or keywords, where the index has three-layered hierarchical structures, with the first layer having a list: Imaging method, Tutorial, Brain function, Task, Stimulation, Brain area, Temporal and frequency component, Model, Technology, and Link.

Furthermore, we are also developing convenient visualization functions, which are useful for neuroimaging database. They are capable of an easy-to-use display of 3D brain images, and a function of search by pointing locations on the images.

NIMG-PF content registration: Until now, visualization software, bibliographies of research papers, books, tutorial videos and instructions for beginners, and documents and related materials of research reports have been registered. In addition, there is a plan of registering MEG multi-dipole analysis software and raw data of MRI and MEG.

Conclusions: In NIMG-PF, any users can search, view, and use contents as well as register their original contents to make them open. We hope that NIMG-PF will become a site where useful information gathers. [4]

[PF MEMBERS: Ryoji Suzuki, Kazuhisa Niki[1], Norio Fujimaki[2], Shinobu Masaki[3], and Kazuhisa Ichikawa[4]. ([1]National Institute of Advanced Industrial Science and Technology, [2]National Institute of Information and Communications Technology, [3]ATR-Promotions, and [4]Kanazawa Institute of Technology)]

2.9 Neuroinformatics Common Tools PF

The Neuroinformatics Common Tools (NICT) PF aims to share mathematical theory, analytical tool and NI-supporting environment. We believe that sharing common base technology for neuroscience may promote studies for not only theoretical neuroscientists but also experimental neuroscientists. In addition, by making the several analytical tools specialized for neuroscience available, it is expected that collaborated studies can be rapidly and seamlessly conducted on the Internet. At present, software tools using mathematical theories and NI-supporting environment developed for neuroscientists are being registered.

NICT-PF is now playing another role on neuroscience. Frequently, tools, source codes used for plotting result published in papers are lost because of researchers' retirement etc. To keep and share such precious treasures, we are creating laboratory digital archives on NICT-PF. We believe that this feature of NICT-PF provides further promotion of neuroscience.

The tools developed by the Laboratory for Neuroinformatics at RIKEN BSI are: 1) Customizable base platform; XooNIps, 2) Personal database software; Concierge, 3) System analysis total environment; SATELLITE, and 4) Visualization tools; Samurai-Graph. (http://platform.ni-tech.neuroinf.jp/)
[PF MEMBERS: Hiroshi Ishikane, Nilton Kamiji[1], Tomokatsu Kawakita[1], and Yoshihiro Okumura[1]. ([1]RIKEN BSI)]

3 Conclusion

NI has initiated the ground that neuroscientists are concerned with the integrating aspect of their research as well as their specific research. NIJC seeks to (1) identify the major domestic field of neuroscience for the development of platforms, (2) disseminate relevant data, and (3) develop the standard for common terminilogies and data production. The J-Node portal has expanded its platforms with increasing users of each platform. We will continue to make these efforts for the substantiality and sustainability of the NI research.

References

1. Sato, A., Morita, N., Sadakata, T., Yoshikawa, F., Shiraishi-Yamaguchi, Y., Huang, J., Shoji, S., Tomomura, M., Sato, Y., Suga, E., Sekine, Y., Kitamura, A., Shibata, Y., Furuichi, T.: Deciphering the genetic blueprint of cerebellar development by the gene expression profiling informatics. In: Pal, N.R., Kasabov, N., Mudi, R.K., Pal, S., Parui, S.K. (eds.) ICONIP 2004. LNCS, vol. 3316, pp. 880–884. Springer, Heidelberg (2004)

2. Ikeno, H., Kanzaki, R., Aonuma, H., Takahata, M., Mizunami, M., Yasuyama, K., Matsui, N., Yokohari, F., Usui, S.: Development of invertebrate brain platform: Management of research resources for invertebrate neuroscience and neuroethology. In: Ishikawa, M., Doya, K., Miyamoto, H., Yamakawa, T. (eds.) ICONIP 2007, Part II. LNCS, vol. 4985, pp. 905–914. Springer, Heidelberg (2007, this volume)
3. Usui, S.: Visiome: Neuroinformatics research in vision project. Neural Networks 16(9), 1293–1300 (2003)
4. Suzuki1, R., Niki, K., Fujimaki, N., Masaki, S., Ichikawa, K., Usui, S.: Neuro-imaging platform for neuroinformatics. In: Ishikawa, M., Doya, K., Miyamoto, H., Yamakawa, T. (eds.) ICONIP 2007, Part II. LNCS, vol. 4985, pp. 895–904. Springer, Heidelberg (2007, this volume)

Neuro-Imaging Platform for Neuroinformatics

Ryoji Suzuki[1], Kazuhisa Niki[2], Norio Fujimaki[3], Shinobu Masaki[4],
Kazuhisa Ichikawa[5], and Shiro Usui[6]

[1] Kanazawa Institute of Technology, 7-1 Ohgigaoka, Nonoichi, Ishikawa 921-8501, Japan
[2] Neuroscience Research Institute, National Institute of Advanced Industrial Science and
Technology, 1-1-1 Umezono, Tsukuba, 305-8568 Japan
[3] Biological ICT Group, National Institute of Information and Communications Technology,
588-2, Iwaoka, Iwaoka-cho, Nishi-ku, Kobe, Hyogo, 651-2492 Japan
[4] Brain Activity Imaging Center, ATR-Promotions, 2-2-2 Hikaridai, Seika-cho, Soraku-gun,
Kyoto, 619-0288 Japan
[5] Department of Brain and Bioinformation Science, Kanazawa Institute of Technology,
3-1 Yatsukaho, Hakusan, 924-0838 Japan
[6] RIKEN Brain Science Institute, 2-1 Hirosawa, Wako, Saitama, 351-0198 Japan
`suzuki@his.kanazawa-it.ac.jp,niki@ni.aist.go.jp,`
`fujimaki@po.nict.go.jp,masaki@atr.jp,`
`ichikawa@his.kanazawa-it.ac.jp,usuishiro@riken.jp`

Abstract. We organized the Neuro-Imaging Platform (NIMG-PF) committee, whose members are drawn from 18 Japanese research sites, as an activity of Neuroinformatics Japan Center (NIJC) at RIKEN, and are constructing a database of non-invasive brain function measurements for beginners and specialists. We are gathering the content related to various neuroimaging technologies such as MRI, MEG, EEG, PET, and NIRS, and their integrations: bibliographies of research papers, tutorial materials, software content, experimental data, and related information. About 200 pieces of content have already been registered. NIMG-PF is constructed on a base-platform, XooNIps, on which users can search contents by selecting indices, items, or keywords. Furthermore, we are developing convenient tools for visualizing 3D-brain images and for information searches that work by the user pointing to locations on the images. In NIMG-PF, any user can register their original content and use content if they accept the permission conditions. NIMG-PF will open later this year.

Keywords: neuroimaging, database, visualization, tutorial.

1 Introduction

Brain imaging has become one of key technologies for studying human brain mechanisms, despite arguments portraying brain imaging as neo-phrenology. Recent studies show the possibilities of brain imaging technology not only as a tool to get anatomical information, but to get insight into brain mechanisms. Brain imaging technology is expected to be able to elucidate dynamical aspects of brain functions, if and only if the brain imaging experiments are conducted based on computational models and powerful analytical methods. Furthermore, together with cellular and genetic methods, brain

M. Ishikawa et al. (Eds.): ICONIP 2007, Part II, LNCS 4985, pp. 895–904, 2008.

imaging may lead to a unified view of how the human brain supports the mind. Thus we believe that brain scientists should have a platform that they can access through a network and get useful experimental data, analytical methods of brain imaging, and/or mathematical modeling. To this end, we have organized the Neuro-Imaging Platform (NIMG-PF) committee as an activity of the Neuroinformatics Japan Center (NIJC, http://nijc.brain.riken.jp) at RIKEN [1]. There are many resources in Japan that can be incorporated in NIMG-PF, and researchers throughout Japan have joined this activity. The committee has just started to design the PF. The details of our work are described below.

2   NIMG-PF Content

2.1   Survey of Databases

The world has many databases. To get an idea of what content they hold, we and other NIMG-PF committee members selected 43 that were closely related to neuroimaging. NIJC did a survey collecting statistical data on their content (Fig. 1) [2]. The results show that the major databases have 0 to 1000 bibliographies of research papers, except for PubMed, which has more than ten million, 0 to 15 items for software, and 0 to several hundred related links. The software includes visualization tools which are important for brain imaging, for example, "Search & View" of BrainMap, Brede, Brain Voyager, "CARET" of Van Essen Lab, and Free Surfer. They can be operated on-line or be downloaded. There are only few sites that have raw data related to human brain functions (e.g., BrainMap, Brede, and fMRIDC). In particular, it's rare to find tutorial materials on neuroimaging methods other than MRI, standard protocols for measurement and analysis, and stimulus and measurement tools. In addition, we failed to find simulation models for massive neural activation, or experimental data such as stimulus data and programs or scripts. Free offers of such content may be limited by organizations of contributors who want to protect intellectual property rights. However, registration of content in public databases has advantages because it enables world-wide distribution and can encourage researchers to register their own content. We believe this would be helpful for many users.

2.2   Focus on NIMG-PF Content

We wanted to include original and useful content that no other databases have. In particular, we thought that tutorial information would be helpful, because neuroimaging technologies have recently been used by researchers in other fields for applications such as quantitative evaluation of human responses to products and circumstances (neuroeconomics), and brain-computer interfaces.

Based on the above survey and discussions with NIMG-PF committee members, we decided to focus on collecting the following kinds of content related to neuroimaging technologies such as MRI, MEG, EEG, PET, NIRS, and their integrations, for newcomers as well as specialists.

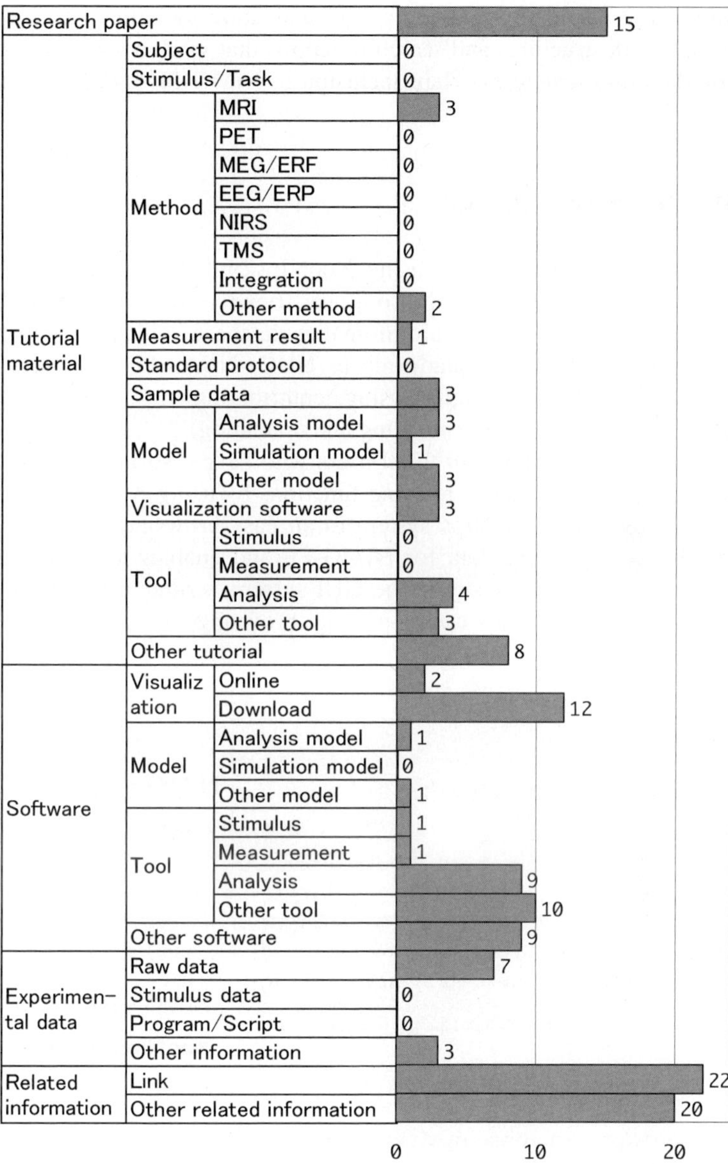

Fig. 1. Number of sites having content based on the data in reference [2]

- Bibliographies of major and recent research papers
- Tutorial materials such as measuring technologies, standard protocols for measurement and analysis, and sample data
- Software for brain visualization, models, and tools
- Experimental data including raw data, stimuli, and program/scripts
- Related information and links

A neuroimaging database ought to have visualization tools that offer easy-to-use displays of 3D brain structures and search functions that work by the user pointing to locations on the brain structures. Their inclusion in NIMG-PF is described in section 3 and 6.

3   NIMG-PF System Design

NIMG-PF, which is constructed by using XooNIps and Ajax, is designed as a research archive (NIMG database) and also a user-friendly viewer for the NIMG database. The core of NIMG-PF is a neuroinfomatics database, which is compatible with other neuroinfomatics database platforms at NIJC. NIMG-PF will have standard XooNIps' functions for searching/browsing, contributing via a web interface, and sharing research resources (by downloading and uploading).

To make NIMG-PF more useful to all users who have a strong interest in the human brain, we created its "easy" browsing functions by using Ajax method. Figure 2 shows how to extend the XooNIps system to an easy-browsing GUI; XooNIps extended system extended meta-data for NIMG-PF and enables to access the NIMG database from a XooPs GUI system. The GUI system, written by using XooPs language and Ajax methods, offers a user-friendly browsing function for searching the NIMG database.

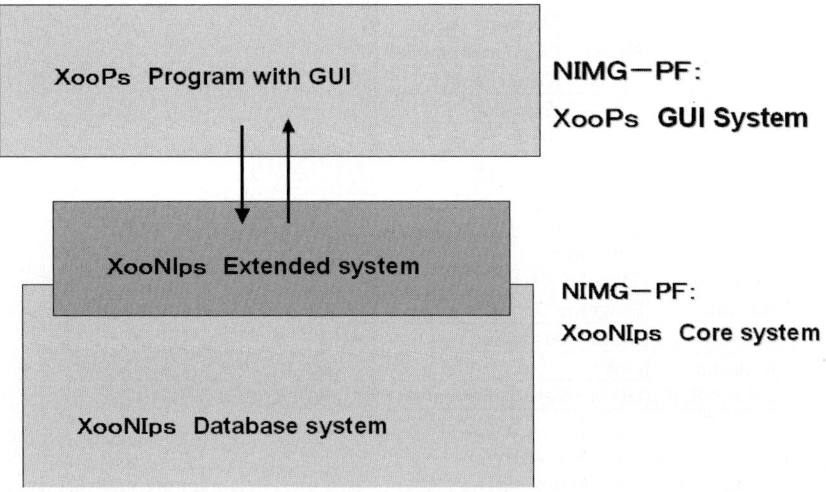

Fig. 2. Extending the XooNIps system to NIMG-PF's easy-browsing GUI

Figure 3 shows the top page of the extended NIMG-PF. We can browse NIMG database by using brain figures from the user point. We will report how we extended XooNIps to realize the easy browsing function after NIMG-PF opens.

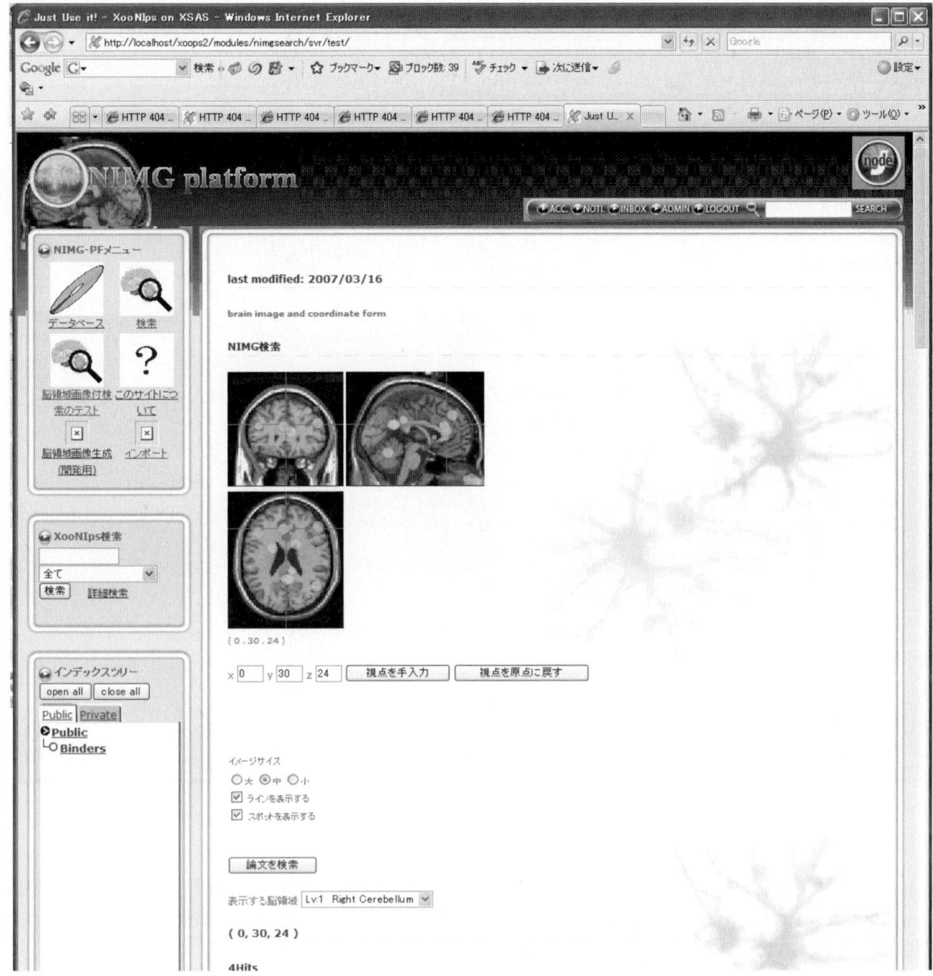

Fig. 3. NIMG-PF supports easy browsing of NIMG database using brain figures

4 NIMG-PF Index

The data in the DB should be able to be easily retrieved. An index tree is one way to do this. An index tree can also offer users, especially beginners, a global view of brain imaging research. The index tree of NIMG-PF DB was constructed as shown in Fig. 4. Content (papers etc.) in each index appears on the right side of the same page. By clicking on content, detailed information about it will appear.

The NIMG-PF index tree is composed of three levels. The 1st level includes Imaging Methods, Tutorial, Brain Function, Tasks, Stimulations, Brain Areas, Temporal and Frequency components, Models, Technologies and Links. The 2nd and 3rd levels

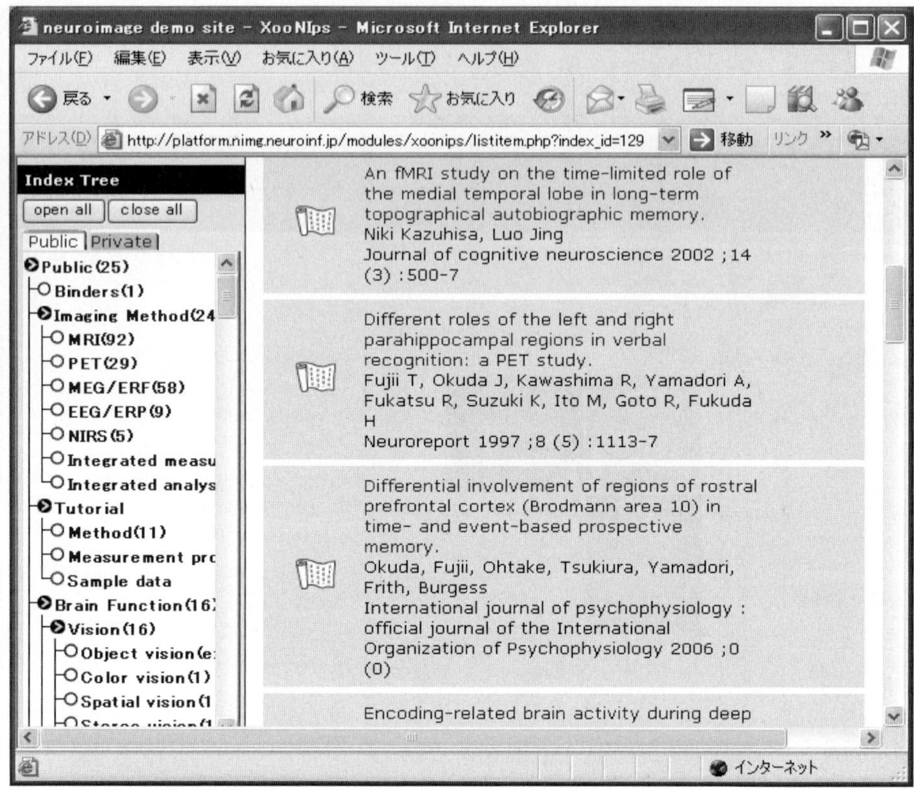

Fig. 4. Index tree at the left side of the top page of NIMG-PF DB

have detailed indexes. The "Tutorial" index seems to be a little odd but NIMG-PF DB emphasizes tutorials, and so the Tutorial index was created with searching in mind. Here you can find typical stimuli and protocols for brain imaging.

We did not intend that the NIMG-PF index tree would show a comprehensive view of brain imaging research. Rather it categorizes content so that you can find what is and is not included in NIMG-PF DB.

5   Registration of Content

5.1   Data Input

Neuro-imaging researchers all over the world can voluntarily register content in NIMG-PF. Here, we briefly introduce the data registration procedure.

As described in the previous section, you can enter data for items such as "Book," "Data," "Model," "Paper," "Tool," and "Url." For example, if you want to register a "Paper", you should fill in the required information in all fields including author(s), journal title, and paper title. If you know the "PUBMED ID," you don't need to enter all of the data. All you have to do is to enter the ID number in the appropriate field. Then, the rest of the information is automatically filled in from the database itself.

During registration, you are required to choose key words listed in the "index tree" to characterize the data itself. The three layers of key words in the "index tree" are always displayed on the left side of NIMG-PF's homepage (Fig. 4). Note that selecting suitable key words improves the usability of the database. Appropriately selected "index tree" key words attached to data can help users to search for information in NIMG-PF.

5.2 Two-Step Data Registration

Registration of data consists of two steps. The first step is to input the data in the "Private" quotas provided to all NIMG-PF users. When you fill in the information as presented above, the data is registered in the "Private" quotas. During this step, only the user who registers the data can refer to the information.

The second step is to publish the data. When you put data in the public area, all NIMG-PF users can access it. Currently, publication is performed after permission is granted by a NIMG-PF moderator.

Such permission is required to maintain the quality of the database. The moderator works not only to prevent inappropriate information from being registered but also to prevent the double registration of the same data.

5.3 Protection of Intellectual Property

The registered data should able to be accessed by all users for the purpose of sharing information. On the other hand, the information provider's intellectual property rights to the data should also be protected. The base platform of NIMG-PF has a built-in function for this, and NIMG-PF uses a system whereby data are registered, and non-exclusive rights to use the data are transferred with some rights reserved of the following six patterns or with all rights reserved.

(1) Attribution
(2) Attribution-NoDerivs
(3) Attribution-NonCommercial-NoDerivs
(4) Attribution-NonCommercial
(5) Attribution-NonCommercial-ShareAlike
(6) Attribution-ShareAlike

A short explanation of these rights is as follows.

Attribution: The user must attribute the work in the manner specified by the author or licensor

NonCommercial (=Noncommercial): The user is not allowed to use the content for commercial purposes.

NoDerivs (=No Derivative Works): The user is not allowed to alter, transform, or build upon this work.

ShareAlike: If the user alters, transforms, or builds upon the contents, he/she may distribute the resulting work only under the same or similar license to this one.

These restrictions are based on the conditions provided by a non-profit organization named Creative Commons (http://creativecommons.org/licenses).

5.4 Promoting Data Registration

NIMG-PF organizers and committee members were involved with data registration in the development phase during fiscal 2006. The current situation is that the registered data is not as large the neuron-imaging database. Voluntary registration is essential to enlarge the content and to improve the quality of the database. If you would like to submit content related to neuron-imaging research, please contact us by E-mail (NIMGcontents@po.nict.go.jp), or visit our NIMG-PF (http://platform.nimg.neuroinf.jp).

6 Registered Content

6.1 *sBrain*

The present version of NIMG-PF does not support 3D views of brain images and viewing Brodmann areas on 3D brain image. We developed free software called "*sBrain*" for viewing 3D brain images and content (papers, etc.) relating to the selected brain area on the 3D image. You can register your own content in *sBrain*, and this can help you to perform meta-analysis using *sBrain*.

The brain areas selected from the list on the right in Fig. 5 are shown in the transparent 3D brain image. This viewing mode is very useful for beginners to find 3D locations

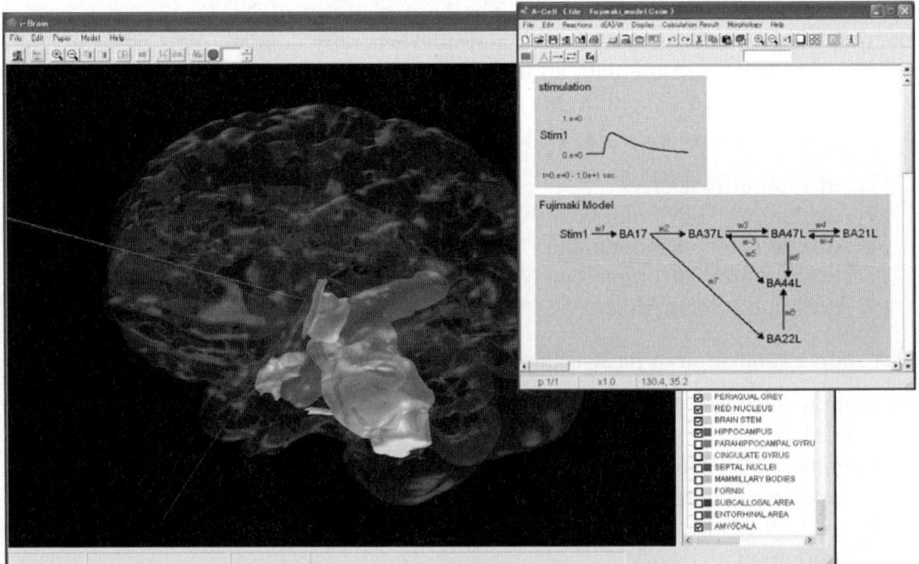

Fig. 5. *sBrain*

in the brain, especially areas in the brain stem. If you click on the 3D image, its coordinate will appear on the screen together with the Brodmann area name. In addition, papers relating to the brain area are displayed in the window. On the other hand, if you select the registered paper(s), the brain areas dealt with in the paper(s) are displayed on the 3D image.

The most distinguishing feature of *sBrain* is its modeling and simulation capability. You can construct a macroscopic model of brain area activation. The model can be simulated on *sBrain*, and brain activation dynamics can be viewed on the 3D image. The modeling and simulation UI and algorithm are the same as in A-Cell [3], [4]. The modeling window is shown on the right in Fig. 5.

Some of the functions of *sBrain* will be enabled on NIMG-PF in the future. At present, several functions are only available on *sBrain*. The personal meta-analysis capability together with the modeling and simulation capability will offer users their own tools for brain image research. The *sBrain* software can be downloaded from the NIMG-PF DB.

6.2 Other Content

NIMG-PF has tutorials on neuroimaging technologies, which cover operations, practical aspects of measurements, and analysis methods. For example, tutorial videos (lasting 10 minutes) include "For creative brain research", which introduces brain research at NICT: "Searching brain information processes", which introduces measurement instruments and methods of MRI, MEG and NIRS. They have a Japanese version, a Japanese version for students, and an English version.

Furthermore, original documents including instructions on measurement systems and recent research reports related to linguistic brain functions in power point or pdf format have been registered for the use of specialists.

In addition, we are planning to register experimental data such as MRI structural data, fMRI functional data, MEG measurement data, and two analysis methods for solving MEG inverse problems. One is the selective minimum norm (SMN) method, which estimates neural sources by minimizing the L1-norm on the condition that number of active dipoles is limited so that unknown dipole parameters can be solved using measured data. The other one is an fMRI-constrained MEG multi-dipole analysis method. It estimates neural sources, whereby dipole locations are determined from fMRI active locations, while dipole moments are determined from MEG data. The spatial resolution of this method is limited to a few cm, but it is robust because no arbitrary mathematical assumptions are used. It can be used in combination with SMN, which serves to complement fMRI-invisible dipoles.

7 Conclusion

We should emphasize that brain imaging technology has great potential as a tool for studying human brain functions. We hope that NIMG-PF will benefit research on brain functions.

Acknowledgments

This work was partially supported by JSPS KAKENHI 198072.

References

1. Usui, S. et al.: Japanese neuroinformatics node and platforms. presented in this conference
2. Usui, S., et al.: Survey Report on the International Activities of Neuroinformatics and Related Databases (in Japanese) NIJC at RIKEN BSI (March 2007), `http://nijc.brain.riken.jp/`
3. Ichikawa, K.: A Modeling Environment with Three-Dimensional Morphology, A-Cell-3D, and Ca2+ Dynamics in a Spine. Neuroinformatics 3, 49–64 (2005)
4. Ichikawa, K.: A-Cell: graphical user interface for the construction of biochemical reaction models. Bioinformatics 17, 483–484 (2001)

Development of Invertebrate Brain Platform: Management of Research Resources for Invertebrate Neuroscience and Neuroethology

Hidetoshi Ikeno[1], Ryohei Kanzaki[2], Hitoshi Aonuma[3], Masakazu Takahata[3],
Makoto Mizunami[4], Kouji Yasuyama[5], Nobuyuki Matsui[1],
Fumio Yokohari[6], and Shiro Usui[7]

[1] University of Hyogo, 1-3-3 Higashikawasaki-cho, Chuo-ku, Kobe 670-0092, Japan
[2] The University of Tokyo, 4-6-1 Komaba, Meguro-ku, Tokyo 153-8904, Japan
[3] Hokkaido University, N10W5, Kita-ku, Sapporo 060-0810, Japan
[4] Tohoku University, Katahira 2-1-1, Aoba-ku, Sendai 980-8577, Japan
[5] Kawasaki Medical University, 577 Matsushima, Kurashiki 701-0192, Japan
[6] Fukuoka University, 8-19-1 Nanakuma, Jyonan-ku, Fukuoka 814-0810, Japan
[7] RIKEN, 2-1 Hirosawa, Wako 351-0198, Japan
`http://platform.invbrain.neuroinf.jp/`

Abstract. Various kinds of analysis and mathematical models based on neuroscience are developing in the neural network study. In the research, experimental data and knowledge so far obtained are essential resources to deepen their consideration of neuronal systems and functions. In order to utilize the accumulation of expertise and research effectively, it is important to integrate various resources, such as bibliography and experimental data. The managing and sharing of research resources are absolutely imperative for future development in both experimental and analytical studies. Various scientific fields need a new method to obtain precise information, because the amount of experimental data and publications has increased rapidly due to innovations in measurement, computers and network technologies. Under this situation, an effective resource-managing based on CMS (Content Management System) is introduced here for the laboratory use. We are providing functional modules to manage research resources for neuroinfomatics. As a practical use of these modules, a database system for managing image data of invertebrate neurons measured by Confocal Laser Scanning Microscope (CLSM) is developed. Furthermore, these modules are implemented for management of contents in the Invertebrate Brain Platform.

Keywords: Neruoinformatics, Content Management System, XOOPS, Invertebrate, Neuroscience, Neuroethology.

1   Introduction

In order to utilize the accumulation of expertise and research effectively, it is important to integrate various research resources, such as bibliography and experimental data, from individual laboratories to international portal sites [8].

M. Ishikawa et al. (Eds.): ICONIP 2007, Part II, LNCS 4985, pp. 905–914, 2008.
© Springer-Verlag Berlin Heidelberg 2008

The sharing of these resources and the integration of knowledge are absolutely imperative for future development in both experimental and computational neuroscience fields. Several vigorous neuroniformatics projects for the integration of research resources have been implemented, after the recommendation of OECD [3]. In various scientific fields, it is highly important to obtain precise information more quickly and easily with the help of database system, because amounts of experimental data and publications have been rapidly increased by innovations in measurement, computers and network technologies. However, it has still not been easy to setup and manage database systems without comprehensive technical knowledge and experience. In order to improve current situation of data sharing in the neuroscience field, International Neuroinformatics Coordinating Facility (INCF) was organized in 2005.

Similar problems arise in WWW system management, that is, engineers skilled in web, database and network systems are needed for the stable operation and updating of portal sites. In order to solve this problem, Content Management System (CMS) have become widespread in the construction and management of WWW portal sites. CMS usually combines WWW servers, database and script languages, to provide a unified methodology for site and resource management. XOOPS (The eXtensible Object Oriented Portal System) and XOOPS Cube are widely used open source CMS, coded in PHP script language. XOOPS can be run under Apache for WWW server, MySQL for database and PHP for script language [14,15].

In our platform project, in order to construct an effective resource managing environment in the laboratory and Internet, we developed two database modules: CosmoDB and PubMedPDF [2,9]. These modules are able to provide data integration and sharing capabilities, for bibliographical resources and archived data files. Their effectiveness was then evaluated by applying the modules to our laboratory studies of the management for physiological/behavioral experimental data and for bibliography construction [5]. Several internet portal sites for neuroinformatics have been developed under the INCF Japan-node (http://www.neuroinf.jp/index.php?ml_lang=en) in a collaborative project with NIJC (Neuroinformatics Japan Center at RIKEN BSI). These modules are currently being used for constructing websites, Invertebrate Brain Platform: IVBPF [6], for sharing such resources as the physiological and behavioral data from insects and other invertebrate animals.

2   Data Management and Sharing in the Laboratory

World Wide Web (WWW) must be the most powerful data integration and sharing system in the world. It is consisted with WWW servers, network and clients. Hyper text transfer protocol (HTTP) is used for transmission of text and binary data from server to client. Recently, WWW server environment are constructed and operated with database software in order to update, manage and maintenance their contents easily.

Under this situation, it is considered that the web system is one of the most general and efficient ways for resource sharing on the Internet. In order to reduce the costs of building and maintaining a web portal site, CMS such as Plone, PHPNuke, XOOPS and XOOPS Cube, are extensively used as powerful management tools for websites and web content. XOOPS Cube is an object oriented CMS, written in PHP and widely used for creating various scale of web systems including commercial sites. It can be run with a coalition of relational database (MySQL) and web server (Apache). It can provide useful basic functions for management of user account, content, page layout and design. Other functions for operating portal site (for example, news, forum, link lists and so on) are provided as basic and custom modules.

Furthermore, various plug-in modules, such as a scheduler or blog, have been created and provided for customization of web site by volunteer developers. CosmoDB and PubMedPDF, were developed as the XOOPS Cube module for the management of research resources in laboratories. Their effectiveness would be extended by use in combination with other XOOPS Cube modules (Fig. 1).

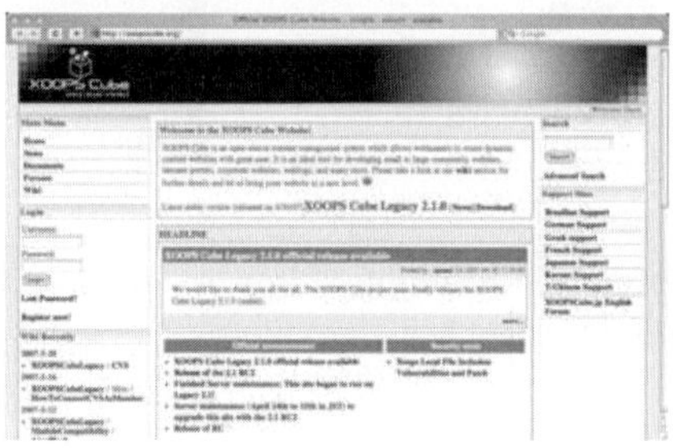

Module	Function
AntiDoS-P	protect from DoS attack
backpack	backup MySQL table data
BluesBB	bulletin board
myaddress	address book
piCal	calendar and scheduler
TinyD	contents management
WordPress ME	blog tool
X_movie	movie contents
Xoops WebMail	Web Mail
XoopsHP	e-learning

Fig. 1. XOOPS Cube official site (*http://xoopscube.org/*) and useful XOOPS Cube plug-in modules for laboratory works

2.1   Multipurpose Database Module: CosmoDB

This module has the capability of managing various kinds of data files, such as images, experimental data and model programs. Almost every operation for data management and mining can be done through web browsers, such as Internet Explorer and Firefox. Database contents (experimental data, model description and so on) can be registered by uploading a file or archive file into upload directory tree in the content registration page. Registered content consists of data labels, comments, thumbnail images and data files. A page corresponding to the content, called data sheet, is automatically generated by this registration process.

In the example, Fig. 2, the datasheet contains several items, such as, basic information about content, thumbnail images, keywords. Items for display and layout in this page are described in HTML by format descriptions, which can

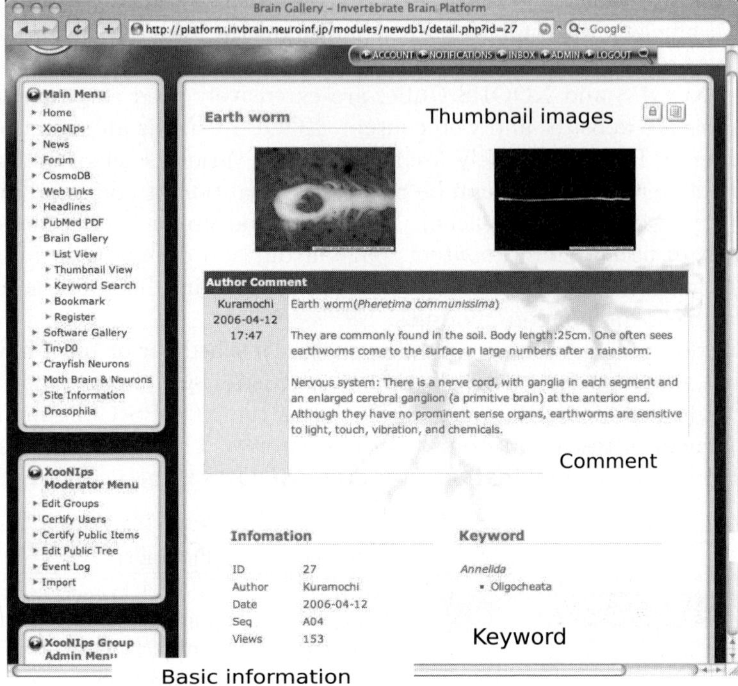

Fig. 2. Detail information of content, Basic information, thumbnail images, comment and keyword, are registered and displayed on the data sheet

be modified by an administrator. All or selected registered data, can be listed in the form of text index or thumbnail images. Each data sheet can be opened by clicking on its data label in the index pages. Basic manipulations for content management (registration, removal and modification), browsing (reading/adding comments, downloading data files) and searching (by keyword, author, registered date or by full-text search) are provided by basic functions of this module. If it is necessary to execute a program for data processing when content is registered, application software can be executed as a background task by including description files written in PHP. The cosmoDB module has been developed as open software and has been distributed through its official site [2] and sourceforge Japan site (*http://sourceforge.jp/cosmodb*).

2.2   PubMed Linked Bibliography Module: PubMedPDF

Bibliographic information is an essential resource for scientific research activities. Many of the articles in both medical and biological fields are indexed by a unique number (PMID) in PubMed (*http://www.pubmed.gov*). It was shown that these numbers are extremely useful for managing bibliography even in the laboratory. We have developed a XOOPS module for automatically accessing the PubMed site and making indexes based on PMID. In this module, the registration of literary information can be performed by inputting a PMID or uploading a PDF reprint file, previously named gPMID.pdfh. The module then accesses the PubMed site with a PMID and downloads an XML file, which has detailed literary information.

Literature information without PMID is also registered and used by this database. On the top page of this module, the literature is indexed by publishing year, author and journal (Fig. 3). Organized listing of registered bibliography is accessed from these index term, then detail information is shown by other page. User can define the shortcut to any page from top page for direct access.

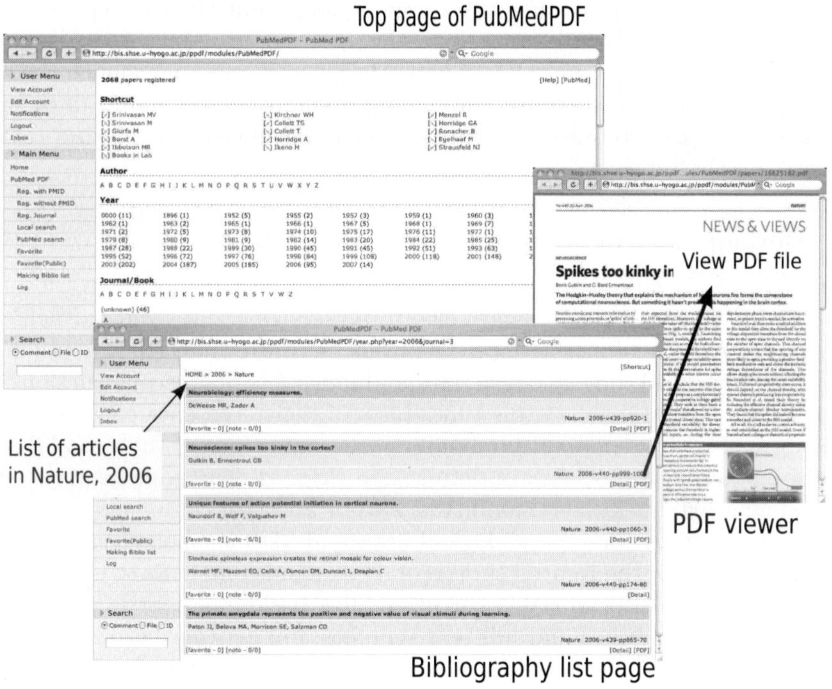

Fig. 3. Bibliography database system by PubMedPDF module

The module also provides several functions, such as the attachment of notes to each article, keyword or full-text search ability and an output of the bibliography list. Registered users can make their own bookmark folders, which are collections of literature on a special topic. Bookmark folders can be assigned as gprivateh or gpublich for the purposes of access rights. These folders can help to organize the masses of information available on the internet in a variety of dimensions. In addition, bookmark information can be both exported and imported, making it easy to share. For example, creating a gsocial bookmarkh folder, which contains a list of selected papers or other organized information by an outstanding scientist would provide helpful information for students and young scientists.

The PDF file management by literature database is quite effective in the laboratory, because PDF reprint files of papers and articles tend to be available from many publishers and academic organizations, through the Internet, now. This PubMedPDF module can provide a database environment for bibliography without any additional cost to the laboratory. This module has also been developed as open software and is being distributed via the official site[9] and sourceforge Japan site (*http://sourceforge.jp/ppdf*).

3   Resource Management System by XOOPS Cube

XOOPS Cube is extensively used for a lot of web sites in these days. We are planning to use it for providing a resource management environment in various size of data sharing, from personal to the Internet use. In this section, it is presented two examples of XOOPS Cube based resource management system. Neuron database is constructed for management of experimental data in the laboratory and Invertebrate Brain Platform is developed for sharing research resources on the Internet.

3.1   Development of Neuron Database

In an example of laboratory use, we used the CosmoDB module to develop a database for morphological images, electrophysiological data and mathematical model specifications of insect (moth) neurons [5]. More than 1,000 neuronal images taken by CLSM, physiological data and morphological reconstructions were registered in the database at this time. Lists of registered data can be reviewed in the form of text index and thumbnail images. Additionally the actual data file can also be accessed on the data detail page (Fig. 4). The page displays superimposed neuronal images as thumbnails, author and user comments, links to the LSM scanned image files, physiological data and 3D morphological reconstructions in a format for the Neuron simulator. Notes and comments to the registered data can be added after initial registration. The basic functions of database operations, such as keyword and full-text searches, linking to other content/URLs and the updating of registered data, are provided by module functions. Under the environment of Microsoft Windows, the directory path to registered LSM images is transferred into the clipboard from the data sheet. LSM scanned image file then can be accessed by application software through the paste manipulation.

Neuronal 3D structures can be reconstructed by tracing morphologies in and across slice images of CLSM. However, this process is quite time-consuming, even if limited to simple neuron structures. More importantly, such reconstructions are extremely difficult to perform on neurons which have numerous branches and complex structures. Several software packages have been developed and used for semi- or fully- automatic structural reconstruction of neurons [13,10]. For example, Rodriguez et al. proposed an automatic reconstruction tool from CLSM images, recently. Their method would be good at manipulation and integration of neuronal structure, because neuronal structure is represented in the form of polygonal surfaces.

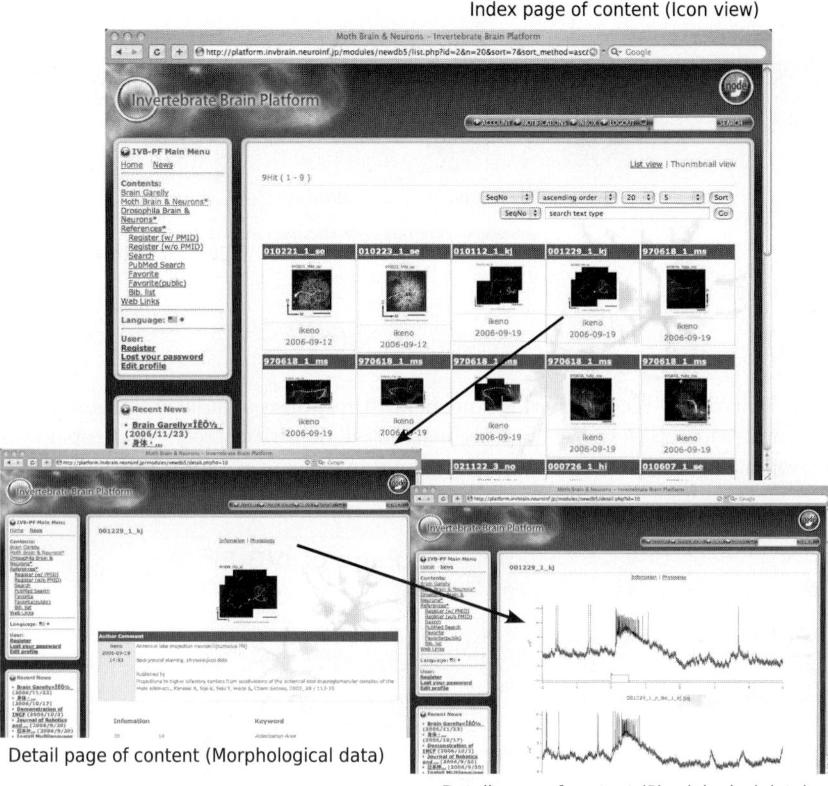

Fig. 4. Neuron database system by CosmoDB module

We also present a novel software for automatic reconstruction of neuronal 3D morphological structure from CLSM tomographic images [17]. Our software contains several image processing functions for detecting neuronal regions, and extracting dendritic branching structure using the Single-Seed Distance Transform (SSDT) method [18], which was applied for reconstruction of blood vessel structure in the lungs. Morphological data is then automatically transformed into a compartmental (or segment) model. In order to analyze electrical response properties of reconstructed neurons, output can be obtained as a model description for the neuronal simulator, NEURON [4]. The effectiveness of our system is shown through reconstruction of interneurons in antennal lobes of silkworm moths (Fig. 5).

3.2   Development of Invertebrate Brain Platform

Invertebrate Brain Platform (Fig. 6) was developed and operated based on XOOPS Cube with Linux operating system. Many valuable functions for managing portal site, such as scheduler and message board, are available as open source

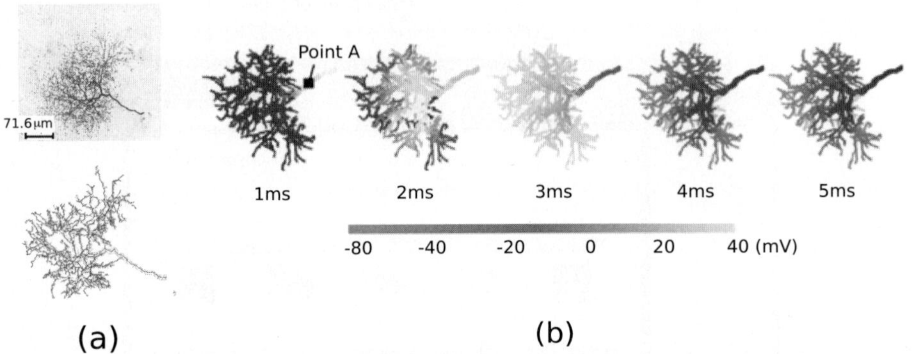

Fig. 5. Result of 3D reconstruction and neurall response simulation of antennal lobe interneuron, (a) CLSM image and reconstructed dendritic tree, (b) Propagation of neural response by injection of current at Point A

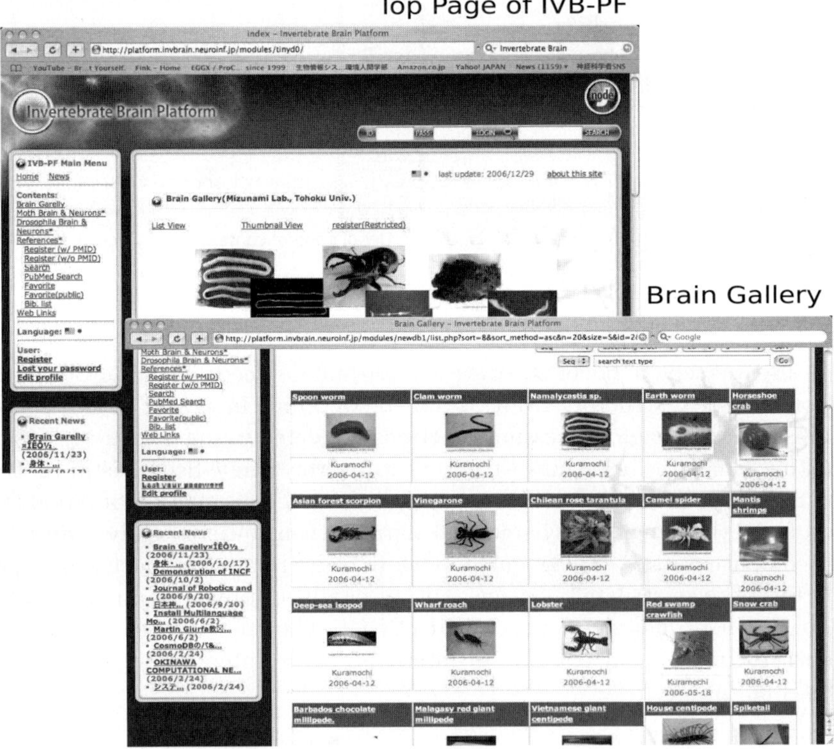

Fig. 6. Top page of Invertebrate Brain Platform and Brain Gallery page in this site

modules on the Internet. The XooNIps module (*http://xoonips.sourceforge.jp*) which is developed by NIJC is applied for management of user accounts because the original XOOPS user accounting system was not sufficient for the sitefs operational policy (more information about the user was required by the site).

Our originally developed modules, CosmoDB and PubMedPDF, manage the contents of the site. For example, Invertebrate Brain Gallery, which is a collection of images of nervous systems in various invertebrates, is constructed and managed by the CosmoDB module. Literary information about invertebrate behavior and physiology is collecting and managing by the PubMedPDF module. Original image data of invertebrate neurons, for example, interneuron of antennal lobe of moth brain, are collected on the site.

In near feature, we will provide data transfer functions from XOOPS Cube based laboratory database to the IVB-PF. It would be very important to integrate and publish various contents on the platform. XML based descriptions, such as NeuroML, will be applied to use as a common language to connect between private and public database systems.

4   Conclusion

In this paper, it was presented application of XOOPS Cube and their modules for laboratory database and portal site. Most of XOOPS modules have been developed as open source software and are provided through the official and related sites. We are developing other tools and packages for neuroscience, such as being able to transform CLSM images from company oriented original format into a common format, like OME (Open Microscopy Environment) and then automatically registering them into the database [7,11]. It could be very useful for experimentalists because they wouldnft need to consider data transformation and management in order to register into database.

Development of the IVB-PF began last year as one of the platform under the Japan-node. At that time, it was important to construct a stable server environment and collect high-standard research results in the field of invertebrate science. We believe that the aggregation and sharing of research resources can accelerate the progress of science. Improvement of these database tools and applications in the neuroscience fields can become cornerstone for research undertaken with information technologies.

References

1. Apache Friends: `http://www.apachefriends.org/en/`
2. CosmoDB XOOPS module official site: `http://cosmodb.sourceforge.jp/en/`
3. Eckersley, P., et al.: Neuroscience data and tool sharing: a legal and policy framework for neuroinformacs. Neuroinformatcs 1, 149–165 (2003)
4. Hines, M.L., Carnevale, N.T.: The NEURON simulation environment. Neural Comput. 9(6), 1179–1209 (1997)
5. Ikeno, H., Nishioka, T., Hachida, T., Kanzaki, R., Seki, Y., Ohazwa, I., Usui, S.: Development and application of CMS-based database modules for neuroinformatics. Neurocomputing 70, 2122–2128 (2007)

6. Invertebrate Brain Platform: `http://platform.invbrain.neuroinf.jp/`
7. Open Microscopy Environment: `http://openmicroscopy.org/index.html`
8. Pittendrigh, S., Jacobs, G.: NeuroSys: a semistructured laboratory database. Neuroinformatics 1, 167–176 (2003)
9. PubMedPDF XOOPS module official site: `http://sourceforge.jp/ppdf`
10. Rodriguez, A., Ehlenberger, R., Kelliher, K., Einstein, M., Henderson, S.C., Morrison, J.H., Hof, P.R., Wearne, S.L.: Automaged reconstruction of three dimensional neuronal morphology from laser scanning microscopy images. Methods 30, 94–105 (2003)
11. Rueden, C., Eliceiri, K.W., White, J.G.: VisBio: a computational tool for visualization of multidimensional biological image data. Traffic 5, 411–417 (2004)
12. van Pelt, J., van Ooyan, A., Uylings, H.B.: The need for integrating neuronal morphology database and computational environments in exploring neuronal structure and function. Anat. Embryol (Berl) 204, 255–265 (2001)
13. Weaver, C.M., Hof, P.R., Wearne, S.L., Lindquist, W.B.: Automated algorithms for multiscale morphometry of neuronal dendrites. Neural Comput. 16(7), 1353–1383 (2004)
14. XOOPS: `http://www.xoops.org/`
15. XOOPS Cube: `http://xoopscube.org/`
16. XSAS: `http://xsas.sourceforge.net/`
17. Yamasaki, T., Isokawa, T., Matsui, N., Ikeno, H., Kanzaki, R.: Reconstruction and simulation for three-dimensional morphological structure of insect neurons. Neurocomputing 69, 1043–1047 (2006)
18. Zhou, Y., Kaufman, A., Toga, W.: 3D skeleton and centerline generation based on an approximate minimum distance field. Visual Comput. 14, 303–314 (1998)

ICA-Based Spatio-temporal Features for EEG Signals

Sangkyun Lee and Soo-Young Lee

Brain Science Research Center and Department of Bio & Brain Engineering,
Korea Advanced Institute of Science and Technology
373-1 Guseong-dong, Yuseong-gu, Daejeon 305-701, Korea
sylee@kaist.ac.kr

Abstract. The spatio-temporal EEG features are extracted by a two-stage ICAs. First, a spatial ICA is performed to extract spatially-distributed sources, and the second ICA is introduced in temporal domain for the coefficients of spatial sources. This 2-stage method provides much better features than spatial ICA only, and is computationally more efficient than single-stage spatio-temporal ICA. Among the extracted spatio-temporal features critical features are selected for the given tasks based on Fisher criterion. The extracted features may be applicable to the classification of single-trial EEG signals.

Keywords: Brain-Computer Interface, Independent Component Analysis (ICA), single-trial EEG, Spatio-Temporal filter.

1 Introduction

The Brain-Computer-Interface (BCI) has attracted a lot of attention recently [1] [2] [3] [4] [5]. For accurate recognition of EEG signals it is important to have noise-robust and neurophysiologically-relevant features. In this paper, we focus on unsupervised feature extraction in both spatial and temporal domains for the single-trial classification of EEG signals.

In BCI systems, each electrode measures a mixture of many neuronal sources, which are diffused through inhomogeneous brain medium. Therefore, many papers have described the spatial filtering to extract relevant spatial features from these mixtures [6] [7] [8] [9] [10]. In addition, it is also necessary to obtain temporal filters [3]. This is required because the neurophysiological features such as Event-Related-Desynchronization (ERD) and Event-Related-Synchronization (ERS) occur in specific frequency bands. For temporal filtering a fixed-frequency bandpass filter was used in [7] for upper-alpha and beta bands. However, especially for single-trial classification of BCI, it is important to take into account of subject-dependency on the temporal frequency bands.

The spatio-temporal features may be extracted by a 2-dimensional ICA, which requires extensive computing and is sensitive to noises due to the large number of unknowns. In this paper, we present a 2-stage method, where the spatial and temporal features are extracted in sequence using Independent Component Analysis (ICA) with user-specific fine-tuning.

M. Ishikawa et al. (Eds.): ICONIP 2007, Part II, LNCS 4985, pp. 915–920, 2008.

2 ICA-Based Spatial Features

EEG signals are diffused with volume conduction in inhomogeneous brain medium, and naturally mixed together. A popular spatial filtering method is the Surface Laplacian (SL) method [11], which is basically a spatial high-pass filter. In contrast, ICA looks for statistical independence and is naturally robust on diffusion effects. If given EEG signals are linear mixtures composed of several sources, independent sources may be obtainable by ICA.

The observed mixed signal vector $\mathbf{x}(t)$ is represented as a linear summation of independent sources, and denoted by a multiplication of mixing matrix $\mathbf{A}$ and source signal vector $\mathbf{s}(t)$

$$\mathbf{x}(t) = \mathbf{A}\,\mathbf{s}(t) \tag{1}$$

where $\mathbf{x}(t)$ is measured EEG signals composed of n channels from n electrode positions, $\mathbf{s}(t)$ is neural signals composed of n independent sources, and $\mathbf{A}$ is an n-by-n matrix. Each column vector of $\mathbf{A} = [\mathbf{a}_1 : : : \mathbf{a}_n]$ is a statistically-independent spatial map, i.e., the spatial distribution of an independent source. Due to the fast speed of electromagnetic waves we assume instantaneous mixing without time delays. Also, the mixing assumed to be stationary with a constant matrix $\mathbf{A}$.

The estimated source $\mathbf{u}(t)$ is denoted by the multiplicative form of the demixing matrix $\mathbf{W}$ and the observed signals $\mathbf{x}(t)$ as

$$\mathbf{u}(t) = \mathbf{W}\,\mathbf{x}(t), \tag{2}$$

where the demixing matrix $\mathbf{W}$ may be obtained by ICA learning rules.

The spatial maps may be sorted by the covariance of coefficients $u_i(t)$. If the measured data are labeled by a class variable C, the mutual information between $u_i(t)$ and C may denote the significance of the coefficient $u_i(t)$ for the classification and used for the sorting and feature selection.

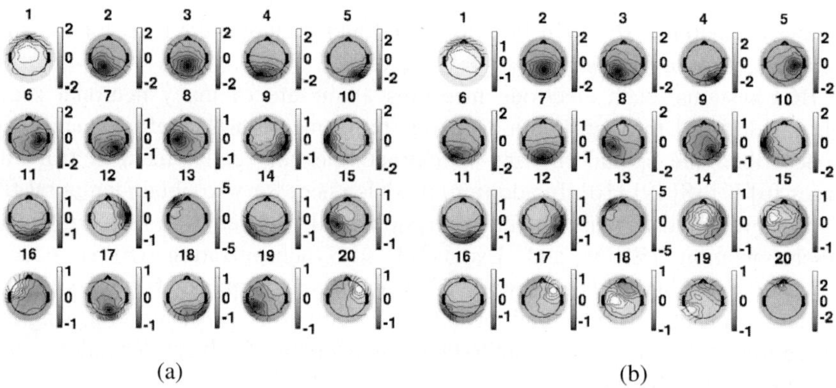

(a)   (b)

Fig. 1. ICA-based EEG spatial maps obtained from the binary class tasks of subject *aa*. The spatial maps are sorted in descending order according to the signal intensity of sources, and the top 20 spatial maps are shown. (a) Left hand vs. right hand imagery. (b) Right hand vs. foot imagery.

In Figs. 1(a) and (b), the 20 ICA-based EEG spatial maps are shown for a subject. In Fig. 1(a), the task was to imagine left and right hand movement. Among several spatial maps, a few maps are closely related to the task, while the others may come from artifacts in either experimental paradigm or measurements. In Fig. 1(a), the 6th spatial map shows the neural activity distribution related to the left hand imagery, while the 8th and 15th spatial map represents the right hand imagery. In Fig. 2(b), the 2nd and 8th components are related to the right hand and foot, respectively.

3 ICA-Based Temporal Features

After obtaining new time signals for each spatial feature, it is useful to look for temporal features. The neurophysiological phenomena such as ERD and ERS are used for classifying motor-related tasks, and mainly appear in particular frequency bands. Therefore, both temporal filtering and spatial filtering are required for effective classification. [12] Although Fourier or Wavelet analysis has been used to analyze the frequency characteristics of EEG of a subject, here we use ICA to obtain subject-dependent temporal bandpass filtering with unsupervised learning.

In the ICA-based temporal filtering, ICA is used separately in each spatial source. For each $u_i(t)$ from $\mathbf{u}(t) = [u_1(t) \ . \ . \ u_n(t)]^T$, where n is the number of sources, ICA-based temporal filtering is performed for framed samples in a moving time window as [13]

$$\tilde{\mathbf{u}}_i(t) = [u_i(t) : u_i(t-1) : ... : u_i(t-m+1)]^T \tag{3}$$

where the frame length m is the number of time steps needed to contain sufficient temporal information. Again, $\tilde{\mathbf{u}}_i(t)$ is represented as a linear combination of basis vectors, and the temporal features and corresponding coefficients may be obtained by ICA learning algorithms.

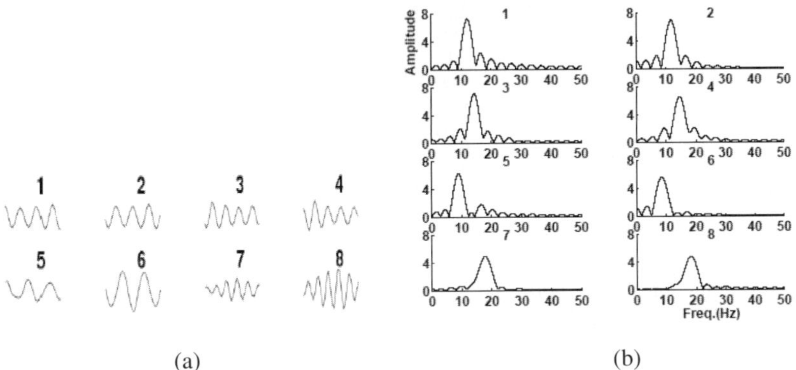

(a)   (b)

Fig. 2. Top 8 temporal bases from the 15th spatial IC of Fig. 1(a) when a subject is given a binary task, i.e., left hand vs. right hand movement imagery. (a) Temporal bases in time domain, i.e., impulse responses of FIR filters. (b) Frequency spectra, i.e., FIR filter transfer functions.

Fig. 2 shows the ICA-based temporal filters in (a) time domain, i.e., impulse responses, and (b) frequency domain, i.e., transfer functions. Since we are interested in the frequency band of 8-30Hz, m is set to 30 to obtain 300ms time windows which correspond to 2.4 cycles of the lowest frequency component with 100Hz sampling frequency. The temporal features are sorted by the signal variance.

In Fig. 2, the top 8 temporal bases are plotted from coefficients corresponding to the 15th spatial map in Fig. 2(a) when a subject is given a binary task, i.e., left or right hand movement imagery. This map is localized spatially in the left hemisphere, and some temporal bases corresponding to this spatial IC are located on the alpha band. Since ERD may be generated in the alpha band over these regions for right hand imagery, it is well matched with known neurophysiological facts.

It is well known that the standard ICA algorithm is not able to extract shift-invariant features, and some of the temporal bases are actually shifted version of other bases. However, Fig. 2 and 4 clearly demonstrate that the temporal basis components are localized in the frequency domain, especially in the alpha and beta bands.

4 Feature Selection

In this study, we performed experiments by assuming different numbers of sources and select relevant features thereafter by Fisher score. By applying Principal Component Analysis (PCA) we reduced the vector dimension to 10, 30, 50, 70, 90, and 110 from 118 channels [14]. Then, for each case Fisher scores are calculated for each spatial maps, and the spatial maps with larger Fisher scores are considered as critical sources. It turns out that 50 to 90 spatial maps show higher Fisher scores, and are used for subsequent experiments. In temporal ICA, 10, 20, and 30 independent components are assumed. Then, Fisher scores are calculated for each spatio-temporal features.

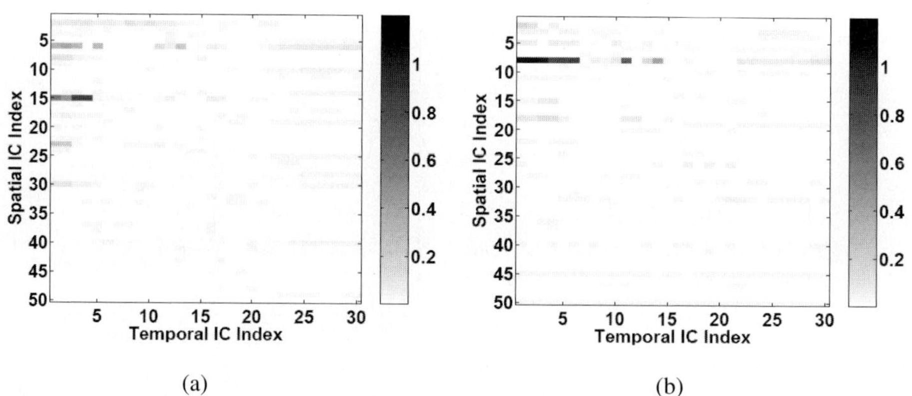

(a)   (b)

Fig. 3. Fisher scores of the ICA-based spatio-temporal features when subject *aa* is given binary asks. (a) Left hand vs. right hand movement imagery. (b) Right hand vs. foot movement magery.

Fig. 3 shows the Fisher scores for 50 spatial ICs with 30 temporal ICs each. In Fig. 3(a), the 15th and 6th spatial components are dominant. As shown in Fig. 1(a), the 15th and 6th spatial components are dominant on the left and right motor cortex, respectively. Although the 8th spatial map is similar to the 15th map and may be selected by simple insights [7], it is less effective for the binary discrimination.

In the temporal ICA, the temporal bases in the upper alpha band have higher Fisher scores. In Figs. 2 and 3(a), the 3rd and 4th temporal bases are located in the upper alpha band, and they have a higher score. Fig. 3(b) shows the Fisher scores for right hand vs. foot imagery, and the 8th spatial map is dominant. As shown in Fig. 1(b), the 8th spatial map has dominant activation on the left hemisphere. When a right hand movement is imagined, ERD in the left hemisphere is dominant. Also, when a right foot movement is imagined, ERS occurs in the left hemisphere [15].

After the ICA-based spatial and temporal filtering for data from a subject, we can select a few critical spatio-temporal bases according to the Fisher scores. This analysis is intended to be implemented for each subject and extract features fine-tuned to specific subject for better recognition of single-trial EEG for BCI applications

5 Discussion

For BCI systems based on motor imagery tasks, especially for single-trial EEG systems, ERD and ERS generated in particular brain area and frequency band are good features. In previous studies, efforts have been made to obtain spatial maps from EEG data [6] [7] [9] [10]. However, temporal filtering is also required to extract ERD/ERS features. Although fixed alpha band (8-13Hz) and beta band (16-24Hz) may be used [7] [10], these bands may be fine-tuned to users for better classification in this study.

The ICA-based spatio-temporal filtering proposed in this paper is capable of extracting dominant features of the ERD and ERS for each subject, and results in much better recognition rates with smaller personal variance. The spatial ICs correspond to independent neuronal sources with spatial maps, and temporal ICs are obtained for each spatial IC. Several dominant temporal ICs are located in the alpha and beta bands.

Since the number of features is not known in priori and the measured data are quite noisy, it is also important to select only a few critical features from many self-organized features. The Fisher score is one possible criterion to select subject-dependent spatial maps and frequency bands. Recently the mutual information (MI) between the class label variable and features are used for the feature selection with some success. However, the MI calculation needs joint probability density function, which is difficult for multivariate variables. The statistical independence of ICA-based features allows to use only MI between the class variable and a feature variable.

The user-adaptable self-organized features and feature selections may be extremely important for single-trial EEG classification with huge personal and trial variation. By filtering EEG signals with those dominant spatio-temporal features we are working on confirming ERD and ERS for certain motor imagery tasks, which coincides well with neurophysiological understanding.

Acknowledgments. This research was supported as Brain Neuroinformatics Research Program by the Korean Ministry of Commerce, Industry, and Energy. We are grateful to Drs. Klaus-Robert Müller, Benjamin Blankertz and Gabriel Curio for providing us with their data.

References

1. Birbaumer, N., Kubler, A., Ghanayim, N., Hinterberger, T., Perelmouter, J., Kaiser, J., Iversen, I., Kotchoubey, B., Neumann, N., Flor, H.: The thought translation device (ttd) for completely paralyzed patients. IEEE Trans. Rehab. Eng. 8, 190–193 (2000)
2. Donchin, E., Spencer, K.M., Wijesinghe, R.: The mental prosthesis: assessing the speed of a p300-based brain-computer interface. IEEE Trans. Rehabil. Eng. 8, 174–179 (2000)
3. Makeig, S., Enghoff, S., Jung, T.P., Sejnowski, T.J.: A natural basis for efficient brain-actuated control. IEEE Trans. Rehabilitation Eng. 8, 208–211 (2000)
4. Pfurtscheller, G., Neuper, C., Flotzinger, D., Pregenzer, M.: EEG-based discrimination between imagination of right and left hand movement. Electroenceph. clin. Neurophysiol. 103, 642–651 (1997)
5. Wolpaw, J.R., McFarland, D.J., Vaughan, T.M.: Brain-computer interface research at the wadsworth center. IEEE Trans. Rehabil. Eng. 8(2), 222–226 (2000)
6. Muller-Gerking, J., Pfurtscheller, G., Flyvbjerg, H.: Designing optimal spatial filters for single-trial EEG classification in a movement task. Clin. Neurophysiol. 110, 787–798 (1999)
7. Naeem, M., Brunner, C., Leeb, R., Graimann, B., Pfurtscheller, G.: Seperability of four-class motor imagery data using independent components analysis. J. Neural Eng. 3 (2006)
8. Cichocki, A., Shishkin, S.L., Musha, T., Leonowicz, Z., Asada, T., Kurachi, T.: Eeg filtering based on blind source separation (bss) for early detection of alzheimer's disease. Clinical Neurophysiology 116, 729–737 (2005)
9. Ramoser, H., Muller-Gerking, J., Pfurtscheller, G.: Optimal spatial filtering of single trial EEG during imagined hand movement. IEEE Trans. Rehabil. Eng. 8(4), 441–446 (2000)
10. Dornhege, G., Blankertz, B., Curio, G., Muller, K.-R.: Boosting bit rates in non-invasive EEG single-trial classifications by feature combination and multi-class paradigms. IEEE Trans. Biomed. Eng. 51(6), 993–1002 (2004)
11. McFarland, D.J., McCane, L.M., David, S.V., Wolpaw, J.R.: Spatial filter selection for EEG-based communication. Clin. Neurophysiol. 103, 386–394 (1997)
12. Tsai, A.C., Liou, M., Jung, T.P., Onton, J.A., Cheng, P.E., Huang, C.C., Duann, J.R., Makeig, S.: Mapping single-trial EEG records on the cortical surface through a spatiotemporal modality. NeuroImage 32, 195–207 (2006)
13. Lee, J.H., Lee, T.W., Jung, H.Y., Lee, S.Y.: On the efficient speech feature extraction based on independent component analysis. Neural Processing Letters 15, 235–245 (2002)
14. Duda, R.O., Hart, P.E., Stork, D.G.: Pattern Classification, 2nd edn. John Wiley & Sons, Chichester (2001)
15. Pfurtscheller, G., Brunner, C., Schlogl, A., da Silva, F.H.L.: Mu rhythm (de)synchronization and EEG single-trial classification of different motor imagery tasks. NeuroImage 31, 153–159 (2006)

Dynamical Nonstationarity Analysis of Resting EEGs in Alzheimer's Disease

Charles-Francois Vincent Latchoumane[1], Emmanuel Ifeachor[2], Nigel Hudson[2], Sunil Wimalaratna[2], and Jaeseung Jeong[1,*]

[1] Korea Advanced Institute of Science and Technology (KAIST), Dept. of Bio and Brain Engineering, Daejeon, South Korea
jsjeong@kaist.ac.kr
[2] Department of Computer Science, University of Plymouth, Plymouth, UK

Abstract. The understanding of nonstationarity, from both a dynamical and a statistical point of view, has turned from a constraint on application of a specific type of analysis (e.g. spectral analysis), into a new insight into complex system behavior. The application of nonstationarity detection in an EEG time series plays an important role in the characterization of brain processes and the prediction of brain state and behavior such as seizure prediction. In this study, we report a very significant difference in the mean stationarity duration of an EEG over the frontal and temporal regions of the brain, comparing 22 healthy subjects and 16 patients with mild Alzheimer's disease (AD). The findings help illuminate the interpretation of the EEG's duration of dynamical stationarity and proposes to be useful for distinguishing AD patients from control patients. This study supports the idea of a compensatory activation of the fronto-temporal region of the brain in the early stages of Alzheimer's disease.

Keywords: Alzheimer's disease, EEG, dynamical nonstationarity, nonlinear system analysis.

1 Introduction

1.1 Early Detection of Alzheimer's Disease Using EEG Time Series

With an increase in life expectancy, dementia-related disorders such as Alzheimer's disease (AD), Parkinson's disease (PD) and vascular dementia (VAD) are having an increasing impact on socio-economic issues and affected over 29 million people worldwide in 2005, with over 4 million new cases every year [1]. Alzheimer's disease has in particular been working to understand the underlying causes and early disturbances of the brain functions due to the progressive course of the disease; the pathological findings include disturbances in the acetylcholine system [2] and deposition of amyloid plaques and neurofibril tangles [3]. Indeed, patients suffering from AD who are detected early are more likely to receive appropriate treatment to slow the progression of the disease, thereby reducing the cost of their treatment as well as reducing the healthcare system expense. Several methods are now available to

M. Ishikawa et al. (Eds.): ICONIP 2007, Part II, LNCS 4985, pp. 921–929, 2008.

help diagnose AD, including cognitive tests [4], neuro-imaging [5, 6], electro-physiological tests [7, 8], and as a final resource, post mortem analysis of amyloidal plaques and neurofibrillary tangle depositions. In light of the advanced age of the average patient suffering from AD, non-invasive and low-cost methods are preferred, hence the recent interest in EEG analysis the clinical evaluation and diagnosis of early-stage AD.

1.2 Quantitative Study of EEG: Linear and Nonlinear Approaches to Stationarity

Previous studies that have applied quantitative analysis of EEGs in patients with AD can be divided into two approaches: linear and nonlinear methods (see [9] for review). The linear method principally based on spectral, temporal, and spectro-temporal analyses have successfully characterized AD patients in terms of a slowing of the EEGs [10] (i.e. increase in delta and theta powers, and decrease in alpha and beta powers). These findings support the theory of brain reconfiguration in AD patients as the disease progresses, and have also been confirmed by connectivity studies [11, 12]. The characterization of the brain as a nonlinear, deterministic system has justified the application of "nonlinear" methods based on both statistical and dynamical methods extracting associated invariants of the EEG time series [13]. Both linear and nonlinear methods have encountered the well accepted "high nonstationarity" of EEGs as a major limitation to their application. However, the nonstationarity of EEG time series, an intrinsic property of brain electrical signals, appears to be an interesting feature for characterizing brain regimes [14] or state transitions [15].

1.3 Dynamical Nonstationarity Analysis

The current investigation of the EEG time series has revealed several closely related properties that are common to complex dynamical systems (i.e. scaling, complexity, and nonstationarity) and fundamental for interpreting brain (micro/macro) states [15-17]. It was demonstrated that EEGs at rest present a long range correlation and a scale-free set of properties within the alpha and beta bands [18], which is thought to be a hallmark of complex systems with plasticity and multi-time scale correlations (i.e. self-organization) [19]. Statistical nonstationarity (i.e. temporal changes in weak stationary propertics such as the mean, variance, or power spectrum) is a consequence of the multi-scale spatio-temporal interaction within the brain, whereas the dynamical nonstationarity (i.e. temporal change in the dynamical parameter of the system) might be both a consequence and facilitator of the spatio-temporal complexity of the brain signals. In this study, we investigated the potential for dynamical nonstationarity to be a viable observation point to differentiate the control brain from AD brain signals during the resting state at a defined scale, which is constrained by the sampling frequency (128 Hz), the window size (W = 250 data points), and the decision threshold (CUT) used in this analysis.

This paper is structured as follows. In Section 2, we briefly introduce the dissimilarity measures that were used as indexes to observe the change in dynamical nonstationarity. We propose a method based on clustering and outlier identification in order to detect combinations of dissimilarity (i.e. in the two-dimensional space of dissimilarity) that represent dynamical change or transitions. In Section 3, we apply the method to the identification of AD patients when compared with control subjects, in a resting state. Finally, the study is concluded with a discussion of possible clinical applications of the new index to the early detection of AD patients. The aim of this paper is to enhance the understanding of dynamical nonstationarity as meaningful feature of the EEG time series; the issue of temporal/spatial scaling in our method is not addressed, although the interpretation and parameter choice (e.g. length of segments) greatly depend on this factor.

2   Materials and Methods

In this section, we describe the algorithm used to detect the point of changing dynamics (i.e. the dynamical nonstationarity point), as well as the settings of the EEGs and a description of the subjects studied.

Phase Space Density Distribution and Global Dynamical Model. To characterize the nonstationarity of a time series, it is necessary to use dissimilarity measures that are able to distinguish different dynamical regimes. Numerous methods have been proposed to detect nonstationarity transitions of a time series [20-22], but only a few have demonstrated good performance against noise and with a low number of data points (< 1,000). In this study, the density distribution of the phase space [23] and the global dynamical model based on distance polynomial coefficients [24] are used as dissimilarity measures. The details of the computation of these two dissimilarities can be found in the Appendix. The dissimilarities will be calculated for two sets of segments of the original time series comparing temporally successive segments, as explained in the following section.

Segmentation and Clustering. Each time series studied was divided into a first set containing segments of 250 data points (~2 sec) and a second set similar to the first one, but consisting of 125 points (50%). The dissimilarity measures were computed for each set of segments and averaged to form a single, contrasting set of values for each measure, corresponding to the variation in the time of the dissimilarity. The two dynamical indexes of dissimilarity were used as two-dimensional, time dependent (i.e. referring to the comparison of two segments at a given time) coordinates to characterize the temporal variation of the dynamical dissimilarity. The dynamical nonstationarity points form a set of points that have dissimilarity values above the average. Then, we clustered the set of points representing the temporal, dynamical dissimilarity using affinity propagation [25], and the set of nonstationarity points were identified by the clusters with a mean distance to other centers above the threshold θ, defined in Eq. 1:

$$\theta = \mu + CUT * \sigma \tag{1}$$

where μ and σ are respectively the mean and the standard deviation over the inter-center distance, and CUT is a parameter used to modulate the threshold. We also verified that the cluster of nonstationarity points satisfied a sufficient distance to the origin of the dissimilarity space, so that the chosen clusters are outliers and have high dissimilarity values. We demonstrated that for CUT values ranging from 0 to 1.25, the performance of this method against noise was very satisfying [15].

2.1 Subjects

In this study, we used a group of 16 patients with mild Alzheimer's disease (8 men and 8 women, age = 77.6+10.3) and a group of 22 healthy controls (9 men and 13 women, age = 69.5+11.4). The subjects received full cognitive tests, but neuro-physiological information was unavailable for this study.

2.2 Task and EEG Recordings

The EEG time series were digitalized at a sampling frequency of 256 Hz and downsampled to 128 Hz, using 19 leads on a modified Maudsley system (equivalent to the international 10-20 montage) with the reference at the earlobes. The EEGs were recorded for four minutes during a resting condition with various states: awake, drowsy, and alert, with periods of the eyes closed and open. Hence, this recording is representative of a resting state with spontaneous changes in the state of the subject.

2.3 Statistical Analysis

To compare the controls and AD patients, we first examined the effect of the main factor "diagnostic group" and the within-subject factor "channel" using a repeated measure ANOVA. For the post-hoc analysis, we first performed a Kolmogorov-Sinai test to verify the normality of the mean duration of stationarity, followed by a one-way ANOVA with Welch correction for nonequality of variance. Also, the correction for multiple channels using a Bonferroni correction of the p-value is discussed. All statistical analyses were performed using the statistical package for social sciences (SPSS 13.0).

3 Results

The main effect was only found in the "diagnostic group" (F = 8,596, df = 1, p = 0.006), although the "channel" factor was nearly significant (F = 1.839, df =7.585, p = 0.074, Huynh-Feldt correction). No iteration of the "group X channel" effect was found.

Alzheimer's Disease Patients vs. Controls. In this subsection, we present the results found for the parameters S = 10, d = 3, tau = 30, and W = 250 data points; similar results were found for S, d and tau in the range of {5,10}, {3.4} and {20,30}. We found that the AD patients had a shorter duration of stationarity over all channels compared with the controls. The topographic plot of the mean duration time over all leads is presented in Fig. 1.

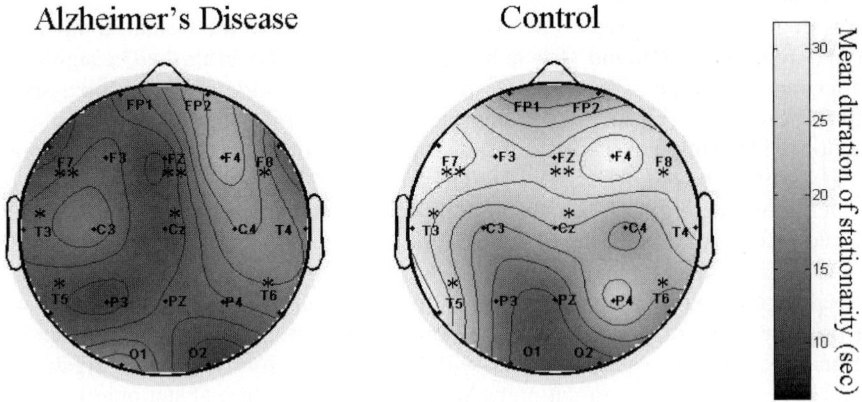

Fig. 1. Topographic plot of the mean duration of stationarity (sec) for Alzheimer's disease patients and control subjects. The leads with significant difference in mean are marked with * (p < 0.05) and ** (p < 0.01).

We found that the difference in the frontal region was highly significant for leads F7 (F(1,26.519) = 9.885, p = 0.004) and Fz (F(1,26.839) = 9.813, p = 0.004), and significant for lead F8 (F(1,23.435) = 5.948, p = 0.023). The temporal region also exhibited significant differences for leads T3 (F(1,28.387) = 5.613, p = 0.025) and T5 (F(1,2.441) = 5.835, p = 0.024) in the left hemisphere, and for leads T6 (F(1,21.962) = 4.301, p = 0.050) and Cz (F(1,23.975) = 4.621, p = 0.042) in the right hemisphere. It can be seen that if the Bonferroni corrections were applied, the new p-value would be set to p = 0.0026, and none of the differences would be considered significant. The Bonferroni correction in this case might be too conservative and could result in a type II error.

We did not have access to the cognitive tests results, so the correlation between the severity of AD disease and the mean duration of stationarity could not be calculated.

Complexity Results. From our previous study [8], we had found that AD patients had a significantly lower complexity (p < 0.05) than the controls for the posterior region of the brain, including the parietal, temporal, and occipital regions. The complexity measures used were the Fractal Dimension (FD), Hjorth Index (HI) and Zero Crossing Interval Distribution (ZCI) [8], and various combinations of those three methods.

4 Discussion

We found the mean duration of dynamical nonstationarity in the EEGs of AD patients significantly shorter than those of the controls in the frontal and temporal regions. The subsequent, significant activation of the two central leads, Fz and Cz, support the existence of a default mode during the resting state [26]. However, since the resting state was somewhat mixed with different states, and also given that other regions were found to be involved in results, caution should be with this conclusion. The early stages of Alzheimer's disease have been thought to involve the frontal, temporal, and parietal regions. We found that a bilateral region of the brain had a significantly shorter mean duration of stationarity, involving the activation of the region associated with the executive (F8, $p < 0.05$) and memory (bilateral temporal region, $p < 0.05$) functions. This supports the idea of a disruption of normal activities in those regions in the early stages of AD [27, 28]. This result could be interpreted as a form of compensatory activity of the fronto-temporal regions, resulting from a cell-loss-induced reconfiguration of the brain network [28].

The decreased complexity found in AD patients was primarily located in the parietal region and to a smaller extent in the temporal area [8]. In this paper, we do not propose a correlation between the complexity results and the mean duration of stationarity; however, such analysis will be a subject for future investigation. We would expect a positive correlation between the short duration of stationarity and high complexity, synonymous with brain activation. Still, it remains unclear how the complexity and nonstationarity are linked. For instance, our previous study on Attention-Deficit and Hyperactivity Disorder (ADHD) supports dynamical nonstationarity being better related to attention change in the brain and a short duration of nonstationarity being more related to a stronger brain activation [29].

In this study, the resolution of the dynamical stationarity was limited by the low sampling frequency of recordings. We will investigate the scaling effect and the influence of the window size, as well as the threshold parameter (CUT), on the mean duration of stationarity for each population in future research. A clear investigation of the relation between the complexity and mean duration of stationarity would be of great benefit to interpret future findings related to those measures.

Acknowledgement. The first author would like to thank the Minister of information and Technology of South Korea, Institute of Information and Technology Advancement (IITA) for their financial support.

References

1. Wimo, A., Winblad, B., Jonsson, L.: An estimate of the total worldwide societal costs of dementia in 2005. Alzheimers & dementia 3 (2007)
2. Lleo, A., Greenberg, S.M., Growdon, J.H.: Current pharmacotherapy for Alzheimer's disease. Annu. Rev. Med. 57, 513–533 (2006)
3. Braak, H., Braak, E.: Neuropathological stageing of Alzheimer-related changes. Acta Neuropathologica 82(4), 239–259 (1991)
4. Locascio, J.J., Growdon, J.H., Corkin, S.: Cognitive test performance in detecting, staging, and tracking Alzheimer's disease. Archives of Neurology 52(11), 1087–1099 (1995)
5. Fox, N.C., Crum, W.R., Scahill, R.I., Stevens, J.M., Janssen, J.C., Rossor, M.N.: Imaging of onset and progression of Alzheimer's disease with voxel-compression mapping of serial magnetic resonance images. The Lancet 358(9277), 201–205 (2001)
6. Jelic, V., Nordberg, A.: Early diagnosis of Alzheimer disease with positron emission tomography. Alzheimer Dis. Assoc. Disord. 14(suppl. 1), S109–113 (2000)

7. Woon, W.L., Cichocki, A., Vialatte, F., Musha, T.: Techniques for early detection of Alzheimer's disease using spontaneous EEG recordings. Physiol. Meas. 28, 335–347 (2007)
8. Goh, C., Ifeachor, E., Henderson, G., Latchoumane, C., Jeong, J., Bigan, C., Hudson, N., Besleaga, M., Capostosto, P., Wimalaratna, S.: Characterization of EEG at different Stages of Alzheimer's disease. In: Proc. International Congress in Clinical Neurophysiology (ICCN 2006), Edinburgh, Scotland (2006)
9. Jeong, J.: EEG dynamics in patients with Alzheimer's disease. Clin. Neurophysiol. 115(7), 1490–1505 (2004)
10. Pucci, E., Belardinelli, N., Cacchio, G., Signorino, M., Angeleri, F.: EEG power spectrum differences in early and late onset forms of Alzheimer's disease. Clin. Neurophysiol. 110(4), 621–631 (1999)
11. Wada, Y., Nanbu, Y., Kikuchi, M., Koshino, Y., Hashimoto, T., Yamaguchi, N.: Abnormal functional connectivity in Alzheimer's disease: intrahemispheric EEG coherence during rest and photic stimulation. European Archives of Psychiatry and Clinical Neuroscience 248(4), 203–208 (1998)
12. Jeong, J., Gore, J.C., Peterson, B.S.: Mutual information analysis of the EEG in patients with Alzheimer's disease. Clin. Neurophysiol. 112, 827–835 (2001)
13. Jeong, J., Kim, S.Y., Han, S.H.: Non-linear dynamical analysis of the EEG in Alzheimer's disease with optimal embedding dimension. Electroencephalogr Clin Neurophysiol. 106(3), 220–228 (1998)
14. Dikanev, T., Smirnov, D., Wennberg, R., Velazquez, J.L., Bezruchko, B.: EEG nonstationarity during intracranially recorded seizures: statistical and dynamical analysis. Clin. Neurophysiol. 116(8), 1796–1807 (2005)
15. Latchoumane, C.-F.V., Chung, D., Kim, S., Jeong, J.: Segmentation and characterization of EEG during mental tasks using dynamical nonstationarity. In: Proc. Computational Intelligence in Medical and Healthcare (CIMED 2007), Plymouth, England (2007)
16. Wackermann, J., Lehmann, D., Michel, C.M., Strik, W.K.: Adaptive segmentation of spontaneous EEG map series into spatially defined microstates. Int. J. Psychophysiol. 14(3), 269–283 (1993)
17. Lehmann, D., Strik, W.K., Henggeler, B., Koenig, T., Koukkou, M.: Brain electric microstates and momentary conscious mind states as building blocks of spontaneous thinking: I. Visual imagery and abstract thoughts. Int. J. Psychophysiol. 29(1), 1–11 (1998)
18. Linkenkaer-Hansen, K., Nikouline, V.V., Palva, J.M., Ilmoniemi, R.J.: Long-Range Temporal Correlations and Scaling Behavior in Human Brain Oscillations. Journal of Neuroscience 21(4), 1370 (2001)
19. Ulanowicz, R.E.: Complexity, stability and self-organization in natural communities. Oecologia 43(3), 295–298 (1979)
20. Cao, Y., Tung, W.W., Gao, J.B., Protopopescu, V.A., Hively, L.M.: Detecting dynamical changes in time series using the permutation entropy. Phys. Rev. E Stat. Nonlin Soft Matter Phys. 70(4 Pt 2), 046217 (2004)
21. Gao, J.B.: Detecting nonstationarity and state transitions in a time series. Phys. Rev. E Stat. Nonlin Soft Matter Phys. 63(6 Pt 2), 066202 (2001)
22. Schreiber, T.: Detecting and Analyzing Nonstationarity in a Time Series Using Nonlinear Cross Predictions. Physical Review Letters 78(5), 843–846 (1997)
23. Hively, L.M., Gailey, P.C., Protopopescu, V.A.: Detecting dynamical change in nonlinear time series. Physics Letters A 258(2), 103–114 (1999)
24. Gribkov, D., Gribkova, V.: Learning dynamics from nonstationary time series: Analysis of electroencephalograms. Physical Review E 61(6), 6538–6545 (2000)

25. Frey, B.J., Dueck, D.: Clustering by Passing Messages Between Data Points. Science 315(5814), 972 (2007)
26. Greicius, M.D., Krasnow, B., Reiss, A.L., Menon, V.: Functional connectivity in the resting brain: A network analysis of the default mode hypothesis. Proceedings of the National Academy of Sciences 100(1), 253–258 (2003)
27. Bookheimer, S.Y., Strojwas, M.H., Cohen, M.S., Saunders, A.M., Pericak-Vance, M.A., Mazziotta, J.C., Small, G.W.: Patterns of brain activation in people at risk for Alzheimer's disease. N. Engl. J. Med. 343(7), 450–456 (2000)
28. Nestor, P.J., Scheltens, P., Hodges, J.R.: Advances in the early detection of Alzheimer's disease. Nat. Med. 10, S34–41 (2004)
29. Latchoumane, C.-F.V., Lee, D., Lee, K.H., Jeong, J.: Dynamical nonstationarity of the EEG in adolescents with attention-deficit/hyperactivity disorder during cognitive task. In: Proc. European Medical & Biological Engineering Conference (EMBEC 2005), Prague, Czech Republic (2005)
30. Takens, F.: Detecting strange attractors in turbulence. Lecture Notes in Mathematics 898(1), 366–381 (1981)
31. Gautama, T., Mandic, D.P., Van Hulle, M.M.: A differential entropy based method for determining the optimal embedding parameters of a signal. In: IEEE International Conference on Acoustics, Speech, and Signal Processing, 2003 Proceedings (ICASSP 2003), vol. 6 (2003)

Appendix: Dynamical-Based Dissimilarities

Phase space density distribution. Phase space density distribution: the dynamical study of a complex time series often yields a phase space reconstruction, which, under the proper conditions, is able to resituate the geometrically defined, dynamical behavior of the system. The characterization of the phase space by its density distribution [23] is able to extract the dynamical invariants (and to some extent the statistical invariants as well [14]) of a time series and has demonstrated a capacity for detecting slight variations in dynamical parameters of a given deterministic system. Given a time series X, we describe the computation of the dissimilarity measure based on the phase space density distribution and between two segments of X, X1 and X2 as follows:

1. The time series X is normalized into S bins as in equation 1:

$$0 \leq s(x(i)) = floor\left(\frac{S*(x(i) - x_{min})}{x_{max} - x_{min}}\right) \leq S - 1 \qquad (2)$$

   Where the floor is a function returning the next lower integer of its input, and xmax and xmin are respectively the maximum and minimum of X.

2. For the two segments X1 and X2, we perform the reconstruction of the phase space using the delay coordinate following Takens' theorem [30]:

$$V_{i,1/2} = \{s(i), S(i + \tau), ..., S(i + (d-1)*\tau\}$$
$$i = 1, .., N - (d-1)*\tau \qquad (3)$$

Where Vi,1/2 is a d-dimensional vector for the time i corresponding to the segment X1 or X2. N is the number of points of each segment X1 and X2, and d and τ are the embedding parameters, namely the embedding dimension and the time delay.

3. For each of the reconstructed and partitioned (through binning of X) phase spaces of X1 and X2, we calculate the point density in each unity volume (or space partition). We obtain the spatial density distributions of the reconstructed phase spaces D1 and D1, respectively, of X1 and X2.

The dynamical dissimilarity is obtained by comparing the two distributions D1 and D2 using a chi-square method:

$$\chi^2(D_1, D_2) = \sum_{l=1}^{B} \frac{(D_1(l) - D_2(l))^2}{D_1(l) + D_2(l)} \tag{4}$$

Where B is the total number of bins of the distributions D1 and D2.

We estimated the embedding parameters using Kozachenko-Leonenko (K-L) based differential entropy [31] and found that (3,30) and (4,20) for the (d, τ) values were suitable for our EEG data sets. We found that S ranging from 5 to 10 gave a good contrast of dissimilarity, especially against noise [15].

Global dynamical model. As an additional measure of dissimilarity, we used the Euclidian distance between the coefficients of a global dynamical model. This distance between two segments has been consequently used in [14, 24] and demonstrated a capacity for identifying dynamically changing points for appropriately chosen polynomial orders. A time series segment can be reconstructed using a recurrent form:

$$x_{n+1} = f(x_n) \tag{5}$$

Where f is a polynomial function of order p as described in equation 5:

$$f(x_n) = \sum_{i=0}^{p} \alpha_i x_n^i \tag{6}$$

The distance between two segments can be defined as the Euclidian distance between the coefficients of the two segments' model:

$$d = \sum_{i=0}^{p} (\alpha_{i1} - \alpha_{i2})^2 \tag{7}$$

Where $\alpha i1$ and $\alpha i2$ are the model coefficients of segment 1 and 2, respectively. We found that polynomial models of an order higher or equal to 6 were sensitive to small changes of dynamical parameters. We chose p = 6 for all analyses.

Computational Modeling of Circadian Rhythms in Suprachiasmatic Nucleus Neurons

Hyoungkyu Kim and Jaeseung Jeong

KAIST (Korea Advanced Institute of Science and Technology), Dept. of Bio and Brain
Engineering, 335 Gwahak ro, Yuseong-gu, Daejeon, South Korea
jsjeong@kaist.ac.kr

Abstract. The suprachiasmatic nucleus(SCN) is a self-sustaining circadian
rhythm generator in mammals. SCN neurons exhibit irregular and complex
firing activity, but their firing rates display well-defined deterministic behavior
with a periodicity of 24 hours. Their underlying mechanisms are still unclear. In
this study, we aim to develop the computational model using NEURON, a
software package for biological neuron simulation, to examine channel
contributions to circadian rhythms. We found that SCN neurons produced
circadian rhythms of firing activity through an interplay of various channels,
including the potassium and sodium channels.

Keywords: suprachiasmatic nucleus, computational model, potassium channel,
sodium channel.

1   Introduction

The suprachiasmatic nucleus(SCN) is a self-sustaining circadian rhythm generator in
mammals [1]. The rhythmicity of the SCN originates in the negative feedback loop of
clock genes that interact with the gene expression cycle of each other [2]. The
internal molecular oscillations create circadian change of physiological signals, and
thus produce high-frequency firing during the day and low-frequency firing at night.
These diurnal patterns of electrophysiological properties may exert control over the
circadian activities of organs, body temperature and locomotion. Therefore, a
considerable amount of experimental research has investigated the circadian firing
activity of SCN. However, it is difficult to experimentally measure every parameter at
the same time and it is barely possible to control several components simultaneously.
At present, these problems are best overcome by using computational modeling.

1.1   Circadian Activity of SCN Neurons

Spontaneous firing patterns of the SCN can be divided into regular and irregular
types, based on the interspike interval histogram and the membrane potential
trajectory between spikes. SCN neurons exhibit either regular or irregular activity, or
can be silent [3, 4]. The average firing rate of individual neurons ranges between 0
and 15 Hz. Regular-firing neurons generally have higher firing rates than irregular

M. Ishikawa et al. (Eds.): ICONIP 2007, Part II, LNCS 4985, pp. 930–939, 2008.

ones [5]. Applied depolarizing currents are known to convert an irregular pattern into regular firing, and hyperpolarizing currents can convert regular to irregular activity [3, 6]. This physiological property feature is an important clue for understanding the underlying mechanism of SCN firing. However, the mechanisms responsible for these different patterns of electrical activity and their role in the circadian rhythms of the SCN and its targets are presently unknown.

1.2   Ion Channels and Electrophysiological Properties in Circadian Activity

The modulation of basal membrane potential and regulation conductance in spike production are important components of spike frequency change in the SCN. Therefore, various experiments were performed to account for the spontaneous firing and day/night firing rate oscillation of SCN in ionic mechanisms supporting spike frequency rhythms and several ionic properties contributing to regulate membrane currents have been recently proposed. Slowly inactivating persistent sodium currents are one of the important sources of the repetitive spiking as the depolarizing current drives the cell toward the spike threshold [7, 8].

Many kinds of neurons in the mammalian central nervous system have a non-inactivating component of the tetrodotoxin-sensitive Na current, commonly referred to as persistent Na current (INa,P) [9]. This current has a low threshold for activation, is thought to play an important role in the control of neuronal excitability, and could serve as a driving force in spontaneous firing. A pharmacologically similar Na current that exhibits slow inactivation (INa,S) has been found in SCN neurons [10]. It has been suggested that INa,S participates directly in spontaneous firing in SCN neurons, because INa,S has a large amplitude during the interspike interval. Furthermore, riluzole, a specific inhibitor of INa,P, inhibits INa,S and suppresses spontaneous firing in these neurons [11]. In principle, all three could originate from a single population of channels, because some models of sodium channel gating kinetics predict slow and incomplete inactivation of macroscopic current of depolarizations into subthreshold voltages [12]. However, some of the previous studies have classified the subthreshold sodium current as a slowly inactivating component of the sodium current distinguishable from both conventional fast-inactivating sodium current and persistent noninactivating sodium current [8, 10]. Therefore, we inserted fast and slow inactivation sodium channels and persistent sodium channel separately into our model.

A sufficiently rapid repolarization in the falling phase of the spike is also required for repetitive spontaneous spiking. Voltage-dependent potassium currents are closely correlated with this property. Potassium currents are a large and diverse family of voltage regulators, and previous studies have characterized a number of intrinsic voltage-gated potassium currents in SCN neurons. Recently, the fast delayed rectifier (FDR) potassium current that contributes to circadian spike frequency regulation was characterized in SCN neurons [13]. The possibility of diurnal or circadian modulation of these potassium currents has not, however, been reportedly explored in any detail, nor the mechanism for regulating the daily rhythm by the frequency of action potentials.

The control of basal membrane potential is mostly mediated by leak potassium currents. Long-term intracellular recordings from the circadian pacemaker neurons demonstrated that circadian rhythms in the firing rate were driven by daily changes in basal membrane potential. During the day phase of the circadian cycle, SCN neurons are continuously depolarized by approximately 10 mV relative to their basal membrane potential during the night phase [4]. These changes are mediated primarily by a daytime decrease in the conductance of potassium currents in SCN neurons [14].

Calcium activated potassium (BK) currents also contribute to changes of the firing rate with rhythmic oscillation of the expression of channel proteins. BK channels mediate repolarization following an action potential. They participate participates in the falling phase of spikes, as well as in producing the after-hyperpolarization (AHP). The daily expression of the large conductance BK channel in the SCN is controlled by the intrinsic circadian clock. A rhythmically expressed transcript in the SCN encoding the large conductance BK channel is highly expressed during the subjective night, when SFR is low. BK channels are implicated as important regulators of the SFR, and it has been suggested that the SCN pacemaker governs the expression of circadian behavioral rhythms through SFR modulation [15, 16].

The other form of intrinsic drive-to-threshold in SCN neurons comes from depolarizing calcium current oscillations mediated by L-type voltage-dependent calcium channels. These oscillations cause the membrane voltage to fluctuate around the spike threshold and are regulated in a diurnal manner, being active only during the day time. They contribute modestly to high SCN neuron spike rates during the day phase and are not the primary cause of physiological rhythmicity. The K current-mediated rhythms in basal membrane potential and input resistance persist during acute blockade of high-frequency calcium oscillations by L-type channel blockers and blockade of sodium currents by tetrodotoxin [17]. In addition, day-night differences in intracellular calcium levels within SCN neurons have been observed [18, 19], and complete removal of calcium from the extracellular medium or simultaneous blockade of multiple calcium channel isoforms apparently halts the circadian clock in the SCN [20]. Thus, whereas calcium currents may have a limited role in actual spike production in SCN neurons (above), they may nevertheless provide a key feedback link from membrane events to the intracellular oscillator mechanism.

1.3 Previous Studies with Computational Models

Over a period of many years there have been several different attempts to construct computational models of the SCN. Mathematical models for circadian rhythms have been proposed for Drosophila [21] and Neurospora[22]. These deterministic models, based on experimental observations, predict that in a certain range of parameter values, the genetic regulatory network undergoes sustained oscillations of the limit cyclic type corresponding to circadian rhythmic behavior, whereas, outside this range, the gene network operates in a stable steady state. Stochastic simulation showed the circadian rhythms remain robust with respect to molecular noise [23], and the deterministic model incorporated the regulatory effects exerted on gene expression by the PER, CRY, BMAL1, CLOCK, and REV-ERB proteins, as well as posttranslational regulation of these proteins by reversible phosphorylation, and also light-induced Per expression[21]. A model of physiological spike firing, however, has not been reported.

1.4 Significance and Aims of the Study

There are many experimental studies of single channel properties which help explain various aspects of the physiological properties in SCN neurons. However, these individual results are hard to incorporate with each other. It is almost impossible to control every variable and estimate the innate relationships of the channels. That is the reason why the underlying physiological mechanism and relationship between the components of the contributing channels are still unknown. In addition, the study of a physiological model with computational simulation had not previously achieved sufficient progress to be effective due to a lack of experimental data. Based on the accumulation of newly discovered results in the various part of SCN neuron, we developed a biologically faithful model of circadian activity in SCN neurons. We constructed a computational model of spontaneous firing SCN neurons by inserting individual channel models into single SCN neurons and estimated the parameters from the information of previous experimental studies. After the model construction we reproduced the experimental finding in previous studies using the model. We tested the spontaneous firing and regular/irregular firing pattern changes in the model. We also checked whether the functional role of each channel is similar to reported experimental results. After verification of the model, we investigated the spontaneous firing rate (SFR) with variations of conductance in specific channels mainly contributing to SFR change. Simulation of channels correlated with SFR and reconstruction of day/night circadian rhythmic firing rate change was able to reveal the underlying principles of physiological mechanisms in SCN neurons.

2 Channel Selection and Parameter Estimation for Modeling

The NEURON 5.6 simulation environment (Hines and Carnevale, 1997) was used for neuronal modeling and simulation. The morphology of SCN neurons was based on the observations by Hofman, et al. (1988). A single neuron structure was built with a simulator by using cable theory. In the standard condition, the specific membrane resistance (Rm), and specific membrane capacitance (Cm) were uniform and set to 20 kΩ/cm2 and 1μF/cm2, respectively. Axial resistivity was 11.5 mS/cm, and membrane capacitance was 1μF/cm2. Temperature for simulations was 23°C. Passive leak conductance, gleak, was calculated to give the matched average value of Rin in real tonic neurons when tested with TTX present. The transient sodium (INa,S , INa,F) and delayed rectifier potassium (IKFDR, IKSDR) currents were described by the Hodgkin-Huxley model. These sodium and potassium channels were modeled as described by Wang et al. (1998), Traub et al. (2003), and Hodgkin and Huxley (1952).

Other active currents (M-type potassium (K(M)), L-type calcium (Ca(L)), calcium-dependent potassium (K(Ca)), persistent sodium (NaP)), were described by the Hodgkin–Huxley formalism. All channel mechanisms were obtained from the web-accessible Model DB and implemented without modification.

With the currents, membrane capacitance Cm (mF/cm2), and the passive leak conductance (L), membrane potential V was given by the equation:

$$C_{\mathrm{m}}\frac{\mathrm{d}V}{\mathrm{d}t} = -I_{\mathrm{Na}} - I_{\mathrm{K}} - I_{\mathrm{K(A)}} - I_{\mathrm{Ca}} - I_{\mathrm{K(Ca)}} - I_{\mathrm{NaP}} - I_{\mathrm{L}}$$

We estimated biologically plausible channel conductance ranges from experimental data reported in previous studies [7, 13, 15, 17, 19, 24]. The basic estimated values of conductance were calculated from the I-V relation and input resistance data. We only used experimental data of the mouse and whole cell patch-clamping method was the first experiment considered, then cell attached experiments. We estimated the range from calculation of day/night channel conductance changes, as in the experimental studies already presented. The unknown parameters, however, (e.g. leak potassium current and persistent sodium current) were estimated by subtracting the conductance values already known from entire sodium or potassium conductance values. The values in parentheses are the ranges that the model maintains appropriate spike firing rates during the trials of the model simulation. The parenthesized values are stable ranges in the model simulation trials.

Table 1. Conductance range of specific channels in the SCN neuron model

Biologically Plausible Conductance Range (mS/cm^2)			
Leak potassium current	0.00001~0.0003 (0.00001~0.0001)	Fast delayed rectifier K current	0.0015~0.0045 (0.002~0.0042)
Fast inactivation s odium current	0.01~0.0947 (0.02~0.078)	Slow delayed rectifier K current	0.001~0.002 (0.001~0.003)
Slow inactivation sodium current	0.01~0.0947 (0.02~0.078)	Calcium activated K current	0.003~0.0105 (0.0005~0.0018)
Persistent sodium current	0.0005~0.006 (0.0006~0.0032)	L-type calcium current	0.001~0.00295 (0.001~0.0022)

3 Verification of the Model

3.1 Reproduction of Spontaneous Firing

Although there has been a great deal of experimental data gathered in previous studies, the parameters were obtained from conditions of different species, life stages, instruments and drugs used in the experiments. In addition, it is almost impossible to know the relative contribution ratio of each of the channels or the proper combination of usable data in a single experimental case, because each experiment is limited to monitoring only one or two channels at the same time. Therefore, the recording conditions also exert a heavily influence on the values of the parameters, even in experiments for the same ion channel. For example, the conductance estimation of a single slow inactivation sodium channel was one-fifth compare with another study [24]. To determine accurate values the model was simulated with various conductance values for every channel within the biologically plausible range.

We chose conductance values so as to reproduce spontaneous spike firing and spike shape in the SCN neurons without an environmental input signal. Regular high frequency firing and irregular low frequency firing were reproduced (in figure 1). The spike firing rate (SFR) of the model is high and regular with high persistent sodium current and fast delayed rectifier potassium current, and low leak potassium current and calcium-activated potassium current. Low and irregular SFR was simulated with opposite conductance values. The spike shape is the same as the Hodgkin-Huxley type neuron spike.

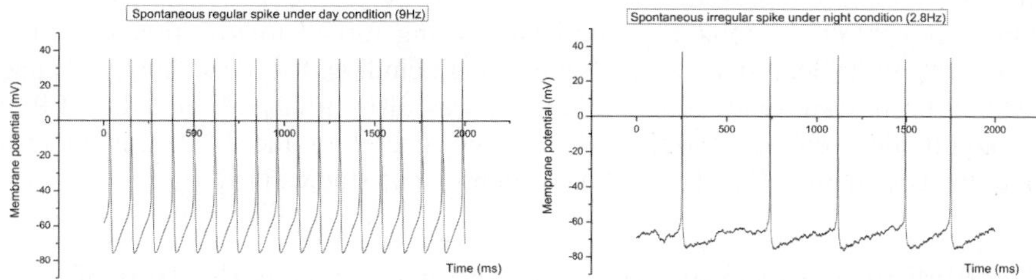

Fig. 1. Regular and high spike (left) and irregular and low spike generation (right)

We also compared spike shape and interspike intervals (ISIs) of the regular and irregular firings. The outcome was very similar with the result of a previous study on the mechanism of irregular firing in SCN neurons [25]. In addition, the asymmetry (skewness) of the ISI values in each state were largely different (regular state < 1.3, irregular state > 2.5) as in previous studies [25].

3.2 Reproduction of Channel Functions in Spike Firing

There are a number of studies on channel activities in SCN neurons using channel blockers. Each channel has been blocked with a specific channel blocker in brain slices or dissociated SCN neurons to estimate channel conductance, and the channel contribution during spike firing verified. We simulated our model by excluding important channels associated with spike firing. The SFR and spike amplitude are

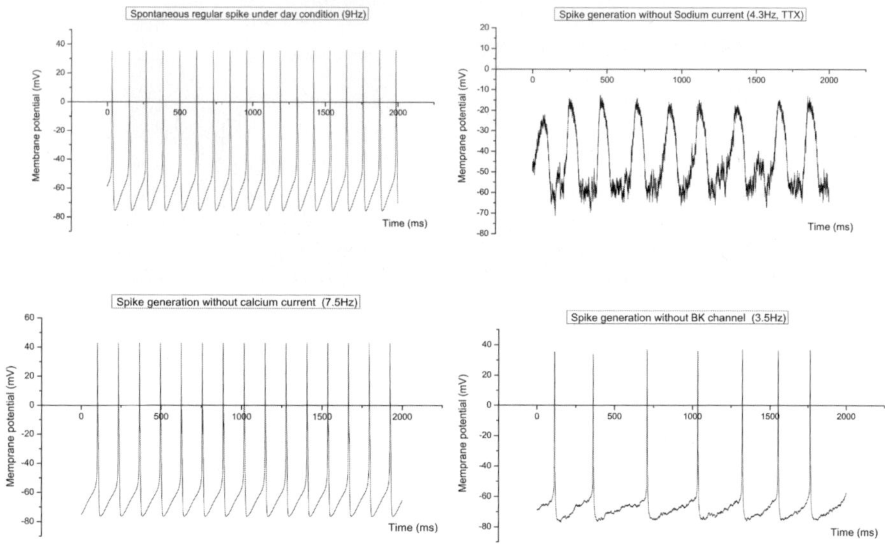

Fig. 2. Spike generation without channels

strongly reduced in the presence of TTX [17], and we reproduced this model without sodium currents. The regular high frequency firing turned to low frequency firing with an amplitude less than zero (figure 2). Excluding L-type calcium channels, which can be blocked with nimodipine [17] was also simulated, and the SFR and spike amplitude were decreased (9Hz-7.5Hz). Therefore the SFR was increased without the BK channel (2.8Hz-3.5Hz) , as in previous studies [15].

4   Prediction of Physiological Properties for Reproduction of Circadian Activity

4.1   Mechanisms of SFR Determination

Persistent sodium currents appear to be a main component in the regulation of the SCN neuron firing rate [8]. As well as the persistent sodium currents which regulate the SFR of SCN neuron, leak potassium currents and fast delayed rectifier potassium current are also expected to be important parts of the firing activity of SCN [13]. We simulated our model with various combinations of conductance using these channels. Increasing persistent sodium current and fast delayed rectifier potassium (KFDR) current pushed the SFR to a high frequency. On the other hand, increasing leak potassium current induced low frequency though both the KFDR and leak currents are related to potassium ions. When the leak current is too much higher than the persistent sodium current, the SCN neurons did not exhibit an action potential.

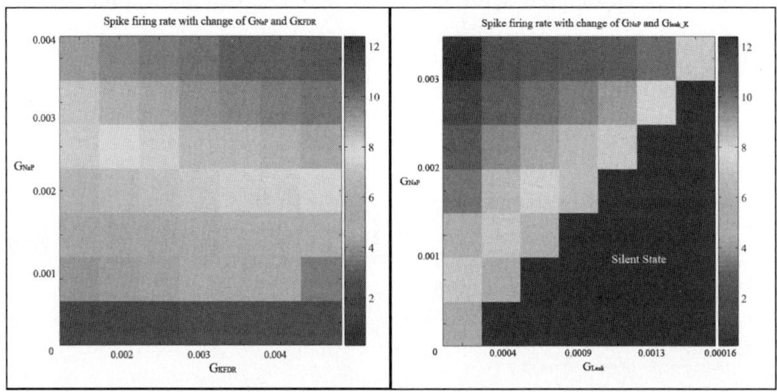

Fig. 3. Color map of SFR with conductance changes

4.2   Channel Contribution in Circadian Rhythm Generation

We examined the SFR with changes in the conductance of persistent sodium current with the assumption that the conductance is modified into a triangle and sinusoidal shape over time. The circadian change of SFR, however, was not a sinusoidal shape, as has been shown previously [26]. Therefore, we changed the regulated shape of the conductance change to a cuspidal shape.

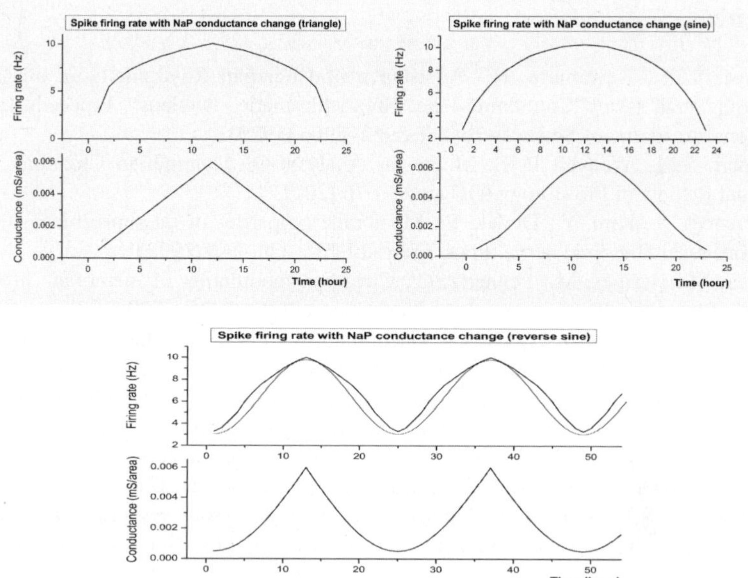

Fig. 4. Circadian change of SFR linked with the conductance shape of the NaP channel

As shown in figure 4, the circadian SFR became much more similar with a sinusoidal curve (red). We propose that the circadian change of channel conductance to be a cuspidal shape. The change in NaP conductance, however, could not create a realistic circadian rhythm, because the conductances of the other channels were fixed.

5   Discussion

SCN neurons evoke spontaneous firing activity and are mainly involved in subthreshold sodium and potassium currents [7, 25]. Because the membrane current oscillation is proportional to each channel conductance, there were many investigations of day/night changes in channel conductance which have sought to make clear the mechanism of circadian rhythm generation. The conductance value and SFR with time flow, however, are hard to measure in the course of experiments because the life-time of the patched cells is not sufficiently long to check for circadian change. We were able to estimate the appropriate conductance shape time and propose the shape to be a cuspidal curve. This is reasonable because the subunits of the NaP channel can rapidly combine with each other as the concentration of subunits is higher.

The circadian rhythm of SFR differs from an exact sinusoidal curve only with the NaP channel conductance change shown in figure 4. The differences emerge along with the other channel properties. At midnight, KFDR and CaL channel conductance decreases and BK and leak channel conductance increases [10, 15, 27]. All of these changes indicate a lower SFR in proportion to the amount of changes. In addition, the reduced calcium concentration and hyperpolarized resting membrane potential are also reasons for the decreasing SFR[17]. The circadian SFR rhythm is reproduced by means of a summation of the contribution of all of the channels.

References

1. Inouye, S.I.T., Kawamura, H.: Persistence of Circadian Rhythmicity in a Mammalian Hypothalamic"Island"Containing the Suprachiasmatic Nucleus. Proceedings of the National Academy of Sciences 76(11), 5962–5966 (1979)
2. Reppert, S.M., Weaver, D.R.: Molecular Analysis Of Mammalian Circadian Rhythms. Annual Review of Physiology 63(1), 647–676 (2001)
3. References, S., Kim, Y., Dudek, F.: Membrane properties of rat suprachiasmatic nucleus neurons receiving optic nerve input. J Physiol 464, 229–243 (1993)
4. de Jeu, M., Hermes, M., Pennartz, C.: Circadian modulation of membrane properties in slices of rat suprachiasmatic nucleus. Neuroreport 9(16), 3725–3729 (1998)
5. Thomson, A.M., West, D.C., Vlachonikolis, I.G.: Regular firing patterns of suprachiasmatic neurons maintained in vitro. Neurosci. Lett. 52(3), 329–334 (1984)
6. Thomson, A.M., West, D.C.: Factors Affecting Slow Regular Firing in the Suprachiasmatic Nucleus In Vitro. Journal of Biological Rhythms 5(1), 59 (1990)
7. Jackson, A.C., Yao, G.L., Bean, B.P.: Mechanism of Spontaneous Firing in Dorsomedial Suprachiasmatic Nucleus Neurons. Journal of Neuroscience 24(37), 7985–7998 (2004)
8. Kononenko, N.I., Medina, I., Dudek, F.E.: Persistent subthreshold voltage-dependent cation single channels in suprachiasmatic nucleus neurons. Neuroscience 129(1), 85–92 (2004)
9. Reppert, S.M., Weaver, D.R.: Coordination of circadian timing in mammals. Nature 418, 935–941 (2002)
10. Pennartz, C.M.A., Bierlaagh, M.A., Geurtsen, A.M.S.: Cellular Mechanisms Underlying Spontaneous Firing in Rat Suprachiasmatic Nucleus: Involvement of a Slowly Inactivating Component of Sodium Current. Journal of Neurophysiology 78(4), 1811–1825 (1997)
11. Kononenko, N.I., Shao, L.R., Dudek, F.E.: Riluzole-Sensitive Slowly Inactivating Sodium Current in Rat Suprachiasmatic Nucleus Neurons. Journal of Neurophysiology 91(2), 710–718 (2004)
12. Taddese, A., Bean, B.P.: Subthreshold Sodium Current from Rapidly Inactivating Sodium Channels Drives Spontaneous Firing of Tuberomammillary Neurons. Neuron 33(4), 587–600 (2002)
13. Itri, J.N., Michel, S., Meijer, J.H., Colwell, C.S.: Fast delayed rectifier potassium current is required for circadian neural activity. Nature Neuroscience 8, 650–656 (2005)
14. Kuhlman, S.J., McMahon, D.G.: Rhythmic regulation of membrane potential and potassium current persists in SCN neurons in the absence of environmental input. Eur J Neurosci 20(4), 1113–1117 (2004)
15. Meredith, A.L., Wiler, S.W., Miller, B.H., Takahashi, J.S., Fodor, A.A., Ruby, N.F., Aldrich, R.W.: BK calcium-activated potassium channels regulate circadian behavioral rhythms and pacemaker output. Nature Neuroscience 9, 1041–1049 (2006)
16. Pitts, G.R., Ohta, H., McMahon, D.G.: Daily rhythmicity of large-conductance Ca 2-activated K currents in suprachiasmatic nucleus neurons. Brain Research 1071(1), 54–62 (2006)
17. Pennartz, C.M.A., de Jeu, M.T.G., Bos, N.P.A., Schaap, J., Geurtsen, A.M.S.: Diurnal modulation of pacemaker potentials and calcium current in the mammalian circadian clock. Nature 416, 286–290 (2002)
18. Colwell, C.S.: Circadian modulation of calcium levels in cells in the suprachiasmatic nucleus. European Journal of Neuroscience 12(2), 571–576 (2000)

19. Ikeda, M., Sugiyama, T., Wallace, C.S., Gompf, H.S., Yoshioka, T., Miyawaki, A., Allen, C.N.: Circadian Dynamics of Cytosolic and Nuclear Ca2+ in Single Suprachiasmatic Nucleus Neurons. Neuron 38(2), 253–263 (2003)
20. Lundkvist, G.B., Kwak, Y., Davis, E.K., Tei, H., Block, G.D.: A Calcium Flux Is Required for Circadian Rhythm Generation in Mammalian Pacemaker Neurons. Soc Neuroscience (2005)
21. Leloup, J.C., Goldbeter, A.: Toward a detailed computational model for the mammalian circadian clock. Proceedings of the National Academy of Sciences 100(12), 7051–7056 (2003)
22. Smolen, P., Baxter, D.A., Byrne, J.H.: Modeling Circadian Oscillations with Interlocking Positive and Negative Feedback Loops. Journal of Neuroscience 21(17), 6644 (2001)
23. Gonze, D., Halloy, J., Goldbeter, A.: Deterministic Versus Stochastic Models for Circadian Rhythms. Journal of Biological Physics 28(4), 637–653 (2002)
24. Kononenko, N.I., Dudek, F.E.: Noise of the slowly inactivating Na current in suprachiasmatic nucleus neurons. Neuroreport 16(9), 981–985 (2005)
25. Kononenko, N.I., Dudek, F.E.: Mechanism of Irregular Firing of Suprachiasmatic Nucleus Neurons in Rat Hypothalamic Slices. Journal of Neurophysiology 91(1), 267–273 (2004)
26. Gillette, M.U., Medanic, M., McArthur, A.J., Liu, C., Ding, J.M., Faiman, L.E., Weber, E.T., Tcheng, T.K., Gallman, E.A.: Intrinsic neuronal rhythms in the suprachiasmatic nuclei and their adjustment. Ciba Found Symp 183, 134–144 (1995)

Incremental Knowledge Representation Based on Visual Selective Attention

Minho Lee[1] and Sang-Woo Ban[2]

[1] School of Electrical Engineering and Computer Science, Kyungpook National University
1370 Sankyuk-Dong, Puk-Gu, Taegu 702-701, Korea
[2] Dept. of Information and Communication Engineering, Dongguk University
707 Seokjang-Dong, Gyeongju, Gyeongbuk, 780-714, Korea
`mholee@knu.ac.kr, swban@dongguk.ac.kr`

Abstract. Knowledge-based clustering and autonomous mental development remains a high priority research topic, among which the learning techniques of neural networks are used to achieve optimal performance. In this paper, we present a new framework that can automatically generate a relevance map from sensory data that can represent knowledge regarding objects and infer new knowledge about novel objects. The proposed model is based on understating of the visual what pathway in our brain. A bottom-up attention model can selectively decide salient object areas. Color and form features for a selected object are generated by a sparse coding mechanism by a convolution neural network (CNN). Using the extracted features by the CNN as inputs, the incremental knowledge representation model, called the growing fuzzy topology adaptive resonant theory (TART) network, makes clusters for the construction of an ontology map in the color and form domains. The clustered information is relevant to describe specific objects, and the proposed model can automatically infer an unknown object by using the learned information. Experimental results with real data have demonstrated the validity of this approach.

Keywords: Incremental Knowledge Representation, Visual Selective Attention, Stereo Saliency Map, Incremental Object Perception.

1   Introduction

Recent research has been directed toward developing a more human-like machine with an autonomous metal development mechanism [1, 2, 3, 4]. In order to develop such a model, we need to consider an efficient method that represents knowledge in complex visual scenes by incremental mode. The human visual system can efficiently process complex visual information by the systematic cooperation of visual selective attention, object perception, knowledge acquisition and inference. Since the human visual cortex can be understood as an efficient organ, the proposed knowledge representation model is based on understanding the visual pathway in our brain. In this paper, we present a new method that can automatically generate a relevance map from sensory data.

M. Ishikawa et al. (Eds.): ICONIP 2007, Part II, LNCS 4985, pp. 940–949, 2008.

In order to implement an incremental knowledge representation model, first, we consider a selective attention model. Previous attention models, including Itti, Koch and Ullman's proposed model, are based on "feature integration theory" [5]. This is done by using color, intensity, and orientation as bases, in order to make a saliency map [6]. Navalparkkam and Itti proposed a goal-oriented attention guidance model that estimates the task-relevance of the attended locations in a scene [7]. Walther, Itti, Riesenhuber, Poggio, and Koch proposed a combined attentional selection model for spatial attention and object recognition [8]. Tsotsos et al. proposed a biologically motivated attention model for detecting movement [9]. Sun and Fisher proposed hierarchical selectivity for object-based visual attention [10]. Conventional approaches are restricted to sensory data and object-based fields, while our model leads sensory data to knowledge representation. Recently, Fei-Fei showed a knowledge transfer framework via one-shot learning [11].

Our motivation is to mimic and understand the mechanism that is involved in autonomous mental development with human interaction. We propose a new knowledge inference scheme, by using the topology information of a selected object, to represent knowledge.

In order to extract and represent features of an arbitrary object by an attention model, we considered the convolution neural network (CNN), which has an ability to characterize and recognize variable object patterns directly from pixel images without the need for preprocessing.

Also, we propose a new growing fuzzy topology adaptive resonance theory (TART) network that makes knowledge clusters in an incremental mode. Finally, the growing fuzzy TART makes clusters.

The main contribution of this paper lies in a new framework for knowledge representation regarding object and knowledge inference based on the preference attention of a natural scene. Furthermore, a new method is developed that uses the proposed growing fuzzy TART to create a knowledge representation model hybrid, with ontology maps for color and form information. Knowledge inference about new objects from previously-perceived data, in conjunction with the perception of color and form, can autonomously and incrementally be processed.

The paper is organized as follows: In Section 2, the proposed knowledge representation model will be described, in which its biological background and the bottom-up saliency map model are explained. In addition, the knowledge representation model, based on the selective attention mechanism, is outlined. Computer simulation results will follow. Concluding remarks and the direction of future research are presented in Section 4.

2 Proposed Model

2.1 Bottom-Up Selective Attention

Figure 1 shows an object preference bottom-up saliency map model [12]. In order to model the human-like visual attention mechanism for a static input scene, we use edge, intensity, and color information. Feature maps ($\overline{I}$, $\overline{O}$ and $\overline{C}$) are constructed by the center surround difference and normalization (CSD & N) of the three bases, which mimic the on-center and off-surround mechanism in our brain. Among the feature maps, the orientation feature map is generated using features that are extracted using Gabor filters from the edge feature, which mimics the orientation selective activation of simple cells in the V1. Moreover, the symmetry feature map is constructed from symmetry features that are obtained by a noise tolerant generalized symmetry transformation (NTGST) algorithm from the orientation features, which mimic the higher-order analysis of complex cells and hyper-complex cells in the V1. By considering symmetry features, this bottom-up attention model has object preference attention. Since most objects normally have symmetry features. The constructed four feature maps ($\overline{I}$, $\overline{O}$, $\overline{S}$, and $\overline{C}$) are then integrated by an independent component analysis (ICA) algorithm, that is based on entropy maximization [12].

Barlow's hypothesis is that human visual cortical feature detectors might be the end result of a redundancy reduction process [13]. Sejnowski argued that the ICA is the best way to reduce redundancy [14]. After the convolution between the channel of the feature maps and the filters obtained by ICA learning, the SM is computed by integrating all feature maps for every location [12]. The LIP provides a retinotopic spatio-feature map that is used to control the spatial focus of attention and fixation, which does this mean the spatial focus is able to integrate feature information in its spatial map. As an integrator of spatial and feature information, the LIP provides the inhibition of return (IOR) mechanism that is required here to prevent the scan path returning to previously-inspected sites [12].

2.2 Object Representation Using CNN

The CNN architecture has the ability to characterize and recognize variable object patterns directly from pixel images without the need for preprocessing. This is done by automatically synthesizing its own set of feature extractors from a large data set [15]. Figure 2 shows the proposed feature extraction model using a CNN. CNN consists of a set of layers. Each layer contains one or more planes. Multiple planes are usually used in each layer so that multiple features can be detected. The input features of the CNN are obtained from a selected salient object area that is automatically decided by the bottom-up saliency map model described in Section 2.1.

In the CNN model, HIS (Hue, Intensity, Saturation) information that is transformed from the RGB input image is used as color input features. Typically, convolutional layers are followed. A convolutional layer is typically followed by another layer that performs local averaging and sub-sampling operations. Log-polar operation can obtain size and rotation invariant representation for a selected object area that has an arbitrary size [16]. Finally, the color features of an object are represented by a 96-dimension vector that consist of six feature maps each of which has 4x4 dimensions.

For the form representation of an input object, eight directional Gabor filters are used to extract initial features. As the input of Gabor filters, we consider the winner-take-all of edge information for each feature which contains feature map reflected parts of dominant pixel in salient regions. We use the same procedure for Garbor features by applying convolution and sub-sampling process. The form features of an input object are represented by a 144-dimension vector that consists of 36 feature maps (2x2 sizes). Therefore, each object is represented by a 240-dimension vector; 96 and 144 dimensions from color features and form features, respectively.

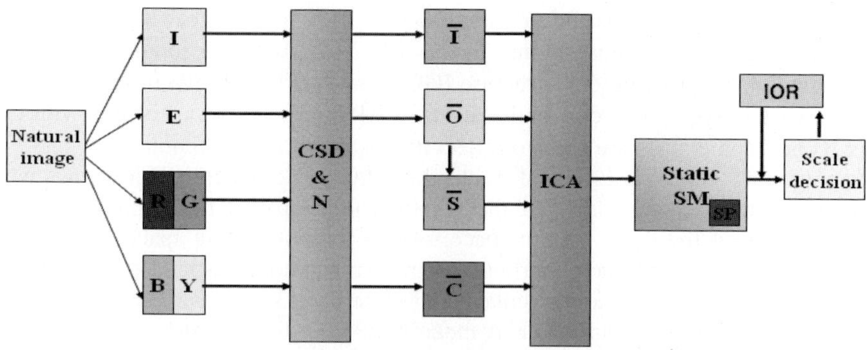

Fig. 1. An overview of the proposed biologically-motivated object selective attention model, in conjunction with an incremental object perception model (I: intensity feature, E: edge feature, RG: red-green opponent coding feature, BY: blue-yellow opponent coding feature, LGN: lateral geniculate nucleus, CSD&N: center-surround difference and normalization, $\bar{I}$: intensity feature map, $\bar{O}$: orientation feature map, $\bar{S}$: symmetry feature map, $\bar{C}$: color feature map, ICA: independent component analysis, SM: saliency map, SP: salient point)

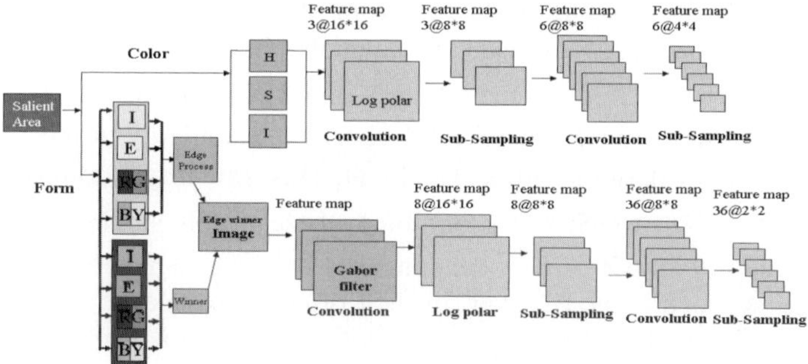

Fig. 2. A convolution network model for extracting form and color features of an object (H: Hue, S: Saturation, I: Intensity)

2.3 Knowledge Representation Using Growing Fuzzy Topology ART (TART)

In exploring the results related with functions in the brain, it is well known that color and form perception can be used for object representation, and knowledge representation module always interacts with the inference module. All of these modules are related with the functions of the prefrontal cortex and they have a close relationship with working memory. The bridge between the sensory data and knowledge representation lies in the motivation to mimic and understand autonomous mental development through human interaction.

The knowledge representation model, based on visual information processing, is described in Figure 3. After natural images are inputted into the system, the saliency point was selected by the bottom-up saliency map model. Features for a selected area are generated by the CNN.

The color and form perception were implemented by the growing fuzzy TART which is integrated the conventional fuzzy ART [17], with the topology-preserving mechanism of the growing cell structure (GCS) unit [18] as shown in Figure 4. Each node in the F2 layer of the conventional fuzzy ART network was replaced with GCS units. Topographic maps are used to reflect the results of the GCS unit.

Topographic maps are related with the idea of competitive learning which incorporates the winner node and the neighborhood around the winner node. The transformation of the input pattern space into the output feature space preserves the topology. Neurons in the neighborhood of the winner node respond to similar input feature. Neurons are tuned to particular input patterns in such a way that they become arranged with respect to each other. A meaningful coordinate system for the different input features is created and spatial locations signify intrinsic statistical features of the input patterns.

The inputs of the growing fuzzy TART consist of the color and form features obtained from the CNN. These features are normalized and then represented as a one-dimensional array X that is composed of every pixel value a_i of the four feature maps and each complement a_i^c is calculated by $1 - a_i$, the values of which are used as an input pattern in the F1 layer of the growing fuzzy TART model. Next, the growing fuzzy TART finds the winning GCS unit from all GCS units in the F2 layer, by calculating   the Euclidean distance between the bottom-up weight vector W_i, connected with every GCS unit in the F2 layer, and X is inputted. After selecting the winner GCS unit, the growing fuzzy TART checks the similarity of input pattern X and all weight vectors W_i of the winner GCS unit. This similarity is compared with the vigilance parameter ρ, which is the minimum these results similarity between the input pattern and the winner GCS. If the similarity is larger than the vigilance value, a new GCS unit is added to the F2 layer. In such situation, resonance has occurred, but if the similarity is less than the vigilance, the GCS algorithm is applied. The detailed GCS algorithm is described as the following [18]:

For initialization, one GCS unit in the F2 layer is created with three nodes n_1 , n_2 , n_3 for its topology and randomly initialized the weight W_i. C, as the connection set, is defined as the empty set $C = \varnothing$.

For each node i in the network, the GCS calculates the distance from the input $\|X - W_i\|$.

The GCS selects the best-matching node and the second best, that are nodes s and t $\in$ A, such that

$$s = \arg \min_{n \in A} \|\xi - W_n\| \qquad (1)$$

$$t = \arg \min_{n \in A/\{s\}} \|\xi - W_n\| \qquad (2)$$

where W_n is the weight vector of node n.

If there is no connection between s and t, a connection is created between s and t.

$$a = \exp(-\|X - W_s\|) \tag{3}$$

If activity a is less than activity threshold a_T, a new node should be added between the two best-matching nodes, s and t.

First, GCS adds the new node r

$$A = A \cup \{(r)\} \tag{4}$$

GCS creates the new weight vector by, setting the weights to be the average of the weights for the best matching node and the second best node

$$w_r = (w_s + w_t)/2 \tag{5}$$

Edges are inserted between r and s and between r and t

$$C = C \cup \{(r,s),(r,t)\} \tag{6}$$

The link is removed between s and t

$$C = C /\{(s,t)\} \tag{7}$$

Adapt the positions of the winning node and its neighbors, i, are adapted to nodes to which they are

$$W_s = \in_b {}^* (\xi - W_s) \tag{8}$$

$$W_i = \in_n {}^* (\xi - W_i) \tag{9}$$

Our approach hopefully enhances the dilemma regarding the stability of fuzzy ART and the plasticity of GCS [17, 18]. The advantages of this integrated mechanism are that the stability in the convention fuzzy ART is enhanced by adding the topology preserving mechanism in incrementally-changing dynamics by the GCS, while plasticity is maintained by the fuzzy ART architecture. Also, adding GCS to fuzzy ART is good not only for preserving the topology of the representation of an input distribution, but it also self adaptively creates increments according to the characteristics of the input features.

As shown in Figure 3, inferences can be induced from the learned information facts which consist of object labeling/naming, the color abstract representation and the form abstract representation. We can use the extracted information from the perceptions of both the color and form feature domains that to represent knowledge of objects. Color abstract representation and form abstract representation can be regarded as the bases for inferring new objects, while labeling/naming can be designated by the human supervisor or by some given reasoning rules. Furthermore, it can be concluded that ontology maps can be generated through the conceptual scheme by the given relevance between represented objects and its components, as well as by the inferred novel object and there constitutive elements.

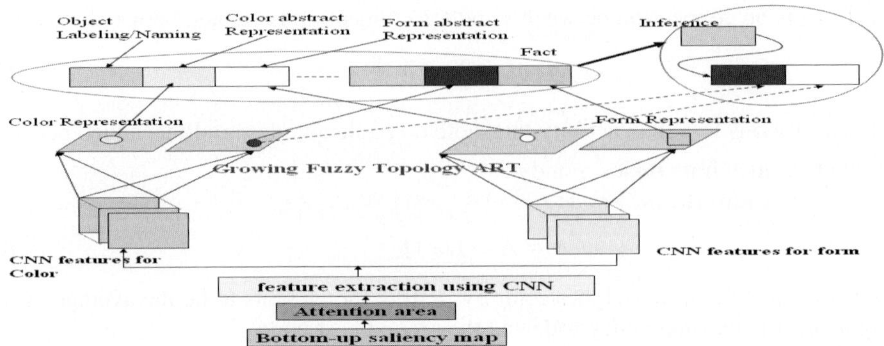

Fig. 3. A knowledge representation model based on visual information processing

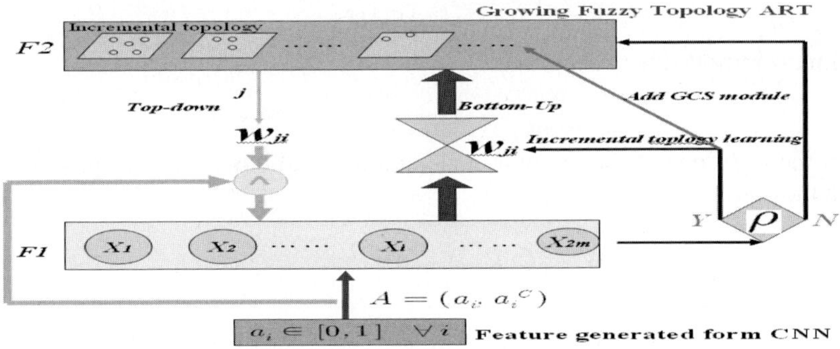

Fig. 4. Growing fuzzy topology adaptive resonance theory (TART) network

3 Experiments

Figure 5 shows the experimental results of the proposed bottom-up selective attention model. The saliency map (SM) model generates candidates of interesting regions using the ICA filter with bottom-up saliency features such as intensity, orientation, color and symmetry.

Figure 6 shows the extracted features generated by the CNN for a selected object area in conjunction with the bottom-up SM model. Figures 6a-c show an input image, the scan path generated by the bottom-up SM, and the corresponding saliency map for an input image, respectively. Figures 6d and 6e present the color features and form features for the first salient area in Figure 6b, which are extracted by the CNN, respectively. In Figures 6d and 6e, the top row offers extracted features such as HSI for color information and the winner-take-all image of Gabor features for form information, respectively. Feature maps corresponding to convolution and sub-sampling layers can be seen in Figure 6d and 6e in the subsequent rows, below the top row.

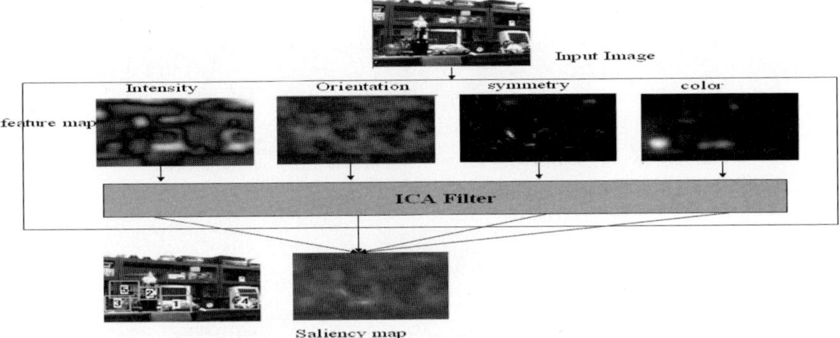

Fig. 5. Experimental results of bottom-up selective attention

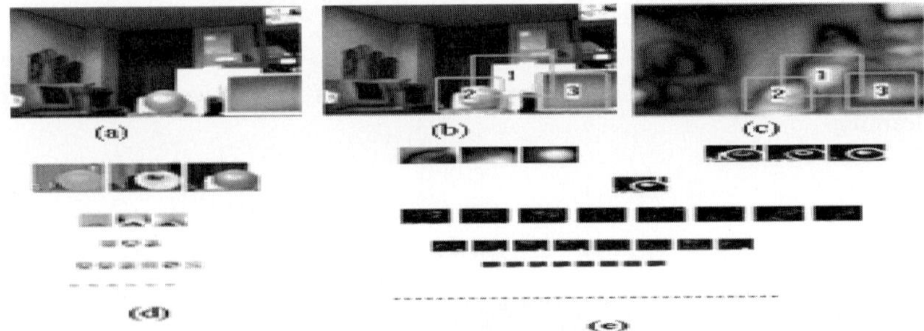

Fig. 6. Experimental results for feature extraction using a convolution network: (a) Input image, (b) the visual scan path of the input image, (c) saliency map for the same input image, (d) and (e) extracted color features and form features for the second salient area by a convolution network, respectively

Figures 7a and 7b present the consecutive training results of the proposed growing fuzzy TART, in which the saliency map detects a red ball in Figure 7a and a blue box in Figure 7b. The CNN results of the colors and the shapes in the selective attention regions are used as input for the growing fuzzy TART. After finding the winner GCS in each object, a new node is added between a winner node and a second winner node through GCS learning process.

Figure 8 shows that the proposed knowledge representation model can successfully generate new object knowledge by simple inference when a red box appears as a test object after learning a red ball and a blue box as shown in Figure 7. This is done by using a combination of learned factors of both color and form information. The representation for the test data can be combined to comprise inferences of new objects using the learnt color and form information of an object. As shown in Figure 8, the second GCS unit in color perception becomes a winner GCS for a red box, and there exists a winner GCS unit, such as "GCS for rectangular", in form perception for the red box. Then, using the previous knowledge consisting of labeled objects, our model can successfully infer about a new object, such as the "red box".

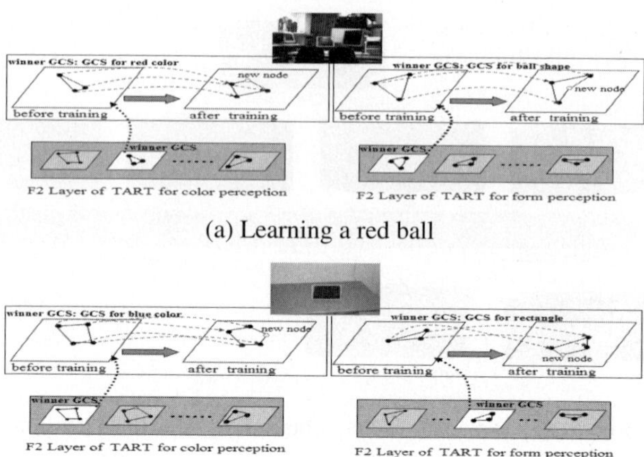

(a) Learning a red ball

(b) Learning a blue box after learning a red ball

Fig. 7. Simulation results that show the growing topology of the F2 layer of the TART during object learning

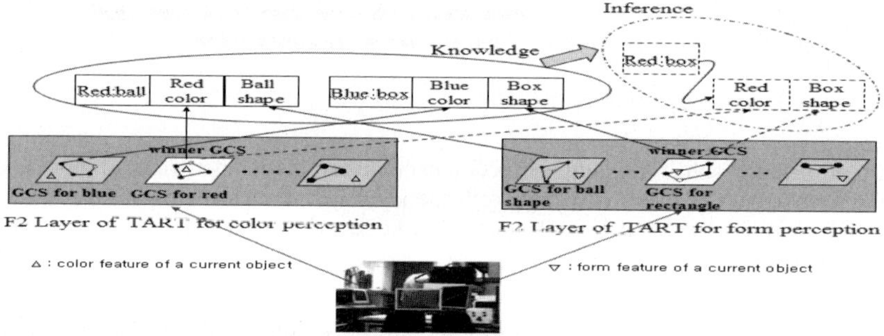

Fig. 8. Experimental results on knowledge inference, by the proposed knowledge representation model, based on TART

4   Conclusions

The proposed knowledge representation model, from sensory data, can be regarded as a framework for autonomous mental development through human interaction, while the proposed attention model can select salient object areas. The approach can automatically generate relevant maps from sensory data and inferences for unknown objects, by using learnt information based on the visual pathway in our brain. The growing fuzzy topology ART structure allowed clusters to construct an ontology map. The proposed model considered an incremental representation framework by taking into account the ontology. This dynamically growing architecture can evolve into a GCS, according to the characteristics of the input data. It, therefore, can provide a new perception of the space we are navigating. Regarding further research, we are considering a Bayesian approach in order to construct a relevant map in ontology.

Acknowledgments. This research was funded by the Brain Neuroinformatics Research Program of the Ministry of Commerce, Industry and Energy in Korea.

References

1. Breazeal, C.: Imitation as Social Exchange between Humans and Robots. In: Proceedings of the 1999 Symposium on Imitation in Animals and Artifacts (AISB 1999), Edinburg, Scotland, pp. 96–104 (1999)
2. Weng, J., McClelland, J., Pentland, A., Sporns, O., Stockman, I., Sur, M., Thelen, E.: Autonomous Mental Development by Robots and Animals. Science 291, 599–600 (2000)
3. Scassellati, B.: Investigating models of social development using a humanoid robot. In: Proceedings of International Joint Conference on Neural Networks, pp. 2704–2709 (2003)
4. Metta, G., Fitzpatrick, P.: Early integration of vision and manipulation. In: Proceedings of the International Joint Conference on Neural Networks, pp. 2703 (2003)
5. Treisman, A.M., Gelde, G.: A feature-integrations theory of attention. Cognitive Psychology 12(1), 97–136 (1980)
6. Itti, L., Koch, C., Niebur, E.: A model of saliency-based visual attention for rapid scene analysis. IEEE Trans. Patt. Anal. Mach. Intell. 20(11), 1254–1259 (1998)
7. Navalpakkam, V., Itti, L.: A goal oriented attention guidance model. Biologically Motivated Computer Vision, 453–461 (2002)
8. Walther, D., Itti, L., Riesenhuber, M., Poggio, T., Koch, C.: Attentional selection for object recognition – a gentle way. In: Bülthoff, H.H., Lee, S.-W., Poggio, T.A., Wallraven, C. (eds.) BMCV 2002. LNCS, vol. 2525, pp. 472–479. Springer, Heidelberg (2002)
9. Tsotsos, J.K., et al.: Modelling visual attention via selective tuning. Artificial Intelligence 78, 507–545 (1995)
10. Sun, Y., Fisher, R.: Hierarchical Selectivity for Object -Based Visual Attention. In: Bülthoff, H.H., Lee, S.-W., Poggio, T.A., Wallraven, C. (eds.) BMCV 2002. LNCS, vol. 2525, pp. 427–438. Springer, Heidelberg (2002)
11. Fei-Fei, L.: Knowledge transfer in learning to recognize visual objects classes. In: ICDL (2006)
12. Choi, S.B., Jung, B.S., Ban, S.W., Niitsuma, H., Lee, M.: Biologically motivated vergence control system using human-like selective attention model. Neurocomputing 69, 537–558 (2006)
13. Barlow, H.B., Tolhust, D.J.: Why do you have edge detection? Optical Society of America Technical Digest 23, 172 (1992)
14. Bell, J., Sejnowski, T.J.: The independent components of natural scenes are edge filters. Vision Research 37, 3327–3338 (1997)
15. Lawrence, S., Giles, C.L., Tsoi, A.C., Back, A.D.: Face recognition: A conventional neural network approach. IEEE Trans. on Neural Networks, 98–113 (1997)
16. Wolberg, G., Zokai, S.: Robust image registration using log-polar transform. In: Proc. IEEE Intl. Conference on Image Processing, Canada (2000)
17. Carpenter, G.A., Grossberg, S., Makuzon, N., Reynolds, J.H., Rosen, D.B.: Fuzzy ARTMAP: A Neural Network Architecture for incremental supervised learning of analog multidimensional maps. IEEE Transactions on Neural Networks 3(5), 698–713 (1992)
18. Marsland, S., Shapiro, J., Nehmzow, U.: A self- organising network that grows when required. Neural Networks, Special Issue 15(8-9), 1041–1058 (2002)

Integrated Model for Informal Inference Based on Neural Networks*

Kyung-Joong Kim and Sung-Bae Cho

Department of Computer Science, Yonsei University
134 Shinchon-dong, Sudaemoon-ku, Seoul 120-749, South Korea
kjkim@cs.yonsei.ac.kr, sbcho@cs.yonsei.ac.kr

Abstract. Inference is one of human's high-level functionalities and it is not easy to implement in machine. It is believed that inference is not results of single neuron's activity. Instead, it is a complex activity generated by multiple neural networks. Unlike computer, it is more flexible and concludes differently even for the similar situations in case of human. In this paper, these characteristics are defined as "informality." Informality in inference can be implemented using the interaction of multiple neural networks with the inclusion of internal or subjective properties. Simple inference tasks such as pattern recognition and robot control are solved based on the informal inference ideas. Especially, fuzzy integral and behavior network methods are adopted to realize that. Experimental results show that the informal inference can perform better with more flexibility compared to the previous static approaches.

Keywords: Informal Inference, Neural Networks, Robot Control, Pattern Recognition, Fuzzy Integral, Behavior Network.

1 Introduction

Biological neural networks are composed of a number of modules specialized to a specific task and integrate them for high-level functions. In an engineering perspective, there are three practical problems in realizing this biological anatomy: the selection of appropriate neural network architecture, the learning mechanism for each model and the integration method. It is very important that a solution for each problem has to show the similar characteristics with the biological counterpart. Meanwhile, it also has to be useful in an engineering perspective: the system might satisfy the performance requirement.

Inference is one of the critical brain's functions and many researchers have been attempted to mimic it by using symbolic or connectionist models [1][2]. Using the function, human reaches a conclusion from evidences (observations and facts). Unlike the artifacts, human's inference is not always the same and sometimes it is flexible and dynamic. In short, it is informal. The traditional engineering methods are well defined in the perspective of formality and it is required to adopt a new method for the informality. Figure 1 shows the difference between two inference models.

* This research was supported by Brain Science and Engineering Research Program sponsored by Korean Ministry of Commerce, Industry and Energy.

M. Ishikawa et al. (Eds.): ICONIP 2007, Part II, LNCS 4985, pp. 950–959, 2008.

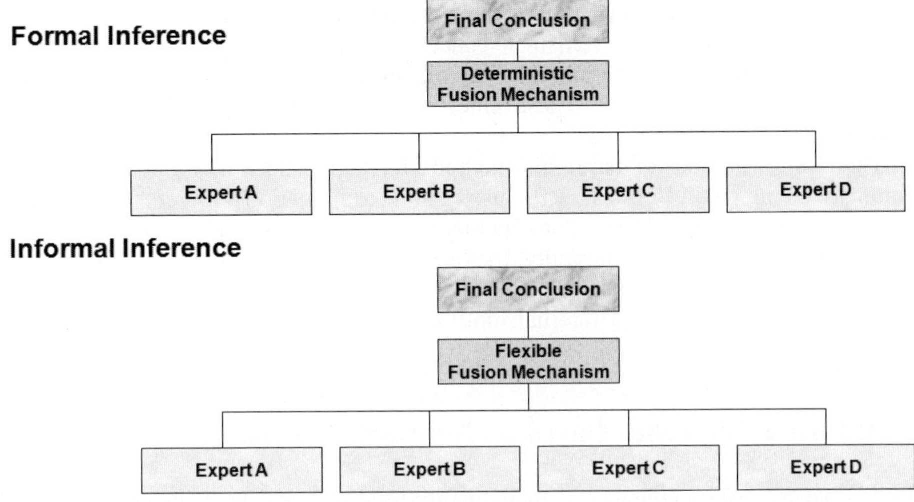

Fig. 1. Comparison of two inference methods

The easiest way to model the informality on a set of neural networks is to derive computational method for the connections among the neural models. Based on [3], the integration within and among specialized areas of human's brain is mediated by effective connectivity. Behavior network is a computational model that is derived from the research of action selection of animals [4]. It connects a number of behavioral modules using symbolic connections and selects the best action for each sensory inputs and motivation by propagating activation through the network. It is more flexible and dynamic than strict rule sets.

Sometimes, a human expert can incorporate his or her subjectivity on the preference of the neural modules and the final inference becomes more informal than one without user's preference. Fuzzy integral is a mathematical model that provides a systematic way to incorporate user's subjective preference on the neural models [5]. It is more flexible than the static combination rules.

In this paper, the behavior network and fuzzy integral are used to realize the informal inference in the real-world applications. They are controlling mobile robot using multiple neural behavior modules [6] and classifying web documents preference based on user's subjectivity on the neural modules [7]. For each problem, we have used different neural models that are integrated with more flexible methods.

2   Related Works

The term "informal inference" is not common word and not frequently used in engineering domain. Traditional symbolic logic is one of the examples of formal logic but it is not flexible to deal with human's generalization capability. There are many works to implement the inference capability using connectionist models like neural networks [1]. In probability theory society, the "informal inference" is used as the same meaning with plausible inference (probabilistic inference) [8]. In statistics education society, the term is used as the concept compared to the "formal statistics" [9]. Usually, adults capture statistical concepts using statistical formula and logics. But it is not easy for children and they use pictures, trends and patterns to grasp high-level statistical information. These inference processes are called as "informal inference."

There are a number of ensemble methods for neural networks and they are well summarized in [10]. Verikas *et al.* used "soft combination" to refer combination methods with more flexibility. They include fuzzy integral as one of the group of soft combination. In robotics community, they tried to incorporate motivation of the agent to the multi-module controller [4]. This allows the ensemble of multiple modules can be flexible to the change of internal motivation and user's subjective preference on each module.

3   Informal Inference Based on Neural Networks

In this paper, two computational methods are used to implement informal inference that shows different behaviors based on user's internal preference and agent's internal motivation. Fuzzy integral combines a number of neural networks with user's preference on each module. Behavior network combines multiple neural networks for high-level behaviors reflecting internal motivation of agents.

3.1   Fuzzy Integral

The definition of fuzzy integral is as follows. Let $C=\{c_1, c_2, c_3,..., c_N\}$ be a set of classes, where binary classification problem has $|C|=2$. Let $Y=\{y_1, y_2,..., y_n\}$ be a set of classifiers. $h_k(y_i)$ is an indication of how certain we are in the classification of web page to be in class c_k using the network y_i. Usually, the $h_k(y_i)$ is assigned as the real value from kth output neuron (normalized from 0 to 1) for the input. $A_i=\{y_1,y_2,...,y_i\}$ is a partition of the set Y. $G=\{g_1,g_2,...g_n\}$ is a set of user's preference value on each classifier. Based on user's evaluation, we calculate λ.

$$\lambda+1 = \prod_{i=1}^{n}(1+\lambda g^i) \qquad \lambda \in (-1,+\infty) \text{ and } \lambda \neq 0. \tag{1}$$

From calculated λ, the fuzzy measure value of each A_i is decided based on following equation.

$$g(A_1) = g(\{y_1\}) = g^1$$
$$g(A_i) = g^i + g(A_{i-1}) + \lambda g^i g(A_{i-1}), \quad \text{for } 1 < i \leq n. \tag{2}$$

The final classification of multiple neural networks is determined based on user's evaluation and the fuzzy measure values for each classifier set.

$$\text{Final class} = \underset{c_k \in C}{\operatorname{argmax}}\left[\max_{i=1}^{n}[\min(h_k(y_i), g(A_{ki}))]\right] \tag{3}$$

For example, each neural network (NN) determines the class label of an unknown document as "0" or "1" (in the binary classification problem). If SASOM$_1$ classifies the document as "0", $h_0(NN_1)=1.0$ and $h_1(NN_1)=0.0$. Supposed that there are three NN's, user evaluates classifiers as g^1, g^2 and g^3, respectively. λ is calculated from g^1, g^2, and g^3. It is easily determined from the 2nd degree polynomial based on (1). For each class k, classifiers are sorted by $h_k(NN_i)$. By the sorted order, they are labeled as y_1, y_2 and y_3. With $g(y_1)$, $g(y_1,y_2)$ and $g(y_1,y_2,y_3)$, the class label of the unknown document is determined using formula (3). Figure 2 shows an example of fuzzy integral calculation

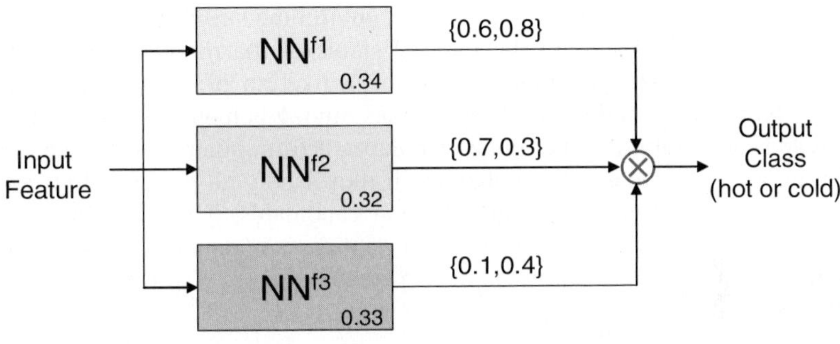

class	$h(y_i)$	$g(A_i)$	$H(E)$	Max$[H(E)]$
hot	0.7	$g(\{y_2\})=g^2=0.32$	0.32	
	0.6	$g(\{y_2,y_1\})=g^2+g^1+\lambda g^2 g^1=0.66$	0.6	V
	0.1	$g(\{y_2,y_1,y_3\})=1.0$	0.1	
cold	0.8	$g(\{y_1\})=g^1=0.34$	0.34	
	0.4	$g(\{y_1,y_3\})=g^1+g^3+\lambda g^1 g^3=0.67$	0.4	V
	0.3	$g(\{y_1,y_3,y_2\})=1.0$	0.3	

Fig. 2. An example of fuzzy integration

3.2 Behavior Network

A behavior network is defined as a set of topology and the parameters. The topology means the relationships among nodes, sensors and goals. If the sensor is the precondition of the behavior, there is a link between the behavior node and the sensor node. It means that the sensor has to be true if the robot wants to execute the behavior. If a behavior is directly related to achieve the goals, there is a link between the behavior node and the goal node. Among behaviors, there are two different kinds of connections and they are called as predecessor and successor links. If one behavior is possible to help the other behavior's future execution, there is a predecessor link between the two behaviors. The successor link is the reverse of the predecessor link if one behavior can help other behavior right now (executable without delay). The topology is manually designed by experts.

The parameter part of the behavior network is related to the strength of the links. For each link type, there is different weight value and it controls the strength of the inputs, goals and the internal relationships among behaviors. The inputs from the environmental sensors are multiplied by ϕ and those from goals are readjusted by multiplying γ to the original input value. The weight of the successor link is defined as ϕ/γ and the one of the predecessor link is 1. The parameters are determined by designer manually.

After constructing the architecture (topology + parameters) of the behavior network, it is required to define the selection procedure based on it. If the architecture is fixed, we can propagate the activation of each behavior. The first step is to input the values from sensors into the behavior through environmental links. After then, inputs from goals that are representing the internal status of the robot are inputted to the behavioral node through goal links. Then, the activation of each behavior node is updated by propagating activation through links among behaviors. Based on the type of link, it adds activation to other node or reduces it from other's one. After finishing all updating, we choose candidate behaviors if they satisfy all preconditions and have larger activation than threshold value. Among candidates, the one with the highest activation is finally selected as a final winner. If there is no candidate, the threshold is reduced by 10% and the activation update is repeated. Figure 3 shows the algorithm in a pseudo code manner.

```
WHILE (1) {
    initialization();
    spreading activation();
    normalization();
    FOR all behaviors {
      IF (all preconditions are true
          && activation (behavior) > threshold) {
            candidate (behavior);
      }
    }
    IF (candidate () = NULL) {
        threshold = 0.9 * threshold;
    }
    ELSE{
        select();
        break;
    }
}
```

Fig. 3. A pseudo code for behavior network action selection

4 Experimental Results

The two methods are tested in different two applications. The first method is evaluated on pattern classification problem which classify HTML document into one of "hot" and "cold" class. "Hot" means that the page is preferable by the user. The dataset is downloaded from UCI benchmakr repository and its name is "Syskill & Webert." There are two different types of groups in HTML webpages: Goats and Bands. The second method is evaluated using robot controlling problem. The controller is composed of multiple neural modules evolved. For each time step, one of modules can get the control of robot and behavior network is used to choose of the multi-modules. Internal goal of agent is modelled in the network of action selection. In both cases, we tried to compare them with static methods (rules and statical combination scheme).

4.1 Web Document Classification

From the UCI KDD database, Syskill & Webert data that have web documents and user's preference value ("hot" or "cold") are accessible. Syskill & Webert data have four different topics "Bands," "Biomedical," "Goats," and "Sheep," among which we use "Goats" and "Bands" data.

"Goats" data have 70 HTML documents and "Bands" 61 HTML documents. Each document has the class label of "hot" or "cold." Each HTML file contains texts related with the topic. Rating file contains file name, rating, URL, date and title orderly. Preprocessing of web documents constructs input vector with selected features and class label. From training data, we extract k important features using three different feature selection methods. Each method ranks all features by different manner. Document $D=<v_1, v_2, v_3,..., v_{128}, c>$ has three different input vectors that are used to train SASOM (Structure-Adaptive Self-Organizing Map) [12].

The problem to solve is to predict unknown documents' classes using known web documents with fuzzy integration of three different SASOM's trained using the input vectors. Experiments are repeated 10 times and the result is the average of them. For comparison, representative combination methods are used. Figure 4 shows the classification accuracy comparison (FI=Fuzzy Integral, BKS=Behavior Knowledge Space, WA = Weighted Average). It shows that the proposed fuzzy integral outperforms the other static combination methods for both dataset. Also, it allows user assign the preference for each classifier.

SOM is very powerful to visualize the classification results as a map of 2D structures and SASOM also has such capability. After training each SASOM, user can watch each SASOM's classification results (clusters) on 2D maps. Based on this, user can give preference on each SASOM. It allows user tune his system by changing preference for each SASOM. This integrated system can progressively improve his performance with the interaction of user. In this context, visualization of classifier's structure and results is quite important.

4.2 Robot Control

In robot control problem, four different modules are used. Among them, following light and avoiding obstacle behaviors are implemented using evolutionary neural networks. The four behavior modules are as follows.

- Recharging Battery: If a robot arrives at a battery recharge area, the battery is recharged. This behavior enables the robot to operate for as long as possible.
- Following Light: The robot goes to a stronger light. This behavior can be used to make the robot go to the battery recharge area, because the light source is located in that area.

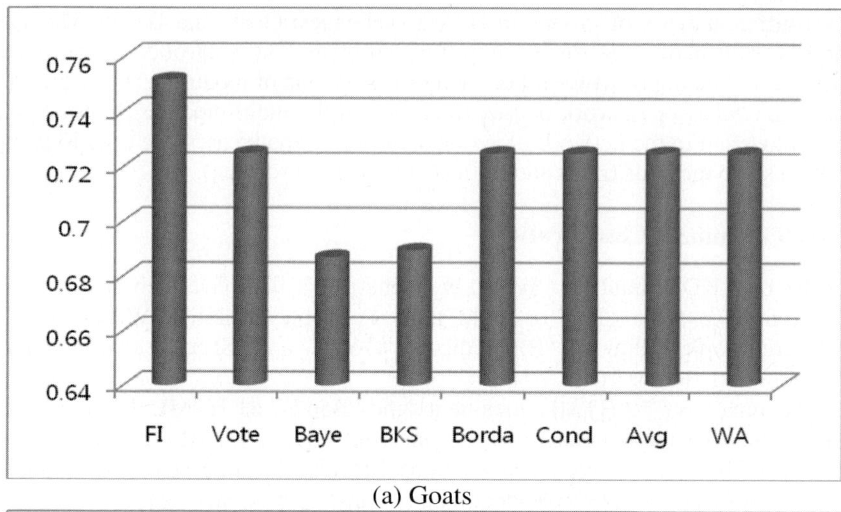

(a) Goats

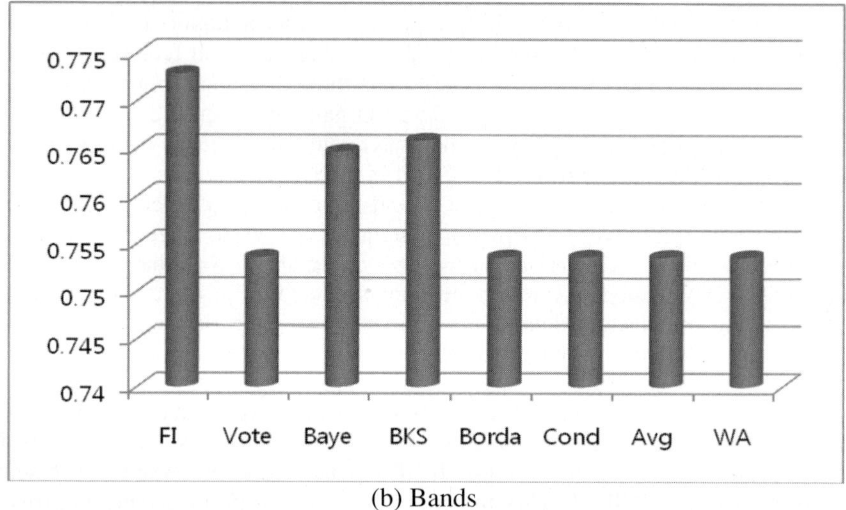

(b) Bands

Fig. 4. Comparison of classification accuracies for both dataset

- Avoiding Obstacles: If there are obstacles around the robot, it avoids them without bumping against them.
- Going Straight: If there is nothing around the robot, it goes straight ahead. This behavior allows it to move continuously without stopping.

The problem to solve is that maintaining robot's life in simulation environment by minimizing bumping to the walls. Robot has initial battery level (2500) and it decreases 1 if it moves. To survive, robot has to go to battery recharge area (upper left area) and executes the battery recharge behavior automatically. The coordination task is choosing one of four behaviors at each time appropriately based on robot's sensory and internal motivation. The robot's motivation is to survive long time by minimizing bumping. In previous research, the coordination task is implemented using rule-based logic [13] and behavior network [6]. In this experiment, we focus on the adaptability of the two coordination methods. In the environment, light source is placed in the battery recharge area (represented as black arc). It allows robot find the area automatically. The coordination mechanism is evaluated in 3 different new environments (figure 5).

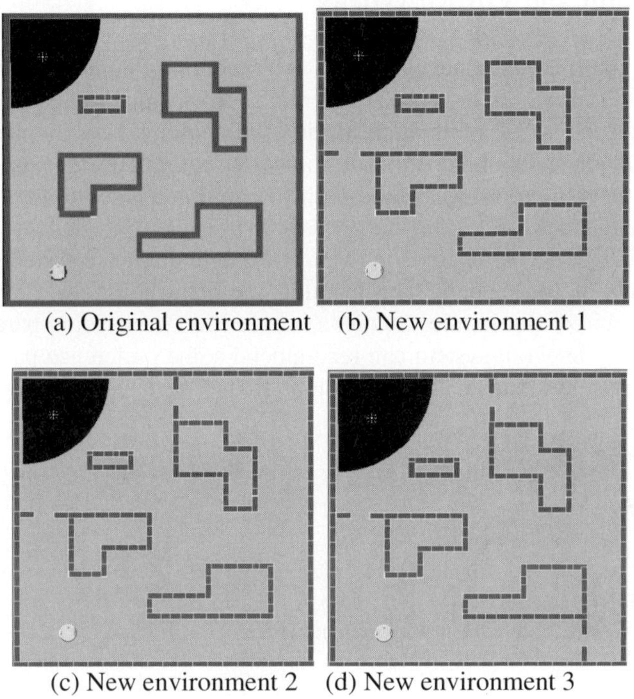

(a) Original environment   (b) New environment 1

(c) New environment 2   (d) New environment 3

Fig. 5. Original and 3 different new environments

Table 1. Comparison of performance for 3 new environments (100 runs for each model, N=Number of cases that recharge battery is done more than 1, A=Average battery usage for the successful cases

		Rule-based Model	Behavior Network
New environment 1	N	3	2
	A	4210.333	5156.5
New environment 2	N	8	10
	A	4293.75	4861.2
New environment 3	N	4	3
	A	4100.75	5104.333

Table 1 shows statistics on the experimental results. Because the environment is changed, the successful rate is not high. For the number of successful cases, there is no significant difference between the two models. However, the average life time (battery usage) is larger in behavior network than one in rule-based model. This shows that the behavior network can work better than the rule-based model in changed environment.

5 Conclusion and Future Works

In this paper, informal inference is defined as a function of human's flexible inference that response differently to the similar external sensory inputs. This is because human has his own preference or motivation inside of his brain. Two computational models are used to simulate this behavior and compared with static models. Experimental results show that the proposed method performs well compared to the rule-based and statistics-based model.

There are still some parameters on forming flexible inference systems and it makes difficult to use of the models. The learning mechanism for the flexible inference models are required to minimize human's intervention in deciding parameters of the system. In fuzzy integral, system can recommend some preference parameters to the user based on some statistical information. It can save user's fatigue to use the system.

References

[1] Browne, A., Son, R.: Connectionist inference models. Neural Networks 14(10), 1331–1355 (2001)

[2] D'Ambrosio, B.: Inference in Bayesian networks. AI Magazine 20(2), 21–35 (1999)

[3] Friston, K.: Learning and inference in the brain. Neural Networks 16(9), 1325–1352 (2003)

[4] Meas, P.: How to do the right thing. Connection Science 1(3), 291–323 (1989)

[5] Cho, S.-B., Kim, J.-H.: Combining multiple neural networks by fuzzy integral for robust classification. IEEE Transactions on Systems, Man and Cybernetics 25(2), 380–384 (1995)

[6] Kim, K.-J., Cho, S.-B.: A unified architecture for agent behaviors with selection of evolved neural network modules. Applied Intelligence 25(3), 253–268 (2006)

[7] Kim, K.-J., Cho, S.-B.: Fuzzy integration of structure adaptive SOM's for web content mining. Fuzzy Sets and Systems 148(1), 43–60 (2004)

[8] Pearl, J.: Probabilistic Reasoning in Intelligent Systems: Networks of Plausible Inference. Morgan Kaufmann, San Francisco (1997)

[9] Rubin, A., Hammerman, J., Konold, C.: Exploring informal inference with interactive visualization software. In: Proceedings of the 7th International Conference on Teaching Statistics (2006)

[10] Polikar, R.: Ensemble based systems in decision making. IEEE Circuits and Systems Magazine 6(3), 21–45 (2006)

[11] Verikas, A., Lipnickas, A., Malmqvist, K., Bacauskiene, M., Gelzinis, A.: Soft combination of neural classifiers: A comparative study. Pattern Recognition Letters 20, 429–444 (1999)

[12] Cho, S.-B.: Self-organizing map with dynamical node splitting: Application to handwritten digit recognition. Neural Computation 9(6), 1343–1353 (1997)

[13] Kim, K.-J., Cho, S.-B.: Evolved neural networks based on cellular automata for sensory-motor controller. Neurocomputing 69(16-18), 2193–2207 (2006)

Serial Processing of Emotional Type and Intensity: Evidence from an ERP Study

Nugraha P. Utama[1,2], Atsushi Takemoto[2], Yasuharu Koike[1], and Katsuki Nakamura[2]

[1] Department of Computational Intelligence and System Science, Interdisciplinary Graduate School of Science and Engineering, Tokyo Institute of Technology, Tokyo, Japan
koike@pi.titech.ac.jp
[2] Department of Animal Models for Human Disease, National Institute of Neuroscience, National Center of Neurology and Psychiatry, Tokyo, Japan
{utama,takemoto,katsuki}@ncnp.go.jp

Abstract. ERP responses were examined while subjects were identifying type of facial emotion as well as assessing intensity of facial emotion. We found a significant correlation between the magnitude of P100 response and the correct identification of type of facial emotion over the right posterior region and that between the magnitude of N170 response and the assessment of intensity of facial emotion over the right posterior and left frontal regions. Finding of these significant correlations from the same right occipital region suggested that the human brain processes information about facial emotion serially; type of facial emotion is processed first and thereafter its saliency or intensity level.

Keywords: P100, N170, emotion type, intensity, face, BCI.

1 Introduction

In our daily communications, we respond to what others say, not only from the verbal content but also from the non-verbal communicative signals, such as facial emotion. Facial emotion can enrich our communication so we can more easily understand the message that other is trying to convey.

Recognizing facial emotion is one of the very skilled ability of humans. Recent ERP studies have supported the hypothesis that the process of facial-expression recognition starts very early in the brain [1, 2]. Many researchers have shown the brain responded to emotionally charged stimuli more than that of the neutrally rated stimuli [3, 4], and only very recently, a few studies have reported the effect of saliency or intensity of facial emotions on ERPs [5-7]. But yet, none of them parametrically changed intensity of facial emotion to examine the psychometric properties of its assessment, and examine its neural correlates. Therefore, neural mechanisms underlying the assessment of intensity of facial emotion are mostly unclear yet.

To address this issue, we used several morphed images of facial emotion as stimuli and examined which ERP components were related to assessment of the intensity. In addition, subjects were required to identify the type of facial emotion and assess its intensity in a single trial in order to determine if different brain regions

M. Ishikawa et al. (Eds.): ICONIP 2007, Part II, LNCS 4985, pp. 960–968, 2008.

simultaneously processed or the same brain region serially processed the two properties of facial emotion. We analyzed brain responses using ERP recording because of its high temporal resolution and convenience, which are crucial properties for BCI techniques.

2   Material and Method

2.1   Subject

Fourteen healthy volunteers (6 females and 8 males) took part in psychological experiment (age 30.8±5.95). Another nine healthy subjects (2 females and 7 males) were participated in physiological experiment (age 27±4.0). All subjects have normal or corrected to normal visual acuity and this study was conducted according to the guidelines approved by the ethical committee of National Center of Neurology and Psychiatry. A written informed consent was obtained from each subject.

2.2   Stimuli and Apparatus

Six basic facial emotions (angry, happy, disgusted, sad, surprised, and fearful) of three male models (EM, JJ, PE) derived from Ekman and Friesen (1976)'s [8] were morphed with neutral face image from the same model using Smartmorph software (http://meesoft.logicnet.dk/SmartMorph/). The images of facial emotions were initially cropped with same outline as its neutral face image to exclude extraneous cues, such as hair, and ears. After normalizing the contrast and luminance of the images of facial emotions to neutral face image, all facial emotion images were put on a uniform gray background (Fig. 1a).

We designated the neutral face as 0% and the original facial emotion as 100% of the intensity. All stimuli were presented using Matlab6.5.1 software and Psychtoolbox [9, 10] at the center of a CRT 21" monitor (1280x1024, 100Hz), and the face images subtended approximately $6° \times 8°$ when viewed at a distance of 70 cm.

Original and transitional morphed images in *ten-percent* increment (Fig. 1) were used as stimuli in psychological assessment to examine how these images were categorized into specific emotional type and evaluated their intensity level of facial emotion by the subjects. As clearly shown in Fig.2, we found the different in shape of the graph between the correct identification of type of facial emotion (thick line) and the assessment of its intensity level (thin line). To examine whether or not there were some ERP components related to the correct identification of type of emotion (TYPE) and the assessment of its intensity (INT), we selected five different morphed images for each type of facial emotion which were presented best this difference for our physiological experiment; happy face (5%, 15%, 40%, 60%, and 100%) and disgusted face (15%, 30%, 40%, 75%, and 100%). For convenience, we named the five different intensity levels as condition 1 to 5 from weak to strong, respectively. To require the subjects to identify one type of emotion among various types, we also used two different intensity levels (75%, 100%) of angry, sad, surprise and fearful expressions as stimuli.

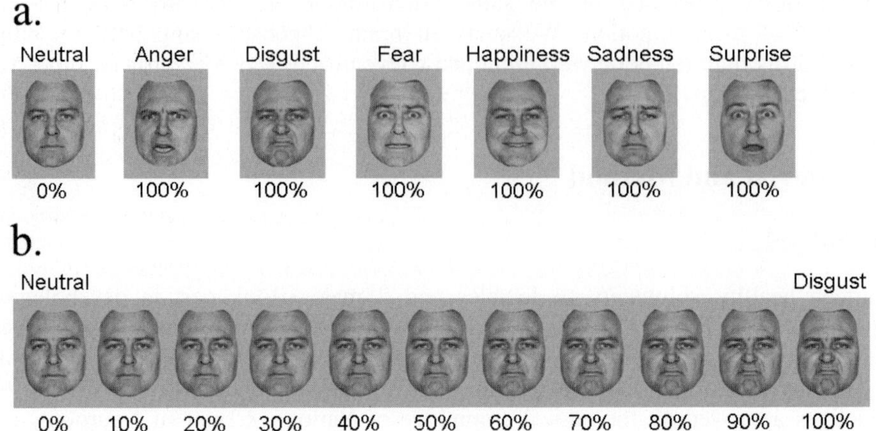

Fig. 1. *a. Prototypical stimuli.* Original images were taken from Ekman and Friesen (1976) which were neutral and facial emotions of anger, disgust, fear, happiness, sadness, and surprise. Images were cropped with same outline. Numbers were designated 0% as neutral expression, and 100% as the intensity of the original images of facial emotions. *b. Sample of morphed images.* Transitional images from neutral to disgust facial emotions, created by Smartmorph computer software, in *ten-percent* increment values.

2.3 Experimental Design

A trial began with the presentation of a white fixation dot on a gray background for 0.75 s. Then a neutral image was presented for 0.65 s, followed by the 0.4 s presentation of an image of a facial emotion of the same model which was randomly selected from the stimulus set. After the presentation of the facial emotion, the white fixation dot was presented again for 0.3 s. The subject was required to categorize the facial emotion as one type and assess its intensity in 10% of trials. The requirement to categorize the facial emotion was signed by the appearance of six circles corresponding to neutral, four basic emotions (happy, disgusted, sad, and fearful), and one named else. After categorizing the facial emotion indicated by clicking one of these six circles, subjects had to assess its intensity level by choosing one of ten circles; labeled from 1 to 10 which corresponded to the weakest and strongest level of intensity, respectively (Fig. 3). There was no feedback to them. Subjects used their right index or middle finger to press buttons in order to move the cursor into their selection, and inputted the answer by pressing other button using their left index finger. To avoid the effects of hand and arm movements on brain activity, no response was required in 90% of trials. The 10% trials were randomly selected. Therefore, the subject could not predict in which trials the responses were required so that the level of attention of the subject could be kept high.

We conducted four sessions of experiment. Each session consisted of five blocks, and each block contained 94 or 95 trials. Five different morph-levels of happy and disgusted facial emotions from three different models, two different intensities from four other facial emotions and one neutral face from each model made 57 different images in total stimuli. All of those images were used as stimuli, and each of them

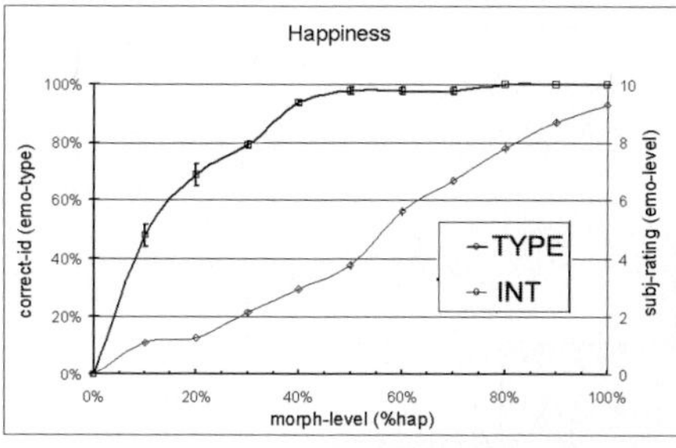

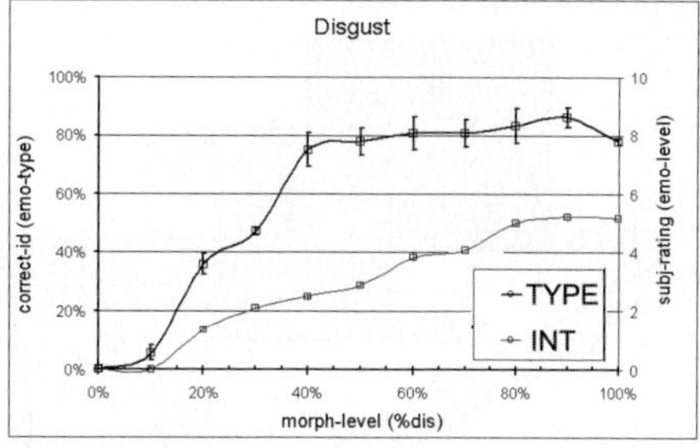

Fig. 2. *Behavioral results.* Results of psychological assessment on happiness and disgust facial emotions. The *thick* line corresponded to the correct emotional-type identification (TYPE) of emotional expression (in percentage) and the *thin* line corresponded to its emotional strength (INT); from 1 as the lowest to 10 as the strongest. X-axis of these graphics was the morph-level.

was repeated forty times in this experiment. One block of training was done before recording the ERPs.

During the experiment, subjects were seated in a sound attenuated, electrically shielded room and were asked not to blink during the images presentation, and breaks were done between blocks.

2.4 Electrophysiological Recordings

Electroencephalograms (EEGs) and electrooculograms (EOGs) were recorded continuously with a band pass filter of 0.05-100 Hz and were digitized at a rate 1,000 Hz. EEGs were recorded from 73 electrode sites (10-10 system) via Ag/AgCl electrodes mounted on a cap using SYNAMPS system (NEUROSCAN) and an acquisition software (SCAN 4.3) with a gain of 2,500, referenced to the nose-tip (impedance < 5kΩ) [11]. Horizontal and vertical EOGs were recorded from two electrode pairs placed on the outer canthi of the two eyes, and the infra and supra orbital ridges of the left eye. Based on the ocular electrodes, artifacts $\geq$ 70 μV were rejected at all electrodes' location after baseline correction was performed.

2.5 ERP Analyses

Continuous ERP data were digitally filtered (0.1 – 20 Hz) with zero phase shift 24dB/oct decrement, and re-sampling with 500Hz sampling rate. Independent Component Analysis was applied to reduce the artifact; especially those were from eye-blink and muscle activities. Data of 500ms epochs (-100 to 400ms) were realigned with the pre-stimulus onset time as the baseline. The time zero was the onset of the presentation of a facial emotion. The data were re-referenced to average reference, to give meaning that the scalp distribution of an ERP component is not influenced by the reference site. All of these processes were done using EEGLab [12, 13]. Only the responses to the happy and disgusted facial images were analyzed.

Experimental Design

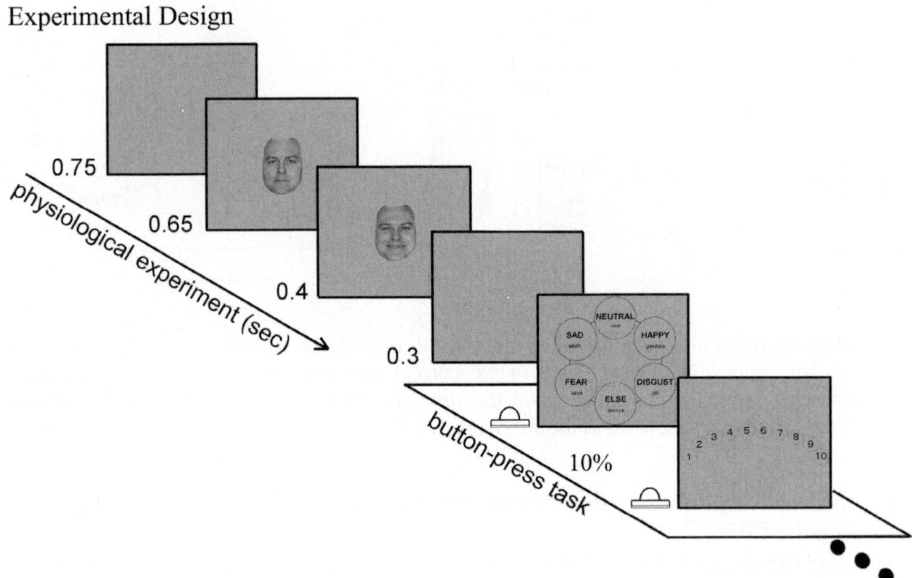

Fig. 3. *Experimental Design.* Time for each presentation is written next to its display [sec].

The final interest of these analyses was related to the detection of the peak-amplitude of the ERPs signals. To search the peaks, data from all subjects were analyzed using k-mean clustering technique [14] and t statistic with multivariate permutation tests [15] which were embedded inside in-house plug-in software. The time-ranges when at least 20 (out of 73) channels were passed the significance level of t statistic ($p<0.05$) were firstly used to determine the period of interest, then the time-ranges obtained from k-mean clustering which were within the period of interest were used to set the exact time-range windows.

To select the significant electrodes, half maximum and half minimum peak-amplitude values at each time-range windows were used as positive and negative thresholds respectively. Electrode which has at least three consecutive amplitude values more than positive threshold or less than negative threshold was selected as "significant" electrode.

The effects of electrodes' location (electrode), morph-level (level), and their interaction (electrode*level) on the ERP response were analyzed for the data from significant electrodes using repeated measurement ANOVA.

3   Results and Discussion

An example of ERP responses to the images of happy facial emotion which was taken from the electrode located at PO8 on the occipital region can be seen at Fig. 4. We assumed the peaks as significant components of ERP response; therefore we searched them at each time-window determined by k-mean clustering (see ERP analyses). As shown in Fig. 4, the peak could be detected in the time-windows 1 and 2. After

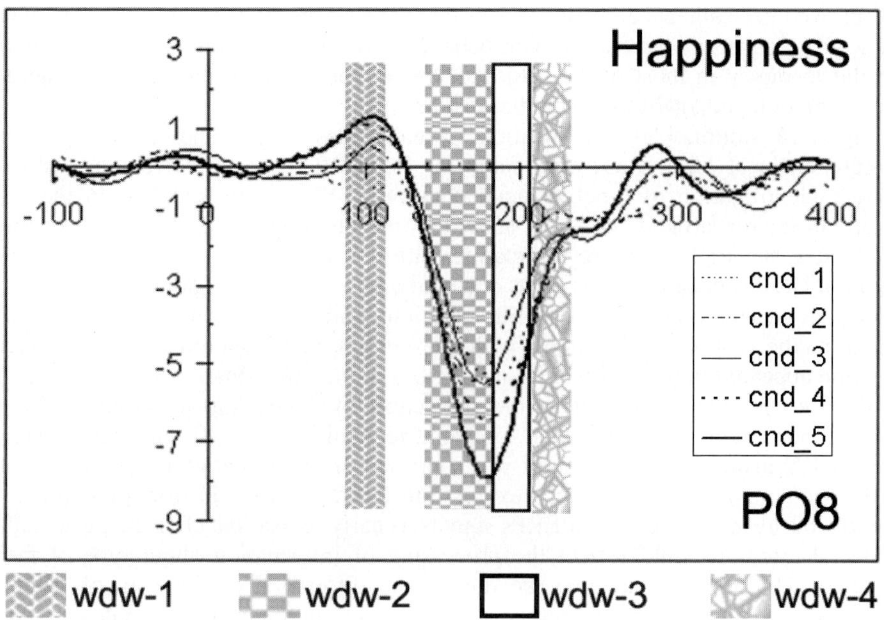

Fig. 4. *ERP signal and time-range window at PO8 location of happiness stimulus.* In this sample location, only at time-range window 1 and 2 the peak-amplitudes are detectable.

HAPPINESS		DISGUST			
wdw-1 (90 ~ 110)ms	wdw-2 (138 ~ 180)ms	wdw-1 (86 ~ 120)ms	wdw-2 (142 ~ 188)ms		● n≥8
				TYPE	
				INT	○ n<8 or N.S

Fig. 5. *The darken area* indicated the locations which have p<0.05 from at least 8 subjects and the rests are for the insignificant or the number of subjects which have significant p-value are less than 8 subjects

getting the peak values, we examined whether or not these values – as the representation of ERP response – correlated to some behavioral results. The peak values at time-window 1 significantly correlated to the subject's correct identification of type of facial emotion (TYPE). By contrast, the peak values at time-window 2 significantly correlated to the subject's assessment of intensity of facial emotion

(INT). An inter-subjects comparison was done to find the locations of electrode which showed a significant correlation with behavioral results in all subjects, and we found similar tendency in most of the subjects. We further analyzed the data for disgusted facial emotion and again found similar results.

Figure 5 summarizes the location of electrodes which showed a significant correlation in at least 8 out of 9 subjects. The ERP response correlating with the correct identification of type of facial emotion (TYPE) appeared first in the right occipital region around 100 ms after the presentation of each facial emotion. Thereafter, the ERP response correlating with the assessment of intensity of facial emotion (INT) appeared in the right occipital and left frontal regions around 170 ms after the presentation of each facial emotion. Only in response to happy facial emotion, the response correlating with the correct identification of type of facial emotion appeared in the bilateral frontal regions at the same time.

Previous studies have stated, the deflection of ERPs signals around 120 ms corresponded to a 'structural code' of facial recognition [16-18], and the deflection around 170 ms after stimulus onset was supposed of an 'expression code' implicated in the decoding of emotional facial expressions [19-21]. Different from these previous reports, our results suggest that ERPs signals as early as 100 ms after the presentation of facial emotion could reflect the processing of information about type of facial emotion. This discrepancy may be due to the difference of the way of stimulus presentation between ours and previous methods. In our study, we presented a neutral face just before a facial emotion to remove the effects of the simple face presentation on the ERP response, i.e., the responses to change in brightness, complex pattern and face perception. Such responses may be so large that the moderate response to facial emotion around 100 ms after the stimulus onset may be covered up.

Our present results indicate that the right occipital region consistently shows the responses correlating with the correct identification of type of emotion and with the assessment of its intensity 100 ms and 170 ms after the presentation of facial emotion. Here we propose that the right occipital region processes information about facial emotion serially; type of facial emotion is processed first and thereafter its saliency or intensity level.

Recent BCI mostly focused on motor movement, like controlling computer cursor, and selecting characters. But the function of a brain is more than just motor movement; therefore we still need to explore also the other function. From our results, we could detect and discriminate the information of recognizing the type of emotion and its intensity level from facial expressions which were seen. Even this information still has to be more manipulated in order to be applicable on EEG-based BCIs, but it can be the basis for emotional decoding. For being able to decode the emotional information, we can isolate them to improve the signal-to-noise ratio of other function, or we can use them for special task. The usage of EEG-based BCIs can be more expanded and it seems to indicate that EEG-based BCIs are likely to continue to offer some practical solutions in the future.

4   Conclusion

This study focused on *how* we can detect the emotional information about the type of the emotion and its intensity level using ERP technique. We addressed the following question. *When* and *where* does our brain process these two features of emotional information, in other words, are these features processed serially in the same brain region or simultaneously in multiple brain regions? Our data indicate that the human brain processes information about type of facial emotion first (around 100ms post stimulus onset) and then information about its intensity (around 170 ms post stimulus onset) in the right occipital region.

Acknowledgment

This research was supported by CREST, JST.

References

1. Bruce, V., Young, A.W.: A theoritical perspective for understanding face recognition. In: Young, A.W. (ed.) Face and Mind, pp. 96–131. Oxford University Press, Oxford (1998)
2. Ellis, H.D., Young, A.W.: Faces in their social and biological context. In: Young, A.W. (ed.) Face and Mind, pp. 67–96. Oxford University Press, Oxford (1998)
3. Fredikson, M., et al.: Functional neuroanatomy of visually elicited simple phobic fear: additional data and theoretical analysis. Psychophysiology 32(1), 43–48 (1995)
4. Balconi, M., Pozzoli, U.: Face-selective processing and the effect of pleasant and unpleasant emotional expression on ERP correlates. International Journal of Psychophysiology 49, 67–74 (2003)
5. Leppanen, J.M., et al.: Differential electrocortical responses to increasing intensities of fearful and happy emotional expressions. Brain Res 1166, 103–109 (2007)
6. Sprengelmeyer, R., Jentzsch, I.: Event related potentials and the perception of intensity in facial expressions. Neuropsychologia 44(14), 2899–2906 (2006)
7. Rossignol, M., et al.: Categorical perception of anger and disgust facial expression is affected by non-clinical social anxiety: an ERP study. Brain Res 1132(1), 166–176 (2007)
8. Ekman, P., Friesen, W.V.: Picture of Facial Affect. Consulting Psychologist Press (1976)
9. Brainard, D.H.: The Psychophysics Toolbox. Spat Vis 10(4), 433–436 (1997)
10. Pelli, D.G.: The VideoToolbox software for visual psychophysics: transforming numbers into movies. Spat Vis 10(4), 437–442 (1997)
11. Picton, T.W., et al.: Guidelines for using human event-related potentials to study cognition: recording standards and publication criteria. Psychophysiology 37(2), 127–152 (2000)
12. Delorme, A., Makeig, S.: EEGLAB: an open source toolbox for analysis of single-trial EEG dynamics including independent component analysis. J Neurosci Methods 134(1), 9–21 (2004)
13. Makeig, S., et al.: Mining event-related brain dynamics. Trends Cogn Sci 8(5), 204–210 (2004)
14. Pascual-Marqui, R.D., Michel, C.M., Lehmann, D.: Segmentation of brain electrical activity into microstates: model estimation and validation. IEEE Trans Biomed Eng 42(7), 658–665 (1995)
15. Blair, R.C., Karniski, W.: An alternative method for significance testing of waveform difference potentials. Psychophysiology 30(5), 518–524 (1993)
16. Pizzagalli, D., et al.: Affective attitudes to face images associated with intracerebral EEG source location before face viewing. Brain Res Cogn Brain Res 7(3), 371–377 (1999)

17. Junghofer, M., et al.: Fleeting images: a new look at early emotion discrimination. Psychophysiology 38(2), 175–178 (2001)
18. Lane, R.D., Chua, P.M., Dolan, R.J.: Common effects of emotional valence, arousal and attention on neural activation during visual processing of pictures. Neuropsychologia 37(9), 989–997 (1999)
19. Ashley, V., Vuilleumier, P., Swick, D.: Time course and specificity of event-related potentials to emotional expressions. Neuroreport 15(1), 211–216 (2004)
20. Blau, V.C., et al.: The face-specific N170 component is modulated by emotional facial expression. Behav Brain Funct 3, 7 (2007)
21. Krombholz, A., Schaefer, F., Boucsein, W.: Modification of N170 by different emotional expression of schematic faces. Biol Psychol (2007)

Estimation of Force Motor Command to Control Robot by NIRS-Based BCI

Tadashi Tsubone, Kiyotaka Tsutsui, Takeo Muroga, and Yasuhiro Wada

Department of Electrical Engineering, Nagaoka University of Technology
tsubone@vos.nagaokaut.ac.jp

Abstract. We consider a possibility for estimating force amplitude and start and end timing of movements based on hemoglobin density by using near-infrared spectroscopy (NIRS). In first experiments, subjects carried out isometric movements of three levels of force amplitude in order to measure EMG, force amplitude and hemoglobin density, and these relationships were investigated. We confirmed strong correlations between these measurements. From these relationships we propose two estimation models; one is to estimate the EMG from hemoglobin density and the other is to estimate the force amplitude from the estimated EMG. We can construct estimation models with high performance by minimizing AIC. Second, we examines the estimation of start and end timing of tapping movement by using NIRS signal around pyramidal area. We show the analysis of regional cerebral blood flow during maximum tapping effort movement and the method to quantitatively estimate start and end timing of movement. Finally, we show an example of a BMI system applying estimation models to control an arm robot.

1   Introduction

Recently, BMIs (Brain Machine Interface) and BCIs (Brain Computer Interface) have been developed by using biological signals from the brain. McFarland et al. [1] reported that a two-dimensional cursor control could be performed by rhythm that can be identified from an electroencephalogram (EEG). In BMI systems, users need to control brain information measured as EEG or BOLD (Blood Oxygenation-Level Dependent) signals. Brain information may be controlled by imagining or by recalling something. This means that brain information might be controlled without the activation of muscles. From the point of view of the possibility that a robot can be controlled without muscle activations, BMI has gotten a lot of attention recently because it has the possibility of becoming a communication tool for a person like an ALS (Amyotrophic Lateral Sclerosis) patient who cannot communicate with others easily. Changes in nervous activities in the brain by moving muscles have so far been analyzed through varieties of tasks by brain information measurement techniques, PET (Positron Emission Tomography) and fMRI (functional Magnetic Resonance Imaging). In squeezing tasks in which sizes of force were set to three stages, Cramer et al. [2] investigated the relation between the fMRI by the BOLD signal and the size of force

M. Ishikawa et al. (Eds.): ICONIP 2007, Part II, LNCS 4985, pp. 969–978, 2008.

and reported that active regions in the sensorimotor area broadened with the size of force, and the level of activation strengthened, too. Dai et al. [3] measured grip forces and EMGs that are considered to be motor commands from the central nervous system, and fMRI images while executing a grasping task, and reported that the grip force and EMG were directly proportional to the BOLD signal level of the cortex region related to motor control. In general, nervous activities in the primary motor area are known from many previous works to become active with an increase in force. In particular, Near Infrared Spectroscopy (NIRS) has recently drawn attention as a brain information measurement technique. The relation between muscle activities and brain activities detected by NIRS are reported [4]. Furthermore, BMI systems using NIRS are achieved. Coyle et al. [5] show that it is possible to recognize three times a minute from oxy-Hb whether a subject imagines a movement. NIRS is expected to become a tool for BMI because NIRS is a small measurement device and can be used noninvasively without constraints of posture. In this paper, we show a NIRS-based BMI system in which a robot arm can be controlled by NIRS signals, that is, hemoglobin density. The NIRS signals are identified as muscle activities, that is, muscle activities are estimated through NIRS signals. The robot arm movement speed can be controlled according to the level of NIRS signals. First of all, we performed experiments with subjects and analyzed the relations between force amplitude (force sensor), muscle activity (EMG) and hemoglobin level measured by the NIRS system. There are few papers that measured forces, EMGs and hemoglobin levels by NIRS at once and discussed relations between muscle activity and brain activity. Since the activation around pyramidal area can be observed relatively strongly during movement [6], therefore, this paper also examines the estimation of start and end timing of tapping movement by using NIRS signal around pyramidal area. By measuring Hb signals during the movement, the increase of Oxy- and total-Hb and the decrease of deOxy-Hb around the motor cortex have been reported [7,8]. While a subject performs tapping movement, Hb signals depend more on muscle activity than movement frequency, and the largest activation was found by maximum tapping effort [8]. First, we analyze the relation between force amplitude and EMG, and the relation between EMG and hemoglobin level by NIRS. Then, we propose an EMG estimation model from hemoglobin density and a force estimation model from the estimated EMG. The EMG estimation model is expressed as a linear summation model in which coefficients are optimized using AIC (Akaike Information Criteria). Second, we examines the estimation of start and end timing of tapping movement by using NIRS signal around pyramidal area. We show the analysis of regional cerebral blood flow during maximum tapping effort movement and the method to quantitatively estimate start and end timing of movement. Finally, we can estimate force levels from hemoglobin signals using the two models. By the models, we show a BMI system in which an arm robot was controlled by hemoglobin signals. We suggest these models can be applied to various BMI systems for force control, speed control, On/Off control, etc.

2 Estimation of Force Motor Command

2.1 Experiments

A. Experimental setup

Eight right-handed subjects participated in the experiments. Informed consent was obtained from all subjects. The experimental set-up is shown in Fig. 1. Subjects sat in chairs adjusted to lift their arms to shoulder level, and their right wrists were supported by a brace. The left arm rested naturally by the side of the body. Subjects performed isometric movements of three levels of force amplitude. A fiber cap for the NIRS measurement was installed on the head, and infrared ray markers for a three-dimensional positional measurement device, OPTOTRAK 3020 (Northern Digital Inc.), and surface electrodes for the EMG measurement were attached to the right arm. In the experiments, hemoglobin signals in the hemispheres of the brain, EMGs on the right arm, and force were measured at once. Oxy-Hb and deoxy-Hb were measured by NIRStation (OMM-3000/8, Shimadzu Corporation). Total-Hb is defined by the sum of oxy-Hb and deoxy-Hb. Ten channels on primary motor areas for each hemisphere of the brain were selected to be measured according to the internationally standardized 10-20 system.

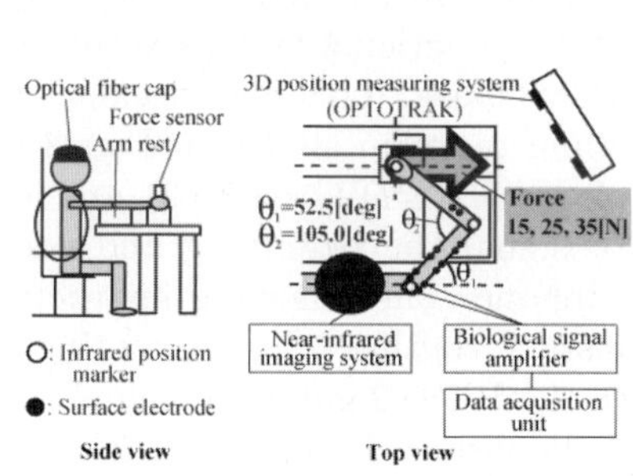

Fig. 1. Experimental setup

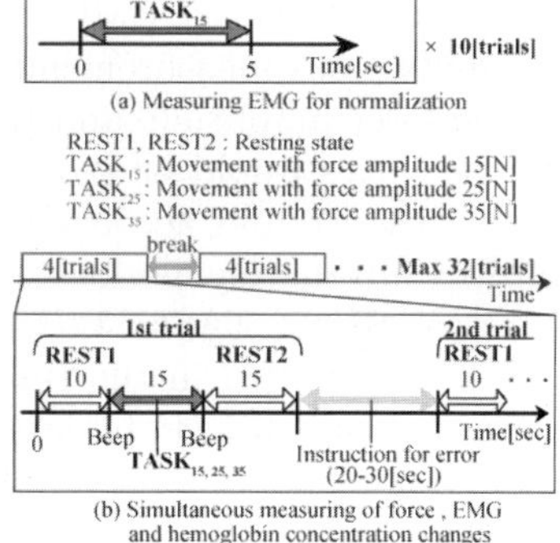

Fig. 2. Timing chart

The sampling period was 70 [msec] and signals for each hemisphere of the brain were simultaneously measured. EMG signals were amplified by using a multi-channel bio-amplifier (MME-3132, Nihon Kohden Corp.), then recorded in a data acquisition device (ODAU IICNorthern Digital Inc.) at 2000 [Hz]. The following six parts on the right arm that are related to two jointsf (shoulder and elbow) movement on the horizontal plane were measured: the brachioradialis, the medial head of the triceps brachii, the two biarticular muscles, the biceps brachii and the long head of the triceps. Forces produced by the right arm were recorded with a six-axis force sensor (Niita Corp.) at 200 [Hz]. OPTOTRAK 3020 was used to measure positions of markers placed on the joints of the elbow and the shoulder. The marker positions were sampled at 200 Hz. Before the experiment, the force sensor position was adjusted like the arm posture shown in Fig. 1.

B. Task Procedure
Tasks were isometric contractions by a right hand as shown in Fig. 1. Three levels of force 15, 25, 35[N] (TASK15, TASK25, TASK35) were given to the subjects. The same posture was required for all tasks. One task per day was performed, and it took three days to finish all tasks. On each day, first, EMG measurements for normalization were performed. Hemoglobin signals, EMGs and force were measured continuously and simultaneously.

C. Measurement of EMG for Normalization
The impedance between the surface electrode and the adhesive part are different every experiment day. Therefore, it was necessary to normalize the different muscle outputs because the measured total EMG of six muscles was adopted as an index of EMG. EMG for normalization was calculated from EMG when the smallest load TASK15 was executed. The subject performed the force generation in the direction indicated in Fig. 1 by 15N for five seconds on the signal of the experimenter, who monitored the force on the display. The cursor corresponding to the force vector projected on a horizontal plane was indicated on the display. The subject repeated force generation ten times.

D. Measurement of Force, EMG, and Hb signal
In the simultaneous measurements of force, EMG, and Hb density, the subject learned the force amplitude and the direction by practicing tasks several times because their eyes would be covered with an eye mask. This measurement was done after practice and according to the timing diagram shown in Fig. 2 (b). The subject alternately performed states of rest (REST1, REST2) and task execution (TASK15, TASK25, TASK35). To signal the beginning and end of a task, a beep sounded in the subjectfs headphone. The following instructions were given to the subject: breathe with constant rhythm while executing the task, and do not correct force amplitude until the REST2 go-ahead signal rings. The instructions for the size and direction of the force generated by the subject such as "Too large" and "The direction swerves here" were given after each trial, then the subject tried to succeed in the force generation. When the successful trials numbered 20 on each experiment day, that dayfs experiment was over. However, the experiment also ended if the subject performed a total of 32 trials even without 20 successful ones.

2.2   Analysis

A. Processing of measuring data - Force
The vector that consisted of two axis elements on horizontal planes except the element of perpendicular direction was treated as a force vector generated by the subject. The length and angle deviation of the force vector were calculated, and it was judged whether it was a successful trial. A successful trial was assumed to be a trial that met the following two requirements concerning the error margin

of the first 2-15 seconds of force. (1) The size of the force error margin to the targeted value must be less than 4N. (2) The size of the direction error must be less than 20 deg. The number of successful trials did not reach 20 trials though there was the maximum number of 32 trials. We added an insufficient number of trials from the failed trials. The added trials were sequentially selected from the small error trials. Finally, twenty trials were analyzed.

B. Processing of measuring data - Hb density
To remove the influence of breath and heart rate, the fourth Butterworth filter of 0.01-0.70Hz was used. Afterwards, the mean value of the first two seconds of each trial was assumed to be a baseline, and it was subtracted from the original signal.

C. Processing of measuring data - EMG
In the measurement experiment, the band-pass filter of 20-1000Hz was passed through EMG by the bio-amplifier in each muscle. A moving average with 11 points was conducted to the absolute value of each muscle five times. Afterwards, each muscle was normalized by using EMG for the normalization of each muscle described in the following. Finally, the normalized total of all six muscles was assumed to be an index of EMG.

$$EMG_{sum}(t) = \frac{1}{e_{sum}} \sum_{ch=1}^{ch_{max}} \left\{ \frac{1}{e_{ch}} EMG_{ch}(t) \right\}. \tag{1}$$

D. Calculation of EMG for normalization
The moving average was processed to EMGs that were obtained by task for normalization. Next, the mean value of each muscle for two to five seconds was averaged for each trial. It was assumed to be the EMG for the normalization of each muscle. ch shows the EMG measurement channel and $trial$ shows the trial number. TASK15 was assumed to be a standard of the EMG of each muscle by e_{ch}. Next, the total of six muscles was taken after the mean value of two to five seconds was normalized with e_{ch}, and the averaged value over the trials was assumed to be a normalized constant. TASK15 was assumed to be a standard of the total EMG by $e_{sum} \cdot e_{ch}$ and e_{sum} were calculated every experiment day.

$$e_{ch} = \frac{1}{trial_{max}} \sum_{trial=1}^{trial_{max}} \left\{ \frac{1}{t_2 - t_1} \int_{t_1}^{t_2} EMG_{ch_{trial}}(t)dt \right\}. \tag{2}$$

$$e_{sum} = \frac{1}{trial_{max}} \sum_{trial=1}^{trial_{max}} \sum_{ch=1}^{ch_{max}} \frac{1}{e_{ch}} \left\{ \frac{1}{t_2 - t_1} \int_{t_1}^{t_2} EMG_{ch_{trial}}(t)dt \right\}. \tag{3}$$

$$(ch_{max} = 6, trial_{max} = 10, t_1 = 2.0[\text{sec}], t_2 = 5.0[\text{sec}])$$

E. Correlation between Force, total EMG, and Hb density
To examine the relations among force, total EMG, and Hb density, Pearson's product moment correlation coefficient was calculated. Mean value in REST1 (20 points in each targeted value, and 60 points total) and TASK15, 25, 35

(each 20 points and 60 points total) of force, total EMG, and Hb density (oxy-Hb, deoxy-Hb, total-Hb) were used.

F. Regression model for total EMG estimation using Hb density
We propose an EMG estimation model by using the Hb density. The model was assumed to be a linear regression model of the Hb density shown in Eq. (4). $\overline{EMG}$ shows the estimation value of total EMG, and Hb_{ch} shows the amount of the Hb density and ch shows the channel index, respectively. Hb_{ch} and ch_{max} show the number of measurement channels. $L_{max}+1$ points of each channel were used to estimate. A best estimation model was selected by AIC.

$$\overline{EMG}(t) = a_0 + \sum_{trial=1}^{trial_{max}} \sum_{ch=1}^{ch_{max}} a_{L \cdot ch} \cdot Hb_{ch}(t - dt - L). \qquad (4)$$

G. Estimation of force from estimated total EMG
Force was estimated from total EMG estimated from the Hb density. The force estimation model is represented by a regression model shown as Eq. (5). a and b are regression parameters.

$$\overline{force}(t) = a \cdot \overline{EMG}(t) + b. \qquad (5)$$

2.3   Result

A. Result of measurement As for the mean value of force in 2-15, the main effect of the task was significantly different in three conditions (TASK15, 25, and 35N) ($p<0.01$) for all subjects as a result of one factor analysis of variance. In addition, significant differences were observed between tasks as a result of Tukey-Kramer multiple comparison ($p<0.01$) for all subjects. Therefore, we confirmed that force data were divided at three levels by all subjects. B. Correlations between force, total EMG, and Hb density Strong correlations of more than 0.9 were observed between force and total EMG in all subjects. Moreover, there was a very strong linear relation. Next, a significant, positive correlation between total EMG and oxy-Hb, or total-Hb were observed in both hemisphere channels. As for total EMG and deoxy-Hb, the correlation was weak; a significant correlation was observed with some channels, but the sign of the correlation was not consistent. The correlation coefficient was compared with oxy-Hb, deoxy-Hb, and total-Hb. Deoxy-Hb was obviously small. Oxy-Hb and total-Hb were almost the same. However, it is rather clear that the correlation coefficient of total-Hb is larger in the little difference. Next, correlation coefficients of total EMG and total-Hb were compared between the left hemisphere and right hemisphere. There were four subjects with a strong correlation to the left hemisphere. There were four subjects with a strong correlation to the right hemisphere, and a consistent tendency was not seen. We understood that total-Hb is better as a signal to predict total EMG. The correlation of total EMG and total-Hb on the left hemisphere is shown in Fig.3. On the other hand, the reaction of the right and left hemispheres was almost the same for oxy-Hb and total-Hb. There are a lot of reports about

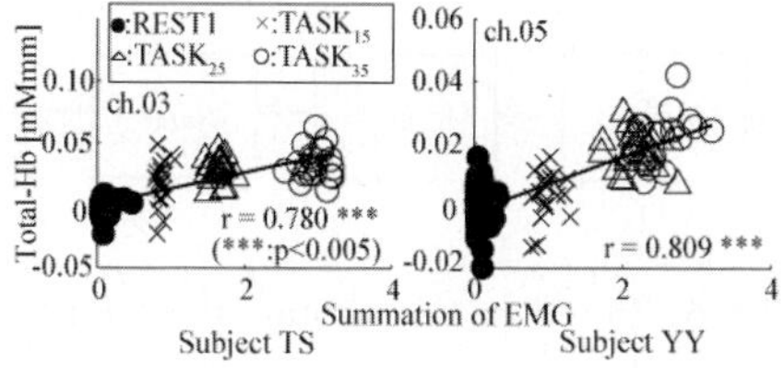

Fig. 3. The correlation of total EMG and total-Hb

the brain image in the human muscle output task. In general, it is known that the motor area in the opposite-side hemisphere activates. However, there are reports of activation in the same-side hemisphere. Cramer et al. [2] reported that the activating area has increased as force increases, though the activating area of the same-side hemisphere is narrower than that of the opposite-side hemisphere. Dai et al. [3] reported that activating level and area were observed in the same side hemisphere as well as the opposite-side hemisphere. It can be said that our result denotes the same tendency observed by these two reports. C. Total EMG estimation by Hb density The total EMG is predicted by the regression model using total-Hb of the left hemisphere. Estimation in REST1 tended to become a higher level than the measurement level. There was not much difference between total EMG estimations in REST1 and in TASK15. On the other hand, estimations for TASK25 and TASK35 were highly accurate. Results of measurements and model estimation are shown in Fig. 4. D. Estimation of force from estimated

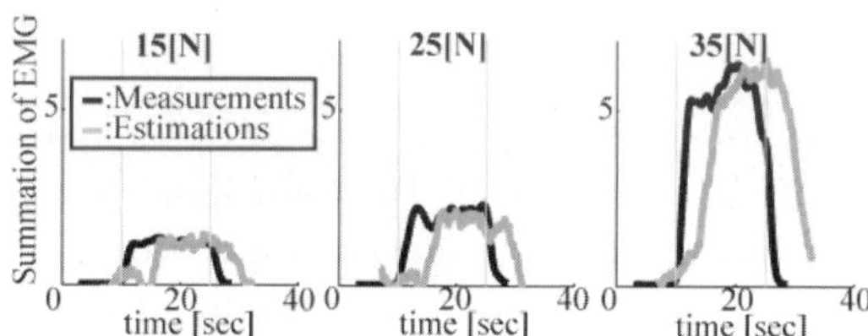

Fig. 4. Results of measurements and model estimations

total EMG Force was estimated from the estimated total EMG by using the regression model. Here, mean values of power in TASK15, 25, 35 were compared by measurements and estimation. As for the correlation between measurements and estimation, a significant, positive result in all subjects except subject KN was observed. The slope of the regression line became more than 0.5 except for some subjects. There are small differences between estimations and measurements of force. However, a rough, linear relation was confirmed. It appears to be able to predict force from estimated EMG. V. ROBOT CONTROL SYSTEM BY HB DENSITY Force prediction by the proposed models can be achieved. Here, we show a system that controls an arm robot by using the force estimation model using Hb density. In the system, control parameters of the robot depend on the

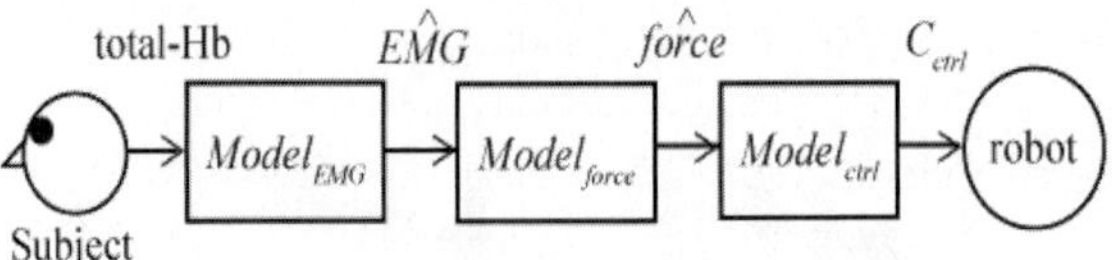

Fig. 5. The flow from total-Hb to force

estimation value of force from Hb density. $Model_{EMG}$ is the model that predicts total EMG from the Hb density shown by Eq. (4). $Model_{force}$ indicates the force estimation model from the estimated total EMG (Eq. (5)). The flow from total-Hb to $\overline{force}$ is shown in Fig. 5. $Model_{ctrl}$ is a model that decides the value of control parameter C_{ctrl} given to the robot. For instance, $Model_{ctrl}$ becomes the model shown in the next equation.

$$C_{ctl} = G\left(\frac{1}{T_2 - T_1}\int_{T_1}^{T_2}\overline{force}(t)dt\right).\tag{6}$$

That is, C_{ctrl} is decided according to the average of the prediction of force. G is a kind of function for deciding the robot parameter value. Actually, C_{ctrl} can represent force amplitude, movement duration, etc. Thus, there is a possibility that a system controlled by the robot can be achieved using the Hb density.

3   Estimation of Start and End Timing of Movements

3.1   Method

A. Subject & Motor tasks

Four right-handed men, in age from 20 to 33 years participated. The subject sat in a chair with his body fixed by a belt. His right hand was placed on the desk and his left on his thigh. A sign was marked on a white curtain. The size of the sign is about 10 cm. The movement was tapping of the right hand. He was requested to give maximum amplitude and speed. While resting, the subject was asked to gaze at the sign without thinking about anything.

B. Time sequence

One trial consisted of 60 seconds (10 s: rest, 20 s: action, 30 s: rest). The subject practiced for a few minutes before the experiment began. He was informed about start and end of movement times by a beep and instructed to gaze at the sign while resting and close his eyes during the movement. The number of trials was 28.

3.2   Measurement Results

Fig. 6(a) shows an example of Hb signals in the activated region. Let us focus on the Hb signals of the activated part. We observed the following typical activation: increase of Oxy and total-Hb and a slow deOxy-Hb decrease in a few seconds from the start of movement. Then Hb returned to the resting signal level after the end of the movement. Total-Hb is a summation of Oxy/deOxy-Hb and the noise of total-Hb is smaller than the other Hb. Also, we can observe that activation tendencies of the premotor area (PM) and the primary motor area (M1) are larger than that of the primary sensory area (S1). And, following tendencies of total-Hb at M1 and PM were observed with time; Hb increased within 10 s from the start of movement, decreased within 10 s from the end of movement, and had no variation at rest (except within 10 s from the end of movement). Hence, we use total-Hb of 1, 2, 4, 5, 8 and 9ch around M1 and PM.

3.3   Estimation of Start and End Timing of Tapping Movement

We examined the estimation of start and end timing of movement by classifying the states into three types: "Hb increase," "Hb decrease," and "no variation Hb." Namely, the feature quantity to classify the state is the differential of an Hb time series data. In order to classify them, we use a simple Neural Network which is a three-layer multilayer perceptron discussed in [9]. The data obtained from the six NIRS channels are inputted to the six units of input layer. The output layer outputs almost three level states corresponding to "Hb increase," "Hb decrease," and "no variation Hb." Input signals are diffrential values of total-Hb obtained from each channels. The number of input units, hidden units and output unit are 6, 6 and 1, respectively. The input unit functions are linear functions, and

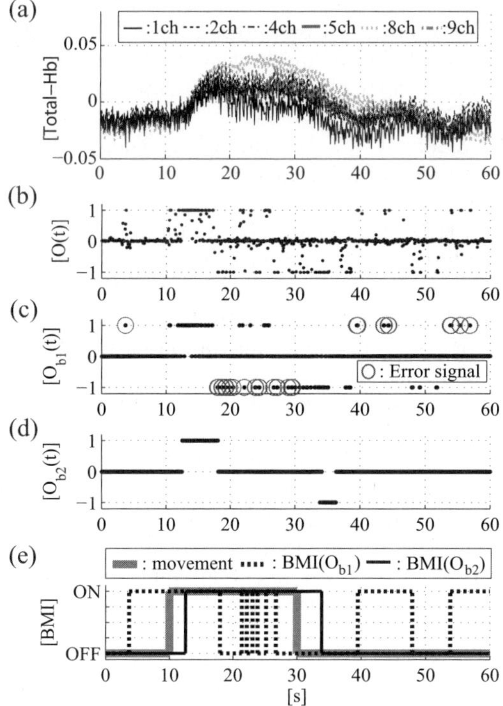

Fig. 6. Time series data

the hidden and output unit functions are sigmoid functions. Back propagation method was used for learning. The detail is shown in [9]. The output of final stage of Neural Network is to be as Fig. 6(d). "+1" can be observed within 10 seconds from the start of movement. "−1" can be observed within 10 seconds from the end of movement . Therefore, start and end timing of movement are estimated by using the network. ON/OFF control is accomplished as the solid line in Fig. 6(e). In the case of a subject T. S., the success rate is about 78%. In the case of other three subjects, the success rate is grater than 70%.

4   Conclusion

In this paper, First, the relations between force, EMG, and Hb density were found through a right arm movement experiment according to three force levels. It appears possible to estimate the actual generated force using the models using Hb density. Second, the estimation method shows the possibility of applications to the ON/OFF control of BCI. Therefore, we may be able to create a robot control system based on Hb density and achieve a NIRS-based BMI.

References

1. McFarland, D.J., Lefkowicz, A.T., Wolpaw, J.R.: Design and operation of an EEG-based brain-computer interface with digital signal processing technology. Behavior Research Methods, Instruments, Computers 29(3), 37–345 (1997)
2. Cramer, S.C., Weisskoff, R.M., Schaechter, J.D., Nelles, G., Foley, M., Finklestein, S.P., Rosen, B.R.: Motor cortex activation is related to force of squeezing. Human Brain Mapping 16, 197–205 (2002)
3. Dai, T.H., Liu, J.Z., Sahgal, V., Brown, R.W., Yue, G.II.: Relationship between muscle output and functional MRI-measured brain activation. Exp Brain Res 140, 290–300 (2001)
4. Huppert, T.J., Hoge, R.D., Diamond, S.G., Franceschini, M.A., Boas, D.A.: A temporal comparison of BOLD, ASL, and NIRS hemodynamic responses to motor stimuli in adult humans. NeuroImage 29, 368–382 (2006)
5. Coyle, S., Ward, T., Markham, C., McDarby, G.: On the suitability of near-infrared (NIR) systems for next-generation brain-computer interfaces. Physiol, Meas. 25, 815–822 (2004)
6. Dechent, P., Merboldt, K.-D., Frahm, J.: Is the human primary motor cortex involved in motor imagery? Cognitive Brain Research 19(2), 138–144 (2004)
7. Huppert, T.J., Hoge, R.D., Diamond, S.G., Franceschini, M.A., Boas, D.A.: A temporal comparison of BOLD, ASL, and NIRS hemodynamic responses to motor stimuli in adult humans. NeuroImage 29(2), 368–382 (2006)
8. Kuboyama, N., Nabetani, T., Shibuya, K., Machida, K., Ogaki, T.: Relationship between Cerebral Activity and Movement Frequency of Maximal Finger Tapping. Journal of Physiological Anthropology and Applied Human Science 24(3), 201–208 (2005)
9. Tsubone, T., Muroga, T., Wada, Y.: Application to robot control using brain function measurement by near-infrared spectroscopy. In: Proc. of the 29th Annual International Conference of the IEEE EMBS, pp. 5342–5345 (2007)

Decoding Syllables from Human fMRI Activity

Yohei Otaka[1,2], Rieko Osu[2,3], Mitsuo Kawato[3], Meigen Liu[4],
Satoshi Murata[3], and Yukiyasu Kamitani[3]

[1] Department of Rehabilitation Medicine, Tokyo Bay Rehabilitation Hospital
[2] National Institue of Information and Communications Technology, Keihanna Science City,
Kyoto, Japan
[3] ATR Computational Neuroscience Laboratories, Keihanna Science City, Kyoto, Japan
[4] Department of Rehabilitation Medicine, Keio University School of Medicine
otaka119@mac.com

Abstract. Language plays essential roles in human cognition and social
communication, and therefore technology of reading out speech using non-
invasively measured brain activity will have both scientific and clinical merits.
Here, we examined whether it is possible to decode each syllable from human
fMRI activity. Four healthy subjects participated in the experiments. In a
decoding session, the subjects repeatedly uttered a syllable presented on a
screen at 3Hz for a 12-s block. Nine different syllables are presented in a single
experimental run which was repeated 8 times. We also specified the voxels
which showed articulation-related activities by utterance of all the syllables in
Japanese phonology in a conventional task-rest sequence. Then, we used either
all of these voxels or a part of these voxels that exist in anatomically specified
ROIs (M1, cerebellum) during decoding sessions as data samples for training
and testing a decoder (linear support vector machine) that classifies brain
activity patterns for different syllables. To evaluate decoding performance, we
performed cross-validation by testing the sample of one decoding session using
a decoder trained with the samples of the remaining sessions. As a result,
syllables were correctly decoded at above-chance levels. The results suggest the
possibility of using non-invasively measured brain activity to read out the
intended speech of disabled patients in speech motor control.

Keywords: decoding, brain machine interface, syllable, speech, rehabilitation,
functional Magnetic Resonance Imaging (fMRI).

1   Introduction

Speaking is one of the most complex skills that humans perform. The variety of
articulations and phonemes are one of the distinct ability of the human species that
lead to the evolution of language. In our everyday communication, we convey
thoughts, and ideas through spoken languages. Since language plays essential roles in
human cognition and social communication, technology of reading out speech using
non-invasively measured brain activity will have both scientific and clinical merits.

Humans produce speech by dexterously controlling the non-rigid vocal tract using
multiple muscles. However, neurological, psycholinguistic, and perceptual-motor

M. Ishikawa et al. (Eds.): ICONIP 2007, Part II, LNCS 4985, pp. 979–986, 2008.

processes behind these movements have not been well understood due to biomechanical complexities and lack of animal model. Aside from its complexities, speech has a distinct character, as compared to other domains of motor control such as locomotion or upper limb movement. This distinct character of speech is in the form of its end-products. The forms of end-products of speech are not continual scales but categorical forms, e.g. syllables. Therefore, it is feasible to decode speech rather than other limb movement witch has non-categorical end-products. Among end-products of speech, we focused on syllable which plays an important role in the production and the understanding of spoken language, as well as in language acquisition. Here, we demonstrate that each syllable can be decoded from human fMRI activity by using machine learning algorithms for pattern classification.

2 Methods

2.1 Participants

Four healthy adults without neurological deficits participated in the experiments (25–34, years of age, all Japanese male and native speakers of Japanese). Each participant gave informed written consent before the experiment. The experimental procedure was approved by the local institutional review board.

2.2 Experimental Setup

Participants performed speech tasks while lying supine in an MRI scanner. Head movements were restrained by vacuum beanbag pillows (Engineering system Co.) surrounding the head and neck. Through a tilted mirror, a rear-projection screen outside of the scanner was visible to the participants. The target syllable(s) was displayed on the screen. The experimenter continuously checked whether participants uttered correct syllables by monitoring participants' voice through a microphone.

2.3 Speech Tasks

The fMRI experiment consisted of a decoding session and a ROI session. The decoding session consisted of eight experimental run. The participants repeatedly uttered a syllable presented on a screen at approximately 3Hz for a 12-s block. After a 4-s rest, another syllable was presented. Nine different syllables (/ma/ /sa/ /ka/ /me/ /se/ /ke/ /mo/ /so/ /ko/) were presented pseudo-randomly in a single run. The syllables were selected based on Japanese phonology. In a ROI session, the participants uttered 40 syllables of the Japanese kana syllabary ("aiueo", "kakikukeko", and so on) in a conventional task-rest sequence (12-s each, 8 blocks) so that articulation-related regions were specified. The ROI session consisted of two to four experimental runs. Participants were trained outside of the scanner until they could perform the tasks properly.

2.4 MRI Acquisition

Scanning was performed on 1.5-Tesla MRI scanner (Shimadzu-Marconi) at Brain Activity Imaging Center, ATR promotions. To measure BOLD contrast, standard

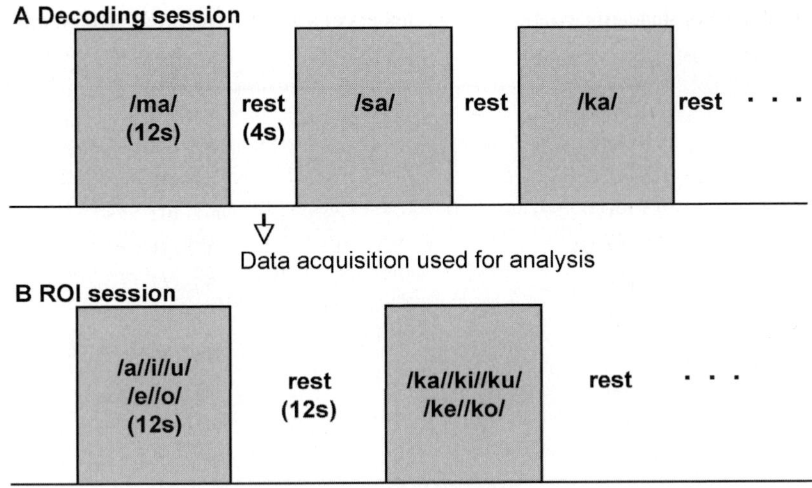

Fig. 1. Experimental design

gradient-echo echoplanar imaging parameters were used to acquire 40 slices (TR = 4000 ms, TE = 50 ms, flip angle = 90, voxel size 3×3×4 mm). A high-resolution three-dimensional T1-weighted anatomical scan (FOV 256 × 256, 1×1×1 mm resolution) was acquired for each participant. A T2-weighted anatomical scan was also acquired in each session (FOV 192 × 192, 0.75×0.75×4 mm resolution).

2.5 fMRI Data Preprocessing

We used SPM5 (Wellcome Department of Cognitive Neurology) for fMRI data preprocessing for both decoding and ROI sessions. First, motion artifacts in all functional images were removed by realigning images to the first functional image of all the sessions for each participant. Second, all the functional images were co-registered to T2-weighted anatomical images, and then to three-dimensional anatomical images followed by re-slicing. Third, the data were smoothed spatially with a Gaussian kernel of 8 mm full-width at half maximum (FWHM).

Then, we selected voxels for decoding analysis within anatomically specified ROIs. Anatomical ROIs were chosen based on previous literatures that showed speech-related brain activity[1-4]. They were motor area (BA 4, 6), somatosensory area (BA 1, 2, 3), dorsolateral prefrontal cortex (BA 9), opercular and triangular sections of the inferior frontal gyrus incuding Broca's area (BA 44, 45), insula (BA 13), auditory area (BA 41, 42), posterior part of superior temporal gyrus including Wernicke's area (BA 22, 39), supramarginal gyrus (BA40) and cerebellum. First, these ROIs were specified on the standard brain by using WFU PickAtlas (The Functional MRI Laboratory Wake Forest University School of Medicine). Then, we transformed specified anatomical ROIs onto individual brain using Deformation-toolbox of SPM. And we masked SPM results of the ROI sessions using those anatomically specified ROIs. Voxels in each ROIs were selected in the order of highest t-value until the number of voxels reached 1001 in the ROI session for each

Table 1. Mean and standard deviation of the numbers of voxels in each ROI across participants

ROI	Num. of voxels
BA (1 2 3 4 6)	1201±159
BA (4 6)	866±154
BA (1 2 3)	334±30
BA (9)	461±102
BA (44 45)	175±41
BA (13)	358±27
BA (41 42)	76±8
BA (22 39)	536±126
BA (40)	243±50
Cerebellum	3681±138
White matter	241±79.2

BA: Broadman's area

subject. If the number of the voxels in a certain ROI was smaller than 1001, all of the voxels were used (Table 1). As a control ROI, we manually specified white matter region on a EPI image of each subject using MRIcro.

To avoid the movement-induced artifacts [5][6], the MRI signal intensity of each voxel during 4-s rest period was used as the data samples for decoding analysis. Because hemodynamic delay was about 4 seconds, the activity during the rest period reflects the utterance of the preceding task period. We also normalized the voxel intensity within each volume to remove signal baseline draft. Each data sample was labeled according to its corresponding syllable that was uttered in the preceding speech task block, and served as input to the syllable decoder analysis.

2.6 Decoding Analysis

Decoding was performed based on a pattern classification method described in Kamitani and Tong [7]. We used linear support vector machines (SVM) to calculated linear discriminant functions for pairs of syllables. Using a training data set, a linear SVM finds optimal weights and bias for the discriminant function. After the normalization of the weight vectors, the pairwise discriminant functions comparing one syllable and the other syllables were simply added to yield the linear detector function.

To evaluate syllable decoding performance, we performed a version of cross-validation by testing the fMRI samples in one run using a decoder trained with the samples from all other runs. This training-test set was repeated for all runs ("leave-one-run-out" cross-validation). We used this procedure to avoid using the samples in the same run both for training and test, since they are not independent because of the normalization of voxel intensity within each run.

We used two different methods to decode the nine syllables. In one method, we decoded three vowels (a, e, o) and three consonants (m, s, k) separately and combined those results to predict the nine syllables, since the syllables consist of consonants and vowels. In the other method, we decoded the nine syllables at once.

3   Results

3.1   Articulation-Related Regions

We examined articulation-related regions individually in ROI sessions. Bilateral sensory-motor cortex were activated in all participants, cerebellum, insula and superior temporal gyrus were activated in some participants (Fig.2). These areas were included in the anatomical ROI.

3.2   Decoding Vowels, Consonants and Syllables

We examined if consonants (m, s, k) or vowels (a, e, o) can be decoded by decoders trained uisng 9 syllables. For vowel decoding, we considered /ma/ /sa/ /ka/ as (a), /me/ /se/ /ke/ as (e) and /mo/ /so/ /ko/ as (o). For consonant decoding, we treated /ma/ /me/ /mo/ as (m), /sa/ /se/ /so/ as (s) and /ka/ /ke/ /ko/ as (k). Table 1 shows the ROIs that had the top five average prediction rates over all participants for each decoding. The predictions of both vowels and consonants were above chance level (33.3%). The best prediction rates scores of vowels and consonants across participants were 57.4 % by

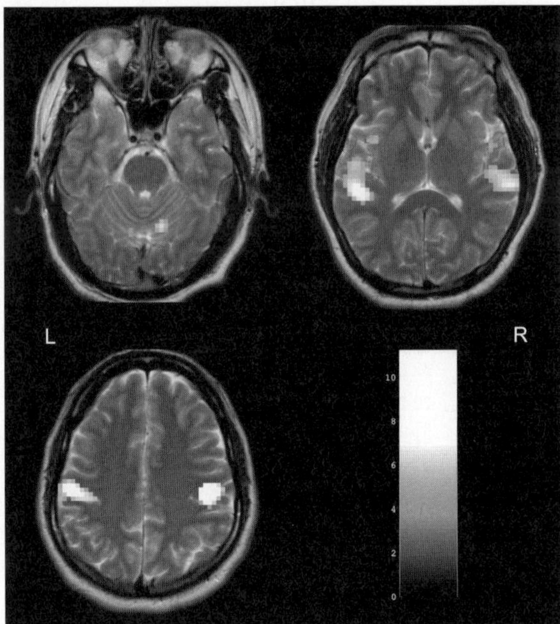

Fig. 2. Hemodynamic response evoked by utterance of 40 syllables in Japanese Kana syllabry in a conventional task-rest sequence of participant D (p < 0.05 corrected). Activations were observed in bilateral sensory- motor cortex, cerebellum, insula and superior temporal gyrus.

Table 2. Mean and standard deviation of prediction rates across participants that showed top five decoding performance for vowels, consonants and syllables

Rank	Vowels		Consonants		Syllables	
	Performance(%)	ROI	Performance(%)	ROI	Performance(%)	ROI
1 st	43.5±7.5	BA (22 39)	49.5±10.9	Cerebellum	18.1±7.3	BA (13) R
2 nd	42.6±14.1	BA (1 2 3 4 6) L	48.6±7.6	BA (1 2 3 4 6) L	18.1±6.9	BA(1 2 3 4 6)
3 rd	41.2±2.3	BA (1 2 3) L	47.7±8.3	BA (1 2 3 4 6)	17.7±3.1	Cerebellun
4 th	40.7±8.8	Cerebellum R	46.8±13.7	Cerebellum L	17.4±3.7	BA (22 39)
5 th	40.3±6.7	BA (1 2 3 4 6)	46.3±11.4	BA (13)	17.4±6.7	BA (4 6) R
Control	33.8±4.1	White matter	32.9±1.8	White matter	13.2±6.2	White matter

BA: Broadman's area   L: Left   R:Right

left sensory motor cortex activity of participant C and 63.0 % by cerebellum activity respectively of participant C. We also decoded nine syllables using a single decoder. The prediction rates were above chance level (11.1%).

3.3 Prediction of 9 Syllables by the Combination of Vowel and Consonant Decoders

Table 3 shows the combination of the ROIs that had the top five average prediction rates over all participants. On average, the combination of sensori-motor cortex showed good prediction performance (Table 3). The prediction rates were above chance level (11.1%).

Table 3. Mean and standard deviation of prediction rates across participants that showed top five decoding performance for 9 syllables by using the combination of vowel and consonant decoders

Rank	Performance(%)	ROI	
		Vowels	Consonats
1 st	22.6±9.1	BA (1 2 3 4 6) R	BA (4 6)
2 nd	22.2±6.5	BA (4 6) R	BA (4 6)
3 rd	21.5±9.0	BA (1 2 3 4 6) R	BA (1 2 3 4 6)
4 th	21.2±6.4	BA (4 6) R	Cerebellum
	21.2±12.1	BA (4 6)	BA (4 6)

BA: Broadman's area   L: Left   R:Right

3.4 Comparison between Two Methods

We compared decoding performances of those two methods to decode 9 syllables. For three of four participants, predictions by the combination of vowel and consonant decoders were superior to those by a single decoder.

Table 4. Comparison of the best decoding performance between the two methods

Participant	Decoding at onece		Combination of consonants and vowels	ROI	
	Performance(%)	ROI	Performance(%)	Vowels	Consonants
A	22.2	BA (1 2 3 4 6)	38.9	BA (4 6)	BA (1 2 3 4 6)
B	27.8	BA (13) R	36.1	BA (22 39)	BA (4 6) R
C	27.8	BA (1 2 3 4 6) R	25.0	BA (13) BA(41 42)	BA (4 6) BA (4 6) R
D	20.8	Cerebellum	26.4	BA (13)	Cerebellum

BA: Broadman's area   L: Left   R:Right

4 Discussions

In the present study, syllables were decoded from fMRI data of articulate-related brain regions at above-chance levels. There have been several reports that certain category of sensory information was successfully decoded from fMRI activities. Cox and Savoy [8] reported that they classified fMRI activation evoked by the visual presentation of various categories of objects at above-chance level using multivariate statistical pattern recognition methods, including linear discriminant analysis and support vector machines. Kamitani and Tong [7] also reported that they successfully decoded the perception of edge orientation from fMRI data using support vector machines. Moreover, they reported when subjects had to attend to one of two overlapping orthogonal gratings, feature-based attention strongly biased ensemble activity toward the attended orientation. Those reports suggested that multivariate analyses can take advantage of the information contained in activity patterns across space, from multiple voxels. Such analyses have the potential to greatly expand the amount of information extracted from fMRI data sets. To our knowledge, however, there were no reports about decoding process of motor control from fMRI activation.

The successful decoding would be dependent on the functional localization of human cortex. Since the speech require dexterous control of multiple muscles similarly to hand manipulation, the articulate related region occupies relatively large areas in human cortex.

In the present study some participants showed good decoding performance through auditory area like BA 41, 42 and speech perception area like BA 22, 39. It is possible that this area was coding the perceptual signal and what was decoded was not on speech production but speech perception. Since we always hear what we speak, it is difficult to segregate perception from production. It is also well known that the specific motor circuits are delicately involved for speech perception as well as production. For example, Pulvermüller F and co-workers [9] found involvement of sound-related somatotopic activation in precentral gyrus not only when subjects spoke the lip- or tongue-related phonemes but also when subjects listened to the lip- or tongue-related phonemes. We also found good decoding performance though insula (BA 13) for some participants. This is reasonable since insula is reported to have strong relation to articulation [1][4][10] .

Syllables in Japanese phonology consist of one consonant and one vowel. So, we tried a unique method besides normal decoding technique that classified the nine syllables at once. Namely, consonants and vowels were separately decoded first, and then those results were combined to lead the prediction of final nine syllables. It was interesting that the decoding performance was improved when decoding process were divided into two steps. Although, it is uncertain whether this improvement of decoding performance has some relation to physiological mechanism of speech production, this result provides new insight for the methodology of decoding technique.

For fMRI studies of speech production, movement-induced artifact has been as a significantly limiting factor. The motion-induced artifact associated with fMRI studies of human speech production comes from both direct and indirect sources. Direct source of motion artifact comes from head movement. Indirect source of motion-induced artifact is more problematic. Birn RM and co-workers [5] showed that motion of speech alter the susceptibility-induced magnetic field distribution at the brain slice images. To avoid the influences of motion artifacts mentioned above, we only used data of rest blocks. So, there were little possibilities results were influenced by motion artifacts. And, functionally correlated results itself also supported successful decoding of brain activities related speech motor control.

This technique has potential to help understanding underlying mechanisms of speech disorders as well as normal speech. Furthermore, the results suggest the possibility of using non-invasively measured brain activity to read out the intended speech of disabled patients in speech motor control.

Acknowledgments. We thank Y. Aramaki for his advice for fMRI analysis. This research was partly supported by SCOPE.

References

1. Wise, R.J., Greene, J., Buchel, C., Scott, S.K.: Brain regions involved in articulation. Lancet 353, 1057–1061 (1999)
2. Guenther, F.H., Ghosh, S.S., Tourville, J.A.: Neural modeling and imaging of the cortical interactions underlying syllable production. Brain Lang 96, 280–301 (2006)
3. Sakai, K.L.: Language acquisition and brain development. Science 310, 815–819 (2005)
4. Dronkers, N.F.: A new brain region for coordinating speech articulation. Nature 384, 159–161 (1996)
5. Birn, R.M., Bandettini, P.A., Cox, R.W., Jesmanowicz, A., Shaker, R.: Magnetic field changes in the human brain due to swallowing or speaking. Magn. Reson Med. 40, 55–60 (1998)
6. Gracco, V.L., Tremblay, P., Pike, B.: Imaging speech production using fMRI. Neuroimage 26, 294–301 (2005)
7. Kamitani, Y., Tong, F.: Decoding the visual and subjective contents of the human brain. Nat Neurosci 8, 679–685 (2005)
8. Cox, D.D., Savoy, R.L.: Functional magnetic resonance imaging (fMRI) brain reading: detecting and classifying distributed patterns of fMRI activity in human visual cortex. Neuroimage 19, 261–270 (2003)
9. Pulvermuller, F., Huss, M., Kherif, F., Del Prado Martin, F.M., Hauk, O., Shtyrov, Y.: Motor cortex maps articulatory features of speech sounds. Proc Natl Acad Sci USA 103, 7865–7870 (2006)
10. Fox, P.T., Huang, A., Parsons, L.M., Xiong, J.H., Zamarippa, F., Rainey, L., Lancaster, J.L.: Location-probability profiles for the mouth region of human primary motor-sensory cortex: model and validation. Neuroimage 13, 196–209 (2001)

Prediction of Arm Trajectory from the Neural Activities of the Primary Motor Cortex Using a Modular Artificial Neural Network Model

Kyuwan Choi[1], Hideaki Hirose[2], Yoshio Sakurai[3], Toshio Iijima[2],
and Yasuharu Koike[1]

[1] Precision and Intelligence Laboratory, Tokyo Institute of Technology
[2] Graduate School of Life Sciences, Tohoku University
[3] Graduate School of Letters, Kyoto University
`kwchoi21@hi.pi.titech.ac.jp`

Abstract. First, we reconstructed 9 muscle tensions (filtered EMG signals) from 105 neurons in the arm region of the primary motor cortex, then estimated arm movement in four degrees of freedom in the shoulder and the elbow from the reconstructed 9 muscle tensions. The reconstructed arm movement showed good correlation with the actual arm movement.

Keywords: BMI, EMG, Neural activity, M1, arm movement.

1   Introduction

In recent times, interest in the field of brain machine interfaces has been rising and many papers have been published. Brain machine interfaces is a technology for paralyzed people who cannot move their arms due to damage to their bodies from an accident or a disease. The main goal is to allow paralyzed people to interact with society more freely by giving them control over an external device such as a robot arm or a mouse cursor from the brain signals through a mathematical model.

Since 1999, when Chapin et al. [1] controlled arm movement of a robot in one degree of freedom from the neural activity of the motor cortex of a rat, much development and research has been done in this field. Carmena et al. [2] succeeded in reconstructing arm movement of a robot in three degrees of freedom and grip force from the neural activity of the premotor cortex, primary motor cortex and posterior parietal cortical area of a monkey. In addition, Musallam et al. [3] extracted high level signals, such as the goal of a movement, the preference and motivation of a subject from the neuron signal of the parietal reach region (PRR) and area 5 which are the major pathways of visually guided movement. Recently, Hochberg et al. [4] succeeded in controlling a computer cursor on a 2 dimensional display from the signal of the primary motor cortex of the brain of an actual human.

In order to implement a brain machine interface system similar to a human arm, reconstructing the position and force information of the arm from the

M. Ishikawa et al. (Eds.): ICONIP 2007, Part II, LNCS 4985, pp. 987–996, 2008.

neural activity of the brain is necessary. For example, if we consider when a human picks up an object, the human moves his arm to the object position from the original position, then gives proper force depending on the weight of the object. Like this the reconstruction of the force information is an important factor in the implementation of brain machine interface system. We used EMG signals to reconstruct the position and force information, simultaneously. EMG signals reflect muscle tensions, so, we can reconstruct arm posture, joint torque and stiffness from the EMG signals, precisely.

In this study, first we reconstructed 9 muscle tensions (filtered EMG signals) from the neural activity of 105 neurons in M1 by using a linear regression method, then estimated joint angles in four degrees of freedom related to the shoulder and the elbow from the reconstructed muscle tensions using a modular artificial neural network model.

2   Materials and Methods

2.1   Behavioral Task

We trained a Japanese monkey (Macaca fuscata; male, 7.4kg) to do a continuous arm reaching task. The task, as shown in figure 1, consisted of pushing the buttons Hold-C-A-B, Hold-C-D-B, Hold-D-B-A, and Hold-D-C-A. Here we will explain only Hold-C-A-B sequence, as the others have similar patterns. First the monkey pushes the hold button for 1 second when the hold signal turns on. If the monkey succeeds in pushing the hold button for 1 second, then the C button turns on and the monkey has to push the button within 1 second. After pushing the C button, the A button turns on. As in the case of the C button, if the monkey pushes the button for 1 second, then finally the B button turns on, the monkey should push the button for 1 second. The monkey received juice rewards if the task was completely succeeded. All procedures were approved by the Tohoku University Animal Care and Use Committee.

2.2   Recording Neural Activity in the Primary Motor Cortex

After the monkey became sufficiently skillful in the task, a stainless steel recording chamber (diameter 20mm) was installed around the primary motor cortex of left hemisphere under aseptic conditions. Using a glass-insulated Elgiloy alloy microelectrode, the neural activity of the upper part of the body region in the primary motor cortex was measured by the conventional chronic single-unit recording method. The main recording target was the neurons located in layer V. In controlling the microelectrode, an electronic stepping microdrive (MO-81, Narishige) was used. The neural activity was measured at 1kHz sampling rate. In order to search which muscle is linked to each neuron measured in the primary motor cortex, we used the intracortical microstimulation (ICMS). We identify the muscle that moves or contracts, to the neuron when a train of 12 cathodal pulses of 0.2ms duration at 300Hz was applied at each neuron under the intensity below 40uA.

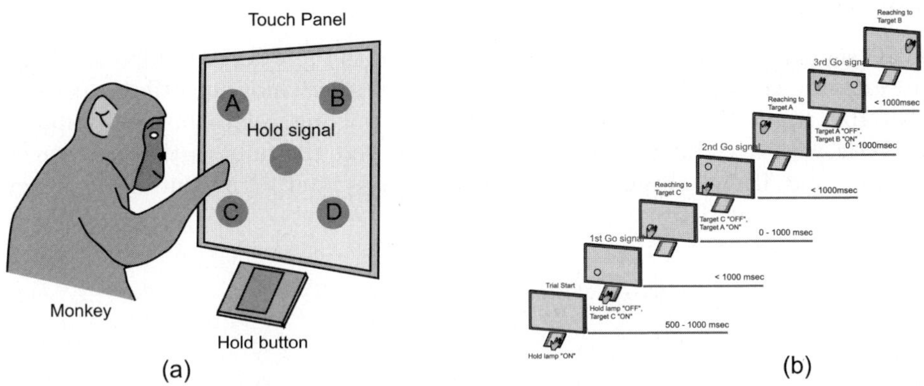

Fig. 1. (a) Behavioral task: The monkey sat in a primate chair with its head fixing and facing a touch panel equipped with five lamps and five buttons,was trained to do a continuous arm reaching task. (b) A sequential arm reaching task (C-A-B trial).

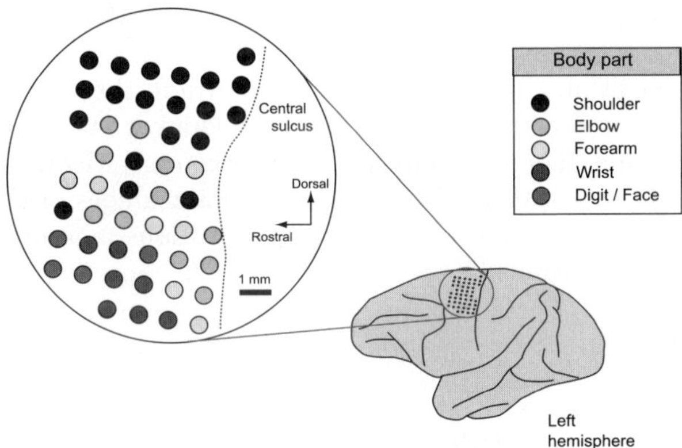

Fig. 2. The recording area of the primary motor cortex of left hemisphere. Each circle represents each recording site. The circles imply the body representation, which was defied as the body part that moved or in which muscle contractions were visually observed when intracortical micro stimulation was applied.

161 neurons were measured in the primary motor cortex (figure 2). Among these neurons, the number of the neurons related to the shoulder muscle were 66, and the number of the neurons related to the elbow muscle were 39. The others were the neurons related to the wrist and finger. In this study, we used 105 neurons in 31 places, which are related to the shoulder and elbow muscle to reconstruct arm posture. The neural activities measured at 1kHz sampling rate were summed within non-overlapping 30ms time bins. On average, neural activities were measured 10.88 trials at each neuron, and we used the half of the data as training data and others as test data.

2.3 EMG Signal Processing

EMG signals were measured in 9 muscles related to the 4 degrees of freedom [13]. To measure the EMG signals, we used a silver/siver chloride surface electrode (NE-102, Nihon Kohden). After differentially amplifing, each signal was sampled at 1kHz with a 12-bit resolution. The signals were digitally rectified, averaged for 5ms, and filtered through a 2nd-order low pass filter with a cut-off frequency of approximately 3Hz.

$$f_{EMG}(t) = \sum_{j=1}^{n} h_j EMG(t - j + 1) \tag{1}$$

$$h(t) = 6.44 \times (exp^{-10.80t} - exp^{-16.52t}) \tag{2}$$

The coefficients h_j in equation 1 can be acquired by sampling h(t) in equation 2 discretely. The resulting signal is very similar to the actual tension; hence, it is called quasi-tension [8].

2.4 Kinematics

To measure the position of the shoulder, the elbow and the wrist of the monkey, we attached an infrared marker on the arm of the monkey and measured each position of them using a 3D position measurement system (MacReflex, Qualisys). The sampling rate was 120Hz. To calculate the joint angles of the four degrees of freedom in the shoulder and elbow from the positions measured, we used the inverse kinematics equations [5].

3 Results

3.1 The Estimation Result of the Filtered EMG Signals from the Neural Activity of the Primary Motor Cortex

The estimation of the filtered EMG signals is obtained by simply linearizing the neural activities of the primary motor cortex with a linear regression method.

$$fEMG_i(t + \delta t) = \sum_{j=1}^{m} \omega_{ij} n_j(t) + bias \tag{3}$$

Here, $fEMG_i$ and n_j describe the i th filtered EMG signal from j th neuron. δt is the delay between the neuron activity of the primary motor cortex and the EMG signals. The weighting-factor ω_{ij} represents the strength influence from neuron j on the muscle i.

We estimated the filtered EMG signals from 105 neurons in the primary motor cortex using equation 3. To decide the delay time parameter, we used the Intracortical Micro Stimulation Method (ICMS) that we shocked 9 locations of the primary motor cortex 275 times by electrocity, and searched the time that

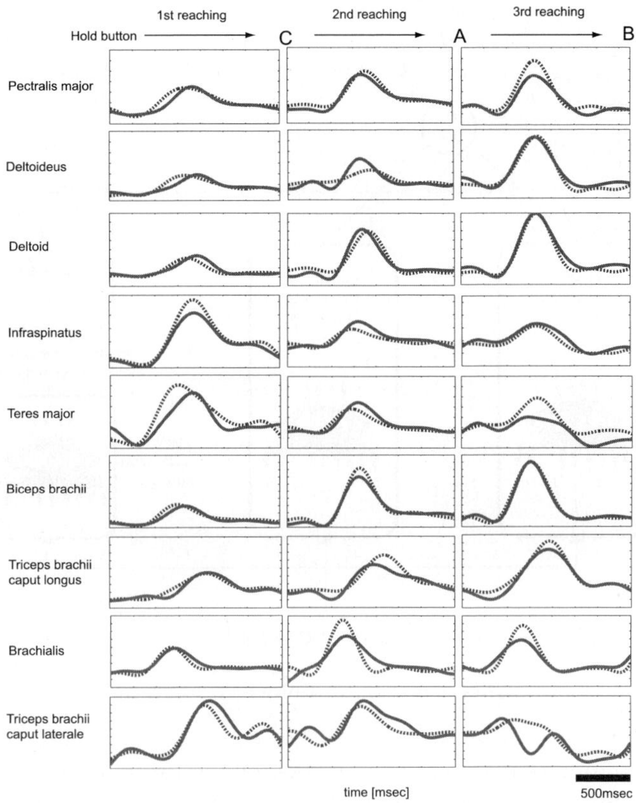

Fig. 3. The reconstruction of the filtered EMG signals using the ensemble of 105 neurons of the primary motor cortex. The dotted lines represent the actual filtered EMG signals and the solid lines show the reconstructed filtered EMG signals.

the EMG signals are occurred. As a result, the delay time was 16.57 ± 3.46msec. So, we set to 17msec. when we estimate the filtered EMG signals from the neural activities of the primary motor cortex.

Figure 3 represents the result of estimation from the neural activities to the filtered EMG signals. The estimated filtered EMG signals have a correlation coefficient of 0.93 with the actual EMG signals.

3.2   Estimation of Joint Angles from the Filtered EMG Signals

To estimate joint angles from the filtered EMG signals, we used a modular artificial neural network [9], as shown in figure 4. Training the data of posture and movement in different network will improve the accuracy of the estimation of joint angles as compared to training the whole data in the same network since the muscle tension is different in the two mentioned cases. If training is done well, gating network selects one of two expert networks by its input signal.

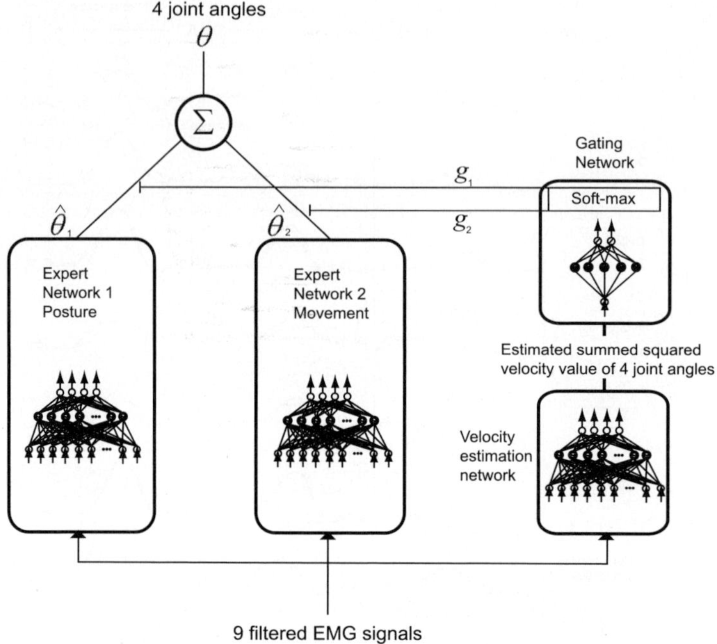

Fig. 4. Joint angle estimation model which has a modular architecture

In this case, among two expert networks, one is for posture and another is for movement. Since the gating network decides the output ratio for each expert network depending on its input signal, the sum of the outputs of the gating network should always be 1.

To make this, as shown in Eq. 4, the output g_j of gating network, which corresponds to jth expert network is normalized using the "soft max" activation function.

$$g_j = \frac{e^{x_j}}{\sum_{i=1}^{N} e^{x_i}} \tag{4}$$

Here, x_i is the value determined by the input signal of gating network and N is the total number of the outputs of the gating network. The total output is calculated by that the output of gating network is multiplied to the output of each expert network and then the result is summed, like Eq. 5.

$$\theta = \sum_{i=1}^{N} g_i \hat{\theta}_i \tag{5}$$

Gating network and each expert network are trained to maximize the likelihood function lnL (Eq.6) by the back propagation algorithm [11].

$$lnL = ln \sum_{i=1}^{N} g_i e^{\frac{-||\theta - \hat{\theta}_i||^2}{2\sigma_i^2}} \tag{6}$$

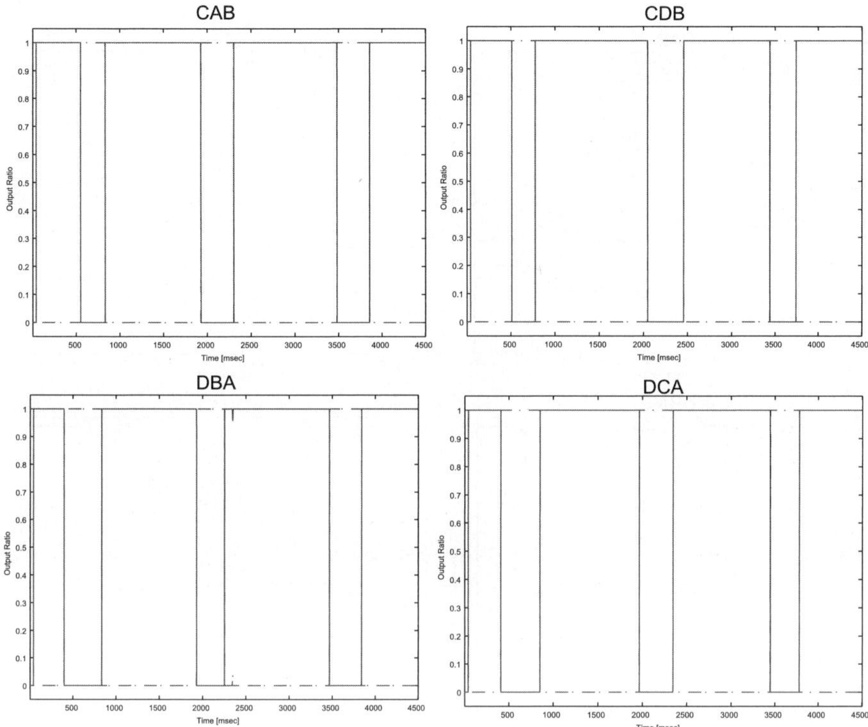

Fig. 5. The output of the gating network. (The solid line represents the moment of posture and the dotted line shows the moment of movement).

The filtered EMG signals of 9 muscles were used as the input of each expert network model. And, the summed squared velocity value of 4 joint angles was used as the input of the gating network since the summed squared velocity value discriminates easily the moment of posture and movement. After measuring 30 trials of the EMG signals and movement trajectories of the arm of the monkey, we used 29 trials as training data and one trial as test data. The number of training data is 522348 samples ($29trials \times 1kHz \times 4.503sec \times 4cases$) and the number of test data is 18012 samples ($1trial \times 1kHz \times 4.503sec \times 4cases$). In the case of gating network, the network was trained by the summed squared velocity value of 4 joint angles. However, since the summed squared velocity value of 4 joint angles cannot be used as test data, we estimated the velocity values of 4 joint angles from the filtered EMG signals. Figure 5 shows the outputs of gating network when the estimated squared acceleration values of 4 joint angles were inputted. And, figure 6 represents the estimated 4 joint angles from the neural activity of the primary motor cortex. The correlation coefficient between the estimated joint angles and the actual joint angles was about 0.92.

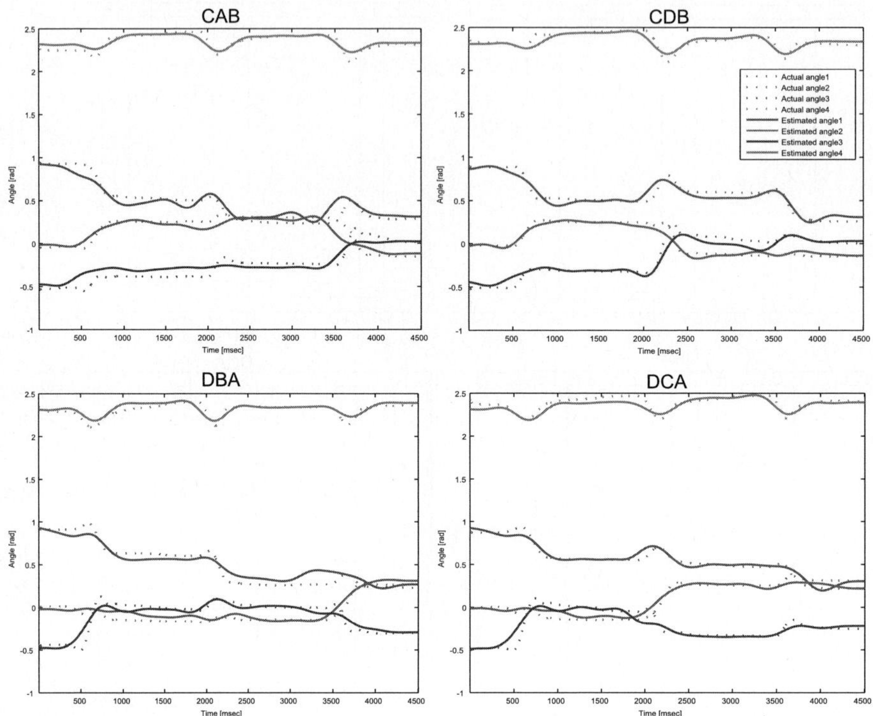

Fig. 6. The estimated joint angles from the neural activity of M1. The dashed line represents the actual joint angles and the solid line shows the estimated joint angles.

4   Discussion

We reconstructed muscle tensions from the neural activity of the primary motor cortex related to the shoulder and the elbow. Then, we estimated the joint angles from the reconstructed muscle tensions. When reconstructing the muscle tensions from the neural activity, we could determine the delay time by examining the correlation coefficient between neural activity and EMG signals. But, the EMG signal is a simple waveform which has one or two peaks, and the neural activity is also similar. So, to determine the delay time by correlation coefficient is very difficult. Therefore, in this study, after determining the delay time by ICMS, we fixed the δt when reconstructing the muscle tensions from the neural activity of M1.

The reason why we do not directly estimate arm posture from the neural activity of the primary motor cortex, and instead use the muscle tensions is that since anatomically muscles are linked to M1 by 2 or 3 neurons through the spinal cord, we can get a signal that is highly correlated with M1. And, when a human takes a posture, the brain stabilizes the posture by controlling the muscle tensions. So, by using muscle tensions, we can reconstruct arm posture more precisely than the existing method that directly reconstructs arm posture from the neural activity of M1. And, If EMG signals are reconstructed from the neural activity of M1, there is a possibility that a paralyzed person can control his arm by himself using the estimated EMG signals as command signals for the Functional Electrical Stimulation system.

We used the modular artificial neural network model when reconstructing joint angles from muscle tensions. The reason is that in the case of isotonic movement where force is outputted with changing length of the muscle, the tension is different depending on the velocity that the muscle flexes or extends. In the case that a muscle flexes, the tension will decrease as the flex velocity increases. And, in the case that muscle extends, the tension will increase as the extension velocity increases. We could improve the estimation performance of joint angles by training two networks with tension values, which changes depending on the velocity rather than training the data in the same network, we used one network for 0 velocity and the other for movement velocity.

Acknowledgments. This work was supported by grants from the Ministry of Education, Science, Sports and Culture, Grant-in-Aid for Scientific Research (B), 16360169 and JST CREST Program to Y.Sakurai.

References

1. Chapin, J.K., Moxon, K.A., Markowitz, R.S., Nicolelis, M.A.L.: Real-time control of a robot arm using simultaneously recorded neurons in the motor cortex. Nature neuroscience 2(7), 664–670 (1999)
2. Carmena, J.M., Lebedev, M.A., Crist, R.E., O'Doherty, J.E., Santucci, D.M., Dimitrov, D.F., Patil, P.G., Henriquez, C.S., Nicolelis, M.A.L.: Learning to control a brain-machine interface for reaching and grasping by primates. PLoS Biology 1, 664–670 (2003)
3. Musallam, S., Corneil, B.D., Greger, B., Scherberger, H., Andersen, R.A.: Cognitive control signals for neural prosthetics. Science 305, 258–262 (2004)
4. Hochberg, L.R., Serruya, M.D., Friehs, G.M., Mukand, J.A., Saleh, M., Caplan, A.H., Branner, A., Chen, D., Penn, R.D., Donoghue, J.P.: Neuronal ensemble control of prosthetic devices by a human with tetraplegia. Nature 442, 164–171 (2006)
5. Koke, Y., Kawato, M.: Estimation of arm posture in 3D-space from surface EMG signals using a neural network model. IEICE Trans. Fundam. E77-D 4, 368–375 (1994)
6. Koke, Y., Kawato, M.: Estimation of dynamic joint torques and trajectory formation from surface electromyography signals using a neural network model. Biol. Cybernet. 73, 291–300 (1995)
7. Koke, Y., Kawato, M.: Estimation of dynamic joint torques and trajectory formation from surface electromyography signals using a neural network model. Biol. Cybernet. 73, 291–300 (1995)
8. Basmajian, J.V., DeLuca, C.J.: Muscles Alive. Williams and Wilkins (1985)
9. Jacobs, R.A., Jordan, M.I., Nowlan, S.J., Hinton, G.E.: Adaptive mixtures of local experts. Neural Computation, 79–87 (1991)
10. Mannard, A., Stein, R.: Determination of the frequency response of isometric soleus muscle in the cat using random nerve stimulation. J. Physiol, 275–296 (1973)

11. Rumelhart, D., Hinton, G., Williams, R.: Learning representations by back-propagation errors. Nature, 323, 533–536
12. Wiener, N.: Cybernetics: or control and communication in the animal and the machine. MIT press, Cambridge (1948)
13. Choi, K., Hirose, H., Iijima, T., Koike, Y.: Prediction of four degrees of freedom arm movement using EMG signal. In: 27th Annual international conference of the IEEE engineering in medicine and biology society (EMBC 2005), CD-Rom No. 1018 (2005)

Prediction of a Go/No-go Decision from Single-Trial Activities of Multiple Neurons in Monkey Superior Colliculus

Ryohei P. Hasegawa[1, 2,*], Yukako T. Hasegawa[1,2], and Mark A. Segraves[2]

[1] Neurosci. Res. Inst., AIST, Tsukuba, Ibaraki 305-8568, Japan
[2] Dept. Neurobiol. and Physiol., Northwestern Univ., Evanston, IL 60208, USA
{hase-p@ni.aist.go.jp}

Abstract. The purpose of this study was to develop an algorithm capable of transforming neural activity to correctly report behavioral outcome during a cognitive task. We recorded from small groups of 2-5 neurons in the superior colliculus (SC) while monkeys performed a go/no-go task. Depending upon the color of a peripheral stimulus, the monkey was required to either make a saccade to the stimulus (go) or maintain fixation (no-go). In order to replicate the progress of the decision-making process and generate a virtual decision function (*VDF*), we performed a multiple regression analysis, with 1 msec resolution, on neuron activity during individual trials. Post hoc analyses by *VDF* predicted the monkey's choice with nearly 90% accuracy. These results suggest that monitoring of a limited number of SC neurons has sufficient capacity to predict go/no-go decisions on a trial-by-trial basis, and serves as an ideal candidate for a cognitive brain-machine interface (BMI).

Keywords: Saccade, Superior colliculus, Decision-making, Prediction, Brain–machine interface, Go/no-go.

1 Introduction

We have recently focused on monitoring single trial activities in single SC neurons, and developed an algorithm to provide a good prediction of go/no-go decisions [1]. In this study, we extended the algorithm to predict these decisions from the activities of multiple neurons, recorded simultaneously in the SC.

1.1 Decision-Making and the Superior Colliculus

The oculomotor system is frequently chosen as the model system for investigating the neural substrates of simple decision-making. The superior colliculus (SC), located on the dorsal surface of the midbrain, is an important component of this system [2]. Several studies have looked at the role of the SC in decision-making [3] [4] [5]. In addition, the SC receives substantial input from areas of parietal and prefrontal cortex

---

* Corresponding author.

M. Ishikawa et al. (Eds.): ICONIP 2007, Part II, LNCS 4985, pp. 997–1006, 2008.

known to have activity related to decision-making [6] [7] [8] [9] [10] [11] [12] [13] [14]. An important component of movement control is the ability to withhold movements when appropriate. Recent experiments have looked at neural activity in the frontal eye field [15] and SC [1] in decision-making tasks that require the active suppression of saccade eye movements. These experiments suggest that many neurons in the oculomotor system exhibit selectivity for go/no-go decisions, that is, plans to make a saccade or to maintain fixation.

1.2 Single-Trial Based Prediction for the BMI

The decision-making process is entirely internal and does not necessarily produce motor behavior. Studies on techniques to read out such an internal signal are closely related to brain-machine interface (BMI), especially cognitive BMI that might provide useful communication tools for patients with difficulty in expressing their intentions. Unfortunately, most previous studies on decision-making are based upon comparison of neural activity averaged across many trials. We recently addressed the issue of how well the activity of single SC neurons can predict, for individual trials, a monkey's decision to make a saccade or to maintain fixation in response to a peripheral cue [1]. We found that our methods correctly predicted the monkey's decision on about 83% of the trials. In this study we hypothesized that simultaneous recording of multiple neurons might improve the accuracy of prediction, and applied our decoding methods to the ensemble activity of SC neurons.

2 Methods

2.1 Animal and Surgery

Two adult female Rhesus monkeys (Macaca mulatta) were used for this study. Each monkey received preoperative training followed by an aseptic surgery to implant a subconjunctival wire search coil, a plastic cilux recording cylinder aimed at the superior colliculus, and a titanium receptacle to allow the head to be held stationary during behavioral and neuronal recordings. All of these methods have been described in detail elsewhere [9]. Surgical anesthesia was induced with the short-acting barbituate thiopental (5-7 mg/kg IV), and maintained using isoflurane (1.0-2.5%) inhaled through an endotracheal tube. Northwestern's Animal Care and Use Committee approved all animal protocols, which were in compliance with the NIH Guide for the Care and Use of Laboratory Animals.

2.2 Behavioral Task

We trained each monkey on an oculomotor go/no-go task (**Fig. 1**). A trial was initiated by fixation of a central fixation spot (white spot; 0.5° diam.). Next, the fixation spot disappeared and simultaneously a peripheral stimulus ("cue"; 1° by 1° square) appeared. The monkey was trained to respond differently to the stimulus depending upon the color of the cue, that is, either make a saccade toward the stimulus within 800 ms (green cue; go trial) or maintain fixation for longer than 800 ms (red cue; no-go trial). A correct response was rewarded with a drop of water.

During training, we presented the green or red cue at 24 locations that were in 8 directions (45° spacing) at 3 eccentricities (5, 10 and 15° away from the fixation point). All conditions were run in a pseudorandom fashion. During the recording sessions, we first presented all of these possible conditions to define the response fields of isolated neurons. Then, we presented the green/red cue only at the preferred location (near the center of the response field) and at the opposite location (rotated 180° with the same amplitude). This reduction of the number of conditions allowed us to record more trials with the responses of interest (usually more than 20 trials for each condition).

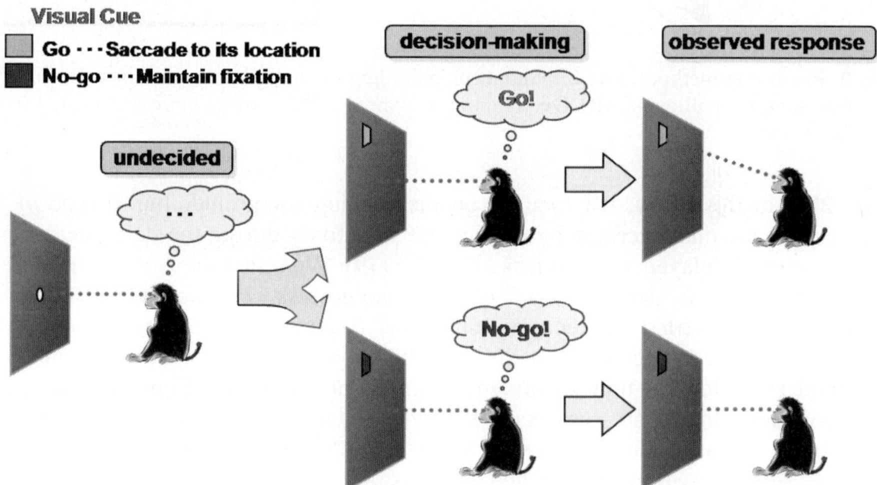

Fig. 1. Oculomotor go/no-go task. Go (saccade) or no-go (maintenance of fixation) response is required immediately following the appearance of a peripheral cue. The concurrent disappearance of the fixation spot signals the time for a response. The color of the cue is green (go) or red (no-go). Dashed line indicates desired direction of gaze.

2.2 Electrophysiological Recording

When the monkey's performance reached the criteria (>85% over 3 successive days) in overall training history, we started recording from the SC. The location of the SC was confirmed by stereotaxic coordinates, the response properties of isolated neurons, and the characteristics of its topographically organized visual/motor map (**Fig. 2A**). The recording of single and multiunit activity was done with tungsten microelectrodes (A-M Systems, Inc.) introduced through stainless steel guide tubes that pierced the dura, using a Crist grid system [16]. For multielectrode recordings, electrodes were introduced through separate guide tubes. These electrodes were manipulated by one or two separate Narishige microdrives. A 16-channel Plexon System was dedicated to accepting the electrode input, and could isolate 2 neurons' waveforms from each of those electrodes. We usually used 2-4 electrodes for recording maximally from 8 neurons. Nearby neurons recorded from the same electrode or from two different electrodes in adjacent grid holes had response fields with similar spatial properties

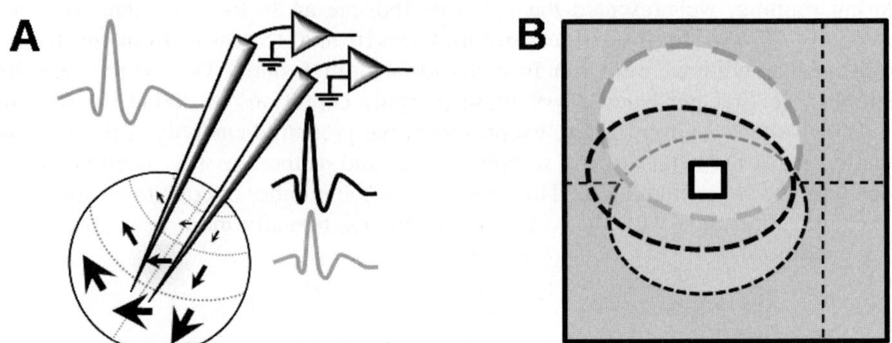

Fig. 2. Recording methods. **(A)** Simultaneous recording of multiple neurons located nearby in the right superior colliculus. **(B)** Overlapping response fields of those neurons, located in the left visual field.

(Fig. 2B). In this study, we focused on the buildup (or prelude-burst) type of SC neurons that are characterized by an increase in activity during the delay period of a visually-guided delayed saccade task [17] [18] [19]. We tested the isolated neurons in separate blocks of a "delay-version" of the go/no-go task (with an additional 800 ms response delay inserted between cue onset and fixation spot disappearance). Those blocks were mixed together with the regular "no-delay" blocks. The neurons were classified as buildup if they exhibited a significant (Wilcoxon Sign-Rank test, P < 0.05, compared to the pre-cue fixation activity) increase in delay period activity on the delayed go task. We used the REX system [20] running on a Dell Pentium II computer for behavioral control and eye position monitoring. Visual stimuli were generated by a second PC, which was controlled by the REX machine and rear projected onto a tangent screen in front of the monkey by a CRT video projector (Sony VPH-D50, 75Hz non-interlaced vertical scan rate, 1024 x 768 resolution).

2.3 Data Analysis

We analyzed data offline using programs written in Matlab. We modified the prediction methods for single neurons [1], and performed a multiple regression analysis on the ensemble activity of SC neurons in order to generate a virtual decision function (*VDF*), which reflected the progress of go/no-go decision making. For each neuron we first calculated a spike density function by convolving single trial activity with a Gaussian kernel [21] with a sigma of 10 ms (36 ms spread of the spike density function). We measured the activity over a 500 ms interval, starting 100 ms before the cue onset and ending 400 ms after it. We used a linear model for each millisecond (t) of ensemble activities:

$$y(t) = \frac{2}{1 + \exp(c(t) - \sum_{i}^{n} w_i(t) x_i(t))} - 1 \tag{1}$$

where independent variables, $x_i(t)$ were discharge rates of simultaneously recorded neurons (i, neuron ID; n, total number of neurons), $w_i(t)$ were unstandardized partial regression coefficients (weights), and $c(t)$ was a constant term at the moment of t. Dependent/predicted variable, $y(t)$ was a desired go/no-go score; its actual data (type of trial), z was set to either 1 on go trials or to -1 on no-go trials, and was held constant throughout a given trial.

$$z = \begin{cases} 1 : & \text{go trial} \\ -1: & \text{no - go trial} \end{cases} \tag{2}$$

A set of appropriate weights of the model were determined by the least square method which minimized the sum of the squared regression errors.

$$S_E(t) = \sum_{j=1}^{m} \left(z_j - y_j(t)\right)^2 \tag{3}$$

where z_i and $y_i(t)$ were respectively z (actual data) and $y(t)$ (fitted data) on each trial (j, trial ID; m, total number of trials). $S_E(t)$ represents the variation which is unexplained by the regression equation. On the other hand, the sum of squared errors from the mean represents the total variation.

$$S_T(t) = \sum_{j=1}^{m} \left(z_j(t) - \overline{y}(t)\right)^2 \tag{4}$$

The fitness of the model was evaluated by the coefficient of determination (R^2)

$$R^2(t) = 1 - \frac{S_E(t)}{S_T(t)} \tag{5}$$

which represents the proportion of variation that is explained by the model. R^2 may vary from 0 (no predictive power) to 1 (perfect prediction).

In this study, we repeated this analysis over the 500 ms interval beginning 100 ms before cue onset to determine weights x_i, constant c and R^2 at a time t (sampled at 1 kHz). We used $R^2(t)$ as well as $y(t)$ to produce a $VDF(t)$ that was designed to reflect a single trial-based decision-making process for go (saccade) or no-go (maintenance of fixation) time-locked by the appearance of cue stimulus.

$$VDF(t) = y(t)R^2(t) \tag{6}$$

R^2 represents how well the expected data fit the real data. It can be a good index for the confidence level of prediction but R^2 itself does not indicate the essence of the prediction (go vs. no-go). Instead, $y(t)$ is the actual predictor although it lacks the information about "how well". Therefore, y(*t*) and R^2 complement each other when those functions are multiplied.

To evaluate the success or failure of a prediction on each trial, we used a pair of criteria for "go decision" and for "no-go decision" (e. g., +0.3 for go and -0.3 for no-go). If the *VDF* reached either criterion, it was considered that the neurons had made a prediction. If the neuronal prediction matched the observed behavior, that is, the monkey's decision, the trial was considered to be one with a good prediction. For each recording session, we set the criteria by simulations; out of 19 candidates of a pair of criteria (i.e., ±0.1, ±0.15, ±0.2 ...±1.0), we chose the "optimal" pair so that the number of good predictions was maximized. We defined *decision time* as the first moment when the function reached either the go or no-go criterion. A mismatch of neuronal prediction to actual behavior or (rarely) a trial where no neural prediction was made was considered to be a trial with a bad prediction. It was also incorrect if the *VDF* became 1 or -1 before the cue was presented, since it was unlikely that the monkey formed a decision before the instruction was presented. Therefore, we counted those trials (including the trials with the neural prediction made within 50 ms after the cue onset) as bad ones. We also set a time limitation of up to 400 ms after the cue presentation for inclusion of neuronal data in the analysis.

3   Results

3.1   Application of Regression Analysis on Neuronal Activity

In total, 59 neurons were recorded during 23 recording sessions in 2 monkeys. As described in a previous study [1], most SC neurons exhibited higher activity on go versus no-go trials after the initial response to the cue onset. We addressed the issue of how well the activity of the neurons could predict the monkey's decision, on each trial, whether the monkey made a saccade or suppressed it. To test this, we used the activity (spikes/sec) of small groups of neurons as independent variables and a binary decision outcome (1 for go and -1 for no-go) as a dependent variable. First, we repeatedly applied the regression analysis to the ensemble activity over all trials with a time step of 1 ms and duration of 500 ms ranging from 100 ms before to 400 ms after the onset of the cue. This process produced basic results about the regression for every millisecond, including partial regression coefficients (*w*), constant term (*c*), and coefficient of determination (R^2).

The *w* value became higher after the cue onset (between 100-300 ms), indicating that the neuron's higher activity was linked to a higher probability of a go decision. The *c* value was decreased during the same 100-300 ms time period, reflecting the nonselective response of this neuron to the visual cue onset regardless of the go/no-go decision. These parameters directly contributed to the calculation of the predictor variable (*y*). On the other hand, R^2 indicates how much of the total variation in the dependent variable can be explained by the regression equation. The R^2 values became higher between 100-300 ms after cue onset, indicating that prediction during this time was more reliable than during the preceding period. For each recording session (with n trials), we prepared a template (database for prediction) which consisted of these three parameters. For the prediction above, we used one of cross

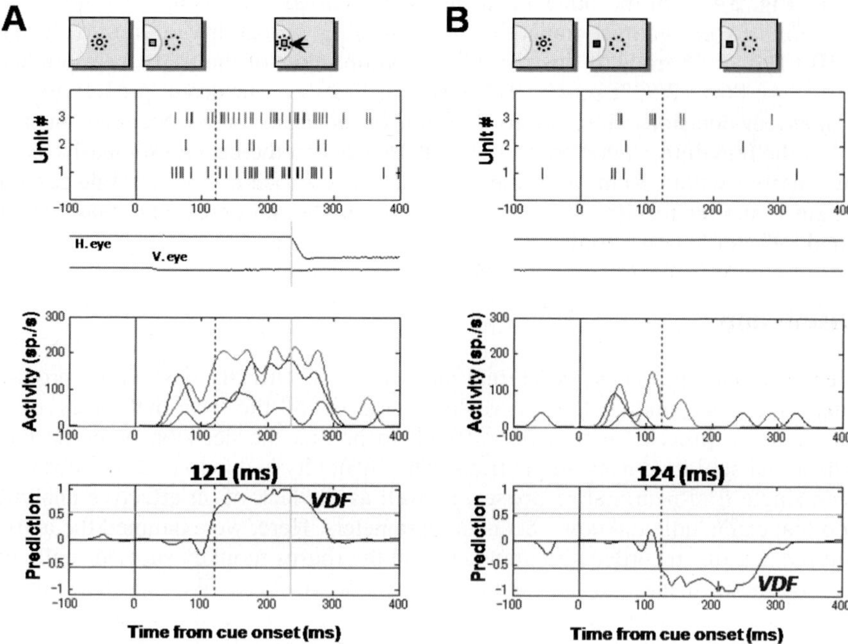

Fig. 3. An example of recording session data and trial-by-trial prediction of the monkey's go/no-go decision. Representative trials are shown for correct predictions of 'go' **(A)** and 'no-go' **(B)** decisions. Single trial activity of three neurons is shown by raster (top row) and spike density histogram (middle row) aligned to cue onset at time = 0. A virtual decision function (VDF, bottom row) was calculated by a linear combination of the responses on a given trial and a set of coefficients (weights and R^2) that were derived from the multiple regression analyses. A vertical dashed line indicates the decision time where the **VDF** reached the criteria for 'go' (+0.55) or 'no-go' (-0.55). The vertical line (colored cyan) in the left column indicates the beginning of the saccade.

validation methods, "leave-one-out method", in which we removed single trials from the template (n-1) to construct the model and tested the model against the removed trial. This procedure was repeated n times.

3.2   Go/No-go Prediction by the Virtual Decision Function (VDF)

After we prepared the templates for all trials in each recording session, we returned to the analysis of single trials to verify the predictability of the go/no-go decision based upon the template. We generated a **VDF** on each trial which was designed to reflect the progress of the go/no-go decision time-locked to the appearance of the cue. To calculate the **VDF** we multiplied a predictor variable (y), which was calculated for each millisecond of a trial by a linear regression model, with R^2 (see Methods). **Figure 3** shows typical examples of successful "go" and "no-go" predictions. The **VDF** tended to stay near 0 at the beginning of each trial, indicating that a decision had not been made. Later, however, the value of **VDF** started increasing toward 1 on a go trial around 100 ms after the cue onset, indicating an increasing probability of a go decision (**Fig. 3A**). On the other hand, the **VDF** started decreasing on a no-go trial with a similar time course, indicating a decreasing probability of no-go decision (**Fig. 3B**). For all 46 trials of this recording session, most of the trials were predicted correctly (go: 96%, 22/23; no-go: 91%, 21/23). For the 3 incorrect predictions, two were incorrect decisions (i.e., no-go decision on go trials or go decision on no-go trials). In the remaining incorrect trial, the **VDF** reached the criteria too early (before the cue onset or within 50 ms after the cue onset). For a total of 23 recording sessions, we obtained similar results. The average correct prediction percentage was 88% for "go" and 89% for "no-go" trials.

4   Discussion

The decision-making process is internal and we cannot directly observe its progress. Although previous studies have revealed evidence of the neuronal basis of the decision-making process, it remains difficult to predict the decision outcome based upon neuronal activity during single trials. This difficulty is due to both the variability between single trial neuronal responses, as well as the lack of an effective analytical method that can handle unknown decision parameters. Here, we examined the activity of multiple neurons recorded simultaneously in the rhesus monkey superior colliculus during the performance of an oculomotor go/no-go task. We applied multiple regression analysis to the responses of ensemble activities and produced, *on each trial*, a virtual decision function that was designed to reflect a decision-making process for go (saccade) or no-go (maintenance of fixation) time-locked by the appearance of a cue stimulus. Decisions were successfully predicted by this function at a level of nearly 90% of trials, which was better than the results of prediction by single neurons of the same population (83%) [1]. The results of this study support the hypothesis that a small number of SC neurons can provide sufficient information to make accurate trial-by-trial predictions of a monkey's decision.

4.1   Activity of SC Neurons as a Predictor of Oculomotor Behavior

The primate SC is an important structure for the generation of saccadic eye movements, integrating multiple cortical inputs and providing an oculomotor command to the premotor burst neurons [2]. The deep layers of the SC primarily contain two types of neurons related to saccade execution: buildup and burst neurons. Previous studies have shown the activity of SC neurons, particularly buildup neurons, to be related to the selection of saccade targets from among multiple candidate stimuli during a variety of tasks [3] [4] [5] [17] [18] [22] [23]. These studies suggest that the activity of SC neurons reflects not only the generation of a motor command but also the cognitive process for decision-making related to saccades. Our attempt to extract a prediction signal from the SC is an extension of these earlier studies demonstrating a reliable SC signal for target selection.

Moreover, recent studies suggest that the SC is also involved in the inhibitory control of saccades during an antisaccade task [24] and a countermanding task [25]. These tasks are similar to our go/no-go task in that the subject is required to suppress a saccade toward the stimulus location. Our results are also consistent with these studies in which SC neurons exhibited less activity on antisaccade/stop trials than prosaccade/control trials. Based upon the knowledge about such a differential activity, we hypothesized that monitoring of SC signals should make the single trial prediction of a go/no-go decision possible.

4.2 Prediction of Go/No-go Decision-Making by SC Ensemble Activity

Previous studies of BMI demonstrated that neural signals from motor-related areas could serve to control robot arms or computer cursors [26] [27] [28] [29]. In addition to the outer devices, it has been shown that muscle activities of subjects were reliably reconstructed by a small number of neurons recorded from the primary motor cortex [30] [31]. While these studies focused on the prediction of either kinematic parameters of movements (such as hand position and joint angle) or muscle activities related to them, our main goal in this study was to predict cognitive decision making by monitoring the ensemble activity of a small number of SC neurons. Techniques for decoding a categorical decision-making process hold promise for patients with dysfunctions in communication. Our experiments have demonstrated that the combination of SC neurons' ensemble activities with the go/no-go saccade-decision task provides a good model for a cognitive form of BMI with the capacity to decipher categorical thought ("neural mind reading").

Acknowledgment

We thank for Drs. Ken Ohta, Kenichiro Miura, Takio Kurita, Narihisa Matsumoto for comments on this article, Angela Nitzke for technical assistance, and the staff of Northwestern's Center for Comparative Medicine for Animal Care. This study was supported by the NIH (EY08212), MEXT of Japan (KAKENHI 18019048 and 19500289), and the Sumitomo Foundation (Grant for Basic Science Research Projects).

References

1. Hasegawa, R.P., Hasegawa, Y.T., Segraves, M.A.: Single trial-based prediction of a go/no-go decision in monkey superior colliculus. Neural Netw 19, 1223–1232 (2006)
2. Sparks, D.L.: The brainstem control of saccadic eye movements. Nat. Rev. Neurosci. 3, 952–964 (2002)
3. Horwitz, G.D., Newsome, W.T.: Separate signals for target selection and movement specification in the superior colliculus. Science 284, 1158–1161 (1999)
4. Ratcliff, R., Cherian, A., Segraves, M.: A comparison of macaque behavior and superior colliculus neuronal activity to predictions from models of two-choice decisions. J. Neurophysiol. 90, 1392–1407 (2003)
5. Ratcliff, R., Hasegawa, Y.T., Hasegawa, R.P., Smith, P.L., Segraves, M.A.: Dual diffusion model for single-cell recording data from the superior colliculus in a brightness-discrimination task. J. Neurophysiol. 97, 1756–1774 (2007)
6. Segraves, M.A., Goldberg, M.E.: Functional properties of corticotectal neurons in the monkey's frontal eye field. J. Neurophysiol. 58, 1387–1419 (1987)
7. Hanes, D.P., Wurtz, R.H.: Interaction of the frontal eye field and superior colliculus for saccade generation. J. Neurophysiol. 85, 804–815 (2001)
8. Sommer, M.A., Wurtz, R.H.: A pathway in primate brain for internal monitoring of movements. Science 296, 1480–1482 (2002)

9. Helminski, J.O., Segraves, M.A.: Macaque frontal eye field input to saccade-related neurons in the superior colliculus. J. Neurophysiol. 90, 1046–1062 (2003)
10. Schall, J.D.: Neural basis of deciding, choosing and acting. Nat. Rev. Neurosci. 2, 33–42 (2001)
11. Leon, M.I., Shadlen, M.N.: Exploring the neurophysiology of decisions. Neuron 21, 669–672 (1998)
12. Hasegawa, R., Sawaguchi, T., Kubota, K.: Monkey prefrontal neuronal activity coding the forthcoming saccade in an oculomotor delayed matching-to-sample task. J. Neurophysiol. 79, 322–333 (1998)
13. Hasegawa, R.P., Matsumoto, M., Mikami, A.: Search target selection in monkey prefrontal cortex. J. Neurophysiol. 84, 1692–1696 (2000)
14. Hasegawa, R.P., Blitz, A.M., Geller, N.L., Goldberg, M.E.: Neurons in monkey prefrontal cortex that track past or predict future performance. Science 290, 1786–1789 (2000)
15. Hasegawa, R.P., Peterson, B.W., Goldberg, M.E.: Prefrontal Neurons Coding Suppression of Specific Saccades. Neuron 43, 415–425 (2004)
16. Crist, C.F., Yamasaki, D.S., Komatsu, H., Wurtz, R.H.: A grid system and a microsyringe for single cell recording. J. Neurosci. Methods 26, 117–122 (1988)
17. Basso, M.A., Wurtz, R.H.: Modulation of neuronal activity in superior colliculus by changes in target probability. J. Neurosci. 18, 7519–7534 (1998)
18. Glimcher, P.W., Sparks, D.L.: Movement selection in advance of action in the superior colliculus. Nature 355, 542–545 (1992)
19. Munoz, D.P., Wurtz, R.H.: Saccade-related activity in monkey superior colliculus. I. J. Neurophysiol. 73, 2313–2333 (1995)
20. Hays, A., Richmond, B., Optican, L.: A UNIX-based multiple process system for real-time data acquisition and control. In: WESCON Conf. Proc., vol. 2, pp. 1–10 (1982)
21. Richmond, B.J., Optican, L.M., Podell, M., Spitzer, H.: Temporal encoding of two-dimensional patterns by single units in primate inferior temporal cortex. I. Response characteristics. J. Neurophysiol. 57, 132–146 (1987)
22. McPeek, R.M., Keller, E.L.: Saccade target selection in the superior colliculus during a visual search task. J. Neurophysiol. 88, 2019–2034 (2002)
23. Krauzlis, R., Dill, N.: Neural correlates of target choice for pursuit and saccades in the primate superior colliculus. Neuron 35, 355–363 (2002)
24. Munoz, D.P., Everling, S.: Look away: the anti-saccade task and the voluntary control of eye movement. Nat. Rev. Neurosci. 5, 218–228 (2004)
25. Pare, M., Hanes, D.P.: Controlled movement processing: superior colliculus activity associated with countermanded saccades. J. Neurosci. 23, 6480–6489 (2003)
26. Wessberg, J., Stambaugh, C.R., Kralik, J.D., Beck, P.D., Laubach, M., Chapin, J.K., Kim, J., Biggs, S.J., Srinivasan, M.A., Nicolelis, M.A.: Real-time prediction of hand trajectory by ensembles of cortical neurons in primates. Nature 408, 361–365 (2000)
27. Taylor, D.M., Tillery, S.I., Schwartz, A.B.: Direct cortical control of 3D neuroprosthetic devices. Science 296, 1829–1832 (2002)
28. Serruya, M.D., Hatsopoulos, N.G., Paninski, L., Fellows, M.R., Donoghue, J.P.: Instant neural control of a movement signal. Nature 416, 141–142 (2002)
29. Wolpaw, J.R., McFarland, D.J.: Control of a two-dimensional movement signal by a noninvasive brain-computer interface in humans. Proc. Natl. Acad. Sci. USA 101, 5430–17849 (2004)
30. Morrow, M.M., Miller, L.E.: Prediction of muscle activity by populations of sequentially recorded primary motor cortex neurons. J. Neurophysiol. 89, 2279–2288 (2003)
31. Koike, Y., Hirose, H., Sakurai, Y., Iijima, T.: Prediction of arm trajectory from a small number of neuron activities in the primary motor cortex. Neurosci. Res. 55, 146–153 (2006)

Diverse Evolutionary Neural Networks Based on Information Theory*

Kyung-Joong Kim and Sung-Bae Cho

Department of Computer Science, Yonsei University
134 Shinchon-dong, Sudaemoon-ku, Seoul 120-749, South Korea
kjkim@cs.yonsei.ac.kr, sbcho@cs.yonsei.ac.kr

Abstract. There is no consensus on measuring distances between two different neural network architectures. Two folds of methods are used for that purpose: Structural and behavioral distance measures. In this paper, we focus on the later one that compares differences based on output responses given the same input. Usually neural network output can be interpreted as a probabilistic function given the input signals if it is normalized to 1. Information theoretic distance measures are widely used to measure distances between two probabilistic distributions. In the framework of evolving diverse neural networks, we adopted information-theoretic distance measures to improve its performance. Experimental results on UCI benchmark dataset show the promising possibility of the approach.

Keywords: Information Theory, Neural Network Distance, Fitness Sharing, Evolutionary Neural Networks, Ensemble.

1   Introduction

There is a work using structural difference as distance criteria for neural network [1]. If two neural networks are the same in their topological properties, their behaviors will be the same. However, small deviations in their topological structure result in big different in their behaviors (Figure 1). This makes difficult to use structural difference as a measure of distance in neural networks. Instead of this, it is common to use output response of two neural networks as a measure of distance. In this approach, it is important the way to interpret the output of neural networks. If it is regarded as a numerical value, Euclidean distance and other distance measures can be used to calculate their numerical distance. However, it can be also interpreted as a probability [2][3]. In this view, the input to the neural network is the prior knowledge of conditional probability and the neural network outputs posterior probability.

Previously, mutual information is used to measure distances between two neural networks [4]. In this work, the output of neural network is interpreted as random variables and they attempt to find the model of the random variable's behavior using

* This research was supported by Brain Science and Engineering Research Program sponsored by Korean Ministry of Commerce, Industry and Energy.

M. Ishikawa et al. (Eds.): ICONIP 2007, Part II, LNCS 4985, pp. 1007–1016, 2008.

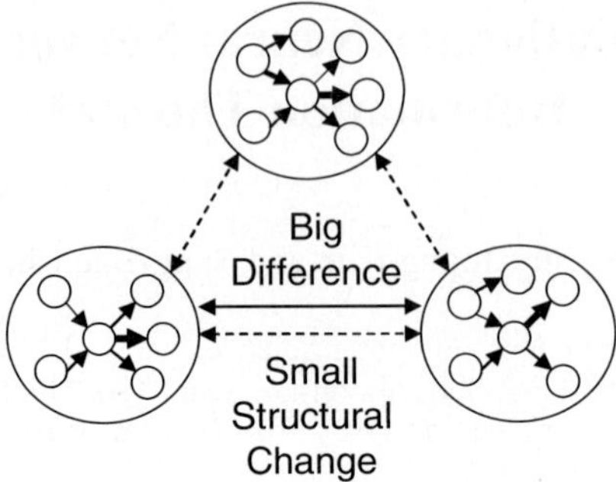

Fig. 1. The problem of using structural deviation as a measure of distance

Gaussian distribution (Figure 2). Calculating mutual information between two Gaussian distributions from neural networks is a way to measure distance. In this paper, we interpret the output of neural network as a posterior probability given the prior knowledge (input pattern). The straightforward approach measuring the distance between two probability distributions is Kullback-Leibler entropy [5] and it is adopted.

Evolving artificial neural network has been one of the hot topics and gained much interest from neural network community [6]. Because it maintains a number of neural networks simultaneously, it is interesting to use them for better performance. If there are more diverse neural networks in the population, more performance gain can be expected when they are used together as an ensemble [7]. Usually, genetic algorithm suffers from the premature convergence and it is called as genetic drift [8]. To avoid the premature convergence, it is important to calculate distances among individuals and use it in a diversity promotion mechanism.

This paper applies the distance idea to the problem of constructing multiple neural networks. It uses genetic algorithms with fitness sharing to generate a population of ANN's that are accurate and diverse. The Kullback-Leibler (KL) entropy method measures the difference between two ANN's using entropy theory. The combination of diverse classifiers is done with the Behavior Knowledge Space (BKS) method [9]. Experimental results on UCI benchmark dataset show that the proposed method can perform well compared to not only the other distance measures but also previous works.

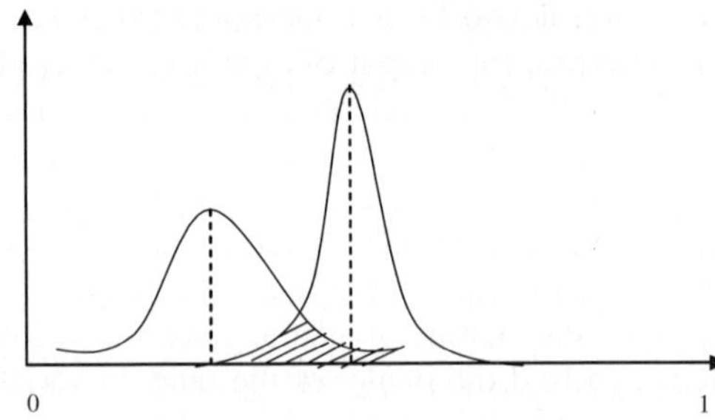

Fig. 2. Interpretation of neural network output as a random variable with Gaussian distribution. The dashed area is shared by the two distributions.

2   Related Works

Table 1 summarizes works related to the Kullback-Leibler (KL) entropy distance measure. This method is not only computationally more efficient than the similarity measure based on mutual information, but also produces comparable accuracy in multi-modal image registrations [10]. Do *et al.* showed that using a consistent estimator of texture model parameters for the feature extraction step, followed by computing the KL distance between the estimated models for the similarity measurement step, is asymptotically optimal in terms of retrieval error probability [11]. Gruner *et al.* proposed a method for quantifying neural response changes in terms of the KL distance between the intensity functions for each stimulus condition [12]. The use of the KL distance to determine the roundness of rock particles has been investigated [13]. In a general framework for self-organizing maps, which store probabilistic models in map units, the distance between a probabilistic model and a data point itself has been defined using the KL distance [14].

A method called the Behavior Knowledge Space aggregates the decisions obtained from the individual classifiers and derives the best final decisions from a statistical point of view [9]. Roli *et al.* analyzed the generalization error of the BKS method and proposed a simple analytical model that relates the error to the sample size [15]. They pointed out that the fusion method could provide very good performance if large, well-distributed datasets were available. Otherwise, over-fitting is likely to occur, and the generalization error quickly increases.

Table 1. Summary of KL entropy distance measure research

Authors	Usage
Chung *et al.* [10]	Multimodal image registration (3D clinical magnetic resonance angiograms)
Do *et al.* [11]	Texture image retrieval (MIT vision texture database)
Gruner *et al.* [12]	Quantifying neural response changes
Drevin [13]	Determining the roundness of rock particles
Hollmen *et al.* [14]	Winner search in self-organizing maps (user profile clustering)

3   Evolutionary NN Ensembles with KL Distance Measure

Figure 3 summarizes the algorithm of evolving multiple neural networks. Each neural network is represented as a matrix. Half of the matrix is used for representing connection of each node and another half is for connection weights. After initializing neural networks, they are trained using backpropagation algorithm using training data. To avoid premature convergence, the training's epoch number is set as small number. The fitness of this evolution is the classification accuracy on validation data set. Because the purpose of this evolution is to generate multiple diverse neural networks for better ensemble performance, diversity is promoted by using fitness sharing scheme (Figure 4).

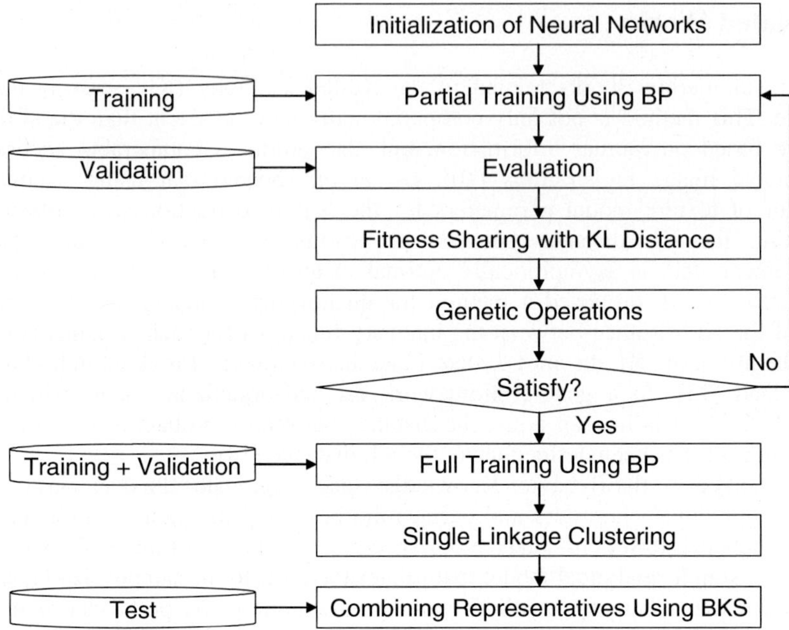

Fig. 3. Flowchart of algorithm

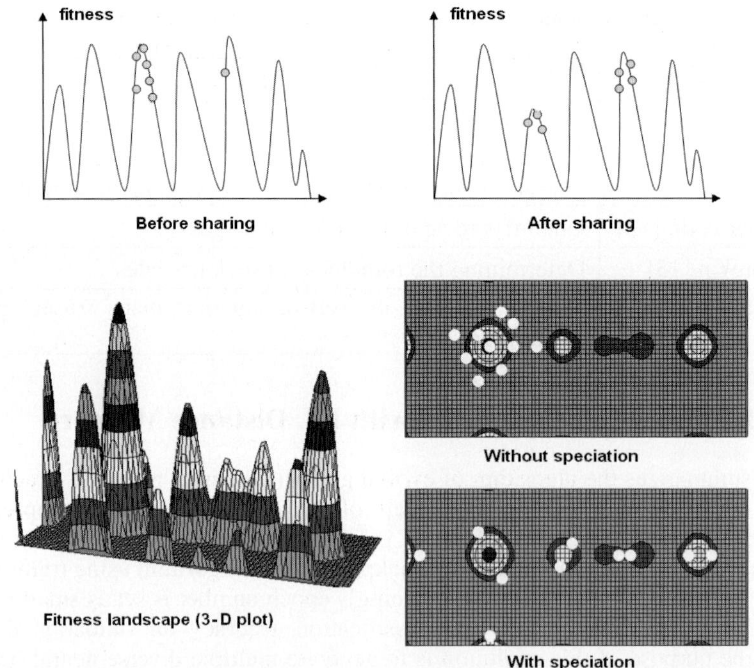

Fig. 4. The effect of fitness sharing in 2D and 3D fitness landscape

Sharing scheme calculates population density in the landscape using distance measures and readjusts their fitness based on the density. If there are many similar individuals with high fitness value, their fitness can be shared by each other and decreases too much. On the other hand, although its fitness is low, the one with low density can survive to the next generation because there is no negative readjustment of the fitness. In this stage, KL distance measure is used to calculate similarity between two neural networks.

Based on the readjusted fitness, roulette-wheel selection, crossover and mutations are sequentially applied to the matrix. Simple matrix genetic operations are used. If there are successful individuals in the population, the evolution stops. Instead of combining all neural networks in the last generation, their clustered results are used to choose the representatives among them. Single linkage clustering is used and the best one for each cluster is combined using BKS method. Finally, the performance of the ensemble is evaluated using test dataset.

3.1   KL Distance Measures

Let one discrete distribution have probability function p and the other discrete distribution have probability function q. Then the relative entropy of p_k (k is a random variable and p_k represents the probability of specific values of k) with respect to q_k, also known as the Kullback-Leibler distance, is defined by:

$$d = \sum_k p_k \log\left(\frac{p_k}{q_k}\right)$$

Although relative entropy does not satisfy the triangle inequality and is therefore not a true metric, it satisfies many important mathematical properties [16]. For example, it is a convex function of p_k, always non-negative, and equal to zero only if $p_k=q_k$. Relative entropy is a very important concept in quantum information theory, as well as statistical mechanics [17]. However, relative entropy is not a true distance because it is not symmetric, i.e., $D(p, q) \neq D(q, p)$. To remedy this problem, the modified Kullback-Leibler entropy measure is used.

$$D(p,q) = \frac{1}{2}\sum_k (p_k \log\frac{p_k}{q_k} + q_k \log\frac{q_k}{p_k})$$

Modified Kullback-Leibler entropy measures the difference of two ANN's. Let p and q be the output probability distributions of two ANN's. p and q represent output probability distributions given input evidences (a vector of attribute values of a specific sample). The ith output node provides the likelihood of a sample with respect to the ith class. When the estimation is accurate, the network outputs can be treated as probabilities. The total KL distance between the two neural networks is the sum of the KL values for all samples and output nodes. Actually, the integral over all input combinations is not possible, and the summation of the samples is taken.

Then, the similarity of the two ANN's is calculated as follows:

$$D(p,q) = \frac{1}{2}\sum_{j=1}^{m}\sum_{t=1}^{n} (p_{jt} \log\frac{p_{jt}}{q_{jt}} + q_{ij} \log\frac{q_{jt}}{p_{jt}})$$

where p_{jt} means the jth output value of the ANN with respect to the tth training data. The two ANN's are more similar as the symmetric relative entropy decreases. Figure 5 shows an example of probabilistic function approximation using output for training patterns.

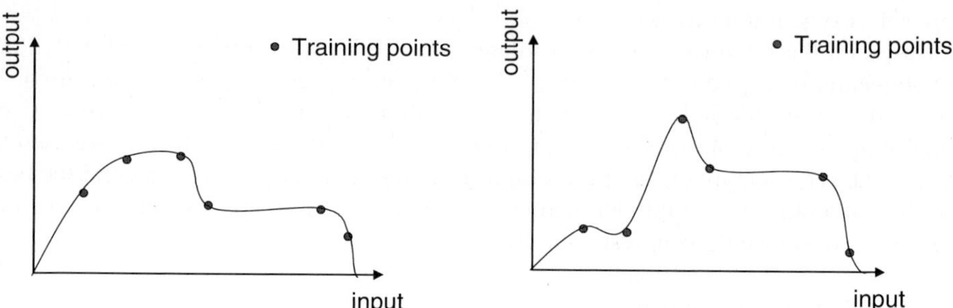

Fig. 5. Approximation of real probabilistic function with the outputs on training dataset

3.2 BKS Combination

To combine the speciated neural networks, we adopted the Behavior Knowledge Space method of the "multinomial" rule [9]. This fusion method is well-known for providing good performance if a large and representative dataset is available [15]. Methods for fusing multiple classifiers can be divided into three levels: the abstract level, the rank level and the measurement level. In abstract-level outputs, every possible combination of abstract-level classifier outputs is regarded as a cell in a look-up table [15]. The BKS table is derived from training and validation sets. Each cell contains the number of samples characterized by a particular value of class labels and the most dominated class is chosen for the cell. In this method, the term "cell" is used to represent a space for storing behaviors of the ANN. BKS is a set of cells, where the M^K cells are required to store the necessary information of the K classifiers with the M classes. $BKS(e_1(x),...,e_K(x))$ is a cell with index $(e_1(x),...,e_K(x))$.

$$BKS = \text{a } K\text{-dimensional behavior-knowledge space.}$$

$BKS(e_1(x),...,e_K(x))$ = a unit of BKS, where the 1st classifier gives its decision as $e_1(x)$, ..., and the Kth classifier gives its decision as $e_K(x)$.

$n_{e_1(x)...e_K(x)}(m)$ = the total number of incoming samples belonging to class m in $BKS(e_1(x),...,e_K(x))$

$T_{e_1(x)...e_K(x)}$ = the total number of incoming samples in $BKS(e_1(x),...,e_K(x))$

$$= \sum_{m=1}^{M} n_{e_1(x),...,e_K(x)}(m)$$

$$R_{e_1(x)...e_k(x)} \quad = \quad \text{the} \quad \text{best} \quad \text{representative} \quad \text{class} \quad \text{of}$$

$$BKS(e_1(x),...,e_K(x))$$

$$= \{ j \mid n_{e_1(x),...,e_K(x)}(m) = \max_{1 \le m \le M}(m) \}$$

The combination function of BKS is defined as follows:

$$F(e(x)) = \begin{cases} R_{e_1(x)...e_K(x)} & \text{if } T_{e_1(x)...e_K(x)} > 0 \text{ and } \dfrac{n_{e_1(x)...e_K(x)}(R_{e_1(x)...e_K(x)})}{T_{e_1(x)...e_K(x)}} \ge \lambda \\ M+1 & \text{otherwise} \end{cases}$$

λ is a threshold value to decide whether the result is rejected or not. For each class, there is a $\dfrac{n_{e_1(x)...e_K(x)}(m)}{T_{e_1(x)...e_K(x)}} \times 100$ percent probability to class m. If rejection is not allowable, then the class with the highest probability is the best and the safest choice as the final decision.

4   Experimental Results

From UCI benchmark data, breast cancer dataset is downloaded. It is divided into training, validation and test dataset with the ratio of 2:1:1. The number of neural network inputs is the same with number of attributes of the dataset. The population size is set as small value to minimize computational cost. Crossover and mutation rates are set from empirical trial-and-error. The experimental results are the average of 10 runs. Table 2 summarizes the parameters and settings of this experiment.

Table 2. Parameters of experiment

Dataset Name	Breast Cancer
# of classes	2
# of inputs in NN	9
Training/Validation/Test	349/179/175
Population size	20
Crossover rate	0.3
Mutation rate	0.1
# of runs	10

Figure 6 shows the prediction accuracy on test dataset of the proposed methods and other works (EPNET [18]). Average output (AO) and Pearson correlation (PC) measures are used for the comparison. Average output measures Euclidean distances between two average values of output values from the two neural networks. Pearson Correlation also uses the average and standard deviation of each output neuron's output. Table 3 summarizes statistical test results among the best three methods (BKS+KL, BKS+AO, BKS+PC). The statistical test is done by using t-test. T-value is calculated using the below formula.

$$t = \frac{\mu_A - \mu_B}{\sqrt{\dfrac{\sigma_A^2}{N_A} + \dfrac{\sigma_B^2}{N_B}}}$$

where, μ_A represents the average test accuracy of neural network A and σ_A is standard deviation of the multiple runs. N_A is the number of runs of the experiment. In this case, N_A is 10. If t-value is derived from the averages and standard deviation of the two methods, it is compared with the value in t-table. Degree of freedom is $N_A + N_B - 2$. If the t-value is larger than the value in the table, it is statistically significant. Table 3 summarizes the statistical significance test results among the best three methods. It shows that the BKS+KL method performs better than other two methods with statistical significance. However, the difference between BKS+AO and BKS+PC is not statistically significant.

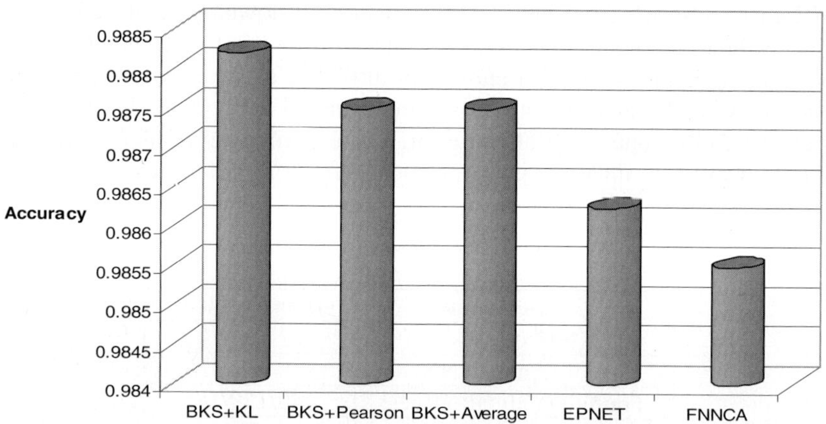

Fig. 6. Comparison with other works

Table 3. Statistical t-test ($p=0.1$) (AO=Average Output, PC=Pearson Correlation) (+: statistically significant)

	BKS+AO	BKS+PC	BKS+KL
BKS+AO		-	+
BKS+PC	-		+
BKS+KL	+	+	

5 Concluding Remarks

In this paper, the outputs of neural networks are interpreted as posterior probability and the difference between two models are calculated using Kullback-Leibler entropy measure. It is applied to the evolutionary neural ensemble framework to promote diversity in the evolutionary process. Experimental results on UCI benchmark dataset shows that the proposed methods perform better than other candidates with statistical significance. As a future work, it is required to evaluate the method to the other datasets. Also, it is interesting to find other applications of this distance measures.

References

[1] Stanely, K.O., Miikkulainen, R.: Evolving neural networks through augmenting topologies. Evolutionary Computation 10(2), 99–127 (2002)

[2] Richard, M.D., Lippmann, R.P.: Neural network classifiers estimate Bayesian a posteriori probabilities. Neural Computation 3, 461–483 (1991)

[3] Lippmann, R.P.: Neural networks, Bayesian a posteriori probabilities and pattern classification. From Statistics to Neural Networks-Theory and Pattern Recognition Applications (1994)

[4] Liu, Y., Yao, X.: Learning and evolution by minimization of mutual information. In: Guervós, J.J.M., Adamidis, P.A., Beyer, H.-G., Fernández-Villacañas, J.-L., Schwefel, H.-P. (eds.) PPSN 2002. LNCS, vol. 2439, pp. 495–504. Springer, Heidelberg (2002)

[5] Kullback, S., Leibler, R.A.: On information and sufficiency. Ann. Math. Stat. 22, 79–86 (1951)

[6] Yao, X.: Evolving artificial neural networks. Proceedings of the IEEE 87(9), 1423–1447 (1999)

[7] Brown, G., Wyatt, J., Harris, R., Yao, X.: Diversity creation methods: A survey and categorization. Information Fusion 6, 5–20 (2005)

[8] Rogers, A., Prügel-Bennett, A.: Genetic drift in genetic algorithm selection schemes. IEEE Transactions on Evolutionary Computation 3(4), 298–303 (1999)

[9] Huang, Y.S., Suen, C.Y.: Recognition of unconstrained handwritten numerals. IEEE Transactions on Pattern Analysis and Machine Intelligence 17(1), 90–94 (1995)

[10] Chung, A.C.S., Wells III, W.M., et al.: Multi-modal Image Registration by Minimising Kullback-Leibler Distance. In: Dohi, T., Kikinis, R. (eds.) MICCAI 2002. LNCS, vol. 2489, pp. 525–532. Springer, Heidelberg (2002)

[11] Do, M.N., Vetterli, M.: Wavelet-based texture retrieval using generalized Gaussian density and Kullback-Leibler distance. IEEE Transactions on Image Processing 11(2), 146–158 (2002)

[12] Gruner, C.M., Johnson, D.H.: Calculation of the Kullback-Leibler distance between point process models. In: International Conference on Acoustics, Speech, and Signal Processing, pp. 3437–3440 (2001)

[13] Drevin, G.R.: Using entropy to determine the roundness of rock particles. In: 5th International Conference on Signal Processing, pp. 1399–1404 (2000)

[14] Hollmen, J., Tresp, V., Simula, O.: A self-organizing map for clustering probabilistic models. In: Ninth International Conference on Artificial Neural Networks, vol. 2, pp. 946–951 (1999)

[15] Raudys, S., Roli, F.: The behavior knowledge space fusion method: Analysis of generalization error and strategies for performance improvement. In: Windeatt, T., Roli, F. (eds.) MCS 2003. LNCS, vol. 2709, pp. 55–64. Springer, Heidelberg (2003)
[16] Cover, T.M., Thomas, J.A.: Elements of Information Theory. Wiley-Interscience, Chichester (1991)
[17] Qian, H.: Relative entropy: Free energy associated with equilibrium fluctuations and nonequilibrium deviations. Physical Review E 63, 042103/1–042103/4 (2001)
[18] Yao, X., Liu, Y.: A new evolutionary system for evolving artificial neural networks. IEEE Transactions on Neural Networks 8(3), 694–713 (1997)

Diversity-Based Feature Selection from Neural Network with Low Computational Cost

Md. Monirul Kabir[1], Md. Shahjahan[3], and Kazuyuki Murase[1,2]

[1] Department of Human and Artificial Intelligence Systems, Graduate School of Engineering
[2] Research and Education Program for Life Science
University of Fukui, Bunkyo 3-9-1, Fukui 910-8507, Japan
[3] Department of Electrical and Electronic Engineering
Khulna University of Engineering and Technology, Khulna 9203, Bangladesh
{kabir,murase}@synapse.his.fukui-u.ac.jp,
jahan@mail.kuet.ac.bd

Abstract. This paper presents a new approach to identify the activity of input attributes efficiently in the wrapper model of feature selection. The relevant features are selected by the diversity among the inputs of the neural network and the entire process is done depending on several criteria. While the most of existing feature selection methods use all input attributes by examining network performance, we use here only the attributes having relatively high possibilities to contribute to the network performance knowing preceding assumptions. The proposed diversity-based feature selection method (DFSM) can therefore significantly reduce the size of hidden layer priori to feature selection process without degrading the network performance. We tested DFSM to several real world benchmark problems and the experimental results confirmed that it could select a small number of relevant features with good classification accuracies.

Keywords: Diversity, feature selection, neural network, classification.

1 Introduction

Selection of relevant input attributes (features) is of primary importance to construct a Neural Network (NN) with good accuracy and generalization ability. The computational cost to find the minimum relevant attributes should be low in addition. Feature selection requires a search strategy to select candidate subsets and an objective function to evaluate these candidates. Two different general models are commonly considered, the filter model and the wrapper model [1][2]. Researchers have indicated that the wrapper model always outperform filter model [1], because it evaluates the effect of the feature subset on the performance of the mining algorithm. A number of works have been proposed based on the wrapper model [1]-[8] and two search techniques have been introduced in wrapper model, forward search and backward search [2].

It is stated that, wrapper model always suffers from two problems: high computational cost [2], and instability due to changing weights randomly [7]. A method (NNFS) proposed by Setiono [3] has succeeded to select relevant features but failed to reduce computational cost as a NN with 12 hidden units is used in their

M. Ishikawa et al. (Eds.): ICONIP 2007, Part II, LNCS 4985, pp. 1017–1026, 2008.

process throughout. In contrast, the Guan's method (ICFS) [4] performed feature selection by training each attribute separately and used separate network for each attribute while the required number of hidden units are dynamically adjusted. Experimental results show that, to implement the entire process, ICFS needs a huge number of hidden units, which indicates high computational cost. The Dunne's method [7] also suffer from the same problem, because their solution is based on the aggregation of several runs of a sequential search process.

According to our best knowledge, no algorithm exists for solving the high computational cost problem in wrapper models. We here propose a new backward feature selection approach, called the diversity based feature selection method (DFSM) using coherence training and pruning. As backward search outperforms forward search [7], we implemented two aspects in it, the coherence training by using positive correlation learning (PCL) [9] and the feature selection by their diversity. Firstly, we remove the unnecessary hidden units (HUs) based on correlation criterion. Secondly, we delete the irrelevant attributes based on the combination of two criteria, the training error and correlation among the HUs during training. This combination leads to generate relevant features with less computational cost.

Unlike Abe's method [5] where the contribution of each attribute is computed, we instead selected only the attributes that are more diverged among the others. This resulted in much faster computation as well as the compactness of the network. To evaluate DFSM, we applied it on several real world classification problems such as breast cancer, diabetes, and glass problems. Experimental results exhibited that the DFSM works well and generates a small number of relevant features providing low computational cost.

The remainder of this paper is organized as follows. Section 2 gives new stopping criteria used in DFSM. In Section 3, details of DFSM are described. Experimental results and comparison to other methods are reported in Section 4. A short discussion and conclusions are given in Section 5 and Section 6, respectively.

2   New Stopping Criteria Used in DFSM

In this proposed method, we used a feedforward NN that is trained by the PCL algorithm [9] and new criteria for early stopping are adopted to improve generalization ability and reduce training cost.

2.1 Stopping Criteria (SC)

Stopping criteria used in DFSM are summarized in this section. The details are available in [11]. The flowchart of DFSM is shown in Fig. 1.

The training error function is defined by,

$$E = \frac{1}{2} \sum_{n=1}^{P} \sum_{k=1}^{K} (o_k(n) - t_k(n))^2 \tag{1}$$

where, P and K are the total number of input patterns and number of output units, respectively. $o_k(n)$ and $t_k(n)$ are actual output and target output at the nth pattern presentation.

The minimum error on training set $E_{\min}(t)$ is defined to be the lowest validation set error obtained in epochs up to epoch t: $E_{\min}(t) = \min\limits_{t' \le t} E_{va}(t')$ where, $E_{va}(t')$ is the error on the validation set after epoch t'.

2.1.1 Stopping Criterion for Removing Hidden Units

During removing the HUs, the SC is $cor' < cor_{th}$ which means that, reduction of optimum correlation due to the deletion of last HU is less than 1% of cor_{opt}.

2.1.2 Stopping Criterion for Removing Irrelevant Features

During the course of removing the features, the SC are $(cor'' < cor_{th}) AND (E' > E_{th})$. It means that, during removing the last feature, the maximum correlation cor'' is less than 0.1% of cor' and the minimum error E' is larger than 0.1% of $E_{\min}$, are both satisfied.

3 The Proposed Method

3.1 Parameters Used in DFSM

Before describing the proposed algorithm, we define some parameters used in the algorithm such as correlation, attribute distance, and network connection.

3.1.1 Correlation (CR)

To estimate the CR among the hidden units, we compute the CR between the hidden unit i and the hidden unit j in epochs t by,

$$Cor_{ij}(t) = \frac{\sum_n (h_i(n) - \bar{h_i})(h_j(n) - \bar{h_j})}{\sqrt{\sum_n (h_i(n) - \bar{h_i})^2 \sum_n (h_j(n) - \bar{h_j})^2}}(t), \tag{2}$$

where, $h_i(n)$ and $\bar{h_i}$ are the value of HU i at the nth training pattern and the average value of HU i over all training patterns, respectively. Now, the average CR among all HUs, Cor_{avg}, is calculated by the following equation,

$$Cor_{avg}(t) = \frac{1}{\binom{H}{2}} \sum_{i=1}^{H-1} \sum_{j=i+1}^{H} Cor_{ij}(t) \tag{3}$$

where, H is the total number of HUs. The above equation is used to determine the maximum correlation, Cor_{max} between the HUs that is mentioned below.

$$Cor_{max}(t) = \max\limits_{t' \le t} Cor_{avg}(t') \tag{4}$$

where, the Cor_{max} is defined to be the highest Cor_{avg} obtained in epochs up to t.

3.1.2 Distance Measurement of Attributes

In order to identify the attributes that are more important for the network, we compute the distance of each attribute into three steps. Firstly, we calculate the average distance (AD) of all weights in the input layer from the reference point zero.

$$AD = \frac{1}{L \times H} \sqrt{\sum_{i=1}^{L} \sum_{j=1}^{H} (0 - w_{ij})^2} \tag{5}$$

where, L and H are the total number of attributes and HUs, respectively. After that, we determine the distance of each attribute (D_i) from AD for i=1 to L.

$$D_i = \frac{1}{H} \sqrt{\sum_{j=1}^{H} (AD - w_{ij})^2} \tag{6}$$

The most irrelevant one can be distinguished by the following equation,

$$D_{\max} = \max(D_i) \tag{7}$$

3.1.3 Calculation of Network Connection

The number of connections (C) of the final architecture of the network can be calculated in terms of the number of existing input attributes (x), number of existing hidden units (h) and number of outputs (o) as follows.

$$C = (x \times h) + (h \times o) + h + o \tag{8}$$

3.2 The Framework of DFSM

In this proposed approach, we use a three-layered feedforward NN with one input layer, one hidden layer and one output layer. The PCL algorithm [9] is used for weight adjustment of all units in the network during training except bias unit. In this framework, DFSM comprises into three main steps: (a) deletion of HU, (b) attribute distance calculation and backward elimination, and (c) subset validation. These steps are dependent each other and the entire process has been accomplished one after another depending on particular criterion.

3.2.1 Deletion of Hidden Unit

It is reported that, during the course of training using PCL, all the unnecessary HUs are correlated with necessary ones in a positive sense. Therefore, we can delete the unnecessary ones depending on a particular criterion mentioned in 2.1.1 subsection. However, to describe the working procedure of this context we incorporate it into five steps below and the flow chart is shown in Fig. 1.

> **Step a:** Initially create an initial three-layered NN architecture. Numbers of input and output units are equal to those of input and output of the problem, respectively. The number of HUs is decided for the large number. The weights are initialized to random values between [+1.0, -1.0], set the value of learning rate, η between [0.1, 0.3], strength of positive correlation, λ depending on the characteristics of the problem as well.

Step b: Train the network by using PCL and motivate the HUs to be correlated in maximum among each other by Eq. (4). Measure and save the maximum correlation cor_{max} and then go to step **c**.

Step c: Delete one HU in each step and then retrain the network. Try to correlate between the remaining ones in maximum again and save the correlation cor'.

Step d: If the SC described in Section 2.1.1 is not satisfied, then repeat the step **c**. Otherwise, go to step **e**.

Step e: Restore the deleted HU with associated all weights and correlation values. Measure the training error, E and save it for using in a certain section.

3.2.2 Computation of Attribute Distance and Backward Elimination

This section describes a searching method that has been employed to generate relevant features. It is a heuristic search, because the irrelevant features are sequentially deleted using one new technique, i.e., computation of attribute distance. The above adaptation is utilized using the weight decay property of PCL. The details of this context are divided into two steps, step f & g. These are mentioned below and also shown in Fig. 1.

Step f: To attain the fare selection of feature subset, compute the maximum attribute distance, D_{max} among the existing ones by Eq. (7). Delete the attribute from the network, retrain the network to achieve the minimum training error, E' while correlation should be less than or equal to the user defined threshold of cor' at step **e**. The procedure to calculate E' has been described in Section 2.1.

Step g: If the stopping criterion mentioned in subsection 2.1.2 will not be satisfied, then, repeat the step f. Otherwise, go to next step.

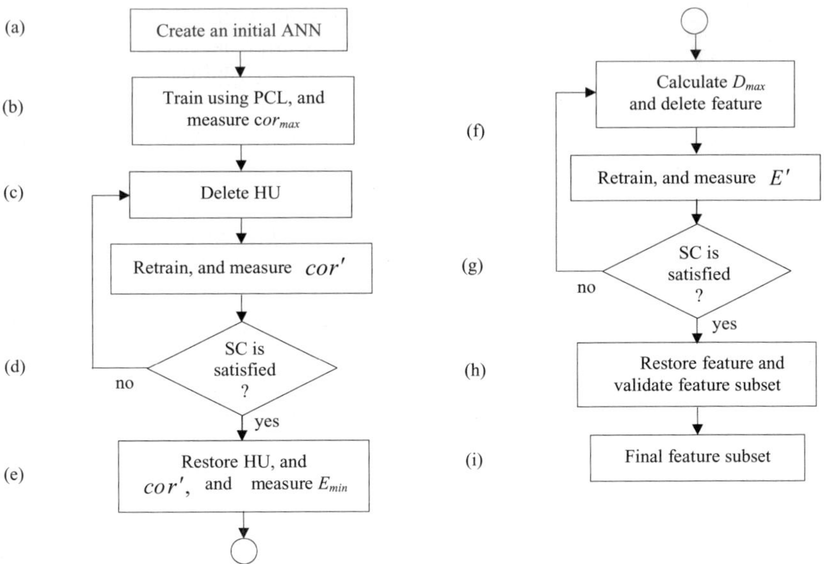

Fig. 1. Flow chart of DFSM, adapted from [10]

3.2.3 Subset Validation

The final best subset is used to validate the performance on the unseen real world dataset. No prior knowledge about the data was given during the training period. This subsection is consisted by two steps, step h & i of Fig. 1.

> **Step h:** Restore the last deleted feature with all associated components. In order to justify the classification performance of the newly generated subset, apply them to unseen datasets of the problems.
> **Step i:** Finally, the final feature subset is obtained.

4 Experimental Analysis

To evaluate the performance, DFSM was tested on three well-known benchmark problems. These are Breast cancer (BCR), Diabetes (DBT), and Glass (GLS) problems. Detailed descriptions of the datasets are available at the UCI web site [12]. Table 1 shows the characteristics of data sets.

In this study, the total number of examples in a data set is divided into three sets. The first 50% of a data set is selected as a training set to train the network, the second 25% as the validation set to check the condition during training, and the last 25% as the test set to test the network. The test set completely remains unseen to the network during training. The total partition of each dataset is mentioned in Table 2. Each experiment was carried out 10 times and the presented results were the average of these 10 runs.

4.1 Experimental Results

Table 3-5 exhibit the average results of DFSM where the number of selected relevant features, network performance, and number of HUs and so on are included for BCR, DBT, and GLS problems. In these tables, CA refers to the classification accuracy, and ITN to iteration. For clarification, training error we measured by the Eq. 1 and CA is the ratio of classified examples to the total examples of the particular dataset.

In each experiment, DFSM produced lower numbers of relevant features with good CAs as well as less numbers of HUs. In Table 3, it can be seen that, for example, a network with an average of 3.74 relevant features with 3.25 HUs for BCR data set was obtained with 97.86 testing CA. Similarly, for DBT (Table 4) and GLS (Table 5) dataset, we can be seen that, DFSM can select smaller numbers of relevant features with good CAs as well as reduces the numbers of HUs.

We performed another task to be calculated the average number of connections from the final network by the subsection 3.1.3. Table 3-5 exhibit the results in this regard for the above-mentioned three problems. The numbers are relatively smaller and we can conclude that DFSM generates relevant features with low computational cost.

4.2 Comparison with Other Methods

In this part, we compare the results of DFSM to those obtained by the methods reported in [3] and [4]. The results are summarized in Tables 6-9. A caution should be taken because different technique has been involved in these methods for feature selection.

Table 1. Characteristics of Benchmark Datasets

Name	Examples	Classes	Input Attributes
BCR	699	2	9
DBT	768	2	8
GLS	214	6	9

Table 2. Separation of the examples into training set (TS), validation set (VS), and test set (TS)

Name	TS (First)	VS (Middle)	TS (Last)
BCR	349	175	175
DBT	384	192	192
GLS	108	53	53

Table 3. Results of BCR problem. Numbers in () are the standard deviations.

	Before FS	After FS
No. of	9	3.74
Features	(0.00)	(1.25)
Training Error	3.58	3.25
(%)	(2.20)	(1.79)
Training CA	96.35	96.75
(%)	(1.60)	(1.55)
Testing CA	95.95	97.86
(%)	(2.16)	(1.64)
No. of HU	3.25	
No. of ITNs	182.5	
No. of Connections	23.90	

Table 4. Results of DBT problem. Numbers in () are the standard deviations

	Before FS	After FS
No. of	8	2.81
Features	(0.00)	(2.42)
Training Error	22.60	21.35
(%)	(2.41)	(2.03)
Training CA	76.14	76.40
(%)	(3.05)	(2.74)
Testing CA	74.25	75.33
(%)	(3.15)	(2.20)
No. of HU	4.55	
No. of ITNs	205.5	
No. of Connections	28.43	

Table 5. Results of GLS problem. Numbers in () are the standard deviations

	Before FS	After FS
No. of	9	5.10
Features	(0.00)	(1.06)
Training Error	34.95	33.86
(%)	(1.64)	(2.03)
Training CA	63.82	63.98
(%)	(1.50)	(1.25)
Testing CA	63.54	67.62
(%)	(2.40)	(1.32)
No. of HU	6.30	
No. of ITNs	212.2	
No. of Connections	82.23	

Table 6. Comparison on the number of relevant features for BCR, DBT, and GLS data sets

Prob	DFSM	NNFS	ICFS (M 1)	ICFS (M 2)
BCR	3.74	2.70	5	5
DBT	2.81	2.03	2	3
GLS	5.05	-	5	4

Table 7. Comparison on the average testing CA (%) for BCR, DBT, and GLS data sets

Prob	DFSM	NNFS	ICFS (M 1)	ICFS (M 2)
BCR	97.86	94.10	98.25	98.25
DBT	75.33	74.30	78.88	78.70
GLS	67.62	-	63.77	66.61

Table 6 shows the ability to discriminate the relevant features among all the features. In case of BCR, DFSM is quite good in respect to two methods of ICFS but not so good to NNFS. In contrast, for DBT and GLS problems the results of DFSM

Table 8. Comparison on the average number of hidden units for BCR, DBT, and GLS data sets

Prob	DFSM	NNFS	ICFS (M 1)	ICFS (M 2)
BCR	3.25	12	33.55	42.05
DBT	4.55	12	8.15	21.45
GLS	6.30	-	62.5	53.95

Table 9. Comparison on the average number of connections for BCR, DBT, and GLS data sets

Prob	DFSM	NNFS	ICFS (M 1)	ICFS (M 2)
BCR	23.90	70.4	270.4	338.5
DBT	28.43	62.36	42.75	130.7
GLS	82.23	-	756	599.4

are comparable. In Table 7, the results of DSFM for BCR and DBT are better comparing to that of NNFS, and for GLS it is better than that of ICFS (Method 1 & Method 2).

The major comparable aspect for DFSM with NNFS and ICFS is the smaller structure of the final network consisted by less numbers of HUs and connections. The results in this regard are shown in Table 8 & 9 for all problems. For example, BCR problem of DFSM (Table 8), the number of HUs is 3.25, while the numbers in NNFS, ICFS (Method 1), and ICFS (Method 2) are larger, 12, 33.55 and 42.05, respectively. Similar results are obtained for the other problems. The number of connections that is existed after feature selection in the network architecture is shown in Table 9. For BCR problem of DFSM, the number of connections is 23.90 in DFSM, which is much smaller than 70.4, 240.4 and 338.4 by NNFS, ICFS (Method 1), and ICFS (Method 2), respectively. Similar results are also obtained for the other problems. We can therefore conclude that DFSM gives comparable generalization ability and subset that is contained by the smaller number of relevant features. Such type of compact architecture illustrates that DFSM has an ability to perform the feature selection with less computational cost.

5 Discussion

This paper describes a new method DFSM for feature selection that generates relevant features in less computation. The main reasons why DFSM provides less computational cost are: (i) DFSM can create diversity among the input attributes during training so that it is easier to discriminate the relevant features from the original ones. We instead introduced only the attributes that are more diverged among the others. This resulted in compactness of the network and faster training. (ii) In backward elimination, the steps for the removal of attributes are as same as the number of rejected features instead of all features, and (iii) Removal of unnecessary hidden units. The results shown in Table 3-5 exhibit that DFSM generates subset with small number of relevant features.

DFSM used the coherence training using PCL, which removes HUs based on correlation criteria. Consequently, it quickened training and saved the computational cost. The experimental outcomes of DFSM in summary are: 1) the number of HUs was significantly reduced due to the coherence training, and eventually a compact architecture was obtained. DFSM could generate much less number of connections

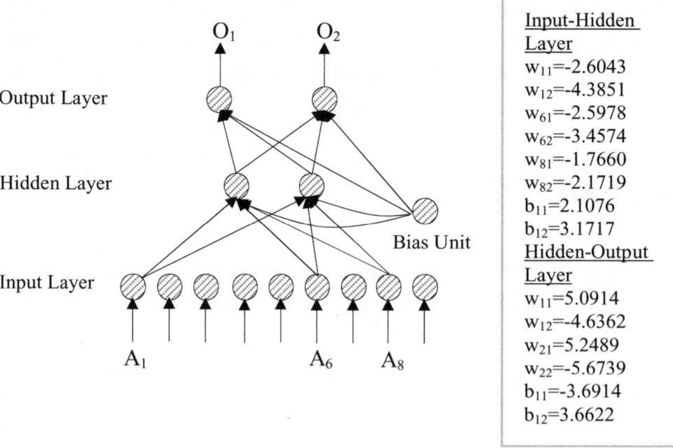

Fig. 2. An example of the NN obtained by DFSM for breast cancer problem

than other methods and that's why DFSM is much faster and computationally less expensive. 2) DFSM generates smaller components of subsets and comparable generalization ability to other methods.

Numbers of connections in the final network obtained by DFSM for different problems are shown in Table 3-5. DFSM apparently has enough capability to reduce computational cost as it can achieve a network with limited structure. In Fig. 2, a representative example of network obtained by DFSM in breast cancer problem is illustrated. The classification accuracy of this network was 98.28% with this simple structure.

Using PCL, the cross-fertilization of weight coherence and coherence between HUs enhance the utility of this method. PCL guarantees the convergence of smaller coherent weights and HUs as well. Therefore, smaller distances of weight from zero were taken as an evidence for filtering the attributes.

Extracting rules from NN is important to interpret the way how the network works. For this purpose, a network with a compact structure is desirable. As DFSM can give support to fulfill the requirements, rule extraction from NN is the further task by using DFSM.

6   Conclusion

In this paper we propose a new approach for feature selection called DFSM based on diversity of input attributes. Actually, in course of training of the network using PCL, the input attributes become diversed according to their dissimilar activities. After that, a straightforward computation is performed to recognize the features, which are not significant for the network performance. In the latter part, that features are deleted during training without degrading the network performance. Thus, a set of relevant features is generated. The entire process is accomplished by using several criteria. One foremost aspect of DFSM is that, it can significantly reduce the size of the hidden layer priori to feature selection process. It provides the more compactness of the network architecture. Moreover, to evaluate the DFSM, it was applied to three standard benchmark problems. The results confirmed that DFSM has a strong capability of feature selection, and it can select feature subset with low computational cost and produces good generalization ability.

Acknowledgements

Supported by grants to KM from the Japanese Society for Promotion of Sciences, the Yazaki Memorial Foundation for Science and Technology, and the University of Fukui.

References

1. Kohavi, R., John, G.H.: Wrappers for feature subset selection. Artificial Intelligence 97, 273–324 (1997)
2. Liu, H., Tu, L.: Toward Integrating Feature Selection Algorithms for Classification and Clustering. IEEE Transactions on Knowledge and Data Engineering 17(4), 491–502 (2005)
3. Sateino, R., Liu, H.: Neural Network Feature Selector. IEEE Transactions on Neural Networks 8 (1997)
4. Guan, S., Liu, J., Qi, Y.: An Incremental approach to Contribution-based Feature Selection. Journal of Intelligence Systems 13(1) (2004)
5. Abe, S.: Modified Backward Feature Selection by Cross Validation. In: Proceedings of the European Symposium on Artificial Neural Networks, April 2005, pp. 163–168 (2005)
6. Bontempi, G.: Structural feature selection for wrapper methods. In: Proceedings of the European Symposium on Artificial Neural Networks, April 2005, pp. 405–410 (2005)
7. Dunne, K., Cunningham, P., Azuaje, F.: Solutions to Instability Problems with Sequential Wrapperbased Approaches to Feature Selection. Journal of Machine Learning Research (2002)
8. Stracuzzi, D.J., Utgoff, P.E.: Randomized Variable Elimination. Journal of Machine Learning Research 5, 1331–1362 (2004)
9. Shahjahan, M., Murase, K.: Neural Network Training Algorithm with Positive Correlation. IEICE Trans.Inf. & Syst. E88-D(10), 2399–2409 (2005)
10. Monirul Kabir, M., Shahjahan, M., Murase, K.: A Backward Feature Selection by Creating Compact Neural Network Using Coherence Learning and Pruning. Journal of Advanced Computational Intelligence and Intelligent Informatics 11(6) (2007)
11. Prechelt, L.: PROBEN1-A set of neural network benchmark problems and benchmarking rules. Technical Report 21/94, Faculty of Informatics, University of Karlsruhe, Germany (1994)
12. Newman, D.J., Hettich, S., Blake, C.L., Merz, C.J.: UCI Repository of Machine Learning Databases. Dept. of Information and Computer Sciences, University of California, Irvine (1998), Available: http://www.ics.uci.edu/~mlearn/MLRepository.html

Reconstruction of Temporal Movement
from Single-trial Non-invasive Brain Activity:
A Hierarchical Bayesian Method

Akihiro Toda[1], Hiroshi Imamizu[2], Masa-aki Sato[2],
Yasuhiro Wada[1], and Mitsuo Kawato[2]

[1] Nagaoka University of Technology, Niigata, 940-2188, Japan
[2] ATR Computational Neuroscience Lab, Kyoto, 619-0288, Japan

Abstract. We tried to reconstruct temporal movement information (position, velocity and acceleration) from single-trial brain activity measured using non-invasive methods. While human subjects performed wrist movement in eight directions, brain activity was measured by functional magnetic resonance imaging (fMRI) and magnetoencephalogram (MEG). To reconstruct the movement information, we used cortical currents estimated by hierarchical Bayesian method for each subject. Correlation coefficients between reconstructed position and actual position ranged from 0.45 to 0.6. Although accuracy of our method is inferior to those in a previous study, our method is based on cortical current that is tightly coupled with anatomical regions, and thus would be a useful tool in neuroscience if the accuracy could be improved.

1 Introduction

Recently, basic studies for brain computer interface have become popular. Georgopoulos et al. [1] predicted continuous joystick movements from MEG sensor signals with accuracy of correlation coefficients ranging from 0.8 to 0.9. However, it is difficult to understand neurophysiological meanings of MEG sensor signals without appropriate source localization in anatomical regions. Sato et al. [2] have proposed hierarchical Basyesian methods for MEG source localization. Their method utilizes combined advantages of MEG (good temporal resolution) and fMRI (good spatial resolution) using a hierarchical prior that can effectively incorporate both structural and functional MRI data. We can estimate current sources on subjects' cortical surface using this method. Here, we tried to reconstruct movement information from cortical current sources in sensorimotor regions rather than MEG sensor signals.

2 Experimental Procedure and Data Acquisition

Four adults from 21-45 years of age, averaging 29.5 years old, participated in the experiment. All subjects were right handed. A written informed consent was obtained from each subject. The experimental protocol was approved by the

M. Ishikawa et al. (Eds.): ICONIP 2007, Part II, LNCS 4985, pp. 1027–1036, 2008.

ethical committee of the Communications Research Laboratory and Advanced Telecommunications Research (ATR) Institute.

Subjects conducted out-and-back wrist movement using their index finger. Wrist movements were made towards eight directions with constant movement time. Neutral position was at the center of the region where the tip of the index finger reached. Movement in a trial was out-and-back movement from neutral position to peripheral position targets. Moving distance and movement time was about 100 [mm] and 400 [msec]. We instructed subjects not to their eyes blink before movement 2 [sec]. Fixation point blinked to determine frequency of the movement. Visual feedback of the trajectory was displayed at 1000 [msec] after movement. The subjects made wrist movements toward one of the eight targets in a random order (block randomized) in 12 sessions (10 [min] per session). The subjects randomly selected a target in each trial.

Brain activity was measured in separate sessions, in the fMRI where subjects performed the same task as in the MEG. The fMRI data was used to hierarchical prior in hierarchical Bayesian method. In the fMRI experiment, the same visual stimuli were presented on the screen in a rest condition to subtract brain activity evoked by visual stimulus. Functional images were collected using an echo-planar imaging (EPI) sequence. A total of 90 multi-slice images were acquired during wrist movement task. Imaging parameters were TR=3.5 [sec], TE=65 [msec], Flip Angle=90 [deg] and in-plane resolution=3.4 [mm] ($64 \times 64 \times 44$ voxels). Subject's high-resolution anatomical image was T1-weighted structural image.

MEG signal for current source estimation were measured at sampling rate 2000 [Hz]. The high pass filter of the cutoff frequency 200 [Hz] and the low pass filter of the cutoff frequency 0.01 [Hz] were applied to the MEG signals. Hand position was measured at sampling rate 60 [Hz]. Electro-oculogram (EOG) and electrocardiogram (ECG) were measured at sampling rate 2000 [Hz]. EOG and ECG were measured to reject artifacts caused by eye movements and abnormal cardiac rhythm.

Brain activity was measured using a 1.5 Tesla MRI scanner (Shimadzu-Marconi scanner GNEXECLIPSE 1.5T) and a 208-channel axial gradiometer MEG system (Yokogawa-MEGvision PQ1400R 208ch) in the ATR Brain Activity Imaging Center. Hand position was measured by position tracking system using a color image (OKK-QuickMAG4 type2).

3   Brain Activity Data Analysis

3.1   MEG Preprocessing

Movement onset time was defined as 5% of maximum velocity in a trial. Baseline MEG signal was obtained before onset (-1000 $\sim$ -500 [msec]) of the movements. MEG signal drift was corrected by first order linear regression. Trials and MEG sensor were rejected if the EOG exceeded 100 [μ V] or if the MEG signal exceeded 1000 [fT].

3.2   fMRI Analysis

Functional images were analyzed with SPM2 statistical parametric mapping software (http://www.fil.ion.ucl.ac.uk/spm/spm2.html). Functional images of all subjects were realigned to the first image of each session as a reference. The functional images of each subject's brain were transformed to the Montreal Neurological Institute's reference brain (MNI; Montreal, Canada). The data was spatially smoothed with a Gaussian kernel by a 6 [mm] full width at half maximum (FWHM). The high pass filter of the cutoff frequency 0.002 [Hz] and the low pass filter of the cutoff frequency 0.25 [Hz] were applied to the fMRI signals. We statistically analyzed the active regions in the wrist movement condition in comparison to the rest condition.

3.3   Current Source Estimate of MEG Signal by Hierarchical Bayes Method

Sato et al. [2] combined the advantages of MEG and fMRI by introducing a hierarchical prior that can effectively incorporate both structural and functional MRI data. A structure of the cortical surface was constructed based on individual MRI image. This method is capable of appropriately estimating the source current from the MEG data supplemented with the fMRI data.

When neural current activity occurs in the brain, the relationship between the source current $\boldsymbol{J}(t) = \{J_n(t) \mid n = 1 : N\}$ in the brain and observed magnetic field $\boldsymbol{B}(t) = \{B_m(t) \mid m = 1 : M\}$ is given by

$$\boldsymbol{B}(t) = \boldsymbol{G} \cdot \boldsymbol{J}(t), \tag{1}$$

where $\boldsymbol{G} = \{G_{m,n} \mid m = 1 : M, n = 1 : N\}$ is the lead field matrix [3]. The lead field represents the m-th magnetic field produced by the n-th unit dipole current. The MEG inverse problem is to estimate the source current $\boldsymbol{J}(t)$ from the observed magnetic field $\boldsymbol{B}(t)$. A dipole source current $\boldsymbol{J}(t)$ is assumed to be in each vertex point on the cortical surface.

Although the number of dipole currents, N, was reduced by introducing fMRI constraint, N is still larger than the number of sensors M. As fMRI data reflect temporally averaged neural activities during movement in this study, the signal strength of fMRI data may act as a prior for the variance of the current amplitude. In the hierarchical Bayesian method, the current $\boldsymbol{J}(t)$ and its variance $\boldsymbol{\alpha}^{-1}$ are simultaneously estimated with a hierarchical prior. The current $\boldsymbol{J}(t)$ is given by

$$\boldsymbol{J}(t) = \boldsymbol{L}\left(\boldsymbol{\Sigma}_{\alpha}^{-1}\right) \cdot \boldsymbol{B(t)}, \tag{2}$$

$$\boldsymbol{L}\left(\boldsymbol{\Sigma}_{\alpha}^{-1}\right) = \boldsymbol{\Sigma}_{\alpha}^{-1} \cdot \boldsymbol{G}^{T} \cdot \left(\boldsymbol{G} \cdot \boldsymbol{\Sigma}_{\alpha}^{-1} \cdot \boldsymbol{G}^{T} + \beta^{-1}\boldsymbol{I}_{M}\right)^{-1}, \tag{3}$$

where $\boldsymbol{L}\left(\boldsymbol{\Sigma}_{\alpha}^{-1}\right)$ is the inverse filter, $\boldsymbol{\Sigma}_{\alpha}^{-1} \equiv \mathrm{diag}\left(\boldsymbol{\alpha}^{-1}\right)$ is the current variance matrix and $\beta^{-1}\boldsymbol{I}_M$ is the noise covariance matrix. The inverse current variance parameter $\boldsymbol{\alpha}$ is estimated by introducing an Automatic Relevance Determination (ARD) hierarchical prior [4],

$$P_0\left(\boldsymbol{\alpha}\right) = \prod_{n=1}^{N} \Gamma\left(\alpha_n \mid \bar{\alpha}_{0n}, \gamma_{0n}\right), \tag{4}$$

where $\Gamma\left(\alpha_n \mid \bar{\alpha}_{0n}, \gamma_{0n}\right)$ represents the Gamma distribution with mean $\bar{\alpha}_{0n}$ and scale parameter γ. Intuitively, the hyper-parameters γ_{0n} represent confidence of the hierarchical prior. $\bar{\alpha}_{0n}$ is assumed to be proportional to the fMRI activity at the n-th vertex. Because of the hierarchical prior, the estimation problem becomes nonlinear and cannot be solved analytically. Therefore, we employed the Variational Bayesian(VB) method [5]. In the VB method, $\boldsymbol{J}(t)$, β and $\boldsymbol{\alpha}$ are iteratively updated from some initial values of $\boldsymbol{\alpha}$.

According physiological knowledge with regard to distribution of neural current activity, we assumed a spatial smoothness constraint on the current distribution along with the cortical surface. We employed a smoothing filter matrix $W_{ij} \propto \exp(-d_{ij}^2/R^2)$, where d_{ij} is the distance between i-th and j-th current dipoles along cortical surface. The smoothing radius parameter, R, was set to 6 [mm]. By introducing an internal current $\boldsymbol{Z}(t)$ and letting

$$\boldsymbol{J}(t) = \boldsymbol{W} \cdot \boldsymbol{Z}(t), \tag{5}$$

eq. (1) can be replaced by

$$\boldsymbol{B}(t) = \tilde{\boldsymbol{G}} \cdot \boldsymbol{Z}(t), \tag{6}$$

where $\tilde{\boldsymbol{G}} \equiv \boldsymbol{G} \cdot \boldsymbol{W}$ is a smoothed lead field matrix. Therefore, $\boldsymbol{Z}(t)$ can be estimated by using the smoothed lead field matrix $\tilde{\boldsymbol{G}}$. After estimating $\boldsymbol{Z}(t)$, the current $\boldsymbol{J}(t)$ is calculated using eq. (5).

4   Reconstruction of Movement Information

4.1   Linear Sparse Regression Algorithm for Reconstruction

The linear regression model to predict movement information (position, velocity and acceleration) is given by

$$\boldsymbol{Y}(t) = a + \sum_{i=1}^{N_{source}} \sum_{j=1}^{N_{time}} b_{ij} \cdot S_i(t-j), \tag{7}$$

where $S_i(t)$ is a subset of the source current signal $\boldsymbol{Z}(t)$ in the cortical surface. $\boldsymbol{Z}(t)$ is sub-sampled in 20 [msec] interval, and normalized in limited anatomical area(see Sect. 4.2). $\boldsymbol{Y}(t)$ is time series of movement information. N_{source} is the number of current source used in the prediction. N_{time} is the number of time delayed samples. The regression coefficient can be calculated by MSE (Minimum Squared Error) estimation. Since the number of parameters is very large, it is necessary to selecte small set of parameters in order to increase the generalization ability for unknown data. Therefore, we used Bayesian sparse linear regression, which is derived by using Variational Bayesian method. In the sparse linear regression, the regression coefficients b_{ij} of eq. (7) are calculated as

$$b = \sigma T \langle Y \cdot S^T \rangle \cdot \Sigma_b^{-1}, \tag{8}$$

where $\langle \rangle$ represents the expectation value over time period, and T is the number of time samples. Reguralized input covariance matrix Σ_b is given by

$$\Sigma_b = \sigma T \langle S \cdot S^T \rangle + \Lambda, \tag{9}$$

where $\Lambda \equiv \mathrm{diag}(\lambda)$ and λ is the precision parameter for each input dimension. The noise variance σ and λ are estimated as

$$\sigma^{-1} = \tfrac{1}{N} \left\langle (Y(t) - b \cdot S(t))^2 \right\rangle \\ + Tr \left(\Sigma_b^{-1} \cdot \langle S \cdot S^T \rangle \right), \tag{10}$$

$$\lambda^{-1} = \frac{1}{N} \mathrm{diag} \left(b^T \cdot b \right) + \mathrm{diag} \left(\Sigma_b^{-1} \right), \tag{11}$$

where $\mathrm{diag}(\Sigma)$ represents the diagonal component of a matrix Σ. In the learning process, the estimation of the regression coefficient b, eq. (8) and eq. (9), and the estimation of σ^{-1} and λ^{-1} are alternately updated. For irrelevant input dimension, λ_{ij} becomes infinity and effectively eliminates the corresponding coefficient b_{ij}.

4.2   Reconstruct Analysis

A training data comprised 70% (the average number of trials across the subjects was 672 trials, 84 trials per direction) and a test data comprised 30% (the average number of trials across the subjects was 287 trials, 35 trials per direction) of all trials. Using the hierarchical Bayesian estimation, a inverse filter for the cortical currents was calculated using all training data set. An N_{source} of eq. (7) corresponded to 500 vertex sources which are the strongest source currents in the movement-related regions (supplementary motor area(SMA), premotor area(preMotor:BA6), motor area(M1:BA4), sensory area(S1:BA1,2,3), parietal region(BA5,7,39,40)). N_{time} of eq. (7) was 200 [msec].

We divided eight directions of data set into three categories (cross direction (CR : four directions), oblique directions (OB : four directions)Call directions(ALL : eight directions)). Because we are interested in generalization ability in similar directions ($<45°$), four directions were combined into the same category, CR and OB. The regression coefficient b was estimated for each category (tran-ALLCtran-CR and tran-OB) using corresponding training sets. Additionally, different models are estimated for prediction position, velocity and acceleration in each category.

To estimate generalization ability for predicting hand movements, we calculated position, velocity and acceleration for test data sets using trained models described above. Correlation coefficients between actual signals and predicted signals (movement information) were calculated to measure prediction accuracy. We also examined distribution of b on cortical surface.

5   Results of Movement Information Reconstruction

5.1   Current Sources Estimated by Hierarchical Bayesian Method

Cortical currents for each subject were estimated with the recorded MEG data using the hierarchical Bayesian method [2]. Fig. 1A shows results from the fMRI experiment for a typical subject (HI). According to an analysis of difference between movement and rest condition, significantly activated areas were found bilaterally in the motor areas and interparietal regions. The contralateral motor area was particularly activated.

A polygon model of the cortical surface was constructed based on individual MRI image using Brain Voyager software (Brain Innovation, Netherlands). The regions for cortical current estimation convert the whole brain. The average number of cortical current across subject was 5060 ± 372(mean $\pm$ SD). The cortical currents in left anatomical regions (Fig. 1C) was used to construct the regression model. Anatomical regions were determined according to a template of Brodmann area(BA) and Automatic Anatomical Labeling(AAL) maps in MRIclo software.

We estimated that the pattern of cortical activity from 500 [msec] before movement onset to 1000 [msec] after movement onset. Fig. 2 shows time series of estimated cortical current by training data set for a typical subject(HI). Fig. 2A shows current $J(t)$ averaged across trials. Movement onset time is 0 [msec] in this figure. Peaks of cortical currents in Fig. 2A were found at -170 [msec] , 90 [msec] and 160 [msec]. Fig. 2B illustrate the activity of Fig. 2A. The three peaks of Fig. 2A correspond to the three activity peaks (M1 and S1) at each side of the

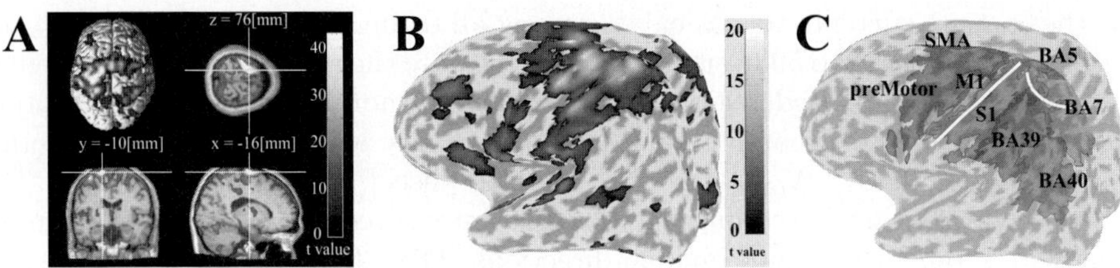

Fig. 1. (A) fMRI activity(uncorrected p<0.001) for 8-direction task for a typical subject(HI). cross point is most activate point. (B) fMRI activity map to polygon model of the cortical surface. (C) Movement-related anatomical regionDsupplementary motor area(SMA), premotor area(preMotor:BA6)Cmotor area(M1:BA4), sensorimotor area(S1:BA1,2,3), parietal region(BA5,7,39,40).

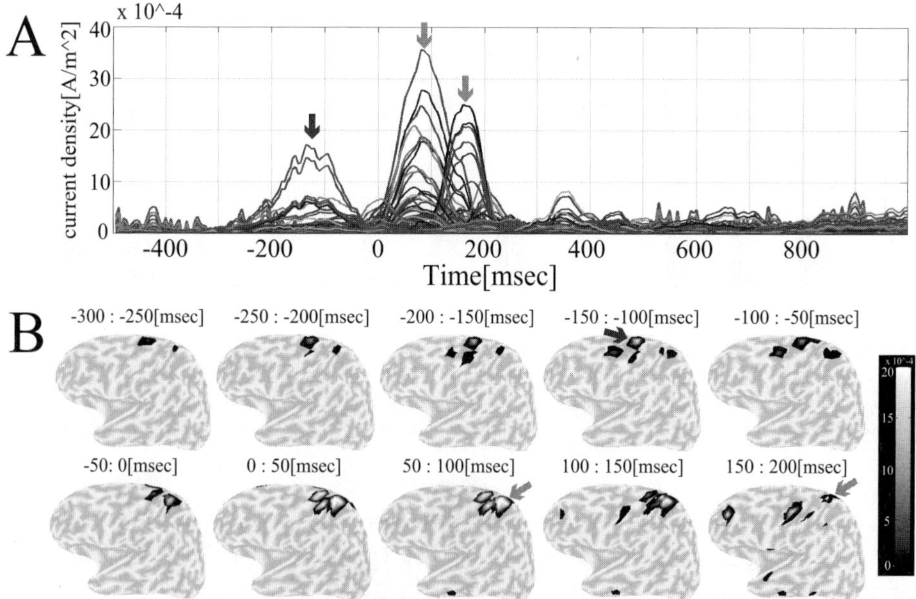

Fig. 2. Time series and spatial map of estimate current $J(t)$ for a typical subject(HI). (A) All vertex current wave form (5044vertex). Averaged across all training data set (756trials). (B) Estimate current spatial map from 300 [msec] before onset to 200 [msec] after onset. Spatial map is averaged across 50 [msec].

central sulcus. Peaks of spatial pattern exist in -150:-100 [msec], 50:100 [msec] and 150:200 [msec] of Fig. 2B. The estimated current peak at -150:-100 [msec] was located in the primary motor area(M1), and the peak at 50:100 [msec] and 150:200 [msec] were found in the sensory area(S1). A peak in M1 is thought to be activity related to motor control. The first and the second peaks in S1 may reflect input signals from the thalamus and feedback signals from higher-order somatosensori regions, respectively. Double peaks in S1 are also found in Kitada et al. [6] investigating MEG response to sensory stimuli.

5.2   Reconstruction of Temporal Movement

Averaged movement duration across the subjects in eight-direction task was 515 ± 79 [msec] (mean±SD) . Source currents are assumed to be the top 500 current with highest estimated amplitude in region of Fig. 1C.

The regression model was estimated by eq.(8)-(11) using the training data set (tran-ALLCtran-CR and tran-OB). Fig. 3 shows correlation coefficients between the actual movement and the predicted movement. The predicted movement was calculated by using the trained regression model with the estimated current of the test data sets(test-ALLCtest-CR and test-OB) as the input signal. Prediction accuracy was evaluated in each category using correlation coefficients.

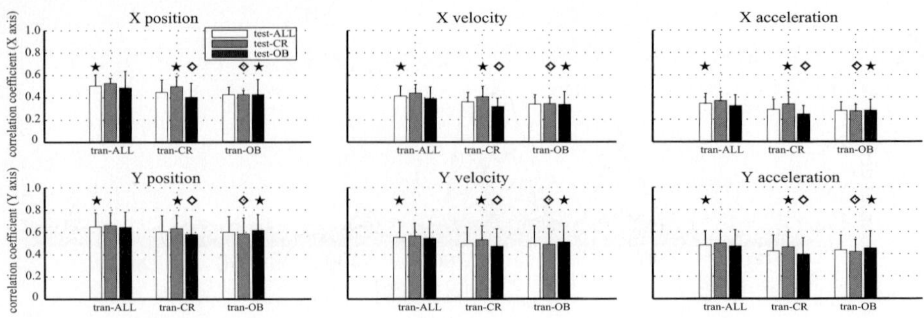

Fig. 3. Results of cross-validation. Averaged correlation coefficient across subjects.

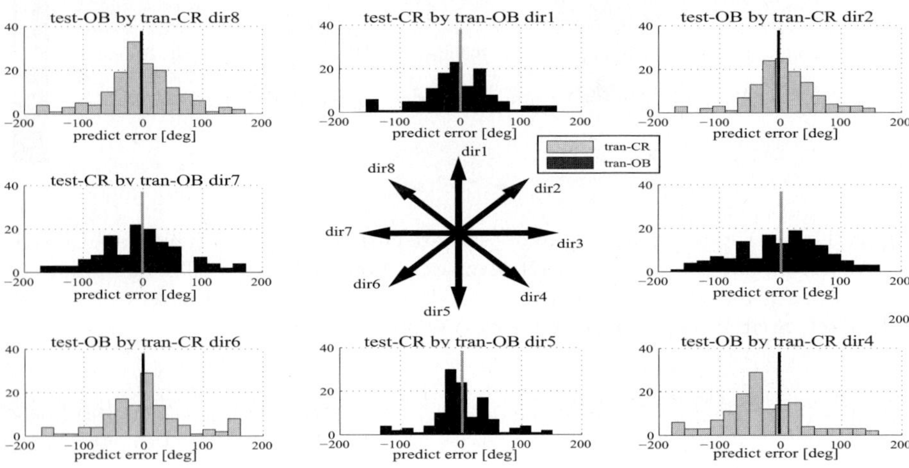

Fig. 4. Histogram of predicted angle for all subjects. A "test-OB by tran-CR" estimated test-OB by tran-CR (gray bar). In contrast, a "test-CR by tran-OB" estimated test-CR by tran-OB (black bar).

Correlation coefficients were calculated for predicted movement of x-y coordinates of position, velocity and acceleration. The upper panel in Fig. 3 shows results regarding x-coordinate (position, velocity and acceleration). The lower panel shows results regarding y-coordinate. As shown in Fig. 3, prediction accuracy in x-coordinate was 0.45 and accuracy in y-coordinate was 0.6. Coefficients for velocity and acceleration were lower than position. When the direction category of the test data sets are different from that of trained set(ex, test-CR by tran-OB), it is indicated by . When the direction category of the test data sets and the trained data sets are the same, it is indicated by . When comparing the same direction categories (in Fig. 3) with the different direction categories (in Fig. 3), we could not find remarkable difference. Therefore, generalization between directions was found.

To examine prediction accuracy for each direction, Fig. 4 shows a histogram of the predicted angle in each direction. The predicted angle was measured using neutral position and the farthest position from neutral position in predicted trajectory. In Fig. 4, the horizontal axis indicates the error in the predicted angle for each direction. One bin of histogram represents 22.5 [deg]. Predicted angle was obtained from cross-validation analysis based on the data in other directional categories. As shown in Fig. 4, distribution of the directions of the predicted trajectory can be fitted by Gaussian distribution centered at the target direction.

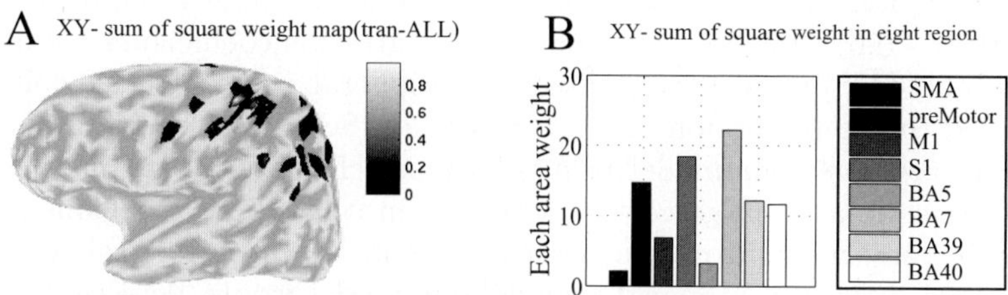

Fig. 5. Prediction weight map and weighting factor for each area prediction. (A) prediction weight map for a typical subject(HI). Weights were calculated tran-ALL for X-Y positionDThe weight map was sum of square of XY-weight. (B) Weighting factor for each area, averaged across subjects mapped.

Fig. 5A shows estimated regression coefficients that were mapped to cortical surface. Mapped regression coefficient estimated for position using tran-ALL data. Because, b_{ij} was estimate for time series as eq. (7), the map shows $b_i = \sum_{j=1}^{N_{time}} |b_{ij}|$. As shown in Fig. 5A, large regression coefficients exist in sensorimortor region. In this region, high amplitude cortical current was estimated by hierarchical Bayesian method. Fig. 5B shows regression coefficient averaged across the subjects in the eight regions. There were large coefficients in premotor area (preMotor), sensory area(S1) and BA7(intraparietal sulcus). In contrast, coefficients in other two regions (SMA and BA5) were small. We also tired prediction of the movements using small cortical currents located in visual regions (BAs 17 and 18) but the accuracy ranged from 0.3 to 0.4.

6 Summary and Conclusion

In our study, we estimated the current sources on the subject's cortical surface using hierarchical Bayesian estimation for MEG inverse problem developed by Sato et al [2]. Furthermore, we tried to reconstruct the movement information from a single-trial non-invasive brain activity. As shown in Fig. 2, hierarchical Bayesian method could estimate the brain activity with fine temporal and spatial resolutions. As shown in Fig. 3, generalization between directions was found. Correlation coefficient between predicted and actual positions ranged from 0.45 to 0.6. As shown in Fig. 4, distribution of the direction of the predicted trajectory can be fitted by Gaussian function centered at the target direction. According to the cross-validation analysis, generalization between directions could be identified. These results suggested that signals used for predictions (cortical current) contain information for movement control in the brain. As shown in Fig. 5, large regression coefficients exist in sensorimortor area. In this region, high amplitude cortical currents were also estimated.

To compare our result to that in Georgopoulos et al. [1], we also tried prediction of the wrist movements using MEG sensor signals in the similar fashion to their study, and got correlation coefficients raging from 0.5 to 0.7. Thus, accuracy of prediction was better when using sensor signal than when using cortical current (0.45 - 0.6). However, our analysis of regression coefficients revealed that signals obtained from sensors located in peripheral parts of head coil largely contributed to the prediction. These sensors are far from sensorimotor cortical regions. In contrast, our model using the hierarchical Bayesian method could successfully estimated large cortical currents in sensroimotor regions and predicted wrist movements from the cortical currents. Because cortical currents are tightly coupled with anatomical regions, our model would be a useful tool in neuroscience if the accuracy could be improved. This is a merit of our methods.

Because the value of estimated coefficients was large at vertices in motor-related region, we think that signals used for the reconstruction were derived from neural activity related to motor cortex. Such analysis can be done only through hierarchical Bayesian method that estimates current source on the cortical surface.

Acknowledgment

We thank Hirokazu Tanaka for commenting on an earlier version of this paper.

References

1. Georgopoulos, A.P., Langheim, F.J., Leuthold, A.C., Merkle, A.N.: Magnetoencephalographic signals predict movement trajectory in space. Exp. Brain. Res. 167(1), 132–135 (2005)
2. Sato, M.A., Yoshioka, T., Kajihara, S., Toyama, K., Goda, N., Doya, K., Kawato, M.: Hierarchical Bayesian estimation for MEG inverse problem. Neuroimage 23(3), 806–826 (2004)
3. Hamalainen, M., Hari, R., Ilmoniemi, P., Uutila, J., Lounasmaa, O.: Magnetoencephalography theory, instrumentation, and applications to noninvasive studies of the working human brain. Rev. Mod. Phys. 65, 413–497 (1993)
4. Neal, R.M.: Bayesian learning for neural networks. Springer, New York (1996)
5. Sato, M.: On-line model selection based on the varidational Bayes. Neural. Compt. 13, 1649–1681 (2001)
6. Kida, T., Wasaka, T., Inui, K., Akatsuka, K., Nakata, H., Kakigi, R.: Centrifugal regulation of human cortical responses to a task-relevant somatosensory signal triggering voluntary movement. Neuroimage 32(3), 1355–1364 (2006)

Subject-Adaptive Real-Time BCI System

Han Sun and Liqing Zhang

Department of Computer Science and Engineering,
Shanghai Jiao Tong University, Shanghai 200240, China
`jeremiah@sjtu.edu.cn, zhang-lq@cs.sjtu.edu.cn`

Abstract. Brain Computer Interface (BCI) provides people with motor disabilities a new channel for communication and control. In this paper, we first introduce a framework of BCI system, consisting of EEG Acquisition, Signal Preprocess, Feature Extractor, Pattern Classifier, Subject Task Generation and Visualization. The system is able to adapt to subjects online and to work in real time condition with high accuracy and short latency. The BCI system is based on analysis of EEG patterns of object's left and right motor imagery. Independent Component Analysis and temporal filter are employed for artifacts removal and noise reduction. Spatial filter and autoregressive model are used as feature extractor, from which feature vectors are classified by SVM. The best classification accuracy of all objects' is up to 99% in offline analysis and 80% in online condition.

1   Introduction

Nowadays, many studies focus on building up an reliable and efficient communication channel between human brain and computer [1]. Among available techniques for brain signal extraction as EEG, PET, fMRI and others, EEG is the most promising candidate for a real time BCI system for its high temporal resolution, portable size, and relatively low cost [2].

A primary task of EEG based BCI system is to identify EEG patterns. In this paper, we focus on discrimination of left and right motor imagery patterns. Researches shown that rhythmic EEG components (such as μ and β rhythms) can be used as analysis basis, since sensorimotor rhythms display an event-related desynchronization (ERD) close to contralateral primary motor areas during hand movement imaginations [3].

Recently, although offline EEG pattern classification had achieved good performance, how to build up an online BCI system is still very challenging.

What makes a good online BCI system? The first requirement is the real-time response. Generally, latency maybe caused by long period routines of complex algorithms, EEG acquisition and transmission, systematic delay and so on. With regard to processing speed, many algorithm such as Common Spatial Spectral Pattern(CSSP) [5] and Common Sparse Spectral Spatial Pattern(CSSSP) [6], despite their satisfactory offline performance, are not advisable in an online system.

M. Ishikawa et al. (Eds.): ICONIP 2007, Part II, LNCS 4985, pp. 1037–1046, 2008.

In this paper, an intergraded EEG recording, transmitting, and interpreting process will be described, of which each trial is achieved within 30 milliseconds. This real-time ability offers low controlling latency and therefore higher band width of BCI[7] [8].

The other requirement is subject-adaptation. In recent years, a number of BCI systems have been developed. For example, in 2000 Wadsworth Center proposed its BCI2000 system based on μ,β rhythm control and P300 detection [4]. BCI2000 system has demonstrated successful in a wide range of applications, such as objects driving and characters selection. However, since its primary basis is the ordinary pattern analysis of μ,β rhythm or P300, and hadn't unified a training procedure, the subjects may take a very long time to learn to fit a constant and generic pattern. In our system, a subject-oriented training procedure is implemented, which will adjust the parameters in every module dynamically, based on the comparison of cross-validations.

To meet these requirements, we developed a full-featured BCI system, with both offline and online analysis capability. There are seven modules in our system: EEG Acquisition, Signal Preprocessing, Feature Extraction, Pattern Classifier, Subject Task Generation, and finally System Console and Visualization System. The details of all modules, methods and experiment results will be shown in the following sections.

2   System Architecture

Most current BCI studies mainly focused on analyzing offline EEG signals. A few BCI systems ([11][4]) could provide online processing and feedback capability, but either choose some simple techniques and algorithms to achieve short online latency, or have relatively simple designs and static structures.

Our BCI system is developed to provide a general platform for research and BCI system design. With an extendable architecture, our system integrates alternative feature extraction methods, classification algorithms, control tasks in different user populations and real-time capability, supporting more flexible experiment schemes and scalability.

In this section, we will introduce the working modes of our BCI system, and the functional modules that support these modes. The general framework of our system is shown in Figure 1.

2.1   Working Modes

1. *Offline Analysis* uses recorded EEG signals as inputs, demonstrates the performance of algorithms in each module.
2. *Online Processing and Real-time Control* processes EEG signals acquired from subject with real-time capability. Then a prediction of subject's motor imagery is generated to deliver a control signal. Within the state feed back, the subject performs online controlling using motor imagery.

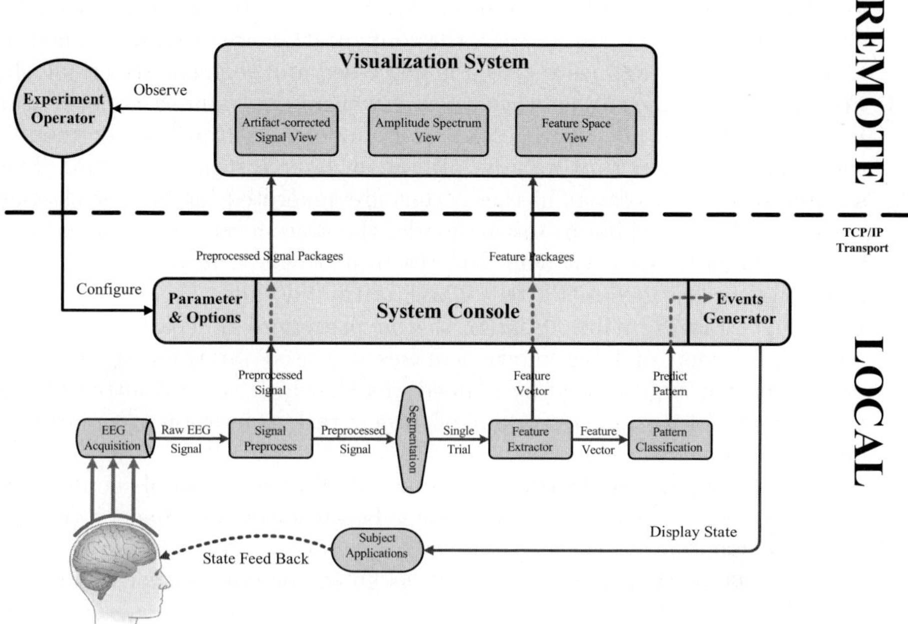

Fig. 1. General framework of our BCI system. It consists of two subsystems. System Console is the main controller of all functional processes with two interfaces. One for configuring to system variables, such as parameters to all algorithms employed in our system and the options for switching working states. The other one is events generation, which controls the states of subject tasks. Its systematical independency allows extended control capability for some generic device. Another subsystem is Visualization System, which provides an observer view for experiment operators. Communications between the two subsystems base on TCP/IP protocol.

3. ***Subject-Adaptation Training:*** Before a subject begins his (her) online controlling, a certain length of EEG signals with stimulus and events are recorded. A group of representation basis and models are trained for later testing procedure. And a set of parameters for feature extraction and classification algorithms are chosen by cross-validation results.

2.2   Functional Modules

Our system consists of six modules that communicate with each other. Each module is to accomplish a certain function that may be implemented by optional algorithms independently.

1. **EEG Acquisition** is an interface to peripheral equipment that scans and transmits EEG signals or a process that loads recorded EEG data.
2. **Signal Preprocessing:** Raw EEG data transmitted from acquisition module is preprocessed here. Because the signal-noise-rate (SNR) of EEG is very

low, an essential task of this module is to denoise and to remove artifacts. The channels that are not contained in the configuration are discarded. Then the EEG data the system has received is processed and segmented periodically.

3. **Feature Extractor:** When the system is working in training mode, Feature Extractor collects all preprocessed trials and labels from former module, then trains a model that may be utilized in later testing procedure. Then a group of feature vectors of these trials are generated for further classifier training. When working in testing mode, the system receives only one trial with unknown labels, extracts features from single trial data and further transmits the features to Pattern Classification module.

4. **Pattern Classification:** Similar to the procedure of Feature Extractor module, a group of label-known features are used for training, or a predicted pattern is generated by trained model, which is transmitted to System Console for further controlling of subject task generation or a peripheral device.

5. **Subject Task Generation:** A simple subject task is implemented that enable subject to drive an object using left-right motor imagery (used in following experiment).

6. **Visualization System:** This module is an important tool for online data analysis. It depicts features in different aspects of EEG signals, including temporal view, amplitude spectrum, and feature space. In order to ensure the real-time capability of our system, this information is transmitted to another computer, processed and displayed remotely.

Integrating these modules we develop a BCI experiment platform with both offline, online analysis and subject-adaptive training capabilities.

3   Methods

Up to the present, a number of methods and algorithms are implemented and tested on our BCI system. In preprocessing module, temporal filtering and cICA are used to artifacts removal. Common spatial patterns and autoregressive model are employed for feature extraction. Finally we use SVM as the classifier in Pattern Classification Module.

3.1   Data Preprocessing

Because the common spatial pattern method is very sensitive to artifacts [13], a two-stages preprocessing is employed.

In the first stage, all EEG channels were filtered through a specific frequency band (8-30 Hz, 8-12 Hz, 19-26 Hz, 30-42 Hz, which contain all μ, β, α, θ rhythms). This band is chosen by cross-validation in training procedure.

Then constrained Fast ICA is used to extract and remove eye-movement and blink artifacts EEG[12].

The cICA deals with the following constrained minimization problem:

$$Maximize: f(w) = \rho[E\{w^T x\} - E\{G(v)\}]^2$$
$$Subject to:\ g(w) \leqslant \{0\}$$
$$h(w) = E\{y^2\} - 1 = 0$$
$$E\{r^2\} - 1 = 0 \tag{1}$$

where $f(w)$ denotes the one-unit ICA contrast function, and $g(w)$ is the closeness constraint, $h(w)$ constrains the output y to have unit variance. And the reference signal r is also constrained to have unit variance. We use EOG and EOG channels as reference(r) to serve as a temporal constraint in the cICA algorithm.

After reconstructing the signals by deflation procedure, we get the artifacts corrected EEG signals as shown in Figure 2.

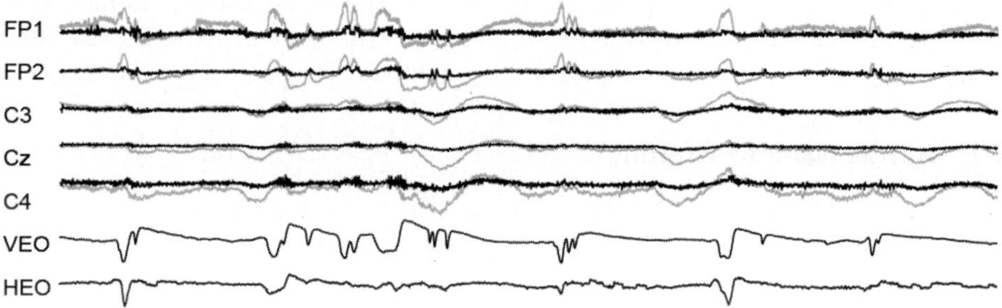

Fig. 2. Figure of temporal filtering and constrained Fast ICA for automatic artifact removal of EEG. Corrected EEG traces (black) without ocular artifacts superimposed on the raw EEG traces (gray) containing blinks and eye movements.

3.2   Feature Extraction

Recently, some approaches used the common spatial patterns (CSP) [14] to extract motor imagery features. The goal of CSP is to design spatial filters that lead to new time series whose variances are optimal for the discrimination of two populations of EEG related to left and right motor imagery [15].

Given n channels of EEG with each left and right trial E, the CSP method gives an $n \times n$ projection matrix W. This matrix is a set of spatial patterns, which reflect the specific activation of cortical areas during hand movement imagination. With the projection matrix W, the decomposition of an trial E can be written as: $Z = WE$.

Only the first and last m rows of Z are used here. The feature vector used for classification is formed by combining the normalizing and log-transforming of the $Z_p(p = 1 \ldots 2m)$ and Z_1, Z_{m+1}'s autoregressive coefficients of order k.

$$f_p = log\left(\frac{var(Z_p)}{\Sigma_{i=1}^{2m} var(Z_i)}\right)$$
$$a_i = AR(Z_i) \tag{2}$$

Then f_p, a_1, a_{m+1} put into one vector to represent the feature of trial E. And the m and k are free parameters to be selected between 4-8 and 5-8 [14].

3.3 Classification and Prediction

We employ the multi-category SVM as the classifier. When system is working in online mode, a sampling window is sliding on the buffer and fetch the corresponding EEG signals for analysis. The window is 3-5 seconds wide and sliding within 200 ms. Every 1-2 seconds our system will make one prediction (the command to applications or devices) based on several windows' classification results.

4 Experiments

In order to demonstrate the performance of algorithms that used in all modules, we integrate them into one system, and set up a number of experiments that enable subjects to control an object falling right or left using motor imagery.

4.1 Subjects and Stimulus

Four male right-handed subjects, aged from 20 to 30 took part in this study. These subjects were seated in an armchair and looked at a monitor placed 1m in front at eye level.

The procedure of an experiment trial is shown in Figure 3. The experiment includes a training procedure consisted of 5 sessions of 60 trials each (about 30 left and 30 right trials) and an online experiment with feedback to the subject.

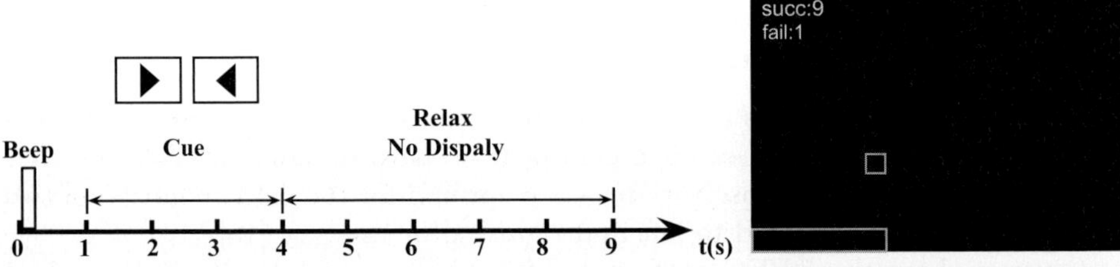

Fig. 3. the left figure shows the procedure and stimulus of training experiments. At beginning, a short "beep" warns subject that a trial is about to start. At 1s, a fixation triangle display on monitor, pointing to the left (right) randomly ("cue"), which instructs subject to imagine a movement(grasps or raises) of the left (right) hand during the cue presentation. This cue lasts for 3 seconds, followed by a 5 seconds' period for subject to relax without any display on monitor. The right figure represents the subject interface of online experiment, in which subject is instructed to drive the falling object to hit the target bar in the bottom of screen, using left (right) motor imagery. The predicted moving direction of the falling object at sight forms a feedback to the subject.

4.2   Data Acquisition

EEG signals were recorded at 500 Hz sampling rate by an ESI-128 Channel High-Resolution EEG/EP Systems (SynAmps2, Neuroscan, at Lab for Brain-Like Computing at Shanghai Jiao Tong University, China). In this experiment 64 channels EEG cap was used. Electrooculogram (EOG) was derived bipolarly using two electrodes, one placed medially above and the other laterally below the right eye.

5   Results

In this experiment, four subjects' EEG signals were recorded for training and analysis, and three of them participated in the following online testing sessions.

Figure 4 shows the most important spatial patterns for the detection of left and right motor imagery, which are extracted by spatial filter.

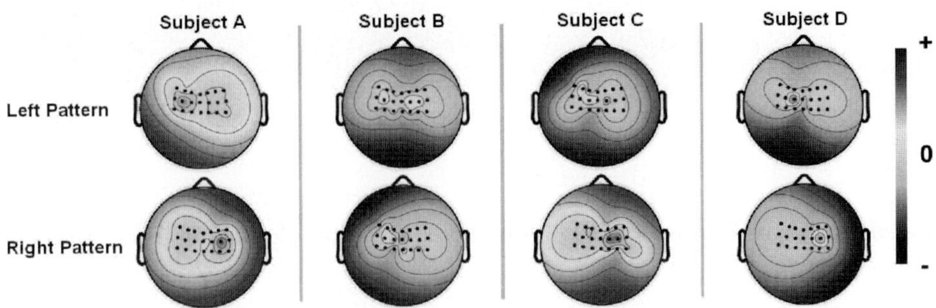

Fig. 4. Figure of most important spatial patterns for the discrimination of left and right motor imagery

Obviously, all subjects' patterns show that imagination of left (right) movement leads to reduced amplitude of sensorimotor rhythms over the right (left) hemisphere. Furthermore, after applying the most important patterns, Figure 5 shows the projection of one left and one right trial in the two most important patterns of each subject.

By comparing these time serials, a high amplitude difference can be observed. These features obtained form spatial filtering were used for further analysis.

Then all feature vectors generated by feature extractor are mapped to two-dimensions space using PCA in Figure 6. There are significant discriminating lines between each class, so it's forseeable that a higher accuracy can be achieved using integrated features in cross-validation.

Table 1 shows the comparison for each subject among different temporal filter bands and lengths of trials. The best accuracy 99.1% is achieved by Subject A, when the band is 8-30 Hz, and trial duration is 2 seconds long. The other subjects also achieve high accuracy from 83% to 92%. However, this result also implies

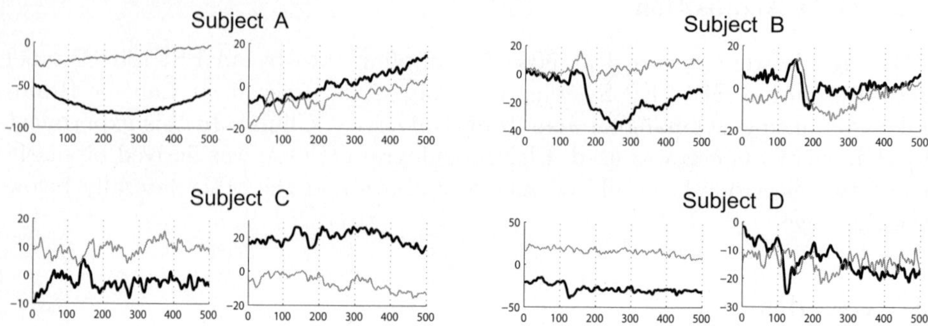

Fig. 5. For every subject, two figures show the projections of trials on the two most important patterns, with left trial plot in black, and right trial in gray

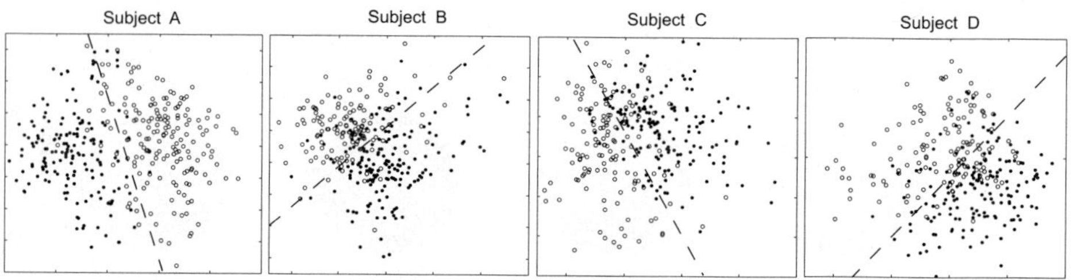

Fig. 6. The feature space of all subjects. Right trials are plotted in circles, with left trials in dots.

Table 1. The offline classification accuracy. For each subject, four frequency temporal filter bands and three different trial lengths are profiled.

Subject A	Trial Length			Subject B	Trial Length		
Bandpass	1000ms	1500ms	2000ms	Bandpass	1000ms	1500ms	2000ms
8-30 Hz	93.9%	94.8%	**99.1%**	8-30 Hz	77.0%	80.0%	81.0%
8-12 Hz	92.2%	95.7%	96.5%	8-12 Hz	71.0%	71.0%	75.0%
19-26 Hz	86.1%	93.0%	90.4%	19-26 Hz	81.0%	78.0%	**83.0%**
30-42 Hz	75.1%	80.4%	78.9%	30-42 Hz	65.0%	70.0%	71.0%
Subject C	Trial Length			**Subject D**	Trial Length		
Bandpass	1000ms	1500ms	2000ms	Bandpass	1000ms	1500ms	2000ms
8-30 Hz	80.0%	78.0%	79.0%	8-30 Hz	70.0%	82.0%	86.0%
8-12 Hz	66.0%	**86.0%**	75.0%	8-12 Hz	64.0%	80.0%	**92.0%**
19-26 Hz	73.0%	80.0%	78.0%	19-26 Hz	69.0%	75.0%	89.0%
30-42 Hz	62.0%	69.0%	65.0%	30-42 Hz	65.0%	70.0%	71.0%

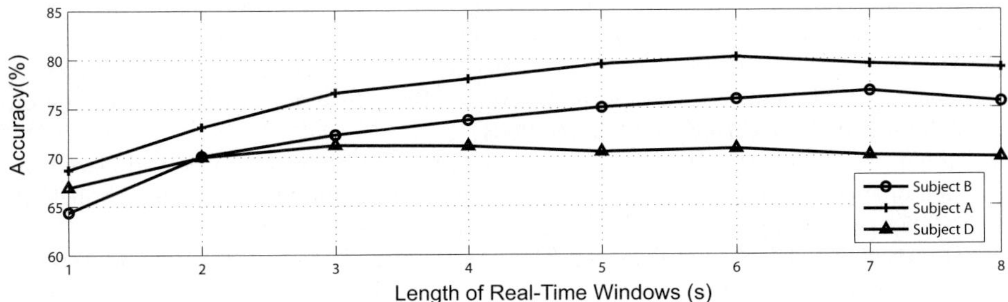

Fig. 7. Online classification result of three subjects

there exists discrepancy between different subjects, since they are adaptive to different trial lengths and frequency bands. This phenomenons maybe caused by physiological distinguish of people. So for each subject, specifically, a set of optimal parameters is chosen for online discriminations.

Figure 7 represents the online classification accuracies of three subject, from which we can see that a higher accuracy (up to 80.2%) can be achieved by increasing the window length. At the same time, it results in the increasing of response time.

In general, an ideal window length for online controlling varies from 3 to 5 seconds.

6   Conclusion

Experiment results have demonstrated the feasibility and performance of EEG feature extraction methods and online controlling capability of our BCI system. BCI research and analysis is a complex and challenging task in neuroscience and neurocomputing field. The main aspect of future research work may focus on including additional feature selection methods, especially nonlinear and temporal-frequency domain combined methods, then enhance the online controlling capability further.

Acknowledgements

The work was supported by the National Basic Research Program of China (Grant No. 2005CB724301) and the National High-Tech Research Program of China (Grant No. 2006AA01Z125).

References

1. Wolpaw, J.R., Birbaumer, N., McFarland, D.J.: Brain-computer interfaces for communication and control. Clinical Neurophysiology 113(8), 767–791 (2002)
2. Wolpaw, J.R., McFarland, D.J., Vaughan, T.M.: Brain-computer interface research at the Wadsworth center. IEEE Trans. Rehab. Eng. 8, 222–226 (2000)

3. Pfurtscheller, G., Neuper, C.: Motor imagery activates primary sensorimotor area in humans. Neurosci. Lett. 239, 65–68 (1997)
4. McFarland, D.J., Hinterberger, T., Birbaumer, N., Wolpaw, J.R.: BCI2000: A General-Purpose Brain-Computer Interface (BCI) System. IEEE Tansactions on Biomedical Engineering 51(6) (June 2004)
5. Lemm, S., Blankertz, B., Curio, G.: Spatio-spectral filters for improved classification of single trial EEG. IEEE Trans. on Biomedical Engineering 52(9), 1541–1548 (2005)
6. Dornhege, G., Blankertz, B., et al.: Combined Optimization of Spatial and Temporal Filters for Improving Brain-Computer Interfacing. IEEE Trans. on Biomedical Engineering 53(11), 2274–2281 (2006)
7. Wolpaw, J.R., et al.: Brain-computer interface technology: A review of the first international meeting. IEEE Trans. Rehab. Eng. 8, 164–173 (2000)
8. Cheng, M., Gao, X., Gao, S.: Design and Implementation of a Brain-Computer Interface With High Transfer Rates. IEEE Tansactions on Biomedical Engineering 49(10) (October 2002)
9. Peterson, D.A., Anderson, C.W.: EEG-based cognitive task classification with ICA and neural networks. In: Mira, J. (ed.) IWANN 1999. LNCS, vol. 1607, pp. 265–272. Springer, Heidelberg (1999)
10. Mason, S.G., Birch, G.E.: A general framework for brain-computer interface design. IEEE Trans. Neural Syst. Rehab. Eng. 11, 70–85 (2003)
11. Bayliss, J.D.: A Flexible brain-computer interface, Ph.D. dissertation, Univ. Rochester, Rochester, NY (August 2001)
12. Hesse, Christian, W.J., Christopher, J.: The Fast ICA Algorithm With Spatial Constraints. IEEE Signal Processing Letters 12(11) (2005)
13. Guger, C., Pfurtscheller, G., Pfurtscheller, G.: Real-time EEG analysis for a brain-computer interface (BCI) with subject-specific spatial patterns. IEEE Transactions on Rehabilitation Engineering 8, 447 (2000)
14. Mller-Gerking, J., Pfurtscheller, G., Flyvbjerg, H.: Designing optimal spatial filters for single-trial EEG classification in a movement task. Electroenc. Clin. Neurophys. (to be published, 1999)
15. Ramoser, H., Mller-Gerking, J., Pfurtscheller, G.: Optimal spatial filtering of single-trial EEG during imagined hand movement. IEEE Trans. Rehab. Eng. (2000)

A Study on Scheduling Function
of a Magnetic Parameter
in a Virtual Magnetic Diminuendo Method

Hiroshi Wakuya and Mari Miyazaki

Saga University, Saga 840-8502, Japan

Abstract. A virtual magnetic diminuendo method proposed recently is originally inspired by the analogy between the Hopfield network and the spin glass. It is a simple and ingenious idea for solving combinatorial optimization problems, because only a threshold of Hopfield network is controlled from a negative value to zero as a magnetic parameter, which is newly introduced in this study. According to the preliminary study, it seems to be clear experimentally that the proposed method is effective. In order to carry out further considerations, a scheduling function of the virtual magnetic parameter is investigated in this study. As a result of some computer simulations with the crossbar switch problem, it is found that changing polarity (negative $\rightarrow$ positive) of the magnetic parameter must be effective to improve the score.

1   Introduction

A combinatorial optimization problem is a task for searching an optimal solution from the plural combinations. A Hopfield network [1], one of the famous neural network models inspired by the spin glass system, is a good tool to solve it, but its major drawback is existence of energy local minima corresponding to spurious solutions. In order to avoid falling into them, various kinds of attempts have been undertaken by a lot of researchers. Since some of them show good performance, they become well-known techniques these days.

Generally speaking, such techniques are divided into two major groups: One is an idea based on an analogy between the Hopfield network and the spin glass system, and the other is just an operation to get better solutions without any physical background. From the viewpoint of the former case, i.e., consideration referring to the original concept of the Hopfield network, a novel search method called a virtual magnetic diminuendo method [2] is proposed recently and its effectiveness is also confirmed through some computer simulations. As the next step to refine this theory, further considerations are carried out in this paper.

2   Virtual Magnetic Diminuendo Method

2.1   Basic Idea

A virtual magnetic diminuendo method [2] is originally inspired by the inclusion relation between the Hopfield network and the spin glass. As can be seen in Fig. 1,

M. Ishikawa et al. (Eds.): ICONIP 2007, Part II, LNCS 4985, pp. 1047–1054, 2008.

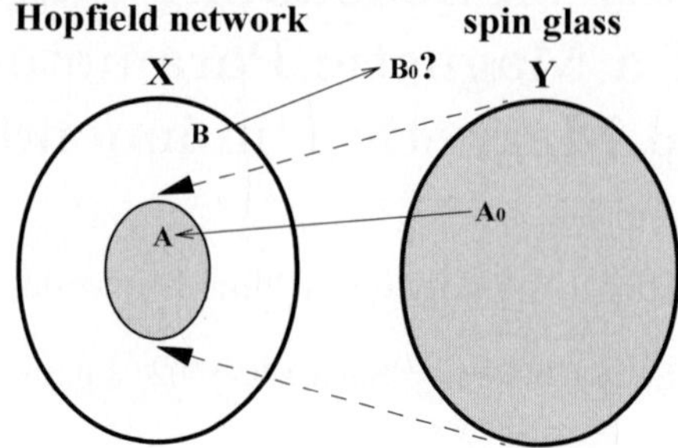

Fig. 1. Inclusion Relation between Hopfield Network and Spin Glass

Table 1. Summary of Correspondence between Hopfield Network and Spin Glass

Hopfield network	spin glass
energy (E)	Hamiltonian (H)
weights (W)	interactions (J)
neuron outputs (V)	spin states (S)
threshold (θ)	magnetic field (h)

it is clear that only the latter region Y is projected into the former region X. This fact suggests that an idea A_0 developed in the field of the spin glass system Y ($A_0 \in$ Y) must be also applicable in the field of the Hopfield network X, i.e., $A_0 \longmapsto A \in$ X. One of the famous methods called a simulated annealing belongs to this category.

Table 1 is a summary of correspondence between the Hopfield network and the spin glass: If neuron outputs (active/quiescent) V are assigned to spin states (up/down) S and weights W are assigned to interactions J, respectively, an energy E of the Hopfield network is defined by the Hamiltonian H of the spin glass system. Usually, a solution of the combinatorial optimization problem is defined as an energy minimum point, so the Hopfield network will change the state toward reducing its energy, and finally it is expected that the state reaches the desired solution automatically.

Taking account of above-mentioned essence, a following thought experiment is plausible. When we apply a magnetic field from outside the spin glass system, all spins in it must be aligned with their orientation. Then, as the magnetic field is reduced gradually, it makes the spin free depending on its interactions with other spins. According to Table 1, it is obvious that the magnetic field h corresponds to a threshold θ of each neuron in the Hopfield network. It is noticeable here that the proposed method controls a position (bias) of the sigmoidal function, while the conventional simulated annealing controls its gradient. Therefore, the principle of the basic idea is completely different.

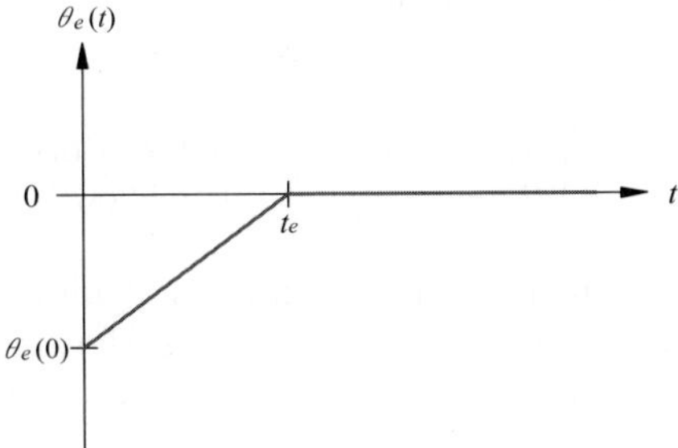

Fig. 2. An Example of Scheduling Function Adopted in the Previous Study

2.2   Formulation

First of all, an energy function E is designed to satisfy task-dependent constraints. Next, through a comparison with the Hamiltonian H, both a weight coefficient W_{xy} from the neurons y to x and a threshold θ_x of the neuron x are obtained. With these parameters, an output of the neuron x in the Hopfield network is defined by the asynchronous manner as follows:

$$V_x\left(t + \frac{\tau + 1}{n}\right) = f\left(\sum_{y=1}^{n} W_{xy} V_y\left(t + \frac{\tau}{n}\right) - \Theta_x(t)\right),\tag{1}$$

$$\Theta_x(t) = \theta_x + \theta_e(t),\tag{2}$$

$$f(z) = \begin{cases} 1, & z \geq 0, \\ 0, & z < 0, \end{cases}\tag{3}$$

where n is a number of neurons and θ_e is a virtual magnetic term, respectively. And τ is a moment each neuron changes its output at time t one by one.

2.3   Scheduling Function of the Virtual Magnetic Parameter

In the primitive study of the virtual magnetic diminuendo method [2], scheduling function of the magnetic parameter (threshold) is quite simple and defined changing with time t linearly as,

$$\theta_e(t) = \begin{cases} \theta_e(0)\left(1 - \dfrac{t}{t_e}\right), & 0 < t \leq t_e, \\ 0, & t > t_e, \end{cases}\tag{4}$$

The virtual magnetic parameter $\theta_e(t)$ is set $\theta_e(0)$ as an initial value at $t = 0$, and disappeared completely at $t = t_e$ as shown in Fig. 2. Since its proposal, the virtual magnetic parameter $\theta_e(t)$ is usually a negative value, so it must be careful that its polarity is opposite to the *normal* case. In the previous study, for example, all parameters are provided as $\theta_e(0) = -500.0$ and $t_e = 5000$, respectively. For the sake of clarity, (4) is rewritten as,

$$\theta_e(t) = \begin{cases} -500 + 0.1t, & 0 < t \le 5000, \\ 0, & t > 5000, \end{cases} \tag{5}$$

Fortunately, even though such a simple definition is adopted, an advantage over the conventional method is confirmed. Then, as the next step to refine this theory, a control strategy of the virtual magnetic parameter is investigated.

3   Computer Simulations

There are many kinds of combinatorial optimization problems in this world. Among them, a crossbar switch problem is adopted, because it is so simple that an advantage of the proposed method must be identified easily. Also, it contains an essence of solving combinatorial optimization problems, and has been applied on the practical business scene such as a task-management problem. It is a task to mark N different areas in the $N \times N$ squares not to occupy more than one at the same time in both vertical and horizontal directions. In other words, it is an N *"rooks" problem* instead of the famous N queens problem.

By the way, only the comparison of the total scores is considered in the previous study with the simple scheduling function changing with time t linearly as (4). Then, in order to make clear its mechanism, a few kinds of further considerations are carried out in this paper.

3.1   Overview: Ratio of Correct Answer

Figure 3 is a summary of the computer simulation results starting from 1000 different initial states. The scheduling function of the virtual magnetic parameter is the same as the previous study and defined by (5). At first glance, it is clear that the proposed virtual magnetic diminuendo method shows much better performance than the conventional method not introducing the virtual magnetic parameter. It is natural that the ratio of correct answer decreases with the number of regions N, because the number of all correct solutions is expressed by $N!$ while the number of all possible combinations is by 2^{N^2}. For reference, the same computer simulation is performed under the condition $N = 80$, the conventional method shows poor performance around 15%. On the contrary, the proposed method still shows good performance of 100%, so it is concluded again that the proposed virtual magnetic diminuendo method is quite effective.

3.2   Dependence of the Initial Value

As a next step, the dependence of the initial value of the virtual magnetic parameter is investigated. It is noticeable here that only the parameter $\theta_e(0)$ in (4) is controlled from the certain negative value to zero while the parameter t_e

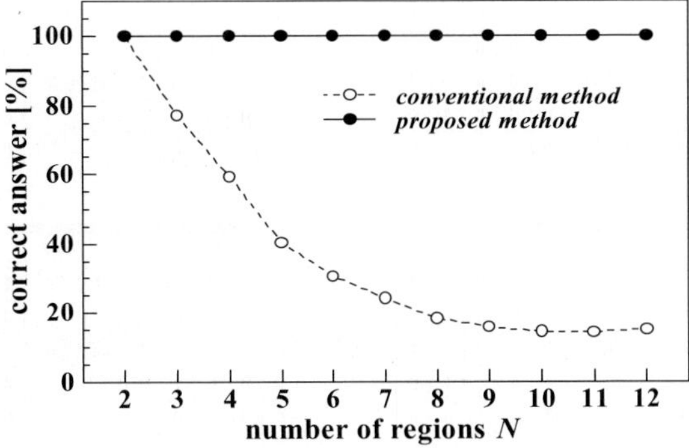

Fig. 3. Results of Computer Simulations [I] — Ratio of Correct Answer

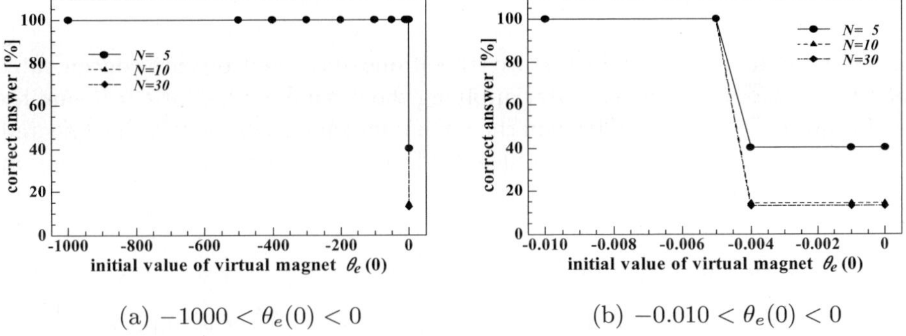

(a) $-1000 < \theta_e(0) < 0$ (b) $-0.010 < \theta_e(0) < 0$

Fig. 4. Results of Computer Simulations [II] — Dependence of the Initial Value

is constant at 5000, and three different conditions of $N = 5, 10, 30$ are adopted. As can be seen from Fig. 4(a), it is confirmed that all of these show a similar tendency. That is a *sudden drop* of the ratio slightly smaller than the point at $\theta_e(0) = 0$. In order to focus on this range, an extended version is also shown in Fig. 4(b). According to this figure, the ratio fallen down from 100% to a certain rate, depending on the number of regions N, is restricted within quite narrow range of $\theta_e(0)$ and extremely close to zero. In other words, an effectiveness of the virtual magnetic parameter will be emerged just a quite small value. Therefore, it is important to apply the virtual magnetic parameter but its initial value seems to be not so significant.

3.3   Temporal Development of Each Neuron

In order to reveal its mechanism, as a third step, temporal development of each neuron in the Hopfield network is investigated. Figure 5 is an example of $\theta_e(0) = -500.0$ and $N = 5$, and the neurons, which change their states from active to quiescent and vice versa, are marked by circles for easy to identify. According to

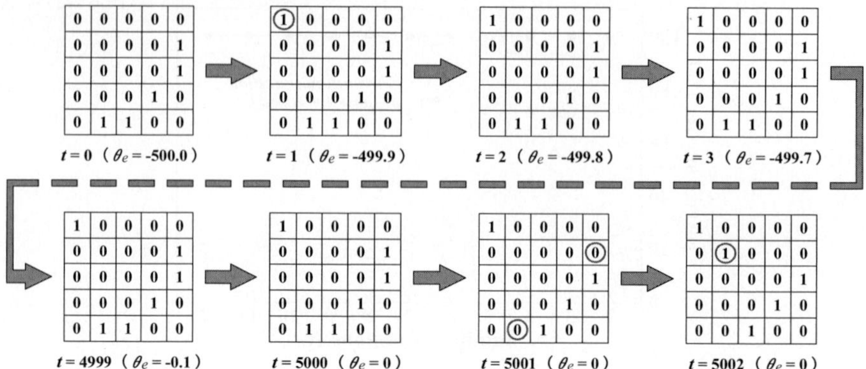

Fig. 5. Temporal Development of Each Neuron in the Hopfield Network. Circles Show the Neurons Which Change Their State.

this figure, it is found that most state transitions of the neurons are concentrated upon two periods: One is just after applying the virtual magnet at $t = 0$, and the other is around $t = t_e = 5000$ when the virtual magnet is completely disappeared. This fact reminds us that no significant effects seem to be observed during an interval between above-mentioned two periods.

3.4   Origin of Mysterious Phenomenon

As can be seen from Fig. 5, the virtual magnetic parameter is applied at $t = 0$, and its effect is reflected at $t = 1$ through calculation for each neuron's state transition. At that time, there is a neuron which changes its state from quiescent to active. It is said generally that a low threshold makes the neuron be easy to fire, this transition supports the theory. Since then, no state transitions have been observed until the virtual magnet is completely disappeared at $t = t_e = 5000$. Because of the same reason mentioned above, disappearance is reflected at $t = 5001$ through calculation for state transition.

By the way, the former case of state transition at $t = 0$ is relatively easy to understand, because an external factor is newly applied to the Hopfield network. But the latter case at $t = t_e = 5000$ is hard to understand, because what disappearance of the virtual magnetic parameter affects the network is uncertain. Then, a detailed analysis of the parameter $\theta_e(t)$ is examined. As a result, it is found that $\theta_e(t)$ is not zero but an extremely small positive value less than the order of 10^{-10}. Generally speaking, all digital computers are working based on the binary coding system, so that all calculations are executed based on the binary system. Taking into account of such difference between our daily life and the computing architecture, it is suspected that an aliquot in the decimal system is not always an aliquot in the binary system, but it might be an aliquant in the binary system. It must be important to address here that an advantage of the proposed method is completely disappeared, if the virtual magnetic parameter

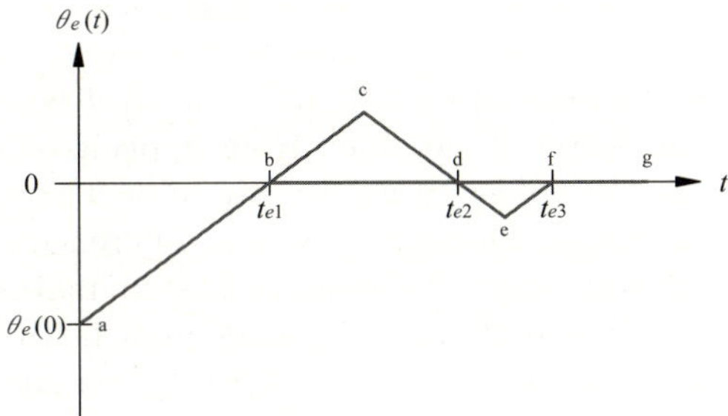

Fig. 6. Some Examples of Scheduling Function Proposed in This Study — Simple, Moderate and Advanced Versions

$\theta_e(t_e)$ is provided not to exceed zero making use of a *conditional sentence* in the computer simulation program. As a result of these considerations, the origin of the mysterious phenomenon must be summarized in changing polarity of the virtual magnetic parameter.

Based on the above-mentioned various facts, a guiding principle for improving the score of combinatorial optimization problems is obtained: The virtual magnetic parameter must be provided starting from a negative value toward a positive. As can be seen from Fig. 6, several versions of application are considered as follows:

1. a simple version :
   negative $\rightarrow$ zero (a-b-d-f-g in Fig. 6) ,
2. a moderate version :
   negative $\rightarrow$ positive $\rightarrow$ zero (a-b-c-d-f-g in Fig. 6) ,
3. an advanced version :
   negative $\rightarrow$ positive $\rightarrow$ negative $\rightarrow$ zero (a-b-c-d-e-f-g in Fig. 6) .

Also, the further advanced versions will be considered in the same manner. As a result of some primitive computer simulations, not shown here for brevity, it seems to be said that ratio of correct answer is improved with the repetition of changing polarity of the virtual magnetic parameter.

4   Discussion

An original motive of the proposed method comes from reconsiderations of the correspondence between the Hopfield network and the spin glass. A trivial question arisen from Fig. 1 led us to the thought experiment mentioned in **2.1**, and it also gave us an inspiration of the virtual magnetic diminuendo method. Even though quite a simple scheduling function of the magnetic parameter is adopted in the preliminary study, the proposed method seems to get a better score than the conventional one. Then, it is said that the proposed method must be worth thinking.

By the way, a virtual magnetic parameter has been provided only starting from a negative value to zero as a scheduling function since its proposal. But there are no significant reasons to persist so. In short, it is also considered that a virtual magnetic parameter is provided from a positive to zero, because a magnetic parameter can be taken either a positive or a negative value. At the present time, it is not certain whether there is a difference between the above-mentioned two cases. But violation of symmetric system makes emerge somewhat of differences. This is why the Hopfield network used in this study is working based on the binary (0/1) mode, not the bipolar (-1/1) mode, as defined by (3).

On the other hand, there is a famous technique for improving the score called a simulated annealing. As mentioned above, its essence is to control a thermal parameter starting from high temperature to low. Although their appearances are similar each other, detailed mechanisms for approaching the desired solution are completely different. If any merits of the proposed method are presented by force, a magnetic parameter can be provided from wide range including a negative value while a thermal parameter can only a positive value. Of course, the proposed method is not consistent with the conventional simulated annealing, but further considerations on performance comparison must be required to refined the proposed method.

5   Conclusions

In this paper, a virtual magnetic diminuendo method proposed recently is investigated. It is originally inspired by the analogy between the Hopfield network and the spin glass, and newly introduced a magnetic parameter. As a result of computer simulations with the crossbar switch problem, it is found experimentally that changing polarity of the virtual magnetic parameter is an excellent strategy to get better score of the combinatorial optimization problems.

References

1. Hopfield, J.J., Tank, D.W.: 'Neural' computation of decisions in optimization problems. Biol. Cybern. 52, 141–152 (1985)
2. Wakuya, H.: A new search method for combinatorial optimization problem inspired by the spin glass system. In: Brain-Inspired IT II, ICS, vol. 1291, pp. 201–204. Elsevier, Amsterdam (2006)

Stereo Saliency Map Considering Affective Factors in a Dynamic Environment

Young-Min Jang[1], Sang-Woo Ban[2], and Minho Lee[1]

[1] School of Electrical Engineering and Computer Science, Kyungpook National University
1370 Sankyuk-Dong, Puk-Gu, Taegu 702-701, Korea
[2] Dept. of Information and Communication Engineering, Dongguk University
707 Seokjang-Dong, Gyeongju, Gyeongbuk 780-714, Korea
ymjang@ee.knu.ac.kr, swban@dongguk.ac.kr, mholee@knu.ac.kr

Abstract. We propose a new integrated saliency map model, which reflects more human-like visual attention mechanism. The proposed model considers not only the binocular stereopsis to construct a final attention area so that the closer attention area can be easily made to pop-out as in human binocular vision, based on the single eye alignment hypothesis, but also both static and dynamic features of an input scene. Moreover, the proposed saliency map model includes an affective computing process to skip an unwanted area and/or to pay attention to a desired area, mimicking the pulvinar's function in the human preference and refusal mechanism in subsequent visual search processes. In addition, we show the effectiveness of using the symmetry feature implemented by a neural network and independent component analysis (ICA) filter to construct more object preferable attention model. The experimental results show that the proposed model can generate more plausible scan paths for natural input scenes.

Keywords: Integrated saliency map, stereo saliency map, affective attention, bottom-up selective attention.

1 Introduction

The human visual system can effortlessly detect an interesting area or object within natural or cluttered scenes through the selective attention mechanism. The selective attention mechanism allows the human vision system to process visual scenes more effectively with a higher level of complexity. The human visual system sequentially interprets not only a static and/or dynamic input scene but also a stereo scene with affective factors based on the selective attention mechanism.

In previous research, Itti and Koch [1] introduced a brain-like model in order to generate the saliency map (SM). Koike and Saiki [2] proposed that a stochastic WTA enables the saliency-based search model to vary the relative saliency in order to change search efficiency, due to stochastic shifts of attention. Kadir and Brady [3] proposed an attention model integrating saliency, scale selection and a content description, thus contrasting many other approaches. Ramström and Christensen [4]

M. Ishikawa et al. (Eds.): ICONIP 2007, Part II, LNCS 4985, pp. 1055–1064, 2008.

calculated saliency with respect to a given task by using a multi-scale pyramid and multiple cues. Their saliency computations were based on game theory concepts. In recent work, Itti's group proposed a new attention model that considers seven dynamic features for MTV-style video clips [5], and also proposed an integrated attention scheme to detect an object, which combines bottom-up SM with top-down attention based on signal-to-noise ratio [6]. As well, Walter and Koch [7] proposed an object preferable attention scheme which considers the bottom-up SM results as biased weights for top-down object-perception [8]. Lee et al. have also proposed a bottom-up SM model using symmetry information with an ICA filter [9, 10] and implemented a human-like vergence control system based on a selective attention model, in which the proposed model reflects a human's interest in an area by reinforcement and inhibition training mechanisms [10].

However, none of the proposed attention models consider the integration of a stereo type bottom-up SM model and a top-down selective attention scheme biased by human affective factors in a dynamic environment.

A human can attend different locations according to his or her affective sense. The human vision system includes an affective computing process to skip an unwanted area and/or to pay attention to a desired area, a preference and refusal mechanism mediated by the pulvinar [11]. Moreover, binocular depth information also plays a role in deciding the attention area [12].

In this paper, we propose a new integrated SM model, which can generate an attention area by considering the dynamics of continuous input scenes as well as including both the human's affective computing process and the stereo vision characteristic in selective attention. Furthermore, even though the SM models proposed by Lee et al. already used symmetry feature information based on generalized symmetry transformation (GST) [9, 10, 13] and also considered an independent component analysis (ICA) filter to integrate bottom-up features, in this paper, we examine through extensive computer experiments using hundreds of test images how important the symmetry feature and ICA filter are in generating a human-like plausible scan path in a visual search.

In Section 2, we present in detail the proposed SM model. In Section 3, we describe computer simulation and the experimental results. The Discussion and Conclusion will follow in Section 4.

2 Integrated Saliency Map Model

Figure 1 shows the simulated biological visual pathway from the retina to the visual cortex through the LGN for the bottom-up processing, which is extended to the limbic system including the pulvinar for the top-down processing. In order to implement a human-like visual attention function, three processes are integrated to generate a stereo SM. One generates static and dynamic saliency in terms of monocular vision. Another considers affective factors for reflecting human preference and refusal, which mimic the function of the pulvinar in the limbic system. Finally, we can build a stereo SM by combining two monocular SMs.

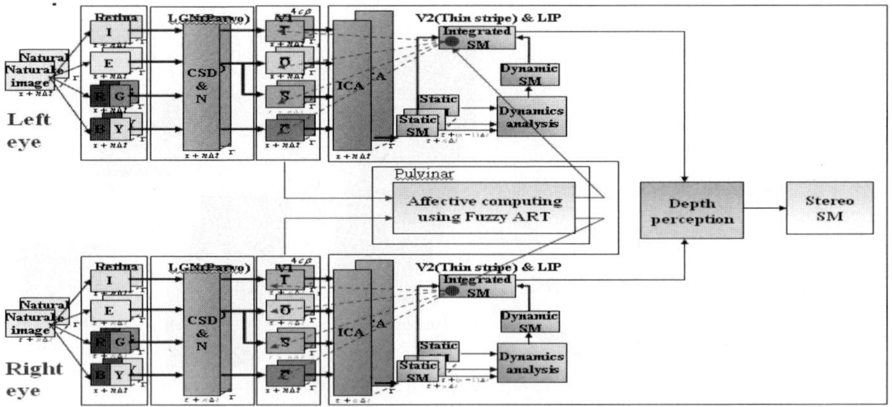

Fig. 1. Stereo saliency map model including dynamic features and affective factors

2.1   Static Bottom-Up Saliency Map with Symmetry Information and ICA Filter

Based on the Treisman's feature integration theory [8], Itti and Koch used three basis feature maps: intensity, orientation and color information [1]. Extending Itti and Koch's SM model, we previously proposed SM models which include a symmetry feature map based on the GST algorithm and an ICA filter to integrate the feature information [9, 10]. In this paper, we investigate through extensive computer experiments how important the proposed symmetry feature map and the ICA filter are in constructing an object preferable attention model. We newly incorporate the neural network approach of Fukushima [14] to construct the symmetry feature map, which is more biologically plausible and takes less computation than the GST algorithm.

Symmetry is a highly salient feature of animals, plants, and the constructed environments. Symmetry is implicated as an important component of direction of visual attention independent of context [15]. Symmetry information is very important in the context free search problem [13]. Duncan suggested that visual attention is deployed at the level of segmented objects [16]. In order to implement an object preferable attention model, we emphasize using a symmetry feature map because an object with an arbitrary shape contains symmetry information, and our visual pathway also includes a specific function to detect a shape in an object [14, 17]. Although the symmetry is obtained by comparison of features in an image through which the feedback from an extrastriate cortical area [15], symmetry information can also be extracted near by symmetry axis, which is obtained from early visual cortex areas [14]. In order to consider symmetry information in our SM model, we modified Fukushima's neural network to describe a symmetry axis [14]. In the course of computing the orientation feature map, we use 6 different scale images (a Gaussian pyramid) and implement the on-center and off-surround functions using the center surround and difference with normalization (CSD & N) [1, 9, 10]. As shown in Figure 2, the orientation information in three successive scale images is used for obtaining the symmetry axis from Fukushima's neural network [14]. By applying the CSD&N to the symmetry axes extracted in four different scales, we can obtain a symmetry feature map. This procedure mimics the higher-order analysis mechanism

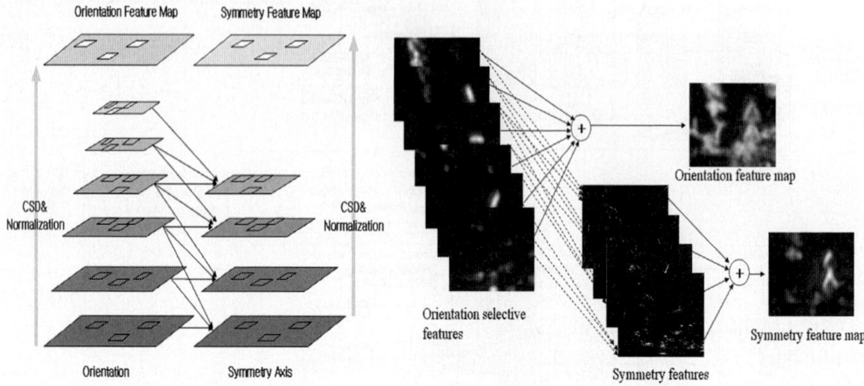

Fig. 2. Symmetry feature map generation process

of complex cells and hyper-complex cells in the posterior visual cortex area, beyond the orientation-selective simple cells in the V1. Using CSD & N in Gaussian pyramid images [1], we can construct the intensity $(\bar{I})$, color $(\bar{C})$, and orientation $(\bar{O})$ feature maps as well as the symmetry feature map $(\bar{S})$.

Based on both Barlow's hypothesis that human visual cortical feature detectors might be the end result of a redundancy reduction process [18], and Sejnowski's results that ICA is the best way to reduce redundancy [19], the four constructed feature maps $(\bar{I}, \bar{C}, \bar{O} \text{ and } \bar{S})$ are then integrated by an independent component analysis (ICA) algorithm based on maximization of the entropy [19]. A static SM, $S(x,y)$, is obtained by summation of the convolution between the r-th channel of input image (I_r) and the i-th filters (ICs_{ri}) obtained by the ICA learning [9] , as shown in Eq. (1) [9, 10].

$$S(x, y) = \sum I_r * ICs_{ri} \qquad for\ all\ i \qquad (1)$$

2.2 Dynamic Bottom-Up Saliency Map

Human beings decide what constitutes an interesting area within a dynamic scene, as well as static images. The dynamic SM part in our proposed model is implemented based on the model proposed by Lee et al. [20]. The proposed dynamic SM model is based on successive static SMs. The entropy maximum is used to analyze the dynamics of the successive static SMs; this is an extension of Kadir's approach [3] since the proposed model considers time varying properties as well as spatial features. Figure 1 shows the procedure to compute a final SM by integrating both the static SM and the dynamic SM from natural input images. For the first frame at time τ , the most appropriate scale x_s for each area centered at location x is obtained by Eq. (2) which aims to consider spatial dynamics at each location:

$$X_s = \arg\max_{s}\{H_D(s, X, \tau) \times W_D(s, X, \tau)\} \qquad (2)$$

where D is the set of all descriptor values which consist of the intensity values corresponding to the histogram distribution in a local region with size s around an attended location X_s in a static SM at time τ, and $H_D(s, X, \tau)$ is the entropy defined by Eq. (3) and $W_D(s, X, \tau)$ is the inter-scale measure defined by Eq. (4):

$$H_D(s, X, \tau) \equiv -\sum_{d \in D} P_{d,s,X,\tau} \log_2 P_{d,s,X,\tau} \tag{3}$$

$$W_D(s, X, \tau) \equiv \frac{s^2}{2s-1} \sum_{d \in D} \left| P_{d,s,X,\tau} - P_{d,s-1,X,\tau} \right| \tag{4}$$

where $P_{d,s,X,\tau}$ is the probability mass function obtained from the histogram of pixel values in a local region with a scale s at position X in a static SM at time τ, and the descriptor value d is an element in a set of all descriptor values D.

The probability mass function for a dynamic scene $PH_{D(X_s,X,\tau+n\Delta t)}$ is obtained from the histogram of the entropy values for a sequence of static SMs in (k+1) frames from τ to $\tau + n\Delta t$ where k is the number of continuous frames and Δt denotes the sampling time. The entropy value at location X is calculated using the histogram of pixel values of the local area centered at X with size X_s in a static SM. Using the probability mass function for a dynamic scene $PH_{D(X_s,X,\tau+n\Delta t)}$, the time varying entropy $T_D(\cdot)$ is calculated by Eq. (5):

$$T_D(X_s, X, \tau+n\Delta t) \equiv -\sum_{d \in D} PH_{D(X_s,X,\tau+n\Delta t)} \log_2 PH_{D(X_s,X,\tau+n\Delta t)} \tag{5}$$

The entropy value $T_D(\cdot)$, at each pixel X, represents a fluctuation of visual information according to time, through which the proposed model can generate a dynamic SM. Finally, the attention areas are decided by a final SM which is generated by integration of the static SM and the dynamic SM. Therefore, the proposed attention model can selectively choose an attention area by considering not only static saliency but also dynamic feature information obtained from consecutive input scenes.

2.3 Affective Saliency

Although the proposed SM model generates plausible salient areas and a scan path, the selected areas may not be considered interesting from the point of view of for human affective factors as the SM only uses primitive features such as intensity, edge, color and symmetry information. In order to implement a more plausible selective attention model, we need to consider affective factors that reflect human preference and refusal for visual features. Attention to particular stimulus features or attributes can suppress or facilitate responses to stimuli falling in receptive field [21]. Top-down modulation of visual inputs to the salience network might facilitate visual search [21]. Modulation of specific classes of visual input based on the human's affective factors could serve to make the entire network more sensitive to particular features according to preference. Lee et al. previously proposed a trainable selective attention model which considers reinforcement and inhibition mechanisms on selective attention regions [10]. In this paper, we extend Lee's research to include a Hebbian learning process for generating suitable top-down bias signals according to human affective factors. According to Picard's research [22], human affective factors are involved in many aspects of the decision process and behavior as well as in attention. In the course of eye movement to pay attention to an interesting area, a human's affective factors bias the saliency results. Humans ignore an uninteresting area even if it has salient primitive features, according to their emotion, and can memorize the characteristics of the unwanted area. We avoid paying attention to a new area having similar characteristics to a previously learned unwanted area by generating a top-down bias signal obtained by a training process. Conversely, humans can pay attention to an interesting area even if it does not have salient primitive features, or is less salient than another area. We propose a new selective attention model using a top-down bias signal that is obtained by a Hebbian learning process. In Lee's trainable selective attention scheme [10], fuzzy ART networks learn the characteristics of unwanted and interesting areas [23], but the training process does not learn suitable top-down bias weight values.

Figure 3 shows the selective attention model with affective factors. The top-down weight values are trained by Hebbian learning between the activation values of the SM and those of each feature map as shown in Eq. (6) and (7).

$$\Delta w(x, y)_{k+} = S(x, y) \cdot YFA(x, y) \quad for\ preference \tag{6}$$

$$\Delta w(x, y)_{k-} = -S(x, y) \cdot YFA(x, y) \quad for\ refusal\ where\ k \in \{I, O, S, C\}\ and\ Y \in \{I, O, S, C\} \tag{7}$$

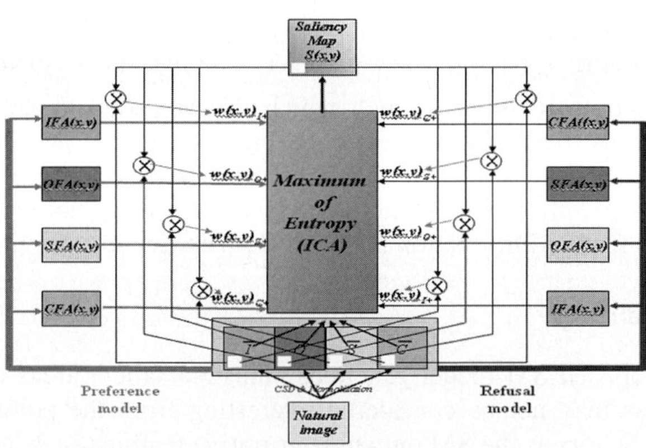

Fig. 3. Selective attention model considering affective factors (IFA: Fuzzy ART for intensity features, OFA: Fuzzy ART for orientation features, SFA: Fuzzy ART for symmetry features. CFA: Fuzzy ART for color features).

2.4 Stereo Saliency

Based on the single eye alignment hypothesis [24], Lee et al. developed an active vision system that can control two cameras using a human-like vergence mechanism [10]. The purpose of Lee's stereo vision system was to use the static selective attention model to implement an active vision system for vergence control [10]. In this paper, we now utilize the depth information obtained by the vergence control vision system to construct the stereo SM model, which can then support pop-outs for closer objects. In our model, the selective attention regions in each camera are obtained from static and dynamic saliency in conjunction with the affective saliency, and are then used for selecting a dominant landmark. After successfully localizing corresponding landmarks on both the left image and the right image, we are able to get depth information by a simple triangular equation [10]. Then, the proposed stereo SM model uses the depth information as a characteristic feature in deciding saliency using a decaying exponential function. The final stereo SM is obtained by $S(x, y) \cdot \exp^{-z/\tau}$, where z is the distance between the camera and an attend region, and τ is a constant.

3   Computer Experimental Results

Figure 4 shows an example in which the proposed SM model generates more object preferable attention by using symmetry information as an additional input feature and ICA for feature integration. The numbers in Figures 4a-c represent the order of the scan path according to the degree of saliency by different SM models. As shown in Figure 4, the symmetry feature map is effective in choosing an attention area containing an object. The ICA filter successfully reduces redundant information in feature maps so that the final scan path does not pay attention to the sky in the input image. Table 1 compares the object preferable performance of three different SM models using hundreds of test images. Considering both the symmetry feature and ICA method, we can achieve the best object preferable attention.

Figure 5 shows that the proposed SM model can generate more reasonable attention results by considering dynamic features as well as static features.

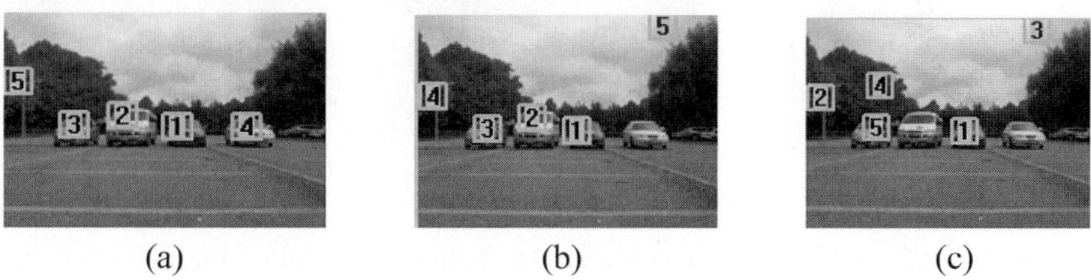

(a)   (b)   (c)

Fig. 4. (a) Salient areas for $\overline{I} + \overline{C} + \overline{O} + \overline{S} + ICA$, (b) Salient areas for $\overline{I} + \overline{C} + \overline{O} + \overline{S}$, (c) Salient areas for $\overline{I} + \overline{C} + \overline{O}$

Figure 6 shows the simulation results using the affective saliency of our proposed model. Figure 6b shows the scan path generated by the static SM model, where the 2nd salient area is deemed a refusal area according to the human's affective factors, and it is trained by the affective SM model for refusal. Figure 6c shows the modified scan path after the refusal processing. The 4th salient area is also changed after training the affective SM model for preference.

1062   Y.-M. Jang, S.-W. Ban, and M. Lee

Table 1. Comparison of three different bottom-up SM models for object preferable attention

Salient area (SA)	I+C+O+S+ICA	I+C+O+S	I+C+O (Itti's model)
1st SA	165	150	143
2nd SA	106	104	103
3rd SA	68	77	64
4th SA	66	57	47
5th SA	46	32	28
Total	451	420	385
(%)	90.2 %	84.0 %	77.0 %

Detail results; ftp://abr.knu.ac.kr/DB/Simulation_Result/SM models_comparison

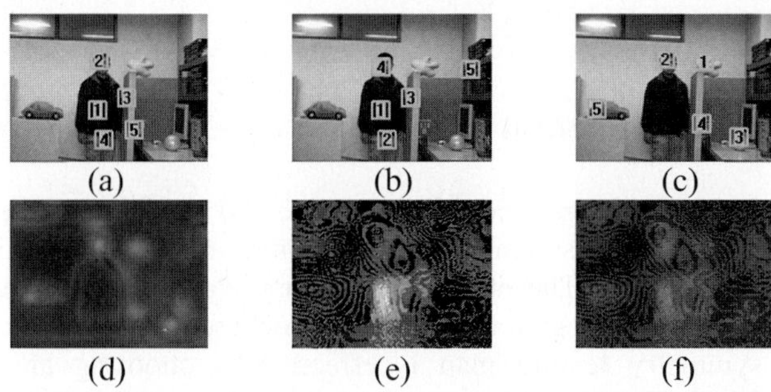

Fig. 5. Comparison of the dynamic SM with the static SM: (a) scan paths generated by the static SM for static image at 4th frames (b) scan path generated by the dynamic SM from τ to $\tau + 3\Delta t$, (c) scan path generated by integration of (a) and (b), (d)-(f) corresponding SMs for (a)-(c).

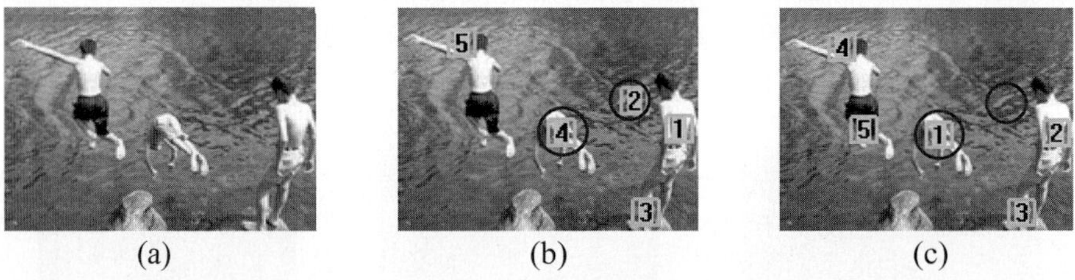

Fig. 6. (a) Natural image (b) Saliency map (c) Salient areas after inhibition of 2nd and reinforcement of 4th salient areas

Fig. 7. Stereo saliency simulation results; (a) Scan path of left image with depth (1st:163.72cm, 2nd:127.78cm, 3rd:130.88cm) (b) Scan path of right camera, (c) Scan path of left camera after considering the depth feature (d) Scan path of right camera after considering the depth feature.

Figure 7 shows a simulation result using stereo saliency. As shown in Figure 7, by considering the depth feature, the proposed model can make closer attended objects mostly pop out.

4 Conclusions

We proposed a new biologically motivated stereo SM model that mimics human-like visual selective attention, emphasizing the importance of a symmetry feature map and ICA filtering, which gives better performance in generating an object preferable selective attention as shown in our computer experiment. Also, our proposed attention model can generate a SM that integrates static and dynamic features as well as affective factors and depth information in nature input scene. In particular, we proposed a Hebbian learning process to generate a top-down bias signal according to human affective factors, and we integrated the stereo dimension of binocular vision to complete the saliency map. For further work, we are considering task specific object biased attention and a new SM with internal dynamics caused by affective factors.

Acknowledgments. This research was funded by the Brain Neuroinformatics Research Program of the Ministry of Commerce, Industry and Energy in Korea.

References

1. Itti, L., Koch, C., Niebur, E.: A model of saliency-based visual attention for rapid scene analysis. IEEE Trans. Patt. Anal. Mach. Intell. 20(11), 1254–1259 (1998)
2. Koike, T., Saiki, J.: Stochastic guided search model for search asymmetries in visual search tasks. In: Bülthoff, H.H., Lee, S.-W., Poggio, T.A., Wallraven, C. (eds.) BMCV 2002. LNCS, vol. 2525, pp. 408–417. Springer, Heidelberg (2002)
3. Kadir, T., Brady, M.: Scale, saliency and image description. International Journal of Computer Vision, 83–105 (2001)
4. Ramstrom, O., Christensen, H.I.: Visual attention using game theory. In: Bülthoff, H.H., Lee, S.-W., Poggio, T.A., Wallraven, C. (eds.) BMCV 2002. LNCS, vol. 2525, pp. 462–471. Springer, Heidelberg (2002)
5. Carmi, R., Itti, L.: Visual causes versus correlates of attentional selection in dynamic scenes. Vision Research 46(26), 4333–4345 (2006)
6. Navalpakkam, V., Itti, L.: An integrated model of top-down and bottom-up attention for optimal object detection. In: IEEE Conference on Computer Vision and Pattern Recognition (CVPR), pp. 2049–2056 (2006)
7. Walther, D., Rutishauser, U., Koch, C., Perona, P.: Selective visual attention enables learning and recognition of multiple objects in cluttered scenes. Computer Vision and Image Processing 100(1-2), 41–63 (2005)
8. Treisman, A.M., Gelde, G.: A feature-integration theory of attention. Cognitive Psychology 12(1), 97–136 (1980)
9. Park, S.J., An, K.H., Lee, M.: Saliency map model with adaptive masking based on independent component analysis. Neurocomputing 49, 417–422 (2002)
10. Choi, S.B., Jung, B.S., Ban, S.W., Niitsuma, H., Lee, M.: Biologically motivated vergence control system using human-like selective attention model. Neurocomputing 69, 537–558 (2006)

11. Ward, R., Calder, A., Parker, M., Arend, I.: Emotion recognition following human pulvinar damage. Neuropsychologia 45(8), 1973–1978 (2007)
12. Hancock, S., Andrews, T.J.: The role of voluntary and involuntary attention in selecting perceptual dominance during binocular rivalry. Perception 36(2), 288–298 (2007)
13. Reisfeld, D., Wolfson, H., Yeshurun, Y.: Context-free attentional operators: The generalized symmetry transform. IJCV 14, 119–130 (1995)
14. Fukushima, K.: Use of non-uniform spatial blur for image comparison: symmetry axis extraction. Neural Network 18, 22–23 (2005)
15. Norcia, A.M., Candy, T.R., Pettet, M.W., Vildavski, V.Y., Tyler, C.W.: Temporal dynamics of the human response to symmetry. Journal of Vision 2, 132–139 (2002)
16. Duncan, J.: Selective attention and the organization of visual information. Journal of Experimental Psychology: General 113, 501–517 (1984)
17. Werblin, F.S., Roska, B.: Parallel visual processing: A tutorial of retinal function. Int. J. Bifurcation and Chaos 14, 83–852 (2004)
18. Barlow, H.B., Tolhust, D.J.: Why do you have edge detectors? Optical society of America Technical Digest 23, 172 (1992)
19. Bell, A.J., Sejnowski, T.J.: The independent components of natural scenes are edge filters. Vision Research 37, 3327–3338 (1997)
20. Ban, S.W., Lee, I., Lee, M.: Dynamic visual selective attention. Neurocomputing 71, 853–856 (2008)
21. Mazer, J.A., Gallant, J.L.: Goal-related activity in V4 during free viewing visual search: evidence for a ventral stream visual saliency map. Neuron 40, 1241–1250 (2003)
22. Picard, R.W.: Affective computing. MIT Press, Cambridge (1997)
23. Carpenter, G.A., Grossberg, S., Markuzon, N., Reynolds, J.H., Rosen, D.B.: Fuzzy ARTMAP: A neural network architecture for incremental supervised learning of analog multidimensional maps. IEEE Trans. on Neural Networks 3(5), 698–713 (1992)
24. Thorn, F., Gwiazda, J., Cruz, A.A.V., Bauer, J.A., Held, R.: The development of eye alignment, convergence, and sensory binocularity in young infants. Investigative Ophthalmology and Visual Science 35, 544–553 (1994)

Inference Based on Distributed Representations Using Trajectory Attractors

Ken Yamane, Takashi Hasuo, and Masahiko Morita

Graduate School of Systems and Information Engineering, University of Tsukuba,
Tsukuba-shi, 305-8573 Japan

Abstract. It is considered that a key to overcoming the limitations of classical artificial intelligence is to process distributed representations of information without symbolizing them. However, conventional neural networks require local or symbolic representations to perform complicated processing. Here we present a brain-like inference engine consisting of a nonmonotone neural network that makes inferences based only upon distributed representations. This engine deduces a conclusion according to state transitions of the network along a trajectory attractor formed in a large-scale dynamic system. It has the powerful capability of analogical reasoning. We also construct a simple inference system and demonstrate its many advantages; for example, it can perform nonmonotonic reasoning simply and naturally.

1 Introduction

It has been noticed that classical artificial intelligence (AI) based on symbolic manipulation has the symbol grounding problem [1] and the frame problem [2]. For those reasons, it does not work well in the real world. In contrast, although animals such as dogs and cats do not seem to have languages or manipulate symbols, they evidently "think" and can deal better with many real-world problems than AI. It is therefore expected that brain-like processing, where information is distributedly represented and manipulated without being symbolized, might overcome some limitations of classical AI. We refer here to such information processing as completely pattern-based processing.

However, few processing systems can form inferences without using symbols. Although artificial neural networks are typical pattern-based processing systems, existing neural network models of inference require local representations; alternatively, they are combined with symbol processing models to form hybrid systems.

In this paper, we propose a completely pattern-based inference engine using a nonmonotone neural network. We then examine its possibilities by constructing a simple inference system.

2 Structure and Dynamics of the Inference Engine

2.1 Nonmonotone Neural Network

The inference engine we propose comprises a nonmonotone neural network [3]: a fully recurrent network of which elements have a nonmonotonic output function.

M. Ishikawa et al. (Eds.): ICONIP 2007, Part II, LNCS 4985, pp. 1065–1074, 2008.

The original model is described by the following dynamics:

$$\tau \frac{du_i}{dt} = -u_i + \sum_{j=1}^{n} w_{ij} y_j + z_i, \tag{1}$$

$$y_i = f(u_i). \tag{2}$$

Here, u_i is the internal potential of the i-th element, y_i is the output, w_{ij} is the connection weight from the j-th element, z_i is the external input, n is the number of elements, τ is a time constant, and $f(u)$ is the output function given as

$$f(u) = \frac{1 - e^{-cu}}{1 + e^{-cu}} \cdot \frac{1 - e^{c'(|u|-h)}}{1 + e^{c'(|u|-h)}}, \tag{3}$$

where c, c', and h are positive constants.

Because the polarity of u_i is important in this model, we consider $x_i \equiv \mathrm{sgn}(u_i)$ ($\mathrm{sgn}(u) = 1$ for $u > 0$ and -1 for $u \leq 0$) and refer to the vector $\boldsymbol{x} = (x_1, \ldots, x_n)$ as the current state of the network. The network state $\boldsymbol{x}$ at an instant is represented by a point in state space consisting of 2^n possible states. It almost always moves to an adjacent point in the state space because x_i changes asynchronously when $\boldsymbol{x}$ changes. Consequently, a continuous trace of $\boldsymbol{x}$ is drawn with the passage of time, which is called the trajectory of $\boldsymbol{x}$.

An important feature of this model is that it can make stable transitions along a given continuous trajectory in the state space; such a trajectory is called a trajectory attractor [3]. By forming trajectory attractors from states S^μ ($\mu = 1, \ldots, m$) to T^μ, we can associate binary (± 1) patterns S^μ with the corresponding patterns T^μ. That is, if S^μ is given as the initial state, the network makes state transitions autonomously and recalls T^μ. We respectively refer to S^μ and T^μ as cue and target patterns.

2.2 Forming Trajectory Attractors

We give a spatiotemporal pattern $\boldsymbol{r}(t)$ changing continuously from S^μ to T^μ as a teacher signal and train the network to form the trajectory attractor. Specifically, we set $\boldsymbol{x} = S^\mu$ and feed $\boldsymbol{r}$ to each element in the form of $z_i = \lambda r_i(t)$ (r_i is a component of $\boldsymbol{r}$ and λ is the input intensity), and allow the network act according to Eqs. (1)–(3). Simultaneously, we modify connection weights w_{ij} according to

$$\tau' \frac{dw_{ij}}{dt} = -w_{ij} + \alpha r_i y_j, \tag{4}$$

where τ' is the time constant of learning ($\tau' \gg \tau$) and α is the learning coefficient. Although α can be a constant, we set $\alpha = \alpha' x_i y_i$ in this study (α' is a positive constant) because the learning performance is improved if α decreases with increasing $|u_i|$.

Intuitively, this learning decreases the energy of the network in the neighborhood of $\boldsymbol{r}$. Accordingly, when $\boldsymbol{r}$ changes successively from S^μ to T^μ, a continuous

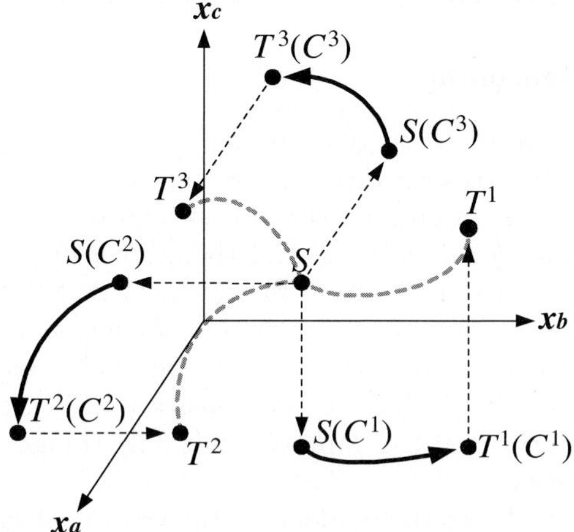

Fig. 1. Schematic representation of the process of context-dependent recall

groove remains in the energy landscape. In addition, because r leads to x, a gentle flow from S^μ to T^μ is generated at the bottom of the groove. By repeating several cycles of learning for all μ, gradually decreasing the input intensity λ of r, the network comes to make autonomous transitions from S^μ to T^μ, or trajectory attractors have been formed.

2.3   Contextual Modification Using Selective Desensitization

The original nonmonotone neural network always recalls a fixed target from an identical cue. For the network to recall various targets according to the "context", we introduce a novel method of modifying the network dynamics: selective desensitization [4,5].

This method desensitizes about half of the elements or renders their output as neutral, depending on a given pattern C, which represents the context. Specifically, assuming that the neutral value or the average output is 0, we substitute Eq. (2) for

$$y_i = g_i f(u_i). \tag{5}$$

Here g_i denotes a variable gain of the element, which usually takes 1 but takes 0 when the element is desensitized. We consider the simplest case, in which C is an n-dimensional binary pattern whose components c_i take ± 1 with equal probability; the gain is given as $g_i = (1 + c_i)/2$.

Through this operation, the modified state of the network is projected onto a subspace comprising active (undesensitized) elements. It also produces transitions according to the dynamics in the subspace. If trajectory attractors [3] are formed in the respective subspaces, the network state reaches different target patterns according to context patterns, as presented schematically in Fig. 1.

3   Pattern-Based Reasoning System

3.1   Method of Reasoning

Assume that a cue pattern S^1 is given to the model in a context C^1 and that the network makes state transitions from S^1 via S^2 to T^1. If the pattern S^1 represents *Sparrow*, S^2 *Bird* and T^1 *can fly*, we can regard this transition as a reasoning process "*Sparrow* is a *Bird*, and therefore *can fly*." In this case, C^1 is regarded as representing the context in which <FLYING ABILITY> is asked. Under this interpretation, we ask a question "Can *Sparrow* fly?" by giving the cue pattern S^1 and the context pattern C^1 to the model, and the model makes an answer "*Sparrow* can fly." Here, we emphasize that S^1, S^2, T^1, and C^1 are not symbols but patterns that can represent not only things or context, but also the relation of similarity.

We must give knowledge to the model to construct an actual reasoning system. That knowledge is given by forming a trajectory attractor, for example, from S^1 (*Sparrow*) via S^2 (*Bird*) to T^1 (*can fly*) in the state subspace specified by context pattern C^1. If another trajectory attractor from S^3 (*Horse*) via S^4 (*Mammal*) to T^2 (*cannot fly*) is formed in the same subspace, the system has gained another piece of knowledge "*Horse* is a *Mammal* and therefore *cannot fly*." In addition, a trajectory attractor from S^1 via S^5 (*Animal*) to T^3 (*move*) in another subspace specified as C^2 (MOBILITY) corresponds to a piece of knowledge "*Sparrow* is an *Animal*; therefore, *moves*."

After acquiring knowledge, the system can infer a conclusion deductively by state transitions along a learned trajectory. Moreover, because of the distributed representation of knowledge and powerful generalization ability of the model, it is expected that the system can infer plausible conclusions even if novel questions are asked.

3.2   Encoding

The reasoning ability of the model described above depends largely on encoding: how to represent information using distributed patterns. In the case of the brain, not only concrete objects but also abstract concepts are represented as patterns of neuronal activity that are structured, which means that related things are represented by similar patterns. We cannot learn from the brain, however, because neither detailed representations nor neural mechanisms of encoding are clear. Consequently, for the experiment described below, we used a convenient method, but not the best method.

First, context and target patterns were generated randomly under the condition that each component took the value $+1$ or -1 with equal probability. Accordingly, similarities (direction cosines) between these patterns were nearly zero, except that context patterns <FLYING ABILITY> and <WING> were set to have a similarity of 0.5, and target patterns <*can fly*> and <*have wings*> were set as identical so that we can investigate the case in which context patterns are similar.

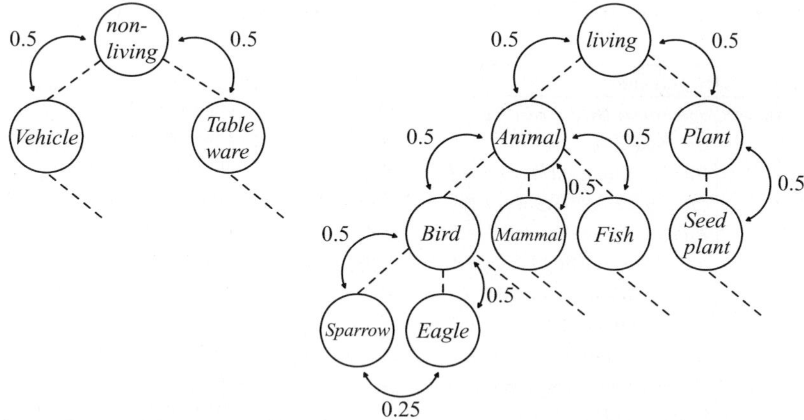

Fig. 2. Hierarchical structure of similarities among code patterns

Second, cue patterns were constructed based on categories. Specifically, the code pattern of an object was generated by adding a certain amount of noise to (flipping a certain number of components of) a pattern representing its category. Patterns representing categories were generated to form a tree structure, as shown in Fig. 2, where the numerical values denote similarities between patterns.

This structure was also used for training; that is, each piece of knowledge was represented as generally as possible using a superordinate concept because such generalized knowledge has a wide range of applications. It is noteworthy that there can exist some exceptions (we can give "*Sparrow* is a *Bird* and therefore *can fly*" to the system although some birds cannot fly), and that the superordinate concept can differ in respective contexts (e.g., "*Sparrow* is an *Animal* and therefore *moves*").

3.3   Simulation Experiment

We simulated the model with $n = 2000$ elements and constructed the system on a computer to examine the reasoning ability of the model. The parameters were $c = 50, c' = 10, h = 0.5, \tau = 5000\tau'$, and $\alpha' = 2$.

For actual operation of the system, some points were noted. First, it is difficult for the system to learn exceptional knowledge because the corresponding trajectory attractors are strongly affected by those corresponding to common knowledge and are therefore difficult to form. We varied the number of training sessions for each piece of knowledge so that all trajectory attractors would be formed securely to cope with this problem.

Second, conventional neural networks must generally relearn acquired knowledge when they learn new knowledge [6]. That relearning is inefficient, however, if

Table 1. Originally given knowledge

Context	Knowledge
FLYING ABILITY	$Sparrow \Rightarrow Bird \Rightarrow can\ fly$
	$Bat \Rightarrow can\ fly$
	$Horse \Rightarrow Mammal \Rightarrow cannot\ fly$
	$Cherry \Rightarrow Plant \Rightarrow cannot\ fly$
	$Airplane \Rightarrow can\ fly$
	$Helicopter \Rightarrow can\ fly$
	$Automobile \Rightarrow cannot\ fly$
	$Bike \Rightarrow cannot\ fly$
	$Boat \Rightarrow cannot\ fly$
	$Cup \Rightarrow Table\ ware \Rightarrow cannot\ fly$
BREED	$Sparrow \Rightarrow Bird \Rightarrow egg$
	$Dog \Rightarrow Mammal \Rightarrow young$
	$Lily \Rightarrow Seed\ plant \Rightarrow seed$
BREATHING	$Pigeon \Rightarrow Bird \Rightarrow lung$
	$Bear \Rightarrow Mammal \Rightarrow lung$
MOBILITY	$Eagle \Rightarrow Animal \Rightarrow move$
	$Dandelion \Rightarrow Plant \Rightarrow not\ move$
	$Bike \Rightarrow Vehicle \Rightarrow move$
	$Fork \Rightarrow nonliving \Rightarrow not\ move$
FEEDING	$Lion \Rightarrow Animal \Rightarrow feed$
	$Azalea \Rightarrow Plant \Rightarrow not\ feed$
	$Spoon \Rightarrow nonliving \Rightarrow not\ feed$
CHLOROPLAST	$Giraffe \Rightarrow Animal \Rightarrow not\ have$
	$Morning\ glory \Rightarrow Plant \Rightarrow have$
	$Pot \Rightarrow nonliving \Rightarrow not\ have$

Table 2. Added knowledge

Context	Knowledge
FLYING ABILITY	$Penguin \Rightarrow cannot\ fly$
	$Tuna \Rightarrow Fish \Rightarrow cannot\ fly$
WING	$Helicopter \Rightarrow not\ have$
BREED	$Trout \Rightarrow Fish \Rightarrow egg$
	$Grayfish \Rightarrow young$
BREATHING	$Salmon \Rightarrow Fish \Rightarrow branchi$
DEATH	$Duck \Rightarrow living \Rightarrow will\ die$
	$Cow \Rightarrow living \Rightarrow will\ die$
	$Apple \Rightarrow living \Rightarrow will\ die$
	$Boat \Rightarrow nonliving \Rightarrow will\ not\ die$
	$Knife \Rightarrow nonliving \Rightarrow will\ not\ die$

the system requires relearning even for a small addition of knowledge. We tested the system before and after additional learning of new knowledge to investigate this point.

The kind of knowledge that was given originally to the system and that which was added afterward are shown respectively in Tables 1 and 2. Initially, we trained the network 10 times on average for each piece of the original knowledge until the system acquired all. Then we asked the system various questions about both learned and unlearned knowledge. Next, we trained the network for the additional knowledge. The number of training iterations was 10 times on average. Then we asked various questions again.

Table 3 shows the results. In this table, shaded regions indicate the part related to additional learning (the question was newly asked or the answer changed); bold face indicates the answer that was given directly in training. We can say that the system gives a suitable answer to unlearned questions if we consider the limited knowledge given to the system.

Table 3. Reasoning results

	FLYING	WING	BREEDING	BREATHING	MOBILITY	FEEDING	CHLOROPLAST	DEATH
Sparrow	**fly**	*have*	*egg*	*lung*	*move*	*feed*	*not*	*die*
Eagle	*fly*	*have*	*egg*	*lung*	**move**	*feed*	*not*	*die*
Swallow	*fly*	*have*	**egg**	*lung*	*move*	*feed*	*not*	*die*
Duck	*fly*	*have*	*egg*	*lung*	*move*	*feed*	*not*	**die**
Penguin	*fly*	*have*	*egg*	*lung*	*move*	*feed*	*not*	
	not	**not**						*die*
Pigeon	*fly*	*have*	*egg*	**lung**	*move*	*feed*	*not*	*die*
	⋮	⋮	⋮	⋮	⋮	⋮	⋮	⋮
Bat	**fly**	*have*	*young*	*lung*	*move*	*feed*	*not*	*die*
Horse	**not**	*not*	*young*	*lung*	*move*	*feed*	*not*	*die*
Dog	*not*	*not*	**young**	*lung*	*move*	*feed*	*not*	*die*
Cow	*not*	*not*	*young*	*lung*	*move*	*feed*	*not*	**die**
Bear	*not*	*not*	*young*	**lung**	*move*	*feed*	*not*	*die*
Lion	*not*	*not*	*young*	*lung*	*move*	**feed**	*not*	*die*
Giraffe	*not*	*not*	*young*	*lung*	*move*	*feed*	**not**	*die*
	⋮	⋮	⋮	⋮	⋮	⋮	⋮	⋮
Tuna	**not**	*not*	*egg*	*branchi*	*move*	*feed*	*not*	*die*
Trout	*not*	*not*	**egg**	*branchi*	*move*	*feed*	*not*	*die*
Grayfish	*not*	*not*	**young**	*branchi*	*move*	*feed*	*not*	*die*
Salmon	*not*	*not*	*egg*	**branchi**	*move*	*feed*	*not*	*die*
	⋮	⋮	⋮	⋮	⋮	⋮	⋮	⋮
Cherry	**not**	*not*	*seed*		*not*	*not*	*have*	*die*
Dandelion	*not*	*not*	*seed*		**not**	*not*	*have*	*die*
Lily	*not*	*not*	**seed**		*not*	*not*	*have*	*die*
Apple	*not*	*not*	*seed*		*not*	*not*	*have*	**die**
Azalea	*not*	*not*	*seed*		*not*	**not**	*have*	*die*
Morning glory	*not*	*not*	*seed*		*not*	*not*	**have**	*die*
	⋮	⋮	⋮		⋮	⋮	⋮	⋮
Airplane	**fly**	*have*			*move*	*not*	*not*	*not*
Helicopter	*fly*	*have*			*move*	*not*	*not*	
		not						*not*
Car	**not**	*not*			*move*	*not*	*not*	*not*
Bike	**not**	*not*			**move**	*not*	*not*	*not*
Boat	**not**	*not*			*move*	*not*	*not*	**not**
	⋮	⋮			⋮	⋮	⋮	⋮
Cup	**not**	*not*			*not*	*not*	*not*	*not*
Fork	*not*	*not*			**not**	*not*	*not*	*not*
Knife	*not*	*not*			*not*	*not*	*not*	**not**
Spoon	*not*	*not*			*not*	**not**	*not*	*not*
Pot	*not*	*not*			*not*	*not*	**not**	*not*
	⋮	⋮			⋮	⋮	⋮	⋮

4   Discussion

The inferential system described above has the following human-like features that most existing systems do not have.

(a) Analogy based on similarity between cue patterns. To many test questions, the system performs analogical reasoning using similarity between patterns. For example, the system answers *"Eagle* can fly" to a novel question "Can *Eagle* fly?" This is because *Eagle* is represented by a code pattern similar to <*Sparrow*>; therefore, the network state is attracted to the trajectory attractor <*Sparrow* → *Bird* → *can fly*>.

(b) Analogy based on similarity between context patterns. The system can perform analogical reasoning when the context is different but similar to a familiar context. For example, if the system knows that X can fly, it is generally inferred that X has wings, even though it learned nothing about wings because contexts <FLYING ABILITY> and <WING> are represented by similar patterns, and trajectory attractors formed in the former context produce flows parallel to them in the subspace corresponding to the latter context.

(c) Nonmonotonic reasoning. In general, inference systems with high ability of analogical reasoning suffer from exceptional knowledge. Inversely, systems which deal excellently with exceptional knowledge require numerous detailed rules and have difficulty in using analogy. The present system, however, solves this dilemma.

For example, although *Bat* is a *Mammal* and is therefore represented by a similar code pattern to <*Horse*>, <*Dog*>, etc., the system replies *"Bat* can fly" to the question "Can *Bat* fly?" because exceptional knowledge has been given. Nevertheless, it performs analogical reasoning to other questions about *Bat* similarly as it does to questions about *Horse* and *Dog* (e.g. *"Bat* bears young"). In other words, the trajectory attractor <*Bat* → *can fly*> in the context <FLYING ABILITY> does not much affect the flow from <*Bat*> toward <*Mammal*> in other contexts because the influence of trajectory attractors toward <*Mammal*> in various contexts, such as <*Horse* → *Mammal*> in <FLYING ABILITY> and <*Dog* → *Mammal*> in <BREED>, is stronger.

For the same reason, the influence of exceptional knowledge in the same context is limited and does not impair the ability of analogical reasoning as long as the knowledge is exceptional. For example, when a novel cue pattern with equal similarities to <*Bat*> and to <*Dog*> is given in the context <FLYING ABILITY>, the network state moves to <*cannot fly*> through the neighborhood of <*Mammal*>. Such an inference can be regarded as a kind of common-sense reasoning.

(d) Analogical reasoning using a structure of similarities among patterns. A crucial advantage of distributed representations over symbolic representations is that the relation among objects, like that shown in Fig. 2, can

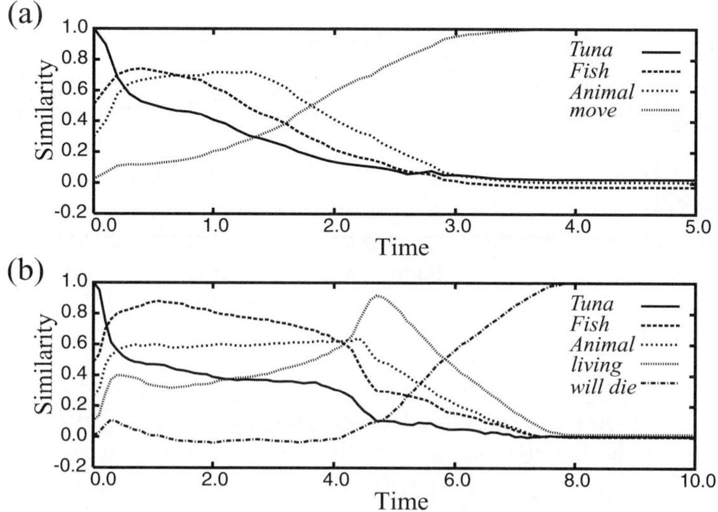

Fig. 3. Process of reasoning using structure of code patterns

be expressed implicitly by similarities or distances between code patterns. The present system can make good use of this advantage for inference.

For example, although the system has learned nothing about *Fish* in the context <Mobility> and has not learned explicitly that they belong to *Animal* in any context, it drew the conclusion that "*Tuna* moves." The process of inference is shown in Fig. 3(a), in which the time course of similarities between the network state x and individual code patterns is shown (the abscissa is scaled by the time constant τ). As this graph shows, the network state moves initially from <*Tuna*> toward <*Fish*> and <*Animal*> as a result of the influence of various trajectory attractors to them. Then it is attracted to the trajectory attractor <*Animal* → *move*>, which was formed when the system learned "*Eagle* is an *Animal*; consequently, *moves*."

Similarly, the system infers "*Tuna* will die", as depicted in Fig. 3(b), where the network state is carried by a flow along <*Tuna* → *Fish* → *Animal*>. It is then attracted to a trajectory attractor formed when the system learned "*Duck*, *Cow* and *Apple* are *living*; thus, *will die*."

(e) Addition of knowledge. Conventional multilayer neural networks confront the serious problem that previously acquired knowledge is disrupted suddenly in the process of learning a new set of knowledge, which is called catastrophic interference [6]. The present system is, however, robust to additional learning of new knowledge.

In the above experiment, for example, addition of knowledge about *Fish* caused no error in inference as to acquired knowledge because <*Fish*> is distant from other code patterns. Similarly, additional learning in a novel context <Death> had little influence on acquired knowledge.

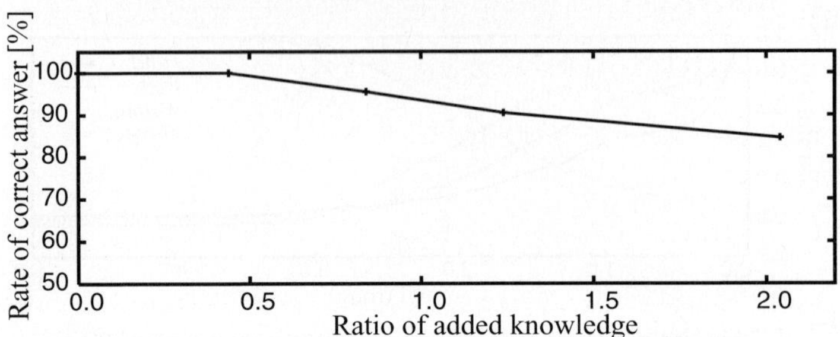

Fig. 4. Interference to learned knowledge by additional learning

Although addition of exceptional knowledge can interfere with related general knowledge, the interference is actually limited. For example, even after the system additionally learned *"Helicopter* has no wings"*, it can infer by analogy that *"Eagle* has wings" and *"Car* has no wings."

To examine the interference effects more specifically, we gradually increased the amount of additional knowledge in the experiment described above, while maintaining the ratio of exceptional knowledge around 20%. Figure 4 shows the result in which the percentage of correct inferences as to original knowledge is shown as plotted against the ratio of added knowledge to the original. That figure illustrates that the rate does not decrease rapidly; it remains higher than 80%, even when a double amount of knowledge is added. This result indicates that the system can accumulate knowledge merely through occasional relearning.

Although the present system leaves much room for improvement and although there remain many subjects for future study, the features described above suggest the great potential of our model, which might engender an important breakthrough in neural computation and artificial intelligence.

References

1. Harnad, S.: The symbol grounding problem. Physica D 42, 335–346 (1990)
2. McCarty, M.: Some philosophical problems from the standpoint of artificial intelligence. Machine Intelligence 4, 463–502 (1969)
3. Morita, M.: Memory and learning of sequential patterns by nonmonotone neural networks. Neural Networks 9, 1477–1489 (1996)
4. Morita, M., Murata, K., Morokami, S.: Context-dependent sequential recall by a trajectory attractor network with selective desensitization. In: Proc. of the Third International Conference on Neural Networks and Artificial Intelligence, pp. 235–238 (2003)
5. Morita, M., Matsuzawa, K., Morokami, S.: A Model of context-dependent association using selective desensitization of nonmonotonic neural elements. Systems and Computers in Japan 6, 73–83 (2005)
6. McCloskey, M., Cohen, N.: Catastrophic interference in connectionist networks: The sequential learning problem. The Psychology of Learning and Motivation 24, 109–164 (1989)

Task Segmentation in a Mobile Robot by mnSOM and Clustering with Spatio-temporal Contiguity

M. Aziz Muslim, Masumi Ishikawa, and Tetsuo Furukawa[*]

Dept.of Brain Science and Engineering, Kyushu Institute of Technology, Japan
aziz-muslim@edu.brain.kyutech.ac.jp, ishikawa@brain.kyutech.ac.jp,
furukawa@brain.kyutech.ac.jp

Abstract. In our previous study, task segmentation by mnSOM implicitly assumes that winner modules corresponding to subsequences in the same class share the same label. This paper proposes to do task segmentation by applying various clustering methods to the resulting mnSOM without using the above assumption. Firstly we use the conventional hierarchical clustering. It assumes that the distances between any pair of modules are provided with precision, but this is not exactly true. Accordingly, this is followed by a clustering based on only the distance between spatially adjacent modules with modification by their temporal contiguity. This clustering with spatio-temporal contiguity provides superior performance to the conventional hierarchical clustering and comparable performance with mnSOM using the implicit assumption.

1 Introduction

Task segmentation in navigation of a mobile robot based on sensory signals is important for realizing efficient navigation, hence attracted wide attention. Tani and Nolfi [4] proposed 2-level hierarchical mixture of recurrent experts (MRE), which is an extension of the network architecture proposed by Jacobs et al.[3]. Wolpert and Kawato [7] proposed MOSAIC architecture for motor control with the soft-max function for assigning responsibility signal to each module.

In the conventional competitive learning, only a winner module or unit is highlighted, accordingly the degree of similarity between modules or units, and interpolation among them are not taken into account. There are two types of "interpolation": one is creating an output which is an interpolation of outputs of multiple modules, and the other is creating a module which is an interpolation of multiple modules. Let the former be called "output interpolation" and the latter be called "module interpolation". Our study focuses on the latter.

The soft-max [7] is an improvement over the conventional competitive learning in that the output interpolation is possible based on the responsibility signals produced by the soft-max function. Similarity between modules, however, is not

---

[*] Corresponding author.

M. Ishikawa et al. (Eds.): ICONIP 2007, Part II, LNCS 4985, pp. 1075–1084, 2008.

explicitly represented. Furthermore, the soft-max function and segmentation do not generally coexist; only when the soft-max function is asymptotically equivalent to winner-take-all, segmentation is possible at the sacrifice of interpolation.

Self Organizing Maps (SOM)[5] is a popular method for classification and visualization of data, while preserving topological relationship between data. The resulting topological maps demonstrate the unit interpolation among units on a competitive layer of SOM. In contrast to SOM with a vector unit as its element, a modular network SOM (mnSOM) uses a function module as its element to increase its representation and learning capability [2]. Owing to competitive learning among function modules, mnSOM is capable of segmentation. Owing to topographic mapping of function modules on a competitive layer, neighboring function modules tend to have similar characteristics. Hence, interpolation among function modules becomes possible. Simultaneous realization of segmentation and interpolation is unique and unparalleled characteristics of mnSOM. mnSOM also has an advantage of computational stability in contrast to competitive learning due to careful assignment of learning rates to modules and classes.

We proposed to use mnSOM for task segmentation in navigation of a mobile robot [8][9]. In case of a mobile robot, however, the standard mnSOM is not applicable as it is, because it is based on the assumption that class labels are known a priori. In a mobile robot, however, only an unsegmented sequence of data is available. Hence, we proposed to decompose it into many subsequences, supposing that a class label does not change within a subsequence. Accordingly, training of mnSOM is done for each subsequence in contrast to that for each class in the standard mnSOM.

Our previous studies [8][9] demonstrated the segmentation performance, supposing that winner modules corresponding to subsequences in the same class share the same label. This is based on an implicit assumption that these modules have similar characteristics for subsequences with the same label. In this paper we propose to do task segmentation by applying various clustering methods to the resulting mnSOM without using the implicit assumption. First use the conventional hierarchical clustering. It assumes that the distances between any pair of modules are provided with precision. However, since mnSOM training adopts neighborhood learning as in SOM, the distance between a pair of far apart modules tends to be meaningless. Accordingly, this is followed by a clustering method based on the distance between only the spatially adjacent modules with modification by their temporal contiguity. This is what we call a clustering with spatio-temporal contiguity.

2   Task Segmentation and Clustering

2.1   Task Segmentation Using mnSOM

Data Segmentation. Task segmentation, here, is to partition the entire movement of a robot from the start position to the end position into a sequence of primitive movements such as a forward movement or a right turn movement. Experiments are carried out using a Khepera II mobile robot moving in robotic fields in Fig.1(a)(b). It has 8 infra-red (IR) proximity sensors, from which the robot gets information about current field, and 2 separately controlled DC motors. Robot movement are determined by wall following behavior. In case of robotic field in Fig.1(a), task segmentation and environmental or space segmentation is almost equivalent. Generally speaking, forward movement corresponds to straight corridor in a robotic field, right turn movement corresponds to L-shaped corner, and so forth. In case of Fig.1(b), however, task segmentation and environmental segmentation are different, especially at T-junctions. Fig.1(c) shows an example sequence of sensory-motor signal for the path of robotic field 1. For later evaluation of training and test results, the whole dataset are manually segmented into 9 sequences based on motor commands as in Fig.1(c). Sequences 1, 3, 5, 7 and 9 correspond to a class of forward movements, sequences 2 and 4 correspond to a class of left turns, and sequences 6 and 8 correspond to a class of right turns.

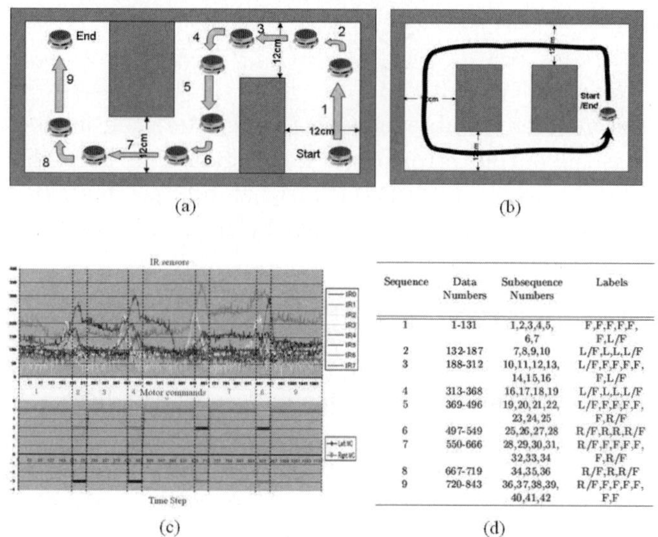

Sequence	Data Numbers	Subsequence Numbers	Labels
1	1-131	1,2,3,4,5, 6,7	F,F,F,F,F, F,L/F
2	132-187	7,8,9,10	L/F,L,L,L/F
3	188-312	10,11,12,13, 14,15,16	L/F,F,F,F,F, F,L/F
4	313-368	16,17,18,19	L/F,L,L,L/F
5	369-496	19,20,21,22, 23,24,25	L/F,F,F,F,F, F,R/F
6	497-549	25,26,27,28	R/F,R,R,R/F
7	550-666	28,29,30,31, 32,33,34	R/F,F,F,F,F, F,R/F
8	667-719	34,35,36	R/F,R,R/F
9	720-843	36,37,38,39, 40,41,42	R/F,F,F,F,F, F,F

Fig. 1. (a) Robotic Field 1 (b) Robotic Field 2 (c) Data from the Robotic Field 1 (d) Example of data division in Robotic Field 1

The whole dataset is split into many subsequences with the uniform length as in Fig.1(d). Details of data segmentation method is in [8][9]. By relating table in Fig.1(d) with Fig.1(a), we have rough spatial segmentation of robotic field 1. Each subsequence has its own label. As a consequence of uniform splitting, some subsequences stretch over two consecutive sequences (i.e., a forward movement sequence and a left turn sequence). They are called "transition" subsequences, and constitute virtual classes.

The mnSOM. To deal with dynamical systems, recurrent neural networks (RNN) are employed as a function modules in mnSOM [2]. Fig.2 illustrates the

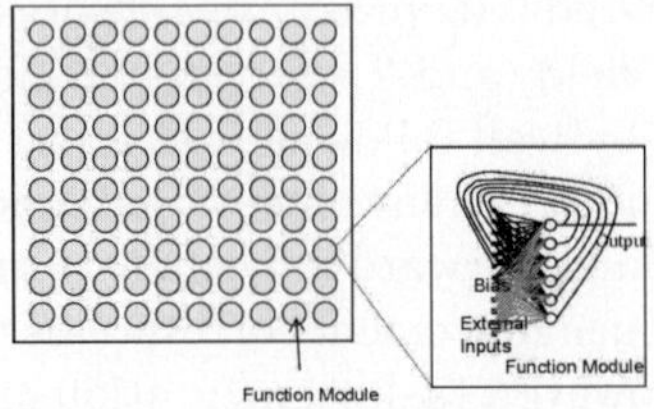

Fig. 2. Array of modules in mnSOM and the function module as its element. The function module is a fully connected RNN.

architecture of mnSOM and the function module as its element. Each mnSOM modules is trained using backpropagation through time (BPTT) [6]. Accordingly, connection weights of module $k,\mathbf{w}^{(k)}$, are modified by [2],

$$\Delta w^{(k)} = \sum_{i=1}^{M} \Psi_i^{(k)}(t) \left(-\eta \frac{\partial E_i^{(k)}}{\partial E^{(k)}} \right) \tag{1}$$

where M is the number of subsequences, t is the iteration number in mnSOM learning, $E_i^{(k)}$ is the output error of the k-th module for the i-th subsequence, and $\Psi_i^{(k)}(t)$ is the learning rate of the k-th module for the i-th subsequence. This Learning rates are carefully assigned by using the following normalized neighborhood function:

$$\Psi_i^{(k)}(t) = \frac{\phi\left(r\left(k, v_i^*\right); t\right)}{\sum_{i'=1}^{M} \phi\left(r\left(k, v_i^*\right); t\right)} \tag{2}$$

Here, neighborhood size decreases as time increasing as follows

$$\phi(r; t) = \exp\left[-\frac{r^2}{2\sigma^2(t)} \right] \tag{3}$$

$$\sigma(t) = \sigma_{min} + (\sigma_{max} - \sigma_{min})e^{\frac{-t}{\tau}} \tag{4}$$

where $r(k, v_i^*)$ stands for the distance between module k and the winner module v_i^*, ϕ is a neighborhood function, σ_{min} is the minimum neighborhood size, σ_{max} is the maximum neighborhood size, and τ is a neighborhood decay rate. These learning rate selection mechanism will improve modules prediction ability for a certain type of subsequence. mnSOM terminates when connection weights converge and the resulting mnSOM becomes stable.

2.2 Clustering

Hierarchical Clustering. A procedure of hierarchical clustering [1] is the following.

1. Let each module form a separate cluster.
2. Merge two clusters with the minimum distance.

3. Recalculate the distance between clusters.
4. Repeat steps 2 and 3 until the minimum distance between clusters exceeds a given threshold or the number of clusters reaches a given number of clusters.

An essential issue in clustering is the definition of the distance. Suppose that

$$m_i = \arg\min_k MSE(k, i) \tag{5}$$

where $MSE(k, i)$ stands for the mean square error of module i given input subsequence k. The distance between modules i and j is defined by:

$$d_{ij} = \sqrt{(MSE(m_i, j) - MSE(m_i, i))^2 + (MSE(m_j, i) - MSE(m_j, j))^2)} \tag{6}$$

The inclusion of only the subsequences m and n in the definition is to prevent the distance from being blurred by many less relevant subsequences. We then define the distance between clusters I and J. Suppose that the cluster I is composed of modules, $M_{I1}...M_{IR_I}$, and the cluster J is composed of modules, $M_{J1}...M_{JR_J}$. The distance between these two clusters is defined by,

$$D_{IJ} = \frac{1}{R_I R_J} \sum_{i=1}^{R_I} \sum_{j=1}^{R_J} d_{ij} \tag{7}$$

where d_{ij} is the distance between two individual modules i and j as in Eq.(7).

Clustering with spatial contiguity. In mnSOM the neighboring area shrinks as learning proceeds. This suggests that the distance between modules are meaningful only within neighboring modules. On the other hand, hierarchical clustering assumes that the distance between any pair of modules is given and meaningful. Considering this issue, we propose the following clustering method with spatial contiguity.

1. Calculate the distance between any pair adjacent modules. For module (i,j), adjacent modules are $(i,j-1)$, $(i,j+1)$, $(i-1,j)$ and $(i+1,j)$.
2. Rank order adjacent distances in increasing order.
3. Merge a pair of adjacent modules with the minimum distance.
4. Calculate the number of clusters formed by the merger.
5. Repeat steps 3 and 4 until the predefined number of clusters is obtained.

Clustering with spatio-temporal contiguity. In mobile robot data, temporally contiguous subsequences tend to have the same label. Accordingly, winner modules corresponding to temporally contiguous subsequences tend to have the same label. To take temporal contiguity into account, we propose to modify Eq.(6) as follows

$$d_{ij} = \sqrt{(MSE(m_i, j) - MSE(m_i, i))^2 + (MSE(m_j, i) - MSE(m_j, j))^2}$$
$$* \left(1 - \exp\left(-\frac{|m_i - m_j|}{\tau}\right)\right) \tag{8}$$

where τ is a time constant for temporal contiguity, and m_i and m_j are subsequence numbers. In contrast to Eq. (6), the second term in Eq. (8) will reduce the distance between winner modules by taking into consideration the temporal contiguity of subsequences. This modified definition of the distance is expected to have the tendency that these modules have the same label.

3   Experimental Results

3.1   Task Segmentation

mnSOM modules learn internal models of nonlinear dynamics of robot-environment interaction by minimizing mean prediction error of sensory or sensory-motor signals at the next time step, given the past sensory-motor signals. After training, the resulting mnSOM provides a label to each module by a procedure in [8][9], supposing that winner modules corresponding to subsequences in the same class share the same label. Given a subsequence, either experienced or novel one, one of the modules becomes a winner. The label of the winner module provides task segmentation for each subsequence. Fig. 3 depicts the resulting task map for robotic field 1 and robotic field 2. To evaluate the segmentation performance of the task map, training datasets as well as novel dataset are given to them. Fig. 4 illustrates the resulting labels for test subsequences for robotic field 1 and robotic field 2. The numbers written in the mnSOM module are subsequence numbers won by corresponding mnSOM module. Comparison Fig.4(a) and the table as in Fig.1(d) gives rough relationship between locations of a robot and the corresponding winner modules.

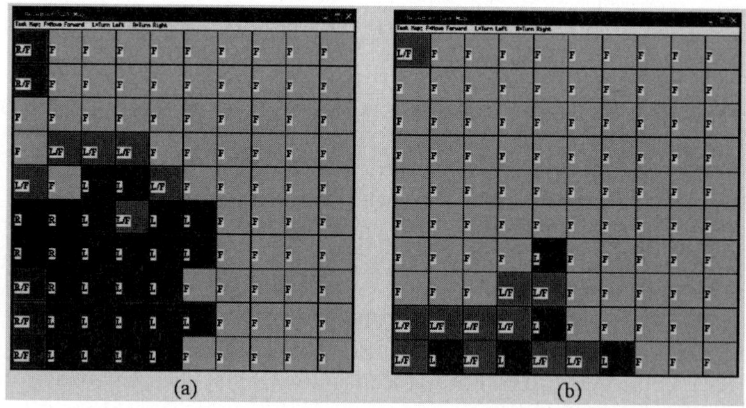

Fig. 3. Resulting Task Map: (a) for robotic field 1, (b) for robotic field 2. Labels "F", "L", "R", "L/F", and "R/F" stand for forward movement, left turn, right turn, the transition between forward movement and left turn, and the transition between forward movement and right turn, respectively.

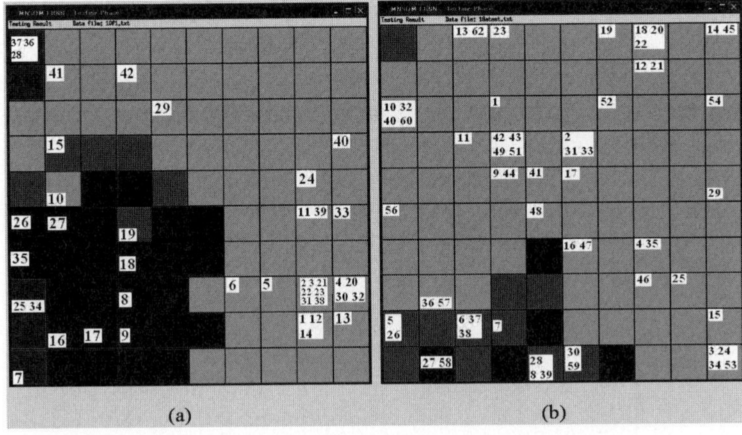

Fig. 4. Resulting labels for novel subsequences based on mnSOM (a) for robotic field 1, (b) for robotic field 2

3.2   Clustering

We propose to do task segmentation by applying various clustering methods to the resulting mnSOM without using assumption that those winner modules corresponding to subsequences with the same label have similar characteristics. Fig. 5 illustrates the resulting segmentation of a novel dataset by hierarchical clustering for robotic field 1 and robotic field 2. The task maps used in Fig. 5 are similar to those by mnSOM in Fig.3 to some extent.

Table 1 gives summary of segmentation performance by various methods. Table 1 shows that mnSOM has the best performance with the correct segmentation

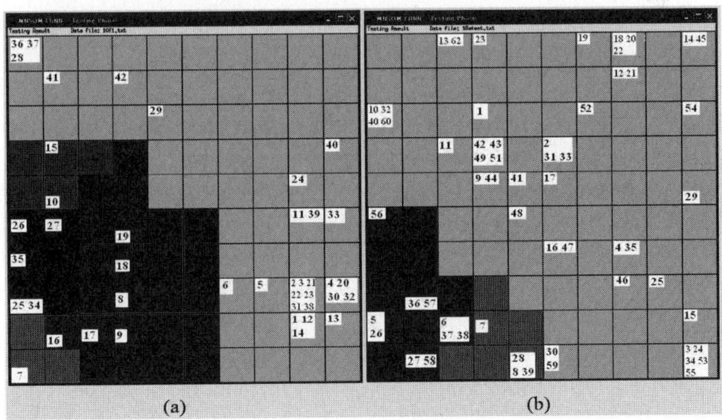

Fig. 5. The Resulting Segmentation by Hierarchical Clustering: (a) for robotic field 1, (b) for robotic field 2

Table 1. Correct Segmentation rate (%) by mnSOM and by various Clustering Methods. "Tr1", "Tr2", "Tr3", "Tr4" stand for training dataset 1, 2, 3 and 4, respectively. "Ave" stands for the average over 4 datasets. "Novel" stands for novel dataset.

Robotic Field	Data-set	mnSOM	Hierar-chical	Spatio-temporal contiguity					
				$\tau \approx 0$	$\tau=2$	$\tau=7$	$\tau=11$	$\tau=15$	$\tau=19$
1	Tr1	94.4	85.71	86.9	86.9	88.1	78.6	67.9	67.9
	Tr2	96.4	85.71	82.1	82.1	84.5	67.9	66.7	52.4
	Tr3	94.0	91.67	78.6	78.6	83.3	71.4	75.0	54.8
	Tr4	100	90.48	80.9	80.9	83.3	63.1	65.5	53.6
	Ave	96.2	88.4	82.1	82.1	84.8	70.3	68.8	57.1
	Novel	94.0	92.9	83.3	83.3	86.9	82.1	70.2	67.9
2	Tr1	97.6	88.7	86.3	86.3	94.4	91.1	91.1	93.6
	Tr2	96.0	88.7	83.1	83.1	86.3	86.3	86.3	91.1
	Tr3	99.2	85.5	91.1	91.1	92.3	92.7	92.7	90.3
	Tr4	98.4	91.1	87.1	87.1	89.5	89.5	89.5	89.5
	Ave	97.8	88.5	86.9	86.9	90.6	89.9	89.9	91.1
	Novel	95.2	92.7	80.6	80.6	87.9	87.9	87.9	93.6

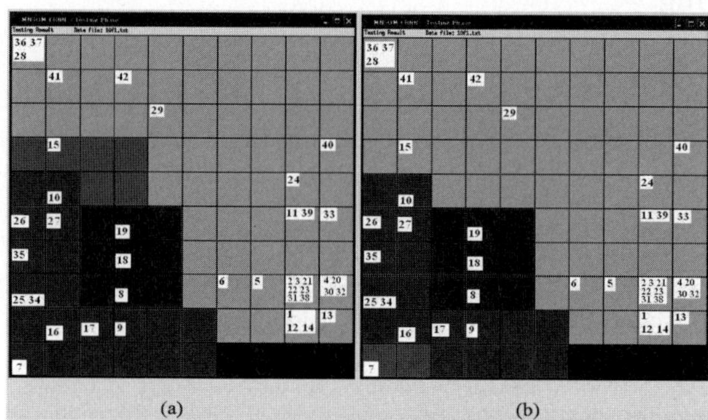

Fig. 6. Resulting Segmentation by Clustering with Spatio-temporal Contiguity for Robotic Field 1, (a) $\tau=2$, (b) $\tau=7$

rate of 94.05% for robotic field 1 and 95.16% for robotic field 2. This is reasonable because it uses additional information provided by the implicit assumption. In clustering with spatial or spatio-temporal contiguity, the performance of clustering depends on a time constant parameter, τ, in Eq. (9). $\tau=0$ corresponds to clustering with spatial contiguity and positive values of τ correspond to clustering with spatio-temporal clustering. Table 1 shows that for robotic field 1 the performance is best for $\tau=7$, while for robotic field 2 the performance is best for $\tau=19$. Larger τ deteriorates the performance. Clustering with spatio-temporal contiguity is superior to clustering with spatial contiguity. In robotic field 1, however, the performance of hierarchical clustering is superior to that of

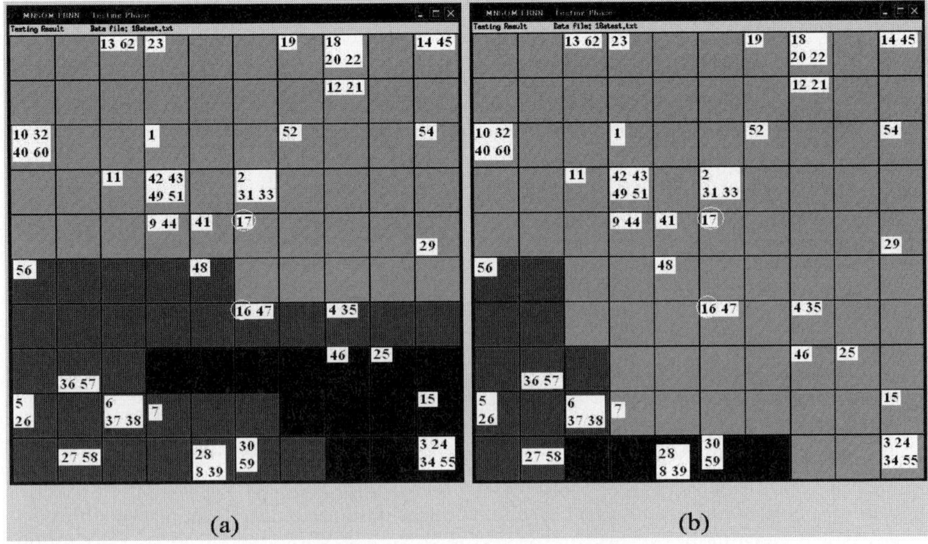

(a)   (b)

Fig. 7. Resulting Segmentation by Clustering with Spatio-temporal Contiguity for Robotic Field 2, (a) $\tau=2$, (b) $\tau=19$. Subsequences 16 and 17 (circled) which are lied on separated cluster in (a) became on one cluster in (b).

clustering with spatio-temporal contiguity. The reason for this is left for immediate future study.

Figs. 6 and 7 illustrate that proper value of τ moves the cluster borders, so as to make results several winner module corresponding to adjacent subsequences (e.g. subsequence 16 and 17 in Fig.7) in the same cluster.

4   Conclusions and Discussions

In this paper task segmentation by applying various clustering methods to the resulting mnSOM without using the assumption that winner modules corresponding to subsequences in the same class share the same label is proposed. Firstly we use the conventional hierarchical clustering. This presupposes that the distances between any pairs of modules are provided with precision, but this is not exactly true. Accordingly, this is followed by a clustering method based on the distance between only the spatially adjacent modules with modification by their temporal contiguity.

mnSOM uses unrealistic assumption, hence it is no wonder that its segmentation performance is superior to those without this assumption. In the Robotic Field 1, the proposed method is superior to hierarchical clustering only in Tr1. In the Robotic Field 2, however, clustering with spatio-temporal contiguity is superior to hierarchical clustering on the average. These results indicates the superiority of the proposed method in some cases.

Acknowledgments

This research was partially supported by the 21st Century COE (Center of Excellence) Program and by Grant-in-Aid for Scientific Research(C)(18500175) both from the Ministry of Education, Culture, Sports, Science and Technology(MEXT), Japan.

References

1. Duda, R.O., Hart, P.E., Stork, D.G.: Pattern Classification. Wiley-Interscience, Chichester (2001)
2. Furukawa, T., Tokunaga, K., Kaneko, S., Kimotsuki, K., Yasui, S.: Generalized self-organizing maps (mnSOM) for dealing with dynamical systems. In: Proc. of NOLTA 2004, Fukuoka, Japan, pp. 231–234 (2004)
3. Jacobs, R., Jordan, M., Nowlan, S., Hinton, G.: Adaptive Mixtures of Local Experts. Neural Computation 3, 79–87 (1991)
4. Tani, J., Nolfi, S.: Learning to perceive the world as articulated: an approach for hierarchical learning in sensory-motor systems. Neural Networks 12, 1131–1141 (1999)
5. Kohonen, T.: Self-Organizing Maps. Springer, Heidelberg (1995)
6. Williams, R.J., Zipser, D.: Gradient-based learning algorithms for recurrent networks and their computational complexity. In: Chauvin, Y., Rumelhart, D. (eds.) Backpropagation: Theory, Architectures and Applications, pp. 433–486. Lawrence Erlbaum, Mahwah (1992)
7. Wolpert, D.M., Kawato, M.: Multiple paired forward and inverse models for motor control. Neural Networks 11, 1317–1329 (1998)
8. Aziz Muslim, M., Ishikawa, M., Furukawa, T.: A New Approach to Task Segmentation in Mobile Robots by mnSOM. In: Proc. of 2006 IEEE WCCI (IJCNN2006 Section), Vancouver, Canada, pp. 6542–6549 (2006)
9. Aziz Muslim, M., Ishikawa, M., Furukawa, T.: Task Segmentation in a Mobile Robot by mnSOM: A New Approach To Training Expert Modules. Neural Computing and Application, Springer (to appear, 2007)

Author Index

Printing: Mercedes-Druck, Berlin
Binding: Stein+Lehmann, Berlin